EUROPEAN WRITERS

The Twentieth Century

EUROPEAN WRITERS
The Twentieth Century

GEORGE STADE
EDITOR IN CHIEF

Volume 12

GEORGE SEFERIS

TO

YANNIS RITSOS

Charles Scribner's Sons
NEW YORK

Collier Macmillan Canada
TORONTO

Maxwell Macmillan International
NEW YORK   OXFORD   SINGAPORE   SYDNEY

Library of Congress Cataloging-in-Publication Data
(Revised for volumes 10–11)

European writers.

Vols. 5– . Jacques Barzun, editor, George Stade, editor in chief.
Vols. 8– . George Stade, editor in chief.
Includes bibliographies.
Contents: v. 1–2. The Middle Ages and the Renaissance:
Prudentius to Medieval Drama. Petrarch to Renaissance
Short Fiction—v. 3–4. The Age of Reason and the
Enlightenment: René Descartes to Montesquieu.
Voltaire to André Chénier.—v. 5–7. The Romantic
Century: Goethe to Pushkin. Hugo to Fontane.
Baudelaire to the Well-Made Play—v. 8–9. The
Twentieth Century: Sigmund Freud to Paul Valéry.
Pío Baroja to Franz Kafka. v. 10–11. Yevgeny Zamyatin
to Pär Lagerkvist. Walter Benjamin to Yuri Olesha.
v. 12–13. George Seferis to Yannis Ritsos. Jean Anouilh
to Milan Kundera.
1. European literature—History and criticism—
Addresses, essays, lectures. I. Jackson, W. T. H.
(William Thomas Hobdell), 1915–1983. II. Stade,
George. III. Barzun, Jacques.
PN501.E9   1983   809'.894   83–16333

ISBN 0–684–16594–5 (v. 1–2)   ISBN 0–684–17916–4 (v. 10)
ISBN 0–684–17914–8 (v. 3–4)   ISBN 0–684–18798–1 (v. 11)
ISBN 0–684–17915–6 (v. 5–7)   ISBN 0–684–19158–X (v. 12)
ISBN 0–684–18923–2 (v. 8)   ISBN 0–684–19159–8 (v. 13)
ISBN 0–684–18924–0 (v. 9)

Charles Scribner's Sons   Collier Macmillan Canada, Inc.
Macmillan Publishing Company   1200 Eglington Ave. East
866 Third Ave.   Suite 200
New York, New York 10022   Don Mills, Ontario M3C 3N1

1 3 5 7 9 11 13 15 17 19   B/C   20 18 16 14 12 10 8 6 4 2

PRINTED IN THE UNITED STATES OF AMERICA

The paper in this book meets the guidelines for permanence and durability of
the Committee on Production Guidelines for Book Longevity of the
Council on Library Resources.

ACKNOWLEDGMENTS

The following pamphlets in the Columbia University Press Series Columbia Essays on Modern Writers are here reprinted, in revised form, by special arrangement with Columbia University Press, the publisher:

Brodin, Dorothy: *Marcel Aymé*
Copyright © 1968 Columbia University Press

Frohock, W. M.: *André Malraux*
Copyright © 1974 Columbia University Press

Guicharnaud, Jacques: *Raymond Queneau*
Copyright © 1965 Columbia University Press

The Cesare Pavese and Elio Vittorini essays were originally published in *The Modern Italian Novel: From Pea to Moravia* by Sergio Pacifici. Copyright © 1979 by Southern Illinois University Press. Revised and reprinted by permission.

LIST OF SUBJECTS

Volume 12

Volume 13

CONTRIBUTORS TO VOLUME 12

LUCILLE F. BECKER
Drew University
GEORGES SIMENON

ANN M. BEGLEY
Columbia University
SIMONE WEIL
MARGUERITE YOURCENAR

THOMAS G. BERGIN †
Yale University
SALVATORE QUASIMODO

HARALDUR BESSASON
University of Akureyri, Iceland
HALLDÓR LAXNESS

MARILYN JOHNS BLACKWELL
Ohio State University
EYVIND JOHNSON

DOROTHY BRODIN
*Emerita of Lehman College,
City University of New York*
MARCEL AYMÉ

JUDITH BUTLER
The Johns Hopkins University
JEAN-PAUL SARTRE

DORIS L. EDER
ANDRÉ MALRAUX

W. M. FROHOCK †
ANDRÉ MALRAUX

JACQUES GUICHARNAUD
Yale University
RAYMOND QUENEAU

LOUIS KIBLER
Wayne State University
ALBERTO MORAVIA

BETTINA KNAPP
Hunter College
NATHALIE SARRAUTE

ANNE McCLINTOCK
Columbia University
SIMONE DE BEAUVOIR

KOSTAS MYRSIADES
*West Chester University
of Pennsylvania*
YANNIS RITSOS

SERGIO PACIFICI
*Queens College, City
University of New York*
CESARE PAVESE
IGNAZIO SILONE
ELIO VITTORINI

JOHN REXINE
Colgate University
GEORGE SEFERIS

LEIF SJOBERG
*State University of New York
at Stony Brook*
GUNNAR EKELÖF

WALTER H. SOKEL
University of Virginia
ELIAS CANETTI

RALPH TARICA
University of Maryland
ANTOINE DE SAINT-EXUPÉRY

EWA M. THOMPSON
Rice University
WITOLD GOMBROWICZ

ALBERTO TRALDI
University of Puerto Rico
IGNAZIO SILONE

EUROPEAN
WRITERS

The Twentieth Century

GEORGE SEFERIS

(1900–1971)

THE ANNOUNCEMENT on 24 October 1963 by the Swedish Academy that the Nobel Prize for literature had been awarded to a Greek poet and diplomat for his remarkable lyric poetry aroused the curiosity of the literary world. At the time of the Nobel announcement George Seferis—whose poetic work was comparatively slight in quantity but extraordinary in quality and content—was virtually unknown in the United States, though better known in England and Europe. His poetry was considered the most representative of any living Greek poet, combining a consciousness of the classical Greek past, the modern Greek world, and the Western European literary tradition. It had been publicly admired by his contemporaries Archibald MacLeish and T. S. Eliot. The British classicist C. M. Bowra and the translator and poet Cecil Day-Lewis had both proclaimed Seferis to be one of the most important poets of his time.

In the *Saturday Review* of 30 November 1963, translator Kimon Friar provided an overview article to go with a cover that featured Seferis. In it he compared the poet with his compatriot Nikos Kazantzakis, noting, "They are the positive and negative poles between which flows the electric current of Greek literary talent." Seferis belonged to the so-called Generation of 1930, a generation that included such literary masters as Elias Venezis, George Theotokas, Stratis Myrivilis, Nikephoros Vrettakos, and the literary critic and patron George

K. Katsimbalis. The Nobel award indicated the admission of this modern Greek literature into the mainstream of modern European literature. (The poet Odysseus Elytis became Greece's second Nobel Prize winner, in 1979.) The Swedish Academy appeared at the same time to be showing a recognition of other modern Greek authors, such as Kostes Palamas, Constantine Cavafy, Kazantzakis, and Angelos Sikelianos, who were likewise worthy candidates for international acknowledgment.

In the introduction to *Poems* (1960), Rex Warner's selected translation of Seferis' poetry into English, Warner writes:

> Seferis, eminent as he is as a European poet, is preeminently a Greek poet, conscious of that tradition which shaped, and indeed created, the tradition of Europe. . . . Throughout the poetry of Seferis one will notice his profound consciousness of the presence of the past, and its weight. There is also to be observed an extraordinary freshness of vision. Objects, recognised and felt to be extremely old, are seen suddenly, as for the first time.
>
> (pp. 5–6)

Seferis was not merely conscious of the literary and cultural past; he was clearly and profoundly influenced by modern historical and literary events and developments. He spent his adult life in the diplomatic service, a career that culminated in his appointment as

Greece's ambassador to Great Britain, a position he held from 1957 to 1962. In his Nobel Prize acceptance speech, a brief address given (and translated into Greek by Seferis in his *Dokimes* [Essays], 2, pp. 159–161) at the official dinner in the Stockholm City Hall following the Nobel Prize ceremony on 10 December 1963 (he also delivered a longer lecture to the Swedish Academy on the afternoon of 11 December), he expressed his own vision of his achievements and concerns:

At this time I feel that I am myself a contradiction. Truly, the Swedish Academy has decided that my effort in a language widely spoken for centuries but of limited use in its present form was worthy of this high distinction. It wished to honor my language, and here I am, expressing my thanks in a foreign language. I ask forgiveness of you, as I ask, first of all, from myself.

I belong to a small country, a rocky promontory in the Mediterranean with no other assets than the struggle of its people, the sea and the light of the sun. Our country is small, but its tradition is vast, and what characterizes this tradition is that it has been conveyed to us through the centuries, without interruption. The Greek language has never ceased to be spoken. It has undergone the changes that any living thing must undergo, but there is no break in its course. Another characteristic of this tradition is its love for humaneness; its rule for justice. In ancient tragedy, which is organized with so much precision, whoever exceeds the measure must be punished by the Erinyes. The same law is valid even where physical phenomena are concerned: "The Sun," says Heraclitus, "will not overstep his measures; if he does, the Erinyes, the handmaids of Justice, will find him out."

It is not unlikely, I believe, that a modern scientist might profit by considering this aphorism of the Ionian philosopher. As far as I am concerned, what moves me the most is to observe that the sense of justice had so deeply permeated the Greek soul that for them it had become also a rule of the world of nature. And one of my teachers wrote, at the beginning of the last century, "We shall be destroyed because we did wrong." This man was an illiterate; he learned to write only at the age of thirty-five. But in modern Greece oral tradition is as deeply rooted as the written tradition. The same applies to poetry. It is important to me that Sweden should wish to honor this poetry, as well as poetry in general, even though it springs from a small nation. For I believe that this contemporary world in which we live, tormented by fear and anxiety, does need poetry. Poetry has its roots in human breathing—and what would happen to us if our breath were to fail? It is an art of trust—and God knows whether most of our ills are not due precisely to our lack of trust.

Last year around this table it was pointed out that there is a great difference between the discoveries of modern science and literature; it was also observed that between an ancient Greek drama and a modern one the difference is small. Yes, human behavior does not seem to have changed much. And I must add that man has always felt the need to hear this human voice called poetry. This voice is ever in danger of extinction for lack of love and is always born anew; when threatened, it knows where to find shelter; when denounced, it instinctively finds new roots in the most unexpected places. For poetry there are neither large countries nor small. Its domain is in the hearts of all men on earth. It has the grace always to avoid mechanization of habit. I am grateful to the Swedish Academy for having felt all this, for having sensed that languages of so-called limited use should not be turned into barriers behind which human heart throbs are stilled. I am also grateful because the Academy has proved itself an Areopagus adept: "to judge with solemn true life's ill appointed lot"—to quote Shelley, who, we are told, inspired Alfred Nobel, a man who found a way to redeem inevitable violence through the greatness of his heart.

In this rapidly shrinking world each one of us needs all the others. We must seek out man wherever he may be.

When on the road to Thebes Oedipus met the Sphinx and was given an enigma to solve, his answer was *man*. This simple word destroyed the monster. We have many monsters to destroy. Let us consider Oedipus' reply.

(*The Charioteer* 27 [1985], pp. 25–27)

Rarely do we have from the pen of a poet such a clear and unequivocal statement, expressed with such brevity and eloquence, of what he is about. Seferis distinguishes himself in his concern for the Greek language: for the continuity of that language and literature; for the primacy of poetry in the Hellenic tradition; for a view of the world that is anthropocentric, humanistic, Hellenocentric, and tragic but is at the same time a vision always concerned with order and justice, disorder and injustice. In her excellent book *Love and the Symbolic Journey in the Poetry of Cavafy, Eliot, and Seferis*, Carmen Capri-Karka notes the importance to Seferis of the Aeschylean notion of justice and adds, "In his prose writings, too, Seferis refers to the Aeschylean idea, which can be traced back to Anaximander, that the moral law of justice is an expression of the fundamental law of nature" (p. 199).

In this connection it is interesting to note that the "teacher" to whom Seferis refers in his Nobel acceptance speech is General Yannis Makriyannis, hero of the Greek War of Independence (1821–1827) and leader of the popular insurrection that gave Greece the Constitution of 1843, who later found himself imprisoned under Greece's first king, Otto I, and his Bavarian court. Seferis notes a passage from Makriyannis' *Apomnimonevmata (Memoirs)*; at the beginning of the revolution in Arta one of the local beys says to his friends:

> Pashas and beys, we shall be destroyed, destroyed! For this war is not with Moscow nor with the English nor the French. We have wronged the Greek infidel and taken away his wealth and his honor. And this darkened his eyes and he rose up in arms. And this Sultan, this beast of burden, does not know what is happening. He is deceived by those around him.
>
> (*On the Greek Style,* p. 58)

Seferis compares the above statement, put in the mouth of the enemy Turk with the statement Aeschylus put in the mouth of another Greek enemy—the Persians—in his play *The Persians:* "We shall be destroyed because we

did wrong." Makriyannis' words were spoken in 1821 and recorded in 1829; Aeschylus fought at the Battle of Salamis in 480 B.C. and his *Persians* was presented in 472 B.C. Seferis embraces this very classical Greek sense of the cosmic order. As he observes in his "Letter on 'The *Thrush,'*"

> It is my belief that in the Greek light there is a kind of process of humanization; I think of Aeschylus not as the Titan or the Cyclops that people sometimes want to see him as, but as a man feeling and expressing himself close beside us, accepting or reacting to the natural elements just as we all do. I think of the mechanism of justice which he sets before us, the alternation of Hubris and Ate, which one will not find to be simply a moral law unless it is also a law of nature. A hundred years before him Anaximander of Miletus believed that "things" pay by deterioration for the "injustice" they have committed by going beyond the order of time.
>
> (*On the Greek Style,* p. 104)

Throughout his life George Seferis was haunted by the Asia Minor disaster (known simply as the *Katastrophi* to the Greeks), an uprooting that affected his family, the Greeks of Asia Minor, and the Greeks of the mainland and that made of him and his experience, both cultural and diplomatic, a virtual Odysseus and Odyssey. Seferis was born George Seferiades on 29 February 1900 in the Asia Minor city of Smyrna, the firstborn son of Stelios and Despo Tenekides Seferiades. His very name is etymologically rooted in the Arabic word for journey, *safariy* (which emerges in Swahili as *safari*). His whole life was, in fact, a journey, and the symbolic journey is very much a part of his work and a major theme in his poetry. He used the shortened form Seferis without the patronymic *-iades* that identifies his Ionian Greek roots.

In 1906 the young Seferis learned his first letters, at the Lyceum of Christos Aronis. From the beginning of his education he learned Greek and French simultaneously, as did his brother and sister. During vacations he spent time in the family summer home at Skala Vourla, the ancient Clazomenae. In 1914 Seferis wrote his first verses and at the beginning of World War I the Seferiades family moved to Athens, where in 1917 Seferis graduated from the Model Classical Gymnasium of Athens. In 1918 Despo Seferiades, her two sons (the younger son was named Angelos), and her daughter Ioanna (who later married Constantine Tsatsos, president of Greece from 1975 to 1980) moved to Paris, where her husband had taken employment as an attorney. It was in November 1918 that Seferis first read the French poet Jules Laforgue (1860–1887), who was to have a formative influence on his own poetry.

Seferis studied at the University of Paris until 1924; he did both his undergraduate and graduate work there, ultimately receiving a doctorate in law, but his correspondence reveals that his real interest was poetry. His study of law had been urged upon him by his father, an expert in international law who later served as a judge at the Permanent Court of International Justice at the Hague and drafted the Treaty of Sèvres of 1920. Seferis' father had first translated the poetry of Byron into modern Greek and himself composed poetry.

In 1924 Seferis went to London for the first time, to perfect his English in preparation for the examinations for employment with the Greek Ministry of Foreign Affairs. On 25 December of that year he composed the poem "Fog." He remained in England for more than a year, returning to Athens in the winter of 1925.

Seferis read the *Memoirs* of Makriyannis for the first time in 1927, the year he was appointed an attaché to the Ministry of Foreign Affairs. Also in 1927 his mother, who had been entirely devoted to her family, died. After enduring the Smyrna catastrophe of 1922 she had written about it to her son; she also had arranged to salvage much of the Seferiades property in Asia Minor from the Turks.

In July 1928 a translation into Greek of Paul Valéry's essay "Une soirée avec Monsieur Teste" was published in the prestigious Greek literary journal *Nea Estia* under the signature of George Seferiades. The next month his "Gramma tou Mathiou Paskali" ("Letter of Mathios Paskalis") appeared.

Seferis accompanied the French statesman Édouard Herriot on his trip to Greece in October 1929 and that fall began writing "Erotikos logos" (Song of Love), which he finished in December 1930. "Leophoros Syngrou, 1930" ("Syngrou Avenue, 1930") was dedicated to George Theotokas, and in the same year Seferis began "Aiolia," which he finished in 1931.

The publication of Seferis' *Strophe* (*Turning Point*) in 1931 marked a turning point for modern Greek poetry and for the poetic career of Seferis. *Strophe* meant more than a turning point in prosody; it meant a new form of expression that freed Greek poetry of artificial embellishments and that recognized developments in European lyricism. Seferis used fresh, new images and a bold way of expression. In September 1931, the eminent Greek poet Kostes Palamas' letter about Seferis' *Turning Point* was published in *Nea Estia*. This first collection (which appeared under the nom de plume George Seferis), as well as all other books that Seferis produced until 1945, was published at his own expense.

In the summer of 1931 Seferis became vice-consul at the Consulate General in London, where he later became director; he remained there until 1934. Seferis produced major work during this period. He published "Pantoum," with the title "Mia nichta stin akroyialia" ("A Night on the Beach") in *Nea Estia* in January 1932; in October *I sterna* (*The Cistern*) appeared. In 1933 an article on Seferis by Tellos Agras appeared in *The Great Greek Encyclopedia,* and Aristos Kambanis mentioned Seferis in the third edition of *The History of Modern Greek Literature.* Also in 1933 the poet's father, Stelios Seferiades, was elected a member of the Academy of Athens. Seferis never became a member of the Academy, although he greatly desired the honor.

In December 1933 Seferis began writing *Mythistorema* (a title intended to evoke in its meaning both myth and history), which he finished a year later. The collection's publication in 1935 marked the initiation of modernism in Greek poetry. Seferis had returned to Athens from London in 1934, and in the course of that year two events in particular made a lasting impression on him: One was his introduction to the paintings of Theophilos G. Hajimihail, who died that same year. Theophilos represented for Seferis a man of the people who was a source of life for contemporary Greek painting and who offered a different way of viewing art. The other was his discovery of T. S. Eliot's *Marina,* which exemplified a new way of looking at the world through poetry that emphasized the contemporaneity of the past. The publication of *O poietis Giorgos Seferis* (The Poet George Seferis) by literary critic Andreas Karandonis in 1934 identified Seferis as a leading Greek poetic voice and established him as a foremost figure in modern Greek literature.

The literary journal *Nea Grammata* printed Seferis' poem *The Cistern* in its premiere issue of January 1935, beginning a collaboration with the poet that would last for the next several years. In September 1935 the review published Seferis' translation of T. S. Eliot's poem "Difficulties of a Statesman" and in November his rendering into modern Greek, from the English translation by Ezra Pound, of Rihaku's "Letter of an Exile." That fall Seferis had completed his writing of *Gymnopaidia,* consisting of the poems "Santorini" and "Mycenae"; the volume's title, explained in an epigraph, connotes the lyrical dances performed on Santorini at a time when the island was the center of an ancient religion.

On 30 May 1936 Seferis completed the introduction to his book *T. S. Eliot,* which was published in July and dedicated to George K. Katsimbalis, whom Henry Miller later called "the Colossus of Maroussi." In the same year Seferis was appointed consul in Koritsa, Albania, a lonely but, for the Greeks, very sensitive and important post close to the Greek-Albanian border. He remained there until 1938.

On 13 February 1937 Seferis published in *Neohellenika Grammata* a letter having to do with the state of the demotic language, which he loved and was to promote all his life, even though in the diplomatic corps he was obligated to use the *katharevousa,* or classical, "purist" language. His memorial article on Constantine Katsimbalis appeared in *Nea Grammata* in April 1937, and in November in the same periodical Seferis translated Henri Michaux's "Je vous écris d'un pays lointain" ("I Write to You from a Distant Place"). The first translation into French of a poem by Seferis was published in 1937 by Elli Lambrides in *Revue internationale des études balkaniques.*

At the beginning of 1938 Seferis was transferred to Athens as head of the Bureau of the Foreign Press in the Department of Press and Information. He left an essay on Cavafy half-finished but published in *Nea Grammata* a translation of Archibald MacLeish's "American Letter." In June of the same year, in the *Link* of Oxford, the first translation into English of a poem by Seferis was published by Nicholas Bachtin, with the collaboration of Samuel Baud-Bovy. Seferis' translations of a chapter of a book by Roland de Reneville, *L'expérience poétique,* and of Paul Éluard's "Sans age" ("Without Age") appeared in *Nea Grammata* in July.

In August 1938 Seferis completed his "Dialogos pano stin poiesi" ("Dialogue on Poetry"), written in response to an essay by Constantine Tsatsos titled "Prin apo to xekinima" (Before the Start). Tsatsos' essay addressed the nature of philosophy and its relation to poetry and had been published in the periodical *Propylaea* in April. *Nea Grammata* published this reply by Seferis, and also his "Defteros dialogos i monologos pano stin poiesi" ("Second Dialogue on Poetry") in May 1939. Public discussion between the two men continued until December, when *Nea Grammata* ran two letters, one from Seferis and one from Tsatsos, under the title "To telos enos dialogou" (End of a Dialogue).

In December 1938 *Nea Grammata* had carried a number of Seferis' poems, including "To fillo tis lefkas" ("The Leaf of the Poplar"), "O dhikos mas helios" ("Our Sun"), and "Allilengie" ("Mutual Guarantee"). In 1939 Seferis met André Gide; he also traveled with T. K. Papatsonis to Romania. Throughout 1939, *Nea Grammata* continued to feature Seferis' work: in March the journal published his translation of Pierre Jean Jouve's "Les quatre cavaliers" ("Four Horsemen"); in June, his translation of three cantos by Ezra Pound; and in December, several of Seferis' own poems—including "Aphigisi" ("Narration"), "Proi" ("Morning"), and "I apophasi tis lysmonias" ("The Decision to Forget")—along with translations of "The Ship of Death" by D. H. Lawrence and Marianne Moore's "The Monkeys" and "In a Snail."

March 1940 marked the publication of *Tetradio gymnasmaton* (*Book of Exercises*), which collected Seferis' poems of 1928 through 1937. In April there appeared *Imerologio katastromatos* (*Logbook I*), and in May a volume titled *Poiemata* (Poems I), collecting the poems of *Turning Point, The Cistern, Mythistorema,* and *Gymnopaidia.*

Seferis married Maria (Maro) Zannou on 22 April 1941 and the couple followed the Greek government to Crete as the Nazis occupied mainland Greece. On 16 May they arrived in Egypt and remained in Alexandria until July. That August, Seferis was dispatched to South Africa—first to Johannesburg and then to Pretoria, where he served the Greek embassy until April 1942.

In March 1942 Seferis published, with a prologue, an important edition of the *Lyra* of Andreas Kalvos. In April he was transferred to Cairo, to the Greek government's Office of Press and Information. Despite his full-time diplomatic service with the Greek government-in-exile in Egypt, Seferis found the time and the audience to continue his literary activities during his stay in North Africa. He lectured on General Makriyannis and on Palamas in Alexandria, produced a photolithographic edition of the manuscript of his *Imerologio katastromatos B* (*Logbook II,* 1944), and inaugurated exhibits in Alexandria on the occasion of the Nazi occupation of Greece. But with the libera-

tion of Greece from German rule, he returned to Athens on 23 October 1944 and soon found himself director of the political bureau of the Regent Archbishop Damaskenos, a position he held until 1946.

Following the advice of T. S. Eliot, Seferis never gave up his diplomatic career to pursue a literary career full-time, and it seems that his active diplomatic life nourished his creative poetic and literary aspirations. *Logbook II* was published in the periodical *Tetradio* in 1946, a year of intense political activity. Early in the year Seferis had labored over a lecture on the seventeenth-century Cretan masterpiece *Erotokritos;* this epic poem remained a concern of the poet's throughout his life (its use of the demotic language was very much of primary interest to him). But it was the leave he received in October 1946—the first one since the summer of 1937—that would give him two months on the island of Poros and enable him to produce his important poem *"Kichle"* (*"Thrush,"* 1947). After returning to Athens, he delivered his famous lecture comparing the poets Cavafy and Eliot, later published as one of his most influential essays.

Seferis was awarded the coveted Palamas Prize on 26 February 1947, but he shared the award with I. M. Panayotopoulos and was himself the subject of considerable controversy in Greece at the time. Critics were aware that Seferis was a significant literary figure, but they were not sure how important he was, and they were concerned that he was breaking away from what they were familiar with as traditionally Greek.

Seferis' time in Turkey as counselor to the Greek Embassy in Ankara, from 1948 to 1950, also was the time during which "O vasilias tis Asinis" ("The King of Asine," from *Logbook I*), considered his masterpiece by some, appeared in an English translation by Bernard Spencer, Nanos Valaoritis, and Lawrence Durrell as *The King of Asine and Other Poems* (1948), with a preface by Rex Warner. Though Seferis had all of his formal European education in France and was much influenced by French symbolist poets, he was increasingly drawn to the British for inspiration and guidance in the direction of his own poetry. His friendship with Rex Warner, for example, became lifelong, and his admiration for T. S. Eliot was manifested in Seferis' translations of *The Waste Land* and *Murder in the Cathedral* into modern Greek. The Greek publisher Ikaros brought out his book *T. S. Eliot: I erimi hora kai alla poiemata* (*The Waste Land and Other Poems*) in August 1949, and the influence of Pound's *Cantos* was indicated by the translation of a short article on the *Cantos* by Seferis in a commemorative volume on Pound. Seferis' debt to Lawrence Durrell and Bernard Spencer was noted by Kenneth Young in an article in *Life and Letters* (January 1950).

Seferis spent the better part of 1950 traveling in Turkey; among the places he visited was Smyrna, the city where he had been born and raised, and which had been burned to the ground in the Asia Minor catastrophe of 1922. These travels produced essays (included in *Dokimes*) that were much more than reminiscences; they were attempts to recapture the ancient, medieval, and modern Greek past of Anatolia for himself and his compatriots.

Seferis' transfer to London in May 1951, as counselor to the Greek Embassy, brought him into direct contact with Louis MacNeice and Rex Warner as well as with the British literary public. His subsequent appointment as (joint) ambassador to Lebanon, Syria, Jordan, and Iraq, in April 1952, elevated him to the highest rank in the Greek foreign service and brought him into direct contact with Cyprus, its problems, and its cultural heritage. Three trips to Cyprus resulted in considerable literary output—"Salamina tis Kypros" ("Salamis in Cyprus"), "Agianapa I," "Agianapa II," "Treis moules" ("Three Mules"), "Leptomereies stin Kypro" ("Details on Cyprus"), "Epikaleo toi ten theon" ("I Surely Call upon God"), "Apo to imerologio tou '46" ("From the Diary of '46"), "Eleni" ("Helen")—which Seferis collected as *Imerologio katastromatos C* (*Logbook III*) in 1955. The collection was reprinted by the pub-

lisher Ikaros the same year, and titled with the epigraph from Seferis' first edition, as *Kypron, ou m'ethespisen* (*To Cyprus, Where Apollo Foretold Me*).

Both of Seferis' careers—his diplomatic service and his literary activity—continued to flourish. In the summer of 1956 Seferis returned to the Ministry of Foreign Affairs in Athens. He remained there until 1957, and in February of that year was at the United Nations for discussion of the Cyprus problem. The crowning of his diplomatic career occurred in May 1957, when he was appointed ambassador to Great Britain. In England, Seferis received the kind of recognition that he craved. Cambridge University awarded him an honorary doctorate of literature in June 1960, and in March 1961 he received the William Foyle Prize for poetry—the first time that award had gone to a foreigner. In July readings of Seferis' poetry took place at the Mermaid Theatre in London, in English translation and also in Greek by Seferis himself.

Works about Seferis continued to be published in various languages. A monumental volume commemorating the thirtieth anniversary of *Turning Point* appeared in 1961. Further editions and translations of his poems and essays circulated. Seferis retired from the diplomatic service, and returned to Greece for good in August 1962. When he received the Nobel Prize for literature in October 1963, the event was hailed in Greece with national celebration and was followed in April 1964 with the award of an honorary doctorate by the University of Thessaloniki. In June of the same year Seferis received an honorary doctorate from Oxford. This was followed by an honorary doctorate from Princeton in June 1965 and honorary membership in the American Academy of Arts and Sciences in March 1966.

Elected a member of the Institute for Advanced Study at Princeton in 1968, Seferis that fall traveled to the United States, where he was invited to teach at Harvard but declined. It was the period of the Greek military junta (1967–1974), when Greek authors were unable to express themselves freely, and Seferis—who held a diplomatic passport at that time—made a point of saying so.

The French Institute of Athens in December 1966 published a Greek edition of Seferis' *Tria krypha poiemata* (*Three Secret Poems*); in January 1969 Walter Kaiser of Harvard published the volume in a bilingual edition. In March 1969 Seferis issued a terse statement condemning the Greek military junta for what it was doing to Greece and the Greek creative spirit. His own contribution to *Dekaohto Keimena* (*Eighteen Texts: Writings by Contemporary Greek Authors*), published by Kedros of Athens in 1970, contained veiled but stinging criticism of that same government, which had withdrawn his diplomatic passport.

George Seferis entered the Evangelismos Hospital in Athens at the beginning of August 1971 to undergo surgery. He never recovered. He died on 20 September at daybreak.

Seferis' life was very much the story of an Odysseus, of a man wandering from place to place, and indeed Seferis embodied the Greek tradition that Odysseus so powerfully represents. Many critics see Odysseus, the most complex and contradictory of the Greek heroes, as the unifying symbol of Seferis' poetry. To cite Kimon Friar, "Seferis uses Odysseus as a symbol of inner tension: the eternal wanderer forever seeking the Land of Heart's Desire—the Lost Paradise lying somewhere behind the mysterious smiles of archaic statues" (*Saturday Review*, 30 November 1963). But although the breadth of human experience that Odysseus characterizes has made him an enduring figure in the Greek literary tradition, the poetry of George Seferis is more complex than such an assessment of Odysseus' role would imply.

One can look, for instance, at Seferis' use of another Homeric figure, Elpenor. As Edmund Keeley points out,

> Odysseus is the poet's persona, the first-person voice of the poem. He speaks as a man who is striving for spiritual liberation, but who finds his aspiration constantly frustrated by his weaker companions. The latter are represented by Elpenor, the youngest of the crew, who wins the coin at dice and typically disappears as the others set off again with their broken oars. If the Ghost of Odysseus is the principal narrator of Seferis' modern *Odyssey*, Elpenor is the principal subject of his narration: the typical "companion" on the voyage, the figure who reveals the weakness of spirit that so frustrates his captain and that makes the voyage agonizing and endless.
>
> ("Seferis' Elpenor: A Man of No Fortune," *Kenyon Review* 28 [1966], pp. 380–381)

Keeley goes on to argue that "Elpenor is the figure who most clearly demonstrates Seferis' talent for making myth dramatic—that is, for representing the truths myth has to offer through characters in action" (p. 381). He calls Elpenor a subhero, that is, "both a minor character in Homer and a man of little substance." Elpenor was Odysseus' oarsman; he had gotten drunk, fallen off Circe's roof, and broken his neck. When Odysseus visits Hades in Book 11 of the *Odyssey*, he meets Elpenor's *psyche,* which has not been granted admission to the world below because it has not had a proper burial:

> There, O my lord, remember me, I pray,
> do not abandon me unwept, unburied,
> to tempt the gods' wrath, while you sail for home;
> but fire my corpse, and all the gear I had,
> and build a cairn for me above the breakers—
> an unknown sailor's mark for men to come,
> Heap up the mound there, and implant upon it
> the oar I pulled in life with my companions.
>
> (*Odyssey* 11. 71–80, Robert Fitzgerald trans.)

Seferis sees Elpenor as a man to be pitied, as a man who is "sympathetic, sentimental, mediocre, wasted," who is obsessively hedonistic and has not learned to control his animal appetites, but who also knows that he is "wasted." These are words that the poet himself uses to describe Elpenor in his comments on *"Thrush"* and they identify, both in Homer and in Seferis, an Elpenor who is trying to escape from the stranglehold of memory but for whose whole being memory is now virtually all he has left. He, like all of us, wants to be remembered for something. Elpenor represents the common man: he is an oarsman, but even an oarsman wants to be remembered for his oarsmanship. The great Homeric heroes all possessed *arete;* they were *aristoi* (aristocrats) who performed *aristeia* (deeds of valor). Elpenor does his job, as so many common men do. *Arete* also conveys the meaning of "excellence," and Elpenor is good at his oarsmanship. He does not wish to be forgotten, nor do his men, the often nameless Argonauts. The poet has the responsibility of recalling for us the burden that such individuals carried: in celebrating the ordinary man with all his faults, he celebrates life itself.

Contrary to the reputation Seferis has acquired as a poet of tragic pessimism—a poet who, in the words of George Arnakis, sees "all-devouring death everywhere, even in the country of light and rebirth" (*The Texas Quarterly 7* [Spring 1964], p. 58)—he is also a poet of light, love, and life. His vision, though based on the centuries-old tragic history of the Greek people, interprets that history through the symbol of the journey—a symbol that goes back to the Odyssey, a symbol of Seferis' own journey through life and every individual's journey through human experience. Seferis' poetry reminds us that despite centuries of tragedy and suffering, there have also been centuries of achievement and of continued creative life.

At a time when Greek poetry was in a state of decline, Seferis brought to it something new. Kostes Palamas, the grand old man of modern Greek poetry, had declared that Seferis' *Turning Point,* published in 1931, was indeed a turning point for modern Greek poetry. *Turning Point* shows us a genuine, gentle lyric voice that is at the same time spiritually tormented by the constant anxiety of man in search of deliverance. For example, the last poem of the collection, "Erotikos logos" (Song of Love), is a tender expression of lyrical sentiment and philosophical thought, an interaction of material sensation and spiritual contemplation of love. This love motivates and elevates the soul, reveals a broader perspective on life, renews the value of things, and transforms their contents.

The Cistern, published in 1932, stands as one of the most moving and most tragically centered of Seferis' poems. It confronts the reader with human suffering and the ravages of time, the role of memory and desire, the sad realization that death constitutes the finality from which there is no recall. The "we" of the poem represents the voice of the individual as well as that of humanity. The cistern is Seferis' first important symbol. The poet and critic Andonis Decavalles has said it stands for "consciousness as it accumulates the experience of losses, personal and historical. The simple natural beauty of Greece is haunted by the ghosts of unfulfilled dreams and longings."

In both the *Turning Point* and *Cistern,* Seferis retained the external forms of traditional modern Greek poetry, namely, rhyme. Few modern Greek poets have been able to write such harmonious and musical decapentasyllabic (fifteen-syllable lines) verses as Seferis did in "Erotikos logos."

Much more important for modern Greek literature and for Seferis' own development was *Mythistorema* (1935). Here he abandoned the traditional forms and with an original and expressive use of free verse and unforced development of subject revealed his personal style. The late historian of modern Greek literature Linos Politis said:

Here we meet the Seferis we will come to know. He has definitely abandoned strict meter and rhyme, to create his own personal style in free verse. This collection consists of twenty-four poems or, rather, a poem in twenty-four parts. These were critical years for Greece and for Europe, over which, unresisted, hung the heavy shadow of totalitarianism. The poet found refuge in new researches or new conflations in *myth* and *history* (in Greek myth and Greek history). No other collection is so weighted with classical recollections. The tragic element, as the Greeks first conceived it, returns with tormenting insistence;

a permanent element, like a counterweight to the tragic decay of our time.

(Linos Politis, *A History of Modern Greek Literature,* 1973, p. 232)

Mythistorema enriched modern Greek poetry with new ways of expression and new combinations of words—plain, unadorned words. Feelings and ideas emerge clearly, in no uncertain terms, full of natural simplicity and economy, reflecting life itself with all its hopes, conflicts, and agonies. Poem number 3 from *Mythistorema,* in the now-standard translation of Edmund Keeley and Philip Sherrard,[1] provides a good sample of the style, imagery, and themes that Seferis employs:

> Remember the baths where you were murdered.
> Aeschylus, *The Libation Bearers,* 491

I woke with this marble head in my hands;
it exhausts my elbows and I don't know where to put
    it down.
It was falling into the dream as I was coming out of
    the dream
so our life became one and it will be very difficult for
    it to separate again.

I look at the eyes: neither open nor closed
I speak to the mouth which keeps trying to speak
I hold the cheeks which have broken through the
    skin
I haven't got any more strength.

My hands disappear and come toward me
mutilated.

The above selection powerfully recalls the importance of the classical past to the present, of the archaeology of Greece that is a permanent part of the contemporary landscape and that Seferis sees in relation to human psychology. Costas G. Papageorgiou has noted that the "statues symbolize nothing else but the human

bodies which have been hardened by insensitivity and are bent by love or mutilated by the waste of time" ("Notes on the *Three Secret Poems,*" *Charioteer* 27 [1985], p. 128).

The reader will find stones throughout much of Seferis' poetry. It is thus appropriate to go on to *Gymnopaidia* (1936), which consists of two poems, "Santorini" and "Mycenae." These poems reflect the realization that somehow nothing belongs to us anymore, that oblivion erases everything. Indifference, ignorance, and injustice all produce a frightening view of life. Man is abandoned to a tragic role in a suffocating world where miracles no longer exist. Inanimate powers like fire and time destroy the works of human beings.

"Mycenae," here quoted in full, deserves pondering:

Give me your hands, give me your hands, give
    me your hands.

I have seen in the night
the sharp peak of the mountain,
seen the plain beyond flooded
with the light of an invisible moon,
seen, turning my head,
black stones huddled
and my life taut as a chord
beginning and end
the final moment:
my hands.

Sinks whoever raises the great stones;
I've raised these stones as long as I was able
I've loved these stones as long as I was able
these stones, my fate.
Wounded by my own soil
tortured by my own shirt
condemned by my own gods,
these stones.

I know that they don't know, but I
who've followed so many times
the path from killer to victim
from victim to punishment
from punishment to the next murder,
groping

[1] All translations of Seferis' poetry given here are from this volume: *George Seferis: Collected Poems, 1924–1955.* Princeton, 1967; enl. ed. 1981.

the inexhaustible purple
that night of the return
when the Furies began whistling
in the meager grass—
I've seen snakes crossed with vipers
knotted over the evil generation
of our fate.

Voices out of the stone out of sleep
deeper here where the world darkens,
memory of toil rooted in the rhythm
beaten upon the earth by feet
forgotten.
Bodies sunk into the foundations
of the other time, naked. Eyes
fixed, fixed on a point
that you can't make out, much as you want to:
the soul
struggling to become your own soul.

Not even the silence is now yours
here where the millstones have stopped turning.

The stones are more than mere stones for Seferis. They are the stones of the past that weigh upon his present. They are a part of the present, as they will be a part of the future. In literal terms Greece is 80 percent rock, and stones, marble fragments, silent statues color the poetic landscape of Seferis just as they characterize the actual Greek landscape. Anthony N. Zachareas in his article "George Seferis: Myth and History" (*Books Abroad* 42 [1968]) has rightly put it this way:

These grounds littered with ruins, ancient marine kingdoms, empty harbors, the trail of arid mountains, slow-moving ships, abandoned homesites, together with the Aegean Sea, the bright sun, and the maddening wind are woven into a symbolic net, the tangled web of the Hellenic experience. Moreover, the Hellenic experience embraces the moral conflicts and existential doubts that characterize much of the problematic literature of our times. The poet usually gazes at the stone images and searches for more identity with past values, but statues do not always reveal their hidden truths and man must face the mystery alone, maimed, as it were.

(p. 190)

In *Book of Exercises* (1940), the real aim of the collection is in the search, in the wandering; these poems wander among human feelings and problems, from the most typical to the most improbable, from the most prosaic and ordinary to the most solemn and ritualistic. *Book of Exercises* is marked by bitterness and irony—gentle but caustic irony—and a feeling of dissatisfaction toward the continuous endeavor of searching after a goal that has ceased to be a goal. Many messages are condensed in a single verse. Unusual combinations of ideas and words arouse a multitude of emotions and images. Here again is Seferis' sense of the bitter finality of everything, of desolation, of the anguished inquiry under the empty pedestals of the statues of the gods that have once more been demolished by time. These lines from "Enas logos gia to kalokairi" ("A Word for Summer") are representative:

We walked together, shared bread and sleep
tasted the same bitterness of parting
built our houses with what stones we had
set out in ships, knew exile, returned
found our women waiting—
they scarcely knew us, no one knows us.
And the companions wore statues, wore the naked
empty chairs of autumn, and the companions
destroyed their own faces: I don't understand them.
There still remains the yellow desert, summer,
waves of sand receding to the final circle
a drum's beat, merciless, endless,
flaming eyes sinking into the sun
hands in the manner of birds cutting the sky
saluting ranks of the dead who stand at attention
hands lost at a point beyond my control and
    mastering me:
your hands touching the free wave.

Logbook I was published in April 1940. World War II had already begun, and it was obvious that Greece would soon be involved. The expectation of war runs through the poems in this collection. A climate of gloom is evident in them, not of panic but of an agony full of determination and boldness. It was an almost prophetic book for Greece, a book that was al-

2265

ready talking about the war and the bitter days that followed. Even the title and the prosaic sentence of the first page—"We remain in this position awaiting orders"—assume a special significance. *Logbook* records the course of that historical period. Linos Politis has said: "His heart beats together with the heart of the nation, with the heart of the world." One poem of special note in *Logbook,* "I teleftaia mera" ("The Last Day"), was written at Athens in February 1939. Even though the great moment had not yet arrived, and no decision had been taken, the air was heavy with threatening meaning. The poet knew that by the next morning all would be lost, and the poem poses the questions: "How are we going to die?" "How does a man die?"

The last poem in *Logbook I* is perhaps Seferis' most famous. Some would consider it his best poem. One word in Homer's *Iliad* 2.560, in the so-called catalogue of ships, accounts for the title of the poem, "The King of Asine." The catalogue of ships offers a list of the Greek forces that set out for the war against Troy (as well as a list of the Trojan forces). This Homeric reference to the men sent by Asine, *Asinen te,* provided Seferis with the inspiration for this poem. In Seferis' words, from a BBC III program of 12 July 1959, we learn:

> The King of Asine is mentioned by Homer in the list of those who sent ships against Troy—as he says. We know the remains of his palace near Nauplion; but about him nothing at all; just a name. Years after my visit to Asine a small terracotta was discovered, which was christened the King of Asine. The find disappointed me. Then I felt that it was perhaps our total ignorance about him which attracted me. I could add that this poem taught me something on the unconscious ways of poetry. When I started writing it the poem could not advance. After many attempts I had to abandon it; my manuscript was lost in the meantime. Two years after I wrote it without any difficulty in one night.

Civilizations have come and gone, and the archaeologist's spade has been able to bring to light for us evidence of cultures that we never knew. In the case of Asine, near the modern village of Tolos on the coast of the Argolid, Swedish archaeologists were able to bring to light a place preserved in historical and literary memory only by Homer. Seferis, in a way, through his poetic masterpiece, demonstrates how the poet—both ancient and modern—is responsible for the preservation of human memory and the rediscovery of human achievement:

We looked all morning round the citadel
starting from the shaded side, there where the sea
green and without luster—breast of a slain
    peacock—
received us like time without an opening in it.
Veins of rock dropped down from high above,
twisted vines, naked, many branched, coming alive
at the water's touch, while the eye following them
struggled to escape the tiresome rocking,
losing strength continually.

On the sunny side a long open beach
and the light striking diamonds on the huge walls.
No living thing, the wild doves gone
and the king of Asine, whom we've been trying to
    find for two years now,
unknown, forgotten by all, even by Homer,
only one word in the *Iliad* and that uncertain,
thrown here like the gold burial mask.
You touched it, remember its sound? Hollow in the
    light
like a dry jar in dug earth:
the same sound that our oars make in the sea.
The king of Asine a void under the mask
everywhere with us everywhere with us, under a
    name:
"*Asinen te . . . Asinen te . . .* "
                        and his children statues
and his desires the fluttering of birds, and the wind
in the gaps between his thoughts, and his ships
anchored in a vanished port:
under the mask a void.

Behind the large eyes the curved lips the curls
carved in relief on the gold cover of our existence
a dark spot that you see traveling like a fish
in the dawn calm of the sea:
a void everywhere with us.

And the bird that flew away last winter
with a broken wing
the shelter of life,
and the young woman who left to play
with the dogteeth of summer
and the soul that sought the lower world squeaking
and the country like a large plane-leaf swept along
    by the torrent of the sun
with the ancient monuments and the contemporary
    sorrow.
And the poet lingers, looking at the stones, and
    asks himself
does there really exist
among these ruined lines, edges, points, hollows,
    and curves
does there really exist
here where one meets the path of rain, wind, and
    ruin
does there exist the movement of the face, shape of
    the tenderness
of those who've shrunk so strangely in our lives,
those who remained the shadow of waves and
    thoughts with
the sea's boundlessness
or perhaps no, nothing is left but the weight
the nostalgia for the weight of a living existence
there where we now remain unsubstantial, bending
like the branches of a terrible willow-tree heaped in
    permanent despair
while the yellow current slowly carries down rushes
    uprooted in the mud
image of a form that the sentence to everlasting
    bitterness has turned to marble:
the poet a void.

Shieldbearer, the sun climbed warring,
and from the depths of the cave a startled bat
hit the light as an arrow hits a shield:
"Asinen te . . . Asinen te . . . " Could that be the
    king of Asine
we've been searching for so carefully on this
    acropolis
sometimes touching with our fingers his touch upon
    the stones.

No one who has seen the golden Mycenaean death masks in the National Archaeological Museum in Athens can help but be haunted by this poem. One can almost see the mask and hear the voice coming through it, saying, "Under the mask a void." We look in vain to find the king behind the mask, but there is no king to be found—only the mask. The king is dead. The heroes are gone. "The King of Asine" was written in a period of bankrupt leadership, as people looked desperately for heroes, but there were no heroes. There was no Odysseus to guide those seeking leadership back home. This is a magnificent poem in which the classical past and the contemporary present are integrated to bring home an unmistakable message.

Logbook II, written during World War II in places of exile, is inspired by the loneliness of exile and the desire to return home. In these poems Seferis recalls the experience of war and occupation, the military defeat of the Greek nation, and the agony of a Greek from the vantage point of an outsider. It is a poetry dramatic in character, profoundly moving, anguished, almost desperate. For example, the poem "Enas gerontas stin akropotamia" ("An Old Man on the River Bank") could be described as a kind of apology. It is a reassessment of past life and its accomplishments. It is a poem that raises questions about the use of our physical, intellectual, and critical faculties. The poem reflects bitterness and doubt, but it also leaves room for the possibility of a new life order, the hope of restoring humaneness to humanity.

Another poem from *Logbook II,* "Teleftaios stathmos" ("The Last Stop"), was written on 5 October 1944 in Italy at Cava dei Tirreni. The poem takes the form of a protest, and has even been described as the revolt of the soul that refuses to accept the horror of a life that will be repeated without regaining what has been lost. "The Last Stop" is a frightening and nightmarish picture with amazing dramatic frankness, composed at Seferis' last stop before the return to his liberated land.

Two years later, on the island of Poros, Seferis wrote his enigmatic poem *"Thrush."* A ship that sank during World War II off the coast of Poros, the *Thrush* becomes a symbol of the black ship that carried Odysseus down to Hades. On his way down, Odysseus becomes transformed into Oedipus at Colonus and then into the symbol of self-integration, Antigone, upon coming into the light. Its deeper meaning, according to the poet's own explanation, consists in the antithesis, the collision of absolute light with the poet's own life, the life of his country, the life of the whole world. Alexandros Argyriou has said that it is Seferis' most personal poem: "What is attempted in it is a retracing of the past and a vindication of it, leading finally to a general conception of life, a testimony of the poet about all that he has lived through, suffered and faced" ("Suggestions About The 'Thrush'," *Charioteer* 27 [1985], pp. 58–59). Seferis lets his mind wander into the secrets of life and death and into the other side of light, which is darkness:

Light, angelic and black,
laughter of waves on the sea's highways,
tear-stained laughter,
the old suppliant sees you
as he moves to cross the invisible fields—
light mirrored in his blood,
the blood that gave birth to Eteocles and Polynices.
Day, angelic and black;
the brackish taste of woman that poisons the
    prisoner
emerges from the wave a cool branch adorned with
    drops.
Sing little Antigone, sing, O sing . . .
I'm not speaking to you about things past, I'm
    speaking
about love;
decorate your hair with the sun's thorns,
dark girl;
the heart of the Scorpion has set,
the tyrant in man has fled,
and all the daughters of the sea, Nereids, Graeae,
hurry to the radiance of the rising goddess;
whoever has never loved will love,
in the light. . . .

We need to hurry to live, says Seferis, before we are enveloped by the black light, darkness. He sees a metaphysical dimension of the light that is the human presence: this is the good light, of life, the angelic light. Love is the purest light, the positive element of life on which a better future can be built.

A decade would elapse before Seferis' next poetic production, *To Cyprus, Where Apollo Foretold Me* (1955), better known as *Logbook III*. In the poet's own first edition, he observes: "The poems of this collection, except for two ("Memory" I and II), were generated in me in the autumn of 1953 when I visited Cyprus for the first time. It was the revelation of a [new] world, and it was the experience of a human drama, which, whatever may be the expediencies of everyday happenings, measures and judges our humanity. . . . It is strange to say this today. But Cyprus is a place where miracles still take place."

Cyprus was also a place in which George Seferis particularly felt the deeply rooted presence of Hellenism. It was 1955 when Cyprus began fighting for its independence and Seferis, appreciating the agony of that struggle, wrote sixteen poems for the island, not of the usual patriotic, rhetorical, conventional type. He expressed the feelings of one who had gone through the frustrating experience of two wars and the sense of betrayal which accompanied that experience. It is interesting that Seferis, a product of the lost Hellenism of Ionia, recognized and was touched by the Hellenism of Cyprus—at Agianapa, at Platres, at Kyrenia, at Salamis, and at Engomi. He saw and heard Greece and the Greek presence. From the dead and the living, from the inanimate and animate, he constantly heard an undying groan, a cry that overwhelmed him. Again in "Salamis in Cyprus" Seferis expressed his hopes and aspirations about Cyprus.

"Helen" is one of the most important poems in this collection. It is charming and warm, hovering between reality and magic, painfully contemporary in sensitivity and purpose. The bitter futility of fighting for the sake of an illusion, for the phantom Helen of Troy—as depicted by Euripides in his *Helen* and Seferis in his—is compared to the sacrifices Greece has made for the West and the ungratefulness of her allies when, in their turn, it comes to helping ensure justice for Cyprus.

The poem's most memorable words may be those of Teucer, the brother of Ajax:

And my brother?
     Nightingale, nightingale, nightingale,
what is a god? What is not a god? And what is there
  in between them?

These words are illustrative of Seferis' use of symbolic language, in which there is continuous correspondence between myth and reality, with the added motif of deceit and betrayal.

In Seferis' last volume of new poetry, *Three Secret Poems,* there are some faint echoes, in theme and technique, of *The Cistern* and *"Thrush."* More stress is now laid on the theme of light. In fact, the poem "Pano se mia himoni-atiki ahtina" ("On a Ray of Winter Sun") reads: "Years ago you said, / 'In essence, I am a matter of light.'" The *Three Secret Poems* are also much more tightly woven and epigrammatic, "secretive" and suggestive. Here Seferis' poetry reaches its peak in simplicity and bare essentials. In the foreword to his translation of these poems, Walter Kaiser writes: "Even in translation, however, it is possible to perceive the shorter lines, the extraordinary economy of means, the compressed lyric intensity, and the greater general austerity of this latest work. Poetry here has been stripped to its naked essence. . . . It is just this quality of utmost simplicity and candor . . . which gives these *Three Secret Poems* their special luminosity and places them among Seferis' most profoundly moving, most intensely personal utterances" (pp. viii–ix). In these poems the reader can detect much more hope, even a hint of joy. Kaiser concludes: "The miracle of these poems . . . is that they encompass so much suffering and so much despair and yet appropriately end on this note of ultimate affirmation" (p. xviii).

Although Seferis' international reputation must necessarily rest on his reputation as a

poet, he also earned considerable esteem as a literary critic, essayist, and translator in the Greek-speaking world. His superb prose style is exhibited in his *Dokimes* (Essays, 1944; translated as *On the Greek Style*), which deal with authors like Constantine Cavafy, Andreas Kalvos, and T. S. Eliot; with history and language (especially the continuity and the proper use of the Greek language); with poetry and philosophy; and with Seferis' travels to ancient and Byzantine sites. Seferis also applied his talent for language to translations of Eliot, Yeats, Pound, MacLeish, Gide, and others into Greek, and to his *metagraphes* (as he called them), transcriptions of the biblical Song of Songs and book of Revelation into modern Greek.

Through Greek suffering and tragedy, Seferis sees the tragedy and suffering of the human race. Through Greek history he sees the continuity of the human experience. At the same time, Seferis is a modern poet who, though much indebted to the French symbolists, is essentially a Greek poet in the best classical tradition. His aim was to be Greek, contemporary, and universal. Like Euripides, he paints men as they are—often stiff and unfeeling like stones and statues—but midst all the destruction, wars, conflict, and tragedy, there remains the creative force of love, and Seferis loves humanity.

Seferis was a human being of unusual sensitivity. Though very much a Greek of the diaspora, he agonized over the tragic nature of Hellenism. The citation of the university orator at Princeton University's 218th commencement (15 June 1965), when Seferis was granted the honorary degree of doctor of letters, may very well encapsulate his life and work:

Like his countrymen of the Golden Age, [Seferis] serves the twin mistresses of art and state, *poiesis* and *polis.* The wisdom and sure sensitivity that he brought to the arts and diplomacy are reflected in the maturity of his poetry, which is as sharp in color, as sparse in ornament, as austerely beautiful as the enduring landscape it so often invokes. The long continuity of the classical spirit glows in his images that reflect the mood of modern man by calling upon the legend and the history of the land he loves and nobly represents, the cradle of Western civilization.

Selected Bibliography

EDITIONS

INDIVIDUAL WORKS

POETRY

Strophe. Athens, 1931.
I sterna. Athens, 1932.
Mythistorema. Athens, 1935.
Imerologio katastromatos. Athens, 1940.
Tetradio gymnasmaton. Athens, 1940.
Imerologio katastromatos B. Alexandria, 1944.
"Kichle." Athens, 1947.
Imerologio katastromatos C. Athens, 1955.
Tria krypha poiemata. Athens, 1966.

PROSE

Dokimes. Athens, 1944; 3d ed., 1974.
Treis meres sta monasteria tis Kappadokias [Three Days at the Monasteries of Cappadocia]. Athens, 1953.
Delphi. In *O tachydromos.* Athens, 1962.
Discours de Stockholm. Athens, 1964.
He glossa sten poiese mas [Language in Our Poetry]. Thessaloniki, 1965.

TRANSLATIONS BY SEFERIS

Antigraphes [Copies]. Athens, 1965.
I apokalypsi tou Ioanni [The Apocalypse of Saint John]. Athens, 1966.
Asma asmaton [The Song of Songs]. Athens, 1966.
T. S. Eliot: Dolophonia stin eglisia [*Murder in the Cathedral*]. 2d ed., Athens, 1965.
T. S. Eliot: I erimi hora kai alla poiemata [*The Waste Land and Other Poems*]. Athens, 1949, 1965.

TRANSLATIONS

Eighteen Texts: Writings by Contemporary Greek Authors. Edited by Willis Barnstone. Cambridge, Mass., 1972.
George Seferis: Collected Poems 1924–1955. Translated and with an introduction by Edmund Keeley and Philip Sherrard. Princeton, 1967; enl. ed., 1981.
The King of Asine and Other Poems. Translated by Bernard Spencer, Nanos Valaoritis, and Lawrence Durrell. Introduction by Rex Warner. London, 1948.
On the Greek Style. Translated by Rex Warner and Th. D. Frangopoulos. Introduction by Rex Warner. Boston, 1966. Selected essays from *Dokimes.*
Poems. Translated, with an introduction and notes, by Rex Warner. London, 1960; Boston, 1961.
Six Poets of Modern Greece. Translated, with an introduction and notes, by Edmund Keeley and Philip Sherrard. London, 1960; New York, 1961.
Three Secret Poems. Translated by Walter Kaiser. Cambridge, Mass., 1969.

BIOGRAPHICAL AND CRITICAL STUDIES

Capri-Karka, Carmen. *Love and the Symbolic Journey in the Poetry of Cavafy, Eliot, and Seferis.* New York, 1982.
———. *War in the Poetry of George Seferis.* New York, 1986.
———, ed. *The Charioteer: An Annual of Modern Greek Culture* 27 (1985). Special issue on George Seferis.
Daskalopoulos, Demetres. *Ergographia Seferi (1931–1979): Bibliographiki dokime* [The Writings of Seferis: A Bibliographical Essay]. Athens, 1979.
Giatromanolakis, Giorgos, ed. *Metagraphes* [Transcriptions]. Athens, 1980.
Karandonis, Andreas. *O poietis Giorgos Seferis* [The Poet George Seferis]. Athens, 1934; 2d ed., 1976.
Keeley, Edmund. *Modern Greek Poetry: Voice and Myth.* Princeton, N.J., 1983.
Labrys 8: George Seferis. April 1983.
Nea Estia. 15 October 1972. Issue dedicated to George Seferis.
Savidis, G. P., ed. *Gia tou Seferi* [For Seferis]. Athens, 1961. Essays commemorating the thirtieth anniversary of *Turning Point.*

Sherrard, Philip. *The Marble Threshing Floor: Studies in Modern Greek Poetry.* London, 1956.

Tsatsos, Ioanna. *My Brother George Seferis.* Translated by Jean Demos. Minneapolis, 1982.

Vayenas, Nasos. *O poietis kai o horeftis: Mia exetasi tis poietikis kai tis poiesis tou Seferi* [The Poet and the Dancer: An Examination of the Poetics and the Poetry of Seferis]. Athens, 1979.

Vitti, Mario. *Phthora kai logos: Eisagogi stin poiesi tou Giorgos Seferi* [Destruction and Discourse: Introduction to the Poetry of George Seferis]. Athens, 1978.

JOHN E. REXINE

IGNAZIO SILONE

(1900–1978)

ANY DISCUSSION OF the work of Ignazio Silone should begin by acknowledging one extraordinary fact: until the 1950's, when he had completed the best and most memorable part of his creative work, Silone enjoyed a solid reputation and a large following in almost every country in the world except his own. He occupied a place in the hearts of the European intellectual community while remaining little known or, what is worse, neglected or eschewed by Italian critics. Those who read his books and knew something of his life were aware of the almost legendary nature of this unusual man. Along with such brilliant poets and novelists as Arthur Koestler, André Malraux, Stephen Spender, and George Orwell, he had been an active member of the Communist party for a number of years, contributing to the strength and charisma enjoyed by communism during the dark, confusing, and hopeless period following the end of World War I. For many intellectuals, communism came to represent the most viable road to peace and well-being for the millions of farmers, factory workers, and working people everywhere, promising to put an end once for all to those conditions which had bred injustice, economic exploitation, political repression, and one war after another.

Unfortunately, our historical perspective has all too frequently been distorted by a kind of hysterical reaction toward most political systems that we have suspected to somehow threaten "the American way of life" (a curious euphemism for "economic interests" of greedy business leaders). This posture has produced an incapacity to understand, for example, that if many people from all walks of life, particularly from the intelligentsia (Silone among them) espoused communism for a time, it was because they believed it to have high on its agenda a vast program of social, political, and economic reforms other ideologies had failed to deliver. Once the excessive zeal and the hunger for power and control of the Communist leadership became evident, the initial enthusiasm of many early converts cooled considerably. Many prominent members of the party became so disillusioned that, like Silone, they broke away from communism, much to the consternation and embarrassment of the Soviets. The experience of these disaffected followers was subsequently recorded in various essays, the best of which were collected in the anthology *The God That Failed* (Richard H. S. Crossman, ed. [London, 1950]).

Silone's break with communism took place relatively early in his life, less than a decade after he, along with Palmiro Togliatti and Antonio Gramsci, had founded the Italian Communist party at Leghorn in 1921. The experience of this break was to prove central in Silone's life. He set himself to give shape and reason to the way he perceived history, politics, and the place of the individual in relation to the state, always trying to reach a more complete understanding of the significance his own political experience had had for his personal life. As we shall see, politics had an enormous impact on his fiction and nonfiction alike. Key themes and issues of his encounter with communism form the substance of every one of his novels, which may be read as a kind of sui generis record of the changes and development of his political education. His resignation from the party and his subsequent criticism of communism and his own church made him an isolated person, as he himself acknowledged more than once: "I consider myself a socialist without a party and a Christian without a Church." His stand as an anticommunist socialist was bound to be unpopular in his country; his status as a literary outsider, a man without strong connections with literary groups or schools, and without a strong, resourceful publisher to develop his work and increase his readership, did not help matters.

Many critics felt that Silone's work did not give much evidence of stylistic or thematic development, a lack turning him into a monotonous writer, a description Alberto Moravia accepted (in a positive way) for his own work: "Good writers are monotonous, like good composers. They keep rewriting the same book. That is to say, they try to perfect their expression of the one problem they were born to understand" ("Ricordo degli *Indifferenti*," *L'uomo come fine* [Milan, 1964]). Silone seemed to echo this idea when he candidly confessed:

The reason that in more than thirty years as an author I have published so few books is, first, that I write very slowly and with great difficulty, but more important, that if it depended on me alone I would forever rewrite one book all my life, just as some painters in the Middle Ages kept painting new versions of the same picture. It is a pity that material considerations force writers to write a book every year, pretending that it is a new one, when it is almost always the same dressed up differently. Fundamentally, most writers have got only one book in them, but for economic reasons they have to assume a prolificness they don't have.

(Quoted in Allsop, p. 49)

Even the experience of writing has been deromanticized by Silone and described more realistically as a demanding, frustrating job. "For me," he confessed on another occasion, "writing has never been, except in a few rare moments of inspiration, a serene aesthetic pleasure. Rather, it has been the painful and solitary continuation of a struggle, after separation from my good friends in the party."

The oddities of what has been called correctly, yet too vaguely, "il caso Silone" (since practically every writer in Italy seems to be a "case," or worthy of special attention for one reason or another!) do not stop here. In a country almost totally Catholic, and yet without a real tradition of a Catholic novel (as in France), Silone managed to weave subtly political and religious themes into most of his novels while remaining profoundly skeptical of the capacity, or will, of the two great institutions, the church and the state, to resolve any of the pressing problems of war and peace, employment, education, and the welfare of the poor and dispossessed. He kept his focus on his native land and yet avoided being parochial, giving the suffering endured by his characters a stamp of universality: "Everything I have written, and probably I may still write, is only concerned with the *small* piece of land that can be seen at a glance from the house where I was born." By the same token, he made the little world of the Marsica, and the region itself, symbols of human endurance. As he wrote in the opening section of *Fontamara* (1933):

All poor farmers are alike in every country. They are men who cause the earth to bear fruit; they suffer from hunger; and whether they are called fellahs, coolies, peons, muzhiks or *cafoni*, they form their own nation, their own race and their own church all over the world, even though no two are exactly alike.

(Fergusson trans., pp. 3–4)

And because life under such conditions is unbearable and unnatural, and since society is generally opposed to any drastic change that will improve the lot of the poor, the possibility of revolution becomes more urgently pervasive. "Revolution," affirms Murica, a young student in *Pane e vino* (*Bread and Wine*, 1937), "is the need to cease to be alone. It is an attempt to remain together, and not be afraid anymore."

Although politics is one of the major components of his work, Silone always maintained that he was apolitical. His chief ambition, in the words of R. W. B. Lewis, Silone's most original and perceptive critic, was "to show, or try to show the age and body of the time its form and pressure." He sought to re-create in his books certain pivotal historical events in a way that would shed light on their significance without ever betraying his own commitment to "truth and hope." Perhaps we have been wrong to view him as a traditional novelist, as Nicola Chiaromonte suggested in a review article of Silone's novel *Una manciata di more* (*A Handful of Blackberries*, 1952), published in 1954:

Rather than novels, Silone's books are apologues and fables. Their theme and their style are those of an educated peasant who speaks so as to be understood by other peasants, who speaks himself through homely and familiar examples; and he must do so in a manner which they understand.

(Nicola Chiaromonte, "Return to Fontamara," *Partisan Review* 21 [1954]: 309)]

Knowing Silone's past, and particularly his experience as a journalist at the age of eighteen, one must realize that whatever he wrote, no matter what form it took, aimed largely at elaborating or reinterpreting his ideas and experience in another period of his life. At one time, when events made it impossible for him to act, he made literature a substitute for action, or even a call for action, accepting all risks involved in such a choice. He insisted that every human being should have freedom, not as a special gift or privilege but as a natural right. In an essay in *Uscita di sicurezza* (*Emergency Exit*, 1965), he offered a partial definition of freedom in these terms: "Freedom is the possibility of doubting. . . . [It is] the possibility of making a mistake, the possibility of experimenting, of saying no to any authority, literary, philosophical, religious, social, or political."

Silone's view of the world reserved a special place for "the need for effective brotherhood, an affirmation of the priority of the human person above all the economic and social mechanism that oppresses him." He was equally demanding about a writer's qualifications and responsibility in today's world. "Writers," Silone observed, "have not only the obligation, but the moral duty to enlighten public opinion on the issues they have studied and analyzed." As he perceived it, the writer's function was becoming increasingly important. He belonged to society, not to the state. "The individual writer must decide for himself whether to 'commit' himself or not—by that, I mean whether or not he takes part in political action. But his duty remains: to defend the individual's rights against invasion and erosion by the State."

The freedom to speak, however, just like the freedom to listen or to address himself to controversial issues and policies, carried a heavy price. Silone was forced to spend almost fifteen years in exile, during which, much like Dante, he wrote his most powerful and moving books. In 1944, the war almost over, he was free to return to his native country and begin a new life with his wife, Darina (née Laracy), a former correspondent for the *New York Herald Tribune*, whom he had met in Switzerland, his home away from home. By 1978, when he passed away in a Swiss clinic, he had written eight novels (of which the last was left incomplete), six collections of essays ranging from autobiography to politics, and scores of editorials and other articles. He was also active in various political and cultural fields.

Yet Silone always thought of himself first and foremost as a writer, and specifically a writer of fiction, an activity that was his special love. He cared deeply about the art of story-telling, as shown by the way in which he care-fully revised, corrected, and even reshaped his novels before they appeared—at long last!—in Italy, in their definitive form. Indeed, he was persuaded that only through fiction could he deal with what he saw as the central themes of his native land, bathing history in the miracu-lous waters of poetry. Object as one may to his perceptions, it is impossible not to admire the honesty and genuine simplicity he dis-plays even when recounting the most trying crises of his life. "It is not pleasant to talk about one's mistakes and follies," he once ob-served, "about one's own hysteria: it is not amusing to live those years of oppression over again, even if only in recollection; but it is our duty to testify."

Just who was this man who spoke with such understanding and compassion about the pain of existence and the problems, personal and universal, close to his sensitivity? He was born Secondo Tranquilli (a name he was obviously to change) on 1 May 1900 in the small village of Pescina, in the central-southern region of the Abruzzi, where for centuries, he wrote, there had been

> no buildings worth looking at but churches and convents, no illustrious sons but saints and hew-ers of stone. The human condition has always been hard . . . and for those whose spirit has been roused, the most acceptable forms of rebellion against their destiny have always been either the Franciscan or the Anarchist.
>
> (Origo, p. 86)

His father was a small landowner; his mother, a weaver. From his earliest years he became aware of the reality and effects of poverty and the pain most people must endure, as in the case of the tragic earthquake of 1915, in which, in just a few seconds, some thirty thousand people died and hundreds of homes simply disappeared. It was a shocking experience, but also shocking were the daily occurrences of social injustice which, unlike the unpredict-able forces of nature, could be rectified. As Silone reached that understanding, there de-veloped in him a sense of outrage and indigna-tion that accompanied him throughout his life and turned him into a kind of activist novelist. He thus joined the group of writers that in-cluded Malraux, Sartre, and Camus. An exam-ple of experiences of this sort was the arrest of some three hundred women and children who had objected to the arrest of three soldiers guilty of a slight offense. Ignazio, barely six-teen, served as a kind of spokesman for the group by making speeches denouncing first the injustice of the action taken against the sol-diers and then, when the case reached the court, the system itself.

Then there was the shocking experience, re-counted in *Emergency Exit,* that took place one Sunday, the day when Italian men and women stroll in their best clothes up and down the boardwalks, the parks, or the main streets of town, to see and to be seen. As he was crossing the street with his mother, Silone witnessed

> the stupid and cruel spectacle of a local young man of good family sicking his dog on a little seamstress as she came out of church. The poor woman was thrown to the ground, badly hurt, and her clothes were ripped to shreds. There was indignation throughout the village, but discreet indignation. No one ever understood where the poor woman got the unfortunate idea of suing the young man, since it had the predictable result of adding the farce of official justice to what she had already gone through. She had the sympathy of everyone, as I have said, and was secretly helped by many; but she could find no one who would testify before the judge, nor a lawyer that would take her case. But the young man's lawyer (considered to be of the left) and some bribed witnesses perjured themselves, swearing to a grotesque version of the incident, accusing the woman of having provoked the dog. The judge, a

worthy and honest man in private life, acquitted the young man and ordered the poor woman to pay the costs of the trial.

(Fergusson trans., pp. 47–48)

Several months later the judge, who happened to be a friend of the Tranquillis, called on them, and while expressing his regrets about the case, he remarked that despite his personal feelings, the decision had been legally correct. Thereupon Silone's mother observed: "What a horrible profession [the judge's]." "Son," she said to Ignazio, "when you grow up be anything, but don't be a judge."

The schools, staffed by priests, offered no alternative to a way of life that had managed to avoid confronting such moral (if not legal *strictu senso*) perversion of justice. The students were instructed in the "truth" of the church, but their answers had to match the questions on the state exams, thus creating a kind of intellectual schizophrenia. Young Ignazio felt that there simply had to be an alternative, and that he must somehow help society change its ways. In 1914 his father passed away, and one year later the earthquake struck the region, a calamity that, strangely enough, rekindled hope in the boy's heart. Long after, again in *Emergency Exit,* he told of how that tragic event had furthered his understanding of the corrupt bureaucratic apparatus of the state. It also persuaded him that society could begin to change only after it had found, through a disaster of considerable magnitude, the bond that unites all of mankind:

What surprised me most was to see with what matter-of-factness the people accepted this tremendous catastrophe. In an area like ours, in which so many injustices went unpunished, the frequency of earthquakes seemed so plausible a fact that it required no explanation. On the contrary, the surprising thing was that earthquakes did not occur more frequently. In an earthquake, everyone dies: rich and poor, learned and illiterate, authorities and people. An earthquake accomplishes what words and laws promise and never achieve: the equality of all. An ephemeral

equality, for when fear had died down, collective misfortune became the opportunity for even greater injustices.

What happened afterward was therefore no surprise, and that was the reconstruction by the State. Because of the way it was done, because of the intrigue, fraud, embezzlement, favoritism, scheming and thievery of every sort to which it gave rise, it appeared a far greater calamity than the natural cataclysm. From that event dates the origin of the popular belief that if humanity is bound to get thoroughly skinned some time or another, it will be not in time of earthquake or war, but in a post-war or post-earthquake period.

(pp. 59–60)

With just a younger brother, Romolo, left (his five brothers and sisters having died of tuberculosis, though Silone later said they died in the earthquake), Ignazio, still in his teens, left for Avezzano and the beginning of what was to be an unusually stormy political career. Persuaded of the inequities of capitalist societies, he pinned his hopes of vast social reforms first on socialism and then on communism, whose programs were promising, if not always adequate. He served for a while as secretary to the Abruzzi Federation of Farmers, then moved to Rome, where he became a member, and then a representative, of the Socialist Youth League. His position allowed him to travel extensively to France, Spain, and Switzerland, and eventually to the Soviet Union. A well-informed politician and a brilliant ideologue, Silone seemed destined to play an important role in the political life of his country. He became chief editor of the Roman Socialist periodical *L'Avanguardia,* and later of the Communist daily *Il Lavoratore* of Trieste. In 1925 Mussolini's government outlawed all political parties except the Fascists. Even before then, Silone reminded his readers that "calling oneself a Socialist or a Communist" meant risking everything, breaking with one's relatives and friends, and not being able to find work.

The political experience of this period culminated in Silone's cofounding of the Italian

Communist party in 1921. In 1927, after being named head of the Interior Office of the party (a position second only to that of Togliatti, who was its secretary), Silone left for Moscow. His stay there proved to be a turning point in his political life. One of the chief items he became involved in there was a controversial report by Leon Trotsky, "Problems of the Chinese Revolution," which addressed the role played by Chiang Kai-shek. To arrive at an honest determination of whether Trotsky should be censored required a careful reading of the report, a move deemed unthinkable by Joseph Stalin. Silone (and Togliatti) agreed that no vote on the question of Trotsky's culpability could or should be taken until all documents in question were released.

The matter, properly muddled by all parties, was eventually resolved just as Stalin had planned. It became clear to Silone and others that at issue was not so much a notorious document as an attempt to control the party's machinery, and eventually the decision-making process of international communism. The mistrust, irritation, and annoyance at Silone's conduct during the "trial" left an indelible mark on all parties involved. Silone later confessed in an interview:

> It was a great crisis in my life, and that, I suppose, has left scars. Although I tried to be an efficient Communist, I was never a good one, because I thought that Communism was something that it is not. It took me longer to find that out than it should have, but all during that period one was so busy in the day-to-day activities that one had no time to scrutinize the true nature of Communism.
>
> (Quoted in Allsop, p. 49)

The political crisis was accompanied by more personal crises. From the time the Italian government had banned all political parties, Silone's name had been prominent among those wanted for questioning and criminal prosecution for illegal activities against the state. His brother, Romolo, was also wanted for questioning, even though he had never been politically active. As Romolo was passing through the northern town of Como, on his way to meet someone who was to furnish him with a false passport and other papers that would permit him to cross over into Switzerland, he was stopped by the police and charged with plotting to murder King Victor Emmanuel III. Only a few hours before his arrest, a bomb had gone off in Milan, shortly before the arrival of the king, who was to open the International Fair. The king escaped unhurt, but several dozen innocent bystanders were killed or injured.

It was simple for the police to construct a case against the brother of a well-known left-wing organizer. Romolo was dragged to the police precinct, interrogated at length, and brutally beaten. Even the horrified reaction of a number of influential persons who protested the arrest and vouched for Romolo's innocence was of no avail. Brought to trial, Romolo stated that he was a Communist, even though he was not. As he later wrote to Ignazio, he had tried to act as he thought Ignazio himself would have acted in his place. He was sentenced to twelve years in prison, of which he served only four, dying of tuberculosis and other infirmities in 1932.

Meanwhile Ignazio, now safe in Switzerland but suffering from tuberculosis so severely that he was almost resigned to not surviving yet another bout with his illness, entered a well-known clinic in Davos. His illness, however, could not curb his intense will to depict and be a witness to the inhuman working conditions of his fellow men, who were always being used and exploited by one evil segment of society or another: the landowners, the bankers, the politicians, or the bureaucrats. So strongly did he feel the urgency of his undertaking that he made it a central theme of his work, a major statement regarding a reality far too compelling to be ignored. In the "Note" to *Fontamara*, he wrote:

Since I was alone there—a stranger with an alias to evade the efforts of the Fascist police to find me—writing became my only means of defense against despair. And since it did not appear that I had long to live, I wrote hurriedly, with unspeakable affliction and anxiety, to set up as best I could that village into which I put the quintessence of myself and my native health so that I could at least die among my own people.

(Fergusson trans., p. x)

And in *Emergency Exit,* he added:

So, driven by homesickness and by a passion for politics that could find no other outlet, I began to write *Fontamara,* that story of poor southern peasants in which I tried to recount the vicissitudes of the clash, at once tragic and grotesque, between their as yet semifeudal mentality and the new form of exploitation and tyranny to which they were being subjected.

(p. 157)

Writing a first novel is seldom an easy undertaking. Writing a story that deals with men and women living in abject, shockingly poor places while living in comfortable, safe surroundings was a tremendous challenge to Silone. That he succeeded so magnificently is a tribute to him not only as a man but also as a novelist whose memory and imagination worked together to invent a village and a story that is profoundly human and, despite its tragic content, filled with robust humor.

Once the work was completed, the search for a publisher began. Because of its political content, however, the search proved to be more difficult, not to say exasperating, than anyone might have imagined. Meanwhile, the novel in manuscript form was read by a Bavarian woman, Nettie Sutro, who found it so beautiful that she began translating it into German. Three years after its completion, the novel appeared, not in the original but in Sutro's translation, with the author and some eight hundred subscribers subsidizing the cost of printing.

Shortly afterward, in 1934, *Fontamara* appeared in English, under the imprint of Harrison Smith and Robert Haas, and then in some two dozen other languages. Its success was immediate and greater than anyone could have imagined. Its theme, its simple style and structure, the manner in which the author presented a picture of Italy so completely different from the traditional romantic one cherished by the majority of readers, yet did so with restraint and compassion, were the first qualities that captured the sympathy of the international reading public.

Italians, on the other hand, had to wait until 1944 for the book to be available in the original language. It appeared in serial form in the Roman magazine *Il Risveglio,* and in book form in 1947, under the imprint "Il Faro." Two years later, Italy's largest publisher, Mondadori of Milan, signed Silone as one of its authors, bringing out a second, thoroughly revised edition of *Fontamara,* followed shortly by a school edition and by several routine reprints at regular intervals of a few years; then, in the 1960's and 1970's, there were paperback editions that turned *Fontamara* into an extraordinary success (at least for those days), with more than 200,000 copies sold. Why did the book fare so well in Italy? How did it manage to say something fresh and new about the condition of its poor while simultaneously breaking off from the native tradition of the novel in Italy? A closer look at the book provides the answers to these and other questions.

A book's first problem is invariably stylistic: In which special way is the writer going to communicate with his readers, and will the style and form be sufficiently effective to enhance his personal view of the world? The problem is far more complicated than it may seem, particularly in a culture that, unlike American culture, has a long history of conflict between the written and the spoken language. It has often been noted that an Italian is born into two languages: his native dialect (mastered in his earliest years, before beginning grade school) and the official language, taught in every school, spoken nationally, and used by all media. (It should be noted here that radio and television, and the new mobility Italians have been enjoying since the end of World War II, have resulted in a dramatic decrease in the importance of dialects.) The question of the lingual difficulties facing a writer is taken up at the very beginning of the novel by the author-narrator himself:

> In what language should I tell this story?
>
> Don't think for a moment that Italian is spoken at Fontamara. It is for us a language learned at school, like Latin, French or Esperanto. It is a foreign tongue for us, a dead language whose vocabulary and grammar have grown apart from our way of acting and expressing ourselves.
>
> Naturally other southern peasants have spoken and written Italian before me, just as we put on shoes, collars and ties when we go to town. But you can tell at a glance how awkward we are. When it shapes our thoughts the Italian language can only mangle and cripple them, so that they appear to have been badly translated. And translation is never direct expression. If it is true that one should learn to think in a language before expressing oneself in it, the trials we go through to speak Italian evidently mean that we cannot really think in it. The Italian culture has always been school culture for us.
>
> (pp. 13–14)

The title of the novel itself is highly symbolic. Fontamara, the name of the town where the action takes place, is a compound noun made up of *fontana* and *amara* (bitter fountain). The fountain is the spring, or force of life, in that barren, mountainous part of the Abruzzi, a region where water is scarce and therefore particularly precious to the life of the *cafoni*, the heroes of Silone's tale.

What exactly is a *cafone?* In contemporary Italian, the term connotes a person who is ill-mannered and boorish, or even a would-be elegant person who behaves like a peasant (in the worst sense). But in the world of Silone, a *cafone* is part of a subclass at the bottom of the

human heap, a "piece of flesh accustomed to suffering," as he writes in *Fontamara.* The animal often, if not exclusively, associated with the *cafone* is the donkey, his constant companion with whom he seems able to communicate. At one point the *cafone* is called "a donkey that reasons" and "an arguing donkey." In a manner strongly reminiscent of Giovanni Verga's masterpiece *I malavoglia* (translated as *The House by the Medlar Tree,* 1881), we learn that the *cafone* has chosen to be "baptized like his donkey with a thrashing." And "he who is born like a donkey, dies like one. Regularly beaten, the evidence of cruel treatment is easily seen in the swollen shoulders, the bad state of its knees, the hairless tail, [and] other signs of everyday living, common to poor people."

Ironically, there are striking differences between a donkey and its master: "A donkey usually works until he is twenty-four, a mule until twenty-two, a horse until fifteen. But the wretched human being works until he is seventy and more. Why has God pity toward animals and not toward man?" For the *cafone,* life is but a punishment that cannot be lessened by tears, prayers, or even hope. Nature and the state are seen as conspiratorial agents bent on making his lot more miserable than it already is. There is no one he can trust: not the lawyer, to whom he often runs for help when he has saved a few coins; not the padrone of the land he works; not the priest. He trusts no ruler, knows that the cards are stacked against him from day one of his life, comes to believe that even thinking is useless, and withdraws into a state of fear and resignation that prevents even the chance of change. This is particularly true of politics, which change nothing except, occasionally, the appearance of things. His only means of self-protection (insofar as his ability to bear life is concerned) are humor and evasion. Laughter helps relieve the pain of tragedy; evasion merely postpones our awareness of the desperate nature of our predicament. Both are temporary and ineffective means to resolve a problem: the music must be faced, our obligations (however unfair or unreasonable) must be discharged, and the chain of sorrow remains unbroken.

If these are, briefly, the main traits of a *cafone* as seen by an observer, it remains for one of the characters, Michele Zompa, to give a direct, realistic characterization of how a *cafone* looks at himself:

> "God is at the head of everything. He commands in Heaven. Everybody knows that.
> "Then comes Prince Torlonia, ruler of the earth.
> "Then come his guards.
> "Then come his guards' dogs.
> "Then nothing.
> "Then more nothing.
> "Then still more nothing.
> "Then come the peasants.
> "That's all."
>
> (pp. 30–31)

The world of the *cafoni* is one that demands our empathy, but it is also one we can hardly love—nor does Silone himself wish that, for it is pitiable and grotesque. It is a world of ignorance, superstition, and abject poverty as permanent conditions—a thought hard to accept by a society like ours, which is founded on the premise, however illusory, of change and improvement—that have pushed the *cafoni* off into a corner of history. Precisely because of this situation, from his very first novel Silone chose to make them conspicuous symbols and constant reminders of neglect and moral failure, never romanticizing the nature of their plight. His only commitment is to understand and help us understand. Only honest representation of things as they are provides some hope, tenuous as it may be, of change.

The novel proper opens with a stark announcement: "On the first of June Fontamara was without electricity for the first time. . . . Fontamara continued to do without electricity. It kept on like this for days and months, until Fontamara got used to moonlight again." Having neglected to pay their electricity bills for far too long, Fontamarans now find themselves having to live without another great miracle of modern technology. At the same time, a visitor riding a bicycle comes to speak with the *cafoni*. At first, they think he is another tax collector. Finally, he succeeds in persuading them he is not. The purpose of Cavaliere Pelino's visit is to ask the Fontamarans to sign a petition (the text of which is not available). Since no new tax is involved, the peasants cheerfully sign.

Little do they know that they have given permission "to change the course of the stream to the lands of the town, 'whose proprietors can invest more capital,'" thus presumably creating new, badly needed jobs for the Fontamarans. The truth is quite different, for the scheme will benefit only the Trader, a clever businessman who also happens to be the mayor of the town. When the purpose of the "petition" becomes clear, a protest takes place and a riot is barely averted. A compromise is worked out between the Trader and the people of Fontamara, with each party agreeing to get three-quarters (?!) of the water for a period of time that is never clear to the Fontamarans. One of the people involved in the negotiations is a lawyer:

> Don Circostanza, who was also known as the People's Friend, had always—as he so constantly reminded us—had a special place in his heart for Fontamara; he was our protector, and it would require a long litany to do justice to him. He had always defended us, but he had ruined us as well. All the lawsuits of Fontamara came through his office, and most of Fontamara's hens and eggs had been ending up in his kitchen for the last forty years as payment to the People's Friend.
>
> (p. 61)

Like much of the book, the episode has an essentially choral quality about it, much like Verga's masterpiece. Silone makes no effort to present his characters in depth by means of traditional techniques. What we learn about Fontamara and its people is conveyed to us through the comments and observations made by the characters themselves. Silone respects the autonomy and sense of privacy of the creations of his imagination. Three people—a man, his wife, and their son—narrate the events of *Fontamara*. With the help of an underground man, dedicated to fighting a tyrannical government, they are making their way into another country, fleeing from Fontamara, which is about to be destroyed by the Fascists in retaliation for having plotted a "revolution: against the State." The tale they tell is one in which they have participated—a story of suffering and injustices in which every peasant is indeed a hero.

Fontamara does not have a central protagonist until the second third of the book. Berardo Viola's towering figure can be fully appreciated only after the qualities of the town and its people have been firmly sketched out. Berardo enjoys the respect and affection of his peers for more than one reason: he is unusually strong, motivated, honest, and resolute in his simple yet ambitious dream for his future. Knowing that he could never live in Fontamara (especially after having been betrayed by a dear old friend), he has decided to emigrate to South America, make his fortune, and never set foot in Fontamara again. He sells a plot of land that had provided the livelihood for his family for many years and buys himself passage on a steamer, only to discover that a recently passed law has suspended all emigration:

And so Berardo had to stay at Fontamara, like an unleashed dog that doesn't know what to do with its freedom and desperately circles around the good thing it has lost.

Nobody thought he was wrong. How can a man of the soil resign himself to the loss of his land? The land had belonged to Berardo's father, and Berardo had worked on it since he was ten years old. Where we live, and probably in other places as well, the relationship between the farmer and his land is a long, hard business, not unlike marriage. It's a sort of sacrament. Just buying land doesn't really make it yours. It gets to be yours after long years of sweat, tears and exhaustion. If you have land you don't sleep nights when the weather is bad; even if you're dead tired, you can't

sleep, for you don't know what's happening to it. In the morning you run to see how it is. If someone else takes your land, even if he gives you money for it, it's always a little as if he had taken your wife. Even when the land is sold, it carries for a long time the name of the man who first had it.

(pp. 78–79)

One day Berardo realizes that his dream of going abroad will never materialize, and decides to settle down to his former life as a farmer. He seeks help from Don Circostanza, and his mother requests that the land the lawyer bought from her son be sold back to him. But Don Circostanza, never minding the sweet proposition, refuses the request. When Berardo becomes incensed and almost violent, Don Circostanza offers him financial assistance in purchasing a small plot of land not far from Fontamara. Once again, nature unleashes its force, and after a frightening storm, the topsoil is washed away and the land is no longer productive. Berardo is at the end of his wits, and senses that his fate has been sealed: try as hard as he can, he will never succeed, at least as a farmer. His latest disaster embitters him even more, and radicalizes his view as to what sort of action is likely to gain concessions from the landowners. His experience has made it abundantly clear that it is impossible to have faith in the prevailing system of justice, because "the law is mad and interpreted by judges who are all townsmen, and is interpreted by lawyers who are all townsmen. How can a farmer ever be right?" Gradually, he becomes an articulate and persuasive exponent of violence—out of a reasoned conviction that those who set the work rules for their farmhands come to understand and accept the idea of an accommodation with their workers only when their comfortable way of life and their property are threatened.

The mounting number of examples of unjust treatment of the poor citizens is dramatically and yet soberly conveyed in chapter 6, which constitutes a sui generis summation of the scandalous behavior of government officials and their reprehensible policies:

> Soldiers had come to Fontamara and raped several women. This was an outrage, nevertheless an understandable one. But that it had been done in the name of the law and in the presence of the chief of police was not understandable at all.
>
> At Fucino the rent of the small tenants had been raised and that of the large tenants lowered, and this was more or less natural. But the proposal had come from the representatives of the small tenants, and this was completely unnatural.
>
> The so-called Fascists had several times beaten, wounded and even killed people who had done nothing but annoy the Trader, and even this might seem natural. But the thugs and assassins had been rewarded by the authorities, and this was entirely inexplicable. In short, it could be said that everything that had happened to us recently was not new and had ample precedents in the past. But the way everything happened was absurd, and we could find no explanation at all for this.

(pp. 152–153)

The list by no means stops here, for it includes examples of the way in which certain businessmen use privileged, sensitive information to reap huge windfall profits at the expense of the farmers. When the government decides to change its wage policy (in order to stimulate capital building and thus reduce unemployment), the *cafoni* are again exploited by being made to pay their debts with their labor, compensation being reduced by a staggering 60 percent. "At least one thing was clear: new laws were coming out every day in favor of the landowners. But only the old laws that were in favor of the peasants were being abolished, the ones that were unfavorable remained."

Life in Fontamara gets no easier with the passing of time: the intensity of exploitation increases each day, and violence escalates accordingly. First electricity is cut off; then there is a ban on discussing what is happening in town ("After all," the podesta cynically points

out, "all peasants' troubles comes [*sic*] from arguing"). Then there is the raid on the town and the raping of the women, followed by the charade of the protest meeting, topped by new government work and emigration laws. It is no wonder that Berardo begins thinking of violence, especially when his fiancée, Elvira, narrowly escapes unhurt thanks to having hidden in the church's bell tower. Without a husband, Berardo realizes, she will never be safe. Having no land nor money, he must go to Rome and find a difficult, even dangerous, well-paying job that no one wants, and marry Elvira with his pride intact. After he leaves, however, he receives word that she has died of mysterious causes. (Her death has a highly sacrificial quality, since she offered her life to God for Berardo's salvation.)

In Rome, meanwhile, Berardo and a friend (one of the narrators of the story) wait in vain for the offer of a job. Broke, they are evicted from their room and head home. At the train station, by chance they meet "the man from Avezzano," a man Berardo had met before. Stopped by the police for a routine check, they are about to be allowed to go when a package containing anti-government propaganda is found nearby. The "man from Avezzano" happens also to be the "Solitary Stranger," a "criminal" wanted by the police because of his subversive work. Berardo, taken to jail, makes it possible for the "man from Avezzano" to be released by confessing that it is he who is the "criminal." Interrogated at length, he refuses to answer any question, and for this he is brutally beaten and dies after much suffering. His death has both religious and political significance: it is, first of all, described in a manner analogous to Christ's death. Just as the Son of God died on the cross so that man might be redeemed, so Berardo dies both to save the "Solitary Stranger" and to allow him and others to carry on the struggle against the tyranny of fascism.

Inspired by his death, a small group of Fontamarans initiate an underground paper. Entitled *What Can We Do?*, it is dedicated to opposing the injustices and abuses of the government, an admirable objective that carries a heavy price: many of those involved in this activity are arrested and killed, while the town itself is destroyed as a warning to others.

The story ends not on a tragic note but with a haunting question:

> With the help of the Solitary Stranger, we've come abroad. But obviously we can't stay here.
> What can we do?
> After so much suffering, so many tears, and so many wounds, so much hate, injustice, and desperation—
> WHAT CAN WE DO?

The important element is that, at long last, questions are being asked even if no solutions are being offered. The people's consciousness is being raised. A struggle against evil can be waged, if only after Berardo has given his life. His act is shining proof that love is a most powerful force capable of bringing about the rebirth of hope and of a sane, decent, humane existence in a world where mankind believes in the concept of brotherhood.

It is easy to see why *Fontamara* was so enthusiastically received by the most disparate audiences and what some of the reasons for its wide success were. To begin with, the nature and quality of the novel helped make it immediately accessible to all readers. Its plot has an almost classical simplicity (good versus evil); its structure is uncomplicated and unpretentious. Silone's approach to—and treatment of—his material is refreshingly candid, with no trace of paternalism. Readers acquainted with Italian literature know that Silone's is no mean achievement. Simplicity of form and content is enhanced by humor, one of his best resources, which he uses with a consummate artistry and sense of timing. His is a special kind of humor, deeply rooted in the life of his native land and the values of its people. No mere ornament to this or other works, it is, as R. W. B. Lewis perceptively notes,

never wit (the humor of the cities), and rarely gaiety; it consists rather of an inexhaustible awareness of the droll and the grotesque in human conduct. . . . He recreates the humor in the mouths of his characters and then circumscribes it with his own vision—a tragic vision turned gentle and faithful, a compelling sanity that measures the most hopeless failures within a dimension of wisdom.

(p. 113)

The purpose of Silone's humor varies greatly: it may lend a special flavor to a comment by the novelist, or it may relieve tension that has been building up, or it may contribute yet another layer of meaning to the character involved. This may explain why so many characters are named after someone in the Bible or in history. Other character names offer a synthesis of what the characters are: Sorcanera (Black Cunt) is a sexually active war widow who will not give up her government pension just for sex; Don Circostanza is a lawyer streetwise in the art of accommodation based on circumstances. Then there are the various scenes, such as the one depicting the Fontamarans being asked questions by the police that are aimed at determining their political allegiance, with most of them ending up as "refractory." There is also the quietly funny opening visit by the Cavaliere Pelino, who comes to collect the signatures of the Fontamarans, asserting that his visit is proof of the state's interest in the rights of its citizens. Of course, he has conveniently forgotten to bring the petition. It does not matter: so long as no new tax is involved, they will sign almost anything. The humor does not hide the fact that the issue at stake is political, a theme obviously fraught with dangers and pitfalls, particularly in view of the ever-present possibility, or temptation, that the author will use the medium to make political points.

The question of Silone and the political novel has been discussed with admirable clarity and thoughtfulness by Irving Howe, who finds Silone's work less exciting and far less rewarding than that of Conrad or James. Silone's shortcomings are to be found in what is also his strength: a rare simplicity, an ability to present complex issues in terms everyone can understand, an almost total absence of literary pretension. As practiced by Silone, the art of the novel is based on anecdotes, humble talk, and folk stories. Yet, his success as a persuasive painter of the condition of the *cafone* with his curious mixture of ignorance and wisdom, his poverty of things and his riches of human decency, can hardly be denied. Silone's Berardo is at once a dispassionate portrayal of a man and, as Giuliana Rigobello writes, "of the very soul of Fontamara, not just the person who inspires the revolt, but the Fontamaran par excellence, who reflects the mentality and virtues of the peasant from the Abruzzi, simple and unpolished: his seriousness, his endurance, his dignity."

Aside from being a good novel, full of insights into the condition of man, *Fontamara* is also a prime document tracing or, better still, narrating in fictionalized form its author's anguished experience with communism and his gradual political awareness. (It must be clear by now that Silone makes of his personal political *via crucis* the very stuff of all his work.) *Fontamara* presents only the stage of its author's search for the ideal political order. From there, we move to the second, crucial phase reflecting Silone's serious misgivings about the party's structure and its leaders' excessive personal ambition. *Bread and Wine,* Silone's second, and probably best, novel, the second of the "trilogy of the exile," deals with this important personal experience.

Bread and Wine is a powerful and memorable book, "possibly," writes R. W. B. Lewis, "the most representative novel of his generation." We think the book is to the political situation of Fascist Italy in the 1920's and 1930's what Moravia's *Gli indifferenti* (*The Time of Indifference,* 1929) was to the moral climate in the early years of Fascism, and what Elio Vittorini's *Le donnne di Messina* (*The Women of Messina,* 1949) was to the hopes for a gentler,

more just, and humane world that typified the years immediately following World War II.

Bread and Wine was written in Switzerland (mostly in Zurich) during 1935 and 1936, with the echoes of Italy's war against Ethiopia foreshadowing the outbreak of an inevitable conflict that would involve most of the world's nations. But while Silone remains faithful to his grand theme, the two novels are strikingly different both in scope and in style. Thus, while *Fontamara*'s style is lean and staccato, with most sentences consisting of just a few words, *Bread and Wine*'s is fuller, more robust, more rounded (one is almost tempted to say "literary"), as befits the theme. While still lacking the tightness and depth of a first-rate novel, the book moves with a surer pace toward its denouement, which some critics have found forced and unnatural. Conceived, according to Silone, as an attempt "to paint a certain society," the work may seem "at first glance . . . a bewildering haphazard novel, a collection of anecdotes held together loosely by the presence of a chase—a stumbling tale that for all its many philosophical meditations seems to descend to the pointless antics of cops and robbers."

The hero of the story is not a *cafone,* but a middle-class intellectual by the name of Pietro Spina who, after spending many years in exile (his last country of residence is Belgium), is returning home to his native Marse to resume his anti-government political activity. The years abroad have hardly been good for him: he is lonely, in poor health, and not altogether sure of how his mission can be carried out most effectively. As the book opens, a small group of people are gathered to celebrate the seventy-fifth birthday of Don Benedetto. They are men in their thirties, whose respect and affection for their former teacher is at once evident. For some time he has been living in his modest home, after having been dismissed from his teaching position—in a private religious school catering to the best families of the region—for being "primitive and crude," which means intellectually independent, incapable of hypocrisy, and morally irreproachable, traits that have endeared him neither to his church nor to the state. Notwithstanding the fact that he is retired, Don Benedetto retains a strong interest in his former students, among whom Pietro Spina is the one he remembers most fondly for his unusual intellect and, more than that, for his unusual spiritual and ethical qualities.

The opening section of the book presents Spina before he actually makes his appearance. Don Benedetto remembers Pietro's outstanding qualities, especially his love of his companions: "The most severe punishments he received during all his years in school were invariably provoked by his protests at what he believed to be undeserved punishments inflicted upon others." He also recalls Pietro's greatest desire, here expressed in Pietro's own words:

> If the prospect of being displayed on altars after one's death, and being prayed and worshipped by a lot of unknown people, mostly ugly old ladies, were not very unpleasant, I should like to be a saint. I should not like to live according to circumstances, environment, and material expediency, but I should like, ignoring the consequences, in every hour of my life to live and struggle for that which seems to me to be right and good. This is why Pietro, dissatisfied with the stance of his church vis-à-vis contemporary politics in his country, saw fit to become more directly involved in helping his fellow men improve their miserable condition.

The ailing Spina seeks shelter from an old friend, Mulazzo Cardile, whom he had met in France years before, and who remembers with a mixture of admiration and affection how the two used to meet after work to talk. Concerned with his friend's health, Mulazzo asks Dr. Nunzio Sacca, a former fellow student of Spina's, to help. To protect him from the police, who had already been notified of his impending return, his friends ask Spina to assume another identity: henceforth he will be Don Paolo Spada, a priest from the archdiocese of Frascati, who is

there for a period of rest and cure. Wearing a cassock, Don Paolo takes a room at an inn run by a widow, Berenice Girasole. It is there that Don Paolo experiences his first crisis. He is urgently summoned to the bedside of a young woman, Bianchina, who is in critical condition after having performed an abortion on herself, and who now requests the last sacraments, which Don Paolo is not authorized to administer. But his kind, reassuring words have an extraordinary effect on Bianchina (who eventually undertakes certain assignments at Spina's request). She heals well enough to begin contributing to the saintly reputation of Don Paolo. The irony of the situation begins emerging: Pietro Spina, member of the Communist party, underground man, and political activist, is wearing the robes and playing the role of a priest, whose church supports the very regime he is fighting.

In Pietrasecca, where he has moved into the inn of Matalena, Don Paolo grows more comfortable in his role every day, and he begins dedicating himself to observing and familiarizing himself with the *cafoni,* striving to reach a deeper understanding of their predicament and to increase their sense of their fate as human beings, a fate that need not be as devastatingly hopeless as it has been. His experience with the *cafoni* is not very hopeful. They are resigned to their lot, and it is extremely problematic to show them that there is a way in which, in a climate of freedom and democracy, they could participate in governing their lives. This bleak state of affairs is partially redeemed by Don Paolo's friendship with Gioacchino, a modest, humble, and compassionate friar with whom he shares his dream of a Kingdom of Heaven that awaits man. The other person with whom Don Paolo establishes a unique bond of friendship is a young woman from one of the most affluent families in town, Cristina Colamartini, a shy, religious, sensitive soul who offers him consolation and encouragement in his self-appointed mission without knowing the political side of his undertakings.

Circumstances make it difficult and dangerous for Don Paolo to accomplish very much, and he realizes the necessity of making contact with the Communist cell of nearby Fossa. However, when the party's demands begin showing a pervasive insensitivity to the worth of the individual person, he realizes that he may no longer be able to work within the structure of the party. This awareness becomes a central theme as the story progresses, informing the book with a moral and intellectual substance that helps create a kind of polemic or, better still, an ideological conflict that gives *Bread and Wine* much of its relevance and vitality.

All this activity makes it more urgent for Don Paolo constantly to re-evaluate his life, his values, and his thoughts about his mission and the formidable obstacles he must surmount if he is to contribute to improving the condition of the peasants. The central dilemmas facing him are emotional and ideological. He is increasingly uneasy about his relationship with Cristina, a relationship that cannot be genuine if he continues playing the part of a priest. He is also deeply troubled by his growing realization that the interests, values, and uniqueness of each human being must never succumb to the trappings of party ideology. He asks himself at one point:

> Is it possible to participate in political life, put oneself at the service of a party and remain sincere? Has not truth become, for me, the truth of party, justice, the justice of party? Interest in the organization, has it not ended with overpowering, even in me, all moral values disparaged as petit bourgeois prejudices and has it itself become the supreme value?
>
> (David and Mosbacher trans., p. 179)

Don Paolo yearns for more time with Cristina, and that feeling is mutual; but, like their physical attraction, it must always be checked and repressed. Aside from their self-discipline, what helps the situation to stay within the boundaries of accepted behavior is the visit to Pietrasecca by Cristina's spiritual adviser. At the request of a nearby convent, he has come to remind Cristina that the nuns and the staff of the convent are waiting for her to keep a vow, made long ago, to enter religious life.

Much work remains to be done. Don Paolo, realizing the importance of re-establishing personal contacts with Communist cells in Rome, leaves for the capital, where the Fascists are busy organizing "spontaneous" demonstrations supporting the imminent invasion of Ethiopia. Among the few persons visited by Don Paolo is an old fellow university student, a violinist by the name of Uliva, who has been an active party member. The two have a spirited debate about many issues of a philosophical and political character. Later that same evening, Don Paolo learns of the deaths of his friend and his wife, who have taken their lives by using the gunpowder with which he was planning to blow up a church scheduled to be visited by several high-ranking Fascist officials. Despite the brief part Uliva has in the story, he is important in that he articulates his profound disappointment with the intellectual and moral character of the party leadership. But beyond this, he also makes some telling comments about what happens when the ideals of a revolution are drowned by hunger for personal power and control, and what the fate of an intellectual proves to be when dissent becomes evidence of betrayal of the dreams of the revolution:

> I read and studied in my privations, and sought for at least a promise of liberation. I found none. Every revolution, every single one, without exception whatever, started as a movement for liberation and finished as a tyranny. For a long time I was tortured by the fact. Why has no revolution escaped that destiny? . . . You have not yet won, you are still an underground movement, you have already become simply a group of professional revolutionaries. The regenerating passion by which we were animated in the student group, has become an ideology, a network of fixed ideas, a cobweb. That is the proof that there is no escape for you, either. And you are only the beginning of a parabola. That is the destiny of every new idea. It is crystallized in formulas so that it may be

propagated. It is entrusted to a body of interpreters so that it may be preserved. That body is prudently recruited, sometimes specifically paid for its task, and is subject to a superior authority whose duty it is to resolve doubts and suppress deviations from the line indicated by the masters. Thus every new idea invariably ends by becoming fixed, inflexible, parasitical, and reactionary. And if it becomes the official doctrine of the state, no more escape is possible. A carpenter or a laborer can perhaps adapt himself even to a regime of totalitarian orthodoxy, and eat, digest, procreate in peace; but for an intellectual there is no escape. He must bend the knee, and either enter the ranks of the dominant clerks, or resign himself to hunger and defamation and be killed off at the first favorable opportunity.

(pp. 180–181)

Back in his native region, Don Paolo decides to pay a visit to Don Benedetto, his former teacher, who has been forced into silence by a church that has grown complacent with its power and authority, and that is too little involved with the spiritual and emotional, not to say economic, problems of its flock. The two share a deep commitment to the cause of the poor people and a strong anti-Fascism rooted in their love of freedom of thought and their belief in the concept of life as a constantly enriching experience.

Their deeply moving meeting is followed by a visit from a young man, a former underground man and a Communist, who tells Don Paolo the story of his life. His parents had made many sacrifices to see him acquire an education, but at a certain point, they were no longer capable of giving him more financial help. Aware of this situation, the secret police had recruited him as a paid political informer, a position for which he had ample qualifications, having many anti-Fascist friends. He had soon realized that he could not continue living an existence of betrayals, and had moved to the country.

Now Don Paolo learns from another underground man that Luigi Murica has just died. Just three days before, he had been searched by the police, who found a piece of paper on which he had written: "Truth and brotherhood will reign among men in the place of hatred and deceit; living labor will reign in the place of money." Taken to the police station, Murica is ridiculed, kicked, and otherwise physically abused until he dies, two days later, after being forced to wear a chamber pot on his head in an irreverent and graphic re-enactment of Jesus' tortures before his death. (Don Benedetto, too, meets a sacrificial death: the Fascists put poison in the sacramental wine, and he falls dead while celebrating mass.)

The story comes to its conclusion after Murica's funeral, during which his friends and relatives eat bread and drink wine, symbolizing a new ideological communion. All of them are anti-Fascist and profoundly Christian (although not in the official Catholic sense of the word). During the funeral, Pietro Spina is told that the police are aware of his true identity. He must run away, leaving a diary in which he has recorded his feelings and thoughts on many aspects of his life, and which he now leaves to Cristina as proof of his love. He then flees, taking the road to the snow-covered mountains. Cristina attempts to follow him, but she becomes lost in a fierce snowstorm and is devoured by a pack of wolves.

For all the thematic similarities of Silone's first two novels, the differences are numerous and profound. Both books deal with the poverty of the *cafoni,* and their exploitation by the state and the middle class that supports it in order to protect its own interests. But *Fontamara* focuses on the gradual emergence of a consciousness that the injustice and repression of Fascism must be brought to an end, through a revolution, if need be. By contrast, *Bread and Wine* proposes the possibility of resolving the problem not through an armed confrontation but through brotherhood and love. The final haunting question asked by the Fontamarans, "WHAT CAN WE DO?" changes in the second novel into a broader, more universal and philosophical question on the very nature of man and the meaning of life. Trying to attempt to deal with, much less answer, this question necessitates a reassessment of our values, an examination of the efficacy of the use of violence, even in order to regain our freedom.

The experience of the book tells us that if force and intellectual persuasion often fail us, love, as *caritas,* never will. Central, in this respect, is the episode of Don Paolo's encounter with a deaf-mute young man, Infante, in chapter 6. Don Paolo is trying to get to know the peasants better, but his "casual encounters left him dissatisfied." He decides to talk to them on an individual basis, so as "to inspire confidence and have confidence." Among the peasants returning home, one, a youth whose "hair ruffled over his brow gave him a wild look, which contrasted with his kind eyes, which were like those of a tame domestic dog," approaches him, and Don Paolo begins to sing his praises of the situation of the working class in Russia.

At the wretched, filthy hovel where he lives, Infante begins preparing a modest meal of corn bread, tomatoes, and an onion, which he shares with the priest. When Don Paolo is told by Matalena, who is summoning him to supper at the inn, that Infante can neither hear nor speak, he is speechless. It is evening by now, and the sickly Don Paolo coughs. The youth fetches his blanket and puts it around the priest's shoulders. In less than three pages Silone conveys in an utterly moving way the universal need for companionship and the ritual of giving to others, of sharing what we have, a profoundly human ritual that has its application to politics as well.

The episode is thus turned into a metaphor of that ideal condition to which Silone aspires. It is only through this way of life, he seems to say, that man can overcome the tragic situation that threatens to render human life a meaningless and cruel hoax. And this is also the way to overcome the apathy and resignation of the masses, the abandonment by some of the old companions of a commitment that should transcend all other earthly preoccupations. Ultimately, as Murica indicates, this kind of existential responsibility for others must be preceded by a moral rebirth of the individual. In the fine novel *Conversazione in Sicilia (In Sicily,* 1938), its author, Elio Vittorini, conveys a similar message through one of his characters, the Great Lombard, who states: "I think precisely this . . . I believe [man] is ripe for something else, for new and different duties, it is this that we feel, I believe, the want of other duties, other things to accomplish for the sake of our conscience in a new sense" (*A Vittorini Omnibus,* p. 21). Silone's Pietro Spina clearly anticipates, in spirit if not in the same words, the feelings expressed by Vittorini's spokesman.

Spina correctly perceives that the importance of a well-phrased political program has traditionally been overemphasized at the expense of truth and morality. Now it is time to show the necessity of persuasion through personal example. Honesty, generosity, compassion—these are the qualities people understand and value far more than empty slogans or manifestos. Communism, much like fascism, is overly preoccupied with propaganda and power: what is needed is exemplary action that occurs at a level most people can understand and that will benefit them without undue delays. And so he turns to Christianity as an inspiring, rich source of the love, care, and concern the poor peasants so desperately need. But Spina's is a Christianity completely divested of its institutional apparatus, the pomp and spectacle that accompany many of the church's activities, which explains the appropriate presence of Jesus in the novel. He is "present," as Irving Howe remarks, "not in His resurrection, but in His agony"; he is a Jesus, therefore, figured in human terms as "the first, and perhaps last, fully human being."

Like Jesus, Pietro seeks to inspire by his example, to show that it is irrelevant to speak of personal sacrifices unless we ourselves are ready to make them; that it is useless to speak of courage unless people see it and recognize it in their leaders; that we can demonstrate what we mean by a fairer distribution of the resources and wealth of our country by putting an end to our traditional attachment to, and craving for, material possessions. Like Silone himself, Spina reaches this understanding only after much suffering and reflection. His growth as a man is made possible by his friendships with Bianchina and Cristina, both of whom awaken in him a love of life per se, and a need for being committed to a cause even when personal experience makes him skeptical of, and ultimately estranged from, the ideals and program of his party.

Just as the theme of *Bread and Wine* is richer than that of *Fontamara,* the same is true with respect to the richness and diversity of the characters. We are no longer locked exclusively in the world of the *cafoni,* and the author's focus has markedly shifted to the middle class—appropriately enough, in view of the original intention to offer a study of a certain society. Yet more than that, *Bread and Wine* is really a novel of dilemmas, the most important being the dilemma of the state versus the individual, and the individual's shrinking power to maintain his intellectual independence and freedom whenever he is perceived to have views that differ from, and therefore threaten, the views and interests of the state. What we remember long after we finish the book is less the re-creation of the social and political scene of the 1930's (absorbing and accurate as it may be) than the ideological, moral, and intellectual struggle taking place in Pietro's mind between the different forces that have formed his values: training, education, and experience, particularly in the areas of politics, religion, and ethics. And these are the new focuses of Silone's next novels.

The third novel of Silone's "trilogy of the exile," or "anti-Fascist cycle," is *Il seme sotto la neve (The Seed Beneath the Snow,* 1941), which was written in 1939 and 1940, and published in many other languages beginning in 1941. The novel appeared in Italy in 1945, the first Silone brought out after his return, which in itself is a strong indication that this was his favorite work. (He later declared that this was "perhaps my most important book, the only one of which at times I reread some passages.") Although *The Seed Beneath the Snow* does not rank as high as the first two novels in literary worth or in critical acclaim, the fact that the work was of primary importance to its author justifies a detailed examination of it, in order to understand Silone's motives in writing it.

The story begins where *Bread and Wine* left off. Pietro Spina is again fleeing from the police. He decides not to take the difficult route through the snowy mountains of wintertime Abruzzi. The word has now spread that he has died, and the finding of human bones bears this out. Actually, these remains belong to Cristina. For the time being, Pietro finds shelter in a stall hewn in the rocky slope of a mountain, near a farmhouse that belongs to Sciatáp. (Sciatáp had spent many years in New York working as a carter, and got his nickname from the interjection "Shut up," which he learned in America and keeps repeating to his fellow villagers.)

Pietro shares the straw floor of the stall with a donkey, who warms him in a setting resembling the stable at Bethlehem. It is here that he meditates on the human condition as he talks to the donkey. And it is here that he observes the growth of a seed near the wooden structure of the stall—a seed that is clearly allegorical indicating a new life developing from pain and difficulty. Later on, as he recalls this experience, Pietro realizes that it was here that he began to detach himself from worldly interests, or at least from active politics in a traditional sense. He feels more and more that he belongs to a tiny minority of human beings, to an "underground world," and he is tempted to yell at the police who are looking for him: "But can't you see, you fools, that I am not one of your kind? . . . I'm one of those whose kingdom is not of this world."

Sciatáp (the first peasant in Silone's novels who proves capable of bourgeois opportunism) threatens to denounce the fugitive Pietro to the Fascist authorities. Then he delivers him for a handsome transportation fee (for the carter he is) to Pietro's octogenarian grandmother, Maria Vincenza, a proud woman with deep loyalties to her family and to old-fashioned values. Undaunted by the lack of support from her family, especially from Pietro's uncle Don Bastiano, she tries to arrange the granting of a pardon to her grandson. The government is willing to decree an official pardon on the condition that Pietro ask for it and thus renounce his opposition to the regime—a condition that he finds unacceptable.

The chase must go on. Whereas in *Bread and Wine* Pietro posed as a priest to evade the police dragnet, he now poses as a former army officer, sporting the uniforms, medals, and documents belonging to his late uncle Don Saverio (who had died in Libya, fighting for his country's efforts to establish an African foothold). The fugitive moves to the nearby town of Acquaviva, and then to an abandoned mill that belongs to Simon-the-Polecat (called Simone the Weasel in another translation). He begins associating with a number of people, all alienated from the government and its policies, who have turned their energies to establishing inner freedom for themselves and deep bonds of friendship and affection for each other. They spend less time theorizing on or preparing for a future revolution and the politics of change than they do on developing their little group, which may be termed an ideal community based on a mixture of anarchist and early Christian principles. One understands why Severino, a member of the group, satirically remarks: "This is the real revolution of our era . . . the collapse of friendship." The members of the group are "companions" with whom one can share more than simply the "bread" (*panis*) that is part of the etymology of "companion." They can also share aspirations and all the essential elements of a spiritual life.

Pietro no longer has the goal of achieving salvation for society, but only for individual human beings. He finds a renewed emphasis on the rejection of material possessions (in a manner reminiscent of Saint Francis of Assisi) and on building a bond of love and concern for other human beings. In fact, Pietro spends much of his time with Infante, the deaf-mute we met in *Bread and Wine*, and struggles to teach him some rudimentary words to express his feelings and needs. This is a hard job, and one from which no financial benefit is to be derived. The presence of the little group is especially effective in the novel because it is developed against a backdrop of the colorless, materialistic life of "others," the affluent middle class who are busy improving their status through connections with the ruling Fascists and filling their coffers with "gold." Yet Silone's talent as a storyteller is too strong to let this work turn into a "novel of ideas" of limited narrative development. On the grotesque level he adds the scatological story of Aunt Eufemia, satirizing the pursuit of riches. For years Eufemia has been amassing, in metal containers, the "remains of her digestion," and when she dies, she wills to her relatives and friends a massive supply of filth in sealed buckets.

The themes of friendship and unselfishness are also exemplified in the final setting of the novel, a farm owned by Cesidio. There Pietro, Simon, and Infante work as sharecroppers without receiving any pay, only food and lodging. They are happy living close to nature and to each other, and enjoying the local wine and food. Cesidio is also a pacifist and an anti-Fascist. During the war against Ethiopia, he goes to the railroad station to greet a friend who is leaving for combat duty, and, being a little drunk, he has no qualms about shouting at him: "Bring back, if you can, a pair of clean hands unstained by blood."

Also on the subject of money, Silone added an important episode in the revised version of this novel. In a flashback, we learn that Pietro's mother had been buried alive in the earthquake of Avezzano in 1915. Pietro's uncle Bastiano had found her corpse under the fallen house and committed the heinous crime of stealing her billfold. But, overtaken by remorse, he did not dare to spend the money. He kept it for twenty years, after which he decided to return it to Pietro and to confess his guilt. Pietro "took the billfold from the ground cautiously, with the same disgust he would have had for a nest of vipers," and burned the banknotes, murmuring "Damned money." This detail is partly autobiographical. When Silone was fifteen years old, his mother was buried alive in the Avezzano earthquake.

Obviously this tragic event may have favored in the youth the formation of a weltanschauung of sorrow and of violent, sacrificial death, which later surfaced in his fiction. It is also interesting to note that Silone used the occurrence of the earthquake to shroud the truth about other tragic deaths in his family. Silone's father and his five brothers and sisters died of tuberculosis. Since many Italians considered tuberculosis an "unmentionable" disease, Silone apparently spread the story that both his parents and his five brothers and sisters had died in the 1915 earthquake. In fact, only his mother died then. (See Alberto Traldi, *Fascism and Fiction* [Metuchen, N.J., 1987], pp. 138–139).

The earthquake is also important because it links the major character Faustina with Pietro's family. Having been left destitute and without any surviving relatives, Faustina is forced, after the earthquake, to live with a male relative of Pietro's, and consequently she is wrongly considered to be a loose woman. Instead, she is a devout Catholic and a deeply honest, spiritual being, very much reminiscent of Cristina in *Bread and Wine*. In an episode added in the revised edition of the novel, we learn that she is so religious and prone to sacrifice that as a child she had asked Jesus to share his crown of thorns with her. Since then she has been plagued with atrocious headaches that no medicine has ever cured; sometimes she can distinctly feel the thorns piercing her brain.

Faustina and Pietro are bound by a platonic, highly spiritualized, and deeply romanticized love. In another addition to the revised version, Silone has Pietro swoon over Faustina and tell her, "I don't know if it's been from this instant or for centuries that I've loved you. . . . I couldn't live in the desert of your absence." The two share a room during some of Pietro's wanderings, although they sleep separately—Faustina in the bed, Pietro on the floor. Then Silone brings in a tragic complication that seals the fate of the main character both as a political fugitive and as an idealistic lover. While Faustina is away for a few days, Infante's father returns from the United States and wants his son, whom he had abandoned as a child, to come and live with him. The deaf-mute does not understand the situation and, terrified by the thought of leaving Pietro and his friends, stabs his father to death. Pietro realizes that the deaf-mute's action was the result of a strong attachment to Pietro himself, and feels responsible for what has happened. He turns himself in to the police, stating that he is the killer, and the novel ends as he is led to jail by two carabinieri.

It must be stressed that in *The Seed Beneath the Snow* the political elements are secondary to the plot and theme. Fascists are no longer bloodthirsty, as in Silone's previous novels; in fact, they are inclined to forgive Pietro if he will only ask for an official pardon. Other political elements are of a grotesque nature. Lice and bedbugs attack a Fascist leader in a flophouse while leaving the other clients alone. Infante learns how to write only question marks, and he goes around painting them on posters and signs; the effect is particularly humorous when he adds them at the end of the Fascist slogans. Silone also injects religion into political themes. For instance, the local ideologue, Marcantonio, wants the carpenter Eutimio to make a combination cross-*fascio,* that is, to superimpose the Fascist bundle of rods on the trunk of the cross and to add an ax to its upper extremity. The carpenter refuses to do so, arguing that Jesus would then have no way to rest on the cross, since the Fascist ax would be exactly where his head is (and because, the carpenter adds, according to a local legend Jesus is still alive and suffering on the cross).

Simon joins in to oppose the project, and sacrilegiously suggests that the Fascists create a symbol by placing a dishful of spaghetti on the cross. He thus pokes fun at the Fascists' opportunism in reaping material advantages from religion, and at their saddling people with a heavy cross to bear.

The denouement of the novel is especially puzzling because Pietro turns himself in to the very police from whom he had been so laboriously trying to escape, and because he relinquishes his much-sought-after freedom to save a deaf-mute who killed his father. There is little doubt that Pietro's final decision must have an allegorical—indeed, a spiritual—meaning. The deaf-mute Infante may symbolize mankind, and Pietro's sacrifice may symbolize the attachment we must feel for any fellow human being, no matter how lowly, if we want to strengthen the bonds of human kinship without which society cannot survive.

Probably the most bewitching aspect of art is the possibility of a pluralistic interpretation of a text. Pietro Spina may be viewed as a paradoxical combination of Stoic philosopher, Christian hermit, and modern existentialist, who makes a decision to live in a Fascist jail with his own kind of unhampered freedom and spirituality, rather than to live like a fugitive in a politically and morally evil society. In other words, he may be a revolutionary who has understood that all political revolutions will fail until each human being has carried out a personal revolution through meditation, honesty, and sacrifice. At the same time, Pietro may want to prove that, as Fascism is everyone's fault, so was the murder of Infante's father, for the human bond unites us in both good and evil; he may thus want to redeem himself and his friends from a political and moral "original sin" that demands expiation. (It must not be forgotten that Silone himself recognized that the character of Pietro Spina—and, earlier, that of the Unknown Hand or the Solitary Stranger—has a strongly Christlike component.) Finally, Infante's murder of his own father, which precipitates Pietro's decision, may itself be symbolic of the genocide of World War II, since the work was written at the outset of the conflagration.

What is most important here is to ascertain that Silone found a spiritual, symbolic way to end the trilogy, which began with the rebellion against Fascism in *Fontamara,* continued in *Bread and Wine* as a search for moral or religious reasons for anti-Fascism, and completed its trajectory in *The Seed Beneath the Snow,* arriving at the theme of a spiritual bond between friends and ultimate sacrifice for the sake of friendship.

It seems proper at this point to examine in at least a cursory fashion the response to the three novels written by Silone during his exile, both because they probably are his best novels and because there later developed the "caso Silone," that is, the case of an author who for years was quite successful abroad and rather unsuccessful at home.

The three novels went through scores of translations and editions all over the Western world; inasmuch as they could not be published in Fascist Italy, editions in Italian were brought out in France and England. Silone enjoyed particular success, both popular and critical, in England and the United States. *Fontamara* and *Bread and Wine* became bestsellers. Graham Greene was so mesmerized by *Fontamara* that, with scant feeling for history (or with little prophetic sense), he recommended it in *The Spectator* as a convincing text for "all who believe that there are different brands of Fascism, and that the Italian trademark is any better than the swastika." (There were also some dissonant notes: Mark Van Doren on the American scene, and the *Times Literary Supplement* on the British, considered *Fontamara* a hackneyed piece of propaganda.)

The Seed Beneath the Snow, however, failed to become a best-seller, probably because, at the beginning of World War II, it was advocating abandonment of political activity in favor of an individual quest for moral introspection.

It elicited some favorable reviews in England, where the *Times Literary Supplement* extolled its "bitter satire aimed at . . . the cheap and windy bombast that for Ignazio Silone is the distilled essence of the Italian Fascist régime." In America, however, it drew strongly unfavorable comments. William Phillips wrote in the *Partisan Review* that Silone showed "foolish heroics . . . lack of will to action," and Malcolm Cowley stated in the *New Republic* that Silone was "groping in darkness." The author responded with a letter to the *New Republic,* "The Things I Stand For," which explained that he had meant to explore "the ethical concepts of Socialism" and which shifted the blame to Marx (whom he accused of having misunderstood the farmers) and also to Ernest Hemingway and Malraux (whom he accused of indulging in Marxist portrayals of "men of steel and action").

When he returned to Italy from Swiss exile and began publishing his works there, Silone was either snubbed or condemned. One reason for this was that his novels had been written several years earlier for a foreign audience and therefore, despite many revisions, appeared quite dated when they were published after the fall of Fascism in Italy. Another was that Italians appreciate moralistic fiction less than Anglo-Americans do, and conversely, they appreciate elegant writing and literary traditions much more. This was a double disadvantage for Silone, who was long on moralism and ideology, and short on literary tradition.

A few examples will suffice. Francesco Jovine (who was still tied to Silone by ideological and regional affinities) castigated his "uneven, dissonant" manner of writing and accused him of having disregarded Verga's teaching. Giuseppe de Robertis commented that in *Fontamara* "nothing happens on time; order and measure are lacking." Giorgio Pullini and Luigi Russo saw Silone's success abroad as having had either political or sociological causes, and argued against his literary or artistic excellence. Emilio Cecchi ventured the hypothesis

that his books read better when translated into another language.

Fontamara did achieve one immediate, though nonliterary, success. Its depiction of the exploitation of the Abruzzi peasants was instrumental in bringing about, in 1950, the expropriation of lands that the Torlonias had acquired by drying up the Fucino lake, and the division of the estate among many farmers.

Rehabilitation came about gradually. Geno Pampaloni praised especially the "moral paradigm, religious suggestion and peasant myth" of *Fontamara,* and the "irony" of *The Seed Beneath the Snow;* the latter novel, having indicated Silone's detachment from politics, pleased Italian (and British) critics much more than it did their American counterparts. Although recognizing that some of Silone's characters are portrayed in a "utopian" light, Ferdinando Virdia stressed the political and even historical merits of Silone's works and attempted to place him in the mainstream of the neorealist current. In 1971 Luce d'Eramo published a survey of nearly one thousand book reviews, interviews, and essays written on Silone that had appeared in publications around the world. Furthermore, she advanced the hypothesis that his works were appreciated in many languages because his prose possessed a "semiological" simplicity that lent itself to translation.

Silone waited more than a decade to publish his next work of fiction. The primary reason for the delay was that, contrary to the idea of disengagement he had expressed in *The Seed Beneath the Snow,* he had gone back into active politics in 1940, just as he was finishing the novel. Under the pressure of the advent of World War II, he became the director of the Swiss-based headquarters of the Italian Socialist party (the same party he had bolted from in 1921 to become a Communist). In this capacity, Silone authored a series of pronouncements so strongly anti-Fascist and anti-Nazi that Mussolini's government asked (in vain) for his extradition from Switzerland. In October

1944, while the war was still raging in northern Italy, he boarded an Allied plane with his wife, Darina, and returned to his native country. For about a year Silone was the managing editor of the Socialist daily *Avanti!* in Rome, and he was also elected to the National Assembly that drafted the new constitution. In the early 1950's, however, he again began to detach himself from active politics.

Another probable reason for his delay in writing new fiction was that Silone preferred, at first, to edit the three novels he had published abroad, making minor plot changes and literally thousands of stylistic revisions. Having seen his works met by snubs and open criticism, he may have been hesitant to write and publish a new novel.

When he finally wrote his next novel, Silone followed the rule that most writers of fiction repeat many of their usual themes. The main concession to novelty in *A Handful of Blackberries* was that it was set in contemporary time, in 1945, after the end of World War II. The main theme, however, is very much reminiscent of *Bread and Wine;* its protagonist, Rocco, returns to his native Abruzzi while breaking away from communism. (Rocco, too, is slightly autobiographical; he has been an active Communist since 1930, and he has even traveled to Soviet Russia.) Silone represents him as a visionary, utopian character, who from the very beginning of the novel refuses to attend the party meetings, and then openly talks against its programs, policies, and leaders. Unfortunately, one may feel that Rocco is anachronistic in complaining about the lack of ideological freedom within the party, and the persecution of dissenters and deviators from the party line. These problems existed within communism long before 1945.

The anticommunist theme is not strong enough to support the plot, partly because Silone fails to find a consistent ideology to substitute for communism. He most likely wanted to avoid a repetition of the themes of *Bread and Wine,* in which Pietro Spina turned from com-

munism to a recovery of an early Christian spirit. Silone does make Rocco declare that his main tenet is a "choice of the poor as comrades," but this latter theme is hardly developed. The only significant action that Rocco engages in to help the poor (and Silone fails to describe it to its completion) is encouraging unemployed farmers to occupy the untilled land in the area.

A few connections are made between communism and the fallen Fascist regime, mainly through the secondary character of Don Alfredo. After amassing quite a fortune as the town's Fascist tax collector (having been appointed by Mussolini because he could pluck a live chicken, feather by feather, without its uttering a single cry), Don Alfredo gives his allegiance to the Communists when he realizes that Fascist Italy is losing the war. His main contribution to his new party is the creation of a Communist Indulgence Office, which metes out fines to former Fascists who want to trade the black shirt for the red flag.

In this work it is clear that, although Fascism is gone, Italy still has its share of problems. The farmers suffer from poverty and neglect. The landowners are greedy and insensitive. All that is done for veterans and destitute farmers is to give token gifts to be distributed through the local Communist cell, which in return agrees not to create problems for the landowners. In a sense, the Communists have become conservative and bourgeois—a charge leveled at them more and more often in modern Italy and elsewhere.

Another important point about *A Handful of Blackberries* is that Silone here dares to carry out one of the few examples in Italian fiction of a portrayal of Communist partisans as savage killers. Silone states that while Rocco commanded a Communist unit, he tried to save people from the firing squad, in particular a soldier who had been drafted into the pro-Fascist army and then captured by the partisans as he was returning home. The Communists killed him, and later, when Rocco began to move away from the party, they unjustly blamed him for the shooting of the soldier. Silone mentions this episode chiefly for its anti-Communist value, but this charge is indirectly leveled at the whole resistance movement, of which the Communist party was the main component; moreover, it must be borne in mind that up to 1952 the ideology of the anti-Fascist resistance was the official ideology of the various government cabinets.

One new element that Silone introduced in this novel—and that had been sorely missed in his previous ones—was the presence of a full-fledged mistress for his main character. Rocco is the lover of Stella, an Austrian Jewish girl who had escaped the Nazis with the help of the charitable mountaineers of the Abruzzi—a relationship that is much gossiped about. Stella, too, is involved in the Communist party, so much so that its leaders attempt to use her to bring Rocco back into the fold and to retrieve papers he had written criticizing the party. As their efforts end in failure, both Stella and Rocco are expelled from the party.

A subplot of the novel, one that also helps to create a denouement, involves the symbol of a trumpet. The trumpet, which, according to Silone, was actually used during the Fascist regime to announce rallies of the Socialist Farmers' League, had been hidden in a monastery by the peasant Lazzaro to prevent the Fascist police from seizing it. Now it is kept hidden because the Communists want to seize it in order to bolster their own rallies. At the very end of the novel the old shepherd Massimiliano, holding his staff and flanked by his dog, harangues an "invisible audience" as he stands in front of the town hall. He announces that the trumpet will be seized from its hideout by an angel and blown to signal the doom of the "worms and vermin" who have tried to snatch it from the peasants (which may mean either the ruling class, or the Fascists, or the Communists). Stella asks him when all this is going to happen, and Massimiliano answers: "Maybe next year, or twenty or five hundred years from now."

Even in this uncertain, fragmentary novel, Silone proves himself a gifted writer by interspersing delightful plot episodes and by giving us felicitous secondary characters. Besides reaching a high level of grotesque irony in his portrayal of Don Alfredo and his Communist Indulgence Office, Silone consummately renders a few other minor characters. It should suffice to mention only Zaccaria, the crippled innkeeper, who takes advantage of the "liberation" by the Allies to set up a band of brigands and smugglers under the guise of an "independent Soviet," and Don Nicola, the old priest who defends the Communist Rocco and his unbaptized, sexually uninhibited girlfriend against his sister's prejudices.

In *Il segreto di Luca* (*The Secret of Luca*, 1956), the peasant's capacity for spirituality is heightened to an extreme level—although outside of the political realm. Luca is a peasant who has been jailed for forty years for a crime he never committed. Although he could easily have defended himself at his trial by revealing that he had spent the night of the crime in a rendezvous with a married woman (to whom he was bound by platonic love), he remained silent to protect her reputation. The woman paid tribute to his loyalty by leaving her husband and spending her life in a convent. The spirituality of the story is heightened by Silone's frequent comparisons between the innocence and suffering of the peasant and that of Jesus.

Using a technique he had never used before (and which illustrates his exceptional talents as a narrator), Silone here employed the devices of a mystery story. The innocence of Luca and the reasons for his silence are unfolded gradually by Andrea, a former teacher who had been banished from the town for his anti-Fascism. Andrea is certain of Luca's innocence because, as a child, he wrote letters to Luca on behalf of his illiterate mother, and read Luca's letters out loud to her—all of which testified to Luca's honor.

Silone's next work of fiction, barely a novelette, was derived from an old short story of his. *La volpe e le camelie* (*The Fox and the Camel-*

lias, 1960) is the story of a "good Fascist," the only one in all of Silone's works. The secret agent Cefalu has been sent from Italy to Switzerland in order to uncover a network of Italian Socialist émigrés who are engaged in anti-Fascist activities. He is severely beaten by a member of the Socialist group named Agostino, who is the hapless suitor of Silvia, the group leader's daughter. There follow a few contrivances that may be considered excessive by some standards. In order not to have his wounds arouse the suspicions of the border guards, Cefalu fakes an automobile accident in Swiss territory, and then asks for shelter on a farm—which turns out to be the farm of the anti-Fascist leader, Daniele, and the hideout of the network. Cefalu is kindheartedly given hospitality, which gives rise to another contrivance: Daniele's daughter Silvia, obviously unaware of the secret agent's identity, falls in love with him, while the latter, similarly unaware of the family's staunch anti-Fascism, reciprocates her feelings.

After things have progressed to the point of a probable engagement of the couple (which causes obvious discomfiture for Agostino), the secret agent accidentally discovers anti-Fascist literature in Daniele's studio, along with a list of the network's members. He is caught in a tragic dilemma, which he solves quite precipitously and dramatically by committing suicide. Silvia and her parents thus become aware of the man's identity, but this only increases their admiration for his desperate attempt at redemption. Although Silone does not give ideological reasons for the suicide, it is made clear that the Fascist agent must have possessed good qualities because he came up against a moral and political impasse (and also because he deserved the love of Silvia, a deeply sensitive, honest girl).

Silone here used the plot of a short story he had published in 1937, but the new version is drastically different. In the story, not only did the Fascist agent not commit suicide but he passed on to the authorities the information he gathered about the underground network, and

had several émigrés arrested when they returned to Italy. It should be added that the novelette includes artistic traits that redeem the many contrivances of the plot. In particular, Silone created a clever metaphor for the agent's activities: a trap that Daniele sets for a fox that has been decimating his poultry.

These brief summaries illustrate that the three novels Silone wrote in Italy fall short of those he wrote during his exile. It is reasonable to assume that the anti-Fascist urgency of his previous works had given an added scope to his fiction, greatly firing his powers of imagination. Once the Fascist question had receded after World War II, Silone played down that theme, and was unable to find a valid substitute in either the anti-Communist slant of *A Handful of Blackberries* or the sentimental puzzles of *The Secret of Luca* and *The Fox and the Camellias.*

The critical reception of these novels in Italy ranged from fair to mediocre; there were neither the devastating critiques nor the uncommon words of praise that his previous works of fiction had elicited. A much more drastic change occurred in opinions abroad. Reviewing *A Handful of Blackberries,* and assessing it along the trajectory initiated by *The Seed Beneath the Snow,* Stephen Spender openly criticized Silone for his lack of a sociopolitical commitment and saw a cause-and-effect relationship between this fault and his loss of prestige. In a review of *The Fox and the Camellias,* V. S. Naipaul similarly cited the paucity of ideological elements and concluded that "the book gives an impression of great weariness and boredom, the sadness of a writer deprived of his cause." This latter remark prompted an impassioned defense by a contributor to the *Times Literary Supplement* (authoritatively identified as Isabel Quigly), who retorted that Silone was instead "an outstanding social historian" who "has not lost his cause, because in the deepest and most humane sense he is a moralist, and every person, every action, every agent, is judged morally" in his fiction. Many more critics voiced their dissatisfaction with

Silone's narrative. Irving Howe and Angus Wilson concurred that he had entered a decline in popularity. Leslie Fiedler and Donald Heiney went so far as to recognize Silone's lack of literary refinement, a fault that had been generously ignored in earlier critiques.

Within a few years, however, Silone's fortunes in Italy saw a marked improvement. In 1965 he published the collection of memoirs and essays, *Emergency Exit,* which brought him national prestige for the first time. Since the essay on his break from Marxism had caused bitter argument with the Communist leader Togliatti, the book was rather unfairly excluded from the runners-up for the Viareggio Prize (which had largely pro-Marxist predilections). Partly to offset the furor that arose from this controversy, Silone was soon awarded the renowned Marzotto Prize, named after the textile manufacturer. Ideological arguments and literary prizes being exceedingly important in the Italian cultural scene, the publicity afforded the author (and the fact that Italy was then enjoying a boom in paperback editions) made it possible for many of his novels to be reissued in the next few years by Mondadori in the popular Oscar series. Editions ran into hundreds of thousands of copies, quite respectable figures in the Italian publishing industry.

Silone's next work of fiction—which was also the last to appear in his lifetime—was written in the form of a play (although of a particularly Italian genre, to be read as a novel rather than to be staged). Oddly enough for Silone, the play was set in the thirteenth century. It was *L'avventura d'un povero cristiano* (*Story of a Humble Christian,* 1968), its protagonist being Fra Pietro da Morrone, the hermit from the Abruzzi who founded a monastic order and who, at the age of eighty, was elected pope—only to become within a few months the first man to abdicate the papacy.

Silone wanted to indicate that he had not been strictly historical. His preface to the play stated that the portrayal of this extraordinary pope had allowed him to illustrate both a resistance to the temptations of power and the moral, spiritual, and utopian character of the Christian message. Furthermore, this hermit-pope character had given him a chance to show the "peasant ecumenical spirit" that binds the *cafoni* of the Abruzzi to peons, coolies, and fellahin of all times, and also the relationship between medieval hermits and contemporary "advocates of social revolution" such as those who had populated his previous works of fiction. (The book has an appendix of a historical nature, which suggests a markedly different interpretation to the whole story.)

The play opens with a monologue by the weaver Concetta, in which she complains about the sorry state of religion. She reminds the audience that, the time being May 1294, the cardinals have been arguing for over two years and have been unable to elect a new pope. There follows a conversation between several Spiritual Franciscans and Morronese friars (the latter being the order founded by Fra Pietro) regarding the plight of their humble congregations in relation to the established orders and hierarchies of the church. One friar issues a stern condemnation of any Christian groups involving more than a handful of people, saying that "a large community is a dangerous, almost diabolical machine, even for those who are part of it," because of the inevitable "compromises and adjustments" required for it to hold and increase its power. Another friar poses the disturbing question of whether "a man can sin even when he is alone," thereby subtly circumscribing the evil within an individual's soul. Silone fails to respond in a modern, existential way, but instead has another friar answer that a good Christian is never completely alone, because when he prays he is with God.

It must be noted, to Silone's credit as a narrator, that he lightens the burden of these ideological remarks by including several humorous characters. For example, the clownish Cerbicca offers a farcical talk on the subject of evangelical contempt for riches. Having heard that money is considered "filth," he volunteers to haul away any such filth that the parish priest may possess. Kicked out of the sacristy, he goes into the church and seizes the alms box, since he interprets the sign "For the Poor" as meaning for himself.

The news soon arrives that the cardinals have agreed to elect Fra Pietro to the papal see. It is brought by a messenger from the king of Naples who comes to the cave on Morrone mountain, where the old hermit lives. Yielding, with reluctance and doubt, to the offer of the supreme religious title, Fra Pietro tries to follow the rule of evangelical poverty: wearing the simple habit of his order, he rides to town on a donkey. Unfortunately, trouble starts as soon as he is crowned pope under the name of Celestine V and takes up residence in Naples. He is angered at the priests and congregations—including those of his own order—who ask for special rights, donations, dispensations. Celestine is disgusted to find out that the church levies taxes on bordellos and that the priests behave like servants of the ruling governments, blessing whatever war is being fought. He finds out that kings (especially the French one) meddle in the administration of the church, which in turn meddles in politics.

Cardinals and secretaries try to explain to Celestine that, in order to survive, the church must abide by the rules of temporal governments. He soon comes under the influence of crafty Cardinal Caetani, who at first tries to control him and then tries to convince him to abdicate. He is told that he must accept the "pretenses" by which any state must abide, and that "man longs for command more than for liberty and virtue." The hermit-pope vainly counters that Christianity should rest on morality and conscience, and that a bishop or pope should not give up "those very qualities that won him respect and the election."

Silone has Celestine V work out the abdication on two levels. Privately, the hermit-pope reaches the conclusion that "the defect lies not so much in the individuals as in the system" of the church, and that he cannot attempt to salvage the church because "the disease has spread to many parts of the body." Publicly, however, he explains his unprecedented desire to abdicate from the papacy with his "lack of doctrine," his physical weakness, his need to return to the simple life of a hermit, and "the wickedness of the world."

The former pope now assumes the name of Pier Celestine and returns to his cave in the Abruzzi. Cardinal Caetani is elected pope with the title of Boniface VIII, and has his predecessor arrested. In a final confrontation, the old hermit reiterates his belief in the "apparent absurdities" of Christianity—that is, in the love of poverty, charity, meekness, and spirituality—while the new pope reiterates that these "heroic commandments" cannot be made into a "rule of government." The old hermit soon dies in jail, amid rumors that he has been put to death by his captor.

There follow some fifteen pages of historical notes, written—or at least approved—by Silone. The reader will find much useful information in them, including the similarities between the Franciscan Spirituals and the Morronese friars, and the proclamation of Pier Celestine as a saint. (He was given this honor largely to vent the hatred of the French king for Boniface VIII.) For the purpose of the present survey, the most important information is that which allows an interpretation of Celestine V different from—and historically more accurate than—the one expressed in the play. He is portrayed as lacking political and cultural qualities to the extent that "it was impossible for him to be aware of the crisis of his time, caused by the break-up of the old feudal world and *Christianitas,* and the rise of the new social needs." These historical notes also give several divergent interpretations of Pier Celestine, as quoted from Italian scholars ranging from Petrarch to Dante's commentators. The former considered him divinely inspired and praised his longing for a peaceful life. The latter identified him with the unnamed "slothful" placed by Dante in the vestibule of *Inferno* as "he who out of cowardice made the great refusal."

It should not be difficult to perceive that the ideological elements here overwhelm the artistic ones (although the latter are considerable), and that the author merely transposed some of his favorite themes into the thirteenth century. The creation of the hermit-pope probably comes closer than any of Silone's other characters to the painting and repainting of the same portrait of Jesus by medieval monks, which Silone used as an example of his writing and rewriting on the same subject. Pier Celestine and his friars are, to some extent, "spiritual revolutionaries" of the type of Pietro Spina, and are also Abruzzese peasants of the type of the Fontamarans. It may be added that Silone's inspiration is greatly drawn from a sharp Manichaean dichotomy between virtuous losers (such as Pier Celestine and his friars, or Pietro Spina and his friends) and violent rulers (such as Boniface VIII or Benito Mussolini), with substantial similarities that transcend the centuries between. It is also possible that when Silone had Cardinal Caetani talk about the "pretenses" by which a state must abide, or about man's greater longing for power than for virtue, he had Machiavelli in mind. Although *The Prince* was published in the sixteenth century, Machiavelli espoused a pessimistic view of mankind and Christianity that would have made a sharp contrast with the utopian, naive views of the hermit-pope.

The story struck a responsive chord in the Italian public, not only because it involved the church and the relationship between morality and papal authority, but also because it dealt with the very re-examination of Catholicism that had been started a few years earlier by Pope John XXIII. It is not surprising that this became Silone's first work of fiction to be "blessed" in Italy (the pun may be excused in light of the subject matter) by critical acclaim, large sales, and a highly prestigious literary prize, the Campiello of Venice.

A few excerpts from favorable reviews will suffice to give an idea of the response. Guido Piovene wrote that "it is time to recognize that Silone . . . is one of our few living writers endowed with greatness." Geno Pampaloni praised the "outrageously moral truth" of Celestine's dramatic plight. Gabriele Sartorelli pointed out that Silone had taken some liberties with historical evidence, but that it was precisely because of these liberties that he dealt with "the old and new themes of the Church" at the level of the papacy, and not simply at the level of the parish priests of his previous works of fiction. Father Alessandro Scurani excused another shortcoming, this one in the realm of religion, by pointing out that Silone had availed himself of the "popular" rather than of the scholarly body of Christian thought, and that his condemnation of the papacy could be more easily accepted if seen within the "two aspects" of the church: human and divine.

Needless to say, there were some negative reviews as well. The anonymous literary critic of the pro-Communist *Paese Sera* castigated the play largely because it was based on a "renunciation" of social change and improvements. Father Domenico Grasso, S.J., criticized it because Silone blamed the system of the church and too easily forgot the "original sin" that, according to church doctrine, affects all individuals.

The response in English-speaking countries was modest in terms of sales but slightly favorable in terms of literary critiques. The anonymous reviewer of the *Times Literary Supplement* remarked that Silone was "not exactly a novelist or historian or essayist, but all three," and that "the hopeful upheavals of the present-day Church . . . give an added point to this personal view of history." Writing in the *New York Times Book Review*, Irving Howe termed the play "a moral fable" told "with an ear for peasant speech." The American Catholic periodical *Commonweal* carried a rather unfavorable review by Father James Gaffney. Silone is described as an "undisguisedly didactic writer," and the play as "historical fiction" about "the most blundering and inefficient of popes." For once, the "Silone case" had somewhat reversed itself. Now his ideology favored a success in Italy, but not abroad.

Old and suffering from recurrent bouts of tuberculosis, Silone wrote very little during the last decade of his life. When he died on 22 August 1978, at the age of seventy-eight, his wife, Darina, took up the task of completing the novelette *Severina* (1981), which he had left in a badly unfinished state. She filled in whole chapters, using the notes enclosed with the manuscript and remembering their conversations about the story. The novelette has the distinction of being Silone's only work of fiction to have a female protagonist.

Severina is a teacher-nun who lives in the Abruzzi in the 1970's and breaks away from the church for political and moral reasons. The change in her attitude comes through a chance event. She happens to witness a savage beating by the police of a hapless youth who had participated in a leftist rally against the government. The youth dies, and the police claim that he was beaten by unknown assailants. When the nun steps forward to accuse the police, her superiors warn her of the implications of her testimony, and discourage her from setting herself against the government and abetting the leftist opposition groups. Insistent on her loyalty to truth, the nun becomes disgusted with the opportunism and hypocrisy of her superiors. She leaves both the order to which she belongs and the school in which she teaches. Severina even loses her faith in God, retaining just a hope of being able to recapture it. She then joins a student protest group, is mortally wounded by police fire during a demonstration, and, before dying, donates her body for transplant use.

Whereas *Severina* cannot be properly assessed at the literary level because it was largely written by Silone's wife, the novel may be assessed at the ideological level on the basis of its story. Silone clearly indicates that political oppression of dissenters and police brutality continued in post-Fascist Italy with the consent of the ruling classes, and even of the Catholic hierarchy. Things were not as bad as under the Duce, but they were still bad. Moreover, although the general sentiment is definitely pro-leftist, no mention of any leftist party or organization is to be found in the novel. It must be stressed that the story clearly shows the author's detachment from religious structures. Silone may insist on the importance of Christian principles, but he does not want to belong to any existing church. In a way, the novel was an attempt to render, on a narrative plane, his own position, which in the last years of his life he often referred to as being that of "a Christian without a Church and a Socialist without a party."

In the preface and in extensive notes to the book, Darina Silone describes the manner in which she had completed the manuscript, adding that Silone had meant to pattern his heroine after the French Christian existentialist Simone Weil. The last months of Silone's life are also described, and a reproduction of his will is included, in which he asked to be buried without religious ceremony, under a rock with no name or epitaph on it, near the bell tower of the church of St. Berardo in his hometown of Pescina dei Marsi. (Berardo was the main character of *Fontamara*.) It should be noted that, as he neared death, Silone felt a taste of poverty, a condition he had often ascribed to his heroes. His last best-seller, on Celestine V, already dated some ten years back, and reissues of his previous works were yielding very low royalties. The president of the Italian republic, Sandro Pertini, who had been Silone's comrade in the Socialist party, personally intervened to offer state money.

A few more words should be said concerning some of Silone's works that have not been included in the present survey.

In 1938 Silone published *La scuola dei dittatori* (*The School of Dictators*), a combination Machiavellian treatise and Socratic dialogue on the subject of Fascism. (Appearing initially in German translation, the work was not published in Italian until 1962). It is basically an essay, and as such it remains largely outside the scope of the present work, which is devoted to Silone's fiction. Yet its "frame" is of a fiction type. The dialogues are spun by three main characters: Thomas the Cynic, an Italian émigré who lives in Switzerland, and the Americans Mr. Double You and Professor Pickup, who aspire to establish a Fascist dictatorship in the United States. The basic theme is ironic. Thomas the Cynic (who obviously is the author's mouthpiece) deeply despises Mussolini, Hitler, and their like, and yet he sadly acknowledges that Nazi fascism is the proper form of government for the masses of bourgeois opportunists who infest the world. However, at the same time, he prefers to belong to the tiny and powerless elite of anti-Fascist nonconformists.

Also in 1938, Silone published *Mazzini* (*The Living Thoughts of Mazzini*), which consisted of an essay on the Italian patriot and excerpts from his writings. In 1944 he published the play *Ed egli si nascose* (*And He Did Himself*), which is based on the novel *Bread and Wine* and shares most of its main characters. In 1958 he published *Un dialogo difficile: Sono liberi gli scrittori russi?* (*An Impossible Dialogue Between Ivan Anissimov and Silone*), consisting of the letters he exchanged with the Russian writer Anissimov, and of comments about the limitations of freedom for literary writers in the Soviet Union.

There are also the hundreds of articles and essays that Silone wrote throughout his life for political or cultural publications. The cultural reviews he either founded or directed were *Information* (founded in 1931 in Zurich), *Europa Socialista* of Rome (which he directed in the late 1940's), and *Tempo presente,* also of Rome (founded in 1955, and codirected with Nicola Chiaromonte until its demise in 1968). Silone also directed cultural institutions, such as the Italian branches of the PEN Club and of the Movement for Freedom of Culture.

Of paramount importance in Silone's fiction is the fact that he successfully exploits the principles of morality and of early Christian spirituality. This is true not only of novels of a political nature, or what Italians call "romanzo-saggio" (novel of ideas), but also of novels for general consumption (such as *The Secret of Luca*) and of the historical play *The Story of a Humble Christian.* Italian literature is generally quite impoverished in this respect, so much so that, in order to find suitable derivations in this realm, we have to go back to the Romantic period or to writers like Alessandro Manzoni, Francesco Guerrazzi, and Antonio Fogazzaro.

Another great virtue of Silone is the unsophisticated quality of his message. His themes are deep and yet extremely simple, and they are rendered in his typically unadorned, sincere style, which runs contrary to the literary refinements usually practiced in Italy. Indeed, with his pervasive simplicity, Silone gives us one of the finest examples of harmony between content and form, between the qualities of his heroes and the natural, emotionally charged way in which they talk. He may be compared to a spinner of folktales, or to the artists who carved the softly hued bas-reliefs that adorn old churches in Italy and the wooden statues of saints that still show the knots and grains of the wood. It was his fate that his books were, at first, appreciated much more abroad than at home; but Italians have a satirical adage according to which foreigners appreciate and know Italian art better than Italians do.

This abundance of moral elements and paucity of literary refinement are prime reasons for the slights and snubs suffered by Silone at home. To these two reasons we must add, both as cause and as effect, that throughout his life Silone remained very much an isolated writer. He broke away from the political and religious organizations that make up much of Italy's cultural life. And he also kept away from the literary circles of Rome, in which writers influenced likes and dislikes, and carried out an elusive interplay between themselves and critics or prize panelists. Much like the heroes of his novels, Silone preferred either solitude or the company of a few friends. His behavior falls in line with clichés about the people from the Abruzzi, according to which they are "forti e gentili" (strong and gentle) and suspicious of those who are not either neighbors or trusted friends. Moreover, they are quite stubborn, and prefer sincerity, simplicity, and modesty to the showy ways of outsiders. (Little wonder that, possessing these characteristics, Silone could not long remain in politics, where the rule was ostentation, demagoguery, and duplicity.)

Through a combination of moral, religious, and highly individualistic elements Silone creates the fundamental dichotomy inherent in his thematics or poetics: the rulers are violent, mass-organized Cains who oppress the individualistic, nonviolent Abels. Bringing this discourse a step further, one may notice that Silone favors a utopian solution, in which his ideal society is formed by communities of innocent, childlike, philosophizing friends who carry very little, if any, power.

This outlook is double-edged. On the one hand, it undoubtedly advocates morality and social justice, thus combating the sadly typical form of Italy's—or any country's—authoritarian, inefficient, rhetorical, corrupt government. On the other hand, by advocating individual responsibilities and individual solutions, it also risks advocating a most pernicious trait of Italian society, namely, the temptation of anarchy, the fragmentation into myriad individuals or groups.

To Silone's eclectic literary derivations we may thus add both the timeless fables of God and Satan, and the works of political science fiction such as Evgeny Zamyatin's *My* (*We*, 1924), Aldous Huxley's *Brave New World* (1932), and Orwell's *Nineteen Eighty-Four* (1949), whose old-fashioned, morally superior heroes are oppressed by materialistic rulers. This dichotomy of "good" and "bad" allows Silone to effectively portray two struggling groups and makes him one of the foremost novelists to deal with fascism. But at the same time it causes excessive abstraction and idealization by simplistically dividing characters into "good guys" and "bad guys" and eliminating any chiaroscuro of virtues and vices within any single individual. It follows that Silone veers toward moralism and a novel of ideas (and perhaps even toward satire or surrealism), which indicates the need for a change in perspective about his works similar to that which has been proposed for other writers of the so-called *neorealismo* group (such as Cesare Pavese and Elio Vittorini, in whose works substantially nonrealistic elements were later detected).

The defects and excesses of this ethical-ideological division are ultimately responsible for the wide meanings of Silone's narratives. The deformations and nonrealistic elements of his work allow these portrayals to reflect not only on the plight of the Abruzzi people, but on the plight of all oppressed minorities. Silone wanted to show through his characters that one might exert the wisdom, courage, and strength that Italians needed to resist an encroaching autocracy, and that any society needs in order to rebel against its oppressors.

Finally, there can be seen in Silone's works a great vindication of the overwhelming power of fantasy over reality, which occurred at the very onset of *neorealismo,* a movement to which he had been rightly connected as an early member. In the 1940's *neorealismo* was assessed basically as a true-to-life tendency in fiction, as shown in the works by Vittorini, Pavese, Vasco Pratolini, and Silone. However, starting in the mid 1950's, Italian literary critics reassessed the mixture of realism and fantasy present in the works of this movement, detecting substantial doses of fantastic elements, especially in the realm of lyricism and moralism.

It is hard to deny that Silone, who more than any other major Italian novelist knew intimately the intricacies of—and shared in the power of—contemporary politics, gave us some of the most fantastic, idealized, and even romanticized novels about Italian political and historical events. Indeed, he represents one of the very best examples of fiction as a complement to history, of the writer's imagination availing itself of its knowledge of human aspirations to fill the gaps that scholarly works leave in the portrayal of human events. Therefore, rather than writing as a politically accurate author, Silone wrote as a disgruntled moralist and a gloomy prophet. Rather than being a chronicler of historically limited periods, he made his works into allegories of the eternal fight between good and evil, and thereby extended their meaning to reflect on the history of our own troubled society.

Selected Bibliography

EDITIONS

Fontamara. Zurich and Paris, 1933; rev. ed., Milan, 1949.

Pane e vino. Lugano, Switzerland, 1937; rev. ed., *Vino e pane.* Milan, 1955.

Il seme sotto la neve. Lugano, Switzerland, 1941; rev. ed., Milan, 1950.

Ed egli si nascose. Zurich and Lugano, 1944; rev. ed., Milan, 1965.

Una manciata di more. Milan, 1952.

Il segreto di Luca. Milan, 1956.

La volpe e le camelie. Milan, 1960.

La scuola dei dittatori. Milan, 1962.

Uscita di sicurezza. Florence, 1965.

L'avventura d'un povero cristiano. Milan, 1968.

Severina. Edited by Darina Silone. Milan, 1981.

TRANSLATIONS

And He Hid Himself. Translated by Darina Laracy Silone. New York and London, 1945.

Bread and Wine. Translated by Gwenda David and Eric Mosbacher. New York, 1937. Rev. ed. translated by Harvey Fergusson II. New York, 1962.

Emergency Exit. Translated by Harvey Fergusson II. New York, 1968.

Fontamara. Translated by Michael Wharf. New York, 1934. Rev. ed. translated by Harvey Fergusson II. New York, 1960.

The Fox and the Camellias. Translated by Eric Mosbacher. New York, 1961.

A Handful of Blackberries. Translated by Darina Silone. New York, 1953.

The School of Dictators. Translated by Gwenda David and Eric Mosbacher. New York, 1938. Rev. ed. translated by Harvey Fergusson II. New York, 1961.

The Secret of Luca. Translated by Darina Silone. New York, 1958.

The Seed Beneath the Snow. Translated by Frances Frenaye. New York, 1942. Rev. ed. translated by Harvey Fergusson II. New York, 1962.

The Story of a Humble Christian. Translated by William Weaver. New York, 1970.

BIOGRAPHICAL AND CRITICAL STUDIES

Agnello, Nino. "Silone e Pirandello: Sanità senza santi." *Ipotesi* 12–13 (3–1):56–63 (1984–1985).

Alei, R., ed. *Socialista senza partito e cristiano senza chiesa.* Rome, 1974.

Allsop, Kenneth. "Ignazio Silone." *Encounter* 18:49–51 (1962).

Annoni, Carlo. *Invito alla lettura di Silone.* Milan, 1974.

Aragno, Piero. *Il romanzo di Silone.* Ravenna, 1975.

Bergin, Thomas G. "From Revolution to Freedom." *Saturday Review,* 24 October 1953, 62–64.

Bocelli, Arnaldo. "Itinerario di Ignazio Silone." *Nuova Antologia* 487:25–33 (1966).

Canfield, Dorothy. "Fontamara." *Book-of-the-Month Club News,* October 1934, 4.

Caserta, Ernesto G. "The Meaning of Christianity in the Novels of Silone." *Italian Quarterly* 16 (62–63):19–39 (1972).

Cassata, Maria Letizia. *Gli uomini di Silone.* Gubbio, 1967.

———, ed. Introduction to *Paese dell'anima.* 2d ed., Milan, 1968.

Circeo, Ermanno. *Da Croce a Silone.* Rome, 1981. Pp. 105–141.

Cowley, Malcolm. "Donkey Town in Italy." *New Republic,* 10 October 1934, 247.

———. Foreword to *Fontamara.* Rev. ed., New York, 1960.

D'Eramo, Luce. *L'opera di Ignazio Silone: Saggio critico e guida bibliografica.* Milan, 1971.

Esposito, V. *Ignazio Silone: La vita, le opere, il pensiero.* Rome, 1979.

Fadiman, Clifton. "Fontamara." *The New Yorker,* 22 September 1934, 101.

Falconi, Carlo. "La letteratura italiana ispirata al Marxismo." *Humanitas,* May 1950, 512–542.

Falqui, Enrico. "Ignazio Silone. 'Una manciata di more.'" *La Fiera Letteraria,* 11 April 1954, 3-4.

Reprinted in *Novecento Letterario. Vol. 3.* Florence, 1961. Pp. 522–528.

——— . "I settant'anni di Silone e i quarant'anni di *Fontamara." Il dramma,* May 1970.

Georges, Robert A. "Silone's Use of Folk Beliefs." *Midwest Folklore* 12:197–203 (1962).

Guerriero, Elio. *L'inquietudine e l'utopia: Il racconto umano e cristiano di Ignazio Silone.* Milan, 1979.

Heiney, Donald. "Silone: Emigration as the Opiate of the People." In *America in Modern Italian Literature.* New Brunswick, N. J., 1965. Pp. 114–125.

Howe, Irving. *Politics and the Novel.* New York, 1957. Pp. 217–226.

——— . Book review of the revised edition of *Fontamara. New Republic,* 12 September 1960, 27.

——— . "Ignazio Silone: Politics and the Novel." In *From Verismo to Experimentalism: Essays on the Modern Italian Novel,* edited by Sergio Pacifici. Bloomington, Ind. 1970. Pp. 120–134.

Krieger, Murray. "Ignazio Silone." In *The Tragic Vision: Variations on a Theme in Literary Interpretation.* New York: 1960. Pp. 72–85.

Lewis, R. W. B. "Ignazio Silone: The Politics of Charity." In *The Picaresque Saint.* Philadelphia, 1956. Pp. 109–178.

Lombardi, Olga. "Ignazio Silone." In *Novecento.* Vol. 8. Milan, 1982. Pp. 6959–6985.

Lucente, Gregory. "Signs and History in *Bread and Wine:* Silone's Dilemma of Social Change." *Novel: A Forum in Fiction* 16:230–245 (1983).

Marabini, Claudio. *Gli anni sessanta, narrativa e storia.* Milan, 1969. Pp. 259–274.

Mariani, Mario. "Ignazio Silone." In *Letteratura italiana: I contemporanei.* Vol. 3. Milan, 1969. Pp. 371–390.

McAfee-Brown, Robert. "Ignazio Silone and the Pseudonyms of God." In *The Shapeless God,* edited by Harry J. Mooney, Jr., and Thomas F. Staley. Pittsburgh, 1968. Pp. 19–40.

Mitgang, Herbert. "A Talk with Ignazio Silone About *Bread and Wine." New York Times Book Review,* 21 October 1962, 4.

Origo, Iris. "Ignazio Silone: A Study in Integrity." *Atlantic Monthly* 219:86–93 (1967).

Pacifici, Sergio. *A Guide to Contemporary Italian Literature from Futurism to Neorealism.* New York, 1962; repr. Carbondale, Ill., 1972. Pp. 121–124.

Pampaloni, Geno. "L'opera narrativa di Ignazio Silone." *Il Ponte,* January 1949, 49–58.

Petrocchi, Giorgio. "Vent'anni di Fontamara." *Humanitas* 4:759–758 (July 1949).

——— . "Il romanzo italiano di Ignazio Silone." In *Poesia e tecnica narrativa.* Milan, 1962.

Petroni, Guglielmo. "Testimonianza a Silone." *La Fiera Letteraria,* 11 December 1949, 1–2.

[Quigly, Isabel.] "Moralist with a Cause." *Times Literary Supplement,* 18 August 1961, 543.

Radcliff-Umstead, Douglas. "Animal Symbolism in Silone's *Vino e pane." Italica* 49:18–29 (1972).

Rawson, Judy. "Silone's Early Fiction and Its Abruzzo 'Subsoil.'" *Italian Studies* 40:93–104 (1985).

Rigobello, Giuliana. *Ignazio Silone.* Florence, 1975.

Schneider, Franz. "Scriptural Symbolism in Silone's *Bread and Wine." Italica* 44:387–399 (1967).

Scott, Nathan A. "Ignazio Silone." In *Rehearsals of Discomposure.* New York, 1952. Pp. 66–111.

Scurani, Alessandro. *Ignazio Silone: Un amore religio per la giustizia.* Milan, 1969.

Silone, Darina. "The Last Hours of Ignazio Silone." *Partisan Review* 51(1):79–90 (1984).

Spender, Stephen. "Village Soviet of the Barefoot Band." *New York Times Book Review,* 18 October 1953, 4.

Tarola, L. *Trilogia siloniana: I romanzi dell'esilio.* Avezzano, 1978.

Taylor-Gatti, Marisa, and Steven M. Taylor. "Eschatological Christianity in Dostoevsky and Silone." *Renascence* 34:131–143 (1982).

Virdia, Ferdinando. *Silone.* Florence, 1967; 2d, enl. ed., 1979.

Viti, G. *Il romanzo italiano del novecento.* Florence, 1978.

Weatherhead, Kingsley A. "Ignazio Silone: Community and the Failure of Language." *Modern Fiction Studies* 7:157–168 (1961).

SERGIO PACIFICI
ALBERTO TRALDI

ANTOINE DE SAINT-EXUPÉRY

(1900–1944)

FOR MANY READERS, Saint-Exupéry is the quintessential "heroic" writer of the first half of the twentieth century, a novelist who, as Germaine Brée has remarked, looks more like the hero of a novel. As a pilot, he participated in the new age of aviation during those pioneer days when to fly was an adventure, and again in wartime as a fighter against the invaders of his country. As a writer he set down in a spare, lyrical prose that would become the hallmark of his style his compassionate view of mankind and the record of his adventures, discoveries, and reflections. Not surprisingly, these have more to do with the psychological and moral nature of man than with geography or technology, because for Saint-Exupéry a man's chosen *métier*—his craft in life—was above all an instrument for achieving an awareness of the self and of the world. The two facets of his life— the active and the reflective, the adventurous and the literary—together constitute something more than a man: they make up a legend that continues to attract modern readers through the impact of its unique humanistic perspective.

Antoine Jean-Baptiste Marie Roger de Saint-Exupéry was born in Lyons on 29 June 1900. His parents could trace their aristocratic origins on both sides far back into the proud traditions of France; the town of Saint-Exupéry, which lent its name to his father's family, is in the department of the Corrèze. His father died when Antoine was barely four years old,

leaving his mother to raise her five children as best she could: Antoine, his two older sisters, Marie-Magdeleine and Simone, a younger brother, François, and a younger sister, Gabrielle.

His mother, Marie de Fonscolombe, herself of the Provençal aristocracy, managed to provide a beautifully warm and secure environment for her "tribe," as Antoine would refer to his family, despite the heaviness of her burden. Saint-Exupéry would retain virtually no memory of his father, but his abundant references to his family and to childhood are thoroughly imbued with the dreamy, romantic tinges of a golden age. His maternal grandmother and great-aunt each owned an estate, one not far from Lyons, at Saint-Maurice-de-Rémens, the other at La Môle, inland from Saint-Tropez. Antoine spent much of his childhood in these two family châteaus, playing with his sisters and brother, exploring the gardens, becoming familiar with plants and animals, and enjoying the security furnished by the gentle presence of his mother and the governesses who helped look after them.

His mother, who held a diploma in nursing and could write poetry, paint, sing, and play the guitar, provided an atmosphere that fostered creativity in the family. Antoine, or the "Roi Soleil," as he was called because of his blond curls, flourished here; he wrote bits of poetry, dabbled at the violin, and joined his brother in devising mechanical inventions, including an attempt to create a flying machine by attaching wings to a bicycle.

In 1909, Antoine's mother moved her family to Le Mans and enrolled her two sons in the Jesuit school that their father had attended. Antoine would remain here until 1914, enduring, as best as might be expected for a somewhat restless and easily distracted boy, a kind of discipline for which he had not been prepared. He wrote poetry and won recognition from his teachers for his literary talents. On vacation at Saint-Maurice, in 1912, he was given his first airplane ride at the Ambérieu aerodrome and wrote his first aeronautical poem (of which three verses are still extant).

When war broke out in 1914, Antoine's mother moved her family to Ambérieu to take on the post of head nurse in the local hospital. Her sons adjusted poorly to the local school and so were sent back to Le Mans to finish out the year. The following year they were sent to a Marist college in Fribourg, Switzerland. While Antoine would reject the teachings of church dogma, the emphasis placed on the cultivation of individual responsibility was one that suited his own temperament and would serve him well for the rest of his life. He later remembered his two years spent there with a sense of satisfaction that his teachers had communicated the right ideals of heroism. Indeed, he was called upon to put those ideals to the test sooner than expected. His brother, François, developed a serious case of rheumatic fever. Antoine had barely passed his *baccalauréat* examinations in June 1917 when François died, leaving Antoine the only remaining male member of the family.

In the fall of 1917, Antoine left for Paris to begin his preparatory studies for entrance into the naval academy in Brest. He passed his written exams in 1919, only to fail the orals that June. Having exceeded the age limit for taking the exam, he was effectively excluded from entering the navy. For the next two years he essentially marked time as a student in the architecture department at the École des Beaux-Arts. Meanwhile he had developed strong friendships that would last him a lifetime, and benefited from the excellent contacts opened to him by his aristocratic Parisian relatives.

In April 1921 he was called up for his two years of military service. In a fateful act that would determine his future career and the shape of his life, he chose the Second Air Force Regiment in Strasbourg. Assigned to the ground crew to work in the repair shops and to teach aerodynamics, he began almost immediately to yearn to fly, and so he took private lessons at a civilian station that shared the Strasbourg airfield with the military. Events moved in a rapid, decisive manner from this point on. By early summer he had completed his first solo flight and, despite a dramatic landing with full engines smoking, was granted his civilian license. His unit sent him to Morocco to continue flight training, and by December he had received his military pilot's license. Back in France, he was sent to the pilots' school in Avord in April 1922. By October, Corporal Saint-Exupéry had completed his training, been promoted to second lieutenant, and given his choice of assignments. In the brief interim from April 1921 to October 1922 he had thus had his first taste of the desert—a setting for which he would develop a deep and abiding attachment—and had made strong friendships with several fellow pilots: Marcel Migéo, Jean Escot, Marcel Reine, and, most notably, Henri Guillaumet. He had also developed an art form that gave him much pleasure, the pencil sketches with which he now illustrated his letters; they would finally be given official status in *Le petit prince* (*The Little Prince*, 1943/1946).

Saint-Exupéry completed his tour of duty at Le Bourget. The proximity to Paris allowed him many social pleasures, not least of which was the company of Louise de Vilmorin, later to become a well-known writer and social figure. The Vilmorin family was not pleased with the prospect of this match, however, and even less so after he suffered a fractured skull in a crash early in 1923. He would clearly have to choose between a career in aviation and marriage to

Louise. Upon leaving the military, he chose Louise.

The period from June 1923 to the fall of 1926 forms a bleak interlude in the life of Saint-Exupéry. Blessed with an essentially optimistic nature, he nonetheless made choices that turned out to be the wrong ones for him. The Vilmorin family had found him an office job at a tile factory. When that left him unsatisfied he turned to a job selling trucks, but managed to sell only one truck in his eighteen months there. His engagement to Louise, further, did not last long. Sensing that the relationship did not hold great promise, or perhaps conceding to her family that he was not her best choice, Louise simply stopped seeing him. Finally, in 1926 his life was once again touched by a tragic loss with the death of his sister Marie-Magdeleine.

His time in Paris was relieved, however, by some important consolations. He would fly as often as he could at Orly, for that had become a joy upon which he could always rely, but increasingly his thoughts turned to another serious preoccupation: writing. In his letters to family and friends he made references to a novel he was working on, and began giving thoughtful critical judgments on contemporary writers and on the art of writing. The twenty-five-year-old Saint-Exupéry, in a classic example of a visible maturation process, expresses his distrust for the superficial and for mere verbal trickery; he identifies good writing with the honest attempt to come to grips with oneself, with real experience as transformed by studious reflection. Finally, in the April 1926 issue of Jean Prévost's short-lived journal *Le navire d'argent,* Saint-Exupéry's first published effort appeared. Entitled "L'aviateur" ("The Aviator," published in *A Sense of Life*), it is a short story describing episodes in the life of a pilot, Jacques Bernis.

Saint-Exupéry's time of floundering eventually came to an end when he was introduced to the head of the newly founded Latécoère Aviation Company. Offered an office position in Madrid, he would settle for nothing less than a flying job. His persistence paid off, as it would many times again in his life: he was assigned to the main operations station in Toulouse.

He began his new job in October 1926. His supervisor, Didier Daurat, was probably the single most influential shaping force in Saint-Exupéry's life as a pilot, and undoubtedly the model for the imposing character Rivière in the novel *Vol de nuit* (*Night Flight,* 1931). Daurat immediately put the novice to work on airplane engines so that, like any other pilot of the time, he would be able to serve as his own mechanic in case of trouble. Within a few months' time Saint-Exupéry was flying the regular company flights from Toulouse to Spain and on to Morocco and Dakar. In his letters he now expressed a sense of profound personal satisfaction in being joined with his pioneering comrades on the line.

Later in 1927, Daurat assigned him to direct the airport at Cape Juby, in the Spanish Sahara colony of Río de Oro. This was one of the ten regular stops between Casablanca and Dakar, but it was a particularly difficult post (as even Daurat was well aware), for the French company had to deal with Spanish military personnel who were frequently at odds with rebellious desert tribes just inland from the coast. Nevertheless, with his considerable personal charm and naturally outgoing manner, Saint-Exupéry had soon befriended the Spaniards as well as a number of Muslim tribesmen in the area, from whom he even learned some Arabic. He gained their respect by himself respecting their culture, and developed enough of a following among them to carry off several rescue missions of French and Spanish pilots who had been forced down in rebel country and taken hostage in exchange for an anticipated ransom. His extraordinary feats at Cape Juby were sufficient to win him the Legion of Honor award in 1930.

The strong impact of this desert mission on Saint-Exupéry's sensibilities would be revealed in his writings. He discovered his talents for diplomacy in dealing with people and their problems, a natural outgrowth of his feelings of respect and affection for people of all cultures. The sense of danger that came not only from his sporadic dealings with hostile tribesmen but—more regularly—from the ever-present menace of airplane accidents sharpened his appreciation for the things he valued most in life. Finally, the life of severe simplicity and monastic poverty that he and his men were obliged to lead in the desert opened him up to the spiritual wealth hidden in the emptiness of wind, sand, and stars. Where other Westerners might have discovered frustration and suffering, Saint-Exupéry found the necessary distance for reflection and a fertile terrain in which his affectionate curiosity for mankind and nature could grow. It was during these eighteen months that he wrote *Courrier sud* (*Southern Mail*, 1929).

This first novel was the fruit of a talent that had slowly been maturing in the young man's mind. That he was gifted in the use of language had already been demonstrated in his school years. That he had a strong need to express his thoughts and attitudes through the written word was also made clear in his abundant correspondence over the years with his mother (published as *Lettres à sa mère* [Letters to His Mother], 1955) and to Renée de Saussine, sister of his friend Bertrand (published in 1953 in two versions, *Lettres de jeunesse* [Letters of Youth] and *Lettres à l'amie inventée* [Letters to the Invented Friend]). These letters contain statements of literary attitudes that perhaps only someone who is thinking of becoming a writer would make, in preparation for establishing his own models of literary style and worth. Meanwhile, Saint-Exupéry had already published a sort of trial version of his novel in the story "L'aviateur," consisting of eight fragments recounting "L'évasion de Jacques Bernis" (The Escape of Jacques Bernis). More recently, Saint-Exupéry's friend and admirer Jean Prévost had introduced him to the publisher of the *Nouvelle revue française,* Gaston Gallimard, who published *Southern Mail* in 1929.

This novel weaves two narrative threads in the life of Jacques Bernis: his experiences as a pilot delivering the mails from Toulouse southward along the line, and his love affair with Genevieve, a childhood playmate now married and living in Paris. The narrator, an old friend and fellow pilot, awaits Jacques's arrival at Cape Juby. He possesses the omniscience that will allow him to tell us what Jacques has done, thought, and felt, either through a real knowledge of the facts or through a kind of sympathetic imagination that allows him to identify with Jacques.

The image we have of Jacques is that of a dreamer who has not given up his childhood love of exploration. Having chosen the world of aviation, he has simply exchanged the childhood mysteries of garden and house for the adventurous world of a pioneer airman. His state of mind is that of a young man dissatisfied with ordinary people and restlessly seeking some undefined realm beyond. Both the narrator and Jacques can be seen as projections of the author himself, who takes the two roles of observing subject—the sympathetic, rational commentator—and his observed object, the rather romantic seeker of something not yet fully grasped.

The story is divided into three sections. The first is supported by a number of details drawn from Saint-Exupéry's personal experiences. The narrator, awaiting the arrival of Jacques's flight, describes the sensuous pleasures of night in the desert at Cape Juby and focuses our attention on the stages in Jacques's journey: dressing for flight, taking orders from the chief, takeoff, meditation during flight, and landing at his first stop in Spain. In the course of his meditations he recalls his most recent trip to Paris, two months earlier. These last recollections—a flashback recounting his affair with Genevieve—constitute the second part, the core of the story.

If Genevieve bears a special significance for Jacques now, it is essentially because she played an important part in his childhood. Earlier he had described himself to the narrator as "the water-diviner whose rod trembles and who moves it over the world to the treasure"—though a treasure unknown, in a quest not yet understood—until he finds Genevieve again: "I have found the spring. Do you remember her? Genevieve. . . ." During their play as children Genevieve seemed to possess a key that allowed her to unlock the secret meaning of things. Upon Jacques's return to Paris, on leave from his duties at Cape Juby, he will rediscover Genevieve and find in her an antidote to his dissatisfaction with the ordinary people he finds there, whose lives seem devoid of meaning to him.

Genevieve, too, is dissatisfied with the way her life has turned out. Married to a man who is the stereotype of the insensitive and uncaring husband, she finds in Jacques a renewed hope for emotional fulfillment. After her child falls ill and dies, she goes off with Jacques hoping to find a new meaning in life with him. But she suffers from her separation with the familiar world she had organized for herself, and Jacques, realizing she needs that stability to be happy, lets her go. Once alone, Jacques attempts to find consolation for his unhappiness. A visit to the cathedral of Notre-Dame convinces him that religion will not furnish him the answers he needs. His Paris leave now over, he takes the train to return to his post at Toulouse.

In the last part of the novel, the two narrative threads come together. Arriving finally at Cape Juby, Jacques recounts to the narrator his last sight of Genevieve, but in the altogether different mode of a tragic fairy tale. Stopping on his way to Toulouse at the town where Genevieve is staying, he is guided along to her place by dreamlike guardian figures who recognize in him the necessary qualities that allowed Orpheus to pursue his search for the woman he loved. When he arrives Genevieve barely recognizes him, as she is now on the threshold of death. Leaving her for the last time, he understands that he has lost that precious gift by which meaning was bestowed upon things.

When he finishes this strange story, Jacques then flies on to another stop on the company line, and at one point his plane disappears over the desert. The narrator sets off after him and finds him alone on the desert dunes, his arms stretched out as though crucified, his face turned toward the stars. The narrator laments the death of his companion in a poetic ending that prefigures the pilot's lament in *The Little Prince* upon the death of the boy. By contrast, the official wire message tells us simply, "Pilot killed plane broken mail intact. Stop."

In examining how Saint-Exupéry has structured the story of the love affair in such a way as to doom it to failure, it is not difficult to find the deeper explanation of his attitude toward domestic happiness as opposed to his growing attachment to the extraordinary world of aviation. Jacques's love for Genevieve is clearly grounded on something that will not work. In endowing Genevieve with her mystical gift, Saint-Exupéry appears to be stressing not so much her understanding of the natural world as the joys of the past. For Genevieve is the person who allows Jacques to rediscover the precious world of his childhood. To pursue his affair with Genevieve would in a sense be to revert to that protected world, and, like the character Franz de Galais in Alain-Fournier's classic neoromantic tale *Le Grand Meaulnes* (*The Wanderer*, 1913), to live out his life in a perpetual state of childhood. By having Genevieve's child die, Saint-Exupéry has given us the real reason why the affair cannot go on. It is as though the death of the literal child signals the necessary death of childhood for Genevieve and Jacques. They cannot continue their affair because they are no longer children, and they must somehow reorder their lives in conformity with a framework of meanings that pertain to the adult world.

The final depiction of Genevieve dying in the manner of some romantic heroine strengthens the reader's reluctance to give her serious consideration as a real character in her own right. Genevieve is Saint-Exupéry's only attempt at developing a female character in some depth, and she no doubt demonstrates his limitations in this respect. In bestowing mystical powers upon her, and in casting her story in a legendary mode, he has deprived her of the opportunity to become a flesh-and-blood character. She is a foil for Jacques, existing above all as an object of Jacques's spiritual needs. She is a symbol, and to the extent that her significance is based on Jacques's perception and understanding of that symbol, her death simply duplicates the death of her own child. It will confirm the message that Jacques must not count on reliving the comforts of his childhood; the precious qualities of childhood must somehow be metamorphosed into a state that can exist comfortably within the adult.

Like other first principal works of blossoming writers, this novel should be judged on the basis of what it gives us of the future writer at his best. Saint-Exupéry never repeated his attempt to write a love story, and on the whole reduced the sentimental element in his future work. His interest in childhood was henceforth focused on children, whether real or imaginary, and not on recollections of past childhood. But many of the qualities and themes upon which his reputation later rested are already here. *Southern Mail* depicts in subtle detail the process by which an ordinary man is transformed into a special being through his chosen field of aviation, and it documents the heightened state of awareness that aviation bestows upon him. It describes the particularly close bonds of comradeship of men who participate in the same heroic enterprise. And it makes consistent references to those elements of the natural world that become part of the central poetic stock of language found in all his work: wind, sand, stars, water, and the night.

Back in France after his successful eighteen-month period on the Africa line, Saint-Exupéry took an advanced aerial navigation course in Brest. He had a strong aptitude for mathematics and science, and would invent and even patent a number of mechanical devices for the airplane over the next few years. Yet despite this practical streak, at Brest he developed something of a reputation for being absent-minded, and made a poor showing on his final examinations. Daurat took him back without reservations, however, to serve the recently formed Compagnie Générale Aéropostale, another pioneering venture in commercial aviation—this one linking France with a new aerial network in South America. Within two weeks of his arrival in Buenos Aires, in October 1929, Saint-Exupéry was named director of the Aeroposta Argentina, a subsidiary of the main company. There he established a number of new airfields linking Buenos Aires with towns toward the west and the south, so that by April 1930 the mail could be flown the entire length of the region of Patagonia. But his domain was only a small part of the greater pioneering adventure that was taking place and that he would soon consecrate in *Night Flight*. His old friend Jean Mermoz had already developed night flights as the chief means to gain time in the delivery of the mails. Mermoz now accepted Daurat's request to run the first transatlantic crossing from Dakar, on the western tip of Africa, to Natal, at the eastern tip of Brazil. From there a relief race run by Saint-Exupéry's fellow pilots took the mail onward, to Rio, to Buenos Aires, and to Santiago. By 15 May 1930, the complete circuit from Paris to the Pacific was down to four and a half days.

It is no exaggeration to say that these men were continually risking their lives. To cross great expanses of land, sea, and mountain ranges in the fragile flying machines of the 1920's, subject to the storms and powerful gusts of wind that could come up unpredictably, and without the benefit of visual contact with any land objects other than occasional lights at night—these were truly death-defying feats that tested the courage of the men Saint-Exupéry writes of in the collection *Terre des hommes* (*Wind, Sand, and Stars*, 1939), which relates several such episodes. The best depiction of the struggle between man and the elements, however, and the meanings that can be derived from engaging in this struggle, come across most clearly and dramatically in his second novel, *Night Flight*, which he began during the summer of 1930. In a severe attempt to reduce the lyrical element—perhaps in acknowledgment of some of the criticism *Southern Mail* had received—he cut the final version from over four hundred pages to less than two hundred. The result is a spare and sober novel, very much in the French "classical" style of elegant simplicity, with a sharp focus on the central element: the moral drama taking place within the mind of the chief character, Rivière.

The story is told through the progress of three mail planes flying toward Buenos Aires: one from Chile, another from Paraguay, the last from Patagonia. Upon arrival, their various cargoes will be transferred to a plane bound for Europe. The movements of the three planes are being monitored by the French team at the airport, presided over by Rivière, who runs the entire operation as though it were his personal empire. This empire is essentially a commercial one: by cutting mail delivery to the shortest possible time, the company hopes to maintain its advantage over other, competing means of transport. Yet at no point do commercial preoccupations come to the fore. This is a story about the courageous struggle of pilots and their director to win a race against time, in a combat pitting human determination against a multitude of hostile natural forces.

Saint-Exupéry weaves his plot in such a way as to create a strong dramatic tension. Suspense is heightened through the constant forewarnings of the dangers of flying, especially stormy weather, which requires the total concentration of a pilot's resources to keep control over his machine, and flying at night, when his only sense of security is provided by the lights down below. The pilot coming in from Chile flies through the forbidding, snow-covered peaks and crags of the Andes without incident, only to have to contend with a storm on the other side. Nonetheless he arrives safely, as does the pilot flying in from Paraguay. It is Fabien, the pilot advancing northward from Patagonia, who serves as the tragic focus of the reader's attention. Flying through calm skies, he suddenly comes upon a storm that has appeared without warning. Unable to maintain control of his craft against the powerful buffeting, he catches a sight of a star overhead and allows his plane to rise up over the cloud cover. Now hopelessly lost and with little gas left in his tank, he is doomed.

The point at which it becomes clear that Fabien cannot be saved would appear to be the climax of the story, but in fact is not. For the narrator now shifts our view away from the final moments of Fabien to the thoughts of Rivière. As head of the operation he is ultimately responsible for this loss; hence he will have to reevaluate the goals of his enterprise. He is also the one who will have to deal with the grief of Fabien's wife. It is therefore not so much the pilot who demands our attention but rather Rivière, who must bear the consequences of the enormity of this event. In like fashion, the personal drama of each of the pilots pales before the much greater drama that is at stake in Rivière's attempt to create a special order over and beyond the demands of human happiness, represented here through the pilots' wives. In short, character parts in this drama can be reduced to three main roles: the pilots—all the pilots, whether specifically named or not; their wives—again, all their wives, representing that other existence of pilots when they are merely ordinary men seeking unheroic happiness; and finally Rivière, who must bear the drama of these differences and find a satisfactory justification for the superhuman endeavor he is promoting.

The pilots are clearly men who are set apart. While not arrogant, they are keenly aware of their special calling in forgoing the pleasures of ordinary men in order to exercise their taste and talent for risk-taking beyond the ordinary. A pilot in his plane is depicted as a sort of knight on his steed, so that pilots together form a new sort of knight-errantry for the modern age. What these men hold in common is a particular myth—"myth" taken in the sense of a shared set of beliefs that validate life: the myth of the *métier.* This French word suggests at the same time the notion of profession, vocation, craft, or, more simply, a job taken seriously. The myth applies to men at lower levels as well. Among the ground crew, for example, Rivière admires Leroux, an old-timer who looks back on his life with "the happy tranquillity of a woodworker who has just smoothed a good board."

These men are joined in a brotherhood of shared work. As in any mythic system, the rewards may be considered in both personal and universal terms. At the personal level, the common goal provides them with a ready-made path of achievement that has been socially validated, allowing each to direct his energies toward a well-defined goal. When well accomplished, the job will bring satisfaction and even the sense of exaltation found in victory. This state of spiritual well-being is such that individuals may be willing to pay the price of suffering and even to risk death along the way. At the universal level, the myth demands of each member his obedience and his honest and generous service for the good of all. These men do not often speak; they do not need to: "A strong sense of brotherhood allowed them to do without words."

An important motif illustrating this expectation of common service runs throughout the novel. The pilots are essentially participants in a relay race. When one lands, it is so that another may take his place to cover the next lap, and so on. This continuity exists on earth as well: "A man was at work somewhere so that life could remain continuous, so that human will could remain continuous, and in this way, from one stop to the next, so that the chain stretching from Toulouse to Buenos Aires should never be broken." Lights on earth serve as guideposts provided for the pilots' benefit to show them the way. Likewise, radio operators pass on information about the weather in chain fashion to guide them safely home. Shared work thus provides personal satisfaction and social usefulness: it creates human bonds and provides a vehicle for justifying an individual human being's existence.

The second role is played by the wives of the pilots. They are relatively minor characters (only two are shown in some detail: the wife of the pilot who must be awakened to prepare for his flying mission, and Simone, the wife of the doomed pilot). Together they portray a universal condition. Taken as realistic depictions of women they appear superficially weak, destined to lead a life of eternal sacrifice because their husbands will always go off to face untold dangers. But woman for Saint-Exupéry also incarnates an age-old archetype, the provider of comfort, and therein lies her real strength. She is the keeper of the hearth and the port of refuge to which her loved one can come home when the dangers of the day are over. Underneath this stereotypical depiction of woman we can glimpse the archetype of the protective mother threatened with imminent bereavement; one cannot help but suspect that the true model here is Saint-Exupéry's conception of his own mother. If this model is present here, it is to represent a view opposed to Rivière's notion of heroic action. But if these women cannot be said to have fully developed personalities, the same can be said of the pilots as well. The important thing is to demonstrate two differing notions of what life is supposed to mean, and to furnish Rivière with intellectual justification for espousing one view over the other.

The likely model for Rivière was Saint-Exupéry's own supervisor, Didier Daurat, and once again what is important in this character sketch are not his specific qualities but the typical qualities of a leader of men. He is a solitary figure who chooses not to show his love for his men and the pity he often feels for their human frailties, so that the will required to maintain the spirit of his group enterprise will not be weakened. The chief frailties are carelessness and fear. Rivière will go so far as to cast shame on his men when that is what is necessary to get them to shake off their fear and self-pity, or to avoid mistakes. To underscore this point, Saint-Exupéry has created a foil for Rivière in the character of Inspector Robineau, a frankly mediocre man who admires Rivière but does not seem to have learned any of the duties of leadership from him. His hunger for friendship is so great that he invites a pilot to have dinner with him, blind to the fact that fraternizing will only create expectations that can interfere with the efficacy of his authority. Rivière will make Robineau find some pretext by which to punish the pilot so as to restore the necessary relationship.

Rivière recognizes that the task of organizing his men will always be a Sisyphean struggle against forces exceedingly more powerful than man. He expresses these as "events" that must be controlled, associating with them two types of metaphor. When human frailty shows itself, he thinks of it as a *mal,* a sickness or evil that must be eradicated. After he fires a workman for having performed a dangerously careless piece of work he thinks:

> If I fired him in such a brutal way, it is not because of him but because of the evil—for which he may not even have been responsible—that was passing through him. Events *have* to be controlled . . . and then they obey, and one can create. And men are pitiful things, and one can create them too. Or else you move them out of the way when evil passes through them.
>
> (p. 83)

This metaphor expresses an internal danger; Rivière uses another type of metaphor to express the external danger as well. When men let go, events take over, like jungle growth swiftly reclaiming its rights over great monuments that have been abandoned. Even a gardener working his lawn, for example, is engaged in a perpetual struggle to prevent the soil from producing the primitive forest it contains within itself.

Readers may be tempted to see in Rivière something of a sadistic martinet or, in view of the fact that Saint-Exupéry was an enthusiastic reader of Nietzsche, some tyrant of the Will; but this is not what the author means to convey. Rivière is a fifty-year-old man obsessed by the fragility of human life in the face of those enemies that consume life: time and death. Man's dream, for Rivière, is "to endure, to create, to exchange his perishable body." The only way to overcome his human condition is through a transcending of his individual life in the name of something greater: the human race, which will continue to exist beyond his individual death. He recalls that an engineer once told him that people continue to build bridges over rivers despite the inevitable construction accidents that occur. Rivière had answered: "If human life is priceless, we always act as though something surpassed human life in value. . . . But what?" This quality, whatever it may be, must be worth the price of snatching men away from their lives of simple happiness.

In the final analysis, the question of human happiness in this novel is focused on the pilots, who are offered two separate and competing paths to follow. Their wives offer warmth, comfort, and love—but nothing that can stand up against the natural fear of death. Rivière offers a heroic, dynamic value that is higher than happiness—higher because it involves more than individual men and projects the meaning of their existence into the future. In Rivière's empire some men must die, but in the system of domestic happiness represented by the wives all men will eventually die anyway. At least in Rivière's system the notion of a heroic humanity transcending individual death will live on.

Rivière virtually admits that his system is a blind gamble when he thinks to himself, "We don't ask to be eternal but, rather, not to see our acts and things suddenly lose their meaning." And again: "Our goal may not justify anything, but action frees us from death. These men endured through their machines." Perhaps, then, the illusion of an eternal meaning is sufficient if it allows his men to achieve an unsuspected height of human potential. But so far as the pilots are concerned, the conflict over two opposing systems is not really an issue. They do not have to choose sides, but rather profit both from the benefits of domestic happiness as provided by their wives and from the heroic action of their knightly brotherhood as organized for them by Rivière. At the end of the novel, Rivière's ideology will hold sway. In spite of death and grief, the flights will go on.

Saint-Exupéry brought the manuscript for the novel back to France with him in 1931, and Gallimard published it later that year. It became an immediate success. André Gide read it and was sufficiently impressed to contribute a preface extolling the nobility of human achievement represented within its pages, the spirit of self-sacrifice, and the important moral lesson it gave on the need to accept responsibility as a duty. By the end of the year the novel had won one of France's most prestigious literary awards, the Prix Fémina, and henceforth Saint-Exupéry was assigned to the ranks of the most important current authors.

The manuscript was not all Saint-Exupéry had brought back to France from Argentina, however. At a reception of the Alliance Française, he had met Consuelo Suncín, the widow of an Argentine journalist. With her vivacious Latin charm and somewhat temperamental personality, she was not exactly the type of woman one would have expected him to marry, yet they were indeed wed shortly after his return to France. Relatively little has been written of their relationship, but it is known that they frequently broke up and lived apart despite the obvious signs of mutual attachment and affection they shared.

Meanwhile, changes were taking place in Saint-Exupéry's world of aviation, some of which had begun to make themselves painfully evident to him at about the same time *Night Flight* was published. During a dispute between the Aéropostale and the French government, Daurat had been called upon by the government to keep the flights going, and he accepted. As the dispute developed, some of Saint-Exupéry's comrades turned against Daurat, Saint-Exupéry's subsidiary company was abolished, and Daurat himself was fired. The company was merged with others into a larger one: the movement toward commercial efficiency was accelerating, and the pioneer spirit

seemed to be fading into the past. Meanwhile, Saint-Exupéry was distressed to learn of the reaction of a number of pilots to the success of his recent book: he was now being looked upon as an amateur aviator who had somehow broken the brotherhood's code of honor by writing of it for outsiders.

Finding himself without his old job, he was obliged to take on various piloting positions and for a while became a test pilot for seaplanes being produced by Latécoère. On one testing mission at Saint-Raphaël, in 1932, he crashed into the sea and very nearly drowned. In 1934 he joined the recently formed company Air France to serve as a publicity specialist, making a number of lecture trips within France and abroad, and traveling as far as Indochina.

In view of the rapid strides taking place in the field of aviation, he was determined not to abandon the heroic spirit of adventure of the earlier days. When Pierre Billon decided to make *Southern Mail* into a movie in 1934, Saint-Exupéry joined his team on location in Morocco and performed the stunt-flying for the actor playing the role of Bernis. Soon after, he secured a plane for himself, a Simoun model, and on 29 December 1935 set off together with his mechanic Prévot on a Paris-to-Saigon long-distance run in an attempt to beat the record. At one stage of their North Africa leg, they set off from Benghazi eastward to fly over the desert, without the benefit of lights or radio contact. They were soon lost and through a fatal judgment of altitude crashed into the heart of the desert, about two hundred kilometers west of Cairo. The ordeal of survival in this unforgiving landscape, the men's fateful decision to walk eastward despite their mistaken belief that they were already east of Cairo, and the miraculous encounter with the Bedouin caravan that would save them—all these adventures were later recounted in detail in *Wind, Sand, and Stars.* In 1935 he proposed a race to set a new world record, this time from New York to Punta Arenas, at the southern tip of South America. Together with Prévot, in his Simoun, Saint-Exupéry sailed for New York in

January 1938 and in February began his race southward. Upon takeoff from Guatemala City, the two men experienced their worst accident yet. Prévot suffered a broken leg, and Saint-Exupéry a brain concussion and multiple fractures from which he would never fully recover. After spending a month in a Guatemalan hospital, he was taken back to New York for a long convalescence. There, in a borrowed apartment with a view of the East River, he began organizing his texts for *Wind, Sand, and Stars.*

Some of these texts were pieces Saint-Exupéry had written earlier. Since publishing *Night Flight* he had not tried his hand at fiction other than to complete a filmscript begun in Argentina. Rather, he had become increasingly interested in developing his skills as a writer of articles and short essays, eyewitness accounts, character profiles of friends, personal reminiscences, and similar types of anecdotal sketches that permitted him to elaborate a personal journalistic style, whereby he could blend moral observation with philosophical meditation, and employ a spare prose with poetic sensitivity. As a publicity agent for Air France, he contributed several pieces to their official flight magazine. In 1935 he was asked by the newspaper *Paris-Soir* to go to Moscow to give an account of the new Russia from a human perspective. In 1936 another Paris journal, *L'Intransigeant,* published his account of his crash in the Libyan desert, and sent him to Spain to report on the fighting there. More articles were commissioned by *Paris-Soir* in 1937 and 1938, before and after his crash in Guatemala, and meanwhile he was being asked to write prefaces and introductions to works relating to the aviation world, including Anne Morrow Lindbergh's *Listen! the Wind* (1938). Some of these pieces found their way, faithfully reproduced or in somewhat revised form, into *Wind, Sand, and Stars.* Others eventually appeared, posthumously, in *Un sens à la vie* (*A Sense of Life,* 1956), an anthology of diverse pieces. Still others appeared periodically in the French aviation magazine *Icare,* and have never been anthologized.

Of all these pieces, the collection to which Saint-Exupéry attempted to give a unified form was *Wind, Sand, and Stars.* Even here we face the problem of having to deal with two different versions, the American and the French. While in New York he gave the manuscript of some of the pieces to his translator, Lewis Galantière, for preparation of the American edition. Back in France, however, he continued editing the work, adding a few passages not found in the American edition and cutting others. The French version begins with a brief statement that provides the unifying message of the book: Man can discover himself only when he measures himself against an obstacle. For this he needs a tool, and herein lies the significance of the *métier.* Although the texts do not stress the superiority of the airplane as a tool, they make it clear that the plane can offer an original and particularly instructive vantage point: the view of all mankind down below. What that view reveals to Saint-Exupéry is the essential unity of all men, but also one's obligation to speak to others, in the face of so much mutual hatred and hostility, of the need for unity.

The first chapter describes the metamorphosis of an ordinary young man into a new type of human being when he becomes a pilot. The pilot is an exemplary man because he lives in a state of awareness that will allow him to fulfill his own potential while serving the needs of mankind. The second chapter then gives us profiles of two such exemplary figures, chosen from among the great veterans of the early days that he knew personally. The first is Mermoz. After surviving incredible feats of flight-pioneering on so many fronts—across the ocean, over mountain ranges and deserts, and through the night—one day he does not return from one of his flights. What we consider heroism is simply acting as though the odds did not exist, until one day one can act no more. The second is Guillaumet. Crash-landing in the Andes, he survives his ordeal by simply going on, oblivious to what everyone had said to be impossible, and goes through—as he puts it—what no animal would ever have gone through.

In the chapters following, Saint-Exupéry takes up the theme of the airplane as an instrument of individual self-knowledge and also of knowledge of the human experience in the cosmos. Having once seen the earth from above, when the pilot lies on the desert sands below he understands that the earth is like a ship, bearing each of us with the force of its gravity. The distances the plane allows man to cover reveal the exotic differences among people and also their essential similarities. In "Oasis," for example, he tells of the peasant family who take him in when he is forced to land on a stretch in Patagonia. The two daughters who sit shyly judging him over dinner test his reactions by announcing that the strange movements coming from below the table are caused by snakes that live in a hole there. These girls behave like his own sisters, who, he recalls, would call out mysterious numbers to each other when young male guests were invited, making use of a secret code that summarily ranked the worth of the guest on a scale from one to twenty.

In the chapter "Dans le désert" ("Men of the Desert") Saint-Exupéry gives us glimpses of cultural exchange between two groups considered alien to each other: Europeans and Muslim tribesmen of the desert. The latter are truly scornful of the French, no matter what their material accomplishments, because they are Christians who do not have God on their side. Those Muslims who have been to France (according to the American edition) are unimpressed by buildings, radios, locomotives, or even the Eiffel Tower. But they do admit to their great attraction for circus women who can jump standing from one galloping horse to another. Above all they are impressed by the forests, the waterfalls, and greenery. These men who have made their religion "out of a fountain" are puzzled by the irony of a mysterious God who has been so much more generous to the French than to the Moors.

But even desert tribesmen share our essential brotherhood, as Saint-Exupéry demonstrates at the end of the next chapter, "Au centre du désert" ("In the Center of the Desert"). Here he describes his accident in Libya according to the classic formula of the adventure tale. Beginning with his original desire to prove his own valor to himself by means of a record-breaking race, the text moves through the early stages of the trip to the central terrain of hardship, the fateful event, the ordeal in the desert, the discovery in the wreckage of the plane of an orange that provides a miraculous respite from hunger and thirst, and finally the unhoped-for encounter with the desert caravan. Here is the embodiment of a human society forever vigilant to come to the rescue of fellow men. He thinks of the Arab who first sees him: "You are Man and you appear before me with the face of all men at once."

By this point the thematic emphasis of the book has shifted from the privileged insights of the pilot to the pressing need for human unity and brotherhood. The final chapter, "Les Hommes" ("The Men"), gives us Saint-Exupéry's views on the Spanish Civil War. What is important here is not the description of battles or the temporary victories of one side over the other, but the impassioned plea to men to stop fighting each other and move together toward a common goal. The profile sketch of an old army sergeant serves as the example of a man discovering his need to find a truth he is willing to die for, so long as he shares the fight with his companions. The only problem is that he and his companions are eager to fight and kill other men who are fighting for *their* truth. Saint-Exupéry therefore calls for the abandonment of political ideology. Both sides have a truth, and in the ultimate sense that a truth is what gives meaning to life, their truths are identical (the author would, of course, receive some sharp attacks for failing to distinguish the nature of the respective truths). In an uncharacteristic foray into sociohistorical analysis, he explains that if the Europe of the 1930's is suffering such widespread anguish, it is because the industrial age has stripped men of their peasant identities and thrown them into ghettoes, and because they are made to learn the narrowest of trades instead of human culture. Meanwhile hope is fading for the bulk of humanity. The book ends on a memory that comes back to him from a train trip he once took through Poland: the scene of a beautiful young boy sleeping between his working-class parents, and doomed to spend the rest of his life in the same sort of misery as they, despite all the promise he carries within him of a future Mozart. He is the image of a Mozart murdered in the bud, a new rose that will not be cultivated because there is no gardener for mankind. He is a symbol of what must not be allowed to happen to modern man.

Wind, Sand, and Stars was released virtually simultaneously in France and America early in 1939 and achieved instant success in both countries. In France it received the Grand prix du roman de l'Académie française; in America it was chosen as the Book-of-the-Month Club selection for June and received the National Book Award and other honors as well. Saint-Exupéry had clearly become something of a national—and increasingly international—celebrity. In May he was awarded the rosette of the Legion of Honor, in a ceremony at which Guillaumet also received the Legion award. As though to underscore the worthiness of the message of his book, Saint-Exupéry and Guillaumet broke the transatlantic record returning from New York to France on Bastille Day. He returned almost immediately to New York to participate in the honors being bestowed upon him by his American public.

But amidst these personal glories he had begun to turn his mind to the signs of war, which were growing increasingly ominous late that summer. He returned to France in August and reported for military duty at Toulouse as a captain assigned to flight training. Pressing his request for reassignment to active flight duty, he attained his goal in short order. Despite the fact that he was technically over the age limit, and against the advice that he was not medically in shape as a result of his Guatemalan accident, by early November he was transferred to Reconnaissance Group 2/33, stationed north of Paris at Orconte. Here he recapitulated the earlier pattern of his life by developing a tight network of emotional ties with a brotherhood of men serving a common cause, and sharing life in the monastic ambiance of a military barracks. The group was involved in carrying out dangerous missions over enemy-held territory to photograph military operations. One such mission, over Arras on 22 May 1940, was to become the subject of his next book, *Pilote de guerre* (*Flight to Arras,* 1942); but he would not write that book until France had lost the fight and he was in America.

With the defeat of the French military in June 1940, the officers of Saint-Exupéry's group were sent to Algiers to carry on the struggle from North Africa. With the signing of the armistice later that month, resistance collapsed, and by the end of July his group had been demobilized. Sharing the shock and bewilderment of so many of his countrymen, he spent the next few months deciding what his best course of action should be in view of the fall of the Paris government and the installation of the puppet regime in Vichy. Friends had been urging him to go to the United States to represent the voice of free France. Opposed to working with the Vichy government, not sufficiently attracted to de Gaulle to cast his lot with the general, and encouraged by his American publishers to come to New York, he made his decision to go to the United States.

At no point did Saint-Exupéry think of himself as either an emigrant or an immigrant, but rather as a traveler whose duty was to represent his country in the best light while waiting to return home. He was happy to have occasion to come in contact with the French community living in exile, a number of whose members he had personally known in France, but he was dispirited by their tendency to indulge in partisan politics. Some were for Vichy, others for de Gaulle, and both camps solicited his allegiance. This factionalism did not diminish the ordeal of France, which was uppermost in his mind, rendered all the more painful for him by the widespread public view that France had somehow been shamed by not having fought harder against the Germans. His American publishers pressed him to write a book that would speak for France. He therefore decided to interrupt his efforts to get on with the book he had long projected as his major work, *Citadelle* (*The Wisdom of the Sands*, 1948), to write *Flight to Arras.*

It would be difficult to classify this work by literary genre. It clearly combines the two major types of writing that Saint-Exupéry had thus far elaborated in his career as an author—autobiographical reminiscences and the novel form. The main story line gives an account of his reconnaissance flight to Arras in the north of France, now occupied by the Germans, culminating with the arrival of his plane over that town in a hail of shellfire. Hence there is a strong element of suspense as the reader is left wondering whether the plane will reach its destination without incident, take the aerial photographs it has been sent to get, and make it back safely. Although based entirely on fact, the story has been shaped into a dramatic tale and given a universal perspective by the personal memories and reflections that come to the narrator's mind during and after his flight.

The fighting group to which Saint-Exupéry belongs bears an unmistakable resemblance to the brotherhood of knights he had described earlier in *Night Flight.* Daurat, now dead, has been replaced by Major Alias, playing the set role of commanding officer. Each of Saint-Exupéry's comrades-in-arms (to whom the book is dedicated) is each given a distinctive character sketch that brings him to life for the reader: Dutertre, Israel, Gavoille, and a cowardly gunner referred to simply as T., who dies while trying to parachute out of a plane headed into enemy territory. Given the overwhelming military superiority of the Germans, the French effort to resist invasion remains hopeless. The question keeps recurring like a refrain: Why are the men of Saint-Exupéry's unit being called upon to risk their lives conducting reconnaissance flights when it is understood by everyone that the photographs they bring back

are absolutely useless? The answer is that such are "the rules of the game." An overpowered army must continue to fight on, and men must continue to perform their duties even in the face of defeat. The absurdity of their gesture is never felt more keenly than when their planes must fly directly into the path of antiaircraft batteries determined to do them in. But the rules of the game are still good rules because they spring from the need to give meaning to life. These men are united in the common cause of saving France, and even when their goal is doomed to failure they are still engaged in an endeavor that gives their own lives meaning. In trying to save France they are therefore affirming a transcendental value that nourishes them all.

To view this attitude merely as blind patriotism would constitute a serious misreading of the text. Taking to heart his role as spokesman for France, Saint-Exupéry's purpose will be to justify her in defeat. When the critics of France say that French military resistance was insufficient, they have overlooked the very real differences between, as he points out in a hyperbolic example, a nation of 80 million industrial workers and a nation of 40 million farmers. And yet, as France's critics have apparently not understood, the French have continued to play by the rules of the game by fighting on. Of the twenty-three air reconnaissance crews in Saint-Exupéry's unit, seventeen were shot down in what could, in the cold light of reason, be judged to have been a totally absurd sacrifice. To counter the critics who say the French gave in too quickly in order to avoid suffering, Saint-Exupéry gives us a picture of a France rapidly disintegrating before his weary eyes. Villages are burning and people streaming southward by the millions, sporadically bombed and strafed by the enemy for no apparent reason. Roads are hopelessly blocked; order has broken down. France has not avoided suffering.

Given the chaos and the tragic turn of events, who can sit in judgment of France? It is clear that Saint-Exupéry has summoned his arguments in defense of France to persuade the Americans in particular. In a section containing some of his most strongly polemical language he writes that if France is fighting for democracy, then it is the duty of the democracies, and in particular the most powerful one, to join the fray. In preaching democracy, he has in mind not so much a set of principles as a set of desires: that men be brotherly, free, and happy. His "patriotism" is in fact a form of humanism. He may love France, where people are free and happy to be French, but he loves men of other nations as well and respects their right to be free and happy within their own national identities.

Never before had Saint-Exupéry developed his arguments on the spiritual dimensions of the human adventure—everything that would constitute his humanistic message in all his subsequent works—in such ample detail and with such assurance. What defines man, in his view, is his spirit, and the key to understanding him is the action that he brings to bear in a social context. Saint-Exupéry speaks often here of the web of human relationships that together form a "civilization," giving a "density" to individual lives. A Dominican friar at prayer, Pasteur looking into his microscope, Cézanne motionless before his easel, or Saint-Exupéry in his room at Orconte—these are all examples of men imbued with a culture that gives their lives meaning, much as the *métier* gives meaning to men. Further, to be a human being is to be a participant and not a spectator. Because he is woven in a web of relationships with his comrades, Saint-Exupéry achieves his own density through fulfilling his obligations toward them; for he is a part of his men, just as they are a part of their country.

While flying through fire over Arras, Saint-Exupéry relates, his plane is struck but, miraculously, does not go down. He then joyfully anticipates returning home to his web of relationships, which must forever be cultivated and renewed. Upon his return he goes to have dinner with a farmer's family, and feels he has reestablished his ties with all humanity.

When the farmer's niece smiles, "her smile was transparent for me and, through it, I saw my village. Through my village, I saw my country. Through my country, I saw other countries. For I am of a civilization that has chosen man as its keystone."

At the end of the book Saint-Exupéry offers his Credo, an extraordinary document of religious humanism that marks the transition to a new, more didactic and consciously rhetorical style, one that will characterize much of his subsequent work. Individual men have no meaning except through a transcendental notion of Man, just as a pile of stones does not take on meaning until it is formed into a cathedral. While Saint-Exupéry was never a particularly observant Christian, his humanism is clearly founded on a respect for the values espoused by the Western Christian tradition. Modern democracy is the heir of that tradition. Men cannot be brothers nor can they be equal except *in* something, and that something is essentially Saint-Exupéry's definition of God. The notion of responsibility is the heir of the traditional value of bearing the sins of others, and what is called charity is the sacrifice granted to man in order that he may find personal fulfillment.

Flight to Arras appeared in New York early in 1942. It was greeted by critics in America as one of the great testaments to the abiding spirit of hope for a liberated France. Henri Peyre wrote that it was "the finest prose work that World War II seems as yet to have produced." Through some curious misreading of the text, permission was granted for its publication in Vichy France later that year, with only four words censored. That error was caught soon after and the book was banned, but clandestine versions continued to circulate. Meanwhile Saint-Exupéry, now joined by his wife, Consuelo, in New York, continued to write at a rapid pace. He prepared an article, "Message to Young Americans," for a national high school magazine, sharing his message that war requires the best of each individual. His "An Open Letter to Frenchmen Everywhere" appeared in the *New York Times Magazine* soon after the Allied invasion of North Africa, late in 1942, and was broadcast to France as "Lettre aux Français." Here he formally recognized de Gaulle—somewhat belatedly, in the view of the general's followers—as a figure fully capable of leading the French cause.

By early 1943, Saint-Exupéry had completed and published two additional works in New York, *Lettre à un otage* (*Letter to a Hostage*) and *Le petit prince* (*The Little Prince*). The first takes up the ideological threads of *Flight to Arras* in a renewed call for the urgent defeat of the Nazis. The second, variously known as a whimsical fairy tale for adults or a hauntingly sad story on the loss of childhood, remains by far the work upon which the author's popularity is most firmly established. Despite their apparent differences in structure, tone, and intent, at a deeper level the two works reflect elements of kinship, for in both we find the tone of loss, nostalgia, and tenderness expressive of a man whose emotional roots have been violently wrenched from their nourishing earth.

This nourishing earth, in *Letter to a Hostage,* is France and the friends he has left behind as hostages of the German occupation. He writes in particular to one of his very close friends, Léon Werth, who as a Jew bears the brunt of the tragedy in a particularly poignant way. There are six sections in the letter, each intricately woven of memories and feelings expressed in a spare, elegiac manner.

The book begins by portraying Saint-Exupéry as a reluctant voyager as he is about to set sail from Lisbon to New York, surrounded by refugees—for the most part well-to-do—who instill in him a sense of guilt at leaving his friends behind. But the memories of these friends move him to begin preparing his return even as he is about to depart. He compares exile to a magnetic field: his friends, his memories, and his loyalties are the poles, pulling so strongly at him that he can think of himself only as a temporary voyager. One of those memories then comes to life. One day when he

and Léon Werth were picnicking by the river, they invited two nearby boatmen, one Dutch, the other German, to join them in a drink. The smile that they all shared became a bond of friendship, uniting them in a sort of mystical communion. He then takes up the smile as the motif of universal fellowship. He recalls how, in Spain, his situation was saved one day when, caught by militants who thought he was one of the enemy, he asked one of them for a cigarette, gave a smile, and received a smile in return. And he also remembers the smile of the Arab whose caravan party rescued him and his mechanic from certain death in the Libyan desert.

Saint-Exupéry then turns to the more immediate matter of why the Nazi enemies must be defeated. The war can be reduced to a struggle between two fundamentally different attitudes: one that respects individual persons and allows them to find their own path of "ascension," the other that refuses "creative contradictions" and forces all men to fit the totalitarian model. Saint-Exupéry's political idealism shows through: as long as men maintain a fundamental respect for the notion of Man, it does not matter which political system dominates. What matters in a civilization is not its form but its substance. Reflecting on his friend Léon Werth, in the last section, he affirms his belief that their friendship is all the stronger because each is different, while respecting the differences of the other. If he fights again, he promises to fight for Werth's truth as well as his own, to recover the smile he needs from his friend. All Frenchmen, being of the same tree, must be free to sink their roots into the same land. As a testimony to friendship as a fundamental value in a free society, Saint-Exupéry's little book thus turns the expression of personal feeling into a political statement.

As for *The Little Prince,* one is tempted to ascribe its popular success in no small part to the fact that for years it was used as a reader for teaching French in American schools; but of course it has been read widely in many other countries and other contexts as well, and its charm has been universally acclaimed. It is the only book of its sort that Saint-Exupéry wrote, and the only one in which he finally put his talents as an illustrator to the test. The combination of text and illustrations proved to be a winning one, and Saint-Exupéry was himself very fond of the book. He had begun making sketches of the Little Prince as early as 1939, but began to write the book only in 1942 in response to his New York publisher, who encouraged him to produce a children's book after seeing one of his little drawings.

The story tells of a small boy who lives alone on a tiny planet, to which the narrator assigns an asteroid number to satisfy his adult readers' impatience for scientific classifications. The boy performs regular chores: he sweeps out the three volcanic chimneys of his planet and uproots the baobab-tree seedlings that could overrun the planet's surface if allowed to take hold. When he feels melancholy he turns his chair to watch a rapid series of sunsets. He would be happy if he could count on the love of a rose that grows there, but she is not reliable in her affection and makes unreasonable demands upon him until, one day, unable to bear the emotional strain any longer, he decides to leave his planet by latching onto a flock of migratory birds traveling through space.

He then stops briefly at six tiny planets, each of which is inhabited by a single human being caught in some characteristic act. The King is delighted by the boy's arrival, as it provides him with a subject for him to rule over; the Vain Man, eager for an audience, asks that that the boy applaud him in his various posturings; the Drunkard cannot escape from the vicious circle in which he is trapped, feeling shame for his drinking and then drinking in order to forget his shame. The fourth planet is the home of the Businessman (Saint-Exupéry uses the English term), who sits at his desk counting stars in the belief that he owns everything he counts. The Lamplighter, whose job it is to light his planet's lamp each night and extinguish it the following morning, finds him-

self growing increasingly weary as his planet rotates faster and faster. The Geographer does not go off on explorations himself but sits at his desk taking notes on the discoveries reported to him by others.

All of these figures may be presumed to be allegories of human types based on the author's experience with men. Essentially they give a critique of false values in the modern world. The common denominator for establishing a scale of moral values here would appear to be the quality of human relationships toward other men and the world. At the negative pole one would find the Vain Man, the Drunkard, and particularly the Businessman, who represents the extreme perversion of relationship as quantifiable possession. At the positive extreme the Lamplighter performs his duties—his *métier*—with admirable faithfulness, despite his perception that the task has become absurd; moreover he actually *does* something, and does not scribble at a desk. But we must not forget that these views are supposed to be those of a child looking at "serious" adults, as imagined by an adult who has great sympathy for the way children see the world. A reader who goes much further in pressing meanings out of types created with such playful whimsy runs the risk of being taken for a "serious" adult himself.

The Little Prince finally arrives on the seventh planet, Earth, and meets the narrator, Saint-Exupéry playing himself in a somewhat altered account of his crash in the Libyan desert. Working hard at his plane repairs like any serious adult, he is challenged by the boy to reconsider his notions of what is truly serious in life. One of the major themes of the book, then, is that adults are impoverished by having lost their capacity to view the world through a child's eyes. The pilot prides himself in his belief that he is exempt from that charge; he understands, for example, that a particular drawing illustrated in the book represents not a man's hat lying on the floor but rather a boa constrictor that has swallowed an elephant. He also succeeds in calming the boy's anxieties about a certain sheep on his planet that might very well eat his beloved rose, by drawing a container in which to safely pen the sheep. The narrator is thus here to partake of the boy's experience and to communicate it to the reader in a manner that is affectionate and lighthearted, but at the same time grave and profound. Above all he accepts the responsibility to speak to adults of the benefits of looking at the world, and themselves, through the fresh perspective of a child.

While he is on Earth, the Little Prince makes many discoveries, and eventually attains the wisdom that allows him to understand that what he truly desires is to return to his rose. In one way or another, all the lessons he learns have to do with love. On his planet the Little Prince's rose was unique, and so he is astonished to find on Earth a garden filled with roses, all alike, that make his own rose seem merely ordinary. Weeping in the grass, he is approached by a desert fox who will serve as his mentor figure (Saint-Exupéry had himself described an encounter with a desert fox in *Wind, Sand, and Stars*). The Little Prince would like to be his friend, but the fox explains that they must first "tame" each other (the French word *apprivoiser* carries the sense "to make more sociable"). People who tame each other come to need each other; they become unique for each other. This process is slow, requiring patience and ritualized gestures rather than words. The fox also teaches him to strengthen the ties of love through sensuous and poetic associations, to see with his heart rather than his eyes, and to understand that the object thus tamed—that is, the loved one—is also the object for which one becomes responsible.

The Little Prince shares these lessons with the narrator, and teaches him to see the special beauty of an object that is needed. The narrator then understands, for example, the true value of water found in a desert well: "This water was much more than nourishment. It was born of my walk beneath the stars, of the song of the pulley, of the efforts of my arms. It was, like a

gift, good for the heart." Indeed, the Little Prince becomes both the tamer of the narrator and his mentor, offering him one aphoristic truth after another, each a variation on the same essential cluster of themes: men rush about but do not know what they are looking for; the most important things in life are invisible, and to find them requires the patience of indirect action and vision.

Finally, understanding that to return to his planet he must dispossess himself of his physical body, the Little Prince goes out to meet the serpent who had earlier promised to help him die. Before he goes, however, he bestows a farewell gift. The pilot had loved to hear the boy's laughter; now, through the magic powers of association, that laughter will sound like the tinkling of bells emanating from the Little Prince's planet and stretching across the vast expanses of space. And so it comes to pass. Six years later the narrator can see stars, "hear" their tinkling and the boy's laughter beyond; but he also wonders if the Little Prince has managed to save his rose from the sheep.

One cannot dismiss the claim that this book is a fairy tale of sorts, but it clearly has a density of thought that goes beyond the ordinary children's tale, and a melancholy tone that may not even be understood by children. Some readers will be tempted to see the book as a roman à clef and look for biographical clues: the rose refers to Saint-Exupéry's wife, or perhaps to Louise de Vilmorin; the Little Prince is the son the author never had; the death of the boy alludes to the death of Saint-Exupéry's young brother; the dispossession of the physical body is an allusion to the Christian notion of resurrection, which had an appeal for the writer; and so on. In one sense the visit of the Little Prince as an extraterrestrial traveler can be seen as a pretext for social observation and satire, albeit of a very elementary and playful sort. But all critics seem agreed that the Little Prince is considerably more than a pretext for satire; as an externalized projection of the author's psyche, the boy embodies Saint-Exupéry's profoundest attitudes toward childhood, affection, love, and death. It is no doubt this very richness of interpretive potential, in addition to its undeniable charm for children and adults alike, that has guaranteed the work a place as a classic of modern literature.

During the few months between the publication of *Letter to a Hostage* and *The Little Prince*, Saint-Exupéry found his chance to end the melancholy burden of his passive exile and to return to active duty. The Allies had debarked in North Africa in November 1942; by April 1943, Saint-Exupéry found himself passage on an American troop ship headed for Algiers. Despite his age, his persistence in pursuing his goal led to success. He was given the rank of major and was assigned to the unit of his choice, his old Reconnaissance Group 2/33, now stationed at an American base in North Africa. Henceforth he would fly the Lockheed Lightning, which was considerably larger and more sophisticated than the planes he had known before the war. Within a few weeks he had made his first reconnaissance flight over France and was overjoyed finally to see his land once again, even from such a great height. But at the end of July, returning from his second mission, he made a bad landing, damaged his craft, and was grounded by the American commander. He spent the next several months in Algiers at the home of his friend Dr. Georges Pélissier, in a state of profound gloom as a result of having lost his chance to fight with his comrades so soon after reentering the fray.

During this period he continued working on the manuscript of *Citadelle* (*The Wisdom of the Sands*). It was also then that he very likely wrote his "Lettre au Général X" ("Letter to General X"), discovered among his papers after his death. This manuscript contains statements astonishing in their pessimism for someone who had so consistently expressed his hope in man: the airplane has become merely a transportation device; while improvements in our material existence have become increasingly visible, man's spiritual life has been impoverished to an extent hitherto unknown; totalitarian governments, whether fascist or Marxist, have become propaganda machines transforming individual citizens into robots and cattle; once the Germans have been defeated, the fundamental question of the meaning of man will still remain unanswered; and so forth. Saint-Exupéry's demoralized state can certainly be understood in view of his gnawing anxieties over the fate of relatives and friends still living under the heel of the Nazi occupation. The fact that some of de Gaulle's advisers were still harboring a grudge against him for not having sided with the general while in New York did not help matters. The only antidote to his depressed state was active service and not a desk job as a reservist in Algiers.

He finally saw another chance in April 1944, when he was given a new assignment as commander of a bombing squadron stationed in Sardinia. Again, after incessant pleadings to carry out reconnaissance missions himself, and despite the maximum age limit of thirty-six for piloting fighter planes, he was granted permission by his American commander to rejoin his old group, now stationed in Corsica, and to conduct five additional missions. Only then was Saint-Exupéry satisfied, sharing the rigors of military life with his old friends and flying over his native land, particularly the Alpine corridor leading north to the Annecy region that he knew so well. Only then, when risking his life under extremely dangerous circumstances, did he feel truly fulfilled.

And so he went on beyond the five missions he had been allotted, over the anxious objections of his friends. They finally managed to work out a discreet scheme with the American authorities to ground him for his own good. Their plan would have taken effect on the evening of 31 July. Meanwhile, Saint-Exupéry had been granted permission to fly a mission—his ninth—on the morning of 31 July. This did, indeed, prove to be his last mission, for he flew off and was never heard of again. The official military report would record simply: "Mapping east of Lyon . . . No pictures. . . . Pilot did not return and is presumed lost." The most plausible theory was that he had been shot down by

German fighter planes off the coast of Corsica on his way northward to the Annecy area. His comrades waited for his return for a long while. They continued to wait for news that he had somehow survived a crash over France, as though in fulfillment of the romantic legend of a charmed existence that had come to be associated with him. But this time he did not return; he had disappeared without leaving a trace. In November of that year Saint-Exupéry was awarded a posthumous military citation for his qualities of daring and skill, signed by de Gaulle. On 12 March 1950, he was again awarded a citation, carrying the Croix de Guerre, with palm, for having made "French wings shine with a new brilliance" and for having expressed "his taste for action and the generosity of his ideals in literary works ranking among the most important of our time and celebrating the spiritual mission of France."

Among the writer's papers was found a short piece that would be published in 1948 as "Seigneur berbère" (not translated into English), telling of an old Berber chieftain and his stronghold empire in the desert—a subject that was perhaps surprising in its exoticism and certainly quite different from the sort of thing Saint-Exupéry had written up to that point. His immense attraction to the desert dated back, of course, to his earliest years as a pilot in North Africa, and he considered himself reasonably well-informed on the customs and beliefs of the Muslim tribesmen of the region. The Berber lord examines his power over his subjects; he is a despot, but a benevolent one, caring for the well-being of each individual through the creation of bonds of responsibility, a unified state, and subservience to a silent God. In its broad outline, then, this text of about ten pages can be seen as a trial version of Saint-Exupéry's last great work, where he would again place his ideas on political leadership, man's moral nature, God, and other themes in the mouth of a desert chieftain rather than in that of a Rivière type of Westerner.

The most voluminous packet of manuscripts found among his papers was the work that was published posthumously as *The Wisdom of the Sands.* There is some irony in the notion that it is a "posthumous work"; Saint-Exupéry himself jokingly referred to it as such, claiming it would need another ten years for completion. He had begun in 1936 to take notes for it in his notebook, later published in French as *Carnets* (1953). The bulk of its typewritten pages were probably composed in New York. He carried it with him to North Africa, where he continued working on it up to two months before his death; a separate folder containing a thick sheaf of handwritten pages was found together with the typescripts.

Saint-Exupéry often spoke to his friends about his book in progress and thought of it as his most significant literary achievement; indeed, he is quoted as having stated that next to this work all his other books were "mere exercises." The problem of editing the work according to the presumed intention of the author would therefore appear to have been a crucial one. We must remain content with the resulting close approximation, however, for the editors had little way of knowing where the supplementary pages were to be added or what the precise order of the chapters should be; moreover, some the handwriting was virtually illegible. Further, given our knowledge that Saint-Exupéry had cut out more than half the bulk of his draft of *Night Flight* in its final editing, in order to achieve the succinctness and tightly knit structure for which it is justly famous, the question remains as to what the total length of the work would have been. Even after final excisions of obvious redundancies, the French version still contains 219 chapters and 527 pages. The American version, with its 123 chapters and 350 pages, presents a distinctly more manageable text.

Critics frequently choose to refer to *The Wisdom of the Sands* as a "work," as though hesitant to call the book a novel. At least in the formal sense, however, it can be considered a novel of the fictional-memoir type. A desert chieftain, the Great Caid, delivers his meditations to the reader in a prose style reminiscent of certain portions of the Bible where a universal perspective of human society is stated with simple grandeur and rolling cadences, with fervor and feeling. (The true model may in fact have been Nietzsche's *Also sprach Zarathustra*.) There are virtually no characters and no plot in the usual sense. The narrator is a relatively young man who tells of the lessons he has learned from his recently assassinated father and the lessons he has himself mastered from the practice of ruling over his empire. Specific events are recounted and particular persons described as examples of the way people behave, and these in turn become pretexts for explaining and justifying how a ruler should use his knowledge to shape the state in the name of the common good. Thus, despite the exotic setting and the very different format chosen, the work contains many of the major themes that Saint-Exupéry elaborated over the years.

Saint-Exupéry was not a "philosopher" in any formal sense, and it is clear that he distrusted any logical system not tempered by the heart. One is reminded of the seventeenth-century writer whom he greatly admired, Blaise Pascal, who eventually came to the realization that logic and reason could carry man only so far in his search for truth, beyond which only the heart and faith could serve as satisfactory guides. In choosing to communicate his ideas through parables rather than logical demonstrations, Saint-Exupéry ran the risk of structuring contradictions into his work, and these may well puzzle the reader. As a desert patriarch—presumably Muslim—the chieftain combines qualities that may appear contradictory: the leadership ability of a King David, the wisdom of a King Solomon, the thirst for adventure and the aloofness of a legendary Alexander or Cyrus, but also the ruthlessness of a tyrant. Like his father, the chieftain metes out punishments that are harsh and cruel, but he also performs acts of charity and speaks of his subjects with fraternal tenderness. For, while authoritarian, he is aware of his own imperfections, and while noble, he is not arrogant. Punishments carried out for the good of the culprit, or as an example to society, are reminiscent of Rivière's methods in *Night Flight* and, as critics have often noted, demonstrate a Nietzschean influence in Saint-Exupéry that is difficult to reconcile with the Christian notions of humaneness that he also espouses. Would he have clarified these ambiguities in a final editing, or would he have left them as an integral part of the fabric of the book? To use one of his recurring images, the work is still imbedded in its *gangue*—its matrix—like a sculpture only partially released from the marble in which it is imprisoned.

The "citadel" of the French title suggests a city that must be safeguarded. In its wider sense it represents a total civilization composed of the sum of relationships of all its citizens: relationships with one another, with their material world, with their past history and traditions and with their future as well, as the civilization itself takes on a transcendental value that gives meaning to the life of each individual and to all those yet to come. The role of a political leader is to promote the defense and development of this citadel, and to "found" it in the heart of each citizen.

In its broad outline, the Caid's "wisdom of the sands" constitutes nothing less than the sum of Saint-Exupéry's humanistic philosophy. Man is not simply a physical presence on earth but a sum of values—values that must be constructed, then strengthened, and finally defended against the internal and external forces that are disposed to weaken and demolish the structure. In this struggle, authority of a paternalistic or feudal type is essential to impose constraints on the people for their own good. While such notions as justice, equality, and individual freedom are important and have their place, the notions of discipline, fraternity, and responsibility hold a higher rank in the hierarchical value system of this empire; for whatever *creates* Man must take precedence over that which merely allows an individual to enjoy life, since to create Man is to give him spiritual meaning. Human beings find their greatest fulfillment when they "barter" their ephemeral existence on earth for eternity by performing acts that will outlast them and become part of the heritage of the civilization itself. As the Caid says:

> For I respect above all that which endures longer than man, and thereby saves the meaning of their barter, and constitutes the great tabernacle to which they entrust everything of themselves. . . . They shall gladly barter themselves for that which is more precious than themselves. Thus are born painters, sculptors, engravers and carvers. But hope not for man if he work for his own life and not his eternity.
>
> (p. 38)

The material, utilitarian world may serve as a means to attain that end, like steps leading to a temple, but the ultimate goal of a civilization is to create and strengthen a knot of relationships. In this system God is defined as the "essential knot of diverse acts," or—to use Saint-Exupéry's architectural analogy—the keystone in the arch supporting the entire structure. But this God is beyond our reach. By his very nature—one might say his noble nature, for Saint-Exupéry often reveals an aristocratic bias—God will not respond to prayer, nor should our turn of mind be so utilitarian as to expect him to do so. Throughout *The Wisdom of the Sands*, Saint-Exupéry appears ripe for a mystical experience leading to true faith, but that faith never fully asserts itself. He undoubtedly felt nostalgia for his early Catholic upbringing; what he retains of it primarily, however, is a respect for ritual, authority, and the "Christian" values of Western civilization, but where Christ is only the palest of shadows. Ultimately, his God is an ideal deistic notion that imbues human life with the spiritual meaning necessary to foster creative acts, ties of love, and the steadfast acceptance of social duty.

Saint-Exupéry read the first few pages of the work to Drieu La Rochelle and Benjamin Crémieux, two friends whose judgment he re-spected. They did not hide their disappointment. For them, he was the poet of action, an enthusiastic, virile writer of whom they were expecting new stories of adventure. Their reservations undoubtedly stemmed from the marked abstractness of the ideas expressed in the book and its immense distance from the concrete world to which they had become accustomed in their friend's work—the world of the pilot, of discovery, of courage, and of warm friendships. While *The Wisdom of the Sands* can count several strong supporters among Saint-Exupéry's critics, others tend to view it as ponderous or as an anomaly in the canon of his works, occupying a questionable place in that canon because it does not bear the author's final imprimatur.

A summary glance at Saint-Exupéry's total literary production will show that there is a gradual evolution in the writer's choice of literary forms, paralleling his search for a personally satisfying ideological base. This evolution is marked by three phases. In the first, his attraction to the novel form of a traditionally realistic type gives us two very different kinds of thematic material. In pursuing its focus on the past—childhood, love, consolation—his first novel, *Southern Mail,* depicts a quest for something not yet known; the meanings are uncertain, and the reader is left with the impression of a romantic longing that cannot be satisfied. In *Night Flight,* the goal is clearly sighted: civilization itself is a value system that will allow men to fulfill themselves through giving their best. What is important, then, is to barter the ephemeral nature of an individual life for the enduring values of human structures; and the right path is that of duty, responsibility, courage, and a Nietzschean shaping of the self through the agency of a *métier.*

The principal literary form of the second phase is a type of eyewitness journalistic reporting that becomes increasingly autobiographical (*Wind, Sand, and Stars; Flight to Arras; Letter to a Hostage*). Here Saint-Exupéry focuses on what he perceives to have gone wrong in the modern world. Materialism has triumphed over the spiritual and brought on a reign of mediocrity, efficiency has replaced courage, political hostilities have corrupted friendship and love, state-sponsored conformism has obliterated the diversity that fosters creativity, and young Mozarts are being murdered in the bud. His response is to hold up images of Man's unending potential through examples of courageous men he has known; to cultivate the smile of friendship among men of all nations and cultures; to deny victory to the Nazi invaders despite their overwhelming strength, by stubbornly fighting on in the name of civilization itself, which will ultimately triumph.

In his third phase, he returns to fiction, but in the nonrealistic tradition of fable and parable (*The Little Prince, The Wisdom of the Sands*). Here the author has moved still further in the direction of giving sharp definition to the spiritual insights and rules of moral conduct that he had slowly been formulating from his earliest period onward. His writing is never so frankly didactic as in this last phase. The aphoristic lessons of *The Little Prince* and the codification of ethical and political rules in *The Wisdom of the Sands* bespeak a writer who not only has found the right spiritual path to follow but now accepts the responsibility of bringing his message to the readers of his troubled times.

On balance, however, the relative artistic success or failure of each of his works does not depend so much on the choice of literary form or the elaboration of philosophical ideas as on certain distinct characteristics of his style. One is the concreteness of his inspiration. Saint-Exupéry is probably never better than when he writes of the joy of the pilot in his plane, fully aware of his existence and in a privileged position to cast new perspectives on the meaning of the human adventure taking place on earth. At the other extreme we sense that the representation of certain types of point of view—that of a woman, or of a desert chieftain, or of men choosing sides in a political battle that is not their own—may be too remote from the au-

thor's own experience to allow his text to come to life with the same vigor or his arguments to be made with the same conviction. When Saint-Exupéry deals with what is most familiar to him, his gift for bringing thematic material to life through simple and striking imagery is at its most impressive. His vocabulary is studded with a number of concrete poetic images, key words radiating symbolic ideas relatively complex in their meaning yet easily graspable: *to tie, to tame, to barter, bonds, thirst, métier, cathedral, tree, fountain, smile, house, ship, stars,* and so forth. By contrast, some of the terms found primarily in his last work have a decidedly more abstract cast: *to found, slope, matrix, empire, domain.*

Finally, there are opposing tensions in much of Saint-Exupéry's work, and these work to greatest advantage when they are clearly identified and then left in an unresolved state. The power of *Night Flight* is attributable in large measure to the fact that each of the opposing sides in the debate is recognized as having a value that should not be canceled by the other. A woman's love and a pilot's right to private happiness are too important for a Rivière to achieve a final and definitive triumph—as Rivière is himself aware. We may admire Rivière's strength of character and the ultimate societal benefits of his ideology while fully recognizing, as he does, that his victory must remain a provisional one; the debate remains in a state of creative nonresolution. Similarly, the Little Prince's decision to return to his beloved rose signals the beginning of his metamorphosis into a "serious," responsible adult, a shift that is further dramatized by the death and disappearance of the child; but the fact that Saint-Exupéry wrote the story proves the adult author's need to remain in a situation of creative dialogue with the vulnerable child he would always carry within.

To reduce Saint-Exupéry's search to a few ideological formulas, or even to think of him principally as a purveyor of philosophical ideas, is to ignore the true value of his writing as the expression of a vigorously affirmative attitude toward life—the attitude that life itself is a never-ending adventure. First and foremost, he was a poet with an unflagging passion to live life to the fullest in the company and service of his comrades. His talents of observation served as the vehicle for expressing his vitally curious and compassionate attitudes toward men and the world, with a sense of wonder and spiritual concern, but also with deep affection and gentle humor. Critics are correct in viewing his career, both as writer and as adventurer, as a quest; for the notion of "quest" assumes a forward-looking orientation and a positive, even heroic, turn of mind that readily applies to Saint-Exupéry. In his works, life is seen less as a problem than as a mystery. His message to us today is that the spiritual meaning is there, but that it is not visible because it has been obscured by the dehumanizing materialism of our age. Given this outlook, the task of the writer is to pursue paths that will lead to a perception of spiritual meanings. In this endeavor it is not so much the ultimate answer that matters as the search itself, which will allow human beings to be joined to something greater than their individual selves.

Selected Bibliography

EDITIONS

INDIVIDUAL WORKS
Courrier sud. Paris, 1929.
Vol de nuit. Paris, 1931.
Terre des hommes. Paris, 1939.
Pilote de guerre. New York, 1942; Paris, 1942.
Lettre à un otage. New York, 1943; Paris, 1945.
Le petit prince. New York, 1943; Paris, 1946.
Citadelle. Paris, 1948.
"Seigneur berbère." *Table ronde* (July 1948): 1091–1101.
Un sens à la vie. Paris, 1956.
Écrits de guerre, 1939–1944. Paris, 1982.

COLLECTED WORKS
Oeuvres. Paris, 1959.

NOTEBOOKS

Carnets. Paris, 1953.

CORRESPONDENCE

Lettres de jeunesse, 1923–1931. Paris, 1953.
Lettres à l'amie inventée. Paris, 1953. (Same letters as above, with illustrations by Saint-Exupéry.)
Lettres à sa mère. Introduction by Saint-Exupéry's mother. Paris, 1955.

TRANSLATIONS

Airman's Odyssey. New York, 1942. (A trilogy comprising *Wind, Sand, and Stars*; *Night Flight*; and *Flight to Arras.*)
Flight to Arras. Translated by Lewis Galantière. New York, 1939.
Letter to a Hostage. Translated by John Rodker. In *French Short Stories.* New York, 1948.
The Little Prince. Translated by Katherine Woods. New York, 1943.
Night Flight. Translated by Stuart Gilbert. New York, 1932.
A Sense of Life. Translated by Adrienne Foulke. New York, 1965. (Includes "The Aviator," "An Open Letter to Frenchmen Everywhere," "Letter to General X," and other pieces.)
Southern Mail. Translated by Stuart Gilbert. New York, 1933.
Wartime Writings, 1939–1944. Translated by Norah Purcell, with an introduction by Anne Morrow Lindbergh. New York, 1986.
Wind, Sand, and Stars. Translated by Lewis Galantière. New York, 1939.
The Wisdom of the Sands. Translated by Stuart Gilbert. New York, 1949.

BIOGRAPHICAL AND CRITICAL STUDIES

Berghe, Christian van den. *La pensée de Saint-Exupéry.* New York, 1985.
Bréaux, Adèle. *Saint-Exupéry in America, 1942–1943.* Rutherford, N.J., 1971.
Brée, Germaine, and Margaret Guiton. *The French Novel from Gide to Camus.* New York, 1962.
Cate, Curtis. *Antoine de Saint-Exupéry: His Life and Times.* New York, 1970.
Chevrier, Pierre. *Antoine de Saint-Exupéry.* Paris, 1959.

Delange, René. *La vie de Saint-Exupéry,* followed by Léon Werth, *Tel que je l'ai connu.* Paris, 1948.

Estang, Luc. *Saint-Exupéry par lui-même.* Paris, 1956.

Forsberg, Roberta J. *Antoine de Saint-Exupéry and David Beaty: Poets of a New Dimension.* New York, 1974.

Ibert, Jean-Claude. *Antoine de Saint-Exupéry.* Paris, 1960.

Knight, Everett W. *Literature Considered as Philosophy: The French Example.* London, 1957.

Major, Jean-Louise. *Saint-Exupéry: L'Écriture et la pensée.* Ottawa, 1968.

Monin, Yves. *L'esotérisme du Petit Prince de Saint-Exupéry.* Paris, 1984.

Ouellet, Réal. *Les relations humaines dans l'oeuvre de Saint-Exupéry.* Paris, 1971.

Pélissier, Georges. *Les cinq visages de Saint-Exupéry.* Paris, 1951.

Peyre, Henri. *French Novelists of Today.* New York, 1967.

Quesnel, Michel. *Saint-Exupéry; ou, La vérité de la poésie.* Paris, 1964.

Robinson, Joy D. Marie. *Antoine de Saint-Exupéry.* Boston, 1984.

Rumbold, Richard, and Margaret Stewart. *The Winged Life: A Portrait of Antoine de Saint-Exupéry, Poet and Airman.* London, 1954.

Simon, Pierre-Henri. *L'Homme en procès: Malraux, Sartre, Camus, Saint-Exupéry.* Neuchâtel, 1949.

Smith, Maxwell A. *Knight of the Air: The Life and Works of Antoine de Saint-Exupéry.* New York, 1956.

Vercier, Bruno. *Les critiques de notre temps et Saint-Exupéry.* Paris, 1971.

RALPH TARICA

NATHALIE SARRAUTE
(b. 1900)

JEAN-PAUL SARTRE, in his preface to Nathalie Sarraute's *Portrait d'un inconnu* (*Portrait of a Man Unknown,* 1948), referred to the work as an "anti-novel," one in which primacy was given to the "platitude" and the "inauthentic." According to Sartre, Sarraute's experimental fiction encourages readers to peer into every nook and cranny of the sensate and amorphous worlds, to observe those insalubrious "protoplasmic" inner spheres that lie hidden behind facades and surfaces.

Sarraute was not the originator of the stylistic innovations contained in her novels and plays. Joyce, Proust, and Dostoevsky, whose works she had read and studied, were her mentors, and revealed to her a microscopic view of the world. They taught her how to look into beings and things and how to explore an invisible dimension, thereby expanding her notion of reality. The novel, viewed by her as a constantly renewing force, thus becomes the perfect vehicle to probe and disclose unknown worlds. Writing turns into a quest; and language, with all of its evocative, sonorous, and rhythmic qualities, is the instrument called upon to give the visual experience verbal meaning without losing any of its elusive reality.

Like the "New Novelists" or the "New Realists" (Michel Butor, Alain Robbe-Grillet, Claude Simon, Claude Ollier, and Robert Pinget—a loosely defined group of writers with whom Sarraute has frequently been identified), she broke with traditional creations of fictional plot, characterization, locale, chronology, and dialogue. Sarraute does not tell a story, nor does she invent characters; she rejected, as did the New Novelists, the well-worn techniques of Balzac, Stendhal, Flaubert, and Zola, with their structured plots, psychologically oriented flesh-and-blood human beings, and realistic descriptions. Certainly, these writing conventions were innovative in their time; today, they are ossified. According to the New Novelists, to continue churning out "old-fashioned" nineteenth-century-type novels would be to perpetuate the parasitic relationship between reader and author. A casual reader of conventional fiction generally laps up the exciting events, the conflicts, and the passions of the characters. Such reading, the New Novelists maintain, is facile, no more than a pleasant past-time. Sarraute and the New Novelists, however, despised the facile and obvious. For them, reading is to be looked upon not as a diversion but rather as a labor, a puzzle, requiring the utmost concentration and mental effort.

Despite these points of agreement, Sarraute's writings differ from those of the New Novelists. In an interview, she remarked:

Each of us writes in his own personal way, and very differently. Robbe-Grillet, for example, describes the exterior world: things, objects as seen from the outside. I, on the other hand, describe inner movements. His universe is more or less immobile whereas mine is in perpetual motion—

in a state of constant transformation. One could in fact say that our ways of writing are diametrically opposed both in terms of temperament and vision.

(*Off-Stage Voices*, p. 168)

Sarraute, for example, did not approve of the emphasis placed by the New Novelists upon abstraction, nor did she approve of their meticulously detailed depictions of the physical properties of exterior objects, or their use of these objects as catalysts to narrate patterns of behavior or experiences. An object for Sarraute is not a "linguistic" instigator; it is a "sign" that suggests internal human processes.

In *L'Ère du soupçon* (*The Age of Suspicion,* 1956), which consists of four critical essays, Sarraute explores the works of famous authors of the past in terms of her own literary vision. She discerns that behind the "solid reality" that Balzac offered his readers burned a mysterious hidden dimension, and she says that imitators of Balzac's literary technique have deadened what had been innovative in his time. Sarraute also notes that the role of "inauthenticity," which was so dear to her, was magnificently enacted in Flaubert's *Madame Bovary* (1857) in the series of trite images and traditional emotions that underlie Emma Bovary's dreams— themselves platitudes of Romanticism. Important as well was Flaubert's thematic view of fiction. "What I should like to do," she quotes him as saying, "is to compose a book about nothing . . . a book with almost no subject or at least where the subject was almost invisible, if possible." According to Sarraute, contemporary fiction must take this cue; the novel must be about nothing, must be divested of themes, characters, plots, doctrines, and messages so as to preserve its quality as a pure work of art. From Dostoevsky she learned to observe the abnormal world with its complex of opposites and its shadowy mental states, the subterranean world within which real drama exists. Proust and Joyce, using their finely discerning eyes and ears, invited her to experience

a world observed through a "microscope" and simultaneously to listen to the continuous conversations and sub-conversations of perpetually changing characters. Virginia Woolf also paved the way for the introduction of a fresh psychological reality, one cut off from the traditional conventions of time, place, and character.

By furnishing no details concerning a character's name, age, background, milieu, or any other physical or personal traits, Sarraute divests her fiction of all those familiar props that western readers have come to depend upon implicitly to find their bearings. Such technical devices she deemed to be unimportant remnants of a superficial and misleading way of viewing life and the creative process; they merely cater to readers' laziness by providing them with "security blankets" to grasp and hold onto. Instead, Sarraute dives directly into *someone's* thoughts while maintaining that individual's facade of anonymity. Nor are the creatures of her fantasy flesh-and-blood human beings. Proper names, she asserts, serve to confuse and to destroy any real communication between herself and the inner being whose sensations and thoughts she seeks to penetrate, extract, and reveal to the reader. Most frequently, Sarraute uses third-person narration (referring to characters as "he," "she," or "they") to define the trajectories of those beings whose sub-worlds she charts. She seeks to disorient her readers by compelling them to leap directly into those "inner movements" that lie at the core of speech and gesture and that she calls "tropisms." Disconcerted, the reader must adjust to this fragmented and chaotic reality and bathe, both physically and intellectually, in its perpetually innovative and restorative waters—or become lost in the attempt.

In *The Age of Suspicion,* Sarraute defines the tropisms or inner meanderings that lie at the heart of her literary vision:

They are undefinable movements which glide very rapidly to the limits of consciousness; they are at the root of our gestures, our words, of the feelings we manifest, which we believe we feel and which we can define. They seemed to me and still seem to me to constitute the secret source of our existence.

When these movements are in the process of formation, they remain unexpressed—not one word emerges—not even in the words of an interior monologue; they develop within us and vanish with extreme rapidity, without our ever really perceiving them clearly; they produce within us frequently very intense, but brief, sensations; these can be communicated to the reader only through images, thereby giving them an equivalent and enabling them to feel analogous situations. These movements had to be decomposed and allowed to extend into the reader's conscious mind in the manner of a film in slow motion. Time was no longer experienced in terms of the workaday world, but rather in a distorted and aggrandized present.

(Jolas trans., p. 8)

Tropisms are the sum and substance of Sarraute's intellectual and aesthetic credo. These "sub-movements," as she calls them, are inscribed in each of her novels and theater pieces, in a lush and rich, yet extraordinarily precise vocabulary, and they bombard and bewitch both the readers and the anonymous beings upon whom she focuses in her novels. The sensations aroused by these mysterious and hidden tropisms are perceived by the sensitive observer behind the most banal conversations and the most rudimentary gestures.

Enfance (*Childhood*, 1983), a loosely autobiographical work that describes Sarraute's life up to her school years, is, for the most part, made up of sequences of images and sensations rather than detailed factual narration. *Childhood* is one of the few statements Sarraute made concerning her personal life. She refused to reveal personal details of her life, as do such diarists as André Gide, Simone de Beauvoir, Anaïs Nin, Julien Green, Claude Mauriac, Thornton Wilder, Sylvia Plath, and so

many more. To persistent and inquiring newspaper reporters, scholars, and admirers, Sarraute doled out as few facts as possible. What was important to her was her oeuvre, not her person, because the former, as a true work of art, lives on eternally, while the latter, a finite and temporal entity, goes the way of all mortals.

Nathalie Sarraute was born Nathalie Tcherniak on 18 July 1900 in Ivanovo-Voznessensk, Russia. Her parents, Ilya Tcherniak and Pauline Chatounowski, were university students in Geneva when they met. (Under the reign of Nicholas II, Jews were prevented from studying at Russian universities, so families intent upon educating their children were compelled to send them abroad. This was the case with both of Sarraute's parents.) After receiving his doctorate of science in chemistry, Ilya went back to his native land, married Pauline, and started a dye factory in the textile town of Ivanovo.

Nathalie, two years old when her parents divorced, left Russia for Paris with her mother and subsequently visited her father for two months every year. Traveling between the two countries during her childhood enabled her to become fluent in both French and Russian. Nathalie's mother remarried in 1906, returned to Russia, settled in St. Petersburg with her historian husband, and spent her time writing short stories and novels and working on a literary review. Nathalie returned to Paris in 1908 to live with her newly remarried father, who had moved to Paris earlier and had started a dye factory in his new homeland. Politically oriented, Ilya had returned to Paris after an earlier visit to organize a group that would help fight the extradition of his brother, a revolutionary who had, along with others, attacked the tsarist government and escaped to Sweden.

The Tcherniaks lived within an enclave of Russian intellectual emigrés. Nathalie benefited from her surroundings: she learned German and English from her stepmother's mother, a highly cultured woman, while also spending a good deal of her time reading the

Russian and European classics. She loved school, studied hard, and was awarded many prizes for her consistently high grades. Her father's constant encouragement gave her the self-confidence she needed to pursue her career.

After earning a *certificat d'études* from a small community school on the rue d'Alésia, Sarraute was enrolled at the Lycée Fénelon, where she studied physics, among other disciplines, and received her baccalaureate degree in 1914. After preparing a *licence* in English at the Sorbonne, she moved to Oxford in 1920, where she studied for a B.A. From 1921 to 1922 Sarraute attended the Faculty of Letters in Berlin, specializing in sociology. The next academic institution she attended was the Paris Law School. She was admitted to the Paris bar in 1925. It was in law school that Nathalie met a fellow student, Raymond Sarraute, whom she married; they had three daughters, Claude, Anne, and Dominique.

Sarraute's extraordinarily fine education served her in good stead as a writer. It increased her understanding of human beings and broadened her technical acumen and vocabulary, thus largely accounting for her verbal artistry as novelist, playwright, and essayist. Her works are veritable feasts of words, full of incredible pictorial images and their accompanying intonations and rhythmic patterns. Her training as a lawyer developed her ability to reason to an extreme degree. Quietly and calmly, as if with a scalpel, Sarraute probes ever more deeply into the myriad layers of her characters' inner worlds, concretizing their tropisms in an incisive meta-language that transcends the usual function of language. As sensation upon sensation becomes impacted in endlessly interlacing spoken and narrative discourses, the multifaceted visions of her creatures are experienced by the reader in ever-fluid, crystallized forms. Each sequence, a mini-drama in itself, is endowed with catalytic power; each tropism is ready and able to withdraw or to parry, aggress, violate, or defend; the image-sequences in the tropisms

are endowed with energy that affects the reader like arguments or verbal confrontations with increasingly deepening and well-defined orbits.

As far back as Sarraute could remember, she had wanted to write fiction. She authored a novel when she was seven years old, but when she showed it to a writer friend of her mother's, she was utterly dismayed to hear that she should learn to spell before undertaking the writing of a book. So strongly embedded in Sarraute's psyche was her feeling of rejection at this rebuke that it may have been instrumental in preventing her from sending her first volume of literary sketches, *Tropismes* (*Tropisms*), to another publisher at this time. Although it was composed in 1932, *Tropisms* was not published until 1939.

Tropisms consists of a group of unrelated fragments that delineate separate tropistic movements. Within them, in seminal form, is the sum and substance of everything that Sarraute wrote subsequently. Undefinable in terms of traditional literary designations, these sequences may be referred to as "microdramas" or "prose poems." Each is a vignette depicting some slight incident in the life of an ordinary person: an easily disturbed housewife who speaks derogatorily of everyone she knows; a grandfather who holds his grandson's little hand with great tenderness as the two cross a street, believing he is protecting the boy from harm; a group of ladies chatting over their tea, a means, perhaps, of filling the void and the deep silence that corrodes their lives. However, the reader will never be able to visualize these beings as individuals; rather, they are scientific or zoological and sociological species: groups of *lieux communs* (commonplaces) whose complex thoughts and sensations are concretized in sequences of Sarrautian tropisms. From Tropism 1, we read her description of an amorphous mass, referred to at first as "they," who are later recognized as a crowd of people observing shop windows in the street:

They seemed to ooze from everywhere, hatched in the warmish moisture of the air, they streamed out gently as if exuding from the walls, the railed-off trees, from the benches, the squalid pavements, and the squares.

They stretched into long, dark clusters amongst the dead facades of the houses. From time to time, in front of the fronts of shops, they formed more compact, motionless knots, causing some swirling, some slight congestions.[1]

Satiric, but always objective, Sarraute uses her tropistic literary technique to emphasize the weaknesses in human behavior. As if she were writing a report, she does not take a stand; she is not politically *engagé* in her writing, as were André Malraux and Sartre. She merely comments on what she observes: a world of banalities, platitudes, and clichés, beneath which, and hidden from view, exists a sphere of turmoil and anguish. Her terse and concentrated portraits of faceless and anonymous beings, divested of the usual time, place, and character references, gain a universal quality.

Tropisms are experienced in image form. They come into being as consciousness is brought into existence, prior to their verbalization. Sartre has called Sarraute's visions "protoplasmic" because they delineate organic substances with utmost accuracy and finesse, with Cartesian precision and geometric method. The clarity of the observations, with their emphasis on microscopic details, creates a series of eidetic images, each imposed and superimposed upon the other in seemingly infinite layerings. These stratifications are never static. On the contrary, amoeba-like, they are in a state of perpetual flux, altering in form and content, substance and point. In Tropism 2, concerning the relationship of an old man with a child, we read:

And the child felt something weighing down on him, paralyzing him. A soft suffocating mass, which someone was forcing him relentlessly to absorb, using a gentle but unyielding pressure, lightly pinching his nose to make him swallow, without any possibility of resistance, was flowing into him, while he trotted along quietly and properly, docilely giving his little hand to hold, nodding his head very sagely, and while it was being explained to him how necessary it was to move with great caution and look carefully, first right, then left, and to take care, great care, for fear of an accident, while crossing the street.

Sarraute's tropisms are unlike Joycean interior monologues, which flow through one's conscious mind. They are preconscious incisions, pre-interior monologues clothed in a vocabulary as sensual as Proust's and as incisive as Samuel Beckett's.

In *Portrait of a Man Unknown*, Sarraute takes the reader into the world of a penurious father, similar to Balzac's Grandet, and his spinster daughter. In this miasmic sphere of sub-surfaces, beings are described in meticulous detail: their attitudes, emotions, and sensations are incised in a vocabulary replete with colorations and alternating rhythms. Character types did not interest Sarraute. They did not exist as real beings for her: they were not even "presences," to use Robbe-Grillet's appellation. Sarraute called them "envelopes," imprisoned in their masks, subservient to the role assigned to them by the writer. Dostoevsky, Sarraute wrote in her essay "From Dostoevsky to Kafka" (in *The Age of Suspicion*), exteriorized the inner essences and systems of his characters in "the most minute variations of a current, its subtle movements, hardly perceptible, fugitive, contradictory." Dostoevsky also succeeded in translating and then articulating sequences of hidden "subjacent movements" within the heart and soul of his creations, while with Kafka, "all feeling disappeared, even disdain and hatred," leaving "only an immense empty stupor." Sarraute probed the void unearthed by Dostoevsky and then used it as a basic element in her work.

Rejecting "surface reality," which she defined as what everyone sees effortlessly, Sar-

[1] All translations by the author except as noted.

raute, the true realist, sought, more like the naturalist, to observe inner meanderings through external referents, in what could be alluded to as a human semiology. The author becomes a kind of listener, and, like the reader, witnesses the event as it is happening or being experienced. Distances are maintained by the author so as to retain as much objectivity as possible. Previously, novelists manipulated their characters as they saw fit, through their actions, names, milieux, and so forth. Not Sarraute, since she has no characters; she catapults fragmented essences within the event and the thought, which is then concretized in variegated tropisms.

Portrait of a Man Unknown, like all of Sarraute's subsequent works, has neither plot nor characters in the traditional senses of the words. Viewing such structures as artificial, she banished them from her aesthetic universe. Proust, she remarked, was the first writer to demonstrate the perpetual modification characters undergo in living out their histories. His are not static figures. At the end of *Remembrance of Things Past* (1913–1927), Proust's protagonists have become, in a manner reminiscent of Sarraute's tropistic views, totally different from what they had been at the outset.

In *Portrait of a Man Unknown,* an anonymous narrator, speaking in the first person, discloses his trepidations. Unlike the customary authoritative and strong narrator, Sarraute's figure, a victim of self-doubt, hesitates constantly. He may be seen as a paradigm of the author herself as she ferrets out ways of seeing and feeling into situations and people through modification of the very essence of conventional structures.

Although no facts are given in *Portrait of a Man Unknown,* the reader feels drawn into the narrator's world of banalities as he articulates his feelings each time he meets the egotistical miser, either alone or with his neurotic daughter. Although one is never allowed to perceive the narrator as a person, he explores the miser's and his daughter's world through his own consciousness, and in the process he discloses in detail what he has observed and is observing, depicting the hidden underpinnings of these people in tenuous subterranean movements—or tropisms. As a result, multiple modes come into view: the timbre of the daughter's voice, for example, described as "atonal," sounds out an inner climate divested of love and feeling. Such sonorities may refer to her present situation, living ascetically with a penurious father, or they may convey the anguish resulting from an emotionally deprived childhood. The father's fears that his daughter may milk him dry are experienced by the narrator in colorful expressionist forms as well as in representational images such as that of a muscle flexed in readiness for the fight or for the leap about to be taken. Sarraute uses descriptions of insects and animals throughout her writings, epithetically, analogically, and symbolically. The reference, for example, to the father as "a giant spider," ever ready to catch a fly, indicates his ever-vigilant attitude toward money and things. The allusion to the daughter at times as a hyena intimates her alertness. She, too, is ready to do battle if necessary. The narrator, identified with a crab in its hole, fearful lest he be hurt in some way, is a perfect visualization of timorousness and escapism. Beneath these and other images lies a world of repressed desires, where father and daughter, like "two enormous dung beetles," exist in a state of undeclared war.

The narrator's world consists of his reactions to the father-and-daughter duet. He wants to know them plainly, to understand the meaning of their inner pulsations, those that their presence activate within him. They are the sum and substance of his existence; because they are the object of his scrutiny, he follows them everywhere, attempting in this way to ferret out more and more information concerning their motivations and feelings. When he is barred from approaching them for one reason or another and is therefore no longer able to register the inner movements that give him a sense of life and a raison d'être, he feels himself losing touch and becoming cut off from the world of the living. Solitude and loneliness invade his being. To fill the void within, he sometimes succeeds in conjuring them in his mind's eye. When, on other occasions, he meets the daughter in a restaurant or sees her with her father at home, his observations pursue their course directly, incisively, and forthrightly. After multiple disappointments and the pain these people elicit in him when he feels himself to be an outsider to their world, the narrator eventually realizes that he can never really know a person fully.

At the novel's conclusion, the daughter introduces the narrator to her fiancé, Louis Dumontet, whose profession and physical qualities are described. Resorting to such conventional depictions—including a proper name and other details concerning this person—is experienced as a defeat for the narrator. To have recourse to proper names is to yield to a facile view of reality, to old-time novelistic techniques, thereby putting an end to the tropisms that were the narrator's great preoccupation. When the daughter leaves with her fiancé, the narrator and the old man remain together. No longer are they immersed, as they once were, in the tropistic world of internal movement, of protoplasmic reality; rather, they have returned to old, worn ways and obsolete forms. Even linear time takes over as the father, growing old, reasons that it is best for his daughter to get married. The reign of the "inauthentic" has begun, and with it the conventional categories of the traditional novel.

Sarraute uses the narrator's continuous search to capture and encapsulate the father's and daughter's essences as a way to question and challenge the very structure of the novel form. His successes and failures create the novel's momentum, its suspense and drama. As for the narrator's obsessions, they are, to some extent, mirror images of the author's own preoccupations with the act of writing.

Although the narrator considers himself defeated at the conclusion of *Portrait of a Man Unknown*, the author does not, since Sarraute used the same interrogative mode of narration as a probing or sounding board in her next novel, *Martereau* (1953). In this novel the narrator lives in a cloistered environment with his aunt, uncle, and cousin. Highly sensitive to the tropisms he discovers within himself and within those who surround him—as was the narrator in *Portrait of a Man Unknown*—he differs from the latter at first, in that he remains an observer only. His personality, feelings, and sensations are constantly cast in the background. The picture changes, however, the moment an intruder—his friend Martereau—enters the family compound.

The drama in *Martereau* revolves around a banal incident: the uncle's purchase of a house and piece of land. To avoid paying certain taxes, the uncle gives Martereau cash to purchase the property in his name. Because Martereau fails to give the uncle a receipt for the cash, he is thought to be dishonest. Conflict is born within the family, each member taking sides, for a variety of reasons, with or against the intruder. The personality struggle between the family members arouses such uncertainty that the resulting malaise reaches out and affects the reader as well. The narrator is also unnerved by Martereau's apparent deception, until, at the novel's conclusion, Martereau's receipt finally does arrive and all thoughts of his dishonesty are dispelled for the time being. Although nothing has changed, everything has altered. The narrator views him in an altogether different manner, as do the family members.

The plot in *Martereau* is unimportant. What is significant are the inner movements or tropisms the protagonists generate within each other and their impact upon the individual family members and the family as a whole. The narrative, as in *Portrait of a Man Unknown,* is related by a first-person narrator who views the events he records. The reader is situated within his consciousness. Unlike the narrator in *Portrait of a Man Unknown,* however, he is characterized as "nonproductive," since he has never achieved status in his field. Referred to as an interior decorator, he has never developed a sense of color or a feel for furnishings or decor, nor does he feel obsessed, as did the narrator in *Portrait of a Man Unknown,* by a desire to penetrate the essence of the family members. The narrator's great preoccupation revolves around his need to be accepted and liked and to be involved in the family. So sensitive is he to the reactions of others, so persistent is his fear of annoying people—his uncle in particular, whom he is afraid of alienating—that he constantly observes them all, spies on them. Indeed, he inspects their every intonation, thought, and gesture, endeavoring to detect any little sign or symptom of incipient rejection.

In every way possible, he tries to get closer to the family, even if this means entering into complicity with each of them. Yet, despite his need, and perhaps in conflict with it, the narrator paradoxically tries to remain on the outside of things. There are times when he cannot. Eventually, he must take sides for or against Martereau, the "bloodletting games of the arena" making it impossible for him to remain aloof. When he is drawn into battle by his aunt and cousin, his uncle views his vacillating attitude with distaste, seeing it as a paradigm of "degrading promiscuity." In part to heal his own hurt, and also to quell his uncle's annoyance, he goes to Martereau's house, inquiring as to why he has not furnished his uncle with a receipt for the money. Martereau is deeply hurt by the family's lack of confidence in his integrity. The narrator, reacting to his friend's pain—real or feigned—returns home and tries to convince the family of his friend's sterling character. The uncle sees things differently: he believes that Martereau has taken the money and moved into the house himself. As the narrator ponders the various interpretations of the situation, analyzing and replaying them in his mind, his relationship with and his view of Martereau changes. In the end, although Martereau turns out to be a dependable fellow, he is no longer the person the narrator had thought him to be at the outset.

Relationships, like an interplay of mirrored reflections, lead at times to a loss of bearings.

Fissures and cracks and defects, although not always visible at first glance, are potential in every being. The novel's name, *Martereau,* from "martyr" and from the French word *marteau,* meaning hammer, suggests the painful blows experienced with the birth or eruption of knowledge and the breaking up of an illusion and the consequent pain.

Some critics have alluded to the constant bickerings and struggles taking place between Sarraute's creatures, manifested in her myriad sparring, martial, and animal visualizations, as evidence of a perpetual struggle between active and passive individuals. Her world, then, seems to be made up of those who seek to dominate and those who yield. In an interview, Sarraute countered this impression:

> I would not call it a struggle between the active and passive beings, but rather between various types of tropisms and appearances. There is always the kind of individual who seeks to delve deeply into himself so as to perceive those tropisms I have mentioned and others who prefer not to see them, but take great pains to mask them. A state of flux always exists, therefore; constant play between the exterior and interior worlds, visible and invisible reality.
>
> (*Off-Stage Voices,* p. 165)

Herein also lies the drama of *Le planétarium* (*The Planetarium,* 1959), where surface descriptions vie for supremacy over internal movements. The title itself indicates the antipathies involved, for a planetarium reveals an artificial rather than a real sky. So, too, are the beings who live out their anxieties in their secret insalubrious spheres endowed with masks that others seek to penetrate by burrowing like termites through infinite surface pulsions.

The plot, if in fact there is one, revolves around an old aunt, Berthe, who is obsessed by her apartment and her furniture. Eventually, these are to be willed to her nephew, Alain, for whom she has played the role of surrogate mother since the death of his own when he was very young. It was Berthe who always assuaged his fears and wiped away his tears whenever his father disappointed him for one reason or another. Was it she, as well, who encouraged a certain weakness—now a flaw—in his character? Alain, who is in the process of writing a dissertation on painting, thinks of himself as quite an art connoisseur. He and his wife, Gisèle, both love furniture—particularly aunt Berthe's. Alain has his eye on her apartment, and Berthe, who feels she is close to the end of her life, is prepared to give it to the young couple.

The opening image features Berthe, who is annoyed with the workman who is redoing an oak door in her apartment. As Sarraute focuses on every detail of that door, rich and lush images, metaphors, and similes emerge so fully that the reader's love of that oak door and hostility for the workman whose work is so slipshod are made to parallel the aunt's. There follows a minute description of the apartment, its furniture and knickknacks. Gisèle's mother comes into the picture: she wants to give her daughter and son-in-law two "superb leather armchairs." They, however, want two antique *bergères* (Louis XV–style easy chairs). Alain goes to see Germaine Lemaire, a well-known writer, to ask her which would be more suitable for the apartment, the leather chairs or the two *bergères.*

Meanwhile, the aunt has changed her mind, or so rumor has it. She no longer wants to give her apartment to Alain and Gisèle but prefers to remain there, where memories of her whole life are embedded. Furthermore, she wants to remain in the neighborhood she has always lived in. At the same time, Alain grows more and more possessive and obsessive about her apartment and its contents. He even threatens his aunt. Gone is the loving mother image with which he has always identified her; instead, she has taken on the countenance of a "hideous hag." Soon, Berthe experiences episodes of breathlessness; she feels herself suffocating. Will she die? Is Alain manipulating her? Some say no; he adores his aunt. Other friends and acquaintances see his relationship

in a different light. Finally, the tug of war becomes too stressful. Berthe yields and gives her apartment to Alain. She will live in a modern apartment.

Although *The Planetarium* revolves around seemingly banal themes, the tropisms pulsating beneath the surfaces and concretized in Sarraute's extraordinary imagery generate a whole series of questions concerning Alain and his relationships with his aunt, with Germaine Lemaire, with Gisèle, and with her mother. Gisele's attitudes toward Alain, her mother, Berthe, and Germaine Lemaire are also called into question. Does Berthe try to dominate her nephew? Was Gisèle's mother intent upon having her way when she offered the couple the two leather chairs? Are young and old pitted against each other? Do these people focus obsessively on the material world? Wasn't it Berthe who inculcated in Alain a love for possessions? Or could Alain's obsession be called cupidity? What are the hidden behavior patterns behind this family's moves? Do they consist of love, hate, repulsion, attraction? Are spiritual and moral values completely absent?

As in *Martereau,* a material entity—this time the apartment—sets the stage for the tense ensuing battle of emotions and wit. As these impulses and emotions become manifest, they break up, splatter, and scatter. People are not seen as whole beings but rather as disparate or fragmented entities that regroup continuously in Sarraute's tropistic world, forever creating other incidents, arousing fresh sensations and ideations. In *The Planetarium,* as in Sarraute's previous novels, the continuously appearing and disappearing beings bobbing up and down in her novel are no more than transparencies that make their way in and out of situations, as they move about the world of objects (a piece of furniture, a book, a door, a *bergère*), or about the human beings with whom they must contend. (For example, Martereau takes on life through the money the uncle gives him to buy property.) The endless conversations about furniture, decors, colors, and Berthe's apartment further reveal the inner worlds of

Sarraute's beings, their tics and attitudes acting as facades for their lies and fantasies.

Tropisms take on life within the context of human relations: there they expand and grow like so many fungi. In *Tropisms,* readers see a variety of forms walking about, sitting and chatting, playing, being called to dinner, or being taken across streets, each form performing the sequence of rituals implicit in his or her character or life-style. In *Portrait of a Man Unknown,* the narrative focuses upon father and daughter; in *Martereau,* uncle and nephew; in *The Planetarium,* mother, daughter, aunt, and nephew. Each is linked to the other. Articulated or silent, a repressed world exists, but is barely sensed, guessed at through tropisms; these nascent spheres come into being through the wizardry of Sarraute's incredible imagination and unique sense of reality. In this unformed tropistic sphere, individuals depend upon each other for existence, though there are moments in *The Planetarium* when Sarraute's essences, or figurations, wish they could divest themselves of friends and relatives, and at other moments their inner rage is so great that they meditate upon ways of killing the person they consider their enemy. How can Alain rid himself of his obsession? Is he a victim of greed?

Are there autobiographical elements implicit in Sarraute's novels in general, and in *The Planetarium* in particular? Did Sarraute project herself upon Aunt Berthe? Martereau? the father and daughter duo? Sarraute addressed these questions in an interview as follows:

> Autobiographical elements exist everywhere in my works just as they do in everybody else's. In my case I never write anything that I have not truly experienced or have not known anyone else to have experienced. This does not mean that I extract situations from my own life. I have never known a more generous person than my own father; yet I have described an avaricious father. I have never really used autobiographical ele-

ments or situations but simply sensations, impressions scattered here and there.

> (*Off-Stage Voices,* p. 166)

The Planetarium, Sarraute's most popular book, offers more of a plot than her previous works. Incidents and people are interconnected; there is a progression in the action and a chronological order in the circular patterns of events depicted. However, these vestiges of old-fashioned literary techniques may be traps or artifices set by Sarraute to lure the reader into other paths, to arouse different sensations. Tropisms always lurk beneath and behind every glance, stance, gesture, sensation, and inner dialogue. Indeed, just as Sarraute gave birth to a new aesthetics, so too did her insistence on tropisms elicit a fresh psychological approach, giving her access to the collective and anonymous side of the beings peopling her work. Nevertheless, she remarked in an interview that she was not trying to compete with scientists:

> I merely want to translate certain impressions which are actually poetic. But it is very difficult to define in words exactly what one feels—what poetry per se tries to express. When the reader begins to feel what I have been trying to say, when the sensations have been transmitted to him, I believe I have succeeded at this particular moment in my endeavor. I try to depict a way of feeling and of seeing things which is my own, but which many other people feel in a similar manner.

> (*Off-Stage Voices,* p. 167)

Sensations and impressions, and shifting moods and feelings, are made visible and exciting in a vocal, visual, and rhythmic metaphorical language replete with crescendos and diminuendos, presented in alternating paces. Aunt Berthe's pleasure at the installation of a new and beautiful oak door is felt so keenly that deep stress takes over moments later when she notices that the worker has put an ugly nickel-plated doorknob on it, thereby destroying its elegance. So excruciating is her pain that her emotional equilibrium seems to be disturbed; she begins to think that the worker has deliberately set out to ruin her door. The metaphor Sarraute uses to convey this emotion could not have been better chosen: that of an advancing army destroying Aunt Berthe's world. Visible, then, is the dichotomy between the relatively trivial incident and the affective nature of the tropism it generates. Logic, reason, and control have all but disappeared. The instinctual layer of being alone has been activated.

Sarraute also uses symbols with felicity. The leather club chairs, which apparently stand for bourgeois stability and conventional views, are gifts of a mother to a daughter. Discussions have taken place as to whether the chairs really do represent solid bourgeois ideals, in which case the mother's intent is to protect her daughters from the vagaries of fortune, or whether they may stand for the mother who seeks to dominate her children, thereby divesting them of their independence. The antique bergères, on the other hand, may represent the creativity, beauty, and harmony implicit in Alain's and Gisèle's marriage.

Sarraute's way of shifting her views of family members and inviting the reader to observe people from multiple vantage points is fascinating. Germaine Lemaire, for example, is seen as "ugly" and "beautiful," depending upon the moment and upon the person describing her as a presence. Arguments also elicit myriad tropisms, depending upon the subjective reactions of the observer (or reader). At times disputations trigger affective reactions disproportionate to the incident. The feelings of uncertainty resulting from so many optical illusions is Sarraute's way of accentuating the complex and fluid nature of reality. Just as there is no single fixed pictorial image that serves to delineate a person once and forever, so there is no answer to a problem, no universal precept, no unique palliative. Everything—be it human or nonhuman—is in a state of flux,

changing, altering, erupting, breaking up, and renewing itself.

The Planetarium concludes with the breaking up of a world. Alain, who may be labeled Sarraute's central consciousness, no longer considers Germaine Lemaire to be his ideal. He sees her more realistically—as a woman with foibles, faults, and cracks. She is not the all-good mother figure, the one to whom he must constantly turn to for advice, for comforting, for assurance. Nor will he and Gisèle, at least temporarily, have recourse to labels and classifications with respect to their future relationships. They will try to see people as they are.

The world of art that Sarraute emphasizes in her later novels, such as Les fruits d'or (The Golden Fruits, 1963) and Entre la vie et la mort (Between Life and Death, 1968), is already present in incipient form in The Planetarium. Aunt Berthe, though not an artist or an aesthetician, is interested in home furnishings and decor. Alain is an art student writing a dissertation on painting. (The reader never really discovers what his subject is nor whether he will ever complete his volume.) Why is he drawn to art? Not because of his enjoyment of beauty exclusively, but also because, during his meditations, he gives the impression of wanting to be the focus of the admiration and envy of the untutored. As for Germaine Lemaire, she questions the value of her own writing after receiving some unfavorable reviews. She begins to assess her work: her prose is no longer resonant with fresh, active, and living forces. Instead, leaden qualities dominate: "It's all dead. Dead. Dead. Dead. Dead. A dead star." But no sooner do her admirers return than she feels rejuvenated and recovers her self-esteem. She yields to compliments rather than dealing directly and objectively with her own reactions to her writings.

Sarraute goes a step further in the depersonalization process in The Golden Fruits. Not only is there no plot, but there is no central or even semi-central consciousness. Nor is the author present in the guise of a narrator. Despite its fragmented, dispersive, and explosive quality, *The Golden Fruits* is unified: it focuses on a novel entitled "The Golden Fruits." Tension is created through Sarraute's depiction of the fictional readers' reactions to the fictional novel: at first, they admire "The Golden Fruits," but then they reject this same work. Each swell of excitement or slackening of it, revealed in constantly renewing wavelike tropisms, generates the novel's drama.

Some critics have noted a diminution of images in *The Golden Fruits* and an increase in the scenic play and dialogue. Although Sarraute rejected the former assessment, she did acknowledge the latter:

> I have the impression that there are as many images in *The Golden Fruits* as there are in *The Portrait of a Man Unknown.* There are, in fact, only images in these works; but they are not introduced by means of comparisons. I do not say, for example, "He was like a man who had known military degradation." I *show* military degradation. I do so by means of images. In the course of one conversation in my work concerning a book, one has the distinct impression that one of the interlocutors is undergoing the actual pain of military degradation. That is certainly an image. There are many such images in the novel *The Golden Fruits.*
>
> I am forever looking for images as I write. Yes, it is quite true—there is more dialogue in *The Planetarium*, in *Martereau*, in *The Golden Fruits* than there is in *Portrait of a Man Unknown.* This is the case because in the latter work, the featured character was never present at the crucial scenes. There was, therefore, less dialogue.
>
> (*Off-Stage Voices*, p. 162)

As one might expect, then, the image is the vehicle Sarraute uses in *The Golden Fruits* to make a sharp distinction between what is said about a book and its true worth as determined by a genuine appraisal of the author's talent. Sarraute's microscopic eye focuses on Jacques and his wife, active members of the Parisian literary or so-called cultivated milieu. They and their coterie of friends are snobs. Yielding to fads, they follow the trajectory of the rise and fall of the best-seller.

Not people, but essences—or disembodied voices—parade before the reader. As each takes center stage, he or she is silhouetted and caricatured. Readers, however, are not the only butt of Sarraute's parodic insights in *The Golden Fruits*—writers and journalists also enunciate their banal reactions concerning the book in vogue at a particular time. It must be noted that these beings—readers, writers, and critics—who appear and disappear throughout the work, do not create the plot. Rather, they are created by the fictional novel's destiny. Their reactions, and therefore their presences, come into being when a book is being read and reread and reacted to by those who want to be up to date—to be in the know. As a result, phrases, sentences, epithets, and analogies that have been pronounced by readers and critics alike are constantly bobbing up and down in Sarraute's text, sometimes repeated in toto, at other moments rephrased or repositioned, with a word missing here and there, or placed elsewhere. These clauses or fragmented sentences, occurring like a refrain throughout her work, may be seen as leitmotifs in the verbal, visual, and musical composition that is *The Golden Fruits.*

Sarraute's technique of depersonalization applies not only to her novel *The Golden Fruits* but also to the novel bearing the same name being scrutinized by the readers within the book. Only the book's name is given—no details concerning its contents. Once published, it no longer even belongs to its author. It has entered the public domain and, to use Sartre's phrasing, becomes part of the "common substance" or "common patrimony," the "common mass." The tropisms, which are continuously being born and vanishing only to be reborn anew, are catalyzed by the individual's relationship with "The Golden Fruits" and with his or her "cultured" acquaintances.

To have used an inanimate object, such as a book, for the central consciousness of her novel; to have substituted for plot the excitement of that book's rise to fame and subsequent decline; to have identified the imagistic world of tropisms with a mixture of disembodied voices, as Sarraute has accomplished in *The Golden Fruits*, is brilliant. The confusion that arises in the reader's mind between Sarraute's novel *The Golden Fruits* and the fictional novel "The Golden Fruits" is designed to underscore the similarity among all bestsellers, which are designed to appeal to an accepting and naive audience. This is Sarraute's way of casting aspersions on those people who never think for themselves but instead follow fads, nomenclatures, and systems.

Although the satire is perhaps more pointed and directed in *The Golden Fruits* than in Sarraute's previous works, value judgments are not given, nor are theories enunciated. What is offered instead is the constant flow of human interplay as involved in the battle of the books. Not only does Sarraute mock the cultured group, but she also berates the world of critics—be they professionals or the homegrown types—who thoughtlessly repeat what others have already written. Superficial and flippant, they make their impact on society by praising what seems to catch the public's attention, only to change their minds weeks later, when a novel no longer seems titillating and has fallen into oblivion. Critics, like authors, also require praise and constant adulation to make up for their lack of self-confidence, or worse, their unconscious feelings of vacuity.

The battle of the books gives birth to factions, hatreds, fear, aggression—emotions of all types—and arouses no end of tropisms. Feelings and unarticulated thoughts are thereby concretized in the image and in the ensuing dialogue or bits of sentences enunciated by and between the members of a constantly swelling, diminishing, emerging, and vanishing group of readers. During these tension-filled moments, distinctions may be made between those who reveal a genuine and those who reveal an inauthentic reaction to the artistic work. The first group includes the sensitive

and thoughtful people—those with integrity, who give free rein to their spontaneous reactions while also rejecting the stereotypical. They are individualists and do not court the up-to-date faddists. Those in the latter group pay lip service to collective value judgments based on what others say, feel, and think; to act in this way guarantees them acceptance by the so-called intellectual elite.

The Golden Fruits begins with a gathering of cultured snobs. The ecstatic exclamations of some as they praise a painting by Gustave Courbet that they have seen in an art gallery are as sonorous, as heated, as excited—and as banal—as those they enunciate when referring to "The Golden Fruits." When this elitist group later realizes that the book they had praised so highly has achieved recognition by the majority, these very same "bleating sheep" feel compelled, in order to maintain their elitist stance, to abandon their previous stand and to refrain from further comments upon "The Golden Fruits." Other groups enter the melee by reacting differently to "The Golden Fruits" or to the Courbet painting or to other art objects. Platitudes fly high and brilliantly—like so many flags wafting in the wind.

The group dominates the proceedings in *The Golden Fruits.* Like the godhead, it has its faithful, its heaven, and its hell. Its hierarchy of spokesmen are made up of critics: these are its priests, pastors, or shamans, who constantly verbalize their credos and rule their flock dictatorially. They are the ones who determine what is considered acceptable and what is not. Conversion to their points of view necessarily leads to the extermination of any rival stance. The votaries of this group are its readers, who either adore or execrate the book of the moment. In this regard, one may suggest that "The Golden Fruits" takes on the power of a fetish. Belonging to a group may confer some sense of needed support, but it also requires a sacrifice of individuality and of one's own views. People may fail to stand up for their beliefs; they must not be loners. In many cases, however, such a divestiture is meaningless, for some people have never probed or questioned their thoughts or feelings authentically and thus consider their surface reactions entirely satisfactory. They therefore extol with lavish praise such accepted French writers and artists as Verlaine, Gide, and Courbet, for doing so reinforces their sense of belonging both to the group and to their homeland.

Nevertheless, there are a few persons who express their genuine reactions to "The Golden Fruits." Being an individualist, however, takes courage and might result in expulsion from the group, forcing one to live out one's existence as a pariah. A woman who does not agree that "The Golden Fruits" is "the best book written in fifteen years" is considered "mad" and is exiled from the group. The majority of opinions are enunciated by those who, fearing that their personal views might alienate members of their group, repress them, and even go so far as to adopt those of the majority. A few remain silent on the subject of "The Golden Fruits," thereby arousing suspicion in the minds of the rest. What are his or her *true* ideas? Does he or she agree with the majority opinion or not? Plurality of opinions concerning the intrinsic value of "The Golden Fruits" arouses antagonisms, creating a virtual call to arms and a sadomasochistic verbal battle. One reader who feels beyond the reach of adverse forces finds pleasure "in the effectiveness of his blows." He watches his victims writhe and groan in pain, for they are unprepared to counter his sudden and brutal attack.

At the height of the popularity of "The Golden Fruits," the members of the group analyze its wealth of tonalities, rhythms, and images in sequences of hyperboles. So extreme is their praise that they are convinced that this work of genius will change the course of world literature. Intolerance and authoritarianism mark their valuations, and "nobody dared to budge." If anyone were to convey the slightest notion of disagreement, he would be looked upon with contempt, considered unfeeling, abnormal, retarded.

No sooner does the popularity of "The Golden Fruits" wane than the author himself is taken to task. Although he is idolized at first, his peculiarities are now underscored: he is vain and arrogant. Gossip has it that he behaved in a cowardly way during a mountain-climbing expedition. At the height of his fame, he was thought to be a creative genius and the generative force behind a new brand of literature. His works were considered the finest written since Stendhal's and Benjamin Constant's. No one wrote better. After his eclipse, he is considered a derivative writer and is compared to others in an unfavorable light. To express the continuous wavelike movement implicit in Sarraute's work, she presents sequences of disembodied voices articulating their vacuous opinions, either alone or followed by others in polyphonic or fugal sequences: "Admirable . . . Higher . . . Nothing in our literature which is comparable . . . Higher still and higher . . . The finest thing written since . . . Ever higher, the huge peaks unfurl. . . ." Finally, at the conclusion of Sarraute's novel, the members of the group are disenchanted, realizing that nothing is new under the sun and that the author of "The Golden Fruits" has not made any world-shaking statement in his book.

Sarraute's arrows also strike hard at the members of hermetic literary cults who hide behind a facade of jargon. Although not named, the structuralists and deconstructionists, as well as other literary-political schools that may be seen as enforcing an autocracy of the mind through their systems, credos, and priestly hierarchies, are mocked and berated. Few of their followers understand the meaning of the words used and promulgated by these intellectuals; fewer still attempt to probe and question their ideologies. These "sheep," like the snobs taken to task in Sarraute's previous tropistic sequences, merely follow the crowd—whatever the group in question may stand for. In Sarraute's view, tyranny and victimization are in the offing for anyone who is caught up in a fad.

When, at the conclusion of Sarraute's work,

accolades go to another novelist and no longer to the author of "The Golden Fruits," a lone voice stands out in the crowd. He does not want to be a mirror image of the group; he seeks to experience his own reactions, his own sensations.

> It's something like what you feel in the presence of the first blade of grass that timidly sends up a shoot . . . a crocus not yet open. . . . It's that perfume they smell of, but it's not yet a perfume, not even an odor, it has no name, it's the odor of before odors. . . . It seems to me that it's that. . . . It's something that takes me gently and holds me without letting me go . . . something untouched, innocent . . . like a child's slender fingers clinging to me, a child's hand nestling in the hollow of my own.
>
> (p. 218)

The idea expressed by this single voice, which certainly parallels Sarraute's own, contains a refusal to be swayed by success or failure and a concerted attempt to search out the book's qualities by returning to the text. Truth, for Sarraute, lies in a constant reappraisal of the work of art and a perpetual reevaluation of the thoughts and feelings revolving around it and triggered by it, a process figured forth, in the passage above, in terms of nature's continuous renewal. Absolutes do not exist, any more than fixed principles or guarantees. There are no permanent criteria of values. They shift, as does everything else. Categories, judgments, and philosophies create impulses that are initially alive and exciting but in time turn into ossified systems, deadened and arid frames of reference. Sarraute writes in *The Golden Fruits:* "The dead, those recently dead, and those who died long ago, arranged in categories, the major and the minor, each one resting in his place. Look how we have arranged them. We have had autopsies done on them" (p. 211).

The inadequacy of language is another theme of *The Golden Fruits.* A distinction is made between what one seeks to express and what one actually does express. Such a dichotomy and the polarities evidenced by it pave the way for moments of authentic anguish on the writer's part—authentic in that they may, on occasion, give birth to new ways of seeing and feeling things as well as to a fresh manner of capturing sensations and thoughts. Questions are also posed throughout *The Golden Fruits.* What does a subjective or an objective approach to a fictional universe imply? While formulating one's reactions to a work of art, when does an individual require the approval of others? What is art? What does success imply? To articulate an opinion is to deform or destroy a previous one. Likewise, to write an innovative book is to destroy a previously stable and fixed set of literary values. Indirection may lead to direction, truth to a lie, sincerity to hypocrisy.

Between Life and Death, Sarraute's most profound and greatest work, explores the notions of creativity and the creative process. Unlike *The Golden Fruits,* whose protagonist is the novel "The Golden Fruits," in *Between Life and Death,* the Writer is the focus of Sarraute's attention. The reader is shown how the uncreated work of art, embedded in the *prima materia,* or the great void, is concretized in book form. The multiple stages of the Writer's literary trajectory are viewed as a struggle to transmute the amorphous word into the concrete glyph on the blank sheet of paper. Pain and anguish accompany the birth of the created work, here alluded to as the "thing" or the "object." The attitude of the successful Writer also comes under Sarraute's scrutiny. Is he the kind who postures and panders to his public? Or does he become aware of the increasing void within him and, to remedy his sterility, dig deep into the real living substance within him, thereby triggering the rebirth of his creative élan? Like the ancient seer, or *vates,* Sarraute's Writer is also a miracle worker able to inject life into what had previously been dead or uncreated—that is, the written word. How is such a sleight of hand accomplished? How does the process of transforming words from the realm of the uncreated to the concrete realm of the empirical affect both the Writer and the reader in *Between Life and Death*?

Descriptions of the creative process per se have been undertaken by many poets and novelists in their writings: for example, Nerval, Rimbaud, Goethe, Baudelaire, Woolf, Joyce, and Gide, to mention only a few. Sarraute's approach is different from theirs. She concentrates on the word alone—the sensations, feelings, and ideations that make for its livingness or its deadness. In so doing, she organizes, on a verbal, conscious level, what might be called polyphonic musical compositions emerging from the interweaving of successive voices from the unconscious into single or double oft-repeated themes. Sarraute's images and vocal devices in *Between Life and Death* take on a fugal quality as they impose themselves—amplified or diminished—at various stages during the creative process.

The creative process, as viewed by Sarraute in *Between Life and Death,* transcends temporal philosophical, aesthetic, and sexual schemes. Values and demarcation lines have changed. Heretofore, the notion of giving birth—be it to an object or an infant—has almost always been linked to the Great Mother, since she is the bearer of life, nourisher and devourer, and is identified with Eros, the principle that brings things together in nature and within the psyche. Spiritual and intellectual factors—Logos—have usually been associated in the west with the male. Sarraute's Writer, however, is androgynous. Although alluded to as masculine, since the masculine personal pronoun *il* is uded to identify him, he is neither male nor female. He is a component of both sexes, an archetypal composite of opposites, as is the creative spirit in general. He transcends polarities and reaches beyond the empirical into eternal realms. Pierre Teilhard de Chardin's remark in his *Hymne de l'univers (The Prayer of the Universe,* 1961) with regard to the creative process is applicable to Sarraute's androgynous Writer: "Everything in the Universe is made by union and regeneration—by the coming together of elements that seek out one another, melt together two by two, and are born again in a third."

Sarraute's Writer is not only androgynous; he is also physically unidentifiable, sexless, and torsoless, as were the disembodied voices in *The Golden Fruits.* Aside from a few appendages (hands, fingers that gesticulate and mime every now and then), he is all head. As a kinetic object dramatizing his emotional experience, he is forever distorting, foreshortening, expanding, rotating, and shifting spatial and sensorial illusions. Nor does this metaform convey much feeling; love, warmth, tenderness are virtually banished in his nonrelationship with others or even with himself. Interaction exists only on an intellectual and sensorial level.

Thinking is the Writer's dominant function. His rational capabilities enable him to structure and synthesize data by means of categories, concepts, abstractions, and generalizations. As a sensory being as well, he is able to perceive and adapt to external reality through his sight, hearing, touch, taste, and smell. He is introverted to the extreme; his world revolves around his creative output, and later, when he becomes famous, around the admiration his works elicit from his reading public. Like a hypersensitive instrument, the Writer is forever monitoring his internal environment by means of his mind, perceptions, and bodily sensations, which relay information concerning external situations to his inner world and thereby affect his entire system, including his nerve endings or receptor neurons. There is little that is human about the Writer. Like Athena, he is all intellect, all mind, all thought; he knows how to develop good tactics during moments of conflict, think clearly when challenged, and avoid personal entanglements.

Similarly to Sarraute's other novels, *Between Life and Death* has no real plot. It centers around a controlled or contrived situation—in the Writer's case, the creative process. The essence of the work concerns words as individual entities, as universal, recurring images or patterns of behavior. One word interacts with another, affecting the Writer and his listeners or readers and drawing energy and power to itself from other words, letters, or figures of speech. In the process, the pace alternately slackens and increases, thereby altering the meaning, weight, emphasis, substance, rhythm, sensations, and impact of clauses, sentences, paragraphs, and pages. This makes for the narration's sharp and frequently brutal dramatic effects.

Sarraute's kinetic, dynamic literary technique brings the unactualized into being. The creation of her novel occurs through combinations of letters, words, and numbers—a technique used in an ancient cabalistic text, the *Sefer Yetsirah* (the *Book of Creation,* which predates the second century A.D.), and in other mystical tracts. Repetitions, flashbacks, reworkings of words and syntax, and positional shifting of clauses are used by Sarraute in *Between Life and Death* to create emotional experiences and to alter pitch, pace, and orientation, thereby influencing concentration, perception, and affect.

To bring forth the word from nothing, as Sarraute's Writer does, may be looked upon as paralleling a cosmogonic event. The word arises from the Beginning, the Void, Chaos; it then undergoes a transfiguration, from Nothingness to Something (or Being). The cabalists have illustrated this transformation linguistically, wrote Gershom Scholem in *Major Trends in Jewish Mysticism* (1941), by means of the Hebrew words *ain,* which means "nothing," and *ani,* defined as "I." A mere rearrangement of the same letters alters the meaning of the words. Such a change implies, symbolically, the passage from a gap of existence, or the Void (Nothingness), to existence. It is this instant of transformation and what leads up to and follows it that Sarraute's Writer attempts to understand and to convey.

Some words and letters—idea forces— emerging from the Writer's collective unconscious are endowed with substance, energy, rhythm, and patterns of behavior. A certain word or letter becomes capable of fomenting a dynamic process, which puts into motion a feeling, an imagining, or an action. Once the letters or words are written, or even thought or sensed by the Writer, they take on contour, becoming at once concretion and abstraction, sign and symbol; they also have the potential to develop virtualities and possibilities in time and space. Words in Sarraute's orchestrated prose achieve a scale of nuanced timbres, intonations, and amplitudes that at times triturate, lacerate, exacerbate, striate, bombard, and sear the Writer and reader as well. Or they may work their charms on listeners by means of velvety, mellifluous, endearing, siren-like harmonics, depending upon their connotations, their positionings in a sentence, and their juxtaposition with other words of the "tribe," to use Sarraute's term.

Cases in point are plentiful. When, for example, the Writer hears a woman at the next table in a restaurant say to her son, "Armand, if you continue, your father will prefer your sister," the power of the words he has just heard affects him deeply; they cut and dig into his flesh, insidiously and mercilessly. On another occasion, the Writer's mother unabashedly accuses him of "ruminating," of literally and figuratively chewing his words, swallowing, masticating, pulverizing, and regurgitating them as he probes their origin, meaning, and effect upon him during his word-play sequences. She does not understand him—the artist in him— and for this reason is forever attempting to normalize him. She would like him to be just like the others. Once he has achieved fame, however, she makes a swift turnabout. She swells with pride—the pride of a mother who has given birth to a genius. He was "predestined" to become a great writer, she now claims. The minute he was brought to her in his swaddling clothes, "*J'ai su*" ("I knew"), she states with authority—as the Virgin *knew* the Annunciation, or as the priests instinctively chose the child who was to be the Dalai Lama.

Between Life and Death begins as the Writer attempts to convey to his audience the stages involved in the creation of his book. Sarraute's use of verbal and gestural language in the opening scene is arresting. It offers the reader a mirror reflection of the Writer's unconscious and conscious attitudes—a world of tropisms:

> He shakes his head, puckers his lids, his lips . . . "No, positively no, that won't do." He stretches out his arm, bends it again . . . "I tear out the page." He clenches his fist, then his arm drops, his hand relaxes . . . "I throw it away. I take another sheet. I write. On the typewriter. Always. I never write by hand. I reread . . ." His head moves from side to side. His lips are pouting . . . "No, no, and again no. I tear it out. I crumple it. I throw it away. And so, three, four, ten times I start over . . ." He puckers his lips, frowns, stretches his arm, bends it again, lets it drop, clenches his fist.
>
> (Jolas trans., p. 7)

Sarraute has portrayed her Writer in a series of studied poses. But are they really studied, as in a planned photograph? Or are they spontaneous, as in a candid shot? Ambiguity and mystery lie at the core of Sarraute's figurations throughout *Between Life and Death*. Each time she repeats the above sequence in one form or another, she repositions certain words, omitting others or adding some new ones, and as the reader questions her reasons for repetition, her technique comes to seem as mysterious as is the human psyche. Thus drama is heightened in the pantomimic sequence.

The image of Sarraute's Writer becomes unforgettable as we see him nodding, frowning, rising, sitting, extending his arm, then bending and lowering it, tearing a sheet of paper out of his typewriter, clenching his fist, opening his hand, grabbing another sheet of paper, inserting it into the machine, typing, reading what he has just written, deciding it's not quite right, tearing it out again, crumpling it up, throwing it away, and so forth. There are times, he remarks in another sequence, when he reaches such a peak of frustration—becomes so preoccupied with finding the specific word that will evoke the right idea or sensation— that he leaves his study in a sweat, oblivious to all outside noises or presences. Then, for no apparent reason, the very word or letter he is searching for incarnates itself in his mind's eye, and he transcribes it "on the white page and sentences form. Miracle. How do we do it? It's a great mystery."

The very mystery behind creation heightens the Writer's fascination with the transformational process, the transmutation from nothing to being. As he pursues his self-interrogation, even awakening at night in his continuous struggle to find the right word—that single power that will encapsulate meaning and sensation—his obsession imposes upon him a stinging torment. "Why my God, why?" he asks—as if experiencing excruciating martyrdom. The Writer's continuous quest for the word, which he dredges up once he sinks into his unconscious or which ejaculates into his consciousness without any apparent rhyme or reason, may be considered a kind of transformational ritual. The gestural language used by Sarraute in the opening episode (quoted above) takes on a religious flavor, accompanied as it is by specific signs: punctuation, figures of speech, and other literary devices. (Religion here is to be understood in its original sense, derived from the Latin *religio*, "link"—that which unites.) The numinous formality of the opening ceremony, increased each time it is repeated during the course of the narrative, discloses an ontological need on the Writer's part to repeat symbolically the original act of Creation.

Since to reactualize is to renew, and thus to destroy linear time sequences, the reactualization of a cosmogonic act serves several purposes. It regenerates time for the Writer, lending the entire novel a cyclical scheme and, therefore, a mythic dimension. In such a scheme, time is reversible, and the Writer can regress to his childhood, becoming linked with events that have faded out of his consciousness and that he brings back to a present reality. The repeated transformations of the opening episode also commemorate the primordial conflict: the passage from chaos to cosmos, which parallels his struggle to articulate the word and to give substance to the amorphous.

In reexperiencing childhood and bringing forth language, the Writer experiences a sense of fulfillment and joy, a raison d'être. The written word—indeed, the entire creative process—acts as a compensatory device for the Writer. It takes him out of his world of unbearable loneliness, which is caused in part by his inability to relate to people on a human level. Later, when his readers describe his torment using the simplistic and banal term "unadaptable," they believe they have resolved the entire unresolvable problem. Mystery for them is an open book.

Examples of the Writer's extreme sensitivity to language and to the impact of meanings, rhythms, sonorities, sensations, and variations of form and pronunciation are given early in the book. As a child, he had questioned the many meanings of the verb *faire* (which include "make," "do," "play a role," and "give the appearance of being") and had felt completely disoriented. He recalls the time when he was in school and one of his teachers, noticing that he was reading James Fenimore Cooper, remarked: "*Tiens vous faites de l'anglais?*" ("So you're doing English?") The verb is used here idiomatically and actively, as well as ironically, as when referring to someone doing the marketing, the ironing, and other chores. *Faire* is also used passively, as in "*Je fais une pleurésie*" ("I have pleurisy") or "*J'ai fait une crise cardiaque*" ("I had a heart attack").

The question remains as to why the young boy felt physically and emotionally bruised by the multiple uses of this word. Why did he sense danger ahead for him? His reactions are not so outlandish as they might at first seem. The teacher's question (and the many examples of the use of *faire* given by Sarraute) aroused heretofore unknown sensations in the highly intuitive lad. The discovery that no one word has just one definition was like stepping into quicksand. He sensed that just as *faire* has many meanings and can be used in multiple ways, depending upon the context, so varied options and courses were open to him in the life experience that was his writing. The straight and narrow path had disappeared; barriers had vanished, and with them the security he had thought existed in the empirical domain of words. Gone were the fixity and solidity—the very foundations—of his psyche and aesthetics. Everything existed in a state of flux; anything could become something else and be transformed, altering its own consistency and scope.

Like Proust's narrator, Sarraute's Writer learns in time that he is not even one person, so to speak, but is the sum total of all the people and events he has experienced, both passively and actively, during the course of his life. As Sarraute remarks in *The Age of Suspicion*, there is no single extreme bottom or depth in anyone; everyone is endowed with "multiple depths; and these rise tier upon tier to infinity." As the multiple selves inhabiting the Writer increase in dimension and scope, so, too, do his feelings of confusion, to the point that he sometimes wonders who he is. Today we label such anxieties identity crises.

As previously mentioned, for the seven-year-old child words were playthings, toys that he set in motion or immobilized whenever the spirit moved him. These treasures, which stimulated further verbal associations and incredible fantasy images, are presented by Sarraute in a spectacular display of active imagination during a train trip the young lad takes with his mother. As the train rolls through bleak and snowy countryside, the lad turns inward, entertaining himself by pronouncing homonyms and homophones in rhythm to the sound of the turning wheels. As each word comes into consciousness, irregular images form, removing him increasingly from his circumscribed and referential world and plunging him more deeply into vaster, more nebulous spheres.

The lad's starting point for his periods of active imagination are words that spurt forth homophonically: "*Hérault, héraut, héros, aire haut, erre haut, R.O.*" Words and their accompanying images hurtle forth almost simultaneously, and together they make up an entire story. The child's creative and pleasurable pastime is, in his view, forever being interrupted by his mother, seated in the same compartment, who criticizes him for "ruminating." Not for one moment does she realize that her son is exploring the magical world of imagination—a domain where wholeness exists. A world of secret desires and compensatory states of being emerges during his periods of active imagination. The homophones for *Hérault* (the name of a department in France), meaning herald, hero, an eagle's nest, a wanderer on high, and R.O., evoke white landscapes, a lavender horn, a knight followed by others riding a richly caparisoned charger, fog breaking out, dark skies lit by flickering stars. The *R* evokes a bulldog standing erect with his legs firmly set on the ground. The *O* symbolizes the closed circle: "Everything closes and we start over again."

What do these images disclose about the child's needs and his personality? Does he see himself as herald, hero, or wanderer? The words he uses imply aggressivity, power, and energy. He is struggling to be heard, to be understood, and to penetrate areas that will require of him a show of heroic strength. The charger that forges ahead into untraveled, snow-covered terrain will help him achieve his goal. A medieval atmosphere is conjured up as a spectacular battle scene unfolds before him: flags, horses, and men arrayed in brilliant tonalities, each bearing the heraldic symbol of his family or master, pursue their heated struggle. This is violent, cruel, and electrifying action painting at its height.

The train in which the lad is riding is also both sign and symbol. As it speeds across the snow-covered landscape, activating his imagination, normal time expands and mythical time is born. The boy feels himself living in the medieval period; in his imagination, the charger is festooned in colorful array, and the knight, strong and virile in his coat of mail, bears his heraldic symbols for all to see. Since the train represents the mechanistic world of objects, the boy is also part of the linear time scheme in a contemporary world, which functions scientifically and with the accuracy of a clock. Inflexible in its order, disciplined, con-

trolled, and punctual to the extreme, the train is unconcerned with any human factor. It is a link in a complicated communication network that connects a variety of areas and time schemes. Like a human artery that carries the blood from one part of the body to another, it also functions as part of its own vast circulatory system, relocating travelers and merchandise in a continuous round. A train physically and psychologically imposes its laws and rhythms on the human being, since it determines the individual and collective destinations of all those within its metal frame.

Although the woman in the train is the young boy's mother, she may also be seen as a negative, collective mother figure with a decidedly disturbing, provocative, and irritating quality that the Writer encounters in various avatars in the novel—in restaurants, at gatherings, and at lectures. As an interlocutor who never lets him rest in the serenity of his creative imaginings, she plays the role of devil's advocate, constantly challenging him while he is at play and criticizing him for his laziness. She rebukes him for his futile meanderings, his overly introverted ways, his inability to see outside of himself, and his spasmodic span of attention. At the conclusion of *Between Life and Death,* the famous Writer reveals, tropistically, his unwillingness to continue pandering to his public, and he realizes that he is not alone, as he feared he would be if he took a firm aesthetic stand. Rather, he is surrounded by what could be labeled his "word-protagonists." As an androgynous principle, he is endowed with two selves, the traditionally "feminine" creative force—and the traditionally "masculine" analytic force, and from these is born the third—the work of art.

In *Vous les entendez?* (*Do You Hear Them?,* 1972), the reader is plunged into the world of the art lover—a person who responds to and delights in a static and conventional view of the creative work. A small stone animal figure is this man's object of veneration. His children, whom he loves deeply, do not share his traditional approach to art. They look upon the object with disgust, as a piece of old and crumbling stone. Rather than admire the fixed values this object represents, the children opt for a spontaneous and free expression toward the creative principle.

Do You Hear Them? opens in a country home. The father and a friend are seated opposite one another on either side of a low table upon which has been placed a stone statue. Both contemplate this primitive and rough-hewn sculpture with awe, deriving aesthetic pleasure and a sense of harmony from it. The children, meanwhile, beg to be excused. They go upstairs, ostensibly to bed. Soon, peals of laughter emanating from the upstairs room descend in waves and sheets of cascading sonorities. Tonalities and rhythms vary: prolonged and short, high and low sonorities, stopping suddenly only to continue more hilariously than ever. The father wonders: What does this laughter imply? Are his children ridiculing his treasured work of art, and, by extension, him? Or is it simply an innocent outburst on their part—pure fun? Each peal of laughter is imagined by the father as an encounter, an aggressive act demolishing his standard formulations and definitions.

The father's self-doubt, his self-conscious and tenuous inner voice responds continuously to the laughter floating toward him—the mysterious flow that subsides only to burst forth again and then to be followed by an equally enigmatic silence. He never knows what his children are thinking. The multiple reflections that invade his being, conveyed in the usual Sarrautian tropisms, reveal a variety of emotional reactions: the love he feels for his children, his fear and anguish at the thought that they may be desecrating his values, taste, and judgment, and his mounting scorn and rage at the thought that his views are being threatened and made impotent by the younger generation.

Sarraute again uses recurring religious symbolism, as she had in *The Planetarium* and in *Between Life and Death*. Reference is made to the father's "sacred object," which his children

are supposed to look upon "reverently," in "religious silence," and "steeped in devotion." Sarraute uses religious language in such a way as to suggest that the father uses conversion techniques on his children, but he fails to "convert" them to his old-fashioned concepts of beauty and love of art. Finally, children and father reach out to one another in what is thought to be a "togetherness" but that in fact implies the father's capitulation. The father gives them the stone animal. After his death, they donate the "family heirloom" to the Louvre. When visiting this august sanctuary and bending over respectfully to read the inscription, they recall the past: "You remember when one of us called it [the statue] unthinkingly a Cretan sculpture? What a crime! My father was ready to kill him. . . . Ah, poor Papa. . . ." Then, peals of laughter, and "a door had closed up there. . . . Then nothing more."

"disent les imbéciles" ("*fools say,*" 1976), perhaps Sarraute's most hermetic novel, consists of dialogue and sub-dialogue and plays on pronouns revolving around a first person engulfed by rapidly sequential disembodied voices. These include clauses emitted by a pregnant form at a funeral, by cats who might be "playing" at being cats, and by children, a grandmother, and more. The word, used as a tyrannical force, is manipulated by Sarraute with great expertise. In the opening image of "*fools say,*" a woman's grandchildren, who idolize their grandmother, call her "cute" (*mignonne*). One of the children refuses to apply this epithet to the grandmother, feeling that to do so would be to label her and therefore to view her as an inanimate object. The others grow anxious: Should they try to force him to conform?

What is significant in "*fools say*" is that the individual is considered, paradoxically, as a collective entity and as an infinite and contourless microcosm. Throughout the novel, this entity is portrayed observing others, looking upon them either as simple beings or as multifaceted emanations, knowing all the while that he is being viewed by them in like manner. They project their feelings, sensations, and ideations upon him as he does upon them. The drama consists in the continuous interplay between a central consciousness—who really is a composite of those he observes—and the others. During the interchange, structurations and classifications are formed. Hierarchies are born, such as the dichotomy between the "supremely intelligent" and the "imbeciles."

L'Usage de la parole (*The Use of Speech*, 1980), another Sarrautian exploration, takes the form of ten mini-dramas or mini-comedies that sound the tropistic universe buried in the deepest recesses of individuals. In "Ich sterbe" ("I Am Dying"), a kind of meditation upon death, Sarraute introduces her readers to the first-person pronoun *Ich* ("I") in the German phrase "Ich sterbe." Since Sarraute does not at first inform her readers about what the "Ich" refers to, they are left in a quandary, wondering what the story is all about. We are told, after a bit, that Anton Chekhov uttered these words in 1904 while on his deathbed at a German spa. Thus the stage is set for Sarraute's profound discussion concerning death.

"À très bientôt" ("See You Soon"), in this same volume, depicts the periodic meetings of two friends in a restaurant. As they exchange views, talking about everything and nothing, they give the impression of enjoying each other's company. Soon each seems to have developed a personality of his own. The first has rushed to the rendezvous, arriving out of breath. The other, relegated to virtual silence, sits and listens. Does his smile indicate approval? The enigma remains. If *The Use of Speech* is, as some maintain, a poetic development of her first texts in *Tropisms*, then Sarraute has come the full circle.

Sarraute's work for theater is as unique as her novels. It defies classification. It is neither guerrilla theater nor theater of the absurd nor theater of cruelty, hysteria, or panic—nor is it political or philosophical. It is a theater of her own invention—a personal construct that may be labeled a "theater of tropisms."

Like her novels, Sarraute's plays have no real plots. They center around a controlled or contrived situation: a conversation or a series of conversations; silences revolving around the manner in which certain words are pronounced, thereby giving them the power to alienate or attract people; the success or failure of a novel; the problems actuated by the creation of a work of art. The tropisms or visualizations that emerge from these conversations and sub-conversations frequently unmask the participants and reveal hidden relationships among them as they interact or clash with one another during the short periods of a get-together. The tropism is the mechanism Sarraute uses to set her play in motion. The detail referred to by the performers, which creates the suspense and brings forth the climax, is buried within these closely knit images and is clothed in a sparse but rambling dialogue. The spectator must catch the detail and absorb it if he seeks to follow the dialogue.

Her characters, like those in her novels, are not flesh-and-blood creations but rather faceless beings without identity—they are so many presences, not in the old sense of the word, not endowed with form and substance, but rather transparencies based on an ever-altering world of images. These presences are actualized feelings, concretized sensations, with the fluidity and variegated transparencies of a jellyfish. Her creatures are like clusters or groups of vocal emanations, voices with variegated tonalities and infinite nuances in their timbres and intonations. In *Le mensonge* (*The Lie*, 1967), they have first names. In *Le silence* (*Silence*, 1967), only one character is known, Jean-Pierre; the others are Women 1, 2, 3, and 4 and Men 1 and 2. In *Isma* (*Izzum*, 1970), He and She emerge; the other characters are Men 1, 2, and 3 and Women 1, 2, and 3. In *C'est beau* (*It's Beautiful*, 1973), we are made privy to a mother-father-son triangle in which the One is pitted against the Two in an ever-shifting combination. *Elle est là* (*It Is There,* 1978) revolves around an idea buried in the deepest recesses of someone's head. *Pour un oui ou pour un non* (At the Drop of a Hat, 1984) calls attention to the fact that H^2 was insulted by the tone used by his friend H^1 when the latter pronounced a certain phrase. Divested of personal histories, of plot, atmosphere, decors, and psychology in the conventional sense of the word, Sarraute's beings lead us into a penumbra—an inner domain of hidden and billowy movements where everything is sensed and experienced on the most instinctual level. Although Sarraute's theater might seem to be lacking in drama, in fact it may be considered active and dramatic in scope, in that the tropism is the catalyst for the tension of each work. When the tropism comes into being, it mystifies at first, then delights; later it hurts and may attract or repel, anger or pacify. Sarraute's world of tropisms is a realm of perpetually shifting, heaving, diminishing, and swelling sensations.

Unlike Antonin Artaud's theater of cruelty (which seeks to bludgeon the viewer into participation by means of psychedelic lights, harsh and brutal noises, and shocking dialogue), Fernando Arrabal's "panic theater," which blasts his audience with pornography and sadomasochistic scenes aimed to shock, Jean Vauthier's symbolist dramas, with their flamboyant and brutal images, Jean Genet's mythical works, or Liliane Atlan's cosmic theater, Sarraute's theater, more like parlor comedy, initiates her viewers slowly, by degrees and with dignity, into a controlled and subtly alluring private world. Once she has enticed her prey into a realm of intrigue, she abandons them there—in a psychologically and spiritually spaceless area where they are left to flounder with a group of unidentifiable beings.

Sarraute's theater is both realistic and unrealistic. It is microscopically precise in that she describes the stage happenings in minute detail. But it is unreal in that the outside realm is virtually nonexistent. The power of Sarraute's

objectivity rests on a kind of "alienation" technique like that employed by Bertolt Brecht. She believes that distance must be maintained in the theater between the event, the memory of it, and its entrance into the conversation, as well as between the protagonists themselves, each one of whom is a victim of a powerful solitude that cannot be thrust off. Distance must also exist between the protagonists and the audience. As Sarraute builds her constructs in an alternately rapid and slackening rhythm, depending upon the sensation implicit in the situation, she creates empathy between the presences on the stage and those in the audience. Feelings of annoyance, anger, pain, joy, or hatred are aroused, only to be destroyed seconds later as she repels, alienates, and cuts them off by changing the topic of conversation.

Interestingly enough, both the viewer and the dramatist participate in the event as it occurs—the latter as author, the former as participant in the action. Detachment permits an intellectual understanding of the arguments, whereas identification allows the protagonists and audience alike—and the interplay of all concerned—to undergo the anguish, disgust, joy, or hate implicit in the inner landscape. Such sequences of detachment and identification are experienced in a state of constant flux, in a hierarchy of disturbing moods, as one eidetic sequence follows another and replaces it.

Silence introduces audiences to a mundane group. One man has just finished telling his friends about a trip he has taken, and they are delighted with his narration. However, a single person in the group voices no reaction, and the others cannot fathom his silence. Is it a timid, angry, jealous, or insulting silence? The drama revolves around each person's growing desire to break contact with the rest of the group and to seal himself in his own world.

The Lie concentrates on Simone and her friends, who are playing a parlor game. They decide, during the course of their conversation, that one person is going to tell a lie, and the others are to ferret out the guilty party. Simone casually tells her friends that she spent the war years in Geneva, but Pierre believes that she spent them in France. He discerns her lie. Pierre is tortured with the uncertainty of it all and declares that he will no longer believe anything she says. Tensions reach a nerve-racking pitch. Thus, the little lie, even when uttered in the spirit of fun, provokes tropisms and as a result assumes tremendous proportions that in turn constitute part of the play's action.

The Lie, as is the case with *Silence,* could take place anywhere at any time. There is no decor, no details concerning the participants' life histories, nothing that could identify them with any group or ideology. Communication between actors and spectators is experienced only through the images—tropisms— that arise in the conversations and through the sensations Sarraute captures, intensifies, aggrandizes, and subdues. Her characters "live at the level of the movements that are produced at a level where ordinary people refuse to descend."

The conversations in *Izzum* take place after dinner, when the guests begin "denigrating" a couple, the Dubuits, who have just left. Silence, they feel, must be avoided at all costs when couples get together; it is the sign of an unsuccessful party. What better way is there of spending the evening than to gossip about others, particularly when the couple discussed are not present to defend their reputation? Woman 2 has a pang of conscience and wants to find another topic of conversation. Thus, in an attempt to change the subject, she broaches an impersonal topic, and the group discusses Dante, Gide, and Paul Valéry. Banalities ensue as each character voices a literary opinion, an intellectual idea that seems to give him or her some feeling of superiority. Moments later, however, the conversation returns to the Dubuits. Like carnivorous animals, the guests now tear the couple apart. The Dubuits are unpleasant, *antipathiques,* revolting. But why? Each protagonist wants to analyze his or her own feelings. What factors in the Dubuits' per-

sonalities repel them so? Is it their actions? Their conversations? They are utter bores, of course. "What you feel about the Dubuits is vague, inexpressible. . . ."

Trying to maintain their calm and objectivity, the guests remember the Dubuits' attitude about certain ideas and their intonations of certain words. The protagonists seem to be coming close to an answer. The clue: their reactions stem from the "dry" way in which the Dubuits pronounce certain words, the stress they place on suffixes, such as "*isme.*" For example, instead of "*capitalisme*" they say "*capitalisma,*" and they deform other words, such as "*syndicalisma,*" "*obscurantisma,*" "*romantisma.*" The addition of the *a* sounds "brutal"; it unnerves others. Pronunciation and enunciation are a sign of some inner climate. How can one help but hate such people? The more the guests mention the "detail of pronunciation," the more their anger rises. Feelings of hatred bulge and dilate, engulfing the entire group and the audience. Each in the theater is now a participant—a "torturer" and an "executioner."

It's Beautiful introduces audiences not to the "cult of false individuality," nor to hypocrisy, nor to a group of snobs, but to a drama in which the generation gap is adroitly unmasked. Unlike Roger Vitrac's *Victor* (1929) or Jacques Borel's *Tata* (1967), in which parents are verbally mutilated in an overt and flashy manner, Sarraute's weapon—language—excoriates in a controlled manner. She cuts through the mask of ordinary conversations and through her usual "pre-dialogue" or "subconversation" to expose feelings, sensations, and thought patterns. Language is the catalyzing agent, the "detonator," the trenchant instrument that emasculates and devastates.

It's Beautiful introduces audiences to a family nucleus: mother, father, and son. Two milieus, two cultures, and two viewpoints are exhibited: the parents, representatives of an arid, disintegrating society, and the son, whose values are new and, at least to him, exciting.

The father would have liked his son to be the image of himself on a more modern scale. He had gone to libraries and museums when he was young, but his son enjoys comics and watches television. Language vibrates as confrontation begins. Sensations of anger and disgust emerge from both quarters. Then are spoken the terrible, banal words that represent a dead past: "It's beautiful." Innocuous enough, they give rise to feelings of humiliation. As the son looks at his father, his presence weighs upon the older man; his son's gaze degrades him. "It's beautiful" had been spoken in the father's generation each time anyone saw a painting, heard music, or attended a play. But to the son these words signify nothing. He considers them representative of an attitude that is no longer valid, whereas his parents had been nurtured on such banalities. A series of flashbacks enlighten the situation, revealing that the parents had dominated the family and had imposed their values on the son. The mother had coddled her baby boy and had created a secret alliance between him and her in opposition to the father. The father blames the mother for the son's wayward behavior, but the mother returns the accusation. Both finally admit that they treated "their baby" not as an equal but as a "superior" from the time he was toilet-trained. In time, the child attempts to affirm his identity, and hostility is then born. The son creates his own slogans. Are they any better? Do they offer an answer to humankind's yearnings and insecurities? It is apparent now that the father can barely pronounce, "It's beautiful." He chokes on the words, gasps. The son has the last word in this sequence when he accuses his mother of covering her ears so as to block out reality.

In *It Is There,* two businessmen are deep in discussion. Earlier, the collaborator or associate of one of the men had not offered an opinion on a certain topic that arose during their discussion. Now that she is gone, he probes the situation. Although she said nothing, he is certain that she did not agree with his idea. As a result, his peace of mind has come to an end. His partner tells him that he must not waste his time thinking about such details, but he can't help himself. It has becomes an idée fixe: he wants to know whether she agrees with him or not. He has the silent woman return, with the thought of discovering her conviction. He finds an ally in the audience—who, like him, is intolerant of anyone with a differing opinion. When the single word "in-tole-rance" is uttered on stage, it becomes obvious that the insalubrious, shadowy, and silent inner realms in each being are fertile fields for the germination of terrorism, totalitarianism, and violence.

Pour une oui ou pour un non features three nameless men and one nameless woman. The tension, always subtly manipulated in Sarraute's ultracerebral theater, stems from the fact that M^2 was offended by the manner in which M^1 had pronounced, emphasized, and accented certain congratulatory words. They discuss the implications, in the process suggesting a panoply of subtle, negative innuendo.

Sarraute's novels and plays take us directly into the inner world of her still brute protoplasmic emanations. From this vantage point, she extracts and then structures the substance out of which she molds her remarkable mini-dramas. Each of Sarraute's novels and plays revolve around the commonplace, the collective aspect of the human experience: people's dependence upon one another, their need to belong, their cruelty, vanity, hypocrisy, and immorality as well as their creative instincts. The mechanism of the tropism, which became Sarraute's convention, permits readers and audiences to understand and react to the intricacies and artifices that people build up out of fear, insecurity, solitude, or pain. This mechanism masks what they seek to hide and what is sickly within them; it also is used as a means of regressing into solitary or dark realms. As Sarraute burrows deeply into the substructure of those protoplasmic beings of her confection, she extracts the full import of an experience, each element of which is detected by her infallible antennae, then concretized in the dazzling verbal gyrations that are her tropisms.

Selected Bibliography

EDITIONS

FICTION

Tropismes. Paris, 1939. Sketches.
Portrait d'un inconnu. Paris, 1948. Novel.
Martereau. Paris, 1953. Novel.
Le planétarium. Paris, 1959. Novel.
Les fruits d'or. Paris, 1963. Novel.
Entre la vie et la mort. Paris, 1968. Novel.
Vous les entendez? Paris, 1972. Novel.
"disent les imbéciles." Paris, 1976. Novel.
Enfance. Paris, 1983. Autobiographical fiction.

THEATER

Le silence suivi de Le mensonge. Paris, 1967.
Isma, Le silence, et Le mensonge. Paris, 1970.
C'est beau. Paris, 1973.
Théâtre: Elle est là; C'est beau; Isma; Le mensonge; Le silence. Paris, 1978.
Pour un oui ou pour un non. Paris, 1984.

CRITICISM

L'Ère du soupçon. Paris, 1956.
L'Usage de la parole. Paris, 1980.

TRANSLATIONS

All titles are translated by Maria Jolas unless otherwise noted.
The Age of Suspicion. New York, 1965.
Between Life and Death. New York, 1969.
Childhood. Translated by Barbara Wright. Paris, 1984.
Collected Plays. Translated by Maria Jolas and Barbara Wright. New York, 1981. Includes *It Is There, It's Beautiful, Izzum, The Lie,* and *Silence.*
Do You Hear Them? New York, 1973.
"fools say." New York, 1977.
The Golden Fruits. New York, 1964.
Martereau. New York, 1959.
The Planetarium. New York, 1960.
Portrait of a Man Unknown. New York, 1958.
Silence and The Lie. London, 1969.
Tropisms. New York, 1963.
The Use of Speech. Translated by Barbara Wright. London, 1983.

BIOGRAPHICAL AND CRITICAL WORKS

Allemand, André. *L'Oeuvre romanesque de Nathalie Sarraute.* Neuchâtel, 1980.

Bernal, Olga. "Des fiches et des fluides dans les romans de Nathalie Sarraute." *Modern Language Notes* 88 (May 1973).

Besser, Gretchen R. *Nathalie Sarraute.* Boston, 1979.

Blanchot, Maurice. "D'un art sans avenir," *Nouvelle Nouvelle Revue Française* (March 1957).

Bouraoui, H. A. "Sarraute's Narrative Portraiture: The Artist in Search of a Voice." *Critique* 14, no. 1 (1972).

Butor, Michel. "*Le planétarium:* Le jeu compliqué des paroles et des silences." *Arts* (3–9 June 1959).

Cagnon, Maurice. "*Le planétarium:* Quelques aspects stylistiques." *French Review* 40 (February 1967).

Calin, Françoise. *La vie retrouvé: Étude de l'oeuvre romanesque de Nathalie Sarraute.* Paris, 1976.

Coenen-Menremeier, Brigitta. *Der Roman im Zeitalter des Misstrauens: Untersuchungen zu Nathalie Sarraute.* Frankfurt, 1974.

Cohn, Ruby. "Nathalie Sarraute's Subconversations." *Modern Language Notes* 79 (May 1963).

Cranaki, Mimica, and Yvon Belaval. *Nathalie Sarraute.* Paris, 1965.

Eliez-Ruegg, Elisabeth. *La conscience d'autrui et la conscience des objets dans l'oeuvre de Nathalie Sarraute.* Berne, 1972.

Jaccard, Jean-Luc. *Nathalie Sarraute.* Zurich, 1967.

Knapp, Bettina L., ed. *Off-Stage Voices.* Troy, N. Y., 1975.

———. "Nathalie Sarraute: A Theatre of Tropisms." *Performing Arts Journal* (Winter 1976).

Micha, René. *Nathalie Sarraute.* Paris, 1966.

Minogue, Valérie. *Nathalie Sarraute and the War of the Words: A Study of Five Novels.* Edinburgh, 1981.

Newman, Anthony S. *Une poésie des discours: Essai sur les romans de Nathalie Sarraute.* Geneva, 1976.

Picon, Gaëtan. "*Le planétarium.*" *Mercure de France,* no. 1151:491–494 (1959).

Pingaud, Bernard. "Le personnage dans l'oeuvre de Nathalie Sarraute." *Preuves* 154 (December 1963).

Régy, Claude. "Nathalie Sarraute: Un théâtre d'action." *Cahiers Renaud Barrault* 83 (1973), pp. 80–89.

Temple, Ruth Z. *Nathalie Sarraute.* New York, 1968.

Tison Braun, Micheline. *Nathalie Sarraute; ou, La recherche de l'authenticité.* Paris, 1971.

Vineberg, Elsa. *Au delà des tropismes: Études des romans de Nathalie Sarraute.* Irvine, Ca., 1973.

Wunderli-Müller, Christine B. *Le thème du masque et les banalités dans l'oeuvre de Nathalie Sarraute.* Zurich, 1970.

BETTINA L. KNAPP

EYVIND JOHNSON

(1900–1976)

HAD EYVIND JOHNSON written in one of the more popular European languages, it is almost certain he would be read today with the same attention and respect afforded James Joyce, Thomas Mann, and Marcel Proust, with all of whom he had something in common. He too was a tireless experimenter with novelistic form who struggled to reproduce and to create the means for accurately reflecting what might superficially be called the dilemma of modern man. An abiding interest in and extensive experiments with form characterize the entirety of Johnson's work, for which he was awarded an honorary doctorate from the University of Gothenburg (1953), election to the Swedish Academy (1957), the Nordic Council's Literature Prize (1962), and the Nobel Prize for Literature (1974), shared with his compatriot Harry Martinson. The last of these awards occasioned some surprise in European and American literary circles, owing solely to the lack of familiarity with Johnson's novels. The brilliantly innovative works in which he investigated twentieth-century consciousness of the problems of ontology, cognition, aesthetics, and politics merit a wide audience.

Eyvind Johnson was born on 29 July 1900 near the city of Boden in Sweden's northernmost province of Norrbotten. Important primarily as a railroad junction linking the main line from Stockholm with the ore-bearing trains from inland Sweden, Boden provided Johnson with ample exposure to the poorest of working-class Swedes and the social injustices that were visited on them daily. Because Johnson's father was poor, very ill, and given to certain mental aberrations, he was raised from the age of four by his maternal aunt. Since his aunt and her husband lived across the road from his parents, whom he saw daily, Johnson experienced this situation as very bewildering: "I went away although I was going home and went home although I was going away." This and similar terse statements about his childhood reflect the confusion of having two homes and yet none. The early feeling of homelessness became vital to his artistic development, for he experienced firsthand the essential rootlessness and searching so characteristic of his generation.

At the age of thirteen, Johnson left what home he had and for the next five years took a variety of jobs in Norrbotten, at a lumber camp, a brick kiln, a sawmill, a movie theater, and construction sites; his adolescent sensibilities were greatly affected by the misery and exploitation he encountered. In 1919 he moved to Stockholm, where he joined the Young Socialists and became a regular contributor to the revolutionary periodical *Brand*. Disillusioned, like many of his compatriots, by the postwar angst and pessimism that permeated Europe, in 1921 he stowed away on a ship bound for Germany. He spent most of the next decade on the Continent. On a trip to the Bay of Biscay in

1926, he experienced a kind of epiphany as he observed the crashing walls of water and the endless sandy beaches. The ocean as a metaphor for human consciousness, while not original with Johnson, has seldom been given such intensity of poetic expression as in his novel *Strändernas svall* (*Return to Ithaca*, 1946).

Johnson described his journey to the Continent as "a continuation of a striving outward, a striving outward which in some respects was an escape." This traveling or escape entailed growth and intellectual development. His belief in "the experienced world, the ability of change to impart knowledge about the world," as Setterwall notes, emphasizes the juxtaposition of experience and knowledge for a self-educated writer striving to create a rich and multifaceted mode of artistic expression. In his article "Något om material och symboler" (Something on Material and Symbols, 1959), Johnson noted that objective reality, the external world, is a source of knowledge, but it is the movement in and out of this reality that provides the ambiguity necessary for an accurate and truthful artistic vision (25):

> The dilemma of the author can upon occasion be that at the same time that he wants to penetrate into his own time in order to comprehend and understand its essence, he also wants to protect himself against that time, at least to the extent that he has enough strength left to bear forth his own testimony.

The rootlessness that was such an integral part of Johnson's youth was reflected in his later narrative concerns: in a focus on the function and role of the narrator and a constant shifting in narrative stance.

Like his fellow Scandinavians Henrik Ibsen and August Strindberg, Johnson seemed sometimes to find his native land too small, too confining. From 1921 to 1923 he lived mostly in Berlin, where he encountered such figures as Oscar Kokoschka and Ernst Toller and became involved with groups of political refugees. After a brief return to Sweden, Johnson went back to the Continent in 1925 and lived for the next five years in or near Paris, barely making a living on money from journalistic pieces he wrote for Stockholm papers. During this French sojourn he met and married his first wife, Aase Christoffersen, who helped impart a sense of peace and calm to his otherwise hectic and volatile life. He returned to his homeland in 1930 and devoted himself fulltime to his writing. When Aase died in 1938, he married Cilla Frankenhaüser. After a selfimposed exile first in Switzerland and then in England from 1947 to 1950, Johnson lived in Sweden until his death on 25 August 1976.

It is hardly surprising that Johnson's travels should open up new literary as well as geographical vistas. During his wanderings about the Continent in the 1920's he read voraciously and widely—Sigmund Freud, Henri Bergson, Knut Hamsun, Proust, Joyce, Ovid, Homer, Goethe, Shakespeare, Gide, and Strindberg, to name but a few.

But even as Johnson submerged himself in his readings and travels, he nurtured a deep and abiding concern for social issues. In his work he adheres to the basic tenets of European humanism in its specifically social manifestation. The theme clusters of freedom / violence and utopia / reality figure prominently in his novels, but these concerns are almost always presented in terms of problems of communication, of narrative form and linguistic limitations. As Meyer points out, Johnson typically investigates the claims of action versus passivity and the limits of man's private world in relation to society at large; within the private sphere we find such cognitive and existential problems as the ability of consciousness to gain knowledge about the past so that it is capable of influencing the present, and the relationship of the conscious to the unconscious as a function of time (26).

Johnson made many explicit and implicit comments on the place of literature and the role of the author in society. Language, because it is the source of knowledge and the means whereby the individual forges his own reality, is both a public and a private phenomenon, a way both to achieve social contact and to exercise power over others. As Johnson said in a 1931 article entitled "Romanens inbillade förfall" (The Imagined Decline of the Novel), the most important task for a novelist is "to produce human documents."

This concern with contemporary life and social issues did not entail an escape from or a negation of the past. On the contrary, few novelists of our century have been so concerned with the role of history in human consciousness. In "En författare i sin tid" (An Author in His Time, 1962), Johnson asserted: "An author's reading of history need not indicate an escape from the reality of the present; it can instead be a searching for means and forms in an attempt to interpret the meaning of our own times." In this respect he pointed the way to the modern function of the historical novel: "the past as a receded and thereby actualized present, the present as reexperienced, the past revitalized." History represented for Johnson a shortcut of a kind to the truths for which he was striving, because it allows access to temporally nonspecific truth. It is the immutable nature of man that Johnson sought to uncover in his works. In "Metoden Bovary" (The Bovary Method, 1931), he indicated precisely this universal quality as distinguishing great literature:

> It is the universally human qualities of a work and man's eternally recurring dreams which impart to it the validity which extends through the centuries. The vitality of a poetic work is not contingent upon the startling newness of the truths it thunders or whispers to us but rather on the radiance and power of its metaphor, the universal relevance of its choice of images.

Because of this conviction, Johnson's work is suffused with myth, legend, history, and symbol, repositories of experience that allowed him access to the human unconscious as well as to the possibility of rendering concrete and palpable much that is difficult or ostensibly inaccessible. Myth, symbol, and dream represent a kind of poetic shorthand to Johnson, an intermediate stage between fact and memory.

All these ideas are embodied in Johnson's work through daringly innovative formal techniques. The narrator is a medium through which the reader may encounter worlds of experience both essentially different from and essentially the same as his own. Johnson's narrators are often ironic and self-reflective, pointing up their own imperfect knowledge of the events they recount. The narrator becomes, therefore, both reflector and person reflected. As Johnson said in "Vi slipper inte undan ett val" (We Cannot Avoid a Choice, 1952): "The author, great or insignificant, beginner or established, is an instrument. He is simultaneously the reflecting surface and the reflection which the surface casts."

Despite his belief in permanently valid psychological truths and his profound ongoing social commitment, Johnson was skeptical about the possibility of effectively communicating these concerns. He is perhaps above and beyond all else an author of ambiguity. As he said in "Anteckningar om romanförfatteri" (Notes on Writing Novels, 1950), "How can one achieve clarity in what one wishes to say without sacrificing much of living and life-giving ambiguity?"

Johnson's narrator is situated somewhere between objective reality and subjective experience in the artwork, in part because of the author's ambivalent position toward language, which in his view has both a creative and a destructive potential. Johnson simultaneously distrusts the power of language to describe human states accurately and relishes its resilience and waywardness. In a text that delights in its own complexity, where aspects of form carry an extra-textual significance, the narrative must necessarily be vastly different from a straightforward recital of events (Setterwall, 7). Indirectly responding to the literary critics who advised him to compose "tighter, more cohesive texts, Johnson said in reference to Balzac, Stendhal, Joyce, and Thomas Mann:

"The dependent clauses, which according to the 'concentrated' method are unnecessary and weighty, are the very life of these works."

Setterwall shows that Johnson probes through layers of meaning in search of a core that evades ordinary verbalization by being always one layer away, but that may be related through circumspection, by expansion and elaboration of form. His method focuses on the writer himself as a craftsman of verbal expression and as a reflector of the social, political, and ideological climate of his time. The rootlessness of Johnson's life is expressed as an ontological rootlessness, a movement and mobility necessary to ensure experience, knowledge, and a clear overview; he searches for truth in the juxtaposition of fact and imagination, of analysis and sensual impressions; he employs language as a way to formulate the inexpressible (7, 9).

Johnson's perception of man's ambiguous position in the world and his formal virtuosity clearly link him to the mainstream of the modernist tradition. He was extraordinarily well read, an autodidact of the highest order. The critic Örjan Lindberger has written in "Eyvind Johnson" of the various sources that Johnson may well have drawn on:

It would be a long list, beginning with the German expressionists and Hamsun, continuing with French surrealism, then with Bergson and Proust, Gide and Joyce, containing too examples of crosswise cutting such as Dos Passos' *The 42nd Parallel* or Döblin's *Berlin Alexanderplatz*, the lessons of Thomas Mann and Hesse, and more recently a debate with existentialism. Behind all this now and then we would catch a glimpse of the shadow of Henry James (1958: 2–3).

In "Romanfunderingar" (Thoughts on the Novel, 1945), Johnson said he found in Proust, Gide, and Joyce "new ways of observing man and his circumstances, new ways of describing the acquired experiences. Each of them has in his own way opened the eyes of others to new or latent possibilities in the novel." In Gide's *The Counterfeiters* (1926) he singled out "noble French classicism in conjunction with a new knowledge of man, a modern understanding, and a ruthless analysis of human beings, with modulations of voices, elements of mysticism and a striving toward the ultimate limits of thinking, and an alternately calm, alternately trembling, not judgment, but observation of the phenomenon of man." He valued Proust's extensive descriptions and circumlocutory style as well as his "careful investigations of the contents of memory." He also adapted Joyce's much-celebrated "stream-of-consciousness" technique in his own novels to give an immediate and efficacious impression of a character's range of expression or mode of thought. Johnson is an artist of ambiguities and dichotomies, in terms of both his biography and his literary proclivities. As the critic Gavin Orton put it: "His roots are deep in the Swedish people . . . but he is also, by education, a European intellectual. Norrbotten and Paris: it is a surprising but exceptionally powerful combination."

Johnson's early novels, as Meyer has noted, belong to the so-called autodidact literature of the 1920's and 1930's, a literary development that heralded the serious acceptance of proletarian authors and working-class themes in Swedish literature. For these proletarian authors, literature was a cultural bastion to be conquered at the same time that it represented the possibility for the liberation of the masses. Johnson portrayed the bourgeoisie and its internal dissolution in novels rather more sophisticated and aesthetically complex than was then the norm in Sweden. It was Johnson who helped introduce into Swedish literature recent European cultural developments, such as the revolutionary discoveries of psychoanalysis and the literary use of interior monologue (143). His protagonists find themselves outside the mainstream of society less as a result of choice than of intellectual and temperamental proclivity. They are outsiders, drifters, characters Johnson came to call "Hamlet figures" because they are unable to act or to direct their fates; victims of impulses, of vagaries of thought and will, they embody the cultural paralysis that gripped so much of Europe after World War I.

Johnson made his literary debut with *De fyra främlingarna* (The Four Strangers, 1924), four "human documents" dealing with some aspect of hunger, either physical or political. Together they form a scathing indictment of contemporary Swedish society. Each story describes an instance of social humiliation, but while remarkable for intensity of feeling, they lapse into melodrama and are therefore primarily of historical interest.

Johnson's next work, *Timans och rättfärdigheten* (Timans and Justice), was published a year later. This novel also presents a socially alienated protagonist, but this character is the son of a wealthy factory owner, a young man who experiences a deep sympathy for the plight of his father's exploited workers but who nonetheless is powerless (or rather experiences himself as powerless) to effect any significant change. This son, Stig, is one of Johnson's most paralyzed Hamlet figures from the 1920's; the narrator says of him:

> The greatest loneliness is that of a young man. Its boundaries are mist through which the noise of the world penetrates, tempting and frightening, in beckonings and howls. And he lives in a circle which follows him wherever he goes; wherever he wanders the emptiness follows, the world recedes and flees. Action and woman reside in the unattainable. He knows them only in his timid dreams.
>
> (p. 38)

As this quote indicates, Johnson posits an opposition between the Hamlet figure, the doubter, and a realm of action, immediate experience, and passion embodied in the primi-

tivism that was sweeping Europe and that found its most articulate exponent in D. H. Lawrence.

Johnson's next novel, *Stad i mörker* (City in Darkness, 1927), represents a considerable honing of his craft. While *Timans och rättfärdigheten* consists of brief narrative fragments, the structure of *Stad i mörker* centers on fewer but longer episodes, allowing for the more leisurely and circumspect style that characterizes Johnson's best work precisely because it is suited to the rendering of a reality both elusive and uncertain. The outsider in *Stad i mörker* is able to come to terms with the society he feels has so wronged him by virtue of his embracing a philosophy perhaps best called existential humanism. He is able to make the journey from the mind to the heart through a kind of humanistic resignation. The complex reconciliation that obtains between the outsider-protagonist and the society in which he lives is also evident in Johnson's style; irony conjoins with lyricism to produce an aesthetic equivalent of the philosophical and social harmony that reigns within the text.

In contrast to the precocious balances and harmonies of *Stad i mörker*, Johnson's next novel *Stad i ljus* (City in Light, 1928), reasserts the primacy of chaos. The plot centers around a young Swedish author who wanders through the streets of Paris observing and absorbing impressions and experiences. Like previous Johnson protagonists, he is socially alienated and seems buffeted about by a hostile fate. Although *Stad i ljus* is probably one of Johnson's least successful (and certainly least cohesive) works, it remains interesting for its vitality and for the intensity of its images.

Minnas (Remembering, 1928) is largely significant because it represents one of Johnson's first attempts to weave together disparate narrative threads. The themes of memory, repressed and active, of passion, latent and manifest, of social involvement, rejected and embraced, are central to this novel. Although the work is flawed by its rather facile characterization, its failure to completely intertwine the two narratives, and its not always successful forays into irony, it embodies in rough form those qualities which raised Johnson's work to world stature.

Kommentar till ett stjärnfall (Commentary on a Falling Star, 1929) presents a kind of amalgam of contemporary life in Stockholm. While nihilistic in tone and content, the work is far more sophisticated in its subtle interpolation of plot lines than the earlier novels and represents the high point of this period in Johnson's career. Working again with the issues of primitivism and social criticism, Johnson depicts characters who illustrate the bankruptcy of bourgeois society and its economic and cultural values, and who are cut off from the most essential sources of human strength: personal and cultural memory and the regenerative powers of nature (Orton, 31). One character, Magnus Lyck (his last name is associated with the Swedish word for luck and destiny), embodies the author's Hamlet problem. Magnus is "the *eye*, the powerless eye that followed everything but could not intervene." But his essential passivity is tempered by his involvement with nature; alone on an island in the middle of a great lake, he builds a fire and exclaims:

> We dig down into the earth with our questions, deeper and deeper. And it's fortunate that we can ask, that we can make grand gestures and hurl our question marks at the vault above us. Perhaps all progress depends upon a new, a more intelligent, a more ingenious way of asking. . . . There is hope in every question, and a man who hopes looks to the future.
>
> (p. 312)

Although the passivity of the Hamlet figure is not laudable, he makes his contribution to the future by asking questions and searching for the truth. Magnus' speech to his own man-made fire and to the nature around him marks the culmination of a period of restless—

sometimes agonized—introspection in Johnson's work (Orton, 30).

Avsked till Hamlet (Farewell to Hamlet, 1930) represents, as its title might indicate, a coming to terms with the Hamlet problem. It is also the first of five novels that share the character of Mårten Torpare. The series is devoted to a consideration of various relevant social problems and employs Mårten Torpare as a kind of authorial alter ego. *Avsked till Hamlet* depicts a young man torn from his working-class environment and disoriented by the new bourgeois world in which he finds himself, until he is able to return to and derive social and spiritual sustenance from the world that he left. He is thus able to overcome his essentially passive, Hamlet-like stance and commence a course of positive action: "Civilization . . . is ennobled nature, the discipline of instincts, the will to justice, the knowledge of justice. The most important element in civilization at the moment is the workers' movement, because it has the will without which everything is dead."

Johnson's work during the 1930's began under the sign of social commitment, in a belief in the salutary effects of personal action. On returning from his lengthy sojourns abroad, Johnson found himself in the middle of a proletarian renaissance in Swedish literature and soon assumed a prominent place in its literary debate. As is evident from the many pieces he wrote for the radical Stockholm paper *Arbetet* (Work), he began at this time to abandon his anarchistic convictions in favor of more moderate political views, as a result of which he aligned himself with the Social Democrats. But he was far from seeing a deep preoccupation with formal values as bourgeois or reactionary self-absorption (as appears increasingly to be the case with literary critics today). On the contrary, Johnson felt that formal experiments were an integral part of the changes which must be wrought in decadent capitalist literature. He perceived himself to be allied with Proust, Joyce, Gide, and Mann in changing literature, but he did not see them as capitalists or decadents. He proclaimed in *Arbetet* (17 November 1932):

> The novel has the greatest prospects for being a mirror of its time. For a serious novelist, that is to say one who . . . would attempt to reproduce his own time as truthfully as possible, for him there is a problem in the medium of expression itself: he must revolt against that form whose deficiencies he acknowledges and attempt to create a literary form for the reality which he experiences and which he would describe.

It is this new literary form that Johnson attempted to create in one of his most important novels of the 1930's, *Bobinack* (1932). While *Avsked till Hamlet* concentrates on one character, this novel revolves around a group of people who are related to each other by social or familial ties. *Bobinack* is Johnson's contribution to the literary and cultural debate that raged in Europe at the time. It depicts and revolts against traditional bourgeois society and issues a clarion call for a "new" literature, a new perception of society and of human consciousness. As Monica Setterwall pointed out in "The Unwritten Story":

> The conventions of the realistic novel—the autonomous closure-provided text, the sequential arrangement of events bound in time by cause and effect, the solid character development, and the omniscient author—are replaced by momentary insights into a life situation, broken up time sequences, glimpses of various levels of consciousness, avoidance of closure, and above all, a narrator who observes, speculates on, and questions his own presentation (73).

This critic continues to note that *Bobinack* is in many respects a very modernist text. It presents the bustling city life so beloved of the modernists and contrasts it with the other side of the modernist coin, primitivism. The preoccupation with the vitality of natural forces is evident in the characters' unconscious impulses, in their dreams and memories of an uncomplicated existence, in the exoticism of the jungle, and in Bobinack's laughter. Johnson ridicules psychoanalysis as a method of exorcising the unruly primitivistic currents of the human mind and posits a view that stagnant bourgeois culture is doomed to extinction and that out of its ashes will rise a new type of human being and a new society (73–74).

The modernist striving for rich and full experience is expressed in the opposition of convention to instinct. Johnson devastatingly depicts the state of modern European culture, attacking its religious hypocrisy and advertisement culture, its Americanization and social indifference, and pits these forces against one of his most vital and intriguing protagonists, Bobinack. Each of the characters in the novel comes to confront Bobinack and through him to acknowledge in some way the primitivistic content of life.

The enigmatic figure of Bobinack embodies this primitivistic life force in his very being. If the Hamlet figure is the lodestar for Johnson in the 1920's, then Bobinack, in his capacity as a kind of Pan figure—an idea that can probably be traced back to Johnson's admiration for Hamsun and especially his 1894 novel *Pan*—dominates his works of the 1930's. This fascinating figure is both "God's messenger on earth" and "the devil himself," the adversary of a decadent culture and immorality, a character reminiscent of Gide's Lafcadio. He radiates a kind of pure, unadulterated joy. When the other characters in the novel meet to kill him, they are deeply affected by his laughter, which is described as "a great wave of mockery and joy, evil and warmth, madness and wisdom" and which effectively paralyzes them, for they can no more destroy him than they can the life force that he represents.

The structure of the novel also reflects the fundamental conflict between the irrational and the conventional. A traffic accident begins the narrative *in medias res* and functions as a point of intersection for all the characters. The technique of employing a single event to bring together widely disparate characters and narrative strands, a technique that imparts cohesion and focus to otherwise ostensibly disjointed texts, is one that Johnson consistently used throughout his career.

Narratively, too, *Bobinack* is the most sophisticated of Johnson's early works. As Setterwall, the novel's best critic, explains, he employs a self-conscious strategy through which a character, Mårten Torpare, ridicules the narrator as a busybody who wants to know everything about everybody, a pompous manipulator who is guilty of trying to enclose the vital and amorphous flow of life in the confined format of a novel. Mårten Torpare claims that his own book about these same events would be a "charmingly lovely book," suitable for reading aloud in Sunday school. In other words, the narrator is by definition alienated from the life stream he is trying to portray. Although he is a necessary vehicle for the narrative, he is incapable of impartiality. His own values infiltrate the creative and reflective process through the selection and presentation of the material.

Language, as the medium through which artistic content is conveyed, also comes in for serious consideration by Johnson. In the conflicts that create the dramatic tensions in the novel, characters are defined by the mastery they possess over words. Cederquist commits suicide struggling for words that will articulate his dilemma and formalize it so that it can be dealt with rationally. Only those outside society, those who are a part of the life stream like Lydia and Bobinack—who, respectively, embody passion and the demonic—are capable of effectively communicating.

Bobinack, Johnson's experiment with the primitivistic aspect of modernism, has a text in which objective reality is relative rather than absolute, characters fragmentary rather than well rounded, and the narrative open-ended rather than closed. Bobinack is the focal point against which individuals are forced to reas-

sess their relationship to society and to themselves. Johnson here posits the possibility of escape from imprisonment because imprisonment is seen as a social and cultural phenomenon, whereas later Johnson sees imprisonment as an essential part of the human condition, grounded in consciousness.

The novel is remarkable for its openness to a variety of readings not only by the reader but also by the narrator himself, as he searches for new combinations of form and content to represent fictional reality. Johnson establishes a self-directed criticism that investigates the validity of its own premises, implicitly contending that the form of the narrative should be versatile enough to reflect all the facets of its content, just as society as a cultural form should answer to the needs of ambiguous, multifaceted human beings. *Bobinack* is Johnson's first novel in which metaform appears as a deliberate attempt to bring the narrator's ambiguous position into relief, a narrative technique that became more pronounced in his later work (114–116).

Unfortunately, Johnson's next novel is not up to the standards of *Bobinack. Regn i gryningen* (Rain at Dawn, 1933) describes an individual's attempt to achieve middle-class respectability and his subsequent rejection of the bourgeois life for an existence in nature. His affair with a country girl, whom he calls Harmony, takes on Lawrencian overtones but cannot prevent the novel's ultimate failure, for it adds up to little more than a simplistic paean to the more hackneyed aspects of primitivism.

But Johnson's next project, *Romanen om Olof* (The Novel About Olof, 1934–1937), is arguably his greatest work before *Return to Ithaca* and represents a milestone in Swedish and Nordic literature. *Romanen om Olof* is actually a tetralogy consisting of *Nu var det 1914* (*1914,* 1934), *Här har du ditt liv!* (Here Is Your Life!, 1935), *Se dig inte om!* (Don't Look Back!, 1936), and *Slutspel i ungdomen* (Finale in Youth, 1937). This massive undertaking is a semiautobiographical *Künstlerroman* (novel of artistic education) that traces the development of the young Johnson (here called Olof Persson) from the time he took leave of his foster parents at the age of thirteen to his departure from Norrbotten five years later. The novel also serves as a sometimes eloquent and lyrical description of the social, cultural, and topographical environment of Norrbotten. Johnson depicts with savage clarity the totality of this miserable world—the work, the camaraderie, the bragging and blustering, the workers' sexual lives. But the narrative expands from description to social criticism; he says of the lumbermen: "The day they stood up, put their hands on their chests and said: 'Now I see clearly'—that day would be their last. They could not bear the terrible truth, that their life was a frozen or sweaty hell and nothing more."

The theme of the novel series is human consciousness and its development through the processes of socialization. Olof Persson progresses from an introverted and almost mute boy to an individual with greater and greater knowledge of the world and its people. Mjöberg argues cogently that Ofof's problem is in part a timeless, private one—to become an adult and learn more about the world—and in part a concrete, social one—the dilemma of a working-class boy who wishes to storm the cultural barricades erected by bourgeois society. The extensive global knowledge he seeks is not to be found among the poor working class of his native Norrbotten—there he finds only a meager peasant culture in the process of dissolution. Rather he must search in books for his knowledge, in Strindberg, Alexandre Dumas *père,* and the *Odyssey*—in other words, in the literature of a class to which he does not belong.

This is the problem of the autodidact, a problem that plagued an entire generation of Swedish proletarian authors but is by no means limited to one period or one country: how one is to conquer and assimilate the language of the dominant, educated class and at the same time keep one's own experiences as a member of the working class intact. That

Olof succeeds, or rather will succeed, is apparent, but he must pay the price of isolation. His solitary reading isolates him from his peers, and the abyss that develops between them grows even wider. But Olof attains a new insight about himself that includes those whom he has left behind in his quest for knowledge, and that of necessity has certain consequences for his perception of society and his political thought (144–145):

> Every human being is alone and you will never connect with the others—and all people belong together and are humanity, and you belong to it. . . . Everything depends on you—but you cannot live alone in the world and you must believe in the worth and dignity of the other people—and you must believe in the majesty and holiness of man and his great mission to create happiness out of misery—and you stand here and are you and cannot come any further. You are you but you must stand together with the others who are not you . . . but you are perhaps you precisely through them.
>
> (*Slutspel i ungdomen,* p. 341)

Olof discovers that although experience cannot be adequately articulated in language, life depends on precisely this articulation. The pathway to freedom traverses language:

> Now I am sitting here and they can't get any words out of me. I have no words now. Further on I will probably get words, *otherwise I cannot live!* But then the words may not be able to reach out and tell how I once sat on a sofa and thought about them like this.
>
> (*Slutspel i ungdomen,* p. 28)

Olof's involvement with language as a literary medium is also manifest in the role that fairy tales play in the tetralogy. Each volume contains at least one fairy tale. Orton points to the fact that in the third volume Olof is no longer reading or listening to fairy tales; he is himself composing them: from the passive stage of listening, he proceeds to the active stage of artistic creation. And in the last volume there is an intimate blending of literature and life. Literature colors Olof's interpretations of his experiences at the same time that his experiences are expressed through literature. The fairy tale is rendered in the form of a fevered dream he has while ill, in which he adopts a variety of roles in his adventures—he is alternately Vicomte Olof of Ultima Thule in a Dumas novel, Buffalo Olof of the Wild West, Olof Hamlet, Olof Werther, King Olof of the Sagas, and Olof Odysseus. Even the literary style of his fairy tale is imitative: blank verse for Hamlet, hexameters for Homer (63–64). This sequence represents the first clear statement of one of the major contentions of Johnson's work, his unshakable conviction of the inseparability of life and art. He does not merely hold that a life without art is impoverished; he asserts that a life without art is impossible.

Later in his career, as a kind of continuation of *Romanen om Olof,* Johnson wrote *Romantisk berättelse* (Romantic Tale, 1953) and *Tidens gång* (The Course of Time, 1955). Like most of his postwar oeuvre, the novels depict several different temporal levels. The narrator describes how he wrote the novels during the early 1950's, while the events they recount— the protagonist's sojourn on the Continent— took place some thirty years before. The two time frames are additionally complicated by the fact that the narrator purports to base much of his text on written documents—diaries and letters—that have come into his possession. This kaleidoscopic technique has the effect of forcing the reader to perceive the text as a kind of reality-within-a-reality-within-a-reality rendered yet more complex by the various time frames.

What is perhaps most significant about these books—for they are relatively unsatisfying aesthetically—is Johnson's altered perception of his semiautobiographical protagonist. Whereas he is called Olof Persson (or person) in the Olof novels, he is here called Olle Oper. Olle is a nickname for Olof, but Oper, as one character suggests, might well be interpreted

as a shortened form of *opersonlig,* "impersonal." Indeed, Johnson's attitude toward his protagonist in these novels is much more detached and ironic than in the Olof novels.

In the late 1930's the world's attention was increasingly focused on the threat of German political expansionism. Always a socially conscious author, Johnson was alarmed by what he observed, all the more so because of his liberal-radical political convictions. In the prewar years and all through the atrocities of the conflict itself, Johnson relegated his more purely aesthetic narrative concerns to the background, concentrating instead on the enormity of the threat that fascism posed.

His next work, *Nattövning* (Night Maneuvers, 1938), although artistically uneven, demonstrates the depth of his convictions. It recounts a rather fantastic story of an organization of Swedish Nazis who are engaged in smuggling arms and will stop at nothing, including the murder of their countrymen, to forward their schemes. Whatever its literary failings, the novel succeeded in bringing into focus the sympathies, both latent and manifest, of a large part of the Swedish middle class for Germany and its Aryan ideal, as well as the country's widespread indifference to Nazism, an indifference meretriciously dignified by the term *neutrality.* Johnson is finally forced to "the bitter, desperately repellent conclusion that perhaps violence must be fought with violence; that life is so fantastic that bombs must tear apart human bodies in order that humanity shall achieve the possibility of happiness."

It is significant, too, that the character of Mårten Torpare, who resurfaces in *Nattövning,* should no longer be the contemplative, doubting Hamlet figure. In a crisis of this magnitude the luxury of disinterested inquiry is unthinkable. Rather, Torpare issues to all humanity a clarion call for active resistance. When considering a book he intends to write, Torpare concludes that it must be very different from *Regn i gryningen*: "Perhaps too many people have walked through the forests in Scandinavian literature." He condemns his thought of the past as too insular: "A kind of faith in blood, in grass, in clouds, in rain, in uninhibited experience. How far away this was after a few years! 'The face of the world has changed so quickly,' he said. 'The individual's fate matters so little now.'"

The final Mårten Torpare novel, *Soldatens återkomst* (The Return of the Soldier, 1940), carries the same intensity of political conviction as its predecessor, but is more aesthetically even. With a kind of filmic technique, it develops the thoughts of "Scandinavia's soldier," who has come back from the Spanish Civil War, the winter war in Finland, and the spring campaign in Norway. On his way home, he is attacked by a man named Sander (Alexander), who represents all the political evil that derives from a lust for power. The soldier says that he has fought for "freedom and the happiness that is created through freedom" but also for decency:

> Decency is freedom. We are defending decency; one can also call it free culture. Here in Scandinavia and in the Western world there is the possibility of decency; in the east and the south lives its enemies. They are trying to eradicate the human features from the face of time. They form pacts in order to do this.
>
> (p. 198)

This statement is a reference to the pact between Germany and the Soviet Union of August 1939. Although the story takes place within a relatively short time period—a few early morning hours—the characterization achieves fullness and richness primarily through Johnson's use of interior monologue, a technique he raised to veritably Joycean standards in his later works.

Throughout the war years Johnson continued vehemently to oppose the tide of German expansion and to dedicate himself to thwarting the enemy through every means in his power. He was bitterly disappointed when Russia invaded Finland in 1939 and the Scandinavian countries took no action, and again, when

Germany occupied Norway and Denmark and Sweden still insisted on remaining neutral. Too old to enlist, Johnson turned to his pen as a way of fighting the enemy. He was the person legally responsible for the Norwegian resistance newspaper *Et Håndslag* (A Handclasp, 1942–1945), for which he wrote most of the editorials along with Willy Brandt, then an unknown German of Norwegian extraction. But it was primarily through his Krilon trilogy that Johnson hoped to awaken his countrymen to their responsibilities.

This trilogy, composed of the novels *Grupp Krilon* (Krilon's Group, 1941), *Krilons resa* (Krilon's Journey, 1942), and *Krilon själv* (Krilon Himself, 1943), is a massive literary enterprise systematically depicting a social overview of neutral Sweden. Rich in stylistic experiments, the novels begin by treating a small discussion group in Stockholm and develop into what Johnson called "a complete picture of the world as I myself saw it." As Orton points out, it is an account of man's eternal struggle against evil and, more particularly, of the Allies' struggle against Nazism (17).

The seven members of Krilon's discussion group meet every Sunday evening to discuss some literary, philosophical, or social issue. But two business rivals of Krilon's set about undermining his friendships, an action that results in their social and personal destruction and that of Krilon as well. It is significant that these rivals are named G. Staph and T. Jekau; as the former informs us, his name is to be pronounced "Gestapo," and the Swedish pronunciation of the latter makes it a variant of the Swedish transcription of Stalin's secret police, the Cheka. G. Staph is further assisted by a triumvirate called Görgöhö—Gören, Göben, and Höllén, individuals who bear a striking resemblance to Goering, Goebbels, and Himmler. Krilon himself, although less directly representative than the other characters, can be identified with Winston Churchill, and he is helped in his efforts by an American friend, Frank Lind, who can be similarly identified with Franklin D. Roosevelt. The members of Krilon's group are likened to individual European countries that are one by one swallowed up by the evil G. Staph. And Frank Lind and Krilon go out into Lake Mälaren in a boat "painted in the gray-blue color of a battleship" to form their own "Mälar Charter."

Krilon, whose initials are J. K. (Swedish "Jesus Kristus"), is a short, stout, not very prepossessing Stockholm estate agent, but he represents the political ideal of democracy. As Mjöberg notes, he believes, like his creator, that man is a noble being of unshakable integrity; he believes in the power and the ultimate victory of the human spirit, in loyalty to one's ideals, in social solidarity and the goodwill of mankind. He dreams about a "kingdom of decency" on earth (307).

Meyer observes that if the Olof tetralogy poses the problem of how an individual can progress from the world of action and work to that of education and knowledge, the Krilon trilogy poses the opposite question: how education, culture, and abstract moral values can be transformed into action. Through the crises the characters experience, they come to the insight that the struggle between freedom and oppression does not take place in some remote "political" sphere, but rather is played out constantly in everyday life. Johnson mobilizes the entirety of Europe's cultural heritage in the various novelistic techniques he deploys as arms in the struggle against evil.

Krilon reminds the discussion group of the cultural human context they are on the point of forgetting, which finds its roots outside the elitist values traditionally associated with "culture." He talks extensively about life in the countryside, peasant crafts and culture, even the cultivation of tulips—all of which represent values threatened by "the new age" valorized by dictatorships (146–147). Johnson is now positing a synthesis between his earlier poles of experience and consciousness, insofar as the former is embodied in the peasants' proximity to nature and the latter in the cultural heritage of Europe.

The Krilon novels also evince the style that became standard in Johnson's mature works: a syntactically complex, convoluted, and rather exhaustive manner of presentation. In an effort to be accurate, he spares no elaboration. As he said in an interview:

> The whole thing is an attempt to describe a human being as thoroughly as possible. I don't know how well I have succeeded as far as that is concerned. And perhaps people merely think it is strange when, for example, I describe a face in six printed pages. But I wanted to be exhaustive.
> (*Dagens Nyheter*, 7 December 1943)

Truth, for Johnson, is not directly apprehensible, but rather can be achieved only through digression and circumlocution. Krilon's manner of speech reflects Johnson's digressive description of him, while G. Staph expresses himself in a terse, direct prose that embodies his conviction that he has a shortcut to the truth. But for Johnson there are no shortcuts to truth, only a long, difficult, and often circuitous uphill climb to insight, both political and personal. A number of critics have noted the influence of Mann on this style. Erik Linder, for example, contends that Krilon is described "with an exhaustiveness and in a formal style that Johnson has adapted from Thomas Mann's novel about Joseph and his brothers."

Johnson also experiments in the Krilon novels with narration, by injecting a distinctly self-conscious narrator as well as a consideration of the act of writing itself:

> The re-narrator's role is to re-narrate, perhaps not exactly as he sees it, but so that what he sees can reach other people as pictures of what is real or likely. . . . Often he is only the supplier of the raw material—reality, dreams. His work can consist of handing it out, or handing out bits of it. In this way he can determine the high or low calorie and vitamin content and provide a recipe for its preparation, while the receiver, the reader, the person seeing it at second hand, can fry, boil, spice, and thicken it himself.
> (*Krilons resa*, pp. 310–311)

The author must also, Johnson claims, if he is to be honest, admit his imperfect knowledge of his fictional reality, so that the reader may engage in his own processing of it. In the text of the novels, the protagonist discusses the problem of literary realism and literary fantasy in terms of the liquidation of the Jews of Poland and Lithuania: "Of all the gigantic horrible mass of reality, there remain only fragments, figures, data, names of German executioners and places in Lithuania and Poland" (*Krilon själv*, p. 522). Such a naked factual reality, Orton notes, cannot affect the reader; instead he must be made to reexperience the reality behind the statistics. Art can assist in the mediation of this reality (81):

> If someone who has tried to reexperience such things in his soul can snatch a single living picture out of this compact block of suffering . . . then the whole reality appears before his eyes. . . . He can see it, he can reproduce it, convey it in a picture, in words that provoke a picture in us. By transforming, changing, compressing reality, he can carry the truth about it further.
>
> (*Krilon själv*, p. 523)

The Krilon novels argue that, in order for man to act consciously, he must become aware of the fact that the route from knowledge to action is both indirect and tortuous. In all the postwar novels, Johnson transforms his earlier contention that imprisonment arises out of repressive political systems into the idea that enslavement, grief, and suffering are essentially products of man's consciousness.

After the conclusion of the war, Johnson continued to examine such social issues as violence versus freedom and reality versus utopia, but through the format of the quasi-historical novel, for he was interested in how the past and human history help to comprise human consciousness:

> No one period of time on its own forms our present. I mean, the experiences of the past mingle with our daily life, the daily life of those now living, just as our present, what is present at the moment, will in its way mingle with the life of the future.
>
> ("En författare i sin tid," p. 121)

Like Joyce's *Ulysses,* Johnson's masterpiece, *Return to Ithaca,* reconstructs the events of the *Odyssey* in a modern framework: both authors see the "eternal" nature of the Odysseus motif and impart to their narratives a dimension of mythical depth by playing them out against a background of the patterns of the ancient epic. For both Joyce and Johnson, the static symmetry of the traditional self-contained plot can no longer be imposed on the dynamic formlessness of life, which they experience as a variable flowing rather than as an unchanging being. But while in *Ulysses* the action takes place in contemporary time and the novel only alludes to the latent pattern, Johnson transfers the action to Odysseus' own time. Thus the technical method for achieving mythical timelessness is more complicated for Johnson than for Joyce. Johnson follows Homer in the general details of the plot and in constant shifts between the hero's travels and his life on his homeland, Ithaca, but the novel is unmistakably modern both in its philosophical implications and in its treatment of time, memory, and narration, for Johnson posits narration as the single most significant human activity.

Deeply fascinated by classical Greek literature from an early age, Johnson is at intellectual and literary odds with most of his fellow proletarian authors; unlike his compatriots Jan Fridegård and Ivar Lo-Johansson, who treated almost exclusively the bitterness and deprivation of rural Swedish poverty, Johnson is concerned with the totality of timeless human experience and consequently seeks a unity of both temporal experience and literary expression, a unity to be found in the act of narration. For him the works of Homer and Xenophon especially are revelations of the fundamentally unchanging nature of man and history. The classical material is, however, filtered through the antirationalistic tradition that extends from Schopenhauer through Nietzsche to Freud and Bergson. Like Mann, Johnson strives to present a view of life that stresses the individual's organic connection with a living tradition, a living past.

Odysseus' experiences of narration develop in conjunction with the progress of the narrative text to reveal Johnson's view of narration as a realization of human identity. Odysseus' journey is a voyage toward the past in order to reconquer it as reality and make it live again in his own consciousness, but this triumph is to be achieved only through the magical act of narration. *Return to Ithaca* is a novel in part about the process of socialization, about the necessary development of the individual in society. It depicts how a social reality is created through linguistic designations, and how the reality created through this process expands to embrace and enclose human will and consciousness.

The conflict between classic and modern comes alive in Johnson's protagonist Odysseus, who, instead of embodying the heroic qualities of his namesake in *The Odyssey*, is a hero in spite of himself. In recounting to Calypso his reasons for going off to the Trojan War, he tells her, "I was perhaps more of a farmer than a prince, a seaman, or a warrior." Indeed, he tells her that he went to war only in order to be able to come home again.

The disparity between the presentation of Odysseus as hero in Homer and the portrait of him as anti-hero in Johnson compels us to contemplate the connections between the two texts. With certain reservations we might say that *Return to Ithaca* is a kind of critical commentary on Homer's epic. This critique is expressed through the Re-narrator, the implicit embodiment of Johnson's presence in the novel, who occasionally surfaces with his doubts about the veracity of the facts in Homer. The novel is, therefore, a metatext, a questioning of the implications of narration. Johnson further juxtaposes reality and myth by having Odysseus appear as a narrator who recasts his reality into myth, at the same time that he, through his Re-narrator, tries to penetrate the myth and find the reality behind it. *Return to Ithaca,* then, presents us with an account of the creation of Homer's epic.

For Johnson the process of narration is inextricably linked with that of time and history. He does not so much describe the present through the past as show that the two are identical, because man finds himself in essentially the same situation in every historical epoch. Myth and history give us access to quintessential human experience, which remains fundamentally unchanged. In Johnson's 1951 novel *Lägg undan solen* (Put Away the Sun), the protagonist addresses this problem: "By historical I don't mean so much Gibbon or Macaulay as Frazer. . . . In Frazer the events are perhaps the same, but he seeks more deeply for the sources. . . . *The impelling forces are exposed more to the reader. The depths* [of history] *yield their currents.*"

That the subtitle of *Return to Ithaca* is *A Novel About the Present* is therefore not surprising, for it is a novel about the present on numerous levels. The events it portrays all superficially refer to events occurring in the time in which the novel was written, the years during and immediately after World War II. In an article from 1949, Johnson claimed that his intention with the novel "from the first moment" was "to try to create an image of modern man. Not in his entirety, that's impossible, but in one of his most difficult situations . . . : the necessity of using violence to combat even greater violence" ("*Strändernas svall,*" in *Röster i radio,* no. 10, 1949). Repeatedly the characters in the novel break out of their historical framework to give their ideas and comments, an anachronistic device by means of which a double perspective is brought to bear on the event. For example, when Odysseus and the swineherd Eumaeus discuss whether it is right to take up arms and kill the suitors in order to regain power on Ithaca, they do so in a way that makes it clear that the discussion is simultaneously concerned with a problem of great urgency to the author and his contemporaries: Can democracy be defended by violent means against threats from totalitarian movements? The suitors are divided into two groups: those who want to rule the world because they think they were born to it, chosen by the gods, and those who say they want to rule in the name of the people but in reality merely want power for themselves. The analogies to the Nazis and the Communists are obvious attempts to expand the temporal boundaries of the work.

But *Return to Ithaca* is a novel about the present in other respects as well, for in the act of reading we experience the past (the preterite) as present. In keeping with the epic theory to which *The Odyssey* adheres, the novel begins *in medias res,* on Calypso's island; all earlier events are recounted as memories or narratives. As in Homer the external action spans only that part of the twenty years of Odysseus' absence during which he leaves Calypso and returns home to wreak vengeance on the suitors. Because of internal textual obfuscations, precisely how long that time is cannot be reckoned exactly, but it is safe to say that it is somewhere between three and six weeks.

In this brief period are present all the twenty years that have passed since Odysseus left Ithaca as a twenty-five-year-old. They are present in part in the external transformations the years have wrought in the characters, transformations the author emphasizes in his description of Odysseus' body in the first chapter. But the years are also present in terms of the inner experiences of the characters. Stored in Odysseus' unconscious are both those experiences he wants to remember and those he would rather forget, the latter symbolically concentrated in his obtrusive thoughts of Astyanax, whom he has killed.

The novel is therefore not only about a relatively short "present" in the narrative, it is also about a kind of perpetual present, the combination of past, present, and future that makes up any present. Recurrent episodes and motifs that offset the inherent chronology of the narra-

tive also force us into a constantly expanding, ever richer and deeper present. Thus narration has the power on the supratextual level to reclaim for us our mythic and historical past and transform it into a present.

The present of the text is also established by a kind of double perspective through which events and people are perceived. The focus shifts between historical and present time; these dissolve into a synthesis in which the distinction between then and now seems irrelevant and arbitrary. This approach is crystallized in Odysseus' conversation with Eumaeus; Odysseus is looking for a solution to the situation in Ithaca that would not entail having to kill the suitors:

> My lord . . . there is no choice for him. I have heard of other people, far away, people who can choose. There it is considered a great shame, a stain on one's honor and a crime against the gods, to kill people. But now we are in reality, Traveller—we are in the present! We are in the civilized world! There is no choice.
>
> (p. 479)

In "the civilized world" man still has no choice but to kill. Reality then and reality now are fundamentally the same. The 3,000 intervening years are an abstraction: Odysseus' sense that he is a powerless victim of the whims of outside forces is not temporally specific. Johnson communicates the simultaneity of then and now; through narration the two images of time fuse together into one.

Language is a vital part of this process, for it is a medium for encapsulating and reproducing experience, a stratagem for releasing oneself from the prison of subjectivity; in order to master the past one must tell about it, share it with another person. Narration becomes an act of self-affirmation, a means of orienting oneself in reality.

But if Odysseus must conquer time and the past in order to narrate, so too must Johnson triumph over the spatial and temporal gaps that divide both him and his material from the reader if he is to reclaim both history and fiction for us. This problem is the major concern of the five chapters that alternate depictions of Odysseus' life on Ogygia with presentations of life on Ithaca. Basing his ideas in large part on those of Bergson, Johnson develops two different concepts of time that we might call simultaneity and reiteration.

The idea of simultaneity has a psychological origin and is based in an analysis of human consciousness. It involves the notion that, as regards the individual experience of time, no clear boundaries can be drawn between times and events; present and past merge in consciousness and different moments exist side by side. The idea of simultaneity is formulated by Johnson as an aesthetic problem; the merging of different elements in the flow of consciousness cannot be directly related in language, which is by its very nature chronological and discursive and describes a movement *from* one thing *to* another. However much the writer may split up and subdivide the course of events in the story, he is still bound by the fixed order of words.

Johnson copes with this problem in much the same way as do Joyce and Proust, by expanding small blocks of time so as to give an impression of fullness and continuity within the limits of the unit of time chosen. He deliberately sacrifices speed and the interest caused by movement and change in order to achieve a closer correspondence between the pace of living, or more truly, of thinking and feeling, and his depiction of it. In this way Johnson impresses on us that the greater part of the novel is occurring in the present—a present, however, that is rich with memories and reverberations of the past. This simultaneity is juxtaposed to the chronology of Odysseus' departure from Ogygia and his trip home; he moves forward in time, while time to some extent stands still for those on Ithaca awaiting his return.

The concept of reiteration in *Return to Ithaca* derives from the idea that the same situations and trains of events constantly recur in history. Mankind and the fundamental situa-

tion of mankind have not changed in the course of 3,000 years. This line of thought clearly corresponds with Johnson's notion of the simultaneity of past and present; in each event all other events that form a repetition of the same pattern are present in an abstract sense. Narration, then, can recapture our collective cultural past and render it as present experience.

Despite the fact that Johnson's view of time as a constant pattern of reiteration may in some ways seem pessimistic, simultaneity tempers that pessimism by allowing us a particular richness and fullness of experience. Man can transcend the limits of his individual existence by being implicated in the collective experiences and memories of humanity, even when these experiences are grim and brutal ones. We have, Johnson implicitly contends, only to listen to and remember our pasts to defeat the gods who would enslave us. In this view there exists a note of humanistic optimism and a conception of constantly increasing knowledge about man and his condition. Just as the waves of violence that Odysseus sets in motion when he kills the suitors will roll on forever, so too will the narrative continue far into the future with ever new narrators who communicate *their* view of reality; narration, for Johnson, ultimately leads to an ever-improving understanding of reality and consequently to morality.

Johnson's works after *Return to Ithaca* are more strictly historical novels, more exact in their historical perspective, even though Johnson refused to call them historical novels in the usual meaning of the term. In all of them Johnson avails himself of his "objective" historical material to consider a whole range of problems centering on human consciousness and cognition. By using historical subjects, Johnson achieves both distance from and proximity to the fictional material. It is hardly surprising, then, that these novels represent the high point in Johnson's postwar novelistic achievements, while the narratives that are enacted in the present are less successful.

Drömmar om rosor och eld (*Dreams of*

Roses and Fire, 1949), *Molnen över Metapontion* (The Clouds over Metapontion, 1957), *Hans nådes tid* (*The Days of His Grace,* 1960), and *Livsdagen lång* (Life's Long Day, 1964) are remarkable novels that, while not as masterful as *Return to Ithaca,* merit extensive critical attention. All are tales of people engaged in a quest for love, even as their political and social worlds subvert that quest. Victimized by political power struggles, they strive valiantly to maintain, however tenuously, their essential humanity.

Dreams of Roses and Fire takes place in a period of historical transition and depicts a group of people in a small, unnamed French town who are drawn into the world of international power politics. The specific incident on which the novel is based is the trial and burning of a Jesuit priest, Urbain Grandier (Grainier in the novel), in the city of Loudun in 1634. Accused of witchcraft, Grainier is a pawn in the power struggle of Cardinal Richelieu, who has ordered the destruction of the city walls of Loudun because they serve to harbor a stronghold of Huguenot heretics (an action the historical Grandier opposed). Aldous Huxley also found this historical incident to be of interest, as his *The Devils of Loudon* (1952) attests; his version of the events largely coincides with Johnson's.

There are no fewer than three narrators in *Dreams of Roses and Fire:* the assessor Daniel Drouin, the prioress of the cloister Jeanne de Beaucil (whom Grainier is said to have enchanted), and the canon Jehan Minet. The narrative is further complicated by two parallel plots, one centering on Grainier's fate and the other on the dispute over the city walls. Grainier is as complex and intriguing a character as Bobinack, whom he resembles in his capacity to both attract and repel, and in his enormous vitality. The walls are essentially as ambiguous in their function as is Grainier in his character; just as he is said to be attractive to both men and women, interested in political gain but deeply devout, so too the walls provide protection against the outside world while con-

taining demons within. This essential ambiguity suffuses all the characters, including the three narrators, and is based on a conflict between inner, irrational forces—largely sexual in nature—and external social, religious, and political realities.

Meyer, who reads the novel very persuasively, points to its polyphonic composition and narrative technique. Images crowd next to each other and are sometimes obscured by or superimposed on other images—as when the "objective" narrator comments on what is happening within the consciousness of another character. In this way the narrative forces us to keep a certain distance from the text, to evaluate, to resist the illusion and the temptation of identifying with any given character. We are constantly directed to focus our attention on the relationship between what is said and what remains unsaid. The time perspective becomes a kind of "all-time" in which both we and the narrators are observers and sufferers.

Both implicit and explicit in *Dreams of Roses and Fire* is a consideration of the role language plays on an individual and a political level. Both Johnson himself and his protagonist take on a variety of roles that the conscious manipulation of language helps them to fulfill. In this sense language functions as a necessary but forever provisional means to achieve a specific goal: namely, the establishment of contact between individual human consciousness and the outer social world. The novel investigates the relationships between language, truth, and illusion. Language both produces and reproduces an image of the world, an image of external reality as well as of human consciousness.

The narrative technique is subordinated to a larger problem of cognition that constitutes a dominant motif in the work; even the "objective" narrator expresses his doubts about the possibility of complete knowledge, yet claims to seek it, as do the characters who narrate smaller segments. Johnson develops the action through the consciousnesses of various characters; our attention is directed to those processes through which consciousness distinguishes something as foreign, a process in which the concept of time plays a decisive role.

The essential ambiguity of reality appears as a tension between the narrators' conscious memory and a subtext that communicates something different; the initial omniscient narrator gives way to a polyphony of narrative voices, a kaleidoscopic reality in which different versions of the same event are arrayed so that the narrative as a whole appears as a series of cognitive rings, each ring intersecting others, each with its own center in an individual character. In this fashion Johnson demonstrates his contention that art can impart only one of the possibilities of what the truth might be (30–55).

In *Molnen över Metapontion* Johnson returns to the authors of antiquity who were so significant to his intellectual development. The novel takes as its starting point Xenophon's *Anabasis;* Johnson follows the career of one of the characters from this work, Themistogenes, who participated in the campaign that Xenophon recounts. Themistogenes' fate is paralleled by that of a modern Swede, Klemans Decorbie, who has occasion to retrace the Greek's footsteps through southern Italy in the 1950's on a quest for his own past.

Three different periods of time coexist in Decorbie's consciousness: the present, the age of Themistogenes, and a period during the war when he was a prisoner in a German concentration camp. He first learned about Themistogenes from a fellow prisoner; while in the camp he also fell in love with another prisoner, Claire, whom he is now seeking in Italy. By emphasizing the ways in which the protagonist experiences all three of these time periods as one, Johnson creates the illusion of simultaneity for which he strives in all his historical works. But the two plot lines also intersect spatially as Decorbie treads the same soil Themistogenes walked so many centuries before, and the two characters share the further trait that each seeks a physical and spiritual escape

from the pain and suffering Johnson deems fundamental to the human condition.

This extremely intricate novel derives its complexity from the various narrative planes that flow into, out of, and over one another; events in Themistogenes' life, for instance, are told in the concentration camp by one individual and recounted ten years later by another. Themistogenes' life is told by contemporaries and by later historians, who are in turn read and commented upon by Decorbie. Meyer again explicates the novel's epistemology: the many layers of the narrative underline the essentially fictive nature of the material before us. We are never granted any secure viewpoint from which we might begin to identify with characters or to suspend disbelief, for every narrative plane is constantly pointed up as fictional. Only the fiction of the main character, Klemens Decorbie, remains intact, and even that is undercut by his self-conscious irony. To Johnson's primary theme of the ungraspable nature of man as both subject and object is added the secondary theme of narration as a means to attain insight: the extensive parallels between the characters on the various fictional planes and their conjunction in time and space bring home the realization that man in the past and the present is essentially unchanging.

As in Johnson's two preceding novels, language plays a vital role in *Molnen över Metapontion.* The culturally weighted, refined, but static language of the rulers and the undeveloped, searching, inaccurate "slave language" of the ruled are set in opposition. The former is capable only of reproducing the atrophied state of consciousness in which it originates, whereas the latter, while dynamic and organic because it is based on experience, is also powerless because of its lack of articulation. Nonetheless, this is the language of protest, even though the protest remains latent because it is private and cannot be communicated. The individual remains isolated because of his imperfect linguistic system.

Decorbie and Themistogenes are both on a

quest that remains forever beyond their reach, ending only in frustration. During their travels the world of man comes to appear foreign, impenetrable, and static, a power outside human consciousness; this is the case especially but not exclusively with language (61–75). But like one of his sub-narrators, Johnson sees in history a means of "learning more about the conditions under which mankind lives on earth and its prospects for combatting suffering." Increased knowledge and increasingly wide perspectives can lead us to the *possibility* of something better.

Johnson's next novel, and some would argue his greatest, *The Days of His Grace,* is his longest and most complicated work. It continues the concerns of his earlier novels in that it investigates the ways in which the individual absorbs social norms and conventions through society's language and also examines language as a creative process through which norms for what is real are created. It treats problems of narration as well as the individual's and society's possibilities for liberation through conscious action.

The novel is set in Italy during the reign of Charlemagne, "His Grace" of the title, and it centers not on the Holy Roman Emperor but rather on the lives of his victims, the Lupigis family of Lombardy. As these ordinary people are drawn into the net of power and intrigue that surrounds Charlemagne, their lives are rendered painful, anguished, and wretched, a state of being only intermittently alleviated by ephemeral interludes of joy. Love, pure and uncompromised, despite assaults from a corrupt world, appears as man's only consolation. Here, as in earlier Johnson novels, the perspective is that of the victims, those defeated by power and violence, those who ask nothing of life but love and an unattainable dream. These characters live, as the motto of the novel indicates, "on an aspen leaf," insecure, battered about, unconscious of their precarious position in reality.

The themes are familiar: the relationship between a powerful society and the powerless individual, between memory and forgetfulness, between captivity and freedom, between war and peace. These themes, as Meyer notes, are presented through two image clusters: one, representing light, treats the moon and the stars and has an aura of eternity, of secure and overwhelming immutability; the other, indicating eruption, deterioration, and change in human life and in nature, includes water, storms, and avalanches (97). Thus history has its correspondences in the natural world, where death and eternal renewal, the storm of the novel's central metaphor, ravage life but also ensure perpetual change.

The style of this novel, as Söderberg notes, differs somewhat from that of Johnson's preceding works: the sharp dissonances and unmediated contrasts are reconciled into a grand, cohesive, calm, and clear vision of man's life in a stormy world. But there is still considerable stylistic variety—rapid shifts from elevated literary language to formal and precise chronicle style, from simple dramatic realism to prosaic rhetoric (9, 34). Myths, storms, and legends abound, functioning as potential interpretive models and as commentaries on the fictionality of the work.

The Days of His Grace contains a number of short narratives that are subsumed and ultimately negated by a larger, ostensibly "objective" narrative, which is in turn invalidated by a series of self-conscious linguistic devices that reveal its inadequacy. The novel is a narrative about Agibertus' reproduction of and commentary on Johannes Lupigis' own notes from a period many years earlier; considering the overall text, we are then four times removed from reality.

As in most of Johnson's novels, there are multiple narrators at work here. The delineation of perspectives and narrative stances creates a dizzyingly complex text that is undermined by irony and ambiguity. On occasion it is even unclear which of the narrators is speaking; this makes us yet more unsure about the text we are encountering. There is no single, ideal point from which we can view the whole, and we are therefore compelled to join in the creative process, to speculate about these characters and events in such a way that their reality becomes our reality.

Other factors that complicate the novel are its shifting chronology, interpolated stories and poems, and constant allusions to events in the future and the past. This self-reflexive narrative technique means that we must constantly re-evaluate our interpretations of certain events, at the end of which process everything appears to mean something other than what is specifically stated. This is especially manifest in the coalescing and fragmenting of character, which makes us perceive humans as both mutable and unchanging, specific and universal.

Just as the character Anselm tries through the act of narration to bridge the gap between the larger political world and the everyday private world of the Lombardians who are his audience, so Johnson attempts to bridge this abyss with his text, to create a truly authentic language. The character Warnefrit, like Cederquist in *Bobinack,* is literally destroyed because of his inability to express himself in language; for Johnson, that which is inarticulated can never be exorcised. As Meyer explicates, language in *The Days of His Grace* is an instrument for creating and communicating an alienated consciousness; that is, all consciousness is alienated, cut off from true knowledge. Genuine reality is without language, which implies that human action occurs blindly, outside of consciousness. Thus language is not a part of action but a distorted reflection of it.

Consciousness becomes in this novel a protection *against* experience; active memory is a bewitching repetition of disparate and statically isolated elements in the past, an obstacle to the non-disparate time that contains the possibility of greater knowledge. The enslavement of consciousness is a consequence of this separation from experience: a prerequisite for man's ability to act meaningfully and effectively in relationship to the present is that he understand the past as a dynamic process leading to the present and not as discontinuous points of fixed, static time.

The central problem for the protagonist is his attempt to reconquer the past and preserve it as a dynamic experience. The present exists as a product of events in the past and also as an entity that can be altered through actions, both individual and social. In contrast to this relatively optimistic vision, consciousness is no longer posited as a means—in spite of everything—to acquire knowledge; rather, because of its very nature, it is an obstacle to the true knowledge synonymous with continuous time. The most essential function of consciousness is to cut off the human mind from a dynamic sense of time. Consciousness arises after action and is a false reflection of it. But by way of compensation for unsuccessful, outwardly directed activity, man's private, personal life is prized. Memory, while private and unable to provide man with any insight into the outer world, can form the basis for an inner truth, a perception that links up with Johnson's earlier primitivism and its emphasis on a richness of experience (101–117).

Livsdagen lång is to a great extent both a consummation of and a conclusion to Johnson's previous work, on which it sometimes self-reflexively comments. Its seeming simplicity belies an extraordinary complexity; multitudinous plot lines are juxtaposed with a single, recurring pattern of human striving to produce a rich and profound novel. Like many of its predecessors, the novel is constructed around two narrative strands that are brought into conjunction by our active participation. The first focuses on the Narrator—who bears certain striking resemblances to Johnson himself—and a number of situations in his life between the 1920's and the 1960's, which are in turn linked, however obliquely, with his interest in the lovers Donatus and Astalda, the two main characters in the second, historical narrative. The Narrator wants to find these two characters and longs to know "who they were."

In a series of narratives from the ninth to the sixteenth century, all of which are variations and refinements of the others, Donatus seeks Astalda and finds her in a number of disguises. They recognize and avow their love for each other, but each time Astalda eludes the hero, who falls into a pit from which he escapes to continue on his quest to find her. These episodes vary in time and place, but the presence of the two lovers and the necessity of Donatus' continuing on his search are common to all of them. Individual historical circumstances may differ, but our essential condition remains unchanged.

Livsdagen lång is also a narrative about narrative. Its format is based in the fiction of the frame story: the Narrator is recounting this material to a group of friends who traipse about from one Italian restaurant to another. The narrative complexity is carried further when the characters in one fictional episode appear to be cognizant of their counterparts in the rest of the novel, sometimes even doubting exactly who they are.

The novel is a radical experiment with the nonchronological experience of time and history. As Stig Bäckman observed, there is, on the one hand, an endeavor to dissolve the limits of time and space and to allow vastly different events to fuse and cohere in our consciousness, and, on the other hand, a sober, objective narrative posture that imparts careful explanations as to precise dates, places, and circumstances. The latter tendency is best exemplified by the Narrator's friend, the Historian; together they enter into lengthy discussions of the differing demands of their professions, of their contrasting approaches to historical subject matter.

In these conversations, the Narrator maintains his right to deviate from the historical facts if he finds it necessary in order to give shape to

the deeper, intuitively felt truth that he wishes to communicate to the reader. To the Narrator, history is not something past, but something present, a series of ideas in his consciousness, inseparably interwoven with his personal experiences and memories. (196)

This subjective view of history is also embodied in the structure of the novel: the narrated events of the past are contiguous with the Narrator's own experiences and memories. Donatus' experiences through time are a mirror image of the Narrator's life. Thus the two narratives cohere into one. As Donatus realizes while he is in the pit (a kind of human grave from which he is born again as well as a distinctly Neoplatonic impulse in the work): "Men die, man lives eternally. Through man, men always survive the Day of Judgment." Individual lovers may die, but the lover as an embodiment of the essentially human lives on. Donatus likens himself to the river, the dominant symbol in the novel: "The past runs into the present and the present mixes with a past that in this way continues to live." This conception of time is obviously very closely linked with Bergson's concept of *durée,* or duration, in the flow of individual consciousness. At the end of the novel the two narrative strands cohere in the Narrator's vision as he suddenly realizes that he and Donatus are one and that Astalda is a woman whom he himself once lost "and whose name I had forgotten."

As Bäckman has noted, the novel shares many striking similarities with the work of Mann. In their concern for the workings of time and the opposition between movement and stasis, and in their use of a cumulative novelistic structure and a mythical interpretation of characters and events, the writers are kindred artistic spirits (197).

Livsdagen lång also reveals the development of Johnson's perception of the act of narration. While his earlier narrators are joined with their listeners in a quest for knowledge or memory, here the two are united in the simple enjoyment the narration creates. The "meaning" of the narrative lies in the aesthetic pleasure it provides for others.

The Narrator is a part of the pattern of human history. While his story will certainly survive him, he becomes a part of a great chain of narrators:

[The characters] would be rediscovered by someone wanting to see their faces, be sought the livelong day by someone not this narrator, but a younger, a new narrator. This narrator too would become silent, step aside . . . when the narrator of his age, when the narrator of many ages, would long since have become dumb and have vanished, all their words only whisperings of a seedling grass on a distant coast.

(pp. 329–330)

Because it does not belong to the genre of the historical novel, in which Johnson's best postwar work was done, we have postponed the discussion of *Lägg undan solen,* which depicts one day in the life of war refugees who meet in the Alps to await their opportunity for escape. One of Johnson's least successful works, it offers little of literary or intellectual merit, presenting a pastiche of his thoughts about political action and literary time, although it is here that he directly defines the concept of simultaneity that he had already artistically used in better novels:

One of the most difficult aesthetic problems of our time is precisely the problem of simultaneity, the impression of omnipresence in space and time; only pictorial art can do this. Authors cannot succeed here, for however splintered and rearranged the events may be presented, still one word must follow the other; the images that the word imparts glide, sweep along, move along lines that go from now to then and from then to now and between proximity and distance, the individual and the communal.

(pp. 54–55)

Johnson's penultimate novel, *Favel ensam* (Favel Alone, 1968), describes the thoughts of an elderly man over a period of several hours; the narrative, while lacking in external plot, is rich in memories and fantasies that coalesce in an inner, constantly associative and shifting experience of time that has little contact with the outside world. The novel is not far removed from the French *nouveau roman,* with its free narration, independent of time and space. It takes for its subject contemporary Europe (which is, for Johnson, Europe throughout its history), more exactly, the philosophical tradition of European idealism and the necessity for some kind of political commitment even though the frustrations of that commitment are overwhelming.

The title of Johnson's final novel, *Några steg mot tystnaden* (Some Steps Toward Silence, 1973), stands in ironic juxtaposition to the fact that it was indeed his last and that soon he would be entering the very silence of which he wrote. Subtitled *A Novel About Captives,* it is constructed around three narrative threads: the honeymoon of a young couple on the Swiss border in 1946, the murder of the duke of Enghien on Napoleon's orders in 1804, and the subsequent trial of André-Saturnin Colinet-Guenole. These narratives are mediated by two main characters who for different reasons are personally interested in the events they recount. As in earlier novels, the two narrators and the three narratives overlap and permeate each other. Various other historical events are also invoked, all of which conjoin with fictional episodes to produce in the act of reading an experience of simultaneity that transcends space and time. In this kaleidoscopic reality Johnson completely abdicates any responsibility for or attempt at mimetic representation. In this way he reiterates his frequently voiced contention that any narrated account is not a final product, but is instead only an impetus for other narratives.

The characters and narrators all join in a search for reality, for the growth and development that constitute their essential humanity. For all the depth and insight of Johnson's vision of mankind and human consciousness, he is still able to take his steps into silence with a kind of joyous resignation, for as one of his narrators comments: "It is the case with narratives . . . that they end. But new ones of course will always arise, if only there are narrators who can extract them out of life, out of the world, out of the past, out of the dreams of what we experience—out of us here and now perhaps."

Throughout Johnson's career, his style developed from a youthful if nihilistic ebullience in the early works, to the juxtaposition of a wretched proletarian reality with the fantasy of fairy tale in the Olof tetralogy, to the reserved, cerebral prose that characterizes his best postwar work. His persistent concern with man's social and political reality, his never-flagging perception of the inherent dignity of man, and his subtle and complex vision of human consciousness place him squarely in the mainstream of the European humanist tradition, a position that has not been sufficiently acknowledged by virtue of his having written in one of the less frequently spoken languages. While Johnson addresses explictly and implicitly many issues that lie at the heart of both contemporary and timeless human experience, perhaps his greatest contribution to world literature lies in the profound and eloquent testimony of his work to the essential inseparability of life and art.

Selected Bibliography

EDITIONS

De fyra främlingarna. Stockholm, 1924.
Timans och rättfärdigheten. Stockholm, 1925.
Stad i mörker. Stockholm, 1927.
Stad i ljus. Stockholm, 1928.
Minnas. Stockholm, 1928.
Kommentar till ett stjärnfall. Stockholm, 1929.
Avsked till Hamlet. Stockholm, 1930.
Natten är här. Stockholm, 1932.
Bobinack. Stockholm, 1932.
Regn i gryningen. Stockholm, 1933.
Än en gång, kapten! Stockholm, 1934.
Nu var det 1914. Stockholm, 1934.
Här har du ditt liv! Stockholm, 1935.
Se dig inte om! Stockholm, 1936.
Slutspel i ungdomen. Stockholm, 1937.
Nattövning. Stockholm, 1938.
Soldatens återkomst. Stockholm, 1940.
Den trygga världen. Stockholm, 1940.
Grupp Krilon. Stockholm, 1941.
Krilons resa. Stockholm, 1942.
Krilon själv. Stockholm, 1943.
Sju liv. Stockholm, 1944.
Strändernas svall. Stockholm, 1946.
Pan mot Sparta. Stockholm, 1946.
Dagbok från Schweiz. Stockholm, 1949.
Drömmar om rosor och eld. Stockholm, 1949.
Lägg undan solen. Stockholm, 1951.
Romantisk berättelse. Stockholm, 1953.
Tidens gång. Stockholm, 1955.
Vinterresa i Norrbotten. Stockholm, 1955.
Molnen över Metapontion. Stockholm, 1957.
Hans nådes tid. Stockholm, 1960.
Livsdagen lång. Stockholm, 1964.
Favel ensam. Stockholm, 1968.
Några steg mot tystnaden. Stockholm, 1973.

SELECTED MODERN EDITIONS

Än en gång, kapten! Stockholm, 1976.
Bobinack. Stockholm, 1960.
Drömmar om rosor och eld. Stockholm, 1974.
Grupp Krilon. Stockholm, 1966.
Hans nådes tid. Stockholm, 1963.
Här har du ditt liv! Stockholm, 1963.
Krilon själv. Stockholm, 1966.
Krilons resa. Stockholm, 1966.
Natten är här. Stockholm, 1969.
Nattövning. Stockholm, 1971.
Nu var det 1914. Stockholm, 1974.
Se dig inte om! Stockholm, 1965.
Slutspel i ungdomen. Stockholm, 1966.
Strändernas svall. Stockholm, 1964.

JOURNALISM

"Anteckningar om romanförfatteri." In *Författaren och hans arbetsmetod*. Stockholm, 1950.
"Anteckningar vid läsning i Gustaf Hedenvind-Erikssons verk." *Svensk litteraturtidskrift* 2, no. 2 (1939).

"Att hoppas trots allt." *Röster i radio* 27, no. 52 (1960), pp. 14–15, 63.

"Den nya franska litteraturen." *Signalen,* 5 August 1926.

"Diktaren—samhället." *Svensk litteraturtidskrift* 7, no. 1 (1945), pp. 145–156.

"En författare i sin tid." *Modersmålslärarnas förenings årsskrift* (1962).

"Jag och den andre: Eyvind Johnson och Olof." *Hörde ni?* 2 (1949), pp.

"Kring en roman." *Garm* 29 (1952), pp. 3–6.

"Kring några namn." *Fronten,* 1931, pp. 4–6.

"Metoden Bovary." *Nya dagligt allehanda,* 17 May 1931.

"Möten." *Svensk Litteraturtidskrift* 29 (1966): 1–6.

"Något om att författa: Ett stycke prosa." In *Tarjei Vesaas 1897–20 aug. 1967.* Oslo, 1967.

"Något om material och symboler." *Svenska litteratursällskapet i Finland* 371 (1959).

"Om diktens förvandlingar." *Bonniers Litterära Magasin* 31 (1962).

"Om ursprung och miljö." *Svenska Dagbladet* 15 (January 1949).

"Om verkligheten i en roman." *Vintergatan* (1937).

"Optimism—eller vad?" *Hågkomster och livsintryck* 13 (1932).

"Personligt dokument." In *Ansikter.* Stockholm, 1932.

"Reflexioner kring André Gides sista roman." *Ny Tid,* 9 September 1927, 20 September 1927, and 14 October 1927.

"Resa hösten 1921." *Vintergatan* (1940–1942).

"Romanens inbillade förfall." *Fronten* 1 (1931): 9–11.

"Romanens verkliga förfall." *Fronten* 1 (1931): 4–6.

"Romanfunderingar." In *Ansikter.* Stockholm, 1945.

"Ur Eyvind Johnsons dagbok." *Röster i Radio* 32, no. 8 (1965): 29–31.

"Vändpunkt?" *Vintergatan* (1965–1966).

"Vi slipper inte undan ett val." In *Mellem Håb og Frygt,* by Sigurd Hoel, Eyvind Johnson, and Paul LaCour. Copenhagen, 1952.

TRANSLATIONS

The Days of His Grace. Translated by Elspeth Harley Schubert. London, 1968.

Dreams of Roses and Fire. Translated by Erik J. Friis. New York, 1984.

1914. Translated by Mary Sandbach. London, 1970.

Return to Ithaca. Translated by M. A. Michael. New York and London, 1952.

BIOGRAPHICAL AND CRITICAL STUDIES

Ahnlund, Knut. "Möten med Eyvind Johnson." *Svensk Litteraturtidskrift* 40 (1977): 17–20.

Bäckman, Stig. *Den tidlösa historien.* Lund, 1975.

Bergengren, K. "Motståndsmännen Johannes, *Krilon,* och *Hans nådes tid." Läste ni?* 1 (1962).

Björklund, C. J. "Eyvind Johnson:, Intelligens, artist, verklighetsskildrare och poet. In *Orädda riddare av pennan.* Stockholm, 1960.

Blomberg, Erik. "Bobinack, djävulen, och Ivar Krueger." In *Stadens fångar.* Stockholm, 1933.

Böhm, A. "Die Heimkehr des Odysseus in Eyvind Johnsons *Strändernas svall."* In *Estrato di Annali.* Vienna, 1970.

Bolckmanns, Alex. "Roman och film: Några funderingar kring Eyvind Johnsons roman *Hans nådes tid." The Seventh International Study Conference on Nordic Literature.* Uppsala, 1966.

Brandell, Gunnar. "Eyvind Johnson." In *Svensk litteratur 1900–1950.* Stockholm, 1967.

Carlson, Stig. "Eyvind Johnson summerad." *Morgontidningen,* 17 and 18 May 1947.

Carlsson, Leif. "Vid läsningen av *Bobinack." Ergo* 31–34 (1954–55): 57–66.

Claudi, Jörgen. *Eyvind Johnson: En karakteristik.* Copenhagen, 1947.

Granlid, Hans. *Då som nu: Historiska romaner i översikt och analys.* Stockholm, 1964.

Göransson, Sverkar. "Berättartekniken i Eyvind Johnsons roman *Molnen över Metapontion." Samlaren* 83 (1962).

Gustafsson, Lars. "'Mer än sagor': Antikt mönster i tre moderna diktverk." *Svensk litteraturtidskrift* 29 (1966): 14–23.

Hallberg, Peter. "Eyvind Johnson: Ordet och verkligheten." *Bonniers Litterära Magasin* 7 (1958).

Harrie, Ivar. "Eyvind Johnson: Före *Krilon."* In *In i fyrtiotalet.* Stockholm, 1944.

Hedberg, Oscar. "Eyvind Johnson." *Folket i bild* 4 (1937): 8–36.

Hegerfors, Torsten. "Tre moderna svenska antikromaner." *Modersmålslärarnas förenings årsskrift* (1966): 100–118.

Helén, Gunnar. "Eyvind Johnson." *Röster i Radio* 14 (1947): 6–7, 28.

Hemmel, Lars. "Eyvind Johnson och existentialismen." *Studiekamraten* 53 (1971).

Hirn, Yrjö. "En fransk häxeriprocess år 1634." In *Den förgyllda balustraden och andra uppsatser från åren 1949–1952.* Stockholm, 1953.

Jaensson, Knut. *Nio moderna svenska prosaförfattare.* Stockholm, 1943.

Jonsson, Bernt. *"Hans nådes tid*—och Karl den Stores." *Svensk Litteraturtidskrift* 40 (1977): 78–98.

Kuntzel, Hans. "Eyvind Johnson." *Biblioteksbladet,* August 1932.

Lassen, Carl C. "Eyvind Johnson." *Litteratur* 3 (1945).

Lindberger, Örjan. "Berättarteknikens utveckling från Hjalmar Söderberg till Eyvind Johnson." *Modersmålslärarnas förenings årsskrift* 90 (1939): 94–117.

———. "Eyvind Johnson och antiken." *Studiekamraten* 39 (1957): 195–202.

———. "Eyvind Johnson." *The Second International Study Conference in Nordic Literature.* Lillehammer, 1958.

———. "Eyvind Johnsons möte med Proust och Joyce." *Bonniers Litterära Magasin* 29 (1960): 554–613.

———. "Människan, trädet, och elden: Om *Kommentar till ett stjärnfall." Svensk Litteraturtidskrift* 40 (1977): 29–43.

Linder, Erik Hjalmar. "Eyvind Johnson." *Fem decennier av nittonhundratalet: Ny illustrerad svensk litteraturhistoria.* Stockholm, 1966.

Meyer, Ole. *Eyvind Johnsons historiska romaner: Analyser av språksyn och världssyn i fem romaner.* Copenhagen, 1976.

Mjöberg, Jöran. "Eyvind Johnson: Förmedlaren, berättaren, moralisten." *Samtiden* 57 (1948): 295–308.

Munk-Neilsen, C. A. "Eyvind Johnson und Thomas Mann." *Orbis Litterarum* (1958).

Munkhammer, Birgit. "30-talets perspektiv." *Svensk Litteraturtidskrift* 40 (1977): 55–77.

Nygård, Bjarne. "Berättelsens makt och vanmakt." *Horisont* 11 (1964): 19–22.

Orton, Gavin. *Eyvind Johnson.* New York, 1972.

Pagrot, Lennart. "Eyvind Johnson och Thomas Mann." Proseminar essay, University of Stockholm, 1951.

Rinman, Sven. "Djävularna i Loudun." *Göteborgs Handels—och sjöfartstindning,* 21 January 1953.

Rud, Nils Johan. "Eyvind Johnson." *Vinduet* 1 (1947): 207–212.

Runnquist, Ake. *Moderna svenska författare.* Stockholm, 1959.

———. "Ett handslag." *Bonniers Litterära Magasin* 29 (1960): 583–586.

Setterwall, Monica. "The Unwritten Story: A Study of Meta-Form in Three of Eyvind Johnson's Novels." Ph.D. diss., University of Wisconsin, 1979.

Sjöberg, Leif. "Eyvind Johnson." *American-Scandinavian Review* 56 (1968): 369–378.

Söderberg, Barbro. *Flykten mot stjärnorna: Struktur och symbol i Eyvind Johnsons "Hans nådes tid."* Stockholm, 1980.

Stenström, Thure. "På djävulens tid." *Svenska Dagbladet,* 14 August 1971.

———. "Perspektiv på Eyvind Johnson." *Svenska Dagbladet,* 4 May 1973.

———. "Existentialism and Swedish Literature in the 1940s. *The Tenth International Study Conference for Nordic Literature.* Reykjavik, 1975.

———. *Romantikern Eyvind Johnson.* Lund, 1978.

Stolpe, Sven. "Eyvind Johnson." In *Det svenska geniet.* Stockholm, 1935.

Thunander, M. "Symboler och komposition i Eyvind Johnsons *Drömmar om rosor och eld."* Proseminar essay, University of Stockholm, 1968.

Wamberg, N. B. "Eyvind Johnson." In *Fremmede Digtere i det 20. Århundrede,* edited by Sven Møller Kristensen. Copenhagen, 1967.

Warme, Lars. "Experiment and Innovation in the Contemporary Swedish Novel." Ph.D. diss., University of Lund, 1952.

———. "Eyvind Johnsons *Några steg mot tystnaden:* En Apologia." *Scandinavian Studies* 49 (1977): 452–463.

Westholm, Carl Axel. "Skollärar Andersson, parlamentarismen och 'det ovanliga': En studie kring Eyvind Johnsons *Stad i mörker." Ord och Bild* 46 (1957): 535–547.

Wiman, Gunnar. "Den inre monologen i Eyvind Johnsons *Kommentar till et stjärnfall."* *Modersmålslärarnas förenings årsskrift* (1956).

MARILYN JOHNS BLACKWELL

SALVATORE QUASIMODO

(1901–1968)

IN 1960, a few months after being awarded the Nobel Prize for 1959, Salvatore Quasimodo wrote a summary of his career.

He was born, he said, in Syracuse on 20 August 1901, the son of a railroad employee. His grandmother was from Patras, Greece. After an elementary education in Gela, he attended technical schools in Palermo, studying to become an engineer. Subsequently he went to Messina, where he began to write verse.

In 1919 Quasimodo moved to Rome, where he attended the Politecnico and supported himself as, successively, a technical designer for a large construction company, a salesman for an ironworks, and a clerk in a large department store. His involvement in organizing a strike caused him to neglect his schooling and got him into trouble with the carabinieri. Quasimodo then joined the Civil Engineering Service and was assigned to Reggio Calabria. Between the ages of fourteen and twenty he had written poems but, dissatisfied with them, had stopped. Now, at the age of twenty-seven, he resumed writing.

Quasimodo reported going to Florence in 1929 in order to join Arturo Loria, Alessandro Bonsanti, Eugenio Montale, Gianna Manzini, and Vieri Nannetti, a group of writers and intellectuals associated with the review *Solaria*, of which Bonsanti was the editor. He left three of his poems with Bonsanti, who published them in March 1930. Soon afterward Quasimodo was asked to prepare a volume of his works; *Acque e terre* (*Waters and Lands*[1]) appeared that same year.

From then on, Quasimodo was a frequent contributor to *Solaria, Circoli,* and *Letteratura.* The poems published in those reviews were collected in 1932 in the book *Oboe sommerso* (*Sunken Oboe*). By 1931, transferred to Imperia, Quasimodo was spending weekends in Genoa with Montale and Adriano Grande, Camillo Sbarbaro, and Angelo Barile. Throughout his stay in Imperia, Quasimodo sought to return to Milan, and eventually he obtained a transfer to the Lombard capital. There he spent his evenings among painters, writers, journalists, sculptors, and musicians.

Erato e Apòllion (*Erato and Apollyon*) was published in 1936. Two years later Quasimodo left the Civil Engineering Service and became secretary to Cesare Zavattini. He ended up working on a magazine of comics, *Settebello*, selecting the jokes for the comic strips. Zavattini began publication of *Il Tempo* in 1939, and Quasimodo subsequently became editor.

Over a period of time Quasimodo had been translating lyrics of the Greek poets; they appeared in 1940 as *Lirici greci* (Greek Lyric

---

[1] The English titles used here and below are those adopted in Jack Bevan's translation of the *Complete Poems.* Except as noted, however, all translations in this essay are the work of the present writer.

Poets). In 1942 his *Ed è subito sera* (*And Suddenly It's Evening*) was published. During the war Quasimodo worked on translations of the *Odyssey*, the poems of Catullus, *Oedipus Rex*, and the Gospel of John.

The poet's account of his career (summarized above), while mainly in keeping with the facts, is susceptible to some revision and calls for considerable amplification. His statement that he first saw the light of day in Syracuse is inaccurate; he was in fact born in Modica, in the province of Ragusa. The misstatement is significant; Quasimodo was proud of his Greek heritage, and Syracuse has a resonance of Hellenism that humble Modica cannot claim. A like motivation may perhaps be observed in the poet's pronunciation of his name. His father was known as Quasimódo, but very early in his career the son chose to be called Quasímodo; possibly the dactyl seemed to him more Greek, or at least more exotic.

Further, the brief curriculum vitae is all but barren of personal data. Quasimodo may have thought, like Giambattista Vico before him, that such matters are irrelevant to the life story of a writer or an intellectual. The poet's personal life story, however, particularly his *carrière sentimentale,* was rich, intense, and at times tempestuous. Throughout his life he was never without feminine solace, which no doubt invigorated and refreshed his muse, although overt love poems as such are relatively rare in the catalog of his lyrics. His relationship with Bice Donetti, "the Emilian woman" memorialized in one of his later verses, began immediately after his move to Rome. Subsequently it was legitimized by marriage. Bice died in 1946, but husband and wife had gone their separate ways well before that date. During Quasimodo's residence in Lombardy in the mid 1930's, he divided his affections between Bice and a married woman, Amelia Spezialetti, whom he had met in Imperia in 1931 and who, four years later, bore him a daughter, Oretta—an event that seems to have somewhat dismayed the young father. ("And have you really had a daughter?" Montale wrote him, adding a little cynically, "From what source?"). Bice, who did not embrace the notion of sharing her husband with another woman, worked behind the scenes to get the Civil Engineering Service to transfer him to Sardinia. It is not clear whether, on his return from banishment a few months later, the relationship with "la Spezialetti" was resumed. It seems unlikely, however, for in 1936 he met the classical dancer Maria Cumani, who immediately captured his wayward heart. His published letters to her cover the years 1936 to 1955 and are of considerable interest, revealing as they do the poet's activities and attitudes over two decades of professional and intellectual life. They span the years of prewar tension in Italy, the war itself, and its confusing aftermath; these are also years of achievement and recognition for the poet. By Maria he had a son, Alessandro, of whom he speaks with touching tenderness in his letters. In 1948, two years after Bice's death, he married Maria. There were other liaisons as well. The published correspondence *A Sibilla* (1983) documents an intense if brief affair in 1935 with Sibilla Aleramo. At that time, the renowned feminist novelist was twenty-six years older than the poet and had already made an imposing number of conquests (or surrenders), involving the poets Vincenzo Cardarelli, Piero Rebora, and Michele Campana, the world-famous Giovanni Papini, and at least half a dozen other prominent men of letters. Quasimodo's dedication to her endured for only nine months, and he seems to have broken with her in a rather brutal fashion. Nor did the poet, in the words of his friend Giancarlo Vigorelli, "disdain occasional love affairs" (one-night stands, as the phrase goes), about which, in the company of friends he would discourse with ironic complacency.

The years in which Quasimodo came to maturity and published the poems that brought him prominence in the Italian world of letters were also the years of the high tide of Fascism.

Mussolini's dramatic march on Rome occurred only a few years after Quasimodo had taken up residence in the North, and the regime was at its zenith through the 1930's. It seems clear from his own testimony and that of his contemporaries that the poet was never in sympathy with the dictatorship. Few writers were, although such prominent figures as Giuseppe Ungaretti and Massimo Bontempelli were good Fascists. However, technically at least, Quasimodo must have been enrolled in the party; his employment by the state would have required lip service to the cause. And it was under the sponsorship of the poet Angiolo Silvio Novara, a member of the Fascist Accademia d'Italia, that Quasimodo obtained his transfer to the Office of Civil Engineering in Milan in 1934. On the other hand, it was Elio Vittorini, husband of Quasimodo's sister, who brought him into contact with the group of writers in Florence associated with *Circoli* and *Solaria* who launched him on his career; and in the years 1936 to 1938, Vittorini wrote *Conversazione in Sicilia* (*In Sicily*, 1938), a novel of anti-Fascist thrust. Like the vast majority of Italian men of letters in those trying years, Quasimodo seems simply to have adapted himself to the exigencies of the moment but with no commitment to the Fascist philosophy or course of action.

After the conclusion of the war, he would—again, like so many of his confreres—become for a short time a member of the Communist party, though with no very strong attraction to Marxist principles. Undeniably he had great admiration for the Russian people and some sympathy for the Soviet experiment. This feeling was intensified by the circumstances attending his visit to Moscow in 1958; there he suffered a serious heart attack. The care bestowed upon him by his nurse, Varvara Alexandrovna, is gratefully acknowledged in a poem dedicated to her in his last volume of verse. Fundamentally Quasimodo was not a political animal; he was, however, responsive to the currents of his times, just as he was in literary matters. In his discourse "The Poet and the Politician," given on the occasion of his receipt of the Nobel Prize, his credo is summarized in the following somewhat opaque paragraph:

> Can there be any coordination between politician and poet? Possibly where there are societies in process of formation, but never on the plane of absolute freedom. In the contemporary world the politician assumes various aspects but an accord with the poet will never be possible since the one concerns himself with the internal order of man and the other with the ordering of men. In a given historical period the internal order of man may coincide with a desire to order and construct a new society.
>
> (*The Poet and the Politician,* p. 40)

These remarks hardly answer such basic questions as the preeminence of order over freedom or vice versa, the right of the state to intervene in social matters, or the preservation of individual liberties that are not always consistent with the collective welfare. As many poets are, and perhaps should be, Quasimodo was a man of intuitional responses rather than firm ideological convictions.

As in the sphere of politics, so in the realm of the Muses, Quasimodo's coming-of-age was a time of crisis. In the 1920's and 1930's poets were turning away from the aulic verses of Giosuè Carducci and the flamboyance of Gabriele D'Annunzio. Each in its own way, the successive schools of the early century—the plaintive *crepuscolari* (twilight poets), the mischievous and blatant *futuristi,* and the sober, classical *rondisti*—exemplified this rejection of the old masters and the groping for a new and more genuine kind of poetry. All such movements were, however, in process of yielding to the new school of hermeticism, launched formally by Giuseppe Ungaretti and cultivated perhaps more seriously by Montale, whose *Ossi di seppia* (*Cuttlefish Bones*) had appeared in 1925. Eschewing eloquence, ornament, and to some degree even emotion, the hermetics aimed for a kind of idealistic austerity, set forth in a symbolic language that is highly subjective and not always easy to follow. On the nature and direction of this new movement Aldo Bernardo writes:

> [The term is] derived from Hermes Trismegistus, reputed author of several works on symbolism and the occult. The term refers generally to poetry using occult symbolism . . . and in particular to a phase or "school" of early and mid-20th-c[entury] poetry having a direct line of descent from the poetry and theories of Novalis and Poe as modified in the works of such Fr[ench] symbolists as Baudelaire, Mallarmé, Rimbaud, and Valéry. Notwithstanding the international flavor of the term, . . . its denotation of a specific phase of recent poetry has peculiarly It[alian] roots. It was first fully defined in 1936 by Francesco Flora in his study *La poesia ermetica,* which traces its primary sources to Baudelaire, Mallarmé, and especially Valéry, and singles out Giuseppe Ungaretti as the chief It[alian] exponent. . . . [The new poetry] was in part an attempt to arrive at "naked poetry" by concentrating all the lyrical potential in the individual word deprived of its decorative or logical elements.
>
> (*Princeton Encyclopedia of Poetry and Poetics* [Princeton, N.J., 1974], p. 345)

Hermetics do not affirm anything; they suggest or evoke; they contend that the world of poetry has no connection with the everyday world of experience. It is an ideal world toward which every poet gropes in his own way, following inner illumination, a highly subjective vision.

One might add that although the hermeticism of our times may have the sources and sponsors cited by Bernardo, the concept of hermeticism has had its niche in the human psyche over many centuries. It has an affinity with the approach of the metaphysical poets, and before them with the *trobar clus* of the troubadours. One might say that the *vers* of William of Poitou, composed over eight centuries ago— "I'll make a verse of nothing at all"—is quintessentially hermetic. With regard to the recent movement, some critics have seen it simply as a reaction against Romanticism, with its overt and often undisciplined emotional element

and its substance reflecting historical or contemporary events or the poet's own vicissitudes. To be sure, all poetry is based on experience, whatever claims the poet may make for his emancipated muse, but with the hermetics experiences and memories are sublimated, abstracted beyond recognition. It should be noted, however, that if the movement is a reaction against romanticism, it by no means signifies a return to classicism, if by classicism we mean formalized discipline in manner and prescriptive or ironic comment on the social order. If it is classicism, it is of a very special Platonic sort.

One also may add that, as touching the Italian hermetics, no transalpine influence could be expected to make an Italian poet forget the legacy of Giacomo Leopardi; the more recent example of D'Annunzio, repudiated but persistent; or the abiding presence of Dante and Petrarch. Indeed, in his lectures Quasimodo indicates his respect for the great masters of Italian letters whom every Italian reads in the formative years. Of Dante's style he remarks: "A difficult style and it is the language of great poetry, from Homer on down. . . . It is the reality of man; his life in the symbols that reveal it." Another essay is dedicated to Petrarch and "the sentiment of solitude," a sentiment or condition essentially hermetic. Such observations are not meant to deny the hermetics their meed of originality or the distinctive nature of their school but, rather, to point out that the hermetic muse has an ancient and honorable lineage.

Quasimodo's first book of verse, *Waters and Lands,* is undeniably hermetic. If it is not the first affirmation of the new school—we have noted the precedence of Ungaretti and Montale—it may be said that, in a sense not easy to define, true hermeticism came into being with Quasimodo's contribution, exploiting the "cult of the word" more consciously and more effectively than his predecessors. And it is also proper to note that although he was familiar with the works of the older members of the hermetic trio, his inspiration, manner, and substance are truly and recognizably his own.

Waters and Lands won enthusiastic critical acclaim. In the year of the book's publication Quasimodo was awarded the Antico Fattore Prize, given in Florence by a group of patrons of the muse. The financial reward was insignificant—a mere thousand lire—but the prize was prestigious. Quasimodo's cause was promoted by his friends in Florence who were connected with *Solaria,* and his most energetic champion, with the possible exception of his brother-in-law Vittorini, was Montale, at that time director of the Vieusseux Library. His published letters to Quasimodo during that period attest to the warm affection and high esteem that the author of *Cuttlefish Bones* had for his younger colleague. Indeed, Montale had labored to have the Antico Fattore Prize given to Quasimodo a year earlier, but ironically the jury had conferred it on Montale himself for his poem "La casa del doganiere" ("The Coast Guard's House"). Quasimodo's "Vento a Tindari" ("Wind at Tindari") was runner-up. During the 1930's the relationship between the two poets was very cordial; Montale wrote frequently to his friend, who for a number of years was living in Lombardy, to keep him informed about the Florentine circle.

"Wind at Tindari," the first item in *Waters and Lands,* merits attention not only as the poem that, more than any other, announced a new voice in Italian poetry but also as a work exemplifying the nature of Quasimodo's hermeticism. We shall give the original and a literal translation:

Tindari, mite ti so
fra larghi colli pensile sull'acque
dell'isole dolci del dio,
oggi m'assali
e ti chini in cuore.

Salgo vertici aerei precipizi,
assorto al vento dei pini,
e la brigata che lieve m'accompagna
s'allontana nell'aria,
onda di suoni e amore,
e tu mi prendi

da cui male mi trassi
e paure d'ombre e di silenzi,
rifugi di dolcezze un tempo assidue
e morte d'anima.

A te ignota e la terra
ove ogni giorno affondo
e segrete sillabe nutro:
altra luce ti sfoglia sopra i vetri
nella veste notturna,
e gioia non mia riposa
sul tuo grembo.

Aspro è l'esilio,
e la ricerca che chiudevo in te
d'armonia oggi si muta
in ansia precoce di morire;
e ogni amore è schermo alla tristezza,
tacito passo nel buio
dove mi hai posto
amaro pane a rompere.

Tindari serena torna;
soave amico mi desta
che mi sporga nel cielo da una rupe
e io fingo timore a chi non sa
che vento profondo m'ha cercato.

Tindari, gentle I know thee
between broad hills pending on the waters
of the sweet isles of the god; today you assail me
and lean into my heart.

I climb heights, aerial precipices,
absorbed by the wind of the pines,
and the band that lighthearted accompanies me
goes off into the air,
wave of sounds and love,
and you take me,
from whom wrongly I withdrew,
and fears of shadows and silences,
shelters of sweetnesses one time assiduous,
and soul's death.

To you unknown is the land
where every day I drown
and nourish secret syllables;
another light unleafs you above the windows
in your nocturnal dress,
and joy not mine reposes
on your lap.

Harsh is exile,
and the quest that I ended in you
for harmony today is changed
into precocious anxiety of dying;
and every love is a screen against sadness.
Silent I pass into the darkness
where you have set for me
bitter bread to break.

Tindari returns serene;
a gentle friend awakens me
that I may lean into the sky from a cliff,
and I feign fright to one who knows not
what deep wind has sought me out.

Tindari is the name of a promontory rising from the sea not far from Messina; in antiquity it was the site of a small town named Tyndaros. Thus the poet's aerial flight has a terrestrial *point de partir.* Furthermore, the poem records an identifiable moment in Quasimodo's life. Giuseppe Zagarrio tells us that in 1926, when Quasimodo, as an employee of the Civil Engineering Service, was posted to Messina, he resumed writing poetry, which he had abandoned for some years. He adds that in 1929 Quasimodo completed his first manuscript, assisted and encouraged by friends in Messina, who visited him every Sunday, listening to his verses and discussing them with him. His friend Salvatore Pugliatti provides an affectionate reconstruction of those early days:

At that time the Sunday pilgrimages of the poet from Reggio to Messina began. Gradually a small group gathered around him. Almost every Sunday there would be the surprise of new compositions. We would wait a while in expectation and then Quasimodo would cautiously draw from his pocket his little pages and the rite would begin. He would read one poem, then another; they would be the objects of lengthy commentary. The archivist [presumably Pugliatti] at the end of the day would collect the little pages (he still keeps them); every once in a while with greedy joy he would count and weigh them. Some times we would take trips, almost always to Tindari, and

on one of these occasions "Vento a Tindari" was born.

(Zagarrio, *Quasimodo* [Florence, 1969], pp. 129–130)

Given this clue, the writer may follow tolerably well the craggy itinerary of the poem. Revisiting scenes familiar to him in his childhood and recalling not only his own youth but also his Greek heritage, the poet regrets his abandonment of his native land ("wrongly I withdrew") and the consequent anxieties of his life "in exile" ("where every day I drown"). Tindari no longer solaces his daily cares, which are relieved only by his almost furtive cultivation of the Muse ("I nourish secret syllables"). He seems almost to resent Tindari (for reminding him of happier times?), but the conclusion, if not optimistic, is at least resigned. Tindari preserves its serenity and a kind friend arouses the poet from his reverie, not knowing what emotions have shaken him.

Such is the "message" of the poem, conceding that it also carries some ambiguities and enigmatic passages. And the message, viewed from the perspective of today, is in itself hardly very "hermetic." Indeed, it is yet another version of a time-honored motif—nostalgia, *Heimweh,* exile—very familiar to the Romantics, as is the pathetic fallacy that personifies Tindari. In substance the poem has much in common with Leopardi's "Le ricordanze" (Memories).

Yet this is only half of the story. A new dimension, one might say a new level of poetic vitality, is achieved through a revolutionary technique employing ellipsis, catachresis, and inversion to shock and sometimes tease the reader—or listener. This tactic brings into sharp relief certain isolated phrases, giving them a life and significance of their own, sejunct from the development of the theme. Herein perhaps we may observe the cult of the word, or at least of the phrase.

To cite a few examples: the opening line—dactylic, alliterative, and musical—makes

SALVATORE QUASIMODO

an immediate impact, fortified by the strong stress on the last syllable, somewhat unusual in a language whose normal rhythm is characterized by an unstressed ending. The syntax is irregular, too, not only reversing the order of prose but also elliptical in structure. In line 12 the ambiguity of "di cui male mi trassi" has taxed translators. (Critics may serenely ignore such puzzles, but translators do not have that privilege.) The phrase is susceptible of two interpretations: Jack Bevan translates it "from whom I drew evil"; William Weaver's version is "from whom I mistakenly withdrew." Logically it is hard to understand why the poet should draw evil from a place that is dear to his memory and, furthermore, is described as "gentle" or "mild"; yet in the following lines "fears of shadows and silences" and the "soul's death" could refer to *male* in the sense of "evil." Perhaps "mi trassi" ("drew for myself"; "I withdrew") is serving a double purpose; the sense may well be "my withdrawal [abandonment] brought me fear of shadows and silences and the soul's death." But the ambiguity, assuredly deliberate, is bound to intrigue and thus capture the reader. Again, in line 28, is "passo" a noun meaning "step" or a verb, as in "I step"? The last lines have their problems, too: Are "torna" and "desta" imperatives, as Bevan would have it, or third-person indicatives, as Weaver prefers? Assuredly no professor of rhetoric would give Quasimodo high marks for clarity, yet undeniably such transgressions are effective. The strength of hermeticism derives to a considerable degree from its willful and challenging disregard of syntactical precision.

One cannot leave the poem without remarking on the magic of its music. Alliteration and assonance are managed with rare mastery; lines such as "onda di suoni e amore," "segrete sillabe nutro," and "amaro pane a rompere" are little musical gems.

Such ingredients of matter and manner will be persistent through all the lyric production of the poet, in which they will be consistently combined with a very special artistry that gives the verses a unique character. Finally "Wind at Tindari" reveals an appreciation of nature, spontaneous and instinctive, that will characterize the poems yet to come.

Another poem in *Waters and Lands* that may help us to appreciate, and certainly will increase our enjoyment of, the Quasimodian muse is "I ritorni" ("Homecomings"). A literal translation will suffice here:

Piazza Navona, nighttime, on the benches
I would lie supine in quest of quiet,
and my eyes, following straight lines and whirls
    of spirals,
would pull the stars together,
the same stars that I followed as a child
stretched out on the pebbles of the Platani,
spelling out my prayers in the darkness.

Under my head I crossed my hands
and remembered my homecoming:
smell of fruit drying on the frames,
of wallflowers, ginger, lavender;
when I would think of reading to you, but softly
(you and I, Mamma, in a shaded corner),
the parable of the Prodigal Son
that followed me always in the silences
like a rhythm that opens with every stride
without wanting to.

But to the dead it is not given to return,
and there is no time even for one's mother
when the road calls;
and I would go off again, veiled in the night
like one fearing to stay for the dawn.

And the road would give me the songs,
that taste of grain swelling on the stalk,
of the flower that whitens the olive groves
between azure of flax and jonquils;
resonances of the eddies of dust,
plainsong of men and creaking of carts
with lanterns wanly swaying,
giving hardly more light than a firefly.

As with "Wind at Tindari," so in "Homecomings" the poet's ascent to "aerial cliffs" starts from a clearly identified launching pad, the Piazza Navona in Rome, where the young exile spent some lonely and difficult years. As in "Tindari" and many of Quasimodo's other verses, the genesis of the poem is in nostalgia and reminiscence. If "Homecomings" is not so moving or so popular as "Tindari," this is perhaps because it is less challenging and its motivations are more obviously displayed. It lacks the ingredients of wrenched, and therefore arresting, syntax and autonomous musical passages that give "Tindari" its appeal. Unashamedly sentimental, "Homecomings" might even be called a "crepuscolare" effusion; the allusion to the poet's mother and the immersion in childhood memories were stock materials for Quasimodo's wistful and plaintive predecessors two decades in the past.

But "Homecomings" is not without its virtues. A particularly attractive aspect of the poem is the brief catalog of sights, sounds, and smells from the South that the exile has left behind him. Such evocations and images, frequent in Quasimodo's work, are a kind of trademark, whether they be genuine personal memories or, as some critics have suspected, sensations drawn from the narratives of Giovanni Verga, Sicily's greatest novelist. It does not greatly matter; the image of the peasants' carts, for example, as they return from their labors, lanterns swinging in the dark, is beautifully and economically depicted. Perhaps even more effectively than any lines in "Tindari," the evocative passage gives evidence of the consistent current of natural piety that runs through the Quasimodian lyric, which it is not too much to call a religious element.

Several other poems in this rather scanty first volume (it contains only twenty-five items) offer more examples of this natural piety, anthropomorphic and obsessive. So in "Terra" ("Earth") we find the exordium:

Night, serene shadows,
cradle of air,
the wind reaches me if I spread myself within
you,
with the sea smell of earth

where my people sing on the shore
to sails, to nets,
to children before dawn awakens.

In "Dolore di cose che ignoro" ("Sorrow of Things I Do Not Know" he writes:

Thick with white and black roots
cut off from the waters
the earth smells of yeast and earthworms.

And the short poem "Rifugio d'uccelli notturni" ("Night Birds' Refuge") bespeaks an almost Franciscan participation:

On high stands a twisted pine;
intent, it gives ear to the abyss
with its trunk bent like a crossbow.

Shelter for birds of the night,
in the deepest hour it resounds
with a rapid beating of wings.

My heart, too, has its nest
suspended in the darkness, a voice;
it, too, stands listening through the night.

Save for "Tindari" and "Homecomings," the poems in *Waters and Lands* are all very short; brevity is the hallmark of the hermetics, following the example of Ungaretti, whose economy of words and lines is almost exhibitionist. Quasimodo's shortest poem, which in later printings was used to introduce *Waters and Lands,* though it is somewhat later in composition, is the celebrated terzina:

Ognuno sta solo sul cuor della terra,
trafitto da un raggio di sole:
ed è subito sera.

Everyone stands alone on the heart of the earth,
transfixed by a ray of sunshine:
and suddenly it's evening.

This is the best-known and most widely quoted of all Quasimodo's verse, arguably also of all the verses of the hermetic school. Herein lies a certain irony, for in fact the lines are not hermetic at all. Their substance is hardly novel; it is as old as Ecclesiastes, and some critics have even called it banal. This is unfair. The little poem has a powerful impact, brought out shrewdly by subtle alliteration and half rhyme. It is in essence banal and may remind some readers, although the author would not rejoice in the association, of Giosuè Carducci's "Congedo."

Whatever may be our judgment today, the poet's contemporary public was charmed by *Waters and Lands.* The slender volume seemed to the critics to herald a new and eloquent voice in the chorus of contemporary singers.

Sunken Oboe was published in 1932, a year after Quasimodo's transfer to Imperia, which brought him into contact with the Genoese literary circle. The book contains thirty-eight poems, most of them written between 1930 and 1932. The title is, one might say, programmatically hermetic. What could be truly more ineffable, more "out of this world," than the notes *in posse* of an instrument forever beyond the range of audibility? The opening poem, from which the book takes its title, establishes the tone and the mood for the collection. We supply the original Italian and a prose translation:

> *Amara pena, tarda il tuo dono*
> *in questa mia ora*
> *di sospirati abbandoni.*
>
> *Un òboe gelido risillaba*
> *gioia di foglie perenni,*
> *non mie, e smemora;*
>
> *in me si fa sera:*
> *l'acqua tramonta*
> *sulle mie mani erbose.*
>
> *Ali oscillano in fioco cielo,*
> *labili: il cuore trasmigra*
> *ed io son gerbido,*
>
> *e i giorni una maceria.*

Miserly pain, late comes your gift
in this hour of mine
of longed-for renunciations.

A frigid oboe re-scans
joy of perennial leaves,
not mine, and grows forgetful;

within me evening falls;
water sinks to its setting
on my grassy hands.

Wings oscillate in a pallid sky,
prone to fall;
my heart migrates,
and I am fallow,

and my days so much rubble.

Through these willfully enigmatic lines and strange images the reader can do no more than deduce that the poet is unhappy, not pleased with the world or himself, and lonely. In fact, the sense of solitude in this collection comes to replace its cousin nostalgia. In one way at least the poem reveals a further step into the cavern of hermeticism, for it supplies no links with the actual world, such as Tindari or Piazza Navona or the Platani. All references and images are austerely remote from any contingent reality. This detachment is emphasized by verbal innovation. "Risillaba" (line 4), "smemora" (line 6), and "gerbido" (line 12) are words not commonly found, and "tramonta" (line 8) is normally used only with reference to the sun. The grammatical ambiguity of "tarda" in the first line (is it imperative or indicative?) is of course a device we have seen before. Yet it must be conceded that somehow the poem works; the sense of discontent and alienation is successfully and even movingly conveyed. Such phrases as "gioia di foglie perenni" and "il cuore trasmigra" have a musical magic; why the poet's hands should be "erbose" (grassy) is not clear, but the image is striking.

Motifs encountered in *Waters and Lands* reappear in this second collection—usually, however, with a more sophisticated elusiveness that is more cunningly achieved. A poem somewhat more "open" than its fellows and perhaps more appealing is "Isola" ("Island"), meaning, of course, Sicily. Prefaced by the lines "I have naught but you, / heart of my race," the poem reads:

> Love of you brings me sadness,
> land of mine,
> when evening disperses
> dark perfumes of oranges,
> or of oleanders, serene,
> the brook runs with roses
> reaching almost to its mouth.
>
> But if I come back to your shores
> and a sweet voice in song
> calls timidly from the road,
> be it childhood or love I know not,
> yearning for other skies turns me,
> and I hide among lost things.

This is the message, if we may call it that, of "Homecomings" in *Waters and Lands,* but more compactly and elliptically expressed and free, for better or for worse, of the Romantic residues of the earlier lyric. So, too, the strain of pantheistic piety is still with us, though set forth in a new, leaner language; witness the poem "D'alberi sofferte forme" ("Suffered Forms of Trees"):

> Now first fruit of the sun
> the light matures that wakened all around
> suffered forms of trees,
> and a sighing of waters
> that the night confused with words,
> and shadows now upraised
> lean over the hedges.
>
> Useless day,
> you take me from suspended spaces
> (quenched deserts, renunciations),
> from quiet woodlands
> bound with golden hemp
> whose sense is not changed by the onslaught of
>   winds
> impetuously crashing,
> nor circling of stars.

You uncover my subterranean heart,
which has roses and rocking moons
and wings of predatory beasts
and cathedrals from which dawn tries to scale
the heights of the planets.

> Unknown you rouse me
> to life on earth.

The poet's identification with nature and its manifestations and operations, troubling or consoling but always mysterious, finds frequent expression. In "Senza memoria di morte" ("Without Memory of Death"), which begins as a love poem, the final lines read:

> Changed into a bough,
> my hand
> burgeons on your side.

"Preghiera alla pioggia" ("Prayer to the Rain") opens with the terzina:

> Good smell of the sky
> on grass,
> rain of the early evening.

In "Autunno" ("Autumn") the poet calls the season "mansueto" ("mild" or "docile") and affirms:

> Harsh pain of coming to birth
> finds me conjoined with you:
> and in you I am broken and healed again.

Such intuitions lead to a condition that is truly mystic and even in the orthodox Christian tradition, as for example in "La mia giornata paziente" ("My Patient Day"):

> My day of patience
> I deliver to you, Lord,
> sickness not healed,
> knees broken by tedium.
>
> I yield, I yield;
> ululation of springtime,
> in my earthen eyes
> a forest is born.

And the volume ends on a note that, ironic though it may be, must be defined as truly religious:

> You have not betrayed me, Lord;
> of every sorrow
> I am made the firstborn.

Before the end of the decade Quasimodo published two more volumes of verse, *Erato and Apollyon* in 1936, and *New Poems* in 1938. Although the interval between their publication dates is short and their substance is not strikingly dissimilar, there are some notable differences in manner and matter that may to some extent reflect the nature of the times in which they were written. The late 1930's were certainly trying times for Italy and for the world. The great economic depression persisted throughout the decade, accompanied by mounting international tensions that culminated in the outbreak of World War II in 1939. Italy entered the war in the following year when Mussolini, having annexed Ethiopia to his new empire, invaded a stricken France. The year of *Erato and Apollyon*, 1936, was full of dark portents: it was the year of the proclamation of the Rome-Berlin Axis and of the beginning of the Spanish Civil War; and in the Orient, Chiang Kai-shek declared war on Japan. Such matters, however, were of little concern to hermetic poets, and there is no allusion to them in the verses of *Erato and Apollyon*. Nor do those verses refer to the poet's own experiences, although these experiences were varied and significant: in 1935 his daughter was born, and the relationship with Maria Cumani began in 1936, when he was probably pondering the move from engineering to journalism. His renown was growing, and his assignment to Lombardy enabled him to make the acquaintance of two respected critics, Luciano Anceschi and Carlo Bo, who promptly enlisted in his corps of admirers. Quasimodo, in spite of his frequent complaints of neglect or vilification, always had a good press; in personal relationships he could charm when he chose to, as his triumphs in the lists of Venus attest.

The title *Erato and Apollyon* suggests an erotic or at least an amatory content. Erato for Quasimodo would signify the beneficent, inspirational aspect of human love; Apollyon, its destructive potential. Yet of the nineteen lyrics composing the volume, very few could be called love poems. Perhaps the only one that a reader might recognize as such is "Nel giusto tempo umano" ("In the Right Human Time"):

> She lies in the wind,
> the beloved of the time of doves.
> Of me, of waters and of leaves,
> you alone, among the living, my dear one,
> speak; and the naked night
> your voice consoles with shining ardors and
>   delights.
>
> Beauty deceived us and the slipping away
> of every form and memory,
> the fleeting movement revealed to affections
> reflecting inner splendors.
>
> But from your deep blood,
> in the right human time,
> we shall be reborn without grief.

Overall, however, the strains, motifs, and attitudes of *Erato and Apollyon* are those with which the preceding collections have made us familiar, set forth with the usual grace and economy but perhaps with less striking imagery. "Ànapo" ("The Ànapo") celebrates the Sicilian river of the author's childhood:

> On the banks the water dove,
> my Ànapo; in memory groans
> at its grieving
> a lofty rustling.

And the note of natural piety returns in "Airone morto" ("Dead Heron"), which reads in part:

> In the warm swamp, fixed in the mud,
> dear to insects, within me grieves
> a dead heron.

I am swallowed up in light and sound;
beaten into squalid echoes
from time to time moans a gust
now forgotten.

Or again, in the well-wrought lines of "Sovente una riviera" ("Often a Coastland"):

> Time of bees: and the honey
> is in my throat
> still fresh with sound.
> A crow circles at noon
> above gray wading birds.

Of particular interest as giving evidence of the poet's immersion in Greek verse at this time is *Lirici greci* with its allusions to classical mythology. One poem is entitled "Ulisse" ("Ulysses"); and in "Sardegna" ("Sardinia"), on which island Quasimodo spent a few months of exile, the figure of the wounded Cyclops is evoked:

> the ancient islander,
> lo, looks for his one eye
> on his forehead
> lightning-struck,
> and tries his arm,
> master in the throwing of rocks.

In his preface to *Erato and Apollyon*, the critic Sergio Solmi praises the new poets for their efforts to free their verses from the eloquence and rhetoric of their predecessors (he has in mind Carducci, Giovanni Pascoli, and D'Annunzio) and to seek for pure poetry. In this quest he thinks that Quasimodo has been more faithful, "even at the cost of saying too much or too little, or of contortions and dazzling obscurities." For *Erato and Apollyon* and its predecessors Solmi's observations are valid. But by the time his remarks were reprinted in *Ed è subito Sera* (*And Suddenly It's Evening*), in which *Poems* is republished under the title *New Poems*, some alterations in the Quasimodian vision are perceptible. Opening the volume, one is immediately struck by a formal innovation. A substantial number of items are written in the traditional Italian hendecasyllable; the short, often dactylic, thrusts that characterize the earlier poems are much less in evidence. In consequence, the syntax is much less irregular than of old; one might say legato comes to prevail over staccato. One is bound to speculate on the reasons for this new direction which is followed in the poet's later publications. It is not unlikely that the phenomenon is at least in part a product of Quasimodo's intense study of the Greek poets. Although in his versions he did not follow the classical metrical schemes, yet the disciplined patterns of the ancients may have left their mark on his muse. Greek metrics are rarely fragmented or capricious, and one may even say that the nature of Greek verse is hardly hermetic.

We may properly here digress, leaving *New Poems* for further comment, and consider *Lirici greci*, the contents of which, though not original compositions, were regarded by many Italian readers as an important and all but unique contribution. They were read probably by a wider public than that which relished the poet's own verses. And to Quasimodo himself the venture had special significance. He liked to think of himself as a "siculo greco" (Greek Sicilian), and his anthology is an affirmation of his heritage. He took great pains to get authoritative texts, and in the main his versions are literally accurate. But recast in his own prosodic idiom, they are hardly line-for-line translations. It was his hope to make them living poems, to make the reader feel that he was not reading translations, which is of course why they often sound like Quasimodo. How far such a procedure is justified or makes for a "true" translation is of course a matter of opinion. Eighteenth-century English poets cheerfully translated Homeric hexameters into iambic rhymed couplets, and were applauded for their efforts. Of *Lirici greci* the critic Pietro Mazzamuto observed:

> Quasimodo's choice of the items translated was dictated by his own emotional preoccupa-

tions. . . . In every poet he translates, one catches at once the timbre of Quasimodo, his voice somewhere between the realistic and the magical, the harsh and the pleasing, the bound and the free; and one notes too, in themes above all, a clear congeniality in the poems he worked on.

(p. 34)

And Mazzamuto quotes, in support of his thesis, passages from Homer, Anacreon, and Theognides that do indeed display the essential Quasimodian elements of nostalgia, angst, and exploitation of nature. However, one may suspect that even as he was "making new" the substance of the ancients, the classical originals may, in turn, have left their mark on the translator. So it may be that their infectiousness is at work not only formally but in the somewhat more open nature of the poems written in these years. This is not of course to deny the impact of contemporary sociopolitical circumstances. Some adumbration of the postwar verses in *Giorno dopo giorno* (*Day After Day*, 1947) may be postulated, at least with the illumination of hindsight.

To be sure, not every page of *New Poems* reveals rents in the hermetic veil. But, as a tolerably good example, we may cite "Dolce collina" ("The Gentle Hill"), which is set forth in conventional iambics:

Birds in the distance, open in the evening,
quiver above the stream. The shower persists,
with whispering of poplars that the rain
illuminates. Like every far-off thing
you come back to my memory. Your dress
of weightless green is here among the plants
scorched by the lightning where the gentle hill
of Ardenno ascends, and where is heard
the kite over the swaying millet fields.

It may be in that flight of compact spirals
that my betrayed homecoming placed its trust,
the harshness, and the Christian piety
defeated, and this naked pain of grief.
You wear a coral flower in your hair.
But your face is a shadow, never changing
(such is death's usage). I am listening
beside the darkened houses of your town

to hear the Adda or the falling rain,
or possibly a halting human step
among the tender reeds that line the banks.

In the original all lines are hendecasyllabic; the intervention of five- or seven-syllable lines, frequent in earlier compositions, is absent. Metrically at least the poet is not trying to shock his reader. Notably, too, the syntax is what we might call normal. Adjectives are where one would expect to find them; sentences, save perhaps for the parenthetical intrusion of line 16, contain no elliptical surprises. Admittedly, the privacy of the poet's vision is preserved; it is not immediately clear why his homecoming ("ritorno") is betrayed ("deluso"), and the reference to "the harshness, and the Christian piety / defeated" seems to have a life of its own. But, generally speaking, "The Gentle Hill" is of orthodox structure and its substance is not especially obscure. Happily, the virtues of the younger Quasimodo—the instinctive pantheism, the sharp, sensitive appreciation of natural things like wind, air, living creatures—are constants. And time, place, and mood are poetically captured.

Another fine poem in which the old ingredients are modified and adapted to the new manner is "Strada di Agrigentum" ("Street in Agrigentum"):

Still blows the wind there I remember burning
the manes of horses coursing on the plains
and cutting oblique paths—a wind that stains
the while it gnaws the sandstone and the heart
of the lugubrious telamones, reversed
upon the grass. With that wind you return,
O ancient spirit gray with grudges, sniffing
the delicate moss mantle that encloses
the giants long ago cast down from heaven.
How lonely is the space that's left to you!
And sadder still you feel to hear the sound
with deep notes fading as it nears the sea
where over morning Hesperus now paints
his stripes. A jew's harp's mournful strain vibrates
within the carter's throat as he ascends
the hill rinsed by the moonlight. Saracen
olive trees rustle, murmuring in the night.

Noteworthy and novel in this poem is its impersonality. The poet is not describing his own predicament or experiences (save as a point of departure in the first lines) nor dwelling on his own angst. He is in effect painting the portrait of a town, noting its sights and sounds and giving it a fourth dimension by allusions to its past. The Agrigentum of today is set before us in impressionistic detail—wind, sea, the carter and his mouth organ—and a kind of eternal Agrigentum is suggested by the telamones of antiquity, the olive groves planted by the Arabs, and the brooding spirit of the past that watches the dawn of a new day. This is an example of a genre that the poet will cultivate frequently in later works.

So too the lyric "Già la pioggia è con noi" ("The Rain Is Already with Us") may be seen as an essentially descriptive piece, although the last lines are commentary—not, however, strictly personal:

> Now the rain is with us,
> shaking the silent air.
> The swallows skim over the weary waters
> flanking the little Lombard lakes,
> flying like sea gulls over tiny fishes;
> from enclosed gardens comes the scent of hay.

> And so another year is burned away,
> without complaint, without a cry upraised
> to win for us an unexpected day.

Nine years were destined to pass between the publication of *New Poems* and the poet's first postwar collection of lyrics. But in 1942, under the air raids, Mondadori brought out, in the prestigious series *I poeti dello specchio* (Poets of the Mirror), the omnibus volume *And Suddenly It's Evening,* which contained all the poet's previously published verses. Aside from testifying to the popularity of Quasimodo's verse, the appearance of the collection signified a recognition of his stature. As we have noted, Solmi's laudatory introduction to *Erato and Apollyon* was reprinted, with slight changes, to present the new publication.

Day After Day, with an introduction by Carlo

Bo, appeared in 1947, five years after the publication of *And Suddenly It's Evening.* During those years the political and social structure of Italy had undergone drastic changes. Fascism had disappeared from the scene with the collapse of the Salò republic; in 1946 the monarchy had gone the way of the dictatorship that it had so shamefully, and unwisely, supported. The six parties that had collaborated with the Allies during the resistance had all dissolved their bonds and gone their own ways; three of them, once the votes were in, faded into insignificance. It was clear that the people of Italy, having put Fascism behind them, were not eager for radical innovations. Although the Communist and Socialist parties showed strength, it was the Christian Democrats, moderately conservative but pragmatic and by no means doctrinaire, who came to power and, under the guidance of the shrewd Alcide de Gasperi, took over the direction of the country's future. Free for the first time in a generation to express their views and vote their preferences, Italians participated enthusiastically, not to say passionately, in the game of politics. Such fresh winds were bound to dissipate the solipsistic mists of hermeticism, which amid the miseries and anxieties of the war had already begun to seem irrelevant. Intellectuals and writers, for years cautious about expressing their views, emerged from their private retreats and strolled freely in the marketplace. In the field of poetry hermeticism lost its momentum; in prose narrative the neorealists—Vittorini, Vasco Pratolini, Cesare Pavese—came to the fore. A poet as sensitive to his ambient as Quasimodo could hardly stand aloof. The ivory tower, a poor bomb shelter in wartime, would also be an inappropriate residence in a country now dedicated to social reconstruction.

In this connection Carlo Bo's preface makes interesting reading. He begins by asserting firmly that in *Day After Day* we shall find the same Quasimodo as ever, but as he goes on, he makes numerous qualifications. In fact, while it is true that the aroma, the color, and assuredly the magic of the old Quasimodo are still present, the content and what one may call the intention are far from what confronted the dazzled and sometimes puzzled reader of *Waters and Lands* or *Sunken Oboe.* Titles are eloquent in this connection. Where *Sunken Oboe* is mysterious and haunting, *Day After Day* is matter-of-fact, prosaic; it might signify a humble diary. In short, what had been adumbrated in *New Poems* is now patent; to borrow Allen Mandelbaum's terminology, Quasimodo has moved from his "hermetic" to his "public" phase.

The first poem of *Day After Day,* "Sulle fronde dei salici" ("On the Willow Boughs"), not only reveals the new direction but also indicates the poet's all but aggressive allegiance to it:

*E come potevamo noi cantare
con il piede straniero sopra il cuore,
fra i morti abbandonati nelle piazze
sull'erba dura di ghiaccio, al lamento
d'agnello dei fanciulli, all'urlo nero
della madre che andava incontro al figlio
crocifisso sul palo del telegrafo?
Alle fronde dei salici, per voto,
anche le nostre cetre erano appese,
oscillavano lievi al tristo vento.*

And how could we sing
with the stranger's foot on our heart
among the dead left lying in the squares
on the frozen grass, under the lamblike
bleating of children, hearing the dark scream
of the mother going toward her son
crucified on the telegraph pole?
On the boughs of the willows, as votive offerings
our lyres too were hanging,
lightly swaying in the breeze.

The catalog of shocking spectacles (perhaps observed by the poet himself) is a kind of neo-realism in verse. The use of the first-person plural makes it clear that the poet is not speaking only for himself, and probably not only for his fellow poets, but for all his compatriots as well. The images are nicely mingled; some starkly naturalistic, some symbolically suggestive, such as "the stranger's foot on our heart" and the concluding vision of the poets' lyres (hermetics?) not only silent but "lightly swaying," which is to say serving no purpose, irrelevant. In keeping with the practice begun in *New Poems,* the metrical pattern is the traditional hendecasyllable. One hermetic (or Quasimodian) characteristic remains: the images are evoked with economy and no unnecessary rhetoric.

The poem that gives its name to the collection is at once personal and social:

Day after day: accursed words and the blood
and the gold. I recognize you, my similars, monsters
of the earth. At your bite pity has fallen
and the gentle cross has left us.
And I cannot again return to my Elysium.
We shall raise tombs by the shore of the sea, on the
   ravaged fields,
but not one of the sarcophagi that designate heroes.
With us death has frequently played:
we could hear in the air a monotonous beating of
   leaves
as in the marsh when under the blast of the sirocco
the swamp moorhen rises to the clouds.

Here, as so often with Quasimodo, the image drawn from nature, attractive in itself, has something more than ornamental value. *Day After Day* is rich in such suggestive figures: in "Lettera" ("Letter"; probably to Maria Cumani) he writes: "O my sweet gazelle, / I ask you to remember that flaming geranium / on a wall riddled with bullets"; in "The Wall" (another love letter) he speaks of "lizards flashing, lightninglike," in the fissures of the stadium wall, and of "frogs returning to their ditches"; in "The Ferry" he sees

. . . the ravenous dogs
rushing toward the river following the scented
   traces;
on the other shore,
luminous with blood,
the weasel laughs in scorn.

While it is true that the hermetic Quasimodo would often launch his flights from a specific time or place (Tindari or Piazza Navona, for example), that tactic is much more evident in *Day After Day* and is in fact a device more appropriate to the "public" style. A number of poems bear titles that, as it were, memorialize a specific date or site: "19 January 1944," "Milan, August 1943," and "By the Adda." Such dates and places have connotations not only for the poet but for his countrymen.

Bo concludes his preface by quoting from the lyric "O My Gentle Beasts" (or, more literally, "sweet animals"), which to be savored must be reproduced in toto:

Now autumn spoils the green of the hillside,
O my sweet animals. We'll hear again
before the night comes down the last lament
of birds, the call of the gray meadowland
withdrawing as it goes to meet the deep
roar of the sea. And then the smell of wood
under the rain, the odor from the lairs,
how sharp it is among the houses here
and among men, O my sweet animals.
This face that turns slow eyes, this hand upraised
directed at the sky, wherein we hear
the thunder rumbling—they are yours, my wolves,
my foxes scorched with blood. Yes, every hand
and every face is yours. And you would tell me
that everything has been in vain, our lives,
our days corroded by assiduous waters
while from the garden rises to our ears
the song of children. What then now, so far
remote from us? But in the air like shadows
the notes fade out. This is your voice. And yet
perhaps I know that all has not yet been.

Bo picks up the last line:

. . . a state then that absolves the quality of the past, and re-proposes for the future our condition, the act of life, the possibility of spiritual growth, the extent of our commitment. You see how we find ourselves confronting an infinite discourse. I do not think I have ever left Quasimodo in the presence of a book so rich in possibilities. Truly "everything has not been."

(*Tutte le poesie*, pp. 225–226)

It is not surprising that Bo, an aficionado of the hermetic school, should be able to read so much into the cryptic conclusion of the lyric. Other readers may find the sweet animals more pleasing to contemplate. In any event, it is likely that with *Day After Day* the poet took his first step toward the Nobel Prize. En route he was in 1950 awarded the San Babila Prize in Milan, and three years later he shared the international Etna-Taormina Prize with Dylan Thomas.

The nine poems published in 1949 under the title *La vita non è sogno* (*Life Is Not Dream*) are of the same nature as those of *Day After Day*, which is not surprising since they are the products of the same postwar years (1946–1948). Even more pointedly than in the case of its predecessor, the title seems almost polemically anti-hermetic. The poems too are more open (and many more discursive) than any we have yet encountered. Unabashedly autobiographical topics are the substance of such poems as "Epitaffio per Bice Donetti" ("Epitaph for Bice Donetti") and "Lettera alla madre" ("Letter to My Mother"), in which the raw emotion reminds us of the self-conscious sentimentalism of the *crepuscolari*. Bice Donetti, it will be recalled, was the poet's first wife, whose death in 1946 left him free to marry Maria Cumani. There is honest if somewhat rhetorical mourning in the concluding lines of the epitaph:

O you who passed by, called by others among the
    dead
before the grave numbered eleven-sixty,
stay a moment to salute her
who never complained of the man
who remains here, detested, with his verses,
one like so many, a fabricator of dreams.

Details of the poet's childhood are called on to enrich the tender letter to his mother:

At last, you will say, a few words
from that boy who ran away one night in his short
    jacket

and a few verses in his pocket. Poor lad, so ready of
  heart
they will kill him somewhere, some day—
"Of course I remember, it was from that gray
  platform
for the slow trains that carried almonds and oranges
to the mouth of the Imera, the river full of magpies,
salt, eucalyptus. But now I thank you,
this I want to do, for the irony you put
on my lips, mild as your own.
That smile has saved me from tears and grief.
And now it does not matter if I have a few tears for
  you,
for all those who like you are waiting
for they know not what.
Ah, gentle death,
do not touch the clock that ticks on the kitchen wall;
all my childhood has passed on the enamel
of that dial, on those painted flowers:
do not touch the hands of the old, nor their
  heart."

In other lyrics the poet takes it upon himself
to speak, as he did in *Day After Day,* for his
country and his fellow citizens as well as for
himself. In "Il mio paese è l'Italia" ("My Country Is Italy"), after touching on the horrors of
Buchenwald and Stalingrad and the tribulations and atrocities of the war, he concludes:

My country is Italy, O foe and foreigner;
  and I sing of her people and likewise the
    lamentations
  covered by the sound of her sea,
  the limpid mourning of her mothers. I sing of her
    life.

Although the rhetoric is of a different tone, the
posture of the bard is Carduccian—patriotic
and aggressive. Effective too is the short poem
"Anno Domini MCMXLVII," linked to a specific
moment in the turbulent chronicle of the times.

You have done now with beating your drums
in a cadence of death from every horizon
behind the coffins pressing on the banners,
with dealing out wounds and tears born of pity
in cities obliterated, ruin on ruin.
No longer is the cry heard: "My God,

why hast thou forsaken me?" No longer does honey
or milk pour from the pierced breast. And now
that you've hidden the cannon among the
  magnolias,
allow us one day unarmed on the grass,
hearing the murmur of running waters
and of fresh leaves of marsh reed twined in our hair,
while we embrace the woman that loves us.
Let the hour of curfew be not suddenly
rung out before nightfall. One day, if only
one day for us, O masters of the earth,
before iron and air fall again to rumbling,
before a splinter sears us full in the face.

The poet who speaks for his country may
speak also for his more intimate homeland.
The poem "Lamento per il Sud" ("Lament for
the South") expresses the regional loyalty that
we have already remarked in this Greek Sicilian but that was never before so openly
expressed:

The red moon, the wind, your color
of a woman of the North, the expanse of snow. . . .
My heart is now on these prairies, in these waters
  shadowed by mists.
I have forgotten the sea, the heavy
shell blown by Sicilian shepherds,
the singsong of the carts along the roads
where the carob quivers in the smoke of the stubble,
I have forgotten the passage of herons and cranes
in the air of the green uplands
for the lands and the rivers of Lombardy.
But a man may cry out anywhere for the fate of a
  homeland.
No one will take me back again to the South.

Oh, the South is weary of dragging the dead
along the shores of malarial swamps,
it is tired of solitude, tired of fetters,
it is tired in its mouth
of the blasphemies of every race
that has shouted death with the echo of its wells,
that has drunk its heart's blood.
For this its children go back to the mountains,
hobble their horses under blankets of stars,
eat the acacia flowers along the trails
again red, still red, always red.
No one will take me back to the South.

And this evening heavy with winter
is still ours, and here I repeat to you
my absurd counterpoint of sweetness and rage;
a loving lament without love.

It is clear that no one will ever take the poet back to his homeland because in fact he has never left it. One has the impression that the images of home, no novelties in the poet's verses, are here consciously cataloged rather than subconsciously recalled. Part of the catalog is composed not of images but of historical abstractions, not without political overtones.

During the late 1940's and through the following decade Quasimodo's prestige continued to grow. He had by now become a prominent member of the literary establishment. Undoubtedly the substance of his verse and its more approachable manner widened the circle of his readers, while at the same time he retained the respect of the critics who had applauded his hermetic contributions. The range of his activities also enlarged considerably during these years. In 1948 he undertook for a magazine called *Le Ore* the writing of a weekly column dealing with the contemporary theater; in the same year the column moved to *Il Tempo.* His translations of plays of Aeschylus and Sophocles, published in these years, gave him some claim to comment on theatrical matters. He served on juries for the awarding of sundry literary prizes. In 1958 he was himself awarded the Viareggio Prize, and the succeeding year witnessed his supreme triumph when the Nobel Prize was bestowed upon him in Stockholm. He was the first of his countrymen since Luigi Pirandello to receive this distinction and the first Italian poet to be so honored since Carducci, more than half a century before. The choice of Quasimodo by the Nobel committee aroused lively debate in Italian literary circles. Though all were pleased that the honor had gone to an Italian, many thought that it might more properly have been given to Ungaretti, a pioneer among hermetics, or to Montale, like Ungaretti older than the winner and, in the opinion of some good critics, a bet-ter poet. If Quasimodo himself never entertained any doubts about the propriety of the award, it must be granted that he had some warrant. He had been enthusiastically recommended by two of Italy's most highly regarded critics, Francesco Flora and Carlo Bo.

For this parade of glories, culminating in international recognition, the poet paid a heavy price. The demands on his energy and time during these busy years took their toll. His health suffered and, sadly, his marriage as well. In the same year that he won the Viareggio Prize he suffered a severe heart attack in the course of a visit to Russia and spent some months convalescing in a Moscow hospital. And the year of the Nobel Prize was also the year in which Maria Cumani requested a decree of separation. The poet's letters to her tell the sad story of what seems to have been a deep and sincere attachment, gradually eroded by the pressures of two ambitious careers that required long periods of separation.

In the 1950's Quasimodo published two volumes of verse: *Il falso e vero verde* (*The False and True Green*) in 1954 and *La terra impareggiabile* (*The Incomparable Earth*) in 1958. It was the latter collection that won for him the Viareggio Prize. *The False and True Green* contains only fourteen poems, written between 1949 and 1955. Some are of the public, almost occasional, stamp: "Auschwitz," for example, or an epitaph for a group of patriots slain in the Resistance. Some are more personal: a lament for his dead brother, and one, inevitably, on Sicilian subject matter. A curious one-line verse, "From the golden net are suspended repulsive spiders," seems a throwback to the old hermetic imagery. Perhaps the most interesting part of the volume is the essay "Discourse on Poetry," published as an appendix to the verses.

Written in a somewhat opaque prose that is not always easy to follow (as was the fashion of Italian criticism at that time), the discourse yet makes it quite clear that the writer considered the day of hermeticism to be over. The opening paragraphs are fairly explicit:

Philosophers, the natural enemies of poets, and the methodical cataloguers of critical thought, assert that poetry (and all the arts) like the works of nature undergo no changes during or after a war. An illusion because war alters the moral life of a people. Man, on his return from war, no longer finds measures of certainty in an inner modus of life, a modus he has forgotten or viewed ironically during his trials with death.

War, with its violence, sets up an unrealized order in the thought of man, a greater grasp of the truth; the occasions of reality are grafted in its history. . . . In 1945 silence creeps into the Hermetic school of Italian poetry in the extreme pastoral cavern of metrical phonemes. Since then the time of waiting has been on trial. . . . [Now] we are witnessing the efflorescence of a social poetry, addressing itself to the various aggregates of human society. . . . The poetry of the new generation aspires to dialogue rather than monologue.

(*The Poet and the Politician,* p. 16)

It is interesting and illuminating to note that the poet dates the beginning of the new poetry in a year that coincides with the composition of the poems in *Day After Day.*

The prize-winning *The Incomparable Earth* offers themes and techniques already familiar to the reader. Many of the poems are of the stamp of "Street in Agrigentum" in *New Poems:* descriptions of sites or landscapes of historical or mythological resonance—Mycenae, Delphi, Marathon, and others—without any subjective involvement of the poet. It is in the first of these, incidentally, that Quasimodo describes himself as a "Greek Sicilian." Of autobiographical content is "Al padre" ("To My Father"), in which the poet recalls the scenes of the Messina earthquake that have haunted his memory since early childhood:

Where on the purple waters
once was Messina, among broken wires
and ruins you go along the rails
and switches with your rooster cap of the island.
The earthquake has been boiling for three days, it is
    December of hurricanes
and poisoned sea. Our nights fall
in the freight cars and we infantile cattle

count dusty dreams with the dead
shattered by irons, biting into almonds
and dried apples in garlands. The science
of grief put truth and blades
into the games of the lowlands of malaria
yellow hued and fever swollen with mud.

A few lines later the poet adds with a certain complacency:

Your suncap bobbed up and down
in the small space they always gave you.
For me, too, everything was measured out
and I have carried your name
a little beyond hatred and envy.

Another poem in the anthology that aroused a good deal of comment is the poet's salute to the Russian sputnik, which successfully orbited in 1957. It is called "Alla nuova luna" ("To the New Moon") and reads in full:

In the beginning God created Heaven
and Earth; then in its proper day
set up the lights in Heaven;
and on the seventh day He rested.

After millions of years man,
made in His image and semblance,
without ever resting,
with his lay intelligence
without fear into the serene sky
of an October night put other lights equal
to those that had been spinning
since the creation of the world. Amen.

Here and there in this volume, in spite of the poet's awareness of the change in poetry's function since 1925, a few traces of hermeticism still linger, combined with the enduring penchant for nature and her creatures. "Oggi ventuno marzo" ("Today, the Twenty-first of March") is a good sample:

Today, the twenty-first of March, the Ram steps into
the equinox and butts his tough male head
against the trees and rocks,
and you, love, as he strikes,
shake winds of winter from your ear, intent

on my last words. Upon
the plants film greenish pale in hue
now surfaces and does not disregard
the admonition, and the tidings reach
up to the sea gulls as they meet
among the rainbows. Down they swoop,
sprinkling their patter out in jets
that echo in the grottos. You, beside me,
cover their cries and clear the bridge
between us and the gusts
that nature readies underground
in witless flashes.
You go beyond the thrust of the young buds.
And now the spring is not enough for us.

The note of acceptance, if not quite optimism, that we may detect in this celebration of spring is characteristic of the pervading tone of the collection. In this respect Quasimodo's title for the volume is typically revealing.

The heart attack suffered in Moscow, severe and admonitory, must have sharpened the poet's awareness of his mortality; in fact, he had but a decade to live. But the award of the Nobel Prize at the end of the same year, signifying exceptional international preeminence, cannot but have been invigorating. Quasimodo made the most of his new distinction, which he thoroughly relished. Other honors were bestowed on him, including an honorary degree from the University of Messina in 1960 and another from Oxford seven years later. Translations of his poems were published in many languages. (Allen Mandelbaum's English version of a large selection of poems and two discourses appeared in 1960.)

These years of glory were also years of intense activity. The poet continued his teaching of literature at the Milan Conservatory of Music and also the writing of his weekly column in *Il Tempo.* He gave frequent lectures and traveled extensively, not only in Europe but also in America. He also served on various literary committees and juries. It was in the course of presiding over one such panel in Amalfi that he suffered a cerebral hemorrhage and died in Naples the following day (14 June 1968).

During these years, too, Quasimodo published a number of translations, including two plays of Shakespeare, two from the classical Greek drama, poems of Conrad Aiken, and a substantial selection of the verses of the Romanian poet Tudor Arghezi. He found time, too, for the writing of two librettos for musical works, and he collected and published (in 1960) a number of essays and lectures written over the years, giving the collection the title *Il poeta e il politico, e altri saggi* (*The Poet and the Politician, and Other Essays*).

Quasimodo was a poet and not a critic, but some of the essays deserve attention. The one that gives its title to the book is the lecture delivered on the occasion of the Nobel award. The tone of the essay suggests that the poet felt that his new dignity gave him the privilege, if not indeed the duty, of taking on the role of prophet. His central argument seems to suggest (oracular prose is not always easy to follow) that the poet and the politician (perhaps "statesman" would be a better translation of "politico") are sharers in the direction of mankind, although they are not always in harmony. But perhaps this oversimplifies the thesis of the writer, whose sallies, often perceptive, are not always consistent. He remarks, for example:

> The poet is an irregular and does not penetrate the shell of a false literary culture full of towers as in the time of the Communes; he perpetuates his own forms even while seeming to destroy them; from the lyric he passes freely to the epic in order to speak of the world and of the meaning of anguish in the world—this through man, measure and emotion. It is here that the poet begins to become a danger. The politician is mistrustful of cultural liberty and strives, working through conformist criticism, to immobilize the very concept of poetry, considering the creative art as outside of time and inoperative, as if the poet were not a man but an abstraction.
>
> (p. 37)

Do these affirmations have eternal validity or do they reflect the speaker's experience under Fascism?

Elsewhere the focus is sharpened:

Can there be any coordination between politician and poet? Possibly, where there are societies in process of formation, but never on the plane of absolute freedom. In the contemporary world the politician assumes various aspects but an accord with the poet will never be possible since the one concerns himself with the internal order of man and the other with the ordering of men.

(p. 40)

However, he adds, "In a given historical period [such as the years following World War II?] the internal order of man may coincide with a desire to order and construct a new society."

The penultimate paragraph, which at first sight seems a defense of hermeticism, may also be the poet's way of telling what kind of a role he has himself played in his times:

The poet is alone. Around him rises a wall of hatred built of stones cast by literary marauders. From this wall the poet observes the world without going forth in the public squares as the minstrels did or even into worldly society as the "literati" do. But from that very ivory tower, so dear to the tormentors of the romantic soul, he arrives among the people not only in its emotional needs but in its intimate political opinion.

(p. 45)

The central thesis of the significant "Discourse on Poetry" is reaffirmed in "Postwar Poetry" (1957):

Something happened around 1945. . . . The poet has found himself all of a sudden cast out of his internal history. The problem of the "why" in life had been transformed into "how" one lives, or if we prefer, into the "why" one lives in a certain way rather than in another, in a way which does not continuously cultivate death as a protagonist of boundless consolation. Thus there was born, not enunciated, a new aesthetic.

(p. 29)

The Poet and the Politician also contains a number of essays, usually brief, on specific poets, ranging from Aeschylus to such medieval Italian figures as Dante, Petrarch, and Jacopone da Todi. For Quasimodo, Petrarch is "the poet of solitude," a thesis developed with some perception, and his comments on Dante provide a veiled gloss on Quasimodo's own trajectory. For him the lyrics of the *Vita nuova* are "hermetic." And he adds:

Through his study of the ancient poets Dante will go beyond the lyric current of the vernacular, apologetic and unchanging in its emotional content. . . . By now Dante's poetry has its feet on the ground and is no longer wandering vaguely over the sea of the *stilnovisti*; it is face to face with man "with his blood and his joints." . . . The discourse of love, the dialect of the stripling years, is overshadowed; by the time it reappears we shall be in the *Paradise,* at the end of the journey, weary in body and wisdom.

(p. 74)

The final paragraph of the essay has some perceptive observations on T. S. Eliot's use of Dante. *The Waste Land,* in Quasimodo's opinion,

contains verses of Dante here and there but no Dantesque verses. In the poem's steep images there is a weight of cultural echoes of remote civilizations and a dry funereal air; it is a world wherein the living are dead. In Dante's *Inferno* the dead are living. Dante could have for Eliot only one lesson: the lesson of language and poetry. But instead Eliot's praise of the *Paradiso* and the *Vita Nuova* is meant to justify the difficult theology of the English poet, his allegory frozen fast in metaphorical meaning only.

We have quoted in another connection Quasimodo's terse comment on Dante's style; he concludes with a remark indicating a somewhat jaundiced view of his contemporaries: "Today in the silence of Italian poetry, in the badly learned art of a tribe of imitators, a return to the realistic world of Dante will drive out the blurred baroque Petrarchism." The essay ends with a somewhat melodramatic asseveration:

"The new generation knows that it is not necessary to plunge into Hell to rediscover man: Hell is here." Written in 1952, when, as the letters to Maria Cumani reveal, the poet was going through a tormented period, the statement probably reflects a passing state of despondency. But Quasimodo's opinion of contemporary society and his fellow man was never very favorable. The ambivalent essay on D'Annunzio, written in 1939, ends on a similar note: "He was the last poet of our country to preempt the solitude necessary to his work, without falling slave to anyone. Poets to-day move about among knives."

In view of the numerous and demanding activities of the poet in the post-Nobel years, it is hardly surprising that he found little time to cultivate the muse. Eight years passed between the publication of *The Incomparable Earth* and the appearance of *Dare e avere* (*Debit and Credit,* 1966), destined to be his last volume of verse. Nor is the lyric harvest very copious: more than half of the book's 128 pages are composed of translations and librettos; the poems number only twenty-three. Many of them are what might be called metrical travel notes, impressionistic evocations of places visited by the poet in this decade of journeys: "Glendalough," "In Chiswick Cemetery," "The Negro Church at Harlem," and the like make up a gallery of sketches, drawn for the most part with a certain detachment. There is, as there should be, a poem dedicated to Annamaria Angioletti, who in 1960, when she was twenty-two years old, took the place of Maria Cumani in the poet's affections and remained by his side until the day of his death. The lines addressed to his nurse during his convalescence in Moscow ("Varvara Alexandrovna") have an appealing warmth:

> I have no fear of death
> as I have had no fear of life.
> Or I think it is someone else who is stretched out
>   here.
> Perhaps if I do not remember love, pity, the earth
> that fragments inseparable nature, the livid

sound of solitude, I can fall from life.
> Your nocturnal hand burns, Varvara
> Alexandrovna, yours are my mother's fingers
> that squeeze to leave long peace
> under the violence. You are the human Russia
> of the time of Tolstoy or Mayakovsky,
> you are Russia, not the landscape of snow
> reflected in a hospital mirror,
> you are a multitude of hands reaching for other
>   hands.

The preoccupation with death is a recurrent theme; the tone of the collection is valedictorian; the title of the volume itself suggests a final balancing of accounts. Yet the closing of the books seems to bring little melancholy; the poem that gives its title to the collection bespeaks rather a kind of aggressive complacency:

> Nothing you give me, you give me nothing,
> you who are listening to me. The blood
> of the wars has dried,
> contempt is a pure desire
> and does not call forth a gesture
> from a human thought
> beyond the hour of pity.
> Debit and credit. In my voice
> there is at least a sign
> of living geometry,
> in yours, an empty shell
> dead with funeral wailings.

In the poem "Solo che amore ti colpisca" ("Only If Love Should Pierce You"), the nature-loving Quasimodo of old reappears, calling on his bestiary to frame and illuminate a statement that might be called an act of faith. In no other poem does the mystic zoophilia of the poet play such a dominant role:

> Never forget that you live among animals,
> horses, cats, sewer rats
> brown like the woman of Solomon,
> terrible as a host with banners displayed,
> don't forget the dog with tongue and tail
> of unreal harmonies, nor the lizard nor the
>   blackbird,
> the nightingale, the viper, the drone. Or you like to
>   think

that you live among pure men and women
of virtue who do not touch
the cry of the frog in love, green
as the greenest branch of the blood.
The birds look down on you from the trees and the
    leaves
know well that the Mind is dead
forever. Its remains smell of burned
cartilage, of rotted plastic: don't forget
to be an animal adept and sinuous,
hot in violence, wanting everything here
on earth before the last outcry
when the body is a cadence of abridged memories
and the spirit rushes to its eternal end:
remember that you can be the being of being
if only love strikes you deep in the guts.

Whether these lines may be considered hermetic or otherwise, whether they constitute monologue or dialogue, they are authentically Quasimodian. The ambiguity of the message— a little obscure but not without hope—is an appropriate and effective valediction.

Quasimodo died at the height of his fame. How enduring the respect for his achievement will be is difficult to predict. The prestige of all poets—and of all artists, for that matter—is inevitably subject to the oscillations of taste. The generations pass, each successive one eager to revise or rectify the verdict of its predecessor. Even giants like Dante and Shakespeare have not been immune to reassessment as the passing years bring with them new aesthetic attitudes and standards of measurement. Sons—at least in the sphere of the muses—having their own gardens to cultivate are prone to find the flowers of their fathers lacking in fragrance. At best such paternal productions will come to seem "dated," even as the hermetics disparaged the verses of Carducci and D'Annunzio. At this time it must be conceded, I think, that the star of Quasimodo has waned a little. The award of the Nobel Prize to his compatriot and sometime friend Montale somewhat overshadowed his glory. It is symptomatic of this reevaluation that in the 1980's at least four full-length studies in English were published on Montale and none on the author

of "Wind at Tindari." Even as early as 1965, with Montale as yet uncrowned, Gianni Pozzi's manual of twentieth-century Italian poetry gave to Quasimodo's contribution considerably fewer pages than to Montale's or Ungaretti's. And of course, aside from the question of precedence among representatives of the same school, the poetry of our times is still awaiting assessment. It is not yet certain whether any poet of the mid twentieth century will have the enduring appeal of Leopardi or even, for that matter, of Carducci or D'Annunzio. Quasimodo's instinctive, and at the same time shrewd, responses to the climate of his times make him more vulnerable to the criticism of posterity. Probably the most eloquent exponent of the hermetic commitment and the most alert to capture the mood of the immediate postwar years, Quasimodo may seem to lack that precious enduring element, transcending contingencies, that gives the voice of great poets—and even some minor poets—a resonance through the years.

Yet it cannot be denied that he has assets that may well secure his survival. His translator, Jack Bevan, summing up such assets and defining the nature of the poet's art, may be given the last word. He writes:

Quasimodo is not in any profound sense an innovator. He helped to modify the language of poetry, as did his two fellow poets, Ungaretti and Montale, as Eliot, Wordsworth and Dante did. But his uniqueness lies elsewhere. [Readers] may agree that he is a different kind of poet from any they have read before, or merely that he evokes responses which are different. In either case, what is striking is that throughout these highly individual poems there runs a unity that binds them together as a collection.

The enigmatic "you" is ever present, sometimes an unseen presence, sometimes himself, or someone from the past, or the person to whom the poem is addressed. These presences fuse together, keep us on our toes, and sharpen our response, so that we read with all our senses alert. Not to do so leads us wildly astray. Strange irradiations run through the fabric. Sometimes dead ones speak, or river gods rise with vegetal growths on them. We see dormice from funeral windows in the "vegetal dark" and enter the poet's dream as if it were our own. Suddenly we are back in his childhood, the dead young woman laid out, and we smell the flowers. Or we hear sounds in the dark, and waken to mysterious modes of our own being. We hear from its bush the last cicada of summer with the siren "deep wailing" its warning over the plain of Lombardy, hear in the winter night the village tower dripping dark, see "dead Solunto" down there among the hare's lentisks. We wake with him in a Chirico streetscape and "follow silent houses where the dead stand open-eyed", and realize that we, too, "shall have voices of the dead." Such images cohere in poems which echo in the memory.

(*Complete Poems*, pp. 23–24)

All of which is to say that we are in the presence of a poet whose manner and language are truly his own and whose imagery has a suggestive richness. Possibly he will be "downgraded"; it is unlikely that he will be ignored or forgotten.

Selected Bibliography

EDITIONS

INDIVIDUAL WORKS

POETRY

Acque e terre. Florence, 1930.
Oboe sommerso. Genoa, 1932.
Erato e Apòllion. Milan, 1936.
Poesie. Milan, 1938.
Ed è subito sera. Milan, 1942.
Giorno dopo giorno. Milan, 1947.
La vita non è sogno. Milan, 1949.
Il falso e vero verde. Milan, 1954; 1956.
La terra impareggiabile. Milan, 1958.
Dare e avere. Milan, 1966.

ESSAYS

Il poeta e il politico, e altri saggi. Milan, 1960.

OTHER WORKS

Billy Budd. Milan, 1949. Libretto.
Conversazione in Sicilia. Milan, 1938.
Orfeo—Anno Domini MCMXLVII. Milan, 1960. Opera-oratorio.
L'amore di Galatea. Palermo, 1964. Myth in three acts.

COLLECTED WORKS

Tutte le poesie. Milan, 1960; 1965.

TRANSLATIONS BY QUASIMODO

Lirici greci. Milan, 1940.
Edipo re. Milan, 1946.
Romeo e Giulietta. Milan, 1948.
Le coefore. Milan, 1949.
Macbeth. Turin, 1952.
P. Neruda: Poesie. Turin, 1952.
Riccardo III. Milan, 1952.
Elettra. Milan, 1954.
La tempesta. Turin, 1956.
Tartufo. Milan, 1957.
e. e. cummings: Poesie scelte. Milan, 1958. Reprinted in *Da Aiken a Cummings.* Milan, 1968.
Otello. Milan, 1959.
Ecuba di Euripide. Milan, 1963.
Antonio e Cleopatra. Milan, 1966.
Eracle di Euripide. Milan, 1966.
T. Arghezi: Poesie. Milan, 1966.
Iliade: Episodi scelti. Milan, 1968.

CORRESPONDENCE

A Sibilla. Preface by Giancarlo Vigorelli. Milan, 1983. Letters to Sibilla Aleramo.
Lettere d'amore a Maria Cumani. Preface by Davide Lajolo. Milan, 1973.

TRANSLATIONS

Complete Poems. Translated with an introduction by Jack Bevan. London, 1983.
The Poet and the Politician, and Other Essays. Translated by Thomas G. Bergin and Sergio Pacifici. Carbondale, Ill., 1964.
Selected Writings. Edited and translated by Allen Mandelbaum. New York, 1960. Contains one hundred poems, published between 1920 and 1960, and two essays: "Discourse on Poetry" and "Dante."

To Give and To Have, and Other Poems. Translated by Edith Farnsworth. Chicago, 1969.

BIOGRAPHICAL AND CRITICAL STUDIES

Angioletti, Annamaria, ed. *E fu subito sera.* Naples, 1969. Contains sixteen essays by various critics and Angioletti's own memoir.

Bowra, C. M. "An Italian Poet: S. Quasimodo." *Horizon* 16 (1947).

Finzi, Gilberto, comp. *Quasimodo e la critica.* Milan, 1975. Contains more than forty essays and articles, covering all of the poet's active years.

Mazzamuto, Pietro. *Salvatore Quasimodo.* Palermo, 1967.

Montale, Eugenio. *Lettere a Salvatore Quasimodo.* Edited by Sebastiano Grasso. Milan, 1981.

Pacifici, Sergio. *A Guide to Contemporary Italian Literature.* New York, 1962.

Pozzi, Gianni. *La poesia del novecento: Da Gozzano ai ermetici.* Turin, 1965. Pp. 187–200.

Zagarrio, Giuseppe, ed. *Quasimodo.* Florence, 1969.

THOMAS G. BERGIN

ANDRÉ MALRAUX

(1901–1976)

A T THE BEGINNING of André Malraux's final novel, *Les noyers de l'Altenburg* (*The Walnut Trees of Altenburg,* 1943), the narrator explains that he is telling this story with the aid of a sheaf of notes to which his father gave the title "My Encounters with Man." As the reader shortly discovers, both the father, an intellectual adventurer whose exploits have made him a legend, and the narrator, a former soldier and writer, represent aspects of Malraux himself. Thus, the "Encounters with Man" must be his own.

"My Encounters with Man" serves as an appropriate title for all Malraux's fiction. During the two decades spanning the late 1920's to the 1940's, André Malraux published six novels, as well as a couple of youthful fantasies. His major works are: *Les conquérants* (*The Conquerors*) of 1928, *La voie royale* (*The Royal Way*) of 1930, *La condition humaine* (*Man's Fate*) of 1933, *Le temps du mépris* (*Days of Wrath*) of 1935, *L'Espoir* (*Man's Hope*) of 1937, and *The Walnut Trees of Altenburg* of 1943. Malraux is often called a tragic humanist because, particularly in novels like *Man's Fate,* he is obsessed with the inherent tragedy of the human predicament. His characters are trapped by the inability to transcend human limitations, beginning with mortality. In his later work Malraux's emphasis changes somewhat: he continues to view our metaphysical situation as essentially tragic but as less dramatic, so that he no longer writes tragic novels.

Malraux thought of himself as a kind of "witness." The word, however, must be taken in a stronger sense than "eyewitness"—in the sense given it by Dr. Rieux in Albert Camus's *La peste* (*The Plague,* 1947), when he declares his need to testify that, when the chips are down, men show there is more good than evil in them. Critics have been bewitched for years by the cliché that André Malraux was a sort of ubiquitous literary Kilroy who was always on the scene when stirring actions took place and who based his fictions on what he had seen. While it is true that *The Royal Way* is based on his personal experience in Indochina, and that *Man's Hope* was written out of his involvement with the Spanish Civil War, there is little evidence that he witnessed the insurrection in Canton before writing *The Conquerors,* and he himself said that he first visited Shanghai several years after the abortive revolution of 1927, which is the subject of *Man's Fate.* Malraux's great gift for describing action as if he had seen it has misled even alert readers, blinding them to the fact that the real events in his novels play a supportive role: they provide the tensions needed to bring out the fundamental nature of the characters.

The meaning of "witness" that is most appropriate here emerges from a consideration of Malraux's *Antimémoires* (*Anti-Memoirs,* 1967). Nothing else can explain the juxtaposition of brilliant passages from *The Walnut Trees* with accounts of interviews with Jawaharlal Nehru,

Mao Tse-tung, and Charles de Gaulle, with a report of Malraux's own somewhat harebrained search for the lost capital of the Queen of Sheba, with a study of the character of the European adventurer David de Mayrena, and with the story of his own imprisonment during the occupation. This disconcerting medley acquires unity from Malraux's gathering of his intuitions about man as confirmed by what he has seen of the potentialities of certain men, many of them exemplary. Malraux's *Anti-Memoirs* are another chapter in his *Encounters with Man*.

Malraux's life is no open book. Though there are now half a dozen biographies of him, none is definitive, for none is a fully documented account based on both private papers and public records. Malraux's efforts to tell the truth about himself were often marred by a tendency to blend fact and fiction.

LIFE

Georges André Malraux was born on 3 November 1901. His parents separated early in his childhood, and he was raised by his mother, while still maintaining warm relations with his father and his father's family, who were shipbuilders and chandlers near Dunkirk. (Members of the clan, thinly disguised, appear in *The Royal Way* and in *The Walnut Trees.*) Malraux won no distinction at school and never took the examination for the *baccalauréat*. If he completed his education at the École des langues orientales vivantes, the evidence has disappeared.

Malraux first captured public attention with *Lunes en papier* (Paper Moons, 1921) and *Le royaume farfelu* (The Bizarre Kingdom, 1921; final form, 1928), two fantasy tales that reveal, above all, a playful imagination. The word *farfelu* is a significant one in Malraux's vocabulary, carrying connotations of the fantastic or farfetched, even of mythomania. In *Lunes en papier,* for example, a group of weird little nonhuman figures set out to find and kill Death but

are frustrated when Death, who has a modern-style aluminum skeleton, commits suicide in a bath of solvent acid.

Malraux had been earning a living as a rare book scout, working the shops and stalls along the Seine, and later in jobs with small publishers. In June 1921 he met and married Clara Goldschmidt, whose prosperous German-Jewish family was displeased by the match. For a short while the couple played the Bourse with success, but when the market collapsed in 1923, they scraped up what money they could and sailed for Indochina.

Malraux had read about the ancient Buddhist temples, covered with precious Khmer high-reliefs, which remained along the old pilgrimage route through Laos and Cambodia; he assumed that those unlisted in the official inventory of colonial monuments were in the public domain. He turned out to be right about the presence of the temples, wrong in assuming that he was free to dismantle one and sell its sculptures. A court of first instance found him guilty of removing public property from a temple at Banteai Srey. Later a court of appeals reduced his sentence to one year and suspended it; later still the court of cassation in Paris threw out the case entirely because the prosecution had placed a defective document in evidence. Malraux returned to Paris, staying just long enough to raise new backing, and left again for Saigon and a brief career in political journalism.

Malraux's paper *L'Indochine* (the first issue of which appeared in June 1925 in Saigon) took an anticolonialist position, supported the local Left-Nationalist "Jeune-Annam" movement, and clashed violently with the colonial establishment. Whether Malraux was also active in the left wing of the Kuomintang is less clear, although he wrote Edmund Wilson, some years later, that he had been secretary of the "Revolutionary Commission." He cannot have held such a post long, however, for after some fevered months he disappeared from Saigon, to reappear in Paris.

Now began a flow of books: *La tentation de*

l'Occident (*The Temptation of the West*) in 1926; *The Conquerors* and the revision of *Le royaume farfelu* in 1928; *The Royal Way* in 1930, and, in 1933 *Man's Fate,* one of the few durable novels ever to win the Goncourt Prize. Malraux became a familiar name and an intimate of the group who published the *Nouvelle revue française.* Simultaneous rumors reported him the darling of the Communists and a millionaire. Although the sale of *The Conquerors* had been banned in the Soviet Union, and despite the Trotskyite tendency of *Man's Fate,* Malraux was invited to Moscow to speak at the Writers' Congress in 1934, where his hearers were either willing to overlook his unorthodoxy or baffled by his rapid French. His sympathies, however, were not in doubt. That same year he went to Berlin with André Gide in an effort to obtain the release of the Communists accused of setting fire to the Reichstag. The effort failed but resulted in another novel, *The Days of Wrath,* in 1935.

When war broke out in Spain, Malraux was among the first foreign volunteers; he helped organize the Republican air arm, flying as a crew member on bombing missions. *Man's Hope* was his response to this experience and the source of the film he made under the same title. He also undertook a speaking tour in the United States and Canada on behalf of the Republicans.

In World War II, Malraux served briefly as a tank soldier, was captured, escaped, and began writing *The Walnut Trees of Altenburg,* first published in Switzerland in 1943. Malraux had gone underground; he emerged, when prospects of an American landing in southern France made resistance practicable, as the leader responsible for welding the diverse groups in the southwest into a cohesive force capable of harassing the retreating *Reichswehr.* Once again captured and wounded, he was released when the advancing Allies reached Toulouse, and took command of the Alsace-Lorraine Brigade, a formation of former Alsatian soldiers who eventually participated in liberating Strasbourg. To the surprise of many who remembered Malraux as the white-haired boy of the Left, he joined de Gaulle and served as minister of information in the short-lived coalition government of 1945, returning to private life when that government fell.

He also returned to his early studies of art—until then known only through occasional articles. *La psychologie de l'art* (*The Psychology of Art*) appeared in three separate volumes during the years 1947–1950. His separate *Saturne: Essai sur Goya* (*Saturn: An Essay on Goya,* 1950) pleased him better than the *Psychology,* which he felt needed revision even before he finished it. Revised and much extended, it appeared in one volume as *Les voix du silence* (*The Voices of Silence*) in 1951. Between 1952 and 1954, Malraux published the three-volume *Le musée imaginaire de la sculpture mondiale* (*The Imaginary Museum of World Sculpture*); yet a further attempt to clarify his views on art is the three-volume *La métamorphose des dieux* (*The Metamorphosis of the Gods*), published between 1957 and 1976.

When de Gaulle returned to power in 1958, Malraux became minister for cultural affairs and for ten years was rarely out of the news. He was constantly dedicating *son et lumiére* installations, visiting overseas departments and foreign capitals, founding "Houses of Culture," planning Bastille Day parades, cleaning the facades of Paris, financing art and theater groups, or guiding Jacqueline Kennedy through art collections.

Malraux's personal life, always jealously guarded, was rarely tranquil. His father's suicide in 1930 upset him deeply. His marriage to Clara Goldschmidt collapsed in 1934, although there was no legal divorce until after World War II. His liaison with Josette Clotis, who bore him two sons, ended when she fell under a moving train in December 1944. His half-brother Roland also died during the war, and Malraux married Marie-Madeleine Lioux, Roland's widow. Malraux's sons were killed in an auto accident. A final love affair, with the poetess Louise de Vilmorin, ended with her sudden death. From 1950 on Malraux himself was plagued by ill health.

There is more continuity in Malraux's career than appears at first blush. He came of age in the cultural climate of the Treaty of Versailles, to which many of his generation responded by revolt: the nihilism of Dada gave way to the abstentionism and alienation of surrealism. Some of Malraux's earliest writings appeared in the little review *Dés,* which also welcomed Dadaist texts, and his fantasy tales, though labeled "cubist" by critics, pleased the surrealists. One of his close friends, Marcel Arland, affirmed in "Sur un nouveau mal du siécle" in the *Nouvelle revue française* in February 1924 that the young were bored to death by everything except a handful of writers, mostly foreign, and perhaps a few interesting crimes. One of their cult heroes was Arthur Rimbaud because he had abandoned poetry and quit Europe in disgust, so they thought, when barely twenty. Friedrich Nietzsche and Feodor Dostoevsky and, sometimes, Karl Marx confirmed their belief that all bourgeois values were tainted. Art was no longer the great palliative it had seemed to the generation of André Gide, Marcel Proust, and Paul Valéry. They were restless and needed action—bullfighting for Henry de Montherlant, flying the mails for Antoine de Saint-Exupéry, exotic adventure and revolution for André Malraux.

Malraux's early involvement in politics was more a means to an end than an end in itself. Revolution offered his imagination a world of violent effort, action, and sacrifice such as Europe after Versailles did not. He said he never held a Communist party card; one may doubt that he could have obtained one if he had wanted to, since the orthodox Communists treated him as a well-disposed bourgeois intellectual. Malraux's political vagaries are most easily explained in negative terms. He sympathized with the Kuomintang because he disliked European colonialism, with Leon Trotsky (in *Man's Fate*) because he disliked the rigidity of Stalinism, with the Spanish Republic because he detested fascism, with de Gaulle be-

cause he feared the monolithic structure that Russian and Chinese communism threatened to become. (His anticommunism relaxed when it became clear that this structure was less monolithic than at first appeared.)

Malraux's literary development is also less inconsistent than at first appears. The juvenile *Lunes en papier* and *Le royame farfelu* are in the avant-garde mood of the early 1920's and as such retreat from reality, exploiting the familiar technique of metamorphosis (of objects into animate beings) and of metaphor-taken-literally that characterize much surrealist work. Malraux later told the critic Nicolà Chiaromonte that he recognized in these techniques a potentially "dangerous" escapism. After his return from Asia he abandoned such fantasies. But the novels exhibit a continuing concern for fantasy through characters who use their fantasy lives, in vain, as a retreat from the reality of the human condition. The character type Malraux calls the "farfelu" turns up in *The Walnut Trees* and is also portrayed in the *Anti-Memoirs.* The unity of Malraux's thought, like that of his career, can be exaggerated—but so can the diversity.

NOVELS

An essay that appeared in 1927, "D'une jeunesse européenne" (Of a European Youth), expressed the disaffection Malraux felt for European life. The previous year *The Temptation of the West,* a fictional correspondence between a young Chinese traveling in Europe and his European counterpart in Asia, concluded with the declaration that while life is absurd—in the sense the existentialists were later to popularize—this fact does not justify living meaninglessly. But how can one force a meaning upon life? Malraux's first two novels picture two alienated young Europeans who have come to Asia in search of an answer in violent action.

The protagonist of *The Conquerors* is a Russo-Swiss named Garine who has become head of police and propaganda for the anticolonialist insurrection in Canton in 1925. His disaffection stems from two events in his own life. For having financed abortions for political colleagues in Switzerland, he stood trial and was condemned to a punishment so disproportionate to the offense, as he sees it, that the whole episode seems unreal. Later, in World War I, he was ordered to wipe out an entrenched enemy position; the knives issued for the assault are so like ordinary kitchen knives that he is overcome by the absurdity of what he has been ordered to do. He deserts and finds an outlet in revolutionary action in Asia, where he becomes a "conqueror," the type who gives meaning to life by engineering revolutions.

The story begins on shipboard, where the anonymous narrator, on his way to join Garine, follows the news dispatches about the insurrection with tense excitement. He joins Garine only to learn that the latter, though winning a revolution, is losing a fight against tropical fever so virulent that his choice lies between returning to Europe in time to save his life or staying on to guide the insurrection to victory. Garine conquers but dies. As in the novels to follow, the cost of giving life meaning is life itself. As W. B. Yeats said, man can embody truth but he cannot know it.

As Malraux uses these words, a "conqueror" is a maker of revolutions, whereas a different kind of revolutionary, the "custodian," is the shaper and guide of the new society set up. The latter's gifts are largely administrative. The "conqueror's" principal trait is an inflexible will. Around Garine cluster an assortment of types who tend to recur in all the novels: Rensky, an archaeologist, whose fantasy leads him to scrawl obscene Sanskrit expressions on monuments, to the bafflement of later scholars; Rebecci, a mentor of young activists who is incapable of the least action himself; Cheng Dai, a Gandhi-like spiritual leader who commits suicide in protest; Hong, a terrorist so committed to direct action and so undisciplined that he must be liquidated; Klein, the German, moving about the world from one rev-

olution to the next; and a sadistic policeman. It may be a weakness of this novel—and even of *Man's Fate*—that these secondary figures are so clearly types and little else; they tend to incarnate abstractions, like two-dimensional allegorical figures.

Nevertheless, the novel is a virtuoso performance. Malraux's nameless narrator is constantly present; his sensitivity and analytic intelligence are established at the beginning, and the action is reported as it comes through his consciousness. At times his sense perceptions and impressions follow one another unlinked by grammatical connectives, so that the style itself conveys the rush of events. Except for one important flashback, necessary because the reader must know about Garine's past, and handled by having the narrator check through an old British intelligence report, time moves forward in a straight line. The pace is set by the dynamics of events themselves: once started, the revolution cannot stop. The extent and ferocity of its violence are conveyed by sudden snatches of vivid detail, as, for example, when the narrator comes upon the mutilated body of his friend Klein and realizes that the eyes seem to stare at him because the lids have been cut off with a razor.

As Leon Trotsky showed in his brilliant article "La révolution étranglée" ("The Strangled Revolution"), which appeared in the *Nouvelle revue française* of April 1931, the people in *The Conquerors* are not models of Communist behavior. Garine shows no interest in the welfare of the coolies he is rescuing from foreign exploitation and no feeling that he is part of a global movement. He serves the revolution only incidentally, for the truth is that he is making the revolution serve him. In short, he is a bourgeois intellectual alienated from his class, leading the insurrection because doing so satisfies a personal need to relieve the existential anguish that follows the realization of the absurd. Malraux's reply to Trotsky's review in the *Nouvelle revue française* was that he was trying principally to write an effective novel.

The Royal Way is a less adept performance

than *The Conquerors.* It was, in fact, the first full-length novel Malraux wrote, although it was published after *The Conquerors.* Narrating now in the third person, Malraux makes young Claude Vannec, a French art student who has chosen to seek adventure in Asia rather than "sell automobiles" in Europe, the center of consciousness, at least throughout much of the book. But there are moments in the story when Vannec cannot know what is in the mind of the other principal character, his companion, Perken; the point of view then shifts to Perken, often without warning. The effect on the reader is one of disconcerting fuzziness.

Vannec, of course, is Malraux under a transparent disguise, and the basic materials are his own adventures in the bush. Vannec wants to find an abandoned temple and sculptures that will make him rich. Perken, whom he has met on shipboard, joins him because he needs money for machine guns to defend the native kingdom he has carved out for himself in the hinterland. He also wants to discover what has happened to another European soldier of fortune, one Grabot, who has disappeared into the jungle like Joseph Conrad's Mr. Kurtz. (Malraux had been much impressed by *Heart of Darkness.*)

Perken is the first of a series of characters in Malraux's work who create their own myths and live by them. He is modeled on the semilegendary Frenchman who, under the assumed name of Mayrena, actually established his own domain in the back country of Indochina before World War I and tried to cede it in turn to France, England, and Germany. Later Malraux was to learn much more about the original, whom he pictures in *Anti-Memoirs* as being weirdly out of touch with reality, but in the novel Perken sounds like a white rajah along the lines of the English James Brooke of Sarawak, who ruled a state in Borneo in the nineteenth century. He may be enough of a mythomaniac to believe his own legend, but he is also one who knows quite well what he is about.

Malraux endows him with an awareness of the absurd like Garine's. Perken is obsessed by death; any weakening of his powers, particularly the sexual, confronts him with what he calls his "human condition." He sees death as the inevitable victory of non-meaning. Yet he revolts against his existential predicament: he will not, as he says in a startling figure, live like a termite in a termite-hill. Instead (again like Garine), he will create his own meaning through the assertion of his will. His "kingdom" is for him what revolution is for Garine, a chance to "participate in a great action," by which to "leave a scar on the map." What each wills is also his own death.

As compared with Malraux's own brief foray into the jungle, theirs is a longer and far more uncomfortable one. They find a temple after hideous days in the dank murk of a forest, where everything oozes or crawls and great leeches hang from the trees. Repulsive insects slither over their hands as they work to loosen the sculptures. Back in the bush lurk savages hardly more human than the insects.

In a hostile native village they find the lost European, Grabot. He has been blinded, castrated, and harnessed like a draft animal to a treadmill. When they release him from his harness, he can neither talk coherently nor stop his monotonous circular pacing. This man, who earlier embodied a willpower like Perken's, is now totally dehumanized.

The game seems to be up, for now that the Europeans know what has happened to Grabot the savages will never let them leave the hut where they have found him. They seem doomed to choose between death in fighting or the mutilation that would follow their being captured alive. But as the natives gather to attack, Perken forces himself to leave the hut and stride across the village compound to face them down, then to bully and trick them into a bargain that will ensure the safety of the expedition. His success marks the essential victory of the human over the inhuman.

However, a wound acquired when Perken tripped over a bamboo war-spike while crossing the compound becomes infected, and by the time they can reach a doctor, treatment is impossible. In a final act of will, Perken insists on trying to get back to his "kingdom" before the railroad being built from Siam can run its tracks across it. He dies on the way.

In an endnote Malraux refers to this story as an "initiation to tragedy." Not all readers will feel that he has endowed Perken with the stature of a tragic hero, but it is not necessary to do so, for the initiation is not Perken's but Vannec's. He has been the neophyte at a ritual from which he has attained new perception: We must live in absurdity, but our humanity will not assent to our living so. We are compelled to revolt, and the tragic trap is such that our revolt brings about our own destruction.

The Conquerors and *The Royal Way* form the first and most elementary of Malraux's "Encounters with Man." He had intended *The Royal Way* to be the first of a series of novels to be called *Les puissances du désert* (The Powers of the Wilderness), but he explains in *Anti-Memoirs* that the idea changed as it ripened and the material went into a single volume, *Man's Fate.* In any event, nothing could be further from concern with wilderness, insects, savages, and the bric-à-brac of adventure than the urban political fiction of *Man's Fate,* set against the background provided by the abortive revolution in Shanghai in 1927.

Several of the major themes of this novel are continued from earlier ones. Man, "the only animal who knows he must die," is trapped in a meaningless and indifferent universe. He may revolt against his predicament, but knows that the revolt is predestined to fail. But in *Man's Fate* the variety of human response to the fundamental situation is much greater, and individual cases are more fully pictured than in the previous novels. Malraux makes one character say that each man's destiny takes the form of his own anguish, that he sees his metaphysical plight through the lenses of his own suffering. And, since each is condemned to be shut up in his own solitude, out of communication with his fellows, each suffers alone. Much later, in *The Voices of Silence,* Malraux remarks that he once wrote a tale about a man who failed to recognize his own voice when he heard it in a recording—his voice as other people heard it—and in an allusion to this, he called his novel *Man's Fate.* The character who has this experience is the hero, Kyo Gisors.

Some ways of facing the human predicament are more satisfactory than others. Ultimate defeat is certain, but a man can choose the manner in which he meets it, through acts that affirm his human dignity; thus, though death is inevitable, humiliation is not. At the end of this story, when Kyo has been captured and is about to swallow his pellet of cyanide, he feels that other revolutionary workers, the world over, are beside him. He finally breaks through his solitude. His comrade Katow, a less imaginative sort, sums up the same emotion of virile fraternity in giving his own cyanide to a fellow prisoner whose nerve has begun to break, thus accepting the worst death his captors can devise. The scene in which he goes out to be executed is intended to be the climax of the tragedy and to evoke appropriately tragic emotions.

The shape of the narrative is simple. Tchen, a terrorist, commits a murder to obtain the paper that will enable the revolutionists to hijack a shipload of arms. The insurrection starts the next morning; the revolutionists overrun the police stations, and after much brutal fighting, only an armored train holds out against them. The victory is supposed to be consolidated by the arrival of Chiang Kai-shek and his troops. But now word comes that the wealthy Europeans in the foreign colony have raised funds and bought off Chiang; he has changed sides. The leaders of the insurrection appeal to the headquarters of the Third International in Hangchow, but the authorities there are unwilling to risk confronting Chiang: the leaders must choose either to dismantle the revolution and go into hiding or to continue the fight unaided, against impossible odds. They choose to go on fighting and are overwhelmed in another brief, bitter battle. Kyo and his friends are hunted down and must either kill themselves or be executed. The revolution has been liquidated and the surviving revolutionaries dispersed.

In outline the story conforms to an idea of tragedy originally propounded by Kenneth Burke. The protagonists undertake an action that, in the light of what they then know, appears possible. But new knowledge reveals that the enterprise cannot succeed. The protagonists are impelled to continue, however, and move on to a disastrous climax. (Oedipus, determined to cleanse Thebes, learns that he will do so to his own cost, but persists in finding the source of the plague—himself; Kyo and his friends begin their revolution, learn it must fail, but continue to fight anyhow.) The reader's feeling of exaltation comes from recognizing that, while the protagonists have been beaten down, they have also transcended the ordinary limits of the human condition. In death Kyo and Katow make us proud to be human.

Malraux uses an unidentified narrating voice that is free to assume various points of view as need arises. The action is concentrated into two periods measurable in hours, with a lull separating them while the leaders go to Hangchow; the episodes take place either simultaneously or so closely in time that no single eye could plausibly observe them all. For a novel in which each character's "destiny" is equated with his particular angst, Malraux avoids the two-dimensional, somewhat allegorical effect some readers find in the novels preceding *Man's Fate*. Each tortured character, in other words, can be viewed through the eyes of various other, equally tortured ones, and made to appear more nearly in the round.

Thus young Tchen, once he has killed his man, feels himself condemned to live in the special world of the murderer. When he tries inarticulately to explain this feeling to his mentor, the elder Gisors (Kyo's father), he fails. The pair are exact opposites: Gisors can teach other men to act, but is completely incapable of taking the least action himself, whereas Tchen is consumed by an imperative need to perform violent deeds, not for the sake of the revolution

but for his own inner relief. But it is Gisors alone, of all the people who deal with Tchen in the story, who perceives that the boy is obsessed by a death wish and will not rest until he accomplishes his own death—as he finally does in an attempt to assassinate Chiang Kaishek. In another episode, in which Tchen is involved in heavy fighting and each man's life depends on someone else, the narrator takes Tchen's own point of view; what the character feels is not a desire to die but his total loneliness. Later still, during the Hangchow interlude, Tchen tries to explain himself to Kyo Gisors, who has learned to identify his personal satisfaction with the success of the revolution; the story assumes Kyo's point of view, and although Kyo has suffered from loneliness, the nature of Tchen's escapes him. The total effect of such a novelistic procedure is complex: what the reader learns is not about Tchen alone, but also about the character who happens to figure with him.

Malraux is fully as interested in the other principals as he is in Kyo and Katow. Several are modeled on people he had actually known. The elder Gisors, the paralyzed intellectual—already sketched lightly as Rebecci in *The Conquerors*—bears recognizable traits of the notoriously inert German philosopher Bernard Groethuysen; Ferral, the professor turned businessman who raises the money to buy off Chiang, combines a number of real-life prototypes; Baron Clappique, the mythomaniac who knows everyone in Shanghai and whose feckless fascination with a baccarat wheel is the direct cause of Kyo's capture, combines two men Malraux met when he visited Shanghai. Ferral and Clappique even threaten at times to preempt the central roles in the story.

Clappique first appears, on the night before the revolution breaks out, in a nightclub called the Black Cat, entertaining two prostitutes with fantastic tales about himself; the girls are either drunk or drowsy, but Clappique is his own appreciative audience. He has been useful to the revolutionists as a go-between in obtaining arms and will continue to figure as a convenient messenger. Why Malraux gives him so much attention in the nightclub sequence is not apparent until much later in the story, when Kyo's old father charges him with a warning for Kyo that Chiang's police are on his trail. Clappique goes to the familiar nightclub to pass time until he is supposed to meet Kyo. Fantasy takes over: he becomes so absorbed in the dance of the little red ball on the gambling wheel that he cannot even make himself look at his watch, and he remains out of contact with reality until the time for saving Kyo has passed.

Malraux cut Clappique's part drastically in his final draft. In the manuscript Clappique realizes finally what has happened, is overcome by terror, and runs in panic from brothel to brothel, trying to assuage his anxiety with a series of women: in the last of the houses he discovers, too late, that he is performing for a hidden audience of voyeurs. The deleted section (published separately in the weekly *Marianne*) is long enough to suggest that Clappique threatened momentarily to run away with the story. Twenty years later Malraux said he cut the section "for artistic reasons."

Ferral is as much a victim of the will to power as Tchen is of the death wish or Clappique of his fantasies. The enormous consortium of business enterprises he has built in Asia is his way of "leaving a scar on the map." His relief from the anxieties of the human condition comes from imposing his arbitrary will on the people around him. Like Clappique, he threatens to disrupt the novel. Malraux includes two episodes that even favorable critics find extraneous. In one, Ferral retires for an hour with his mistress; they have a clash of wills over whether they will make love with a bright light on the woman's face. Ferral's desire prevails, but in the second episode the woman squares accounts by failing to meet Ferral, sending along instead a rival whom she has told to meet her at the same time and place. Ferral retaliates this time by buying up the stock of a pet shop and releasing all the birds and animals in her room. Even in love, his will to dominate is uppermost.

Clappique's denials of reality and Ferral's domination are equally ineffective escapes from the absurd. We last see Clappique disguised as a sailor, hiding his face behind an armful of brooms as he sneaks aboard a steamer that will carry him to safety; once more, he is playing a role. And Ferral is shown later, back in Paris, pleading with his bankers. He has foiled the revolution, but his business empire has collapsed; he is ruined unless he can obtain help from this circle of faceless old men who sit toothlessly sucking soft caramels and watching him abase himself. These absurd episodes contrast with the final heroic scenes of Kyo and Katow. Though Kyo and Katow have lived in an absurd world too, they have not lived absurdly.

Man's Fate made Malraux an international figure, but it is no more an orthodox Communist novel than *The Conquerors.* The revolution again appears as an escape from personal anguish: the class struggle hardly figures in it; most of the characters are again alienated middle-class intellectuals—certainly not workers. And if a political lesson can be derived from the story, it is that the International sets expediency above human values: the office in Hangchow is willing to let men like Malraux's heroes die rather than risk itself. But with fascism and Nazism gaining strength daily, the Left needed allies, and here was a writer of the first rank who, for all his unorthodoxy, was surely on the side of the angels. On his visit to Moscow in 1934 to attend the Writers' Congress, Comrade Malraux heard much less about his bourgeois dilettantism than he might have at another time.

The success of *Man's Fate* enabled Malraux to gratify his taste for travel. He searched the oases of Central Asia for additional evidence of the temporary fusion of Buddhist with Gothic art. With the aviator Édouard Corniglion-Molinier, whom he recruited when Saint-Exupéry proved unavailable, he flew over the most savage stretches of Arabia in search of the Queen of Sheba's capital. He found examples of the lost art, and his flight with Corniglion was reported in a series of articles he wrote for the Parisian *Intransigeant.*

Europe was moving inexorably toward war. Malraux's trip with Gide on behalf of Ernst Thaelmann and Georgi Dimitrov, the accused arsonists of the Reichstag, did not help the prisoners, but the experience moved Malraux deeply. *Days of Wrath* (1935) is an excellent example of an essentially political emotion transmuted into an aesthetic object. It tells of a Communist imprisoned by the Nazis and of his subsequent escape.

The Communist, one Kassner, has contrived to swallow a list of his political collaborators before his captors could find it, but fears they will torture the information out of him or that he may go insane and babble it. He has no means of committing suicide; fantasies—images of combat during the Russian Revolution—crowd his mind until the urge to withdraw from present reality becomes irresistible. But just as he is losing his battle for sanity, another prisoner taps a message on the wall between their cells. The message is interrupted; Kassner is sure the sender will be tortured or killed, but his need to escape is assuaged by a feeling of fraternity and comradeship.

He soon learns he is being released because another comrade, knowing the value of Kassner to the cause, has persuaded his jailers that he, not the man in the cell, is the real Kassner. Kassner never learns the name of his deliverer or that of the pilot who risks his life to fly him over the mountains to Prague through a violent storm. Feeling as though he has died and been reborn, he wanders through the Prague streets looking for his wife and is finally reunited with her.

Malraux thought of *Days of Wrath* as a "botched job." He tried to reduce this story to the essentials of tragedy, with the hero a kind of Everyman, matching the resources of the human against the inhumanity of the Nazis. But if one analyzes its abstract schematic structure, *Days of Wrath* is strikingly like *The Royal Way:* each pits the human against the

inhuman; the human wins, but the victory is ephemeral in each case. Perken dies of his infection; Kassner will risk a new imprisonment. The central elements of imprisonment and release in *Days of Wrath* are translated into solitude and communion. The French title, *Le temps du mépris,* evokes the theme of humiliation. Uncharitable readers may feel that *Day of Wrath* suffers from incoherence or from cramming too much meaning into too small compass. They will be better satisfied with *Man's Hope.*

This novel is unlike *Days of Wrath* in every conceivable way. It is the most populous and longest of Malraux's fictions and is full of action, interrupted by long and sometimes verbose conversations and marked, according to most critics, by an epic rather than a tragic tone. *Days of Wrath* oscillates between art and propaganda. Some readers may share the opinion that Malraux, by some emotional legerdemain, contrives to substitute a victory for humanity for the defeat of the Spanish Loyalists.

In his earlier novels Malraux had already been aware of two very different strains of revolutionists. Those like the terrorists Hong in *The Conquerors* and Tchen in *Man's Fate,* who find fulfillment only in direct action, are not amenable to discipline because they are unable to subordinate their own needs to those of the group; they cannot abide the kind of organization that alone wins wars. The opposite type, represented by men such as Katow and Kyo, see the end to be accomplished as more important than their own desires. This pattern is basic to *Man's Hope.*

The problem confronting the Spanish Republicans is how to make a functioning army out of two such disparate groups. The anarchists are brave fighters and individually capable of decisive action, but they refuse to take orders from any but their own officers and prefer to die fighting in their own way to winning by following another line. What counts for them is their idea of themselves, and in this they are adamant. As Malraux sees them, they have opted for *being* something rather than *doing* something. As the story moves from the first fighting in Barcelona to the successful defense of Madrid, it becomes increasingly clear that only the Communists have the inherent discipline to "organize the Apocalypse."

To some, who are not necessarily anarchists but who, like them, have committed themselves to the Republic out of devotion to principle and to their idea of themselves, the situation becomes intolerable. Thus Captain Hernandez, one of the rare regular army officers to join the Republicans, discovers that, in order to continue the fight, he must forget his own principles—those of a Catholic—and accept those of the Communists. The sacrifice is too great, and he allows himself to be captured and killed. In contrast, a young moviemaker, Manuel, makes the concession and becomes an increasingly useful officer as the war goes on.

How to win the war without sacrificing the human values one is fighting for becomes the subject of lengthy conversations between the various intellectuals whom the war brings together. *Man's Hope* is a story of carnage and suffering, full of brilliantly graphic passages in which men fight and die. But, as an early critic remarked, "These people talk more than they die," and this loquacity may be the one real weakness of the novel.

In the key episode a Republican plane is shot down and crashes in the mountains above Linares. One crewman is dead; most of the others are wounded and unable to descend the slopes unaided. The officer Magnin learns of the disaster and hurries to the scene to direct a rescue operation, but finds that the local peasants have obeyed an instinctive impulse and organized their own. He watches their tiny column come down the mountain, some of the wounded being able to walk with help, the rest on stretchers. In a long, slow sequence, the procession winds down the slope. There are more peasants than are actually needed for the rescue; those not aiding the crewmen line up along the path, near Magnin, as the column passes and raise their hands in solemn salute.

Malraux's imagination is essentially visual. As early as *The Conquerors* his attention to the lighting of scenes, the planned play of light and shadow, was striking. In the crucial scene of *Man's Fate,* when Katow gives away his cyanide and is led out by his guards, the dominant effect is produced by following his shadow, which mounts the wall as he approaches the door until it is decapitated by the ceiling. By common consent, Malraux's eye is "cinematographic." Because of his intense visual sense and his love of action, Malraux took considerable interest in film.

When he filmed *Man's Hope* (as *L'Éspoir,* 1938–1939), some months after the writing and when it was clear that the Republican cause was lost, his whole script was constructed so as to lead up to this "descent of the mountain" sequence. Even more clearly than in the novel, politics is transcended by the perception of human solidarity. These peasants, the eternal victims of war, are simply too unpolitical to understand what the fighting is really about. What prompts them to help the wounded is both elementary and elemental. Five years later Malraux would find the phrase "fundamental man."

Man's Hope musters most of the themes exploited in the earlier novels, but it is now apparent that from novel to novel the emphasis has slowly changed. Concern about the absurdity of the human lot has largely disappeared. Death is too constant a presence for the participants to brood about it much; man's mortality becomes a given. Taking satisfaction in imposing one's will on others becomes less significant than imposing one's will on oneself. Sex is a casual diversion at most and devoid of metaphysical implications. The characters are doubtless aware of fighting for their essential dignity and against the humiliations of fascism, but most often they leave the fact to be taken for granted.

More strikingly, men contrive to communicate with each other. Two soldiers in a foreign brigade, placed next to each other in a night attack, speak no common language, but in the darkness use bird cries and whistles for effective communication. Critics believe that, once Malraux had experienced a feeling of virile fraternity or comradeship in the Spanish Civil War, the isolation of human beings ceased to impress him. This may be true. What is incontrovertible is that in his intuition of human solidarity he testified to yet another of his "Encounters with Man."

The change in emphasis from brotherhood discovered in revolutionary action to the less exclusive kind of communion revealed in the descent to Linares coincided with Malraux's final alienation from communism—even though World War II intervened to defer the public rupture. His Communist critics have argued, taking some slight liberties with chronology, that it also coincided with the close of his career as a practicing novelist, and they may not be completely wrong: the implication that *The Walnut Trees of Altenburg* is less a novel than a meditation in the form of a fiction can be defended.

The protagonist of this work, the intellectual Victor Berger, becomes an adviser and agent of Enver Pasha and the Turkish insurgents shortly before World War I. He travels through Central Asia in Enver's service trying to arouse the latent energies of what he believes to be the old blood alliance of scattered Turkish tribes. He has reached Afghanistan before an unpredictable incident, in which he is beaten by a madman, brings him to realize that the blood alliance exists only as a myth of his own creation. He drops everything and returns to Europe. It is his intention to attend an international conference of intellectuals that his uncle has convened at the ancestral seat of their family, the old priory of Altenburg, in Alsace. Coming ashore at Marseilles, he experiences the first of a series of epiphanies—the feeling of resurrection that Malraux calls "the return to the earth." After this he learns that some hours earlier his father had killed himself.

The intellectuals are to discuss a somewhat "Spenglerian" question: whether man can be said to have a continuous identity. Berger listens to a great ethnologist, Möllberg, argue that such an identity is a myth (much as Berger's own notion of the Turkish blood alliance was a myth). Deeply troubled by his own experience and by the enigma of his father's suicide, Berger rejects Möllberg's contention instinctively, but without being able to refute his logic. Möllberg sums up his point with an elaborate metaphor involving two sculptures carved from the same local walnut wood but in style clearly deriving from two different cultures. Berger asks whether there is no "fundamental mental wood."

The discussion recesses for tea, and Berger walks out into a sunlit landscape washed clean and dripping from a passing shower. He mounts a slope and discovers two ancient walnut trees, thrusting out of the earth as if they had always been there and would remain forever. Between the trunks are framed vineyards falling away to the Rhine—the eternal work of human hands—and, in the far distance, the cathedral of Strasbourg.

Readers coming to *The Walnut Trees* with *Man's Hope* still fresh in mind will remember that when Magnin watches the peasants bring the wounded down the mountain he is standing near a gnarled and ancient apple tree. In the earlier novel the symbolic association is perhaps understated, but in *The Walnut Trees* one cannot miss the symbol. The trees objectify Malraux's intuition of man's solidarity and identity with himself. Berger has found his answer to Möllberg: the walnut trees are eternally walnut trees; man is what he has always been.

In the next episode Berger, now an officer in the German army on the Eastern front, watches an attack in which poison gas is first used against the enemy. German infantry follow the gas and disappear into the enemy trenches. Suddenly Berger sees monstrously tall shapes emerging from the trenches and retreating toward the German lines: instead of going at the disabled Russians with knives and grenades, each German soldier is carrying one of his foes out of danger on his shoulders. Common humanity has overridden national differences, turning an errand of death into one of mercy. Fundamental man has revealed himself.

In a concluding chapter the narrator, Berger's son, records his own similar "encounter with man." His tank falls into a trap and the crew must wait helplessly for some gun, zeroed in on the trap, to blow them apart. The members of the crew are as different from each other in background, culture, and behavior as France could ever produce, but what emerges, as they wait for death, is their fundamental similarity.

The shell they are expecting never comes, and in the morning the tank escapes the trap and pushes forward into the next village, where Berger's son experiences an epiphany like his father's at Marseilles. They come upon a couple too old to have abandoned the place with the other villagers. The old people tell him that they will stay there till "it"—the war and its attendant horrors—"just wears out." Eternal man endures, as always, what must be endured. Young Berger is filled with the feeling of resurrection, "the return to the earth," believing this is how God must have felt on looking upon the first man.

At least from *Man's Fate* on, each fiction seems to exist for the sake of the moment of revelation, the moment of privileged perception—whether Katow's exit, Kassner's return to Prague, or the "descent from the mountain." The unfinished work, *The Walnut Trees,* is composed almost entirely of a series of such epiphanies.

For Malraux, as for so many of his contemporaries, the novel form seemed to be losing its special status. Before their deaths his friends Georges Bernanos and Antoine de Saint-Exupéry had given up fictional narrative for something closer to the personal essay. Louis-Ferdinand Céline tended more and more toward overt autobiography. Jean-Paul Sartre and Albert Camus seem to have cared more about thematic materials than about forms, working over the same, or closely related, themes in narrative, drama, and essay. Malraux would from this point on turn to another form.

BOOKS ON ART

Malraux had been dealing with art, in one way or another, all his mature life, since well before his first jaunt to Indochina. In the thirties he had staged exhibitions for the Gallimard Gallery, been something of an expert adviser for his publisher, and written a few dispersed essays for magazines like *Verve.* According to his first wife, he rarely missed a museum in their travels. He had a fantastically retentive, if occasionally fallible, visual memory.

With the publication of the first part of *The Psychology of Art* in 1947, it became clear that if Malraux was giving up the novel, he was not giving up his preoccupation with the themes that give his novels their special character.

Malraux's successive books on art may be regarded as one continuing monologue that he corrects and retouches as it develops. The *Psychology* would appear to have grown out of his reflections on the making of films. As he wrote this work, various afterthoughts turned up, to appear as appendixes. The third volume was not yet in print when Malraux began revising for the extended, one-volume version called *The Voices of Silence.* His treatment of what he calls "metamorphosis," the process by which one style replaces another, did not satisfy him and became the central theme in *The Metamorphosis of the Gods.*

Students of and experts on art have always played a privileged role in Malraux's novels. Claude Vannec, the anonymous narrator of *The Conquerors,* the elder Gisors, various of the more talkative figures in *Man's Hope,* and several of the participants in the Altenburg conference are apparently adepts of either art or archaeology. These are the characters Malraux most often permits to see deeply into the human predicament, and they are most likely to be present when the inner nature of man reveals itself.

He argues in his art essays that the present time is privileged as no other has been to read the message of art. Through modern color reproductions we may recognize that the function of art, in its totality, has been to express man's feeling of the "sacred," by which Malraux means whatever men have felt to exist outside, above, or even below the natural world.

Art thus expresses man's feeling of "destiny," his reconciliation with or his alienation from it, his acceptance or his protest. Moments of reconciliation and acceptance, such as the great age of Greece or the Christian Middle Ages, have been few and brief. For the most part, Malraux says, art has been an "anti-destiny," meaning that it has rejected the human situation.

For the history of art, he says, is not the history of the perfection of the artist's eye. Men have always been able to see the external world as it is. The distortions of reality that characterize the "primitive" arts of Africa and the Pacific, or those of "enigmatic" civilizations like the Sumerian, reflect no naive inability to see or represent the surrounding world but a determination to wrack and twist a "sacred" that is out of harmony with the needs and aspirations of man. Similarly, most surrealists could, if they wished, paint perfectly rational, representational still lifes; they simply feel no reason to do so.

Malraux's argument requires rather a special concept of culture. A culture, he believes, is expressed by a characteristic style, and styles are discrete and separate: Romanesque, for example, is not an imperfect stage of Gothic but something entirely different. Each style has its own peculiar form of perfection, which can be apprehended only with reference to what it aspires to express. What the squatness of Romanesque and the perpendicularity of Gothic express is the difference in attitude of two cultures toward the "sacred."

But how does one style disappear and another take its place? Art involves, Malraux implies, a double metamorphosis. Each true artist attains his own originality by a sort of conquest in which he effects a metamorphosis both of the form in which he works and of the external world, which he stylizes according to his own will. The artist lives and works within his own culture, but through his originality he also transcends it; that is how one culture may "metamorphose" into another.

Malraux has been saying something like this since those early essays in which he declared that art is a conquest. Highly qualified art experts and historians have refuted him with authority. What a piece of art expresses is, after all, a matter of individual intuition. There is also some circularity in an argument that makes the identification of a culture depend on what its art is believed to express and then interprets the art as an expression of the culture.

Some critics, including the late Claude-Edmonde Magny, have objected to Malraux's idea of an imaginary "museum without walls," where the testimony of all the art of all times can be viewed at once. In this view, bringing together in the uniform format of a book works of widely varying size, putting enlarged miniatures next to reductions of cathedral windows, for example, constitutes an initial distortion that invalidates Malraux's whole method. Erwin Panofsky contended that the brilliance of Malraux's color reproductions was another distortion, promising nothing but disappointment to readers who later saw the "relatively muddy" originals for the first time.

No one questions the extent of Malraux's knowledge or the keenness of his vision. Some very gifted critics, beginning with Gaëtan Picon, have also insisted that, whatever Malraux's standing with art experts, *The Voices of Silence* is a magnificent poem on the spiritual stature of man. There are excellent reasons for honoring Malraux's achievement. However, they are incidental to the primary purpose of his work, which is persuasion, and it is as a work of persuasion that his long monologue about the functions of art and the artist does not succeed. It fails because by temperament Malraux is indeed a poet, not a master of persuasive prose discourse. An examination of his style reveals that it moves from idea to idea without much help from grammatical connectives, and largely unaided by the conjunctions that link cause and effect. Each thought is a momentary flash of illumination, isolated from those that precede and follow by moments of darkness. The testimony about man that Malraux finds in art is not reducible to logical exposition and is thus incoherent.

METAMORPHOSES OF FACT AND FICTION

Many of Malraux's multivolume projects remained incomplete: *Les puissances du désert* (The Powers of the Wilderness), a series intended to encompass several more Asian novels; *La lutte avec l'ange* (The Struggle with the Angel), an extensive work, of which *The Walnut Trees of Altenburg* is all that remains; and *Le miroir des limbes* (The Mirror of Limbo), the overall title for his *Anti-Memoirs.* One reason is that Malraux's ideas were always evolving and changing shape. Another explanation is that his nonliterary activities constantly interrupted his writing career. His years of soldiering and those spent as an aide of de Gaulle occupied nearly two decades of his life, and he was more than ready at other times to drop what he was working on in favor of some role that promised action. Thus, even when nearing seventy, he was tempted to join the fighting in Bangladesh. He also had a disinclination to resume a work laid down, preferring to start afresh. Still, his writings reveal that, while individual—often grandiose—projects may have broken down, his fidelity to his obsessive, fundamental themes remained constant.

Malraux's *Anti-Memoirs* do not admit readers into his private life and disappoint those who hoped for a reply to the revelations studding his first wife's biography. As Malraux's

use of section titles suggests, his controlling intention is to pull together loose strings; this is a literary and philosophical last will and testament meant to correct the perspective of future readers.

What is omitted may be quite as significant as what is included. As political documents, his interviews with de Gaulle, Nehru, and Mao are disappointing. One is hardly surprised by Malraux's conviction that principle and devotion to an idea underlay de Gaulle's apparent opportunism, or more than mildly impressed by his awareness of the atrophying of the general's private personality to the advantage of his public one. We learn that Malraux respects Mao's accomplishment deeply, is somewhat baffled by him, and is persuaded that Mao feels unable to win a war fought outside of China. We learn nothing if we try to explain in political terms why Nehru is given twice as much space as the other two. The question is why these interviews have a place at all in a book that begins with a reworked section of one of Malraux's novels, *The Walnut Trees of Altenburg.*

It is as "encounters" with exemplary human beings that the interviews with Nehru, Mao, and de Gaulle take their places. Malraux sees each as being irrevocably dedicated to a great movement yet separated from it. This special human situation, which he once thought of as "the loneliness of command," had been in his mind at least since he drew the figure of Manuel in *Man's Hope.* Nehru occupies so much space because he is the agnostic leader of a nation that, to Malraux's mind, is no more a nation than a spiritual climate, and thus offers food for speculation.

Malraux has often alluded to the curious way fact has followed fiction in his own life—how, after inventing events in his novels, he has been called on to experience identical ones in reality. He had never seen a firing squad when he described the execution of Captain Hernandez in *Man's Hope,* but found out later what it was like to face one when the Germans, in a bluff intended to make him talk, stood him before one in Toulouse. Similarly, he had scarcely seen Alsace when he decided to set *The Walnut Trees* there, but three years later, under the name of Berger, he took the Alsace-Lorraine Brigade into Strasbourg. Like T. E. Lawrence, Malraux believed that an imagination that dwells too frequently on a given kind of experience is likely to confront the experience in actuality one day. The line between fact and fiction is so thin—the accuracy of *Anti-Memoirs* when Malraux remembers personal exploits must be challenged by attentive readers—that he finds each equally capable of providing valid "encounters with man."

"What interests me in any man," Malraux writes, "is the human condition; in a great man the form and essence of his greatness; in a saint, the character of his holiness. And in all of them certain characteristics that express not so much an individual personality as a particular relationship with the world." Malraux assumes that the readers of *Anti-Memoirs* are familiar with all his writing, including the essays on art, the novels he has been reluctant to reprint, and even the early fantasy tales. The five sections, each with its own title—"The Walnut Trees of Altenburg," "Anti-Memoirs," "The Temptation of the West," "The Royal Way," and "Man's Fate"—are broken into chapters that are untitled but usually bear dates and the name of a place. Thus the introduction: "1965, off Crete." Sometimes there are two place-names and dates: "1934, Sheba; 1965, Aden." Malraux's chapters follow the itinerary he took in 1965—by ship for reasons of health—as de Gaulle's special emissary to Mao, which in turn retraced the one he followed on his early journeys to the East: Suez, the Red Sea, Aden, the Indian Ocean, Indochina, Singapore, Hong Kong. In instances like the Sheba–Aden chapter, being at Aden inspired him to relive his flight with Corniglion. The organization of the whole book depends upon such associations.

What motivates the associations is not always so obvious. It seems perfectly natural that an account of a long conversation with

Nehru about imprisonment should lead into the story of his own imprisonment by the Germans: the experience of prison has always had symbolic value in Malraux's work. It is equally understandable that in the "Man's Fate" section he should move from the transferral of the remains of the Resistance fighter Jean Moulin to the Panthéon into a story of the Nazi prison camps, which he considered the most effectively vicious means of depriving men of their humanity. But to follow Malraux through the "Anti-Memoirs" section, from his version of his first meeting with de Gaulle to the events of 1958 and the new constitution, and from these to his visits to the Antilles on behalf of the General, on from there to his contacts with Nehru, and finally to his own experience of prison—this requires a reader most alert in detecting inexplicit relationships.

Fortunately, Malraux kept his old habit of sprinkling his pages with allusions that catch the eye of an initiate and remind him of major themes. For example, his remark "I thought of the ring of dead walnuts back there in Alsace" recalls a detail in the chapter from *The Walnut Trees* that leads to the central symbol of the trees. Malraux's memory of his thematic materials is elephantine; except for his early concern with the erotic, not a single theme of his is absent from the *Anti-Memoirs.* The absurd and its antidote of meaningful action, art as man's protest against his predicament, alienation and loneliness, humiliation and human dignity, mythomania and the feeling of the ever-renewed reality of life, death and the fear of physical decline that is death on the installment plan, anxiety and the dreadful human eagerness to embrace any way of escaping it—all are present either directly or by allusion. Malraux is here recapitulating his lifework.

Nothing but a desire for completeness in this respect could explain the awkward and apparently irrelevant intrusion into this book of reminiscences of his work on a movie script on the life of David de Mayrena. This forms the section entitled "The Royal Way," dated 1965 and purportedly written in Singapore. This digression is needlessly complicated by the device of reviving Baron Clappique from *Man's Fate* to narrate the script. Clappique spends an evening and uses up more than ninety pages of print telling Mayrena's story. Mayrena was Malraux's model for Perken in *The Royal Way* and a model of the "farfelu," the charismatic adventurer or mythomaniac who casts a spell over others but may well succumb to romantic self-delusion himself. Malraux recognized the "farfelu" in himself but spent a lifetime taming it.

There is a theory that Malraux's novels exercised a therapeutic function, that the fictional exploration of certain obsessive themes externalized his neurotic needs and relieved them. Without a fully documented biography and his personal correspondence, such psychoanalytical interpretations remain hypothetical. However, it is instructive to analyze parallel patterns in his work and in his public behavior.

In each of Malraux's stories there occurs a journey to a distant place, or a sojourn in one, which becomes the scene of some kind of struggle, analogous to a tragic agon, which in turn leads to some kind of enlightenment or moment of revelation. Even in the fantasies someone goes somewhere and learns something. Claude Vannec in *The Royal Way*, the unnamed narrator in *The Conquerors*, Magnin, who seems to be Malraux's surrogate in *Man's Hope*, and Vincent Berger are all men who have made a journey and participated in a struggle. Each is a witness to the struggle; his role is to receive and transmit the enlightenment that ensues. What the enlightenment consists of is more clearly articulated as the novels proceed, but in no case is it articulated completely; to some extent, the oracle must always be interpreted. Malraux told his friend and translator Haakon Chevalier that a critic who had observed that his work was shamanistic was *astucieux,* (shrewd or insightful).

What makes a shaman a shaman is an experience not unlike that repeatedly outlined in Malraux's novels. A character of intense temperament disappears from his normal haunts and reappears later to report that he has been through some struggle or undergone some ordeal that has made him, in both his eyes and those of his tribe, the possessor of special knowledge communicated in some supernatural or super-rational way. This initiation conforms to Arnold Toynbee's familiar pattern of withdrawal, enlightenment, and return. It entitles the initiate to the respect of those around him, for the knowledge he has acquired is of extreme value.

Malraux's own career follows a similar pattern. His withdrawals are represented by his absences in the Orient and Spain; the struggles are the violent actions he has either imagined or actually taken part in; his returns are the books in which his enlightenments have been inscribed. His special knowledge, which is his testimony about man, comes from a super-rational source. This could well be why his novels succeed as his essays on art do not: his witness is not reducible to rational, discursive exposition.

Malraux's equipment for writing novels was unusual. Social relationships, the normal pabulum of his great predecessors, meant little to him. He was not interested in the slow evolution of character; with the one exception of Manuel in *Man's Hope*, none of his people grow in the course of their stories. They are too enclosed in themselves—Malraux would say in their "destinies"—for the story to develop out of the grinding of one character against another. Given his feeling of time as an absolute limit within which individual destinies must be worked out, any such development would be impossible. And for Malraux motivation is a mere datum, since it is indistinguishable from neurosis.

He said that his novels grow not out of characters but out of situations. By situation he means crisis: he places people where they must take immediate, decisive, and irrevocable action; each acts according to the particular form of humanity he manifests. After each manifests his form of humanity and provides, directly or indirectly, his own insight into the nature of man, Malraux is finished with him. (We are never told whether Victor Berger survives when gas from the enemy trench is blown back on his position by a change of wind.) What counts is what we learn from these surrogates of ourselves about ourselves and about our metaphysical predicament. That is why some credit Malraux with having invented the "metaphysical novel."

In the final account the novels stand as Malraux's major achievement. In one of his studies of Malraux, Gaëtan Picon has written that for the generation just coming to literary maturity at the time, the impact of these novels was like "a slap in the face." Doubtless they do not have the same shock value for us, nor will they for our children, especially now that literary taste everywhere has turned against the elevated style—Malraux's style is elevated to the point of seriousness bordering on solemnity. Our current sensibility is not tragic, and few of us think or write about man with a capital letter. Further, the historical events that are Malraux's backdrops have lost their immediacy. Yet for all this Malraux's novels do something that had not been done before and that probably will not be done again. They bear vital testimony to their times and to man's eternal spirit.

Selected Bibliography

EDITIONS

INDIVIDUAL WORKS

Lunes en papier. Paris, 1921.
La tentation de l'Occident. Paris, 1926.
"D'une jeunesse européenne." In *Écrits.* Paris, 1927.
Le royaume farfelu. Paris, 1928.
Les conquérants. Paris, 1928.
La voie royale. Paris, 1930.
La condition humaine. Paris, 1933.
Le temps du mépris. Paris, 1935.
L'Éspoir. Paris, 1937.
Les noyers de l'Altenburg. Lausanne, 1943.

Esquisse d'une psychologie du cinéma. Paris, 1946.
La psychologie de l'art. 3 vols. *Le musée imaginaire,* vol. 1; *La création artistique,* vol. 2; *La monnaie de l'absolu,* vol. 3. Geneva, 1947–1950.
Saturne: Essai sur Goya. Paris, 1950.
Les voix du silence. Paris, 1951.
Le musée imaginaire de la sculpture mondiale. 3 vols. *La statuaire,* vol. 1; *Des bas-reliefs aux grottes sacrées,* vol. 2; *Le monde chrétien,* vol. 3. Paris, 1952–54.
La métamorphose des dieux. 3 vols. *Le surnaturel,* vol. 1; *L'irréel,* vol. 2; *L'intemporel,* vol. 3. Paris, 1957–76.
Antimémoires. Paris, 1967.
Le triangle noir. Paris, 1970.
Les chênes qu'on abat. Paris, 1971.
Oraisons funèbres. Paris, 1971.
La tête d'obsidienne. Paris, 1974.
Lazare. Paris, 1974.
Hôtes de passage. Paris, 1975.
Le miroir des limbes. 2 vols. Paris, 1976.
L'homme précaire et la littérature. Paris, 1977.

COLLECTED WORKS

Oeuvres complètes. 7 vols. Geneva, 1945.

TRANSLATIONS

Anti-Memoirs. Translated by Terence Kilmartin. New York, 1968.
The Conquerors. Translated by Winifred S. Whale. Boston, 1956. Translated by Stephen Becker. New York, 1976.
Days of Hope. Translated by Stuart Gilbert and Alastair McDonald. London, 1938. Also published as *Man's Hope.* New York, 1938.
Days of Wrath. Translated by Haakon M. Chevalier. New York, 1936. Also published as *Days of Contempt.* London, 1936.
Felled Oaks: Conversations with de Gaulle. Translated by Irene Clephane. New York, 1971.
Lazarus. Translated by Terence Kilmartin. New York, 1977.
Man's Fate. Translated by Haakon M. Chevalier. New York, 1934. Also published as *Man's Estate.* Translated by Alastair McDonald. London, 1948.
The Metamorphosis of the Gods. Translated by Stuart Gilbert. New York, 1960.
Picasso's Mask. Translated by June and Jacques Guicharnaud. New York, 1976.

The Psychology of Art (*The Museum Without Walls, The Artistic Act, The Twilight of the Absolute*). Translated by Stuart Gilbert. New York, 1949–1951.

The Royal Way. Translated by Stuart Gilbert. New York, 1935.

Saturn: An Essay on Goya. Translated by C. W. Chilton. New York and London, 1957.

The Temptation of the West. Translated by Robert Hollander. New York, 1961.

The Voices of Silence. Translated by Stuart Gilbert. New York, 1953.

The Walnut Trees of Altenburg. Translated by A. W. Fielding. London and Toronto, 1952.

BIOGRAPHICAL AND CRITICAL STUDIES

Blend, Charles D. *André Malraux: Tragic Humanist.* Columbus, Ohio, 1963.

Blumenthal, Gerda. *André Malraux: The Conquest of Dread.* Baltimore, 1960.

Boak, Denis. *André Malraux.* London, 1968.

Boisdeffre, Pierre de. *André Malraux.* Paris, 1952.

Carduner, Jean. *La création romanesque chez Malraux.* Paris, 1968.

de Courcel, Martine, ed. *Malraux: Life and Work.* New York and London, 1976.

Delhomme, Jeanne. *Temps et destin: Essai sur André Malraux.* Paris, 1955.

Domenach, Jean-Marie, and others. *Malraux.* Paris, 1979.

Dorenlot, Françoise E. *Malraux; ou, L'Unité de pensée.* Paris, 1970.

Duthuit, Georges. *Le musée inimaginable.* 3 vols. Paris, 1956.

Ellis, Elizabeth A. *André Malraux et le monde de la nature.* Paris, 1975.

Fallaize, Elizabeth. *Malraux: La voie royale.* London, 1982.

Fitch, Brian T. *Les deux univers romanesques d'André Malraux.* Paris, 1964.

Flanner, Janet. "The Human Condition." In her *Men and Monuments.* New York, 1957.

Frank, Joseph. "Malraux's Image of Man." In his *The Widening Gyre.* New Brunswick, N.J., 1963.

Frohock, W. M. *André Malraux and the Tragic Imagination.* Stanford, 1952.

Gaillard, Pol. *André Malraux.* Paris, 1970.

———. *Les critiques de notre temps et Malraux.* Paris, 1970.

Galante, Pierre. *Malraux.* Translated by Haakon Chevalier. New York, 1971.

Gannon, Edward. *The Honor of Being a Man: The World of André Malraux.* Chicago, 1957.

Gaulupeau, Serge. *André Malraux et la mort.* Paris, 1969.

Greenlee, James W. *Malraux's Heroes and History.* De Kalb, Ill., 1975.

Harris, Geoffrey T. *André Malraux: L'Ethique comme fonction de l'esthétique.* Paris, 1972.

Hartmann, Geoffrey H. *Malraux.* London and New York, 1960.

Hewitt, James Robert. *André Malraux.* New York, 1978.

Horvath, Violet M. *André Malraux: The Human Adventure.* New York and London, 1969.

Jenkins, Cecil. *André Malraux.* New York, 1972.

Kline, Thomas Jefferson. *André Malraux and the Metamorphosis of Death.* New York and London, 1973.

Lacouture, Jean. *André Malraux: Une vie dans le siècle.* Paris, 1973. Translated into English by Alan Sheridan as *André Malraux.* New York, 1975.

Langlois, Walter G. *André Malraux: The Indochina Adventure.* New York, 1966.

Lewis, R. W. B., ed. *Malraux: A Collection of Critical Essays.* Englewood Cliffs, N.J., 1964.

Madsen, Axel. *Malraux: A Biography.* New York, 1976.

Malraux, Clara. *Les bruits de nos pas.* 6 vols. *Apprendre à vivre,* vol. 1; *Nos vingt ans,* vol. 2; *Les combats et les jeux,* vol. 3; *Voici que vient l'été,* vol. 4; *La fin et le commencement,* vol. 5; *Et pourtant j'étais libre,* vol. 6. Paris, 1963–79.

———. *Memoirs.* Abridged and translated by Patrick O'Brien. New York, 1967. First two volumes only.

Marion, Denis. *André Malraux.* Paris, 1970.

Mauriac, Claude. *Malraux; ou, Le mal du héros.* Paris, 1946.

Moatti, Christiane. *"La condition humaine" d'André Malraux: Poétique du roman d'aprés l'étude du manuscrit.* Paris, 1983.

———. *Le prédicateur et ses masques: Les personnages d'André Malraux.* Paris, 1987.

Nouvelle revue française 295 (July 1977).

Payne, Robert. *A Portrait of André Malraux.* Englewood Cliffs, N.J., 1970.

Picon, Gaëtan. *André Malraux.* Paris, 1945.

————. *Malraux par lui-même.* Paris, 1953.

Righter, William. *The Rhetorical Hero: An Essay on the Aesthetics of André Malraux.* New York, 1964.

Tannery, Claude. *Malraux: L'Agnostique absolu; ou, La métamorphose comme loi du monde.* Paris, 1985.

Tarica, Ralph. *Imagery in the Novels of André Malraux.* Rutherford, N.J., London, and Toronto, 1980.

Thompson, Brian, and Carl A. Viggiani, eds. *Witnessing Malraux: Visions and Re-visions.* Middletown, Conn., 1984.

Vandegans, André. *La jeunesse littéraire d'André Malraux: Essai su l'inspiration farfelue.* Paris, 1964.

Wilkinson, David. *Malraux: An Essay in Political Criticism.* Cambridge, Mass., 1967.

Yale French Studies 18 (Winter 1957). Entitled *Passion & Intellect; or, André Malraux.*

BIBLIOGRAPHIES

Langlois, Walter G. *André Malraux: Essai de bibliographie des études en langue anglaise consacrées à André Malraux (1924–70).* Paris, 1972.

————. *André Malraux: Malraux Criticism in English, 1924–70.* Paris, 1972.

Talvart, Hector, and Joseph Place. *Bibliographie des auteurs modernes de langue française,* vol. 13. Paris, 1956. Pp. 176–195.

PAPERS

Malraux's papers are at the Bibliothèque Nationale and the Fonds Jacques Doucet, in Paris; there are also some papers at the Harry Ransom Humanities Research Center at the University of Texas, Austin.

W. M. FROHOCK
Revised and updated by DORIS L. EDER

MARCEL AYMÉ

(1902–1967)

SINCE THE TIME of Cardinal Richelieu, France has honored its greatest writers by electing them to the Académie française. There have been some notable exceptions, of course, such as Molière in the seventeenth century and Marcel Aymé in the twentieth. In the latter case the fault was not that of the Académie; Aymé simply refused to be a candidate, just as he had refused all other public honors. He was a modest man who disliked pretense and looked upon official awards as either undeserved or superfluous, and therefore useless in any case. He valued friendship and loyalty above all else, and he lived without fear and without envy, writing in absolute freedom exactly what he wished to write.

In a country where most writers belong to the intellectual classes, Aymé did not conform to the general pattern. He was not shaped by the classical and humanistic disciplines, or fashioned according to the usual university mold; and he steadfastly refused to be considered an intellectual or to belong to any literary school or movement. His experience of the world and his transposition of this experience were always essentially pragmatic and strikingly individualistic, but he appeals to readers of all kinds because of his vivid and unusual style, his extraordinary ability to put words through their paces, and especially because of the fresh and unexpected quality of his vision. His imagination created a new and wonderful world that allows a momentary escape from the one we know. Then we can come back to reality somehow refreshed and perhaps see it in a new light, and therefore appreciate it better.

Some see in Marcel Aymé an amusing author of improbable and risqué tales, whereas more serious readers and critics describe him at times as an indulgent moralist whose work is a mixture of irony and tenderness or, on the contrary, as a bitter spectator of the human comedy whose caustic humor spares neither men nor institutions, however sacred. He has been called a leftist because of his anticlericalism and his attacks on smug bourgeois conformists; others have accused him of fascist leanings because of his friendship with Louis-Ferdinand Céline and Robert Brasillach. The truth is that he cannot be labeled or pigeonholed. He wrote under the inspiration of the moment, and moments are many and varied.

Marcel Aymé was born on 28 March 1902 in Joigny, where his father worked as a blacksmith. Because of his mother's death he was raised by his grandparents and his aunt, spending most of his youth in and near Dôle, a small town of the Franche-Comté region. There he successfully completed secondary studies at the local lycée that left him vivid, if unpleasant, memories.

After his military service Aymé went to some of the larger cities, where he tried a variety of trades and professions, including journalism. He failed as a reporter, perhaps because he was too outspoken, but the experience proved valuable, for through it he discovered that he enjoyed writing. Later, while convalescing from an illness, he turned to fiction and, in 1926, brought out his first novel, *Brûlebois.* His early works, largely based on childhood memories, were novels about small towns (*Brûlebois*) or the country (*La table-aux-crevés,* 1929; translated as *The Hollow Field,* 1933). The success of *La jument verte* in 1933 (translated as *The Green Mare,* 1955) enabled Aymé to make a career of his avocation and to devote his time to composing short stories, novels, essays, and plays. He also became connected with the world of the motion picture: several of his works were adapted for the screen, and he collaborated in writing the French script for Walt Disney's *The Living Desert.* His adaptation of Arthur Miller's *The Crucible* was filmed in France under the title of *Les sorcières de Salem* (1955).

Aymé had other contacts with American milieus, and even visited the United States in 1950 when, after the considerable success obtained by *The Barkeep of Blémont,* the translation of *Uranus,* he was invited by *Collier's* magazine to spend a few months in that country.

He returned to Paris, which had become his home, but although he became a well-known figure in his beloved Montmartre, he always retained something of the Franc-Comtois peasant. Unaffected by his growing fame and the realization that he was one of the accepted leaders in the world of fiction, Aymé continued to be unassuming, rather shy, and always extremely kind and generous. When he died at the age of sixty-five, on 14 October 1967, the press unanimously mourned the passing of a great writer and a good man.

Some critics have described Aymé as essentially a fabulist. He did, in fact, like Jean de La Fontaine and Charles Perrault, often use allegory and fable to speak of the world and its inhabitants. His *Contes du chat perché* (1939; translated as *The Wonderful Farm,* 1951) is a collection of ironical tales of children and animals on a typical French farm. Through the device of a nonrealistic, purely imaginative story, the fabulist pokes fun at prejudices and conventions, and indirectly, almost casually, points up a lesson.

Although Aymé's world is not the "comédie aux cent actes divers" (the hundred-act comedy) that we find in La Fontaine, we nevertheless can discover in his animal kingdom the image of a human world with the stratification, preconceived ideas, clichés, and pomposity of men engaged in the postures of social relations. To that world and society children bring the freshness of doubt. They are not convinced by the teaching of adults. They do not believe that the donkey is stupid, the wolf necessarily bad, or the panther something other than an overgrown, playful cat. The adults are wrong when they attach labels to God's creatures; yet, at the same time, they are not entirely wrong, since even the worst prejudices and platitudes have some basis in truth.

Some of Aymé's fables and apologues suggest strongly that people should not aim beyond their talents. This is one of the several meanings of "Les boeufs" (The Oxen), in which the good little girls Delphine and Marinette impressed by a traditional speech on the benefits of education, want the oxen to reap those benefits. They are children and can be excused for not understanding that what may be appropriate in some cases is not necessarily appropriate in others. As for the white ox who takes seriously to the idea of learning, he is like the main characters in Aymé's unfinished novel *Bouvard et Pécuchet,* who accumulate knowledge without making any headway in the direction of wisdom or culture. Although somewhat proud and ambitious, he has been a good, hard-working ox. With his introduction to the world of books and arithmetic, however, his inherent faults begin to develop. It is dangerous to be too proud and too ambitious, or to acquire an education unsuited to one's real capacities. The children are flexible enough to realize their mistake and, after the white ox has found refuge in a circus, they carefully refrain from teaching the other animals to read, for they have learned that oxen do not benefit from education. But are their elders equally wise? It would seem that there are many who still do not understand that what may be helpful for a future engineer can perhaps prove useless or even harmful for an ox; and so countless bovine students continue to ponder problems of the "if two faucets fill a hundred-gallon container . . ." type in countless classrooms all over the world.

"Le petit coq noir" (The Little Black Cock) is a fable that tells of the revolt of the poultry against their masters. The well-meaning, but naive and conceited, little black cock leads the other barnyard denizens to accept as true the fox's promise that they will acquire teeth if they live in the forest, far away from their owners. The conclusion of the story, of course, is the triumph of the truism that hen's teeth are indeed rare. We behold the return of the prodigal fowls, or at least of those which have not been eaten by the fox, and witness the fate of the leader of the insurrection, who ends his life as a "coq au vin." The apologue points out the moral that there is no safer—or surer—happiness than to be eaten by one's masters. But the real lesson of the fable, insofar as there is a lesson, is perhaps that a leader should not lightly expose his troops to complete annihilation.

In "Le nain" (The Dwarf, 1934), another of Aymé's tales, the dwarf of the Barnaboum Circus, in defiance of the laws of medicine, suddenly grows to normal size and can no longer win easy applause as a freak. As a normal man he has to work to deserve applause. He wants to be something more than what he was as a dwarf. He wants to be a great artist, a great performer. But he fails. It is not enough to decide to be great. Talent and a sense of responsibility are also necessary.

Some of Aymé's longer works could also be considered fables. The author himself stated that *Gustalin* (1937), for instance, is a fable of field mice and city mice. The city mice—Victor and Sarah Jouquier—pay a visit to their country cousins, Hyacinthe and Marthe. Sarah tries to bring to the village the ways of the city. She overpays the maid; she invites villagers to tea; she has literary and philosophical discussions with the curé. She instructs Marthe as to the nature of her rights as a woman; introduces her to the joys of tea, idle talk, Ping-Pong, and the phonograph; and advises her to rebel against her environment. She persuades the country woman that women, all women, must be constantly on the alert to protect themselves against men who are all too ready to "wallow in their lives," letting their mates do all the work, carry all the responsibility. Marthe, who was unsatisfied but at least resigned, now becomes a kind of Emma Bovary, a deeply frustrated woman ready to exchange her husband and children for the mirage of comfortable city living. In short, unintelligent or insensitive people who fail to understand what is or is not appropriate can cause fully as much harm as those who deliberately set out to do mischief.

In another novel, *Aller retour* (Round Trip, 1927), a small, timid, unhappily married bureaucrat, Justin Galuchey, suffers a face wound in an accident. He shaves his mustache and with his change of expression acquires a different personality and outlook on life. He becomes bold, speaks with authority, gambles, and finally succeeds in winning the love of Raymonde, a good-looking, rich young woman for whose sake he prepares to leave his ugly, stupid wife. Unfortunately his uncle, who does not like the idea of Justin's seducing Raymonde, shows her a ridiculous portrait of Justin and his wife on their wedding day. That photograph is enough to determine the "return trip" of *Aller retour.* Justin, faced with what he was and what he still is, takes refuge in flight and returns to the bleak, monotonous life he had known before the accident. He has not truly changed.

The final lesson of *Aller retour* notwithstanding, this book and many of Aymé's stories teach that one's nature is often the result of a certain physical appearance, superficial perhaps, yet much more than skin deep since it is the source of the image that the outer world has of us. That image has a profound influence on our destinies. It was, after all, because of an accident of appearance that Cyrano de Bergerac could not imagine himself accepted as the great lover he really was; it would seem true that in order to play a part convincingly, if only to express one's inner self, one must look the part. Clothes often make the man.

In *La belle image* (1941; translated as *The Second Face,* 1951), Aymé tells the story of Raoul Cérusier, who has quite suddenly been blessed, or cursed, with a new appearance, that of a young and handsome man. Soon he develops an entirely new personality, the reflection of the effect he now produces on the people around him. Habit and security are devoutly to be sought, however, and finally Cérusier, like the hero of *Aller retour,* goes back to his former stable and unadventurous existence, happy to retrieve his own middle-aged, homely face.

In the course of a human life there may be an opportunity for a radical transformation of one's existence, but in general men prefer to avoid change. When forced into it by some ironic turn of fate, they may find that their old ways were happier or, at least, more comfortable. This does not mean that change is impossible for everyone, or even that it is ever too late to try. Dreams and ambition, however, are not enough; one must also have courage, talent, and a willingness to accept the consequences of the change and to construct another life based on a firm belief in the reality of one's new existence.

Aymé's theater also offers moral lessons. *Vogue la galère,*[1] for instance, takes up in a slightly different way the theme of change, of freedom, and of the tendency we have to sacrifice them for the animal comfort of knowing what is expected of us and what the next day will bring. In this play mutinous slaves who have listened to an idealistic young Protestant, Lazare de Barrals, a nobleman condemned to the galleys for religious reasons, are unable to follow his incomprehensible ideals or to control their elemental passions. They are happier when one of their number enslaves them anew, and they readily do from habit and fear what they could not bring themselves to do in the name of freedom and human dignity. The idealistic young man is sacrificed as an offering to the gods of hypocrisy, and will be executed at the same time as the dispossessed tyrants against whom he led the rebellion. The play, besides being a commentary on man's reactions to freedom and change, suggests that a society cannot subsist without discipline, common sense, and a kind of moderate conservatism. The idealism of Barrals, who preaches friendship and brotherhood, not only dooms his mutiny to failure because of his basic ineffectiveness; worse than that, it nearly causes the loss of the galley with all on board. By his well-intentioned bungling, the young man causes more bloodshed and death than the brutally efficient convict who finally takes over and salvages the ship and its crew.

In another play, another dramatic fable, Aymé shows us that miracle workers and scientists can go wrong if they pursue their course blindly. Valentin, in *Les oiseaux de lune* (*Moonbirds,* 1956), has the amazing faculty of changing people into birds; but with the new moon some of his miracles miscarry, and the victims are changed into snails instead of birds. Intoxicated with power, Valentin would like to continue his experiments, for he has lost sight of everything but the interesting aspects of his achievements, and, as one of the other characters points out, his "honnêtes métamorphoses" are ruthless and inexcusable, as senseless as the atom bomb.

Aymé consistently derided "progress" seen in terms of increasingly efficient means of destruction or increasingly ugly cities where men become numbers and disappear into poured-

[1] *Vogue la galère* (Come What May! 1944) is a play on words. It translates as "come what may," or "let the chips fall where they will." The verb *voguer* means to row or sail. The play deals with the uncertainty of mutiny and command, and also takes place on a galley, so that the title can also be interpreted literally as "row the galley" or, considering *vogue* as a subjunctive, "let the galley sail on."

concrete beehives. His last play, *La convention Belzébir* (The Belzébir Decree, 1967), takes us into the future, to a time when men wealthy enough to buy a hunting license can kill other men, and do so with the government's blessing and society's admiring approval. The absurd and revolting laws of that future time are finally abrogated when the government is forced to declare war and everyone—rich and poor—can kill with impunity.

Men as individuals or men in society, whether through ignorance, stupidity, malice, or selfishness, can deform or flout certain natural laws, and in so doing engender suffering. Most of Aymé's fables contain this truth. He presents these natural laws, which should govern human relations and which must enter into account if men and societies are to be saved, in a cosmos often quite different from that of our daily lives. Indeed, the supernatural and the mechanisms of science fiction and of surrealism are frequently the chief ingredients of his universe. His characters move in a world where reality extends beyond the limits we usually assign to it. There animals and human beings undergo varied and striking metamorphoses. A little white hen is asked by Delphine and Marinette to play the part of an elephant, since there is no elephant available on the French farm that is their home; the hen does it with such vigorous sincerity that in some essential way she really becomes an elephant, creating practical problems as she moves about the house. The little girls, as well as their animals, travel freely in the realm of imagination. If they wish sincerely to become a donkey or a horse, they wake up to find the transformation accomplished. Their thoughts and concepts give shape to the world in which they move. If they paint a four-legged animal and grant it only two legs, the live animal becomes a biped also. Oxen one day stop existing except for their horns because that is all the girls have painted. Creatures repeatedly change size with respect to each other because the young artists have represented "a horse not quite half as big as a rooster" or a dog of absolutely monstrous size.

There is a reality created by the artist that is independent of our everyday experience. In "Oscar et Erick," a story in the collection *En arrière* (Backward, 1950), Aymé tells of an Icelandic painter who is derided and ruined by his countrymen because he paints cacti and banana trees, which they have never seen and therefore consider absurdities. The academic, literal people around him insist that a painter has no right to represent anything he does not actually see, whereas Oscar believes that "if God had created only what He saw, He would not have created anything." The super-reality seen by the gifted artist may very well be reality itself. In Aymé's world supernatural beings exist and mingle with "ordinary" creatures in a society where everyone accepts this situation as normal. A young centaur, for instance, falls in love with Mademoiselle Godin, a little provincial bourgeoise, and they become engaged ("Fiançailles"). In rural France a divinity of the waters, a supernatural being called La Vouivre, is seen walking through the woods accompanied by her attendant serpents; but she also stops off at the local café, as would anyone in need of refreshment, and she makes love to Arsène, a young peasant who does not believe in the supernatural (*La vouivre,* 1943; translated as *The Fable and the Flesh,* 1949).

Fictional characters often develop a life of their own in Aymé's world. They move in and out of reality to mingle with living beings. An anonymous burglar escapes from between the pages of a detective story and accidentally finds his way to the house of his long-lost parents, but, having forgotten to ask them his real name, he goes back into "an excellent detective story and various great novels of love and hatred" ("La clé sous le paillasson" [The Key Under the Doormat], in *Le nain*). Other characters meet their author, and at a literary cocktail party one of them, rejuvenated by a beauty treatment, is so attractive that the publisher falls in love with her ("Le romancier Martin" [Martin the Novelist], in *Derrière chez Martin* [Behind Martin's], 1938). (Woody Allen may or may not have read Aymé's stories, but in some ways he is a kindred spirit of the French author: in *Side Effects* (1981) he tells of a college professor who teaches a course on *Madame Bovary* and is so interested in his subject that he actually gets into the book, to the dismay of his students, who cannot understand how he happens to appear in the novel.)

The miracles that occur so frequently in Aymé's world are not all of the same kind or of the same duration. Some are pseudo-miracles like the "death" and "resurrection" of Messelon, the old Republican anticlerical mayor of *The Green Mare,* who comes back to life when he has been kissed by the statue of Marianne.

At other times the miracle is in a sense a real one but stems from the poetic vision and deep compassion of the author. Such is the lovely moment in "Le paon" (The Peacock) when the ridiculous young pig who has been starving himself to death in an effort to be as beautiful as the peacock is assured by the children that he need diet no longer because he has already reached his goal; he makes a tremendous effort and, as he looks over his shoulder, "the rainbow suddenly came down and rested on him in colors so tender, but also so vivid, that the peacock's feathers would have seemed grayish in comparison." Such is also the ending of the story "Les bottes de sept lieues" (The Seven-League Boots), in which a little boy has managed to buy a pair of boots for which the rich boys of the neighborhood have tried to outbid him, because all the children think the boots are magic seven-league boots. At night, when he is supposed to be asleep, he puts them on and, with absolute faith in their supernatural properties, a faith that the reader might not have shared until now, he leaves for the ends of the earth in order to bring back a present to his old and tired mother, a large bouquet of the first rays of the sun that he lays on her bed, where they light up her careworn face and make it seem less weary.

The miracles are not all of the same duration and need not be permanent, for Aymé often abandons the supernatural as soon as he has made his point. Delphine and Marinette, in spite of their many adventures, always return to being real little girls on a real farm. The man who could travel through walls suddenly finds this strange faculty gone, and he is trapped. The hero of *The Second Face* eventually must return to his old face, to his middle-aged wife, and to his house slippers.

Reality exists and exercises its rights, but even when people and events seem most ordinary, their existence may have more meaning than meets the eye. Aymé created certain characters who seem quite real and move in realistic situations, but whose role is nevertheless quasi-allegorical. Perhaps the most striking of these is the little barber in the novel *Travelingue* (1941; translated as *The Miraculous Barber,* 1951). A seemingly unimportant member of the common people, he is in fact the power behind the government. He summons ministers to his home, distributes rewards and decorations, and settles financial matters of international scope. This vivid example of a petit bourgeois, with his colorful speech and pat political thinking, controls the destiny of the nation. There is a strong suggestion here that society does not obey its apparent leaders but reacts to obscure, unknown powers. Reality is not the appearance that things and events present; reality is *l'absurde.*

Aymé was primarily concerned with man and with the society and relationships man has created. Whether he presented his characters in a world of fantasy and the supernatural, where imagination rules and makes its own laws, or whether, on the contrary, he had them move in the ordinary world we know, he always expressed through them his interest in mankind. He looked about him and described what he saw, often in very amusing terms, sometimes with caustic and bitter irony or under the guise of "black humor." In his first books his verve was exercised mostly at the expense of peasants and artisans, castigating the mores of those who live in small towns and villages. Even in his later works (*The Green Mare, The Fable and the Flesh*), country people were the target of a good deal of his banter.

Aymé showed peasants as simple, patient, and resigned human beings preoccupied with hard work and unrefined amusements like drinking and lusting. They were not exactly avaricious but, by necessity, parsimonious; they did not like to throw away money or clothes. Their women, in general, were neither beautiful nor very clean, but worked almost as hard as they did, sometimes harder, like the "dévorante" (devouring) Germaine Mindeur (*The Fable and the Flesh*), who knocked off "the work of several steam engines." They were usually honest, although peasant servants occasionally took some of their masters' food home to their parents. They were creatures of instinct, endowed with minds often led by their flesh, but most of them were, nevertheless, "fairly virtuous."

Their children were precocious in sexual matters, but neither the parents nor the public authorities were overly concerned, since real property values were not involved. Aymé himself was amused by the feeling expressed today that young people have become excessively free in their manners and actions. As he said in the last article he wrote (*Le Figaro Littéraire,* October 1967), this has always been true among the children of the peasant and working classes.

Aymé gently ridiculed peasants, or their wives, who had ambitions for their children; who were proud of their academic success; who wanted them to become civil servants, teachers, army officers, or tax collectors; and who expressed their peasant aspirations in bourgeois terms.

Sunday in the country was a day for socializing, for wearing shoes rather than sabots, and for showing off one's finest clothes. As for religion, it was considered suitable for women and children. Catholicism for a good many of these peasants was somewhat like a farm. The characters of *The Hollow Field* and *The Fable and the Flesh* imagine God as the owner who distributes the work. The saints are the team leaders. The Virgin is a good woman who is pleasant and outgoing in spite of her Son's re-

nown. The Demon is symbolized by a cabaret with a nickelodeon. Jesus is not easy to place in the setting of a model farm, and at least one of the characters would have liked to ignore the problem He presents.

The peasants believe in God, and they all go to church on important occasions. In general, however, their minds turn to the immediate problems of the moment, for these are real and much more certain than those they may have to overcome in an afterlife. In moments of lesser stress, peasants are not averse to turning to the supernatural for help, or to calling on religion in order to satisfy private interests.

Religion, in short, is a reality to be recognized, interpreted, and used according to one's sex, social position, and needs. It is also a force to be reckoned with in all phases of political life. Politics at the village level, while usually possessed of religious overtones, also represents, more often than not, a family quarrel. It is a *chamaille,* or feud, rather than any ideological struggle, that pits clan against clan (Mindeurs against Museliers in *The Fable and the Flesh,* Malorets against Haudouins in *The Green Mare,* etc.). How inane village politics can be is brought out through the ironical contrast between the energy expended by some villagers and the unimportance of the issues involved.

When the vicissitudes of Aymé's career led him to leave the country scenes of his childhood for work in the city, he observed other types of people quite different from the peasants and small-town workmen he had known. His writing was to reflect the change in his surroundings. From country settings he passed to stories with the city as a background; and, as he began to concentrate on the bourgeoisie, his attitude became more caustic. Unlike Guy de Maupassant, who also had satirized both peasants and city dwellers, Aymé did not create a cohesive universe based on a naturalistic and pessimistic point of view. He merely described the people he saw and remembered.

In such works as *Le moulin de la sourdine* (1936; translated as *The Secret Stream,* 1953) and *Uranus* (1948; translated as *The Barkeep of Blémont,* 1950), Aymé dealt with the petite bourgeoisie of small towns; in *Maison basse* (1935; translated as *The House of Men,* 1952), *The Miraculous Barber,* and *Le chemin des écoliers* (1946; translated as *The Transient Hour,* 1948), he dealt with that of big cities. There dull people meet and discuss dull subjects. They strive to attain "useful" kinds of perfection. They marry without love and without joy. The bourgeois marriage is a marriage of reason, and the young people's principal duty is to save money. In this class of society, a young wife looks upon marriage as a Christian obligation to be met after a girl has earned her school certificate. Bourgeois parents have been known to put money above their children's happiness and to consider their daughter's marriage a business transaction that must be evaluated in terms of profit and loss. This attitude does not make for love between generations, but it creates a sort of understanding. A young woman, for instance, calmly takes for granted the unconcealed dislike of her parents-in-law because she is aware of their concept of marriage (*The House of Men*). Divorce in a rich bourgeois family can be a catastrophe, not because of the emotional suffering it entails but because it displaces money.

Members of the bourgeoisie are conformists whose practice of religion is conditioned by their ambition and grows with their prosperity. They have the cult of external appearances and deem it better to be well thought of by one's concierge than by the Creator. Their hypocrisy, from childhood to old age, was one of Aymé's favorite targets. In the play *Clérambard* (1950) the old lawyer, Galuchon, hides a photograph of a prostitute in his volume of canon law. Three times a week this paragon of respectability secretly visits La Langouste, a prostitute. In *The Miraculous Barber,* Lasquin, the industrialist, hides the photographs and letters of his mistress in an album labeled "Taxe à la production."

The bourgeois, and for that matter almost any Frenchman who owns anything, likes his possessions. He bemoans their loss or his bad investments longer than the death of his loved ones or the defloration of his daughter. His inordinate love of money is ridiculed in many of Aymé's works. The landlord, an incarnation of bourgeois rapacity, is often the butt of the author's sarcasm. In "L'Huissier" (The Bailiff) a character is sent back to Earth after his death and is given the chance to save his soul by performing one good deed. At last he is successful and returns to Heaven, his mission accomplished: he, a process server by profession, has died a second time, while defending a poor woman against the greedy brutality of her landlord and shouting, "Down with landlords!" God is impressed.

Middle-class snobbery and pseudo-intellectualism are also strongly satirized in *The Miraculous Barber* and *Le confort intellectuel* (Intellectual Comfort, 1949). Because of an affair with a lady of artistic tastes, M. Lasquin, in *The Miraculous Barber,* adopts a Freudian vocabulary and consequently fits into the bourgeois salons where people indulge in foolish discussions of Sigmund Freud and Karl Marx. Anaïs Coiffard, M. Lepage's governess, in *Le confort intellectuel,* is the archetype of today's intellectual bourgeoise. Her speech is a parody of the language of contemporary snobs who speak of Faulkner, Picasso, Kafka, de Sade, and others as "formidable" and "madly beautiful."

As for the aristocracy, whether old or new, wealthy or poor, it is only occasionally the subject of Aymé's satire. *Clérambard* shows the ridiculous aspects of a class that has outlived its usefulness and feeds on illusions and glorious memories. Hector de Clérambard has established in his "château" a factory for knitted goods that is as unrealistic as the vision he will have of Saint Francis. He is the only aristocrat fully portrayed in Aymé's work, but other members of his class make fleeting appearances. The Marquis and Marquise de Valorin and their son-in-law, the Baron de Cappadoce, are seen in the short story "Fiançailles." Very proper, they address each other as "vous," and the bemonocled marquis shows a poise worthy of his station in society at the critical moment when a young centaur calls him "Papa." These members of the nobility, however, are only minor characters. Like others, such as the Baroness de Fanfol in the play *Les maxibules* (1962) or the Countess Piédange in *The Miraculous Barber,* they are briefly sketched or are simply mentioned as members of the fauna surrounding the protagonists. They seem irresponsible and useless, but the fact of their having a title is incidental. Aymé did not systematically satirize the aristocracy. He almost always dealt with representatives of the peasant class and of the "petite" and "grande" bourgeoisie.

Aymé also turned his attention to members of various professions. As could be expected, clerics were natural targets for his irony, as they had been for a long line of satirists before him.

There are two kinds of priests in Aymé's world, the strong and the weak. The strong are the virile "décrasseurs de paroisse," those who try to wash away the dirt of their parish. Such is the curé of Claquebue (*The Green Mare*), a man so honest and indiscreet as to be thoroughly impossible at times. His kind is hard to live with, but the sensible farmers prefer strong clerics to the "saint rétrécis" (shrunken saints). The peasants are willing to accept a real man, a real priest who knows how to eat and walk and tell a few lies, and who can put the fear of God into the womenfolk.

The second category, far more bitingly satirized, comprises thin, lymphatic, and bookish would-be men, as exemplified by the intellectual curé in *Gustalin* whose monotonous voice and basic incompetence exasperate the farmer Hyacinthe. This poor priest, a virtual stranger in his parish, participates in lengthy abstract discussions but is unaware that the roof of his church needs repairs. Other "weak" priests are the worldly clerics who consider the truths of the Church primarily as symbols and see in Catholic ritual only the outward signs of a kind of moral discipline. This category also includes those members of the hierarchy, often in exalted positions, who encourage the sort of sterilized Catholicism found in the writings of certain so-called Catholic or Jansenist authors whose "liberalism" allows for better relations with heretics and freethinkers.

The army fares a little better than the clergy in Aymé's world. His *adjudants* follow the well-known pattern of the loud, slow-witted, and tyrannical career men whose thankless task it is to train the soldiers and, by dint of drills and penalties, make them into the organism that the commanding officers demand. The *adjudant,* like the master sergeant, his American counterpart, is an easy target of ridicule. He has been stereotyped by countless storytellers and, as delineated by Aymé, he runs true to type.

The *adjudant* is the link between the working army and its leaders, chief of whom, of course, are the generals. General d'Amandine (*Le boeuf clandestin* [The Clandestine Steak], 1939), a man whose "undisputed importance" always places him above common opinion, makes such statements as "Give me two weeks of dictatorship and I'll decentralize France for you with some well-placed kicks in the pants."

Adjudants and generals, the noncoms and the higher-ups at either end of the military chain of command, come in for their share of ridicule, but are nevertheless treated with sympathy and a certain gentleness. Aymé saw them as simple souls, the wooden and unimaginative victims of a particular kind of training. There is no evil in them other than that which is inherent in the well-constructed mechanism—unfortunately a lethal one—of which they are the highly specialized parts.

This is not quite the case with the administrators, bureaucrats, and *fonctionnaires* (civil servants) who are frequently the butt of Aymé's satire. A bureaucrat is often ridiculous, the more so when he regards his job as a sacred mission, "feeling a religious pleasure in handling papers, distributing his signatures like blessings." At once pretentious and inane, M. Lécuyer, the assistant office manager in "Le passe-muraille" ("The Walker Through Walls," 1943), makes "sweeping reforms" that consist merely in changing the introductory terms of a business letter into a "more American" form. A civil servant behind his window is "the dog of rich people and of big corporations." In times of war he profits from the black market; in times of peace he is open to corruption; at all times he is petty and unpleasant.

The various representatives of the law were bound to be disliked by a nonconformist like Aymé. He found them lacking imagination and ideals and deplored their attachment to "realities." In *Moonbirds,* when certain human beings have been changed into birds, the men who investigate the case are more interested in finding a corpus delicti for the legal necessities of the case than in learning the real fate of those who have disappeared.

Rural policemen (*gardes-champêtres* and *gendarmes*), more often than not, are simple souls, blind to the supernatural, who demand only that property and authority be respected. The *gendarme's* morality is essentially a matter of appearances. If he sees a centaur, he is shocked, because he feels that somehow the centaur is making a mockery of law and order. Fantasy and humor must be excluded from the society he understands, for they sap the very foundation of the minutely structured—and thus easily recognized—organization that is at once the reason for his power and its safeguard. A city policeman, on the other hand, is more responsible and more involved than his rural counterparts in real problems of right and wrong. His position and authority confer upon him certain privileges and legitimize his very mistakes. He has the legal right to be wrong. Thus policemen can do whatever they wish and can give a suspect the third degree without regard for his rights. In "Le faux policier" (The False Policeman, 1947) a man is shown spitting out several of his teeth after an interrogation because he has committed the unforgivable crime of impersonating a police officer. The fact that he is actually guilty of more than one murder is incidental.

In Aymé's books politicians are often qualified for their jobs not by their talents but by their capacity for drink. Municipal elections are settled in cafés and through the influence of local barkeepers. Wine and politics command one another, and are inextricably intertwined, "budding and blooming on one another. Wine led to politics and politics to wine, in a generous and raucous symbiosis."

All parties and professional politicians are equally bad or ridiculous. Aymé, although he probably preferred *républicains* to *cléricaux, laïques* to *calotins* ("priest lovers"), *radicaux* (not radical in the English meaning of the term but fairly conservative, albeit anticlerical) to *réactionnaires,* made fun of both extremes in his country novels. In the later works rightists and leftists received equal treatment. Aymé's detachment caused him to look down upon the weaknesses of all. In *Le nain* and *Le vin de Paris* (Paris Wine, 1947), he showed how radical and conservative candidates for the municipal council often present the same illusory platform. Communist militants are as bad as rich conservatives or reactionaries. They are so confident, they are so certain about everything, that they are no longer men and cannot recognize the common man when they see him.

In *The Barkeep of Blémont* there is an intellectual Communist, Jourdan, who defends and even exalts a criminal's violent and irresponsible acts, calling them a magnificent "revolt" against his lot. Jourdan plays politics without the slightest consideration for human values or the fate of the working classes. He is hateful and hated by all, even by his "comrades."

If politicians are bad, those charged with administering justice are worse. To begin with, people in authority are ready, as a matter of principle, to place respectability before justice. In *Silhouette du scandale* (1938) Aymé emphasizes that juries are less apt to punish murder than threats to private property. The very people whose duty it should be to protect the lives and interests of the collectivity sometimes commit the most serious inequities. Such is the bigoted sheriff in the play *Louisiane* (1961), who neatly and legally kills a black man for the "crime" of being loved by a white woman and then states that he has saved him from being lynched.

In Aymé's many commentaries on human "justice" there is also the suggestion that in our society men may be convicted not because of their crimes but because of their brutish appearance, their name, or their reputation. In *The Secret Stream,* when Madame Marguet's maid is found in a pool of blood, mutilated and stripped of her clothes, everyone immediately suspects the ugly "monster" Troussequin, whom Maître Marguet had employed as a house painter on that day. Troussequin is arrested. The *commissaire* (constable) and the examining magistrate have already decided that he is guilty and are prepared to prove it.

Judges are terrified by whatever might harm their career. The story "Dermuche" makes this point. When, through a miracle, a condemned man is replaced in his cell by a newborn babe, the representatives of the law see in this wonder only a "deplorable example" to prospective criminals, an easy (!) way of escaping the consequences of one's crime. Miracles cannot be allowed to interfere with the law and its administrators. The innocent baby is duly executed, and the final irony is that justice miscarries doubly, since the lawyer later finds the "assassinated" victims very much alive.

In *Le confort intellectuel* mention is made of two perjured witnesses arrested not for their crime of perjury but for their "fascist" opinions. Ironically, it is this concern with their political leanings (and not the innocence of the man they have denounced) that finally causes justice to triumph.

But it is the play entitled *La tête des autres* (Other People's Heads, 1952) that contains the most violent and bitter satire against those who administer "justice" in courts of law where the guilt or innocence of a defendant seems to be totally irrelevant as brilliant lawyers compete for the plaudits of the audience in a frightful contest, a lethal game played for the head of the accused. The protectors of society appear as cynical and venal sycophants. The policeman, who takes pride in arresting a suspect, and the district attorney, who takes pride in his power to sway a jury, come to consider the verdict a personal triumph or defeat. A murder trial is a tournament of eloquence during which opposing lawyers revel in flamboyant oratory. Each has a coterie of admirers and graciously accepts their congratulations after playing the game or presenting the show.

Although magistrates and lawyers have been portrayed by French authors ever since the Middle Ages, their profession has certainly not been the only one satirized. The disciples of Hippocrates have consistently come in for their share of ridicule. Aymé too found doctors amusing and, like Molière, mocked the technical jargon, the posturing, and the pompous phrases they often use to impress their patients and conceal their own ignorance. He portrayed a profession in which ability and knowledge are much less important than the patronage of influential people. The "good" doctors are those who prescribe expensive remedies and uphold the values of society by calling "insane" a man like Clérambard who shows "an abnormal regression of the ownership instinct." Like Molière's doctors they believe in authority and refuse to accept any phenomenon not attested by medical writings. If they have not read of the existence of green mares, they will refuse to admit that a green mare exists even after they have seen it; and since no one grows after the age of twenty-five, they suppress all information about the case of the Barnaboum Circus dwarf who began to grow when he was thirty-five.

Aymé saw doctors as possibly dangerous, through ignorance rather than malice and in proportion to the prestige they enjoy. He considered specialists more of a peril than other doctors, and psychiatrists the most frightening of all.

There is often this type of progression in Aymé's satire. When he spoke of the world of education, for instance, he was relatively gentle in his treatment of primary-grade teachers, naive and honest *instituteurs* like Humblot (*The Fable and the Flesh*), who liked children, his job, gardening, fishing, and the Republic. Secondary-school teachers, on the other hand, he depicted as prejudiced and intolerant petty tyrants ready to fight and hate over the pronunciation of Latin words (-*us* or -*ous*), students' marks, and the importance of their subject compared with those taught by their colleagues. They strive for "fairness" and are apt to build up minor incidents into a Dreyfus case. They tend to live in an unrealistic world, seeing life in purely literary terms. As he leaves the subway at the Clichy station, Josserand, a character in *The House of Men,* thinks of himself as the poet Vergil coming out of Hades. He finds it difficult to answer his seventeen-year-old daughter's questions about love because his own concept of love is conditioned, in equal parts, by his admiration for the great classical tragedies and by his honestly conservative prejudices. He thinks in quotations, favoring Latin texts over those written in French.

Teachers know their subjects and teach them conscientiously, but their knowledge is too frequently secondhand information gleaned from scholarly works by commentators and pedants. Chabert (*Moonbirds*), a former teacher of philosophy who has become, for economic reasons, the director of a *boîte à bachot* (examination mill), confesses to his daughter that he has never read Plato, although he has lectured extensively on Plato's works. To compensate for this, he makes his daughter read Plato.

Aymé derided university professors for their formalism, pedantry, vanity, and arrogance. Contrasting self-taught people and the so-called scholars, one of his characters suggests that the latter too often let themselves be hypnotized by questions of pure form and seduced by "the velvet of words." An illustration of this statement can be found in *Gustalin*: Victor Jouquier, the former Sorbonne professor, writes two pages of footnotes on one sentence of a new edition of Pascal, hoping that "all his notes would make people somewhat forget Pascal's text."

Writers are not spared Aymé's irony. They are often presented as naive and egotistical. They are shocked when their importance is not recognized. They are immodest and think of themselves as more important than any other category of people. And the worst are undoubtedly the members of the Académie française.

Some writers are fantastically ingenuous, like the poet who during World War II, when France was occupied by the Germans, composed undecipherable cryptograms but told his wife and friends (and probably believed) that he was going to be shot by the enemy because of his courage in expressing his views. Moreover, snobbishness and naïveté can go hand in hand. This is true, for instance, in the case of Jouvedieu, the "surrealist-statistician" poet of *Le vaurien* (The Good-for-Nothing, 1931).

Aymé also ridiculed the "prophets," writers who utter messages and speak of the "fate of the universal values." He showed "Catholic" writers in a particularly unflattering light. Pontdebois, one of the least prepossessing characters in *The Miraculous Barber,* considers himself a "thinker" but expresses himself in the most abominable clichés. This "Jansenist" novelist and future Academician has just written a novel on divine grace that, as summarized by Aymé, is a parody not only of François Mauriac's books but also of the language of Mauriac's admirers.

"Proletarian" writers are even more fiercely satirized in *The Miraculous Barber.* Milou, a prizefighter supported by a homosexual, is encouraged by his friend to become a writer. The latter tells him that he should succeed in "la carrière des lettres" because, first of all, he photographs well and, second, his father was a funeral director.

Nor did newspapermen escape Aymé's satire. Journalists ascribe an enormous, absurd importance to people who have money or status—princes, movie stars, bankers, oilmen, homosexuals. Interviews can be dishonest, indiscreet, and stupid. There is a parody of this kind of interview in the play *Les quatre vérités* (The Four Truths [also a colloquial expression for "plain truth"], 1954) when Noel Bélugat, representing a paper called *La Lanterne Libérée,* questions Olivier Andrieu, the young scientist whose discoveries seem likely to provide good copy. He asks him a series of inane "human interest" questions about his taste in sports and his opinion of Winston Churchill's painting. In the same play a journalist very frankly states that in his profession it is simply impossible to tell the truth.

On the other hand, Aymé was generally kind to artists, although he held up to ridicule the pseudo-artists who work mainly at "enriching their personalities in the Montmartre cafés" and live on a reputation enhanced, especially where women are concerned, by a manner of dress that constitutes a sort of disguise.

As for speculators and businessmen, they fare worse than people in the liberal professions. In *Le vaurien,* Aymé created the character of M. Jiquiaud, a cynical and ruthless executive who boasts to a young disciple that he is going to ruin thousands of investors and their families. Jiquiaud's conscience is perfectly clear because he feels that speculation is not only licit but highly moral, since it helps redistribute the wealth of this world. But whereas Aymé was able to laugh at Jiquiaud's ironic economic theories, in his postwar novels he treated with unmitigated harshness the corrupt members of the wealthy classes, swindlers like Lormier and his partner in *Les tiroirs de l'inconnu* (1960; translated as *The Conscience of Love,* 1962), or profiteers like M. Monglas in *The Barkeep of Blémont,* who made fortunes during the war, often by collaborating with the Germans and playing both ends against the middle. These characters are among the author's most unpleasant creations, but Aymé did not single out speculators and businessmen in order to study their machinations. Unlike Honoré de Balzac or Émile Zola,

he was not particularly interested in their techniques. Rather, he considered them part of the social scene at a certain period in history. When they make a quick fortune through black market operations, or corner the stock of a company in order to satisfy a lust for power, their activities merely highlight their character. They are also a phenomenon of history, an integral part of that particularly painful era which the author wrote about in such novels as *The Barkeep of Blémont* and *The Transient Hour.*

The objective quality of laughter probably makes it easier to deride collectivities and general types than individuals, for as soon as the individual becomes more than the example of some abstract entity, there can intervene that measure of human identification which sparks our sympathy. On the other hand, the great institutions that give solid foundations to a society become unwieldy and ridiculous whenever they achieve a monstrous existence of their own, whenever they are admired and nurtured for their own sake rather than for the good of the society that has created them. These institutions have ever been subjects for the satirist's barbs.

Aymé mocked classes and professions; he wrote also about institutions. He spoke of marriage, of the family—that microsociety—of the system of education that prepares men for civic life, of government offices and ministries that organize society's choreography, of the official rewards and sanctions that are set up and codified to express society's approval or blame.

Marriage and the family were frequently the easy targets of the writer's irony. One of the characters in *The Conscience of Love* asserts that a man has to marry in order to drain the cup of human misery. Aymé showed the sacred institution of marriage, as well as the virtue of chastity, to which all but the most shameless at least pay lip service, as systematically flouted in all classes of society—frankly and with a certain animal gusto by the earthy peasants, secretly and in more complicated ways by the city denizens and the bourgeoisie.

Many of the married women in Aymé's novels, tales, and plays forget their conjugal vows at the first opportunity; but the unmarried women are just as unconventional. Marguerite Maloret (*The Green Mare*) is the mistress of Deputy Vautier and tries to seduce Honoré Haudouin; the Dulâtre girl (*Le boeuf clandestin*) is pregnant before her marriage; Marie-Anne Archambaud (*The Barkeep of Blémont*) has a lover; Valérie (*The Conscience of Love*) sleeps with her fiancé's brother; and Léna, "une fille pleine de bonté, de douceur et de mensonge" (a young woman filled with goodness, sweetness, and illusion), has, besides Porteur, two other lovers at the same time.

The family as an institution is not all light and love, but a complex of painful relationships between people who do not understand or even like each other. Parents are exasperating. They are always ordering children to do unpleasant things and telling them it is for their own good. They force children to wear clothes that satisfy their own egos and sense of the aesthetic, not realizing the implications and values that exist within the dimensions of a child's world. Lucien's mother (*Gustalin*) makes him wear a sailor hat inscribed in gilt characters with the ship's name, *Jeanne d'Arc.* To her it seems expensive-looking and proper. To Lucien it is torture and inevitably results in his being called "Jeanne d'Arc" by his schoolmates. He fights a dogged battle to get rid of the hat, trying to lose it, have it fall in the well, and finally, in desperation, burying its ribbon at his grandfather's grave; but he is never able deliberately to destroy it or to explain to his mother why he hates it so. His relationship with his mother does not allow for explanations, since she slaps him long before he has time to clarify a situation. Where understanding and communication are concerned, the two live in entirely separate worlds.

There is active warfare between the generations. In *The Wonderful Farm* Aunt Melina scratches and pinches her little nieces and forces them to eat moldy bread and cheese, and in *The Green Mare* a child seeks relief for his pent-up rage by praying for his father's death.

Parents constantly lie to their children and to themselves, invoking the "sacrifices" they have made. Some of them joyfully and sadistically persecute and humiliate their children, claiming all the while that they are doing their duty as educators. But then, what is education?

In *The Wonderful Farm* Aymé shows the effects upon the white ox of applying himself to typical problems of school arithmetic and implies that learning is not necessarily a blessing. Education can even ruin people who might have been contented and good if left alone. As for the much-praised "culture générale" that French schools strive to impart, it comes in for Aymé's irony in several of his works. Its possible superficiality and pretense are shown by characters who discuss great writers whom they have never read—but about whom they read in class. The studies that should lead to a greater appreciation of one's intellectual heritage can be distorted and lead, on the contrary, to false values and to substituting appearances for reality. And the diplomas and degrees that purport to be the signs that the process of education has been successfully undergone and has left its tangible and beneficial mark become, on the contrary, the reality to be sought. Losing sight of what an educated man should be, everyone has an inordinate taste for something called "education" and especially for the material or social advantages it promises.

Aymé, in dealing with education, satirized the French habit of regulating by law and by innumerable decrees the content and relative importance of the various parts of the *baccalauréat.* In "Pastorale" (1932) he even imagined a future time when the government would institute as part of that *baccalauréat* an examination in obstetrics with a coefficient of importance of 27!

Generally speaking, the state, the administration, and the ministries come in for a giant share of the author's mockery. Members of the government are derided as puppets, extras, or nonentities, such as the character in *The Conscience of Love* who is a member of most of the *combinaisons ministérielles* of the Fourth Republic and heads such "unimportant" departments as Commerce, Health, and Public Works. His absolute lack of ability is proverbial, but "deputies [representatives] liked him." The deputies themselves, moreover, are shown as a sorry tribe; often pompous and didactic, they speak in clichés and are concerned only with being re-elected.

Members of the government are the ones who distribute the bits of colored ribbon with which Frenchmen like to adorn the lapels of their suits. Aymé frequently scoffed at decorations, particularly the Palmes académiques and the Légion d'honneur. To obtain the coveted red ribbon, it is not really necessary to perform acts of heroism or civic virtue; having the right connections and knowing influential people is a much easier way. Medals and decorations are often awarded unjustly or even by mistake, but so great is their prestige that, in almost all classes of French society, men will go to any lengths to obtain them. Some even see in them a guarantee of respectability powerful enough to overcome all social prejudice. In *Le vaurien*, for instance, a young suitor whom the family of the girl he loves finds unacceptable because he has only one arm becomes a welcome son-in-law when he receives a decoration that suddenly transforms his empty sleeve into some glamorous sign of bravery. Men keep substituting the symbol for the thing signified; they mistake diplomas for learning and medals for the civic virtues that they are intended to reward.

Aymé did not speak only of France and French society. As he glanced at other nations, he noted their salient traits, those which seemed ridiculous and lent themselves to caricature. In most cases he dealt summarily with his subject.

Of England he evoked the sense of tradition and pageantry, as well as the cherished ceremonies and privileges that surround royalty, by imagining that a certain Lord Burbury, a descendant of John Lackland and his mor-

ganatic wife Ermessinde de Trencavel, was granted the unusual right of opening his umbrella (and his wife, her parasol) in the royal apartments. Of Hitler's Germany, Aymé had little to say, except that it was a militarized land whose people had been robbed of their human personality. The prewar novel *The House of Men* showed the Germans as unhappy individuals trying to forget their unhappiness in the crowd. Nor was the Soviet concept of life completely overlooked by Aymé. Although he had never visited the USSR, he was familiar with the clichés of its propaganda and ridiculed them in *The Miraculous Barber,* which describes a "typical" Russian film, a kind of girl-meets-boy-meets-tractor romance.

On the subject of America, Aymé was much more prolific. Fundamentally he admired that country, and he realized that what he disliked was not so much "Americanism" as its bad European imitation. Yet the United States presented many traits he found amusing, unpleasant, or simply impossible to reconcile with his own attitude toward life. Of course, to a Frenchman there is something absolutely monstrous in the idea that a country could freely vote to outlaw alcoholic beverages. At the time when his first novel, *Brûlebois,* was published, that is, more than twenty years before he visited the United States, Aymé had written, "To the tiresome sermons carried by the dry wind of America, Brûlebois opposes his incomparably winy breath." Shortly after that, in "Pastorale," which takes the reader into the distant future, he showed the government of the United States bent on collecting arrears on the annual payments "which France had been making for 1,700 years." Thus, long before crossing the Atlantic, Aymé considered America the country of prohibition, puritanism, and false values based on an inordinate love of money.

After his stay in the United States, in the days of the McCarthy investigations, the author wrote two plays (*La mouche bleue* and *Louisiane*) and a short story ("Le Mendiant" [The Beggar]) that had America as their setting. This country appears as a land where ridiculous and bigoted sects abound, where people have lost (or perhaps never discovered) the art of living, where you can hear the Moonlight Sonata played as hot jazz and visit synthetic Renaissance castles, the land of capitalism, McCarthy witch-hunts, and soul-destroying automation. As the translator of Arthur Miller's play *The Crucible,* Aymé knew full well that many American voices were raised against the same abuses. He was aware that the term "air-conditioned nightmare" had been coined by an American, and he realized that it is difficult for one country to understand another. He portrayed Americans, however, as particularly provincial and uninformed about the rest of the world. They group together the English, the French, the Egyptians, "and other Zulus." They are sure that their way of life is the most civilized in the world and are particularly shocked by the French, who practice adultery openly and seem to enjoy love. To them France is the land of "prostitution, popery, cheap baubles, open-air urinals, and colonialism."

In *La mouche bleue* (The Blue Fly, 1957), a broad comedy about the world of big business and wealthy suburbia, the characters are shown as beset by fears ("the blue fly") and neuroses. Everyone is afraid—afraid of public opinion, of love, of life, of death. Death, incidentally, is never mentioned, and the threat it holds is concealed through the organized services of specialized firms bearing such names as *Douceur de l'Au-delà* (Charm of the Beyond) or *Passage dans un monde meilleur* (Journey to a Better World). Men are afraid of sex and of women—of their mothers, their wives, their daughters, the whole female clan that terrorizes them, spending their money faster than they can earn it. And money itself is the greatest generator of fear, for, in the Hell it creates, the more you earn, the greater your debts and the more afraid you are of losing the job on which the whole infernal cycle depends. Fear is exorcised through heavy drinking and the practice of religion, which raises morale by the judicious use of edifying and optimistic words pronounced by its official representatives.

Aymé was interested in American attitudes toward religion and amused by the ease with which unconventional sects can become popular. His short story "Le mendiant" (The Beggar), an extremely funny and irreverent parody of the Christmas story, tells about the founding of a highly mechanized cult, La Grande Église motorisée (the Great Motorized Church), based on the worship of an automobile. Another sect is described in the play *Louisiane,* where one of the characters belongs to the Gospel Walkers, whose members go on hikes and, just before turning back, pause to read a passage from the Bible. They once prayed that justice might triumph, and American forces were victorious in the Korean War. Then they thanked God for having made their nation just and powerful enough to be heard by all the peoples of the earth.

Louisiane, which deals with racial conflict, is by far the most interesting of Aymé's texts about the United States. What may well strike the American reader of this play is the degree of forbearance and discernment shown by the author in his treatment of a highly complex problem. Whereas the characters of *La mouche bleue* often seem like unreal caricatures, those of *Louisiane* come to life. They are human beings subject to pressures and ethnic forces that make their action understandable if not excusable. Almost all of them, Northerners and Southerners alike, must bear some of the blame for the bigotry and intolerance that cause the final tragedy. Perhaps it was this very effort to go beyond appearances and seek out the true motives of men and women that caused *Louisiane* to be received coolly by the public. It is by no means a great play, but it is quite as good as many others that have met with success.

On the whole, although Aymé's irony is particularly sharp when it is directed against self-satisfied moralists who consider themselves the allies of Providence, what he criticized in American civilization, he criticized everywhere. The "justice" meted out by the racist sheriff of *Louisiane* and the "justice" portrayed in *La tête des autres* are very much alike in that they are mockeries of justice. Aymé mistrusted and disliked power, powerful individuals, and powerful collectivities. Cruelty, smugness, and hypocrisy are the same the world over, although they take on specific forms in specific cultural settings. As for bad taste, Aymé did not consider it an American monopoly. He was as critical of Europe's bad imitations of good American architecture as he was of America's imitations of Renaissance castles. He realized also that noise, speed, and technology are inherent parts of the modern world; but he wistfully expressed the hope that they would not completely dehumanize mankind.

Aymé was perhaps even less sanguine when he discussed nationalism and war, for he saw in them the outgrowth of basic human defects—vanity, smugness, pettiness, as well as savagery and the urge to kill—that have characterized men throughout the centuries and will probably continue to do so in that future era portrayed in *La convention Belzébir*. Aymé stated clearly that he felt neither animosity nor contempt for foreign nations, for any nation including his own France. He did, however, detest the concept of "national honor" that leads to carnage. War, he believed, is often the result of some ridiculous incident that is blown up into an international crisis for which the little people of all the countries involved have to pay. There is something to be said for the times when war was waged by the noblemen who took pleasure in it; the common man seldom enjoys the game. But today wars have become increasingly inhuman, and those of the future may well be worse, necessitating the kind of drill described in *The Conscience of Love*: Eight soldiers sit facing "a metal stanchion on which there is a dark-colored button." Their officer gives the command, " 'Tenshun! Ready . . . thumb! Push . . . button!"

Aymé paid little attention to matters of foreign policy. In international affairs right and wrong do not exist; they are merely a question of opportune time and place, or matters of divergent points of view, highly relative at that.

National honor and the sacrifices it demands may be important to politicians and rulers, but for the common man it is far too costly.

It may be true that nations, social classes, and institutions are not merely the sum of their parts but have an identity of their own. Their existence, however, depends on those who have created them and, even more, on those who maintain and support them. Like most satirists, Aymé wrote about and against man's vices and illusions. He denounced envy, vanity, pride, prejudice, snobbery, bigotry, egoism, lack of charity, foolishness, all the inner evils that plague mankind. He was especially outspoken against moral blindness and hypocrisy.

In *The Wonderful Farm* Aymé's principal targets are the animals who are envious; those who, like the bad gander, are ridiculously vain and bully others; those who are proud and boastful like the little black rooster, or greedy like the wolf and the fox; those who, like "la Cornette," betray others or inform on them. The human beings portrayed in these tales are also far from perfect. The parents and the sadistic aunt of Delphine and Marinette are derided for their harshness, their penny-pinching materialism, their prejudices, their lack of charity and generosity; and the neighboring farmers are castigated for their dishonesty.

Animals may be cruel, or vain, or envious. They may present all the defects common to men, but they are generally true to their own nature, and this is a saving grace. We cannot really condemn the wolf for his voracity, nor the peacock for his vanity. There is a certain guilelessness in the animals' conduct even when it is most reprehensible.

Human beings, on the other hand, far from measuring up to their real or imagined dignity, seem to spend much of their time and energy deluding themselves and deceiving others. They speak in terms of morality, but their real concern is with what people will say. In the play *Lucienne et le boucher* (Lucienne and the Butcher, 1947) the maid is fired by her respectable employers not because she was raped but because her screams attracted attention. Like Lucienne and her husband, whose bourgeois values lead them to forbid their daughter's marriage with the butcher's pleasant and well-educated son, other snobs entrenched in the "virtuous" middle class consistently base their moral judgments on caste. Parents who tenderly watch over their daughter are tolerant of the lascivious attentions paid her by an elderly general because, after all, he has an exalted rank (*Le boeuf clandestin*). Perhaps the worst snob and hypocrite of all is Yolande, who appears in *The Conscience of Love* and in *Les maxibules,* the play derived from that novel. By nature she tends to love all men, but her education usually leads her to go after businessmen, capitalists, and aristocrats. Hiding behind pious platitudes, she wallows in puritanism and sex, taking a morbid delight in confessing her sins.

Respectable and pious people may honestly be what they appear to be, but there are many whose thoughts and motives resemble those of Tartuffe. Prudish and ugly women condemn springtime because of excesses they gleefully imagine. Men who consistently try to appear better than they are hide their prurient thoughts behind loud denunciations of concupiscence. Ferdinand Haudouin, the reputable veterinarian and petty politician of *The Green Mare,* sends his children to good schools and scrupulously checks on their progress. His obsession with good behavior, however, and his outrage at his brother's uninhibited love of life are the result of a dirty mind, violently repressed feelings of guilt, and sexual curiosity. As for his daughter, Lucienne, her education in the genteel school her father has chosen is a programmed course in middle-class pietistic hypocrisy. She learns to commit a reasonable number of venial—but not insignificant—sins so that she can discuss them in class, thereby earning good marks and a reputation for having a sensitive and alert conscience. While her father is worrying about the pernicious influence on his children of their earthy country cousins, Lucienne's highly "moral" upbringing

is, in fact, forcing her to sin so that she will not seem callous or self-righteous.

People not only are confused about moral values, but are often completely unaware of them. They consider honesty a purely personal matter quite irrelevant to the domain of business relations. Compassion they deem a sign of weakness if it is more than a sentimental reaction. A scholar's wife, for instance, can be deeply dissatisfied with her husband's "harmless" occupation when she compares him with the prestigious magistrate who has the power to inflict the death penalty (*La tête des autres*). Many of Aymé's characters, usually women, lie as they breathe, without necessity and for the simple reason that truth has no importance or even meaning for them. Such is Tatiana Bouvillon in *The Conscience of Love,* or again Nicole, the heroine of *Les quatre vérités.* But the inability to tell or even discern the truth is not an exclusively feminine attribute. Some men actually live their lies, like the "vegetarian" in *Le boeuf clandestin* who has managed to convince the people around him that it is somehow noble and virtuous not to eat meat, but who takes advantage of the times when he is alone to eat large portions of steak with gusto. He basks in the admiration of his family and, by urging others to enjoy their dinner while he makes a great show of eating carrots, draws attention not only to his own asceticism but also to his tolerance of weakness and self-indulgence in others. He is a liar and a pharisee.

Aymé repeatedly attacked hypocrisy in its myriad forms, and did so with increasing indignation as he wrote of its large-scale public manifestations. In *The Secret Stream* he showed a whole community living under the rule of hypocritical notables and thoroughly contaminated in its language and behavior. In the novel *The Barkeep of Blémont,* which has been called "a mirror of modern hypocrisy," almost every character is a hypocrite, but it is among those who are leaders in their social or political sphere that the vice is best exemplified and indeed becomes a way of life. Only one man, Professor Watrin, has by a trick of fate been transformed and regenerated, so that he sees the world with an entirely new vision and is true to himself and to others. In his case, however, sincerity seems to be the quality of those too stupid, too vile, or too desperate to conceal their thoughts.

The Barkeep of Blémont is a bitter work bristling with the author's indignation at the events that followed the German occupation of France: the Liberation, with its tainted atmosphere of civil war, denunciations, purges, and reprisals visited in the name of justice not only upon collaborationists but also upon persons who had been merely outspoken, weak, or unlucky. Aymé's works had appeared in some collaborationist weeklies and, although he was not among those tried and condemned, he suffered from the necessity of keeping silent while other writers, some of them personal friends, were punished by the postwar tribunals. He stated that he found nauseating the fact that a writer should be arrested for his opinions, for any opinion whatever.

The postwar novels and plays of Aymé are often savagely sarcastic and contain gruesome accounts of stonings, lynchings, hideous massacres of helpless people, brutal and useless acts committed under the mantle of patriotism. The author, when asked about the shocking scenes he described, said that he had not invented them, and indeed could not have done so; that "civilized" men and women had in fact sadistically participated in those violent events or stood by without protest while the mob killed its victims, because they "wanted to be on the side of morality." Cowards and hypocrites all!

The footnote biographies in The Transient Hour give the impression that Aymé is interested in all his characters, even those who flash through the story and are merely mentioned in one or two lines. The biographies, however, need to be examined in another light, for they are generally cruel little vignettes showing the characters in question as helpless marionettes manipulated by a blind and uninterested puppeteer. Like The Barkeep of Blémont this novel gives the impression that during the occupation society was made up principally of profiteers, traitors, and pseudo-heroes; that corruption was universal; and that there was no real difference between heroes and cowards. Human behavior was the result not of character or reason but of unforeseeable tricks of fate.

Critics, shocked by these works, remembered that many of Aymé's earlier novels and short stories had also contained a degree of violence and cruelty. They accused him of subscribing to a "morale de l'indifférence" and of seeing only self-interest, hypocrisy, depravity, and hatred in an absurd world where norms and values are either inexistent or false. Such a reaction to his work is understandable, but it is as unjustified as the equally one-sided view that he was no more than a tender and amusing storyteller. The truth is more complex. Criticism of hypocrisy and evil in the societies, institutions, and professions of men has been traditionally the affair of writers through the ages; Aymé's satire cannot fairly be singled out as more violent a denunciation than most. Bitterness, moreover, is far from being the only element to be found in his work. It must be remembered that in The Barkeep of Blémont, for instance, there appears the luminous character of Watrin, and that even in Silhouette du scandale, a book that contains some of the author's most indignant statements, there is the thought that we human beings are not absolutely shockproof but can at length be roused from our "morale de l'indifférence," our lethargic acquiescence, when events become scandalous enough.

However caustic Aymé may have been when he spoke of the smug pharisaical powers of society, he always dealt gently with the humble, unpretentious creatures whose candor and occasional stupidity make us laugh. His sympathy went to animals, children—especially country children and poor children—and those adults who are true to their own nature. He could understand and forgive weakness, and he pitied men and women who are sometimes led by their senses but are redeemed by their capacity to love. Perhaps it is Professor Watrin who best expresses Aymé's thoughts when he says that there is nothing more beautiful than man, and that life is a magnificent river which may carry along in its course all sorts of unpleasant things, but also has enchanting sights along its banks. Generosity, humility, and sometimes innocence can disarm evil.

Whereas Aymé's popularity can undoubtedly be attributed to the richness of his imagination and his ability to tell even the most fantastic and unbelievable tale convincingly and entertainingly, he was much more than a popular author of entertaining books and plays. He could bring to vigorous life all sorts of characters, ranging from the most commonplace to the most extraordinary. He possessed, moreover, a wonderfully supple and vivid style, a brilliantly inventive and amusing way of writing. He used all kinds of literary devices, freely inventing new words and spellings and indulging in many forms of verbal acrobatics.

Aymé's names and titles are particularly evocative. "Les Sabines" tells of Sabine, who has the gift of ubiquity and can also multiply herself ad infinitum. Her name is famous from the story of the rape of the Sabine women. *Le chemin des écoliers* is a story of teenage racketeers. Its literal title derives from the expression "to take the schoolboys' way," which means to take a roundabout approach. *Les quatre vérités* is a story about journalism, specifically its foibles and the lies of interviewers. It translates literally as "the four truths"; its colloquial meaning, however, is to call someone to account. *Les tiroirs de l'inconnu* uses *tiroir* in the literal definition of a drawer in a piece of furniture; it also refers to the recesses in the minds of the characters. And *Travelingue* is a play on the word *traveling* that translates as "traveling camera platform." This is a fitting name for a novel about people interested in the motion-picture world.

Many characters, like the *académicien* Per-

ruque, the Countess Piédange, and M. Caracalla, who is probably a tyrant at heart despite his mild appearance, have names that immediately suggest their true personalities. Other names, on the contrary, are amusing precisely because they are so ill-suited to the status or qualities of the persons they designate. A highly individualistic painter is called Théorème, while M. Poulet-Bichon ("chicken-lapdog" [*poulet* being also a derogatory term for a policeman]) turns out to be a tycoon. The hero of "Le passe-muraille," whose family name, Dutilleul, is inevitably reminiscent of linden tea (*tilleul,* a weak tea considered the beverage of ladies), is known to the underworld as Garou-Garou (the Werewolf); the combination Garou-Garou Dutilleul is somehow the résumé of his whole amazing adventure. Even an ordinary name like Martin, no less common in France than Smith in America, can provoke laughter when it is used for so many different characters that they finally become the multiple incarnation of the common man. In *Derrière chez Martin* and in some of his novels, Aymé called nearly everyone Martin, even the Algerian Abd-el-Martin, and gave the tongue-in-cheek explanation that he "liked the name."

Place-names of Aymé's invention are no less interesting. The action of *The Green Mare* occurs in the town of Claquebue, whose combined syllables immediately prepare the reader for the atmosphere of farce and the lusty activities of the novel. Another invented town is Cstwertskst, the setting for "Légende Poldève," and we know that this terrifying word is pronounced as one syllable because the soldiers of the town's garrison sing "Le hussard de Cstwertskst," a parody of a well-known song, "L'artilleur de Metz."

An author can, of course, enjoy complete freedom in inventing fictitious proper names, and Aymé did so with particularly good results. Nor did he hesitate to go beyond the existent vocabulary and coin words whenever the need arose. He used all sorts of nouns and modifiers of his own making that are almost always quite easy to understand but cannot be found in any dictionary. His stories about the underworld also contain a liberal amount of real and invented slang.

At times Aymé achieved striking effects through lists and enumerations, malapropisms, misunderstandings, and the deliberate association of incongruous terms or incongruous acts. He was very apt to use parody, imitating with signal success all types of literary styles in prose and poetry. In France the pastiche, or literary imitation, has long been a favorite genre employed by many famous writers. Aymé's works contain innumerable examples of his extraordinary talent in this domain. Among them are typical *explications de texte,* detective stories of the Arthur Conan Doyle variety, fabliaux and Rabelaisian bawdy tales, schoolgirl verses, popular romances, heroic tirades like those found in *Cyrano,* "difficult" symbolist poetry like that of Stéphane Mallarmé, and other incomprehensible but high-sounding poetry in the modern vein. Having been a journalist, Aymé also found it easy to write in various journalistic styles, presenting articles like those of conservative clerical weeklies or anticlerical leftist newspapers. In each case he would place the accent on the particular axe that the "editor" wanted to grind, and thus achieved highly amusing results. He liked to take over the point of view of others, of animals (dogs and wolves and pigs, or even a green mare) and of people (murderers and judges, soldiers, civil servants, children, hypocrites, and saints).

Perhaps the most famous and the most fully developed of Aymé's accounts made from the vantage point of someone else's outlook are the "Propos de la jument" (The Mare's Comments) scattered through *The Green Mare.* The miraculous portrait of the green mare looks down on the lives of the Haudouin family and psychoanalyzes their sexual mores and opinions as well as those of all of Claquebue and the other cities she has visited. She classifies men and women as "continent" or "generous." The former, who practice continence in order to become rich and respectable, are inhibited and belong to

the clerical reactionary group; the latter are poor but uninhibited and belong to the anticlerical progressive party. The mare also distinguishes between the city people, who satisfy their desires through the vicarious thrills provided by books and the theater, and the country people, who find in sex the cause, explanation, and validation of everything that happens; religion and political ideas are the expression of various attitudes toward love. This analysis, seriously presented not by the author but by the green mare, is extremely funny.

Aymé had a highly developed sense of the incongruous and the paradoxical, creating a world of the absurd that functions according to its own very special brand of logic. In the story "La grâce" (in *Le vin de Paris*), for instance, a young Breton girl becomes a streetwalker on the Boulevard de Clichy because she cannot bring herself to go into service in a socialist atheistic household. And in *La convention Belzébir* it is war that removes the unjust law which made killing the exclusive prerogative of the rich.

Aymé was primarily a man of imagination. Freely he created new situations where the laws of our cosmos are abrogated or suspended. His creatures move about with an imperturbable logic of their own, forcing our assent. We are freed from our hidebound concepts of time and space, cause and effect; and we can appraise characters and events with a fresh outlook. Like La Fontaine, Aymé composed fables and apologues; like Jonathan Swift and Lewis Carroll, he invented strange new worlds. There are in his work distant echoes of many famous writers, and critics have often compared him with the great authors of the past, with Rabelais and Voltaire in his use of language, with Molière, Balzac, Stendhal, Proust, and others because of his interest in society and the human comedy.

Although comparisons with other authors seem inevitable, they bring out not only resemblances but also evident differences. The principal divergence usually lies in the fact that what is a conscious and systematic process with a Balzac or a Rabelais or a Raymond Queneau is incidental and transitory with Aymé. He may be a novelist of mores, but he is not a sociologist; and if his works often possess documentary value, it is because of his remarkably keen perception of significant traits. Like Queneau he coined new and amusing words and resorted to unconventional spellings, but there is no such thing as a theory of language in his works. He wrote in one manner or another, according to the necessities of his subject, and although he himself did not deny the possibility of having been influenced by his readings, that influence, if it did exist, was largely unconscious. He was above all an individualist, curiously old-fashioned at times in his attachment to the values of individualism itself. He was perfectly capable of rising in anger at the abuses he saw about him, but he was unable or unwilling to sustain his indignation in the manner of a true satirist. Bitterness and anger mark only part of his work. He was undoubtedly mercurial and outspoken, but there was about him a gentle quality more often reminiscent of La Fontaine than of Voltaire.

Much of the time Aymé appears primarily as a witty, entertaining writer who thoroughly enjoyed his life and his work, but most of what he wrote is essentially human and therefore timeless. His plays, especially *Clérambard,* continue to be produced in French and in translation. His stories have not lost their popularity, and while *The Wonderful Farm* continues to delight children and, even more, their parents, "The Walker Through Walls" and "La traversée de Paris" (made into the film *Across Paris* in 1956) have certainly established Aymé's place as a master of the short story. Aymé the novelist, however, will probably be best remembered for *The Green Mare,* often referred to as a "classic," a term the author would probably have rejected.

The 1980's have seen a renewal of interest in Aymé's work. On 12 September 1986, thirty-five years after its first performance, *Clérambard* was again produced at the Théâtre des Champs-Elysées, where it had opened in 1950.

In literary circles 1989 was proclaimed a Marcel Aymé year. There was a Marcel Aymé festival on French television, during which adaptations of three of his short stories and ten of his plays were shown.

Numerous translations of Aymé's works, doctoral dissertations on various aspects of his writing, limited "art" editions of the stories about Delphine and Marinette on their wonderful farm, and even a deluxe edition of Aymé's complete works illustrated by Topor, a popular contemporary artist, all bear witness to the author's continued vitality and presence on the literary scene. In fact, today the society Amis de Marcel Aymé unites many of his admirers who believe that he should be given his rightful place in the rich history of French literature.

Aymé cannot easily be classified. Perhaps this is a weakness in that his very versatility, his lack of identification with any single genre or "school," may lead some readers to think of him as a pleasant literary dilettante rather than a serious analyst and critic of his times. But if the purpose of art is to touch and to please, Aymé was certainly an artist, and a good one. Neither a realist nor a surrealist, he sometimes described the world in bitterly ironic terms, but in general he looked at life with tolerant amusement. He varied his style and his approach with his particular mood and the needs of the story he wished to tell. His bittersweet, tragicomic world contains a wealth of gaiety, imagination, and lusty good fun.

Selected Bibliography

EDITIONS

INDIVIDUAL WORKS

NOVELS

Brûlebois. Paris, 1926, 1930.
Aller retour. Paris, 1927.
Les jumeaux du diable. Paris, 1928.
La table-aux-crevés. Paris, 1929.

La rue sans nom. Paris, 1930.
Le vaurien. Paris, 1931.
La jument verte. Paris, 1933.
Maison basse. Paris, 1935.
Le moulin de la sourdine. Paris, 1936.
Gustalin. Paris, 1937.
Le boeuf clandestin. Paris, 1939.
La belle image. Paris, 1941.
Travelingue. Paris, 1941.
La vouivre. Paris, 1943.
Le chemin des écoliers. Paris, 1946.
Uranus. Paris, 1948.
Les tiroirs de l'inconnu. Paris, 1960.

COLLECTIONS OF SHORT STORIES

Le puits aux images. Paris, 1932.
Le nain. Paris, 1934.
Derrière chez Martin. Paris, 1938.
Les contes du chat perché. Paris, 1939.
Le passe-muraille. Paris, 1943.
Le vin de Paris. Paris, 1947.
Autres contes du chat perché. Paris, 1950.
En arrière. Paris, 1950.
Derniers contes du chat perché. Paris, 1958.
Soties de la ville et des champs. Paris, 1958.

PLAYS

Vogue la galère. Paris, 1944.
Lucienne et le boucher. Paris, 1947.
Clérambard. Paris, 1950.
La tête des autres. Paris, 1952.
Les quatre vérités. Paris, 1954.
Les oiseaux de lune. Paris, 1956.
La mouche bleue. Paris, 1957.
Louisiane. Paris, 1961.
Les maxibules. Paris, 1962. Based on the novel *Les tiroirs de l'inconnu.*
Le minotaure Paris, 1967. Published with *La convention Belzébir* and *Consommation.*

COLLECTED WORKS OF FICTION

Romans de la province. Paris, 1956.
Romans parisiens, suivi d'Uranus. Paris, 1959.
Marcel Aymé illustré par Topor: Oeuvres romanesques, 6 vols. Paris, 1986.

ESSAYS AND MISCELLANEOUS WORKS

Silhouette du scandale. Paris, 1938.
Le confort intellectuel. Paris, 1949.
Antoine Blondin. La Parisienne, nos. 11–20 (Nov. 1953–Sept. 1954).

Les sorcières de Salem (adaptation of *The Crucible* by Arthur Miller) Paris, 1955.

TRANSLATIONS

"Across Paris" and Other Stories. Translated by Norman Denny. New York, 1958.
The Barkeep of Blémont. Translated by Norman Denny. New York, 1950.
Clérambard. Translated by Norman Denny. English version by Alvin Sapinsley and Leo Kerz. New York, 1958.
The Conscience of Love. Translated by Norman Denny. New York and London, 1962.
The Fable and the Flesh. Translated by Norman Denny. London, 1949.
The Green Mare. Translated by Norman Denny. New York, 1955.
The Hollow Field. Translated by Helen Waddell. New York, 1933.
The House of Men. Translated by Norman Denny. London, 1952.
The Magic Pictures: More About the Wonderful Farm. Translated by Norman Denny. New York, 1954.
The Miraculous Barber. Translated by Eric Sutton. London, 1950.
Moonbirds. Translated by John Pauker. New York, 1959.
"The Proverb" and Other Stories. Translated by Norman Denny. New York, 1961.
Return to the Wonderful Farm. London, 1954.
The Second Face. Translated by Norman Denny. New York, 1951.
The Secret Stream. Translated by Norman Denny. New York, 1953.
The Transient Hour. Translated by Eric Sutton. New York, 1948.
"The Walker Through Walls" and Other Stories. Translated by Norman Denny. London, 1972.
The Wonderful Farm. Translated by Norman Denny. New York, 1951.

BIBLIOGRAPHICAL AND CRITICAL WORKS

Brodin, Dorothy. *The Comic World of Marcel Aymé.* Paris, 1964.
Cathelin, Jean. *Marcel Aymé ou le paysan de Paris.* Paris, 1958.
Dumont, Jean-Louis. *Marcel Aymé et le merveilleux.* Paris, 1967.

Lord, Graham. *The Short Stories of Marcel Aymé.* Nedlands, Australia, 1980.

Robert, Georges, and André Lioret. *Marcel Aymé insolite.* Paris, 1958.

Scriabine, Hélène. *Les faux dieux.* Paris, 1963.

Vandromme, Pol. *Aymé.* Paris, 1960. Contains extensive bibliographical material.

DOROTHY BRODIN

HALLDÓR LAXNESS

(b. 1902)

IN 1955 HALLDÓR LAXNESS received the Nobel Prize for literature for his "lucidly descriptive writings, which have revitalized the grand Icelandic art of storytelling."

Halldór Laxness is a towering figure in modern Icelandic literature, combining a rare intellectual genius with unrelenting self-discipline. The quality of his novels has brought him international fame, and the mere quantity of his writing is astounding.

Halldór Guðjóusson was born in Reykjavík on 23 April 1902. While still a child he moved with his parents to the farm of Laxnes in the district of Mosfellssveit, a short distance from Reykjavík. As a grown man he adopted the surname Laxness, by which he has since been known. He attended senior secondary school in Reykjavík, but the school atmosphere did not agree with him and he left without completing the final examination in the spring of 1919. In the same year he left Iceland for an extended stay in Europe, having first completed the manuscript of his first novel, *Barn náttúrunnar* (Child of Nature), which was published in Reykjavík in the fall of 1919. In this novel the seventeen-year-old author contrasts the virtues of an idyllic life on an Icelandic farm with the pursuit of wealth, which brings death and disaster. Although this youthful and romantic work does not quite anticipate Laxness' major novels, it nevertheless reflects his view on the detrimental effects of ill-gotten gain.

Having traveled widely in western Europe and observed the ruins and the confusion after World War I, the young Laxness found himself by the end of the year 1922 at the Benedictine monastery of St. Maurice de Clervaux in the Grand Duchy of Luxembourg. Shortly afterward, on 6 January 1923, he was baptized and confirmed in the Catholic faith at a solemn Mass in the monastery, taking at the same time the Christian names Kiljan Marie Pierre and adopting Laxness as a surname. At St. Maurice, Laxness took part in daily religious practices and studied ecclesiastical writings and contemporary literature. Here he also had the opportunity to improve his command of various languages and to practice monastic discipline. And he continued writing in Icelandic and produced three works: *Rauða kverið* (The Red Booklet, extant only in a fragmentary manuscript), *Nokkrar sögur* (A Few Stories, 1923), and *Undir Helgahnúk* (By the Holy Mountain, 1924, in fragmentary form; second edition with an epilogue by the author, 1967). In 1925, his *Kaþólsk viðhorf* (From a Catholic Point of View) appeared. By the time he published his first major novel two years later, Laxness had broken with the Catholic church and become a socialist.

Vefarinn mikli frá Kasmír (The Great Weaver from Kashmir; hereafter *Vefarinn*), Laxness' first major novel, was published in 1927. According to his epilogue to the second edition (1948), at the time of its conception he had been torn between two entirely opposite poles—"between God's creation itself and that which had not yet been created, . . . between man and his God, between love for the creation, on one hand, and hatred of it, on the other" (p. 381).[1]

Laxness adopted the Roman Catholic faith and took up serious studies of theology, and he apparently decided to seek his own salvation in monasticism. During this period he spent nine months in Luxembourg as a guest of the holy brotherhood of St. Maurice de Clervaux, and his subsequent attendance at a Catholic institution of theology in Rome reinforces the impression of a very serious spiritual religious quest, which is clearly reflected in the novel. Yet in the 1948 epilogue, Laxness states that, having concluded his novel, "I suddenly realized that through my writing I had broken with Christendom" (p. 381).

When *Verfarinn* was written, Laxness had been an observer of the ruins of western Europe after World War I. He had studied a wide range of contemporary literature and sought answers to the pressing dilemmas of his day in the works of philosophers, both modern and ancient. He had achieved proficiency in several languages, published three novels in his native tongue, and for a while contributed articles to a newspaper in Copenhagen. In the novel the principal character undertakes a desperate quest for salvation, a quest that ends only when he makes up his mind to join a monastery, concluding that "everything is deception but God" (p. 376).

Vefarinn has distinct autobiographical overtones, which have been adequately dealt with by critics (Hallberg, pp. 27–51). Its chaotic element—the quest itself—reflects to a considerable degree Laxness' own search for personal salvation. This aspect not only puzzled early critics of the novel but led some of them to dismiss it as worthless, and to this day many

of its structural qualities have eluded the attention of literary scholars. Nevertheless, they represent the first stage in Laxness' socialistic writing and therefore deserve further scrutiny.

The narrative span of the novel is of relatively short duration, beginning at about the close of World War I and ending about a decade later. Its geographic setting extends from Iceland to the Mediterranean. Not only is its main character, Steinn Elliði, a restless young poet and intellectual in constant search of man's ultimate goal in life, he is also a man in constant motion, by boat or by train. Now he is in Iceland; now in London, Paris, or Rome. At times his journeys have an unclear destination, a feature that parallels his frantic quest. On closer inspection, this chaotic movement forms a basic structural element, one that can be seen as the functional opposite to a deep and orderly component, behind which there is a clear moralistic purpose.

Vefarinn is not easy to summarize. The greater part of the book consists of Steinn Elliði's own verbal effusions. In part these take the form of dialogues. Elsewhere monologue prevails. Certain chapters are narrated, while others are without a narrative voice. Letters written by Steinn Elliði are inserted in which stream of consciousness alternates with surrealistic elements, such as the dreamlike description of Steinn Elliði's apparent suicide attempt, from which he escapes unscathed (p. 281). In an early chapter he vows "never again to open his soul to anything but joy from the spiritual beauty of things"; he adds that he "is wedded to the beauty emanating from the aspect of things" (p. 36). At first glance this statement appears to anticipate the subsequent quest for the kind of beauty that ensures permanence.

Yet we must wonder whether Laxness sees here the quality of beauty as an individual attainment or as a common good. The novel repeatedly alludes to this dilemma. On a train ride through France, to give but one example, Steinn Elliði points out in his conversation

---

[1] Unless otherwise indicated, all references are to first editions, and all English translations are the work of the present writer.

with a learned member of the canonical order that all the essential qualities of life have been denied to the masses. At the same time he defines human wisdom as "the world's grimmest force, which is molding the masses into sharp-edged weapons with which the head will be sliced off the last enemy of mankind" (p. 144). He believes that this is exactly what has taken place in Russia, and that "in every country there are wise men who, in preparation for the final battle, are sharpening the edges of their weapons, that is the masses themselves, to bring about a total revolution" (p. 36). He likens the church to absolute monarchy based on God's will and Christ's contention that the emperor must receive his due. In his conversation with the monk, Steinn Elliði claims that the church has been "an indefatigable defender of the so-called nobility, which in earlier times grew in strength and power at the end of every war," and "that whatever definition sacred lore may attribute to God's will, one must face reality" (pp. 143–144).

The monk's reply, in summary, is that even if we gain fame through our performances on rooftops or effect revolutions of states and kingdoms, such doings are only engagements in things external and are not to be confused with the conquest of the kingdom of God. "One Pater Noster said in the middle of the night when others are asleep is a more important event than the Russian Revolution" (pp. 150–151).

Other examples could be given to suggest that Steinn Elliði's yearning for social justice outweighs his faith in individual salvation. With this in mind we find it quite perplexing when, in the end, our protagonist turns his back on the world. Not only is this final decision in obvious contrast to his ideas on capitalist exploitation, which he has consistently condemned, but it contravenes as well Steinn Elliði's earlier appraisal of the powers inimical to man, of which, as has been noted, he claims the church is a part. Yet it must be remembered that the quest element of the novel is highly chaotic and full of contradictions. As a whole

it contrasts with another component, very orderly and well-structured, that requires further discussion.

In the opening scene of the novel the reader is introduced to the summer house of Steinn Elliði's family in Iceland. It is elegant, situated on a lake in the southern part of the country in the district of Thingvellir, where, in the early tenth century, the Icelanders founded their legislative assembly. Two swans have just been seen flying in an easterly direction, with the purple skies as their backdrop. A short distance away are the mountains, which have borne the same names for more than a thousand years. The birch trees in the surrounding lava field emit a pleasant scent. Cleanliness and stability prevail in this area, where, in the remote past, the Icelanders laid the foundation of their nationhood. A young lady appears on the balcony of the house and "stretches her neck like a ptarmigan, waiting for the stillness to be broken . . . fair and innocent like a character in a myth who has always lived among the white-fleeced sheep of the forest" (p. 7). Even though her name, Diljá, has no specific meaning, it has a mythical quality. She is an indivisible part of the environment and, at the same time, a mythological extension of it. In this context, the reference to the swans evokes thoughts of Old Norse Valkyries in their ambivalent role as representatives of the divine will and messengers of death.

The scene abounds in allusions to history and myth, all of which reinforce a vertical dimension in which immutable laws of reality prevail. Diljá herself represents this reality. She is in part mythical but at the same time a human being capable of love and suffering. She has been raised by the Ylfing family, the owners of an influential commercial establishment in Iceland. The very name Ylfing, known in Old Norse legend and meaning "wolf pup," has sinister overtones. The names of the two brothers and company directors, Grímúlfur (masked wolf) and Örnólfur (aquiline wolf), are also significant. Nor does it escape one's attention that their mother, a widow and the matriarch of the company, bears the name Valgerður, which is reminiscent of a mythological Valkyrie. These names remind us that, in a metaphorical sense, the members of the Ylfing family must be endowed with some wolflike qualities.

Steinn Elliði, Grímúlfur's son, never becomes an active participant in the family company. His ties with it are of a biological nature. Intellectually he remains an outsider. Therefore, it is only reasonable to believe that his middle name, Elliði, which literally means "lone traveler," has been chosen intentionally by Laxness.

Within the Ylfing family one discerns a hierarchy, with Ylfingur & Co. at the apex. A large fleet of boats belonging to the company dominates the Icelandic fishing banks and a large share of the national export market. The Ylfing matriarch, Valgerður, is the spokesperson for this powerful enterprise and is prepared to defend its policies against any existing or potential disruptions. Her two sons, the company directors, are constantly on the move at home and abroad to ensure material success through the maintenance and expansion of profitable markets.

For further analysis at this stage we may use the structural pattern of Old Norse myth as an analogy, with its three descending levels: sovereignty, enforcement, and fecundity (George Dumézil, *Gods of the Ancient Northmen,* ed. Einar Haugen [Berkeley, 1973], pp. ix–xliii). Following this scheme, the Ylfingur and the matriarchal Ylfing mother represent the sovereign power, and her two sons the enforcement. The third level, which we would expect to be identified with happiness and prosperity, is never realized. Instead, the enforcers bring about ruin and devastation. Although their salient physical features are described, the character delineation of the two brothers is deliberately quite vague. Grímúlfur, Steinn Elliði's father, is now in England, now in Italy—a man obsessed with his business but without a destination in life. To some extent his travels parallel his elder son's continuous search for salvation. The younger brother, Örnólfur, emerges as a ruthless enforcer of the company's business ethics. We are not allowed to observe his actions. Rather, their consequences are discussed in the public media of the day. According to these public discussions, members of the Icelandic cabinet and legislative assembly are no more than "scarecrows in the nesting grounds of Ylfingur and Co." (p. 217). Örnólfur is said to have used the monopolistic position of his company to bring about the capitulation of the entire Icelandic nation to "the merciless claws of capitalism" (ibid.).

We are informed that when the social-democratic forces of the country protested against the prevailing economic injustice, "groans of suffering" (ibid.) were heard from those who had been placed under Örnólfur's yoke of relentless exploitation. Many more accusations of corruption are added, such as charges of bribes given to members of the legislature and ultimatums given to cabinet ministers. Having thus compromised the people in question, Örnólfur is reputed to have made the polite suggestion that the banks empty their coffers into those of his company in order to avert national bankruptcy, an idea that might be construed as an attempt to pick the pocket of every Icelander. The same man is also supposed to have bribed journalists to write damaging reports on honest people in the country, concocted "disgraceful lies about Soviet Russia, and extolled the generosity of American millionaires" (pp. 218–219).

From the context, it is quite clear that although Ylfingur has its home base in Iceland, the company is in essence an integral part of the forces that, in World War I, laid waste large portions of Europe. In one of his lengthy letters Steinn Elliði claims that "the time has come when people in general have realized the full meaning of every war slogan thrown at them during the war," and that "the sovereign is a combination of a sinister decoy and a holy sacrament that the parliamentary system has placed on display for the proletariat. . . . By the same token, this form of government will reveal itself as no more than a mask for a few adventurers bent on grabbing the profit of the world's produce" (pp. 165–166).

We can now extend the analogy with Old Norse myth and demonstrate how the final stage of a three-level hierarchy is the very antithesis of what analysts of myth have designated as the ultimate goal of fecundity. In the novel this stage is one of devastation. With the exception of the young lady, Diljá, all the characters of the novel move within the space of two concentric spheres. The inner sphere contains those members of the Ylfing family who are firmly tied up with their company, their functions and destiny. Within these narrower limits, they go about their business of accumulating wealth without any higher goals. Their pursuit is generated by an abstract and indefinable sovereign force that maintains itself on the principle of continuously expanding exploitation. In the end, the exploiters themselves—the active members of the Ylfing family—suffer an even more tragic fate, in that they are gradually consumed by their own enterprise, in both a literal and a metaphorical sense. Thus, devastation finally prevails within the inner sphere of the novel.

Even though Steinn Elliði belongs to the Ylfing family in the conventional sense, he rejects the entire Ylfing establishment at an early age. As an intellectual with a clear poetic bent, he has nothing in common with his parents, his uncle, and the political-business circles in which these people move. In fact, we can deduce that the sinister and sterile atmosphere surrounding them plays an important part in his decision to seek his fortune elsewhere.

In the final chapter of the novel, Diljá, Steinn Elliði's first and only love, has journeyed from Iceland to Rome, where she finds Steinn at a monastic center on the Via Romagna. He has abandoned earlier thoughts about socialism as the highest attainment for man and made up his mind to submit to the severe discipline of asceticism. Diljá, despite her brief marriage to one of the Ylfing directors, is not in any real sense a member of the Ylfing family and is the

novel's only character who does not fall victim to destructive forces. In the final scene in Rome she still possesses the same mythical qualities as before. Although she has had to endure much, she has retained her innate wisdom intact. This quality does not lend itself to further psychological analysis, but would be best described as common sense or the ability to recognize reality:

> God does not want you to cast me away after all I have endured on your account. . . . He does not want you to persist forever in this agonizing pursuit, and thus waste your life. Steinn, allow me to set you free from the bondage in which these men have placed you.
>
> (p. 497)

This is Diljá's final call of reason before the doors of the monastery close behind Steinn Elliði and the wall between them becomes impenetrable. The surroundings are alien to her as she watches two nuns walking through the Porta Angelica, praying to the Holy Ghost and the Virgin Mary. The two sisters symbolize a total submission to the Roman Catholic Church—an institution founded on man's own interpretation of divine principles. They can also be seen as a significant contrast to the two swans in the opening scene of the novel, whose flight in a certain direction is determined by the ineluctable laws of nature. It is tempting to sum up the total meaning of the novel as a binary opposition of delusion and reality. The text itself does not, however, invite a simplistic interpretation. Rather, we have here, as in many of Laxness' subsequent novels, an intriguing juxtaposition of characters and events. From these we are justified in making certain assumptions about the validity of such divergent forces as prevail in the lives of individuals and the world in which they live. In this instance, Diljá and Steinn Elliði are juxtaposed. Despite her fair share of tribulations, Diljá has not succumbed to the erosive forces around her. Rather, we get the impression that, through various tests of endurance, she has gained strength and the ability to recognize and resign herself to reality. In the first and the final scenes she epitomizes stability and reason. We may say that, in the novel, the course along which she moves is one of linear progression.

Steinn Elliði's course is the very opposite. Having removed himself from the inner sphere of the novel, he becomes trapped in its outer sphere. We see that his decision at the end to submit to monasticism is in clear contradiction to one of his earlier expositions on the Catholic church as a part of the world's capitalistic forces. Thus, in the end, Steinn Elliði himself joins an establishment that is in essence the same as the one from which he originally recoiled for spiritual and ethical reasons.

Although the preceding identification of the two concentric spheres, as opposed to a linear progression, may seem somewhat arbitrary, it may be taken, if accepted, as a testimony of Laxness' early ability to achieve a universality of expression by means of a deeply embedded structure. This feature, coupled with subtle allusions to myth, amply justifies the assessment of *Vefarinn* as a work of enduring artistic merit.

Salka Valka, Laxness' next novel, was published in two parts with the subtitles *Þú vínviður hreini* (O Thou Pure Vine, 1931) and *Fuglinn í fjörunni* (The Bird on the Beach, 1932). The time frame of the novel extends from 1910 into the 1920's. Its setting is a small fishing village in Iceland called Óseyri. On a snowy winter evening a lady by the name of Sigurlína Jónsdóttir arrives in the village by the mail boat with her young illegitimate daughter, Salvör Valgerður (Salka Valka). They are on their way to Reykjavík but cannot afford to travel any farther. The only thing we learn about their origin is that they have come from the north. Their first appearance shows up clearly contrasting attributes. Sigurlína is sick from the voyage, helpless and thoroughly confused. Her daughter, on the other hand, is full of energy and vigor. They have no place to go and do not know anyone in the village. In addition, we are told that the villagers are reluctant to accommodate those who are likely to become a burden on them. In her first evening at this strange place, Sigurlína is therefore forced to take her daughter to the local headquarters of the Salvation Army, where she immediately falls victim to the hypnotic atmosphere of the Salvationists' evening concert. After hearing their testimonies and emotional outpouring she presents her own testimony and gives herself to God.

Upon Sigurlína's arrival at Óseyri, we are told that never before had "such an insignificant woman come ashore in such an insignificant village" (1.13–14). From this we not only draw certain conclusions about Sigurlína's own status but also can deduce that a number of the people at Óseyri are not much better off. These people are exploited by Jóhann Bogesen, the village merchant and representative of vestigial Danish power in Iceland. Nature in this part of the country is harsh, with cold winds that blow from the barren mountains above the village. The sea on which the villagers depend is rough and dangerous, claiming at random its toll of human lives. A stark reality where inclement natural elements complement an inimical social structure thus prevails in the world of Óseyri. The village itself is depicted as the larger world in miniature form, without territorial confines. Salka Valka, the dominant character in the novel and to some extent a mythological extension of her environment, is intuitively aware of its perils, and she reacts to these perils with strength and determination, always prepared to defend herself.

Having in vain sought employment with the most prominent people in Óseyri, Sigurlína has no alternative but to accept an offer from the village drunkard and ruffian, Steinþór Steinsson, to move with her daughter into his run-down cottage. A fisherman and sailor of brutish strength and insatiable desires, Steinþór clearly belongs to the mythological sphere. Indeed, he is keenly aware of this himself, as we learn from his drunken pontifications, in which he assures the mother and her young daughter that he is "the sea that beats upon the coast" and "the storm that swirls around the mountain peaks" (1.19). He invites them to place their trust in his strength, adding that he is "their only hope" and is "prepared to drown all their sorrows" (ibid.). Attracted to the unbridled elemental force of this man, Sigurlína soon accedes to his sexual advances and, in the fullness of time, bears him a son. Their conduct causes much consternation in the moralistic sector of the village, but in reply to the pastor's admonitions, Steinhór once again alludes to his elemental nature, retorting that he is the roaring sea and the storm, and that the pastor could hardly expect either of these forces to assume any moral responsibility. The blood in his veins, he adds, "rises and falls like the waves of the ocean" (1.271).

The preceding analogy is indeed appropriate, in that all social conventions and morality are quite alien to Steinhór, who takes orders from none but his own tumultuous emotions. Yet he is not depicted as an altogether sinister character. The occasional abatement of the wind from the mountains and of the roaring surf on the coast finds unpredictable parallels in moments of humaneness on Steinhór's part. We may even attribute a degree of compassion to his decision to offer the two destitute women shelter in his cottage, although all such sentiments appear to vanish once they have arrived there. Not only does he impregnate Sigurlína, but he also makes advances to her daughter, whose vigorous disposition and physical energy he finds irresistible.

Salka Valka and Steinhór share certain qualities. Their disrespect for conventionalism is one of these. Yet their attitudes in this respect must be differentiated. Even as a child, Salka Valka is consciously at odds with society. With the genuineness of a child she recognizes the antagonistic elements in her immediate environment and reacts to them in conscious opposition. This early awareness is the very premise for her intellectual development and, later, her active involvement in the affairs of her commu-

nity. Steinhór, on the other hand, reacts to the world around him only on impulse. Accordingly, the sojourn in his cottage is fraught with tragedy and disaster for the mother and daughter. After he attempts to rape the girl, Steinhór departs from the village into a prolonged and self-imposed exile. Although young Salka Valka finds employment at Jóhann Bogesen's fish-processing stations and is thus able to establish limited credit in the Bogesen store, the home is without basic necessities. Poor housing and malnutrition result in the lengthy illness and eventually the death of the little boy Sigurlína has borne to Steinhór.

To his mother, the boy's agonies have been reminiscent of Christ's torments—only one instance of many in which this downtrodden and helpless woman makes a feeble attempt to seek an explanation for suffering in the realm of fantasy. In a previous conversation with her daughter, she ascribed her own weaknesses to the will of God, which she has no right to disobey (1.213–214). Unable to comprehend the anti-life forces to which she has fallen victim on every level, Sigurlína seeks an imaginary relief in her own confused ideas of Christ's redemption.

One day, quite unexpectedly, Steinhór returns to Óseyri. He is a reformed character insofar as he has sworn off alcohol, but in other ways he remains unchanged. Sigurlína accepts him back, and in order to formalize their union a "hallelujah wedding" is arranged at the Salvation Army. At the last moment, however, the bridegroom disappears from the village and the wedding is called off. Sigurlína's Salvationist sisters try to console her with songs about God's overabundant love, "the continuous and ceaseless flow" (1.295) of which, as Hallberg has noted, finds a parallel in "the relentless irony of her destiny" (Hallberg, p. 77). However, Sigurlína is impervious to the hymn-singing. Her submissive nature has, at this point, been strained to the breaking point. Suicide by drowning is her final act, and on a chilly Easter Sunday her body is found on the seashore near Óseyri. The scene is at once macabre and deeply moving. In her hand the dead woman holds a pair of shoes for her little boy that she has taken with her into eternity "in case she should find him there with no shoes on" (1.304). This final testimony of her faith shows both her deep love for her dead child and her evident conclusion that poverty, which had plagued her in life, might follow her into the hereafter.

With Sigurlína's death the question of human suffering is, of course, placed before the reader (Hallberg, p. 79). Perhaps we should also attach some significance to Easter Sunday, the day of the Resurrection, on which her body is discovered. The bitterly ironic element in her death is that, despite her naive attempts to embrace a steadfast faith in the Lord and her Savior Jesus Christ, she succumbs to a most bizarre fate. Yet this episode invites a more positive interpretation. The text of the novel reveals that Sigurlína's misfortunes not only distress her young daughter but tend, in addition, to sharpen her awareness and understanding of the social structures to which such misfortunes can be traced. Moreover, it is quite obvious that, in the long run, the mother's tragic suicide lends immeasurable strength to her daughter's determination to combat the oppressive and life-threatening elements in society.

Sigurlína's suicide occurs at the end of the first volume of the novel. To the first part of the second half, Laxness has given the subtitle *Annar heimur* (Another World). In this part he describes the incipient class struggle of Óseyri, with Salka Valka in the forefront. To a degree, the daughter becomes, at this stage, an image of her "resurrected" mother. Death on the day of the Resurrection, therefore, reinforces the notion of sacrifice and the elevation of human life to a nobler level.

In this cryptic survey, the focus has been on Sigurlína, who, together with her daughter, is given a commanding role. Considerations of space preclude a discussion of a number of vividly drawn characters who either complement the mother and daughter or stand in contrast to them. Character delineation, a wide range of imagery, and deep psychological insights not only set this novel apart from Laxness' earlier works, but also anticipate the further development of the artistic skills so evident in his subsequent novels.

Fuglinn í fjörunni, the second volume of the novel, opens with an idyllic scene at Óseyri: a few young girls enjoying the beauty of spring, dancing and singing about "the bird on the beach." They sing about the bird's crest, which is "of silk and pink in color" (2.7). Ironically, the bird, which the song refers to as "your brother," is a seagull, a non-migratory bird with distinct scavenging, predatory instincts. Here we have an ambivalent symbol that, at least in part, directs our attention to human plunderers who, in their inconspicuous ways, have kept the young singers, their homes, and their entire village in a state of unrelenting poverty.

In this part of the novel, the class struggle comes to Óseyri. Young Arnaldur Björnsson, Salka Valka's childhood friend, returns as an enlightened socialist from a prolonged stay abroad. The two of them lay the foundation for the unionization of the fishermen in the village, in opposition to the omnipotent merchant Jóhann Bogesen. Their struggle in this politically primitive place, where most people are incapable of comprehending economic theory or social systems, flounders and lacks firm direction. Nor does the collaboration between the two young leaders have a firm basis. Arnaldur, whose apparent belief in social reform is dogmatic and has the overtones of missionary fervor, places the main emphasis on the theoretical framework of social revolution. At the same time, his political convictions clash with his own pragmatic view of humanity, a cleavage that, in the final analysis, renders him incapable of leadership. Having as a young boy become quite attached to the imaginary world of folklore, where supernatural characters are convenient substitutes for humans, he later fails to adjust himself to the real world. Salka Valka, on the other hand, proceeds more by instinct than by theory. Arnaldur is keenly aware of this difference between them as he likens himself on one occasion to all things that are ambivalent, and Salka Valka to those things that, simply, are (2.149).

In one sense the difference between Arnaldur and Salka Valka lies not only in their contrasting qualities of character, but also in their divergent views of humanity. Hence, their common objective is as unclear as the means of its attainment. A brief love affair between the two is beset by uncertainties, and in the end, it brings them sorrow rather than happiness. We get the impression that their search for personal happiness mirrors the struggle they must engage in on behalf of their community.

On the whole, the task facing the two socialist leaders is made increasingly difficult by the incongruity of socialist theory with the state of preparedness of those for whom it is intended. This incongruity is precisely what Laxness uses to accommodate a number of scenes ranging from deeply touching incidents to the bizarre, all of which testify to the resistance of society to systematic attempts toward change. In Salka Valka's mind many problems require immediate attention. Her constant awareness of the individual needs of her neighbors, rather than a strong faith in theoretical and distant goals, is what sets her apart from Arnaldur. Under the prevailing circumstances she therefore emerges as more practical and less idealistic than he. To give an example, Arnaldur sees it as nothing more than an act of sentimentality when Salka Valka takes personal charge of four helpless orphans, an act he considers tantamount to pouring a little water into Hell (2.192).

The first attempts to unionize the people of Óseyri against the monopolistic sway of merchant Jóhann Bogesen are not successful, in that they only achieve solidarity among the fishermen in the village who have managed to buy shares in a boat. Even though this move is sufficient to break the merchant's power, it places the newly unionized boat owners in a monopolistic position. Being the sole provid-

ers of materials for processing, the boat owners, at least temporarily, gain control of the wages of the workers at the processing stations on land. Despite all the hardships previously brought on these people by the merchant, they had nonetheless been able to rely on enough credit at his grocery store to keep themselves above the level of starvation. With the merchant bankrupt and a new class of oppressors on the scene, the workers on land are left in a serious plight. A union of fish workers is founded at Óseyri and a strike called against the boat owners.

At this time, Steinhór Steinsson quite unexpectedly surfaces at Óseyri once again. He becomes an independent entrepreneur, using his ill-gotten capital to achieve a monopolistic position in the village comparable with the one held earlier by Jóhann Bogesen.

It is important to recall that the first half of the novel is set in the period when Iceland, to all intents and purposes, won its independence from Denmark. Against this historical background, merchant Bogesen, whose ties with Denmark appear to have strengthened his position, represents to some extent a colonial power. We may therefore wonder whether the class struggle at Óseyri, in addition to representing a trend toward socialization, does not also contain an ironic comment by Laxness on generally held and time-honored notions about the attainment of political independence. Hallberg (pp. 69–70) has drawn particular attention to a declaration made by Arnaldur Björnsson, one of the novel's principal characters, to the effect that in 1874, when Danish authorities granted Iceland control over her own financial affairs, the robbers simply changed their ethnic identity (2.257). In view of this, we may assume that, at least in part, Steinhór's replacement of Bogesen is a similar kind of transfer. The wider implication is then that a nation's economic and political autonomy is a mere illusion as long as the traditional means of exploitation have not been eliminated.

In his novel, Laxness depicts the embryonic stages of the labor movement in early-twentieth-century Iceland. Young Salka Valka, who plays the central role in this movement, has had neither the upbringing nor the training to define in unambiguous terms the aims and objectives of a political movement. Instead, she relies on her own common sense and ideas of justice in refusing to accept economic inequality as a viable marker of social distinction. Her main quality reveals itself as a robust and enduring humanity. Within the structural context of the novel, she is reminiscent of Diljá in *Vefarinn,* in that her entire development is linear. Conversely, the other principal characters are, to a greater or lesser degree, the victims of circularity. They either lack the moral strength to recognize justice or are opposed to it. In this way Laxness has established a powerful contrast between the protagonist of his novel and its subsidiary characters, a feature that enhances its artistic merit immeasurably.

The reference above to contrasting elements must now be qualified. At the end of the novel, for example, when Steinhór and Salka Valka alone dominate the scene, it is more appropriate to say that two of the principal characters are placed in a juxtaposition to establish a clear thematic focus on polarity. A dichotomy of good versus evil, or of liberating powers versus the forces of oppression, would yield a far too simplistic meaning. Even though both Salka Valka and Steinhór represent different social forces, they are, in the final analysis, members of the human community with all its complexities and, as is frequently stated in the novel, must therefore share certain qualities with the natural elements and be a part of the same reality.

Steinhór, who at the outset is the physical oppressor of Salka Valka and, in the end, returns as a tangible political force against which she must brace herself, has, we must remember, repeatedly presented himself as a mythological representation of the inclement aspects of nature. Therefore, we should be prepared to consider the possibility that some of the propensities of human nature—as, for example, the tendency of man to exploit man—may have the same ingredients of permanence and the same resistance to change as do the threatening forces of the natural environment.

In the concluding passages of the novel we see another seagull, and now it is one of the "birds of winter" (2.362). It is a chilly day in the autumn, and the bird is depicted as "indifferent and with a broad span of wings" (ibid.). The non-migratory seagull serves here as a powerful unifying symbol. Like man, it is a living creature. On the other hand, it is an integral part of nature and is governed by the same inexplicable laws that determine the rotating seasons, the softness and tranquillity of spring, and the devastating onslaughts of winter. The polarization that Laxness leaves us with sharpens our awareness at the same time that it implies that social change must always be seen in relation to its obstacles.

Sjálfstætt fólk (Independent People, 1934–1935), in two volumes, almost immediately followed *Fuglinn í fjörunni.* This powerful epic covers approximately the first two decades of the twentieth century and is set in rural Iceland. The principal character, Guðbjartur Jónsson, referred to by the abridged name Bjartur, has just bought a small patch of land from his longtime employer Jón of Útirauðsmýri (the abridged form Mýri is frequently used in the text to designate this farm), a prosperous farmer and district administrator. A farmhand at Mýri for eighteen years, Bjartur has managed to build up his own flock of eighteen sheep and to save enough money to buy the remote and virtually uninhabitable holding. He is engaged to marry a young woman by the name of Rósa, who also has been in the employ of Jón. These are the circumstances under which Bjartur starts his new career as an "independent" farmer on his own private property.

There are, however, other significant aspects to Bjartur's hard-earned independence. A man of epic proportions, he is steeped in the time-honored heroic tradition of his country. Having adopted the principles of ancient Icelandic literature, according to which Viking heroes never bowed to the commands of others, Bjartur is determined to fight it out, even against the heaviest of odds, with the same vigor as the warriors of the eddas and the sagas. To these men the question of life and death was always secondary to the concept of honor and unswerving adherence to a rigid set of clearly defined principles. Headstrong as he is, Bjartur is a highly ethical and honorable man who in words and actions will brook neither lies nor dishonesty. He believes in a measure of optimism and thus does not accept the old name Veturhús (Winterhouses), which has long been attached to the site of his farm, renaming it Sumarhús (Summerhouses).

He has now become "Bjartur at Summerhouses," a heroically independent man in a remote and heroic environment near one of the moors in the interior of Iceland. The surrounding terrain, although majestic and beautiful under the sunny skies of summer, can be harsh and menacing in winter, and on the moor the weather is known to be changeable year round. Nonetheless, we know that owing to his experience in the area, strong determination, and immense physical fortitude, Bjartur's chances of succeeding on his desolate farm should be better than those of the average man.

Bjartur's almost fanatic admiration for the lives of legendary heroes of ancient times who fought, conquered, and died with honor is simplistic and unrealistic. Yet this attitude endows him with a clear time dimension. He is in fact an extension of about thirty generations of small farmers who have preceded him in the Icelandic countryside and been subject to the same laws as he. He is also presented as a universal figure representing those subjected to exploitation of any kind. Yet his Icelandic idiosyncrasies are clear and unmistakable.

Bjartur's favorite kind of poetry is the rhymed ballad, with themes derived mostly from medieval heroic poems, which formed a popular literary genre that for about six centuries proved to be as impervious to change as those who cultivated it. In the rhymed ballad

honorable conduct, courage in the face of adversity, and glorification of the superhuman being (a military leader, king, or killer of dragons) represent the noblest vision and the highest attainment. Even though we have here a case in which Bjartur may in fact learn ethics and draw vicarious strength and enjoyment from legend, the entire ideological framework within which the world of legendary kings and warriors exists nevertheless forms a powerful enough contrast with the reality surrounding Bjartur to produce, in the given context, the essence of bitter satire.

Clearly, destitute farmers like Bjartur have little hope of ever achieving victory. We may also expect, with such overwhelming odds, that any move on their part will bring further defeat and disaster as long as they fail to come up with a new strategy. This ultimate defeat is even easier to predict in the case of Bjartur, who, in the complete absence of any outside support, continues his fight against enemy forces that he does not fully understand.

From the opening chapters of *Independent People*, we begin to suspect that "Bjartur at Summerhouses" is one of the vanquished, and that the society into which he was born will not come to his support. Given the circumstances under which he must labor, we also know that the pre-Christian concept of self-reliance, so firmly embedded in the Elder Edda, will not by itself ensure any degree of independence for a man of Bjartur's station. Despite noble intentions and integrity, his vision of independence is an illusion because he is the victim of merciless exploitation.

Laxness introduces us to a handful of other small farmers in the district. In scene after scene they have their humorous but nonetheless revealing conversations on the problems of the day as they see them. These are the characters who, from the literary point of view, complement the protagonist Bjartur and give him an appropriate synchronic dimension.

In *Independent People* the exploitation theme can be dissolved into many strands, which in combination form an impressive artistic unity. On the purely synchronic level there are the two farms, Mýri and Summerhouses, placed in diametrical opposition to symbolize capitalistic domination. Both Bjartur and his wife, Rósa, have toiled long at Mýri without achieving any economic gains. When Bjartur finally obtains possession of his desolate holding, where he builds a most primitive crofthouse, he and his wife are forced to live like virtual indigents without prospects of improvement. We gradually learn that the couple's marriage has a weak foundation, for which they themselves are not really to blame: the district administrator of Mýri and his wife tricked Bjartur into marrying Rósa early in her pregnancy by their unscrupulous son, Ingólfur.

This physical exploitation and its subsequent immoral concealment quickly destroy any prospects of a love relationship and happiness for the couple at Summerhouses. The celebration of their wedding is a highly ironic anticipation of this tragedy. On this occasion the "Madam of Mýri," the district administrator's wife, despite her knowledge of Rósa's pregnancy, proposes a highly animated and hypocritical toast to the bride and the groom on their bright future and noble role as pioneers in the countryside of Iceland (1.36–41).

At Summerhouses, the remote croft by an inland moor and the inimical and life-threatening forces of nature are particularly menacing to people with nothing to depend on but poor housing and primitive technology. We see time and time again how Bjartur and Rósa have to endure difficulties or outright calamities as a result of the onslaughts of nature, against which they are as defenseless as they are against the oppressive forces of society. These two elements often seem to work in conscious combination to bring about their demise. An early chapter of the novel entitled "Dry Spell" exemplifies this. After days of continuous rain the weather finally clears up long enough for the couple to gather the hay from the meadows. The dry spell, however, turns out to be a mixed blessing for them, since a raging storm from the interior tears down the hay ricks

and blows away the dry meadow grass. Yet as soon as the wind subsides, they struggle round the clock to move the remaining portion of the crop to the main stack at home. Bjartur appears undaunted, but Rósa collapses from fatigue and malnutrition, just as the last truss is carried home.

"Dry Spell" is, in one sense, a masterful picture of Icelandic nature in which the devastating force of the storm is contrasted with the reflections of the moon on a small, tranquil pond. The gentler features of nature are seen through Rósa's eyes, and in the area of Summerhouses, these are just as impermanent as any other fleeting moments of beauty she has been allowed to experience. These rare glimpses, however, do not obliterate reality, since the graceful phalaropes on the moonlit pond evoke the thought in her that they would make a nice meal.

Conversely, Bjartur has much in common with the storm that sweeps away his hay. He holds his own in any encounter with the elements. In this chapter the almost continuous fight against threatening rain and ravaging storm is alternately designated as "Bjartur of Summerhouses' war of independence" and "a world war," the winning of which fails to bring Rósa any joy. In her exhaustion she shares the universal feeling that "no one who is victorious in a world war is ever happy" (1.76).

"Dry Spell" presents a wealth of imagery, sharp contrasts, and classic delineations of character, all of which lend strength to the narrative. The text repeatedly alludes to the universal aspects of the battle fought on the meadows of Summerhouses, which not only has engaged Bjartur and Rósa but is, in a broader sense, a "world war" involving everyone in a similar position. The irony of this hopeless struggle is that it is universal and has been going on since time immemorial. In the background of the narrative we nevertheless detect beauty and lyricism that convey Laxness' own humanity and deep compassion for the characters he places here in the world of illusions to fight an invincible enemy.

Although Bjartur and Rósa are allowed a temporary victory over the elements, more severe tests await them. During a prolonged search on the moor for a lost sheep, Bjartur has an unexpected encounter with a bull reindeer and is carried by the beast across one of Iceland's most hazardous rivers. He returns from these adventures to find his wife dead from childbirth and a newborn baby girl in the care of his bitch. This bizarre event brings out Bjartur's superhuman mental and physical strength and, in the artistic sense, places him on a level far above that of ordinary mortals. Without any evident signs of grief, he makes the necessary funeral arrangements and, in the fullness of time, remarries. His deceased wife lives on, as it were, in her daughter (begotten, as previously noted, by the unscrupulous Ingólfur), whom Bjartur affectionately names Ásta Sóllilja (Sun Lily).

Through his relations with Ásta Sóllilja we come to know the human side of Bjartur, for whom the daughter is a subtle foil. She has the same lyrical qualities as her mother and is just as defenseless against the vicissitudes of life. The final scene of the novel, with Ásta Sóllilja near death in the arms of Bjartur, is particularly moving when we recall the lonely death of her mother in the out-of-the-way croft with the family dog as her only company.

Following Bjartur's second marriage, a number of significant characters appear on the scene, such as Bjartur's son Nonni. Nonetheless, the tragedy continues. Bjartur's eldest son loses his life in a mysterious way, and young Nonni emigrates to America. World War I brings temporary relief in the national economy, and improved prospects lead even Bjartur to be persuaded by the same people who originally placed him on his farm to borrow money for its expansion. Then, suddenly, the prices of farm products fall and Bjartur, no longer able to meet his payments, is forced to put his farm up for sale at an auction. Ironically, the buyer is Jón of Mýri, the district administrator and Bjartur's long-time oppressor, who purchases the property at a scandalously low price. Bjar-

tur, altogether destitute, is thus forced to leave for the nearest village in search of a new livelihood. This heroic and dedicated man has, despite all his strength of purpose, been driven away from his own home by the diverse inimical forces that have surrounded him from the time of his birth. Laxness' description of his final departure from Summerhouses speaks for itself:

Once again they had destroyed the lone farmer's holding because the conditions of the lone farmer continue to be the same through centuries of generations. Foreign wars may bring him occasional support but this is both superficial and delusory. The lone farmer continues to exist in misery and affliction as long as man, instead of protecting his fellow man, is man's worst enemy. The life of the farmer, the independent man, is in essence a flight from other men who want to kill him. From one ramshackle night-lodging he heads for another that is in even worse condition. One family of a crofter moves house. The members of this family, four in number, span the last four of thirty generations that have given continuity to life and death in this country for a thousand years—but for whose benefit? Not for themselves, at any rate, and their descendants. They looked very much like fugitives in a land devastated by prolonged wars—hunted outlaws they were—but on whose territory? Not their own, to be sure. In foreign books there is a legend about a man who reached perfection by sowing in the field of his enemy for one night. The story of Bjartur of Summerhouses is one of a man who all his life sowed in the field of his enemy. Such is the story of the most independent man in the country.

(1.345–346)

In the second from the last chapter Bjartur and his son find themselves in the coastal village of Fjörður. This is at the time of the Russian Revolution, the repercussions of which have reached even such distant places as Iceland. There is unrest in the village as a result of a strike by construction workers at the village harbor. Father and son fall in with the young strikers, and much against his will Bjartur accepts a slice of bread from them despite his knowledge that it is stolen—an act that flies in the face of his principles and causes him deep remorse.

This final episode evokes the fleeting thought that, at last, Bjartur may be considering the abandonment of his time-honored heroic principles, that his strategy may be about to change from that of individual combat to joining others to form a united front. From the point of view of both logic and psychology, however, such a conversion would be far too simplistic. Instead, the heroic Bjartur and the striking workers are juxtaposed, adumbrating perhaps new avenues of attack and new defenses for man in his struggle toward a respectable existence. Even though we must attach significance to the fact that Bjartur's son joins with the striking workers at Fjörður, Bjartur himself still remains the representative of Iceland's working people, the oppressed but resilient small farmers or crofters whose lot has been unchanged from the beginning of Icelandic history and will remain the same as long as the oppressors have not been deposed. Returning then to Laxness' account of Bjartur's final departure from Summerhouses, we note that his destination is his mother-in-law's old abandoned farm, an even more remote and desolate place than Summerhouses, where he intends to set up house a second time. Bjartur's own principles force him to continue the fight he has already lost. To him victory and independence will continue to be illusions that he can neither discern nor comprehend.

Despite the preceding account of Bjartur's plight, we must realize that, taken by itself, the social context of *Independent People* does not adequately express its broader character. Peter Hallberg has pointed out that it may be surprising that this feature "does not thrust itself more directly forward in the finished work" (Hallberg, p. 102). Hallberg adds that the "chief reason for this is probably that the social motif has expanded to mythical proportions of universal applicability" (ibid.). In this context

it is appropriate to comment on Laxness' use of motifs from Icelandic folklore and Norse mythology.

In the opening chapter of the novel, Laxness creates his own folktale with fictitious references to ancient Icelandic chronicles and Latin sources on the Irish settlers in Iceland who are said to have practiced sorcery and been driven from the country by the Norsemen who settled there in the latter half of the ninth century. Kólumkilli, the leader of the Irish and a sorcerer of high repute, took vengeance on the Norse by laying a curse on them, swearing that they would never prosper in their new land. Then there is mention of the great upheaval in Iceland when, shortly after the time of settlement, the Norse gods were deposed and new gods and new saints introduced in their place.

In this story Laxness has in mind the Christianization of Iceland in the year 1000, when the heathen gods of the Norsemen were formally renounced and legends and myths about them went underground, to be gradually transformed into folktales in which disguised divine characters of heathen legend often assumed sinister aspects. In all the confusion surrounding the adoption of a new faith and the rejection of an old one, it would have been entirely logical for some characters from the ancient legends of the Irish to accompany the Norse divinities on their downward journey. The Irish were in Iceland before the Norsemen, and in addition, the heathen Norse settlers brought with them a number of Irish people in bondage.

The Irish had of course been Christians for centuries, but one could hardly expect the uninformed Icelandic public to distinguish between the intertwined Christian legends from Ireland and the heathen lore from Norway that reached Iceland before Christianity was legislated by the Icelandic Althing (national assembly). Yet a vague awareness of a distinction between these two sources may well have lingered on.

Icelandic folktales have their roots in the collective consciousness of ordinary people, and they convey the experiences of these people in the form of metaphors and images. Accordingly, it is a reasonable assumption that ghosts and other folktale figures symbolize not only dethroned divinities of an earlier culture, but also the oppressive social and environmental powers that preyed upon the creators and bearers of the folktales.

With this in mind we must accept the truth of Laxness' story about the Irish sorcerer Kólumkilli and the vampire-like witch Gunnvör, who venerated him. In the early reformation era she lived at Albogastaðir on the Moor, where she took up the practice of chanting to Kolumkillí, drank human blood, and satiated her hunger for human marrow.

Evil though Gunnvör was in life, she was twice as cruel after death, refusing to stay put and sparing neither man nor beast. As a ghost she might take on the form of a troll, a serpent, or some kind of sea monster. "According to some accounts, she destroyed the farmhouse at Albogastaðir three times. Others say this happened seven times" (1.13).

This ghost story acquires an additional dimension when we learn that Bjartur has built his farm, Summerhouses, on the ancient site of Albogastaðir. If we wish to believe the folktale, his new realm of independence has remained under the spell that Kólumkilli cast on the Norse settlers of Iceland.

On the level of legend, this powerful preface to *Independent People* anticipates the life and career of Bjartur and his family at the same time that it strengthens the vertical structure of the entire novel. Icelandic folklore has it that mischievous conduct like Gunnvör's ultimately turns an individual into a monstrous character. Yet Bjartur refuses to place any credence in stories about ghosts and monsters. Being a rationalist, he labels them as "nonsense that old women let their heads be filled with" (1.23). Nonetheless, his home is laid waste by sinister forces. Although these do not manifest themselves in the form of folktale characters, they nevertheless seem to reside

everywhere and to be prepared to strike out an infinite number of times. They always have been so and always will be so. The bitter irony of the situation is that, while rejecting the legendary monsters, Bjartur fails to see or comprehend the ones that pose a direct threat to his existence.

Although the preceding example shows Laxness' skill in using motifs from Icelandic folktales to add depth to the main theme of his novel, it is no less important to observe how, on the purely artistic level, he passes beyond folklore to mythology. For example, because of dire poverty the family of Summerhouses, except Bjartur, is showing obvious signs of malnutrition. The livestock consists only of sheep, so that the family has to go without milk. This causes some concern in the district, with the result that the district administrator at Mýri—Ásta Sóllilja's biological grandfather, as noted earlier—has a cow delivered to Summerhouses. "The Sea Cow" is the title of the chapter describing the arrival of the animal. Bjartur is enraged at this imposition, claiming that the cow will eat up the hay intended for the sheep, but he is forced to acquiesce. We are told that the supply of milk brought about a sudden change:

> The brothers did not argue any more or use unbecoming appellations and threats of getting even. Without any signs of lethargy, Ásta Sóllilja finished the vest and began her work on a new pair of knickers with appropriate foresight and industry. From the old grandmother's memory there even came more pleasurable hymns than before and ones less riddled with Latinisms.
>
> (1.284)

Although sea cows frequently crop up in Icelandic folktales, we must agree with Stefán Einarsson's suggestion that Laxness here alludes to the Norse creation myth in *Snorra Edda*, according to which the cow Auðumla supplied milk for Ýmir—the mighty giant from whose body the gods created the world.

(*Skírnir: Tímarit hins íslenska bókmennta-félags* [Reykjavík, 1935], p. 226). But the difference between these parallel stories is quite significant. While the mythological Auðumla makes her appearance as a life-sustaining divinity, Bjartur's cow is sent to him by his oppressor. As it turns out, the cow of Summerhouses brings only temporary relief. A shortage of hay causes an abrupt reduction in the size of his flock of sheep, so that in the end Bjartur has no choice other than to slaughter the cow (1.417).

In succeeding episodes (2.19–22, 30–31), boredom and frustration drive one of Bjartur's sons to create havoc in his father's sheep shed. The son naively expects the incident to be blamed on ghosts. Bjartur reacts in a perfectly rational way, claiming that the shed must be infested with rats, and he acquires a cat to eliminate the problem. Upon its arrival at Summerhouses, the cat inspects the new surroundings with suspicion and "with one paw lifted" (2.24).

The intricate context of mythological overlays that Laxness has so neatly woven into his text allows us to suggest another highly significant mythological allusion. The description of the cat recalls *Snorra Edda*'s famous account of the god Thor's tests of strength and endurance in the home of the deceitful giant Útgarða-Loki. One of these requires the god to lift the giant's cat off the ground. In his unsuccessful attempt he can do no more than lift the cat high enough for one of its paws to be raised off the floor. Having suffered extreme humiliation, Thor finds out that the cat is none other than his archenemy the Midgard Serpent—the monster that extends itself around the whole world. This creature will ultimately effect Thor's own demise when the world comes to an end at the time of *ragnarök* (doomsday).

The concluding chapters of *Independent People* juxtapose Bjartur and the striking workers in the village of Fjörður. As in Laxness' other novels, we are not presented with simplistic solutions. The possibilities of a social system different from the one that destroys Bjartur's world of delusory independence are nevertheless suggested. As noted above, his heroic ethics make it impossible for him to empathize fully with the strikers.

The workers in the village of Fjörður have a long struggle ahead of them because the authorities have taken measures to crush their strike. In this instance, then, the enemy has been flushed out into the open. Again, man is the worst enemy of man.

In the end we learn that, as with the sea cow, every life-sustaining force must be assessed within the context of society, which ultimately determines its quality. We realize that the witch Gunnvör, who in both life and death wreaked havoc on her environment, is a part of reality. So is the Midgard Serpent. It may lie still for a while, but its intentions are evil, and it is forever prepared to carry them out.

Laxness' novels following *Independent People* can be mentioned only briefly: *Ljós heimsins* (The Light of the World, 1937), *Höll sumarlandsins* (The Palace of the Summerland, 1938), *Hús skáldsins* (The Poet's House, 1939), and *Fegurð himinsins* (The Beauty of the Skies, 1940) constitute a four-volume series on Ólafur Kárason, an orphan who in the ordinary sense never succeeds in the world. In this work, which in subsequent editions is collectively entitled *Heimsljós* (*World Light,* 2 vols., 1955), Ólafur makes his way through a life in which society denies him everything. He is abused by everyone except a small circle of friends. Unable to fight back, he retreats into himself at an early age and creates his own world of poetry and beauty. In this world he experiences *Kraftbirtíngarhljómur guðdómsins* (the sonic revelation of the divine—which is also the title of the first part of the novel in the second edition). The gentler features of the Icelandic environment are a significant part of this inner world of Ólafur Kárason. So also are other people whose circumstances have placed them in a position comparable to his. He not only absorbs the beauty of nature but is also capable of deep compassion. All the social injustice of which he is clearly a victim never enters his thoughts. His realm of the divine is therefore impervious to any external threats.

By means of the contrast between Ólafur Kárason's inner world and the real world in which he lives, Laxness introduces a gallery of diverse characters and a vast number of tragicomic incidents, in a world where bitter irony is a constant undercurrent.

Even though the novel is set in Iceland and its main literary sources can be easily identified as Icelandic, it has a deliberately universal scope. On one level it ruthlessly examines the plight of the creative artist in a hostile environment. In another sense it reflects Laxness' reactions to international and contemporary political developments, such as the rising threat of the fascists, whose conduct finds a parallel in Ólafur Kárason's tormentors. Finally, dialogues in the novel often revolve around the basic problems facing all humanity. Particular attention may be drawn to discussions between Ólafur Kárason, who despite his role as protagonist remains entirely passive throughout, and his socialist friend Örn Úlfar. A poet who has destroyed all his poems, Örn Úlfar perceives no beauty in a world "where life is a continuous crime" (2.125). Ólafur Kárason, on the other hand, ultimately reaches the point where "beauty alone will prevail" and meets death at a place where the ice-capped peak of the mountain blends imperceptibly with the skies.

The lyrical quality of Laxness' description of Ólafur Kárason's death is impressive. Yet its deeper layers of irony thrust themselves upon us as we contemplate the poet's discovery of eternal beauty. Society has imposed on him a total alienation, and paradoxically his recognition of his own defenselessness provides him with his only defenses. It is therefore logical for him to proceed on the level of folklore and legend to his death, which, as so often in supernatural tales, takes place in a context that conflicts with the real world, where suffering is still the only alternative for people of his station.

Laxness' next novel was the trilogy *Íslandsklukkan* (Iceland's Bell, 1943), which is also the collective title of the trilogy; *Hið ljósa man* (The Fair Maiden, 1944); and *Eldur í Kaupinhafn* (Fire in Copenhagen, 1946). This powerful epic is set in the late seventeenth and early eighteenth centuries, when Iceland was under the absolute monarchy of Denmark and subject to a Danish trade monopoly. Iceland and Copenhagen provide the main settings, with Jón Hreggviðsson, an Icelandic farmer, Snaefríður Eydalín, the daughter of a representative of Danish authorities in Iceland, and Professor Arnas Arnæus, a collector of Old Icelandic manuscripts, as the principal characters.

Jón Hreggviðsson, an indigent farmer from south Iceland, is wrongly charged with the murder of His Majesty's executioner and sentenced to death. He breaks out of jail in Iceland and gets on board a Dutch fishing vessel bound for Rotterdam. Abroad, this totally inexperienced man encounters a long and incredible sequence of misadventures. When he reaches Denmark, Jón is no longer able to evade the law; he is incarcerated and plans are made for his execution. A remarkably obstinate man and disrespectful of all authority, he somehow manages to survive constant humiliation, adversity, and torment. In his own primitive way, he is able to draw strength from his own cultural and literary heritage. His awareness of Iceland's heroic past, when one of his forefathers "stood twelve ells" and owned a spear that in the north produced "the most wonderful song ever heard" (1.194), is the very premise of his survival. Thus, Jón symbolizes the poor agrarian Icelandic communities of his time, in which, in the face of extreme oppression by Danish authorities, people made life more tolerable by cultivating their heroic themes in the form of rhymed ballads (*rímur*).

Íslandsklukkan therefore examines in great detail the unbroken continuity of Iceland's literary heritage and what this heritage has meant to the Icelandic people. The prototype for Arnas Arnæus is Árni Magnússon (1663–1730), who on behalf of the Danish government collected an immense hoard of Old Icelandic vellum manuscripts and brought them to Copenhagen, where he founded the world-renowned Arnamagnaean Manuscript Institute.

On the purely academic level Arnas is totally devoted to Iceland's literary heritage. Nevertheless, he eventually sees himself as a man whose loyalties are divided between his native Iceland and Denmark, under whose government he has accepted the post of royal commissioner. Deep down he knows that the manuscripts he has removed from Iceland represent the soul of the nation, its classical age, and the inexplicable primitive strength of its peasantry. Arnas' pragmatism prevents him from deriving the same kind of strength from his heritage as does Jón Hreggviðsson. His personal relations with Snaefríður Eydalín, who to a very large degree symbolizes Iceland, come to a tragic end, and the greater part of his manuscript collection perishes in a fire (an incident based on historical fact).

Having at least temporarily prevented the Danish authorities from selling Iceland to the town of Hamburg, Arnas finally obtains an acquittal for Jón Hreggviðsson, an innocent man whose bitter struggle with the Danish judiciary has lasted for thirty years. Undaunted by this extraordinary experience, Jón prepares to depart for Iceland. For Arnas himself his work as a scholar and collector of manuscripts has failed to bring him lasting fulfillment. Eventually, he feels as if his only redeeming act in life has been that of obtaining the release of Jón Hreggviðsson, whom he asks to "show his old ruffled head at the Althing" (3.201). Cut off from its sources, the literary heritage of Iceland loses its meaning even though attempts may be made to place it in the ivory tower of academe. In the end, Arnas is an alienated and exhausted man, spiritually neither a Dane nor an Icelander. On the other hand, the ex-convict

Jón Hreggviðsson remains an Icelander. On a mundane level he symbolizes Icelandic literature. He has drawn his strength from it and it is an inextricable part of him. For centuries peasant folk like him have maintained the continuity and been the source of this literature. Having chanted his rhymed ballads before his executioners and tormentors, Jón has shown himself to be unassailable. He is a representative of values that, despite their simplicity, can neither be erased nor put up for sale on foreign markets. "Bring them the message that this time Iceland has not been sold," Arnas remarks to Jón as the two finally part in Copenhagen (3.201).

In style and idiom, *Íslandsklukkan* reflects the historical and literary sources on which it is partly based. The text abounds in Latinisms and borrowings from Danish—two distinctive features of Icelandic officialese in the seventeenth and eighteenth centuries. Nonetheless, its coherence and immediacy make it modern. This ingenious temporal adjustment of style is strongly reinforced by Laxness' transposition of earlier sentiments evoked in the Icelanders by Denmark's oppressive rule of their country to the highly relevant context of the 1940's, when Iceland declared its full independence from Denmark and became an "independent" republic despite the Allied occupation and the presence of some 50,000 American troops on Icelandic soil. In these times of political upheaval, Laxness presented his nation with *Íslandsklukkan.*

Atómstöðin (The Atom Station, 1948) is a satire on Icelandic politics in the 1940's in which the 1946 decision by the Icelandic Althing to grant the United States the right to control the air base in Keflavík receives due prominence. The young woman Ugla Falsdótir and Dr. Búi Árland, a member of the Althing and a shrewd businessman, are the main characters. Ugla, much like Diljá and Salka Valka in Laxness' earlier novels, is both observant and intelligent. She has come to Reykjavík from a rural area in the north in order to study and to work as a domestic servant. She epitomizes the cultural stability of Icelandic agrarian communities, while her employer, the highly sophisticated Dr. Árland, represents the upper middle class with its rapidly disintegrating moral values. Like Diljá in *Vefarinn mikli frá Kasmír,* Ugla in *Atómstöðin* progresses linearly and thus forms a marked contrast to the other characters of the novel, most of whom follow a circular route.

Gerpla (The Happy Warriors, 1952) is written in the language and style of a medieval Icelandic saga, with Þorgeir Hávarsson, the poet Þormóður Kolbrúnarskáld, and Saint Olaf, king of Norway, as the principal characters. On one level the novel analyzes the time-honored concept of heroism. In Þorgeir Hávarsson we find an individual so totally obsessed with heroic ethics that he becomes an absurdity and a nuisance in a society where the principles of courage, fortitude, and revenge no longer obtain. We get the impression that, despite the almost thousand-year-old setting of *Gerpla,* Laxness in this novel has unleashed his heroes on modern society and in so doing has deromanticized heroism by variously depicting it as insanity and violence.

As mentioned earlier, Laxness received the Nobel Prize for literature in 1955. Literary critics have suggested that this important event in his literary career marks a somewhat abrupt change in his literary orientation (Hallberg, pp. 180–181). We may tentatively agree with this observation, in that Laxness' novels published after 1955, such as *Brekkukotsannáll (The Fish Can Sing,* 1957), *Paradísarheimt (Paradise Reclaimed,* 1960), *Kristnihald undir Jökli (Christianity at Glacier,* 1968), and *Guðsgjafaþula* (A List of God's Gifts, 1972), lack the political thrust so apparent in some of his earlier novels. No identifiable social system figures in these works as a significant point of reference. Rather, Laxness is here deeply concerned with human decency, which is brought into sharp relief by means of striking contrast with its opposite.

Thus, while the deeper literary focus of these books remains the same as in earlier works, Laxness in his later writings has reached the point of being no longer bound by the constraints of political theories. In fact, this marks the culmination of a gradual transition, which extends back to *World Light,* in which leftist politics are far less conspicuous than in the preceding novel, *Independent People.*

This change is attributable in part to Laxness' own search for new literary techniques. As well, we can detect his growing disillusionment with socialism as seen in practice. This we can infer not only from his literary works but also from numerous essays in which he has been quite critical of socialism and even has retracted some of his earlier statements on the subject (Hallberg, pp. 183–184).

None of the novels discussed in this survey offers any final solutions to the sociopolitical problems they so forcefully present. Rather, they reflect Laxness' own realistic views on the persistent disharmony between theory and practice. Indeed, we may detect an anticipation of a subsequent shift of focus away from political models to human values that transcend them.

On Laxness as a poet, playwright, and writer of short stories as well as essays and articles on a great variety of topics, we refer the reader to the bibliography. Many of his novels have been dramatized, and at least three have been turned into films.

On 15 June 1916 the Icelandic children's magazine in Winnipeg, *Lögberg,* published a letter from a fourteen-year-old boy in Iceland. The letter, which is addressed to the children of Icelandic immigrant families in North America, describes Iceland and the customs of the Icelandic people. In a reference to his own literary interest, the boy claims to have read all the old Icelandic family sagas at the age of eleven. The following excerpt (reprinted in Höskuldsson, p. 13) shows his eagerness to have young North American Icelanders share his experiences:

> If you really do not love your country but wish to do so, then this is the method: read the Icelandic sagas and they will inspire you with patriotic love. I do not fully understand just how the reading of these works has increased my love of my country. Nonetheless, it has. So I must tell you that the method surely works.

Needless to say, the author was Halldór Guðjóusson, who later became famous as Halldór Laxness. The letter marks the beginning of a long publishing career and attests to Laxness' early interest in the old classical literature of his nation and his affection for Iceland. Of course, his literary interests were gradually to expand, but his debt to the Icelandic sagas is obvious. He was for quite a long time Iceland's most controversial writer and intellectual. Even though a few literary critics were quick to recognize his genius, there were many who claimed that because of their political overtones, their style, and their unflattering image of Icelandic society, his writings constituted a direct threat to the Icelandic language and culture. In this context, it is fruitless to wonder if such adverse criticism would have put an early end to the career of a writer of less stamina. It was precisely Laxness' moral courage and strong convictions that caused the controversy, and it was under the tense circumstances of such controversy that he wrote the novels that subsequently brought him international fame.

In recent years Laxness has published several volumes of memoirs, limiting himself largely to the era that led up to his career as the leading writer in Iceland. Opinions on his writings have long since ceased to be divided. At the age of eleven he had steeped himself in Iceland's classical age of literature. During his long and extraordinary career as a writer he has, more than anyone else, elevated the literature of modern Iceland to a level comparable in quality with the great works that first informed his creative talent.

Selected Bibliography

EDITIONS

INDIVIDUAL WORKS

NOVELS AND SHORT STORIES

Barn náttúrunnar. Reykjavík, 1919.
Nokkrar sögur. Reykjavík, 1923.
Undir Helgahnúk. Reykjavík, 1924.
Vefarinn mikli frá Kasmír. Reykjavík, 1927.
Þú vínviður hreini. Reykjavík, 1931. Part 1 of *Salka Valka.*
Fuglinn í fjörunni. Reykjavík, 1932. Part 2 of *Salka Valka.*
Fótatak manna. Akureyri, 1933.
Sjálfstætt fólk. 2 vols. Reykjavík, 1934–1935.
Þórður gamli halti. Reykjavík, 1935.
Ljós heimsins. Reykjavík, 1937. Part 1 of *Heimsljós.*
Höll sumarlandsins. Reykjavík, 1938. Part 2 of *Heimsljós.*
Hús skáldsins. Reykjavík, 1939. Part 3 of *Heimsljós.*
Fegurð himinsins. Reykjavík, 1940. Part 4 of *Heimsljós.*
Sjö töframenn. Reykjavík, 1942.
Íslandsklukkan. Reykjavík, 1943. Part 1 of the trilogy of the same title.
Hið ljósa man. Reykjavík, 1944. Part 2 of *Íslandsklukkan.*
Eldur í Kaupinhafn. Reykjavík, 1946. Part 3 of *Íslandsklukkan.*
Atómstöðin. Reykjavík, 1948.
Gerpla. Reykjavík, 1952.
Heiman eg fór. Reykjavík, 1952.
Smásögur. Reykjavík, 1956.
Brekkukotsannáll. Reykjavík, 1957.
Paradísarheimt. Reykjavík, 1960.
Sjöstafakverið. Reykjavík, 1964.
Dúfnaveislan. Reykjavík, 1966.
Kristnihald undir Jökli. Reykjavík, 1968.
Guðsgjafaþula. Reykjavík, 1972.

ESSAYS AND ARTICLES

Kaþólsk viðhorf. Reykjavík, 1925.
Alþýðubókin. Reykjavík, 1929.

Í Austurvegi. Reykjavík, 1933.
Dagleið á fjöllum. Reykjavík, 1937.
Gerska æfintýrið. Reykjavík, 1938.
Vettvanqur dagsins. Reykjavík, 1942.
Sjálfsagðir hlutir. Reykjavík, 1946.
Reisubókarkorn. Reykjavík, 1950.
Dagur í senn. Reykjavík, 1955.
Gjörningabók. Reykjavík, 1959.
Skáldatími. Reykjavík, 1963.
Upphaf mannúðarstefnu. Reykjavík, 1965.
Íslendíngaspjall. Reykjavík, 1967.
Egill Skallagrímsson og fjernsynet. Oslo, 1968.
Vínlandspúnktar. Reykjavík, 1969.
Innansveitarkronika. Reykjavík, 1970.
Yfirskygðir staðir. Reykjavík, 1971.
Af skáldum. Reykjavík, 1972.
Þjóðhátíðarrolla. Reykjavík, 1974.
Í túninu heima. Reykjavík, 1975.
Úngur eg var. Reykjavík, 1976.
Seisseijú, mikil ósköp. Reykjavík, 1977.
Sjömeistarasaga. Reykjavík, 1978.
Grikklandsárið. Reykjavík, 1980.
Við heygarðshornið. Reykjavík, 1981.
Og árin líða. Reykjavík, 1984.
Af menningarástandi. Reykjavík, 1986.

PLAYS

Straumrof. Reykjavík, 1934.
Snæfríður Íslandssól. Reykjavík, 1950.
Silfurtúnglið. Reykjavík, 1954.
Strompleikurinn. Reykjavík, 1961.
Prjónastofan Sólin. Reykjavík, 1962.
Úa. Reykjavík, 1970.
Norðanstúlkan. Reykjavík, 1972.

POETRY

Kvæðakver. Reykjavík, 1930.

JOURNAL

Dagar hjá munkum. Reykjavík, 1987.

TRANSLATIONS

The Atom Station. Translated by Magnus Magnusson. London, 1961.
The Fish Can Sing. Translated by Magnus Magnusson. London, 1966.
The Happy Warriors. Translated by Katherine John. London, 1958.

The Honour of the House. Translator unknown. Reykjavík, 1959.
Independent People. Translated by J. A. Thompson. New York, 1946.
"Lily: The Story of Nebuchadnezzar Nebuchadnezzarson in Life and in Death." Translated by Axel Eyberg and John Watkins. In *Icelandic Poems and Stories.* Edited by Richard Beck. Princeton, 1943.
New Iceland. Translated by Axel Eyberg and John Watkins. Reykjavík, 1960.
Paradise Reclaimed. Translated by Magnus Magnusson. New York, 1962.
A Quire of Seven. Translated by Alan Boucher. Reykjavík, 1974.
Salka Valka. Translated by F. H. Lyon. London, 1936.
World Light. Translated by Magnus Magnusson. Madison, 1969.

BIOGRAPHICAL AND CRITICAL STUDIES

Guðmundsson, Halldór. *"Loksíns, loksíns": Vefarinn mikli og upphaf íslenskra nútímabókmennta.* Reykjavík, 1987.
Hallberg, Peter. *Den store vävaren.* Stockholm, 1954.
———. *Halldór Laxness.* Translated by Rory McTurk. New York, 1971.
———. *Skaldens hus: Laxness' diktning från Salka Valka till Gerpla.* Stockholm, 1956.
Höskuldsson, Sveinn Skorri. "Sambúð skálds við þjóð sína." In *Sjö erindi um Halldór Laxness.* Reykjavík, 1973.
Hróarsson, Sigurður. "Eina jörð veit ég eystra." In *Halldór Laxness og Sovétríkín.* Reykjavík, 1986.
Johannessen, Matthías. *Skeggræður gegnum tíðina.* Reykjavík, 1972.
Jónsson, Eiríkur. *Rætur Íslandsklukkunnar.* Reykjavík, 1981.
Karlsson, Kristján. *Halldór Kiljan Laxness.* Reykjavík, 1962.
Keel, Aldo. *Innovation und Restauration: Der Romancier Halldór Laxness seit dem Zweiten Weltkrieg.* Basel and Frankfurt am Main, 1981.
Kristjánsdóttir, Bergljót. "Romantechnik und Gesellschaftsbild im Roman *Gerpla* von Halldór Laxness." Dissertation, Ernst-Moritz-Arndt University, Greifswald, 1987.
———. "Um beinfætta menn og bjúgfætta, kríngil-

fætta og tindilfætta." *Tímarit Máls og Menningar* 49(3):283–300 (1988).

Kristjánsdóttir, Dagný. "Aldrei gerði Kristur sálu Þorelfi, vorri moður . . . : Um ástina og óhugnaðinn i *Gerplu.*" *Tímarít mals og Menninigar* 49 (3):301–321 (1988).

Ólason, Vésteinn. "Að éta óvin sinn-Marxisminn og Sjálfstaett fólk." In *Sjötíu ritgerðir helgaðar Jakobi Benediktssyni,* vol. 2. Reykjavík, 1977.

Sigurjónsson, Árni. *Den politiske Laxness: Den ideologiska och estetiska bakgrunden till Salka Valka och Fria Män.* Stockholm, 1984.

———. *Laxness og þjóðlifið I: Bókmenntir og bókmenntakenningar á árunum milli stríða.* Reykjavík, 1986.

———. *Laxness og þjóðlifið II: Fra Ylfingabúð til Urðarsels.* Reykjavík, 1987.

Sønderholm, Erik. *Halldór Laxness: En monografi.* Copenhagen, 1981.

BIBLIOGRAPHY

Bibliography of Modern Icelandic Literature in Translation. Compiled by P. M. Mitchell and Kenneth H. Ober. Ithaca, N.Y., 1975. Pp. 164–186.

HARALDUR BESSASON

GEORGES SIMENON

(1903–1989)

GEORGES SIMENON'S PRODUCTIVITY has been a source of amazement to critics and often has diverted them from a consideration of the literary merits of his work. After writing his first novel, *Au pont des Arches* (At the Arches Bridge, 1919), at the age of sixteen, he published more than 200 potboilers under seventeen pseudonyms, 102 novels and short stories devoted to the cases of Commissaire Maigret, 114 additional short stories, 116 novels, 25 autobiographical works, 30 series of articles, and a ballet scenario. Simenon's work has been translated into fifty-seven languages, and estimates have been made that over 600 million copies of his novels have been published. Fifty-four movies, 112 works for television (including several series built around Maigret), and six theatrical works have been made from his novels.

Even more remarkable than the quantity of Simenon s work is its generally superior quality. His novels are marked by an extraordinary blend of narrative skill and psychological insight. His incisive probing into the tragedy of human existence caused François Mauriac to characterize his work as a "nightmare described with unbearable artistry."

It would be impossible to deal with Simenon's vast literary production within the scope offered by the present study. The novels discussed, however, will serve to illustrate the qualities that have won him worldwide acclaim and that prompted André Gide to call Simenon the greatest modern French novelist.

Simenon observed that he had retained a stereoscopic memory of his first twenty years and was able to reconstruct even the most trifling events in their precise chronological order. For him this period is the most important in a man's life:

> I think that a man only absorbs substance, only grows, until he is about eighteen years old. What you have not absorbed at eighteen, you will no longer absorb. It's over. You will be able to develop what you have absorbed. You will be able to make something of it or nothing at all. . . . For the rest of your life, you will remain . . . the slave of your childhood and early adolescence.
> (Parinaud, p. 381)

The record of Simenon's childhood and adolescence found in his autobiographical works supports his contention, for we find there the themes and characters of his novels. His prodigious memory seems to function in the manner of an encyclopedia, from which he borrows a name, a tic, a gesture, an atmosphere. Using this as a starting point, he goes beyond it, integrating it into a new reality, which is the novel.

When Simenon, at the age of thirty-seven, was told by a doctor who had misread his chest X rays that he had two years to live, he decided to write the story of his childhood in the form of a letter addressed to his two-year-old son, Marc. He sent the first hundred pages to André Gide, who advised him to rewrite the work in the third person, in the form of a novel. The original autobiographical pages of *Je me souviens* (I Remember, 1945) were incorporated into the first part of the novel *Pedigree* (1948). In the preface to this work, Simenon wrote: "*Pedigree* is a novel, thus a work in which imagination and re-creation play the greatest role, but this does not prevent me from admitting that Roger Mamelin, the protagonist, has a great deal in common with the child I once was" (pp. 12–13).[1]

In the novel Simenon presents, through a series of flashbacks, a portrait of a city, a class, and a family during the early years of the twentieth century. The lives of the characters are played out against the background of the major political and social events of the time: the Agadir crisis, anarchist bombings, general strikes, the German occupation, the armistice, and the revolutionary intrigue brought to Liège by impoverished students from eastern Europe. These events, however, are important only as they affect the characters in the novel.

Simenon re-creates the whole sensory world of his childhood as he evokes the sounds, sights, and smells of the city of Liège with its houses, streets, canals, barges, seasons, and changes of climate. He is particularly interested in the familiar, imprecise, fragmentary aspects of the city:

> . . . sidewalks in the rain, the rumbling of the streetcars . . . , dawn over the market places, the appearance of . . . [crêpes] on Christmas Eve and the warm wine to accompany them, the horse-drawn barges, fog over the canals, the wagons filled with vegetables, and the cries of the tradeswomen, the flowers in the open air

stalls . . . the alleys filled with the smell of French-fried potatoes, the casseroles of mussels, and the large glasses of beer . . . the odor of gin, of tar, of ginger, of leeks and cloves.

> (Vandromme, p. 15)

Using Liège as a setting, whether busy with its peacetime pursuits or occupied by the Germans, torn by strikes and riots or caught up in the magic of the Exposition Universelle, Simenon describes the life of a class, the petite bourgeoisie, blindly struggling against its mediocrity. The world of the petite bourgeoisie was that of practicing Catholics, and the festivals and holidays Simenon describes are religious in nature. There are also continual references to this Catholic atmosphere, allusions to church buildings and liturgy, images borrowed from religion: clouds look like angels, rooms smell like sacristies, and women are as forbidding as theological virtues. Despite this, religious questions are absent from Simenon's work, as are political considerations. Religion, Simenon maintains, is a question that is too personal, too intimate, to be dealt with in a novel.

In *Pedigree* Simenon presents an unforgettable portrait of his mother, the dominant influence on his life and work. Henriette Brüll (Elise in *Pedigree*, and referred to by that name here) was of German and Flemish parentage, the youngest of thirteen children. Her father had occupied the prestigious post of dike master in Holland before his alcoholism brought ruin on him and his family. Elise and her mother went to Liège, where they lived in desperate poverty. When her mother died, Elise became a domestic in the home of one of her wealthy, married sisters, left her sister's home to become a salesgirl, and then left this position to marry Désiré Simenon, head clerk in an insurance company.

Elise's background explains her dreadful fear of poverty and her insatiable need for security. Simenon felt great resentment for his mother, whom he portrays as the most tormented of individuals, subject to nervous cri-

---

[1] Although the English titles of Simenon's books are used hereafter in citations, all quotations consist of the author's translations from the French editions; all page references are to these original volumes and not to the translated versions unless otherwise noted.

ses and gratuitous crying fits. Because she has an abnormal fear of finding herself without means once again, she converts her home into a boardinghouse for foreign students. Elise's temperament, her obsessions and ambitions, her tics and virtues, are found in many of Simenon's fictional wives and mothers, but she is one of the few to be analyzed in depth. Women, in all of Simenon's other novels except *La vieille* (*The Grandmother*, 1959) and *Betty* (1961), serve merely as catalysts, provoking the reactions of the males, because, for Simenon, it is the destiny of the male that is important.

Simenon inherited from his mother her anxiety and her hypersensitivity, but not her lack of dignity and her hypocrisy, of which he was ashamed. It was his father whom he adored and respected. Désiré Simenon, the thirteenth child of a Walloon family, was very different from Elise. From his father, Simenon inherited the contemplative side of his nature, his feeling of kinship with the world, his sensitivity to the quality of the air, to far-off sounds, and to moving spots of sunlight. Désiré lends his dignity, his quiet courage, his taste for a calm, regular, contemplative life, and his family feeling to many of Simenon's protagonists, especially Maigret.

In *Pedigree* Simenon tells not only the story of his immediate family but also that of two clans, the Walloon Mamelins (Simenons) and the Flemish Peterses (Brülls), the twenty-four uncles and aunts, their spouses, and the sixty first cousins with whom he grew up. The Mamelins are pure Walloons, attached to their city and the working-class Outremeuse district of Liège in which they live. The Peterses, on the other hand, had once been rich. They are less united as a family; almost all are merchants, and self-interest and jealousy often set them against one another. These restless, anguished, maladjusted members of his mother's family, seeking to escape through drink, vagabondage, and power, serve as prototypes for Simenon's characters.

Elise's oldest brother, Léopold, who is thirty years older than she, remembers the years of wealth and tells her stories about their enormous home in Holland. At that time Léopold was a handsome young man who was studying at the university and socializing with the nobility. Suddenly he decided to become a soldier, although the number he had drawn exempted him from service. For some inexplicable reason he sold himself to replace another recruit, and subsequently married the canteen girl of his regiment. This terrible scandal provoked a rupture between Léopold and his family. In between stints as a waiter he would disappear for six months or a year at a time, and no one, including Eugénie, his wife, would hear from him. She would get a job, and when he returned he would put an ad in the newspaper to find her. She never reproached him, and they would resume life together until his wanderlust got the better of him, and he would disappear once again.

One day Léopold disappears forever; he dies of cancer of the tongue (a sickness that will reappear continually in Simenon's work, as will his Aunt Cécile's dropsy and his father's enlarged heart). A few weeks after his death, Eugénie's body is found in her room, where she has starved herself to death: "Eugénie, the canteen girl, had let herself die for love at the age of sixty, a few weeks after the final departure of Léopold, who had left so often before" (*Je me souviens,* p. 110). This love, which Simenon considers the greatest he ever encountered, was to inspire one of his few portrayals of true love and one of his best novels, *Le grand Bob* (*Big Bob,* 1954).

Léopold is also at the origin of a very important theme in Simenon's work, the theme of flight. He is the prototype of those who have total scorn for all social life and all socially acceptable behavior. For Simenon, "There is something great about the strength of character to accept daily humiliation, or rather, not to feel that humiliation" (Pardinaud, p. 389). He maintains that the true tramp is a more complete man than others and that, like Léopold, he is a nonconformist who lives without making any concessions, existing according to his own personal canons (*Simenon sur le gril,* p. 11).

Several of Simenon's maternal aunts inspired cycles of novels. Aunt Marie (Aunt Louise in *Pedigree*) had a grocery store–bar on the quai de Coronmeuse, where she supplied the boatmen whose crafts were moored above the locks. The memory of that neighborhood and the life of the bargemen remained stronger and more vivid for Simenon than the neighborhood in which he grew up and served as a background for many of his novels. Another sister, Aunt Marthe, the wife of a wealthy wholesale grocer, Hubert Schroefs, provided inspiration for a long line of alcoholic women who periodically went on binges, referred to as "novenas" in the family's lexicon. Schroef's lineage included the wealthy, arrogant, cruel individuals found in *Le riche homme* (*The Rich Man,* 1970), *Le bourgemestre de Furnes* (*The Burgomaster of Furnes,* 1939), and *Oncle Charles s'est enfermé* (*Uncle Charles Has Locked Himself In,* 1942).

Marthe is not the only one of Elise's sisters who drinks. Félicie, also an alcoholic, is married to the owner of a bar who torments her and beats her and finally drives her mad. Roger is present when they take her in a straitjacket to the hospital—where she will die of delirium tremens—while her husband is led off to jail. The protagonists of *Malempin* (*The Family Lie,* 1940) and *Faubourg* (*Home Town,* 1937) witness similar scenes.

Alcoholism, this insatiable form of self-destruction, this effort made by many of his maternal aunts and uncles to flee from themselves, is one of Simenon's principal themes. In *Quand j'étais vieux* (*When I Was Old,* 1970), a journal that Simenon kept for the years 1960–1962, he wrote that of all the dangers he ran in the course of his life, alcoholism was undoubtedly the most serious. In a series of novels, set in both the United States and France, Simenon deals with the world of the alcoholic—a world in which certain preoccupations disappear and the importance of things changes.

In addition to the members of the Mamelin and Peters clans there were others who served as models for many of Simenon's fictional characters. A good number of the young students whom Elise had taken in as boarders, in her desperate drive for financial security, appear in Simenon's novels. These young men and women came from eastern Europe to study in Liège because it was the least expensive of the French-speaking university cities. Some of them also were there to pursue revolutionary activities. Many of them were medical students, and they introduced Simenon to the study of medicine and psychology. The medical books he read at that time, including Jean Testut's *Traité d'anatomie humaine* (*Treatise on Human Anatomy*), gave him the biological knowledge of man that is one of the keys to his work. When asked whether he could have been anything other than a novelist, Simenon replied that he could have been a doctor—a diagnostician, not a specialist. He felt that the doctor and the novelist are similar in that they are the only ones to examine men closely.

While the first two-thirds of *Pedigree* is dominated by the figure of Elise, the last third presents a highly detailed portrait of Roger, who is to a great extent the young Simenon. The author stated that, other than in *Pedigree,* he never put himself into his novels. Roger has always been ashamed of his mother, of the way she cheats her boarders, of her constant whining and complaining, of her calculating treatment of others depending on their social status, of her lack of pride, and of her hypocrisy. Coupled with shame is the feeling of impotence experienced by the small boy before the domineering woman, and the desire to free himself. His mother's emasculating nature will leave an indelible imprint on him and affect his judgment of all women, whom he will regard as adversaries. While Roger's humiliation takes the form of an inferiority complex, he begins to adopt an increasingly aggressive attitude toward his mother.

Roger's rebellion against his mother occurs at the same time as his sexual awakening and causes a psychic crisis that will have a profound effect on the portrayal of women and sexuality in Simenon's work. "Woman is both the enemy and the desired object. In order to be possessed, she must also be humiliated to be brought down to the level of the male. Therefore, he wants a woman who has been soiled" (Parinaud, p. 217). This is why there are so many men in Simenon's work who are impotent other than with whores, many who even marry whores, and others who become infatuated with fallen women. Sexuality in Simenon's work is almost always described with the pitiless crudity of this adolescent vision.

There is also a masochistic side to Roger's rebellion against his mother. He is obsessed by a desire to sink further and further into vice. His despair leads to an attempt at moral suicide—he steals, he sells black-market merchandise, he frequents German soldiers and whores, and he delights defiantly in his shame. While the rebellious Roger is the prototype of the adolescents in Simenon's work who feel the need to escape from the pettiness and meanness of their milieu and to lead violent lives, the Roger who longs for purity and order will be the inspiration for others, like the young Alain Malou (*Le destin des Malou* [*The Fate of the Malous*, 1947]).

It is Roger's father who finally saves him. One morning Roger returns home after a night of debauchery and learns that his father has had a heart attack. In effect, Désiré has become the sacrificial victim who will redeem Roger: "From one minute to the next, everything that a little while ago seemed so fraught with potential tragedy works out" (*Pedigree*, p. 454). The theme of paternal salvation presented in *Pedigree* is found in many of Simenon's novels, among them *Le fils* (*The Son*, 1957) and *La neige était sale* (*The Snow Was Black*, 1948; also translated as *The Stain on the Snow*), and is implicit in all of the Maigrets. Désiré, the father, the comrade, forgives all trespasses and has the ability to exorcise the evil possessing the son. Roger draws back from the edge of the precipice; he will enter the world and seek a place in society. "I am going to be a man, I promise you," he tells his father. The leitmotif of Simenon's work, "It is difficult to be a man," attests to the difficulty of this endeavor.

Simenon said in an interview:

I was born in the dark and the rain, and I got away. The crimes I write about—sometimes I think they are the crimes I would have committed if I had not got away. I am one of the lucky ones. What is there to say about the lucky ones except that they got away?

(Gill, p. 235)

It is Simenon's awareness of the thin line separating the criminal from "those who got away" that governs his refusal to pass judgment. He wants his readers to understand that they, too, could be driven to the limit, and, as a result, to ask themselves the question, "Why he and not I?"

Pedigree ends with the armistice of 1918. Roger is sixteen years old. His father's illness makes it essential for him to leave school and find a job. The details of his remaining years in Liège are found in the novels *Les trois crimes de mes amis* (My Friends' Three Crimes, 1938), *Le pendu de Saint-Pholien* (*Maigret and the Hundred Gibbets*, 1931), and *L'Âne rouge* (The Red Donkey, 1933; translated as *The Nightclub*). In the first two Simenon tells the story of the clique of young poets and painters, calling themselves "The Keg," who met in a room in a ruined house behind the Saint-Pholien church. Every one of Simenon's friends in "The Keg" was to fail in life. At seventy-two, looking back on his life, Simenon wrote that this was one of the reasons why failure became an obsession with him:

I knew too many of them in my adolescence, then later on during my early years in Paris, then even later on, and even today. I was afraid of becoming one of them for years. . . . The failure, for me, is the man who had great ambitions in one field or another, who was enthusiastic, who sacrificed everything, and who, one day, years later, realizes that he hasn't arrived anywhere.

(*Un homme comme un autre* [Paris, 1975], p. 28)

Simenon worked as a reporter for a few years. In 1922 he went to Paris because, as he wrote:

> I realized that only what one has lived oneself can be transmitted to others through literature. I had to know the world from every angle, horizontally and vertically . . . know it in all its dimensions, come into contact with countries and races, climates and customs, but also to penetrate it vertically . . . have access to different social strata, to be as much at ease in a tiny fisherman's bistro as at an agricultural fair or in a banker's living room.
>
> ("Le romancier," in the *French Review* 19:228 [1946])

In the early 1920's Simenon began submitting stories to the newspaper *Le Matin,* edited at that time by Colette. She told him that his stories were too pretentious, that he should avoid striving for literary effect and make his work simple by paring it down to what was absolutely essential. When he followed her advice, which he felt was the most useful he received in his life, Simenon's stories were accepted for publication. Also during these years Simenon began to write pulp fiction. The many popular novels he wrote between 1925 and 1934 under a series of pseudonyms were, for him, an apprenticeship in his craft. Instead of working at another job that would permit him to write, as many writers do, he was working in his own field.

Until the outbreak of World War II, Simenon traveled continually. He followed the canals of France from north to south and from east to west, and journeyed throughout the rest of Europe, Africa, Panama, the United States, Tahiti, New Zealand, Australia, India, Russia, Turkey, and Egypt. All of these countries would provide settings for his novels. However, Simenon maintained that he was not traveling in search of the picturesque and that very few of his novels are exotic. Among these he included *Les clients d'Avrenos* (Avrenos's Clients, 1935), set in Turkey; *Quartier nègre* (Native Quarter, 1935), set in Panama; *Le coup de lune* (Moon-struck, 1933; translated as *Tropic Moon*), set in Gabon; *45° à l'ombre* (45° in the Shade, 1936; translated as *Aboard the Aquitaine*), set on the sea route from Matadi to Bordeaux; *L'Aîné des Ferchaux* (The Elder of the Ferchaux, 1945; translated as *Magnet of Doom*), set in the Congo and Panama; *Ceux de la soif* (Those Who Thirst, 1938), set in the Galápagos Islands; *Touriste de bananes* (*Banana Tourist,* 1938), set in Tahiti; *Long cours* (Ocean Voyage, 1936; translated as *The Long Exile*), set in Panama and Tahiti; and *Le passager clandestin* (*The Stowaway,* 1947), set in Tahiti. Even in these, however, the exotic element does not play a great part, because Simenon maintained that local color is only for people who are passing through. He, on the contrary, was not seeking the sense of being abroad. What he was looking for was what is similar in man, the constant. In several series of articles inspired by his travels, Simenon rid himself of what he didn't want to put into his novels, the picturesque and "some more or less philosophical or political cogitations."

In 1945 Simenon went to the United States, where he met Denise Ouimet, a French Canadian who became his second wife after he divorced his first wife, Régine (Tigy) Renchon, in 1950. Denise was the mother of three of Simenon's four children. Their travels throughout the United States provided the background for a series of novels set in various regions of the country. Simenon and his family returned to Europe in 1955, and in 1957 they settled on a large property near Lausanne. He sold this estate in 1972, nine years after Denise's nervous breakdown and their definitive separation. Their love had over the years turned to mutual hatred, and each of them would blame the other for the suicide of their daughter Marie-Jo in 1978.

Drawn by an irresistible urge to return to his roots, Simenon bought a modest eighteenth-century house with small rooms and a mansard roof. From 1973 until his death in 1989 Simenon lived there with Theresa, his companion of more than twenty-five years, the woman with whom he felt that he found the love he had been seeking throughout his life.

Simenon's last work, *Mémoires intimes* (*Intimate Memoirs*), was published in 1981. In it he examines without reticence his two marriages, his disastrous conjugal life, and the birth and childhood of his four children. He spares no detail, however painful, and glosses over nothing in his effort to determine what happened to make Marie-Jo prefer death to life. Like his fictional detective Maigret, Simenon seeks less to judge than to understand whether her death was attributable either to the influence of her mentally ill, alcoholic mother, or to her father's excessive love for her, or to her incestuous love for him. Was her death perhaps the result of genetic fatality, the inheritance of the tormented Brülls, her maternal grandmother's clan, portrayed in *Pedigree*?

MAIGRET, MENDER OF DESTINIES

Simenon wrote the early Maigret detective novels as a bridge between the popular potboilers he had been writing and the more serious literary efforts to which he aspired and for which he did not consider himself ready. They were, in a sense, an apprenticeship for more ambitious works to come. Not knowing at that time how to shift the action from one location to another, he had the idea of creating a character who could move about freely without requiring justification to do so, and decided that a policeman would answer the purpose very well. He proposed the series to Fayard Publishers and, in 1929, signed a contract with them for eighteen novels. While Simenon originally intended to abandon the genre after fulfilling his contract, he returned to his policeman hero in sixty-five more novels and eighteen short stories, often trying out in them themes and situations he would use later in his more serious works. Before considering the "Maigrets," a word that has passed into current usage to designate Simenon's detective novels, it is necessary to describe the genre in order to

demonstrate the way in which Simenon transformed its rules and techniques and used it to express the most important themes of the twentieth-century novel: guilt and innocence, alienation and solitude.

While the detective novel has been defined in many different ways, all definitions agree that basically it is a fictitious prose narrative of an investigation that reveals to the reader how and by whom a crime was committed. Although Edgar Allan Poe's *The Murders in the Rue Morgue* (1841) is considered by many to be the first of the genre, it was actually preceded by Honoré de Balzac's *L'Histoire des treize* (*The Thirteen,* 1833–1835), which is perhaps the archetype. Thus, the birth of the detective novel, which postulates the existence of a hidden truth to be uncovered, occurred during the height of Romanticism, with its glorification of the forces of darkness and mystery and its fascination with the mythology of the criminal. Romanticism exalted the superman, whether bandit or policeman, both of whom were outside the normal order of society. Both of these figures possessed the extraordinary perspicacity and energy that would characterize detective literature, a literature still dominated by the figure of the superior man.

In the post-Romantic period detective novels changed radically, giving the powers of reason precedence over the powers of darkness. It was Poe who created the detective novel that glorified the intellect and showed that all mysteries can be solved by pure intelligence. He established the format of a type of detective novel that is still popular. It would begin with a seemingly insoluble mystery; then a series of witnesses and suspects would appear who would throw out false clues; finally the detective, by careful reasoning, would arrive at the correct, irrefutable, enlightening, and completely unexpected conclusion.

The next great writer of mystery novels was Arthur Conan Doyle, whose novels are contemporary with the first major advances of modern science. Science brought with it the promise that man would eventually solve all of his problems by applying the scientific method to them. Sherlock Holmes, with his microscopic vision and his impeccable reasoning powers, has been called the scientific detective. His success is based on unerring observation, complete concentration, and encyclopedic knowledge. Holmes's brain resembles a gigantic computer into which all human knowledge has been fed and which can automatically solve all problems by relating cause and effect.

The detective novel was to change again in the wake of the disillusionment with science that followed World War I. At the same time, faith in reason was diminishing as Freud gave primacy to the irrational forces of the unconscious. New methods of investigation that relied on instinct, intuition, and empathy replaced rational deduction. Simenon's Maigret, who has been called the Henri Bergson of the detective novel, illustrates this change in emphasis. Maigret's role, unlike that of Holmes, is not to reason but to understand intuitively.

Maigret's infinite understanding and compassion can be traced to a need Simenon felt in his youth for "a type of doctor who would be a doctor both of the body and of the mind, a sort of doctor who, knowing an individual, his age, his physical characteristics, could tell him to embark on one course or another" (*Simenon sur le gril,* p. 48). It was in that frame of mind that Simenon created the character of Maigret, for that is what Maigret does, and that is why the author found it necessary for Maigret to have completed two or three years of medical studies. Maigret is, according to Simenon, "a mender of destinies."

Maigret's ability "to live the lives of every sort of man, to put himself inside everybody's mind" (*La première enquête de Maigret* [*Maigret's First Case,* 1949], p. 105), remains constant throughout the Maigret cycle, as do Maigret's methods. While the technique remains essentially the same, there is a change in emphasis from the early novels, where Maigret is solely a sympathetic witness, to the later works, in which he occupies the entire novel

and his reactions, rather than the case at hand, hold the reader's attention. Maigret becomes the novelist Simenon, in a sense, and comports himself accordingly. Like Simenon, he seeks to find the man hidden beneath surface appearances; like Simenon, he writes down the principal elements of a case on an envelope; like Simenon, he finds that as a case proceeds, he begins to resemble the characters. Maigret has the novelist's passivity—while other detectives sit and think, he sits and imagines. When he follows a suspect, he is not waiting for him to commit the blunder that will facilitate his apprehension but is attempting to feel with him, to adapt to the rhythm of his life, and to understand him. It is for this reason that in all of his cases, Maigret's investigation centers not on events but on an exploration of personality, since his interest lies more in understanding the criminal than in solving the crime. As his inquiry proceeds, Maigret begins to understand—or rather to feel intuitively—the psychological background of the crime.

Maigret's choice of clues is revealing in this respect, for he never looks for fingerprints, traces of blood, or footprints. Nor does he attempt to interrogate witnesses to pinpoint the exact moment the crime occurred. For Maigret a clue is a gesture, a word spoken inadvertently, a look that he intercepts. His clues are a gradually developing awareness of the pressures exerted by a particular atmosphere that drive an ordinary human being to murder. To solve a case, therefore, Maigret tries to relive the psychological crisis that provoked the crime. Putting himself in the criminal's place, Maigret asks himself whether he would make a certain gesture or say a certain word if he had committed the crime. Simenon presents the precise psychological detail that makes the murderer an understandable, unforgettable human being. To emphasize that the traditional hunt of the "whodunit" is unimportant for Simenon, he frequently reveals the identity of the murderer at the beginning of the novel, devoting the remaining pages to the psychological analysis of the criminal that will convince the reader of the inevitability of his crime. As he discovers the truth in such novels, the reader pities the murderer; he shares the belief of the author that he who murders is an unfortunate being, for every man is capable of becoming a murderer if he has sufficient motivation.

Simenon explains that he transmitted his own attitudes to his fictional detective because, in his opinion, the worst humiliation for a man is to feel rejected by human society. Maigret represents a forgiving society, identifies with the criminal, and, by understanding him, gives him back his self-respect after the confession, permitting him, to a certain degree, to be reintegrated into the community.

When Maigret has finally helped the criminal to effect a catharsis through confession, he must turn him over to the judicial process and the insensitivity of judges and juries. Simenon has often expressed his dismay at what he terms the "archaic quality of the French Penal Code, with laws that take no heed of our medical knowledge, particularly in the matter of the degree of responsibility of the criminal," adding that the first Maigrets were "imbued with the sense, which has always been with me, of man's irresponsibility. It is because of this that Maigret does not judge, but attempts to understand" (When I Was Old, p. 81). He separates unconditionally the policemen's job from that of the judiciary.

It is not only his refusal to judge that sets Maigret apart from the traditional detective. While the detective novel, in general, has remained faithful to the original concept of the detective as a heroic figure, Simenon's works emphasize Maigret's simplicity and bourgeois characteristics. Maigret was all wrong for the classic fictional detective; he is a professional policeman, not an amateur detective, corpulent, happily married, middle-aged. Simenon wrote that when he wanted to create a sympathetic person who understood everything— that is to say, Maigret—he gave him, without realizing it, certain of his father's characteristics (Parinaud, p. 389). Maigret, like Désiré Simenon, loves, understands, and pities his fellow men. He knows that they have killed because they are weak or unhappy, because they feel threatened, because they are frightened. The closer he gets to his prey, the greater his sympathy because he understands him better. Simenon once stated:

> If you succeed little by little in interesting yourself [in a man] you will necessarily come to love him. I have never met anyone, no matter how unattractive he may seem at first sight, whom I did not finally like after having studied him. . . . It seems to me that if men do not like one another it is through lack of knowledge and above all because of fear. We detest what we are afraid of. . . . If then, we attain knowledge, hatred is no longer possible. We are not afraid of what we know.
>
> (Parinaud, p. 392)

Maigret, like Désiré, is in harmony with the world around him. His senses are acute, and each of his cases is intimately linked with both his sensory impressions and the weather. The beauty of the spring day on which *Maigret et les vieillards* (*Maigret in Society*, 1960) opens makes Maigret feel both lighthearted and melancholy, preparing one for the ambivalent mood of the novel:

> It was one of those exceptional months of May such as one experiences only two or three times in a lifetime and which have the brightness, taste, and smell of childhood memories. Maigret called it a hymnal month of May because it reminded him both of his First Communion and of his first spring in Paris, when everything was new and wonderful for him. In the street, on the bus, in his office, he would stop short, struck by a sound in the distance, by a puff of warm air, by the bright spot of a dress that took him back twenty or thirty years.
>
> (*Maigret in Society*, p. 7)

Intimate notations and details scattered throughout the Maigret cycle make him a completely believable human being. Maigret's early years in Paris, his courtship and marriage, and his life in the police department are dealt with in detail in *Les mémoires de Maigret* (*Maigret's Memoirs*, 1951). He describes his various assignments in the streets of Paris—the central market, the docks, the crowds, the department stores, and the brothels—that preceded his promotion to the special brigade. Notations of Maigret's physical strength and infinite curiosity about people and things abound in the series. There emerges from all of this a picture of a quiet, unexcitable man who detests hurry, a stolid, peaceable figure who inspires confidence.

Simenon returns repeatedly to other elements that have become part of the Maigret legend: his pipe, his heavy overcoat, the bowler hat he discards later on, his cherished potbellied stove in his office on the quai des Orfèvres, and the all-night sessions in his office—which, eight times out of ten, end with confessions—interrupted by countless trays of sandwiches and beer ordered from the Brasserie Dauphine. Maigret's associates, carefully differentiated, make up a continually reappearing cast of characters. Among them are the faithful Janvier, devoted to his wife and ever-increasing brood of children; Torrence, who, although killed in *Pietr-le-Letton* (*Maigret and the Enigmatic Lett*, 1931), returns to help Maigret in subsequent investigations; Lapointe, the youngest, who can pass for a student and who is always sent out to interview middle-aged, maternal women; Lucas, the associate with the greatest ability, whose only problem is that his profession is written all over his face; Lognon, whom certain people call "Inspector Ungracious" because of his cranky air, but whom Maigret refers to as "Inspector Unfortunate" because he seems to have a gift for bringing misfortune on himself; Inspector Fumal, whose lack of formal education stands in the way of promotion; Dr. Paul, the police surgeon; and Moers, the ballistics expert.

Equally familiar is Madame Maigret, who represents Simenon's concept of the ideal woman. She is completely devoted to Maigret. She is an expert cook and can prepare Maigret's favorite dishes better than any chef. Maigret knows that he can come home at any hour and find his wife prepared to kiss him and serve him some remarkable dish. She is satisfied with his mere presence. Madame Maigret, Maigret's life, his staff, his friends, his gourmandise, his sorrow at being childless, his constant head colds, all contribute to make him a completely believable human being.

Maigret is one of the few harmonious characters in all of Simenon's work. He is wise and kind. He knows that it is impossible to understand men completely, but he accepts them as they are. He is astonished by nothing and never moralizes. His wisdom restores faith in life. It is his reassuring presence that constitutes the major difference between the Maigrets and Simenon's other novels. Many of the same themes are repeated in both types, and Simenon often deals with subjects in the Maigrets that are more serious than those in his other novels. Despite this, in the Maigrets he takes us only to the threshold of tragedy, which he crosses in the others. This is due to the reassuring presence of Maigret, the father figure, who convinces us that there is an order, a structure, and a meaning to life. In the other novels there is no Maigret to whom the protagonist can confess, there is no one to understand or with whom to communicate, leaving him immured in his solitude, stifled and suffocated by repressed confessions.

PSYCHOLOGICAL NOVELS

All of Simenon's novels are built around psychological investigations. In the Maigrets they are carried out by the detective, whereas in the others they are effected by the novelist rather than his alter ego. In the Maigrets, Simenon observes the characters from a distance at first and then slowly closes in, while in the others he focuses directly on a character from the beginning, then delves deeper and deeper into his psyche to reveal what neither he nor the reader suspected previously. In the Maigrets, Simenon starts with a given situation that he examines in order to discover the psychological imperatives behind it; in the other novels he gradually builds up the pressures leading to the final tragedy. In none of his work, however, does Simenon attempt to provide answers to the problems he presents. Answers, he maintains, are a function of intelligence, and his tool is intuition, not intelligence. While the role of intelligence is to explain, reform, justify, and propose solutions, the role of intuition is to attempt to understand and, through understanding, to sympathize, the only true means of communication for Simenon.

In *When I Was Old* Simenon wrote: "Like the great naturalists, I would like to focus on certain human mechanisms. Not on great passions. Not on questions of ethics or morality. Only to study the minor machinery, which may appear secondary" (p. 43). There are several of these "mechanisms" for which Simenon shows a predilection and which inspire certain basic themes in his work. Through an analysis of these themes as they appear and reappear, with infinite variations and subtle modifications, we may attempt to understand this vast work, one in which an enormous cast of virtually interchangeable characters acts out certain dramas in a series of extremely varied settings.

One of the essential themes in Simenon's work is that of the clan. While the clan provides a defense against solitude, it often exerts a destructive, stifling influence, particularly when dominated by the female, thus compelling the young man to escape its domination. Simenon wrote that he attempted to give an idea of the Brüll and Simenon clans in both *Je me souviens* and *Pedigree*. Although he revolted against both, he undoubtedly remained marked by them.

In all of Simenon's work there is only one clan that exerts a constructive influence on its members. Significantly, it is dominated by a strong patriarch. Omer Petermans of *Le clan des Ostendais* (*The Ostenders*, 1947), one of

the few memorable characters in Simenon's novels, holds his family together under conditions of stress. Because of his strength the clan maintains its cohesiveness, despite the disasters caused by the German occupation, which threaten to destroy it. Although many of Simenon's novels were produced during and after World War II, this novel and *Le train* (1961) are the only two set against a background of war. This is because of Simenon's lack of interest in politics, war, and religion.

The Ostenders begins on a Sunday morning in May 1940. Five fishing boats flying the Belgian flag appear in the harbor of La Rochelle, carrying all the members of a clan of Flemish fishermen as well as the crews and their families. They have fled the German bombardment hoping to find a place where the Germans cannot reach them. In despair, they are forced to join all the other refugees in the area. They wonder whether it has been worth all the trouble to do what they have done.

Neither the French nor the occupying German authorities realize the strength and determination of the leader of the clan, Omer Petermans. Slowly, meticulously, he plans their escape, taking his boats out each day so that this will be accepted procedure the day they decide to leave. He never waivers in his determination, even when three of his boats hit mines. Finally they leave, as he had resolved to do from the beginning, despite stupid rules and the disorders of war. Only his wife knows that he feels like crying because he has paid such a high price for their escape and because he wonders if he really had the right to decide for all: "But he had done the essential, he had done his task as a man . . . he had done what he could do, the best he could do" (*The Ostenders*, p. 230).

Simenon returns continually in his work to the difficulty of maturing emotionally to become a man. Petermans is one of the rare individuals who is able to cope successfully with this difficulty and, as a result, attains the stature of a true hero. Simenon's other protagonists merge into a gray mass, barely distinguishable from one another. Unlike Petermans, it is not they who are important but what happens to them when they are pushed to the edge of their endurance.

The extended clan, as well as the family clan, figures in many of Simenon's works. For him the most effective of all such clans is the small village, because you have there the "coming together of a few people who live side by side as neighbors and have the same needs. You belong to the community and it is reassuring" (Parinaud, p. 383). The American equivalent of the French village is the small town, and it is in a series of interchangeable American small towns that Simenon situates four novels: *Un nouveau dans la ville* (A Stranger in Town, 1950), *La mort de Belle* (*Belle,* 1952), *La boule noire* (The Blackball, 1955; translated as *The Rules of the Game*), and *L'Horloger d'Everton* (*The Watchmaker of Everton,* 1954).

Spencer Ashby, the protagonist of *Belle,* encounters the hostility of a closely knit community in a moment of crisis. Originally from Vermont, he has settled in his wife's hometown in Connecticut, where he teaches in a prep school. When their young boarder is raped and murdered, suspicion falls on Ashby, the outsider. He begins to feel persecuted as even his wife appears to suspect him. The shock provoked by the suspicion around him makes Ashby feel guilty as he begins to suspect his own spiritual integrity. Ashby reflects the new notion of the idea of guilt, which Simenon regards as Dostoevsky's major contribution: "Guilt is no longer the simple, clearly defined matter one finds in the penal code, but becomes a personal drama that takes place in the individual's soul" (quoted in Lacassin and Sigaux, p. 187). The doubt of the others becomes contagious, causing Ashby to wonder whether he might actually have been capable of committing such a crime. He becomes obsessed with this idea and, to free himself of the obsession, commits a sadistic crime almost identical to the first.

Ashby's state of mind is symptomatic of that of the majority of Simenon's characters, very few of whom are at peace with themselves. For Simenon there is no such thing as active happiness; happiness for him is finding a temporary state of equilibrium. Ashby's inability to find a kindred soul or to convince others of his innocence is symptomatic of the lack of communion between individuals, and their resultant solitude and isolation. This theme, which Simenon has treated more than any other, as well as the theme of guilt felt by characters who are pushed to existential limits in crisis situations, places Simenon's novels in the mainstream of modern literature despite his use of traditional plot structure.

Simenon uses foreigners to symbolize man's fundamental solitude and alienation in many of the novels with French settings. M. Hire (*Les fiançailles de M. Hire* [*M. Hire's Engagement,* 1933]), born in France of Russian Jewish parents, becomes the prime suspect when a prostitute is robbed and murdered. He is literally hounded to death by an angry mob while the real murderer watches. Almost twenty-five years later Simenon again took up the character, but more fully developed, in the person of Jonas Milk (*Le petit homme d'Arkangelsk* [*The Little Man from Archangel,* 1956]). Milk, who came to France as a child and grew up there, never forgets that he is a foreigner, a member of another race. He is constantly grateful for the tepid acceptance accorded him by his neighbors and does not resent their innuendos when he marries the town slut, Gina. One evening Gina takes off without notice on one of her periodic escapades. Her brother, who had never liked Milk, begins circulating disturbing rumors, insinuating that Milk could very well have killed Gina and disposed of her body. These unfounded rumors come to the attention of the authorities, who decide to open an inquiry. As the irrelevant questions pile up, Milk realizes that others see him as a foreigner, a Jew, "a solitary man from the other end of the world who had come like a parasite to embed himself in the flesh of the Old Market" (*The Little Man from Archangel,* p. 211). Although a witness who saw Gina take off with her lover comes forward, Milk hangs himself because he sees that he has remained a foreigner to those among whom he has always lived. The unexpected hostility of the neighbors, who he felt were his friends, drives him to suicide.

Suicide and the other acts of violence that conclude so many of Simenon's novels are, to him, tragic consequences of the fact that for many men and women life is sometimes, if not nearly always, unendurable. In the moment of crisis they are driven to affirm themselves, and human society being what it is, they can affirm themselves only through murder, rape, arson, suicide, and the rest of the catalog of crimes.

From the very beginning of *La neige était sale* (*The Snow Was Black*, 1948) the reader knows that the protagonist is violent. Frank Friedmaier's childhood was sordid and tragic. He grew up in his mother's brothel in an unnamed central European country, which is now occupied by the Germans. While most of the population is freezing and starving, Lotte Friedmaier is well supplied by her German customers. Frank is disgusted with himself and with the life he is leading, and turns to crime as a way of avenging himself on a world that does not permit him to remain pure. Motivated by cold, defiant despair, he gratuitously kills a German soldier. When the young violinist who lives upstairs is arrested for the crime, Frank feels no pity, although he knows that the young man's mother will die of grief. He also feels no pity when he murders an old woman (who had been kind to him when he was a child) in order to steal watches from a German general. He perpetrates another shocking crime against Sissy Holst, the daughter of their next-door neighbor. Holst, an intellectual reputed to be in the Resistance, is now an impoverished bus driver. Frank is drawn magnetically to Holst, who represents the father he never had. Because of his need to defile everything in order to externalize his infinite self-hatred, Frank lures Sissy, who loves him, into his bed. As prearranged, he changes places in the darkness with his friend Fred Kromer, a bully, thief, and murderer. The plot misfires

and Sissy runs out into the snow barefoot, screaming Frank's name:

It did not matter. Frank had done what he wanted to do. He had rounded the cape. He had seen what was on the other side. He had not seen what he expected to see. No matter. . . . He was on the other side of the turning and he had nothing in common with them any more.

(*The Snow Was Black*, pp. 95–96)

Sissy is found and brought home by her father and the scandal is hushed up, but Frank is seized by a mania to court danger. "He wanted fate to take notice of him" (p. 122). One morning, without warning, fate gives him a gift. He is arrested by the Germans for crimes that he did not commit and is locked up in a former school that has been converted into a prison. Holst comes to see him in prison, bringing Sissy with him, and places his hand on Frank's shoulder, exactly as Frank always thought a father would do. With this simple gesture that wipes out all sin, he brings Frank peace. By this action Holst becomes a father to Frank, and, like Désiré, like Maigret, he brings the paternal pardon that wipes out solitude. Before he turns away, Holst pronounces the words that express a recurring theme in Simenon's work: "It's a difficult job to be a man." Holst absolves Frank as Maigret absolves the criminals he must turn over to justice because both know that man is not master of his destiny and, therefore, is not responsible for his actions. Maigret and Holst speak for Simenon when they express the belief that there are no guilty men, only victims.

In Simenon's work the discovery of the father is the discovery of "virile love which exalts strength, which gives the desire to build, to found, to protect" (Narcéjac, p. 66). The theme of the father as friend and mentor possessing the power to exorcise evil and despair is developed throughout Simenon's work. Simenon once stated that he noticed that most men have more memories of their fathers than of their mothers, and that paternal love is almost always stronger than maternal love. He added that many women don't know what maternal love is (Toureau, p. 150).

Le fils (*The Son,* 1957) is a confession in the form of a long letter written by Alain Lefrançois to his sixteen-year-old son, Jean-Paul. It was at his father's funeral that Lefrançois had decided to write this letter so that his son would understand why he venerated his father. He cautions Jean-Paul, who had looked upon his grandfather with a certain amount of scorn, against the danger of judging people by superficial appearances. Lefrançois warns his son of the danger of summarily judging not only his grandfather but anyone else. The senile, deformed grandmother Jean-Paul had known was once young and witty, and Jean-Paul's mother had not always been the authoritarian, superficial woman she appeared to be. During the war she had risked deportation and death for her activities in the Resistance. Paradoxically, those had probably been the best years of her life because she had found a field of action to her measure.

Lefrançois reminds his son that each of us needs to be aware of his importance, echoing an idea that explains most of Simenon's work. For Simenon one of the causes of the malaise of our time is the fact that people cannot maintain any illusions about their own worth. An artisan is proud of his professional ability, a country housewife is certain that she makes the best soup in the village, while the interchangeable factory or office worker finds satisfaction only elsewhere, if he ever does find it. It is because Simenon devotes his novels to these interchangeable people that there are so few memorable characters in his work. It also explains, in part, his great appeal, since it is easy for the reader to identify with his characters and to empathize with their inarticulate longings, their desperate desire to be something other than nameless cogs in a machine.

Simenon's characters, immured in their solitude, exemplify his belief that basic human truths cannot be communicated. His characters are particularly unable to communicate because they are creatures of instinct rather than of intelligence. They are unable to organize and formulate their thoughts lucidly. Instead, they are dominated by vague ideas and images. The truths they feel, expressed by the frequently used phrase "he knew what he meant," remain locked within them.

A desperate attempt to escape solitude through eroticism is evident in many of Simenon's novels. Charles Alavoine, in *Lettre à mon juge* (Letter to My Judge, 1947, translated as *Act of Passion*), describes this frantic effort to lose oneself in another: "The more she belonged to me, the more I felt her to be mine, the more I judged her worthy of being mine . . . the more I felt the need to consume her even more. To consume her as I, for my part, would have wanted to merge completely with her" (p. 205). Alavoine's failure is made manifest when he finally kills Martine to exorcise the part of her that is standing between them.

In other novels it is alcohol rather than sensuality that permits the characters to break loose from their everyday lives and breathe at a higher level. It is the means by which Antoine (*Antoine et Julie,* 1953; translated as *The Magician*) desperately seeks to flee the loneliness and boredom of his existence. What he seeks when he drinks is "that contact, that way of looking at humanity and of feeling at one with it" (p. 87). When the effect of one drink wears off, he takes another, which automatically puts him back into the desired state. He decides quite calmly that he knows why so many people don't commit suicide; it is because there comes a moment, if you know how to manage things, when it is no longer necessary.

Antoine's increasing dependence on alcohol precipitates the tragic conclusion of an already foundering marriage. One night Antoine goes out to buy medicine for Julie, who suffers from angina. Instead of going home with it, he stays out drinking. When he finally does arrive, Julie is dead. Thereafter he lives alone; nothing is touched in the house and no one passes through the doors. He stops drinking, and every day, whatever the weather, he goes to the cemetery, where the headstone contains a blank space for his name alongside Julie's.

Antoine's devotion to his dead wife raises questions about the failure of their marriage. They really love one another with a tender love devoid of romantic illusions. Unfortunately, with the best intentions in the world, they act upon one another with disastrous effect. Each would like to make the other happy but, instead, causes only suffering. Antoine wonders why they could not become an exception, but then he furnishes the answer himself: "Why should they be exceptions? Why shouldn't the thousands of men and women who walk up and down the Champs-Elysées have the same sort of problems?" (*The Magician*, p. 84).

That Simenon's characters rarely succeed in linking their lives to another is, he maintains, a faithful reflection of reality; he adds that what people call "love" varies in each individual. All of his characters, according to Simenon, have known one type of love or another. Love plays the same role in his novels as it does in life, and in both, there are very few whose lives are given over entirely to love, and even fewer for whom love is a beautiful thing (Simenon, in Thoorens, p. 147).

Simenon's work contains endless variations on the theme of the failure of a couple to achieve true union, from the sexual bondage of Alavoine, through the misalliance of Antoine and Julie and the hatred of the elderly couple in *Le chat* (*The Cat*, 1967), to the detestation leading to murder in *L'Escalier de fer* (*The Iron Staircase*, 1953) and *Dimanche* (*Sunday*, 1958). A recurring image symbolizing this failure is that of the suddenly empty home. The husband returns one day to find that his wife has abandoned him. At first he is bewildered by this seemingly inexplicable act, but as he begins to reflect, he understands that it is the culmination of a long misunderstanding that only his blindness has hidden from him.

In general there is no open confrontation between husband and wife in Simenon's novels. Marriages break apart soundlessly as husbands and wives sink into a mutually ill-tempered daily existence. At times, however, the silent struggle leads to murderous consequences. *Sunday* opens on the Sunday that Emile has selected to murder his wife, an act he has been preparing for eleven months. Through flashbacks Simenon explains the circumstances that have led Emile, an ordinary man, to this desperate act. Emile is the chef in a small hotel on the Côte d'Azur that belongs to his wife. Her marrying him was the first in a long series of humiliations to which she subjected him. Emile involves himself in an affair with a half-wild servant girl whom he compares to a happy animal:

> She was at once his pet dog and his slave. She did not judge him, did not try to understand him or guess what he was thinking. She had adopted him as a master, just as a stray dog, for no apparent reason, attaches itself to the heels of a passerby.
>
> (*Sunday*, pp. 141–142)

Because he is insecure in his virility, Emile is able to relate only to this "slave." He belongs to the vast fraternity of men in Simenon's work who are unsure of their masculinity. Filled with doubt and self-hatred, they are able to relate only to women to whom they can feel superior. When Emile's wife discovers his liaison, she humiliates him to such an extent that he decides he must kill her: "It is claimed that a man can live a long time without eating or drinking. It is more difficult to live without one's pride, and his wife had taken it away from him" (p. 168).

Successful relationships between men and women stand out in Simenon's work because of their rarity. Maigret's happiness is dependent on the fact that his wife is satisfied to assume a passive role, acting rather like a servant or a paid companion. Her life is one of service and dedication to Maigret. Another successful marriage is that of Omer and Maria Petermans (*The Ostenders*), which is more of an equal partnership because Omer respects his wife's opinions and consults her before making any decisions, even in matters relating to his profession.

Bob and Lulu, the protagonists of *Big Bob,* who were patterned on Simenon's uncle Léopold and his wife, Eugénie, the canteen girl, have also achieved marital happiness. Like Léopold, Bob had many jobs because he was never able to settle down and take life seriously. His favorite expression, "crevant" (hysterically funny), repeated at every opportunity, expressed his opinion of life and its responsibilities. His good humor and gaiety were contagious; he had only to approach people for their faces to light up. Lulu adored her husband, whom she supported by running a hat shop. In their apartment behind the shop, Bob and Lulu received their many friends at all hours of the day and night.

Bob and Lulu's story is told by their friend, a Parisian doctor named Charles Coindreau, who had met them at a fishermen's inn at Tilly on the Seine, where they spent their weekends. One Monday, Charles receives a call from Lulu informing him that Bob drowned the day before, while fishing. As Coindreau makes inquiries into the drowning, he discovers that it was not accidental but a carefully planned suicide: "Having decided to kill himself, Bob was concerned to do so decently. It was in character. He had run through all the forms of suicide, searching for one that would look most like an accident" (p. 71). Coindreau's discovery prompts Lulu to ask him why Bob would have killed himself and whether he thought that it was because of her, despite the fact that she thought all her life that she was making him happy.

As Charles makes his inquiries into Bob's life and death, the story develops on three levels. The mystery surrounding Bob's suicide, the least interesting of the three, is solved by the discovery that he had stomach cancer: "He killed himself not because he was afraid of suffering, but because he didn't want to afflict others with the sight of his suffering and with what he considered to be a downfall" (p. 201).

On another level the novel touches on one of the central themes in Simenon's work, that of a middle-aged man who is prompted by an unexpected event to reassess all that he has previously taken for granted. When Charles reviews the completely honest relationship between Bob and Lulu, he realizes the limitations in his own marriage. He is tempted to tell his wife the truth about his feelings for her and about their marriage, but he decides that it is too late in their relationship for such honesty. Bob was honest with Lulu from the start. Charles begins to understand that the carefree atmosphere of Bob and Lulu's home resulted from their honesty and their ability to recognize what was important in life and worthy of their attention.

The most fascinating aspect of the novel is an examination of the character of Bob. As Charles continues his investigation, he discovers that Bob was the son of the dean of the University of Poitiers. When he was seventeen years old, his ambition had been to become an army priest in the Sahara. Then, one day, he decided that he would never make either a good priest or a good officer, and that, deep down, he lacked religious faith. After he passed his baccalaureate, he entered law school and spent one of his vacations as an unskilled worker on the night shift in the Citroën plant with impoverished foreign workers. When Coindreau reflects on Bob's background, he decides that Bob had first aimed too high, and then too low, and had finally settled into joyful mediocrity.

By all conventional standards Bob was a failure, for, despite his background and education, he spent his life in the bistros of Montmartre, supported by a wife whom he had virtually pulled out of the gutter. But he was a happy man because he led the life he had chosen. One day, when his sister asked him whether he was happy, he told her that he would not have changed his life for any other. "Having wished to be a saint in the desert, then the most humble of the humble, he had finished, quite simply, as he told her, by devoting himself to making one person happy" (p. 180).

Bob had also remarked that if everyone would take it upon himself to ensure the happiness of another person, the whole world would be happy.

Lulu, like Simenon's Aunt Eugénie, can find no reason to live without her love. She tells Coindreau that she has the same dream every night, in which she doesn't see Bob clearly, but only a shadowy form that beckons to her to join him. Then she hears a moan, and she tells herself that he is complaining because she is staying behind too long. Two weeks before Christmas, Lulu kills herself rather than spend it without Bob. On the bed next to her body lie a crumpled photograph of her and Bob taken fifteen years previously and an empty vial of sleeping pills.

Unlike Bob, who would not have changed his life for any other, most of Simenon's protagonists are prompted by a desire to lose themselves in another world. Indeed, the principal theme in the work of Simenon is escape, both physical and psychological. In a group of novels Simenon deals with middle-aged men who, after years of conforming to the standards of society, flee their milieu. There is a pattern common to all of the novels that deal with this theme. A certain event causes the hero to break with his habits, his duties, and the type of life he has led; his break is often consummated by a crime; his evasion brings him adventure and initiates him into a certain seedy side of life; although his liberation is consecrated by a redemption, he fails—either he goes mad or he comes back to his point of departure with a knowledge of the meaninglessness of existence. However, the one who has the courage to take the measure of his life and then return has acquired a form of second sight that helps him to survive.

Before their awakening the lives of all of these men are characterized by mechanical repetition of a series of gestures and actions, almost as if ritual exorcised the misfortune that might otherwise overtake them. The break with routine, or crisis, seems to occur spontaneously, but this is only because the cause is not readily apparent. In such cases, however, it is the culmination of a situation that has been developing for a long time. More often a specific event occurs that causes the protagonist to break with his habits and daily routine.

Dr. Hans Kupérus's rupture (*L'Assassin* [*The Murderer*, 1937]) is caused by an anonymous letter denouncing his wife as an adulteress. Armed with this letter, he returns surreptitiously from his weekly professional trip to Amsterdam and kills his wife and her lover. Ostracized by the townspeople, who suspect him without being able to prove that he committed the crime, he begins to audit his life and discovers that he was jealous not of his wife but of her lover. For fifteen years Kupérus had followed the rules, but his wife's lover had lived without rules and he had succeeded in everything he undertook. This being the case, it was Kupérus who had been wrong, and that was why he had to kill. Kupérus must pay the price for this discovery. He has gone too far in his quest for self-knowledge, and what he has seen is terrifying. Unable to turn back from the brink, he escapes into madness. The descent into madness here and in other novels is the type of conclusion for which Simenon has been faulted. It has been suggested that when it is time to end the novel, he often tacks on arbitrary, hasty conclusions.

Other novels dealing with the theme of flight have less melodramatic conclusions. *La fuite de Monsieur Monde* (*Monsieur Monde Vanishes*, 1945) is representative of this second group, in which the hero returns at the end of the novel with a serenity stemming from an acceptance of his own humanity. M. Monde, Simenon's version of Everyman, is a successful businessman. He gets up every morning at the same time, goes to his office, and does his work there with the solemnity appropriate to the performance of a ritual. However, on the morning of his forty-eighth birthday, as he is walking to his office, he unaccountably looks upward and sees the chimneys of the buildings outlined against a pale blue sky in which a tiny white cloud is floating. From that moment on, he changes. He feels ill at ease in his home and office and realizes that he must leave. Little by little he changes his outer appearance to conform to the changes taking place within him. He shaves off his mustache and exchanges his finely tailored clothes for an ordinary, ill-fitting suit of the type worn by the man in the street. Then, almost automatically, he boards a bus for the Gare de Lyon. Just as automatically he takes a train to Marseilles. When he arrives at the seashore, he begins to cry:

> What streamed out from his being through his two eyes was all the fatigue accumulated for forty-eight years. . . .
>
> He had given up. He no longer struggled. He had hastened from far off—the train did not exist, but only an immense movement of flight—he had rushed toward the sea which, vast and blue, more alive than anyone, soul of the earth, soul of the world, breathed peacefully near him. . . . He spoke without opening his mouth . . . of his infinite fatigue which stemmed not from the train trip but from his long journey as a man.
>
> (*Monsieur Monde Vanishes,* p. 58)

Life seeks Monde out, however, as a young woman in the hotel room adjoining his attempts suicide because she has been abandoned by her lover. He rushes in and saves her life; they go off to Nice, where they get jobs in a nightclub. One night Monde's first wife comes into the nightclub. She is a drug addict, down on her luck. The sense of responsibility Monde feels toward her, although she had abandoned him soon after their marriage, makes him realize that one cannot discard one's past. He had always envied those who were carefree and footloose, and had become like them for a time. Now he knows that he must return to Paris and resume his former life. It seems to those about him that Monde has not changed. They do not understand his new serenity, the serenity of those who have decided to look squarely at themselves and at others, accepting their limitations and inadequacies, those who have "laid all ghosts and lost all shadows" (p. 216). And he is unable to tell them about this change,

for his discovery is one that must be made by each man himself; it is a truth that cannot be transmitted.

While criminal and antisocial behavior are the usual stimuli for the awakening of Simenon's middle-aged heroes, this is not always so. In *Les volets verts* (The Green Shutters, 1950; translated as *The Heart of a Man*) and *Les anneaux de Bicêtre* (*The Bells of Bicêtre,* 1963), the protagonists' illnesses lead them to take stock of their lives.

René Maugras (*The Bells of Bicêtre*), editor in chief of an important French newspaper, is struck with hemiplegia and brought to Bicêtre Hospital. Although his mind has remained unaffected, half of his body is paralyzed and he cannot speak. Acutely depressed, he considers the world to which he no longer belongs and which he now observes as an outsider, wondering whether it was ever worth the trouble it entailed. Like so many of Simenon's protagonists, Maugras questions whether others really believe in their roles, whether they are really satisfied with themselves, or whether their activities, like his own, are merely a form of escape. He attempts to evaluate the results of his fifty-four years, and his pitiful inventory, which includes his drunken father, two unsuccessful marriages, and an unloved daughter, proves to him that life is meaningless. François Mauriac has remarked that it is novels like this that succeed, where Christian sermons have failed, in convincing us of the vanity of life.

Maugras's bitter conclusion is reinforced by the humiliations to which his body is subjected and by his feelings of desperation, outrage, and helplessness as he is reduced by sickness to the status of an object. As he lies in his hospital bed, he can think of only two moments when he seemed to have found a meaning in life, two moments during which he had felt "in harmony with nature. Twice he had almost been absorbed into nature. Nature had pervaded his whole being. He had become part of it" (p. 264). Both of these experiences had been linked to water, sunshine, heat, and fresh smells. And both times he had been afraid, had drawn back. Now he wonders whether twice in a lifetime was enough to justify an existence.

During the eight days in the hospital covered in the novel, Maugras changes from a dying man to a convalescent. He will return to his former life, knowing that for him there is nothing else, but with greater self-knowledge. Like Monde, he has reached no great conclusions, only a modest acceptance of his own inadequate, but terribly human, self.

Only two of Simenon's protagonists lead completely successful lives: one, a life of constant evasion; the other, one of total acceptance and serenity. The bantering smile that lingers on the face of M. Bouvet (*L'Enterrement de Monsieur Bouvet* [*The Burial of Monsieur Bouvet*, 1950]), even in death, bears witness to the success of his life of absolute freedom. When the old man dies, without a murmur, as he is looking at the display of a bookseller on the quai, he is taken to his rooming house, where the concierge lays out his body for burial. When his photo appears in the newspaper, those who once knew him appear, to reveal that Bouvet was the final incarnation of an amazing man who had led many different lives. As the various layers of his life are peeled away, it becomes known that he was born to a wealthy family, that he had studied law in Paris but soon dropped out and lived with a young whore in the Latin Quarter, where he frequented anarchist circles. When the girl's pimp attacked him with a knife for having stolen his livelihood, Bouvet killed him in self-defense and fled to Belgium with the girl. After a year he left her, as he would everyone and everything in turn, and went to England. During World War I he was Agent Corsico, the best-paid spy of the day. In 1918 he turned up in Panama in the guise of an American, married there, and fathered a daughter. He left his wife and daughter and went to Africa, where he amassed a fortune mining gold. Although he continued to send vast sums of money to his wife and daughter, he himself went native until, one day, he disappeared again.

Despite his many flights Bouvet was never able to give in to the temptation to become a tramp—the ultimate flight—because he could not tolerate alcohol. This theme of longing for the street, to be the man who has nothing and who lives solely in, of, and by himself, appears in many of Simenon's novels. He himself was always tempted to emulate those who have the strength to flee completely without caring about what others think of them.

Petit Louis (*Le petit saint* [*The Little Saint*, 1965]) is the antithesis of Bouvet. In 1962 Pierre de Boisdeffre wrote that Simenon's readers were still waiting for him to give them the great novel in which he would show not only the

> infinity of human solitude, but also the grandeur of human communion; not only the *libido* and the *destrudo*, but also the will to make something of oneself; a novel in which man could still be the product of his milieu, but where he would no longer be its prisoner because that choice that he, himself, would make, would, in the words of Sartre, become his destiny.
>
> (Boisdeffre, p. 107)

Simenon produced such a novel when he wrote *The Little Saint* in 1964. When he finished it, he exclaimed that he had finally succeeded in externalizing a certain optimism that was in him, a joie de vivre, a delight in the immediate and simple communion with all that surrounded him. Previously, after the first third or first half, his novels invariably turned to tragedy. For the first time, in *The Little Saint*, he was able to create a perfectly serene character in contact with nature and life. That is why he said that if he were allowed to keep only one of his novels, he would choose this one.

The Little Saint takes its title from the epithet applied to the protagonist by his schoolmates because of his serene detachment and the quiet and almost continuous satisfaction that his smile reflects. He is happy, he watches, he goes from one discovery to another, but he makes no effort to understand. What Louis observes, though transformed by his vision, is the poverty-stricken but vibrant life of the working class on the rue Mouffetard in Paris at the turn of the century. Little Louis lives in one room with his mother and four brothers and sisters, each sired by a different man. The children sleep on mattresses lined up side by side on the floor, separated by a hanging sheet from the walnut bed occupied by their mother and her current lover. Louis likes the room, in which the feeling is one of warmth and security, where they live "with one another as in a burrow, sheltered from the outside world, and come what may, their mother is there to protect them" (*The Little Saint*, p. 118).

Louis observes everything. He doesn't like people to bother him or to ask him questions. He wants to be left alone to observe, smell, and touch everything about him. His preoccupation with visual images prepares him for his metamorphosis into a great painter. The images he stores up will appear on his canvases, including those of the changes going on around him: the introduction of gas lighting into their room, anarchist bombs, construction of the métro, public works all over Paris, electricity being installed everywhere.

The last part of Louis's life is hastily sketched, for it was the development of his character and the discovery of his genius that were important. One of his brothers was killed in the Great War, his sisters became fat and callous, another brother died in prison, and still another brother lived with his wife in Ecuador, spending his time hunting butterflies and birds of paradise. His mother remarried and lived comfortably thereafter. "Had he not taken something from everything and everyone? Had he not used their substance?" (p. 244), Louis would wonder when asked about his success. "He didn't know, he mustn't know, otherwise he would be unable to carry on to the end. . . . 'May I ask you, Maître,' he was asked, 'how you see yourself?' He did not reflect very long. His face lit up for a moment as he said joyously and modestly: 'As a small boy'" (p. 244).

Louis's response provides the key to his harmonious life and explains how he differs from Simenon's other characters. He succeeds because he has never lost the young boy's love of all of life. Almost all of Simenon's protagonists have failed to remain faithful to the children they once were. One day, seized with a longing for a world like the one shown in picture books, they flee in search of innocence and childish purity. Their defeat is thus inevitable. Louis, on the other hand, has never failed to see himself as a young boy, and his joyous vision corresponds to that of an age he has never left behind.

EXOTIC NOVELS

Simenon's protagonists are characterized, in general, by an absence of will. A theme prevalent in his work is that of a man who watches impotently as his life disintegrates. Scarcely does a character appear than he collapses and crumbles away. Everything takes place without him, despite him, or against him; he is destroyed before our eyes and doesn't understand what is happening to him as he is carried off, not by a whirlwind but by the everyday disquiet of an almost immobile existence. Simenon watches his characters go astray and descend toward the abyss without doing anything to restrain them. They do not direct their own lives but stand by helplessly, shunted about by the vicissitudes of life. While this disintegration of the characters takes place in all types of surroundings in Simenon's novels, the unmerciful rain, heat, insects, and diseases of the tropics destroy them more quickly and relentlessly.

Madness is the destiny of Joseph Timar, the ill-fated protagonist of *Tropic Moon*. He arrives in Gabon with the hopes, expectations, and luggage of a young man from a good family. There he discovers that the company that hired him is on the verge of bankruptcy, that the job is a ten-day boat journey away, in the heart of the forest, and that the company's boat is inoperative. Even were he to find a way to get there, his actions would be futile because the post is still occupied by a demented old man who threatens to greet his replacement with a shot in the head.

> Then, it was no longer only the anguish of home-sickness that gripped his heart, it was the anguish of uselessness. Useless to be there! Useless to struggle against the sun that penetrated all his pores. Useless to swallow each evening that quinine, which nauseated him! Useless to live and to die to be buried in a makeshift cemetery by half-naked Negroes.
>
> *(Tropic Moon,* p. 67)

Timar is easily influenced by Adèle, the proprietress of his hotel, who convinces him to use his influence to obtain a lumbering concession for which she will supply the capital. His association with Adèle, whose shooting of a native boy has caused an uproar in the colony, has cut him off from the colonial authorities. He and Adèle go into the interior to the concession, and there heat, drink, fever, and his own lack of will destroy him completely. After denouncing Adèle as the murderer at a trial that had been rigged against a poor native, Timar is shipped back to France, mad, muttering, "But there's no such place as Africa" (p. 221).

While some go mad, others, like Joseph Dupuche (*Quartier nègre*), sink into squalor and alcoholism. When Dupuche, a young, well-bred French engineer, arrives in Panama with his bride of two weeks, he is optimistic about his future. However, he discovers that the company that hired him in Paris has gone bankrupt and his letters of credit are worthless. Alone and penniless in Panama, the couple turn to the white community, which is composed in large part of ex-convicts and shady entrepreneurs. Dupuche's wife, Germaine, is hired as cashier in the French-owned hotel in Panama, while he lodges in the native quarter. Although Germaine's refinement and charm endear her to her employers, Dupuche is unable to win the battle against the sun, fever, and alcohol. He discovers that he likes the poverty of the native quarter and has no desire to return to France. He lives with a young native girl who deceives him shamelessly. He begins to prowl about a section of the beach where, only a few yards from buildings made of reinforced concrete, a group of blacks have returned to the way of life of their ancestors, in huts exactly like those found in the heart of Africa.

Emulating these natives, Dupuche becomes indifferent to everything. "*He lived in himself! He was sufficient unto himself"* (*Quartier nègre,* p. 194). He is uninterested in the rules of society and is happy with his black mistress, whose devotion is like that of a dumb animal. Dupuche dies ten years later of acute blackwater fever after having realized his ambition: "to live in a hut at the water's edge behind the railroad, among the rank weeds and the refuse" (p. 207).

The third tragic destiny offered to the "failures of adventure" is an early death, either by one of the infinite forms it assumes in Africa or by suicide. Oscar Donadieu dies a suicide in *Banana Tourist.* "Banana tourist" is the contemptuous epithet applied to those of all classes and all countries who go to the tropics in search of a different life. However, after a month or two, tired of subsisting on bananas and coconuts, bored with this tête-à-tête with nature, they return home.

Oscar Donadieu, the protagonist of *Banana Tourist,* appeared for the first time in *Le testament Donadieu* (Donadieu's Will, 1937; translated as *The Shadow Falls*), where his flight from the ugliness and corruption of society began. In the second novel he has come to Tahiti to seek innocence, but the sordidness and corruption he discovers there are a parody of what he originally fled from in La Rochelle. Those about him believe that he has become one of them, that he has finally learned to play the game. In reality he has decided that life is no longer possible. Fearing that he will become like the others, Oscar kills himself after spending the night with Tamatéa, a Tahitian prostitute. The hysterical shrieks of Tamatéa, who has awakened in a pool of blood, convey the horror of Simenon's tropical hell, with the ever-present sleazy bar-hotel run by an escaped convict, the colonial club where the colonists drink themselves into daily stupors, the intense heat, tropical fevers, deadly insects, and rats.

THE NOVELIST AND THE ART OF THE NOVEL

Simenon defined the novel as a passion that completely possesses and enslaves the writer, and permits him to exorcise his demons by giving them a form and casting them out into the world. He believed that the popularity of the novel can be attributed to the fact that it satisfies an equally great need in the reader, who is not seeking in it an escape from reality but is attempting to see whether others are prey to the same passions, the same doubts, the same vices, the same temptations, the same discouragements as he. When he discovers that others are like him, he is less ashamed of himself and regains confidence in life. Because people today lack a strong religion and a firm social hierarchy, they are more insecure than heretofore. That is why modern novels do not provide a comforting view of humanity but present it as it really is.

> Other periods have left us the novel of the clothed man, of the man on parade. Will ours give us the portrait of the naked man, the one who looks at himself in the mirror while shaving and has no illusions about himself? . . . Is he less great in his search for equilibrium, in his thirst for truth, than his ancestors who draped themselves in purple and affected a borrowed serenity?
> (Le roman de l'homme [The Novel of Man], p. 92)

The modern novel, for Simenon, is the tragedy of our day and, like those of ancient Greece, poses the basic problem of man's destiny. Simenon has called his novels "romans-tragédie" (tragedy novels), and in them he has adopted many of the rules that governed the ancient tragedies. Like them his novels start at the moment of crisis and lead rapidly and inex-

orably to a tragic conclusion. There are no long introductions or chronological expositions; the past is evoked rapidly in a series of flashbacks. There are few characters and no subplots; action is limited; and attention is focused on the eternal drama of man's existence.

Simenon was trying to produce the quintessential, or "pure," novel, reduced to its basic elements and containing nothing that can be depicted through other media. He believed that the domain of the novel has shrunk, since other means of expression have taken over the picturesque, philosophy, and psychology. Thanks to mass communication, the reader's horizon has become so enlarged that excessive detail is no longer necessary. Having renounced all claims to journalism or teaching, the modern novelist should be able to suggest a setting, evoke an atmosphere with a few brief strokes, and then concentrate on the crisis that pits man against destiny.

Simenon believed that what critics call his atmosphere is nothing more than the impressionism of the painter adapted to literature. Like the impressionists he tried to give weight to his impressions, using concrete rather than abstract words. Simenon excelled in conveying a few decisive sensory impressions that evoke an atmosphere more vividly than any long, itemized description. A spot of sunlight on his desk reminds the burgomaster of Furnes of the jetty at Ostend with its sand "the color of blond tobacco, the changing sea that always remains pale, the parasols, the light dresses on the benches, on the rented chairs, the children running, the large red rubber balls that hit you in the legs" (The Burgomaster of Furnes, p. 226).

Although his images are primarily visual, Simenon often established relationships between diverse sensory impressions. Maigret, tracking a criminal, sees the dawn break:

> He saw the first anglers settle themselves on the banks of the river from which a fine mist was rising; he saw the first barges bottled up at the locks and the smoke that was beginning to rise from the homes in a sky the color of mother of

pearl. . . . It was pleasant after the night he had just spent to walk in the grass that was wet with dew, to smell the odors of the earth, that of the logs that were burning in the fireplace, to see the maid, who had not yet done her hair, come and go in the kitchen.

(*Maigret et son mort* [*Maigret's Special Murder*], 1948, p. 181)

Sensory impressions also are used to express states of being, both physical and mental. Simenon uses olfactory impressions in the following passage to convey the special poverty of the island of Porquerolles:

Perhaps it was true that you could still smell the odor of sweat, but it was mixed with other odors that were both bitter and muted, children's urine and sour milk, the smell of garlic, of fish, at the same time as that odor that came from the pine forests and the arbutus, which was sort of the smell of the island.

(*Le cercle des Mahé* [*The Mahé Family's Circle*], 1946, p. 22)

Climate plays an important role in the creation of Simenon's atmosphere. In northern Europe it rains continually:

It had never rained so much. The drops pattered on the sidewalks like celluloid balls and water came out from everywhere, from the gutters on the roofs, sewers, one might even say from beneath the door, forming sheets of water that automobiles entered with caution. . . . No sky, no depth to the atmosphere, no color. Nothing but icy water.

(*The Burgomaster of Furnes*, p. 93)

On the Côte d'Azur and the island of Porquerolles, "The sun weighs down. Everything requires an effort, an effort to adapt, to understand. . . . The air is thick and heavy. The ground, trees, walls steam, emitting waves of heat" (*Le cercle des Mahé*, pp. 15, 18). Between Hamburg and La Rochelle the climate is changeable, as in all temperate regions. And, in the exotic novels, the intense, debilitating, suffocating sun alternates with the intolerable rainy season, a climate in which you must live in slow motion, calculate your slightest gesture, in order to survive.

In the American novels there is the parched Arizona desert and the "luminous mist that rose from the desert of sand . . . the everchanging colors on the mountains that seemed, far off, to close in the world on all sides" (*La jument perdue* [The Lost Mare, 1948], p. 11). Or the swollen Santa Cruz River, the real protagonist of *Le fond de la bouteille* (*The Bottom of the Bottle*, 1949), during the rainy season when it was "high, already higher than during the night. It formed a dark yellow mass, flowing slimy and thick, heaving in places, breathing like a beast, carrying along tree trunks, empty cans, all kinds of filth" (pp. 28–29). And *Les frères Rico* (*The Brothers Rico*, 1952) provides an unforgettable impression of the sea at sunrise in Miami: "The sea was calm. All he heard was one small wave, the one which, forming not far offshore in a barely perceptible undulation, rolled onto the sand, in a sparkling curl and churned up thousands of shells" (p. 10).

Above all, in more than seventy novels, the setting is Paris in all seasons. The cold November rain falls "from a sky of low, unbroken gray, one of those steady showers that seem wetter and somehow more perfidious, especially the first thing in the morning, than ordinary rain" (*Maigret et les témoins récalcitrants* [*Maigret and the Reluctant Witnesses*, 1959], p. 9).

Simenon brings to the reader his Paris of blood puddings and brioches, les Halles and onion soup, chestnut vendors and anglers on the banks of the Seine, book dealers along the quais, bistros with zinc bars, Notre-Dame and the Île Saint-Louis, the place du Tertre and the place des Abbesses, the Moulin Rouge and Montparnasse, the boulevard Saint-Michel and the boulevard Rochechouart, the odors of café au lait, warm croissants, anisette, the small cafés and the elegant cafés of the Champs-Elysées, the rue Mouffetard and the place Blanche, the whores and the drab hotels of Pigalle, the train stations, the quai des Orfèvres and the Sacré-Coeur, a Paris that is constantly being torn down to provide underground parking for the cars that are strangling the city, a Paris that is struggling against the forces of progress and that will remain intact in Simenon's work when the battle has been lost.

It is this total recall of every mood and every aspect of Paris and of France, of northern Europe, Africa, Tahiti, the Galápagos between the two great wars, that caused George Steiner to remark, "Simenon may be among the last to have taken an entire culture for his verbal canvas" (*Language and Silence* [New York, 1967], p. 211).

Simenon described the way in which he went about writing a novel. The creative process would be set in motion one day when he began to feel great anxiety and realized that he would be virtually ill until he was able to effect a catharsis by means of the novel. At this point he rid himself of all social and family responsibilities for ten days and went off alone, seeking to put himself into what he called a "state of grace," which meant emptying himself of all preoccupations that personally affected him. While in this state he would be receptive to some sensory impression that would recall an atmosphere from his past. For example, on a sunny day he might remember a certain spring in the French provinces or in Arizona. A particular sound, an odor, would plunge him into the past, evoking certain memories. The idea for *Le président* (*The Premier*, 1958) was provided by a visual impression. Simenon saw a black-and-white etching over a mantel that reminded him of Normandy and of a period he had spent there years before with a woman. While this memory could have been the start of a love story, something diverted Simenon, as he also remembered an old house on a cliff that he had seen there and the curiosity he felt about its occupants. For some undetermined reason he then thought of Georges Clemenceau and decided to write about an old man living in such a house, looking back on his life.

After the setting the protagonist was created, generally a composite of many people with whom the author had come into contact. Simenon then gave him a name, a family, and a house; he did this by consulting the more than 150 telephone books for all countries that he kept in his study. Contrary to usual practice, Simenon did not give a name to the Premier because he did not want to use a fictitious name for a supposedly real politician. Generally, however, he wrote the name he had chosen on a yellow envelope—the rites Simenon followed were as rigid as those observed by his protagonists—and added to the name the protagonist's telephone number, his address, his father's age if alive, his mother's age, his children, wife, friends, and so forth. He often also sketched a rough plan of the character's house, for he wanted to know whether he opened the door to the left or to the right when he got home.

Having decided to forgo a name in *The Premier* and refer to the protagonist merely as the Premier, Simenon determined that he should be of peasant stock, born in Évreux, an industrial town in Normandy. Following extensive research on Évreux, Simenon then considered the household the Premier would have. He concluded that the old man would require a nurse, because he was eighty-two years old, as well as a secretary, a cook, a maid, and a chauffeur. The chauffeur would also be a part-time spy, since the government, Simenon felt, would want to keep an eye on such a political "monument." Each of the secondary characters was then given a complete identity, a procedure Simenon always followed, although he usually did not make use of this material.

What does an old man like the Premier do to occupy his time was the next question. Simenon decided that such a man would surely be writing his memoirs. In the novel Simenon has him write them on little pieces of paper, which he hides from his staff all over the house. Such a man would also be jealous of the younger men coming to power. In *The Premier* he is particularly jealous of a man named Chalamont, who had once worked for him and whom he had hoped would be his political heir, but who had long ago betrayed the Premier and his country by revealing to an unscrupulous speculator the government's secret plans to devalue the franc.

The problem that arose next for Simenon in writing a novel was crucial in its development. He had such a man, such a woman, in such surroundings, and then wondered what could happen to oblige them to go to their limit. It could be a very simple incident, but it was something that would change their lives. The incident, or catalyst, triggering this reaction, according to Simenon, was the only contrived part of the novel; the rest followed inevitably.

The fall of the government is the determining event in *The Premier.* Chalamont has been asked to form a new government. The old man can destroy Chalamont's chances with a single telephone call. The Premier deceives himself into believing that his hour has finally come, that Chalamont will come to beg for his silence and his forgiveness. But Chalamont never contacts him, and the disappointed, disillusioned Premier soon understands why. The members of his staff have stolen the single weapon he still possessed, Chalamont's letter of confession. Once his anger has subsided, the Premier realizes that his perspective has changed; he has begun to see the vanity of all human endeavor and to look upon life with detachment. He decides to burn all remaining incriminating papers and looks toward death with serenity.

Here, as in all of Simenon's works, the settling of accounts is a private one. While Simenon has often been compared with Honoré de Balzac, this is the great difference between the two novelists. Balzac's hero would have made the call to Paris to bring about a great scene of "annihilation" or, alternatively, would have brought the two men face to face for a confrontation. An even more significant distinction is Simenon's refusal to pass judgment. While Balzac's readers would have been called upon to join the author in condemning political corruption, Simenon's readers are struck by his refusal to moralize. For Simenon there are only problems, no answers.

CONCLUSION

Simenon's decision in 1972 to stop writing novels provided a rare opportunity to consider the work of a living writer in its entirety. It made it possible, from the perspective of a completed body of work, to study the author's narrative genius as well as his psychological perceptions as they apply to all of his novels. There are, inevitably, weak spots in such a vast literary production, principally certain works that seem to be hastily conceived imitations of earlier novels. *L'Homme au petit chien* (*The Man with the Little Dog,* 1964), for example, is vastly inferior to *Le temps d'Anaïs* (The Time of Anaïs, 1951; translated as *The Girl in His Past*), which it copies closely. Yet even in this work there are unforgettable passages, poetic transmutations of hideous reality that evoke the genius of Baudelaire.

Considered as a whole, Simenon's work is unique in modern literature. There are few contemporary writers who have re-created an entire period as completely as Simenon. He has evoked the atmosphere of France in the first half of the century, portraying its provinces and cities, its people and customs, on a vast canvas that can be compared to Balzac's *Comédie humaine* while, at the same time, imbuing the characters with a universality that transcends time and geographical boundaries. His novels form a bridge between the traditional novel, which sought merely to tell a story, and the modern novel, which has much more ambitious goals.

Like the traditional novelist Simenon keeps to chronological plot structure; his novels start at the moment of crisis—the past is evoked by a series of flashbacks—and work directly to a conclusion. Transitions between dream and reality, between supposition and fact, are clearly indicated, and characters are easily distinguishable from one another. Simenon employs many traditional plot situations in his novels, such as conflict over an inheritance, desperate actions to maintain a privileged position, and sibling rivalry leading to murder. The novels range in mood from tragedy to tragicomedy, to drama, to melodrama. That none of them is a comedy may be attributed to Simenon's view of life, summed up in the words "It's a difficult job to be a man."

Unlike many novelists of the post–World War II era, Simenon excludes from his work religion, politics, war, history, and metaphysical speculation. His aim, using a contemporary, timeless background, is to explore the eternal problems of man's destiny. For Simenon success as a novelist implies being understood by people in all walks of life at all times.

Nevertheless, Simenon's novels are very distinctly products of the twentieth century. His impatience with language, his belief that watching one's language distorts thought and that language is a means, not an end, are attitudes shared by many twentieth-century writers. His novels also express the anguish of the twentieth century, the feelings of alienation, guilt, and expatriation to which the works of Kafka and Camus have accustomed us. Like their protagonists, as well as those of Sartre and Malraux, Simenon's characters find themselves alone in a world without transcendent values and without the social structure and hierarchy that formerly gave order, stability, and meaning to life. They are existentialists inadvertently, for they must find in themselves the answers that were formerly supplied by society and religion; they must act instinctively as they encounter each new situation, for nothing in their past dictates their actions.

Yet Simenon's protagonists go beyond those of Sartre and Camus to join those of Samuel Beckett. Unlike the existentialist heroes, Simenon's characters lack lucidity; they are unable to understand their desperate situation. The existentialist hero assumes his role and, by choosing, creates his essence. Simenon's characters, on the contrary, do not choose but are carried along by forces stronger than themselves; they watch helplessly as they are crushed beneath the weight of pressures too heavy to bear. Like Beckett's characters they are the object, not the subject, of the dramas in which they are involved. In their perplexity and confusion they, too, suffer from a strange amnesia, wondering where they were previously and how long they have been in their present situation. This bewilderment, Simenon remarks, results from an internal fissure, a rending of the inner being.

Modern literature aspires to have man lose his distinguishing characteristics, to upset his chemistry, to destroy what had previously defined him, what made him what he was and what he believed he was. In this process of redefinition, man has lost what had formerly been called his soul. Unable, therefore, to establish values, he is led only by vague forces; he does not initiate his actions but merely carries them out. As a result he is not responsible for what he does, a concept that brings with it the concomitant contemporary thesis of the banality of evil. Simenon's characters murder without thought, as instinctively as they breathe. Their lack of lucidity, their subservience to blind forces, is perhaps the twentieth century's "mal du siècle," more fatal than the nineteenth-century despair over the divorce between ideals and reality. The type of man portrayed in Simenon's work lacks distinctive characteristics and positive values, which explains why there are no great thoughts, ambitions, or passions in his work.

Simenon's evolution as a writer was marked by a desire to serve, to better man's life. He did this by demonstrating to his readers that others are prey to the same weaknesses and vices as they. What he espoused, in effect, was an acceptance of limitations—not a desire to go beyond and overcome them. His compassion for all mankind and his understanding of the difficulty of existence, coupled with his narrative genius, account for the unprecedented popularity of his work. In reading Simenon's novels one is struck by his love of life and the joys it affords. He once remarked: "Despite the seeming pessimism of certain of my novels, I am not pessimistic about life. On the contrary, I enjoy every hour of the day, every spectacle that unfolds before my eyes, every type of weather, sun or rain, snow or hail" (*Un homme comme un autre,* p. 22). His goal was to give people a taste for life and for its small joys, for the rain as well as for a glass of beer savored on the terrace of a café.

Selected Bibliography

EDITIONS

NOVELS

Au rendez-vous des terre-neuvas. Paris, 1931.
Le charretier de "la Providence." Paris, 1931.
Le chien jaune. Paris, 1931.
Un crime en Hollande. Paris, 1931.
La danseuse du Gai-Moulin. Paris, 1931.
La guingette à deux sous. Paris, 1931.
M. Gallet, décédé. Paris, 1931.
La nuit du carrefour. Paris, 1931.
Le pendu de Saint-Pholien. Paris, 1931.
Pietr-le-Letton. Paris, 1931.
Le relais d'Alsace. Paris, 1931.
La tête d'un homme. Paris, 1931.
L'Affaire Saint-Fiacre. Paris, 1932.
Chez les Flamands. Paris, 1932.
Le fou de Bergerac. Paris, 1932.
Liberty-Bar. Paris, 1932.
L'Ombre chinoise. Paris, 1932.
Le passager du "Polarlys." Paris, 1932.
Le port des brumes. Paris, 1932.
L'Âne rouge. Paris, 1933.
Le coup de lune. Paris, 1933.
L'Écluse no. 1. Paris, 1933.
Les fiançailles de M. Hire. Paris, 1933.
Les gens d'en face. Paris, 1933.
Le haut mal. Paris, 1933.
L'Homme de Londres. Paris, 1933.
La maison du canal. Paris, 1933.
Le locataire. Paris, 1934.
Maigret. Paris, 1934.
Les suicidés. Paris, 1934.
Les clients d'Avrenos. Paris, 1935.
Les Pitard. Paris, 1935.
Quartier nègre. Paris, 1935.

Les demoiselles de Concarneau. Paris, 1936.
L'Évadé. Paris, 1936.
Long cours. Paris, 1936.
45° à l'ombre. Paris, 1936.
L'Assassin. Paris, 1937.
Le blanc à lunettes. Paris, 1937.
Faubourg. Paris, 1937.
Le testament Donadieu. Paris, 1937.
Ceux de la soif. Paris, 1938.
Chemin sans issue. Paris, 1938.
Le Cheval-Blanc. Paris, 1938.
L'Homme qui regardait passer les trains. Paris, 1938.
La Marie du port. Paris, 1938.
Monsieur La Souris. Paris, 1938.
Les rescapés du "Télémaque." Paris, 1938.
Les soeurs Lacroix. Paris, 1938.
Le suspect. Paris, 1938.
Touriste de bananes. Paris, 1938.
Le bourgemestre de Furnes. Paris, 1939.
Chez Krull. Paris, 1939.
Le Coup de Vague. Paris, 1939.
Les inconnus dans la maison. Paris, 1940.
Malempin. Paris, 1940.
Bergelon. Paris, 1941.
Cour d'assises. Paris, 1941.
La maison des sept jeunes filles. Paris, 1941.
L'Outlaw. Paris, 1941.
Il pleut, bergère . . . Paris, 1941.
Le voyageur de la Toussaint. Paris, 1941.
Le fils Cardinaud. Paris, 1942.
Maigret revient. Paris, 1942. Includes *Les caves du Majestic, Cécile est morte,* and *La maison du juge.*
Oncle Charles s'est enfermé. Paris, 1942.
La vérité sur Bébé Donge. Paris, 1942.
La veuve Couderc. Paris, 1942.
Le rapport du gendarme. Paris, 1944.
Signé Picpus. Paris, 1944. Includes *Félicie est là* and *L'Inspecteur cadavre.*
L'Aîné des Ferchaux. Paris, 1945.
La fenêtre des Rouet. Paris, 1945.
La fuite de Monsieur Monde. Paris, 1945.
Le cercle des Mahé. Paris, 1946.
Les noces de Poitiers. Paris, 1946.
Au bout du rouleau. Paris, 1947.
Le clan des Ostendais. Paris, 1947.
Le destin des Malou. Paris, 1947.
Lettre à mon juge. Paris, 1947.
Maigret à New York. Paris, 1947.
Maigret et l'inspecteur malgracieux. Paris, 1947.

Le passager clandestin. Paris, 1947.

La pipe de Maigret. Paris, 1947. Includes *Maigret se fâche.*

Trois chambres à Manhattan. Paris, 1947.

Le bilan Malétras. Paris, 1948.

La jument perdue. Paris, 1948.

Maigret et son mort. Paris, 1948.

La neige était sale. Paris, 1948.

Pedigree. Paris, 1948.

Les vacances de Maigret. Paris, 1948.

Les fantômes du chapelier. Paris, 1949.

Le fond de la bouteille. Paris, 1949.

Maigret chez le coroner. Paris, 1949.

Mon ami Maigret. Paris, 1949.

La première enquête de Maigret. Paris, 1949.

Les quatre jours du pauvre homme. Paris, 1949.

L'Amie de Madame Maigret. Paris, 1950.

L'Enterrement de Monsieur Bouvet. Paris, 1950.

Maigret et la vieille dame. Paris, 1950.

Un nouveau dans la ville. Paris, 1950.

Les volets verts. Paris, 1950.

Maigret au Picratt's. Paris, 1951.

Maigret en meublé. Paris, 1951.

Maigret et la grande perche. Paris, 1951.

Les mémoires de Maigret. Paris, 1951.

Un Noël de Maigret. Paris, 1951.

Tante Jeanne. Paris, 1951.

Le temps d'Anaïs. Paris, 1951.

Une vie comme neuve. Paris, 1951.

Les frères Rico. Paris, 1952.

Maigret, Lognon et les gangsters. Paris, 1952.

Marie qui louche. Paris, 1952.

La mort de Belle. Paris, 1952.

Le révolver de Maigret. Paris, 1952.

Antoine et Julie. Paris, 1953.

L'Escalier de fer. Paris, 1953.

Feux rouges. Paris, 1953.

Maigret a peur. Paris, 1953.

Maigret et l'homme du banc. Paris, 1953.

Maigret se trompe. Paris, 1953.

Crime impuni. Paris, 1954.

Le grand Bob. Paris, 1954.

L'Horloger d'Everton. Paris, 1954.

Maigret à l'école. Paris, 1954.

Maigret et la jeune morte. Paris, 1954.

La boule noire. Paris, 1955.

Maigret chez le ministre. Paris, 1955.

Maigret et le corps sans tête. Paris, 1955.

Maigret tend un piège. Paris, 1955.

Les témoins. Paris, 1955.

Les complices. Paris, 1956.

Un échec de Maigret. Paris, 1956.

En cas de malheur. Paris, 1956.

Le petit homme d'Arkangelsk. Paris, 1956.

Le fils. Paris, 1957.

Maigret s'amuse. Paris, 1957.

Maigret voyage. Paris, 1957.

Le nègre. Paris, 1957.

Les scrupules de Maigret. Paris, 1957.

Dimanche. Paris, 1958.

Le passage de la ligne. Paris, 1958.

Le président. Paris, 1958.

Strip-tease. Paris, 1958.

Une confidence de Maigret. Paris, 1959.

Maigret et les témoins récalcitrants. Paris, 1959.

Le veuf. Paris, 1959.

La vieille. Paris, 1959.

Maigret aux assises. Paris, 1960.

Maigret et les vieillards. Paris, 1960.

L'Ours en peluche. Paris, 1960.

Betty. Paris, 1961.

Maigret et le voleur paresseux. Paris, 1961.

Le train. Paris, 1961.

Les autres. Paris, 1962.

Maigret et les braves gens. Paris, 1962.

Maigret et le client du samedi. Paris, 1962.

La porte. Paris, 1962.

Les anneaux de Bicêtre. Paris, 1963.

La colère de Maigret. Paris, 1963.

Maigret et le clochard. Paris, 1963.

La chambre bleue. Paris, 1964.

L'Homme au petit chien. Paris, 1964.

Maigret et le fantôme. Paris, 1964.

Maigret se défend. Paris, 1964.

La patience de Maigret. Paris, 1965.

Le petit saint. Paris, 1965.

Le train de Venise. Paris, 1965.

Le confessionnal. Paris, 1966.

Maigret et l'affaire Nahour. Paris, 1966.

La mort d'Auguste. Paris, 1966.

Le chat. Paris, 1967.

Le déménagement. Paris, 1967.

Le voleur de Maigret. Paris, 1967.

L'Ami d'enfance de Maigret. Paris, 1968.

Maigret à Vichy. Paris, 1968.

Maigret hésite. Paris, 1968.

La main. Paris, 1968.

La prison. Paris, 1968.

Il y a encore des noisetiers. Paris, 1969.

Maigret et le tueur. Paris, 1969.

Novembre. Paris, 1969.
La folle de Maigret. Paris, 1970.
Maigret et le marchand de vin. Paris, 1970.
Le riche homme. Paris, 1970.
La cage de verre. Paris, 1971.
La disparition d'Odile. Paris, 1971.
Maigret et l'homme tout seul. Paris, 1971.
Maigret et l'indicateur. Paris, 1971.
Les innocents. Paris, 1972.
Maigret et Monsieur Charles. Paris, 1972.

AUTOBIOGRAPHICAL WORKS

La mauvaise étoile. Paris, 1938.
Les trois crimes de mes amis. Paris, 1938.
Je me souviens. Paris, 1945.
Le roman de l'homme. Paris, 1960.
Quand j'étais vieux. Paris, 1970.
Lettre à ma mère. Paris, 1974.
Un homme comme un autre. Paris, 1975.
Mémoires intimes. Paris, 1981.

TRANSLATIONS

Titles of the French originals are appended in brackets.

Aboard the Aquitaine. In *African Trio.* Translated by Paul Auster and Lydia Davis. New York. 1979. [*45° à l'ombre.*]

The Accomplices. Translated by Bernard Frechtman. New York, 1964. [*Les complices.*]

Account Unsettled. Translated by Tony White. Harmondsworth, England, 1966. [*Crime impuni.*]

Act of Passion. Translated by Louise Varèse. Harmondsworth, England, 1965. [*Lettre à mon juge.*]

At the "Gai-Moulin." In *Maigret Abroad.* Translated by Geoffrey Sainsbury. New York, 1940. [*La danseuse du Gai-Moulin.*]

Aunt Jeanne. Translated by Geoffrey Sainsbury. New York, 1983. [*Tante Jeanne.*]

Banana Tourist. In *Lost Moorings.* Translated by Stuart Gilbert. Harmondsworth, England, 1952. [*Touriste de bananes.*]

Belle. Translated by Louise Varèse. New York, 1954. [*La mort de Belle.*]

The Bells of Bicêtre. Translated by Geoffrey Sainsbury. New York, 1983. [*Les anneaux de Bicêtre.*]

Big Bob. Translated by Eileen M. Lowe. New York, 1981. [*Le grand Bob.*]

Blind Path. In *Lost Moorings.* Translated by Stuart Gilbert. Harmondsworth, England, 1952. [*Chemin sans issue.*]

The Blue Room. Translated by Eileen Ellenbogen. New York, 1978. [*La chambre bleue.*]

The Bottom of the Bottle. Translated by Cornelia Schaeffer. London, 1977. [*Le fond de la bouteille.*]

The Breton Sisters. In *Havoc by Accident.* Translated by Stuart Gilbert. London, 1943. [*Les demoiselles de Concarneau.*]

The Brothers Rico. In *An American Omnibus.* Translated by Ernest Pawel. New York, 1967. [*Les frères Rico.*]

The Burgomaster of Furnes. Translated by Geoffrey Sainsbury. London, 1952. [*Le bourgemestre de Furnes.*]

The Burial of Monsieur Bouvet. In *Destinations.* Translated by Eugene MacCown. Garden City, N. Y., 1955. [*L'Enterrement de Monsieur Bouvet.*]

The Cat. Translated by Bernard Frechtman. New York, 1976. [*Le chat.*]

Chez Krull. Translated by Daphne Woodward. London, 1958.

The Clockmaker. Translated by Norman Denny. New York, 1977. [*L'Horloger d'Everton.*]

The Couple from Poitiers. Translated by Eileen Ellenbogen. New York, 1985. [*Les noces de Poitiers.*]

A Crime in Holland. In *Maigret Abroad.* Translated by Geoffrey Sainsbury. Harmondsworth, England, 1952. [*Un crime en Hollande.*]

The Delivery. Translated by Eileen Ellenbogen. New York, 1980. [*Bergelon.*]

The Disappearance of Odile. Translated by Lyn Moir. New York, 1972. [*La disparition d'Odile.*]

The Door. Translated by Daphne Woodward. Harmondsworth, England, 1968. [*La porte.*]

The Family Lie. Translated by Isabel Quigly. New York, 1978. [*Malempin.*]

The Fate of the Malous. Translated by Denis George. Harmondsworth, England, 1966. [*Le destin des Malou.*]

Four Days in a Lifetime. Translated by Louise Varèse. New York, 1953. [*Les quatre jours du pauvre homme.*]

The Girl in His Past. Translated by Louise Varèse. New York, 1952. [*Le temps d'Anaïs.*]

The Girl with the Squint. Translated by Helen Thomson. New York, 1971. [*Marie qui louche.*]

GEORGES SIMENON

The Glass Cage. Translated by Antonia White. New York, 1973. [*La cage de verre.*]

The Grandmother. Translated by Jean Stewart. New York, 1980. [*La vieille.*]

The Hatter's Phantoms. Translated by Willard R. Trask. New York, 1981. [*Les fantômes du chapelier.*]

The Heart of a Man. Translated by Louise Varèse. London, 1966. [*Les volets verts.*]

The Hitchhiker. Translated by Norman Denny. New York, 1957. [*Feux rouges.*]

Inspector Maigret in New York's Underworld. Translated by Adrienne Foulke. New York, 1956. [*Maigret à New York.*]

Intimate Memoirs. Translated by Harold J. Salemson. New York, 1984. [*Mémoires intimes.*]

The Iron Staircase. Translated by Eileen Ellenbogen. New York, 1981. [*L'Escalier de fer.*]

Justice. Translated by Geoffrey Sainsbury. New York, 1985. [*Cour d'assises.*]

Letter to My Mother. Translated by Ralph Manheim. New York, 1976. [*Lettre à ma mère.*]

Liberty Bar. In *Maigret Travels South.* Translated by Geoffrey Sainsbury. Harmondsworth, England, 1952.

The Little Man from Archangel. Translated by Nigel Ryan. Harmondsworth, England, 1986. [*Le petit homme d'Arkangelsk.*]

The Little Saint. In *The Fourth Simenon Omnibus.* Translated by Bernard Frechtman. Harmondsworth, England, 1967. [*Le petit saint.*]

The Lock at Charenton. In *Maigret Sits It Out.* Translated by Margaret Ludwig. London, 1941. [*L'Écluse no. 1.*]

The Lodger. Translated by Stuart Gilbert. New York, 1983. [*Le locataire.*]

The Long Exile. Translated by Eileen Ellenbogen. New York, 1983. [*Long cours.*]

Madame Maigret's Friend. Translated by Helen Sebba. Harmondsworth, England, 1967. [*L'Amie de Madame Maigret.*]

The Madman of Bergerac. In *Maigret Travels South.* Translated by Geoffrey Sainsbury. Harmondsworth, England, 1952. [*Le fou de Bergerac.*]

The Magician. Translated by Helen Sebba. New York, 1956. [*Antoine et Julie.*]

Magnet of Doom. Translated by Geoffrey Sainsbury. London, 1948. [*L'Aîné des Ferchaux.*]

Maigret Afraid. Translated by Margaret Duff. New York, 1983. [*Maigret a peur.*]

Maigret and the Apparition. Translated by Eileen Ellenbogen. New York, 1980. [*Maigret et le fantôme.*]

Maigret Bides His Time. Translated by Alastair Hamilton. New York, 1986. [*La patience de Maigret.*]

Maigret and the Black Sheep. Translated by Helen Thomson. New York, 1983. [*Maigret et les braves gens.*]

Maigret and the Bum. Translated by Jean Stewart. New York, 1982. [*Maigret et le clochard.*]

Maigret and the Calame Report. Translated by Moura Budberg. New York, 1987. [*Maigret chez le ministre.*]

Maigret in Court. Translated by Robert Brain. New York, 1983. [*Maigret aux assises.*]

Maigret and the Death of a Harbor-Master. Translated by Stuart Gilbert. New York, 1989. [*Le port des brumes.*]

Maigret on the Defensive. Translated by Alastair Hamilton. New York, 1981. [*Maigret se défend.*]

Maigret in Exile. Translated by Eileen Ellenbogen. New York, 1982. [*La maison du juge.*]

Maigret and the Fortuneteller. Translated by Geoffrey Sainsbury. New York, 1989. [*Signé Picpus.*]

Maigret and the Gangsters. Translated by Louise Varèse. New York, 1986. [*Maigret, Lognon et les gangsters.*]

Maigret Goes Home. Translated by Robert Baldick. New York, 1989. [*L'Affaire Saint-Fiacre.*]

Maigret Goes to School. Translated by Daphne Woodward. New York, 1988. [*Maigret à l'école.*]

Maigret Has Doubts. Translated by Lyn Moir. New York, 1982. [*Une confidence de Maigret.*]

Maigret Has Scruples. Translated by Robert Eglesfield. New York, 1988. [*Les scrupules de Maigret.*]

Maigret and the Headless Corpse. Translated by Eileen Ellenbogen. New York, 1985. [*Maigret et le corps sans tête.*]

Maigret Hesitates. Translated by Lyn Moir. New York, 1986. [*Maigret hésite.*]

Maigret and the Hotel Majestic. Translated by Carolyn Hillier. New York, 1982. [*Les caves du Majestic.*]

Maigret and the Killer. Translated by Lyn Moir. New York, 1979. [*Maigret et le tueur.*]

Maigret and the Lazy Burglar. In *A Maigret Trio.* Translated by Daphne Woodward and Robert

Eglesfield. New York, 1983. [*Maigret et le voleur paresseux.*]

Maigret and the Loner. Translated by Eileen Ellenbogen. New York, 1983. [*Maigret et l'homme tout seul.*]

Maigret Loses His Temper. Translated by Robert Eglesfield. New York, 1980. [*La colère de Maigret.*]

Maigret and the Madwoman. Translated by Eileen Ellenbogen. New York, 1979. [*La folle de Maigret.*]

Maigret and the Man on the Bench. Translated by Eileen Ellenbogen. New York, 1979. [*Maigret et l'homme du banc.*]

Maigret Meets a Milord. Translated by Robert Baldick. Harmondsworth, England, 1963. [*Le charretier de "la Providence."*]

Maigret and the Millionaires. Translated by Jean Stewart. New York, 1976. [*Maigret voyage.*]

Maigret in Montmartre. Translated by Daphne Woodward. New York, 1989. [*Maigret au Picratt's.*]

Maigret and the Nahour Case. Translated by Alastair Hamilton. New York, 1986. [*Maigret et l'affaire Nahour.*]

Maigret on the Riviera. Translated by Geoffrey Sainsbury. New York, 1988. [*Liberty-Bar.*]

Maigret Sets a Trap. Translated by Daphne Woodward. New York, 1979. [*Maigret tend un piège.*]

Maigret in Society. In *A Maigret Trio.* Translated by Daphne Woodward and Robert Eglesfield. New York, 1983. [*Maigret et les vieillards.*]

Maigret and the Spinster. Translated by Eileen Ellenbogen. New York, 1982. [*Cécile est morte.*]

Maigret and the Toy Village. Translated by Eileen Ellenbogen. New York, 1987. [*Félicie est là.*]

Maigret in Vichy. Translated by Eileen Ellenbogen. New York, 1984. [*Maigret à Vichy.*]

Maigret and the Wine Merchant. Translated by Eileen Ellenbogen. New York, 1980. [*Maigret et le marchand de vin.*]

Maigret and the Yellow Dog. Translated by Linda Asher. New York, 1987. [*Le chien jaune.*]

Maigret's Boyhood Friend. Translated by Eileen Ellenbogen. New York, 1981. [*L'Ami d'enfance de Maigret.*]

Maigret's Failure. In *A Maigret Trio.* Translated by Daphne Woodward and Robert Eglesfield. New York, 1983. [*Un échec de Maigret.*]

Maigret's Memoirs. Translated by Jean Stewart. New York, 1985. [*Les mémoires de Maigret.*]

Maigret's Mistake. Translated by Alan Hodge. New York, 1988. [*Maigret se trompe.*]

Maigret's Pipe. Translated by Jean Stewart. New York, 1985. [*Le pipe de Maigret.*]

Maigret's Revolver. Translated by Nigel Ryan. New York, 1984. [*Le révolver de Maigret.*]

Maigret's Rival. Translated by Helen Thomson. New York, 1980. [*L'Inspecteur cadavre.*]

Maigret's War of Nerves. Translated by Geoffrey Sainsbury. New York, 1986.

The Man on the Bench in the Barn. Translated by Moura Budberg. New York, 1970. [*La main.*]

The Man Who Watched the Trains Go By. Translated by John Petrie. Harmondsworth, England, 1964. [*L'Homme qui regardait passer les trains.*]

The Man with the Little Dog. Translated by Jean Stewart. New York, 1989. [*L'Homme au petit chien.*]

M. Hire's Engagement. In *The Sacrifice.* Translated by Daphne Woodward. London, 1956. [*Les fiançailles de M. Hire.*]

Monsieur Monde Vanishes. Translated by Jean Stewart. New York, 1977. [*La fuite de Monsieur Monde.*]

The Murderer. Translated by Geoffrey Sainsbury. New York, 1986. [*L'Assassin.*]

A New Lease of Life. Translated by Joanna Richardson. Harmondsworth, England, 1966. [*Une vie comme neuve.*]

The Nightclub. Translated by Jean Stewart. New York, 1979. [*L'Âne rouge.*]

November. Translated by Jean Stewart. New York, 1978. [*Novembre.*]

The Old Man Dies. In *The Third Simenon Omnibus.* Translated by Bernard Frechtman. Harmondsworth, England, 1971. [*La mort d'Auguste.*]

Pedigree. Translated by Robert Baldick. London, 1962.

The Premier. Translated by Daphne Woodward. New York, 1964. [*Le président.*]

The Reckoning. Translated by Emily Read. New York, 1984. [*Le bilan Malétras.*]

The Rules of the Game. Translated by Howard Curtis. New York, 1988. [*La boule noire.*]

The Shadow Falls. Translated by Stuart Gilbert. New York, 1945. [*Le testament Donadieu.*]

The Snow Was Black. Translated by Louise Varèse. New York, 1950. [*La neige était sale.*]

The Son. Translated by Daphne Woodward. London, 1958. [*Le fils.*]

Strange Inheritance. Translated by Geoffrey Sainsbury. London, 1958. [*La voyageur de la Toussaint.*]

Sunday. Translated by Nigel Ryan. New York, 1976. [*Dimanche.*]

The Survivors. Translated by Stuart Gilbert. New York, 1985. [*Les rescapés du "Télémaque."*]

Striptease. Translated by Robert Brain. New York, 1989. [*Strip-tease.*]

Talatala. In *African Trio.* Translated by Stuart Gilbert. New York, 1979. [*Le blanc à lunettes.*]

Ticket of Leave. Translated by John Petrie. Harmondsworth, England, 1965. [*La veuve Couderc.*]

The Train. Translated by Daphne Woodward. New York, 1964. [*Le train.*]

Tropic Moon. In *African Trio.* Translated by Stuart Gilbert. New York, 1979. [*Le coup de lune.*]

Uncle Charles Has Locked Himself In. Translated by Howard Curtis. New York, 1987. [*Oncle Charles s'est enfermé.*]

The Venice Train. Translated by Alastair Hamilton. New York, 1983. [*Le train de Venise.*]

When I Was Old. Translated by Helen Eustis. Harmondsworth, England, 1973. [*Quand j'étais vieux.*]

The White Horse Inn. Translated by Norman Denny. New York, 1980. [*Le Cheval-Blanc.*]

The Widower. Translated by Robert Baldick. New York, 1962. [*Le veuf.*]

The Witnesses. Translated by Moura Budberg. London, 1958. [*Les témoins.*]

The Woman of the Grey House. Translated by Stuart Gilbert. London, 1944. [*Le haut mal.*]

Young Cardinaud. Translated by Richard Brain. London, 1959. [*Le fils Cardinaud.*]

BIOGRAPHICAL AND CRITICAL STUDIES

Becker, Lucille F. *Georges Simenon.* Boston, 1977. (The source for much of the present essay.)

Boisdeffre, Pierre de. "À la recherche de Simenon." In *La Revue de Paris,* 69:96–107 (September 1962).

Eskin, Stanley G. *Simenon: A Critical Biography.* Jefferson, N. C., and London, 1987.

Gill, Brendan. "Profiles: Out of the Dark." *The New Yorker,* 24 January 1953, pp. 35–45.

Lacassin, Francis, and Gilbert Sigaux, eds. *Simenon.* Paris, 1973.

Narcéjac, Thomas. *Le cas Simenon.* Paris, 1950. Translated by Cynthia Rowland as *The Art of Simenon.* London, 1952.

Parinaud, André. *Connaissance de Georges Simenon.* Paris, 1957.

Piron, Maurice. *L'Univers de Simenon.* Paris, 1983.

Raymond, John. *Simenon in Court.* London and New York, 1968.

Richter, Anne. *Georges Simenon et l'homme désintégré.* Brussels, 1964.

Rolo, Charles J. "Simenon and Spillane: The Metaphysics of Murder for the Millions." In *New World Writing.* New York, 1952.

Rutten, Mathieu. *Simenon: Ses origines, sa vie, son oeuvre.* Nandrin, Belgium, 1986.

Simenon sur le gril. Paris, 1968.

Stéphane, Roger. *Le dossier Simenon.* Paris, 1961.

Tauxe, Henri-Charles. *Georges Simenon: De l'humain au vide.* Paris, 1983.

Thoorens, Léon. *Qui êtes-vous, Georges Simenon?* Verviers, 1959.

Toureau, Jean-Jacques. *D'Arsène Lupin à San Antonio: Le roman policier français de 1900 à 1970.* Tours, 1970.

Vandromme, Pol. *Georges Simenon.* Brussels, 1962.

Young, Trudee. *Georges Simenon: A Checklist of His "Maigret" and Other Mystery Novels and Short Stories in French and English Translations.* Metuchen, N.J., 1976.

LUCILLE F. BECKER

RAYMOND QUENEAU
(1903–1976)

CONSCIOUSNESS, DEATH, the meaning of life, nothingness—these are subjects worthy of our consideration. But the weather, potato peelers, the sale of picture frames, the breeding of lice, the art of sweeping—what kind of foolishness is this? An author who writes about the new mathematics in scholarly journals, contributes prefaces to the works of Flaubert and Faulkner, and edits the *Encyclopédie de la Pléiade* clearly belongs to the establishment. But a Saint-Germain-des-Prés songwriter, a virtuoso at punning, the literary father of a kind of virtuous Lolita who says "my ass" to anyone who comes along—can he be worth the trouble? Well, Raymond Queneau represents all those things, and still more.

Of course, he is now recognized as one of the five or six major French writers of the generation born at the beginning of the century. But not until the mid 1950's was he recognized by the academic world and the general public. Although he had been a reader for Gallimard since 1938 and secretary general since 1941, it was not until the end of World War II that substantial articles and critical studies were devoted to him. Moreover, from 1951 on, he was a member of the Académie Goncourt. This recognition was no doubt belated because from the very beginning Queneau committed a sin—at least insofar as he was a contemporary of distinguished writers like Jean Giraudoux and, more especially, of highly serious writers like André Malraux, André Breton, Louis Aragon,

Henry de Montherlant, Jean-Paul Sartre, and, later, Albert Camus. As a matter of fact, his sin was a systematic lack of apparent seriousness—in other words, humor, which Queneau, attributing the words to his Irish creature Sally Mara, defined as "an attempt to purge lofty feelings of all the baloney." Lofty feelings and also lofty subjects, such as consciousness, death, the meaning of life, nothingness. . . .

Indeed, the keynote of Queneau's works is laughter. He himself declared that he did not write to bore people ("jécripa pour enmiélé lmond," he wrote half phonetically in *Bâtons, chiffres et lettres* [Sticks, Numbers, and Letters, 1950]). Queneau was known in Paris for his laugh—a staccato, snuffling laugh that suddenly stopped dead, leaving a silence symbolic of Queneau's second characteristic: deep down, what we may call true seriousness. But, actually, laughter is the immediately perceptible climate of his works. It is a very special kind of laughter that springs from an astonishment at the world. From beginning to end, Queneau's works show surprise at the properties of things, men, and ideas. That the universe is as it is seems to be a perpetual source of delight. But that delight is complex. It goes from the satisfaction of finding his opinion confirmed as to the absurd and the unfathomable stupidity of all things, to a very pure joy, devoid of any value judgment, in the face of certain wonders. It thus includes a Flaubertian satisfaction, and the pleasure, with no ulterior motive, of a curious mind, that of a collector, a scientist, or a jack-of-all-trades. Satisfaction of the first order: hearing, noting down, and re-creating the conversation about the weather between two commuters in a train. Pleasure of the second order: knowing that 1,729 is the smallest number that may be split up into a sum of two cubes in two different ways.

At the junction of satire and wonderment, Queneau saw the world as a vast puppet show—a puppet show worth meticulously observing and then re-creating for the great joy of young and old. Would Queneau, then, give us a lesson in nihilism without tears? We might say that if at the end of laughter he found nothingness, the rainbow of all the colors of being and nonentity were considered with delight. After all, why wouldn't nothingness be as valid a system of reference as this or that being? When, around 1950, André Gillois asked him if he considered mathematics "futile," Queneau replied most laconically: No. Then, questioned about literature, he stated that "the verbal activity of man" is not "complete futility." To avoid all the "isms" that have been surrounding him since the 1950's, let us say that Queneau was expressing a simple truth, which might be summed up as follows: 1,729 is, for all eternity, the smallest number that may be split up into a sum of two cubes in two different ways, but anybody and everybody "croaks" in any case. This is Pascal revised by Flaubert's Bouvard and Pécuchet, or vice versa, and revised also by Rabelais or Joyce, for it is language that is the trap par excellence in which this strange twosome is caught.

Queneau's laughter is thus a philosopher's laughter. If he philosophizes, it's for laughs; but if he laughs, it turns into philosophy. His works abound in allusions, from the pre-Socratics to Hegel—meaning not only artfully integrated quotations but also "inner" allusions that determine the structure of the meaning of individual works. No one really became aware of this until the 1950's (and then in large part only because Queneau himself pointed it out), for the philosophy is carefully transposed into purely literary forms. Or else, if the characters decide to meditate on certain problems, the profundity of their remarks is disguised by the ludicrous contrast between their subject matter (time, history, being and nothingness, saintliness, and so on) and their social position (concierge, café waiter, former soldier turned shopkeeper), as well as the language it implies. The concierge in *Le chiendent* (*The Bark Tree,* 1933) knows more about ontology than Roquentin in Sartre's *La nausée* (in fact, Saturnin came into being five years before Roquentin), but how can he be taken seriously when he writes "nonête" for "non-être"? And one may wonder whether Pierrot, in *Pierrot mon ami* (*Pierrot,* 1942), is not more truly a stranger than Camus's Meursault, or whether the fits of saintliness of Jacques L'Aumône, in *Loin de Rueil* (*The Skin of Dreams,* 1944), and the soldier Brû, in *Le dimanche de la vie* (*The Sunday of Life,* 1952), are not far less allegorical and far more immediately concrete than the attitudes of many righteous heroes in the austere literature of secular saintliness. But here is the real difference: Valentin Brû's saintliness is quite the opposite of a doctor's spectacular sacrifice during an epidemic of the plague; it consists of his

> doing the most bloody awful jobs . . . without calling attention to his devotion; when he manages to perform the thankless duty of cleaning out the crappers daily, without Foinard [a priest] noticing, he congratulates himself on having thus reached a certain degree of abnegation without any fuss.[1]

First of all, the matter of such saintliness lacks dignity; second, its effectiveness is very limited; third, the undertaking comes to nothing, and we go on to something else.

Roquentin and Meursault brought philosophy into the streets, but aside from a few moments of burlesque in Sartre, the reader

---

[1] Translations, unless otherwise noted, are by June Guicharnaud.

never has any doubts as to the solemnity of the message. In Queneau the philosophical message, although remaining essentially serious, does dissolve into an ultimate laugh-provoking truth—the drollery of a world based on the tremendous contradiction between plenitude and nothingness, and in which the touching stupidity of individual destinies unfolds.

Queneau's works include some seventeen novels (one in verse), numerous poems (one a cosmogony of 1,396 lines), a few short stories, a play, some film dialogues, prefaces and various articles, and a few translations. They are all very personal works, not only in style but because the author is obviously present in many respects.

To be sure, Queneau did not write confessions as did the Romantics, but he used himself plentifully. And he often calls attention to himself so that one doesn't forget that he is the poet, the maker of that prose and those verses.

Certain of his texts are in fact closely related to autobiography. His novel in verse, *Chêne et chien* (Oak and Dog, 1937), begins as follows:

I was born in Le Havre one twenty-first of February
in nineteen-o-three
my father owned a dry-goods store, my mother too
they jumped for joy

Nothing could be truer than the first three lines. Queneau then went on to describe his childhood; his father's reactionary and defeatist attitude during World War I; his discovery of the cinema—the first Chaplin films, serials of the *Perils of Pauline* type, dramas of high society; his reading of the Larousse from A to Z; his years at the lycée; and, above all, the development of his complexes—"drama of the lost breast, drama of prehistory," as he said— leading to a period of psychoanalysis (1933–1939), which served as a theme for the second part of the book. As a sign of liberation or of reconciliation, the third part celebrates the "village feast" and ends on the bucolic note of "Keep singing, keep dancing / until the new work of the coming season."

With greater distance and distortion, *Odile* (1937) touches closely on Queneau's private life. He himself tells us (in *Bâtons, chiffres et lettres*) that this novel originated from his break with André Breton in 1929, and that it was only in the "writing of a novel called *Odile*" that he began to get rid of the "impassioned hate" he had felt at the time. The hero of the book is a young mathematician, Roland Travy, who, back from the Rif war, divides his time between a few petty criminals and a literary group led by a certain Anglarès, who is clearly a caricature of André Breton. Queneau, in effect, frequented the surrealist *Centrale* from 1924 to 1929—that is, before and after his military service in the Zouaves and his participation in the Moroccan war. In a photograph taken by Man Ray at the *Centrale*, we see him right next to Breton, in the company of Paul Éluard, Louis Aragon, Robert Desnos, and Roger Vitrac. He was the one who in March 1929 drew up a declaration in favor of collective action during a quarrel that divided the surrealist group and the more or less related coteries. But in 1930 he allied himself with Georges Ribemont-Dessaignes when the latter drafted *Un cadavre*, a violent attack on the pope of surrealism.

Queneau's works are considerably marked by his surrealist experience: in them prime importance is given to dreams, purposeless journeys (not to be confused with the "optimistic" escapism of the writer-travelers of the 1920's), a feeling for mysterious or diabolical characters, surprise meetings, the strange poetry of the landscape and geography of familiar cities (above all, Paris), prophecies, and so forth. But it would seem that Queneau refused to become involved in the hazy metaphysics and the spirit of earnestness that were dominant in official surrealism. In *Odile*, his hero, far more passive than Queneau himself in that venture, took a certain interest in the way his new friends interpreted his mathematical comments in a magic and prophetic sense; but their emphasis on infrapsychism, their wavering with regard to politics, and their little quarrels finally seemed ridiculous. *Odile* is in part a satire on the surrealist group, as the following list of little allied coteries or enemies of Anglarès shows so well:

> The phenomenophile comaterialists . . . the anticonceptional Yugoslavs, the paralyrical mediumists, the irresolute fanatics and advocates of ultrared, the incubophile spirits, the pure asymmetric revolutionaries . . . the anticop fruitarians, the inactive annihilating phenomenologists . . . and thirty-one Belgian groups.

Roland Travy breaks away from the group and devotes himself more and more to a young woman, Odile, whom he marries with the understanding that he doesn't love her. He leaves for Greece, where he has an intuition of what true wisdom is. This illumination brings him back to France, and the novel ends with Odile, whom he loves, awaiting him at the dock in Marseilles. Here we have, of course, the transposition of an intellectual adventure: Queneau tells elsewhere about the profound influence that his trip to Greece had on him, a trip during which he started to write his first novel, *The Bark Tree.*

Queneau's presence in his works is evident not only in his essentially autobiographical transpositions but also in his poems and his apparently most objective novels, by the use he makes of his obsessions—death, which is the substance of his lyricism, and asthma, from which one of the characters in *Les enfants du limon* (Children of the Slime, 1938) suffers, and which becomes, in the poet Des Cigales (*The Skin of Dreams*), an "existential ontalgia." Moreover, his novels are studded with special interests and key objects—filth, to take one example, which he poeticizes through comedy, as Beckett does by means of touching burlesque. As Queneau says in *Chêne et chien:* "I had a taste for muck and filth / images of my hate and my despair." He ends by entrapping it, so to speak, in the dwarf Bébé Toutout (*The Bark Tree* and *Les enfants du limon*), a repulsive and cantankerous little devil, and in the broom (mentioned also in *Chêne et chien:* "I helped sweep out that foul stuff"), which can be seen on a photograph in the hands of Queneau the Zouave, and which takes on epic proportions in *Les enfants du limon* and metaphysical proportions in *The Sunday of Life.*

Another of Queneau's obsessive preoccupations is food. The *choucroute* that Zazie greedily devours in *Zazie dans le métro* (*Zazie,* 1959) is well known. But among his other novels it is rare to find one in which the characters—at least certain of them—do not indulge in some Rabelaisian meal, collectively or quite alone. Throughout his career as a novelist Queneau lovingly described such scenes in great detail, whether the meal takes place in a "de luxe," such as Cidrolin's in *Les fleurs bleues* (*Blue Flowers,* 1965), or consists in an enormous *brouchtoucaille,* the recipe of which is given in *Saint Glinglin* (1948). That obsession with voracious appetites can be explained by the German occupation of France, during which time Queneau drafted his *Une histoire modèle* (A Model History, 1966); one of the main parameters of that "model" (a quantitative explanation of the history of mankind) is the variations of the equation between population and food supply during all time.

The *brouctoucaille* in *Saint Glinglin* is on the order of cuisine-fiction. It is one of the features of that novel-cum-epic-poem in three parts that easily lends itself to a Freudian interpretation (among many others). In it most of Queneau's obsessions become universal in a kind of vast allegory, in which, apropos of the story of a dynasty and in the framework of an imaginary state, La Ville Natale, Queneau introduces very personal themes, using apparently objective and burlesque devices. In contrast to images of woman, linked with primordial life and water, is the image of the petrified father, transformed into a statue, whereas variations on the natural elements—stone, sun, rain—are accompanied by an underlying horror of vegetation comparable to that of another poet of the city, Baudelaire, whose "sanctified vegetables" correspond to

Queneau's "long sheet of boredom and chlorophyll."

Queneau's works are also shot through with signs or signatures. His eyeglasses were famous, and it is no accident, for example, that the first sentence of *Pierrot* reads: " 'Come on, take off your glasses,' said Tortose to Pierrot," or that Vincent Tuquedenne, hero of *Les derniers jours* (The Last Days, 1935)—whose years of study in Paris actually correspond to Queneau's own—is nearsighted. In other novels Queneau introduces himself as a character, as at the end of *Les enfants du limon,* in which the compiler Chambernac gives his manuscript on "literary madmen" to a young author with glasses, who will, as a matter of fact, use it in a novel, and whose name is Queneau. In *The Skin of Dreams* the hero, who has become a great movie star, acts in a film made by the Ramon Curnough Company.

As a lyric poet, Queneau conformed to the rule of the genre: he used the first person a great deal, often addressing a fictional listener, such as the girl in "Si tu t'imagines" (If You Imagine; in *L'Instant fatal* [1977], pp. 181–182). But he had really to feel at home at the heart of his own writings to compose an eight-line poem made up entirely of anagrams of the name Raymond Queneau, the ninth of which is the actual title, "Don evané, marquy" (in *Les ziaux,* 1943).

More subtly, Queneau, without naming himself, even indirectly, intervenes in his novels through remarks that are obviously not made by the characters and consequently must be the author's intrusions. To take an example from *The Bark Tree:* Dominique has informed his son Clovis that he is going to study at the lycée. There follows a lyrical speech addressed to Clovis, holding out bright prospects for his future. It ends with a parenthetical remark that is clearly the author's own: "You shall steadfastly describe this splendid trajectory, Clovis, and nothing will be able to stop you. (Unless he croaks on the way, but we needn't tell him that, he's so easily frightened, he'd get panicky.)" On page 105 of the same novel, in the middle of the narrative, there is a "he says" that would be absolutely unjustified were the "he" not assumed to be the storyteller himself. And at the end of *The Bark Tree* even the characters are surprised:

> "It wasn't I who said that," said the queen. "It's in the book."
>
> "What book?" asked the two roving marshals.
>
> "Well, this one. The one we're in now, which repeats what we say as we say it and which follows us and tells about us, a real blotter that's been stuck on our lives."
>
> "That's a pretty queer story, that one," said Saturnin. "We create ourselves in time and the book snaps us up right away with its little handy scrawlwriting."

Here the author as an occasional presence has given way to the author as creator. But is there a "creator" at this extreme point? We are dealing with writing that produces itself. In any case, before so much erudite criticism was written about either the authorial voice or the authorless text in narrative literature, Queneau, as early as 1933, was showing acute awareness of the problematics implicit in the writing of fiction, as he was to do later on in *Blue Flowers* and *Le vol d'Icare* (*The Flight of Icarus,* 1968).

Finally, Queneau had no qualms about establishing an almost magical relationship between his works and his person. Since etymologically his name comes from two Old French words meaning *chêne* (oak) or *chien* (dog), he entitled his autobiography in verse *Chêne et chien* and a collection of poems *Le chien à la mandoline* (Dog with Mandolin, 1965). Symbolically combining this cipher with his obsession about being hanged, he has the dog Jupiter hanged in *Le chiendent* (another pun on his name, *chiendent* meaning "crab grass"). Then, since he was born under the sign of Pisces, *Gueule de pierre* (Stone Mug, 1934; now included in *Saint Glinglin,* 1948) opens with a long meditation on the "aiguesistence" of fishes. And since his first and last names have seven letters each, the number seven serves as a mathematical ratio for the structure of certain of his novels, especially *The Bark Tree,* the most "egocentric" of his apparently objective works.

From a relatively serious tone to a comic tone, from autobiographical transposition to the more or less dissimulated personal allusion, Queneau thus used all the means possible to indicate that his works are *his* works. But he is certainly not their sole substance or their sole center of interest. Far from it. To some of his adventures and to his presence as a writer he added an infinite variety of materials, the whole baggage of a scholar, a curious mind, an encyclopedist, of a man who has his eyes (and ears) open to what is almost the totality of human experience—all of which obviously implies a keen sensitivity to the things of our time. Before pointing out some of the main fields Queneau drew on, we must stress that, somewhat in the manner of Joyce but more especially in the manner of Flaubert's Bouvard and Pécuchet, he established almost no hierarchies a priori, whence the disparity of his baggage—a disparity that the form of individual works integrates and unifies.

To begin with, the works Queneau read, those that he quotes or alludes to most frequently, include works by certain members of the worldwide literary establishment: Homer, Flaubert, Joyce, Faulkner, Céline, Henry Miller. Their presence is clearly discernible in his writings, and they are acknowledged by him in his articles, interviews, and essays, as in his well-known introduction to *Bouvard et Pécuchet,* where in scholarly fashion he rehabilitates the two antiheroes of Flaubert. But for him literature, "the verbal activity of man," as he puts it, was not limited to great literature. It included the press—newspapers, magazines, and the comics. Queneau was perhaps the first eminent writer in France to include comics in the canon of reputable culture, decades before the BD (*bande dessinée,* or comic strip) fad stormed the country's intelligentsia. "Les pieds-nickelés," a comic strip popular early in the century, was one of his favorites; later came *Le journal de Mickey* and *Robinson,* in which side by side (and speaking French) were "Mandrake the Magician," "Bringing Up Father," "The Katzenjammer Kids," and "Popeye." It was therefore no accident that *Robinson* was the favorite magazine of the soldier Brû (*The Sunday of Life*), who also reveled in *Marie Claire*—the French equivalent of *Glamour*—from which, as a matter of fact, Sally Mara, fictional author of *On est toujours trop bon avec les femmes* (*We Always Treat Women Too Well,* 1947), got her taste for lush undergarments as well as the name of her heroine: Gertie Girdle.

In addition to Queneau the person, Queneau the reader of great and not-so-great books, there is Queneau the scholar. For example, he meditated on the structure of language, indeed of several languages, with the help of the works of Joyce and Céline, Joseph Vendryès's treatise *Le langage* (1921), and probably also, for *Sally Mara,* Vendryès's *Grammaire du vieil irlandais* (1908). He was surprised by the great difference that exists between written and spoken French, compared it to that which exists in Greece between the demotic and the literary language, and came to radical conclusions as to the need for a reform of spelling and even syntax (the latter being, in spoken French, much nearer that of Chinook than that of André Gide; see "Écrit en 1937," in *Bâtons, chiffres et lettres*). However, it would be wrong to overestimate the importance of such research in his works themselves. Queneau wrote his articles, some poems, and most of his novels in literary French. Moreover, he had no intention of reproducing the reality of spoken French as a tape recorder would. The spoken language had to be reworked, transformed, and elevated to a literary form. It then became one of the possible materials for a novel or a poem, like the Homeric style or conventional literary prose. But at any rate, part of Queneau's fame came from his parodic use of "neo-French," such as the well-known "Doukipudonktan," the first sentence of *Zazie,* or the syntax of certain sentences in *The Sunday of Life,* which imitate the specific order of words in today's colloquial French (e.g., "They won't finish filling it up until after the soup, the gravediggers the hole").

Immersed in literature, conscious of the problems of language, Queneau is also one of the few French writers to combine literary culture with a vast scientific culture—which is the very good reason why Gallimard put the author of *Zazie* in charge of the *Encyclopédie de la Pléiade.* First of all, Queneau was a mathematician. For him mathematics was, of all the fields of human endeavor, the least futile, and he managed to keep abreast of all its modern developments. He wrote a great deal on the subject, on the place of mathematics in the classification of sciences, and proposed a "kinematics" of the moves of chessmen (there is a photograph of him playing chess with André Gide, and across from the author of *Corydon,* the author of *Zazie* curiously brings to mind the author of *Lolita*). Numbers, topology, von Neumann's theory of games, Bourbakism—Queneau was as conversant with all these subjects as any amateur and some specialists. In 1964 he became a member of the American Mathematical Society. From mathematics Queneau very systematically went on to the other sciences that proceed from it, not only the physical but the biological and social sciences. Mock-heroic but very learned, his *Petite cosmogonie portative* (Little Portable Cosmogony, 1950) attests to this: it traces the history of the universe from the beginnings of the galaxy to the invention of computers.

After literature and the sciences, philosophy. While he was studying, Queneau received graduate degrees in psychology, the history of philosophy, ethics, and sociology. During the 1930's he attended the École pratique des hautes études as an auditor of the courses of Alexandre Kojève and Henri-Charles Puech. In his writings Queneau was partial to the universalism of Amenhotep IV; he celebrated Ashurbanipal; he had a weakness for Comenius, the seventeenth-century Czech educator—all encyclopedists. He went from there to the pre-Socratics and to all modern philosophy, with Descartes and the phenomenologists probably in the lead. And one critic (Claude Simonnet in *Queneau déchiffré*) has shown what *The Bark Tree* owes to Gnosticism, as well as to Descartes and to Plato's *Parmenides.*

Finally, Queneau would not be a modern writer had he not been fascinated by the cinema. *Chêne et chien* relates the author's first contact with films, before World War I, when he was taken to the movies by his father in Le Havre. In 1944 he published *The Skin of Dreams,* the subject of which is based on the cinematographic play of the imagination. Moreover, his novels are often cut like films. Not only are they constructed as a series of sequences—which is not unique in the mid-century novel (see Malraux's *La condition humaine* [1933])—but their economy of style is based on ellipses that are peculiar to the cinema, or were, until Queneau came along. *The Sunday of Life, Zazie, Blue Flowers,* and *Le vol d'Icare* are distinguished by their lack of conventional transitions and by jumps in time and space, which, in some ways, point to New Wave directors such as Jean-Luc Godard or, for that matter, Louis Malle, who made a film adaptation of *Zazie.* On the other hand, many of the comic effects in his novels recall those of the old American movies, from W. C. Fields comedies to the Marx Brothers.

We thus understand why, in an interview about his quarrel with Breton, Queneau said that although *Odile* does represent a kind of therapeutic testimony of the whole affair, the novel "is not only about that" (*Bâtons, chiffres et lettres*). And one of the more striking characteristics of Queneau's novels is that, in most cases, if one tries to specify what "they are about," the abundance of materials and complexity of the form constantly tempt one to think that they are forever about something else.

It is strange that, more than most novels, Queneau's works are generally almost impossible to summarize, as Claude Simonnet notes in *Queneau déchiffré* or Jacques Bens in his *Ray-*

mond Queneau; the latter, required by the rules of Gallimard's "Bibliothèque idéale" series to give summaries of the novels, found a way out by using the jacket blurbs written by Queneau himself. Most studies of Queneau are allusive and assume that the reader already knows the novels, which are very close to poems, and therefore a summary of the plot, even when possible, can never convey more than a vague approximation of it. There is, however, aside from *Odile,* one novel with a relatively simple story—*Un rude hiver* (*A Hard Winter,* 1939). In Le Havre, in 1916, there lived a war casualty and disconsolate widower, Bernard Lehameau, whose wife had lost her life in a fire; his unhappiness aroused a deep hatred in him for his compatriots but at the same time made him particularly lucid with regard to patriotic propaganda. Lehameau falls in love with an English WAAC stationed in Le Havre; at almost the same time he becomes taken with a very young girl, Annette. He also strikes up a friendship with a certain M. Frédéric, who shares his loathing for French democracy. But Frédéric turns out to be a German spy, who is responsible for the torpedoing of an English troopship, and consequently, perhaps, for the death of Héléna, the WAAC. Lehameau sleeps with Annette's sister, but it is the little girl herself who cures him of his unhappiness and hate; she is his "flame," his "life." Recovered from his wound, he is about to go off to the front, but there is some question of his marrying Annette. In the course of this story, we witness both the development of a character in whom there is a perfect balance of odious and very likable traits, and a kind of "sentimental re-education" that is at once comic and touching. Like *Chêne et chien* and *Odile,* this is, in a way, the story of a cure.

The apparent simplicity of *A Hard Winter* is due to the fact that the novel is centered on one character. But in Queneau's universe the presence of a clearly defined protagonist is not always a guarantee of centrality and the Aristotelian simplicity of traditional plots. *Pierrot,*

for example, is centered on Pierrot, but by itself Pierrot's adventure seems of very small account. Pierrot works at the Fun Palace of Uni-Park; the Fun Palace is closed following a brawl and the beginning of a fire; Pierrot is then employed by a fakir, but faints when he sees his boss stick pins in his cheeks. Pierrot is then given the job of taking a chimpanzee and a wild boar back to their trainer. Meanwhile, he meets the caretaker of a funerary chapel, which houses the remains of a Poldevian prince who died on that very spot, and the caretaker wants to make him his heir; meanwhile, also, he falls in love with Yvonne, daughter of the owner of Uni-Park. Yvonne scorns him and has other lovers. The mistress of the owner of Uni-Park is trying to discover the whereabouts of a young girl who was responsible for the death of her first lover. In fact, her first lover is not dead: he is the wild-animal trainer. Finally, a fire, the cause of which is unknown, destroys Uni-Park. It is replaced by a zoo. Pierrot loses the will given him by the caretaker of the Poldevian chapel. He returns to the caretaker's house, but is greeted by Yvonne. Is the caretaker dead? In any case, Yvonne sends him away. Pierrot walks down the street: "When he got to the corner, he stopped. He began to laugh." Obviously, the novel is more than this strange outline. In the jacket blurb Queneau alludes to an "'ideal detective story,' in which not only does the criminal remain unknown but one has no idea whether there has even been a crime or who the detective is." The explanation is as good as any.

And what is there to say about the plot of *The Sunday of Life*? Here, Julia, a shopkeeper, marries the soldier Brû, who goes off on his wedding trip all by himself, after which Julia inherits from her mother; the couple settles down in Paris, where Brû sells picture frames; Julia secretly becomes a fortune-teller; when she falls ill, her husband discovers this and, disguised as a woman, replaces her. But the war of 1939 is declared and Brû is mobilized. During the phony war he is tempted by saintliness. When the exodus comes, Julia loses track of her husband. She finally finds him in a railway station, just as he is helping young women into an overcrowded train: "Julia choked with laughter: he was doing it so he could goose them." And so ends *The Sunday of Life.*

As for the complex novels, it would take pages to summarize them; for not only are the characters numerous, but the events rush by, one after another. In *The Bark Tree,* for example, after a relatively simple beginning (Pierre decides to observe an unknown man, Étienne, in a throng of Parisians, at the very moment that Étienne starts to become aware of the inauthenticity of his life), relationships multiply between the two protagonists and other characters—women, children, concierges, ragpickers, and the owners and employees of an eating joint—each one motivated by a specific project (seduction, revenge, philosophical undertakings, and the like), all leading up to a kind of treasure hunt (although the treasure is nonexistent), then to a war between the French and the Etruscans, at the end of which we are back to the first sentence of the novel. And most of this takes place in the neighborhood of the Gare St. Lazare and in the western suburbs of Paris. As for *Zazie,* when we say that it is about a little girl from the suburbs who comes to Paris to see the subway but doesn't see it because it's on strike, we are saying nothing, for finally, toward the end of the novel, she is carried on the subway fast asleep, but before that she takes part in a series of frenzied pursuits in the streets of Paris, meets or contrives to meet some highly fantastic characters, finds herself mixed up in an enormous brawl, which somewhat recalls Rabelais or the end of certain Mack Sennett movies; and, everything considered, she is a pure creation of Queneau's imagination, with not much relation to any real little girl—past, present, or future.

In his last two novels Queneau's point of departure is, to all appearances, simple. *Blue Flowers* is built around two characters who are seeking each other: one who is usually a stay-at-home on his barge on the Seine to the west of Paris, the other who is on his way to that barge. But as it happens, the first, Cidrolin, is living at the present time, whereas the life of the second, the Duc d'Auge, begins during the times of the Gauls and crosses not only a part of France but its entire history. Moreover, Cidrolin, who is chiefly interested in eating and drinking (extract of fennel), spends the rest of his time removing the graffiti that is being painted all over his gangway, graffiti for which, as it turns out, he himself is responsible. Each of the two characters appears in the novel when one of them falls asleep and starts dreaming of the other. At the beginning of *The Flight of Icarus,* the situation, although fantastic, is acceptable to the postmodern mentality and perhaps foreshadowed the basic idea of a film like Woody Allen's *The Purple Rose of Cairo:* Icarus, a fictional character imagined by a writer, disappears from the novel he is in. He meets LN, who is no more than two letters in a crossword puzzle (Ellen). Around them, a whole crowd of characters begins to proliferate; the rest is quite simply impossible to summarize.

No, these novels are "not only about that." Apparently insignificant or unrelatable plots and overabundant and extraordinarily diverse materials might have led to works as unreadable and disorderly as those of the "literary madmen" who fascinated Queneau during the 1930's. But it was essentially by his rigorous work on the form—order, organization, and structures—that Queneau managed to orchestrate his knowledge and the fantasies of his imagination, thus giving a meaning to the whole of each of his works.

As he himself energetically affirmed, a novel for him did not consist of "pushing an indefinite number of characters in front of him, like a flock of geese, through a long wasteland of an indefinite number of pages or chapters." For his part, he could not "give in to such abandon" (*Bâtons, chiffres et lettres*). He added, "I established rules for myself as strict as those for the sonnet." That last remark refers to *The*

Bark Tree, whose rigorous structure—a perfect success—"went unnoticed by the critics who chose to speak about it at the time," but which has since formed the subject of Claude Simonnet's detailed and fundamental study.

The Bark Tree's overabundance of events, characters, situations, and plots is corseted by a structure of the whole based on numbers: seven chapters of thirteen sections each. Seven is the number of letters in the author's first and last names; thirteen is a beneficent number, according to Queneau, because it repudiates happiness. The total comes to ninety-one sections, ninety-one "being the sum of the first thirteen numbers, with the sum of its figures being one." In this way Queneau satisfies his "taste for figures" as well as some "personal whimsies." But also he thus balances the whole of his novel. In each chapter the thirteenth section differs from the others by its very subjective nature: dreams, streams of consciousness, and, in the very last section, a reabsorption of the characters by the novel itself. Moreover, since for Queneau a novel was so similar to a poem, this one contains "rhymes" or simple "alliterations"—not of words but of characters and situations. That is to say, the characters are coupled: Saturnin (a concierge) and his brother Dominique Belhôtel (owner of an eating joint), Narcense and Potice (a play on Narcissus—the theme of egocentricity reflected by the private numbers of the novel—and *potence,* or gallows—the theme of hanging), Clovis (Dominique's son) and Théo (Étienne's son), Pierre (the observer) and Étienne (the observed). The themes, or the situations that embody them, also rhyme two by two. As for that favorite theme of Queneau's—hanging, which is mentioned in *Chêne et chien* ("In the wood I saw myself hanged / What uncertain virility")—it is repeated as a "rhyme" in two episodes of *The Bark Tree:* the hanging of the dog Jupiter, guilty of having fallen into an open grave during a funeral, rhymes with the accidental hanging of Narcense seven sections later; and given Narcense (Narcissus) and the dog (Queneau), this rhyme is not at all gratui-

tous. In other words, here "the form expresses what the content is meant to disguise" (*Bâtons, chiffres et lettres*), and the apparently complete objectivity of these burlesque episodes cannot be dissociated from a profound egocentricity.

In this respect *The Bark Tree* is altogether characteristic of Queneau's works. The disciplined novel represents a precise solution to a problem of aesthetics, almost mathematical in nature—that is, a problem of poetry, since the poet must constantly seek for words that correspond to a number of preestablished conditions: a given meaning, a certain number of syllables, the placing of accents, and, when it has to rhyme, a sound pattern fixed in advance. On that score Queneau is something of a classical writer: many of his arts perhaps come close to those of the great *rhétoriqueurs,* but his exigencies link him above all to the tradition that goes from François de Malherbe to Paul Valéry.

Yet there is more to the structure of *The Bark Tree* than numerical rigor and rhymes. The first sentences are identical with the last: "The form of a man stood out in profile; and simultaneously, thousands of them. There were indeed thousands of them." In *Bâtons, chiffres et lettres,* Queneau describes his novel as follows: "*The Bark Tree* may be compared to a man who, after having walked for a long time, finds himself back where he started from." In other words, after a long inquiry, conducted by some of the characters, into life, being, and nothingness; after the complicated schemes of others to appropriate an imaginary treasure; after a war—"everything starts all over again, just as dismal and laughable as it was on the first page, or almost." The structure of the whole is thus a large circular detour, meant to show the vanity of all that sound and fury, which is on the scale of the Paris suburbs but is just as symbolic as more princely sounds and furies.

This cyclical form is discernible in several other of Queneau's novels: *Pierrot, The Skin of Dreams, Zazie,* and *Saint Glinglin,* for example. At the end of each novel the initial situation is reestablished—"or almost." And one may say that, on the whole, Queneau's vision is based on returns, repetitions, or permutations. Consider the novel *The Skin of Dreams*. At the beginning, Jacques L'Aumône as a child goes to a movie theater, where he identifies with the cowboy of the feature; there he meets the poet Des Cigales (perhaps his father). At the end of the novel, Michou, Jacques's son (or perhaps not), sees with Des Cigales a movie starring Jacques (whom he doesn't know), now James Charity—a movie that, as it happens, tells the story of Jacques's life, from his early identification with the cowboy to the moment he acts in the film that is being shown, *The Skin of Dreams*. Added to that is the fact that James's wife is Lulu Doumer, whom we met at the beginning of the novel through Des Cigales, whereas Des Cigales is now the lover of Jacques's former mistress and Michou's mother, Suzanne. Moreover, the novel is punctuated by a leitmotiv—that of lice—apropos of which the most diverse characters say the same things at given points. Such permutations, which clearly spring from Queneau's mathematical studies, take on an obvious philosophical meaning— the everlasting return to the same situations in the human comedy—but they are also an instrument of aesthetic investigation.

In *Les exercices de style* (*Exercises in Style*, 1947), in which Queneau relates the same anecdote in ninety-nine different ways, four of the exercises consist quite simply of permutations of letters, one of metathesis, and so on. This taste for permutation and substitutions governed by fixed numbers later led Queneau to experiments in "Oulipo" (*Ouvroir de littérature potentielle,* or "workshop of potential literature"), such as the following: taking a given text, finding exactly where each noun is in the dictionary, taking the noun that is in the corresponding place in a foreign dictionary, translating it into French, and inserting it in the original text. In his interview with Georges Charbonnier, Queneau thus presented a transcription of the beginning of Genesis, made with a French-German dictionary, which has a certain beauty. The purpose of such work, Queneau added, is "to furnish the writers of today

with new structures, which, in practice, will prove to be *more or less* interesting" (*Entretiens avec Raymond Queneau;* my italics). In his play *En passant* (Passing By, 1944), there is permutation from one act to another: the same situation, almost identical dialogue, but the sexes have been reversed. In one of his last published works, *Morale élémentaire* (Elementary Ethics, 1975), there are fifty untitled poems, based on exactly the same pattern and printed in the same way, made up of four coupled nouns and adjectives, followed by a six-line haiku, and ending with four coupled nouns and adjectives; each poem has an easily identifiable theme, thanks to a subtle game of verbal exercises and oxymorons, a game that might be, and perhaps was, the product of a well-fed computer. Nevertheless, apart from *Exercises in Style,* Queneau's great feat in that realm is the book-object published in 1961 and entitled *Cent mille milliards de poèmes* (One Hundred Thousand Billion Poems), which is "the longest book in the world." It is initially made up of ten sonnets, constructed around the same rhymes; but, in effect, every page is cut into fourteen strips, with one line on each, so that in turning the strips one by one, you get 10^{14}, or one hundred thousand billion different sonnets, or around two hundred million years of reading. This is what one might call "combinative literature."

These last examples represent, of course, an extreme point in Queneau's works. They do not exclude "the other" literature. But they constitute a meditation on the very basis of literary— or, more precisely, poetic—activity, and show that for Queneau the latter was not, at bottom, that far removed from mathematical activity. It therefore perhaps escapes the futility that marks other human enterprises. Moreover, these examples indicate Queneau's desire to give literature an objective status. One thus arrives at, or perhaps will arrive at, certain poetic objects, which are absolutely satisfying and from which the "personal equation" is excluded, though it may be reintroduced eventually. Such research actually shows a kind of confidence in the possibilities of literature: like mathematical research, it is at once detached and fruitful. As early as 1943 the poem *Les ziaux* presented this affirmation. Starting from two real entities—"les eaux" and "les yeux" (waters and eyes)—but fusing them by permuting the genders, Queneau finally produced a third entity, poetically just as real, "les ziaux," at once feminine and masculine, superior to the other two, and called "ziaux de merveille," wondrous "ziaux." Just like these "ziaux," Queneau's works compel recognition as true creatures; they *exist,* but their existence is the very special one enjoyed by the products of a privileged and free imagination.

Strict rules, poetic structure, and the use of mathematics are all applied, as Roland Barthes observed apropos of *Zazie,* to an apparently traditional type of novel, at least in most of Queneau's works. "From the point of view of literary architecture," said Barthes, "*Zazie* is a *well-made* novel." True, it has a beginning, a middle, and an end; and characters are apparently motivated by impulses we understand, even if we don't approve. But all that is a kind of optical illusion. For as Barthes says, "once the whole positivity of the novel is established, Queneau zealously and craftily undermines it with an insidious nothingness, without destroying it directly."

Not destroying it directly, insidious nothingness: indeed, one of the striking characteristics of Queneau's works consists in a permanent shifting of perspective, which leads not, as some are wont to say, to destruction but to an equilibrium—or rather to a constant movement between the real and the unreal that includes both the works and the world, and that in the long run *leads* to an equilibrium.

The author's frequent obvious or underhand presence in his works, both as superior witness and as creator, sets up, of course, a kind of umbilical cord in conformity with the old literary traditions. But that cord grows longer or shorter, breaks or is patched up, in such a way that now it is the fictional objectivity that is called into question by subjectivity, now the

contrary. Earlier I quoted some dialogue from the very end of *The Bark Tree,* in which the characters showed astonishment at being the "prey" of Queneau's writing itself. However, the dialogue is almost directly followed by the eloquent objectivity of the very beginning of the novel. More subtly, a narrative such as *Odile,* whose autobiographical side we have emphasized, is, in depth, based on a very special shift in perspective. The nameless "I" at the beginning makes the novel autobiographical; the first person is, of course, kept all the way through, but it stops being the real Queneau's "I." First, the caricature of the surrealist group transforms the adventure of personal confession into imaginative satire; then, and above all, the "I," which was initially considered the author's, gradually takes on a different identity. As we read on, it becomes Travy, then Roland Travy, and this name slants the narrative toward fiction, which is meant to be altogether distinct from the author's life. But then the end (meditations on the meaning of life, return from Greece) goes back to the tone we are accustomed to in works of personal confession and authentic memoirs. That is to say, *Odile* is very nicely maintained in a realm of literary ambiguity, and by the same token, the reader is kept in a state of doubt, for the subjective is undermined by the objective, and vice versa.

Because of such games of hide-and-seek, with the author's obvious or peekaboo appearances, Queneau's works become a huge question mark—very far from both dadaist negation and artistic pomposity. And doubtless it is from this perspective that his style must be interpreted. What he says cannot be disassociated from the way he says it, and that very revealing way, which is what finally led to his public success, is the vehicle both of a positive content and the basic shifting of perspective we are now discussing. Of course, large chunks of certain novels are written in an "inconspicuous" style, because, as we have already said, it is quite simply the literary style used by most novelists. But that literary style, that language of writers, did not satisfy Queneau. He himself declared (*Bâtons, chiffres et lettres*) that so-called literary French is a dead language, far removed from modern spoken French. (An idea of how the latter can be used may be found in the poems of Jehan Rictus, in the novels of Céline, in the *Canard Enchaîné*'s puns, or in popular songs.) For Queneau this did not mean resorting to slang or even mechanically transcribing the French one hears in the streets; it meant taking spoken French as a basis for style instead of the fixed French of grammar books.

This results, first of all, in the occasional lapses of syntax I mentioned earlier, which does not keep Queneau, in *The Sunday of Life*, from writing almost directly after some startling "Chinook" a literary sentence such as *Eussent-elles parlé, il ne les aurait point entendues,* or—although in English the sophistication of the many various forms of the French conditional is lost—"Had they spoken, he would not have understood them." Thus, by avoiding any unification of style and by constantly setting up contrasts between the "third" French and conventional literary style, Queneau criticizes the one by means of the other and forces his reader to remain conscious of them both. In this respect he differs greatly from Céline, whose use of spoken language is usually constant, so that once the conventional reader's surprise has worn off, it is forgotten in favor of the narrator and his characters. Here, on the contrary, there is a subtle play by means of which the style compels recognition and reveals an even stronger awareness of literature. Whereas, on the level of subject matter, Queneau could say, as he did in his *Petite cosmogonie:*

> We speak of Minos and of Pasiphaë
> of the weary pelican back from a journey
> of the *vierge, vivace,* and *bel aujourd'hui*
> . . . so why not of electromagnetics.
> (1969, p. 128)

He would also seem to say, on the level of style, that we apply the rules of the Académie française, so why not *also* those of concierges, of shopkeepers, and quite simply of twentieth-century Frenchmen involved in their twentieth-century pursuits? By thus going from one language to another, and breaking the monotony of a single, unified style, Queneau, who is a poet, by attracting the reader's attention to the presence of languages as it would be attracted to the presence of characters and themes, becomes akin to the writers he admired, such as Rabelais and Joyce.

Queneau's best-known device for attracting attention to the presence of language as one of the basic ingredients of his works (and of human life) consists in playing with the possibilities of spelling, contrasting the official rules with the phonetic realities. Just as he on occasion uses French syntax as it is spoken, so he sometimes writes French as it is pronounced—but only *sometimes,* even in dialogue. Although in *Bâtons, chiffres et lettres* he expressed the wish that a more or less phonetic spelling be adopted, in his works themselves he uses it very parsimoniously, at given points. Hence the word or phrase written phonetically is grasped by the reader with surprise; it stands, out; it becomes an isolated object, which we don't grow accustomed to, whereas we might, for example, grow accustomed to phonetic signs used constantly, as George Bernard Shaw would have wished. For instance, we know that the first word of *Zazie* is "Doukipudonktan." The eye initially perceives a word that is completely foreign to our vocabulary. This object-word, stripped a priori of all meaning, if read aloud, turns out to be the phonetic transcription of a sentence that would ordinarily be written *D'où est-ce qu'ils puent donc tant?* (literally, "What part of them stinks so much?"). But it is true that, in reality, the ear hears only one vocable, the exact transcription of which is "doukipudonktan." The word invented by Queneau thus conveys more faithfully the lived and perceived reality. But in itself, the transcription, isolated on the page, is totally strange, and one is forced to be aware of both the closer approximation of reality and the comical object that serves as the instrument of that approximation. One may also easily apply this kind of analysis to the other phonetic transcriptions that pop up here and there in Queneau's works: "Polocilacru" for *Paul aussi l'a cru,* or "Paul thought so too" (*Dimanche de la vie*); "Imélamin'hocudlastar!" for *Il met la main au cul de la star,* or "He's goosing the movie star" (*Saint Glinglin*).

Queneau's verbal invention does not stop there. It also includes the interpenetration of words (e.g., *pleuriant* for *pleurant et riant*— "laughing and crying at the same time") and puns. When a character writes *au quai* for "O.K.," it leads to no more than the slight confusion, without any real significance, provoked by a homonym. Nevertheless, the reader's surprise is similar to that caused by the transcription cited above. More interesting is the pun that makes possible a descriptive economy such as that regarding the *buffet style Henri II* (a style that has become a symbol in France of lower-middle-class bad taste) in *Zazie,* described as a "buffet genre hideux." These examples cannot really be considered as far-reaching an attempt at verbal polyvalence as that of Joyce, for Queneau doesn't seem to aim at systematically creating cosmic analogies. Rather, they are means which, by their humor and the way they pop up sporadically and unexpectedly, prevent the reader from completely "losing himself" in the story and point him toward a consideration of the creative power of words.

Of course, there are examples of Queneau's works of verbal creations that take on an almost absolute value, examples in which, as Andrée Bergens says when she draws up a catalogue raisonné of Queneau's devices, "it is a question of words stripped of all meaning, but the grouping and organization of which allow the reader to give a possible interpretation." And before quoting one of Queneau's sonnets made up largely of words that don't exist, Bergens relates it to Rabelais, Joyce, and Henri Michaux. Queneau *did* once translate the very

beginning of *Saint Glinglin* into Joycese, but he stopped after two paragraphs, claiming that the real reason he did it was to help him "fairchtéer" (from the German *verstehen*) *Finnegans Wake.* In his novels and most of his poems the more or less Joycean devices are never systematic, any more than is the use of phonetic spelling. And this absence of *system* is significant. Through its very inconstancy, Queneau's style forces the reader to keep bouncing from one literary universe to another.

We thus come back to a well-known and broader aspect of Queneau's works: their similarity to a body of stylistic exercises. Like a schoolboy who is learning the possibilities of the French language, Queneau constantly seems to have in mind the following object: to relate this or that anecdote in "x" style. In the course of certain novels the abrupt changes in technique demonstrate this. In *Saint Glinglin* and in *Les enfants du limon,* for example, the continuity of the content is forever being broken by an unexpected transition to new forms, which go all the way to the intrusion of chapters in verse. On the whole, Queneau's work's are thus marked by all kinds of signals, reminding the reader of the presence of Queneau-thinking-of-writing-in-this-or-that-manner. Strangely enough, as Bergens so well observed, direct pastiches of already existing literature are rare in Queneau. They are merely extreme points at which the impression of an "exercise" can be attached to a known model. Nevertheless, the impression is almost constant, and is due, of course, to those few pastiches or parodies, to allusions, to the limited borrowing of certain phrases, and so on, but also, and above all, to what might be called a calculated inauthenticity of his general style. That is to say, Queneau writes *as if* he were imitating. In point of fact, he works on the possibilities of the French language itself, starting with linguistic structures he has read or heard.

The title of his *Exercises in Style* must be taken literally. "Exercises" is exactly what these texts are. The interest of the ninety-nine variations on an insignificant anecdote lies essentially in the artist's virtuosity. A young man has an argument with another fellow in a Paris bus; a little later on, the narrator notices the same young man in front of the Gare St. Lazare, in conversation with a friend about a button on his jacket. Without laboring the fact that for Queneau a coincidence of this kind is perhaps as important as an epic encounter, we may say that for the reader this book would seem, first of all, to bear witness to the wealth of verbal expression. Aside from the mathematical permutations we have already mentioned and some rather questionable combinations of letters, most of the variations make the rounds of literary techniques, perspectives, and genres, accepted or possible, or else are presented as examples of the tone of certain types of people taken from reality or from literary tradition.

For example, this anecdote is related by a little Parisian woman, with her comments on the need for using a deodorant or on male attire, her coyness and her untroubled egotism; but it is also given in the form of a three-act play, as a sonnet in alexandrines, and then as the monologue of a reactionary, for whom the anecdote is merely a pretext for recriminations against social reform and the lack of breeding in today's young people. Elsewhere it is told in "précieux" style, and again in the "modern style" of the novelists who were fashionable at the beginning of the century. Each variation bears a title ("Feminine," "Peasant," "Italianisms," "Animism," "Haiku," and so on) that turns our attention away from the anecdote itself and toward the manner in which it is treated. But each style, necessarily considered in relation to the others, is thus relative: it is called into question by the others, just as it calls the others into question. This explains why the book has been accused of being an undertaking to demolish literature. In fact, as Queneau tells us in *Bâtons, chiffres et lettres,* it is concerned with ridding literature of "its various rusts," by some scrupulously careful and detailed work which very much amused him

and which is meant "not to bore the reader too much."

But although the book is correctly entitled *Exercises,* it nonetheless conveys the impression that everything is possible when one writes—an impression both exalting and alarming—and by having accumulated a great number of possibilities, it criticizes each one of them while preserving them all. In the novels themselves and in most of the poems, the "exercise" aspect has an objective that transcends it more clearly. By constantly emphasizing the multiple possibilities of verbal expression, by using a style that is always relative, as it were, Queneau wrote works that may be called "opaque." This opacity should be considered not as obscurity but as the opposite of that transparency of prose spoken of and demanded by Sartre in *Qu'est-ce que la littérature? (What Is Literature?,* 1948). Instead of making us forget the tools that serve the narrative act, Queneau tries to save both the tools and the act they serve. For Queneau is essentially a poet, for whom words—all words, as words—have a life of their own; the sonnet "La chair chaude des mots" (The Warm Flesh of Words; in *La chien à la mandoline*) begins with the following two lines, in which the "words" and the "dog" (= Queneau) correspond:

Take these words in your hands and feel their agile
    feet
And feel their heart beating like that of a dog.

That love of words led Queneau to play with them tirelessly, affectionately, and also a bit sadistically. Coupled, integrated into unforeseen syntaxes, confronting one another, dissected (the poem quoted above ends with "Take these words in your hands and see how they are made"), they are elements in a language that affirms its supremacy, its indisputable existence, by way of a constant criticism of itself.

Obviously, in most of the poems and certainly in the works that are presented as novels, this language expresses something, describes settings or situations, tells stories. Therefore, the constant questioning of expression implies a questioning of the thing expressed, the "reality." It may be, for example, that Queneau launches into a conventional kind of narrative or description, and then suddenly turns our attention toward the hidden absurdity of an innocuous, ordinary sentence, which is correct and accepted by the best writers—a "transparent" sentence. "Along the river . . . it was already dark," we read in *The Bark Tree*. But Queneau suddenly intervenes: "It was also already dark elsewhere, but no matter." This is a method of calling into question a certain way of writing (or speaking), and at the same time the perception of a certain oneness of the night, the absolute way in which we envisage the elements of the world—a question raised about our very awareness of the night.

Among the realities that are so questioned is, more especially, the dialogue of our everyday life. When the parrot Laverdure in *Zazie* repeats at given points, "Talk, talk, that's all you know how to do," he attracts our attention to the very activity of the writer, but also, and above all, to the vacuum of that constant noise by which we think we are communicating and with which we fill the universe. Zazie's favorite phrase, which Roland Barthes calls "the Zazic *clausule*," goes even further: by opposing the remarks of others, their activities, even the city of Paris—which is, as it were, offered to her—with the reply "my ass," she sets up in the face of a group of realities that are thought to be unanswerable an equally strong and unanswerable negation. Each exists in relation to the other. In Queneau, just as style asserts itself by criticizing itself, so reality (and its earnestness) exists through the mockery of reality.

Whence, no doubt, the ambiguous existence of his characters. As puppets, they might be considered the futile reflection of impossible creatures. And yet Bébé Toutout, Mme Cloche, Pierrot, Jacques L'Aumône, Julia and the soldier Brû, Zazie and her uncle Gabriel, Cidrolin, the Duc d'Auge, his attendants, his horses—all

have taken a mythical place in the minds of Queneau's readers, a place similar to that of the so-called living creatures of traditional literature.

Apparently always in danger, skirting the abyss of nothingness, these characters compel recognition for that very reason: beside them or beyond them there is only nothingness. Exceptional, fantastic, as tossed about by their adventures as by the language that imprisons, constitutes, and reveals them, they exist, as it were—dare we use the word?—*dialectically.* Queneau would add (and once did in an article): Well, we have dared to use the word. Or, to continue imitating Queneau, they exist positively at the price of a double negation, just as in mathematics minus times minus equals plus. Thanks to this regained "positivity," they are worth being considered for themselves—without, however, our being able to forget the operation to which they owe their precarious existence.

To begin with, as an urban writer, Queneau was interested in crowds, in the transitory assemblages of anonymous individuals for reasons of some daily routine or some accident or other. Similar to the troops in the ancient epic poems or to the chorus in Greek tragedy, these human conglomerates are maintained midway between the undifferentiated mass, a kind of background for the heroes' adventures, and the juxtaposition of individuals, each representing a possible variant of the common agitation. Such descriptions of secondary collectivities, at a given point, contribute more than a little to adding an epic dimension in the burlesque mode to Queneau's novels. In *The Bark Tree* and *Les derniers jours* it is in relation to the swarming streets of Paris that the protagonists' destinies are fulfilled. Whether the latter be strollers, observers, students, café waiters, or what have you, they rise above the others, not through their great exploits, as in the traditional epic, but through a degree of higher consciousness.

At the end of *Les derniers jours* the higher observer, Alfred the café waiter, both a mathematician and a prophet, sums up the meaning of the crowds—here, the customers of the café and the fauna of the Latin Quarter—and defines them with relation to himself, the lucid character:

> There are the habitués and the new ones, the old, the young, the thin, the fat, the civil and the military. There are those who talk politics and others who gab about literature; there are those who want to found a little journal and others who catch diseases from going with women; there are those who think they know everything and others who seem to know nothing at all. As for me, I just stay there, I serve them cold drinks in summer, hot ones in winter, and alcohol in all seasons. I don't get mixed up in anything and I let everything go on as it will.
>
> (p. 233)

This detachment of Alfred's is the end of a long endeavor, marked by perseverance and obstinacy: after years of more or less magical calculations, he has managed to win the sum of 201,643 francs at the races, exactly what was taken "from [his] father, given the rise in the cost of living and the devaluation of the franc." Having thus fulfilled what he calls his "destiny," he goes back to his job as a café waiter and thereafter peacefully surveys from on high the hustle and bustle of other people's lives.

This Alfred is perhaps not the most famous of Queneau's characters, but he has the distinction of successively embodying the two sets of traits, often opposed, that are shared by the protagonists of most of the novels. First of all is the fixed goal they try to attain with unequaled obstinacy—often with a kind of ferocity; this is encountered especially in the diabolical and feminine characters. Mme Cloche, Julia, and Zazie are driven by gigantic appetites and devote inexhaustible energy to satisfying them— whether it be a question of a treasure, possessing a soldier, or the appropriation of a pair of "bloogenes." Whether their goals are single or multiple, they put everything they have into achieving them—with an indifference to the rest of the world, and an ability to shut the traps of those who try to point out to them that their quest is probably illusory—in a way that somewhat recalls the blind brutality of the passionate quests of certain characters in Molière. In *Blue Flowers* it is by means of generously distributed and brutal kicks that the Duc d'Auge relentlessly crosses through the history of France during the impossible temporal odyssey that leads him to Cidrolin. With more respect for human beings but with the same persistence, Chambernac, in *Les enfants du limon,* belongs to that family, but as an intellectual. What energy and what patient research he devotes to his compilation of "literary madmen"! He even manages to force a "poor devil" into signing a pact with him, making him his slave in that interminable undertaking. In this character Queneau identifies with his obstinate creatures: very large portions of the novel—all of book 5 and all of book 7, in particular—are made up of authentic excerpts from the works of literary madmen (who themselves are as obstinate as anyone) and résumés of their biographies. That is to say, Queneau, after having devoted years of research to those aberrant thinkers, "who had neither masters nor disciples," and not having been able to get his own compilation published, found the means of imposing much of it on his readers by incorporating it into a novel, which—to use his own expression apropos of *Odile*—"is not only about that."

Alfred's victory led him to a new attitude that seems to be the main characteristic of another family of protagonists, mostly male: a mixture of observation and detachment, combined with a kind of gratuitous professional conscientiousness that occasionally verges on puritanism. This race of Quenian men, whether they persist in some type of research or in simply drifting along, is thus generally marked by two traits that may appear contradictory: they do what they have to do in life, at given moments (at least they do their best), and at the same time their being is located at a certain distance from such conscientious action.

But to understand this attitude more clearly, they must be situated socially. The critics have often said that Queneau's protagonists belong to a species of humanity that is not ordinarily encountered in novels. In fact, that particular species can be found in realist or populist literature, which is devoted to individuals who "don't make history." Behind Queneau's characters there are, in certain respects, the common people of Maupassant or the customers of the little cafés in Tristan Bernard (1866–1947)—not to go back so far as to some of Flaubert's characters or even those of Antoine Furetière (1619–1688) and of Paul Scarron (1610–1660). For a long time tradespeople, café waiters, tramps, and ragpickers have appeared in novels and on stage, and no longer surprise us. True, before Queneau, a fakir's assistant in a kind of Coney Island (*Pierrot*) or a "male nightclub ballerina" (*Zazie*) was a rare type. But what counts is that Queneau's choice—whether it has to do with small trades that have already been exploited in literature or with exceptional jobs—is generally directed toward the social situation in which the character has the best chance of experiencing solitude. Indeed, if Queneau's novels contain numerous collective scenes or parodies of unanimism, the protagonists themselves are almost always seen from the perspective of the solitude of their undertakings: no worker heroes in assembly lines, no heroes à la Malraux merging in common action, except perhaps in the mock-epic episode of *Saint Glinglin*. Although involved in a collective movement, the hero of *Odile* finally breaks away from it and chooses a destiny of his own, and this is doubtless the autobiographical key to the choice of solitary heroes in the apparently objective works.

The character who practices a small trade becomes a little isolated planet, conscious of his isolation and therefore in a privileged position, from which he may both participate in the world and judge it from the outside—that is, both live like everyone else on one level (he works, he earns his living, he meets the others in his spare time) and construct a wisdom of his very own. Owing to the force of circumstances, that wisdom is at once convincing and aberrant, for his professional isolation allows him to go all the way with certain ideas.

"Ideas" is no doubt rather a big word for what most often is a general mental attitude, accompanied by a few cryptic remarks, the fruit of meditations unknown to us. Sometimes, however, like Alfred, the characters reveal themselves to us in a traditional way, through their comments or their inner monologue: the concierge Saturnin (*The Bark Tree*), Jacques L'Aumône when he overflows with humility (*The Skin of Dreams*), the soldier Brû when he becomes bewildered by Time or involved in the search for saintliness (*The Sunday of Life*). But in most cases it is the very tone of the narrative or the structure of the novel that conveys the impression of detachment. Indulging with great care in somewhat strange activities, going from one to the other just as diligently and without turning a hair, accepting almost all of life, these characters give the impression of having reached a stage at which they refuse to question the whys and wherefores of things, and they are conscientious with no explicit justification. The soldier Valentin Brû lets himself be married, makes his wedding trip alone, sells buttons or frames, replaces Julia as fortune-teller, and so on, without ever protesting, or at any rate being quite satisfied with a minimum of explanations, which are generally absurd. Julia, claiming that they cannot close the shop at the height of the season "to go on a honeymoon," discusses it as follows:

"Maybe we could put off our honeymoon until our next vacation," suggests Valentin. "But then," objects Julia, "when would we take our vacation?" And there was no answer to that.

They finally came up with a solution, the only possible—the one and only—solution, namely, that Valentin alone would go quite alone on his honeymoon.

(p. 69)

Note that Brû is absolutely bent on a honeymoon—"They're indispensable, honeymoons"—just as he dreams of visiting the battlefield at Jena. But if these little desires of his are deep-rooted, all the decisions in life that are normally considered important he seems to regard with calm indifference, and he lets fate take its course. The title character of *Pierrot* drifts in much the same way from one little job to another, attaching almost no importance to his future, apparently satisfied with his occupation of the moment, and worried only about certain details. And Jacques, in *The Skin of Dreams,* works at breeding lice, at amateur boxing, and at playing walk-ons in films with the same equanimity.

Jacques's equanimity, of course, is understandable, given the gigantic dreams of glory he has had since childhood: he sees himself as a king, a cardinal, a champion, a patron of the arts, but he also knows that life will always fall short of such ambitions. Therefore all real activities become equal. Ironically, as we know, Jacques nevertheless becomes the great movie star James Charity, but his parents, his wife, and his son do not recognize him, and he exists only *indirectly* in the novel—through newspaper articles or the film seen by his son Michou—owing this precarious existence only to the good graces of Raymond Queneau, since the film is produced by the Ramon Curnough Company. In his glory he thus ceases to be a character, as it were, becoming merely one of Queneau's fantasies, and we are retrospectively referred back to his real existence in the previous pages of the novel—that is, to the series of little adventures and little jobs, bogged down in their equality.

On the whole, these characters are in a certain state of grace, which allows them to fulfill the daily tasks offered them by fate without any illusions as to the importance of those tasks. One is more or less as good as the other. And there lies one of the tensions in Queneau's works: in contrast to the attitude of these characters is the voracity or aggressiveness of certain others, with their tireless pursuit of some goal or other, and also the grotesque agitation of the secondary characters, who give colossal importance to what they do.

We should point out that these unwitting "sages" are by no means soft or weak. They accept almost everything—but not a kind of injustice, baseness, or stupidity. They may even chasten some repulsive individual with a good punch in the jaw. In fact, although they give in to their fates, they don't let themselves be taken advantage of. A brawl never frightened Pierrot, and Jacques gets back at a friend with whom, under dangerous conditions, he has made a documentary film about the Amazonian Indians, when the friend begins to betray him by trying to take away his girl, Lulu Doumer:

> Jacques again leaned over toward Rubiadzan.
>
> "Listen here, you jerk," he articulated in English, "if you take one more peek at my doll I break your neck."
>
> But Rubiadzan, who raised his spirits with a few gulps of whiskey, did not take the threat seriously. He continued to ogle Lulu Doumer.
>
> "How do you come to have that kind of talent?" Stahl asked the Borgeiro Indian.
>
> Then Rubiadzan gets
>
> "Even way back when I was a café waiter, I bowled over the customers"
>
> right in the kisser
>
> "by munching lobster claws, snail shells, and even oysters. Except Portuguese oysters I never could."
>
> a terrific
>
> "Even an educated young man who used to come there for lunch compared me to vee-aitch, you know: the poet."
>
> wallop.
>
> He falls down. They pick him up. They sponge off his mug. Then he starts to snivel.
>
> Oncezerwere two old pals six months they had lived together in the virgin forest among the Borgeiro Indians who are specially wild and then just like that for a woman it's over their old friendship, oncezerwere two old pals six months they had lived together in the virgin forest among the

"Change the record," says Lulu Doumer. "Anyway I don't care for that kind of stuff."

"Let's go," Jacques suggests.

They leave together.

Aside from the technical interest of this passage, we are struck by Jacques's composure and efficiency, and above all, by the contrast between the traitor's whining sentimentality and the detached brevity of the last two lines.

Quick to defend himself, Jacques is just as quick to redress certain wrongs provoked by the baseness of others. After having wheedled four hundred francs out of the unknown poet Des Cigales to publish one of his poems, and discovering that it was nothing but a swindle and that the poem was in fact not to be published, Jacques "took a taxi for the rue du Louvre and sent a money order for the 400 francs to Des Cigales. He came back on foot." And he added: "I'm pretty much of an ass, when you come to think of it."

Staunch, fair, and in the end essentially good, these characters are blessed with yet another trait, one that allows Queneau to give them a certain mystery: they are modest about their deep feelings. And this is true not only for the "detached" characters. From Lehameau (*A Hard Winter*) to Gabriel (*Zazie*), Queneau's men are gifted with real sensitivity, which they refuse to expose to others, and which very often even the reader doesn't notice until after the event. Whereas the minor characters show off, brag, and open their hearts—or think they do— the male protagonists never make a spectacle of their innermost being. They fall in love, and although their gestures may be risqué, they refrain from talking too much about their love; some go so far as to deny it, as does Roland Travy in *Odile.* If someone involves them in subtle analyses of their feelings, as Dominique does with Jacques in *The Skin of Dreams,* they prove to be clumsy and the whole business is held up to ridicule. Finally, they suffer deeply when their love is not returned or when they are deceived, but their suffering is revealed by the technique of the novel, not by their own admis-

sion. When, for example, we learn very brutally, at the end of *The Skin of Dreams,* part 2, that Dominique has been "taking in" Jacques, that in fact she has been "sleeping around," Queneau has us jump immediately to the beginning of book 3: "From the top of the hill, they caught a glimpse of San Culebra del Porco." Jacques's state of shock is simply symbolized, without any explanation, by that huge jump in space, which at once leads us to South America.

This modesty about their feelings is due to the shyness of the characters, but it is also one more indication of their attitude toward life— that is, of their accepted and even cultivated solitude. Without making too much fuss, they strive to live, to subsist, by fulfilling as best they can certain inevitable tasks and by secretly absorbing the blows of fate. And it is at the completion of their endeavor, after many detours, that their wisdom is disclosed. It is shown by a gentleness in tone, by the laughter that takes hold of them in the face of their own stupidity, and also by a kind of inner vacuum. An unheroic catharsis, perhaps, the wisdom of Queneau's characters does seem to be the result of a "purging" of the soul—which, if it is to be complete and truly Quenian, must be accompanied by some mocking criticism. For example, after all sorts of adventures, unexpected meetings, and disappointments, Pierrot says to the night watchman of a provincial hotel, who has accused him of daydreaming, "I'm not the type. . . . But I do often think of nothing." And the watchman replies, "Well, that's better than not thinking at all."

In the course of a curious inquiry in reverse, Queneau once asked his readers whether they thought that the main character in a novel was always the author's mouthpiece. To answer such a question is difficult if, for instance, one considers both Pierrot and Zazie. Nevertheless, it would seem that, in many respects, it is the modest, the lucid, and to some degree the detached heroes who most often express part of Queneau's personal philosophy, for, taken as real beings, they are the most attractive and also the most secret of Queneau's characters. And their combination of apparent equanimity and "professional" conscientiousness brings to mind much that we know about Queneau himself. In this regard, even Zazie's "hormosessual" uncle Gabriel, that "male nightclub ballerina," has been seen as a reflection of Queneau's artistic vision. Out of delicacy, his dance number is never completely described in the novel, but Gabriel, the good, conscientious giant, gives away the whole secret of his aesthetic when everyone dwells on how funny his number is: "'Thanks,' says Gabriel. 'Don't forget about art though. Fun is fun, but there's also art.'"

Yet, these funny artists, lucid heroes, and sages can be considered only in relation to the other inhabitants of the novels. Accompanied by ambitious, energetic, and gluttonous women (Marceline, Gabriel's wife, is always gentle and submissive, modest and conscientious; but, as we discover at the end, she is Marcel, a man), they are also surrounded by an infinite variety of minor characters who indulge in an infinite variety of concrete activities. Among the latter, there are a good number of colossal idiots, but also a few disturbing, protean, and actually diabolical creatures. On the most realistic level, M. Frédéric, the spy in *A Hard Winter*, is an evil, parasitic individual of questionable identity. Magnified and carried to fanciful proportions, these traits are found in Trouscaillon, alias Pédro-Surplus, alias Bertin-Poirée, alias Haroum-Arachide, who brags about being the "Prince of this world and several related territories," in *Zazie*. In other words, he is very much akin to the devil. And Queneau had no scruples about introducing a real demon in two of his novels (*The Bark Tree* and *Les enfants du limon*): the dwarf Bébé Toutout. Filthy, gluttonous, and parasitical, he imposes his presence on others by frightening them, by taking advantage of the "crud in the depth of men's souls." In *Les enfants du limon* he lets his disciple take his place—Purpulan, the blackmailing demon with foul breath.

Such characters may be said to embody evil or, rather, a systematic nastiness. But their nastiness is limited to their wanting to annoy people, and somehow they ultimately fail. Even if Bébé Toutout's scheming does set him up in the world, he appears for the last time, in *The Bark Tree*, in a most humiliating situation. The last image we have of him—now manager of his own brothel—is the following: "Bébé Toutout bellowed with rage, for he had just caught his beard in the door of the safe, where he had put away the priest's fifty francs." Trouscaillon lets everyone, including the parrot, get away from him at the end of *Zazie*. Purpulan is quite simply thrown into the Seine by Chambernac, and woefully dissolves in the water. And although Mme Cloche, in *The Bark Tree*, diabolically gets herself up as a priest in order to seize old Taupe's treasure, it just happens that there is no treasure; and as queen of the victorious Etruscans, she is made to regret her past and goes back to being old Mme Cloche, prisoner of a novel by Raymond Queneau, who gives permanence for all eternity to the tale of her blunder regarding the imaginary treasure. As for M. Frédéric, he is probably shot. In Queneau's works evil never wins out.

However, a little diabolism here and there is not without its appeal. For example, if Zazie is a wonderful instrument for calling reality into question, she is, by the same token, as Andrée Bergens points out, inclined to be nasty in ways similar to those of the real demons. This bogus little girl—a utopian character, according to Barthes—is motivated by designs that relate her to Bébé Toutout. Why does she want to become a schoolteacher? "To bitch up the kids . . . the ones who'll be my age in 10 years, in 100 years, in 1,000 years." Why does she also want to become an astronaut? "To go and bitch up the Martians."

If there is a moral universe of Queneau's characters, it would thus seem to be based on a kind of Manichaeism, in which wisdom (or sometimes the attempt to become saintly) is balanced by wickedness, with both being at once fascinating and farcical, and both closely linked in creation itself. For if Pierrot wears Queneau's glasses, Bébé Toutout, by his very name, is also under the sign of Queneau: "toutou," in the lingo of French children, is the word for dog.

Queneau once declared apropos of his characters, "I find that everyone's like that, including myself, naturally"; and another time, "I don't at all think that my characters are simpleminded. One has to feel mighty superior to allow oneself to be contemptuous." To quote the epigraph of *The Sunday of Life,* which is taken from Hegel and could be applied to all Queneau's novels: "Men who are gifted with such good humor cannot be fundamentally bad or low."

"One has to feel mighty superior"; "fundamentally"—these reservations of Queneau's are perhaps a key to all his works: there are people, things, adventures, but at bottom what right have we to go to the bottom? Queneau's works constitute a vast realization about a group of particular phenomena, all more or less equal to each other. As we have seen, literature is a way of constantly peppering them with question marks, which lead to nothing but a lack of answers. Whence the comic aspect of the whole: after all, it's funny that things are as they are, that creatures exist in life or in the imagination or sometimes in both at once, and that we don't manage to see anything behind them—just as there is nothing behind old Taupe's door (*The Bark Tree*).

Once this realization is assimilated, it leads to an attitude now known as 'pataphysics. Defined by Alfred Jarry at the end of the nineteenth century, 'pataphysics, the science of sciences, is characterized by the affirmation that all things are equal, that there are only particular cases, that, as Roger Shattuck put it, "life is of course absurd and it is ludicrous to take it seriously; only the comic is serious." This leads to the equanimity I have pointed out in Queneau's sages. Beyond 'pataphysics there is nothing. The symbol of 'pataphysics is the *gidouille,* a spiral engraved on the belly of Ubu, the stupid, dangerous, and hilarious puppet

invented by Alfred Jarry and elevated to royal dignity in *Ubu Roi* (1896). It is "a symbol of ethernal consciousness circling forever around itself." Circular or spiral, Queneau's novels fit in rather well with these principles: by means of the comic, thanks to it, and resulting in it, a creative consciousness turns around itself and expresses itself in the form of an imaginary universe, 'pataphysically equal to what we pompously call reality. And, like 'pataphysics, these works absorb with equal interest theories, gestures, behavior—mathematical realities, the art of sweeping, phenomenology, the spectacle of a gluttonous little girl devouring sauerkraut and sausages. Computers (*Petite cosmogonie*) become equal to the potato peeler (*The Bark Tree*).

However, Queneau's universe, which is expressed in 'pataphysical terms (from 1951 on, Queneau was a member of the Collège international de 'pataphysique), certainly includes some of mankind's great preoccupations. For example, a serious meditation on history, on which Paul Gayot put great stress, is fundamental in works such as *Saint Glinglin, Blue Flowers,* and of course *Petite cosmogonie,* not to mention the theoretical fragments of *Une histoire modèle:* a cyclical history, history as a spiral, the eternal return, the golden age, and the Iron Age are more than passing themes; they are rather important threads in those Quenian works. In the novels the main characters are divided into those who believe they are "making history" and those who—although not indifferent, but skeptical and wise—observe from a distance while fulfilling the basic duties of mankind.

And of course, there is death: it is brutal; it appears suddenly in Queneau's works, without being announced. Just as the history of France, relived by the Duc d'Auge (*Blue Flowers*), is rectified by a farcical imagination that would seem to lie midway between Alfred Jarry and Mel Brooks or Monty Python, death in Queneau leads to ceremonies and rituals that, all in all, are highly satirical and comical (see *The Bark Tree, The Sunday of Life,* or *Saint Glinglin*).

However, it stimulates, especially in the poems, a few meditations that are not very jolly and that serve as material for a profound lyricism on the decay of beauty and youth (reminiscent of Ronsard) or the putrefaction of dead bodies (reminiscent of Villon).

But irony and humor usually manage to come to the fore as a victory over the awesomeness of such themes. Of course, in French, the best way of conquering *les vers* (worms) of the grave is to identify them with *les vers* (verses, lines) of the immortal poem (see, for example, "Adieu ma terre ronde" [Good-bye, My Round Earth], in *L'Instant fatal*). Thus, restating the classical old commonplaces, Queneau does it with the wink of a man who knows that death is the equalizer of all things, but also knows that at the end of life's efforts there remains a special amused wisdom that, through the very recognition of nothingness, asserts the value of our endeavors:

praiseworthy effort! righteous duty! exemplary
  conscientiousness
    upon which the dead smile for
the fatal moment will come all the same and divert
  us.

                        (*L'Instant fatal,* p. 170)

Perhaps Queneau's works can thus be summed up: a praiseworthy undertaking, the fruit of exemplary conscientiousness, upon which smiles, with skepticism, a profound wisdom, based on the awareness of paradoxes and the precariousness of reality and the human condition. But let Queneau, who died in 1976, speak this last time: here, in *The Bark Tree,* is the dialogue between Saturnin and Ernestine, who is dying:

"If we live, it's because we die, that's what you said, dint you?" [asked Saturnin].

"Yes, I did say that." [Ernestine replied.]

"You might just as well have said the opposite," he observed.

"I agree," replied Ernestine.

"Ah, good," said Saturnin. "That's all I wanted to know."

Selected Bibliography

EDITIONS OF INDIVIDUAL WORKS

Le chiendent. Paris, 1933.

Gueule de pierre. Paris, 1934.

Les derniers jours. Paris, 1935.

Chêne et chien. Paris, 1937.

Odile. Paris, 1937.

Les enfants du limon. Paris, 1938.

Un rude hiver. Paris, 1939.

Les temps mêlés. Paris, 1941.

Pierrot mon ami. Paris, 1942.

Les ziaux. Paris, 1943.

"En passant." *L'Arbalète* (Lyons), no. 8:123–148 (1944).

Loin de rueil. Paris, 1944.

Bucoliques. Paris, 1947.

Les exercices de style. Paris, 1947.

On est toujours trop bon avec les femmes. Paris, 1947. (Under the pseudonym Sally Mara.)

Une trouille verte. Paris, 1947.

Saint Glinglin. Paris, 1948. (Contains a new version of *Gueule de pierre* and *Les temps mêlés.*)

Le cheval troyen. Paris, 1948.

L'Instant fatal. Paris, 1948; repr. 1977.

Bâtons, chiffres et lettres. Paris, 1950.

Petite cosmogonie portative. Paris, 1950.

Journal intim. Paris, 1950. (Under the pseudonym Sally Mara.)

Si tu t'imagines. Paris, 1952.

Le dimanche de la vie. Paris, 1952.

Sonnets. Paris, 1958.

Zazie dans le métro. Paris, 1959.

Cent mille milliards de poèmes. Paris, 1961.

Les oeuvres complètes de Sally Mara. Paris, 1962; repr. 1979.

Bords: Mathématiciens, précurseurs, encyclopédistes. Paris, 1963.

Le chien à la mandoline. Paris, 1965.

Les fleurs bleues. Paris, 1965.

Une histoire modèle. Paris, 1966.

Courir les rues. Paris, 1967.

Battre la campagne. Paris, 1968.

Le vol d'Icare. Paris, 1968.

Chêne et chien suivi de Petite cosmogonie portative. Paris, 1969.

Fendre les flots. Paris, 1969.

Le voyage en Grèce. Paris, 1973.

Morale élémentaire. Paris, 1975.

Contes et propos. Paris, 1981. (Posthumous collection of unpublished or hard-to-find texts.)

TRANSLATIONS

At the Edge of the Forest. Translated by Barbara Wright. London, 1954.

The Bark Tree. Translated by Barbara Wright. London, 1968.

Blue Flowers. Translated by Barbara Wright. New York, 1967. Also published as *Between Blue and Blue.* London, 1967.

"A Blue Funk." Translated by Barbara Wright. In *French Writing Today,* edited by Simon Watson Taylor. London, 1968; New York, 1969. Pp. 25–34.

Exercises in Style. Translated by Barbara Wright. Norfolk, Conn., 1955.

The Flight of Icarus. Translated by Barbara Wright. New York, 1973.

A Hard Winter. Translated by Betty Askwith. London, 1948.

Odile. Translated by Carol Sanders. Elmwood Park, Ill., 1988.

Pierrot. Translated by J. MacLaren Ross. London, 1950.

The Skin of Dreams. Translated by H. J. Kaplan. Norfolk, Conn., 1948.

The Sunday of Life. Translated by Barbara Wright. New York, 1977.

The Trojan Horse. Translated by Barbara Wright. London, 1954.

We Always Treat Women Too Well. Translated by Barbara Wright. New York, 1981.

Zazie. Translated by Barbara Wright. New York, 1960.

BIOGRAPHICAL AND CRITICAL STUDIES

Les amis de Valentin Brû (1977–). Levallois-Perret, France. (Periodical devoted to the works of Queneau.)

Baligand, Renée. *Les poèmes de Raymond Queneau: Étude phonostylistique.* Montreal, 1972.

Barthes, Roland. "Zazie et la littérature." *Critique* 15:675–681 (1959).

Bataille, Georges. "La méchanceté du langage." *Critique* 4:1059–1066 (1948).

Bens, Jacques. *Raymond Queneau.* Paris, 1962.

Bergens, Andrée. *Raymond Queneau.* Geneva, 1963.

Brée, Germaine, ed. *Raymond Queneau: Cahier de l'herne.* Paris, 1975. (Contains an exhaustive bibliography of Queneau's writings, translations of his works, and critical studies to 1975.)

Brée, Germaine, and Margaret Guiton. "Raymond Queneau: 'The Sunday of Life.'" In their *An Age of Fiction: The French Novel from Gide to Camus.* New Brunswick, N.J., 1957. Pp. 169–179.

Charbonnier, Georges. *Entretiens avec Raymond Queneau.* Paris, 1962.

Esslin, Martin. "Raymond Queneau." In *The Novelist as Philosopher: Studies in French Fiction 1935–1960,* edited by John Cruickshank. New York, 1962. Pp. 79–101.

Europe, no. 650–651 (June–July 1983). (Special issue devoted to Queneau.)

Fournel, Paul. *Clés pour la littérature potentielle.* Paris, 1972. (On "Oulipo.")

Gayot, Paul. *Raymond Queneau.* Paris, 1967.

Kojève, Alexandre. "Les romans de la sagesse." *Critique* 8:387–397 (1952).

Mercier, Vivian. "Raymond Queneau: The First Novelist?" *L'Esprit créateur* 7:102–112 (1967).

Queval, Jean. *Essai sur Raymond Queneau.* Paris, 1960.

Queval, Jean, and Nicole Onfroy, eds. *Le chiendent.* Paris, 1975. (Excerpts with commentary and notes.)

Shattuck, Roger, and Simon Watson Taylor, eds. *What is 'Pataphysics? Evergreen Review* 4, no. 13 (May–June 1960).

Shorley, Christopher. *Queneau's Fiction: An Introductory Study.* New York, 1985.

Simonnet, Claude. *Queneau déchiffré.* Paris, 1962.

Temps mêlés: Documents Queneau (1978–). (Journal devoted exclusively to Queneau.)

Thiher, Allen. *Raymond Queneau.* Boston, 1987.

Wright, Barbara, ed. *Les fleurs bleues.* London, 1971.

BIBLIOGRAPHIES

Hillen, Wolfgang. *Raymond Queneau: Bibliographie des études sur l'homme et son oeuvre.* Cologne, 1981. (Most complete bibliography of secondary literature.)

Rameil, Claude. *Les amis de Valentin Brû,* no. 23 (1983). (Bibliography of Queneau's writings.)

JACQUES GUICHARNAUD

MARGUERITE YOURCENAR

(1903–1987)

SINCE THE FOUNDING of the French Academy by Cardinal Richelieu in the first half of the seventeenth century, no woman had ever been elected to sit among the "forty immortals" until March 1980, when Marguerite Yourcenar, née Crayencour, was invited to join the ranks of this distinguished body. This unprecedented historic event, widely reported in the world press, was not without considerable controversy, her nomination having engendered long and acrimonious debate. The reasons for the furor were multiple.

First, she was a woman. It took the efforts of such notables as the president of the Republic, Valéry Giscard d'Estaing, and the eminent politician Edgar Faure to persuade some academicians that denial of membership on the basis of sex in the last quarter of the twentieth century was an unenlightened attitude. In her acceptance speech to the Academy, Yourcenar gently reminded its members of their chauvinistic, though traditional, practice of placing women on pedestals while neglecting to offer them a chair, referring to the forty chairs in the Academy.

Then there was the question of her nationality: when she became a naturalized American citizen in 1947, she was obliged to forfeit her French citizenship. That this was a source of tension is evidenced by the blatant omission of the fact from the detailed chronology of her life given in her collected fictional works, published by the Bibliothèque de la Pléiade, the most respected scholarly press in France. Although her birthplace "happened," as she has put it, to be Brussels, she was brought up in France by her father, a Frenchman, and she wrote exclusively in French, her mother tongue. France's first académicienne, however, had been a resident of the United States for more than four decades. It is not surprising, therefore, that certain academicians regarded her as a foreigner. Nevertheless, as a frequent world traveler Yourcenar returned to France many times over the years. She thought of herself as neither French nor American; rather she espoused a kinship with all humanity: "I have several homelands, so that in one sense I belong perhaps to none" (Les yeux ouverts [With Open Eyes, 1980]). The question of her nationality was easily resolved for the Academy when she acquired dual citizenship, having officially applied for restoration of her French status in 1979.

Her difficulties were further compounded in that she had not presented her own candidacy to the Academy and solicited the votes of the current members to assure her election, as required by protocol. (She was not the first; Henry de Montherlant broke this tradition in 1960.) Instead, Jean d'Ormesson, writer and former editor of the conservative newspaper Le Figaro, after seeking and receiving her permission, proposed her name. She graciously responded in a letter, stating that she "would not be so impolite as to refuse if elected."

Why, it might well be asked, considering all the objections, was this woman sought after and awarded the highest literary recognition France has to offer? Quite simply because this novelist, playwright, short-story writer, poet, autobiographer, essayist, critic, translator, and recipient of numerous prestigious awards combined erudition, scholarship, psychological insight, profound metaphysical meditation, and original genius to produce an art that is remarkable not only in its wide range of literary genres but also in the extraordinary delight and enrichment it affords.

Yourcenar (the surname, an anagram adopted more for amusement than to assure the writer anonymity, became her legal name in 1947) was born on 8 June 1903, the only child of a Belgian mother, Fernande de Cartier de Marchienne, and a father of northern French stock whose lineage can be traced to the early 1500's, Michel de Crayencour. She chronicled their lives at length in *Souvenirs pieux* (Pious Memories, 1973) and *Archives du nord* (Archives of the North, 1977), respectively. At the conclusion of these volumes Yourcenar herself is still only an infant. *Quoi? L'Éternité* (What? Eternity, 1988), the final volume of this autobiography—which is entitled *Le labyrinthe du monde* (The Labyrinth of the World)—has as its theme the strangeness yet banality of life. Contrary to the expectations of some, it does not reveal the writer's own story; Yourcenar does not disclose the "I" that is provocatively absent from most of her writings. This work deals instead with the last twenty-five years of her father's life and with a woman friend of his whose kindness and intelligence were a model for Yourcenar; she herself hardly figures in the book at all.

Yourcenar's mother died of puerperal fever and peritonitis ten days after her daughter's birth; the child was educated entirely at home by governesses and tutors under the guidance of an interested, cultured, adventurous, bon vivant father. At Mont Noir, a château constructed by her great-great-grandfather in Flan-

ders, as well as in family residences in the south of France and in Paris, she grew up in a world of privilege. Multilingual, she read Latin and Greek at an early age, and this was undoubtedly the basis for her later preoccupation with classical themes. It was from Michel (as she called her father) that she received her deep interest in literature and philosophy. At sixteen she received the *baccalauréat,* qualifying her for entrance into the French university system, an option she never chose to exercise.

Although she was baptized a Roman Catholic, her religious education was not extensive. Her main contact with religion was with the superficial, mechanical—almost superstitious—practice of her grandmother, whom she did not admire, which perhaps explains, in part, a certain antipathy she later felt for all formal religions, an attitude that is evident in her writings. Very early on, she espoused a kind of Greek religiosity—an awareness of the unity of everything in matter, an affinity for divine immanence as opposed to the traditional Judeo-Christian tension between a transcendental deity and an immanent, concerned God.

> While still a small child, I came to the conclusion . . . that I had to choose between religion, such as I perceived it around me—that is, the Catholic religion—and the universe. . . . These two aspects of the sacred seemed to me incompatible. One seemed far more vast than the other: the Church hid the forest from my view.
>
> (*With Open Eyes,* p. 41)[1]

Her aversion to the Catholic faith was due largely both to her understanding of it as a series of tedious dogmas and moral constrictions and to her encounter with mediocre, tepid adherents who only served, in her eyes, to discredit it. She chose instead to subscribe to a "mysticism of matter," a world soul, something akin to the *tout* of Denis Diderot. In her eulogy to her predecessor in the French Academy,

---

[1] Except as noted, all translations are by the present author.

Roger Caillois, Yourcenar intoned a kind of hymn to matter, invoking the words of the Apocryphal Jesus—"Break the wood and I am in the sap; lift the stone and I am there"—as well as those of the medieval mystic Meister Eckhart—"The stone is God, but it doesn't know that it is, and it is the lack of this knowledge that defines its nature as stone."

Nevertheless, in *With Open Eyes,* her dialogue with Matthieu Galey, she revealed a satisfaction in her Catholic origins and an affinity for the rituals, imagery, and liturgy of the church. In addition, she was greatly influenced by the beauty and mystery of Eastern mysticism, an interest that pervades much of her work. She did not entertain the slightest thought of renouncing Christ, but still less did she renounce the "wisdom of Tao." Appreciative of Tantrism and Zen as well, she remained above all deeply attached to Buddhist thought. It should be noted that the conflict she initially saw between the love of God and love of the universe, which had haunted her most of her life, she appeared in her later years to have surmounted, reconciling the two. Having turned toward "oriental and Christian myths," she professed an awareness of humanity's constant proximity to the eternal.

When World War I erupted, father and daughter escaped the German invasion of France by sailing away on his yacht, taking their household and other refugees with them to England, where they remained in a London suburb for a year. Since Mont Noir, the family seat, had become the base of operations for the British High Command and was under bombardment by the enemy (it was eventually destroyed), they returned to Paris and finally to the south of France, making periodic trips to other parts of Europe.

When she was fourteen, Yourcenar began writing verse, viewing prose as too formidable for a novice—"an ocean in which one might very quickly drown." Her father arranged for the private printing of her first two books. *Le jardin des chimères* (The Garden of the Chimeras, 1921) is a dramatic adaptation in verse

of the Icarus legend and, in subject matter and motifs, forecasts many of her later works, impregnated as they clearly are by Greek thought, literature, and myths. It was followed in 1922 by *Les dieux ne sont pas morts* (The Gods Are Not Dead), another book of verse, imitative of the symbolists, especially Maurice Maeterlinck, who were in vogue at the time and whose techniques Yourcenar was studying. In reference to her early creative efforts, Yourcenar observed frankly that a beginning writer sometimes has the misfortune of getting into print. Some early literary attempts, she informs us, were "wisely" discarded—namely, the first versions of *Mémoires d'Hadrien* (*Memoirs of Hadrian,* 1951) and a vast *roman-fleuve,* fragments of which were eventually transformed into other works. In the late 1920's her essays and poems as well as some short stories appeared in various literary journals.

It wasn't until 1929, however, with the publication of her first novel, *Alexis ou le traité du vain combat* (*Alexis*), that Yourcenar received the favorable attention of a substantial number of critics. Written in the form of a long letter by the protagonist, Alexis, a sensitive and talented young musician who is a homosexual, to his wife, Monique, whom he loves—ostensibly to explain his abandonment of her and their son, to whom she has just given birth—the book is a profound and moving psychological analysis of a man's unsuccessful attempt to live contrary to the demands of his sexuality and is quite clearly an *apologia pro vita sua.* His only regret, for which he asks Monique's pardon at the end of the novel, is not that he has left her, but that he remained with her for so long. The leitmotif of man's fated existence—that to some extent past events determine the future and mold the individual's life, a theme found in many of Yourcenar's writings—is strikingly present here.

The exploration of homosexuality, a daring theme for its time, coupled with the disassociation of sexual pleasure from love, inevitably evokes the works of André Gide, as does the subtitle, *Le traité du vain combat* (Treatise on a Futile Struggle), which echoes Gide's *Corydon: Traité d'un vain désir* (1924). Both works were drawn, it would seem, from Vergil's "Second Eclogue," entitled "Alexis," in which the shepherd Corydon laments his failure to win the beautiful Alexis. Yourcenar, however, advises us that the works of Gide did not directly influence her writing of *Alexis.* She drew instead on the overview of life that she found and admired in certain works of Rainer-Maria Rilke. The subject of homo- or bisexuality, considered taboo for so long, is handled with delicacy, sensitivity, and artistry; it is at the same time presented in a forthright, frank, and sympathetic manner.

Yourcenar adopted for her first novel the restrained, sparse, sober, precise, disciplined but elegant style of the classicists, the limited-in-scope *récit,* traditionally employed in France, she noted in her preface, by *moralistes* and for "the examination of conscience." The form seems appropriate for the abstract expression of passion and the probing deliberation of the narrator, who, while admitting the importance of the soul, clearly gives prominence to the flesh.

In his confessional letter, Alexis reflects on the painful discovery of the tyranny of his body:

> Perhaps what makes pleasure so terrible is that it teaches us we have a body. Prior to that, it serves us only for living. Finally we are made to realize that this body has a life of its own, its own dreams, its own wills, and that until we die, we shall have to take it into account: give in to it, negotiate or struggle with it.
>
> (*Oeuvres romanesques,* p. 33)

Attempting to understand and accurately reveal his feelings and actions and their underlying causes, Alexis falters as he clarifies an assertion, questions his explanations, attempts to establish a philosophical basis for his conclusions. The tension created by his efforts to lay bare the nuances of awareness of his body's demands in conflict with those of

his conscience and by his search for a language and tone suitable for expression to his young wife parallels Yourcenar's concern to bring us to an understanding of a fact of life that has long been ignored or simply considered with indignation or disdain. She has called *Alexis* the "portrait of a voice." It is an eloquent, haunting, yet reticent voice, eager to express itself but humble in the realization that it may not be understood.

There are those who, with considerable justice, have compared this novel, dense with aphorisms, to the *Essays* of Michel de Montaigne. In fact, all of Yourcenar's work manifests this affiliation. Her exploration of human nature and analysis of man's actions place her within the tradition of the *moralistes.* Her terse observations of the human condition and her reconciliation of apparent contradictions in man's behavior make her the recipient of that Gallic inheritance bequeathed to her from François de la Rochefoucauld, Blaise Pascal, Jean de la Bruyère, Montaigne, Voltaire, and a host of others. Although the sentiments may vary, it is the strains of their voices that Alexis echoes when he remarks that "all of our existence is characterized by infidelity to ourselves" and that "one interprets only one's own trouble: for it is always of oneself that one speaks" or that "pleasure and suffering are two very close sensations."

Alexis' celebration of the body, of sexual pleasure ("I do not see why pleasure should be held in contempt for being only a feeling, when no one holds grief in contempt and that, too, is a feeling"), reflects his creator's view of the sacredness of sexuality, "one of the great phenomena of universal life," as an avenue to transcendent reality. It also reflects her rejection of certain Christian attitudes, permeated with Augustinian philosophy, that view sexual pleasure as an unfortunate accompaniment to the act of procreation.

Homo- or bisexuality recurs as an important motif in Yourcenar's work—notably in *Le coup de grâce* (*Coup de Grâce,* 1939), but also in *Memoirs of Hadrian* and *L'Oeuvre au noir* (*The*

Abyss, 1968), as well as in others. It is in *Alexis,* however, that the subject receives its fullest treatment.

After the death of her father in 1929, Yourcenar traveled extensively throughout Europe and the eastern Mediterranean—to countries that serve as a backdrop for many of her books—making Greece her home in the course of her nomadic wanderings. She had permitted her half-brother (the son of her father's first marriage) to take charge of her legacy, a step she was later to regret. Managing to salvage about a quarter of her inheritance, she resolved to break all family ties, casting off, at the same time, their bourgeois values and conventions. Taking into account money bequeathed to her by her mother, she anticipated having about ten years free of financial concerns.

Employing the same *récit* form as in *Alexis* in her second novel, *La nouvelle Eurydice* (The New Eurydice, 1931), Yourcenar returned to the motif of homosexuality. The main theme of this first-person narration, however, is the impossibility of fathoming the enigma that love is, of understanding the complexity of its various facets, the destructiveness of its driving force, the suffering that inevitably accompanies "the burden of loving somebody." With few exceptions the work was not acclaimed by the critics, and the author, sharing their view, referred to it as a failure.

The following year she published an essay, *Pindare* (Pindar, 1932), written as an adolescent, on the great lyric poet of ancient Greece. This essay was an attempt to express the mystical significance of ritual.

It has often been said that talented novelists make mediocre dramatists and vice versa. For example, one reads Albert Camus's fiction, but not his plays; one reads Jean-Paul Sartre's theater, but rarely his novels. Yourcenar, it is true, has received wide recognition primarily for *Memoirs of Hadrian* and *The Abyss*—both of which have attained the stature of classics among historical novels (they have been translated into sixteen and fifteen languages, respectively), marked as they are by the author's

extraordinary erudition and penetrating psychological analysis. Yet her gifts were such that she had at her command a remarkable range of literary genres. Her theater should not be overlooked. Her plays, rarely performed, were written not so much to be produced on stage as to create a "labyrinth of monologues or dialogues in their pure state." Not as well known nor as successful as her other work, her dramas nevertheless remain important expressions of her analysis of the human condition.

The very short one-act play *Le dialogue dans le marécage* (The Dialogue in the Marsh, 1932) was inspired by the pathetic story recounted in four cryptic lines in canto 5 of Dante's *Purgatory*. As Yourcenar acknowledges in her preface, the play also reflects the Japanese Nō in form and in that the three protagonists echo the Nō characters: the obsessed pilgrim, the Buddhist monk companion (here a Franciscan), and the phantom. It depicts the qualms of conscience of Sire Laurent, a jealous old Italian from Siena, who, having sequestered his unfaithful adolescent wife in a miserable and secluded castle and left her there to die, returns after a twelve-year absence, hoping to be pardoned for his conduct. The obsessed husband, accompanied by Brother Candide, finds his abandoned wife, Pia, well and, to his surprise, content in her prison. In the course of the dialogue it is revealed by Laurent that her lover has died, although Pia insists that he still visits her periodically. Questions arise and remain unanswered. At the conclusion of the play, we are left, as the author intended, unsure as to what has actually transpired, how much of the experience has been real, imagined, or supernatural. The elusive, specterlike presentation of Pia dominates.

La mort conduit l'attelage (Death Drives the Team) received a great deal of praise when it appeared in 1934. It is a collection of three short stories: "D'après Dürer" (According to Dürer), which eventually served as a point of departure for *The Abyss;* "D'après Greco" (According to Greco), a tale of incest later developed into the short story "Anna, soror"

("Anna, Sister") and published years later in the anthology *Comme l'eau qui coule* (*Two Lives and A Dream,* 1982); and "D'après Rembrandt" (According to Rembrandt), subsequently transformed into "Un homme obscur" ("An Obscure Man") and "Une belle matinée" ("A Lovely Morning") for the same anthology. These three short stories have been described as a series of *tableaux vivants* of the Renaissance and the Reformation. They are not biographical sketches, but rather a sequence of dream figures based on historical persons. The corresponding titles were selected, the author asserts, to indicate a similarity of background while setting in relief the contrasts existing between these figures. Although these tales lack the artistry of the mature Yourcenar, they are of interest in that they reveal motifs that reverberate in other works and underline her method of reworking texts.

Stylistically, Yourcenar's novel *Denier du rêve* (*A Coin in Nine Hands,* 1934) represents a departure from the *récit* to a semilyrical narrative form. An attempted assassination of Benito Mussolini is loosely the subject. Set in Fascist Rome in 1933, it is, to be sure, a critique of that political ideology, revealing, "the hollow reality hidden behind the bloated facade of Fascism." But more important, it is the expression of a view of the human predicament: each person, frantically seeking happiness and finding instead misery and death, must deceive not only others but most especially himself into believing that his dreams can and will be realized.

The coin of the title, a ten-lira silver piece, passes from hand to hand nine times, purchasing for an assortment of people, in turn, a momentary escape from reality and despair into illusion and hope, and thus serving as a device to link the lives of all the characters. Yourcenar uses this literary technique to underline the common humanity of her creations: their intrinsic solitude in a world teeming with people, their longing for gratuitous love, their sharp awareness of frustration and misery. Paolo, for example, pays Lina, a prostitute

dying of cancer, for the illusion of love; Lina buys a lipstick with the coin to give herself the appearance of health and vitality; Giulio, unhappily married and unsuccessful in business, exchanges the coin for candles in church in order to obtain temporary peace and hope; Clement Roux, who has suffered a heart attack, tosses the coin into the Trevi Fountain, to wish not for a return to Rome but for the restoration of health, youth, and purity; from there it is retrieved by Oreste to purchase wine, the elixir that will mask reality and create a comforting illusion for a time—by the third bottle, he has buried his mother-in-law, told off his boss, quit his job, removed his enemies from the face of the earth, and proved himself a hero.

Yourcenar integrates dreams and reality—to the extent that at times the line between them is blurred—as a means of conveying a complete overview of life. This is a favored motif, one that is particularly intriguing in *A Coin in Nine Hands.* The book's epigraph is taken from Montaigne: "To abandon one's life for a dream is to know its true value." It is worth noting that the engaging Father Cicca, who also dreams—he yearns for a beautiful gold watch, an electric chandelier for his church, and a car—does not receive the coin that buys illusions; he is nonetheless repeatedly filled with joy from love of God, a mystical gift that is gratuitously granted to him. He has given great value to his life in that he has indeed abandoned it for a dream.

When *A Coin in Nine Hands* was rewritten in 1959, much of the original version was discarded. Numerous changes were made, including a more extensive use of free indirect discourse. Persistently striving after perfection, Yourcenar returned over and over again to her earlier works in order to revise them stylistically, to expand them, to express another viewpoint, or even to recast them in a different form. Each new edition of nearly all her books has been printed with some modifications, if only minor. Some critics find this practice of reworking a text irritating in that it tends to complicate analysis of her achievement. But in the afterword to *The Abyss,* Yourcenar insists that the writer has his own reasons for being more severe with himself than his critics; only he knows what he wishes to accomplish. Feeling a certain responsibility to her art and to her readers, she persisted in making whatever revisions seemed important.

Unlike Samuel Beckett, who absolutely refused to offer insight into any of his work, abstruse as it often is, Yourcenar was genuinely concerned with reader comprehension. For purposes of clarity she guided the reader, making her intentions evident in essays, prefaces, epilogues (some of which are quite lengthy), and interviews, as well as in textual changes. In "Carnet de notes de *Mémoires d'Hadrien*" ("Reflections on the Composition of *Memoirs of Hadrian*"), the postface of her best-known book, she graciously acknowledges readers' comments, thanks them for sharing their reactions to her work with her, and states that any new edition will reflect their discriminating remarks. There is, in effect, another dimension to her work: reader participation.

What may be difficult, or more likely impossible, for readers and critics alike to comprehend fully is that in some arcane, inexplicable way characters take on a life of their own, to some degree independent of their creator. François Mauriac, for example, has commented that one of his characters, for whom he intended a minor role, forced his way to center stage and became, contrary to Mauriac's original intentions, a protagonist. When queried about a particular novel, Graham Greene went so far as to reply that he was not responsible for the words of his characters.

Yourcenar repeatedly asserted that some characters grow and develop over the years and that they refuse to reveal themselves totally until the author has reached maturity. She looked upon her creations as having a life outside the literary framework in which she placed them. To illustrate, included in the text of *Rendre à César* (*Render unto Caesar*, 1961), the dramatic adaptation of *A Coin in Nine Hands*, is a kind of registry directly following the last stage direction, a page headed "Vital Statistics" that provides the dates and places of birth of all the characters in the play as well as the details of their deaths—events that take place long after the curtain has fallen. Upon completion of a work, her fictive figures continued to occupy a place in her mind, to age, to change, and to profit by experiences independent of the author's intention—and to demand, it would seem, to be revealed in their new light to others. For this reason Yourcenar considered writing several sequels to some of her novels. Alexis, for instance, was thinking of returning to his wife, at least for a trial period; and this time it would have been Monique's voice we would have heard. Her characters share her life. "No matter what happens," she remarks in *With Open Eyes,* "when I am dying I am sure to have at my side both a doctor and a priest: Zeno and the Prior of Cordeliers" (characters from *The Abyss*). We are reminded of the dying Balzac, calling for the fictional physician of his novels.

Feux (*Fires,* 1936) has usually been classified as prose poetry or as an anthology of *pensées* (reflections or aphorisms) and short stories. There are elements of the journal as well, the source of most of the *pensées* being the author's diary; the book begins, for example, with the wish, tersely expressed by the persona, that it will never be read. Although Yourcenar describes the volume as "a collection of love poems, or, if one prefers, something akin to a sequence of lyrical prose pieces linked by a certain concept of love" (elsewhere she refers to them as prose poems), she found it appropriate to include them in *Oeuvres romanesques* (Works of Fiction, 1982), a collection of novels and short stories.

The pieces in *Fires,* she declares, are a confession, the product of a love crisis, a kind of exorcism, and at the same time a quest for eternal values. Written in an extremely personal, impressionistic, baroque style ("an almost excessive expressionism") for the purpose of depicting the full complexity and emotional depth of a passion, Yourcenar explains, *Fires* tells the story—sometimes directly, sometimes obliquely (by means of stories based on legends and history)—of a love affair that moves from trust and bliss to disappointment, bitterness, despair, and ultimately to the resolution to rebuild life in a new search for happiness.

The book contains ten groups of *pensées,* which Yourcenar defines in the preface as "theorems of passion," alternating with nine narratives that "illustrate, explain, and often mask" these theorems. Because of the complexity and uniqueness of its structure and because most of the narratives were originally published separately, some critics tend to see a lack of continuity in *Fires.* However, as Edith and Frederick Farrell astutely point out, careful analysis reveals a tightly organized pattern of balanced components that serves to underline the various themes of love and its corollary, suffering.

Excluding Mary Magdalene, all the protagonists of the stories—Phaedra, Achilles, Patroclus, Antigone, Lena, Clytemnestra, Sappho—mythical or real, are associated with ancient Greece. Without exception, they have experienced an all-consuming or "absolute" passion. Their voices interact with each other and with that of the *pensées* in their exploration of love.

Explicating her poems in the preface of *Fires,* Yourcenar comments that total love for someone means inevitable disillusionment, abnegation, and humility. This observation is exemplified in the following revealing *pensées* from *Oeuvres romanesques:*

> Nothing to fear. I've touched bottom. I cannot fall lower than your heart.
>
> (p. 1058)

> Love is an affliction. We are punished for not having been able to remain alone.
>
> (p. 1113)

> Afraid of nothing? I am afraid of you.
>
> (p. 1114)

> A god who wants me to live has ordered you to stop loving me. I don't bear happiness well. Lack of habit. In your arms, I could only die.
>
> (p. 1079)

Considering the terrible suffering that invariably accompanies it, she suggests that love does not merit the exalted place assigned it by poets. Clearly, although the mind and soul have their place in love, in this work the body is perceived as playing the principal role, as a number of *pensées* forcefully expound:

> A heart is perhaps something unsavory. It's on the order of an anatomy table or a butcher's stall. I prefer your body.
>
> (p. 1065)

> Not to be loved anymore is to become invisible. You no longer are aware that I have a body.
>
> (p. 1123)

> You could fall all of a sudden into the void where the dead go; I would be consoled if you would bequeath me your hands. Your hands alone would remain, detached from you, unexplainable like those of marble gods transformed into the dust and limestone of their own tomb. They would survive your actions, the miserable bodies they have caressed.
>
> (pp. 1073–1074)

Still, an all-consuming love, "striking its victim both as a sickness and as a vocation," is, Yourcenar declares, permeated by a kind of mystical force without which it could not survive; a total love is in some way affiliated with the transcendent.

This sumptuous retelling of ancient legends and history, modernized by a twentieth-century orientation as well as by autobiographical associations, evokes the past to set in relief the timelessness and universality of love. A surfeit of joy, love inevitably causes terrible, agonizing pain. This "sickness" can be so all-consuming, as is the case with Phaedra, as to be destructive. Only God's love, it is suggested in the long monologue by Mary Magdalene, is perfect, gratuitous, eternal. Interwoven with cryptic, lyrical fragments, a tapestry beautifully wrought, this volume of prose poems is perhaps the most powerful, the most moving love poetry written in French in the twentieth century.

Yourcenar began her career as a translator due to financial need; she accepted a commission to translate Virginia Woolf's *The Waves* (1931), which was published in 1937 as *Les Vagues.* At about the same time she also translated *What Maisie Knew* (1897) by Henry James, although it did not appear in print until 1947, under the title *Ce que savait Maisie.* Long after money was no longer an issue, she continued to bring out varied and impressive translations for the enjoyment and fulfillment they brought her and also from a desire to be of service—to render into another idiom, for those who might not otherwise encounter them, the complexity and beauty of thought and emotion of other artists.

She transposed into elegant French a collection of Negro spirituals, *Fleuve profond, sombre rivière* (Deep, Dark, Troubled River, 1964), with a preface treating the history of black Americans, as well as black American gospel music, *Blues et gospels* (1984). Among her other translations are the poems of an American friend in a bilingual critical edition, *Présentation critique d'Hortense Flexner* (1969); the play *Amen Corner* (1965) by James Baldwin, published as *Le coin des "Amen"* (1983); and, in collaboration with Jun Shiragi, five plays by Yukio Mishima, entitled *Cinq nô modernes* (Five Modern Nō, 1983).

Since all aspects of Greek culture always occupied a privileged place in her thinking and her work, it is not surprising to find that Yourcenar also undertook to translate Greek poetry. What is striking, however, is that this poetry spans many eras, beginning with the sixth century B.C. *La couronne et la lyre* (The Crown and the Lyre, 1979) is a collection of classical Greek verse. Her choice of poems represents a survey of the changes in Greek civilization through the centuries. Her preferred verse form for the translation of ancient Greek poetry was the alexandrine; some of her translations, authorities have commented, surpass the originals in beauty. In collaboration with the neo-Hellenic scholar Constantin Dimaras, she has also put into ad-

mirable prose the entire poetic output of Constantine Cavafy under the title *Présentation critique de Constantin Cavafy* (1958). Many of the translations are accompanied by valuable critical commentaries.

Yourcenar's aim in translating was to present "an idea, an emotion" as close as possible to what the author intended the reader to feel, even if this meant using an alternate form; it was sometimes necessary "to reach the French reader by another channel." Her objective was to "capture the sound of another spirit." In view of this, it may be said that a translation of this kind is akin to creative writing, that it constitutes, in effect, another genre. A profound knowledge of the two languages involved, essential as it is, is only a technical skill and not at all adequate; what is of primary importance is the innate gift to be able to penetrate the sense of the original text with its emotional depths, to interpret the intentions and feelings of the author, and to present its equivalent in a new linguistic structure. It is generally recognized that Yourcenar attained an exceptionally high level of achievement in this art, which was nonetheless only a marginal part of her creative output.

In the fall of 1937, having accepted an invitation from Grace Frick, an American from Hartford, Connecticut, who was to become her lifelong friend and companion as well as translator of a number of her books, Yourcenar made her first trip across the Atlantic, visiting New England, parts of the South, and Quebec. Returning to Europe in the spring to a rented villa in Capri, she wrote "almost at a single sitting" of some weeks duration the short novel *Coup de Grâce.*

It has always been recognized that we are beings of love; it might be said that love is the secret of our being. The subject of much of Yourcenar's work is this overwhelming power, this remarkable, arcane energy that drives us, this "terrifying force," as she calls it in the preface to *Coup de Grâce,* an account of actual events related to her by the brother of one of the principals involved. This novel, a return to the *récit,* was well received by the critics. It was made into a film in 1977 by Volker Schlöndorff, a director of the new generation of filmmakers in Germany.

Coup de Grâce is a Racinian tragedy in fictional form. Yourcenar pointed out that it observes the classical unities of time, place, and "danger," as Pierre Corneille put it. The story takes place during the Russian Revolution at an isolated anti-Bolshevik outpost in the Baltic province of Kurland. The narrator, Eric, an aristocrat and soldier of fortune who risks his life for causes in which he does not believe, is unable to return the obsessive passion that Sophie feels for him, since he loves her brother Conrad, a comrade-in-arms to whom he has been devoted since childhood. "Why is it," Eric wonders, "that women fall in love with the very men who are destined otherwise, and who accordingly must repulse them, or else deny their own nature?" (The translation is Frick's.) He describes their relationship figuratively as that of executioner and victim, a metaphor that foreshadows the literal occurrence at the conclusion of the novel: Sophie, having been taken prisoner by Eric, is shot by his hand; this is, to be sure, the *coup de grâce* of the title. Such a tragic denouement is one to which, Yourcenar asserts, passion inevitably tends; but, she adds, it generally assumes more insidious or hidden forms in the lives of most people.

The first-person narration, a literary device that Yourcenar often employed effectively to eliminate authorial intrusion, requires strict collaboration, she points out, on the part of the reader, who must be aware that the narration is necessarily a biased one to some extent, and thus may not be reliable. Usually, she notes, a *récit* in the first person favors the speaker; in *Coup de Grâce,* however, it works to the detriment of Eric, who is attempting to understand and judge himself by reviewing his life. Ironically, while scrupulously honest and fearful of deceiving himself, he tends to offer the least favorable interpretation of his actions. Accordingly, it must be recognized that at times a disparity exists between the image of himself that the narrator is creating and the actual person he is, especially given the complex and intense emotions involved.

Like Alexis', Eric's manner is grave; his narration manifests sobriety and restraint, and he views passion somewhat dispassionately. Flattered by Sophie's totally abandoning herself to him—indeed, his vanity becomes dependent on evidence of her passion—he is at the same time repelled and revolted by it. Sophie's consuming need is to give herself, body and soul, to another. Eric's ardent love for Conrad is not just physical nor even sentimental; it includes an idealization of their friendship. The role of the soul in love relationships is considerably more important in this novel than in either *Alexis* or even *Fires.* The book is a moving, penetrating psychological analysis of the anguish of unrequited love; some therefore find Sophie, and not Eric, to be the protagonist.

Although French critics generally consider *Coup de Grâce* to be one of Yourcenar's major works, it has not received the acclaim it deserves in the United States, where the tendency has been to compare it unfavorably with *Memoirs of Hadrian.*

Much of Yourcenar's work is based on or affiliated with myths or legends. Often, even when the characters have a twentieth-century identification, the association is quite explicit; sometimes, however, the comparison is more subtle, depending on stylistic devices or literary tradition to signal the relationship. The Near and Far East furnish the backdrop for most of the *Nouvelles orientales* (*Oriental Tales,* 1938). Although the title evokes the exotic atmosphere of the *Tales of a Thousand and One Nights,* the term *oriental* should be understood in its broad sense, as in Victor Hugo's *Les Orientales* (1829). The tales reveal, as do *A Coin in Nine Hands* and *Fires,* the close connection Yourcenar perceived between myths and reality. Aside from numerous stylistic revisions, the tales (ten in the definitive form of the 1978 Pléiade edition), have remained substantially the same as they passed through five successive editions (besides preprintings and reprintings in sundry periodicals).

"L'Homme qui a aimé les Néréides" ("The Man Who Loved the Néréids") is a liberal interpretation of certain superstitions of modern Greece, in which a man who experiences a supernatural love is not only forever changed by it but also stricken mute so that he cannot communicate his experience to others. "Le lait de la mort" ("The Milk of Death"), a supernatural tale in which a mother, long after she has died, continues to nurse her infant, owes its origin to a Balkan ballad of the Middle Ages. Most of the other stories are derived from authentic fables and legends, ballads, or actual events, both old and contemporary. "Notre-Dame-des-Hirondelles" ("Our Lady of the Swallows"), however, is a fanciful, imaginative account of the origin of an actual chapel bearing that name in Attica. It might be described as a Christian fairy tale; the characters include the mother of Christ and mischievous fairies who prove to be angels to whom God forgot to give wings.

"La tristesse de Cornélius Berg" ("The Sadness of Cornelius Berg"), the projected ending of "that enormous and unruly project" of her "twentieth year," the roman-fleuve that was discarded, is a brief sketch of an aging seventeenth-century Dutch artist turned bitter by the meanness he sees in mankind and by the inevitable decay of all matter with the passage of time. In response to his companion's observation that God is the painter of the universe, Berg retorts, "How unfortunate . . . that God did not limit himself to painting landscapes." "Le dernier amour du Prince Genghi" ("The Last Love of Prince Genji") has as its point of departure a blank page in a Japanese literary text of the eleventh century: the Genghi-Monogotari by Murasaki Shikibu, who recounts in seven volumes the adventures of a Don Juan of the Orient. Characteristic of Japanese refinement of that period, Murasaki chooses not to describe the death of her protagonist; instead she has him retire to a monastery. The blank page that follows is an invitation to the reader to draw his own conclusions. Filling in the lacuna of the Japanese text, Yourcenar imagines what takes place next in the aging Genji's life.

Most of the tales contain elements of the fantastic; all treat the subject of love and its various manifestations. Perhaps the most captivating is "Comment Wang-Fô fut sauvé" ("How Wang-Fo Was Saved"), inspired by an ancient Chinese Taoist apologue that depicts the deep and totally unselfish love of the disciple Ling for his master Wang-Fô, a famous painter. "It was said," the narrator informs us, "that Wang-Fô had the power to give life to his paintings." Enraged at the aging artist because of his ability to create exquisite landscapes ("the only empire over which it is worth reigning"), in comparison with which reality palls, the emperor discloses his plan to have the old man's eyes ("the two magic doors that give him entry to his kingdom") burned out and his hands cut off, but first he must complete an unfinished seascape. Upon hearing this sentence, Ling attempts to assassinate the despot but succeeds only in having his own head cut off. "'I hate you also,'" the emperor sighs, "'because you know how to make yourself loved.'" Wang-Fô does finish his masterpiece, painting Ling and himself into the picture in a small boat disappearing out to sea. This story, so engaging, so different in atmosphere and tone (as are the other Oriental Tales) from so much of Yourcenar's work, reveals nonetheless the same preoccupation with the supernatural, the strangeness and splendor of love, as well as the sure but unfathomable link between time and eternity.

A meditation on the relationship between the unconscious and the aesthetic of dreams, mythology, and poetic inspiration found expression in another work published in 1938, Les songes et les sorts (Dreams and Destinies, 1938), in which Yourcenar relates and analyzes some of her dreams without recourse to the

Freudian approach to dream interpretation or to any of the other dominant theories of the time. Her primary concern is with the aesthetic of the oneiric world rather than the psychological processes at work in the subconscious.

In 1939 Europe was in turmoil and another invitation from Frick brought Yourcenar to the United States for a second visit. Her intention was to remain six months before returning to Greece, but the rapidly expanding German occupation of Europe, coupled with the depletion of her inheritance, forced her to prolong her stay indefinitely. She earned a modest living as a part-time instructor of French literature and art history at Hartford Junior College, where Frick had been appointed head, and at Sarah Lawrence College in Bronxville, New York, to which she commuted from Hartford, Connecticut.

During World War II and the succeeding years, a number of her essays and poems appeared in various French expatriate periodicals in Buenos Aires and Algiers. Three plays, whose subjects are drawn from Greek mythology, date from this period. They were later assembled in the collection *Théâtre II* (1971). For the most part, however, 1939–1948 were years of retirement from literary endeavors, largely due to a difficult teaching schedule, a long commute, and the fact that a divided France made publication there uncertain. Yet in 1943 her dramatic adaptation of a Hans Christian Andersen fairy tale, *La petite sirène* (*The Little Mermaid;* printed in *Théâtre I,* 1971), was produced at the Wadsworth Athenaeum in Hartford, in an English translation by Frick (subsequently lost). Yourcenar subtitled it *Divertissement dramatique* (A Dramatic Entertainment) and repeatedly referred to it as a lyrical drama.

Having vacationed there every summer since 1942, Yourcenar bought a small house with Frick in Northeast Harbor on Mount Desert Island off the coast of Maine, to which they moved in 1950. They named it Petite Plaisance (Small Pleasure). It remained Yourcenar's home until her death; it was here that she studied and wrote, for the most part, although she continued to make frequent trips around the world.

"Just when the gods had ceased to be and the Christ had not yet come, there was a unique moment in history, between Cicero and Marcus Aurelius, when man stood alone." (All translations from *Memoirs of Hadrian* are Frick's.) After this sentence from Gustave Flaubert's correspondence came to her attention, Yourcenar spent many years trying to define and then to depict that man who exists alone and at the same time is closely allied to all being. This project was taken up and abandoned, only to be taken up again, repeatedly during the 1920's and the 1930's. In the epilogue to *Memoirs of Hadrian,* she declared that there are books which should not be attempted before the writer has attained the age of forty; prior to that, the writer is not apt to recognize the "natural boundaries which from person to person, and from century to century separate the infinite variety of mankind."

While going through the contents of a trunk that had been stored in Switzerland during World War II, she came across several sheets of yellowed paper, apparently a letter, that began with the words, "My dear Mark." Wondering what friend or distant relative or love this was whom she could no longer recall, she finally realized that she had in hand the fragment of a lost manuscript of hers. Mark was Marcus Aurelius. It was then, in 1948, that her decision was irrevocably made: Yourcenar would finally write the book and from the point of view of the good Prince, a man who was "almost wise," the aging and infirm emperor Hadrian, who was beginning "to discern the profile" of his "death."

Considering the appropriate literary form to employ, Yourcenar commented that during the Renaissance she would have presented her study of this "great man" in an essay, while the classical age would have called for a tragedy; today, however, the novel is the dominant medium of expression. Her choice of the epistolary novel echoes the taste of the Age of Enlightenment, but in contrast to the fiction of that period, plot does not figure prominently in *Memoirs of Hadrian*. Further, with the exception of Denis Diderot's *Memoirs of a Nun* (1796) and quite possibly Pierre Choderlos de Laclos's *Les liaisons dangereuses* (1782), the narratives of that time were not based on actual histories.

Hadrian's letter to his seventeen-year-old adoptive grandson and heir is ostensibly for the purpose of supplementing Marcus' stoic philosophy with the observations and conclusions his own life, lived to the fullest, has yielded. By means of the emperor's reflections on his twenty-two-year reign and the preceding years, on his approaching death, on the mystery of love and his passion for the handsome Antinous, on statesmanship, on music and art, on the moral systems and religions that contribute to his civilization, Yourcenar provides a richly detailed portrait of the Roman Empire during the second century and of its philosopher-king Hadrian (A.D. 76–138).

Hadrian, predecessor of the Antonines, recalls and examines past events perhaps more for his own benefit than for Marcus' (as do Alexis and Eric in earlier novels), in order to come to a better understanding of who and what man is and who he himself is. An agnostic, he no longer gives credence to the gods who move themselves "neither to warn us nor to protect us nor to recompense nor to punish." Arriving on the political scene in the wake of Trajan's aggressive military exploits in Asia, he fixes the Euphrates as a boundary; his first gift to the empire is the termination of his predecessor's policy of conquest and the establishment of the *pax romana*. A humanist, lover of all that is Greek, patron of the arts, dabbler in astrology and magic, Hadrian distinguishes himself as commander and administrator, traveling throughout the empire making economic reforms, stabilizing the government, and beautifying cities architecturally.

Memoirs of Hadrian is historical fiction at its finest. All events and details, scrupulously and laboriously researched, are carefully documented. Yourcenar spent years reconstructing the emperor's library, reading what he had read and written, holding in her hands objects he had held, traveling where he had traveled, inspecting every available document and artifact of his reign. The novel is accompanied by a biographical note that includes appraisals of an impressive list of sources both ancient and modern, with explanations for any liberties taken. The excellence of Yourcenar's scholarship is such that she has the distinction of being read by historians, and her fictive account is cited in historical bibliographies dealing with Hadrian.

Her main objective was to approach inner reality. She wrote *Memoirs of Hadrian* with "one foot in scholarship, the other in magic . . . in that *sympathetic magic* which operates when one transports oneself, in thought, into another's body and soul." Her most intriguing achievement is the result of the step she took beyond that of the orthodox historian. "Do, from within," she remarks, "the same work of reconstruction which the nineteenth-century archaeologists have done from without." She describes a method she employed "akin to controlled delirium," an intense and continued participation in events of the past to produce another "portrait of a voice," to permit Hadrian to speak insofar as possible without interference from an authorial intermediary. To this end she adapted the *Spiritual Exercises* (1548) of Saint Ignatius of Loyola as well as those of certain Hindu ascetics. Her method consisted of trying to visualize in detail the historical incidents recorded on hundreds of index cards, placing herself in events as a silent observer, eliminating as much as possible all personal beliefs and prejudices, achieving a state of "attentiveness," emptying the mind and leaving it free of everything but the object of interest, capturing and clinging to the feelings thus aroused as a point of contact so as to convey them with fidelity, almost like a medium.

When two texts were in contradiction,

Yourcenar attempted to reconcile them, to regard them as two distinct aspects of the truth or as successive stages of a particular reality rather than give credence to one over the other; she recognized that truth is complex and multifaceted. Living in a symbiotic relationship with Hadrian, at times she had the impression that the emperor was lying—especially on the subject of his election; she ignored this possibility, permitting certain inconsistencies to exist in the text. Although a historical figure, Hadrian has passed through the twentieth-century mind of Yourcenar, resisting manipulation as do her totally imaginative creatures (if such there are) and setting in relief the blurred boundary she constantly sees between reality and fiction.

Although *Memoirs of Hadrian* most certainly meets the requirements for the historical novel—basis in fact, verisimilitude, an instructive text—it is quite clear that this book is much more than a search for lost time or simply entertainment. Rather, like the work of any serious writer, it is an examination of the metaphysical questions that have always absorbed man. Yourcenar described it as a "psychological novel, a meditation on history" and herself, its creator, as "historian-poet and novelist."

The epilogue is a gracious invitation to the reader to step into Yourcenar's study for the purpose of consulting her source material, listening to responses to anticipated questions or objections, observing her creative processes, learning of the birth pangs that brought forth an authentic Roman emperor and the pagan era in which he lived.

The author of *Alexis* had a small following of admirers and interested critics for over two decades. She was convinced, as she worked on *Memoirs of Hadrian,* that neither the man she was portraying nor the book she was writing would please the general public, only the "happy few," since the story line is overwhelmed by philosophical, psychological, and aesthetic reflections reminiscent of Montaigne. Hadrian's rumination on the complex affilia-

tions he sees among freedom, abnegation, license, servitude, and destiny is an illustration:

> Nearly all . . . fail to recognize their due liberty, and likewise their true servitude. They curse their fetters, but seem sometimes to find them matter for pride. Yet they pass their days in vain license, and do not know how to fashion for themselves the lightest yoke. For my part I have sought liberty more than power, and power only because it can lead to freedom. What interested me was . . . a technique: I hoped to discover the hinge where our will meets and moves with destiny, and where discipline strengthens, instead of restraining, our nature. . . . Life was to me a horse to whose motion one yields, but only after having trained the animal to the utmost. Since everything is finally a decision of the mind, . . . and involves also the body's assent, I strove to attain by degrees to that state of liberty, or of submission, which is almost pure.
> (*Oeuvres romanesques,* pp. 317–318)

Never had Hadrian loved anyone more deeply, more passionately than he did the Bithynian youth Antinous; for him alone Hadrian had thrown aside his lucid self-mastery, and yet "the weight of love, like that of an arm thrown tenderly across a chest, becomes little by little too heavy to bear." The emperor's thoughts on the body-soul relationship in love and on sensual pleasure are of interest, particularly in light of views expressed in *Alexis* and *Fires.*

> The cynics and the moralists . . . oblige themselves to scorn their pleasure in order to reduce its almost terrifying power, which overwhelms them, and its strange mystery, wherein they feel lost. I shall never believe in the classification of love among the purely physical joys (supposing that any such things exist) until I see a gourmet sobbing with delight over his favorite dish like a lover gasping on a young shoulder. Of all our games, love's play is the only one which threatens to unsettle the soul, and is also the only one in which the player has to abandon himself to the body's ecstasy. . . . The lover who leaves reason

in control does not follow his god to the end. . . . That mysterious play which extends from love of a body to love of an entire person. . . . The short and obscene sentence of Poseidonius about the rubbing together of two small pieces of flesh . . . does no more to define the phenomenon of love than the taut cord touched by the finger accounts for the infinite miracle of sounds.

(*Oeuvres romanesques,* pp. 294–295)

Contrary to Yourcenar's expectations, *Memoirs of Hadrian* was an immediate and prodigious success when it was published in 1951, winning for Yourcenar international acclaim. The book was awarded the Prix Fémina-Vacaresco as well as Le Grand Prix National des Lettres from the French Academy. The English translation in 1954 by Frick (in collaboration with the author) brought Yourcenar the interest and respect of American readers, making it financially feasible for her to resign her teaching post of nearly six years—"a desperate war expediency." To a large extent, Yourcenar spent the years from 1951 through the early 1960's traveling in Europe, attending academic and literary conferences, rewriting, and doing research for future works.

In the foreword to her two-part play *Electre ou la chute des masques* (Electra; or, the Fall of the Masks, staged in Paris in 1954 and published in the same year), Yourcenar traces the story of this Greek mythological figure from the pre-Homeric legendary epic through the extant versions of the three great Athenian dramatists to Shakespeare's *Hamlet* and the versions of Prosper Jolyot de Crébillon, Leconte de Lisle, and Hugo von Hoffmansthal, to mention only a few, and finally to such modern adaptations as Eugene O'Neill's trilogy *Mourning Becomes Electra* (1931), set in nineteenth-century New England, Jean Giraudoux's *Electre* (1937), and Jean-Paul Sartre's *The Flies* (1942).

According to the myth, Agamemnon, leader of the Greek armies, finding his ships becalmed at Aulis while en route to the Trojan War, sacrifices his daughter Iphigenia to Artemis, thus arousing the maternal wrath of his wife, Clytemnestra, who, together with her lover, Aegisthus, murders her husband in his bath. Orestes and Electra, her two surviving children, slay their mother and her paramour in revenge. Orestes, in turn, is pursued by the Furies.

In his *Oresteia* trilogy, Aeschylus emphasizes the idea of retribution from the point of view of Orestes. In Sophocles' *Electra,* it is a question of justice incarnated in the forceful and masculine image of a young woman. In the *Electra* of Euripides, justice is subordinated to the rancor of the humiliated heroine who has been forced to marry a kindly old peasant; she summons Clytemnestra to their miserable hut on the pretext that she has just delivered a baby, and there and then brother and sister murder their mother.

Contemporary interpretations insist that the leitmotiv of the myth is justice, Yourcenar observes, and suggest sexual motivations, hidden or explicit, for Electra's fury and Orestes' ensuing madness, emphasizing the role of the unconscious in intellectual and moral judgments. The modern poet rejects the ancient attitude toward justice without adopting the Christian one of forgiveness. All terms, psychological or literary, she declares, are merely labels for hatred.

Euripides' version of the myth forms the basis for Yourcenar's innovative treatment of the Greek tragedy, on which she imposes the classic unities of economy and rapidity of action. She raises an intriguing question: What would become of outrage, hatred, and vengeance if it were suddenly discovered that Orestes is not the son of the murdered monarch, but instead that of the assassin and usurper Aegisthus, issue of an adulterous union; and what if it was to protect him, the illegitimate child, that the slaughter of Agamemnon took place? Further, what if Electra's hatred of her mother springs, at least in part, from her love for her stepfather and her consequent jealousy of Clytemnestra? And to further complicate the situation, what if Pylades, in the employ of Aegisthus, is devoted to Orestes? The masks will fall. The play demonstrates "the horrible or sublime insistence of human beings in remaining themselves. . . . Instinct and will make them what they are." Orestes, even though aware of his true identity, nevertheless drives his knife into the body of his father. Pylades, the paid traitor/double agent, does not permit his ambition to damage his relationship with Orestes. Electra remains Electra. The masks, once removed, reveal each individual's destiny; each must be accomplished as was ordained.

As indicated, the story line has been modified by Yourcenar and some interesting overtones introduced: Electra, it seems, is a Catholic; she makes the sign of the cross, enunciating the accompanying formula after referring to the assassination that is about to take place as a "kind of Mass that all must participate in." At the end of the last scene in part one, Electra and Orestes engage in an ironic recitation of the Pater Noster:

ELECTRA: Our father who art in the tomb . . .
ORESTES: Thy will be done . . .
ELECTRA: Thy vengeance come . . .
ORESTES: And forgive us our trespasses . . .
ELECTRA: As we do not forgive those who have trespassed against us.

It is by this deliberate distortion of the most sacred of all Christian prayer formulas, spoken by two murderers seeking to justify their act, that Yourcenar sets in relief the monstrosity that is Electra. The play remains a Greek tragedy in that man's fate is determined and inexorably tragic.

"Once upon a time," begins Yourcenar in her introduction, as she recounts Euripides' version of the legend from which her one-act play *Le mystère d'Alceste* (The Mystery of Alcestis, 1963) is drawn. An oracle having announced the imminent death of the young prince Adme-

tus unless another human being offers to take his place, Admetus searches frantically for a substitute, even imploring each of his parents to sacrifice themselves on his behalf. Only Alcestis, his wife, volunteers to be the sacrificial victim. The evening before the burial a stranger knocks at the door, seeking food and shelter for the night; hospitality being a sacred obligation, he is graciously accommodated and is not told that all in the palace are in mourning. However, after drinking too much, his behavior becomes coarse, and a domestic finally finds it necessary to inform him of the tragic events that have just taken place. Chagrined, Hercules—for that is the stranger's identity—swears to expiate his gross actions by standing guard over the corpse, awaiting the arrival of Death, who will come to take possession of the soul of Alcestis. He enters into combat with this handsome young man with black hair—for it was thus the Greeks envisioned Death—and overcomes him. As promised, he returns Alcestis, veiled and momentarily mute, to her husband. Wishing to test the prince's fidelity he states that his companion is a beautiful slave, the spoils of war, whom he wishes to leave at the castle, since it would be inconvenient to take her with him on his journey. Admetus indignantly refuses to admit another woman into his home. Alcestis is unveiled; she and the prince are reunited to enjoy their happiness "for as long as fragile human creatures are able to."

With these words Yourcenar underlines a theme—secondary in the play to that of death and resurrection—that informs all her work: love, a source of joy, inevitably means suffering. Alcestis is consumed at times with the anguish of jealousy. Pointing out the impermanence of human love, she assures her husband that after her death he will soon console himself with another woman. Nor does the deep love Admetus has for Alcestis satisfy his inner longing. Of particular interest is the concept, found also in Paul Claudel's *The Satin Slipper* (1925), in Graham Greene's *The End of the Affair* (1951), and throughout the fiction of Mauriac, that the primary function of love is to raise man out of himself, to destroy his egocentricity, ultimately to guide man to the experience of infinite beatitude, as Admetus and Alcestis reveal in a dialogue from scene 3:

> ADMETUS: . . . let me see appear in your eyes the light of another world . . .
> ALCESTIS: That's it. I have never been for you anything other than a keyhole through which you might catch a glimpse of the invisible.

In the long commentary that precedes the play, Yourcenar traces the resurrection theme on which the myth is based as far back as the Neolithic period, when human concern for immortality first evidenced itself in the notion that death is not the end of existence, but perhaps a beginning, a kind of birth or passage, a trial that heroes and the pure of heart are capable of overcoming both for themselves and for others. These ideas result either from man's inability to accept his destiny or from intimations of "a mysterious truth that lies beyond the body and perhaps even the soul." In Neolithic times, there arose also the concepts of sacrifice, the substitution of victims, and, consequently, voluntary oblation. Finally, two themes converge: the idea of immortality united to that of a divine savior who conquers death, and the concept of the salvation of an individual by the voluntary oblation of another.

Yourcenar's aim in writing this play, she declares, was to revitalize an ancient myth, to show in a modern setting the tragicomic aspects that invariably accompany mourning—for example, the tiresome and indifferent people always present at a deathbed—and at the same time to show the almost liturgical elements of what is essentially a mystery, the sacred drama of death and resurrection. Death is here personified as a woman in black, an image Yourcenar declared to be more in keeping with contemporary imagination and tradition. The function of the Greek chorus is

performed in her retelling of the myth principally by the wise servant Georgine. Hercules, almost a symbol of virile sanctity for the ancients, is a prefiguration of Christ. Alcestis, "tender" and "good," the "servant of all," "the sacrificial lamb, the chosen virgin," is also clearly a Christ figure. Hercules, "in the service of the weak," triumphs over death, succumbing neither to the fear of death nor to the "appeal of the void." Yourcenar informs us that the mystery of Alcestis is the mystery of Hercules.

Published in the same volume with *Le mystère d'Alceste* is the last of Yourcenar's three plays based on Greek mythology, *Qui n'a pas son Minotaure?* (*To Each His Minotaur*, 1963; translated in *Plays*, 1984), which she labeled "a sacred entertainment in ten scenes." In a very long introduction, "Thésée: Aspects d'une légende et fragment d'une autobiographie," she discloses the origin of the play's composition—a literary game played in the early 1930's with two friends (and revised repeatedly over thirty years). She also reviews various treatments that have been given through the centuries to the story of Theseus, the principal hero of Attica, and his innumerable exploits, among which was the slaying of the Minotaur with the assistance of Ariadne, the lover he subsequently abandoned. After the death of his first wife, the Amazonian queen, he married Ariadne's sister, the formidable Phaedra, whose uncontrollable passion for her stepson Hippolytus has been the subject of many tragedies.

According to Greek legend, the Minotaur, a monster with the head of a bull and the body of a man, was shut up in the Labyrinth on the island of Crete, and was fed every ninth year fourteen youths and maidens, exacted in tribute from Athens. The thread that Ariadne gave Theseus to enable him to find his way out of the Labyrinth has come to be, for hermetists, a symbol of the intellect that guides man, while the Minotaur is one of the oldest symbols for the subconscious. Yourcenar's presentation of the myth is largely an allegorical description of man (represented by Theseus) lost in the innermost recesses of himself (a veritable labyrinth), where he hears voices—sometimes his own from the past, the present, and the future and sometimes those of others he has known—without recognizing that they all conceal one voice to which, unaware, he is prey—"the rumblings of his conscience," as Yourcenar terms it.

The same motifs found in *Le mystère d'Alceste* reverberate throughout this play: man's fear of death and desire for immortality, the voluntary substitution of one sacrificial victim for another, the use of a Christian code, man's innate need for the Absolute, ephemeral human love as the harbinger of a transcendent Love, the unity and indestructibility of all in matter; in addition, there is the notion of divine immanence. The dialogue of the fourteen victims in scene 2 exemplifies some of these themes, echoing Pascal, the Pater Noster, and St. Augustine:

THE TENTH VICTIM: Our sacrifice will mean the salvation of all the others. . . .
THE EIGHTH VICTIM: If He did not love us, He would not have had us seek Him.
THE SEVENTH VICTIM: May His will be done!
THE NINTH VICTIM: . . . Hallowed be Thy name. . . .
THE SEVENTH VICTIM: Our heart is restless, Lord, until it rests in Thee.

Ariadne calls her repentant sister Madeleine and accuses Theseus of being unfaithful to her with Phaedra "under the tree where two mouths have eaten of the same fruit."

This insistent insertion of a Judeo-Christian code in three Greek myths seems to be a sort of leveling process on Yourcenar's part, a statement to the effect that Judaism and Christianity are myths in the strict sense of the term, attempts on the part of anguished man to explain and alleviate the human condition. By fusing the two codes, she underlines man's desperate longing to survive his decayed body and his immutable hunger for the Infinite.

The juxtaposition of human and divine love found in *Le mystère d'Alceste* is repeated in *To Each His Minotaur*. Theseus accuses Ariadne of seeking God in him, to which she replies that most women expect to find God in human form. Later, a character identified by Yourcenar as God informs her: "I am Bacchus. . . . I am the one you were looking for in Theseus, who was only a prefiguration." Theseus' departure, she is told, brought about her encounter with God: he pointed the way; she could not have found it by herself. Similarly, Mauriac insists that all of us, at some point in our lives, put the Infinite in a creature; it is not the essence of our passion that is at fault, but its object. And the heroine of Claudel's *The City* (1892) declares: "I am the promise that cannot be kept and therein lies my grace."

In *Le mystère d'Alceste,* Apollo says that "everything dies, but everything is reborn. . . . Nothing came to be for one time only, except the human soul, and that is why men long so for immortality." And Death advises Hercules: "I am the door that leads to metamorphosis." Toward the end of *To Each His Minotaur,* Ariadne explains that "God" is simply the monosyllabic answer to all man's questions—an easy way out. She prefers the word "Nothing" and argues that she has no need of God to make her immortal; it is a privilege she shares with every atom. God subsequently identifies himself with all matter, declaring that man wrongly insists on making the divinity in his own image. At the conclusion of the dialogue, Ariadne is informed that she is dead and that now her eternal life begins.

Yourcenar's six plays were, for the most part, written to be read, which probably accounts for the fact that they seem to be the least appreciated and least known part of her work; we tend to think in terms of viewing a drama, and hers have rarely been produced on stage. This is unfortunate, since they offer the same psychological insight, metaphysical meditation, and artistry as her other writings.

In 1956 a limited edition of select poems

appeared under the title *Les Charités d'Alcippe et autres poèmes* (*The Alms of Alcippe*). This collection, unlike the poetry Yourcenar had published as an adolescent, was well received. The varied subjects, often highly personal, range from the poet Alcippe, ancient and contemporary artists, death, and love to the sonnet form itself. Some pieces, such as "Poème pour une poupée russe" ("Poem for a Russian Doll"), clearly reveal the influence of Guillaume Apollinaire, while others show a strong interest in the techniques employed by the symbolists.

Becoming increasingly concerned with social and ecological issues, Yourcenar lent her support to civil rights groups and anti-nuclear and peace movements as well as organizations dealing with overpopulation, the protection of animals, and environmental control. Over the years she wrote articles on these subjects for various journals.

Yourcenar is recognized as a brilliant essayist in France; she was awarded the Prix Combat for her work in general and for *Sous bénéfice d'inventaire* (*The Dark Brain of Piranesi and Other Essays*, 1962) in particular. These essays range widely in subject matter: the validity of Roman chronicles of the second to the fourth centuries, a time commonly referred to as the Rome of decadence; religious persecution during the period of the Reformation, her point of departure being Théodore Agrippa d'Aubigné's *Les tragiques* (1616); the successive inhabitants of the Loire Valley château of Chenonceaux, including Diane de Poitiers and Jean Jacques Rousseau; an analysis of the engravings of the eighteenth-century artist Giambattista Piranesi; the works of the Swedish Nobel Prize–winning novelist Selma Lagerlöf (added for the 1978 edition), whom Yourcenar considered one of the greatest women writers of all time; the abtruse Alexandrian poet Constantine Cavafy, engrossed with eroticism and his Hellenistic and Byzantine heritage; and, perhaps her most absorbing study, the novelist Thomas Mann and the

transposition into his fictional world of his intense interest in the occult, demonic powers, and the arcane traditions of hermetists.

After *Memoirs of Hadrian*, *The Abyss* is probably Yourcenar's best-known and most widely translated work, for which she was unanimously awarded, when it was published in French in 1968, the Prix Fémina-Vacaresco (having already received this prestigious prize in 1951 for *Memoirs of Hadrian*). Both are historical novels as well as meditations on existence, death, and the supernatural.

As in the case of Hadrian, the protagonist of *The Abyss*, Zeno—alchemist, philosopher, and physician—had been a long time in gestation; he came into being in the 1920's but grew and matured in Yourcenar's mind over the course of forty years. Originally intended as the first chapter of the *roman-fleuve* of her youth—which was provisionally set aside and which contained the germ of a number of her later books—it was transformed into a short story before it finally evolved into its present form. Unlike the Roman emperor of the second century, however, Zeno is not a historical figure but a composite, to some extent, of a variety of historical persons (Desiderius Erasmus, Leonardo da Vinci, Étienne Dolet, and other seekers after truth) who lived during the turbulent, violent period of mayhem and disorder that was the Renaissance and the Reformation. For all that, he is quite real; long after the completion of the novel, he continued to exist for his creator, who, on one occasion, warmly declared: "I love Zeno like a brother."

In order to give her imagined character that "specific reality conditioned by time and place," Yourcenar drew upon actual persons and events of the sixteenth century. The furor that resulted from Zeno's invention of an improved loom for the local artisans, for instance, is based on an occurrence of the time; his studies and career follow closely what has been recorded about those of Philippus Paracelsus; and the surgical operation on the peasant Han reflects one recounted in the memoirs of Ambroise Paré. To portray Zeno's scientific research and experiments, Yourcenar consulted the notebooks of Leonardo da Vinci and the writings of other historic contemporaries, such as William Harvey and Stephen Hales. Minor characters were also patterned after authentic figures of the period. The Prior's argument against the use of torture was taken from the *Essays* of Montaigne. The details of penal procedures; of trials and lawsuits; of cities stricken with the plague; of political, philosophical, and theological disputes; of military campaigns and social conflicts; and even the names of characters were almost invariably drawn from contemporary chronicles. Yourcenar's exhaustive research and impeccable scholarship, all of which she outlines in the author's note at the end of the book, have resulted in a vivid and convincing portrait of an era.

Across this landscape—one that might have been painted by Brueghel or Bosch—of fierce religious wars, Spanish oppression in the Low Countries, fanatical sects, frenzied Anabaptist peasant rebellions that prompt widespread and cruel reprisals, mass hysteria, and terror (where men bribe the executioner to strangle them before the pyres are set aflame and women are buried alive rather than hanged lest anyone peer lasciviously up their skirts as they swing by the neck) moves the solitary figure of Zeno, whose quest is for the Absolute.

Born in Bruges in 1509, the illegitimate son of a Flemish woman and a dissolute young Italian prelate, Zeno is raised by his uncle, a banker. Abandoning the seminary because he does not experience the Infinite there, he studies medicine, surgery, and herbalism, as well as philosophy, astronomy, engineering, mathematics, astrology and alchemy. A physician and a surgeon, the multilingual Zeno wanders across Europe and North Africa to the East, the sacred home of hermetism and the occult, in pursuit of the truth, universal knowledge of the destiny of man, and ultimate reality.

Alchemy—with all its implications of cosmic unity, perpetual rebirth, evolution without end, restoration after apparent annihilation—is the central motif of the novel. The French title, *L'Oeuvre au noir* (The Work in Black), is the alchemical term used to refer to the first phase of the "Great Work," a structured sequence of operations. This first step, reported to be the most difficult, is the process of separation and dissolution of substance. Most transformations we observe involve material whose characteristics (size, color, shape, and so on) change, while the material remains essentially the same. There are, however, considerably more profound transformations: the transmutation, for example, of ingested dead plants and animals into living flesh and blood. That one substance can be changed into another suggests that material itself is a composite, that there must be a kind of common material or "prime matter." It was the belief in "prime matter" that gave rise to the medieval fascination with alchemy. (The interest for many lay in the hope of changing ordinary metals into gold.)

There is some ambiguity, Yourcenar observes, as to whether the expression "the work in black" designated literal experiments on matter or whether it is simply a metaphor for the mental and emotional distress experienced in the casting off of all forms of prejudice and routine—the disintegration of no-longer-useful ego-consciousness, as Carl Jung puts it, to allow for the growth of a new, harmonious self. This is suggestive of Christ's parable of the seed that must die in order that, transformed, it may engender new life, or of Saint John of the Cross's "Dark Night"—a period of purification that precedes spiritual regeneration.

Experience of the physical world leads to abstract knowledge and eventually, it is hoped, to contemplative union with the Absolute, the Infinite, the Eternal, Ultimate Reality, or God, as the Unchangeable One is variously referred to. In contemplation the soul "knows God negatively," as unfathomable, in the "darkness of the mind." This is the way of mysticism, which requires self-denial ("If you wish to follow me," Christ said, "deny yourself"). All mystics have insisted that the essence of the "Unitive Life" is ineffable; it must be experienced to be understood, for that life does not inhere in the experiences or even in the changed personality of the seeker but in the metaphysical "Wholly Other," the Transcendent which the seeker apprehends.

In the epigraph to part 2 of *The Abyss* is an ancient rule of the alchemists: "Proceed to the obscure and unknown through the still more obscure and unknown." Indifferent to self-enrichment, Zeno's quest is for the Infinite, which he hopes to attain through knowledge of the self in relation to the universe, acquired by means of the dark, labyrinthine processes of alchemy. He is not concerned with the transmutation of base metals and has none of the tools required for this occult practice. Rather, he seeks to be "more than a man," he informs his cousin, Henry Maximilian, as they set out on their separate journeys—the soldier-poet in search of adventure, the philosopher in search of knowledge.

Yourcenar recounts Zeno's efforts to attain the desired goal. Setting aside the theological and moral precepts he has been taught, as well as all conventions and prejudices, he questions the existence of "One who perchance Is." (All quotations from *The Abyss* are in Grace Frick's translation.) He recognizes that man's free will is limited but that he must take responsibility for his own development. A bisexual, he prefers "another body like my own," but he is not tyrannized by the flesh. Having published several heretical treatises, he is obliged to flee Paris, narrowly escaping the Inquisition when his latest book is burned. Assuming another identity, he returns to Bruges, where he doctors the poor and forms a close friendship with the saintly, humanistic Prior of the Cordeliers, who lives in torment and near despair because of the violence and intolerance among

those who profess to be disciples of the Prince of Peace.

Zeno becomes engrossed in the concept of the unity of all matter, the cyclical process of alchemy. Everything begins to reveal its substance to him: wooden objects made by artisans become again only trunks or branches of trees; clothes return to their state of animal fat, milk, blood; shoes, an ox; lard, a pig; and a quill pen, a terrified cackling goose. All transformations imply violence and death. "Everything suffers change" and is in reality something else at the same time. Everything is subject to infinite repetition. This intense meditation on the nature of things, which he likens to mental prayer, actualizes a spiritual transformation in Zeno: a new self is being generated. The "Great Work" has begun.

It is in the chapter "L'abîme" ("The Abyss"), which gives its title to the English translation, that the major transmutations undergone by Zeno are revealed. Gradually, subtle, almost imperceptible transformations begin to take place within him, the result of new habits. He is oppressed by anguish as time and space dissolve and fade. He can feel streaming through his body legions of beings who have already lived on his "point of the sphere" or who are yet to arrive. Time, space, and substance lose their boundaries. The world and he, object and subject, become one.

His philosophy, in the sense that Socrates used the term, is a reasoned mode of living that has as its goal the acquisition of wisdom, a process of purification that liberates the soul to follow its natural tendency toward goodness and truth. Yet it seems to Zeno that he is living in a period when human reason is "trapped in a circle of flames." Perhaps truth is not attainable, not absolute, since "each concept collapses, eventually to merge with its opposite, like two waves breaking against each other only to subside into the same line of white foam."

The freedom Zeno values so highly is also elusive. He comes to realize that one is not free as long as one has desires (the goal of mystics being "holy indifference"), which means, then, perhaps as long as one lives. Disenchanted with the world around him, the temptation to leave this "cumbersome envelope of flesh" presents itself, but he rejects it. He has no fear of death, so familiar to him as a doctor and witness to cities decimated by the plague. Indeed, his inquiring mind almost welcomes it. The epigraph to part 3, from Giuliano de' Medici, expresses Zeno's point of view and foreshadows the inevitable:

It is no villainy, nor from villainy proceeding,
If to avoid a crueler fate someone
Hates his own life and seeks for death. . . .

Better to die, for one of noble soul,
Than to support the inevitable ill
That makes him change both heart and bearing.
How many has death already saved from anguish!
But those who hold the call to death as vile
Do not yet know how sweet sometimes it is.

Gradually Zeno "empties" himself of desire, becomes "detached," as mystics term it. He eats without interest whatever is served to him. Dress he has never heeded. Although he still believes that love is for many the only means of reaching that "fiery realm of which we are perhaps the infinitesimal sparks," chastity now seems to him to be one aspect of his serenity. He has emerged from his dark ordeal.

When his young assistant becomes embroiled in a scandal, Zeno's identity is disclosed and he is brought to trial on charges of sodomy and heresy. Visited in prison by his former mentor, an aged canon who assures him that matters can be arranged—the bishop is in accord—if he will recant, Zeno rejects the offer, refusing to violate truth. The last passage, an extraordinarily moving one, is largely a meditation on death. Condemned to the stake, Zeno chooses instead a "rational exit"—to die by his own hand, by slashing the tibial vein in his foot and the radial artery of his wrist. The description of the slow but progressive change of his physical and mental states, as the fountain of blood spews forth, is totally absorbing. The sober, understated prose provokes introspection and reflection on "that great voyage which inevitably ends for us all, rich or poor, by shipwreck on an unknown shore." The final line recalls the question Zeno once posed: Does the soul survive the "shipwreck" of the body?

Zeno, fearful of the disasters that may result from man's mastery of technology, foresees the possible destruction of the planet, intimating an apocalyptic end. Emese Soos suggests that alchemy functions in *The Abyss* not only as an allegory of spiritual development but also perhaps as a metaphor for the unfolding of history. This is certainly a viable reading considering the unstable, crumbling, fragmented sixteenth-century society depicted, which is comparable to the *nigredo* (black) stage of the alchemical process.

The Abyss was the last book translated by Frick, who died in 1979 after a prolonged illness. Yourcenar continued to receive tributes both in the United States and abroad, age having affected neither her vitality nor her astonishing creative output.

Death, Yourcenar insists in *With Open Eyes*, is "the supreme form of life." She expresses the desire to die slowly, totally aware of what is happening, of an illness whose progress would "allow death to insinuate itself" into her body and then to "fully enfold." She is determined to be completely conscious of "the passage" so as not to miss "the ultimate experience"; Hadrian and Zeno, she reminds us, both die in this spirit—with their eyes open. Although she acknowledges the existence of a natural, instinctive fear of the end of life, she espouses living in constant intimacy with the thought of the inevitable "essential experience," regarding death as a friend, a preparation that may ensure a dignified encounter.

"Imagine your death every morning, and you will no longer be afraid to die," she quotes from a Japanese treatise in her engrossing study of the Japanese writer Yukio Mishima entitled

Mishima ou la vision du vide (Mishima: A Vision of the Void, 1980). She invites the reader to make a choice:

> There are two kinds of people: those who push the thought of death out of their minds in order to live more comfortably and more freely, and those who, on the other hand, feel it is wiser and less stressful to lead their lives while watching out for death in every signal that it sends them via the senses or the hazards of the external world. There is no meeting of the minds on this issue. What some call a morbid mania is for others a heroic discipline.
>
> (p. 109)

Mishima does not fit neatly into either category. Death was for many years his companion, not because he was awaiting its arrival but because he was planning a ritual suicide. Merging chronological biographical detail with literary analysis and significant cultural, political, and sociological factors, Yourcenar—without engaging in value judgments—shows in an expository narrative how and why Mishima arrived at the decision to disembowel himself before being decapitated by a friend. On a table in his office, he left the cryptic message: "Human life is short, and I would like to live forever."

Yourcenar's third collection of short fiction, *Comme l'eau qui coule (Two Lives and a Dream,* 1982), is unquestionably her finest. The French title—Like Flowing Water—is a metaphor for life. "An Obscure Man," set in seventeenth-century Holland, England, and the New World, has as its protagonist the simple, sympathetic Nathanael, who, unfettered by social conventions and philosophical systems, lives in close harmony with nature. Passive—from an intuitive wisdom rather than weakness—and instinctively good, he accepts without question, without protest, whatever life brings him, even when that is death. Serenely facing the end of his life (which may mean the beginning) on a lonely island, he meditates in a beautiful concluding passage on his unity with all of nature.

Lazarus, the twelve-year-old hero of "A Lovely Afternoon," is, Yourcenar advises us in the afterword, the son of Nathanael. An innocent and appealing orphan, he runs away from his grandmother to join a troupe of Shakespearean actors. Telescoping time, the young boy reflects with pleasure and anticipation on all the future roles he will be assigned to play as he grows and matures, underlining his awareness that the passage of time means bodily change and eventual deterioration. When there are no longer any parts for him to play, he muses, he will be the one who lights and extinguishes the candles, as well as the prompter, since he will know all the lines.

The third and final story, "Anna, soror," is perhaps the best of the collection. It is a gripping tale of incest, of an intense and consuming passion between Miguel and Anna, brother and sister, recounted with words, as one critic puts it, of the most burning chastity. One does not choose whom one loves; love strikes like a disease or a tumor that one is powerless to excise—such is the depiction in this tale (as in *Fires* and *Coup de Grâce)* of this "terrible disorder." " 'Why have you not killed me, my brother?' " Anna asks. " 'I thought about it,' " Don Miguel replies. " 'What good would it do? I would still love you, even if you were dead.' " The torrid, suffocating summer heat of sixteenth-century Naples, the pestilence, and the reappearing serpent function as symbols of their irresistible passion. The tension created by the resistance, the struggle of two moral consciences against an overwhelmingly ardent desire, is presented in admirable classical prose.

In "Anna, soror" there is also an intermingling of divine and human love. Miguel is jealous of Anna's devotion to Christ: " 'Do you think I would permit you a lover because he is crucified?' " Anna is led to a full understanding of the situation when she reads the biblical text, pointed out to her by Miguel, in which

2557

Amnon is overcome by lust for his sister Tamar (2 Samuel 13). Finally, on the night of Good Friday, when the sky seems "resplendent with wounds," their love is consummated. Departing after three days of incestuous lovemaking, regretting nothing, Miguel fervently thanks God for this "viatique du départ," which can be translated either as "provisions for the journey" or "viaticum," the last sacrament. And when the priest places the crucifix before the dying Anna, she is heard to murmur: " 'Mi amado' " (my beloved). The narrator comments obliquely, "They thought she was speaking to God, perhaps she was." The fusion of the two codes, the profane and the sacred, sets in relief the author's conviction that there exists a strong affiliation between divine and human love.

Secondary, but related to the theme of love, is the preoccupation with death. Don Alvare, the father of the two lovers, convinced of his own eternal damnation for his sins against chastity, is terrified of dying. A question of justice is subtly raised here regarding eternal punishment to creatures of flesh for a few moments of corporeal joy. At the funeral rites for Miguel, the narrator, functioning as Yourcenar's persona, observes that "the book of creation" has two interpretations, both valid: no one knows whether everything lives only to die, or dies only to be reborn.

Yourcenar's oeuvre tends to resist classification; it does not fall neatly into literary categories. Two of her six novels have been awarded a prize given for excellence in essay writing. A volume of prose poems appears in the Pléiade collection of her fiction. All of her work, without exception, is informed by poetry. What is referred to as her autobiography (in three volumes) is in fact a chronicle of her family lineage, containing polemical commentaries, in which she figures hardly at all. It is in her essays, which also embody imaginative narratives, that she herself is most clearly revealed; they afford us a sharper insight into her perspectives on existence, since in them her usual concern with authorial intrusion is for the most part absent.

Le temps, ce grand sculpteur (*That Mighty Sculptor, Time,* 1983), a series of essays on diverse subjects, reveals her major preoccupations for more than six decades. Time and eternity, traditionally juxtaposed in Western thought, are here presented as a cyclical unity. "There is neither past nor future, only a series of presents, a road, perpetually destroyed and rebuilt, on which we all move forward." In her first article, on the Venerable Bede, the brevity of life is depicted by the image of a sparrow that flies through an open window on a stormy night and across a lighted room to exit through another window. This image symbolizes the unknown on both sides of the "voyage"; the "before life," of which we know nothing, is as important as the afterlife, of which we are equally ignorant.

Diderot wrote: "Everything passes. Everything changes. Only the all remains." It is in this light that Yourcenar views the universe: as continual birth, death, and rebirth, with the divinity immanent in every particle of nature. The passage of time marks destruction and loss. Beauty is ephemeral. In the essay that gives its title to the volume, the sculptor attempts to violate the laws of nature, to immobilize life. But he cannot; the marble statue, no sooner created, is at every moment eroding, reverting back to its original elemental form.

Sexual intercourse manifests in various cultures of both the East and the West a mysterious affinity for the Infinite; it is a symbol, or harbinger, of mystical union with the Eternal— or even a means of spiritual ascent. Yet love also is transitory. "We love," Yourcenar insists, "because we are incapable of remaining alone; we fear death for the same reason." After a few years, or even a few months, she adds, if the dead, no matter how greatly cherished, were to return, they would be looked upon by the living as intruders. Expressing once more her admiration for those who elect to die, she meditates on the two essential characteristics of the Japanese that have made suicide so much a part of their tradition: their passionate love of nature and an "astonishing facility for death." The first trait, she feels, explains the wise and "refined" manner with which they meet the destiny of all creation.

Are we brothers to the animals, cousins to the trees? What is man's destiny? Who, where was he before his parents were united? Have we made God in our own image? Is this "terrible disorder" we call love an obscure and unknowing search for the Absolute? Along with the certitude of inevitable death, a fact many assiduously and desperately thrust from their minds, is a whole network of related ontological and philosophical questions, all of which Yourcenar relentlessly pursues in a line of inquiry that is nothing less than an intellectual adventure. Everything she wrote betrayed her passion for knowledge, her hunger for truth. It is in literature that metaphysics find its most interesting expression.

From the breadth and depth of her erudition, her impressive scholarship, her prodigious capacity for creativity, there may be a tendency to infer, erroneously, that Yourcenar sacrificed living to study and to an unending Flaubertian quest for the "mot juste." In fact, however, her interests were legion. Concerned with the various aspects of the natural world and increasingly preoccupied with the unity of all creation, she, like Roger Caillois, her predecessor in the French Academy, attempted "to listen to stones." Genuinely interested in people of all kinds, her home always open to friends and neighbors, she conscientiously replied to a voluminous correspondence, enjoyed cooking and travel, was actively engaged in efforts to deal with ecological and social problems, and wrote her books, she declared, when she had the time.

After suffering a stroke, Yourcenar was hospitalized for five weeks before she died on 17 December 1987, at the age of eighty-four. She was cremated, and her ashes were buried on Mount Desert Island, her home for more than four decades. Her manuscripts and original editions are in the archives at Bowdoin College in Brunswick, Maine.

Selected Bibliography

EDITIONS

INDIVIDUAL WORKS

FICTION

Alexis ou le traité du vain combat. Paris, 1929. Revised and definitive edition, Paris, 1965.
La nouvelle Eurydice. Paris, 1931.
La mort conduit l'attelage. Paris, 1934.
Denier du rêve. Paris, 1934. Revised and definitive edition, Paris, 1959.
Nouvelles orientales. Paris, 1938. Revised and definitive edition, Paris, 1978.
Le coup de grâce. Paris, 1939.
Mémoires d'Hadrien. Paris, 1951. With "Carnets de notes des *Mémoires d'Hadrien*," Paris, 1953.
L'Oeuvre au noir. Paris, 1968.
Comme l'eau qui coule. Paris, 1982.

NONFICTION

Pindare. Paris, 1932.
Les songes et les sorts. Paris, 1938.
Sous bénéfice d'inventaire. Paris, 1962. With an essay on Selma Lagerlöf, Paris, 1978.
Souvenirs pieux. Monaco, 1973.
Archives du nord. Paris, 1977.
Mishima ou la vision du vide. Paris, 1980.
Les yeux ouverts: Entretiens avec Matthieu Galey. Paris, 1980.
Discours de réception à l'Académie française. Paris, 1981.
Le temps, ce grand sculpteur. Paris, 1983.
Quoi? L'Éternité. Paris, 1988.

PLAYS

Le dialogue dans le marécage. Paris, 1932.
Electre ou la chute des masques. Paris, 1954.
Rendre à César. Paris, 1961.
Le mystère d'Alceste. Paris, 1963.

POETRY

Le jardin des chimères. Paris, 1921.

Les dieux ne sont pas morts. Paris, 1922.

Feux. Paris, 1936.

Les Charités d'Alcippe et autres poèmes. Liège, 1956.

TRANSLATIONS BY YOURCENAR

Les Vagues. Paris, 1937. Translation of Virginia Woolf's *The Waves.*

Ce que savait Maisie. Paris, 1947. Translation of Henry James's *What Maisie Knew.*

Présentation critique de Constantin Cavafy. Paris, 1958. In collaboration with Constantin Dimaras.

Fleuve profond, sombre rivière. Paris, 1964. Revised edition, Paris, 1978.

Présentation critique d'Hortense Flexner. Paris, 1969.

La couronne et la lyre. Paris, 1979.

Le coin des "Amen." Paris, 1983. Translation of James Baldwin's play *The Amen Corner.*

Cinq nô modernes. Paris, 1983. Translation of plays of Yukio Mishima in collaboration with Jun Shiragi.

Blues et gospels. Paris, 1984. Translation of black American gospel music.

COLLECTED WORKS

Théâtre I. Paris, 1971.

Théâtre II. Paris, 1971.

Oeuvres romanesques. Paris, 1982.

La voix des choses. Paris, 1987.

TRANSLATIONS

The Abyss. Translated by Grace Frick in collaboration with the author. New York, 1976.

Alexis. Translated by Walter Kaiser in collaboration with the author. New York, 1984.

The Alms of Alcippe. Translated by Edith R. Farrell. New York, 1982.

A Coin in Nine Hands. Translated by Dori Katz in collaboration with the author. New York, 1982.

Coup de Grâce. Translated by Grace Frick in collaboration with the author. New York, 1957.

The Dark Brain of Piranesi and Other Essays. Translated by Richard Howard in collaboration with the author. Includes "Humanism and Occultism in Thomas Mann," translated by Grace Frick in collaboration with the author. New York, 1984.

Fires. Translated by Dori Katz in collaboration with the author. New York, 1981.

Memoirs of Hadrian. Translated by Grace Frick in collaboration with the author. New York, 1954. With "Reflections on the Composition of *Memoirs of Hadrian,*" New York, 1963.

Mishima: A Vision of the Void. Translated by Alberto Manguel in collaboration with the author. New York, 1986.

Oriental Tales. Translated by Alberto Manguel in collaboration with the author. New York, 1985.

Plays. Translated by Dori Katz in collaboration with the author. New York, 1984.

That Mighty Sculptor, Time. Translated by Walter Kaiser. New York, 1989.

Two Lives and a Dream. Translated by Walter Kaiser in collaboration with the author. New York, 1987.

With Open Eyes: Conversations with Matthieu Galey. Translated by Arthur Goldhammer. Boston, 1984.

BIOGRAPHICAL AND CRITICAL STUDIES

Aubrion, Michel. "Marguerite Yourcenar ou la mesure de l'homme." *Le revue générale* 15–29 (January 1970).

Aury, Dominique. "Marguerite Yourcenar." *La nouvelle revue française* 44 (July 1974): 76–79.

Bernier, Yvon. "Écrits de Marguerite Yourcenar." *Études littéraires* 12 (April 1979): 7–10.

Blot, Jean. *Marguerite Yourcenar.* Paris, 1971.

———. "Marguerite Yourcenar: Le Temps, ce grand sculpteur." *La nouvelle revue française* 375 (April 1984): 115–117.

de Boisdeffre, Pierre. "Marguerite Yourcenar sous la coupole." *Nouvelle revue des deux mondes* (March 1981): 596–605.

Brown, John L. "French: *Le Labyrinthe du monde.*" *World Literature Today* 52, no. 4 (Autumn 1978): 588–589.

Chollet, Bernadette. "*Mishima ou la vision du vide* par Marguerite Yourcenar." *Esprit* 4 (April 1981): 168–169.

Coleman, Alexander. "Essays: *Sous bénéfice d'inventaire.*" *World Literature Today* 53, no. 4 (Autumn 1979): 646–647.

Darbeinet, Jean. "Marguerite Yourcenar et la traduction littéraire." *Études littéraires* 12 (April 1979): 51–64.

Dejaifve, Georges S. J. "Le Démon de Marguerite." *Les études classiques* 50 (1982): 209–224.

Delcroix, Maurice. "*Alexis ou le traité du vain combat:* Un roman épistolaire de Marguerite Yourcenar." *Cahiers de l'Association internationale des études françaises* 29 (1977): 223–41.

———. "Marguerite Yourcenar entre le Oui et le Non." *Marche romane* 31 (1981): 72–80.

Denis-Christophe, Alain. "Sur le suicide de Zénon dans *L'Oeuvre au noir.*" *Études littéraires* 12 (April 1979): 43–50.

de Ricaumont, Jacques. "Inventaire." *Cahiers des saisons* 38 (1964): 297–301.

Farrell, Edith R., and Frederick C. Farrell. *Marguerite Yourcenar in Counterpoint.* Lanham, Md., 1983.

Gendt, Ann-Marie. "Le narrateur et l'imaginaire dans 'L'Homme qui a aimé les Néréides.'" *Lettres romanes* 34 (1980): 193–205.

Guyaux, André. "Le lait de la mère." *Critique* 35 (January–May 1979): 368–374.

Hell, Henri. "Une tragédie racinienne." *Cahiers des saisons* 38 (1964): 293–95.

Horn, Pierre L. "Marguerite Yourcenar's *Le labyrinthe du monde:* A Modern Anti-Autobiography." In *The Writer and the Past,* edited by Donald L. Jennermann, 1–9. Terre Haute, Ind., 1981.

———. *Marguerite Yourcenar.* Boston, 1985.

Kaiser, Walter. "The Achievement of Marguerite Yourcenar." In *European Liberty,* directed by H. R. Hoetink. The Hague, 1983. Pp. 107–137.

Kennebeck, Edwin. "Strange Triangle." *Commonweal* 66 (1957): 574–575.

Kovacs, Laurand. "Marguerite Yourcenar: *Michima ou la vision du vide.*" *La nouvelle revue française* 340 (May 1981): 143–144.

Lebel, Maurice. "Marguerite Yourcenar, traductrice de la poésie grecque." *Études littéraires* 12, no. 1 (April 1979): 65–78.

Magne, Denys. "Deux oeuvres de jeunesse de Marguerite Yourcenar." *Études littéraires* 12, no. 1 (April 1979): 93–112.

Murciaux, Christian. "D'Alexis à Hadrien." *La table ronde* 56 (August 1952): 146.

Nadeau, Vincent. "Du labyrinthe du monde au dédale intérieur." *Études littéraires* 12, no. 1 (April 1979): 79–92.

Roudaut, Jean. "Une autobiographie impersonnelle." *La nouvelle revue française* 310 (November 1978): 71–81.

Rubenstein, Lothar Henry. "Les Oresties dans la littérature avant et après Freud." In *Entretiens sur l'art et la psychanalyse,* edited by André Berge et al. The Hague, 1968. Pp. 224–38.

Salazar, Philippe-Joseph. "Sur *Mémoires d'Hadrien:* L'Idéal narratif." *French Studies in Southern Africa* 10 (1981): 57–67.

Shurr, Georgia Hooks. "Marguerite Yourcenar de l'Académie française." *Laurels* 51–52 (1980–1981): 113–118.

Soos, Emese. "The Only Motion Is Returning: The Metaphor of Alchemy in Mallet-Joris and Yourcenar." *French Forum* 4 (1979): 3–16.

Spencer-Noël, Geneviève. *Zénon ou le thème de l'alchimie dans L'Oeuvre au noir de Marguerite Yourcenar.* Paris, 1981.

Truc, Gonzague. "L'Oeuvre de Marguerite Yourcenar." *Études littéraires* 12, no. 1 (April 1979): 11–28.

Vier, Jacques. "L'Empereur Hadrien vu par Marguerite Yourcenar." *Études littéraires* 12 (April 1979): 29–36.

Whatley, Jane. "*Mémoires d'Hadrien:* A Manual for Princes." *University of Toronto Quarterly* 50 (1980–1981): 221–237.

ANN M. BEGLEY

WITOLD GOMBROWICZ

(1904–1969)

LIFE

WITOLD GOMBROWICZ WAS a Polish writer who spent most of his productive years in Argentina and died in France in 1969. This biographical outline suggests affinities with the expatriate generation of American writers who went to Paris in the 1920's to gain a new perspective on their country. Gombrowicz's exile, however, was not voluntary. Shortly after he landed on Argentine soil in August 1939, World War II broke out and most of the European continent was overrun by the Nazi armies. In September 1939 Gombrowicz became a man without a country, without money, and without a roof over his head. He managed to acquire all three during his twenty-four years in Argentina. And, like the American expatriates, he acquired a new perspective on the country of his birth. But this perspective was born of personal and national misfortune rather than of merely living abroad and being exposed to foreign customs and ways.

The world into which Gombrowicz was born on 4 August 1904 was quite different from the expatriate reality that he was to experience later in his life. He grew up in an agricultural country where millions of peasants toiled for the bare necessities of life and where tens of thousands of landowners and intellectuals lived a life of peaceful refinement. Before World War II life in Eastern Europe was both more and less secure than is life in the United States today. Less, because Gombrowicz's Poland was a poor country and even the class of landowners and professionals to which he belonged was less affluent than an average contemporary American wage earner. Food and servants were cheap, but housing and such manufactured goods as clothing and furniture were scarce and expensive. In addition, Poland was at the center of the tensions and pressures created by the expansionist drives of its eastern and western neighbors, Russia and Germany, whose victorious nationalisms clashed with the nationalism of the Poles.

But within this turbulent world there were other, smaller and more secure worlds of well-rooted social groups. Here life was stable and peaceful: time-honored social hierarchies were cultivated and traditional lifestyles pursued. Gombrowicz spent his childhood and adolescence within one such microcosm. His parents were not titled aristocrats but medium-level landholders who cherished their title of nobility and worked in professions other than farming. Gombrowicz's father was an industrial manager whose friends and acquaintances included lawyers, industrialists, and civil servants. In some ways Gombrowicz's early years resembled the idyllic existence of the well-to-do Southerners before the American Civil War. He lived in a society where being born into a certain family guaranteed access to the best education the country could offer and a circle of acquaintances to which one could always lay claim.

Thus the most prominent feature of Gombrowicz's early years was psychological security accompanied by a modest financial status. This security consisted in taking the ideas of one's ancestors for granted, in knowing that all the people who mattered held opinions that were not radically different from one's own. Being in this milieu entailed possessing the security of never having one's beliefs challenged, and this unanimity of belief stemmed from a worldview that precluded acceptance of a violent change of social structures or religious commitments. It entailed a stability of manners, a gentlemen's agreement about things one could and could not do, and a lack of competitiveness. Indeed, there was little to compete for in an agricultural society. But the security of men and women of Gombrowicz's circle was so fragile that from the perspective of the 1980's it appears tragic. Theirs was the tragedy of peaceful people who were not very imaginative and who possessed many vanities badly in need of revision, but who also were free of resentment and of a desire to destroy others. Many of these people with an old-fashioned sense of honor resembled the noble and ridiculous Major Kobrzycki in *Trans-Atlantyk* (Transatlantic, 1953). Gombrowicz saw the fragility of their existence while he was still in Poland, and perhaps the savage criticism to which he subjected them in his novels was also a way of honoring and pitying them.

Gombrowicz rejected the psychological security of his background while still a teenager. He was never a top student, and was a loner by the time he was in elementary school. According to the testimony of his former schoolmates, he maintained an aloof and sometimes hostile attitude even toward friends. Among his acquaintances at that time were Ted Kępiński and Staś Baliński. In 1974 Kępiński published a book about Gombrowicz in which he attributed Witold's eccentric behavior in school to his morbid vanity and sensitivity. Kępiński also said that Gombrowicz suffered from "an atrophy of tenderness." Baliński was a poet, Gombrowicz's literary adviser, and a rival. Gombrowicz's sarcastic remarks about him in essays and letters span half a century.

In some ways, however, Gombrowicz was not so different from others in his milieu. He shared many features typical of the Polish intelligentsia. His ability to go it alone and search for untrodden paths was inherited from his father, an enterprising and resourceful man. Gombrowicz senior had not gone to college but learned his managerial skills on his own. He was a self-made man, and so was his son.

The same could be said about others from Gombrowicz's circle. When the combined Nazi and Soviet invasion turned the lives of the Polish people into a six-year-long nightmare, some of them emigrated and made new lives for themselves abroad, thus proving that their ability to adapt was considerable. However, Gombrowicz ridiculed his acquaintances both while in Poland and during his stay in Latin America.

After seven lean years in Buenos Aires, Gombrowicz received a job at the Polish Bank, which guaranteed him a steady income. He owed this position to his literary fame (he had already published three books before going to Argentina) rather than his competence as a bank clerk. At that time he worked furiously at his novels and plays and published steadily in the Polish émigré monthly *Kultura* in Paris. He made some friends in Argentine literary circles but, owing to his initial refusal to play the role of a poor relative, he never became a habitué of the dinners and teas at the literary salons of the Argentine patrons of art Victoria Ocampo and Arturo Capdevila. According to his own testimony, he derived more enjoyment from his association with "the other Argentina," which he encountered in the cheap eating houses of Buenos Aires. His study of this "immature" Argentina (as opposed to the ostensibly mature official literary life) confirmed his intuitions about the dialectical relationship between maturity and immaturity in human life. On the basis of these experiences he began to dislike the excessively cerebral quality of modern culture.

In 1955 Gombrowicz's literary fortunes made it possible for him to stop working at the Polish Bank and devote himself fully to writing. This was a remarkable feat because in Argentina he was deprived of his natural audience, which was Polish. Yet he managed to excite enough minds, first in Argentina and then in France, to achieve the reputation of an outstanding twentieth-century writer. Translations of his works began to appear in the 1950's, and several international awards followed. One of them was the Ford Fellowship for Writers, which enabled him in 1963 to leave Argentina and return to Europe. In 1967 he received the prestigious International Publishers' Prize.

In the 1960's Gombrowicz became a celebrity in Polish émigré circles, which numbered several hundred thousand people who had settled in the West after the Soviet occupation of Poland in 1945. In Poland itself a temporary relaxation of political control between 1956 and 1958 resulted in the publication of many of his works, and he became an idol almost overnight. The Polish editions of his works sold out quickly, but the censor's permission for second printings never came. His plays were performed in several Polish cities, and their popularity rivaled that of Sławomir Mrożek's plays. Gombrowicz spent the last six years of his life in Europe. He never returned to Poland but took up residence in France, where he died on 24 July 1969 of respiratory troubles and heart failure.

Gombrowicz is not an emotional writer. His plots are brisk but lack the kind of love stories that, more than anything else, account for the easy readability of some very mediocre writers. The "atrophy of tenderness" of which Kępiński spoke and that was later acknowledged by Gombrowicz in the first volume of his *Dziennik* (*Diary*, 1957–1966) showed itself in his fiction as well.

But while one should not seek a "boy meets girl" plot in Gombrowicz's works, he is neither difficult nor dull. *Ferdydurke* (1937) and *Trans-Atlantyk* (1953) are delightfully funny. *Pornografia* (1960) holds the reader's attention as a detective story. *Kosmos* (1965) is perhaps the least entertaining and most philosophical of his novels. His three plays are humorous in a way that is reminiscent of the theater of the absurd. The three volumes of his *Diary* can be faithful companions for any person interested in literature. In the *Diary* the qualities that made Gombrowicz a misanthrope in his personal life turned out to be supportive of, and encouraging to, an average reader. Gombrowicz addresses himself both to the lonely and to the gregarious, both to those who are alienated from their social background and to those who have accepted it.

WORKS

Placing Gombrowicz

Like most writers Gombrowicz was keenly aware of the influence of ideas on the way men and nations behave. In volume 2 of the *Diary* he said that "the contemporary ideas are the bone structure hidden in the flesh of my novels." He knew, of course, that material existence does influence ideas, but he believed that the reverse is also true and that ideas exert an influence on material existence. He often wrote of the overwhelming and brutal effect of force in the politics of nations and individuals, but he thought that this application of force was itself a result of the ideas cherished both by individuals and by nations. In his works he therefore presented people who won or lost life's battles as a result of the ideas to which they subscribed. Social conditions do play a role in Gombrowicz's works, but ultimately it is the individual who acts and not the conditions into which he was injected by fate.

However, the primacy of ideas in Gombrowicz's works does not preclude his keen interest in the details of physical existence. Because of the abundance of physical details his works at first appear to have little to do with philosophical concerns. His heroes are very much aware of each other's physical appearance, of the objects that surround them, and of the prestige attached to these objects. They pay attention to the physical world rather than to the mental one, and their desires are unashamedly physical. They use and abuse their five senses. Their victories and defeats have a strong influence on their appearance. Their duels begin as debates on issues and end as physical fights, as in the contest between Philifor and anti-Philifor, and sometimes they consist of "making faces" at each other, as in the school scenes in *Ferdydurke.*

Thus Gombrowicz's philosophical proclivity does not mean that his characters engage in debates about ideas with a Dostoevskian passion. Gombrowicz prefers emotional restraint and understatement. His characters are highly stylized, and their partisanship in regard to ideas is much less direct than Dostoevsky's. Nor is Gombrowicz interested in proffering ideology disguised as inquiry into the problems of good and evil. His goal is, rather, to show the differences between the "official" human culture and the "subterranean" culture, between the preferences and desires that are recorded in books and newspapers and those which, in his view, really guide the daily behavior of men and women. Contemporary culture has lost touch with the physical nature of man, according to Gombrowicz. In its totality it addresses a creature who is much more intellectual than real men and women. It underrates the consequences of the physical nature of individuals. One's perception of others and of oneself is heavily influenced by physical factors, yet it is presented in culture as deriving from mental and social factors.

Gombrowicz's novels and plays are reflections of this insight. He tries to show that human carnality cannot be divorced from human mental life, and that mental processes are inescapably dependent on physical characteristics. Human beings never reach the intellectual and emotional maturity that human culture has placed before them as an achievable goal. Like the narrator in Dostoevsky's *Notes from Underground,* Gombrowicz's characters are resentful and petty. The Polish Romantic poet Juliusz Słowacki once bemoaned the fact that in his life he met only men whose chests were "fit for a tailor but not for Phidias." Gombrowicz says that men's chests are indeed made for a tailor rather than for a sculptor, and those who bemoan this fact refuse to face reality. "Everything is honeycombed with childishness," says the philosopher Philifor in *Ferdydurke.*

According to Gombrowicz, the relationship between the human body and social behavior is so intimate that attempts to change it by changing social conditions must be considered ridiculous. In the *Diary* he remarks that any theory that does not take into account human spiritual and intellectual "underdevelopment" (*niedorozwój*) is bound to fail. People are immersed in their physiques even when they are thinking about the most abstract theories. Thus theories can never be considered apart from the needs of the body and from the tremendous importance that individuals attach to their own bodies, to their youthfulness or decrepitude, their beauty or ugliness, health or sickness. People spend a great amount of time observing others' bodies and acting on the knowledge that they acquire from their observations. They also spend a great deal of time thinking about their own bodies. However, such human occupations are virtually ignored by the "official" culture.

Gombrowicz's emphasis on the importance of the human body accounts for his interest in the baroque period in arts and letters. He often spoke with admiration of this era and advised Polish writers and artists to pay more attention to the culture of the Polish baroque. In *Trans-Atlantyk* he followed his own advice and made the characters speak baroque Polish. The novel thus insists that the vital roots of Polish culture go back to the baroque and not to Romanticism. In volume 1 of the *Diary* Gombrowicz said that the attitude of twentieth-century intellectuals toward the baroque will have a decisive influence on contemporary culture. What he meant was that unless artists and writers begin to pay more attention to the sensual part of the human person, their art will continue to lose viewers and readers. Contemporary art is too cerebral and too censorious in regard to the body in spite of all the freedoms it takes with sexuality. It is far too little attuned to human sensuality and to the experience of reality achieved through the five senses. For instance, the sense of touch is virtually neglected by modern art and literature, and bodies in modern art are anything but "touchable." The figures of Rubens, the poetry of John Donne, or the Polish baroque *Pamiętniki* (*Memoirs,* 1656–1688) of Jan Chryzostom Pasek play upon the sense of touch in ways that confirm the physical nature of humanity and cut down to size the importance of those philosophers who disregard the body. The baroque was characterized by ornate complexity and dynamism; baroque paintings show us people who lack the delicate proportions of classical art and instead proudly display their carnality. Thus, Gombrowicz would say, their humanity was revealed. Instead of pretending that they lived by the life of the mind, they openly engaged in the life of the body. They showed off their large bodies as proof that even the most cerebral individuals should not to be confused with disembodied angelic intellects. Only angels live "the life of the mind." Humans live the life of the body, and their thinking is heavily conditioned by it.

It should be clear from the above that Gombrowicz preferred Rubens' ample figures to Marc Chagall's lean ones but that this preference was not a question of personal taste or distaste. He felt that twentieth-century writers and philosophers have not come to terms with human carnality and instead have invented theories that are contradicted by the way people live their daily lives. They ascribe extravagant powers to the mind and shun the real person because, in the words of volume 1 of the *Diary,* that person is "too easy and too simple" for them.

To be sure, Gombrowicz's characters do not merely display their bodies but also use their minds. Gombrowicz insisted, however, that petty concerns about the body are no less characteristic of humans than their thinking and willing. He believed that in the baroque period artists took cognizance of the inextricable unity of the physical and the intellectual but later, in the Enlightenment, the mind began to gain ascendancy and in Romanticism it triumphed. The body was left behind, invisible and contemptible. But this disregard for the body had a price, and it was the falsification of the image of humanity in nineteenth- and twentieth-century art and literature.

Thus Gombrowicz's liking for the baroque is related to his worldview. He belongs to those nineteenth- and twentieth-century thinkers and artists who have turned their backs on the rationalism of the Enlightenment, which originated with René Descartes and his followers. Gombrowicz was deeply skeptical of Descartes's absolute trust in the ability of the human mind to produce knowledge through mental operations only and independently of physical experience. He was skeptical of a retreat of the human mind upon itself.

In taking this position Gombrowicz found himself in the company of men with whom he otherwise had little in common. In the last century or so the autonomy of the human mind has been questioned by thinkers as diverse as Friedrich Nietzsche, Sigmund Freud, Karl Marx, and Jacques Maritain. Nietzsche proclaimed the primacy of the will in human behavior and in the creation of ideas. Freud pointed out the existence of the unconscious, whose intuitions are at odds with those of the conscious mind, and Marx proclaimed the primacy of self-interest in social life and in the life of the mind. Maritain insisted that Descartes looked at human beings as if they were angels who acquired their ideas directly from God rather than from contact with the material world.

In the twentieth century Cartesian rationalism has received further blows from the structuralists, who have emphasized the importance of the hidden patterns in language and society. These patterns signify nothing from the point of view of the rational mind but nevertheless can be perceived by it. The French philosopher Jacques Derrida goes even further in maintaining that all meaning in language is based on a false assumption that there is some center, in the mind or in reality, that gives rise to meaning. There is no such center, Derrida maintains.

Gombrowicz's work is related to all these insights even though he did not identify with any of these philosophers and, in the case of the structuralists, actually preceded them. He agrees with Nietzsche in pointing out the importance of the will in shaping the destinies of individuals and nations; the plots of his novels consist of attempts by individuals to use their will effectively. As was the case with Nietzsche, Gombrowicz's glorification of the will occasionally borders on metaphysics, in that the will becomes for him an entity in itself rather than a metaphor. It acquires a life of its own rather than being a linguistic reflection of life processes, and it overpowers its bearer because it creates "Form," which acts independently on its creator and on those who surround him or her. *Ferdydurke* is largely an exploration of the effects of "Form" on individuals and societies.

Related to these tendencies is the fact that there is no romantic love in Gombrowicz's books. There are parodies of it, as in *Ferdydurke,* but in most cases Gombrowicz's characters display neurotic anxiety over what they perceive to be an unhealthy and criminal sexuality. The narrators in his novels share this attitude and speak of the inhibitions that follow from a suppressed sex drive. In *Ferdydurke,* Siphon and the shy country maiden Isabel are viewed this way; in *Cosmos* the narrator is very much aware of the autoerotism of Mr. Wojtys; and in *Pornografia* the narrator is one of the two middle-aged gentlemen who try to pervert two youngsters, compulsively engage in voyeurism, and end up as instigators of a murder. Indeed, there are hardly any "normal" sexual situations in Gombrowicz's works, and narrators and characters alike carry within them the shame of a sexual impulse that deviates from the normal.

Another way in which Gombrowicz's "bodily" interests manifest themselves is his awareness of the physical nature of the master-servant relationship. There is a scene in *Ferdydurke* in which two servants at a country estate gossip about their masters. It has been said that no man is a hero to his valet, and Gombrowicz's servants amply confirm the accuracy of this observation. They describe the refined customs of their masters in a down-to-earth way and lay bare the masters' physical dependence on their servants. No Marxist writer has done a better job of presenting an exaggerated version of the exploitation of man by man.

However, Gombrowicz's aim is not to encourage class struggle but rather to emphasize the extent to which physical contact between human beings influences their behavior. In *Ferdydurke* the narrator says that masters are "created" by their servants and vice versa, but he has in mind something other than the exchange of goods and services of which Marx spoke. He refers to the poses and the "faces" that the masters assume in front of their servants and that the servants assume in the presence of their masters. A man in his living room is restricted in his behavior by the presence of his servants. He has to sit in a certain way, eat in a certain way, and smoke in a way that will help him to maintain his dignity as master. On the other hand, the servant assumes the dull facial expression of a subordinate in order to relate to his master in the fashion expected by everyone, and he is sluggish and dumb because this is expected of him. His body acts out the qualities that his master wants to see in him. This playing-up to an audience is not, of course, restricted to masters and servants. Gombrowicz uses this case only as an illustration of the ways in which the behavior of our bodies is conditioned by other people or by "Form."

Gombrowicz's concerns are related to, but not identical with, what today is called ideology, or the opinions held by individuals and arrived at not by means of discursive reasoning and the weighing of evidence but unconsciously, as a function of their life situation. Observing those around him, Gombrowicz was struck by the ease with which people slipped into poses prearranged for them by their social and economic status, education, or sex. But in contrast with present-day sociologists, Gombrowicz focused on the psychological influence of one human on another, or the influence that has more to do with ability and volition than with the social position of an individual.

Thus Gombrowicz's novels and plays suggest that in modern times we have inadvertently created a false model of humanity and are now prisoners of this model. We try to adjust ourselves to it and we force it upon others. This model Gombrowicz calls "Form." Being human means living in uncertainty and hesitation. It means never being sure of anything. Real people believe one thing in the morning and another one in the evening. However, owing to the convention of Form, having said something publicly in the morning, they feel that they have to say the same in the evening. Thus a falsity is born, and it in turn produces other falsities. Men cannot express themselves adequately and cannot solve all problems at every turn. Form, or stylization of truth, is thus both undesirable and inevitable.

"I was the first structuralist," Gombrowicz said in an interview published in the French review *La quinzaine littéraire* in 1967. Indeed, the concept of Form, which was first introduced in *Ferdydurke* and then refined in *Cosmos,* bears much resemblance to the "structure" of the structuralists. *Cosmos* illustrates the most radical concepts of the structuralists in that it can be read as an allegory of the physical universe, which is probably meaningless but has been repeatedly interpreted as meaningful because of the structures perceived in it. In the process of interpretation, coincidences are said to be symbols, and scarcity of evidence is glossed over as insignificant. The urge to interpret is illustrated in *Cosmos* by means of the two students' search for the secret meaning of the signs they perceive in and around their vacation home in the Tatra Mountains of Poland. The students live with the family of a retired banking official. Gombrowicz took great pains to present the entire cast of characters as perfectly mediocre. The students perceive mysterious signs around the house of Mr. and Mrs. Wojtys: arrows, a hanged chicken, and so forth. Is someone trying to tell them something? What is it? To what purpose? The minds of the two young men go to work.

In a structuralist reading, the two students represent humanity and its efforts to find meaning in the universe. They seize upon various phenomena that seem to be symbolic of something. But of what? They have no idea. They know that the symbols they perceive around them may be no symbols at all but simply coincidences. The sparrow that was hanged by someone may or may not have something to do with the little twig that was "hanging" on a thread.

Then the narrator (one of the students) hangs a cat. In the morning the dead cat is discovered by the horrified servant. This hanging is of course not the work of the person who was responsible for the earlier ones. Nevertheless, it is a hanging, and so far as Mr. and Mrs. Wojtys are concerned, it falls together with the other strange events. The murders of animals make the possibility of a meaningful mystery even more plausible. Then one of the characters hangs himself. Significantly, it is the level-headed engineer Ludwik, who had previously buried the dead cat and who believed in the possibility of a rational organization of society. Why does Gombrowicz make him die? To discredit his Cartesian turn of mind, of course. His death further stimulates the interpretative urge of the two students. It may be related to the mystery or it may not. Ludwik might have been compelled by some need for symmetry, by some irrational urge to keep up the chain of "coincidences" and kill himself. The students are not sure.

Thus the plot of *Cosmos* seems to illustrate Michel Foucault's theory of history. It is a history without men, a history whose subject matter has been invented by men ex post facto. *Cosmos* is a cheerless parable of a dumb universe in which meanings are invented rather than discovered. However, since *Cosmos* appeared in 1965 and Foucault's major work *Les mots et les choses* (*The Order of Things*) in 1966, the similarity has to be attributed to the spirit of the times rather than to direct influence of one author on another, and Gombrowicz's quip about being the first structuralist is not entirely groundless.

Parallels also can be drawn between Gombrowicz's works and modern Thomistic philosophy, although he has never acknowledged this connection. He was born into a Catholic family but abandoned religion at an early age, and in his *Diary* he spoke bitterly of Catholicism and its adverse influence on the political and cultural life of Poland. In spite of this ostensible rejection Gombrowicz and the Catholic Thomistic tradition meet in their denunciation of the Cartesian brand of rationalism. Since Catholicism in Poland never ranged far from Thomism, it may be that Gombrowicz acquired his skepticism in regard to Descartes through his early exposure to Thomistic Catholicism.

What do Thomistic philosophy and Gombrowicz's strongly secular books have in common? Both reject the assumption that all knowledge originates in the mind rather than in the world of objects. Both claim that the intuitions of the mind cannot be taken for granted but have to be checked and rechecked through the laborious chains of syllogisms in which statements are compared with material reality and judged on that basis before being declared true or false. Both question the self-sufficiency of the human mind and rely on the slow process of reasoning combined with

sense experience to arrive at their conclusions. Both see human beings as motivated in their thinking by much more than "the natural light of reason": the needs of their bodies and sensual impressions combine with feelings and emotions at all junctures of human thinking.

The two philosophical tales inserted in *Ferdydurke* are examples of this influence. In *Pornografia* the narrator says that he dislikes people who smell the flower with their spirit instead of their noses: how very Thomistic! In his *Diary* Gombrowicz remarks that he is less interested in ideas per se and more in the attitude of individuals toward the ideas they hold. In his view the ideas of existentialism, Marxism, and structuralism reside "twenty stories above the real men and women." Humans inhabit the moderate zone rather than the extremes of heat or cold. Similarly, in the realm of ideas the individual should not soar too high lest he lose touch with the physical parameters of existence.

Gombrowicz felt that modern intellectuals have forced upon the rest of us the view that human beings are pure intellects who use their bodies merely as appendices to their minds. Humans do not "think" with their minds only, Gombrowicz insisted. They "think" with their lives. Gombrowicz would certainly agree with Maritain, who said in *Trois reformateurs* (*Three Reformers*, 1925) that the "*denaturing* of human reason . . . remains the secret principle of the break-up of our culture." Reason divorced from nature, or individuals pretending that their thinking is divorced from their physical frailty: here the Thomist Maritain and the agnostic Gombrowicz meet.

Ferdydurke is a novel about the superpose that modern humanity has adopted, the pose of creatures so perfectly groomed externally and internally that they have lost contact with the animal part of their nature. There is in *Ferdydurke* a longing for the kind of open acknowledgment of human clumsiness that was portrayed in Chaucer's *Canterbury Tales,* a longing for a society in which people relate to each other not only in their best-groomed and stage-produced moments but also in their messy and immature moments. It is not so much spontaneity that Gombrowicz's narrator covets as the humility of recognizing that "everything is honeycombed with childishness" and that the poses of psychological maturity are fake even in those who have made great strides toward maturity.

In the same vein, in volume 1 of the *Diary,* Gombrowicz says:

> Do I want humanity to be progressive, to fight against prejudice, to carry high the banner of education and culture, to make sure that arts and sciences develop? Indeed . . . but first of all I want the other man not to bite me, not to spit on me and not to torture me.
>
> (Kultura edition [1971], pp. 43–44)[1]

Thus Gombrowicz can be described as a writer of the body even though he takes ideas very seriously. His work is devoted to the debunking of the myth of spiritualized humanity as it was developed in the works of the great Romantic writers. In his works the intellect is heavily conditioned by carnality, and even his most cerebral characters, such as Frederick in *Pornografia,* are influenced in their thinking by the petty needs of their bodies. These needs cannot be reduced to those of which the Marxists speak. They are pervasive and unavoidable, and have little to do with politics or social change. They are there to stay, and no systemic adjustment can possibly diminish their influence on human actions.

The carnality of Gombrowicz's characters has distinctly Polish overtones. It speaks against the Polish Romantic myth of the individual as primarily a member of a national community. In volume 2 of the *Diary* Gombrowicz said that he "wrote against" those Polish writers who "were concerned with the existence and development of the nation rather than with its citizens, and who spoke of the problems of Poland rather than of the problems of individual Poles." In the works of such writers as Stanisław Wyspiański or Stefan Zeromski, Polishness was prized while Polish individuals were seldom seen as ends in themselves.

Gombrowicz always put the individual before the nation. His characters often face a choice between serving themselves and serving the national cause, and Gombrowicz clearly sympathizes with those who opt for the first. His sympathy is most pronounced in *Trans-Atlantyk,* where the virtuous Major Kobrzycki is presented as ineffective, whereas the homosexual Gonzalez is treated sympathetically. In the *Diary* Gombrowicz said that he was tired of hearing about the heroic Polish people. He wanted writers to find out how Mr. and Mrs. Kowalski lived during World War II and its aftermath. Rather than bemoaning the pauperization of the Polish people after the Communist takeover, he wanted writers and journalists to follow up on individual cases and describe what the Kowalskis and their two children had for dinner on a given day.

In thus proclaiming the primacy of the individual and his or her physical needs, Gombrowicz protested not only against the feverish patriotism of the Poles but also against the myths of race, tribe, and nationhood that have plagued the politics of Poland's eastern and western neighbors, Russia and Germany. In Gombrowicz's lifetime these two nations created totalitarian states based on the idea of racial or class interest conceived by the mind rather than proven in life. Gombrowicz's ironic presentation of "the Fatherland" in *Trans-Atlantyk* contains a warning to those who invoke the shibboleths of national interest and national destiny in their search for power.

Themes

Gombrowicz's grand theme is the dialectic of maturity and immaturity in human life. As early as *Ferdydurke* he noticed the contradictory desires to which most human beings are subject. On the one hand, they want to

---

[1] Unless otherwise noted, all quotations consist of the author's translations from the Polish-language editions.

reach the level of understanding and seriousness that would place them in the "adult" world. They desire consummation and fulfillment, and those who go farthest in fathoming some branch of knowledge or experience are honored by others for their achievement. On the other hand, human beings seem to have an inordinate craving for immaturity. It manifests itself in their adoration of youth and attempts to stay young as long as possible. "The green tree of life" is valued more than the fruits of wisdom that come with old age. In *Pornografia*, Frederick, who comprehends the secrets of reality, abandons them for the sake of youth and inexperience.

Gombrowicz's grand theme is thus a variation on the Faust motif. He is particularly interested in the lack of commitment to either maturity or immaturity in real life and in the oscillation between the two in the works of human culture. In his novels this oscillation manifests itself in the numerous and inconsistent choices the characters make in the course of their daily lives. The final choice is never made, or if it is, it can hardly be identified by the acting subject. Gombrowicz himself is not interested in the metaphysical dimension of the Faustian myth but in the practical consequences of contradictory longings. Thus he brings the Faustian theme back to earth and declares that the dilemma cannot, and would not, be solved except insofar as the consciousness of it is a solution. An inability to commit oneself to either maturity or immaturity is an inescapable human characteristic, and only an awareness of this incapacity can help individuals not to be unconscious dupes of it, he suggests.

Another aspect of the maturity-immaturity dialectic has to do with a certain form of hypocrisy that, according to Gombrowicz, intellectuals routinely practice. In the *Diary* he says that human culture has long overtaken humanity. The culture of humanity is sublime and its resources are huge. Ostensibly, the best-educated men and women have mastered its basic resources and achievements. They have read all the indispensable works of philosophy and literature a cultured person should have read; have seen or heard about all the monuments of architecture worth seeing or hearing about; and have familiarized themselves with the events that have had a decisive influence on human history. This total comprehension is a carefully nurtured fiction, claims Gombrowicz. Most "experts," not to mention ordinary people, do not possess a fraction of the knowledge ascribed to them, and they are far from having a consistent view of human history. However, they have learned to lie to themselves in that regard. The technique of lying and pretending has been perfected in the last century to the point where it has become almost impenetrable to ordinary observers and to the victims of self-deception. People are repeatedly confronted with false experts and told by them how the world runs, and they cannot protest because the cloak of Form surrounding the experts is virtually impenetrable. Underneath the cloak, however, there resides a fleshly bewilderment of monumental proportions.

Such insights run throughout Gombrowicz's works. Professor Pimko, who infantilizes his students in *Ferdydurke*, is a case in point. He and those like him flaunt their fake maturity in front of those who stand naked in their immaturity. But behind the fake maturity of the Pimkos there is a longing for an end to the masquerade, and Pimko's courtship of the high-school student Zutka illustrates this. Pimko drops his pose before Zutka in the hope that she might, after all, like him. A senile lover, he is a caricature of Faust, but his pitiful hopes bring home the notion that the dream of immaturity can overwhelm men and women of all ages.

The lack of attention paid by thinkers and artists to the contradictory drives toward and away from maturity and immaturity never ceased to amaze Gombrowicz. He saw in this dialectic one of the key phenomena of history and felt that it has not been given its due in literature. Human culture is grounded in the premise that man should overcome his craving for remaining unfinished, "green," immature, and dumb, but the contrary is true in real life. The giant mystification thus perpetrated has to do with the failure of art and philosophy to civilize man. While at one level man says "Ripeness is all," at another he hopes that he will never reach it.

Another recurring theme of Gombrowicz's is the dialectic of "younger" and "older" in regard to nations. He keenly perceived a truth that has been glossed over by sociologists and literary scholars: that an individual is inevitably conditioned not only by the kind of social and economic milieu into which he or she is born but also by ethnic origin. Being born in one of the successful nations creates a different kind of individual psychology than being born in an unsuccessful one. Individuals born in the second type of nation develop ways of coping with what is perceived as a collective failure of their culture. They have to go on coping throughout their lives, and often they compensate by trying exceptionally hard to succeed. But their individual successes or failures are heavily conditioned by the national ones, and one may even speak of national neuroses in this regard. Gombrowicz first posed this problem in *Trans-Atlantyk.*

Gombrowicz's background was genteel but it was also provincial. "I am who I am," Gombrowicz's school friend Ted Kępiński once said of himself with the aura of satisfied finality characteristic of persons who are followers rather than leaders. Gombrowicz was bothered by this docile acceptance. He was irritated when he saw Poles and Argentines shopping for English hats, French wines, and German philosophy while hiding their inferiority complex under an accusatory mask. In *Trans-Atlantyk* he articulated the uncertainty and bitterness that often motivate people who belong to the less successful ethnic groups. Owing to the importance in *Trans-Atlantyk* of

ethnic background as a determining factor in one's position in the world, this novel can be called a novel for and about ethnic minorities in any country.

Gombrowicz viewed the problem of being a minority differently than it is often viewed today. He was not interested in the political or economic aspects but in its psychological effects. For him, being a minority amounted not so much to being socially disadvantaged because of skin color or some other attribute of one's physique. Rather, it had to do with belonging to an older or a younger culture. Gombrowicz disagreed with those who mouth platitudes about all cultures being equal but at the same time dictate the terms of intellectual or artistic discourse within their sphere of influence. As a European he was aware that he was a "younger" European and that his country had not impressed its psychological preferences and cultural achievements on other European countries. He knew that a great deal of the influence exerted by the major European nations amounts to an imposition on less successful nations of certain psychological habits that have little value in themselves but that familiarize the rest of the world with Europe: first names of individuals and names of agricultural and industrial products, ways of dressing, and the major languages. It was obvious to Gombrowicz that many nations have to function within a world culture that is a natural home to only a few.

Gombrowicz would say that being a minority is more common than a sociologist might suggest. Any person whose family roots are not part of the dominant culture is a minority and feels like one. In the Western world being a minority means that one's psychological habits and the customs of one's childhood find no confirmation in the cultural mainstream. Even in the First World the small nations are generally subject to this condition, and so, of course, are newcomers from the Second and Third Worlds.

The heroes of *Trans-Atlantyk* are thus victims of a "minority complex." They have a doubly disadvantaged status: as Poles they are the Polish minority in Argentina, and as Argentines they are a minority in the Western world. Polish diplomats know that their country's army has just been defeated, and consequently their status among their fellow diplomats has rapidly declined. Polish writers know that in order to be accepted in Argentina, they must first be accepted in France. Argentine culture occupies a minority position in the marketplace of ideas and it follows the lead of the major European nations instead of relying on its own ethnic resources.

"How to be a minority" is the central question of *Trans-Atlantyk.* Part of the answer lies in the fatherland-sonland metaphor. The novel suggests that one cannot perpetually cling to one's fatherland. Transcending (if temporarily) one's fatherland is a part of growing up. One has to turn away from the security of being a son or a daughter and find one's own way of dealing with the world. This blasting of new paths is what being a minority can mean. It is a state of perpetual discomfort, but it is also a creative state. In the striving for maturity one has to undertake one's own transatlantic journey, which involves insecurity, risk, and doubt. The narrator's friend Gonzalez spells out these insights, and then we are made to expect that Ignatz, the son of Major Kobrzycki, will follow up on them. While the majority of society in the novel clings desperately to the fatherland of its imagination, it is suggested that a few characters, including the narrator, will make their overseas journey at great expense to themselves but ultimately to their own and their fatherland's advantage.

Finally, sadomasochism is Gombrowicz's recurring theme and an object of his incessant fascination. The desire to hurt oneself and others is always present in Gombrowicz's characters, from his early short stories to the last novel, *Cosmos.* The question therefore arises of whether Gombrowicz portrayed himself in his sadomasochistic characters. Part of the answer can be found in the *Diary,* in which the author displays great sensitivity to the suffering of others and true grit in regard to personal misfortunes. At the same time, his curiosity about the torturer's mind is almost obsessive. Just as in Dostoevsky's novels there is the motif of the sexual abuse of a child, a recurrent theme in Gombrowicz's works is human cruelty to other humans and to animals. Unlike Dostoevsky, Gombrowicz does not moralize, choosing instead to dissect this subject in an unemotional way. Instead of asking "What makes this man enjoy his cruel acts?" which Dostoevsky might have asked, Gombrowicz shows men taking pleasure in such acts. In *Ferdydurke,* Professor Pimko derives pleasure from his mental cruelty, and so do Professors of Analysis and Synthesis. In the country mansion the slapping of a peasant's face brings pleasure to the master and his victim. This scene, so vividly parodying Zosima slapping the face of his servant, seems to mock the ease with which the vain and cruel officer of the Russian army became the saintly Father Zosima in *The Brothers Karamazov.* Gombrowicz suggests that the sadistic impulse is far more difficult to eradicate than Dostoevsky's rhetoric makes us believe.

In *Cosmos* the narrator's sexual desire is awakened by the deformity of the maid Katasia's mouth. Part of her face had been crushed in a car accident, and the narrator is morbidly attracted to her deformity. Her past misfortunes and present lowly status evoke in him not pity but a desire to hurt her even more, and his colleague Fuchs joins him in this venture.

One might wonder why Gombrowicz wrote his sadistic fiction for a Polish audience that was hardly used to so heavy a dose of sexual cruelty in imaginative literature. The answer is that precisely because Polish writers had used self-censorship in regard to such impulses, Gombrowicz decided to make them stand out in his work. In the *Diary* he criticized the naturalness of Polish literature. He wanted it to acquire a dose of what was unnatural and abnormal. The difference between Polish literature and, say, the literature of the French, he remarked at one point, was that between raw and cooked food, or between fresh fruit and well-made preserves. Polish literature was up-lifting, natural, and naive. It possessed the in-nocence of a healthy childhood. Gombrowicz wanted to make it less naive, and he was will-ing to pay the price.

Part of the price was that his characters are not lovable. There are no saintly prostitutes or repentant murderers in his novels. Gombro-wicz shows men and women at their shabbi-est moments, and evil is always petty in his works. The desires of the Faustian characters are stunted, and the youth and immaturity they crave come not in the guise of a chaste maiden but in the form of a smelly housemaid. Their crimes are petty rather than grandiose, and their sadism is honeycombed with cow-ardice. Gombrowicz's characters are the tepid ones of the Laodicean church of whom the book of Revelation speaks so negatively. Their sa-dism goes unnoticed and unchecked because they commit their little acts of cruelty in a judi-cious way, without endangering themselves or incurring the wrath of their fellow petty sa-dists. They find excuses for their cruelty, such as the pursuit of a girl (in *Ferdydurke*), an investigation of coded signs (in *Cosmos*), or patriotism (in *Trans-Atlantyk*). In *Pornogra-fia* their main excuse is war. Gombrowicz cer-tainly does not have a flattering view of his characters or, by extension, of humanity in general.

Does he ever encourage his readers to inves-tigate the circumstances in which the cruelty impulse is activated? Let us consider *Porno-grafia*, where World War II serves as a back-ground. In choosing this setting Gombrowicz threw the brutality of Nazi aggression onto the scales on which we, the readers, weigh the actions of the characters. Its weight is so tre-mendous that it has to influence our judgment. Indeed, upon reflection it turns out that in *Por-nografia* sadomasochistic impulses in the characters who lived decent lives before the war are triggered by World War II.

The novel takes place in 1943 in Nazi-occu-pied Poland. All the events in it are related to the war and most of them have been caused by it. Frederick and Witold come to the country manor to work out a black market deal that will enable them to survive for a few months longer. Other characters also have been radically af-fected by war. Under normal circumstances the teenagers would be in school, the resistance officer would farm, landowners such as Albert would practice law, and the peasant boy Olek would work as a field hand.

All the murders and deaths in the novel are generated by war. The murder of the resistance officer stands at the center of the plot; without that murder the crime of the two pornographers could not have taken place. The death of Olek is dependent on this crime, and the sudden outburst of violence in the gentle Lady Amelia is the reaction of a cornered animal who bites indiscriminately because she perceives mortal enemies descending on her from all sides. The schemings of Frederick and Witold are stimu-lated by the unusual circumstances in which they find themselves. The war has "liberated" the worst instincts in people, from Lady Ame-lia's suddenly awakened self-preservation in-stinct to the pornographers' indecent dreams. It has nurtured a sadism that otherwise would have remained latent. *Pornografia* suggests that while the sadomasochistic impulse is widespread, its development or decline de-pends largely on the circumstances. In thus making the war into a decisive factor in the development of sadomasochism in formerly decent people, Gombrowicz departed from the usual ways of presenting armed conflict in lit-erature. Generally novelists who have written of war have divided people into heroes and vil-lains, into enemies and friends. Or they have indiscriminately lumped together aggressors and victims and dropped them all, as it were, into the dark hole of suffering, meaningless-ness, and cruelty. Leo Tolstoy belongs to the first group and Norman Mailer to the second.

Gombrowicz chose another way. He pre-sented the moral effects of war on a society that was not directly engaged in fighting. In *Por-

nografia war tears to pieces the Form that human beings impose on themselves. It nourishes the desire to hurt others and magnifies the desire to dominate. Gombrowicz does not moralize about it, however. No voice in the novel is raised to pass judgment on the characters, and the narrator himself is involved in crimes. The mass that the characters attend has been "polluted" by the narrator's thoughts. The priest is a nonperson; worshipers are a crowd out of which emerge criminals but no heroes. But while there is no explicit condemnation of what is going on, the laconic tone of the narrator strips away the pleasures of sadism and of sexual perversion, and the reader is shown a stark picture of the immature intellectuals acting on their immature desires stimulated by war.

Outside the context of war the sadomasochism of Gombrowicz's characters is one of the ways in which they relate to others. It is a desperate attempt to establish contact while knowing that it is impossible. Most of the characters are misanthropic and extroverted at the same time; they feel the need to reach out to others but profoundly distrust and dislike them. Occasionally they try to attract attention by hurting themselves. Often they cannot communicate except by hurting those with whom they come into contact. Their cruelty is not a form of retribution or vengeance but a way of living.

A related theme is that of pain. In his fictional and nonfictional works Gombrowicz shows concern for pain in general and for the suffering of animals in particular. The *Diary* almost compulsively returns to this theme. While humanity's sadistic motivation in causing pain is highlighted in the novels, in the *Diary* pain itself occupies center stage. In one passage Gombrowicz accuses human civilization, and Christianity in particular, of Olympian indifference to animal suffering. Glimpses of the terrible loneliness of dying animals are plentiful in the *Diary*. We are told of animals dying in winter, abandoned by the herd that moves on to places where food and

security can be found. Animals in the wild cannot afford compassion toward the dying of their own species, and those whose strength has failed are left behind, soundlessly. Then there is the loneliness of a dog in the Argentine pampas who crawls away to die, having been shot by an angry farmer. Other images include the desperation of bugs overthrown by the wind at the seashore and unable to stand on their legs again; the tortures of flies in the flypaper attached to the lamp hanging over the supper table in a country cottage; children whipping frogs to death with little twigs.

These images appear in the *Diary* quite unexpectedly, at the moments when Gombrowicz's personal fortunes seem to have been bright. He displays no trace of sadistic pleasure in recalling them. These incidents indicate that the sense of tragedy that Gombrowicz so acutely felt throughout his life embraced not only human beings, as was the case with Kierkegaard and the existentialists, but all living beings everywhere. Gombrowicz's sensitivity to pain made it impossible for him to accept any philosophy of life that disregards this phenomenon. Like Ivan Karamazov he could not accept a world in which the innocent suffer, but he went farther than Ivan in his rejection. While Dostoevsky's hero spoke of children, Gombrowicz spoke of animals, whose suffering could not be justified by a promise of eternal life. This stark truth made Gombrowicz reject not only the Catholicism in which he was raised but also all Western philosophies that encourage human beings to cope in an imperfect world. Thus, in regard to pain Gombrowicz looked disapprovingly at the indifference of philosophers and the invocation of the mystery of being by theologians, rejecting the rides to eternity offered by both.

The motif of animal suffering also appears in the novels, but there it is presented from the point of view of a sadist and overshadowed by the suffering and confusion of human beings. The narrator in *Ferdydurke* tears off the wings of a fly and leaves the insect in his girl friend's tennis shoe to die. In *Pornografia* the Nazi soldiers shoot and kill tame pigeons just for the fun of it. In *Cosmos* someone hangs a sparrow and a chicken, and the narrator strangles a cat. The world of Gombrowicz's novels is filled with the noiseless cries of animals, birds, and insects being tortured to death by men who likewise suffer. Side by side with the human dramas are the dramas in which the villains never face trial and are never punished. While the characters in the novels look at suffering with indifference or with pleasure, in the *Diary* Gombrowicz is profoundly disturbed by it.

Individual Works

Gombrowicz wrote four novels (*Ferdydurke, Trans-Atlantyk, Pornografia,* and *Cosmos*), three plays (*Iwona, księżniczka Burgunda* [*Ivona, Princess of Burgundia,* 1935], *Ślub* [*The Marriage,* 1953], and *Operetka* [*Operetta,* 1966]), a dozen or so short stories, and the three volumes of the *Diary.* The second and less important part of his creative output includes essays; the detective novel *Opętani* (*Possessed; or, The Secrets of Myslotch,* 1939), which he originally published under a pen name; and an unfinished play.

All his works are highly stylized and belong to the grotesque trend in postmodern literature. Gombrowicz writes about problems that beset many ordinary people, but he clothes his insights in a fantastic and bizarre form. His characters use eccentric language and have a caustic sense of humor. The mixture of high seriousness and humor in Gombrowicz's works exerted a strong influence on Polish literature; the playwright Sławomir Mrożek is the best-known among those who admit to being influenced by him. Indirectly Gombrowicz also influenced the grotesque trend in Soviet Russian literature—for instance, the works of Viktor Erofeev.

Gombrowicz's novels display certain structural regularities. The narrator is a passive person whose participation in the action is arranged by an active companion (Mientus in *Ferdydurke,* Gonzalez in *Trans-Atlantyk,* Fred-

erick in *Pornografia,* and Fuchs in *Cosmos*). In all four novels the narrator is called Witold or Witold Gombrowicz, although he is obviously not identical with the author Gombrowicz.

There are two more recurring types in Gombrowicz's novels. One is a traditional or reactionary type who tries hard but fails to achieve his lofty goals. Such is Siphon in *Ferdydurke,* Major Kobrzycki in *Trans-Atlantyk,* Pani Amelia in *Pornografia,* and Ludwik in *Cosmos.* The other is a passive victim who is seduced or otherwise compromised owing to the machinations of the narrator's friend. Such is the country maiden Isabel in *Ferdydurke,* whom the narrator abducts without intending to marry her; Ignatz in *Trans-Atlantyk,* whom the narrator is ready to deliver to the homosexual Gonzalez; and Henia and Karol in *Pornografia,* who are psychologically coerced to participate in criminal actions. In *Cosmos* the innocent victims are the servant Katasia and Mrs. Kulka's daughter, Lena.

Gombrowicz's first book, a collection of short stories, came as a surprise to many of his friends. They knew that he had tried his hand at journalism and that he was a secretive and ambitious loner, but they did not expect the kind of writing they saw.

Pamiętnik z okresu dojrzewania (Memoir from the Time of Immaturity) was brought out by the publishing house Rój in 1933. When it was republished in Cracow in 1957, the title was changed to *Bakakaj,* ostensibly to commemorate the name of the street on which Gombrowicz lived in Buenos Aires. But the real reason seems to be that some apparatchik had decided that invoking the seasons of human life in a title was not appropriate in a socialist state. "The time of immaturity" suggests that people acquire wisdom slowly and that this acquisition is dependent on age rather than on their social status, which is contrary to the teachings of Marx and Lenin.

The *Pamiętnik* is a presentation in miniature of the themes and style of Gombrowicz's later works. Sadism and suffering, immaturity and maturity, aristocrats and plebeians, minorities and majorities all appear in these succinct, fantastic, and very readable stories. The heroes of the stories live in a world adjacent to that of Kafka and Dostoevsky. They are sickly, secretive, compulsive, and unsure of themselves, and they play up to the audience of other characters. They try to acquire self-esteem and sometimes succeed, but the price they pay is high: all their energies are spent on acquiring self-assurance; nothing is left over for living. They are morbidly sensitive but keep their emotional life under control. When they tell us about their feelings, they do so in a detached way, as if they were not involved in them. They do not appear naked before the public the way Dostoevsky's narrator in *Notes from Underground* does but assume the role of unemotional narrators of their own emotional lives.

In the *Pamiętnik,* Gombrowicz distanced himself from the sentimental and philosophical tone so characteristic of Polish literature of his time. The language of his stories is concise, even though it abounds in unexpected turns of phrase. His verbal inventiveness showed itself at this point in his writing career. Typical of these early stories is "Tancerz mecenasa Kraykowskiego" (Lawyer Kraykowski's Dancer), a first-person narrative in which the Dancer, a man suffering from an inferiority complex, finds an unusual way of overcoming it. He performs actions that individually seem to reinforce the inferiority complex, but their frequency and single-mindedness destroy the self-assurance of the lawyer Kraykowski, with whom the Dancer maintains a love-hate relationship. The hero of this story is a young and sickly man of no distinction who has a small independent income. While trying to buy an operetta ticket without standing in line, he is shoved aside by a distinguished-looking gentleman. Like the narrator of Dostoevsky's *Notes from Underground,* who undergoes a similar experience, the Dancer derives perverse pleasure from this degradation and decides to prolong it by getting in the distinguished gentleman's way on every possible occasion. He finds out the man's name and profession and follows him everywhere, and he urges the woman whom Kraykowski has courted to surrender herself to him. The Dancer desperately wants to acquire self-esteem. He is too weak to accomplish his goal in a traditional way, but he has discovered, with Nietzsche, that one way to acquire self-assurance is to practice resentment masquerading as humility and submission. When the long-anticipated affair between Kraykowski and his friend's wife is finally consummated, the Dancer, who as a Peeping Tom secretly watches the event, experiences supreme ecstasy that climaxes in an epileptic seizure.

Thus we have here all the ingredients of the modern resentful personality: a man without a family, fortune, or fame; another man whom he envies; an attempt to "get even" by forcing his superior to notice him, if only in a disapproving way; and an awareness, on the part of the Dancer, that these determined acts will eventually overcome and destroy Kraykowski. In spite of the lawyer's good looks, his refined taste in clothing and food, his poise, wealth, education, background, and good job, he owes his status to favorable circumstances rather than to his own effort. The Dancer has none of Kraykowski's advantages, but he is determined to force the lawyer to behave in a certain way. The Dancer is a Nietzschean character who by an effort of his will forges his incipient supermanhood, which Kraykowski is unable to break or overcome.

Gombrowicz's first novel, *Ferdydurke,* was an attempt to express the insights of "Tancerz mecenasa Kraykowskiego" in a longer work of fiction. At that time the tone of mainstream Polish prose was one of acceptance. Acceptance of the world, of Poland, of social stratification, of family, of country, of an ideal of nobility of spirit, and of the idea of progress. The labels of good and bad that tradition had affixed to events and attitudes were regarded as permanent, and the vision of the world handed down by the forefathers was considered not merely acceptable but also admirable.

Gombrowicz knew that there was much falsity in such acceptance and that unquestioning surrender to the values of one's forefathers contains a measure of hypocrisy and laziness. He knew that unexamined premises are fragile and cannot withstand the fast pace of modern life. So he mocked all these stock responses and acceptances. In *Ferdydurke* the narrator attacks the cult of the Romantic poets who took the place of the real national heroes Poland lacked at that time. He made fun of the stereotypical attitudes of lovers and described kissing as "offering one's mug to another person," and he spoke ironically of the pure and innocent love that the country maiden Isabel felt for the man she thought she was about to marry. He stressed the role of what he called Form in human life, or a make-believe reality created by the poses people assume vis-à-vis one another.

The title of the novel suggests its style. *Ferdydurke* is an invented word that contains the root of the word *dureń* (a fool) and *Ferdy,* which could be a diminutive of Ferdinand and is ironically suggestive of the fashionable Waldy, the diminutive of Waldemar used by the Warsaw snobs of Gombrowicz's generation.

Ferdydurke's plot is absurd: the thirty-year-old writer Johnnie is forced to adopt a pose of submission toward his mentors, who represent the cultural establishment of the country. His well-intentioned but deadly cultural pedagogues offer unsolicited advice and exert relentless pressure on him, and they force him to adopt the accepted style of the period. The rape of the writer is presented figuratively as Johnnie's forced return to a prep school. A certain Professor Pimko takes him by the hand and conducts him to the best school in town.

At school Johnnie notices how the professors' ideological rigidity affects other students and the society at large. He lives with a family whose goal in life is to conform to intellectual fashions, to be always in step with the times. They are progressive and socially conscious, and they loathe prejudice and mindless traditionalism. But their attitudes turn out to be subtly hypocritical. When confronted with an unusual situation in which their desire to be considered progressive does not find a standard behavioral mold, Mr. and Mrs. Youthful lose their self-confidence and become part of the "wriggling heap" of humanity.

Tucked between Johnnie's adventures are two philosophical tales that look back to Voltaire's *Candide* and Samuel Johnson's *Rasselas:* "Philifor Honeycombed with Childishness" and "Philimor Honeycombed with Childishness." They replay the theme of *Ferdydurke* in a different key. In "Philifor," the Grand Master of Synthesis and the Grand Master of Analysis use the power of their personalities rather than argumentation to impose a view of the world on the public. In "Philimor" an accidental interruption of a tennis game triggers off a chain of events ending in a grotesque scene of the gentlemen mounting their ladies as if the latter were horses.

In *Ferdydurke* people are forced by others to adopt poses inconsistent with their real wishes and needs. Falsification, or Form, suggests Gombrowicz, has a decisive influence on the course of human life. Poses, once assumed, are hard to abandon; they become surrogate selves. Through his presentation of human life as dominated by Form, Gombrowicz attacks the Romantic notion of man as primarily a spiritual being whose mental life can be disconnected from his material conditions. To such Romantic writers as Friedrich Schiller what mattered in man was "the beautiful soul" rather than the behavior of the physical body. Gombrowicz suggests that the truth of Romanticism was two-dimensional and reductive and that it generated false assessments of the ways human beings function in life. In the classroom that Johnnie attends, the teacher mouths platitudes about the great Romantic poets who must be admired. A student points out that nobody reads them except the high-school students who are forced to do so by their teachers. The teacher becomes furious but cannot explain why: the student is telling the truth. At the heart of this controversy, suggests Gombrowicz, is an unrealistic notion of what human beings are and how they behave in their daily lives. The Romantic and neo-Romantic writers dealt in ideas to the exclusion of the "green tree of life," thus courting the danger of being reduced to vapidity by their shallow admirers.

Gombrowicz illustrates his insights by means of the "duel of faces." Two schoolboys, Siphon and Mientus, represent two opposing views of humanity. Siphon is an idealist, worships Romantic bards, and believes in the beautiful soul. Mientus is disgusted with this pose and defiantly flaunts his own: that of a cynic who does not believe in anything and who finds pleasure in sexual and scatological conversations. In their "duel" one of them assumes a facial expression that characterizes his set of beliefs and the other responds with an expression characteristic of his own. The outcome is to be determined by the tenacity of the adversaries in maintaining their poses: whoever gives up first, loses.

The duel of faces in *Ferdydurke* expresses a larger truth, which is that humans first learn to dissemble through their faces. While children's faces are not "prearranged" so as to make the audience forget about the physical needs of a face's owner, adults make efforts to arrange their countenances in such a way that they do not betray their real feelings and needs, but instead express an attitude considered appropriate for the occasion. The face of the public person is meant to express nothing except interest in the ideas currently on the agenda. Such is Professor Pimko's face in his moments of false glory. But we learn later that he is not truly devoted to ideas, and that his interest in the comforts and needs of his body is more powerful than his devotion to the intellectual life he ostensibly represents. His dependence on feelings is real; but for public consumption he distorts his face into expressions of indifference, dignity, or strength, thus helping to forge the hypocrisy of modern life.

In this connection it should be mentioned that the duel between Mientus and Siphon parodies a scene in Dostoevsky's *The Brothers Karamazov.* This great philosophical novel is vulnerable to Gombrowicz's criticism in its naive presentation of Alyosha Karamazov's youth. Like Siphon, Alyosha was pure and idealistic, and he was informed about the facts of life by the schoolboys who forced him down to the floor and shouted obscenities into his ears while he lay there helpless. What in Dostoevsky is meant to be an outrageous act, in Gombrowicz appears as salutary irony directed at Siphon's refusal to face up to the reality of man's carnal life.

Thus the novelistic society of *Ferdydurke* consists mainly of poseurs who try to show off and patronize one another. They combine in a dialectical fashion the function of the tormentors and the tormented as they bring others into submission or are brought to submission by them. The narrator calls the inconsistency and vanity his characters display "immaturity," and he laments the lack of candor with which people treat one another. Professor Pimko, who infantilizes the narrator, is himself immature, although he never admits it to himself. When his disastrous courtship of a girl one-third his age brings the consciousness of it home, Pimko joins the "wriggling heap" of immature men and women. He cannot escape his physical nature even though he tries very hard to give the impression of being immunized against it.

Thus, in *Ferdydurke,* Gombrowicz began creating a new style and new tone in Polish literature. He wanted to replace the unquestioning cult of the past in Polish intellectual life with a critical attitude. Since the tone of post–World War II Polish literature is mostly ironic, one has to assume that his wishes have been fulfilled.

After *Ferdydurke, Trans-Atlantyk* contributed to that development. The action of this grotesque novel takes place in Argentina; its main characters are a group of Poles stranded in a foreign country after the joint Nazi-Soviet attack on Poland in September 1939. The author grafts the social mores of seventeenth-century Poland onto a twentieth-century situation. In the way they behave, the people in *Trans-Atlantyk* resemble those in the world of Jan Chryzostom Pasek, a seventeenth-century Polish nobleman who participated in many wars and wrote his *Memoirs,* a work important for an understanding of that period of history. *Trans-Atlantyk* characters also resemble characters in Chaucer's *Canterbury Tales* and in François Rabelais's *Gargantua and Pantagruel.* They covet simple things, their manners are coarse, and their scheming is naive by twentieth-century standards, but they are warm and outgoing, and ready to talk and listen to others.

Such people are then confronted with the harsh realities of a world war. They find themselves in the situation of men who lived in a skyscraper and woke up one day to see the walls of the building disappear and themselves lying on the verge of a precipice. What should they do? The plot of the novel is built around their clumsy attempts to adjust to their new status as refugees.

In *Trans-Atlantyk,* Gombrowicz combined archaic language and customs with contemporary situations. He went back to the style of the *gawęda,* an old Polish narrative genre that used a highly stylized narrator whose intonations, exclamations, and interjections were an important part of the text. The *gawęda* narrator was usually a petty nobleman who possessed all the shortcomings and virtues of his class: he was conceited, naive, extroverted, sincere, and very warm and human. Gombrowicz's narrator in *Trans-Atlantyk* possesses all these qualities, and his manner of telling the story produces a humorous effect. The work can be described as a spoken novel because it follows the rhythms and turns of phrase of spoken rather than written language, and only through reading aloud can its humorous potential come fully to life. One of the devices that gives *Trans-Atlantyk* its characteristic rhythm is seemingly random capitalization of words in the text. The Polish language uses capitalization sparingly:

only proper names and the letters that begin a sentence are capitalized. In titles only the first word is capitalized. Thus, a narrative in which capitalization occurs in the middle of a sentence is something of a shock for a Polish reader. Such usage drastically changes the rhythm of sentences and the customary associations of words. Instead of subjects and predicates, words that attract the reader's attention in standard Polish—objects, modifiers, and even prepositions and exclamations—become salient; they emphasize the subjective side of the narrative at the expense of the factual one. The characters' unconscious reactions to events become the focus of attention; the reader is exposed not so much to the events as to the effects of the events on the narrator. And this is what the *gawęda* was supposed to convey: not the story itself but the character of the person telling the story. The *gawęda* teller had to know how to hold the listeners' attention. A writer who attempted to write a *gawęda* had to create a credible and amusing narrator first, and then a good story. *Trans-Atlantyk* is successful on both counts.

In this novel Gombrowicz's verbal inventiveness reached its peak. He blended seventeenth-century Polish with contemporary peasant dialects and made the narrator and characters speak a mixture of both, thus combining the charm of archaisms and the simplicity of a lower-class dialect. He added to this mixture his own invention of capitalizing those words whose semantic weight he wanted to emphasize.

The novel's narrator takes a pleasure trip from Poland to Argentina shortly before World War II. The outbreak of the war finds him penniless in an alien country, among people whose language he does not know and whose customs baffle him at every step. His basic problem, however, is a conflict between his acceptance of traditional morality and his desire to break away from the straitjacket of a narrowly understood patriotism. The narrator wants to experience life rather than die on the battlefield for a lost cause. He is tantalized by the possibility of ignoring certain aspects of a sense of duty. Should he choose duty to the fatherland or admiration for the "sonland"? Are sons less important and less worthy than fathers?

In the novel the Polish patriotic tradition is personified by Major Thomas Kobrzycki, an upright man if there ever was one. Kobrzycki never hesitates when he has to choose between honorable behavior, on the one hand, and private interest and pleasure, on the other. His son Ignatz represents the real Poles of those times, including Gombrowicz. Ignatz has been influenced by his father but is still too young to commit himself fully to his father's side, and his youth and naiveté make him a prime target for men immersed in what the studiously naive narrator calls "the unnatural vice." Ignatz, who says little in the course of the novel, is a perfect potential victim of a violent homosexual. When Major Kobrzycki is made aware of the danger to his son, he prepares to kill Ignatz rather than allow him to sink into vice. While the noble father prepares for the murder, the sly and down-to-earth narrator wonders about the pros and cons of inducing the son to kill his father instead. Again the question arises: Why should fathers take precedence over sons? Why should Poles pay for being Polish by having one-fourth of the country's population killed every generation or so? Is it better to be Polish and dead or to embrace Gonzalez' philosophy and live? A contemporary American reader will perceive here a parallel to the "Red or dead" controversy. However, while in America this controversy is conducted by adversaries seated in comfortable armchairs, among Poles it was conducted amid piles of victims. In spite of the grotesque tone the dilemma presented in *Trans-Atlantyk* is bitterly realistic.

When the novel first appeared in an émigré edition in Paris, it offended critics and readers alike, and many persons accused Gombrowicz of treason and immorality. But his aim was hardly to advocate a sellout or a surrender of any kind. He himself was an example of intransigence, of stubbornly clinging to the ideals of his own tradition. He wrote in Polish at a time when the situation of Poland could be perceived as hopeless and when talented opportunists had good prospects of enlisting in some newly powerful language or cause. Gombrowicz passed up all such opportunities. What he wanted to do was to create a perspective from which faithfulness to one's beliefs and ideals could be viewed and practiced. He wanted to eliminate knee-jerk patriotism and promote a reflective one. He wanted to make his countrymen aware of the options and conscious of the costs of remaining uncritically traditional. *Trans-Atlantyk* pleads for openness to experience and for willingness to take risks in order to grow. Traditions have a way of petrifying and impoverishing those who passively cling to them. "Audiatur et altera pars" (let us hear the other side's story), suggests Gombrowicz. Without renouncing responsibility, let us see what the son can accomplish if he abandons his father's house.

In thus leading the reader into territories uncharted by Polish authors of the earlier generations, Gombrowicz could not avoid clashing with them on occasion. *Trans-Atlantyk* parodies two very popular Polish classical authors: the Romantic poet Adam Mickiewicz and the neo-Romantic novelist Henryk Sienkiewicz. Mickiewicz's epic poem *Pan Tadeusz* (*Pan Tadeusz; or, The Last Foray in Lithuania*, 1834) captured the lifestyle and virtues of the Polish nobility in Lithuania during the Napoleonic wars. The heroes of *Pan Tadeusz* are the ancestors of those Poles in *Trans-Atlantyk* who work for the Polish Embassy in Buenos Aires and of those who have settled in that city as refugees. The sleigh ride of *Pan Tadeusz* is parodied in a mock sleigh ride in *Trans-Atlantyk*. The celebrations and festivities of Mickiewicz's poem reappear in a grotesque form in Gombrowicz's novel.

Like *Trans-Atlantyk*, Sienkiewicz's historical novel *Trylogia* (The Trilogy, 1883–1887) borrowed heavily from seventeenth-century language and customs. But while in Sienkiewicz a patina of Romantic ideology was imposed onto the coarse habits of seventeenth-century life, in *Trans-Atlantyk* the porous surface of the Sarmatian (old Polish) lifestyle was exposed without any attempts to make it appear smoother and more refined. Sienkiewicz's noble knights were always ready to defend somebody, to sacrifice their own well-being on the altar of God or country, and to fall on their knees before their princes and ladies. In contrast, the heroes of *Trans-Atlantyk* borrow the stock responses of Sienkiewicz's characters and use them in situations involving no heroism. Thus a mockery is made of expressions and attitudes such as "to fall on one's knees" and "to offer oneself to God."

Trans-Atlantyk, probably the most innovative piece of prose Gombrowicz wrote, is one of the most popular novels in Poland today. However, its language and Argentine-baroque background have frightened English translators. Louis Iribarne tried his hand at rendering it into English but gave up in frustration. *Trans-Atlantyk* can be read in French or German, but as of the early 1990's it still awaits an enterprising English translator.

On the surface *Pornografia* tells an unsavory story of two adults who, in order to satisfy their own sexual cravings by proxy, try to persuade two teenagers to get emotionally involved with each other. This indeed is the stuff pornography is made of. But the motives of the adults are never explicitly mentioned and the teenagers do not even kiss, let alone go to bed. *Pornografia* strips the glamour from the pornographic plot and leaves only an analysis of human motivation and a perception of human fragility and dependence on the material conditions of living. As is the case with Gombrowicz's other novels, sex and sadomasochism appear in *Pornografia* side by side. Frederick and Witold understand the linkage between the two, whereas those characters who do not see that linkage, such as the underground officer Siemian, end up in disaster.

Pornografia is a first-person account of the thoughts and schemings of two intellectuals who have been made superfluous by World War II. They live in Warsaw and support themselves by pitiful black market deals. We meet one of them, Frederick, as he peddles four rabbit skins to other intellectuals, a petty sale that symbolizes the destruction of normal life under the Nazi occupation of Poland.

The narrator is the other intellectual. He calls himself "Witold Gombrowicz," but one should not be fooled by this, since the real Gombrowicz never set foot in Poland during the war. In a manner that smacks of masochism, Gombrowicz assigned his own name to a character whose actions and desires are less than admirable.

The story revolves around a seduction by proxy of the two youngsters, Henia and Karol. What Frederick and Witold actually achieve is not a sexual act but a "pairing together" of the two sixteen-year-olds in the act of murder. Frederick, a former actor, arranges several scenes in which Henia and Karol assume strange poses that have little to do with ordinary sex, but that link them together in the eyes of the onlookers, one of whom is Henia's fiancé, Albert. Frederick wins the youngsters' trust by telling them that such silent pictures are part of a stage production he is contemplating and that he wants to try it with actual people. At one point he asks Henia and Karol to take off one shoe each, and then the stocking (Henia) and the sock (Karol), and then touch each other's soles. The teenagers, who have known each other since childhood, fulfill the request without thinking much of it; indeed, they consider it a joke. But Frederick makes sure that a small and secret audience is watching that scene, which takes place in a garden near a pond.

It should be clear from the above that in *Pornografia* we deal with characters whose sexual and sadomasochistic compulsions are highly developed and frequently practiced. What in *Ferdydurke* and *Trans-Atlantyk* was a timid beginning, in *Pornografia* becomes a way of life for the narrator and his active companion. Throughout his work Gombrowicz tried to show how ordinary people secretly practice sexual and other perversions without incurring the wrath of society for their transgressions.

Pornografia admits of another interpretation, however. It can be read as an extended metaphor of the war itself. It is placed squarely in the midst of World War II, and its plot can be interpreted as a figurative presentation of the sadism and unspeakable injustices of war. If the novel is read this way, the would-be pornographers become analogous to those responsible for the outbreak of war, and the youngsters become the victims-turned-criminals in the deadly conflict.

Wars are usually conceived and planned by adults and executed by young people. They are initiated by the strong, who attack the weak, rather than the other way round; however, such attacks are often camouflaged by claims that the strong were "provoked" by the weak. In wars it often happens that the best men die while the worst survive and even prosper. All these situations are amply present in *Pornografia.*

The planners of violence are the two adults. Henia and Karol are carefree teenagers who could go either way in life: they could become good citizens, or they might choose the life of destruction and crime. They are "weaker" than the adults and in many ways depend on them for survival. They have to follow the orders of adults even when they are told to commit crimes. Amelia and Albert represent human decency, albeit flawed, and they both die. While it turns out that neither of them is immune to the cravings of immaturity, they yield to them only in extreme circumstances. The resistance officer tries to fight a good fight but has a nervous breakdown as a result of long-lasting exposure to danger, and he, too, dies. The peasant boy Olek is killed for a trespass that was so small as not to warrant even a good thrashing in ordinary circumstances. The teenagers Henia and Karol are stigmatized for life by their participation in murder. They are like the two soldiers who joined the army thinking

of the defense of the fatherland and found that the actual business of fighting a war involves more than shooting villains, conquering cities, and receiving flowers from the happy people whose cities have been liberated. Both readings of *Pornografia* leave one with a wealth of suggestions about the dark side of man: the novel is built out of allusions to the secret and disturbing side of man's nature.

Gombrowicz's plays fall outside the realistic convention no less than do his novels. They are directed at viewers who do not wish to subject themselves to the illusion of the fourth wall; they are highly stylized and resemble the theater of the absurd. In the "Author's Commentary" to *Operetka,* Gombrowicz remarked that modern plays are like orchestra scores in that they have to be seen and heard to come alive. This is true not only of *Operetta* but also of the other two plays *Ivona, Princess of Burgundia* and *The Marriage.*

The plots of these plays revolve around princes and princesses, barons and baronesses, and kings and queens, whose security and positions are challenged in some way by the plebeians. In *Ivona, Princess of Burgundia,* Prince Philip courts the commoner Ivona and introduces her to the royal court. To everyone's surprise Ivona generates a feeling of insecurity in the courtiers. In *The Marriage* the two protagonists, Henry and Johnny, witness the undoing of class divisons in war-torn Poland. Henry wants to declare his father king in order to make up for the suffering and humiliation to which the father was exposed under the Nazi occupation. When this scheme fails, he tries to become king himself. In *Operetta* the plot centers on Prince and Princess Himalay, their son, Count Charm, and his friend, Baron Firulet. The revolution comes with a vengeance and destroys their comfortable and mindless way of living.

The aristocratic characters in Gombrowicz's plays seldom speak the language of their social class. Instead, they use words and expressions characteristic of the speech of the uneducated.

Gombrowicz's aim is to show that the "discreet charm" of the upper classes is largely a matter of Form, produced by those who admire it (the commoners) rather than by those who profit from this admiration (the aristocracy). It is suggested that there is no substance to aristocratic mannerisms. After the revolution the fashion designer Fior and the aristocrats to whom he catered become just as unglamorous and uninteresting as the plebeians. In *Ivona, Princess of Burgundia* the King and his Queen use lower-class expressions, which underscores the fact that their anger, delight, and fear are not qualitatively different from the emotions that characterize their low-born subjects. In *The Marriage* the loss of Form is so radical that it destroys those who lose it. War tears off not only the superfluous mannerisms of the aristocrats but also the necessary and vital Form of daily life in society. Henry's destitute parents are forced to work as slave laborers in their former home, an injustice that destroys them psychologically by instilling incurable paranoia in them.

The third characteristic of Gombrowicz's plays is their parodistic nature. Gombrowicz takes to task the popular works of the Polish Romantic theater: Juliusz Słowacki's *Balladyna* (1839) and Zygmunt Krasiński's *Nieboska komedia* (*The Undivine Comedy*, 1835). *Ivona, Princess of Burgundia* and *Balladyna* use the Cinderella theme and then present the transformation of the docile Cinderellas into threatening females. But while in Słowacki's drama Balladyna is ceremoniously punished for her attempt to dominate the male society, in *Ivona, Princess of Burgundia* antifeminism plays no role at all. Ivona is punished by the king and the courtiers not because she is a woman but because she irritates everyone around her. Thus Gombrowicz makes fun of the rigid and naive patriarchy of *Balladyna*.

The Marriage is likewise a parody of what may be called the spirit of Polish Romanticism. The worldview of Słowacki's *Kordian* (1834) was grounded in a dislike of Russian tyranny and devotion to the Polish ideal of fighting "for our freedom and yours." The opening scene of *The Marriage* echoes such attitudes: Henry and Johnny are Polish soldiers who fight the Nazis in France after the fall of Poland. But before the play is over, they abandon their chivalrous pursuits and turn to their private business—an echo of *Trans-Atlantyk*, where Gonzalez urges Witold to behave likewise.

The revolution in *Operetta* parodies the revolution in Krasiński's *Undivine Comedy*. The revolutionaries, whose chief motivation is resentment, destroy the old society, which indeed is corrupt and unworthy. However, the revolution increases the corruption instead of diminishing it; it also wipes out whatever good there was in the old world. While Christianity was invoked in Krasiński's play, Gombrowicz's dramatic society is saved by a destruction of Form and a brief period of human "nakedness." It is suggested that the excessive development of Form made human relations too difficult, and that human beings have an ability occasionally to destroy Form and then begin creating it anew. This is what happens in *Operetta*. At the end of the play Albertine's nakedness rejuvenates both the old society and the revolutionaries, and the play ends on a positive note. The raising of Albertine, however, is due to the efforts of the two petty thieves who first hide her in a coffin and then "revive" her before the eyes of the amazed survivors of the revolution. Albertine is an undistinguished human being, and her chief assets are her youth and beauty. Such qualities were of no significance in the grandiose struggle of ideas that Krasiński had presented. Gombrowicz stresses their triviality while demonstrating the influence they exert on the world of men. Albertine wins, an ironic parallel to the Christ whose resurrection was invoked in Krasiński's play.

Needless to say, these parodies are not meant to discredit either the Gospels or the Polish writers of a few generations earlier. Rather, they are meant to expose the stock responses of Polish readers and stimulate the development of new responses. Gombrowicz's message in the plays seems to be that one of the ways to pay homage to a literary tradition is to provide a counterpoint to it instead of deadening it by docile imitation.

Gombrowicz's best-known play, *Ivona, Princess of Burgundia,* was first performed in Cracow, Poland, in 1957. His foreign theatrical debut took place in Paris, where Jorge Lavelli directed *The Marriage* at the Théâtre Récamier in 1964. The reviews were mixed: Gombrowicz pleased members of the avant-garde but displeased the conservatives (*Le Figaro* gave him a bad review). Lavelli's production of *Ivona* in 1965 was more favorably received. In the same year in Stockholm a production of *Ivona* by Alf Sjöberg was received enthusiastically. A similar reception awaited *The Marriage* in Berlin in 1968. Since that time his plays have been performed throughout Europe and elsewhere. Gombrowicz shares with Samuel Beckett and Eugène Ionesco a predilection for absurd plots, but prefers more ornate and plentiful stage decor than the theater of the absurd; this makes him more palatable to an average audience than the dialogue-only, decor-free dramas of some of the absurdists. Both the first production of *Ivona* and the later productions of this and other plays have been warmly received in Poland.

From the sublime to the trivial, from the spiritual to the scatological: the scope of the three volumes of the *Diary* (which covers the period 1953–1966) is virtually unlimited. The *Diary* is an exercise book in which Gombrowicz laid bare the details of his own life, sketched out the possible plots for his novels, and interpreted his own literary works. In doing so he made sure that the life of the mind did not overshadow the life of the body and that the profound was balanced by the petty. In fact, one of the striking features of the *Diary* is Gombrowicz's obvious desire not to appear "mature," not to play the role of a person whose views have coalesced into hard certainty and who is not subject to the daily bewilderment of a twentieth-century observer of the world and of himself.

Like the other works of Gombrowicz, the *Diary* is characterized by an absence of emotional outbursts. In his early youth Gombrowicz's self-control became his second nature. Neither in public nor in private did he ever display sentimentality of any kind, and reading his novels, plays, and the *Diary* one might think that the part of his brain which generates emotions had been somehow excised. He was like Mr. Spock in the "Star Trek" series, a creature seemingly impervious to emotions.

In the *Diary* Gombrowicz discusses with sympathy and understanding such twentieth-century philosophers as Sartre, Foucault, and Heidegger, only to proclaim his lack of interest in them at other places. This apparent contradiction is a way of saying that, yes, one has to familiarize oneself with the postmodern way of thinking about man and reality, but one also has to know that the philosopher's message is often irrelevant to life. Gombrowicz did not recommend submission to the tyranny of postmodernism. In volume 1 of the *Diary* he remarked that "our libraries had long overtaken our capacity to absorb them," and he believed that any philosophical discussion today should be based on a candid recognition of that fact. What he saw, however, was the opposite: he saw people making pronouncements with fake certainty about matters with which they were only vaguely familiar. Thus an excess of Form was being created that would eventually falsify human relationships until they erupted in conflict.

In a similar way Gombrowicz argued about the younger and older European nations, about poetry and its enemies, and about a multitude of received ideas that many of his generation unconditionally accepted. He was keenly aware that political, social, and intellectual conventions have a way of insinuating themselves into the fabric of society and demanding acceptance similar to that which men and women in the Middle Ages felt obliged to offer to Roman Catholicism. Gombrowicz perceived striking similarities between the compulsive cult of certain ideas today and the dogmatism of the Dark Ages. Long before it became fashionable to do so, he fought against what today is called "the cultural canon" and "the herd of independent minds." He never tired of pointing out that in the three countries he knew well—Poland, Argentina, and France—most people have docilely accepted flawed opinions and judgments from nonelected arbiters of taste. In his skepticism about the present-day cultural establishment Gombrowicz was clearly a libertarian, but in this debunking proclivity he was a typical twentieth-century writer.

Thus, while in some ways he resembled his fellow writers in the Western world, in others he was distinctly an Eastern European. In the *Diary* he said: "The difference between the writers of Eastern and Western Europe consists in that the first know that man can do anything to man." While he was a debunker, his urge to expose and to question was not social, political, or nationalistic, and he cannot be attached to the noisy intellectual movements of our century. What he tried to analyze stemmed from the inner person, a person as a corporeal being, a creature who gets fatigued and goes to sleep, and whose intellect does not function in the same way when he or she is hungry as when sated, when fatigued as when energetic, when sad as when merry. Gombrowicz knew that a major part of history has been created by this intensely private person who escapes definitions and who accounts for the failure of social and political engineering in the postmodern world.

Gombrowicz came from a midsized country whose religious and political traditions have been distinctly European but whose efforts to cling to them have been repeatedly frustrated by forces hostile to Western culture coming from both the East and the West. The knowledge of what happened to his country made Gombrowicz skeptical about the insights of postmodernism in philosophy, politics, and the social sciences, and it made him impatient with the hypertrophy of Form in postmodern Western life. He was painfully aware of what man can do to man, and he felt that twentieth-

century intellectuals have all but ignored this fundamental truth. In exposing the secrets of the private man he expressed his belief in the priority of private life over public. Most of all, he was a champion of individualism. Both his life and his works eloquently argue that it is individuals who make history and not the other way round.

Selected Bibliography

EDITIONS

IN POLISH
Pamiętnik z okresu dojrzewania. Warsaw, 1933.
Iwona, księżniczka Burgunda. Warsaw, 1935.
Ferdydurke. Warsaw, 1937.
Opętani. Warsaw and Radom, 1939. Published serially in *Kurier czerwony* and in *Express poranny* under the pen name of Zdzisław Niewieski, 4 June to 30 August.
Trans-Atlantyk. Ślub. Paris, 1953.
Bakakaj. Cracow, 1957.
Dziennik, 1953–1956. Paris, 1957.
Pornografia. Paris, 1960.
Dziennik, 1957–1961. Paris, 1962.
Kosmos. Paris, 1965.
Dziennik, 1961–1966. Operetka. Paris, 1966.
Rozmowy z Gombrowiczem. Edited by Dominique de Roux. Paris, 1969. Polish text of *Entretiens.*

IN FRENCH
Entretiens de Dominique de Roux avec Gombrowicz. Paris, 1968.

COLLECTED WORKS
Dzieła zebrane. 11 vols. Paris, 1969–1977. Vol. 1, *Ferdydurke;* vol. 2, *Trans-Atlantyk;* vol. 3, *Pornografia;* vol. 4, *Kosmos;* vol. 5, *Teatr (Iwona księżniczka Burgunda, Ślub, Operetka);* vol. 6, *Dziennik, 1953–1956;* vol. 7, *Dziennik, 1957–1961;* vol. 8, *Dziennik, 1961–1966;* vol. 9, *Opowiadania;* vol. 10, *Varia* (contains essays, short stories that previously appeared in periodicals but not in book editions, the novel *Opętani,* Polish translations of interviews with Gombrowicz in the French press, and a bibliography of Gombrowicz's works in Polish, French, German, En-

glish, Spanish, Italian, Swedish, Dutch, Danish, and Norwegian); vol. 11, *Wspomnienia polskie. Wędrówki po Argentynie* (texts of his radio talks and two essays).

TRANSLATIONS

Cosmos. Translated by Eric Mosbacher. London, 1966, and New York, 1969.

Diary. Vols. 1 and 2. Translated by Lillian Vallee. Evanston, Ill., 1988–1989.

Ferdydurke. Translated by Eric Mosbacher. New York and London, 1961.

Ivona, Princess of Burgundia. Translated by Krystyna Griffith-Jones. London, 1969, and New York, 1970.

A Kind of Testament. Translated by Alastair Hamilton. London, 1973, and London and Boston, 1982.

The Marriage. Translated by Louis Iribarne. New York, 1969.

Operetta. Translated by Louis Iribarne. London, 1971.

Pornografia. Translated by Alastair Hamilton. New York, 1966.

Possessed; or, The Secret of Myslotch. Translated by J. A. Underwood. London and Boston, 1982.

Three Novels: Ferdydurke, Pornografia, Cosmos.

Translated by Eric Mosbacher and Alastair Hamilton. New York, 1978.

BIOGRAPHICAL AND CRITICAL STUDIES

Bondy, François, and Constantin Jelenski. *Witold Gombrowicz.* Munich, 1978.

Georgin, Rosine. *Gombrowicz.* Lausanne, 1977.

Gombrowicz, Rita. *Gombrowicz en Argentine: 1939–1963.* Paris, 1984.

Jelenski, Constantin, and Dominique de Roux, eds. *Cahier Gombrowicz.* Paris, 1971.

Kępiński, Tadeusz. *Witold Gombrowicz i świat jego młodości.* Cracow, 1974.

Kurczaba, Alex. *Gombrowicz and Frisch: Aspects of the Literary Diary.* Bonn, 1980.

Merivale, Patricia. "The Esthetics of Perversion: Gothic Artifice in Henry James and Witold Gombrowicz." *PMLA,* 93 (October 1978), 992–1002.

Schmidt, Krystyna. *Der Stil von W. Gombrowicz' 'Trans-Atlantyk' und sein Verhältnis zur polnischen literarischen Tradition.* Meisenheim am Glan, 1974.

Thompson, Ewa M. *Witold Gombrowicz.* Boston, 1979.

Volle, Jacques. *Gombrowicz: Bourreau, martyr.* Paris, 1972.

EWA M. THOMPSON

JEAN-PAUL SARTRE

(1905–1980)

I'm not at ease except in Nothingness—I'm a true Nothingness, drunk with pride and translucid.
—*The War Diaries,* 1940

SHORTLY AFTER THE end of World War II the streets of Paris were once again occupied, this time with the *offensive existentialiste*. In newsreels from the time existentialism is portrayed as a fashionable attitude and life-style, an intoxicating ideology of freedom that promises a release from convention and authority. In its popular form existentialism maintains that human beings, regardless of circumstances, choose their own actions and are therefore responsible for their own fates. And yet there are no objective authorities to dictate which choices are right and which are wrong; those standards are also a matter of choice. Although one can discern the heady implications of such a radical defense of freedom, one can perhaps also sense the dislocation and despair of living in a world where one must choose one's course of action without recourse to any legitimating authority. This quandary is doubtless intensified if the situation in which one must choose is that of war and the consequences involve the fate of other people's lives. Far from a naive defense of freedom, Sartre's existential philosophy acknowledged the difficulty of making choices in a world that is largely beyond one's control, one where the consequences of such choices are grave. Indeed, the tragic brilliance to be found

in Sartre's literary and philosophical work attests to the inherent ambivalence of human choices.

Is it fair, then, to characterize Sartre as a philosopher of freedom, a writer in defense of liberty? From the outset of his intellectual career, he recognized the intransigent character of the world, its opacity, its resistance to alteration by the human will. One may well be free, but what does freedom mean in a world characterized by disorder, irrationality, and catastrophe? Freedom is thus always a tragic mode of being related to a resistant world. And the world's hostility to freedom is not merely the consequence of the historical moment. This tragic relationship is to be found in the very structure of consciousness. An object appears only partially; it resists consciousness. Another human being appears inscrutable; he reminds us of our limits. In 1939 Sartre wrote, "This world is *difficult.* . . . [Difficulty] is there, on the world." The field of objects and other individuals remains strange, opaque, hostile, and inapprehensible until consciousness can find itself expressed in the world that it encounters. In everyday perception, consciousness designates objects and others through negation, through the act that posits things as *not* consciousness. But this antagonism between consciousness and its world does not result in a thoroughly pessimistic conclusion. A consciousness thoroughly knowledgeable about the world, a freedom that finds its limits nowhere—these cannot be produced by everyday perception, but they can be the fruits of a thoroughly imaginary world.

Evident in Sartre's earliest philosophical and literary works is the conviction that the imagination is an experience of freedom unfettered by "difficulty," released from the usual material constraints. Sartre identified the imagination and imaginary works as the locus of a temporary reconciliation between consciousness and world in the two early tracts on the imagination, *L'Imagination* (*Imagination: A Psychological Critique,* 1936) and *L'Imaginaire* (*The Psychology of the Imagination,* 1940). That Sartre never fully forfeited this view becomes clear in his last great work, published in 1971 and 1972, *L'Idiot de la famille: Gustave Flaubert de 1821 à 1857* (*The Family Idiot*).

Indeed, Sartre is not only a philosopher of freedom but, perhaps more descriptively, a philosopher of the imaginary. In an important sense the imaginary—the world of dreams, of images, of fictional works, of visions of the future—attests to the impossibility of fulfillment in a present that is hostile to freedom. The imaginary is freedom postponed and deferred, the vestige of freedom in the face of intransigence. For Sartre, then, to be free is to be caught in a tragic bind: to be unsuited for the world in which one finds oneself, exiled by virtue of one's constitution, as a free being. And yet this sense of existence as rife with irresolution may be either the source of anguish or, significantly, the source of creativity. To create an imaginary world that can suppress the "difficulty" of the world, to create a well-carved reflection of a freedom that endures—this is the task of the imagination caught in existential impasse. Hence, if we are to discover the concrete meaning of freedom in a hostile world, we must look for the capacity to imagine.

It is always questionable to maintain that a writer has only one central insight, and that is not my purpose here. A prolific and diverse writer, Sartre immediately escapes any effort to categorize him in definitive terms. Is he primarily a philosopher? After all, he wrote *L'Être et le néant: Essai d'ontologie phénoménologique* (*Being and Nothingness: An Essay on Phenomenological Ontology,* 1943), which was received internationally as one of the most significant philosophical works of the twentieth century. But perhaps he is more appropriately considered a novelist. Awarded the Nobel Prize for literature in 1964, Sartre was acclaimed as having introduced an absurdist literary genre that typified the modern experience of displacement and solitude. And yet not long after these philosophical and literary triumphs, Sartre embarked upon a career as a political spokesman and essayist, first in his capacity as editor of *Les temps modernes* (a progressive journal that examined the role of the intellectual in French political life), then as a self-identified Communist, and finally as a socialist humanist sympathetic to Maoism.

Reflecting upon this varied and colorful career, one might be tempted to see nothing but discontinuity, sudden shifts, conversions, and changes of directions, and conclude that Sartre was a man of multiple identities for whom no simple categorization would suffice. In a sense that conclusion would be right. Sartre detested categorization in general, fearing that being placed in a category would deprive him of his freedom as an active and changing thinker. And we may understand his sudden shifts of direction and allegiance as so many efforts to escape the rigid categories that others were ready to prepare for him. In a dramatic gesture Sartre refused to accept the Nobel Prize, informing the Swedish Academy that he did not want to become "an institution."

So what are we to make of this elusive Sartre? My suggestion is that we consider his slipperiness as the very attribute that needs to be explained. Even through the shifts of position and politics, Sartre was a thinker and writer who sought to free his thought from the reifying categories of institutionalized academe. Rather than become a thinglike entity, a category or institution, Sartre exemplified his theory of consciousness in his own person, in the career of his own consciousness as an irreducible spontaneity, the manifestation of freedom and individuality. Let us then consider this career as a sustained effort to safeguard freedom in the face of intransigence, to elude the rigid categories of the institutionalized intellect, and to imagine possible ways of transfiguring a hostile world.

Before we can ask who Sartre is, we must, in Sartrian terms, reflect upon the more general problem of how it is possible to understand another human being. In a sense this was the question that preoccupied Sartre, first as a novelist in his efforts to create plausible characters, then as an "existential psychoanalyst" who sought to understand the general structure of the individual in terms of his abiding projects, and then, quite obviously, as a biographer who sought to reconstruct the lives of other human beings through the written remnants of their lives. We cannot attempt a biography of Sartre, but we can perhaps discern the fundamental projects that structured his life. And we can take as our guideline the various inquiries into "self" and "others" that Sartre himself accomplished.

THE NOTHINGNESS OF THE SELF

The hero of *La nausée* (*Nausea,* 1938), Roquentin, discovers in himself a growing awareness of death. Every moment threatens to bring him closer to that inevitable fatality; indeed, every moment promises that death will arrive just that much sooner. And objects, too, appear as so many lifeless things, inanimate and impenetrable, without any reason for existing. This sudden recognition of purposelessness and mortality plunges Roquentin into a series of internal monologues in which he questions the justification for his own existence and concludes that existence is that which has no justification, no intrinsic meaning or necessity. For the duration of the novel, this recognition produces only nausea and dread, the feeling

that everything that exists is superfluous, both "too much" and "unnecessary." Indeed, the material world, including his own body, offends Roquentin, and he recoils at the thought that he is, like an animal or a plant, yet another piece of material subject to the transience of life on earth.

As Roquentin surveys the world of objects about him, he is struck by their contingency. In other words, there is no reason why they should exist rather than not exist. This insight fills him with nausea, the felt sense of endless possibilities. Among the contingent objects he encounters is his own existence, although he is clear that he differs drastically from the objects that surround him. They are dense and solid, material yet contingent, and although his body shares certain material features with theirs, he is distinguished by his consciousness. He *sees* the trees, the garden, the face of the woman he meets on the street; but this seeing, this consciousness, is not a thing among things. Indeed, it is nothing, for it has neither substance nor materiality of its own.

Written in 1938, *Nausea* marks a significant development in Sartre's literary and philosophical career. Roquentin is divided against himself—a material object, mortal, yet also a nothingness, a consciousness, that appears to persist in its own manner as a nonmaterial existence. As a novel *Nausea* is a drama of consciousness not unlike the novels of William Faulkner, Marcel Proust, or James Joyce. As a means of investigating consciousness, *Nausea* is a modernist text, and its hero is an antihero. Roquentin constantly discovers his own limits, and his is the agony of a thoroughly secular vision, one that is, however, not so distanced from the illusions of redemption as not to long for their re-emergence.

At the close of *Nausea,* Roquentin longs for a world of pure forms, a philosophical redemption from transience, in which perfect shapes, like circles, abound. He imagines pure nonmaterial circles, figures with a fully imaginary existence, figures at once complete and infinite, transcending the fatal linearity of human life. But finally Roquentin settles on a slightly different solution and resolves to write the story of consciousness that he has lived, to give it form and hence a second life. In the final pages of *Nausea,* Sartre gives us a theory of literary forms as secular miracles, as if the writing of experience were its redemption from transience. As we shall see, this theory of literature will undergo a number of revisions throughout Sartre's career.

Before writing *Nausea* in the mid 1930's, Sartre traveled to Berlin in the period 1933–1934 to study the work of Edmund Husserl, the leading German phenomenologist. Sartre was interested in an investigation of consciousness, but he sought to avoid idealist theories that would cast doubt on the capacity of consciousness directly to apprehend the reality of things. Tired of philosophical positions that claimed that human beings could know their own representations of objects but never the objects themselves, Sartre understood that phenomenology resolved to return to "the things themselves." Before hearing of Husserl, Sartre had discussed his philosophical notions in private with Simone de Beauvoir, his lover and companion, and Paul Nizan during his studies at the École Normale Supérieure in the period 1924–1929, when he was in his early twenties.

After serving as a meteorologist in the army from 1929 to 1931, he returned to Le Havre to teach philosophy; he was considered a tough and enthusiastic teacher. During that time a famous encounter with Raymond Aron occurred that in some ways resulted both in the writing of *Nausea* and in the early writings on phenomenology. Despite Roquentin's momentary hankering after Platonic solutions, Sartre himself sought a philosophical perspective that would at once resist the conflation of consciousness and world, and yet endow consciousness with the power really to know that which is utterly different from itself. In her memoir *La force de l'age* (*The Prime of Life*), Simone de Beauvoir records the encounter with Aron that eventually propelled Sartre to Berlin:

Raymond Aron was spending a year at the French institute in Berlin and studying Husserl simultaneously with preparing a historical thesis. When he came to Paris he spoke of Husserl to Sartre. We spent an evening together at the Bec de Gaz in the Rue Montparnasse. We ordered the specialty of the house, apricot cocktails; Aron said, pointing to his glass: "You see, my dear fellow, if you are a phenomenologist, you can talk about this cocktail and make philosophy out of it!" Sartre turned pale with emotion at this. Here was just the thing he had been longing to achieve for years—to describe objects just as he saw and touched them, and extract philosophy from the process.

(Peter Green trans., p. 112)

Husserl's phenomenological philosophy disrupted the terms of the usual philosophical debates of the time in France. Because philosophy was taught in universities governed by the state ministry of education, certain philosophical courses of study were required and these tended to support certain kinds of philosophical positions rather than others. The philosophy most acceptable to the state university system appeared to be a kind of neo-Kantianism that centered on the idealist theory of representationalism. According to this theory, one could never get beyond one's own thinking to reach an exterior world. The discovery of German philosophers like Georg W. F. Hegel and Husserl during the 1930's and 1940's permitted philosophers to relate their discipline to concrete historical and personal experiences in the world. In Husserl, Sartre discovered a liberation from representationalism. Objects were no longer mental pictures that were "in" the mind; indeed, the mind was not a repository at all, but rather a relationship to the world. Preferring to call this relationship "consciousness," Sartre learned from Husserl that consciousness was necessarily related to the world, that consciousness had no "being" of its own but was always a consciousness "of" the world.

Roquentin makes a similar discovery in *Nausea.* Nowhere can he find the consciousness that takes in the world, and yet it does effectively apprehend objects and others outside itself. Operating incessantly, an impulsively referential activity, it is not itself a substance. Sartre makes use of imagery to describe the phenomenon of consciousness: it is the "quick, obscure image of a burst," "clear as strong wind," "a sliding beyond itself." Although it is not the same as the objects and the others that it apprehends, consciousness is always related to them. The structure of this relationship is, in phenomenological terms, called intentionality.

In *The Psychology of Imagination,* published in 1940, Sartre suggests that this intentional relation to the world is present in a variety of forms of consciousness: in the imagination, in the emotions, and in perception. These modes of consciousness are not stable, interior structures or faculties of the mind; indeed, they are not interior to anything. They are various modes of being related to the world, spontaneous outbursts toward the world. Loving something, fearing it, loathing it, or needing it—these are all intentional relations to something real. The consequences of this view of intentionality were significant for Sartre. His work on the imagination disputed those theories that held imagination to be nonreferential. In their place Sartre suggested that imagining a thing was a way of being related to it in the mode of de-realization. Images could no longer be understood as meaningless, bearing no relationship to reality; images transfigured reality, and this transfiguration was the very mode of their relatedness.

In 1939 Sartre published *Esquisse d'une théorie des émotions* (*The Emotions: Outline of a Theory*), which argued that emotions, rather than interior disturbances or confusions of some kind, were ways of being related to the world. To be angry is not merely to suffer some chemically induced agitation, but to be angry at something exterior to oneself, or perhaps at oneself. In any case, anger has an object, and the effect of anger is to saturate consciousness with itself in order temporarily to blot out the offensive object. Hence, anger is related to its object in the mode of negation, although the negating is less real than magical. Indeed, for Sartre all emotion has a magical quality. The joyous person waiting for the beloved to arrive on the train jumps up and down in a kind of dance of joy. The dance both anticipates the arrival of the beloved and preempts it—it is as if the time between waiting and the arrival is magically eclipsed by the dance, which magically instates the other person even in his or her absence.

As in Roquentin's quest for an aesthetic redemption of experience, in the structure of the imagination and emotions Sartre pursues a temporary relief from the purely perceptual experience of the world. Although objects appear to us in perception as only partial (they cannot show all of their dimensions at once), they appear complete to the imagination. And although we are powerless to force the train to arrive earlier than it will, we can imagine its presence and effect an emotional incantation of its arrival.

Sartre's novelistic and philosophical pursuits in the 1930's centered on the problem of consciousness, its status as an intentional relationship, its power to transfigure the world through emotional, imaginative, and literary means. But these primarily epistemological studies were restricted to the problems of knowing and apprehending exterior objects. And although Sartre expanded the meaning and scope of consciousness, he was moved to consider an even deeper set of problems. Can we speak about the emotions without first asking who experiences these emotions? Who imagines and who writes? Is there perhaps a single project that is expressed in the intentional structure of consciousness? What kind of being is a human being such that it is constantly apprehending and transfiguring that which is exterior to itself? And what about the apprehension of other human beings? Does that not perhaps have a distinctive structure? Sartre's investigations of epistemology thus turned to more fundamental questions of ontology, and the question of how and what we know gradually became subordinated to the question of who and what we are.

If *Nausea* was a documentation of consciousness, Sartre's ensuing novelistic enterprises tended to be more concerned with character and plot. Just as Husserl's phenomenology offered Sartre a philosophic route into the world of mundane affairs, so his novels expanded their scope and became increasingly concerned with the choices and actions of individuals in complex historical situations. As World War II threatened to become reality in 1938, Sartre began work on *Les chemins de la liberté* (The Roads to Freedom), a trilogy of historical novels situated in France during the advent of war, the experience of occupation, and the drama of liberation. *L'Âge de raison* (*The Age of Reason*), the first novel of the trilogy, published in 1945, depicts a philosophy instructor, Mathieu, who finds that his philosophical defense of freedom is increasingly difficult to realize in his complex personal and political situation. Also published in 1945, the second novel of the trilogy, *Le sursis* (*The Reprieve*), depicts a world more dramatically out of control as the Munich Pact appeared to consolidate the Stalin-Hitler offensive.

Although the first volume treated the characters as individuals faced with the possibility of forfeiting their separate lives for a more collective identity, the second volume attempted to identify the individual fates of the characters with that of France as a nation. Sartre intended the works to be a continuation of *Nausea* and wanted to encourage his readership to consider Mathieu as a Roquentin faced with the prospect of war. If Roquentin discovered himself as a free and contingent consciousness, Mathieu continues that discovery, learning that he is free to lie, cheat, and steal in order to protect himself. As a figure for the French public under occupation, Mathieu presented a contemptible image for the French to ponder. Unsurprisingly, the publication of the novels produced an outraged reaction.

Between the first and second volumes, Sar-

tre worked on *Being and Nothingness,* a philosophical inquiry that brought Husserl's phenomenological method to bear on a theory of freedom and, most significantly, a vision of human beings as a product of their own choices. Written first in a series of notebooks that Sartre kept in the military during the period 1939–1940, *Being and Nothingness* sought to identify the nothingness of consciousness (Sartre's phenomenological insight) with the nothingness of the self (Roquentin's self-discovery). The result was an utterly original philosophical vision—what Sartre termed "phenomenological ontology"—that later became existentialism. As consciousness was a spontaneous outburst toward the world, an incessant referentiality, so human beings could be understood, like Mathieu, as compelled to situate themselves in the world, to be projected toward the world—indeed, to "exist" only to the extent that they commit themselves to various actions.

The doctrine of intentionality was thus replaced by the notion of "a project." Significantly, human beings have no identity—they are nothing—except to the extent that they create an identity through sustained relationships with objects and others outside themselves. Moreover, the only way to sustain these relationships is through the effort of making choices. Hence, the spontaneity of consciousness, its relentless directedness toward exterior objects and others, becomes identified as the choice at the foundation of every human individual; and from now on, consciousness is understood as a manifestation of freedom, and Sartre's epistemological concerns are subordinated to his inquiry into human beings in their primary characterization as free.

How, then, are we to conceive of human beings? What kind of "being" is a human being? Sartre makes clear in *Being and Nothingness* that human reality is not a kind of being but a lack, a void, a nothingness. To be human means not to "be" in any stable sense. Whereas in the case of material objects it is possible to assume a relationship of self-identity (a thing is what it is and, for that reason, not some other thing), human reality poses a quite different ontological situation. As Sartre would put it, human reality signifies a "rift" in being, an ontological scandal. In distinction from self-subsisting, fully actualized beings, human beings are fields of open possibility. Born into a world without a fixed identity or value, human beings must construct themselves, realizing certain possibilities and letting others remain unrealized. The self that emerges in the course of experience is constructed through the series of choices and actions that only retrospectively confer a characteristic meaning upon the agency of those actions. No longer can we refer to a silent, essential self buried in the depths of the soul, as yet unrealized. There is no necessity that we become the kinds of individuals that we eventually do become; in principle, we could become some other kind of individual. There is no mystery to the self that we have; it is our creation and, for that reason, our burden. Nothing is predetermined about our individual existence except that we must choose it in some way; there is no freedom not to choose, for that refusal becomes its own kind of choice. Inasmuch as choice is the realization of possibilities, it is the modality by which an agent brings himself into existence, and yet this choice is not a single event, a self-inception that, once effected, becomes a fact of the past. In a daily sense we choose ourselves again and again; this constitutes the openness and malleability of our existence, but also what Sartre terms "the burden of freedom."

Opposing Freudian psychoanalysis on the grounds that it misunderstood the complexity of consciousness and tended to reduce the individual to primary drives, Sartre developed his own alternative, existential psychoanalysis, which made the notion of choice into its primary explanatory tool. What Freud termed "unconscious," Sartre interpreted as pre-reflective consciousness. Sartre argued that individuals may not always have a lucid understanding of why they are acting in the ways that they do, but that, upon reflective scrutiny, they can realize that they have chosen to act in this way, although the choice may not have been deliberate. In maintaining that there was a significant meaning to a non-deliberate choice, Sartre hoped to account for the occasional opacity of human actions within the terms of consciousness. At stake for Sartre was the autonomy of the individual, something that Freudian psychoanalysis in its bifurcation of the psyche into conscious and unconscious processes appeared to discourage. Moreover, the autonomy of the individual was crucial to the theory of responsibility at the core of Sartre's philosophical program. Only human beings who could recover and appropriate their own motivations in toto could be held fully responsible for their actions.

Sartre insisted that every individual can be understood as a unity of choices. Acts can be traced back to prior choices, and these choices are unified or internally consistent in that collectively they express a unitary project of the individual. This individual project is not identical with the myriad specific choices that an individual makes, although the project is manifest in those choices and only in those choices. As a coherent style or pattern of choice, the project constitutes the specific choices as a unified set. Moreover, in an important sense, the individual's project, what Sartre terms "the fundamental project," is not exclusively his or her own. Every individual, in virtue of being human, strives for the same goal, "the desire to be," which Sartre calls "the original project." Because human reality is nothing save what it makes of itself, it is always craving a substantial identity that it cannot have.

But why should this be the case? Why should individuals wish to resolve their freedom into a substantial, self-identical, objectified reality? Why don't they simply rejoice in their freedom and go on about the business of daily life? Being free, individuals are without a necessary ground or reason to exist; indeed, being free, they are compelled to endow themselves with a reason for existing. This groundlessness produces anxiety that, in turn, gives rise to the desire to achieve fixity, stability, and necessity. Because freedom is burdensome, human beings desire to throw off this burden by assuming a thinglike posture. The conservative moment of all desire, this is the resolve to relinquish desire, to be finally what one is and nothing more, the Sartrian transcription of Thanatos.

Sartre examines this tendency under the rubric of "bad faith." One example he gives is of Pierre the waiter, Pierre who has become a waiter, whose every act and gesture exude his essence as a waiter. One cannot separate him from his identity; he has embodied it with a vengeance, as if it were dictated from birth. Originally a role that Pierre must have practiced, being-a-waiter has become a fixed identity, a necessary existence. Pierre has not stopped choosing his role, but he has also chosen to conceal the reality of that choice. Assuming the role as a necessity, he is, in Sartrian terms, acting in bad faith.

Bad faith, then, is precisely the pretense of being a thing, the transformation of a choosing and dynamic human existence into the semblance of a material object. And yet, bad faith is bound to fail. Because freedom can be concealed but never effectively negated, bad faith is bound to become a dissatisfying project. As much as human beings experience freedom as a burden, they are willing to sacrifice freedom only with ambivalence. Once they are entombed as a thing, ensconced in bad faith, anxiety persists, this time as the anxious desire to be free. Hence, coupled with the desire to be is the desire to be free, and these two desires coexist in continuous tension with one another. This paradox of freedom and necessity is only temporarily resolved through the strategies of bad faith, where bad faith designates either a posture of total necessity or a posture of total freedom (I am *not* a waiter, *not* a Frenchman, *not* any determinate thing, but a pure, elusive freedom). In the former case bad faith dramatizes the self as a self-identical being, a being who is what it is and nothing more, that is, a being who has resolved its

quarrel with freedom and has won. In the latter case bad faith is the posture of pure flight, the dramatization of the self as never being what it appears, a principle of negativity and escape, the triumph of freedom over necessity.

Sartre concludes in *Being and Nothingness* that every individual desires a resolution to this ontological paradox, a reconciliation of freedom and necessity. But this idealized synthesis remains an impossible dream, the purely imaginary object and telos of all human desire. In Sartrian terms this is the "desire to be God," and it is shared universally by every individual.

What would it mean to be "God" in the sense that Sartre intends and why is it impossible? In the first place, to be God would be to choose the facts of one's own situation, the material conditions into which one is born, one's own body, the history that precedes one's own birth. In point of fact, however, these factual dimensions of the world are not the product and expression of individual freedom, but appear instead as brute and resistant otherness, the absolute opposite of freedom. And yet, if human beings could be God, they would be able to ground facticity. Second, one's individual freedom would be the necessary result of one's material and historical station in the world; it would have a purpose and meaning that could be easily derived from the historical and material dimensions of one's existence. In other words, the world in all its facticity would be infused with the human will, its creation and expression.

If human beings are not God, and if they cannot hope to be God, why do they continue, against the odds, to entertain the desire to be God? As if freedom were the vestige of an anachronistic theological dream, the free individual aspires to a kind of efficacy impossible within the material constraints of the world. In a sense freedom acts as God in exile, but insofar as it is human freedom, it is a captive deity, trapped within a resistant material world. Not unlike Sartre's own position in German-occupied France in the early 1940's, the experience of being "outside" a world that one is invariably "in," existence is described as captivity and exile at the same time. But in *Being and Nothingness* the intransigence of the world is its brute facticity, conceived as an existentially invariant feature and not, as yet, a consequence of historical circumstance.

Because there can be no lasting reconciliation between a free consciousness and an intransigent world, there can only be a dream of reconciliation. One can imagine an efficacious transfiguration of the world of facts that would reflect the human will, but that is a vain imagining. Or is it? One who realizes the dream through expression, one who writes the dream and fashions it in aesthetic and communicable form, is an artist who transforms some aspect of the material world to reflect his or her own will. Later we shall see that Sartre considered praxis as a kind of politically informed transformation of facticity and, indeed, sought to subordinate his theory of art to that political program. But first, let us consider the optimism that Sartre entertained with regard to artistic work, especially literary ones, to realize the impossible dream of being God.

SARTRE'S SIDEWAYS EYE ON POSTERITY

One might conclude that Sartre's ontology of human exile is a pessimistic vision but still consider the rich aesthetic consequences of an ontology of human existence that necessitates human beings to be dreamers compelled to realize their dreams. Ontological exile thus becomes the condition of aesthetic creativity. In his biographical studies—*Baudelaire* (1946), *Saint Genet, comédien et martyr* (*Saint Genet: Actor and Martyr,* 1952) and *The Family Idiot*—Sartre combined an inquiry into the fundamental projects of these individuals with an analysis of the ontological sources of aesthetic creativity. In his autobiography *Les mots* (*The Words,* 1964) Sartre is similarly preoccupied with the fundamental project of the literary

writer, with the life that is propelled by the abiding desire to write. In all four cases the original project to be God is manifest in a fundamental project to be an author of compelling imaginary worlds. Intended as concrete examples of his own theory of existential psychoanalysis, Sartre's biographies also aim at uncovering the truth about their subjects. But, considered closely, they reveal traces of a self-analysis as well. What Sartre shares with his biographical subjects is a fundamental desire, an abiding project, to become necessary in and through the written word. After all, Sartre's autobiography is not entitled "Sartre's Life," "Sartre's Words," or even "My Words," but *The Words.* These are words that assume an autonomous and necessary status, eternal or divine words that surpass and sustain the life that creates them.

In 1947, however, Sartre proposed a radically different purpose for literature in his *Qu'est-ce que la littérature?* (*What Is Literature?*). He called for an engaged and committed literature that defended definite political positions and demanded a critical appraisal of contemporary political viewpoints from its readership. Although *Nausea* appeared to defend literature in virtue of its own formal and aesthetic qualities, *What Is Literature?* subordinates the aesthetic value of literature to its ethical or political purpose. The former version of literary works as secular miracles, ways of transcending the transience of life, contradicts the latter version of literary forms as political tools. If one writes in response to a contemporary situation, the relevance of the writing risks being circumscribed by the immediate situation. Indeed, it would be difficult to conceive of such writing as the literary equivalent of a Platonic form.

In *What Is Literature?* Sartre maintains that every writer must ask for whom he writes. But in the case of Sartre himself, the answer is not immediately clear. He was uncertain about his audience, at times directing his works to his contemporaries, and at others writing for the future readers who would guarantee the perpetuity of his name. As early as 1939 Sartre recorded this tension in his literary views; he questioned whether one wrote to escape or to transform one's life. In *Les carnets de la drôle de guerre: Novembre 1939–Mars 1940* (*The War Diaries,* 1983) he writes: "I don't think I'm being over-schematic if I say that the moral problem which has preoccupied me up till now is basically one of relations between art and life." As we shall see, this tension continued to characterize his entire career.

Consider the following dialogue between Sartre and Simone de Beauvoir in 1974, just six years before his death. (The short story "Pour un papillon" [For a Butterfly] was written by Sartre as a child.)

SARTRE: When I originally wrote "Pour un Papillon" (For a Butterfly), I wrote something absolute . . . which was, in short, myself. I carried myself over into an everlasting life. An artistic creation outlives mundane things. If I bring one into existence, it outlasts mundane things and therefore I, the author that it embodies, I outlast mundane things. Behind this there was the Christian idea of immortality—I passed from mortal to immortal life.

DE BEAUVOIR: And it was that notion which came to an end when you reached your committed writing?

SARTRE: It came to an end entirely.

DE BEAUVOIR: There was no idea of salvation anymore? It's never come again? I imagine the very notion has faded away? Not that that means you haven't kept an eye, a rather sideways eye [*un coup d'oeil, un peu en biais*], on posterity.

SARTRE: Until after *Nausea* I had only dreamed of genius, but after the war, in 1945, I'd proved myself—there was *No Exit* and there was *Nausea.* In 1944, when the Allies left Paris, I possessed genius and I set off for America as a writer of genius who was going for a tour in another country. At that point I was immortal and I was assured of my immortality. And that meant I no longer had to think about it.

(Quoted in Simone de Beauvoir, *Adieux: A Farewell to Sartre,* pp. 152–153)

In the same dialogue Sartre explained that once his immortality was assured, he could turn with ease to the mundane world of politics: ". . . it's better not to think of immortality, except out of the corner of your eye [*sauf du coin de l'oeil*], but rather to stake everything on life." And yet, "out of the corner of his eye," Sartre made sure posterity was his. De Beauvoir's playful references to Sartre's wall eye, including the suggestion that he might be able to look in two directions at once, suggest a serious framework for Sartre's dual identity as politician and aesthete. Just as peripheral vision may be said to enhance central vision, so Sartre's immortal sense of self enabled and illuminated his political career.

Sartre's reliance on visual metaphors for describing his relationship to his audience suggests a spectatorial (rather than an engaged) authorship. Indeed, Sartre was watchful of others, somewhat distanced and detached, and especially watchful of the gaze that might be turned on him. The section in *Being and Nothingness* titled "Concrete Relations with Others" argues that the primary relationship between individuals is a mixture of distrust and dependency. Because the self is an immaterial nothingness, it knows itself only when it becomes an object for itself. In rarefied instances it becomes an object when expressed in a literary work. But for the most part self-knowledge requires the presence of other selves who reflect the self in and through their "look." In a significant sense the look of the Other gives the self its objectivity, for the Other can see the self as an object, but the self can become an object for itself, and therefore knowable, only by taking on the point of view of the Other. Sartre capitalizes "the Other" in *Being and Nothingness* because it is a generalized Other, the point of view of anyone who views the self from the outside, anyone capable of this objectifying look.

Because we cannot wholly objectify ourselves, we remain inevitably opaque to ourselves, dependent on others to get a glimpse of how we appear. In *Huis clos* (*No Exit*), a play published in 1945, this point is dramatized through the hellish interaction of three characters, all of whom wield the authority of the "look" to objectify and possess each other. The viewpoint of the Other is, by definition, more comprehensive than that of the self, and the Other can pierce the bad faith of the self, exposing its characteristic ploys and strategies and reducing it to its appearance.

The "look" suggests that human beings stand at a spectatorial distance from each other, that they are separated by a necessary space across which they see one another more clearly than they can ever see themselves. Hence, the look suggests yet another constraint upon individual freedom, a way in which the self is socially constituted against its will. The self may give itself a meaning or value, but the Other, wielding the power of objectification, may refute that self-evaluation and expose that self-definition as a sham. Futile though it may be, the self desires a release from the look of the Other in order to be the source of its own objectivity. But here again, this Godlike project is impossible. Constrained by its own perspective, the self cannot exist fully except under the gaze of the Other, although the Other may not see the self as it would wish to be seen. In other words, the self needs the Other in order to exist, but existence is achieved at the price of freedom and self-definition. This struggle between autonomy and dependence constitutes the battlefield of interpersonal relations and leads Sartre to conclude that "Hell is other people."

But can this hell be transformed? The function of literature for Sartre is to objectify the author in a communicable, aesthetic form and, further, to command the recognition of others who will give that author an objective and enduring existence. In the case of politically committed literature, the author engages others to consider the bad faith in which they live: here the author is the Other whose look, transcribed in the text of the play or novel, exposes the audience for what they are. And yet, even in this version of political art as pedagogy and indictment, the audience still retains the power to "look at" Sartre. But where is he, and what does he show of himself? Does he participate in the world he describes and show himself as an actor in the scenes that he devises? Sartre is not there to be seen but is instead the ever-seeing eye, the pretense of omniscience that looks at everyone but is never seen. Can this grand spectator create an engaged literature and an effective political program? How will he fare as he enters the domain of everyday life?

In *War Diaries* Sartre maintained, "I think with my eyes." In a philosophical critique of Sartre, Maurice Merleau-Ponty suggested that the look was not an adequate concept for explaining interpersonal relations. In *Visible et l'invisible* (*The Visible and the Invisible* 1968), a late and incomplete work, Merleau-Ponty argues (against Sartre) that human beings are not born into the world in physical isolation from one another, that the first and primary mode of interrelatedness is that of touch, not sight. Elaborating on his critique of Sartrian premises, Merleau-Ponty suggests that Sartre overestimates the spectatorial point of view, and that he cannot see or comprehend the interrelations between individuals, or between social and natural existence, precisely because he has already, through the adoption of the spectator role, excluded himself from those domains. As one who watches the world, Sartre never discovers himself as a body among bodies, participating in a sensual universe that binds the individual to the world of others and material objects. In effect, Merleau-Ponty argues that a philosophy of engagement cannot be derived from Sartrian premises, that Sartre cannot relax his watchful eye long enough to enter and engage in the everyday world. In other words, through taking up the position of the spectator, Sartre has deprived himself of the very experience of the world that he wishes to describe. In what follows, we will watch this spectator in the midst of historical events and assess whether Merleau-Ponty was right.

"A STROLLER IN THE PARIS INSURRECTION"

Not until the age of thirty-six did Sartre begin to consider himself a political writer and actor. The year was 1941, and Sartre, on leave from his military post, vowed to Simone de Beauvoir that he must find a more active way to oppose the war. Although Sartre's life was surrounded by world events, he remained aloof from their consequences until the war appeared to impinge upon him directly. He first joined the military at the age of nineteen and learned meteorology. After two years of service, he taught philosophy at the lycée in Le Havre, and in 1933 traveled to Berlin to study Edmund Husserl and Martin Heidegger for a year. After returning to France in late 1934, he continued to teach sporadically, to work on *Nausea,* and to write phenomenological treatises on the emotions, the imagination, and the structure of consciousness. On 1 September 1939, Sartre's budding literary and philosophical career was interrupted by World War II; he was part of a military reserve force that was called up for duty. Assigned to Alsace during the winter of 1939–1940, Sartre enjoyed a prolonged term of leisure because Germany, which had already declared war, waited to invade France until May 1940. This inactive period was called the *drôle de guerre* (Phony War; literally, "joke of a war"), and it provided Sartre with time to write in his diary, which was eventually published as *The War Diaries.*

The diaries contained extensive notes for *Being and Nothingness* as well as early drafts of *The Words,* a project that was to take ten years to complete. Although Sartre wanted his diary to be a war diary, recording the experience of a man in the midst of war, he himself was nowhere near the center of action. Indeed, for him the war meant solitude, leisure, and the uninterrupted time to write. And yet, on leave in 1940, Sartre voiced to Simone de Beauvoir a fear of the impending consequences of European fascism and vowed to supplement his contemplative existence with some more active

form of resistance. Upon return to his post, he was imprisoned by the Germans for nine months and released in March 1941 because of ill health. While in prison he was given a copy of Heidegger's *Sein und Zeit* (*Being and Time,* 1927), and continued to have the time to write.

During the spring and early summer of 1941, Sartre traveled to the south of France to consult with André Malraux and other progressive intellectuals who had sought sanctuary far from occupied Paris. He helped to organize a resistance group called Socialisme et Liberté, which helped to distribute underground literature and participated in producing the underground journal *Les lettres françaises.* Toward the end of the war the group released a number of statements defending the sanctity of freedom, but it never became involved in acts of violence or sabotage.

Although antifascist in his sentiments, Sartre was not prepared to defend communism during the war years. Indeed, he remained committed to his own philosophy of freedom— what became existentialism in the postwar years. Determined to defend his status as a free intellectual and yet to maintain sympathy with antifascist ideologies, Sartre pursued a double course as a defender of freedom and a sympathizer with Communist aims.

Upon his release from the prison camp, Sartre had returned to Paris to find that the publishing houses were either under German control or had made compromising deals with the occupation forces in order to maintain some of their independence. Gallimard, a well-regarded publisher of contemporary philosophical and literary works, had agreed to cease publishing Jewish authors in return for its continued independence. Knowing that Gallimard had agreed to this restriction, Sartre nevertheless published *Being and Nothingness* with the firm in 1943. A year earlier Albert Camus had agreed, under the same conditions, to publish *L'Étranger* (*The Stranger*) with Gallimard. After the war there was some effort on the part of leftist writers to censure those publishers who had struck deals with the German forces. Sartre rose in defense of Gallimard, claiming that what mattered was that such houses were able to publish significant literature because of these deals.

Ironically, the years of the occupation were extremely lucrative for both Sartre and Simone de Beauvoir. Sartre's plays *Les mouches* (*The Flies,* 1943) and *No Exit* were produced without objections by the German censors, and de Beauvoir published *L'Invitée* (*She Came to Stay*). Jewish writers of the time were in prison, underground, or in exile, and other antifascist writers refused to publish or produce their work under the terms of Nazi-occupied France. Sartre agreed, on the other hand, to open *The Flies,* his existentialist version of the *Oresteia,* at the Théâtre de la Cité, which had been the Sarah Bernhardt Theatre before it was "purified" of that actress's Jewish name.

In November 1946 Sartre published *Réflexions sur la question juive* (*Anti-Semite and Jew*), which addressed the problem of anti-Semitism among the French. He argued that the Jew represented the Other for the French bourgeoisie, the projection of their fears and the locus of their bad faith. Clearly intended as a sequel to Marx's *Judenfrage* (*The Jewish Question*), *Anti-Semite and Jew* proposed a socialist democracy in which ethnic differences would be subordinated to the universal rights of human beings. Although the work was an often stunning exposé of the anti-Semite, Sartre's characterization of the Jew was less successful; indeed, his characterizations occasionally tended to affirm the anti-Semite rather than refute him. As a political defense of Judaism, the result was fairly ambivalent.

Sartre's efforts at political analysis more often than not seemed double-edged. While his intentions were invariably progressive (against fascism, against anti-Semitism, for principles of equality and freedom), his methods were less sure. As the war drew to a close, Camus organized a progressive journal, *Combat,* which included Sartre, Aron, Merleau-Ponty, and de Beauvoir on its editorial staff. In one of the first issues Sartre wrote an article

on his experience of the liberation. The title, "Un promeneur dans Paris insurgé" (A Stroller in the Paris Insurrection), expresses Sartre's paradoxical position as the leisurely spectator recounting the joy, the disbelief, and even the anguish of the French as the Allies arrived in Paris.

In the autumn of 1945, Sartre founded *Les temps modernes* with Aron and other leftist intellectuals. In the first few years the journal considered the question of whether independent intellectuals could work in tandem with the Communist party and whether culture and politics were autonomous domains. Often quarrels would erupt between *Les temps modernes* and the Communist newspaper *L'Humanité.* Indeed, at the time the official Communist party was skeptical of Sartre, his popularity after the war, and his defense of "bourgeois freedom." Accusing him of decadence and pseudo-Marxism, the Communist parties in France and in the Soviet Union were indifferent toward Sartre's highly deliberated relation to them. Indeed, a radical break between Sartre and the party occurred in 1949, when Sartre and Merleau-Ponty published reports on the existence of Soviet prison camps filled with political dissidents. They estimated that as many as 10 to 15 million individuals were coercively detained in such camps and further claimed that "there is no socialism when one citizen in twenty is in a camp."

The response was vehement. Sartre was denounced by both *L'Humanité* and *Les lettres françaises,* the latter the very journal that, in its earlier underground form, had been quite sympathetic to Sartre. The following two years saw a radical revision in Sartre's political thinking. Rather than maintain the double course of socialism and humanism, he began to reflect on the necessity of aligning himself unconditionally with the Communist party. In 1951 Sartre publicly accepted Stalinism. In the same year he published the play *Le Diable et le bon Dieu* (*The Devil and the Good Lord*), which rejected the posture of political neutrality and argued that the refusal of a political commitment was itself a commitment to reactionary forces. But, more important, the play showed the futility of purely individual action and suggested that atheism was the necessary ideology of class struggle. "Les communistes et la paix" (*The Communists and Peace*), published between July 1952 and April 1954, might well be read as the theoretical equivalent of *The Devil and the Good Lord.* Published first in *Les temps modernes,* Sartre's essay defends the Communist party as the legitimate representative of the proletariat and assails any position that questions the relationship between them. In an interesting twist of existential theory, Sartre maintains that the only authentic choice for anyone in Sartre's historical situation is the defense of communism.

Sartre's dogmatic defense of communism created a number of controversies at *Les temps modernes.* In October 1951 Camus published *Le revolté* (*The Rebel*), which received a damning review in *Les temps modernes* in July 1952. Clearly unwilling to accept either an unwavering Communist alliance or an uncriticial defense of capitalism, Camus reserved a place for morality above the fray of political quarrels. In a sense *The Rebel* came to exactly the opposite conclusion of *The Devil and the Good Lord.* Camus satirized the Marxist notion of history, charging that there were abuses of human rights on both ends of the political spectrum. The review in *Les temps modernes,* written by Francis Jeanson, charged Camus with political and historical naïveté. Camus's reply appeared the following month, addressed to "Sartre, Monsieur le Directeur," suggesting that Jeanson was but a proxy for Sartre. Camus made it clear that he considered Sartre's new Communist identity to be laughable, especially in light of Sartre's long history of political inaction. Camus remarked that he would no longer receive "lessons in efficacy" from those who "never placed anything other than their armchairs in the direction of history. . . ."

Sartre's differences with Merleau-Ponty also were born of Sartre's increasingly dogmatic defense of communism, particularly in its Stalin-ist form. Merleau-Ponty opposed the Soviet role in the Korean War in 1950 and remained disillusioned as a result of the prison camp revelations. Although he strongly defended Soviet communism in *Humanisme et terreur: Essai sur le problème communiste* (*Humanism and Terror: An Essay on the Communist Problem*) in 1947, Merleau-Ponty forfeited his allegiance to the party as its imperialist designs became more clear. As *Les temps modernes* became increasingly pro-Soviet, Merleau-Ponty and others decided that it was no longer desirable to remain on the editorial board.

In 1955 Merleau-Ponty published *Les aventures de la dialectique* (*Adventures of the Dialectic*), which included a long chapter on Sartre's *The Communists and Peace,* titled "Sartre and Ultra-bolshevism." Challenging Sartre on both philosophical and political grounds, Merleau-Ponty argued that Sartre's philosophy of freedom was incompatible with the social theory and political program that Sartre currently defended. In his defense of communism, Sartre was eager to show that the free subject, the choosing agent, was now embodied or represented by the Party. In response Merleau-Ponty charged that this was the thorough effacement of the existing individual and that the Party, conceived as the sole legitimate Subject, portends dangerous and totalitarian consequences. How, Merleau-Ponty asked, can the individual and his freedom become reconciled with a Party elite that acts as the proxy of the membership and presents itself as a unified collectivity? Is this not an instance of bad faith, consciousness resolving itself into a substance, relinquishing the burden of its own freedom?

Merleau-Ponty further charged that there was a missing link in Sartre's argument that was the inevitable consequence of his faulty ontology. Sartre cannot account for a collective subject (or he can only account for one in mistaken ways) because he has no vocabulary for understanding the social world. Because the individual subject is still an ontological priority, the "I" rather than the "we," Sartre can only imagine the Party as an individual subject writ large. The collectivity now becomes the locus of individual freedom and the real individual is effectively erased. Hence, the project to derive a social theory from Sartrian premises culminates in the denial of those very premises.

In 1955 Simone de Beauvoir entered the fray of political quarrels that *Les temps modernes* included among its pages. In her essay "Merleau-Ponty et le pseudo-Sartrisme" (Merleau-Ponty and Pseudo-Sartrianism), she denounced Merleau-Ponty's criticisms, charging that his theory of the social world was a derivation of Sartre's theory in *Being and Nothingness.* Moreover, Sartre's political positions, she reasoned, were an elaboration of the very theory of commitment that characterized his earlier work. From that point on, the break between Merleau-Ponty and Sartre was decisive, although cordial relations were resumed before Merleau-Ponty's tragic death in 1961. Paradoxically, by the time the first volume of his *Critique de la raison dialectique* (*Critique of Dialectical Reason*) appeared in 1960, Sartre had accepted a good many of Merleau-Ponty's criticisms; and after the latter's death Sartre dedicated a special volume of *Les temps modernes* to his work.

In 1956 the Soviet invasion of Hungary prompted a swift revision in Sartre's pro-Communist stance. He could no longer maintain that the party represented the proletariat when it was clearly the party that suppressed a worker-led insurrection in Hungary. Moreover, Sartre was forced to the conclusion that history was perhaps not as teleologically inclined as he had previously thought. The spirit of socialism was not necessarily embodied in official Communist doctrine or policy, and Sartre conceded that a socialist humanism independent of Soviet communism was necessary.

The period 1956–1957 saw the appearance of two important Sartrian documents, "Le fantôme de Staline" (*The Ghost of Stalin*), an elaborate description and denunciation of the Soviet invasion of Hungary, and "Questions de méthode" (*Search for a Method,* first published

in the Polish journal *Twórczosc* under the title "Marksizmi egzistencjalizm," 1957), reprinted in *Les temps modernes,* and published in 1960 as the introduction to the first volume of the *Critique of Dialectical Reason.* In the former essay Sartre maintained that the Communist party had failed its historical mission and regressed to an earlier stage of its development. Rather than contribute to the universal democratization of humankind, it had constructed a new form of oppressive hierarchy. In *Search for a Method* Sartre questioned the relationship between existentialism and Marxism and concluded that existentialism could only be a subsidiary ideology to Marxism, which was the necessary philosophy for the present historical epoch. While criticizing Marxism for not taking into account the individual's concrete situation, the felt experience of labor and alienation, his concrete choices, Sartre also argued that a purely existential framework could not provide a program for socialist emancipation. Incorporating Merleau-Ponty's criticisms and responding to historical events, Sartre undertook the project to examine the relation between individual actions and collective praxis, that is, between individual freedom and the creation of universal history.

This project was further elaborated in the *Critique of Dialectical Reason* as the theory of ensembles, seriality, the fused group, the function of scarcity and need, and the transformative action of collective praxis. Sartre maintained, however, even in *Search for a Method,* that there was a meaning and integrity to history that signified the achievement of universal socialism in the future. Although Sartre rejected a scientific Marxism that would predict historical change on the model of naturalistic processes, he remained committed to a theory of dialectical materialism that envisioned history as a set of successive, internally unified stages. The problem became twofold: What are the constituent actions of individuals that, executed in tandem, result in a revolutionary praxis, a progressive transformation of one historical state of affairs into another? Secondly, how do we account for the possibility of collective action without forfeiting the individual's freedom in the process? For Sartre the reconciliation of Marxism and existentialism hung in the balance. Moreover, he wanted an answer to questions that had concerned him since the inception of his *War Diaries:* What does freedom mean in the context of adverse historical circumstances, and how does the life of the individual express and recapitulate the historical circumstances in which he lives? In short, how are we to conceive the individual in history?

THE "SINGULAR UNIVERSAL": FROM MARXISM TO BIOGRAPHY

Apart from the few years in the early 1950's when he thought that a dogmatic fidelity to the Communist party was necessary, Sartre was always in tension with official ideologies and institutions, as if the tension itself was what attracted him—and perhaps it was. In *Search for a Method,* Sartre made it clear that he now viewed existentialism as an ideology both spawned and criticized by Marxism. But the Marxism that Sartre defended was hardly conventional. In 1975 Sartre was asked whether he preferred being called an "existentialist" or a "Marxist"; he replied that if a label were necessary, he would prefer to be called an existentialist. Later in that same interview Sartre referred to Marxism as a theory he needed to absorb, but that he now endeavored to go beyond.

The *Critique of Dialectical Reason* represents Sartre's most significant contribution to Marxist theory. The question he wanted to pose stems directly from his earlier philosophical and literary pursuits: How do individuals seize upon their historical circumstances and transform them? If this transformation requires collective action, how are these collectivities formed and how do they get to the stage where they can transform history? One might expect Sartre to answer these questions through a specific historical analysis of group formation and revolutionary collectivities, but instead he describes idealized groups in isolation from any given social context. In this sense Sartre claims a transcendental insight into the invariant structures of social reality—hardly a characteristic Marxist position. Indeed, Sartre poses as a phenomenologist who has wandered mistakenly onto Marxist terrain.

Sartre called for a Marxist method that would integrate the actions and political efforts of individuals with a collective, dialectically achieved historical destiny. That destiny would not be enforced or imposed through totalitarian means; it must be the autonomous commitment of every individual. From Marxism, Sartre accepted a notion of historical necessity, the development of history as both unified and dialectically progressive. Inasmuch as history was progressive, it was considered totalizing, engendering ever more integrated forms of social organization until a universal community of democratic socialism would be achieved. Although Sartre once had seen historical events as so much "contingency" and "arbitrariness," he now conceived this contingent and lawless character of historical events to be the product of an alienated consciousness, evidence of their reified status in a system that conceals the workings of its own interrelationships.

For the Sartre of 1960, then, the world remained "difficult," but this difficulty no longer constituted a limit to intellectual analysis. Indeed, the historical conditions of that difficulty, the historical means of its reproduction, are precisely what the Marxist theorist must examine. Moreover, it becomes impossible to decontextualize the life of the individual or to reduce that life to a set of fundamental and self-generated choices. On the other hand, it is crucial to avoid the reification of history, for no history can develop except through the composite effort of individuals. Hence, history retains its character as a progressively unified experience only inasmuch as individuals vow to create this unity, that is, to create a universal democracy. Sartre's metaphysical assertion of the "unity" of history, then, depends essentially on the successful integration of existential premises into Marxism:

> In short, if there is such a thing as the unity of History, the experimenter must see his own life as the Whole and the Part, as the bond between the Parts and the Whole, and as the relation between the Parts, in the dialectical movement of Unification. . . .
>
> (*Critique of Dialectical Reason,* vol. 1, p. 52)

The *Critique of Dialectical Reason* thus traces the careers of individuals as they assume first an identification with a historical group and then resolve to become part of a collective transformation of history. This journey from the particular to the universal undergoes a series of developmental stages, and the successive chapters of the *Critique* constitute a kind of *Bildungsroman* of the revolutionary.

Rife with examples from everyday life, the *Critique of Dialectical Reason* provides descriptions of how group allegiances are formed, how they are both acknowledged and denied, and how an explicit collective identity is forged. In his discussion of people waiting for the bus in the morning, Sartre describes isolated individuals who are nevertheless joined in their act of waiting, their weariness, their utter subjection to an anonymous transportation system that may or may not deliver a bus in time for any of them to get to work. Although their workplaces and occupations may differ radically, they are joined by the historical necessity that they work. Their anger at each other, their struggle to get first in line, their hostility in getting a seat, the way they look at each other without seeming to—all of this constitutes a negative bond of relatedness. Any one of these individuals is both irreducibly himself or herself and necessarily more than himself or herself, identical or interchangeable with an Other. Rendered interchangeable in virtue of the anonymity of the social system to which they are subject, these individuals also carry the specific anonymity of the Parisian bus system, the specific familiarity of being one of a group of Parisians waiting at the curb. The situation can thus be analyzed in terms of the concrete mediations of individual and general circumstances that constitute the socially specific experience of this "group" and that, theoretically, can be understood in terms of its potentially politicizing effects. Sartre asks not only how this negative bond is at once acknowledged and denied, but also under what conditions this negative bond can be transformed into a positive one. To put it another way, he seeks to know how alienation can produce a collective, self-conscious will.

In Sartre's defense of his own position as a Marxist theorist, he maintains that any given analysis must take place from a prospective point of view, the hypothetical future in which a true collectivity is possible. This is the only way to theorize with a view to change. Only from this point of view of an imagined future, a future dialectically extrapolated from the present, does the potential collectivity stand out in the present situation of waiting for the bus. Only through the adoption of the prospective point of view can the dialectical theorist imagine the individual acting through collective identification and action.

The imaginary thus re-emerges in the *Critique* as a fundamental feature of the theoretical attitude. For Sartre it is impossible to think dialectically without the imagination, for the imagination entertains possibilities and the future is precisely a matter of possibilities rather than realities. And yet, does his imaginary theorizing remain the lone musing of Sartre the individual theorist? Would his speculations on group formation aid the general public in their concrete efforts to form allegiances and act collectively? Can Sartre establish that the unified history, the universal community, that he imagines is a real future possibility for existing individuals and groups?

Sartre proposed to answer this question in

the second volume of the *Critique of Dialectical Reason,* a study he only partially completed. Published in 1985 by his adopted daughter, Arlette Elkaïm-Sartre, the second volume concentrates on an explanation of historical change as a result of conflict and strife. Left unanswered, however, is the question of why the various histories that exist cross-culturally and among different sociohistorical groups and traditions should come together into a single history in the way that Sartre imagines. Although Sartre promised to answer the question, it appears that other philosophical issues and failing health precluded the possibility of an answer. Another perspective, however, emerges in Raymond Aron's critique of Sartre's political philosophy. In his *Histoire et dialectique de la violence (History and the Dialectic of Violence,* 1973) Aron charged that there could be no justification for Sartre's postulation of a single, self-actualizing history. Suggesting that Sartre's argument rested on the transposition of a Spinozistic notion of compulsion and necessity onto historical experience, Aron called this doctrine indefensible. Although it can be shown, perhaps, that under certain conditions of conflict, a more unified social organization can emerge, such an argument cannot predict that it will, of necessity, emerge. And it was this claim that Sartre appeared to make. Moreover, this doctrine of historical "necessity" stands in stark contradiction to Sartre's defense of freedom and "contingency," the insight that Sartre once considered to be his greatest.

Sartre's unwillingness to finish the second volume of the *Critique* may well be related to the problematic character of history in that work. Perhaps with an understanding that proof of his dialectical views would require an analysis of a concrete situation, Sartre wrote the biography of Jean Genet, playwright and poet, thief, homosexual, and occasional prisoner. The biography of Genet was written simultaneously with the *Critique* and published in 1952. Although not a particularly Marxist study, *Saint Genet: Actor and Martyr* does take up one of the *Critique*'s central questions: How do individuals appropriate and reproduce the conditions into which they are born and, through that appropriation, transform their material conditions into a reflection of their own freedom? Although Genet does not prove Sartre's point in the *Critique* that the individual manifests universal history, he does provide the occasion for Sartre to rework his theory of freedom and his view of the imaginary in light of his growing understanding of the effects of historical circumstance. Although unsystematic and highly speculative, *Saint Genet* exemplifies an individual career committed to the relentless transfiguration of historical circumstance. Born into the world without legitimate parentage, Genet seizes his illegitimacy as his identity and reappropriates its meaning in his own terms. Called a thief at an early age, Genet resolves to become a thief and then, later, to write about thieves—indeed, to make writing itself into a scandalous act. Genet is an artist of subversion and reversal, a slick strategist who escapes the definitions that others impose upon him by shifting the very meaning of the terms they use.

In Sartre's obvious fascination with Genet, one can discern his residual faith in the literary experience as the locus of human freedom, the domain of possibility. But Genet is not a hopeless dreamer; he is a writer who produces literary works that are circulated and performed. In other words, Genet institutionalizes his dreams and in that sense produces a new reality. Not unlike the Marxist theoretician who would institute new possibilities through the creation of new forms of praxis, Genet brings possibilities into existence and realizes them through unprecedented literary forms. His works, the labored products of his imagination, are seen by others and have the power to redirect their gaze. No longer a flight from reality, the imagination is the occasion for the realization of a new social experience, the disruption of social conventions, and the subversion of hierarchies.

Sartre's biographical studies of Genet and

Flaubert constitute a bridge between his theory of existential psychoanalysis, outlined in *Being and Nothingness,* and his promise in the *Critique* to display the dialectic in the context of an existence both singular and universal. If the *Critique* can be faulted for its failure to acknowledge contingency, the biographical studies demonstrate that the existential doctrine of choice retains wide-ranging explanatory power. At the close of *Being and Nothingness,* Sartre proposed to demonstrate his theory of existential psychoanalysis in the context of two biographical subjects: Flaubert and Dostoevsky. In 1946 he published a short biographical sketch of Baudelaire, a study that relied on the basic categories of *Being and Nothingness* but lacked a concrete historical dimension, thus raising the question of whether Sartre's interest was in Baudelaire the person and writer or in the demonstration of his own theoretical postulates. In 1954 Roger Garaudy, a Communist and onetime critic of Sartre's existentialism, suggested that he and Sartre both write a biography of the same subject; Garaudy would use a Marxist method while Sartre would employ an existential one. The one work that resulted was Sartre's: a three-volume study of the life and work of Flaubert, Sartre's longest work and his last major publication, which synthesized Marxist, existential, and psychoanalytical interpretive procedures. The final product was not completed until sixteen years later, after three separate efforts to do so: 1954–1955, 1963, and 1968–1970. Sartre proposed a fourth volume that he never completed, and interrupted his study several times to pursue other projects, including the biography of Genet. As an explicit effort to justify the method of existential psychoanalysis, the biography of Flaubert represented an idiosyncratic return to existential themes in 1954, a year in which Sartre's allegiance to communism was at its most firm.

Perhaps he abandoned the project in 1955 precisely because its publication would open him to criticism as a bourgeois thinker preoccupied with bourgeois literary productions.

When he returned to the manuscript, however, it became clear that the biographical study could demonstrate the central claim of the *Critique* that an individual existence could be seen to recapitulate universal history in its own singular way. But even in this last great work, Sartre was deflected from his defense of universal history in favor of a more limited set of historical claims. Flaubert's life and work can be seen to reproduce the particular epoch of French letters and bourgeois culture in which he lived, but there is no effort to link this epoch to a developmental notion of totalizing history. Indeed, that Sartre confidently refers to unified epochs is already cause for hesitation. How are we to decide the parameters of a given historical epoch? When does it begin and end, and from what perspective can its contours be perceived? Has Sartre forgotten the lesson he learned from reading Henri Bergson in the 1930's—that philosophers err when they impose spatial categories on time?

But Sartre's biographical studies are less interesting as philosophies of history than as studies in the historical and existential genesis of literary productions. After all, Sartre's biographical subjects are invariably authors, writers of the imaginary, whose plays, poems, and novels are at once an expression of a singular choice and a transfiguration of an existing situation. As such, they are both the obvious focus of an existential psychoanalysis and the exemplars of Sartre's developing notion of praxis. If there is a continuity between the early and the late Sartre, the existential theorist and the Marxist, it is most likely to be found in these biographical demonstrations, as it were, rather than in the long-awaited second volume of the *Critique of Dialectical Reason* or in the *Cahiers pour une morale* (Notebooks on Morality, 1983).

As late as 1969 Sartre spoke as if there had never been a significant break in his own intellectual project, affirming that the imaginary, the domain of possibility and its unprecedented realization, had always been his central theme. As he said in an interview in the *New*

Left Review that year, "The reason why I produced *Les Mots* is the reason why I have studied Genet or Flaubert: how does a man become someone who writes, who wants to speak of the imaginary?" Questioned why he chose Flaubert, Sartre answered in words that might also explain his choice of Genet: "Because [Flaubert] is the imaginary. With him, I am at the border, the barrier of dreams."

According to Sartre's early theory of existential psychoanalysis, the imaginary is an illusory experience of metaphysical plenitude, the temporary eclipse of freedom by a product of its own making, the concealment of contingency. In the production of a compelling image or a literary experience, consciousness is in the presence of a seamless experience, an uninterrupted presence that is at once its own creation and its manner of hiding its own "lack" from itself. In other words, in the experience of an imaginary world, consciousness is temporarily relieved of its experience of itself, and its ontological struggle to find a necessary ground for its own contingent existence is temporarily put out of play. In this sense the author, once fully established as narrator, assumes the God-like position that is otherwise denied human beings. He creates the world of his experience, transfigures the environment in his own image, and nowhere confronts his own negativity or contingency. As author he is the necessary ground of the world he creates, and as creator he is free.

Clearly, for the early Sartre authorship was one tactic in the struggle to overcome the ontological paradox of human reality. For the later Sartre this meaning of authorship is not wholly gone, but both the structure and the content of creativity are radically altered. Genet does not simply create his fictional worlds ex nihilo; rather, by fictionalizing an already existing situation, he challenges the meanings that the situation already has, releasing new meanings to alter the situation. In other words, the creative act is a reproduction of an existing situation and is, in that sense, always dependent upon an existing situation for its content.

In *Being and Nothingness* desire and choice emerge ex nihilo from the for-itself, but in *The Family Idiot* desire, choice, and the imagination reproduce the historical situation of the individual. And yet for Sartre there is choice in the manner and meaning of reproduction, that is, in the subversions and reversals that reproducing a situation can effect. In Sartre's words, however, "what is important here is to reject idealism—fundamental attitudes are not *adopted* unless they first exist. What is taken is what is at hand."

But how are we to delimit the "situation" of the author? Clearly it involves not only the present circumstances of his life but also his personal history and childhood, the various cultural factors that determine his language and literary history, his class, race, gender, historical location, and political affiliations. Here we can see that Sartre's "search for a method" is fulfilled in the biographical effort to delimit a relevant "situation"; the demonstration of a life as both singular and universal depends essentially on the capacity of the biographer to show the links between these various levels of existence. In *The Family Idiot,* Sartre begins with an examination of early childhood in order to identify those constitutive relations with others that are later reproduced in the characteristic actions of the individual and in his literary works. Choice, once considered an essential determinant of the self, is now understood as an expression and recapitulation of these early relations with others. Hence, Sartre turns to psychoanalysis because "without early childhood, it is obvious that the biographer is building on sand."

For both Genet and Flaubert early childhood was a scene of deprivation; Genet was excluded from legitimate society, while Flaubert was mishandled and poorly loved. Originally victimized by these negative relations with others, both Genet and Flaubert eventually reinterpreted their situations through an imaginary transvaluation of the scene. In Sartre's view these scenes of victimization and exile are invariably reproduced in the works of Genet and

Flaubert, but in reproducing these scenes both authors gain a certain mastery over them that they originally lacked. As a child Flaubert was afflicted with a passive sensibility. Deployed in the service of writing, this passivity constitutes an extraordinarily receptive sensibility, acutely sensitive to details, absorbing whole worlds of experience and recapitulating them in fictional form. The key, for Sartre, is in the act of recapitulation, which ought not to be interpreted as simple repetition or as a conditioned behavioral response. In the recapitulation of the scene is a latent decision or resolve to alter the terms of the scene, especially when the original scene is experienced as a source of suffering. Not unlike the Freudian account of fantasy as a strategy of compensation, Sartre's developed theory of the imagination involves the twofold project to re-enact and, thereby, reinvent the past. Hence, the imagination remains an expression of freedom, but freedom is no longer the unconditioned spontaneity described in *Being and Nothingness.* Still contingent and unjustified, freedom is nevertheless severely restricted in its efficacy. For the Sartre of *The Family Idiot,* one is certainly free, but only to choose one's past again and again, with the hope that the recapitulations will become more creative, more subversive, more promising of possibility.

Sartre delimits the situation of Flaubert in terms of his childhood and adolescence, but also in terms of the Industrial Revolution, the breakdown of feudal relations in France, the history of the bourgeoisie. In this regard Flaubert is the occasion for a dialectical social history of nineteenth-century France, and yet Sartre does not want to say that Flaubert simply represents this epoch in French social history. The epoch produces the career of the individual, but the products of the individual reproduce and alter the very structure of that epoch. Hence, Sartre does not ask what effects the epoch had on Flaubert but, rather, how Flaubert realized this epoch in his own person and work, how this epoch "lived" in the person of Flaubert, and how that singular existence conferred a new meaning on the epoch itself. Nowhere is this dialectical relation between individual and epoch more evident than in those cultural products (such as literary works) that are taken to be both emblematic and transformative. As Sartre states in *The Family Idiot,* "Summed up and for this reason universalized by his epoch, he [Flaubert] in turn resumes it by reproducing himself in it as singularity."

Although Sartre claimed that he gave up his quasi-religious illusions about the immortalizing possibilities of great literary works, it appears that even *The Family Idiot* reflects a fundamental optimism regarding the salutary effects of literary works. If words fail to guarantee immortality, they nevertheless carry the power of inversion that permits the temporary triumph of consciousness over the difficulty of the world. Flaubert may suffer, but by giving words to that suffering, he creates beauty and a temporary redemption. By naming his experience Genet makes himself into a social fact, a public presence, the permanent property of culture, thus reversing his fate as an illegitimate child in exile from society. These literary reversals of experience are not mere fantasies of reparation; as present facts they confer fresh meanings upon the past, carrying that past into the present in a new form. Moreover, the "irreality" of the fictional world allows the transformation of brute facts into fields of possibility; the abandoned or unloved child becomes God over his own past, re-creating it in the image of his desire. Literature thus becomes the occasion of a perpetual reinvention of experience.

As a biographer Sartre makes use of the personal and historical past of his subject in a highly nontraditional way. Rather than find in the past the causes or motivations for future behavior, Sartre understands the past only in terms of the future that the subject projects. In *Being and Nothingness* he made it clear that projects, those fundamental desires which are elaborated in sustained modes of actions, give unity to life. These commitments, which necessarily involve a vision of a future self, confer a retroactive meaning upon the past. Because the subject is always in the process of creating its meaning, the past continually takes on significance in terms of the projected unity of the future self. Hence, the personal and historical past has no intrinsic meaning but requires the project as its necessary context. In this sense the self is a locus of perpetual reinvention and continuous redemption. No single set of facts defines an individual, for those facts must be interpreted, and interpretation is effected through the appropriation of those facts in a current project.

In *The Family Idiot* Sartre is more clearly aware that the interpretation of the personal and historical past is not solely a subjective affair, that the projects which confer meaning upon the past are more often intersubjective in nature. Flaubert is not only what he makes of himself but also what others make of him as he makes himself. Although Sartre emphasized the constituting look of the Other in *Being and Nothingness,* he tended to reduce the complexity of the social construction of identity, the various cultural and linguistic factors that constitute signification and that signify the subject even before the subject interprets himself. The structuralist and poststructuralist critique of Sartre often centers on this problem. A self-reflexive interpretation must make use of language; and subjects do not determine the meanings of a language into which they are born, the language to which they are subject even as they attempt a radical self-definition. Occasionally this criticism is limited to the claim that the Sartrian subject, inasmuch as he does not choose the language that constitutes the possible field of meaning into which he is born, is less free than Sartre himself imagined.

A stronger criticism is sometimes made that the subject is a product of a specific historical system of meaning, a discourse, and is in that sense wholly determined from the outset. Although Sartre generally refused to engage such critics, he knew that they existed, and *The Family Idiot* might well be understood as an effort to defend the self-defining subject even while acknowledging the complex historical and linguistic situation in which it is mired. After all, Flaubert is stuck with an enormous historical and cultural legacy, the history of letters, the Industrial Revolution, the crises of the bourgeois class. But does this situation have only an objective meaning, or does it also remain possible to ask what meaning this history takes on *for him*? Here we are referring not only to an attitude or reflective awareness of the situation but also to a mode of positioning himself in and through the terms of this situation.

The subject may well be constituted by a field of significations of which he himself is not the sole author, or even not the author at all. But this field must be experienced in some way; and that experience, lived as it is by a singular individual from a distinct perspective, a distinct location in space and time, is what constitutes the field as a situation *for him.* Surely it is a situation for others as well, but not in the same way. No one can share the lived experience of that field of significations, because no one can live in the place of anyone else. Moreover, a situation is not passively or contemplatively experienced but is, in Sartre's terms, "existed" in a transitive sense. In other words, experience requires a reflexive act of self-determination, a positioning of oneself, a taking-up of possibilities from that field of significations and a letting-go of others. To experience is to discriminate among possibilities, to act, and therefore to commit oneself in virtue of that act.

Despite the popular characterization of Sartre's philosophy as absurdist, portraying human actions as arbitrary and incoherent, Sartre was concerned with the intelligibility of human actions, their coherence within the life of the individual, and their implicit unity. In *Being and Nothingness* he refers to the reflexive style of the individual, the coherent pattern of choices that come to constitute the self. And in *The Family Idiot* Sartre maintains that Flaubert's life is a unity, a dialectical mediation of the singular and universal features of his experience. In the former work the unity of a life is self-constructed, a unity of desires and choices, and in the latter that unity is an effect of dialectical necessity. In both cases, however, the emphasis on internal coherence and consistency suggests that freedom is not an aimless and arbitrary activity, but retains within itself a normative ideal. This may sound strange as a characterization of an existential philosophy, for existentialism is commonly said to renounce the ascription of any intrinsic normative goals for existence, the latter being the freely chosen projects of each individual. But how then are we to contend with Sartre's insistence that each and every life maintains a unity structured by the desire or necessity to create itself as an internally consistent assemblage of actions? What dictates this unity as a desideratum?

As unified and complete, a given life takes form as a kind of being, a plenum of experience that is achieved through the gradual cultivation of an identifiable self. Being internally consistent, this life masks its own contingency, appearing as a series of choices and actions structured by a unifying theme. Unity is thus a normative ideal toward which any given life strives, but for Sartre it is also a theoretical a priori for the understanding of any given life. As a result the circularity of Sartre's argument precludes the possibility of its demonstration.

But are we to accept Sartre's thesis as true? Is completeness and unity the structure and telos of all human striving? And is Sartre himself clear on where he stands? In the early investigations of the imagination, in *Nausea* and even in *The Words,* literary experience was understood as a kind of vital plenum, a complete and unified experience that masked the contingency and negativity of ordinary experience. In that sense it was an escape from the real, the secularization of absolute presence. Sartre appeared to concur with Nietzsche's *Birth of Tragedy* that life could only be justified as an aesthetic phenomenon.

In *What Is Literature?* Sartre repudiated this version of literature as escape and called for a committed literature that would risk transience for the sake of political efficacy. But the continued insistence on the "unity" of a life in the later biographies suggests that he did not wholly rid himself of the desire for a completed existence, a life that would appear as a work of art, a well-carved reflection of a freedom that endures. At the end of *Nausea,* Roquentin considers that suffering is never transcended but is transformed into melody, a melancholy melody, and that this aesthetic transformation, in its simplicity and completeness, is a kind of temporary redemption. The biography of Genet pursues a similar kind of experience, the beauty of poetic utterance that, Genet says, "reduces the body to a speck of light."

Even though Sartre voiced antipathy for Flaubert, the latter's pursuit of a fully imaginary existence resonates with Sartre's own literary career. In *Critique of Dialectical Reason* Sartre asserts the unity of history but maintains that this unity can be dialectically imagined only in a future synthetically built from contemporary historical experience. Once again the promise of the plenum exists for an imagination that can project the future and then come to believe in the reality of that projection.

But consider the following: the second volume of the *Critique,* which was intended to prove this unity of history, remains incomplete, as does the final volume of *Flaubert,* in which the grand synthesis of singular and universal experience was expected to take place. What rhetorical meaning are we to discern in the incompleteness of these works that argue the case for completeness? It is as if Sartre refused to complete his works, or perhaps his life, by leaving these works open.

In a late interview with de Beauvoir, Sartre stated, "I didn't finish the Flaubert and I never shall." Although colored by a sense of failure, Sartre's penchant for nonclosure also has the air of defiance about it, as if the perfect text were a dangerous thing, inimical to life. Reflecting on his career, Sartre considered *Nausea* and *The Words* to be completed and perfected texts, and yet that kind of writing became increasingly less important to him. He conceded that he no longer wrote very well, and considered *The Family Idiot* to be clumsily composed. The prose is rushed, infused with the speed of experience, and in the *Critique* there is an indifference to beautiful language. Asked why he no longer wrote fiction by the time he took up *The Family Idiot,* Sartre replied that the problem with literary descriptions is that *they are not time.*

And yet, this "problem" was once considered by Sartre to be the source of literature's value, its redemptive power, its capacity to stay time and make the world appear in its absolute presence. The closure of experience seemed less desirable to him as his own life threatened to close. And despite his illness and failing sight, Sartre's uncompleted works suggest a final disenchantment with the imaginary pursuit of plenitude—this, at the threshold of its realization.

Selected Bibliography

EDITIONS

NOVELS
La nausée. Paris, 1938.
L'Âge de raison. Paris, 1945.
Le sursis. Paris, 1945.
La mort dans l'âme. Paris, 1949.

SHORT STORIES
Le mur. Paris, 1939. Includes "Le Mur," "La Chambre," "Erostrate," "Intimite," and "L'Enfance d'un chef."

DRAMA
Les mouches. Paris, 1943.
Huis clos. Paris, 1945.
Morts sans sépulture. Lausanne, 1946.
La putain respectueuse. Paris, 1946.
Les mains sales. Paris, 1948.

Le Diable et le bon Dieu. Paris, 1951.
Kean. Paris, 1954.
Nekrassov. Paris, 1955.
Les séquestrés d'Altona. Paris, 1960.
Les troyennes. Paris, 1966.

LITERARY CRITICISM
Situations. 10 vols. Paris, 1947–1976.
Un théâtre de situations. Edited by Michel Contat and Michel Rybalka. Paris, 1973.

AUTOBIOGRAPHY
Les mots. Paris, 1964.

BIOGRAPHY
Baudelaire. Paris, 1946.
Saint Genet, comédien et martyr. Paris, 1952.
L'Idiot de la famille: Gustave Flaubert de 1821 à 1857. 3 vols. Paris, 1971–1972.

PHILOSOPHY
L'Imagination. Paris, 1936.
La transcendance de l'égo. In *Recherches philosophiques,* vol. 6. Paris, 1937. Reprinted with introduction, notes, and appendixes by Sylvie Le Bon. Paris, 1965.
Esquisse d'une théorie des émotions. Paris, 1939.
L'Imaginaire: Psychologie phénoménologique de l'imagination. Paris, 1940.
L'Être et le néant: Essai d'ontologie phénoménologique. Paris, 1943.
L'Existentialisme est un humanisme. Paris, 1946.
Question de methode. In *Twórczosc* (as "Marksizm i egzistencjalizm"; 1957). Reprinted as introduction to *Critique de la raison dialectique,* vol. 1. Paris, 1960. Reprinted separately, Paris, 1967.
Critique de la raison dialectique. Vol. 1, *Théorie des ensembles pratiques.* Paris, 1960. The second volume, never completed, was published posthumously.

POLITICAL WORKS
Réflexions sur la question juive. Paris, 1946.
Entretiens sur la politique. Paris, 1949. With Gérard Rosenthal and David Rousset.
"Les communistes et la paix." In *Les temps modernes,* 81:1–50 (July 1952); 84–85:695–763 (Oc-

tober–November 1952); 101:1,731–1,819 (April 1954). Reprinted in *Situations,* vol. 6, pp. 80–384.

"Le fantôme de Staline." In *Les temps modernes,* 129–130:577–696 (November–December 1956) and 131: (January 1957). Reprinted in *Situations,* vol. 7, pp. 144–307.

"Le génocide." In *Les temps modernes,* 259:953–971 (December 1967). Reprinted in *Situations,* vol. 8, pp. 100–124; and in *Tribunal Russell.* Vol. 2, *Le jugement final.* Paris, 1968.

Plaidoyer pour les intellectuals. Paris, 1972.

On a raison de se revolter. Paris, 1974. With Philippe Gavi and Pierre Victor.

POSTHUMOUS PUBLICATIONS

Cahiers pour une morale. Paris, 1983.

Les carnets de la drôle de guerre: Novembre 1939–Mars 1940. Paris, 1983.

Critique de la raison dialectique. Vol. 2, *L'Intelligibilité de l'histoire.* Edited by Arlette Elkaïm-Sartre. Paris, 1985.

TRANSLATIONS

The Age of Reason. Translated by Eric Sutton. New York, 1947.

Anti-Semite and Jew. Translated by George J. Becker. New York, 1948.

Baudelaire. Translated by Martin Turnell. New York, 1950.

Being and Nothingness: An Essay on Phenomenological Ontology. Translated by Hazel E. Barnes. New York, 1956.

Between Existentialism and Marxism. Translated by John Mathews. New York, 1974. Originally *Situations,* vols. 8 and 9.

The Communists and Peace. Translated by Martha Fletcher. New York, 1968.

The Condemned of Altona. Translated by Sylvia Leeson and George Leeson. New York, 1961.

Critique of Dialectical Reason, vol. 1. Translated by Alan Sheridan-Smith. Edited by Jonathan Rée. London, 1976.

The Devil & the Good Lord. Translated by Kitty Black. In *The Devil & the Good Lord and Two Other Plays.* New York, 1960.

Dirty Hands. Translated by Lionel Abel. In *Three Plays.* New York, 1949.

The Emotions: Outline of a Theory. Translated by Bernard Frechtman. New York, 1948.

Existentialism and Humanism. Translated by Philip Mairet. London, 1948.

The Family Idiot. Translated by Carol Cosman. 2 vols. Chicago, 1981–1987.

The Flies. Translated by Stuart Gilbert. In *No Exit . . . The Flies.* New York, 1946.

The Ghost of Stalin. Translated by Martha Fletcher. New York, 1968.

Imagination: A Psychological Critique. Translated by Forrest Williams. Ann Arbor, Mich., 1962.

Kean. Translated by Kitty Black. London, 1954. Also in *The Devil & the Good Lord.* New York, 1960.

Life/Situations. Translated by Paul Auster and Lydia Davis. New York, 1974. Originally *Situations,* vol. 10.

Literary and Philosophical Essays. Translated by Annette Michelson. New York, 1955.

Nausea. Translated by Robert Baldick. Harmondsworth, England, 1965.

Nekrassov. Translated by Sylvia Leeson and George Leeson. London, 1956. Also in *The Devil & the Good Lord.* New York, 1960.

No Exit. Translated by Stuart Gilbert. In *No Exit . . . The Flies.* New York, 1946.

The Psychology of Imagination. New York, 1948.

The Reprieve. Translated by Eric Sutton. New York, 1947.

The Respectful Prostitute. Translated by Lionel Abel. In *Three Plays.* New York, 1949.

Saint Genet: Actor and Martyr. Translated by Bernard Frechtman. New York, 1963.

Sartre on Theatre. Translated by Frank Jellinek. Edited by Michel Contat and Michel Rybalka. New York, 1976.

Search for a Method. Translated by Hazel E. Barnes. New York, 1963, repr. 1968.

Situations. Translated by Benita Eisler and Maria Jolas. New York, 1965. Originally *Situations,* vol. 4.

The Transcendence of the Ego. Translated by Forrest Williams and Robert Kirkpatrick. New York, 1957, repr. 1972.

The Trojan Women. Translated by Ronald Duncan. New York, 1967.

Troubled Sleep. Translated by Gerard Hopkins. New York, 1951.

The Wall and Other Stories. Translated by Lloyd Alexander. New York, 1948.

The War Diaries, November 1939–March 1940. Translated by Quintin Hoare. New York, 1985.

What Is Literature? Translated by Bernard Frechtman. New York, 1949. Originally *Situations,* vol. 2, pp. 57–330.

The Words. Translated by Bernard Frechtman. New York, 1964, 1981.

BIOGRAPHICAL AND CRITICAL WORKS

Aron, Raymond. *History and the Dialectic of Violence: An Analysis of Sartre's Critique de la Raison Dialectique.* Translated by Barry Cooper. Oxford, 1975.

Aronson, Ronald. *Jean-Paul Sartre: Philosophy in the World.* London, 1980.

Barnes, Hazel E. *An Existentialist Ethics.* New York, 1967.

———. *Sartre and Flaubert.* Chicago, 1981.

Beauvoir, Simone de. *The Prime of Life.* Translated by Peter Green. New York, 1962.

———. *Force of Circumstance.* Translated by Richard Howard. New York, 1965.

———. *Adieux: A Farewell to Sartre.* Translated by Patrick O'Brian. New York, 1984.

Caws, Peter. *Sartre: Arguments of the Philosophers.* London and Boston, 1979.

Cohen-Solel, Annie. *Sartre: A Life.* Translated by Anna Cancogni. Edited by Norman Macafee. New York, 1987.

Culler, Jonathan. *Flaubert: The Uses of Uncertainty.* Ithaca, N.Y., 1974.

Danto, Arthur. *Jean-Paul Sartre.* New York, 1975.

Grene, Marjorie. *Sartre.* New York, 1973.

Halpern, Joseph. *Critical Fictions: The Literary Criticism of Jean-Paul Sartre.* New Haven, 1976.

Jameson, Fredric R. *Sartre: The Origins of a Style.* New Haven, 1961.

Jeanson, Francis. *Sartre and the Problem of Morality.* Translated by Robert V. Stone. Bloomington, Ind., 1980.

LaCapra, Dominick. *A Preface to Sartre.* Ithaca, N.Y., 1978.

Merleau-Ponty, Maurice. *The Visible and the Invisible.* Translated by Alphonso Lingis. Edited by Claude Lefort. Evanston, Ill., 1968.

———. *Adventures of the Dialectic.* Translated by Joseph Bien. Evanston, Ill., 1973.

Murdoch, Iris. *Sartre: Romantic Rationalist.* New Haven, 1953; London, 1961.

Natanson, Maurice. *A Critique of Jean-Paul Sartre's Ontology.* Lincoln, Nebr., 1951; repr. New York, 1972, and The Hague, 1973.

Poster, Mark. *Existential Marxism in Postwar France: From Sartre to Althusser.* Princeton, 1975.

Schilpp, Paul Arthur, ed. *The Philosophy of Jean-Paul Sartre.* La Salle, Ill., 1981.

Silverman, Hugh J., and Frederick A. Elliston, eds. *Jean-Paul Sartre: Contemporary Approaches to His Philosophy.* Pittsburgh, 1980.

Warnock, Mary, ed. *Sartre: A Collection of Critical Essays.* New York, 1971.

BIBLIOGRAPHIES

Contat, Michel, and Michel Rybalka, eds. *Les écrits de Sartre.* Paris, 1970. Translated by Richard McLeary as *The Writings of Jean-Paul Sartre,* 2 vols. Evanston, Ill., 1974.

Lapointe, François. *Jean-Paul Sartre and His Critics: An International Bibliography (1938–1980).* Annotated and revised 2nd ed. Bowling Green, Ohio, 1981. With Claire Lapointe.

JUDITH P. BUTLER

ELIAS CANETTI
(b. 1905)

ELIAS CANETTI WAS born in Ruschuk, Bulgaria, on 25 July 1905. Both parents came from families of wealthy Sephardic Jews who had emigrated from Turkey. When Elias was six, the family moved to Manchester, England. His primary schooling and introduction to literature thus were in English. After the early death of his father, his mother moved to Vienna with her three sons, of whom Elias was the eldest. He had begun to study at the gymnasium there, when his mother, opposing World War I, took him to neutral Zurich in 1916. Canetti called the five years he lived there his "paradise," from which his mother expelled him to inflation-ridden Frankfurt, Germany. There he completed the Realgymnasium in 1924, and then studied chemistry at the University of Vienna. He received his Ph.D. in 1929 but was never a professional chemist. Personal acquaintance with the Berlin avant-garde—George Grosz, Bertolt Brecht, Isaac Babel, among many others—made him decide to become a writer. Earlier, under the spell of the essayist and poet Karl Kraus, he had fallen in love with a fellow devotee, Venetia (Veza) Taubner-Calderon, who became his intellectual partner, his muse, and eventually his wife (1934).

In the autumn of 1929, Canetti began work on a cycle of novels of which he completed only one, *Die Blendung*, in 1931. (Although this work has been translated as *Auto-da-Fé*, I prefer the original—literally "The Blinding"—for

reasons that will become apparent below.) It was not published until 1935, but on the strength of the manuscript, he became known to the Vienna literary avant-garde. Hermann Broch, author of *The Sleepwalkers* (1932), was particularly helpful. The novelist Robert Musil, interested and sympathetic at first, later turned cool and aloof, offended by Canetti's admiration of other authors. After the Nazi occupation of Austria in 1938, the Canettis moved to London (1939), and years of almost total obscurity followed. Canetti devoted himself ascetically to the writing of a lengthy work of philosophical anthropology, *Masse und Macht* (*Crowds and Power,* 1960), which he considered to be his chef d'oeuvre. For a long time he forbade himself to write anything else, a journal being the sole concession. After the republication of *Die Blendung* in 1963, however, Canetti became gradually known to a wider public. Invitations to give lectures and public readings from his works—Canetti enjoyed a reputation as a most effective and dramatic reader—became frequent, and his growing fame had a fructifying effect upon his literary productivity. A major study of Kafka's *Letters to Felice* appeared in 1968. The journals, essays, and aphorisms were published in several volumes. The appearance of the first volume of his autobiography became the literary sensation of 1977 in Germany. Prestigious prizes were awarded to him in Germany and Austria. Translations of his works into many languages—including English—multiplied. The steep ascent of his reputation culminated in the Nobel Prize, awarded to him in 1981. His first wife died in 1963, and Canetti remarried in 1971. He made Zurich his second (and later his sole) residence.

Canetti's belated fame rests on a relatively slim body of work: one novel; three plays; a philosophical-anthropological study; a small book of travel memoirs from Marrakesh; several volumes of journals, aphorisms, lectures, and essays; a study of Kafka; a study of the Austrian sculptor Fritz Wotruba; a thin volume of imaginary character portraits; and three volumes of autobiography. This preponderance of nonfiction is not unusual in a contemporary author's oeuvre. Canetti was an intellectual author with a bent toward scholarly, critical, and philosophical thought, a voracious—one might even say a fanatical—reader whose reading frequently ignited his writing. Hunger for knowledge and a passionate moral commitment vied in him with the lure of invention. After the early 1950's, nonfiction became the almost exclusive province of his writing. Yet fiction and nonfiction form a close-knit unity in his oeuvre. There are innumerable links between them, and they illuminate each other.

The language in which Canetti wrote was not his native Ladino, the Romance language spoken by the Sephardic Jews of the Ottoman Empire. Rather, the language he chose as his literary medium was German. His mother, a passionate admirer of the theatrical culture of Vienna, insisted, shortly before their move to that city, that her eight-year-old son master German in the shortest period possible. She taught him herself, in a brutally demanding but highly effective way. Thus, German became literally his "mother tongue." He acquired it to keep her love. He saw his proficiency in it as his gift to the mother he adored, who challenged him constantly, and who, as he proclaims in his autobiography, essentially shaped him. He said of himself that he consisted of his mother's conversations with him.

Prior to his mother's lessons, German had possessed the fascination of mystery for Ca-

netti. In memory of their happy youth in Vienna, his parents used German as their secret language, from which the children were excluded. Canetti thus experienced, at a very early age, language as nonreferential, as purely sensory, as inflections of the voice that allowed one to divine emotion but that had no conceptual meaning. He learned to imitate its sounds without knowing their meaning, and was so successful that he could fool his mother, when calling her, into mistaking his voice for his father's. It was in German that Canetti first took his father's place, a role that, in many ways, he was to take on more seriously after his father's early death.

The strange way in which Canetti entered the language that was to become the medium of his work left its imprint on his style and on the significance language as such acquired for him. His style differs markedly from that of most writers whose native tongue is German. It lacks the convoluted syntax, the lyrical pathos, the abstractness, and the linguistic experimentalism that characterize a large part of German literature in his generation and the one preceding it. Canetti's prose does not draw attention to itself. It is straightforward, unpretentious in vocabulary and syntax, clear, close to conversational, and of utmost precision in recording sensory detail. His novel and plays are unsurpassed in the exactness with which they render speech patterns of members of all social classes. Canetti states that certain phrases which characterize Therese, one of the two major characters of his novel, were taken verbatim from the conversation of his Viennese landlady. This acoustic realism seems to apply to all the speeches and interior monologues of his characters even though they show all the earmarks of satirical invention and are by no means "realistically" conceived.

Reading Canetti, one has the impression of an abnormally receptive ear that dictates to an obedient tongue and hand precisely what it hears. Canetti views language as the essence of character. For him, individuals consist of the sentences they speak. Each person has what

Canetti calls an "acoustic mask." It consists of the particular clichés and patterns the speaker uses throughout life. Just as a facial mask both presents and hides the face, so the acoustic mask simultaneously reveals and conceals the person under his or her characteristic commonplaces. For a person's choice of clichés is a distinguishing mark, a signature. The characters of Canetti's novel and plays have such acoustic masks. Their clichéd sentences, used in speech and interior monologue, define them. In the novel it is not the narrator who presents and interprets the characters for us; it is the characters who present themselves in their own words and who, by these words, let us surmise what they conceal and repress.

Of the modern authors in German who influenced Canetti, the most important—next to Kafka—was Karl Kraus. As an indication of Kraus's dominance over his youth, Canetti entitled the second volume of his autobiography *Die Fackel im Ohr* (*The Torch in My Ear*, 1980), referring to the celebrated periodical (*Die Fackel*) of which Kraus was the founder, editor, and practically sole contributor. Kraus dominated the intellectual life of Vienna in the first three decades of the twentieth century by his spellbinding public readings and devastating critiques. His primary concern for the authors and journalists of the day was appropriateness and honesty of language. What appeared to be a stylistic concern, however, was ultimately moral. For Kraus, style revealed character. In the choice of the inappropriate word, in the inconsistency of tone, in the slipping in of cliché, the crooked, pretentious, and commonplace mind revealed itself. Kraus's minute attention to style pointed the way to the examination of morality in public life. He made the deepest impression on Canetti in the aftermath of the burning of the Vienna Palace of Justice by demonstrating Socialist workers on 15 July 1927—an event in which Canetti emotionally participated and that was to provide the seminal image for the novel *Die Blendung*. In a public proclamation that Kraus personally distributed and affixed to the city's billboards, he

brought the charge of mass murder against Johann Schober, the Vienna chief of police, for having given the command to shoot at the demonstrators, thus initiating a bloodbath. Kraus acted completely alone when he dared to challenge the powerful head of police. For this act of civic courage he earned Canetti's unstinted admiration, although his hunger for power dimmed Canetti's admiration in later years.

In the case of Kafka's influence also, the moral example cannot be separated from the stylistic. It was Kafka's severity toward himself that impressed Canetti. This "severity" included Kafka's ascetic desisting from any decorative effect in his writing as well as his scrupulous readiness to find fault with himself. Like Dostoevsky's Underground Man, Canetti suspected all "beautiful writing" as a glossing over of life. The psychiatrist Georg Kien in *Die Blendung*, who in many ways can be considered Canetti's spokesman because he advances views that are presented as Canetti's own in other texts, speaks with contempt of novels that seek to "transpose the ornery painful biting multiplicity of life surrounding us onto a smooth surface of paper across which the reader is able to skim quickly and pleasantly." Such reading is merely a caressing, "another form of making love for ladies and their doctors." Much like Kafka's demand that books should be the ax for the frozen sea within us, Canetti's implicit poetics sees the novel as a wedge that is driven into the reader and splits his sense of identity. Writing should lay the reader open. The writer's hallmark—an extraordinary concern for words—signals moral responsibility. As Canetti explains in his 1976 lecture "Der Beruf des Dichters" ("The Writer's Profession"), words rule our lives in any case. Words prepare future wars. Words threaten nuclear holocaust. Words, therefore, must seek to prevent what they might cause. It is the writer's special task to feel responsible for whatever happens, and to blame himself rather than others for not preventing what he deplores. Canetti's exalted claim for the writer's moral duty calls to mind Shelley's "unacknowledged legislators of the world." Canetti uses the old-fashioned term *Dichter* for writer, a word that has, in recent decades, tended to be discarded as making too special and elitist a claim for the writer. He defends its use programmatically as a call for the writer's return to high responsibility.

What made Canetti choose to be a writer was the fascination that the Berlin intellectuals held for him as "types" or "characters." They all seemed to be monomaniacs, each obsessed with a single idea that was pursued with utmost consistency, to the exclusion of all else. They all seemed mad, but it was a madness that held the young visitor from Vienna spellbound. It revealed to him what he came to see as the modern world, the twentieth century. He immediately planned to write a cycle of novels in the manner of Balzac's *Comédie humaine,* each with a different maniac as protagonist. For a year he worked on several of these novels simultaneously. The world, he felt, was no longer representable from the writer's single point of view. Since the world had fallen apart, a writer depicting it could be truthful only if he had the courage to show it in its chaotic state, without any attempt to harmonize its violent contradictions. No editorial wisdom was to feign a sanity that no longer existed. This did not mean writing chaotic books. On the contrary, characters of the most rigorous consistency should be shown, each restricted to his own fanatical point of view. Subsequently Canetti decided to unite several monomaniacs in a single novel. They were to be grouped around a fanatical bibliophile provisionally called the Bookworm, or simply B.

The concept of character as monomaniac combines a premodern idea with a very modern one. The premodern is the delight in type, and in the richness and variety of character. Canetti stands, in this respect, not only in the tradition of Theophrastus and La Bruyère, but also in that of the Renaissance heteroglossia (to use Bakhtin's term)—the satirical and parasitic countercurrent to traditional and dominant literature—represented by Rabelais and

Cervantes. Its counterpart in painting, the caricaturing style of Matthias Grünewald and Pieter Brueghel the Elder, exerted a profound influence on Canetti. This tradition exaggerates individual traits to the point of caricature and grotesqueness, which Canetti applies with signal success in *Die Blendung.* The strength of this work lies in the profligate inventiveness of incident and situation that presents monomania from ever new angles, and in the consistent clichés of speech and thought by which monomania manifests itself. Essential to the effectiveness of *Die Blendung* is the figural perspective, the view from within the characters, which makes the reader privy to fanatical consciousness.

Here we encounter the modern postrealist quality of Canetti's types. He does not present them from a "sane" authorial point of view as aberrations to be laughed at. The "sane" narrator's communication with the "sane" reader—the authorial address and commentary so typical of the premodern narrative style—is missing. Canetti throws the reader into the warped consciousness of absurd persons and offers no way back to a "normal" (that is, societal) point of view. Here there is no voice of reason, no platform superior to the characters. The grotesques are—and this is Canetti's point when he describes the genesis of his novel—our world. Each character is bottled up in a fixed idea, and fixed ideas—or private ideologies—guide their behavior. The characters see nothing but projections of their own compulsions. They are incapable of entering anyone else's point of view; they cannot share each other's minds. The emotional participation in the other that we conceive friendship and love to be is impossible for them. Canetti's characters see in the other only what their own needs, anxieties, and desires put there. The other is the distorting mirror of the self. Conversations, for these characters, are monologues running past each other. What they hear is what they choose to hear. What they see is part of their schemes, which they confuse with "objective" truth. The characters are so totally alienated from one another that one might call them solipsistic.

Canetti achieves two main effects in his novel: riotous irony, and insight into the workings of the self-deceiving mind. These effects are possible only because he retains one traditional way of orienting the reader that affords the latter a superior or, in Northrop Frye's terms, ironic position vis-à-vis the characters. He retains an omniscient narrator who slips into different minds and thus enables the reader to perceive the characters' failure to respond appropriately to each other and to their situations. Following the narrator into all minds, the reader recognizes the characters' self-deceptions, mutual misunderstandings, and distortions. The plural of subjectivities establishes objectivity.

A related factor of crucial importance is Canetti's scenic mode of representation, which emancipates the reader from the characters' points of view. Irony results, on the one hand, from the flagrant contradictions between a situation shown scenically and the character's response to it and, on the other hand, from the reader's perception of the mutual incomprehension of characters who think they see through each other.

All characters in *Die Blendung,* not merely the protagonist, are obsessed. The difference between him and them is merely that the others suffer from nonintellectual manias, whereas Dr. Peter Kien, a bibliophile and sinologist of independent means, suffers from a hypertrophied intellectuality. Therese, his housekeeper and later his wife, is fixated on vanity and greed. A grotesque-looking woman of fifty-seven, she believes she looks "not a day older than thirty," and that all men gape after her with lusting admiration of her "splendid hips," while in actuality she waddles along. She also lives in fear of a poverty-stricken old age, a fear that drives her to grasp after whatever financial advantage offers itself. The Jewish hunchback Fischerle, a small-time crook and pimp, is a fanatical chess player who dreams of becoming the world chess champion in America. The

panhandler Johannes Schwer, who pretends to be blind, has two obsessions: he must bed as many fat and hefty women as possible, and he must get even with those who throw buttons into his pan instead of coins. The concierge Pfaff's preoccupation is beating people. Even Kien's psychiatrist brother, Georg, the deus ex machina of the plot, displays a mania: he is fascinated by maniacs and collects them in his sanatorium.

In the protagonist, Dr. Peter Kien, Canetti draws a bibliophile who lives entirely in and for books. Kien appears strangely convincing by virtue of his radical consistency. The premise is his need for absolute concentration on his passion—reading. Therefore, it is perfectly logical that he never notices anyone or anything outside his books, and dreads human contact as a mortal danger. To shield himself from all distraction, he has walled up the windows of his library. He has three locks on his door and pays the brutal concierge, Pfaff, a monthly allowance to keep beggars and peddlers away.

The plot is as follows. Kien suddenly marries his housekeeper, Therese, because he has discovered that she is solicitous of books. Terrified, however, of the sexual consummation of the marriage, on their wedding night Kien flees to the toilet and locks himself in. Therese develops an undying hatred of this "skeleton . . . who is not even a man." She gradually outwits him and succeeds in throwing him out of his own apartment. Imagining that he now carries his library in his head, Kien wanders from hotel to hotel to find room for his imaginary books. The hunchbacked dwarf Fischerle joins him, playing the part of Sancho Panza to Kien's Don Quixote. Indulging Kien's fancy, he cheats him of money to indulge, in his turn, an obsessive idea of his own. He plans to use Kien's money to go to America and become the world chess champion; but before he can depart, he is murdered by the panhandler Johannes Schwer because of the button he has put in Schwer's pan. Kien's younger brother, Georg, a psychiatrist, arrives from Paris, gets rid of

Therese, and restores Kien to his library. After Georg's departure, however, Kien sets fire to his books, and himself with them. He dies laughing as he has never laughed before.

Canetti saw the seed of his novel in the following experience. On 15 July 1927, when the Socialist workers of Vienna, demonstrating against a court's outrageous acquittal of Fascist murderers, set fire to the Supreme Court building and several lives had already been lost, Canetti saw a gentleman standing apart, in a side street, lamenting the burning of the court records. Indignant, Canetti could not comprehend how, at a moment when human beings had been killed, someone was capable of mourning the destruction of mere papers. Such an attitude contrasted sharply with his own feelings at that moment. He had felt that he was part of the wave of humanity that had been streaming toward the center of the city. He was a part of the masses, swayed by their will, and had ceased to have a will of his own. It was a feeling that would preoccupy him all his life.

In Canetti's confrontation with the "record man," as he called the bureaucrat who pitied records but not human beings, three elements that play a central role in the novel stand out: the gap between the individual and the masses; the inversion of the value placed on written papers and on human life; and the irresistible appeal of the masses. In the novel Canetti transformed the target of his indignation into a scholar-intellectual. Court records were permuted into literature as that inventory of man's past for which his living present is ignored. Canetti's shift of the target of satire from bureaucrat to bookworm has autobiographical relevance. Kien is first of all a self-caricature of his creator. In his autobiography Canetti portrays himself as a fanatical reader and lover of books. His parents' idolatry of high culture—typical of the Central and East European Jewish bourgeoisie, especially when it tended to look up to German culture—had been transmitted to the child. In particular it was his mother who had inculcated into him, together with the German language, a passionate preoccupation with the classics and a highly emotional interest in the arts and in abstract ideas.

All this was accompanied by contempt of merely practical pursuits. However, in response to the Great War, his mother had a change of heart. An intense social conscience took the place of her earlier devotion to high culture. Preaching active commitment to the betterment of society, she attacked her son's reading mania as frivolous, smug, and unmanly; brutally tore him away from his Zurich "paradise" of books, concerts, and philosophical discussions; and plunged him into the grim environment of a Germany in crisis. Thus Kien is one side of Canetti drawn from a hostile perspective. In fact, Canetti's identification with his protagonist surfaced after the book was finished. He was remorseful for having allowed his hero to destroy his library and himself. Canetti felt he had committed treason against himself.

What is more important, of course, is that Canetti has drawn in his crazy bibliophile a prototype of the Central European intellectual at the dawn of fascism. Only two years after he completed his portrayal of Kien, Germany seemed to follow his example in the Nazi book-burnings of 1933. A society in which intellect had secluded itself from all social and political concern ended by repudiating intellect itself.

Die Blendung is a harsh critique of the gap between rarefied intellect and a society mired in injustice and misery. The novel mourns a split between the individual and the masses, and between mind and body in the individual. Kien is not only the ivory tower intellectual; he is also the purely mental creature, oblivious to and frightened of his body and its needs. The tripartite division of the work reflects, in the titles given to each part—"A Head Without a World," "Headless World," and "The World in the Head"—the mutual alienation of intellectual and society. "A Head Without a World" shows the intellectual separated from humanity, nature, and his own flesh. "Headless World" focuses on the horrors of a society bereft of guidance by mind; it is a world in which mindless self-interest, blind emotion, and beastly prejudice hold sway. The first part shows mind needing world. The second part shows the world in need of mind. The third part, "The World in the Head," shows the invasion of the mind by the world, but also faintly hints at possibilities of bridging the breach.

During the writing of the novel, the protagonist bore the name Kant—a clear signal of a still wider circle of significance. In his hero Canetti satirizes Western man's pride in rationality and knowledge at the expense of imagination and emotion. Reason appears as mere categorizing. The cataloging of Kien's library recalls Kant's categories of reason and the compartmentalization of being he proposed in his three critiques. Knowledge appears as mere encyclopedic embrace of learning. Kien boasts of his phenomenal memory, his instantaneous recall, and his ability to quote entire books verbatim and carry them "in his head," which in his madness he does literally. He prides himself on his impeccable logic. He is a fanatical adherent of order, system, and clarity. Kien divides mankind into two classes: the learned and the ignorant. The latter comprise, for him, the vast majority, and he refuses to have any dealings with them except the few minimal ones that are absolutely necessary. Interest in others is awakened only when he thinks he can detect signs of educability toward the ideal he himself represents. His greatest pride is his "character," his never-changing identity, and his loyalty to his "principles." Kien flatters himself with the conviction that he has always remained the same. His is the Cartesian "I," the subject, pure thought, looking down from its eminence upon the inferior world of physical objects in their ceaseless change and manipulability.

Kien has systematically repressed all bonds to humanity in the flesh by substituting for them a fanatical love of humanity as literature. Created around the time when the French deconstructionist Jacques Derrida was born, Kien might be said to be a satirical representation of the principles of "grammatology" before the fact. He reverses the customary preference for speech over writing as the communication of personal presence and immediacy. For him, reading and writing are the sole activities that matter, and in the light of their overriding importance, companionship is a mere waste of time. Kien's life is dedicated to the texts that he restores, and he despises university teaching as mere rhetoric and, thus, the domain of mediocre minds. He stays away from the scholarly congresses where his presence is eagerly sought, and has never delivered a paper in person. For him, the profession of writing means abstention from personal contact with others; its rigor supersedes the coziness of orality and the frivolity of socializing.

Kien may be compared to Don Quixote. Both replace physical reality with an imagined one derived from books. However, while Don Quixote seeks to make the actual world conform to the ideal world projected in books, Kien is a fetishist of books (in Walter Benjamin's Marxist sense of the term) who does not care what state the human world is in as long as books exist and are protected. Just as reification reduces human beings to things, so fetishism endows things—books, in Kien's case—with humanity. Kien treats books as though they were human, caring for their well-being with tenderness and compassion, while seeing human beings as mere objects of indifference or nuisances. While Don Quixote's imagination revolves around human life as signified by literature, Kien's is obsessed with signification itself. He endows signs with human life and consciousness; addresses his books in an oration; feels deeply for their "misfortunes" if they are neglected, pawned, or exposed to cramped conditions and fire hazards. Whereas Don Quixote's act of setting the state's prisoners free strikes us as noble and utopian, even if misguided, Kien's comparable act of ransoming books from the state pawnshop appears pointless—or, rather, meaningful only to a bibliophile. Unlike Don Quixote's madness, Kien's has its parallel in art for art's sake or in the specialist's dedication to his field regardless of any bearing on human life.

In another way, however, Kien closely parallels the tragicomic aspect of Don Quixote. His concern about the fate of books is a profoundly humane one. It springs from the impulse of love as *caritas;* he feels for and wants to save the victims of a heartless world. Not without some justice can Kien connect his cause with Christ's. The quality and urgency of his involvement are not absurd; they conform to Canetti's demand that the writer feel responsible for all that happens. What is absurd is the deflection of this exemplary impulse to lifeless objects. This deflection leads us to the key image of the work, which is also reflected in its final title, *Die Blendung,* literally, "The Blinding."

The word *blenden* (to blind) runs as a leitmotiv through the work. It occurs for the first time in its past-participle form *geblendet* (blinded), in a dream Kien has early in the novel. He sees a temple terrace on which a man is being slaughtered by two priests dressed as jaguars. As they open the victim's chest, Kien, "blinded" with horror, closes his eyes. He avoids having to see the man's blood spurt forth, and waits for all the blood to be spilled before he opens his eyes again. To his horror, however, he then sees books tumbling out of the victim's chest. The blood has ignited the pile of wood around the altar and has set the books on fire. In indescribable panic, Kien seeks to save the books. He could have lived with human sacrifice, but what he finds unbearable is the destruction of books. Yet he lacks the power to prevent it.

What in fact "blinds" Kien is the sight of socially organized beastliness (the upholders of the murderous ritual of religion are costumed as beasts of prey). Unable to bear the sight of this truth, Kien substitutes books for human beings. His bibliophile obsession appears literally as the consequence of his evasion of humane intervention in the horrible spectacle. Intellectualism takes the place of humanism. With the change of Kien's object of concern from a human being to books, the basic impulse to help and save is made impotent. One could speak in Kien's case of a "sublimation" of the feeling of responsibility. The humane impetus retains its original force, but its object has been deflected, "elevated," like the sexual libido in Freud's concept of sublimation, from involvement in human suffering to the intellectual's preoccupation with monuments of human thought. Thereby compassion and indignation are rendered harmless against the smooth running of a beastly society. In this context we have to recall that Kien employs the sadistic "mercenary" and storm-trooper type, Pfaff, to keep human misery from disturbing his scholarly pursuit.

Blinding, then, is a self-blinding. Canetti excels in presenting varieties of self-deception or bad faith. For instance, Kien would rather be guilty of the murder of his wife than admit to himself that she had beaten and thrown him out. Instead, he insists that he has locked her in the apartment and let her starve to death. Her appearance at the pawnshop, and later at the police station, must, therefore, be hallucination. One of the chief ironies of the work hinges on Kien's obsessive fear of losing his eyesight, which would make him unable to read. Yet he proves himself mentally blind all along, the dupe of his wife and Fischerle, who ruthlessly exploit him. "The Blinding" would thus be a most appropriate English-language title for the work, and would convey a level of meaning that goes beyond the published title, *Auto-da-Fé.*

Auto-da-Fé, on the other hand, is closer to the original title, "Kant Catches Fire," which Canetti had first given to the novel but which Hermann Broch, an admirer of Kant, had made him change. This original title refers (as does the English *Auto-da-Fé*) to the intellectual's self-destruction. By connecting the system-building philosopher's name with fire, the German title expresses the dual nature of the protagonist. The name *Kant* symbolizes a consciousness that seeks to emancipate itself from nature while trying to encompass it through knowledge. Fire, on the other hand, as Canetti points out at length in *Crowds and Power,* is the symbol of the masses. The phrase "Kant Catches Fire" describes the overpowering of character and intellect by the masses erupting from within the individual. Self-destruction is built into the monomania of intellectuality. Kien's fate reflects, as it adumbrates, the fate of Central Europe in the decade that began with the writing of *Die Blendung* and ended with the outbreak of World War II. Its plot describes the pendulum motion from the extreme of intellectualism to its opposite pole—book-burning and chaos. Where books are prized above human beings, they perish in autos-da-fé. Self-destruction is the secret essence of the "bookworm" who has sacrificed life to his single passion. In the fateful split between a worldless head and a headless world, the latter avenges itself through the very mind that had scorned it. Thus the title of the novel's third and final part, "The World in the Head," alludes to the invasion of the mind by the masses.

Left alone in his library, Kien feels himself hounded by mobs and besieged by the police for his "murder" of Therese. This hallucination represents the climax of his subjectivity—his habit of seeing reality according to his obsessions. Substituting Therese's murder for his own humiliation, Kien asserts with it the "Kantian" and "Cartesian" principle that sees the world as a function of mind. By the same token it is also the supreme assertion of the will to power. In his study of the memoirs of Daniel Paul Schreber, the insane ex-president of the Saxon supreme court—a figure made famous by Freud's case study of 1911—Canetti shows the will to power culminating in two forms of madness: megalomania and paranoia. Kien's—or Kant's—end is the end of a paranoiac. He projects enemies and persecutors everywhere. Finally Kien sees even his beloved books rise against him. He cannot keep order among them; they fall apart. Pages loosen from their bindings, lines begin to dance, letters drop out of their lines, and footnotes kick him.

The world that mind has produced—the library, his self objectified—rebels against itself. His books turn into the masses of "racing electrons" of which they are composed. Kien punishes his rebellious books by setting them on fire. To arrest anarchy, he completes it, and with his books he destroys himself.

Kien's deadly hallucination is the eruption of the repressed. Kien represses not only his body and his humanity; he represses the masses in himself. According to Georg, the masses are a collective being, a higher species different from the individuals who compose them. One day all men will be one in the mass. Losing himself in it, the individual participates, even now, in the new species about to be born. The masses are not merely external to the individual; they live within each as an unconscious part of the psyche. We find here echoes of Gustave Le Bon's theory that man in the mass assumes a different nature, of Nietzsche's Dionysian merging of all individuated selves in one universal life, of the *Übermensch* he described in *Also sprach Zarathustra* as a higher species struggling to be born, of Hegel's view that individual consciousness must eventually evolve into universal consciousness, of Jung's idea of the collective unconscious, and of Freud's concept of the return of the repressed. The eruption of the submerged masses within and against the individual is what Georg calls madness. The novel ends with Kien's laugh, a laugh such as he had never laughed before. The laugh signals his repudiation of his entire life, his derision of all the knowledge his library had contained. Yet it is also the laughter of relief and longed-for liberation from an intolerable burden. The intellectual's self-repudiation is his redemption.

This last point illuminates Kien's unconscious preparation for his final act of self-transcendence. This plot runs beneath the "official" text as an implicit process of increasing disloyalty to his "character" and its rigid principles. It manifests itself in acts of reaching out toward the other. The novel begins, in fact, with Kien's deviating from his customary indifference to the life around him. He has started a conversation with a nine-year-old boy whose lively interest in bookstore windows has attracted Kien's attention. Next follows the inveterate bachelor's sudden about-face and decision to marry. Finally, he offers his friendship to Fischerle, in whom he thinks he sees a kindred spirit, chess being a game of which an intellectual does not have to be ashamed. The gradual crumbling of Kien's Chinese wall—his field of specialization, China, is also a symbol of his self—precedes his double immolation of books and self. Kien's enormous concern with book-burnings in history, evidenced also in his dream, presages his own deed.

Images assume the character of symbols in the novel, particularly as they relate to fire. They are transpersonal, going from Peter's dream and apprehensions to his brother. Georg seems to divine the repressed side of Peter that will burst forth in his act of arson. Georg, too, has a dream, one in which he sees Peter associated with an enormous sun. It hurts his eyes as he wakes up, and blinds him. Georg also anticipates Peter's self-destruction in a powerful analogy. As an example of beings who have already evolved into masses, Georg mentions termites, insects that have so successfully overcome individuation, and with it sexuality, that they exist as sexless parts of the colony, the mass. Yet occasionally they suffer a mysterious relapse into their former sexual being that, when they find no outlet, can make the whole colony go mad. Such an eruption, he adds, would be like the unimaginable event of Peter setting fire to his library. The sexual madness of the termites functions as the inversion of Peter's fate. In the termites, madness is the return of their repressed individuation on which sex, as the means of individual procreation, is based; in Kien, on the other hand, madness is the return of the repressed masses that explodes his proud individuation, his "character." The blinding sun, the reawakening of sexuality that now endangers the species— these are images in which life-giving force

merges with destruction. They universalize Peter Kien's end even as they herald it.

Up to a point we can accept Georg as a spokesman of the author, since some of his theorizing anticipates views that Canetti subsequently expressed in *Crowds and Power* and other works. Yet there are contradictions between Georg's statements and what the novel itself shows us; there are also contradictions among these statements themselves. In the plot of the novel, the masses do not appear in nearly so good a light as Georg's enthusiasm would make the reader expect. What we see of mass behavior is horrifying. Its worst example is shown in the trampling to death of a poor hunchbacked woman. In fact, ambivalence is shown in Canetti's own report of his first experiences of the phenomenon that was to become for him one of the foremost problems of human life. The masses appeared to him as a perturbing challenge, a question mark with frightening as well as liberating implications. He anxiously wonders how he could have lost his self-control as a rational being and be so carried away by mass frenzy. This was the question that haunted him and led to *Crowds and Power*.

An important self-contradiction can be found in Georg's view of madness. We have seen that Georg views madness as the eruption of the masses in the self; but elsewhere he calls his mad patients the only true characters and authentic individuals. This contradiction connects with a second one. Georg's enthusiastic views of madness contrast with the largely negative and caricaturing presentation of obviously mad characters like Kien and other monomaniacs in the novel.

These contradictions rest on a distinction between identity and authenticity that is fundamental to the novel but is never made explicit in it. Peter Kien seeks self-identity. He wants to be and to remain himself, a sharply defined character enduring through time. His aim is what Canetti later was to call "the mask," which in Latin is *persona*. Identity is an assertion of the will to endure. The wish for unchanging identity entails a deathly rigidity. It is significant that Kien is held to be dead at one point in the plot, and at another time pretends to have turned into stone in order to make himself insensitive to Therese's blows. As the element of change, fire is the antidote to the mummification toward which identity tends.

What Georg praises in his madmen is not identity but authenticity, that is, their ability to be completely themselves: to speak, to think, to feel, and to act in utterly unprecedented ways. The antonym of identity is change; the antonym of authenticity is convention or routine. Identity is not authenticity. Quite the contrary. Kien, for instance, is receiver and caretaker of the opinions, ideas, and experiences that others have conveyed in books. Georg's admired madmen, on the other hand, are completely original, utterly themselves at any one moment; but they may be unlike themselves at other moments. In their case, therefore, complete faithfulness to the true feeling of any given moment would preclude identity.

The embodiment of Georg's ideal of authenticity is a madman called the Gorilla, in whose presence Georg feels like a bedbug next to a human being. The Gorilla is the exact opposite of Peter Kien in three respects. First, while Kien seeks to embrace the totality of received language in his gigantic library, the Gorilla has invented a language of his own. Second, while Kien wishes to hold on to and perpetuate the amassed learning of mankind, the Gorilla changes the very meaning of his words each time he uses them. And third, while Kien inspires hatred in his wife, the Gorilla inspires love in the woman with whom he lives. In the Gorilla's language, words do not denote objects or refer to concepts; they signify the speaker's momentary emotional relationship to the person or object addressed (he makes no distinction between the two). It is language in which there is no third person, no impersonal referent, but only second-person partners. This language is the opposite of the acoustic masks,

the clichés and commonplaces of all the other characters. In the Gorilla's idiom, language acquires a face. Since his language is his own invention, while its words change their meanings, the Gorilla combines authenticity with metamorphosis, an idea that was to play a very important role in Canetti's later work.

Thus, Georg offers two very different utopian alternatives to the horror of the "real world" depicted in this novel. One is the eruption of the masses; the other is the being of the Gorilla. Only the latter offers a true alternative; the masses offer a deceptive one, as Canetti's subsequent work shows. This relationship becomes clear if we turn from *Auto-da-Fé* to *Crowds and Power,* to which the novel might be said to form a fictional overture.

The seeds of *Crowds and Power* lie in the same experience of the masses to which Canetti traces his novel. Novel and anthropological study are two branches of the same tree. Composed over a much longer period (Canetti worked almost thirty years on it), *Crowds and Power* clarifies the contradictions and brings out various implications of *Die Blendung.*

The opening sections of *Crowds and Power* read as though the problems of Kien had become the human condition. Human beings, *Crowds and Power* holds, dread being touched. They fear physical contact. They have learned to isolate themselves in clothes, build houses to hide in, and create hierarchies to increase distances between persons. In segregating himself from his species, civilized man has evolved into the supreme individual. By the same token, he has shrouded himself in gloom. He longs for liberation from his self-imposed prison. In *Crowds and Power,* the masses no longer offer such liberation. Perhaps in response to the Hitler era, when the masses appeared at their brutal worst, *Crowds and Power* does not hail them as the utopian future of man. Instead, they are traced back to various forms of animal packs and described as embodying man's beastliness. Furthermore, they cannot offer permanent relief to the individual who lives bottled up in his fear of touch. For the mass is nothing but the individual writ large. It is just as mortal, only much shorter-lived. Haunted by the specter of its end, the mass, like the individual, seeks to expand continuously; but eventually it has to disintegrate, and the individuals composing it are thrown back into their isolation. The masses offer no genuine redemption.

Yet it is the universal need for redemption that *Crowds and Power* demonstrates. Canetti paints the universe in the somber colors of Thomas Hobbes—a philosopher who exerted a decisive influence on him. "Eat or be eaten" is the program inscribed into all creatures. The Kienian fear of contact derives from the ancient terror that the predator's claw and maw inspire in its victims. *Crowds and Power* shows, in discursive terms, that beastly foundation of all society which Kien's dream presented in terms of images. "Woe to the victims," which might have been the motto of "Headless World" in *Die Blendung,* turns, in *Crowds and Power,* into a system that shows human civilization as the appendage of a frightful nature.

The world view of *Crowds and Power* is grimly naturalistic. Molded by Darwinism, it eschews all consolation from religion. Canetti views all life as an evolutionary continuum without an essential break between the lower animals and men. In consequence, civilized life appears in terms of the animal kingdom, while animals are considered with a degree of empathy usually reserved for humans. Canetti follows the social instinct back to its biological and physiological antecedents. Like Nietzsche and Freud he is an archaeologist of human behavior. He makes the reader embarrassingly aware of the degree to which the rituals of society derive from practices of the beasts. He uses anthropology to make a connection between the archaic and the contemporary. Since he underlines the constants in evolution rather than the changes, he powerfully suggests the unity of all life but, by the same token, makes evolution appear profoundly ahistorical. Since

Canetti dwells on the persistence of timeless archetypal situations, the insights with which evolution provides him contradict, in a way, the idea of evolution itself.

Our present is for Canetti a "symbol" of our past. It is the reverse of the prefigurations of future salvation that Christian authors saw in the scenes and persons of the Old Testament. For Canetti our institutions are "postfigurative." They point us back to our horror-laden past. Our present is a powerful reminder of our heritage and therefore of our fate. Canetti does not let us forget the repeated holocaust that is our history and the history of life itself. His method is a synthesis of the archaeologist's view of evolution with the phenomenologist's description of the views from which objects and situations appear to consciousness. Thus he shows, for instance, how a hunter or predator sees its living prey, as it flees in deadly panic, as the meat that it intends to eat.

Like Nietzsche, Canetti sees the will to power as the ubiquitous mover of animals and men; but the evaluation he gives to it is the reverse of Nietzsche's. Whereas Nietzsche celebrates the will to power as the creative principle, Canetti, in a sense, writes his entire book to unmask it. He does so in two ways. First, he traces the will to power back not to the desire to master by shaping and forming resistant matter, but to the much less dignified desire to incorporate and digest the other. Second, he shows that the will to power, like vanity and resentment, is a purely reactive quality; this he argues with particular clarity in his essay "Macht und Überleben" ("Power and Survival," 1972), written a year after *Die Blendung.*

A central fact of all higher life, Canetti asserts, is the fear of death. Death is absolute evil. All human beings assume themselves to be immortal, and the encounter with death brings the horror of the inconceivable. However, like the self-deceiving characters of *Die Blendung,* men, to ward off death from themselves, wish it onto others. Surviving others becomes the token of one's own immunity from death. Not trusting in the solidarity of life, and equally threatened by its archenemy, man thinks he can prolong his own life by taking it away from others. He who survives the greatest number of his fellow creatures is considered the luckiest, happiest, and most powerful. He is the hero. Making the wish for survival the foundation of power, Canetti deglamorizes it and throws the will to power from its Nietzschean pedestal.

The stark pessimism with which Canetti paints natural and human history as the calvary of life has as its purpose the mobilization of the reader's empathy with the victims. Making his reader share the victim's perspective, Canetti's descriptions arouse indignation against the victimizers. He provokes empathy as a step to defiance.

In his lecture "The Writer's Profession," Canetti equates empathy with metamorphosis. He states that he prefers the latter term because—as the lecture makes clear—it is the more radical and comprehensive. All empathy is identification with the other, and presupposes the act of temporarily letting go of one's own point of view, one's identity. Only through adopting the other's perspective is it possible to feel what he feels, to "know" him. Empathy is the means by which we change into the other; it is the threshold of metamorphosis.

Metamorphosis, rather than the masses, is Canetti's antidote to both the will to power and death. Metamorphosis differs from mass experience. Both, to be sure, share the element of self-transcendence. The masses, however, accomplish this by abolishing, metamorphosis by multiplying, the individual. Through it one becomes many. At bottom, metamorphosis is the experience of the writer who, according to Canetti's poetics, becomes his characters in creating them. Since they may outlive him, they are his possibilities for immortality. Metamorphosis is the most promising weapon against death. Canetti finds this union of metamorphosis and man's fight against death in *Gilgamesh,* the most ancient epic known. It

begins with Enkidu's transformation from natural to civilized man and continues, after Enkidu's death, with the refusal of his friend—Gilgamesh—to accept it and his search for a "cure" for death. Canetti names the ancient Sumerian epic as the most decisive influence on his life.

Canetti sees in metamorphosis the original theme of all narrative, even as he considers narrative to be the form in which metamorphosis can manifest itself. This is most clearly apparent in the oldest version of narrative myth. Although Canetti, unlike James Joyce, T. S. Eliot, William Butler Yeats, and other moderns, does not rewrite ancient myths in modern versions, he alludes to the myth of Odysseus in his novel and makes the retelling of myths an essential part of *Crowds and Power.* In his autobiography Canetti calls Odysseus a model on whose example he patterned his life. What he loved most about Odysseus was the fact that the Greek hero's life became a story to which he could listen. In the first and most powerful volume of his autobiography, Canetti tells his own life "in the manner of Odysseus," as a sequence of vivid episodes, each of which tends to be a "completed narrative." From *Gilgamesh,* to the *Odyssey,* to the *Śatapatha-Brahmana,* Canetti sees myths teaching, by way of the exemplary tale, that metamorphosis is man's hope. In a postmythic age like ours, it is the writer's task to resurrect to modern consciousness the eternal wisdom contained in myths.

The idea of metamorphosis also plays a crucial role in Canetti's poetics of the symbol. Commenting, in *Crowds and Power,* on the fire dance of the Navaho Indians, Canetti points out that the symbol is a substitute for the object into which one metamorphoses. Using a symbol means to become what the symbol signifies. As the Navahos' dance symbolizes fire, the dancers transform themselves into flames. They aim at abolishing the difference between the sign and the signified. In "The Writer's Profession" Canetti makes the Navahos a model for the writer. The writer, the "guardian of metamorphosis," practices in fiction and drama the art of becoming the other, just as the Navahos become the fire they enact. Merging with his characters through mimicking them, the writer overcomes the difference between writing and being. Canetti seems to arrive at a position quite close to contemporary poststructuralist aesthetics and yet remains at an opposite pole. He affirms "the death of the author," but only to make him live again in his characters. The author is abolished not by language but by the characters he impersonates. The relevance of drama to Canetti's poetics of metamorphosis is clear.

Between the completion of his novel and the publication of *Crowds and Power,* Canetti wrote three plays: *Hochzeit* (*Wedding,* 1932), *Komödie der Eitelkeit* (*The Comedy of Vanity,* 1950 [written in 1934]), and *Die Befristeten* (*The Numbered,* 1964 [written in 1952]). What led him to drama was the same interest in character as type that had led him to the novel. In his dramas Canetti extended this interest to types of social life. This connected his plays with the anthropological interests he was pursuing at the time. However, whereas in *Crowds and Power* he intended an inventory of the human condition, in his dramas—particularly the two later ones—he was engaged in the exploration of unrealized possibilities of human existence. His utopian bent had, of course, already been at work in the invention of the Gorilla in *Auto-da-Fé,* but it was broadened and became the principal theme in the later plays. Even though in his earliest play, *Wedding,* a satirical survey of the actual human condition seems to predominate, the inquiry into the possibility of utopia lies near the heart of all three of his plays.

Wedding presents a dramatic version of the "headless world" of *Die Blendung,* but raises the social level shown from the lower depths to the wealthy bourgeoisie. One is reminded of the equally cynical plays of Canetti's slightly older contemporary Ödön von Horváth. Vanity, greed, snobbery, lust, and unmitigated selfishness characterize everyone's behavior, while speech consists of routinized phrases and clichés that hardly mask the speakers' grasping egotism. The sick, the aged, the dying, and the needy are treated as bothersome nuisances or obstacles to one's enjoyment, if not totally ignored. The voice of utopia is heard in the shrill tones of a moralist with the telling name of Horch (Hearken), who seems to have stepped straight out of the theater of expressionism. Humanity, represented by the wedding party, fails Horch's test. An apocalyptic finale awaits an unregenerate society. In the ruins of the apartment building in which the wedding party had taken place, only the dreary assertion of mere survival is heard at the end. The aged, bedridden landlady announces in her Viennese dialect, "I'm still around. I li——" The truncated form of the word *live* is followed by her moaning and her parrot's endless reiteration "House house house." The principle of property survives the collapse of the society over which it rules.

Vanity, a form of the will to power, had been a prime target of Canetti's satire on Therese. *Comedy of Vanity* shows a utopian society in which the emblem of vanity, the mirror, has been outlawed. However, official suppression by no means eradicates vice. On the contrary, it causes vice to find more vicious forms in which to manifest itself. Its harshest persecutors are its worst perpetrators. Canetti always shows utopia as dystopia. This is particularly true of the most profound of his plays, *The Numbered.*

The Numbered takes issue with a utopian possibility of dealing with Canetti's primary theme—the calamity that is death. The drama shows a future in which the uncertainty of the moment of death has been removed. Thus death seems to have lost its terror, and life is free from fear and trembling. Everyone in this utopian society knows in advance the precise age at which he or she will die. The number of years one has to live serves as his or her name. The predetermined length of life is one's essence. People are named 10, 28, 88, and so on.

Individuals *are* the number of years allotted to them.

Canetti pursues two intentions in this play. He creates a Brechtian or, perhaps more appropriately, Swiftian alienation effect, presenting our habitual way of living and dying, which we assume to be "natural" and inevitable, from an entirely novel perspective. The "natural" is made to appear strange. Thus Canetti forces us to question whether it has to be true for all eternity that we must live as helpless victims of an enemy who may strike us down at any moment. His second intention is to lay bare, beneath a superficially utopian appearance, the features of dystopia. The two intentions merge, of course. Both force the audience to compare two systems of human life and weigh the advantages and disadvantages of each.

Three factors make the world of the numbered a utopian world for us. The first is the elimination of the angst that arises from the possibility that death may strike at any time. The second is the abolition of murder. A totally predetermined and publicly known life span for each person makes any attempt at murder absurd, since it is bound to fail. Third, foreknowledge of the precise length of one's life makes planning it infinitely easier, allows one to calculate the projects that can be undertaken, and immeasurably increases one's control over life. The ignorance in which we have to live our lives seems inconceivable to the citizens of the numbered society. Canetti shows that alternatives to our "unalterable" fate are thinkable, and that what is "natural" to us may, from a different perspective, appear absurd.

Yet the society of the numbered, however disguised it may be as a triumph of individual self-determination, is a totalitarian nightmare. It derives from that prototype of modern dystopia—Ivan's parable of the Grand Inquisitor in Dostoevsky's *Brothers Karamazov.* Peace, contentment, and security are offered in exchange for uncertainty, anxiety, and peril; yet the latter entail freedom, while the former spell enslavement. Like the Grand Inquisitor's society, that of the numbered rests on a "pious" fraud. The number of years of one's life is assigned arbitrarily by the authorities, but a skillful mystique presents the preordained date of death as fate. Each victim's blind faith ensures the smooth working of the system. People die at the moment they are supposed to die because all along they have believed that it is their predestined moment. They uphold the tyranny that tells them when to die.

In the new system death becomes absolute to a degree unknown in our world, where death is subject to randomness and chance. To be sure, the "utopian" scheme eliminates "untimely" deaths; but, much more important, it makes every death timely. Death at the preordained moment has to be accepted without demur. It is hailed as the seal and verification of one's destiny, and proves the marvelous smoothness of the system. The predestined date dooms any attempt to push back the dominion of death by postponing its arrival. By doing away with "premature" deaths, the system bestows on every death the status of an absolute law, which, according to Canetti, death should never be allowed to have. In our world, where death may strike at any time, we always have the chance to contest it, perhaps even to diminish its rule, no matter by how insignificant a margin. The "utopia" of the numbered lives absolves human beings from their perennial task of fighting death. Most important, *The Numbered* exposes power's hidden need for death. In this system death functions, as any ideology does, in the service of political control by a few over the rest of society. Canetti's "utopia" shows that the fight against death is also, and above all, a political and social struggle.

The Numbered is, furthermore, a satire of social inequality. Each citizen's number is a label indicating his or her assigned position in the social hierarchy that the system has created. (Analogies to the Soviet "workers' paradise" cannot be overlooked here.) Life expectancy determines social standing. Low numbers, who have no future, are treated very differently from high numbers, who have much time in which to become important and powerful. The number of years functions in analogy to income and property in Western capitalist society or to the amount of "productivity" contributed by each worker in Stalinist Russia. It is the yardstick of inequality. Those who are destined to live longer are accorded the highest rank. One's place in the hierarchy also determines one's character and outlook. Low numbers are dispirited, lacking ambition, and eager to escape a society in which they stand condemned as practically dead; they are ready to embrace the revolution when it comes. High numbers, by contrast, accustomed to attention and esteem, are conservative and loath to part with a system that has benefited them so handsomely.

In much the same way as the rigorous portrayal of monomaniac types functions in his novel, the extreme consistency with which Canetti traces the ramifications and consequences of the initial premise in *The Numbered* constitutes the strength and the humor of his work. The play resembles an experiment in which an idea is put to the test to let us see how it works and what it would mean to human life. The characters are functional; they merely serve the overall purpose. However, they also behave with mimetically convincing realism. In an unreal context, they speak and act like real people. The plot is episodic. Each scene illuminates a different aspect of the functioning of the societal model. Their sequence shows how the same fundamental pattern applies to the most varied human relationships and situations. Canetti excels in the invention of variations of social situations. At the same time these variations also supply the humor that so strongly marks his work in general. For instance, a woman tells a man whose name is 46 that she prefers men with middling numbers because they have neither the arrogance of men with high numbers nor the resigned air of those with low life expectancies. The scene hu-

morously shows how one's exact place in the social scheme determines one's fate, or, to put it the other way around, that fate is nothing other than one's place in the social hierarchy. It also shows how societal arrangement determines individual character.

The exception in this society is a dissenter named 50, who seems to function as the spokesman of the author, much like Georg in *Auto-da-Fé* or the somewhat satirized expressionist type Horch in *Wedding*. In *The Numbered,* 50 is the one character who refuses to play his assigned role and die at the preordained moment. He does the unprecedented: he questions the system, and thereby brings about its downfall. Daring the unthinkable, the dissenter destroys the mystique on which power rests. His is the messianism of Kien and the uniqueness and authenticity of the madmen whom Georg admires. He lives without precedent.

However, the ensuing revolution reintroduces, along with the uncertainty of the moment of death, the temptation to murder, and the dissenter-spokesman comes to regret his victory. Murders take place, and he wishes he could undo the revolution he has brought about. Canetti is not interested in establishing the superiority of one system over another. He is content to devise an alternative possibility to our own way of life and to show the advantages and disadvantages of each. Unlike Brecht, he does not offer a ready-made ideology. He challenges the audience to think, to reflect, and to debate the possible answers to the questions that are posed but left open by an inconclusive and self-contradictory plot. The audience is made to see that both systems are good in some respects and bad in others. The uncertainty of the date of death, which in our world affects all equally, appears as a paragon of fairness compared with the hierarchy of numbers. However, our way of life encourages murder, while theirs rules it out. In the end, both are condemned, for neither challenges the absolute evil that is the fact of death.

ELIAS CANETTI

In his autobiography, *Die gerettete Zunge* (*The Tongue Set Free*, 1977), Canetti reveals the genesis of his lifelong preoccupation with and combat against death. He presents himself as an intense and high-strung child, overreacting to perceived slights and injustice, and veering toward violence. In a fit of rage at his cousin, who had teased him, he was about to kill her; her life was spared only by their grandfather's intervention. A colossal sense of guilt and dread of the consequences of violence thus arose in young Canetti. Henceforth, all victors and conquering heroes were marked for him by the shame of murder, and the survivor's exultation over his slain victim became the primal scene of abomination to him.

Canetti's autobiography, in three volumes, which must be considered one of his three major works, has to be seen in the light of its late date of composition. Following up on all his other works, it cannot help but be informed and possibly influenced by them. Canetti presents the writing of his autobiography not as a passive recording of a past ready for recall, but as a process of discovering and unearthing a past coming to light in the process of being written. The activity of writing—which takes place in the present—exerts a decisive influence on its subject, which represents the past. It literally shapes it. Thus the writer's current knowledge must play an influential role as he describes his past state of mind. The autobiography consistently shows earliest instances of constellations that, in different forms, appear in Canetti's other works. Canetti's implicit intent seems to be to conjure up the genesis of themes that have preoccupied him throughout his works.

One striking example is his grandfather's curse of his son, Canetti's father, for disobeying, and his father's death soon after the curse. His grandfather never stopped behaving as though he considered himself guilty of his son's death. Canetti paints this sequence of events as an abhorrent example of the triumph of will over love. However, in the context of Canetti's total oeuvre, the linking of the two events dramatically shows how the will to be obeyed—the will to power—sows death. In *Crowds and Power,* Canetti universalizes the family tragedy and makes it the implicit starting point of a phenomenological analysis of command. Every command, Canetti writes, ultimately aims to kill. The death penalty is kept ready for the case of disobedience. For, explicitly or silently, every command enunciates the ominous threat "Or else."

The close analogy between the grandfather's curse and the phenomenology of command—both showing the deadliness of the exercise of power—reveals the mutual illumination of anthropological theory and personal experience. This mutuality is the most characteristic element of Canetti's autobiography. The mythic-historical and the intimate interpenetrate. The public-historical sphere receives deepened significance by its association with details of personal biography. When he read about Napoleon, Canetti tells us, he was reminded of an uncle whom he detested. Conversely, whenever he thought of this uncle, Napoleon came to mind. Canetti's uncle is raised to world-historical rank, and Napoleon is made intimate by reappearing in the uncle. It is his fascination with type—which, as we recall, was the cause of his becoming a writer—that enables Canetti to make the historical and mythic appear in the personal and to give the personal and everyday a superpersonal dimension. Just as his grandfather is part of the archetype that issues death-dealing commands, so his father belongs to the series of dissenter-victims who are Canetti's models.

Influence for Canetti is not merely a stylistic, formal, and technical affair. The word Canetti uses for it—*Vorbild*—implies a particular way of being that becomes inspiration for the conduct of another person's life. Characters of myth, literature, and history as well as artists, writers, and thinkers are among his *Vorbilder,* as are obscure men and women whom he meets on life's way. The first volume of Canetti's autobiography makes plain that his original *Vorbilder* were his father and mother—his father unqualifiedly, his mother dialectically, in a mixture that blended adoration with mutual victimization and eventually led to estrangement. The autobiography shows how the self is formed by the successive incorporations of admired models, or by deliberate decisions not to be like others who might be called negative *Vorbilder,* or by the passionate acceptance of the challenges posed by a third group of *Vorbilder*—Brecht foremost among them. Positively, negatively, or dialectically—the self *is* its models, even as it is the words and phrases that have stayed in it to form its language. The self is thus a living crossroads of traditions that it continues, remakes, and transmits. Canetti sets himself quite deliberately apart from his mother's turn-of-the-century cult of genius as the lonely creator of the absolutely new. He emphasizes not creation ex nihilo but acquisition, re-creation, and transmission.

The organ of transmission is the tongue. Instrument and symbol of speech, it becomes, for Canetti (in sharp contrast with Kien's "grammatological" privileging of writing), witness to and symptom of the integrity of life. This is the meaning of the earliest memory Canetti recounts in his autobiography, which also supplies the title of the opening volume, *The Tongue Set Free.* What Canetti presents as his earliest memory describes a command and threat issued by an adult male to the small child. "Show me your tongue and I shall cut it off!" (The title of the published English translation, *The Tongue Set Free,* fails to convey the threat of destruction that the episode shows and that the German original, *gerettet,* expresses. *Retten* means "to save, rescue, or spare," but not "to set free.") Fortunately, this command was never enforced. The terror issuing from it remained, however; and so did the tongue—to tell about it, to protest it, to defy it, and to proclaim the victim's point of view.

The three volumes of his autobiography trace the history of Canetti's engagement in the cause of life, justice, and literature. Writing for Canetti is the sword with which life battles against death.

Selected Bibliography

EDITIONS

INDIVIDUAL WORKS

PROSE FICTION
Die Blendung. Vienna, Leipzig, and Zurich, 1935.
Der Ohrenzeuge: Fünfzig Charaktere. Munich, 1974.

PLAYS
Hochzeit. Berlin, 1932.
Komödie der Eitelkeit. Munich, 1950.
Die Befristeten. Munich, 1964.

ESSAYS, STUDIES, MEDITATIONS
Fritz Wotruba. Vienna, 1955.
Masse und Macht. Hamburg, 1960.
Der andere Prozess: Kafkas Briefe an Felice. Munich, 1969. (First printed in *Die Neue Rundschau* 79:185–220, 586–623 [1968]).
Alle vergedeute Verehrung: Aufzeichnungen 1949–1960. Munich, 1970.
Die gespaltene Zukunft: Aufsätze und Gespräche. Munich, 1972.
Macht und Überleben: Drei Essays. Berlin, 1972.
Die Provinz des Menschen: Aufzeichnungen 1942–1972. Munich, 1973.
Das Gewissen der Worte: Essays. Munich, 1975.
Der Beruf des Dichters. Munich, 1976.
Hebel und Kafka. Munich, 1980.
Das Geheimnis der Uhr: Aufzeichnungen 1973–1985. Munich, 1987.

SELECTED WORKS
Welt im Kopf. Edited by Erich Fried. Graz and Vienna, 1962.

JOURNALS, AUTOBIOGRAPHY

Aufzeichnungen 1942–1948. Munich, 1965.
Die Stimmen von Marrakesch: Aufzeichnungen nach einer Reise. Munich, 1967.
Die gerettete Zunge: Geschichte einer Jugend. Munich, 1977.

Die Fackel im Ohr: Lebensgeschichte 1921–1931. Munich and Vienna, 1980.

Das Augenspiel: Lebensgeschichte 1931–1937. Munich and Vienna, 1985.

TRANSLATIONS

Auto-da-Fé. Translated by C. V. Wedgwood. London, 1946.

Comedy of Vanity & Life-terms. Translated by Gitta Honegger. New York, 1983.

The Conscience of Words. Translated by Joachim Neugroschel. New York, 1979.

Crowds and Power. Translated by Carol Stewart. London, 1962; New York, 1973.

Ear Witness: Fifty Characters. Translated by Joachim Neugroschel. New York, 1979.

The Human Province. Translated by Joachim Neugroschel. New York, 1978.

Kafka's Other Trial: The Letters to Felice. Translated by Christopher Middleton. London and New York, 1974.

The Numbered: A Play. Translated by Carol Stewart. London and New York, 1984.

The Play of the Eyes. Translated by Ralph Manheim. New York, 1986.

The Plays of Elias Canetti. Translated by Ralph Manheim. New York, 1986.

The Tongue Set Free: Remembrance of a European Childhood. Translated by Joachim Neugroschel. New York, 1979.

The Torch in My Ear. Translated by Joachim Neugroschel. New York, 1982.

The Tower of Babel. Translated by C. V. Wedgwood. New York, 1947.

The Voices of Marrakesh: A Record of a Visit. Translated by J. A. Underwood. New York, 1978.

BIOGRAPHICAL AND CRITICAL STUDIES

Barnouw, Dagmar. *Elias Canetti.* Stuttgart, 1979.

Bartsch, Kurt, and Herbert Melzer, eds. *Experte der Macht: Elias Canetti.* Graz, 1985.

Bischoff, Alfons M. *Elias Canetti. Stationen zum Werk.* Bern and Frankfurt, 1973.

Dissinger, Dieter. *Vereinzelung und Massenwahn: Elias Canettis Roman "Die Blendung."* Bonn, 1971.

Durzak, Manfred. "'Die Welt ist nicht mehr so darzustellen wie in früheren Romanen.' Gespräch mit Elias Canetti." In his *Gespräche über den Roman: Formbestimmungen und Analysen.* Frankfurt, 1976. Pp. 86–102.

Göpfert, Herbert, ed. *Canetti Lesen: Erfahrungen mit seinen Büchern.* Munich, 1975.

Hennighaus, Lothar. *Tod und Verwandlung: Elias Canettis poetische Anthropologie aus der Kritik der Psychoanalyse.* Frankfurt and New York, 1984.

Meili, Barbara. *Erinnerung und Vision: Der lebensgeschichtliche Hintergrund von Elias Canettis Roman "Die Blendung."* Bonn, 1985.

Modern Austrian Literature. 16 (nos. 3–4) (1983). Special Canetti issue.

Parry, Idris F. "Elias Canetti's Novel 'Die Blendung.'" In *Essays in German Literature.* Edited by F. Norman. London, 1965. Pp. 145–166.

Piel, Edgar. *Elias Canetti.* Munich, 1984.

Roberts, David. *Kopf und Welt: Elias Canettis Roman Die Blendung.* Edited by Helga Wagner and Fred Wagner. Munich, 1975.

Sokel, Walter H. "The Ambiguity of Madness: Elias Canetti's Novel *Die Blendung.*" In *Views and Reviews of Modern German Literature. Festschrift for Adolf D. Klarmann.* Edited by Karl S. Weimar. Munich, 1974. Pp. 181–187.

Thomson, Edward A. "Elias Canetti's *Die Blendung* and the Changing Image of Madness." *German Life and Letters* 26:38–47 (1972).

———. *Zu Elias Canetti. Interpretationen.* Edited by Manfred Durzak. Stuttgart, 1983.

WALTER H. SOKEL

GUNNAR EKELÖF

(1907–1968)

THERE ARE CLEAR indications that Gunnar Ekelöf has fared considerably better than his contemporary, the equally great poet and Nobel laureate Harry Martinson (1904–1978), in terms of the number of translations of his work into English, and it is tempting to speculate why. Rhymed poetry and prose with excessive wordplay or new coinages, both typical of Harry Martinson, are difficult to translate felicitously: W. H. Auden, Robert Bly, William Jay Smith, Richard Vowles, and others generally preferred to translate Martinson's free, unrhymed verse. But this leaves some of Martinson's most important contributions untranslated into English, although they have the marks of *Weltliteratur.*

Both poets were great travelers and autodidacts (although of different kinds) who became recognized as "learned men" by their compatriots—Martinson for his interest in natural science, especially astronomy and ecology, Ekelöf for his quite unsystematic studies in antiquity. While Rudyard Kipling, Walt Whitman, Carl Sandburg, Edgar Lee Masters, and their Swedish heir, Artur Lundkvist, were Martinson's early influences, Ekelöf's were surrealists and symbolists, whom he introduced and translated into Swedish. Dreams, nightmares, anguish, and self-mockery; the jocular, the grotesque, the obscene, the ecstatic, and the mystical; nature lyrics, parodies, and puns; allusiveness, complex musicality, and the play of an unusual analytical intelli-

gence—all these are found in Ekelöf's poetry, which achieves its modernity at least partially through a range of personalized borrowings. While Harry Martinson early abandoned private symbolism to study nature, to reach for the "objective," Ekelöf was drawn toward the subjective and the study of the self. If Martinson needed merely a few square feet of nature to describe and observe, to find his way to broad cultural or personal perspectives, Ekelöf needed an archaeological spade and an ancient shard, his collection over the years amounting to a veritable museum of his wishes, fears, and reminiscences.

The question of whether Ekelöf represents the new paradigm and Martinson the old will have to be left unanswered for the time being. As far as international attention is concerned, Ekelöf clearly has the upper hand. Such notable figures as Auden, Bly, Hans Magnus Enzensberger, Rika Lesser, Jean-Clarence Lambert, Leonard Nathan, Giacomo Oreglia, Adrienne Rich, Muriel Rukeyser, and Nelly Sachs have been devoted translators of Ekelöf's poetry.

Whether Martinson, who was honored with half a Nobel Prize, or Ekelöf, who was not, turns out to have been more closely aligned with the future, to use a phrase of Ibsen's, remains to be seen. In any event, a translator of Ekelöf or Martinson is convinced that he or she is dealing with a great poet, one who deserves to be translated. But how can others be convinced that the poet really is "great"? If there is little or no doubt among Swedish poetry lovers that both Martinson and Ekelöf are great, doubt may arise in other readers, who may require convincing proof.

In a survey article on Ekelöf's influence, a young poet, Ragnar Strömberg (b. 1950), admits that he does not know exactly how much he is indebted to Ekelöf, but says, "As a poet?—What a question! [Ekelöf] saved my ass, my ass! I know that he is one of the greatest ever, anywhere. Li Po, Sappho, Homer, Shakespeare, Donne, Dickinson, Dante, Rilke, Pessoa, Vallejo, Char, Rimbaud, Baudelaire. That I know. And that anyone can find out from reading" (Allt om böcker, no. 2 [1984]).

Another young poet, Gunnar Harding (b. 1940), is more ambivalent: "Like most of the [Swedish] poets of my generation I consider Ekelöf to be the greatest Swedish poet of the century. But unlike them I keep away from him. In spite of the fact that no other of our poets has touched me more deeply, he has had no influence on my poetry." To his regret, Harding found that Ekelöf aroused depression and anguish in him when studied for any length of time: "I am not looking for a guide to the underworld, but for a guide out of there." Harding suspects that Ekelöf's personality was "too strong to make him a creative point of departure" and goes on to suggest that reading Ekelöf's poetry for inspiration in one's own work "requires a strong lack of sensibility, an enormous frigidity, two qualities that appear to be growing ever more common" (ibid.). The poet Björn Håkanson (b. 1937) terms Ekelöf's poetic method "a dialectic reductionism, the perfect instrument for a suicidal poetry that does not leave self alone until it stands eye to eye facing Nothing. There are only two alternatives: death or mysticism" (ibid.).

For the novelist Birgitta Trotzig (b. 1929), Ekelöf is "our real and important national poet": he sums up "the great anti-tradition, the black tradition, of Swedish poetry. . . . This tradition: an echo chamber of cultural resonances, borrowed identities, parts. Flowing en-chanted music breaks its way through all the disease. Through the masks the dark radiant icon" (ibid.).

Peter Ortman (b. 1939) recalls that there was a change of mood in Sweden around 1965, which was also the year of deepening American involvement in Vietnam. For a decade Swedish critics had praised everything Ekelöf had written, but after 1965 there were suddenly many "who felt that Ekelöf belonged to the bourgeois baggage that should be abandoned" (ibid.).

It is harder to find statements from Ekelöf's contemporaries. To the fine poet Johannes Edfelt (b. 1904), one of Ekelöf's major reviewers, he was "a stimulus as a human being and as a poet." Edfelt suggests that what united Ekelöf and himself may have been a sense of estrangement from Sweden's bourgeois society and "the same intense apprehension that darkness was falling over Europe at the time of the Fascist and Nazi advance" (ibid.).

In 1968, when Artur Lundkvist (b. 1906) filled Ekelöf's vacant seat in the Swedish Academy, he was among the first to announce some significant reservations about the work of his predecessor. Himself an influential poet, critic, and novelist, Lundkvist intimated in his inaugural lecture that Ekelöf turned away from the world too much and concentrated "one-sidedly" on the problem of self; the result was mysticism, a metaphysics of the ineffable.

According to Lundkvist, Ekelöf achieved his intensity primarily through concentration and reduction, a rigorously pursued line, an often ruthless paring down of his poetry to a statement of his inner battle and his incessant wrestling with personal conflicts. "It was as if the conjuring of a demoniacal world on the border between life and death became more important to him than anything else." To Lundkvist, Gunnar Ekelöf appeared to be tremendously self-centered and at the same time a great master of himself. He was simultaneously "the proudest and the humblest, with one characteristic as the basis for the other. He was close to life by his proximity to death, free by his attachment to his own intricate demands" (Lundkvist, 1968). Noting certain simple and popular features in Ekelöf's work, combined with burlesque, scurrilous, and even scatological elements, Lundkvist views all of them as devices necessary to counterbalance all of Ekelöf's exclusivity and loftiness. Lundkvist did not deny that Ekelöf's inner drama mirrored the outer drama, the tragedy of our time, but he maintained that in this reflection too much is left implicit.

The poet, critic, and biographer Olof Lagercrantz (*b.* 1911) was supportive of Ekelöf, especially after Martinson's *Aniara* had failed internationally (in an infelicitous English adaptation). As an outsider, Ekelöf did not fit into the Swedish Academy. He was not a clubbable man. For years he attended the academy's Thursday meetings only sporadically, though he did maintain frequent contact with his compeer and chief competitor as a poet, Erik Lindegren (1910–1968), with whom he discussed personalities, policies, decisions, and matters of opinion.

In comparing the poets Ekelöf and Lindegren (both renowned translators), Lagercrantz offers some amusing insights. Both were generally short of money, but Lindegren would pretend otherwise by giving his hosts expensive presents, while Ekelöf would come empty-handed—unless he brought his own bottle for his own consumption. Lindegren was lavish with compliments, while Ekelöf very rarely complimented anyone. Lindegren had neither the time nor the strength to take note of others; Ekelöf really saw others and sensed their strengths as well as their weaknesses. "Once in his diabolic humor at a dinner party he went from guest to guest and whispered a word in the ear of everyone, and at once tears burst forth in the eyes of each of them. He had touched their weakest spot" (*Allt om Böcker,* no. 2 [1984]).

As a young man Ekelöf was morbidly self-conscious about his appearance. Why did this awkward and withdrawn being allow himself to be coaxed into becoming a member of the Swedish Academy, where his duties would include rendering judgment and (one would hope) justice in regard to the finest authors of the age? He would be participating in decisions that made Nobel laureates of Salvatore Quasimodo, Saint-John Perse, Ivo Andrić, John Steinbeck, George Seferis, Jean-Paul Sartre, Mikhail Sholokhov (whom Ekelöf did not appreciate), Miguel Ángel Asturias, S. Y. Agnon, and Nelly Sachs (whom he translated and who reciprocated by translating Ekelöf into German). Lagercrantz thinks it possible that Ekelöf saw his election as a unique opportunity to prove himself to his mother, whose early abandonment of him led to guilt, hate, and rage. For a moment he also thought, mistakenly, that becoming one of the "immortals" of the Swedish Academy might help him to cut down on his drinking.

Ekelöf's father, Gerhard Ekelöf (1866–1916), a Stockholm banker with a dazzling career, contracted syphilis from a streetwalker. He received the inadequate treatment then available and in 1906, believing himself cured (although his disease had only gone into remission), married Valborg von Hedenberg (1881–1961), a member of the petty nobility. He failed to inform her of his past, however, and when the disease flared up again, he had to tell her. This revelation of an incurable disease and apparent faithlessness and irresponsibility poisoned their marriage.

Even from this summary description, it is obvious that Gunnar Ekelöf—born in Stockholm on 15 September 1907—came into a family under stress. His father appears to have been a broken man even at the time of Gunnar's birth, and his condition worsened until he was diagnosed as suffering from *dementia paralytica* in 1913. There were, however, intermittent periods of lucidity and improved health, during which contact with his son was possible.

Gerhard and Gunnar Ekelöf seem to have been deeply attached to each other. The dissension between Gerhard and his wife, however, only deepened. On 14 January 1915 Valborg Ekelöf started divorce proceedings, which led to many bitter exchanges and disagreements about the custody of Gunnar. Gerhard eventually died on 1 June 1916, when Gunnar was not yet nine. That same summer Gunnar's thirty-five-year-old mother began seeing a twenty-three-year-old accountant, who later became the boy's stepfather. While Valborg Ekelöf traveled in Norway with her partner, she placed her son in a children's boarding house for the entire summer. It is evident from letters that Gunnar wrote from boarding houses that he had to do without his mother during the next few summers as well. By 1921 she had remarried, and another son was born the same year.

These events coincided with Gunnar's puberty. There is no indication of how he reacted to such changes in the family situation, but, after having qualified for entrance to the university in 1926, he severed contact with his home. It was only after his mother's death in 1961 that Ekelöf, in private, expressed his bitterness against her. He called her second marriage a betrayal of him:

> She was no real mother; she should not even have had children! There was no contact, only something formal, according to the etiquette.
>
> She remarried an inferior person. Then let herself be taken advantage of, disgracefully against herself, disgracefully against me. Under his influence she gradually turned away from all connection with me. . . . She constantly duped me, at times closing me out of what was, very much, my home.
>
> (quoted in Landgren [1971], p. 25)

As a young man Ekelöf traveled a great deal. The summer of 1926 he spent alone in London, where he took one semester of Hindustani at the School of Oriental Studies and frequently visited the British Museum. In a letter written at the time, Ekelöf says he has no roots: "I am the kingdom of G. Ekelöf and nowadays try to live inside myself, within my own borders" (ibid., p. 26). It is possible to infer not only that he felt lonely but also that he had recognized who he was and what he would remain—an outsider.

A materially rich childhood environment facilitated Ekelöf's peculiar educational development, which became unacademic, unsystematic, and without fixed plans or goals. After failing to take any examinations or degrees, Ekelöf studied on his own. He traveled to Paris for extended visits in the summer of 1925 and in 1929–1930; he also visited London, Berlin, Rome, and Greece.

Ekelöf's first marriage (1931–1932), to Gunnel Bergström, ended in divorce, and his affair in 1933 with a young woman named Irma ceased abruptly and under circumstances that he felt were demeaning. Both of these unsuccessful liaisons approached the dimension of personal catastrophes for Ekelöf and added to his feeling of deep despair. He seems to have led a rather peripatetic life until 1943, when he married Gunhild (Nun) Flodquist. He appeared comfortably settled with her until 1951, when he divorced her and married her sister, Ingrid Flodquist. Their marriage lasted the rest of his life. They made their home in the ancient town of Sigtuna, on Lake Mälaren, an hour from Stockholm. Ekelöf had one daughter, Suzanne, by Ingrid.

Calling his approach to literature that of an outsider, Ekelöf stated in his 1941 essay "En outsiders väg" (An Outsider's Way), "Perhaps I was a luxurious phenomenon—even more so than writers in general, but there has been much want in the midst of the abundance, and it is on it that I have lived. Above all: want of opposition" (*Verklighetsflykt* [1958], p. 135).

The outsider produced poetry: his oeuvre includes no fewer than fifteen volumes, plus four published posthumously. His first book, *Sent på jorden* (Late on Earth, 1932), he characterized as "a suicidal book" and as "a death book." Its attitude to life is nihilistic and its attitude to the art of the word is revolutionary; the motto turns on a pun, "crush the alphabitch" (Carl

Fehrman's suggested translation), suggesting the destruction even of the alphabet, as in "Sonataform, Methylated Prose":

> Crush the alphabitch between your teeth yawn vowels, the fire is burning in hell vomit and spit now or never I and giddiness you or never giddiness now or never.
> we start all over
> Crush the alphabitch macadam and your teeth keep yawning vowels, the sweat is running in hell I am dying in my convolutions vomit now or never giddiness I and you. I and he she it. we start all over. I and he she it. we start all over. I and he she it. we start all over. I and he she it. screams and cries: it goes terribly fast what enormous speed in the sky and hell in my convolutions like madness in the air giddiness. screams and cries: he falls he has fallen. it was good it went so fast what enormous speed in the sky and hell my convolutions, vomit now or never giddiness I and you. I and he she it. we start all over. I and he she it. we start all over. I and he she it, we start all over. I and he she it
> we start all over.
> crush the alphabitch between your teeth yawn vowels, the fire keeps burning in hell and spit now or never I and giddiness you or never giddiness now or never.[1]

Turning away from reason and an oppressive reality, Ekelöf in his early poetry associates freely, as though in a dream, as he does in the poem "expansion." The poem "Catacombpainting" was written by a man who had been through a disaster, an unsuccessful marriage. Ekelöf's comment on the poem about 1940 was "suicidal poem plus an almost museum atmosphere.—There rests a thick layer of cultural dust over our lives" (*En röst* [1973], p. 20):

> broken the seal of the dead
> and their love deciphered
> in the cryptograms' cryptogram

---

[1] All translations of Ekelöf's writings are by the present writer unless noted otherwise.

to be equal to each other
to warm each other's corpse under chastity's
lovely curve in eternity's white marble
the gravestone whose oppressive cold forms
over the dream like the smell
over remains or a whisper.

The final poem of the volume, "Apotheosis," states the two alternatives, death or dreams: "give me poison to die or dreams to live." It is in the realm of dreams that Ekelöf feels most at home. Later he maintained that one cannot write poetry "as he dreams," because poetry is composed by the whole person, not just the subconscious part. If it is also true that a poet has to be obsessed by his task and be something of a seer (a view that arose from his interest in the symbolists), Ekelöf did not think there existed a way to "make oneself a seer," to use Rimbaud's expression. Ekelöf was critical of surrealism for its unlimited belief in the resources of the subconscious, which insufficiently emphasized conscious "ability." He looked upon *Sent på jorden* as one of his most original contributions. In terms of its stylistic elements, he emphasized "the Oriental repetition, the pictorial compression of Mallarmé, and the half-surrealistic pictorial expansion and flight of fancy side by side" ("Självsyn" [Self-Appraisal], in *Blandade kort* [1957], p. 163). He claimed that he hardly knew Rimbaud at the time of writing *Sent på jorden*.

Revealing a change of view, Ekelöf's *Dedikation* (1934) appeared with an epigraph from Rimbaud: "I say: one must be a seer, one must make oneself a seer." In his essay "Självsyn" Ekelöf notes that *Dedikation* contains the only purely "surrealistic" poem ("Döden i tankarna" [Death in the Thoughts]) written according to the so-called "automatic method."

Each a formal improvement upon the previous book, *Sorgen och stjrnan* (The Sorrow and the Star, 1936) and *Köp den blindes sång* (Buy the Blind Man's Song, 1938) were later more or less disowned by Ekelöf, who found their approach restricted and idyllic. He particularly ridiculed some of the romanticism and traditionalism in these books and said he could not get through the long, musically inspired poem "The Song of the Singer" without a bottle of port wine at his side. All that Ekelöf was able to tolerate in *Sorgen och stjrnan* was its internationalism and its presentiment of the coming war.

In some respects Ekelöf then returned to the sphere and manner of *Sent på jorden,* with its thoughts and elements from various sources. This allusive technique was developed further in *Färjesång* (Ferry Song, 1941), which he called his breakthrough to himself, although it is actually a composite of thoughts from a great number of sources and beliefs, including Buddhism, Taoism, and mysticism—all early and lasting affinities of Ekelöf's—as well as folklore and modern rationalism. What might appear as eclecticism tended to link Ekelöf's name with Eliot's, but Ekelöf defended himself energetically against charges of imitation.

Since Ekelöf never was in the habit of randomly gathering material for poetic compositions and always sought material with which he was fully able to identify, it seems inappropriate to label him a mere eclectic. Furthermore, the element of elective affinity on a personal basis became increasingly evident in his later poetry, which includes *En Mölnaelegi* (1960).

The title *Färjesång* alludes to the ferryman who carries the souls of the dead across the river Styx; it begins and ends with this riddling reference to death: "I sing of the only thing that expiates, the only practical, for all alike." The last poem of the volume, "Euphoria," presents the sensation of almost ecstatic well-being experienced before a long one-way journey. The poet appears thoroughly prepared for death. He is fearless, calm, almost happy.

A key poem in the collection is "Tag och skriv" (literally "Take and Write"; translated variously as "Open It, Write," "Tolle, Scribe," and "Write It Down"), which alludes to St. Augustine, who said, "Take and read" and "Take for good what you read." In "Tag och skriv" Ekelöf means, "Write, and make it your own; give it your own expression." That is what he succeeded in doing in this poem, in five sections of unrhymed free verse, employing an antithetical technique throughout.

In considering "Tag och skriv," it will prove helpful to keep in mind three of Ekelöf's related poems. The first, also in *Färjesång, is:*

> He who has no hope
> shall be without despair.
> Never can he doubt
> who does not believe
> But he who seeks a goal
> and he who seeks a meaning
> gives venom to the dragon
> and to the knight his sword.

The second is "Samothrace," referring to the statue of the Winged Victory, which appears as a maiden. The third is "Double Entry," from *En natt i Otočac* (A Night in Otočac, 1961), which ends with these lines:

> Balance! O cathedral
> which obliterates yourself:
> Vision and countervision!
> Domain of revocation, not inflation.

This quotation seems to be directly applicable to the view expressed in "Tag och skriv," especially the fifth movement. The key word is "balance" (equilibrium). It is also helpful to recall the St. George legend, and perhaps even Bernt Notke's famous sculpture of St. George and the dragon in the cathedral church (Storkyrkan) of Stockholm, although Ekelöf had only seen pictures of the sculpture and had never visited the church. It is appropriate to focus attention on two essential concepts: the virgin and the combat.

The first variation of "Tag och skriv" begins:

> Of life, of the living,
> Of death, of the dead.
> Of love and hate.
> Of east and west,
> the two that never shall meet
> and never separate

but be aware of the other's nearness,
know and follow the other's movements,
as man must do
in hate and in love.

I sing of the only thing that can redeem,
the only practical, the same for all:
How seldom man holds the power
to renounce power!
To renounce the I and its voice, renounce—
this alone gives power.

Here Ekelöf expresses the paradox that by relinquishing one's self and one's claims, one gains power. Similar ideas had been expressed by Lao-tzu in *Tao-te Ching,* which Ekelöf had read in Alexander Ular's German version.

In the second movement the speaker rises from his ashes and hovers. The "I" has taken the shape of the phoenix, which after a long life sets fire to its nest, out of which arises a new phoenix. While hovering, he can enjoy the bird's-eye view and take in man's predicament: man exists only in his capacity as a witness, an involved spectator, and therefore he has an obligation to record whatever his experience may be.

The next movement of "Tag och skriv" deals with the nature of the self. The "I" is explained as a projection of hallucinated order, generated from fear. Commonplace abstractions such as justice, human dignity, and free will are seen as mere constructions in an ever-expanding system of belief, in which each new extension will eventually be taken for granted, accepted, and assimilated. These beliefs have developed along evolutionary lines during man's fruitless attempts to bridge the inescapable dualism of the self.

Concepts such as salvation and resurrection constitute the core of human wishes, but neither has existence except as highly developed wishful thinking. "In reality you are nobody"— this statement runs through the whole movement like an echo; it is an example of the way in which Ekelöf achieves his simple but effective rhythmic pattern.

It should be remembered that namelessness

and the problem of identity are major themes in Ekelöf. In a draft for a poem from the early 1930's he stated: "Three human names I received at the font, but my body and soul have no names" (quoted in Wigforss [1980], p. 93). When the speaker says, "In reality you are nobody," there is also a connection to Ulysses. As the Cyclops, Polyphemus, asks for the name of Ulysses, the latter says, "Outís [Nobody] is my name" (ibid., p. 94). The poem "O, Holy Death" (in *Färjesång*) invokes Polyphemus and ends, "while the red eye blinks at me, / while the giant's red hands grapple toward me / and finally select another victim. / I knew it" (*Dikter* [1965], p. 131).

Social psychologists agree that "an entirely isolated self is an abstraction not found in real life. The 'I' as such does not exist" (cf. K. E. Lagerlöf, *GHT,* August 10, 1963, p. 194). The individual becomes a carrier of a situation, and the value of the environment speaks with his own voice. Society, the community of shared values, is integrated with his personality. He is a situation that keeps changing in accordance with changes in the external environment. Deep inside he is unique, but he is also a chance creation of external phenomena (ibid.).

The first lines of the fourth variation touch upon the constant struggle between the most fundamental alternatives, which Hindus call Brahma (the creator) and Shiva (the destroyer), and which Freud called the life and death instincts. There is a beautiful truth in its observation "But he who expects redemption, he is unredeemed. He who wills salvation, he is already damned." In his own development Ekelöf reached beyond concern about salvation by courageously facing the human situation as it is. He arrived at a state of independence, so that in this variation he could claim, "I do not lie, there is no lying in me."

Life to Ekelöf is the meeting of antinomies; it is not pure, and it is definitely not what we are told in folktales, where the dragon stands for all evil and the knight for all that is noble. Nor is it in any way convincing to the poet to hear talk about the virgin's hope and trust (religious and moral concepts). The struggle of the opposites lasts forever—and the one to be sacrificed is not a projection like the knight or the dragon, but always the virgin (who is the center between forces).

The poem could have ended here, and at one time it did. However, in a fifth variation, Ekelöf further explores the superb poetical image of the virgin. Her inner attributes are anguish and flight, but these are materialized as in a battle scene: the sword of the knight and the claws of the dragon. Her external attributes—the crown, the mantle, and the clutched hands—are also attributes of the battle, and as such can perhaps be termed inventions of the same type of wishful thinking (salvation and similar concepts) as is expressed in the third variation.

It may help to understand the mystical way in which the virgin functions by recalling the law of contraries in the *Tao-te Ching,* which states, among other things, that "Rest is the lord of motion. What is bent shall be straightened, the empty is what can be fulfilled." Or we may apply Tcheou-tze's philosophy of evolution, which posits the antithesis of movement and rest, dynamics and stress, on which all beings and processes depend. According to this philosopher, whom Ekelöf may have known from his Oriental studies, the highest principles are contained in movement (yang) and rest (yin). Each of these is the basis for the other. In man, yang is the active energy, the good; yin is the passive principle.

Ekelöf denied that he knew much about "this yang-yin business," yet it would seem that he expressed a thought that parallels the opposition of yin and yang—in human life two forces are constantly at variance with each other: in our constant need for generalization we call them good and evil. The continuous struggle between them is what produces the rhythm of life, or evolution. The secret balance of these forces is seen by the poet as the virgin. She can be called virgin because she is in no way yoked with the stereotypical opposites that we routinely confront: life and death, east and west, good and evil, hot and cold, white and black. She is, as Ekelöf wrote in a personal note, "the third, totally independent, and unconnected point of view. That is why, to our conditioned eyes, she seems always wavering" when in rare moments we catch sight of her, in glimpses and pauses. She points to an absolute ideal, toward freedom and independence, beyond good and evil.

Ekelöf uses "you" to address both himself and his reader as directly as he possibly can. The virgin is compared not to a marionette but to a doll, thrown about by children, compliantly resigning herself to meaninglessness. Whoever analyzes the combat as a struggle between two forces automatically discerns the balance point of the struggle, the virgin. Whoever focuses on the virgin (the fulcrum) loses track of her, because she is part and parcel of the combat, and so disappears in the combat.

Ekelöf makes a similar statement in the poem "Det finns någonting" (There Is Something), in *Färjesång:*

There is something that fits nowhere
and yet is not conspicuous
and yet is decisive
and yet remains outside
There is something that is noticed precisely when it
  is not noticeable
(like silence)

and is unnoticed just where it would be noticeable,
for then it is mistaken (like silence) for
something else.

The virgin as the third person is actually a variation of a theme that is the basis of *Färjesång,* one that Ekelöf dealt with continually, up to and including *Vgvisare till underjorden* (*Guide to the Underworld,* 1967), his last book of poetry. She is part of the *udda-mystik,* the mystique of the odd, the third-person mysticism that is found in his "Categories":

The indifferent ones, the antimagnetic.
They are the odd ones.
They who abandon the least,

leaving heart, soul and fate as hostage,
carrying only the uncertain and the indeterminable.

There, on the third side of life,
there is the black, the gray and the white neither
and of the three are created a variety of colors
beyond all truths and lies.

(*Dikter* [1965], p. 127)

Ekelöf's "Du skriker till livet" ("You Scream to Life"), in *Frjesång,* reads:

You scream to life:
Odd or even!—and believe the gauntlet is thrown.
But life takes no risks—and odd wins.
As long as you stand on your right, life will play
    false—and odd wins.
When you give up your right, life plays clean—
    and odd wins:
Odd is one more than even.
Odd and even!—Or was it a question
of fair or false?

(ibid., p. 129)

In "Den enskilde är död" (The Private Self Is Dead), in *Färjesång,* the third reappears:

The private self is dead, long live the private self!
May he live who has the courage to be dead,
    to be what he is: A third,
    something in between,

and yet a nameless outside thing.

(ibid., p. 135)

While Eliot's "third man" refers to Christ, Ekelöf's mystical third force, the virgin (*det udda*), has an identity without "salvation" or dependence on gods. If Ekelöf himself was not a believer, he was anxious to point out that he felt humble, without hubris or arrogance.

The concluding variations further analyze the mechanism of life, leading to the discovery of its secret balance, the virgin, "conscious but unused life." "Tag och skriv" contains an intricate blend of statement, dialogue, lyric, prophecy, meditation, analysis, and vision, all of which turn upon the matter of "the only atone-ment, the only practical, for all alike," which can be interpreted as obliteration. Our excuse is that our nature conditions us to be greedy for power, and we fail to realize that there is a higher type of power, a gentle kind, which fascinated the poet immensely. This power can be attained only by a renunciation of the self and its narrow, egotistical claims.

In *Non serviam* (I Shall Not Serve, 1945—with obvious references to Milton and Joyce), Ekelöf voiced his opposition to the Swedish welfare state, again showing that he was the odd man out, the outsider:

I am a stranger in this land
but this land is no stranger in me!
I am not at home in this land
but this land makes itself at home in me!

I have of a blood that can never be diluted
in my veins a whole glass full!
And always will the Jew, the Sami, the artist in me
seek his blood-kinship: search into the Scriptures
make a detour around the magic rock in the
    wilderness
in wordless reverence for something forgotten
sing an Arctic song against the wind: Savage!
    Negro!—
wail and butt against the stone: Jew! Negro!—
outside the law and beneath the law:
jailed in theirs, the white law, and still
—praised be my law!—within mine!

Om hösten (In Autumn, 1951) presents several rough drafts or early versions of poems that Ekelöf had published previously. Other poems in the volume can be viewed as pilot studies for the nightmarish account of existential loneliness and paralysis called "Voices Under the Ground," in which the self "became the last piece in the jigsaw puzzle / the bit that fits nowhere, the picture is whole without me." In "En verklighet (drömd)" (A Reality [Dreamed]") Ekelöf introduces "this great being," who is related to Emanuel Swedenborg's Maximus Homo, the Greatest Man, in whose enormous body good societies form a harmonious, universal unit:

Every landscape, every change in the
    landscape, contains all possible landscapes
and this life contains all possible lives:
crickets', fireflies', badgers'—all imaginable lives
and it is this life which will continue to exist, which
    continues
even higher and higher up, in other spheres
This life is going on there right now
which is also the life of the invisible, and the dead
    ones
for there is no other life:
All are alive and shall keep on living
and all give their life to all and lend out their light to
    all
and all hide their light from all and live from and
    upon all
and it is not good or bad
It only is.

Swedenborg's mystic concept of Maximus Homo is easily recognized in many of Ekelöf's later poems, such as in this one, in *Strountes* (Tryflings, 1955):

> I am a sperm
> in the Big Man's body
> The meaning is
> that I shall be ejaculated
> As chance and expectation
> in blindness colliding
> shall I live my life
> in this mucous membrane
> that is the world.

If analyzing anguish, cowardice, fear, and powerlessness was considered "correct" in Swedish poetry of the 1940's, with its convoluted style, the 1950's developed a greater sense of optimism and a much simpler style. As an outsider, however, Ekelöf preferred to go his own way, now introducing his anti-aesthetic concept of poetry. This happened in his collection *Strountes* (the title is translated by Muriel Rukeyser as "Tryflings," by Stephen Klass as "Rubbysshe," and by Sven Rossel as "Junque"). This collection marks a new stage in Ekelöf's constant growth, although it opens traditionally with aphorisms by Carl Jonas Love Almqvist, Vergil, and Paul Klee. The poems are less meditative than previously, more whimsical, even absurd or nonsensical. Frequently Ekelöf employs (untranslatable) puns in the manner of Lewis Carroll, Christian Morgenstern, Robert Desnos, and James Joyce. Something of the same is true for his *Opus incertum* (1959), with its ancient Latin graffito (meaning an irregular, somewhat uncertain ancient wall) as a motto, and, to a lesser extent, for *En natt i Otočac,* which—together with *Strountes*—are the centerpieces in Ekelöf's anti-aesthetic and even anti-poetic oeuvre.

What can the reader expect from anti-aesthetic poetry? A semblance of spontaneity, improvisation, and informality. The poems incorporate something of the joy and haste of the work process, the imperfection of the sketch, and they throw out much of the pretentiousness of "learned" poetry.

In Octočac, Yugoslavia, Ekelöf heard a band of Balkan Gypsies for the first time. Their music appeared to him as a series of outbursts, "randomly interfoliated with scherzi and occasional melodies, which in their impassioned 'unattractiveness' relied much more on accent, temperament, and character than on traditional musical values" (*En natt i Otočac,* pp. 79–80). This description could serve, as well, as a characterization of his anti-aesthetic poetry.

This kind of aesthetic program is comprehensive enough to allow the inclusion of almost anything, as long as it serves Ekelöf's larger purpose: his constant and unrelenting search for unity, wholeness, *helhet*.

Ekelöf makes funny transpositions of the letters in his own name; he writes a "perpetuum mobile" with slight variations of one of the letters (or words) in a short phrase; he writes fables, one of them ("Fabel") about an obstinate lamb chop that resolves not to be eaten but that "soon lay full of worms, rotten and forgotten," while its counterpart, the pork chop, takes a different attitude:

> No, sociable and sound
> well done and spiced just right

in every worm's despight
I die for the butcher's hound!

Another fable is about an enormous head of cabbage "thinking, but not of cabbage soup: it thinks of Africa's small bland meatballs, leaping suspended over the savannah":

What does the frank think of?
Its pantry-wrinkles will tell it:
It thinks of the Paleopsychological
p'Institute at Princeton
—And the white pepper and the syrup
the nice Jamaica peppercorns . . .
No, sausages, return to your source!

When the dead are invoked in another poem, "When They Slip Out," it is with sympathy:

When they slip out through the graveyard gates
on Easter night, on Easter night
When the dead go out and look over the town
on a moonlit night, a moon-night
Then eternal homelessness claims its right
its right in all the other dead.

The poem ends thus:

the living often do us evil
The dead do us no harm
The living are the greedy ones
The dead, they are the ones that feed us
The dead are the feeding ones.

Homelessness is a recurrent theme. In "The Land-of-the-Freeze" Ekelöf reacts against the unnaturalness of the super-civilization that the Western world, and especially his home country, has created, compared with the quiet, dignified life of meditation that he would much prefer. The architects have made the clouds rectangular. The hygienic children (never touched by human hands) play "while in spinning parasols around them / the wage-controlled municipal nursemaids hover."

Ekelöf's ironic comments on Western society, which he allegedly failed to escape (on three efforts as a young man to emigrate to India), continue in the same poem: in the evening, the sexless vitamin workers go swarming homeward according to contract and age group, "to their private life, Svea, Mother of Sweden, Queen of hormones / closely guarded by confidence-inspiring bouncers."

When in "Klimat" (Climate) Ekelöf compares the North (Sweden) and the South (Italy), his love-hate for the former is all too obvious:

Farewell order!
Welcome Disorder!
I greet the stink of urine in the alley
the rushing in the pipe at the house wall
and in the background
this damp-stained beauty
I greet, morning and evening
mossy in the overhanging gorge
silence
untouched neighbor to these blatant voices
and that the cats live their cat lives
and the dogs their dog lives
up close to each other
and rich and poor their human lives
up close to each other.

It is striking that several poets in exile of one kind or another are apostrophized in *Opus incertum, En natt i Otočac,* and *Strountes,* among them Ovid, Rimbaud, Rilke, Almqvist (who fled from Sweden to Philadelphia), and, most important, Ezra Pound, to whom Ekelöf dedicated this poem that bears Pound's name:

O voice that came to me
echo of voice that also is vault
vault that is air and space
space that is bloom
Voice I have longed for
how do you ever steal yourself out
of the closed rooms
where they keep you a prisoner
and how is your kind so free!

Has not the sentence set its mark on you
are you so landless?
Truly
you give me the courage again to be that with you

2645

It has been suggested that Ekelöf considered his psychological situation to be somewhat similar to Pound's. In a 1952 draft, Ekelöf even calls Pound "kin" (*syskon*), and he adds: "I pine away / here, like you / there." Clearly Ekelöf admired Pound for asserting his independence in spite of his abjection (cf. Hellström, pp. 68–69).

After Ekelöf had married for the third time, in 1951, he made extended visits to Italy and Greece, adding vastly to his knowledge of Mediterranean cultures. This is reflected in his book-length poem *En Mölna-elegi* (*A Mölna Elegy*, 1960) and his Byzantine trilogy: *Dīwān över Fursten av Emgión* (Dīwān over the Prince of Emgión, 1965), *Sagan om Fatumeh* (The Tale of Fatumeh, 1966), and *Vgvisare till underjorden* (*Guide to the Underworld*, 1967). The chief character of the first volume of this trilogy is not the prince of its title but Digenis Akritas, the hero of a Byzantine romance compiled between the tenth and twelfth centuries. Digenis was the son of an Arab father and a Byzantine mother. When he was captured in battle, he was put into the much-feared jail at Vlacherne, where he was tortured and blinded. In his suffering his main consolation is the Virgin, to whom he addresses his passionate hymns, but she is actually related to the Diana of the Ephesians and thus the Earth Mother, not the Christian Madonna. One song begins thus:

> In the calm water I saw mirrored
> Myself, my soul:
> Many wrinkles
> The beginnings of a turkey-cock neck
> Two sad eyes
> Insatiable curiosity
> Incorrigible pride
> Unrepentant humility
> A harsh voice
> A belly slit open
> And sewn up again
> A face scarred by torturers
> A maimed foot
> A palate for fish and wine
> One who longs to die

> Who has lain with some
> In casual beds—but for few
> Has felt love—a for him
> Necessary love
> One who longs to die
> With someone's hand in his
> Thus I see myself in the water
> With my soiled linen left behind me when I am gone
> (Auden-Sjöberg trans.)

The *Dīwān* was begun in Istanbul in the spring of 1965 and completed within a four-week period. In a note to me, Ekelöf wrote that the *Dīwān* "is my greatest poem of love and passion. I cannot touch it or see it, because I grow ill when I see this blind and tortured man. . . . As far as I can understand, someone has written the poems with me as a medium. . . . Really, I have never had such an experience, nor one as complete."

Sagan om Fatumeh deals with a generous, loving girl who becomes a courtesan and then the beloved of a prince. She bears his child but is deserted by him and is brought to the harem at Erechtheum. She is not allowed to stay there, however; she is abandoned and must move about in misery, selling herself to keep alive. Like Digenis, she is sustained by her visions, for in and through these "ecstatic" poems, despite what has happened and may happen, no disaster shall degrade her soul.

Auden noted that, like Constantine Cavafy, Ekelöf had set these poems in a bygone age. Although their sensibilities were different—Cavafy, ironic and detached; Ekelöf, passionate and involved—neither had chosen the past as an escape: "For both it is a means of illuminating and criticizing the present" (preface to Ekelöf, *Selected Poems* [1971], p. 10). Although Ekelöf was fascinated by Byzantium, he never idealized it. He wrote in a letter:

> Why have I become interested in the Byzantine, the Greek life? Because Byzantine life, traditionally and according to deep-rooted custom, is like the political life in *our* cities and states. I am intensely interested in it because I hate it. I hate what is Greek. I hate what is Byzantine. . . .

Dīwān is a symbol of the political decadence we see around us. *Fatumeh* is a symbol of the degradation, the coldness between persons, which is equally obvious.

As Goethe had done in the *Westöstlicher Diwan* (*West-Eastern Divan,* 1819), Ekelöf managed to present a synthesis of East and West in his *Guide to the Underworld* and, moreover, to give a harrowing history of man's difficulties in the past and in the present. This centerpiece of the trilogy can, perhaps, be considered a counterpart to Dante's wanderings in the underworld and certain ancient accounts of Hades. In *Guide to the Underworld* Ekelöf again returned to the theme of the virgin, in the long poem "The Devil's Sermon," for example, which essentially is written in praise of the virgin. It is not the Christian Virgin to whom he refers, however, but a union of the Panhagía, "the All-Holy One," the Holy Virgin, and Pannychis, "the all-night girl," who is ready for love (coitus) throughout the night (the Latin quotation is from Petronius):

> Ita! Ita! Cur non devirginatur nostra vita?—The
>   Virgin
> must be devirginized to become Virgin once more
> Thus the sex is not simply for coitus!
> She whom Fate purified stands higher
> than Innocence. Higher too stands he
> who took forcibly, who learned something
> about Inviolability: brutality cannot defile!
>
> (Lesser trans.)

Ekelöf's "elective affinities" (the title of a work by Goethe [1809], used in Ekelöf's *Valfrändskaper* of 1960) includes selected translations of such writers as Baudelaire, Rimbaud, Apollinaire, Robert Desnos, André Breton, Paul Éluard, Whitman, Samuel Butler, James Joyce, D. H. Lawrence, W. H. Auden, Friedrich Hölderlin, Nelly Sachs, and Petronius. Among the writers to whom Ekelöf dedicated poems were Angelos Sikelianós and Ezra Pound.

Important commentaries on Ekelöf's view of life in general and on his poetry in particular are found in his books of essays, *Promenader*

(Promenades, 1941) and *Utflykter* (Excursions, 1947), which appeared in a revised version under the title *Verklighetsflykt* (Escape from Reality, 1958). His last collections of essays, *Blandade kort* (Shuffled Cards, 1957) and the posthumous *Lägga patience* (Play at Patience, 1969), also offer art criticism, literary characterizations, and travelogues. The "autobiography" *Gunnar Ekelöf: En självbiografi* (1971) is basically a generous selection of Ekelöf's letters, edited and with an introduction by Ingrid Ekelöf.

Ekelöf stresses repeatedly that the poet's main task is to become himself. He believes not that an individual develops artistically from another artist's influence but, rather, that an artist develops by identifying himself with the spirit of the times and by recognizing the complex patterns that the light of time past casts upon the living screen of the present: "Just as two scientists working apart can simultaneously invent the lightning rod or discover oxygen, so two artists can experience the same basic mood, and under certain conditions, express their perceptions in a similar way" ("Självsyn," p. 170). For Ekelöf saw time as an extraordinarily powerful experience in our lives, as a pervasive influence that could produce homogeneous things in different places. Individualist and outsider that he was, he believed that human production, and especially artistic production, should be considered a collective achievement.

From Ekelöf's very considerable poetic oeuvre, I will discuss the allusive technique in three of his poems in detail: "Jarrama," "Samothrace," and "Absentia animi" (in *Non serviam*). In addition I will trace the theme of time in *A Mölna Elegy*. These works are as representative as they are important; if you know them, you know something about the rest of Ekelöf's poetry as well.

Ekelöf's stay in Berlin during the fall and winter of 1933–1934 was important for his orientation. From 1933 on, he contributed to the leading Stockholm papers and the literary magazines, as well as to the periodicals of the trade union movement and the cooperative movement. It would be impossible, however, to make a strictly "political" writer of Ekelöf on the basis of his literary contributions in the 1930's and the publications in which they appeared.

It is quite unlikely that Ekelöf seriously considered joining the International Brigade of volunteers in 1936 to support the lawfully elected Spanish government in its fight for survival against the Franco insurgents. Ekelöf was not a man of action; in this respect he was similar to Henrik Ibsen, who, when asked why he had not volunteered on Denmark's side in the war against Prussia, said, "We poets have other tasks to perform."

Ekelöf was, as Reidar Ekner has shown, well informed about the Spanish Civil War and sided with the Republican government, which was also supported by the vast majority of the Spanish people. When the idealist lyric poet Erik Blomberg (1894–1965) visited New York a few months before his death, I asked if he did not then consider Ekelöf a conservative writer. Blomberg, an avowed Marxist, answered in no uncertain terms: "Ekelöf is a great poet and is completely outside of the politics of the Left and the Right!"

There is clearly a connection between the poem "Jarrama" and Ekelöf's prose piece "Ett 30-talsöde" (A Destiny from the 30's; in *Promenader*). Apart from the fact that the essay goes a long way toward explaining the origin of "Jarrama," "A Destiny from the 30's" is also a fair example of Ekelöf's prose style. The following is a summary of the piece.

Ekelöf was often with "S.T." (Skoglar Tidström), the subject of the essay and of "Jarrama," during two periods, the first in Stockholm, the second in Berlin during the winter of 1933–1934, yet Ekelöf does not claim to have known him well. "S. T." was in most ways "an ordinary guy," yet there was something strange about him. He was naive, casual, and indifferent. He appeared to take everything in a pleasant, easy way, and that clearly appealed to

Ekelöf. The money "S. T." had inherited he placed in mining concessions for ore deposits in Lapland and in an obscure publishing venture in Stockholm. But the publishing house soon "was in liquidation. The ore deposits rested as they had rested for geological millennia" ("Ett 30-talsöde," p. 19).

To improve in his new interest, photography, "S. T." went to Moscow, where he fell in love with a Russian woman—"very beautiful, very maidenly, very awkward to handle—and a champion in hand-grenade throwing: a Russian amazon" ("Ett 30-talsöde," p. 21). The love affair shook him up. In two months he learned to speak Russian fluently. He distinguished himself at school. And yet, those achievements were not enough. He made his way into the elite of the young intelligentsia, moved in exclusive revolutionary circles, reveled in jokes, and, relaxed and uninhibited, gave inflammatory speeches. He eventually had a nervous breakdown; strangely enough, Isaac Babel (1894–1941), the Russian short-story writer, became involved in placing the young Swede in a Russian institution. After his recovery, "S. T." became a volunteer in the fierce Civil War in Spain, which many writers, including Ernest Hemingway, Auden, Arthur Koestler, George Orwell, and André Malraux, have described. According to Ekner, Ekelöf read Hemingway's *For Whom the Bell Tolls* (1940) and Malraux's *L'Espoir* (Man's Hope, 1937), and his reading of the two novels is evident in "Jarrama." That Ekelöf thought highly of Malraux's work is confirmed by Wigforss (1980, pp. 112–114).

The three stanzas, of sixteen, twelve, and fourteen lines, of "Jarrama" are constructed in two sections in which the motifs are parallel: the first an augmentative simile that has turned into a poem by itself; the other, "carrying a visionary, dreamlike representation of images of those dying or dead, lying on their backs under the spring-winter sky on the battlefield at Jarama, while their inner voices fade away and their consciousness expires" (Ekner [1967], p. 46).

In the first third of the poem, Ekelöf telescopes two worlds, that of Lapland and that of the tropics, in which the drumbeat dominates. The tropical drum is what impressed Ekelöf most strongly from his reading of a travel book about Borneo (the book had been lent to him by his poet-friend Helmer Grundström during a stay in Dorotea, where the Lapps [Sami] were known for their own ritual drums).

The drumbeat, repeated six times, suggests the rhythmic beat of the natives' drum, building up a mood of threat, anguish, and suffering. It "is taken over in the next section by the cannon.—And this cannon is heard equally many times as a background voice, and with a similar rhythmical effect" (ibid., p. 47). The drumbeat, the cannonade, and the heartbeat form a sequence in which all are related. The drumbeat is a reminiscence from reading a travelogue about Borneo, and the cannon comes from Ekelöf's reading of Malraux's Spanish Civil War novel, *Man's Hope*, which Ekelöf translated into Swedish under the title *Förtvivla ej* (Do Not Despair, 1944). The passage where the cannon dominates is toward the end of Malraux's book. The transposition from the cannonade to the arrested heartbeat of the dying is effective. The surreal visions "shimmering black over the eyes' iris is less a weapon than a symbol, feverishly, dialectically alternating between death and victory, in the end settling for the victory symbol" (ibid., p. 47).

Both Pablo Neruda and Rafael Sánchez Ferlosio have treated the heavy fighting at Jarama, in which forty thousand lives were lost: Neruda in the poem "Batalla del Río Jarama" and Sánchez Ferlosio in the realistic novel *El Jarama* (1956). (Note that both employ the traditional Spanish spelling, "Jarama," while Ekelöf uses "Jarrama.")

It is no coincidence that the heavy-artillery battles referred to in the poem are matched by an introductory quotation from Apollinaire's poem "Fusées" (in *Calligrammes*, 1918), which Ekelöf had translated and published: "*Douilles éclatantes des obus de 75 / Carillonnez pieuse-ment*" (Exploding cases of .75 shells / chime piously). In addition to the dedication, "To S. T., killed at Jarrama," the poem originally had an epigraph, "Chopin, Op. 28, No. 17: 68–90," a prelude in which Ekelöf had thought he heard the sound of cannons. The musical concept of the poem played a part in this, but the oblique reference to Chopin may have been included because he was a patriot and a member of the resistance during the Polish uprising against the Russian authorities. As an extension of this civil war we are, indirectly, reminded of the German invasion and occupation of Poland in 1939. (Excluded from Ekelöf's *Dikter, 1932–1951* [1956], the reference to Chopin is included in the collected poems of 1965.)

The poem exhibits a relativism ("On the right side—and the ranks align themselves / the wrong side—and the ranks align themselves") in the face of death that contradicts other statements by Ekelöf. "S. T.," apostrophized in Ekelöf's poem, was in the unfortunate position of having had to fight his own indifference as well as that of the world. But when he was in an ethically clear-cut situation, he had the courage to take sides; and he paid with his life.

Ekelöf does not normally make his characters larger than life, but at the opening of "Jarrama" he refers to "rotting rain-forest giants [lying] on their backs," which parallels the line about the wounded soldiers on the battleground of Jarama: "so we lie here on our backs under the lark." Even if they do not become "heroic," they seem to me to become greatly magnified. Tidström ("S. T.") "apparently appeared to Ekelöf as a symbol of the striving, personally fighting man, suddenly roused to consciousness and his responsibility in a larger context" (ibid., p. 56). In "Jarrama" he is counted among the dead; "in 'Samothrace' he wears down his oarlock, one of the anonymous rowers who has been permitted to leave the foremost bench and has been shifted astern" (ibid.). There are references to "Jarrama" in Ekelöf's visionary poem "Samothrace": "the right side—and—the wrong side—." In the prose piece "Ett 30-talsöde" Ekelöf stated, "It is not always easy to tell who falls in battle on the right side and who falls on the wrong side. I believe that such things are more a consequence of the person fighting than of the idea."

Each poem by Ekelöf has a history of its own. There are many versions left unpublished for a long time, and there are many internal references to other poems, especially his own. Kjell Espmark, appropriately, talks of a dialogue between the texts. There also are various published versions. "Samothrace" appears in three versions, the first in the anti-Nazi daily *GHT* (Gothenburg, 23 August 1941), the second in the leading literary magazine *BLM* (Stockholm, January 1943), and the third in Ekelöf's collection of poems *Non serviam*.

"Samothrace" first carried the significant title "Paian" (Paean), a song in praise of an ancient god but originally intended for magical purposes as an incantation to dispel evil powers. Three of its six stanzas of unrhymed verse consist of thirteen lines, and the remaining ones are of ten, twelve, and sixteen lines. It should be noted that the poem presents alternating chanting between the chief singer and the rowers. In the *BLM* version (1943) the full title was "Samothrace—A Democratic Antiphony." It is dramatic-lyrical and in several musical parts. Aesthetically, the result is less than satisfactory, but it is instructive in terms of Ekelöf's musical intentions.

There is an allusion to Churchill's famous words to his countrymen during Britain's hour of destiny. A fearful voice cries out, "I fear thee, Ancient Mariner," while another answers, "Be calm, thou Wedding-Guest!" The border between life and death and dream and reality is blurred in Samuel Taylor Coleridge's "The Rime of the Ancient Mariner" as well as in Ekelöf's poem. It can be inferred that Coleridge's poem influenced the form of "Samothrace." Tideström has mentioned as another source of inspiration Whitman's "Pioneers! O Pioneers!" —which has a sense of community

with distant ages similar to that of "Samothrace":

> All the prisoners in the prisons, all the righteous
> and the wicked,
> All the joyous, all the sorrowing, all the living, all
> the dying.
> Pioneers! O Pioneers!

An addition to the second version of "Samothrace" (1943) describes how voices respond to the chief singer's exhortation to them to keep their courage up—"some hesitant, others resolute—gradually more and more distant, fading, hardly audible":

> *O Mort, vieux capitaine!*
> Captain! My Captain!
> Coast-brother!
> Sing Sailor Oh!
> *Lettre de Marque!*
> Unknown!
> Nameless!
> Unknown!
> Onelegged, one-eyed!
> Five fathom deep . . .
> In the mast top, always in the mast top . . .
> Leif!
> Es Sindibad!
> Ithaca! Ithaca!
> Phoenicians seeking Ophir . . .
>   (female voice)
> And Saba seeking Solomon . . .
>   (far off)
> Cretans! Minoans!
>   (further away)
> Children of the Nile,
> paddling the ship of death!
>   (cavelike)
> paddling jungle dwellers!

This is, as Tideström and Wigforss have shown, a meaningful mosaic of quotations found in world literature. First we have a line from "Le voyage" by Baudelaire, occasionally referred to as the cloud vendor, part 1 of which Ekelöf, the cloud visionary (as he called himself), had published in *Hundra år modern fransk dikt* (One Hundred Years of Modern

French Poetry, 1934). In "Samothrace" he assimilated one of the first lines of "Le voyage," describing the very moment of departure from life: "O Mort, vieux capitaine!"

Then we have Whitman's cry of "Captain!" from his celebration of the slain Abraham Lincoln (in *Drum-Taps*). "Coast-brother" refers to a contrabandist during the Napoleonic wars, about whom Joseph Conrad has written. "Sing Sailor Oh!" is the refrain from a popular song by the Norwegian genius Henrik Wergeland (1808–1845). "Five fathom deep . . . " is an echo from Ariel's song in Shakespeare's *The Tempest,* also apostrophized in *The Waste Land* by Eliot, whose "Prufrock," "Gerontion," and "Webster" Ekelöf had translated into Swedish in 1941–1942. Brita Wigforss has noted that in an early draft Ekelöf had made the subsequent consoling lines from Ariel's song his epigraph:

> Of his bones are coral made;
> Those are pearls that were his eyes:
> Nothing of him that doth fade
> But doth suffer *a sea-change*
> *Into something rich and strange*
> (italics added)

"In the mast top" is from Harry Martinson's radio play *Lotsen från Moluckas* (The Pilot from Moluccas, 1947), about Ferdinand Magellan (1480–1521), the Portuguese navigator, and his men; "Leif" is the Viking, that is, Leifur Heppni (Leif Eriksson), the discoverer of Vinland, on the North American coast, around the year 1000. Sindibad (Sinbad) the Sailor is the hero who appears in the *Thousand and One Nights.* "Ithaca" is one of the Ionian Islands and, according to tradition, the home of Odysseus. The ancient tale of Phoenicians who traveled to Ophir for gold, ivory, sandalwood, and precious stones for the Queen of Sheba, seeking wisdom, is related throughout the Bible.

In the 1945 version of "Samothrace" the poet silenced these voices by cutting the entire section. Had he reconsidered and decided that he had been too demanding of his readers? Or did

he feel that, although his father had long been dead and buried, it was not "five fathom deep," and not in water? In other words, was Ekelöf dissatisfied with the discrepancy between his love of truth and the quotation as it applied to his own life experience? At any rate, his allusions became increasingly selective and personal in his later poetry. Here we may have a partial answer to the question why his "echo chamber" par excellence, *A Mölna Elegy,* took such a long time to complete; for complicated reasons, his growing need of personal veracity vis-à-vis the borrowed quotations and elements is hard to deny.

Ekelöf often published side commentaries on his poems, including one on the 1943 version of "Samothrace" that is found in the prose piece "Från Västkusten" (From the West Coast [of Sweden]), in *Promenader.* He had visited the fishing village of Mollösund, on the island of Orust, in the fall of 1942 and had seen a funeral procession for a British airman. It had reminded him of a previous occasion, in Stockholm, when he had spontaneously joined a protest march sponsored by *Clarté* (a periodical for "Socialist culture"). His account of the burial begins with words from August Strindberg—that the event "made a strong impression on me." Ekelöf describes the procession in remarkable detail, as if he had special training in observing the traditions surrounding death and the disposal of the dead:

The British Consul, who had traveled here [to Mollösund] for this special occasion, came out of the customs office, shook hands with the minister, the organist, and the notables. Heads were bared.

The crew of the ship which had brought back the corpse carried the coffin and after them came the customs officers with five wreaths. With some effort the coffin was fitted in under the canopy of the hearse, a canopy so low that the fifth wreath had to be shoved on the lid from the rear! The four others were hung on the crosses at the four corners of the hearse as if on clothes pegs.

The small yellowish horse lurched in his trappings and began tractably to struggle with tiny steps. The crowd thinned out, as it began to move: people from the ship blockade, customs officers as honorary guard on each side of the hearse, the consul, next of kin, the parson, organist and local authorities, coast artillerists with their sub-lieutenant, Wacs with flowers, the Home Guards, women with elbows, and ordinary people.

I joined the procession somewhere where all ranking order definitively began to cease. There was still an unfamiliar treading in the too broad lines that had not had time to form with the narrowing road. At some distance one saw the hearse and those at the head, rounding the corner up toward the thickly foliaged old churchyard, and marching in perfect time. . . .

And one was thinking of just nothing, only marching, endeavoring to walk, to a kind of beat [*takt*], to fall in step.

In the last paragraph of Ekelöf's "conscientious funeral report," he reminds his readers that victory at the time was elusive. When the corpse of a German floated ashore on the Swedish west coast a few weeks later, there was no crowd and little or no public sympathy. Things were decidedly different except for official ceremony, which was the same for the Englishman and the German. The German consulate in Gothenburg circulated a news release claiming that there was a general display of flags at half mast and the local population turned out to a man for the German's funeral, an account of which was published verbatim by all Stockholm papers, while only a few lines were given to the English airman's funeral. The right side, the wrong side: Swedish newsmen were hedging their bets. In spite of Sweden's alleged neutrality, Swedish newspapers, in this instance, exhibited a shocking lack of integrity.

The mood of solidarity is the theme of Ekelöf's account, and it helps if the reader detects the same mood of solidarity that pervades "Samothrace," a solidarity embracing vast numbers of the dead:

> ancient Cretans, Hellenes,
> Phoenicians, ancient Egyptians,

> paddling backwoodsmen,
> and further astern
> you crawling, you swimming—

There are various complications in "Samothrace," one of them being the epigraph in the second version: "Navigare necesse, vincere non necesse" (To sail is necessary, to be victorious is not necessary). That is, at certain times it is necessary for us to stand up for what we believe in, even at the risk of losing our lives. This epigraph paraphrases and significantly revises Pompey's drastic dictum in a grain crisis, when his sailors feared the storm and refused to go to sea while the storm lasted: "To sail is necessary, to live is not necessary."

Did Ekelöf remove the epigraph from the third and final version (1945) because it was too explicit? By that time the war was over, and a necessary victory had been won. If the explicit epigraph had served a purpose, the fact that he dropped it would be in line with his deepest aspiration, to produce a poem with universal appeal. As such it could be neither too exhortatory nor too dispirited, as might be expected during wartime conditions. A really good poem, Ekelöf wrote in 1956, "possesses a radioactivity that is weakened and lost only after centuries, perhaps millennia" ("Från en lyrikers verkstad" [From the Workshop of a Poet], in *Blandade kort*, p. 152).

Ekelöf's great fascination with the Mediterranean area, including its people, scenery, art, and culture, past and present, is well known and well documented, and many of his poems are about this area (among them "Ex Ponto," "Monte Chronion," "Tomba dei Tori, Tarquinia," "Pallidula Nudula"). He expressed the idea to me (admittedly in a drunken state), in connection with "Samothrace," that the sea is both a repository of the past and a cradle of human culture. Presumably referring to the sea of "Samothrace," he added, "The Mediterranean is the Sea of Death." He might just as well have said "the Sea of Life."

With this information in mind, it becomes

easier to agree with Tideström's 1947 essay in which the ship in "Samothrace" is associated with a Roman galley manned by slaves. We are allowed to read Ekelöf's thoughts: when his time comes, he will do his share. He is resigned to the fact that he will soon be shifted astern, never to reach a central position (amidships) or to determine the direction by manning the steering oar. His thoughts wander back and forth until finally he begins to wonder if there is such a thing as a steering oar. Resigned to the permanence of his humble seat, he denies to himself (in the name of solidarity?) that he knows any other place and consciously limits his perspective to rowing. The importance of an oarlock to the rower should not be discounted. His oarlock becomes the center around which his sense of solidarity revolves.

There is a curious dialectic operating in his mind, alternating between trust and distrust: "Is there no sail to help?" and "Is there a victory?" Deciding that there is none, he then proclaims with certainty: "The clouds are sails!" In other words, he must sustain himself by his imagination, or faith, alone. The ornamental figurehead of a virgin placed over the cutwater of the ship is seen as the rowers' victory:

> headless and armless
> yet a virgin inviolate
> advancing ahead of us
> through the ranks of monsters
> which the ship's eyes see.

Thus, the figurehead is similar to the Nike of the poem's title. But, as in a dream, Nike changes into something more than a figurehead, and those "who still are rowing in front" and are nearest to the victory feel or imagine that their cheeks are stroked by the folds of her cloak. Nike is then easily associated with the mother-goddess or a virginal cosmic mother. In Erik Lindegren's view, the virgin is a symbol of life's innermost being, its elusiveness and innocence. (See Lindegren's "På väg mot instrumental-lyriken," in Karl Vennberg and Werner Aspenström, eds., *Kritiskt 40-tal* [Stockholm, 1948], pp. 305–310.)

To recapitulate: Glimpsed by the rowers but out of reach, the elusive figurehead on the bow—Nike of Samothrace, the Winged Victory—advances majestically, with the forward movement of the ship of the dead. Their final destination is unknown, and the purpose of their voyage is insufficiently understood or not understood at all. There is no letup in the laborious, unending process of rowing. The rowers are slaves of life, as it were; they know in their bones that they have to continue, even under precarious conditions, since giving up would be an even harder alternative. In their extreme uncertainty the rowers are sustained and inspired by Nike, the Winged Victory, to keep pressing forward.

It is for the reader to decide whether "Samothrace" is an exhortation to continued struggle (Tideström) or a hymn to indomitable human striving for liberty (Wigforss) or a poem dominated more by a life-death theme than by the theme of victory (Brandell). All seem to agree on the importance of rhythm and sonic richness of the Swedish "Samothrace." It is even suggested that Ekelöf "perceives the function of the words essentially as carriers of a musicality, a rhythm" (Stenroth, p. 19). To translate such musicality in Ekelöf is extremely difficult, but the poet is known to have read and approved of the version of "Samothrace" made by Muriel Rukeyser and the present writer. Here are its concluding lines:

> Virgin, you are our victory!
> Who has possessed you?
> Someone, always someone else.
> Yet you are our victory!
> You are our sails and harbor and clouds
> and you are our victory,
> virgin among storm-clouds!
> The beat hold the beat
> holding faith
> we row your ship home.

Comparatists have, naturally, found Ekelöf's great sea poem of considerable interest. Thus an attempt to link the enumeration of seafaring people in Fernando Pessoa's "Ode maritima" (1915) to "Samothrace" has been made (by Lage Lindvall in his "Fernando Pessoas 'Havsode' och Ekelöfs 'Samothrake', " and Stenroth has drawn attention to *Le coffret de Santal* (1873), a peculiar collection of prose poems by Charles Cros (1842–1888), a precursor of symbolism. It is not inconceivable that the prose poem "Le vaisseau-piano" in some measure contributed to Ekelöf's poem. In spite of some parallels with Cros's poem, however, the tone and feeling of Ekelöf's poem appear substantially different and original (Stenroth, pp. 13ff.).

In his youth (in Paris in 1925 and 1929–1930) Ekelöf planned to become a pianist, and throughout his poetry, music and musical conceptions play a large part: leitmotifs, themes and variations, thematic amplification, melodic designs, inversions, repetitions, refrains, and modulations are abundant.

Ekelöf sometimes applies counterpoint. The clouds in "Samothrace" relate to the clouds in "Absentia animi," just as "those eyes are now pearls" in "Samothrace" relate to "the eye of black pearl" in "Absentia animi." The insects around the evening lamp in "Euphoria" are related to those in "Absentia animi," whose blackbird (a poet in disguise!) reappears in *A Mölna Elegy*. The more a reader looks, the more such internal and external references become visible.

Structurally, "Absentia animi" (in *Non serviam*) proceeds from a nature scene (twenty-four lines) to the poet's philosophizing about his poetic activity (thirty-two lines), to an assessment of his situation (nine lines), to identification with a cloud (thirty-nine lines), and finally reverts back to elements in the autumnal scene. (Note: in some published versions the lines are longer, and therefore fewer.)

If "Absentia animi" is musical in conception, it might be possible to suggest the musical key. It is clearly minor. Or is it? Is there even a single key? This uncertainty principle, which is so characteristic of Ekelöf's work, reminds me of how ambiguity spilled over into his mundane world. Once he sent me a telegram inadvertently phrased in such an ambiguous way that it could be understood in two or three different ways!

"Absentia animi" consists of a great number of repetitions; in fact, almost all key words or key sentences are repeated three times. The word "meaningless" appears no fewer than six times, three times with "unreal," and "nothing" (*nada*) appears seven times. To balance this negative set of values, "something else" appears nine times, and, in addition, there is "something" existent / very near / beyond / beyond-near / neither-nor.

There is a snail moving along at a snail's pace, a frayed butterfly "heading to nothing, which is a faded rose / the smallest and the ugliest." By themselves none of these constitutes a poem, but, together with water-filled wheel tracks and rotting mushrooms, they help to sketch an autumnal landscape—and a mental state, a frame of mind.

After all this exposition, center stage is given to a poet of sorts, "an overlooked blackbird" in a treetop. He is the one who fills the landscape with "music." His purpose? He sings "for nothing, for the throat's sake." In other words, when he is in the mood for singing, he cannot do anything else: by inner necessity he is obliged to sing, and in singing he is one with himself. This is not "unreal" or "meaningless"—it is "real," and perhaps even "meaningful."

Ekelöf allows himself some commentary on his art:

he
who *partout* seeks the meaning of all things has
  long since realized
that the meaning of the rustling is rustling.

That there is a discrepancy between his language (the poet's words) and his experience (or reality) is unavoidable. It is as simple as that: "Meaningless—Unreal. / Meaningless." It is meaninglessness that gives meaning to life, Ekelöf says in an autobiographical essay.

The poet wishes himself "far far away," and in the next line his wishes have come true: "I am far away (among the evening echoes)." But then the ambiguous realization: "I am here." How different from the commitment in "Samothrace": "My place is here . . . / I know of no other place!"

If the many repetitions in "Absentia animi" don't indicate intoxication, they surely have to do with some sort of ecstasy. The poem concerns itself with a poet who has found it necessary to transport himself into a certain mental state: he wishes himself "far far away" (among evening echoes), presumably among the ancients in the Mediterranean or Oriental regions (since he finds the present so disagreeable).

This being so, where does the happiness come from? Gunilla Bergsten reminds us that the poet knows magic. He invokes the sacred name of Abraxas (Abrasax) three times: at the beginning, middle, and end of the poem. It is "a symbol of the Divine nature as expressed in the great Cycle of Life, and in the conflict through which the Self passes in its progress through the lower world," says G. A. Gaskell, while C. W. King explains Abraxas as "a speaking type of the *Pleroma,* the *one* embracing *all* within itself" (both quoted in G. A. Gaskell, *Dictionary of All Scriptures and Myths* [New York, 1981], p. 19).

To simplify, no distinction is made here between the poet's persona and Ekelöf himself. While he is in nature, he is connected in numerous ways with what he sees and experiences through his senses. He is a meeting place of feelings of meaninglessness, or even a sense of unreality, conflicts, and contradictions. As in the sense of the Orientals (Arabs, Indians, Chinese), to whom Ekelöf often paid homage, life is occasionally envisioned as an unending, purposeless series of events. It is probably from this source that he originally acquired the concept of infinite process, with different phases, all interrelated to preceding or succeeding ones. The futility of it all is expressed in the lines "series divided by series / of nothing through nothing to nothing."

Ekelöf stresses three significant ideas: first, the fundamental oneness of all things; second, the conflict that the self experiences when passing through the lower world; and third, the sacred aspect of the mystical word "Abraxas." It should then become easier to recognize a formula that ties in with Ekelöf's philosophical idea of "Lord Something Else" as center point, not only in the "reality" of "Absentia animi" but also in Ekelöf's own existence. Readers of Ekelöf are used to encountering "Lord Something Else" in his poems.

"The Gymnosophist" endeavors, like a Hindu philosopher, to come to terms with reality through mystical contemplation:

What I mean
What I wish
is something else
for ever something else—
. . . .
Anytime, but not now
anywhere, but not here
anything, but not this—

What is it I want? What do I mean?
I know what it is—and I don't know!
It has no name, no place, no kind
I cannot call it, cannot explain it
It is what gets a name when I call
It is what gets a meaning when I explain
That's what it is—but before I have called
That's what it is—but before I have explained
It is what still has no name
What has a name is not something else—
. . . .
Holy is Lord Life, holy is Lord Death
on the strength of Lord Something Else
. . . .
unseen, invisible, unpreached in the scriptures
yet everywhere named although unnamed
everywhere known although unknown!
. . . .
but holy, holy, alone holy by means of himself
  is the Lord
the Lord Something Else!

And yet the greatest secret
is kept elsewhere
always elsewhere—
. . . .

Ekelöf's "Lord Something Else" is the kind of discovery (or borrowing from Indian and Taoist precepts) that extends human vision, as well as knowledge of the functions of the world and the mind. By the law of impermanence, everything has to become "Something Else:"

What I want
what I mean
is always something
Else

Such is the logical extension of the thought. As a consequence of this fundamental insight, we can assume that the poet becomes one with himself in a way he has not experienced before. Instead of division and disunity within himself, his insight puts him in full possession of himself. It enables him calmly to endure what goes on around him: the signs of everybody's movement toward disintegration and death. The degree of his awareness achieves peace for him ("the eye—reflects—in happy half-consciousness") as a disinterested observer. This "peace" with the world, however, is paradoxically realized not by *Praesentia animi* (presence, common in classical literature) but by the quite rarely used *Absentia animi* (absence), as the title reminds us. Exactly what that mystical term stands for in Ekelöf's poem would be interesting to know. Meister Eckehart does not employ the expression in any sense other than "separation of body from the soul." St. Augustine uses the term in *De ordine,* and, although Ekelöf alludes to St. Augustine's "Tolle, lege" (or, as Muriel Rukeyser translated the title: "Open It, Write!"), it is unlikely that Ekelöf borrowed the expression from Augustine or from anyone else. It is hard to believe that the title "Absentia animi" signifies no more than "absence of mind"; "inattention to what is going on; failure to receive impressions of what is present, through preoccupation with other matters; involuntary abstraction" (*Oxford English Dictionary,* 2d ed.).

It is tempting to assume that Ekelöf's "absentia animi" is a kind of release of the sort that the mystics sought—a form of ecstasy, in other words, perhaps achieved when "the soul" has absented itself, or moved itself, and has finally planted itself in a civilized ancient sphere to its liking. If so, this can perhaps be considered an early prelude to the extraordinary metamorphoses found in Ekelöf's central poem, *A Mölna Elegy* (to be discussed later). That such devices virtually require multiple personalities can hardly be denied. It is significant that, when dedicating his books to close friends, Ekelöf sometimes signed himself by the names of his created figures: the Prince of Emgión or Alexander (the Great), for example.

With the combination of a treetop and a cloud in "Absentia animi" Ekelöf unobtrusively draws attention to three things: the blackbird in the treetop, the theme of "Lord Something Else," and some of the processes of human perception. It is also his way of saying that we can never reach the ultimate reality. He then defines "something else":

O far far away
swims in the bright sky
over a treetop a cloud
in happy unconsciousness!
O deep down in me
the eye of black pearl reflects from its surface
in happy half-consciousness
the image of a cloud!
Not a thing that exists
It is something else
It is in something existent
but it does not exist
It is something else

O far far away
in what is beyond is found
something very near!
O deep down in me
in that which is near
is something beyond

something beyond-near
in what is near and far
something neither-nor
in what is either-or:
neither cloud nor image
neither image nor image
neither cloud nor cloud
neither neither nor nor
but something else!
The only thing that is
is something else!
The only thing that is
in that which is
is something else!
The only thing that is
in this which is
is that which in this
is something else!
(O the soul's cradle-song
the song of something else!)
    (Rukeyser-Sjöberg trans.)

Ekelöf was a great reader, but also quite unsystematic in his reading, as he said himself. Among his favorite authors were Strindberg and Rimbaud. I shall present evidence of their influence on "Absentia animi":

a frayed butterfly is heading
to nothing, which is a faded rose
the smallest and ugliest.

If the juxtaposition of "nothing" and "a faded rose" appears surrealistic, it is nonetheless from a pre-surrealistic period, and can be attributed to Strindberg. Since the latter's "Indiansommar" (Indian Summer) in *Dikter på vers och prosa* (1883) has thus far not been published in English translation, I venture to offer this version for the benefit of non-Swedish readers:

From the sickroom's chlorine-scented pillows,
darkened from stifled sighs
and hitherto unheard-of curses;
from my night table,
cluttered up with medicine bottles,
prayerbooks and Heine,
I tottered out on the balcony

to look at the sea.
Wrapped up in my flowered quilt
I let the October sun
shine on a bottle of absinthe,
green as the sea
green as the spruce twigs
on a snowy street
where a funeral train has gone by!
The sea lay dead-calm,
and the wind slept—
as if nothing had gone on!
Then came a butterfly,
a brown, horrid butterfly,
that had been a cabbage worm before
but had crawled up now
from a newly made head of leaves,
beguiled by the sunshine
of course!

Shivering from cold
or want of practice
he settled down
on my flowered quilt
And he picked out from the roses
and the aniline lilacs
the smallest and ugliest—
how can you be so stupid!

When the hour was over
and I got up
to go and take in,
he was sitting there still,
that stupid butterfly.
He'd fulfilled his destiny
and was dead,
the stupid devil!

Professor Walter Berendsohn is inclined to view the poem as "a real event." He suggests that Strindberg "probably interprets the butterfly symbolically. Strindberg compares his own way of choosing danger in the vicinity of his beloved to the butterfly's behavior and applied the strongest expression to his stupidity. It is self-irony" (*August Strindbergs skärgårds- och Stockholms-skildringar* [Stockholm, 1962], pp. 252–253).

Strindberg's and Ekelöf's autumnal poems are, to be sure, very different. Yet they have in common a butterfly attracted not to the real thing but to an artificial, quilted rose, "the smallest and ugliest." This butterfly, from Ekelöf's reading of "Indiansommar," has been transformed by Ekelöf into the brittle-legged mosquitoes, which are then called "the stupid devils." In a review of Strindberg's poems, Ekelöf stated that even as a high school student he had taken notice of "Solnedgång vid havet" (Sunset at Sea) and "Indiansommar." He added that he found "Indiansommar" to be "one of the most beautiful descriptions of the sea in Swedish poetry" (*BLM* 10, no. 9 [1941], 7–25). After such a high appraisal, one is not surprised that Ekelöf discreetly inserted a quotation from the poem in his "Absentia animi."

Perhaps Berendsohn's interpretation of the butterfly symbol in Strindberg's poem (it also occurs in Strindberg's "Högsommar" [The Height of the Summer]) is correct. But what can we say about the frayed butterfly in "Absentia animi" apart from the fact that it is related to death in Strindberg's poem? It is noteworthy that while the butterfly incident becomes the main theme in Strindberg (the invalid tottering, the feeble butterfly "shivering from cold / or want of practice" and crawling around on the sick man's quilt), the butterfly in Ekelöf is an image that appears only at the beginning of the poem, in the "concrete" section, where it figures among many en route to disintegration.

In Greek the word for "butterfly" is *psyche,* which also means "soul," but there is no reason to believe that Ekelöf had "the soul" particularly in mind when he introduced the butterfly in "Absentia animi." To an even lesser degree did he have in mind "the immortality of the soul," which is often represented in poetry by the butterfly. "I don't believe in a life after this one. / I believe in this life," Ekelöf declared in "En verklighet (drömd)" in *Om hösten.* The "frayed" butterfly hints clearly that the inevitable destination is approaching fast, that the definitive atomization has begun. Beyond that phenomenon Ekelöf ventured no hope whatever.

The other passage that I would like to discuss is perhaps even more inconspicuous. It is found at the end of the "abstract" portion of "Absentia animi":

> O
> non sens
> non sentiens non
> dissentiens
> indesinenter
> terque quaterque
> pluries
> vox
> vel abracadabra.

Here, as on so many other occasions (for instance, *A Mölna Elegy*), Ekelöf alludes to Rimbaud. But Ekelöf here borrows not from Rimbaud's published text but from a manuscript of "Âge d'or" (Golden Age, 1872). In the margin by the third stanza of "Âge d'or" there is a version that, by Rimbaud's own decision, never saw print:

> Terque quaterque
> Pluries
> Indesinenter.

Both Vergil and Ovid employed the expression "terque quaterque" ("ever and ever again"), so perhaps Rimbaud recalled the phrase from his time at school, when he won prizes for his poems in Latin. While translating or recreating Rimbaud, no doubt Ekelöf checked commentaries and notes on the poems. In the case of "Âge d'or," we can surmise that "terque quaterque" had become a familiar refrain for Ekelöf and was thus included in a modern poem—in spite of (or because of) the fact that Rimbaud had rejected it! Ekelöf then toyed with the words

> non sens
> non sentiens non
> dissentiens

which are suited perfectly to the theme of "Absentia animi," that is, nothingness. As for the words "vel abracadabra," the latter is a magical-mystical expression that nowadays denotes, approximately, "meaningless talk, gibberish, nonsense." The opposites (in the lines quoted from the poem) seem to have merged and achieved a mystical unity: the "I" is both here and far away; "you" is also "I." There is nothing more to wish for. Attaining such a state appears to the poet as something enviable, highly desirable: it is a form of ecstasy, in time but also beyond time.

In a note in *BLM,* Ekelöf wrote that *A Mölna Elegy* "concerns itself with relativity and the experience of time, perhaps also with a kind of attitude toward life. It is not a description of time elapsed but (theoretically) is supposed to occur in one moment. In other words: it is a cross section of time instead of a passage through time" (*BLM* 15, no. 5 [1946], p. 358). The moment occurs "during the transition from Sept. to Oct. 1940" (*sic*). Later he warned against attempts to overemphasize the "one moment." He added (in a personal note to the author):

> Time and time. What is it? It is supposed to occur not in a span of time but outside [of] time, in a mood of passivity and receptivity toward one's self, when everything and anything is possible and nearby. *The ideal psychoanalytical moment* [italics added]. What matter if the hand of your watch has moved one minute or ten from the point when you started summarizing (or memorizing) your situation, your dreams, etc.? It is an instant all the same.

The curious idea of a vertical section of time occurred in André Gide's novel *Les faux-monnayeurs* (*The Counterfeiters*, 1927), which Ekelöf translated into Swedish as *Falskmyntarna* (1932). Gide provides *A Mölna Elegy* with a central theme: "in the past our future is determined." This book-length poem—with a long and complicated history of its own—opens "On Mölna jetty," on the island of Lidingö, close to Stockholm. A person who imperceptibly undergoes a metamorphosis is sitting on the jetty. He is alone and does not interrelate directly with others; in fact, he functions as a passive, experiencing medium. The poet is the author of the protagonist's remarkable transformations.

It is a most peculiar, wonderful, perplexing poem—with anonymous voices from different ages, places, and circumstances mingling with the voices of identified people, including Alexander the Great, Philemon and Baucis, the sibyls, the Gorgon, Ibn al-ʿArabī, Emanuel Swedenborg, Shakespeare, Hieronymus Bosch, Chopin, Rimbaud, Strindberg, Carl M. Bellman, Robert Desnos, Victor Hugo, the Song of Solomon, Homer, Horace, Petronius, Edward Trelawny, Madame de Staël, James Joyce, Edith Södergran, and some of Ekelöf's distant Jewish relatives. They all appear to exchange greetings across the barriers of time and space.

Ekelöf's despair over the Swedish welfare state caused him to turn his back on the contemporary world and look backward, to classical times, to the Mediterranean, to Rome and Greece, to his Jewish ancestors of the seventeenth and eighteenth centuries, to the scribblers of graffiti on the walls of Pompeii and other places in the Roman Empire, and to the incantations from Hadrumetum in North Africa and Charente in France. He never pushed his *alchimie du verbe* further than in *A Mölna Elegy*: "languages—Classical and popular—and the genres—the ditties and the rhetorical—are here twisted like threads, puzzles for philologists, flimmering[*sic*],—fragmentary testimonies of our common life in a Hades as real as the present time" (Åke Janzon).

Regarding the most puzzling part of the *Elegy*, the Latin graffiti, Ekelöf felt compelled to give an explanation. Together the graffiti "make up a tangible Hades." Mommsen has something dry to say about this. The epigrapher C. M. Kaufmann turns his statement in a more expressive and more poetic manner: "Die Innschriften sind nicht Denkmäler der Literatur, sondern des Lebens" ("The inscriptions are not memorials of literature, but of life" as Ekelöf wrote in an end note, adding that "for his part he had endeavored to make the *Elegy* into a commentary on life, albeit incomplete and imperfect.") It is with this in mind that I shall make a horizontal "exagmination" (Joyce's spelling) of Ekelöf's "vertical cut of time" for the benefit of those readers who are new to Ekelöf, indicating biographical connections whenever they have been established with any certainty or where they are of any use.

It would be of considerable interest to study the theme of the four elements (especially fire and water), the theme of the city versus the country, the erotic theme, and the classical or musical elements throughout the *Elegy,* but for practical reasons we shall instead pursue the time theme, and begin with two relevant quotations from Ekelöf's essays. The first one is from *Blandade kort:* "I have always learned from the past and mistrusted those who *teach* the future." Ekelöf expands on his ideas about time in an essay deploring the Western lack of traditions, and offers a plan for a broader kind of education than our schools provide. It should be less compartmentalized, more unified, "because culture is one and indivisible." How can a student profit from being taught mere ideas?

> Instead give him time, its social tone, its costume among high and low, street mud and odors, its carriages and horses, music, even the street ballads, painting, even tavern signs, the sex morality, the shape of glasses, the decor on the plates, food recipes, the cries of the chimney sweep lads, the on dits and bon mots of the day, and give it to him visually.
>
> (p.10)

The second statement that may prove useful in explaining Ekelöf's technique is found in the essay "Modus vivendi," in *Verklighetsflykt:*

> I wish to live associatively, want to find out about myself and the world thus: empirically, through memory and its connections, I want to experience the world *not only in the moment but in the many possible moments of which my now is composed.* The now has no unequivocal directives to offer me. I return to it when it has become memory, in order laboriously, with the help of other memo-

ries, to make a kind of decision, which is hardly more than a divination. But such confirmed divinations can by and by become a vague conviction that will grow clear. *That is my now.* Which was then.

> (p. 143; italics added)

When one reads *A Mölna Elegy* it is rewarding to keep in mind the intimate relationship between time and the self, the identity of which has been scrutinized and questioned in poems such as "Tag och skriv."

Although the self desires to retain a moment of happiness or a moment marking life's culmination, the moment does not linger but fades away into the past, and the situation is already changed, as in a kaleidoscope, when one attempts to capture it. What can be retained is the desire to have seized a particular moment, which automatically passes into a paler sphere than that of the experience itself, into memory, as long as it lasts, or into dream, obsessive or simply occasional, as the case may be. And in dreams the episode of the moment and the mood it created can be experienced in almost hallucinatory intensity, in form as well as color. We speak of an "unforgettable moment," a wonderful or grand moment that is a pleasure to "revive."

One can also think of an "unforgettable" moment of an entirely different kind: the moment that seems impossible to forget, however much one tries, originating in traumatic experiences—moments that have good, bad, or perhaps even dangerous consequences. Before Salvarsan and sulfa were invented, and afterward too, a momentary sexual pleasure with the wrong person could, in time, result in general paralysis and partial or total psychic disorientation—to take a single drastic example.

Do poets and artists relate to the moment differently than people in general? They do, in the sense that they have the courage to try to give shape to it—to be the subject of inspection, viewed by themselves and others. It is easy on the basis of de Maupassant's report to imagine how Monet tried to catch the light and mood of the moment by resolutely walking from one canvas to another, painting on each for a while, until he covered ten canvases, each of which has been painted according to specific positions of the sun and the angle of its rays—or to imagine how Paul Cézanne embarked on painting Mont-Saint-Victoire for the two-hundredth time, in yet another attempt to give shape to the novel sensation he experienced in a unique new light.

Poets of the subjective type presumably do not want to employ the potentialities of photography in their chosen art form. They would rather seek out an individual moment that reveals something of their personality. Pound, for instance, speaks of a "magic" moment; Eliot, of an "unattended" moment; S. H. Vatsyayan, of a "shadowless" moment; Södergran, of a "flying" or "fleeting" (*flyktig*) moment.

It is to the elucidation of such a moment that Ekelöf periodically devoted a large portion of his life, resulting in *A Mölna Elegy*, sections of which appeared in *Ars* (1942), *BLM* (1946), *Prisma* (1949), *Poesi* (1949), and *Ord och bild* (1956) before it appeared as a book-length poem.

If one attempts to write about moments of a traumatic kind, the reason might be self-therapeutic. Such writing might help to get rid of obsessive thoughts by committing them to paper, as Ira Progoff and others have suggested. Ekelöf has several reminiscences that can be included in this category:

> . . . I remember . . .
> the ticked moments, minute minutes tocked,
> slowly lockstepping, slowly
> shoulder-borne—
> I remember the seconds, the dropped moments
> or *the held, riveted ones.*
>
> (311–317; italics added)

Another occasion is kept in remembrance from an episode of ill health:

> And the red ball,
> the high fever-ball, dazzling and inflamed,

came rolling over you, in one moment
of intolerable speed and in the next unendurably
> slow.
And the window's slant suncross on the floor
came relentlessly crawling closer to the bed.
And the wagon came clattering on cobblestones
without ever once stopping . . .
To the suburbs
> they had all gone, or to the country.
>
> (274–283)

To this manuscript, as in many other manuscripts, Ekelöf has added in the margin "respiratory distress," a chronic asthmatic condition. The poet has made an inventory of his indelible memories and has picked out what he could use for artistic purposes. In this instance it is a childhood experience, as Ekelöf has indicated in the manuscripts of his *Elegy*. The same theme reappears in the "Marche funèbre" section:

> The red fever ball that makes me reel
> rolls, tumbles over, rushes
> Fever that slowly
> makes a vault of me, rushing
> dizzying
> rolls me, over me,
> dizzy—
> —la boule rouge qui bouge et roule—
> time arrested, aroused . . .
> And over again . . .
> And over again . . .
>
> (621–630)

Ekelöf acknowledged as his main debts or influences Indian art, Persian and Arabic poetry and mysticism, modern painting and modernistic poetry, Stravinsky's *The Rite of Spring* (1913; this influence is most evident in Ekelöf's first collection of poems, *Sent på jorden*), and, finally, Robert Desnos, "who died at the end of the war, suffering from the aftereffects of the concentration camps Buchenwald and Theresienstadt" ("Självsyn," in *Blandade kort*, p. 163).

Ekelöf described Desnos as being "one of his kind" and "essential to my needs at the time" (ibid.). He reviewed Desnos in *BLM* ([1954], pp. 606–607), and included him in his anthology of translations, *Valfrändskaper* (Elective Affinities, 1960). "La boule rouge qui bouge et roule" (the red ball that moves and rolls), attributed to Max Ernst, was the passage from Desnos that Ekelöf felt aptly described a memorable, painful asthmatic attack in his childhood, and he translated it into Swedish in his anthology of French poetry, *Hundra år modern fransk dikt* (pp. 75–78). Thus, it is a borrowing that clearly played a part in his life.

In the early manuscripts of *A Mölna Elegy* the autobiographical connection was much stronger than it was in the final (book) version. Allusions to Oriental concepts or persons and references to objects seen at the British Museum are found in the manuscripts. When "India" is mentioned in one manuscript, it refers to Ekelöf's escapist dreams of emigrating to India, with whose ancient philosophers he felt so much in harmony.

"It was mysticism that engrossed me during these early years of awakening," he wrote. "I learned to hate Europe and Christianity and during the morning prayer at school I began to mumble 'Om mani padme hum' [The innermost secret is in the lotus flower]" ("En outsiders väg," in *Verklighetsflykt*, p. 127). He discovered A. H. Fox-Strangway's *Music of Hindustan* and *Tarjumān al-ashwāq* by Muḥyi ad-Dīn ibn al-ʿArabī; both became lifelong companions. Ibn al-ʿArabī's voice is heard toward the very end of the *Elegy*, where he says a single word, "Labbayka!" (At thy service!), a phrase from the Islamic pilgrimage ritual.

Scribbled in pencil on a page of "Argument," one of the hundreds of manuscript pages of *A Mölna Elegy*, is the following notation by Ekelöf:

> The whole [thing] is still obscure to me but I have wanted it that way, because I have wanted to work in another light than obscure commonplace clarity. [The *Elegy* is] the result of ten years of stratified work, study, love, disappointments,

coordination, acquired knowledge of physical and psychic heredity, memory.

But, as we know, it took Ekelöf two decades to complete the *Elegy* The book was even advertised by his publisher, Bonniers, as "forthcoming" several times before it actually appeared.

For the young Ekelöf, sunset always had a very special significance, which one can note in his prose pieces "En outsiders väg" and "Solnedgång" both in *Verklighetsflykt*. He recalled:

> That fits a future poet, but I do not know how I happened to become a cloud watcher. The sunset lay heavy over my childhood and I even saw it in my dreams. The intensely brick-red church outside the windows—it was the Johannes Church in Stockholm—threw a hectic, sickly and, as it were, magnified reflection of the sunset deep into the rooms. In this red twilight my father wandered about like a shadow, insane for many years, mumbling and with a vacant, dilapidated face, followed by his nurses.
>
> ("En outsiders väg," p. 124)

Ekelöf's worship of sunset was apparently related to musical excesses ("music is what has given me the most and the best") and to a longing for beauty that he was totally unable to express. In lines 44–46, "The sun setting / glows through fading / greens . . . ," and in line 605, he describes "the sun in perpetual sunset." Both descriptions appear to frame the "moment":

> Time arrested, flailed:
> The sun nailed
> on our bedlam spire
> Silos and towers—
> (30–33)

"In my memory red sunsets and bells are always inseparable," he wrote ("En outsiders väg," p. 124). That line reveals that the reference is to funeral bells in Stockholm, that beloved and hated city. The sunset is thus associated with human extinction. Ekelöf speaks here, as it were, "on the grave of his youth" (as it says in one manuscript). Youth and the experiences of early adulthood were over. Presumably this departure from youth is also the reason why he employs the word "elegy" in the title of his poem, since an elegy recalls what is past.

In *A Mölna Elegy* there is a "symphonic" organization, not one movement but numerous thematic echoes (unlike Eliot's *Four Quartets,* which are defined by four separate movements). The *Elegy* contains "choirs" and "soli," often with simple, clear harmonies, at times with assonances and rhymes or with unrhymed, rhythmic prose, which perhaps can be compared to atonal music.

The *Elegy* abounds in references, comic or horrified, to the tyranny of mindless time. Opposite a page of lascivious Pompeian inscriptions, Ekelöf has placed a modern, hour-by-hour chronicle of bedroom gymnastics:

One o'clock
a young cock.
By cinq heures, the time of the tea dance,
this goat can prance
Then at six
more complex tricks
but not yet! wait,
let's fly at eight.
Two o'clock came
he does the same.
At midnight, by the gate deep in the wood
a piston tight in your cylinder stood.
Three was cried
he came outside.
Ten, in a hotel room at the beach you'll find
a sunburnt couple doing 69.
At one o'clock
this young cock.
Don't forget five p.m.:
Press the button!—

(375–394)

In the "Park Scene" of the *Elegy* an Old Actor has made a date with his Victoria, naturally at a fixed hour; she chooses not to come. The fact that she does not show up does not quench his hopes. He has an appointment with the past, and he will stay on, "waiting for the past." He feels he has cause to consider writing

. . . a memorandum . . .
on the punctuality of ladies . . . —Victoria!
I belong alas also among your captives,
beside the victory chariot—Ha!—surviving captive:
(The sapphire on the little finger, raised,
mouth against crook of cane . . .)

A flying moment—
All of this in the season when the legless sprang
and the fingerless played their guitars till they rang
and the deaf heard it all
and the crippled did not fall
the blind came running to the call.

(80–91)

The waiting scene alludes to Strindberg's Captain waiting, in vain, for his Victoria in *A Dream Play,* but also to Strindberg's literary work in general. A theme running through the entire *Elegy* is evoked by the line "A flying moment—" It is slightly modified from the poem "My future" in *The Land That Is Not* (1916) by the great Finnish-Swedish poet Edith Södergran. In that crucial moment, hopes, aspirations, and expectations for the future were apparently destroyed. Once the capricious moment had been decisive, however unimportant it might have appeared. "The Absurd Ditty" above indicates that the situation is abnormal (a time of deformity, absurdity, and war).

Besides the Pompeian wall inscriptions, Ekelöf has imported into the *Elegy* some Roman funerary inscriptions, on which, in some cases, the year, month, day, and even hour of death are registered, as though the moment of loss were just as important as the loss itself. Ekelöf finds many of these inscriptions moving, and in one or two cases, even "great poetry"; he refers to "Nunc mors perpetua(m) / libertatem dedit" ("Now death / has granted me eternal freedom"; Ernst Diehl, *Vulgärlatein-*

ische Inschriften [Bonn, 1910], 1275). This could have been written by Lucretius, Ekelöf thought. There are also episodes in the *Elegy* that can be pinpointed in time more or less accurately and have received their place in the annals, for example, "Castenhof Tavern 1809" and the "revolutionary" interlude marked "1809" in the left margin, in which Ekelöf's favorite ancestor, Anna Catharina von Hedenberg, née Lewin, participated—even if in a rather peripheral way. Married to King Gustav III's physician in ordinary, she was, of course, expected to keep out of "revolutionary" activity.

The magnificent "Cosmic Occurrence Near the Equator," marked "1786" in the left margin, refers to Anna Catharina's brother, Lieutenant Gustaf Lewin, who for a while worked for a French commercial shipping company involved in the slave trade to the Caribbean islands:

> —Yes, I remember
> a night on circa one degree north latitude.
> The sky stood clear and in godlike majesty.
> On the horizon was seen the well-known light
> which emanates from all the myriad beings
> with which the ocean is so richly endowed.
> I promenaded on deck with the first mate
> when suddenly in the east we saw a great star
> which increased every second in greatness.
> I reported to the captain who soon came up,
> gave orders to summon every man on deck
> to reef the sails, heave to and lash the rudder.
> And then the star or meteor burst open
> into a thousand rays or with the speed of thought
> over the ship the rushing of these rockets
> that covered the whole horizon with a shining
> so dazzling that you could have seen a hair
> if one had been hanging from the masthead!
> Just then arose a hurricane, so violent
> that we dreaded the capsizing of the ship
> and soon after such an abundant rainfall
> that all the water vessels could have been filled
> with what washed over the deck in a few moments.
> This phenomenon lasted hardly forty minutes.
> Air and sky cleared, the stars grew visible,
> the wind the same. The sails set.
> The watch was relieved and allowed to turn in

> and the ship proceeded on the same course
>   as before.
> But in the clarity of night was heard again
> now slack, now strong, as in rhythmically varied
>   choruses
> locked in, below decks, the singing of the slaves . . .
>   (Rukeyser-Sjöberg trans., 231–261)

The exact time, almost to the minute, of Marie Madeleine Brinvillier's death by execution is recorded in Mme de Sévigné's letter of 17 July 1676. Comparable executions took place at the time of the witchcraft and poison epidemic prevalent in Europe and New England in the latter half of the seventeenth century. Mme de Sévigné's diaries were among the books Ekelöf read with attention. He was taken by Brinvillier's fate and devoted both a poem and notes to her. Ekelöf's reasoning about her needs no commentary:

> Whether saint or wild animal, I know not
> or human or only an actress
> Was her revenge real? Or did she become resigned
> and try to get the most out of her role
> that a ruined childhood and a life lived
> under the sign of the abnormal forced on her?
> But what is real, what lacks reality?
> What is sound food, what medicine, what poison?
> And the crowd there that just cried animal
> now cries saint. What is the meaning
> of everything? An abyss opened itself
> in the depths. If heaven now stands open
> the grace is not less fearful than the doom
> and all values are empty in extremis
> and men's riddles questions lives
> hung on nothing
> between the two.
>   (Rukeyser-Sjöberg trans.)

Ekelöf, even more conspicuously than usual, emphasized time and the clock in the *Elegy*. In the "Park Scene" the front gable clock, its hands gone, participates without restraint in a tripartite conversation with the Biedermeier sofa and the blind window, punning in truly Joycean manner: "Trr! Timeworn curses! My watchworks hurt! Clockstroke!"

If the hands had not already fallen off or been removed from the actual clock at Mölna (just outside Stockholm), I suppose Ekelöf would have picked them off, at least in his poem. Why? He was an outsider who, the longer he lived, became increasingly convinced of the disastrous effects and drawbacks of all regimentation. The fact that the clock had lost its hands indicates more than the decrepit state of the place. It also expressly implies that exact chronological time is less important than awareness of how times interchange in life in general, as is evident especially in the main character in the *Elegy*. Above all, Ekelöf wanted to give shape to the experience of time as something relative, something not easy to specify, something protean.

Ekelöf's originality expresses itself in part in his ability to identify with a large number of characters, from the "speaker" in the sections "Alexander" and "Stateira" to the "abortive larvae and lemures" in the section "On Mölna Jetty." His willfully original and meandering educational process must have been decisive for his outlook. He discovered for himself precisely what ancient Indian and Persian philosophers had wondered about: changes and transformations, the impermanence of things and beings, the rise and fall of feelings, "the self same or another I or not I?" (from the end of "Wave Song").

In the section "Leavetaking," Ekelöf repeats the theme of identity from "Wave Song":

> *The same one and still another*
> Your innocence is greatest in disgrace
> —then it emerges, indestructible—
> your voice is at its most clearly audible
> while you are silent . . .
> (654–658; italics added)

Similar philosophical questions regarding the "self" and its identity were raised by the wise men of India 1,400 years before Westerners began to write about the problem. Herakleitos (Heraclitus; *ca.* 540–*ca.* 475 B.C.), known as the "dark philosopher" or the "crying one," had especially emphasized "becoming" and the interplay between "being" and "becoming"; thus the flow, change, "panta rei," "everything is in flux." These thoughts, in turn, attracted young Henri Bergson, who maintained that the past is the all-pervading part of each individual's present, which is ever present in his or her subconscious life.

Bergson's influence on Ekelöf is evident in the manuscripts of the *Elegy,* where the poet's notes on "time" and "la durée" appear. As a result of constant change it is hard, if not impossible, to determine what is and what is not reality. It may actually be a collection of constantly shifting experiences that cannot be fixed for even such small time units as fleeting seconds. Whatever uncertainty Bergson might have sensed, he tried to counter by hypothesizing a more enduring concept, that of "la durée," "the flow of time." Like Proust, Joyce, and Eliot, Ekelöf accepted Bergson's concept of time.

Ekelöf does not refer to time exclusively by means of words:

> Sea-creatures that gape over the ships
> and the Lestrygonians who destroy them
> in wonderful colors
> weathered, half obliterated.
> (468–471)

The sea creatures are seen on maps and drawings, such as those by the Swedish geographer Olaus Magnus in *Carta Marina et Descriptio Septentrionalium* (1539), exhibited in the entrance hall of the University Library, Uppsala. In the next line the scene has moved from Nordic waters to the Mediterranean, to southern shores, where the "Lestrygonians" introduce the well-known myth in the *Odyssey.* Favoring double exposures and certain complexities, Ekelöf refers here to a group of eight antique fresco fragments in the Museo Profano in the Vatican that depict Ulysses as unwelcome among the Lestrygonians, who assembled on the beach and threw stones at him and his crew. On one of the fragments, it looks as though the Lestrygonians have begun to destroy the ships. The sensitive observer of the original, and also (one hopes) the reader of the *Elegy*, should be able to perceive echoes of Homer's billowing waves and sense something of the danger and excitement of seafaring life, Ekelöf thought. Since he strongly appreciated Joyce, and translated some of his poems, he might also have had in mind Joyce's *Ulysses*, chapter 8, which is called "Lestrygonians." A few lines later we find:

> Lithophytes in the deeps:
> Holes and swellings on the limbs of the God
> watered reflections rippling over his face
> waves advancing beautifully from Naxos
> to break at the red palace in Mycenae.
>
> (476–480)

The primary "time-binding" element in this passage is a statue of an ancient god, Poseidon, who has been attacked by lithophytes (stone eaters), which have made holes in his limbs. As a result of a shipwreck at sea, this statue of Poseidon was seen by the eyes of fish rather than humans, until finally it was recovered from the Bay of Baia. The salvaged god can now be seen at Pozzuoli (Puteoli), Italy.

After an interval the theme of the heart appears:

> A man stands there with a heart in his hand!
> A pyre reeks on the beach!
> He squeezes it:
> Quick! Have you other lives?
>
> (*Ord och Bild* 65, no. 9 [1956]: 473)

Since the name Edward Trelawny (a friend of Shelley) appears in a few of the manuscripts of the *Elegy*, he clearly is the man with a heart in his hand. The year was 1822. "This could but does not have to be taken as an allusion to the scene at Shelley's funeral pyre," Ekelöf commented.

The line "Quick! Have you other lives?" from Rimbaud's "Mauvais sang," in *Une saison en enfer* (1873), functions as a bridge to the most

incredible metamorphoses of the *Elegy*'s last few pages: out of the space-time continuum to a spiritual-mystical sphere.

> The voice that cries from the tree's bark
> at the axe bite
> speaking at the point of being cut down
> The kid sucks at the breast of the faun
> or the unicorn seeking refuge
> in the virgin's lap
> O purity, purity!
>
> (487–493)

The voice is that of the dryad, a nymph who lived in the trees and died when the trees died. Eurydice, the wife of Orpheus, was the most renowned of the dryads. The unicorn alludes to the first of the famous tapestries in the Musée de Cluny, Paris, and to the equally famous Unicorn Tapestries in the Cloisters, New York City.

The unicorn, according to legend, was the shiest of all animals and could be captured only by an innocent maid. If and when it encountered such a virgin, it would go to her and place its head in her lap, as it does in this poem. Again, this is proof of Ekelöf's strong affinity for pictures—indeed, one is almost tempted to say, his dependence on artistic images. The fabulous unicorn serves as a "time-binding" device; Ekelöf saw it at the Musée de Cluny, as well as in a seventeenth-century zoology book. The universality of the symbolic unicorn was probably known to Ekelöf through Carl Jung.

"The Fire Song" is partly a description and interpretation of the *Garden of Delights* triptych (Prado, Madrid) by the Dutch painter Hieronymus Bosch, whose name appears as a gloss to the manuscripts of the *Elegy*. On the upper part of the right panel are the fire mills exchanging obscure signals. With the rotating fire mills, the mill symbolism is reintroduced:

> O firerush and glowspray
> Glowrustle firespray
> Flames and these swaying
> fire-mills shifting

obscure signals
significant glances
blinking red beacons
Tornadoes that pluck
flames like locks of hair
tongues that lick
spires and towers—

Glowrush fire spray
fire rustle glowspray
Fire-mills seeing
Fire-dogs peeing
on fire-trees
Devils that fly on ladders
high above the onlookers
unconscious of the fire's threats
those who have beshatten
us in the year of years
How have they seen fit
to see fire? Fire that endures
fire that swinks and sweats?
(494–517)

The expression "Fire-dogs peeing / on fire trees" is probably a reference to the great fire in Stockholm. The great Swedish mystic Swedenborg had a vision of this fire, in which he supposedly saw "elves or other spiritual beings pee at a fence, thereby helping check the fire three houses away from his own, on Hornsgatan." "Devils that fly on ladders" refers again to Bosch's paintings.

An upside-down caricature, with a disproportionate, ungainly head nailed to a saltire, was the poet's own creation (letter to author, 1963). Ekelöf confirmed in a private communication that he was alluding to those who were nailed head down to some wooden structure, but it is unclear whether the reference is to Saint Peter, Spartacus, or others.

It is certain, however, that Ekelöf's next "time-binding" device is complex. It is his employment of quadrigae, teams of four race-horses featured at the Roman circus. The four horses would circle the *meta,* the turning post, at each end of the circus.

Ekelöf selected the names of the horses in the four teams of quadrigae from a long list and attempted to group them according to the ele-ments. However, his plan to order the names this way was only partially carried through. Thus, the first quadriga vaguely suggests fire; the second vaguely suggests air; the third, earth; and the fourth, water. To some extent these suggestions of the four elements correspond to the four elements in the Brinvillier section on the facing page of the *Elegy.* They find another parallel in Carl Jung's volume 5 of *Symbols of Transformation,* which also describes the horses' symbolic relation to the elements in one quadriga:

> The first horse is very fleet. His coat is shining and bears the signs of the planets and the constellations. The second horse is slower and is lit up on only one side. The third goes slower still, and the fourth twists round and round. But there comes a time when the hot breath of the first sets fire to the mane of the second, and the third drowns the fourth with his sweat! *The four horses correspond to fire, air, water and earth respectively,* beginning with the most energetic of the Elements and ending with the most malevolent. *The quadriga, then, becomes a symbol of the universe of space-time.*
>
> (italics added)

By employing the Roman quadriga Ekelöf also introduced a new aspect of time into his *Elegy,* and by building the theme into four separate quadrigae, he added great complexity by means of a simple graphic design.

In the next imaginary scene we are back in Greece, with more references to water. The mythological Gorgon to whom the poem alludes is equivalent to a siren of the seas. The time is that of the Medusa, the Gorgon who had the power to petrify a person by a single glance, but it is also that of the poet, who identifies with the squid, the subject of numerous sea-monster stories:

Wherefrom,
Mother—
Yes, wherefrom have you borne me
my hunger is my strength
my evil is my good

all of us floating here
floating along
O these carcasses that float
that head into the reeds
but rock uncertainly outside.

(576–586)

Both "Marche funèbre" and "Leavetaking" contain easily identifiable references to time. Some characters who are taking themselves out of time are introduced: the front gable clock, whose face is altered by stroke and who speaks a line from *Finnegans Wake* with several allusions to the theater (of life?) and to the hour; the slowly circling Rāgas and Rāginis, Indian male and female tunes, which are also personified in Mogul miniatures as fairies; a genius who transforms himself, according to his wishes, into the one he wishes to be, le Roquefort or le Brie. Rimbaud is the father of these transformations. The jocular genius who keeps shifting his identity fits beautifully into the general theme of metamorphosis. The disabled emanations keep dancing, while chanting, "apple, papple, barries, charries / one and two, one and two: / out goes y-o-u" (697–699). It is possible to read their rigamarole as meaning "outside, excluded, you will be from now on!" Ibn al-ʿArabī's "Labbayka!" indicates the consecrated state. In his autobiographical essay, "En outsiders väg," Ekelöf said that he never could find what he was searching for, until he happened upon *Tarjumān al-ashwāq* by Ibn al ʿArabī, which for a long time was his favorite book. The thrush is also removed from reality, since it is a "heraldic bird; silent, immobile, with its beak up."

Ekelöf apparently wanted once more to invoke the Finnish-Swedish poet Edith Södergran and the Swedish mystic Emanuel Swedenborg near the end of his great mosaic of quotations, allusions, and reminiscences:

—thought that a rocket struck loose up across me,
which sprayed a shower of sparks of beautiful fire:
Love of the sublime.
Perhaps.

(717–720)

That is the end of the Swedenborg quotation about another momentary happening, another metamorphosis: a mystic concerned with dreams is given the last word. Time is again the central theme in the rhymed lines:

From the past's rarely
through now's midway barely
to the future's still lesser
still more rarely.

(721–724)

On the very last page of the *Elegy* the reader is saluted—"Vale viator!" (Farewell, wayfarer!)—just as he was greeted with "Ave viator!" (Hail, wayfarer!) at the beginning of the long "moment." Both expressions are frequently found, one above the other, on gravestones along the Appian Way, which connects Rome with Brindisi. The expression is simple: the dead person both greets and says farewell to the passerby. Ekelöf thought of this as a greeting emanating from Hades, from someone who had already joined the "greater majority," to a poet who was constantly concerned with the netherworld. In a note on one of his copies of *A Mölna Elegy* Ekelöf wrote, "A moment becomes timeless when the itinerant wanderer passes the gravestone and sees its *Vale!* and *Ave!* or the reverse—. Such a fugue should be read both ways, [but] I have not reached as far as that in perseverance."

Below the salutation "Vale viator!" is a picture of archaeopteryx, the prehistoric bird whose fossil remains were discovered in the nineteenth century in Bavaria. The poet Lars Forssell has related Ekelöf's fascination with an old zoology book depicting the fossil remains of the so-called Montmartre bird, "a symbol of the eternal paradox life in death, flight in repose, the hammering heart in the cold stone—" (*All Världens Berättare* 11, no. 12 [1955], 3–7). The fossilized bird, which once strayed hither and thither as uneasily and aimlessly as wandering birds in later eras, is probably above all a reminder of the eons of time and of our connection with the past through endless transformations.

Ekelöf plays in *A Mölna Elegy* with his own caprices, phobias, memories, obsessions, absurdities, idiosyncrasies, and peculiarities, among other things. In his psychic landscape he is attempting to chart a course through a logic of the subconscious: he combines, divides, distorts, and reverses. By adding the subtitle *Metamorphoses* to his *Elegy*, he accurately reflects his collapsing of past and present; of life and death; of heaven, earth, and hell. It is as if Ekelöf wanted to proclaim that all of the disparate elements within the *Elegy* do in actuality constitute a whole that encompasses both man and nature, and the simple as well as the complex.

If the puzzle Ekelöf contrived with such ingenuity and playfulness is intricate in some respects, it is easy in others; but even at its most cryptic and whimsical, it continues to fascinate by testing the reader's imagination and intelligence. Cut free from the usual associations in time and space and compelled to think quite independently, the reader must penetrate the guise of these private or learned metamorphoses and experience the various qualities of existence as facets of a constant in flux. For, to this poet, the individual yields the universal.

Selected Bibliography

EDITIONS

INDIVIDUAL WORKS

POETRY

Sent på jorden. Stockholm, 1932.
Dedikation. Stockholm, 1934.
Sorgen och stjärnan. Stockholm, 1936.
Köp den blindes sång. Stockholm, 1938.
Färjesång. Stockholm, 1941.
Non serviam. Stockholm, 1945.
Om hösten. Stockholm, 1951.
Strountes. Stockholm, 1955.
Opus incertum. Stockholm, 1959.
En Mölna-elegi: Metamorfoser. Stockholm, 1960.
En natt i Otočac. Stockholm, 1961.

Sent på jorden, med Appendix 1962; och, En natt vid horisonten. Stockholm, 1962.
Dīwān över fursten av Emgión. Stockholm, 1965.
Sagan om Fatumeh. Stockholm, 1966.
Vägvisare till underjorden. Stockholm, 1967.
Partitur. Edited by Ingrid Ekelöf. Stockholm, 1969.
En röst. Edited by Ingrid Ekelöf. Stockholm, 1973.
Grotesker. Selected by Roger Fjellström. Luleå, 1981.
Variationer. Selected by Anders Mortensen. Stockholm, 1986.

PROSE

Promenader. Stockholm, 1941.
Utflykter. Stockholm, 1947.
Blandade kort. Stockholm, 1957.
Verklighetsflykt. Stockholm, 1958.
Lägga patience. Edited by Reidar Ekner. Stockholm, 1969.
Gunnar Ekelöf: En självbiografi. Edited by Ingrid Ekelöf. Stockholm, 1971.
Gunnar Ekelöf: Brev, 1916–1968. Edited by Carl Olov Sommar. Stockholm, 1989.

COLLECTED WORKS

Dikter. 3 vols. Stockholm, 1949.
Dikter, 1932–1951. Stockholm, 1956.
Dikter. Stockholm, 1965.
Vatten och sand. Selected by Reidar Ekner. Stockholm, 1966.
Urval. Dikter, 1928–1968. Selected by Olof Lagercrantz. Stockholm, 1968.
Dikter, 1965–1968. Stockholm, 1976.

TRANSLATIONS BY EKELÖF

Falskmyntarna. Translation of *Les faux-monnayeurs* by André Gide. Stockholm, 1932.
Fransk surrealism. Stockholm, 1933.
Kärleken och döden. Translation of three pieces from *Les plaisirs et les jours* by Marcel Proust. Stockholm, 1933.
Hundra år modern fransk dikt. Stockholm, 1934.
En tid i helvetet. Translation of *Une saison en enfer* by Arthur Rimbaud. Stockholm, 1935.
T. S. Eliot: Dikter. Poems selected and edited by Ronald Bottrall and G. E. Stockholm, 1942; 2d ed. 1948.
Förtvivla ej. Translation of *L'Espoir* by André Malraux. Stockholm, 1944.

November. Translation (with Nun Ekelöf) of *Novembre* by Gustave Flaubert. Stockholm, 1946.

Valfrändskaper. Stockholm, 1960.

Glödande gåtor. Translation of *Glühende Rätsel* by Nelly Sachs. Stockholm, 1966.

Arthur Rimbaud: Lyrik och prosa. Edited by Reidar Ekner. Stockholm, 1972.

TRANSLATIONS

Ekelöf's "An Outsider's Way." Swedish Books, no. 4. London and Gothenburg, 1980.

Ekelöf's Later Poetry. Swedish Books, no. 3. London and Gothenburg, 1980.

Friends, You Drank Some Darkness: Three Swedish Poets—Harry Martinson, Gunnar Ekelöf, and Tomas Tranströmer. Translated by Robert Bly. Boston, 1975.

Guide to the Underworld. Translated by Rika Lesser. Amherst, Mass., 1980.

I Do Best Alone at Night. Translated by Robert Bly with Christina Paulston. Washington, D.C., 1968.

Late Arrival on Earth: Selected Poems. Translated by Robert Bly and Christina Paulston. London, 1967.

A Mölna Elegy: Metamorphoses. 2 vols. Translated by Muriel Rukeyser and Leif Sjöberg. Greensboro, N.C., 1984.

Poems: Gunnar Ekelöf. Translated by Brita Stendahl. Cambridge, Mass., 1976.

Selected Poems. Translated by Muriel Rukeyser and Leif Sjöberg. New York, 1967.

Selected Poems. Translated by W. H. Auden and Leif Sjöberg. New York, 1972.

Songs of Something Else: Selected Poems. Translated by Leonard Nathan and James Larson. Princeton, N. J., 1982.

BIOGRAPHICAL AND CRITICAL STUDIES

Allt om Böcker, no. 2 (1984). Special Ekelöf issue.

Bergsten, Gunilla. "Abraxas." In *Samlaren* 85:5–18 (1964).

Brandell, Gunnar, "Samothrake än en gång." In his *Konsten att citera.* Stockholm, 1966.

Ek, Sverker, R. " 'Auditivt focus.' En aspekt på Gunnar Ekelöfs *En Mölna-elegi.*" In *Lyrik i tid och otid. Lyrikanalytiska studier tillägnade Gunnar Tideström 7.2.1971.* Uppsala, 1971.

Ekner, Reidar. "Herren Någonting Annat." In *Ord och bild* 76, no. 7:534–543 (1967).

——— . *I den havandes liv.* Stockholm, 1967.

——— . "Det mörknar över vägen." In *Svensk litteraturtidskrift* 31, no. 3:3–11 (1968).

Enckell, Rabbe. "Gunnar Ekelöfs lyrik." In *En bok om Gunnar Ekelöf.* Edited by Stig Carlson and Axel Liffner. Stockholm, 1956.

Espmark, Kjell. "Ekelöf och Eliot. En studie kring Farjesång." In *BLM* 28, no. 9:773–776 (1959).

——— . *Dialoger.* Stockholm, 1985.

Fehrman, Carl. "Gunnar Ekelöf och traditionen." In *Poesi och parodi.* Stockholm, 1957.

Hellström, Pär. *Livskänsla och självutplåning. Studier kring framväxten av Gunnar Ekelöfs Strountes-diktning.* Uppsala, 1976.

Janzon, Åke. "Gunnar Ekelöfs poesi." In *Svenska dagbladet* (Stockholm), 17 March 1968, "Kultursiden."

Landgren, Bengt. *Ensamheten. Döden och drömmarna.* Stockholm, 1971.

——— . *Den poetiska världen. Strukturanalytiska studier i den unge Gunnar Ekelöfs lyrik.* Uppsala, 1982.

Lindegren, Erik. "På väg mot instrumentallyriken." In Karl Vennberg and Werner Aspenström, eds., *Kritiskt 40-tal.* Stockholm, 1948. Pp. 305–310.

Lindvall, Lars. "Fernando Pessoas 'Havsode' och Gunnar Ekelöfs 'Samothrake.' " In *SLT* no. 1:30ff (1970).

Lundkvist, Artur. *Gunnar Ekelöf.* Stockholm, 1968.

Michl, Josef B. "Franz Kafka och Gunnar Ekelöf." In *Artes* (Stockholm) 12, no. 5:149–155 (1986).

Moberg, Ulf Thomas. *Gunnar Ekelöfs nonfiguration och situationspoesi.* Stockholm, 1982.

Olsson, Anders. "Ekelöfs nej." In *BLM* 49, no. 6:339–347 (1980).

——— . *Ekelöfs nej.* Stockholm, 1983.

Olsson, Bernt. "Gunnar Ekelöf vid tiden för debuten." In *Svensk litteraturtidskrift* no. 1:3–21 (1981).

——— . "Gunnar Ekelöf och språket." In *Svensk litteraturtidskrift* no. 2:3–19 (1981).

Printz-Påhlson, Göran. "Diktarens kringkastade lemmar. Motivisk och metodisk primitivism hos Gunnar Ekelöf." In his *Solen i spegeln.* Stockholm, 1958.

Shideler, Ross. *Voices Under the Ground. Themes and Images in the Early Poetry of Gunnar Ekelöf.* Berkeley, Cal., 1973.

GUNNAR EKELÖF

Sjöberg, Leif. "Gunnar Ekelöf's 'tag och skriv': A Reader's Commentary." In *Scandinavian Studies* 35, no 4:307–320 (1963).

————. *A Reader's Guide to Gunnar Ekelöf's "A Mölna Elegy."* New York, 1973.

————. "How Pleasant to Meet Mr. Ekelöf." In *Nordstjernan-Svea* (New York) 117, no 34:3, 5 (1989). Review article on *Selected Letters, 1916–1968.*

————. "A Life Without Theory: Sommar on Ekelöf." In *Nordstjernan-Svea* (New York) 117, no. 37:3, 11 (1989).

Sommar, Carl Olov. *Gunnar Ekelöf. En biografi.* Stockholm, 1989.

Stenström, Thure. "Icke det heroiske Grekland." In *Festschrift: Gunnar Hansson.* Linköping, 1988. Pp. 134–141.

Stenroth, Ingmar. *Gunnar Ekelöfs Samothrake.* Göteborg, 1981.

Stolpe, Jan. "Latrin och kräkiska. Det antika materialet i Ekelöfs *En Mölna-elegi.*" In *Rondo* 1, no. 1:13–20 (1961).

Thygesen, Erik. *Gunnar Ekelöf's Open-Form Poem "A Mölna Elegy": Problems of Genesis, Structure, and Influence.* Stockholm, 1985.

Tideström, Gunnar. "Samothrake." In *Lyrisk tidsspegel.* Lund, 1947.

Tigerschiöld, Brita. "Samothrakes tema." In *BLM* 28, no. 2:134–142 (1959).

Wigforss, Brita. "Gunnar Ekelöf." In *Columbia Dictionary of Modern European Literature.* 2d ed. New York, 1980.

————. "Mellan riddaren och draken. Gunnar Ekelöfs 'Tag och skriv.' " In *Radix* 3, no. 3–4:68–166 (1980).

————. *Konstnärens hand.* Göteborg, 1983.

BIBLIOGRAPHY

Ekner, Reidar. *Gunnar Ekelöf. En bibliografi.* Stockholm, 1970.

LEIF SJÖBERG

ALBERTO MORAVIA

(b. 1907)

FEW WRITERS HAVE enjoyed longer careers than Alberto Moravia, Italy's best-known and most widely translated novelist of the twentieth century. His first story was published in 1927, and since then he has brought forth a voluminous collection of novels, short stories, essays, plays, filmscripts, travelogues, movie reviews, translations, and—despite his reputation as an erotic writer—even tales for children. Although Moravia has been a literary and cultural force in Italy for more than half a century, he has not been universally admired. Indeed, perhaps no other contemporary writer of recognized stature has incurred as much censure as has Moravia from his countrymen, many of whom have deplored the paucity of his themes, his inelegant style, and his failure to advance the technique of the novel. Foreign critics have been somewhat more favorable, except perhaps toward his most recent works.

It is undeniable, however, that no other writer has presented so complete a picture of Italian life in this century. Moravia has not limited himself to a superficial description of mores and monuments: although most of his works are set in Rome, there is very little local color in his fiction. Instead, he has delved into the substance of Italian civilization in order to examine the problems of its existence, the changes wrought by new ideas, and the effects of historical phenomena such as fascism, World War II, neocapitalism, and the "revolution" of 1968. The skill and imagination with which Moravia has transformed his perceptions into fictional form have resulted in a significant body of work.

LITERARY BEGINNINGS

Alberto Pincherle Moravia was born in Rome on 28 November 1907. His Venetian father was a successful architect and an amateur painter. Carlo Pincherle Moravia was Jewish, but religious observance played no part in his life; his wife, however, was a practicing Catholic, and the young Alberto was baptized in that faith. Moravia's mother was a daughter of the noble de Marsanich family of Ancona. An active woman of strong will, she appears to have overshadowed her shy and quiet husband. It is perhaps significant that, although father figures are rare in Moravia's fiction, strong mothers appear quite often. Three other children completed the Moravia family: Alberto's two older sisters, Adriana and Elena, and a younger brother, Gastone, who died in Libya in 1941.

Most of Moravia's early education was entrusted to a succession of governesses, usually foreign and usually soon dismissed by Signora Moravia. Since the family hoped that young Alberto would eventually enter the diplomatic service, there was strong emphasis on languages. He spoke French before he could speak Italian, and he soon added a knowledge of English to his accomplishments. Although he studied German as well, his progress in that language was slower, and he never completely mastered it. Moravia has often stated that he found his vocation as a novelist at a very early age: when only seven or eight years old, he would tell himself stories in the form of a serial novel, leaving off his storytelling in the evening to take it up at the same place on the following day. As he learned to write, he began setting his stories down on paper.

When Moravia was nine years old, he fell ill with tuberculosis of the bone. (Moravia has always called his disease "tuberculosi ossea"—tuberculosis of the bone. Although osteomyelitis involves similar symptoms, the two diseases are quite distinct. I know of no reason to believe that Moravia suffered from osteomyelitis.) The disease was initially characterized by flare-ups followed by periods of remission that permitted the boy to attend school; however, the relapses became increasingly frequent and prolonged until, four years later, he was confined to bed. Thus began years of seclusion and intense pain: the prescribed treatment of the time was to immobilize the affected parts (in Moravia's case, his legs) in a cast, which caused severe pain whenever the leg muscles contracted. His health deteriorated steadily. Finally, his paternal aunt, Amelia Rosselli, learned of a new treatment practiced at the Codivilla sanatorium in Cortina d'Ampezzo. Over his father's objections, but with the support of Moravia's mother, the boy was taken to the Codivilla in the winter of 1923. He remained there until autumn 1925, even more alone than before but no longer in pain and improving steadily in health.

The author's formal schooling was scanty and uneven. He learned almost nothing about the sciences, and his study of mathematics never reached even the level of long division. Moravia's only academic certificate is a diploma from the *ginnasio,* a mid-level institution oriented toward preparing the student for entrance into the classical *liceo,* a secondary school. To compensate for this lack of school-

ing, to satisfy his early love for literature, and perhaps especially to while away the hours of illness, Moravia read widely among world authors.

Carlo Pincherle Moravia possessed a good library especially well stocked with dramatic literature, and the young Alberto showed an early preference for Shakespeare, Molière, Goldoni, and the classic Spanish and French playwrights. Moravia maintains that it is from these authors that he learned the art of dialogue, and much of his fiction possesses a theatrical structure. Comic writers (Petronius, Apuleius, Boccaccio, Ariosto, Cervantes, Rabelais) also appealed to him, as did certain poets, chief among whom were Giacomo Leopardi and Arthur Rimbaud. The latter's spirit of revolt against middle-class values made an especially deep impression on the boy. Moravia's acknowledged master, however, is Dostoevsky, whose dark passions, complex intrigues, and somber atmospheres are echoed in many of the Italian's works. Of scarcely less importance is Alessandro Manzoni, to whom, according to Moravia, he owes his taste for narration. A wide selection of other novelists, including Defoe, Balzac, Stendhal, Proust, and Joyce, completed Moravia's literary education. When he left the sanatorium, the young man could boast of a solid background in traditional European literature, but he was remarkably ignorant of the contemporary Italian literary and political world. He had no opinions on politics, and he did not even recognize the name of Giovanni Papini, one of the foremost and best-known Italian writers of the twenties.

During his early teens Moravia wrote mainly poetry, which, according to the author, was of a philosophical bent and uniformly mediocre; he later destroyed it. (Many bibliographers attribute to Moravia a collection of poems penned by Alberto Pincherle and published in 1920 under the title *Diciotto liriche* [Eighteen Lyrics]. The Pincherle in question, however, was a Roman professor of religion about ten years older than Moravia.) The young man wrote no more poetry after 1925, and in October of that year, after his release from Codivilla, he began the novel that was to become his first success and his most significant work.

Progress was slow: his illness had left Moravia weak, and he was able to write for only short periods of time. During the three years' writing of *Gli indifferenti* (*The Time of Indifference,* 1929; also translated as *The Indifferent Ones*), the author became acquainted with Corrado Alvaro, who, with Massimo Bontempelli, edited the avant-garde journal *'900* (Twentieth Century). Moravia's first short story, "La cortigiana stanca" ("Tired Courtesan"), appeared in this journal in 1927. The following year he submitted his completed novel to the publisher of *'900,* who rejected the manuscript, saying that it was a "haze of words." The manuscript was later accepted by the Alpes publishing house, with the provision that the author would pay for the printing costs of five thousand lire. Moravia borrowed the sum from his father, and *The Time of Indifference* appeared in 1929. It created among both readers and critics a literary sensation unparalleled in Italy, but no one was more surprised by it than its young author.

Moravia had intended the work to be primarily a literary exercise in applying theatrical techniques to the novel. As the author wrote in 1945 in an essay entitled "Ricordo de *Gli indifferenti*" ("Recalling *Time of Indifference*"):

> I had decided to write a novel that possessed the qualities of both fiction and drama. It was to be a novel with few characters, very few scenes, and with action restricted to a short period of time; a novel in which there would be only dialogue and descriptive narration and in which all the comments, analyses, and interventions of the author would be scrupulously omitted in order to achieve a perfect objectivity.
>
> (*L'Uomo come fine e altri saggi* [*Man as an End: A Defense of Humanism*], p. 63)[1]

---

[1] Except as noted, all quotations from Moravia's works have been translated by the present writer.

Certainly Moravia's early predilection for plays influenced his project, but Joyce's *Ulysses,* with its restriction of time to a single day, was also in the author's mind. The novel that resulted conformed to the plan: it covers slightly more than two days, most of the scenes take place inside rooms or an automobile, entrances and exits are frequent, and there are only five characters.

The story itself verges on melodrama. The widow Mariagrazia Ardengo is about to lose her villa because she cannot pay the mortgage held by her lover, Leo Merumeci, who has spent the previous years not only in her bed but also in her purse. Compounding her worries are the unmarried state of Carla, her twenty-four-year-old daughter, and her son Michele's lack of aim and employment. Of all the characters, Leo alone seems content with his life. He appears to be in complete control of the two elements—money and sexuality—that Moravia, like Balzac, regards as the basic components of human relations. The other characters, however, are almost schizophrenic; their lives are suspended somewhere between what is and what might be. Beset by financial problems, Mariagrazia dreams of sharing Leo's wealth, while Lisa, her friend and Leo's former mistress, deludes herself that she can recapture youth by seducing Michele.

The two young people are more complex and, at least early in the novel, more attractive. Undisturbed by her approaching spinsterhood, Carla is simply bored with the monotonous days in the Ardengo villa and disgusted by her mother's way of life. Like young Rimbaud she dreams of some destructive act that will put an end to her present condition and open the way to a "new life." In desperation she agrees to sleep with Leo, who then unexpectedly proposes marriage to her. And she accepts. Ironically, instead of making an "honest woman" of her, matrimony will make her a dishonest one: at the end of the novel and before her marriage to Leo, she is already fantasizing about her riches and the young lover whom she will take.

It is obvious that her "new life" will not significantly differ from her mother's.

Michele is the most "indifferent" of the characters: he feels detached from the world and those who surround him. There must be, he believes, some action that will be an adequate expression of his feelings and that will establish a bond between himself and the reality outside him. But Michele is the typical Moravian intellectual: he thinks and analyzes until his emotions and beliefs dribble away without consequence, leaving him with no motive for action. Nothing moves him, not even the news that Leo has seduced his sister. Nevertheless, Michele determines to feign anger and outrage. He buys a pistol, confronts Leo in his apartment, aims his weapon, fires—and then realizes that he has forgotten to load the gun. Michele's ironic destiny is as petty and as disappointing as his life has been. His tragedy becomes a farce, and the end of the novel finds him on his way to Lisa's apartment to become her lover and to enmesh himself in the intertwining loves of the wretched group.

The harsh realism of *The Time of Indifference* and its implicit criticism of middle-class Italy attracted immediate attention. In literary as in many other matters, the Italy of 1929 was much more conservative than most European countries. The Catholic church had long exercised a tacit censorship, while the literary establishment, with its respect for tradition and the disproportionate value that it placed on an elegant style, was naturally resistant to works that departed from the usual. Moreover, the puritanical tendency of the Fascist regime was making itself increasingly felt in the arts as well as in society. Although some readers, like G. A. Borgese, recognized the merits of the novel and the promise of its author, most castigated it for its unadorned and sometimes vulgar literary style. Others were offended by its explicit descriptions of sexual and bodily functions. Nearly everyone—and not least the government—was outraged by the pitiless view of an upper middle class permeated by pettiness, egoism, and deceit. The Rome of *The Time of Indifference* contradicted the image of that noble and heroic city cultivated by Mussolini's propagandists. And whereas Il Duce forecast a glorious and hopeful future for the Italian nation, Moravia, so far as the lives of his characters were concerned, was unrelievedly cynical.

Most critics who have written on *The Time of Indifference* have seen it as an anti-Fascist statement, but Moravia himself has always maintained that the political and social criticism implicit in his novel was completely unintentional. Although his cousins Carlo and Nello Rosselli were among the earliest and best-known anti-Fascists (Carlo was the leader and theorist of the Giustizia e Libertà movement; both brothers were assassinated in France in 1937 by Fascist thugs), the young Moravia remained not only politically uninvolved but seemingly even unaware of the profound changes at work in Italian politics. The author's experience during the 1920's was literary and personal, conditioned almost solely by the books that he had read and by his observations of the upper middle class in which he lived. If anything, *The Time of Indifference* attacks not a political regime but a socioeconomic system. This criticism of bourgeois society has been one of the constants in Moravia's works: one finds it in his novels and stories written thirty, even forty, years after the fall of fascism in Italy.

It can also be said that *The Time of Indifference* is the first European novel to come out of Italy: its themes and characters are not peculiarly Italian. Alienation, cynicism, aimlessness—these were the maladies that afflicted a whole generation on both sides of the Atlantic after World War I. Moravia's novel is the first in a long line of fictional works by Elio Vittorini, Ignazio Silone, Cesare Pavese, and others who, by their probing into the problems of the twentieth century, led Italian literature out of regionalism and into the international arena.

This broader effect of *The Time of Indifference* was not immediately noticed: for most critics, the novel remained a *succès de scan-*

dale, the product of an audacious, albeit talented, young man. Like Luigi Pirandello and Italo Svevo before him, Moravia is indebted to French critics for their discovery of many of the implications of his work. One of the earliest of these was Jean Paulhan, who, when Moravia visited Paris in 1948, inquired of the Italian whether he had come to France to visit his existentialist disciples. Dominique Fernandez, in his *Le roman italien et la crise de la conscience moderne* (The Italian Novel and the Crisis of Modern Consciousness, 1958), later characterized *The Time of Indifference,* which poses the problem of the moral justification of action, as the first European existentialist novel.

The Time of Indifference sets the pattern for most of the author's later fiction. It has been said—and with some justification—that Moravia wrote *The Time of Indifference* in 1929 and that he has been rewriting it ever since. Just as he began his first novel "without any precise idea of its meaning, aims, plot, characters, or milieu" ("Recalling *Time of Indifference*"), so has each of his later works evolved almost spontaneously, growing and developing during the act of writing itself. Nor has his style changed in any important way: Moravia's later works reflect the matter-of-fact, almost pedestrian prose of *The Time of Indifference.* His attention to visual detail, reliance on the interior monologue, and skillful use of imagery have remained characteristic of his writing.

Finally, Moravia has continued to explore and develop the themes announced in *The Time of Indifference.* Money and sex, of course, have remained cornerstones of his particular vision, yet, however important they may be, the dominant theme of his work is a moral and philosophical one of which he was not fully conscious when he wrote his first novel. He explained in 1958 in "A Fragment of Autobiography: About My Novels":

The problems of a writer are the problems latent in his epoch, but problems which will only reveal themselves as being of the day and age later, after they have been secretly and darkly manifest in the writer. The writer, by taking stock of these problems, is always in advance of his time.

(*Twentieth Century* 164: 530 [1958], Barbara Lucas trans.)

The problems referred to are those of the years following World War I, which marked a total collapse of the traditional ethics upon which the established scale of values had been founded. The result was a rupture in the relation between man and the reality outside him, an alienation that has endured throughout the twentieth century. This is the crisis experienced by Carla, Michele, and numerous other Moravian characters. He further noted in "A Fragment of Autobiography":

All my books have been worked out in more or less the same way; that is to say, their point of departure has been an effective and objective reality—a reality that I have sought to define and explain and reveal to myself, either so as to be mindful of it or to be free of it, either to sing its praises or to use it as an instrument of knowledge.

(p. 530)

No major new work appeared during the six years following publication of *The Time of Indifference.* Moravia translated some stories of Ernest Hemingway and later of Ring Lardner, Theodore Dreiser, and James M. Cain; but most of his time was spent working as a correspondent first for Turin's *La Stampa,* then for the *Gazzetta del Popolo.* He earned little from journalism, but the work allowed him to satisfy his love of travel; he spent much of the first half of the decade in London and in Paris. Moreover, foreign correspondence was a convenient pretext to escape the growing repression of the Fascist regime. *The Time of Indifference* had not pleased the Fascists, and a sixth printing of the novel was, in effect, prohibited. Although Moravia himself has characterized his opposition to the government as mild, his association with known anti-Fascists made him suspect.

Consequently, Mussolini's Ministry of Popular Culture discouraged, though unsuccessfully, the publication of his next two works, both of which appeared in 1935.

La bella vita (The Good Life) is a collection of eleven short stories, many of which had already appeared in periodicals. Included in the collection is one of the author's best stories, "Inverno di malato" ("A Sick Boy's Winter," 1930). Seventeen-year-old Girolamo is bedridden in a sanatorium and for the previous eight months has shared a room with Brambilla, a middle-aged traveling salesman. Although Girolamo's family has fallen on hard times, Brambilla, whose father was a bricklayer, persistently torments and humiliates the young boy for being a "rich man's son," for belonging to a decadent and impotent bourgeoisie. In contrast, the working class, asserts Brambilla, deals in deeds, not words; it is energetic and virile.

As he boasts of his many sexual conquests, Brambilla chides Girolamo for having had no sexual experience. Seeking to earn the older man's esteem and friendship, Girolamo determines to "seduce" Polly, an English patient three years younger than he is. It has been the custom for some time for the clinic personnel to push Girolamo's bed down to her room so that the two youngsters may keep each other company. During one of his visits Girolamo puts his plan into action and gives Polly a series of kisses. Whether as a result of their behavior or by coincidence, Polly's condition worsens, she becomes delirious, and soon the head of the sanatorium learns what has happened. Girolamo is forbidden to visit her, and the staff is scolded for failing to supervise the two young people. Ironically, instead of gaining the admiration of Brambilla, who is now cured and about to leave, Girolamo receives only his disdain. "Things never change," the salesman says. "Rich men's kids are all the same, they think only of themselves. What do they care if others have to suffer for their foolishness? That doesn't concern them." Brambilla departs, and Girolamo is now completely alone with his guilt for being a bourgeois and his confusion before a world that he does not understand.

Moravia's second novel required more than five years for completion. Begun in the late 1920's, *Le ambizioni sbagliate* (*Mistaken Ambitions*, 1935; also translated as *Wheel of Fortune*) is a long work frankly modeled on a Dostoevskian novel of crime, passion, and greed. The wealthy Maria Luisa seeks the aid of her sister-in-law, Sofia, and her fiancé, Pietro, to bring about a conjugal reconciliation with Matteo, who has taken the beautiful Andreina as his mistress. But Pietro falls in love with Andreina, and, at her instigation, agrees to help steal Maria Luisa's jewels. He balks, however, at her plan to murder Maria Luisa. Undaunted, Andreina eventually strangles her lover's wife in a fit of passion.

Complicated, melodramatic, and very long, the novel is in almost every way unsatisfactory, but its greatest weakness is in the portrayal of its characters. The reasons for Andreina's hatred of Maria Luisa are vague, and the murder seems singularly unmotivated. As for Pietro, who constantly dreams of idealism and innocence, he succeeds only in projecting an image of hypocrisy and self-delusion.

Soon after the publication of *Mistaken Ambitions*, Moravia lost his position with the *Gazzetta del Popolo*, probably because of his antifascism. This event, coupled with his disappointments regarding the acceptance of his second novel, prompted him to leave Italy for a time. Although travel was difficult because of government currency restrictions, Moravia was able to visit the United States with the help of the Casa Italiana at Columbia University. He arrived in New York late in 1935 and, except for a brief trip to Mexico, remained there for about six months. He wrote very little during his American sojourn, but it afforded him the freedom and serenity to reflect more deeply on his political beliefs. His firsthand experience with fascism, combined with the opportunity to observe directly the working of capitalism in America, inclined him toward the ideas of Karl Marx, whose *Das Kapital* he had recently read. Although there was much that the Roman writer admired in the United States, its materialistic values and the wide gap between the poor and the wealthy classes horrified him.

Upon his return to Italy, Moravia began writing a number of short stories that were collected under the title *L'Imbroglio* (The Imbroglio, 1937). The failure of *Mistaken Ambitions* and difficulties with the Fascist regime made publication uncertain, but the volume eventually was brought out by Valentino Bompiani, who has remained Moravia's Italian publisher. When the work appeared in July 1937, Moravia was on his way to China for a visit of about two months. He spent half of the following year in Greece.

Most of the stories that Moravia wrote during the decade from 1935 to 1945 departed radically from his previous realistic stories with their bourgeois settings. At least in part to avoid the censor, the Roman author turned to the surrealistic and satirical tale, in which he could give free rein to his criticism of the Fascist regime. Thus, the title story of the first volume, *I sogni del pigro* (Lazy Man's Dreams, 1940), can be interpreted as a mockery of Fascist fears and ambitions, while that of *L'Epidemia* (The Epidemic, 1944) is clearly a satire on the process of becoming Fascist. "L'Epidemia" is by far the longest of the fifty-four stories in the two volumes; most of the others are brief tales that criticize society and human weaknesses as well as the government. In them Moravia reveals himself as an almost classical moralist in the Italian tradition of Ariosto and Giuseppe Parini. In addition, the allegorical nature of these tales permits Moravia to display his considerable imagination, a quality often difficult to detect in his realistic fiction, where the only outlet for his fantasy is in his frequent descriptions of dreams.

In a similar vein is *La mascherata* (The Fancy Dress Party), published in 1941. Set in a mythical Latin American country ruled by a dictator, Tereso, the novel has all the trappings of a theatrical farce. Cinco, the chief of the secret police, is beginning to lose his hold over Tereso; in order to prove his usefulness, he forms a mock revolutionary group with the aim of staging an attempted assassination of Tereso, which he can then dramatically foil. The only uninformed member of the band is Saverio, who is duped into being the scapegoat. His half-brother, Sebastiano Rivas, is the protagonist of the novel and the lover of Fausta, an opportunistic cynic who has attracted the lustful eye of Tereso. Because of her and not for any political motives, Sebastiano agrees to help Saverio kill the dictator during a masked ball.

Moravia provides us with a scenario worthy of the stage, replete with mistaken identities, masked characters, servants who are in actuality movers of both the novelistic and political plots, and a number of cleverly arranged scenes; in fact, Moravia rewrote the work as a play in 1954. The novel in one sense mirrors accurately Moravia's view of fascism: all is intrigue, hypocrisy, and deceit. Only Saverio and the enamored Sebastiano are sincere and honest, yet both are the hapless victims of events that they do not understand.

Although *The Fancy Dress Party* was written as a satire of Mussolini, it is neither a strong nor an effective political statement. Not only is there little physical resemblance between Tereso and his Italian counterpart, but their characters and policies are very different indeed. The Latin American possesses a "secret and basic modesty" unknown to Il Duce, and he is so beloved by his people that "his government is becoming increasingly benign and paternal," so much so that he is about to sack the odious Cinco. In sum, *The Fancy Dress Party* is the work of a mildly anti-Fascist writer whose attitude is reflected not in the character of Saverio, the idealistic, committed, though naive revolutionary, but in that of his thoroughly apolitical half-brother:

Sebastiano was profoundly bored. . . . His boredom arose from a complete scepticism of the fate of humanity and of his country. Sebastiano had no political experience. But he belonged to a generation that . . . did not believe in anything, neither the state nor the revolution nor freedom nor authority.

(*La mascherata*, in *Romanzi brevi*, pp. 40–41)

Yet however mild the satire, it nevertheless attracted attention; the novel was seized, and Moravia was henceforth forbidden to publish under his own name. He chose the transparent and even defiant pen name of "Pseudo," which continued to appear regularly in Italian publications.

Moravia spent most of the years 1940–1943 on the island of Capri with Elsa Morante, also a writer, whom he married in 1941. He was in Rome, however, in July 1943, when King Victor Emmanuel III and the Grand Council deposed Mussolini, had him arrested, and turned political control of the government over to Marshal Badoglio. With the fall of fascism, Moravia began publishing political articles in the Roman newspaper *Il Popolo*. Unfortunately, this freedom was short-lived; after the 8 September announcement of the armistice between Italy and the Allies, the Germans seized control of most of the country, including Rome. Soon after, the occupying Nazi forces issued an order for Moravia's arrest, but, warned by a friend, the writer and his wife were able to flee the capital.

They boarded a train with the hope of reaching the Allied lines north of Naples. Halfway between the two cities, however, the train came to a halt because the tracks had been destroyed. The two novelists found themselves in the small town of Fondi, which they soon left for the safety of the mountains nearby. They spent the next nine months living in a peasant's hut and foraging in the mountains for food. Moravia has stated that the two most significant events of his life were his childhood illness and the hardships encountered during the winter of 1943–1944. In addition to its influence on his personal life, the latter ordeal also led eventually to a second stage in his literary development.

THE MYTH OF "THE PEOPLE"

Although the story collections *L'Amante infelice* (The Unfortunate Lover) and *Due cortigiane* (Two Courtesans) appeared in 1943 and 1945, Moravia's first important publication after the fall of fascism was the novella *Agostino*. It came out in 1944 and won for its author his first literary prize, the Corriere Lombardo. Agostino resembles in many ways the Girolamo of "A Sick Boy's Winter." He is young (thirteen years old), bourgeois, and totally ignorant of class differences and sex. Agostino has just started his summer vacation at the sea with his young and attractive mother. The two have thus far enjoyed an almost perfect relation founded on tenderness, easy intimacy, and shared pleasures, but the appearance of a young man, Renzo, destroys this idyll. The mother soon neglects her son for the attentions of the other. Her behavior also changes: when Renzo is present, her language and gestures are different, and she mocks Agostino and treats him like a baby until, perplexed and jealous, the boy makes an impertinent remark. The mother slaps him and definitively shatters their past relationship.

Left on his own, Agostino falls in with a band of young boys whose fathers are beach attendants and waiters. The boys' violence, cruelty, and vulgarity make a strong impression on him, but he is most struck—and bewildered—by their knowledge of sex. As they introduce him to its mysteries, Agostino assumes a new attitude toward his mother: no longer is she only his mother, she is also a woman, and he attempts to regard her as such, almost as though she were an object of study. Moreover, he quickly transfers to the boys the allegiance that he had earlier given to his mother and to his middle-class background. He dresses in old clothes, and in one delightful scene he poses as a beach attendant's son and describes the hardships of poverty to a bourgeois and his little boy.

Despite his efforts Agostino cannot integrate himself into the proletariat, nor can he return to unquestioning acceptance of his own class. Similarly, his knowledge of sex is only partial; to remedy this he takes his savings to a whorehouse, but he is chased away because he is too young. At the end of the summer, Agostino finds himself in the limbo of adolescence, no longer a boy but not yet a man. In the final scene his mother has just tucked Agostino into bed: "Like a man, he could not help thinking before he fell asleep. But he was not a man, and many long and unhappy days would pass before he became one."

Although the Oedipal overtones of *Agostino* are obvious (Moravia had read Freud in the 1930's), the novella never has the flavor of a casebook study. On the contrary, it is a simple story that is almost classic in its sober style, subtle imagery, and rigorous composition. In addition, it shows to best advantage the author's sensitive perception and understanding of the critical period of adolescence.

The novelist pursued his study of adolescence in a later work published in 1948, *La disubbidienza* (*Disobedience;* also translated as *Luca*), which, although the characters are different, is often considered a sequel to *Agostino.* Fifteen-year-old Luca is undergoing a crisis: the awkward youth is constantly colliding with objects, and his parents treat him either as a boy or, worse, as though he did not exist: "He felt that the world was hostile toward him . . . and it seemed as though he were waging a continuous and exhausting war against everything that surrounded him." When he discovers that a painting of the Madonna in front of which he has prayed since childhood actually conceals the safe containing his family's wealth, the hypocrisy of his parents causes a profound reaction. The disobedience of the title refers to Luca's decision to reject all bourgeois and materialistic values. He gives away his stamp collection and destroys the money he receives from the sale of his books and toys. His schoolwork deteriorates and finally, in a refusal of life itself, he stops eating and falls

sick. His illness lasts three months, but he does recover with the help of a nurse whose care culminates in physical love, an experience that ends Luca's painful adolescence and effects his reconciliation with the world.

Disobedience confirms Moravia's appreciation and understanding of adolescence. It also places sexuality at the very center of human experience and suggests that it is the most important means of establishing a rapport with reality. Comparison of the novel with *Agostino,* however, is inevitable, and *Disobedience* comes off second best. Laden with symbols and dreams, the novel lacks the natural grace of *Agostino.* Moreover, the later novel does not mark a significant advance in the writer's development as does *Agostino,* which presents the first sustained treatment of the author's new interest in the lower classes.

During the winter that Moravia spent near Fondi, his sympathy with the poor of Italian society, which was indirectly evident even in *The Time of Indifference,* increased to the point of becoming a myth. It seemed to him that the common people—peasants, domestics, small shopkeepers, skilled and unskilled laborers—were free of the problems that afflicted bourgeois intellectuals. The people, for example, felt no alienation from their own class, no guilt at belonging to it; the milieu in which they lived was not perceived as false and hypocritical like that of the middle class. And unlike intellectuals the common people manifested no need to rationalize, to seek out principles that would justify their actions. On the contrary, practical and material concerns aside, they were content with taking life as it came and enjoying being at one with nature and reality. They were, in Moravian terms, authentic.

Moravia's populist tendencies are evident in a long essay published in 1944 under the title *La speranza* (Hope). Like many other Italian intellectuals of his generation, Moravia, in reaction to the perceived moral corruption of the bourgeoisie and the evils of fascism, came to regard Marxism as the most promising system for the future. Christianity, he asserted, had fulfilled its historical role but was no longer an active force; only in communism lay the hope of eliminating materialism, abolishing classes, and creating a just social order. Moravia's conception of communism in *La speranza* contains very few of its economic or political features; in a rather naive way he considers only its humanistic aspects. Although Moravia soon became more critical than laudatory of the practice of communism, he did not abandon his humanistic principles, which he elaborated in an essay written in 1946.

The essay "L'Uomo come fine" ("Man as an End") is a profession of faith in the sacred quality of human beings and in their fundamentally irrational and unknowable character. To apply reason indiscriminately to the lives of men always leads to action, to violence, and to the use of human beings as material, as a means to achieve an end. The proper role of reason, Moravia maintains, is to serve as an instrument to help man "distinguish, know, and evaluate the means and the end. . . . Reason, if it is reasonable, will tell us, as indeed it sometimes does, that the only just and possible end is man himself." Moravia's position is that the authentic humanistic attitude, that is, the recognition of man as an end, lies not in action but in contemplation. The conclusion of the essay is incomplete, for the writer admits that "it is not possible to say at present what kind of contemplation should be practiced in the modern world. Every act of contemplation presupposes an object to be contemplated, and today that object does not exist."

The inconclusive quality of "Man as an End" is typical of many of Moravia's essays. Although the Roman author is interested in ideas and although many of his concerns are philosophical ones, he is not a systematic thinker. Notions that are "in the air," so to speak, are very appealing to him, and as an artist he frequently seizes upon them as material for his fiction. Such is the case with the ideas set forth in "Man as an End," many of which appear in

modified form in *La romana* (*The Woman of Rome,* 1947).

The Woman of Rome is a notable work. Critically and commercially successful in both Europe and the Americas, it was Moravia's first populist novel, his first novel with a female protagonist, and the first work in which he abandoned omniscient narration in the third person in preference for the first person. Defoe's *Moll Flanders* influenced the writing of *The Woman of Rome,* and, like the former, the latter is the fictional autobiography of a prostitute. Adriana lives with her mother, a seamstress, who wants her daughter to take full advantage of her beauty by becoming a model or a dancer. The young girl, however, wishes only to marry her working-class lover, Gino, and have a family. When she discovers that he is already married, she is coaxed into prostitution by one of her girlfriends.

The novel is an investigation of different attitudes toward life, represented by Adriana's various customers. Most are like Giacinti: selfish and hedonistic nonentities from the middle class. Others, however, play major roles in *The Woman of Rome.* Astarita, for example, is a member of the Fascist secret police. He presents a facade of power and self-possession, but behind it is a lonely sadomasochist who wishes he had never been born. In contrast to the crafty Astarita stands the criminal Sonzogno, a brute, unthinking force for whom murder is a natural reaction. He frightens Adriana, and yet there is a strange attraction between them: both are simple creatures, children of nature, though one is gentle and submissive, the other savage. Sonzogno, like Astarita, dies violently.

The most complex of the men in Adriana's life is the one she loves most deeply, Mino. A young intellectual with ideals that he cannot fulfill, Mino bears a strong resemblance to Michele of *The Time of Indifference.* Like his predecessor he lacks a fundamental rapport with reality; words, objects, people have no meaning for him, and he is incapable of transforming abstractions into acts. Although his antifascism leads him into political action, he cannot follow through: when he is arrested and questioned by Astarita, he quickly breaks down and informs on his friends. Mino understands life, but he can accept neither it nor himself, and he ends as a suicide.

Adriana is the touchstone to which all these miserable human beings are compared. Adriana is Eros, the life force of nature opposed to Thanatos, the force of death and chaos. She has a clear and innate sense of what life is and of what she is, and she accepts both. For her, life is concrete, not abstract; it is not what was or will be or should be, but what is here and now. Without passing judgment on those who behave differently, she simply affirms her way of life:

> I have often wondered why sadness and anger are so frequently found in those who try to live according to certain precepts or ideals and why those who accept their own life are usually happy and carefree. I suppose that each obeys not a precept but his own temperament. . . . Mine was to be, at any cost, happy, sweet, and calm; and I accepted it.
>
> (*La romana*, p. 246)

Adriana is Eros incarnate and, like nature, she guarantees the continuity of life: at the end of her story she is bearing Sonzogno's child in her womb.

On 30 December 1948 there appeared in Milan's *Corriere della Sera* a short story, "Un uomo sfortunato" (An Unlucky Man), that set a pattern for Moravia's short fiction for the next ten years. Narrated from the first-person point of view of the protagonist, each of the brief tales presents a sketch of life in the Rome inhabited by workers and small shopkeepers. The basic themes are love, work, and the difficulty of living in a society beset by unemployment, poverty, and inadequate food and shelter. Although social and economic injustice is implicit in the stories, its impact is tempered by humor, pathos, and irony. The stories are not tracts for political or economic reform;

they are social documents whose appearance of authenticity is heightened by the use of dialect words and phrases and especially by the syntactic rhythm of a language that mimics Roman speech. Highly regarded by both readers and critics, 130 of the stories were collected in two volumes, *Racconti romani* (*Roman Tales,* 1954) and *Nuovi racconti romani* (*More Roman Tales,* 1959).

The milieu of the Roman tales reappears in what many regard as the author's best novel, *La ciociara* (*Two Women,* 1957). The novel began to take form in Moravia's mind immediately after World War II, and he wrote nearly one hundred pages of it before he realized that the immediacy of its wartime subject prevented the artistic detachment necessary for producing a work of literature. He took up the project again ten years later, and the novel appeared in 1957. (Like most of Moravia's novels, it was also adapted for the screen. Sophia Loren was awarded an Oscar as best actress for her portrayal of Cesira in Vittorio de Sica's 1961 film version.)

The widow Cesira owns a small grocery shop in Rome. The time is 1943 and Cesira, who is able to get foodstuffs from her relatives in the country, is becoming a well-to-do woman by selling on the black market. Unmindful of the momentous times in which she is living, she divides all her energies between earning money and caring for her daughter, Rosetta, whose innocence, timidity, and religious faith make her seem much younger than her eighteen years.

The war eventually threatens both. When food becomes scarce and bombardments menace Rome, Cesira decides to go live in Vallecorsa with her parents. Upon arriving there, however, they find a deserted city inhabited only by Concetta and her family of thieves. Although Cesira's sense of the inviolability of property makes this group repugnant to her, she and Rosetta pass a few days in their family's house before going to the mountains, where all the other refugees have already fled. The nine months spent in the village of

Sant' Eufemia is a gestation period for Cesira's moral conscience, the seeds of which are planted during long conversations with Michele, an anti-Fascist intellectual. In one of the central episodes of the novel Michele reads the biblical story of Lazarus to the refugees; after upbraiding them for their egoism and moral indifference, he tells them that they are dead and that only consciousness of their state of total putrefaction will effect a resurrection.

Finally, the Allies break through the German lines, and Cesira and Rosetta leave Sant' Eufemia to return to Rome. The road back is painful: after they are raped by a band of Moroccan soldiers, Rosetta becomes cynical, taciturn, and even promiscuous. The despondent Cesira contemplates suicide and later, having sunk to Concetta's level, steals money from Rosetta's murdered lover. But Michele's teachings bear fruit: as they near Rome, Rosetta spontaneously begins to sing and to weep, and the novel ends in an affirmation of hope. Although the two women have experienced cold, hunger, violence, and the inhumanity of their fellow human beings, they have also learned to appreciate the value of human life; their grief has awakened compassion for others, and, like Lazarus, they return to life.

Like all of Moravia's lower-class heroes and heroines, Cesira's point of view is moral, not intellectual. Instead of reasoning, she perceives problems and solutions instinctively, and she expresses the positive message of the novel by means of rather vague sentiments like hope and grief and compassion. As in "Man as an End," negative messages are more concrete: for Cesira, indifference to others, the class system, materialism, sadism, and even sexuality (both she and Michele profess that for them, sex does not exist) are all inauthentic attitudes toward life. *Two Women* is the novel most illustrative of the ideas set forth in "Man as an End"; although written by an atheist, it is almost religious in its messages of faith, hope, and Christian charity.

Despite the importance of many of its char-

acters, the real protagonist of *Two Women* is the Second World War. Although set in Italy, the novel presents an international cast of numerous social, national, and political types: bourgeois and peasant; Italian, German, English, American, Russian, and African; Nazis, Fascists, and Allies. The war consumes some; it transforms all. Atrocities are committed by ordinary citizens as well as by soldiers. The novel is a moving illustration of Cesira's belief that the most horrible effect of war is that it kills pity. Without preaching, Moravia succeeds in demonstrating that war is a sadistic and insatiable beast whose prey is all of humanity.

Moravia's interest in the Fascist mentality, evinced in the character of Astarita in *The Woman of Rome,* was carried to an extreme in *Il conformista* (*The Conformist*), published in 1951. The novel spans about twenty-five years in the life of Marcello Clerici, who takes such pleasure in killing animals as a child that he comes to regard himself as abnormal. As an adult, Marcello reacts by conforming to the sociopolitical norms of the period: he marries the quintessentially middle-class Giulia, and he not only joins the Fascist party but also collaborates with its secret police. Marcello is perhaps Moravia's most despicable character, a creature of egoism and self-delusion. As fascism collapses and with it his conception of normality, Marcello flees Rome, but an Allied warplane puts an end to his misdirected life.

In 1970, Bernardo Bertolucci extracted an excellent film from *The Conformist.* In its literary form, however, the novel has major defects. It presents a facile and unconvincing case study of a psychotic, and much of the plot seems contrived toward a moralistic message. Moravia obviously attempted to depict fascism as a pathological aberration of middle-class values, but the portrayal of Marcello cannot bear the weight of an allegory, nor are his idiosyncrasies and isolated experiences representative enough to account for the characteristics of Italian fascism. *The Conformist* is really two novels: one describing the evils of fascism, the other the mind of an individual. Unfortunately, the two do not fuse.

In two novels, *L'Amore coniugale* (*Conjugal Love*, 1949) and *Il disprezzo* (*A Ghost at Noon*, 1954), Moravia treats the relationship of married couples. The first and shorter of the two established a pattern for much of Moravia's later fiction. The protagonist is an intellectual and an artist whose creative problems are closely related to his life and whose attempts to create lead him to analyze himself and the world about him. The themes of *Conjugal Love* also recur in later works: the relation between sex and creativity, the mysterious force of eroticism, and the apparent impenetrability of the feminine mind.

Silvio Baldeschi goes to his Tuscan villa with the intention of writing a novella. When the words won't come, he concludes that sexual relations with his wife, Leda, are draining his creative energies. They abstain, and he completes a short work of fiction based on his happy married life. When Silvio rereads it, however, the story seems false. After he works late into the night, he goes to Leda's room to discuss his failure with her; she is not in bed. He eventually finds her in a haystack with his barber, the local Don Juan. The discovery is so painful that Silvio considers suicide, but he realizes that her momentary infidelity does not really affect their relationship and that his novella has failed because he does not understand the woman he loves. With renewed appreciation for his wife and his marriage, he sets about rewriting the work, which will be titled *Conjugal Love.*

The narrator of *A Ghost at Noon* is also a writer, but the setting is Rome and Capri, the milieu that of Italy's successful postwar film industry. It was an environment familiar to Moravia, for he had written several movie scripts in the 1940's, and in 1944 he began a long career as a film critic, eventually becoming a reviewer for *L'Espresso* in 1955, a post that he still held in the late 1980's.

In need of money, Riccardo Molteni is an aspiring playwright who has agreed to prepare a filmscript for the producer Battista. The subject of the film, which will be directed by a German, Rheingold, is Homer's *Odyssey*. The three principals, however, have divergent conceptions of the projected work. Battista wants a spectacular film in the manner of Cecil B. DeMille, while Rheingold envisions a Freudian study of Ulysses: he proposes that Ulysses subconsciously delay his return to Ithaca because of marital troubles. As for Riccardo, he wishes to remain faithful to the original; for him, the *Odyssey* is a poem describing a vanished golden age. As he explains to Rheingold:

> The beauty of the *Odyssey* lies in [the Greeks'] belief in reality as it is and as it is manifested objectively, in its form which cannot be analyzed or taken apart, but is simply what it is. . . . Homer belonged to a civilization that had developed in harmony and not in conflict with nature.
>
> (*Il disprezzo*, p. 150)

The main interest of the story is the relationship between Riccardo and his wife, Emilia. After two years of happiness, the wifely love that Emilia had shown earlier has disappeared. Riccardo seems to be pushing her into Battista's eager arms, and Emilia reacts with contempt for her husband. Riccardo regards his actions, however, as the modern, civilized behavior of one who recognizes the necessity of not offending an employer. The finest pages of the novel are those in which the tormented Riccardo attempts to analyze and to understand his wife and the reasons for her disdain. Ironically, the key is to be found in Rheingold's interpretation of the *Odyssey*. He maintains that there is a rift between Ulysses and Penelope that has been provoked by the Greek warrior's long tolerance of his wife's suitors. Penelope is a "primitive" woman who expects her husband, if he is truly a man, to chase them away. When he does not, she can only despise his apparent weakness and willingness to compromise her virtue.

The Greek epic ends in reunion, the Italian novel in separation. Emilia leaves Capri and sets off for Rome with Battista. Later that same day, Riccardo hallucinates and imagines that he sees Emilia, who now tells him that she loves him. But it is only a ghost at noon, for the telegram that arrives later announces Emilia's death in a freak auto accident.

INVESTIGATIONS OF REALITY

The 1950's were an eventful decade for Moravia. He received the Strega Prize in 1952 for his collected stories (1927–1951), published under the title *I racconti* (most of these stories appear either in *Bitter Honeymoon* or in *The Wayward Wife*). The following year, he and Alberto Carocci founded the important politico-cultural review *Nuovi argomenti* (New Topics). He also continued to travel abroad and, for the first time, began writing about the countries that he visited. *Un mese in U.R.S.S.* (A Month in the USSR) appeared in 1958, and other travel volumes at regular intervals thereafter: *Un'idea dell'India* (An Idea of India, 1962); *La rivoluzione culturale in Cina* (*The Red Book and the Great Wall*, 1967); and two books on Africa: *A quale tribù appartieni?* (*Which Tribe Do You Belong To?* 1972) and *Lettere dal Sahara* (Letters from the Sahara, 1981). Although Moravia's critical and popular success grew during this period, it was also a time of crisis in both his personal life and his career. His marriage to Elsa Morante was dissolving, and he was beginning a liaison with Dacia Maraini, a young playwright and novelist. As Moravia later remarked during an interview with Enzo Siciliano:

> At the age of fifty, I went through a severe psychological crisis. . . . I had arrived at a turning point: perhaps I did not like life any longer, and I had the courage to shatter many things which at that time were very dear and meaningful to me. But there was nothing else I could do. . . . That

severance, that rupture produced, I believe, a kind of rebirth.

(*Moravia* [1971], pp. 111–112)

Moravia's art as well as his life was renewed. First, he cast off his fascination with the myth of "the people." Although he did not discard the notion that the lower classes have a stronger bond to reality than does the bourgeoisie, he came to realize that the quality of that relationship is fundamentally different between the classes. The attachment of the people to reality is, Moravia has said, based on the necessities of eating, sleeping, and having shelter. If they do not appear alienated, it is not because they possess a panacea; rather, their basic human needs and their satisfaction of those needs are in balance. "Poverty," Moravia maintained in *The Red Book and the Great Wall*, "is the normal condition of the human being because superfluous wealth does not make him more human than poverty does." Wealth, then, is an abnormal condition that alienates one from reality. Such alienation is characteristic of Moravia's bourgeois characters: bored and dissatisfied, they fail to find any meaning in their lives. Most of them, however, do not recognize that their problem can be traced to a lack of rapport with reality. The task of determining the nature of alienation and giving it a name falls to the intellectual, who is, Moravia claims, the only "positive character" that the bourgeoisie has produced: the intellectual explores his civilization, while the mental efforts of his fellow bourgeois do not extend beyond their personal or professional interests. Since mid 1958 Moravia's fiction has dealt with a bourgeois milieu, and all his novels have been narrated by an intellectual, usually a writer but sometimes a painter or a professor, between the ages of twenty and forty.

The author's concept of the novel also changed. Having so often been accused of writing in the tradition of the nineteenth-century realists, Moravia in the mid 1950's disavowed the relevance of the traditional novel to the contemporary era. His decision was neither a caprice nor a surrender to his critics; it was based on conditions that, in the past, he had perceived intuitively but had never thought through. First, the narrative function of the novel had been preempted by the movies and television. In the description of scenes and in the telling of a story, the novel just could not compete with film, Moravia felt. Consequently, beginning in 1960 with *La noia* (*The Empty Canvas*), there are fewer descriptive passages in Moravia's novels, and the story line is subordinate to other interests. The novel, according to Moravia, should deal with those areas that the movie camera cannot capture or that it can represent only in an awkward way: analyses, for example, or the discussion of ideas. Thus was created what Moravia called the "romanzo-saggio," literally the "essay-novel," but also referred to by Moravia as the ideological or metaphorical novel; in it the writer's personal ideology gives "sense and order to an otherwise senseless and chaotic reality."

Moreover, the relation that existed between the nineteenth-century novelist and the reality he sought to describe has disappeared. In an important essay of 1956, "Note sul romanzo" ("Notes on the Novel," translated in *Man as an End*), Moravia states that the novelist of the last century had no doubt that he was describing an objective reality in a language that was common to all his readers. The twentieth century, however, has recognized that both reality and language are not absolute, but relative: in the contemporary novel, "There is no longer a single reality and a single language, but as many realities and languages as there are novelists." It is from this theoretical stance that Moravia wrote his short stories and his ideological novels of the 1960's.

Moravia's concept of reality became much more complex during this third period in his career. In earlier works the term "reality" seemed to refer rather vaguely to objects and historical or factual events, that which was always "outside" his fictional characters. At this point, however, Moravia had become fully aware that subjectivity—thoughts, imagina- tions, and dreams—constitutes a reality also, and he gave to this subjective reality an importance denied it in earlier works. The exclusive use of first-person narration underscored his changed attitude. The third-person point of view, he maintained, presupposes an objective and knowable reality, whereas the first-person novel implicitly recognizes a multitude of subjective and relative realities. Moreover, the first person is more suitable for the presentation of an ideology; he wrote in 1959 in "Risposta a nove domande sul romanzo" ("Answers to Nine Questions on the Novel," translated in *Man as an End*) that "third person narration permits only the immediate and dramatic representation of the object; the first person allows it to be analyzed, decomposed and, sometimes, done away with." Finally, in *The Empty Canvas* there appeared for the first time in Moravia's fiction the suggestion that, beyond subjective and objective reality, there is a transcendent reality, which imparts to this novel a mystic quality that was present earlier only in the dreams and visions of some of his characters.

The reader familiar only with Moravia's novels of the 1960's and not his short stories will certainly have an incomplete, though not entirely misleading, picture of his third period, for each novel is limited by its focus on a single character and on the world only as it is seen through his eyes. In "Racconto e romanzo" ("The Short Story and the Novel," 1958, translated in *Man as an End*), Moravia contrasted the two genres. The novel, he said, is animated by an ideology; its characters are symbolic, and its analytic method competes with the philosophic treatise or the moral essay. The short story, however, draws its plot from the complexity of life rather than from an ideology, the psychology of its characters is based on events instead of ideas, and it is lyric, not analytic. Above all, the novel should not serve as a social document; this function is proper to short stories, which offer a panoramic vision of a society.

In the quarter of a century following World War II, Italian society underwent profound changes. The postwar hope of many intellectuals for a classless society founded on equality and justice faded before the political and economic realities of the era. A bourgeois-Catholic coalition controlled the dominant Christian Democratic Party, and Italy's rapid change from an agricultural to an industrial economy transformed the individual into a means of production whose needs and desires were dictated by advertising and satisfied by consumer goods. The short stories that Moravia wrote from 1958 to 1970 reflected this neocapitalistic era. Originally published in the *Corriere della Sera,* the stories collected in *L'Automa* (*The Fetish,* 1962), *Una cosa è una cosa* (*Command and I Will Obey You,* 1967), and *Il paradiso* (*Bought and Sold,* 1970) are necessarily brief and of uniform length, with the result that many appear inconclusive; moreover, the variety of themes and Moravia's changing perspectives make the stories seem like microcosmic laboratories in which the author is conducting experiments on language and on society. The majority of his characters, however, are formed in the same mold: they are robots who, in an anonymous and automated system, have become the mindless cogs of neocapitalism. Confusing dreams and reality, they lose their memories, their sense of time, and, eventually, even their identities.

Of the subjects treated in these stories, the most provocative is Moravia's investigation of language and reality. The author poses a central question: Is reality physical or linguistic? That is, do we use words to represent and express reality, or do our words create reality? Although Mino in *The Woman of Rome* had encountered this problem, Moravia's renewed investigation of it derives from his reading in the mid 1950's of Ludwig Wittgenstein's *Tractatus Logico-Philosophicus* (1921). The Austrian philosopher treated the relationship between reality and words and, specifically, the inability of the latter to form an authentic picture of the former. He concluded that often it is not possible to say what a thing is; one can only state tautologically that a thing is what it

is. In extreme cases language fails completely, and the subject must be passed over in silence.

Since Wittgenstein's concerns—language and reality—were those of Moravia the artist, one can understand the appeal of his ideas. It should not be assumed, however, that the Roman writer embraced Wittgenstein's thought in its entirety (even few trained philosophers have done so); rather, he seized upon certain basic concepts presented in the *Tractatus* and used them as a springboard for his literary projects. The first novelistic example of this new direction appeared in 1960, and it won for Moravia the prestigious Viareggio Prize.

Dino, the protagonist-narrator of *The Empty Canvas,* is afflicted with *noia* (boredom), which he defines as "a kind of insufficiency or inadequacy or scarcity of reality, . . . a sickness of objects." An artist who is unable to paint, he slashes the canvas he is working on and begins trying to reestablish contact with objective reality. In the studio of a recently deceased fellow artist, Balestrieri, Dino meets Cecilia, the old man's last and favorite mistress-model. Hoping to pry from her the secrets of Balestrieri's indefatigable will to paint and his close and solid rapport with reality, he becomes her lover. His interest, however, shifts from her relations with Balestrieri to Cecilia herself. Why does she behave as she does? What does she think about? Who, in short, is Cecilia?

In lengthy conversations patterned on a Wittgensteinian approach to language, Dino learns only concrete facts concerning her everyday life. Cecilia herself eludes him, in the sense that her ideas, beliefs, and values remain secret. As the novel progresses, Dino determines with increasing frenzy to destroy her mysterious autonomy and to reduce her to an object of insignificance, not only in order to possess her being, as was his original plan, but also to be rid of her and the obsessive hold that she has on him. He tries many ways to bring Cecilia under his control. He seduces her, he attempts to buy her with money, he even proposes marriage to her. Nothing works. In desperation, Dino tries to kill her, but he stops short when he realizes that death would assure her a definitive autonomy.

Just as the novel begins with Dino's slashing his canvas, so does it end with another violent act: Dino crashes his car into a tree at the edge of the road. He escapes death, however, and regains consciousness in a clinic, where he dispels his *noia* by contemplating a tree growing in the garden. He discovers that he can establish a contemplative rapport with any object, even Cecilia, and he learns that it is not by possessing or changing things nor by analyzing and explaining them that one establishes a rapport, but by recognizing and accepting the freedom and autonomy of their existence. Dino's discovery is comparable to, though more complex than, that of Silvio in *Conjugal Love,* who says that the essential "mystery of all things big and small [is that] everything can be explained except their existence." Given this ineluctable fact, the only authentic rapport with reality must lie in pure and disinterested contemplation, an attitude and a conclusion that are at the same time mystic and aesthetic.

L'Attenzione (*The Lie,* 1965) continues the lines of thought found in *The Empty Canvas.* The three principal themes of the earlier novel are repeated: the relations between a man and a woman, between a man and reality, and between an artist and his material; the last is predominant in *The Lie.* A final connection with *The Empty Canvas* resides in the fact that Dino, at the end of the novel, intends to try again to exercise his creative talents, and *The Lie* is the story of such an attempt.

There are two main threads to the story line. One consists of Francesco Merighi's relations with Cora, his estranged wife, and her stepdaughter, Baba; the other concerns his attempt to write an authentic realistic novel. After nine years as a foreign correspondent Francesco returns to Italy with the manuscript of a novel based on his courtship of Cora. When he rereads it, however, it strikes him as false and artificial or, in his words, "inauthentic." Much

of its inauthenticity can be traced to his not having realized in his marriage the aspirations that impelled him to it: in true Moravian fashion he had married Cora, a petty thief, in the belief that genuine contact with reality lay with the lower classes. Ironically, after their marriage Cora becomes thoroughly middle-class, and their diverging values form a breach between them. Beyond this superficial falseness of the novel, however, Francesco perceives that its inauthenticity resides in the events themselves, and he concludes that the dramatic novel, the novel of action, is by its very nature inauthentic. To determine whether a nondramatic novel, one in which nothing happens, would be more satisfying, he carefully and objectively records the routine and trivial happenings of each day in a diary, which he will then use as notes for rewriting his novel.

But the events Francesco observes are far from commonplace. Indeed, they are the stuff of a soap opera: an anonymous letter, crimes, a terminal illness, attempted seductions, and incestuous passions. Nor is his diary objective. Absolute objectivity is impossible, Francesco realizes, because he cannot record everything. Faced with the necessity of selecting, he decides to use as a criterion the ultimate aim of the diary: he will set down only those things which may be appropriate to his novel. Francesco then goes one step farther and decides to supplement any deficiencies in reality with his own invention and imagination: the diary is thus not simply a chronicle of daily life, but a chronicle of daily life as it is perceived and sometimes changed by the mind of the observer. Subjective reality mingles with objective reality. To view the matter in a different way, the diary is a mixture of actuality and lies. Ultimately, Francesco realizes that his diary is more authentic than any novel that he might be able to draw from it, and he decides to publish the work in its original journal form.

The fruit of much thought, *The Lie* is Moravia's most intelligent and coherent work. Along with *The Empty Canvas,* this novel also serves as a conclusion to the author's long quest for an understanding of reality. He demonstrated in *The Empty Canvas* that objective reality cannot be seized, only contemplated. In *The Lie* he concludes that subjective reality is no less real and that the intention that resides in the imagination of the artist can never be represented faithfully—art is an illusion, a lie, like reality itself.

After publication of *The Lie,* Moravia turned his attention to the theater. Dramatic literature had exercised an early influence on him, and he had already published two plays: a 1954 adaptation of *The Fancy Dress Party* and, in 1958, *Beatrice Cenci,* a historical tragedy set in sixteenth-century Italy. In 1966, together with Maraini and Siciliano, Moravia founded a private theater group in Rome, the Compagnia del Porcospino (The Porcupine Company). The company's first production was Moravia's *L'Intervista* (The Interview), a one-act play based on a satirical short story published nearly twenty-five years earlier in *L'Epidemia.* More ambitious was the two-act *Il mondo è quello che è* (*The World's the World*); written in 1966 and staged that year in Venice, the play offered a rather tedious contrast between the ideas of Marx and Wittgenstein: Should the world be revolutionized through action or could a change in language habits effect a new reality?

Moravia's most complex and successful dramatic work was *Il dio Kurt* (Kurt the God). The 1968 play is set in a Nazi concentration camp whose commandment, Kurt, uses the inmates to stage a production of Sophocles' *Oedipus Rex.* A sadist, he assumes the role of Fate and arranges in reality a parricide and an incestuous mother–son relationship. This blend of personal, historical, and theatrical interests marked the meridian of Moravia's playwriting career, for the convoluted reasoning and the wooden characters of his 1969 play *La vita è gioco* (Life Is a Game), added nothing to his reputation. Despite his long affection for the stage, Moravia did not succeed in transforming his conception of the theater into effective and gripping drama. He wrote in the 1950's that many of the traditional functions of theater,

like those of the novel, had been appropriated by the cinema: movies could more effectively present action, images, and spectacle. Revitalization of the theatrical genre depended on the text and on the pre-eminence of the word. Unfortunately, most of his plays are intellectual constructs in which Wittgensteinian linguistics, word games, and Marxist banalities take on the form of didactic exercises rather than dramatic events. These plays constitute the twilight of Moravia's philosophic period, which had begun with *The Empty Canvas:* he had had exhausted his intellectual approach to the question of reality. At about the same time, political and social upheavals that began occurring in Italy during the late 1960's caused him to give new attention to the society in which he lived.

OBSERVATIONS OF SOCIETY

Although by 1965 Italy was firmly established in the technological and industrial world of the twentieth century, the Italian way of life was not fundamentally different from what it had been fifty years before. There was almost universal respect for the authority of the state, the Catholic church, and the family. Class lines were observed, and a young person was expected to engage in work similar to that of his parents; university education was still largely the privilege of the bourgeoisie. While there were limited opportunities for women outside the home, those women who took jobs were often viewed with suspicion; and at least the appearances of traditional sexual mores were maintained. Much of this ended in 1968, when protests led by student *contestatori* in Italy and elsewhere in Europe threatened revolution. Although political factors were important in the student movement (most of whose members were leftists), the major effect was social: authority was discredited, class distinctions faded, women discovered a new consciousness of self, and sexual expression became freer and more public. Ever sensitive to his civilization, Moravia evaluated and gave literary form to this new and confused world.

Published in 1971, *Io e lui* (*Two: A Phallic Novel*) is the author's only comic novel. Its narrator is Federico (or Rico), a bourgeois screenwriter who, like Silvio in *Conjugal Love*, has temporarily separated from his wife so that sexual relations will not deplete his creative energies; he intends, in Freudian terms, to sublimate his sexual drive. He has failed, however, to take into account the power of his physical and instinctive desires: his intellect is only one half of the pair alluded to in the title; the other half is represented by his outsized sexual member, appropriately dubbed Federicus Rex, with whom he holds long conversations, a dialogue, as it were, between the ego and the id. Rico argues on the side of reason, consciousness, and the abstract, while Federicus Rex supports instinct, sexuality, and the physical. It is not a well-matched contest, for Rico is the usual ineffective and weak intellectual who, in this almost picaresque novel, passes from one mortifying defeat to another.

Rico is preparing the script of a film treating the political activities of a group of *contestatori.* His ultimate aspiration is to be named director of the film, and to this end he attempts first to gain the confidence of the producer and then, when that fails, to seduce the latter's old and ugly wife; but even Federicus Rex rebels at such a distasteful project, and Rico remains a lowly screenwriter. In addition, he must modify radically his original script to conform to the wishes of the student leaders, donate a large sum of money to their cause, and undergo at their hands a humiliating self-criticism of his bourgeois "sins." Finally, heeding the voice of Federicus Rex, Rico renounces his plan and returns to the waiting arms of his wife.

Despite some amusing scenes and the basically humorous premise of a protagonist who communicates with his own sexual organ, *Two* is a disappointing comic novel: many episodes seem superfluous, and the minor characters are tiresome stereotypes. Yet it must be recognized that *Two* is a transitional work in Mo-

ravia's development. In it he makes some of his earlier mentors (Freud, Marx, Wittgenstein) the objects of gentle ridicule, though he stops far short of outright repudiation of their thought. Moravia is less kind toward himself: Rico's rejection of intellectual pretensions and his return to more concrete realities are clear criticisms of the philosophical tendencies of *The Empty Canvas* and *The Lie*. At the same time, two aspects of Moravia's fiction—sexuality and social commitment—receive a new and stronger emphasis that dominates this fourth period of his literary career.

Sexuality has been an integral part of Moravia's fictional world from the time of his very first novel. Some have even called his writing pornographic, and in 1952 the Catholic church placed his works on its Index of Prohibited Books. Yet sexuality is seldom gratuitous in Moravia's fiction; it is not included merely to titillate the reader or to increase sales. The Roman novelist regards sex as a universal phenomenon rooted in the nature of men and women and branching out into all areas of human existence. For the artist it is a means of investigating reality, while for the Moravian character it is often a way of establishing a relationship with others and with reality itself. In none of Moravia's previous novels, however, had the description of sexual acts been as graphic as in *Two*, and in none had sex occupied so central a role. The new permissiveness in Italian cultural life had opened the way for a frankness of expression that before 1968 would have been either unpublishable or found only in books sold clandestinely on street corners. Moravia took full advantage of this new freedom not only to explore the phenomenon of sexuality itself but also to use it as a creative device, as a metaphoric indicator of attitudes toward life.

Two also contains Moravia's first fictional treatment of contemporary social and political matters since the veiled satire of *The Fancy Dress Party*. Of course, he had criticized fascism in *The Woman of Rome, The Conformist,* and *Two Women;* but each of these had been written from a perspective of historical detachment. In the comic novel *Two,* however, the still active student protest movement serves as the background and as the antagonist against which Rico plays out his story.

Despite Moravia's adherence to left-wing causes, the *contestatori* of *Two* are presented in a most unfavorable light. They are depicted as the asexual and spoiled brats of an alienated bourgeoisie. Like robots they mouth slogans and obey without question leaders whose imagination does not extend beyond the competitive and even exploitative methods of the middle class in which they were reared. At least part of the caricatural treatment of the protesters can be attributed to revenge. In 1968 Moravia, sympathetic to the revolutionary aims of the student movement, consented to a debate with some of their leaders. He was scarcely prepared for the accusations hurled at him: he was, charged the *contestatori,* guilty of bad faith, a traitor to Marxism who, while professing populist beliefs, was by birth a bourgeois who had enriched himself by writing for the establishment. In later essays Moravia expressed his disillusion with the results of the protest movement. He lamented that the students lacked intellectual and political maturity; instead of promoting a revolution that would change the very structure of society, they had merely brought about superficial modifications in a few Italian institutions.

Although Moravia has often said that he does not regard himself as a politically committed writer, his participation in political and social movements has been constant. In *The Red Book and the Great Wall,* for example, he excoriates the alienating effect of wealth and neocapitalism by contrasting it to the humanizing influence of Chinese poverty. More recently he has been a frequent endorser of liberal manifestos, and many of his political writings have been collected in *Impegno controvoglia* (Commitment in Spite of Myself, 1980). He has given especially firm support to the women's liberation movement in his native country. Indeed, during the 1970's he published three volumes of short stories, all of which present the woman's point of view and explore her relation to the world in which she lives: *Il paradiso* (*Bought and Sold,* 1970), *Un'Altra vita* (*Lady Godiva,* 1973), and *Boh* (*The Voice of the Sea,* 1976).

Many of Moravia's varied interests converge in *La vita interiore* (*Time of Desecration,* 1978). Desideria is the bastard child of a prostitute who has sold her to Viola, a wealthy middle-class woman with two obsessions: to be a good mother and to engage in erotic acts. The child is a property purchased to satisfy these conflicting desires. In her childhood Desideria is most unattractive; she is a formless blob who is fat because she overeats and vice versa. At puberty, though, like a chrysalis, she undergoes a metamorphosis and emerges as a beautiful teenaged girl. Soon afterward she hears for the first time a disembodied Voice that begins to direct her life. The Voice provides the girl with a specific kind of consciousness, what might be called a consciousness peculiar to youth, for it will abandon Desideria when she ceases to be a virgin and passes into adulthood.

Under the tutelage of the Voice, Desideria lays out a "Plan of Transgression and Desecration" in which she will systematically profane all the accepted values of bourgeois society: property, language, culture, religion, money, love, and even life itself. At the same time the Voice sets for Desideria the positive goal of joining a revolutionary group; for the young girl, this becomes almost a religious quest to which she pledges her virginity. When the long-awaited revolutionary organizer, Quinto, finally appears and Desideria yields to him, she realizes that the life he promises her is scarcely different from the hated middle-class life heretofore represented by Viola. The Voice disappears, and Desideria's story ends unexpectedly soon after.

Like *Agostino* and *Luca, Time of Desecration* is a study of youth and its problems. Unlike them, however, the novel is not a psychological study of an individual adolescent, but an attempt to understand and explain a whole generation of Italian society. "In practical life," says Desideria, "there is real action; but in the inner life, everything happens symbolically." Such is the case in the novel. Although the number and variety of sexual experiences contained in it almost rival those of Richard von Krafft-Ebing's *Psychopathia Sexualis* (1886), they function not as examples of realism but as representations of attitudes toward oneself and toward life. The novel itself (which is in the form of an interview between Desideria and the supposed author) does not observe the usual conventions of fictional closure, for Desideria breaks off the interview before reaching the expected and foreshadowed conclusion to the story line. *Time of Desecration* obeys only its own internal logic, as Desideria obeys her literary, symbolic, and anti-realistic character. To explain her abrupt Pirandellian departure from the work, she tells her interviewer:

> Life does not have nor can it have a conclusion: I will continue to live even after what you and the Voice call the "solution" to my problem, and then my story would never end. But what does the story matter? What matters is me and now you know enough to understand and to explain who I am. . . . At Hiroshima, after the explosion of the atomic bomb, there was left on a wall the imprint of a human body, like a track in the sand. . . . The body that left the imprint had been devoured, annihilated by the fierce heat. So it is with me. Your imagination has incinerated me, consumed me. Ultimately, I will no longer exist, except in your writing, as an imprint, as a literary character.
>
> (*La vita interiore*, pp. 407–408)

At first glance, Moravia's next novel, *1934* (1982), seems to break his stance of commitment to contemporary problems. Lucio, a young scholar of German literature, plans to spend a month on the island of Capri in order to complete his translation of a story by Heinrich von Kleist and to resolve a worrisome question: Can one live without hope and not

desire death? He intends to find some way to "stabilize" his despair so that he can live with it as a normal condition of life. On the boat that is taking him to Capri, he sees his own despair reflected in the eyes of a young German actress, Beate; they exchange glances, and Lucio soon falls in love with her. By coincidence, she too is an admirer of Kleist and is apparently seeking a partner to reenact with her the double suicide of the German dramatist and his mistress. The couple have little opportunity to meet or talk, for Alois Möller, Beate's husband and a Nazi party official, guards her jealously. Before she ends her brief stay in Capri, however, she does manage to tell Lucio that her mother and twin sister, Trude, will be arriving shortly. The young Italian anxiously awaits them with the hope of learning the whereabouts of Beate and then following her.

Trude is physically indistinguishable from Beate, but her character is completely different. Whereas Beate is a shy, intellectual, anti-Nazi romantic, Trude is bold, vulgar, anti-Semitic, and a zealous member of the Nazi party. When the mother, Paula, promotes meetings between the young couple, Lucio exploits them to learn more of his beloved Beate. Trude uses them for other purposes: she offers to play the role of Beate in a lovemaking game and thus to give Lucio the illusion of attaining his desire. The young man, however, decides to leave Capri immediately and to seek Beate in Germany. At this point, Paula confesses to him that all has been a charade: Beate and Trude are really the same person, Paula herself is not a mother but an actress and the lesbian lover of Beate/Trude, and the two women have invented everything as an elaborate Teutonic joke on the self-assured Casanovas who frequent Italian resorts. Strangely, Lucio feels neither anger nor resentment at the deception. On the contrary, it resolves for him the problem that he had posed at the beginning of the novel:

> I realized I was in love not so much with the imaginary Beate or with the imaginative Trude, but with a woman who was at the same time both

Beate and Trude, the invented one and the inventor. This woman was all I could desire. . . . Thus, the joke came full circle and closed to my advantage; Trude and Beate fused in a single person would permit me to realize my project of stabilizing despair as a normal condition of human existence.

(*1934*, p. 237)

Lucio's bliss is short-lived. The date is 30 June, the Night of the Long Knives, during which Hitler purged his party by executing many of its officials. Among those who die is Alois Möller, and the next day Trude and Paula are found slumped in each other's arms, the victims of a Kleistian suicide pact.

1934 is perhaps Moravia's best novel since *The Empty Canvas.* Despite its ambiguities (does one really know all the truth about Beate/Trude?) and certain improbable coincidences, it is an imaginative and well-constructed story. Beate and Trude arouse the reader's interest, while the minor characters enrich the fabric of the plot. Unfortunately, Lucio is the garden variety Moravian intellectual—naive, passive, almost comic; he is an unlikely player for the role of the typical Italian lover that Beate/Trude has in mind as the butt of her joke.

The novel is most successful, however, as a description of the ambiguous atmosphere that enveloped Europe during the Nazi/Fascist years. As in *The Fancy Dress Party* and *The Conformist,* deceit and treachery are its chief characteristics; life itself seems to be a masquerade in which values become deformed and propaganda supplants common sense. In *Time of Desecration,* Desideria formulates her ideology of transgression and desecration by means of what she calls "dialectic binomials"; for example, "property-theft" is a dialectic binomial because the second term negates the first. A similar method is used in *1934,* where Moravia opposes the German character to the Italian, fascism to freedom, Beate to Trude, and literature to life. The tension established between the contrasting terms gives rise to a third and different quality, difficult to define but none-theless perceptible. It is in this manner that Lucio, as we saw above, is able to "stabilize" his despair. And it is with this method of co-existing opposites that Moravia succeeds in evoking a menacing atmosphere of perverted reality, the impression of being a spectator at a comedy destined to end in tragedy.

Though set in a now almost remote past, the world described in *1934* is not unlike the present. Lucio alludes to this when he says: "I did not like living under fascism; but I really would not have wanted to live in any future time because I was sure . . . that the hope of a better world could only be a deception or an illusion." And indeed, for Moravia, modern states continue to harbor the deceit, lies, and hypocrisy he detested under fascism; economic injustice is as rife now as it was fifty years ago; and, if anything, stabilized despair as the normal human condition has now been perpetuated by the nuclear threat, a concern that surfaces in some of the stories collected in *La cosa e altri racconti* (*Erotic Tales,* 1983) and that underlies the structure of Moravia's late novel, *L'Uomo che guarda* (*The Voyeur,* 1985).

The voyeur of the title is Edoardo, a professor of French literature who, in addition to an Oedipal complex and a penchant for voyeurism, is haunted by thoughts of a nuclear holocaust. He passes the first few minutes of each day thinking about the end of the world, and every afternoon he watches the clouds pass above the cupola of St. Peter's cathedral. Occasionally, a mushroom-shaped cloud will be seen to pose briefly above the dome, and Edoardo takes a lugubrious pleasure in imagining that it is an atomic explosion destroying the basilica.

Edoardo's wife, Silvia, is a docile creature. Completely apolitical, she seems strangely out of place in her modern milieu. In fact, her husband maintains that she would be perfectly comfortable in the pre-Risorgimento Rome of 150 years ago. Their sexual life, too, has an antiquated quality; Edoardo regards it almost as a ritual of adoration, with Silvia assuming the role of a compassionate Madonna. Just as Cecilia in *The Empty Canvas* symbolizes objective reality, so does Silvia become the emblem of an ancient and holy civilization.

Because of their poverty, the couple live in two rooms of the large apartment belonging to Edoardo's father, also an academic. Yet despite their kinship and their common profession, one could scarcely imagine two more different people. The son is a humanist and a former *contestatore,* an idealist who in 1968 renounced his bourgeois property rights by deeding to his father a sumptuous apartment he had inherited and that is now standing empty. In contrast, the father is a professor of physics, a renowned and wealthy scientist firmly entrenched in the middle-class establishment; even his way of making love is diametrically opposed to that of Edoardo: the old man is violent, cruel, almost bestial.

As the novel begins, Silvia has gone to live with an aunt. She denies that it is a marital separation and explains that she merely needs some time to reflect on her life. Convinced that she is dissatisfied because they do not have their own home, Edoardo buries his pride and asks his father to return the vacant apartment to him. Then he learns from Silvia that the real issue is her affair with another man. Silvia insists that she is not in love with the man with whom she is having the affair, and she realizes that her behavior is foolish; but like a schoolgirl with a "crush," as she calls it, she yields in spite of herself when she is near him.

Without the knowledge of Silvia or her lover, Edoardo discovers the identity of his rival: it is his father. As in *The Lie* and *Time of Desecration,* incest underscores the ambiguity of relations among the characters of Moravia's world. Does Edoardo hate his father because he is his father or because he is his rival? Eventually, Silvia informs her husband that she and her lover have mutually agreed to break off their affair. Unfortunately, though, the couple cannot afford to maintain the large apartment, and there is no choice but to move back in with Edoardo's father. The young man will thus live

in a state of constant uncertainty very much like Lucio's stabilized despair: he will never know when Silvia may backslide, just as he never knows when the mushroom cloud will appear above St. Peter's dome.

Until the 1960's Alberto Moravia was neatly characterized by almost all critics as a realist whose forebears were the great European novelists of the nineteenth century. Since then, however, and even before Francesco Merighi concluded in *The Lie* that the realist novel was no longer possible, the Roman writer has been elaborating the metaphorical or ideological novel whose themes lie beneath the external "facts" of the work. The difficulty of perceiving the underlying structure of his recent novels has led to varying judgments of their merits. Frequently neglecting to go beyond the surface sexuality of his fiction, American reviewers have been particularly severe toward Moravia. The ambiguities created by his method of dialectic binomials have further obscured his message. Certainly one can identify the general attitudes of the author of "Man as an End": his scorn for the bourgeoisie, his distrust of totalitarian states, his Marxist sympathies, and his pessimism. Yet, especially since 1970, he has offered few unequivocal conclusions or recommendations. Perhaps it is just as well. Those who boldly prescribe remedies are almost always the proponents of narrow ideologies with limited applications and little tolerance for differing opinions. Moreover, for Moravia ambiguity is an integral part of his concept of the novel. As he wrote in "Notes on the Novel:"

> The thought of the [ideological] novelist will thus be the sum of the themes lying beneath the surface of the factual narration, brought to light and reconstructed somewhat like the fragments of a long-buried statue. The result will be an ambiguous and contradictory quality whose ideology will always be hypothetical and will never lend itself to a precise and comprehensive definition.
> (*Man as an End: A Defense of Humanism,* p. 265)

In *The Voyeur* Edoardo compares literature to an act of exhibitionism that permits the voyeur to penetrate into and to observe what are normally the private corners of life. And, as voyeur, the reader is essentially a passive watcher. Unlike Jean-Paul Sartre, Elio Vittorini, or other politically committed writers of his generation, Moravia is unwilling to assume a militant stance toward his society; he presents his thought not as a stimulus for actions that will change history, but as a foundation upon which his reader can construct an idea of the world.

AFTER 1985

The year after the death of Elsa Morante in 1985, Moravia married Carmen Llera, a press officer for a publishing firm. He continues to live in Rome and, despite his age, to write. In 1977, with a somewhat startling change of pace, he began publishing children's fables. Entertaining and often slightly irreverent, the tales feature the cleverly named primeval forebears of many creatures familiar to all today: Pin Guinone (big penguin), An Guilla (Italian for "eel"), O Ran Gu Tang, Pah-dreh-ther-noh (a phonetic rendering of *padre eterno,* God the Father), and many others. Accompanied by the imaginative illustrations of Flavia Siciliano, twenty-four of the stories were collected in *Storie della preistoria* (Prehistoric Stories, 1982).

Moravia has also continued to produce in fields more familiar to him and to his regular readers. *L'Angelo dell'informazione e altri testi teatrali* (The Angel of Information and Other Plays, 1986) includes recent plays—*La cintura* (The Belt) and *Voltati parlami* (Turn Over and Talk to Me)—as well as a reprint of a work originally published in *Nuovi argomenti* in January 1968, *Omaggio a James Joyce; ovvero, Il colpo di stato* (Homage to James Joyce; or, The Coup d'État). The play that gives its title to the collection is a sexual comedy over which hangs the threat of nuclear war, a common though now rather outdated theme of Moravia's during the 1980's.

Passeggiate africane (African Walks) continues the author's series of travelogues on Africa and emphasizes to his readers Moravia's fascination with that continent. It appeared in 1987, one year before his novel *Il viaggio a Roma* (The Trip to Rome). In the latter, Mario, the twenty-year-old protagonist, has been living in Paris for fifteen years when he receives an unexpected invitation from his widowed father to visit him in Rome. The uneasy relations between father and son, the sexual promiscuity of the characters, and the overtones of incest in *Il viaggio a Roma* now seem shopworn and almost commonplace. It is not likely that the novel will add to Moravia's distinction as a writer.

It hardly matters. Alberto Moravia's place in the literature of Italy is secure. None of its writers is so well known both in his own country and abroad, and, though many of his critics may not acknowledge it, he is the yardstick against which other living Italian novelists are measured. More important, he has retained his appeal for succeeding generations: young Italians used to read him in the 1930's; they still do so in the 1990's.

The object of both adulation and invective, no writer has been more controversial than Moravia. His critics complain that he has written too much, that his works are repetitive and laden with superfluous detail and explanations. His style, they say, does nothing to lighten the burden: it is crude, simplistic, and dull—in short, very much like his humdrum characters, the irresolute intellectual and the shallow-minded, promiscuous woman. Lastly, his themes are monotonous. Must everyone be alienated? Is sex the only means of communication?

Although none of these criticisms is without justification, Moravia's virtues outnumber his faults. The quality of his many books is indeed uneven; but if he has sinned, it has been through excess and not, happily, through insufficiency. His direct and unadorned prose is free of the Latinate syntax peculiar to traditional literary Italian, and even his most severe critics recognize Moravia's skills as a craftsman and as a master storyteller. Finally, his defenders regard the limited number of his themes not as evidence of a sterile imagination, but as a sign of the author's seriousness of purpose and of his choice to examine thoroughly just a few questions central to modern life.

Whatever the merit of his work, the man himself is admirable for his strength of will, for his moral and intellectual courage, and for that deeply rooted individualism which manifested itself first, perhaps, in his decision not to complete his formal education but instead to become a writer in a country where writers usually go hungry. Since that time, he has made his way with what R. W. B. Lewis has identified as "stubborn gallantry." By turns passionate and objective, Moravia is a rebel with common sense, critical of all: literary deities and fads, social structures and political ideologies, and, finally, himself and his work, which he has weighed with intelligence and honesty. The author of *The Time of Indifference* has been unwilling to rest on his achievements, and yet, without ceasing to push forward, he has remained faithful both to his art and to his vision of humanity.

Selected Bibliography

EDITIONS

INDIVIDUAL WORKS

NOVELS
Gli indifferenti. Milan, 1929.
Le ambizioni sbagliate. Milan, 1935.
La mascherata. Milan, 1941.
Agostino. Rome, 1944.
La romana. Milan, 1947.
La disubbidienza. Milan, 1948.
L'Amore coniugale e altri racconti. Milan, 1949.
Il conformista. Milan, 1951.
Il disprezzo. Milan, 1954.
La ciociara. Milan, 1957.
La noia. Milan, 1960.
L'Attenzione. Milan, 1965.
Io e lui. Milan, 1971.
La vita interiore. Milan, 1978.
1934. Milan, 1982.
L'Uomo che guarda. Milan, 1985.
Il viaggio a Roma. Milan, 1988.

SHORT STORIES
La bella vita. Lanciano, 1935.
L'Imbroglio, Milan, 1937.
I sogni del pigro. Milan, 1940.
L'Amante infelice. Milan, 1943.
L'Epidemia. Rome, 1944.
Due cortigiane e Serata di Don Giovanni. Rome, 1945.
I racconti. Milan, 1952.
Racconti romani. Milan, 1954.
Nuovi racconti romani. Milan, 1959.
L'Automa. Milan, 1962.
Una cosa è una cosa. Milan, 1967.
Il paradiso. Milan, 1970.
Un'altra vita. Milan, 1973.
Boh. Milan, 1976.
La cosa e altri racconti. Milan, 1983.

THEATER
Teatro: La mascherata. Beatrice Cenci. Milan, 1958.
Il mondo è quello che è. L'Intervista. Milan, 1966.
Il dio Kurt. Milan, 1968.
La vita è gioco. Milan, 1969.
L'Angelo dell'informazione e altri testi teatrali. Milan, 1986.

ESSAYS, TRAVEL LITERATURE, AND FILM REVIEWS
La speranza; ossia, Cristianesimo e comunismo. Rome, 1944.
Un mese in U.R.S.S. Milan, 1958.
Un'idea dell'India. Milan, 1962.
L'Uomo come fine e altri saggi. Milan, 1964.
La rivoluzione culturale in Cina; ovvero, Il convitato di pietra. Milan, 1967.
A quale tribù appartieni? Milan, 1972.
Al cinema: Centoquarantotto film d'autore. Milan, 1975.
Impegno controvoglia: Saggi, articoli, interviste—

Trentacinque anni di scritti politici. Edited by Renzo Paris. Milan, 1980.

Lettere dal Sahara. Milan, 1981.

L'Invierno nucleare. Milan, 1986.

Passeggiate africane. Milan, 1987.

CHILDREN'S LITERATURE

Tre storie della preistoria. Milan, 1977.

Quando Ba Lena era tanto piccola. Teramo, 1978.

Un miliardo di anni fa. Turin, 1979.

Cosma e i briganti. Palermo, 1980.

Cama Leonte diventò verde lilla blu. Teramo, 1981.

Storie della preistoria. Milan, 1982.

INTERVIEWS

Moravia. Milan, 1971. With Enzo Siciliano.

Alberto Moravia: Vita, parole, e idee di un romanziere. Milan, 1982. With Enzo Siciliano.

Il bambino Alberto. Milan, 1986. With Dacia Maraini.

Io e il mio tempo: Conversazioni critiche con Ferdinando Camon. Padua, 1988. With Ferdinando Camon.

COLLECTED WORKS

Opere complete di Alberto Moravia. 17 vols. Milan, 1953–1967.

TRANSLATIONS

Beatrice Cenci. Translated by Angus Davidson. New York, 1966.

Bitter Honeymoon, and Other Stories. Translated by B. Wall, B. G. Smith, and F. Frenaye. New York, 1956.

Bought and Sold. Translated by Angus Davidson. New York, 1973.

Command and I Will Obey You. Translated by Angus Davidson. New York, 1969.

The Conformist. Translated by Angus Davidson. New York, 1951.

Conjugal Love. Translated by Angus Davidson. New York, 1951.

The Empty Canvas. Translated by Angus Davidson. New York, 1961.

Erotic Tales. Translated by Tim Parks. New York, 1986.

The Fancy Dress Party. Translated by Angus Davidson. New York, 1952.

The Fetish, and Other Stories. Translated by Angus Davidson. New York, 1965.

Five Novels: Mistaken Ambitions. Agostino. Luca. Conjugal Love. A Ghost at Noon. Introduction by Charles J. Rolo. Translated by Arthur Livingston, Beryl de Zoete, and Angus Davidson. New York, 1955.

A Ghost at Noon. Translated by Angus Davidson. New York, 1955.

The Indifferent Ones. Translated by Aida Mastrangelo. New York, 1932.

Lady Godiva, and Other Stories. Translated by Angus Davidson. London, 1975.

The Lie. Translated by Angus Davidson. New York, 1966.

Man as an End, A Defense of Humanism:—Literary, Social, and Political Essays. Translated by B. Wall. New York, 1965.

Mistaken Ambitions. Translated by Arthur Livingston, New York, 1955.

More Roman Tales. Selected and translated by Angus Davidson. New York, 1963.

1934. Translated by William Weaver. New York, 1983.

Three Novels: The Conformist. The Fancy Dress Party. A Ghost at Noon. Translated by Angus Davidson. New York, 1961.

Time of Desecration. Translated by Angus Davidson. New York, 1980.

The Time of Indifference. Translated by Angus Davidson. New York, 1953.

Two Adolescents: The Stories of Agostino and Luca. Translated by Beryl de Zoete and Angus Davidson. New York, 1950.

Two: A Phallic Novel. Translated by Angus Davidson. New York, 1972.

Two Women. Translated by Angus Davidson. New York, 1958.

The Voice of the Sea, and Other Stories. Translated by Angus Davidson. London, 1978.

The Voyeur. Translated by Tim Parks. New York, 1987.

The Wayward Wife, and Other Stories. Selected and translated by Angus Davidson. New York, 1960.

Wheel of Fortune. Translated by Arthur Livingston. New York, 1937.

Which Tribe Do You Belong To? Translated by Angus Davidson. New York, 1974.

The Woman of Rome. Translated by Lydia Holland. New York, 1949.

The World's the World. Translated by A. Coppotelli. In *Salmagundi* 14: 39–104 (1970).

BIOGRAPHICAL AND CRITICAL STUDIES

Benussi, Christina, ed. *Il punto su Moravia.* Rome, 1987.

Cottrell, Jane E. *Alberto Moravia.* New York, 1974.

Dego, Giuliano. *Moravia.* New York, 1967.

Fernandez, Dominigue. "Essai sur Alberto Moravia." In his *Le roman italien et la crise de la conscience moderne.* Paris, 1958. Pp. 9–138.

Heiney, Donald. "Alberto Moravia." In his *Three Italian Novelists: Moravia, Pavese, Vittorini.* Ann Arbor, Mich., 1968. Pp. 1–82.

Lewis, R. W. B. "Alberto Moravia: Eros and Existence." In his *The Picaresque Saint: Representative Figures in Contemporary Fiction.* New York, 1956. Pp. 36–56.

Mezzalana, Bruna Baldini. *Alberto Moravia e l'alienazione.* Milan, 1971.

Pacifici, Sergio. "Alberto Moravia: Sex, Money, and Love in the Novel." In his *The Modern Italian Novel from Pea to Moravia.* Carbondale, Ill., 1979. Pp. 200–239.

Rebay, Luciano. *Alberto Moravia.* New York, 1970.

Ross, Joan, and Donald Freed. *The Existentialism of Alberto Moravia.* Carbondale, Ill., 1972.

Sanguineti, Edoardo. *Alberto Moravia.* Milan, 1962.

BIBLIOGRAPHIES

Alfonsi, Ferdinando, and Sandra Alfonsi. *An Annotated Bibliography of Moravia Criticism in Italy and in the English-Speaking World (1929–1975).* New York, 1976.

LOUIS KIBLER

SIMONE DE BEAUVOIR

(1908–1986)

Man, my friend, you willingly make fun of women's writings because they can't help being autobiographical. On whom then were you relying to paint women for you . . . ? On yourself?

(Colette, *Break of Day*)

I

SIMONE DE BEAUVOIR'S life was by all accounts a scandal. Her writing is doubly scandalous, since it is the stubborn celebration of a singular female life. She was born in Paris on 9 January 1908 into a family safely ensconced in the comforts of the imperial *Belle époque*. At the age of seventeen, after a secret apprenticeship in revolt nurtured by forbidden books, she chose to disobey paternal and class decree by becoming a teacher. At a stroke she reneged on her destiny—the "maternal slumber" of bourgeois wife and mother—and crossed at once into what her father and her class regarded as "the enemy territory of the intellectuals" (*Mémoires d'une jeune fille rangée* [*Memoirs of a Dutiful Daughter*], 1958).

"Dutiful daughter" of the French bourgeoisie, she dedicated her life and art to denouncing passionately the "splendid expectations" that had illuminated her childhood. When World War II burst over her, she inherited history in its most terrible form. From then on, her life and work as a writer, teacher, and intellectual bore witness to virtually every major

turbulence of twentieth-century Europe: the Spanish Civil War, the Occupation and Resistance, the rise and defeat of Fascism, the bloody dismantling of French imperialism, the heyday and demise of the French intellectual Left, and the resurgence of French feminism. Her great literary output—five novels, a play, the monumental polemic *Le deuxième sexe* (*The Second Sex*, 1949), her essays, short stories, travel writing and journalism, the radical treatise *La vieillesse* (*Old Age,* 1970), the vast autobiography—would amount to an impassioned and sustained refutation of the alluring promises of bourgeois culture, the delusion of "a happy life in a happy world" for all. In 1963 de Beauvoir gave an intimation of how deep ran her sense of betrayal: "Turning an incredulous gaze towards that young and credulous girl, I realise with stupor how much I was cheated" (*La force des choses* [*Force of Circumstance*]).

It is thus not difficult to fathom the "festival of obscenity" that greeted the publication in 1949 of *The Second Sex*. Flung into the ravaged world of postwar France, it was a hugely erudite, radical, and eloquent rebuttal of the "false certainties" over which the war had raged: the male management of the world, international capitalism, the middle-class family, maternity, and marriage. De Beauvoir was accused, as a result, of every infamy; frigid, priapic, neurotic, she had trampled underfoot everything that was good and beautiful in the world. The Right detested her; the Left lacerated her with contempt. She was blacklisted by Rome. Rumor had it that she danced naked on the rooftops of Rouen. Male friends threw her book across the room. Her open liaison with Jean-Paul Sartre became the subject of public notoriety and vilification.

Yet her revolt also had its paradoxical side. De Beauvoir often denied, in the face of much evidence to the contrary, that her femininity had ever been a hindrance: "No, far from suffering from my femininity, I have . . . accumulated the advantages of both sexes" (*Force of Circumstance*). Certainly, her special position was that she was both an intellectual and a woman. As Mary Evans points out, she thus escaped the two fates of most of the women of the world: poverty and motherhood. De Beauvoir declared with that same "fearless sincerity" she so exalted in life and art: "I have not shared in the common lot of humanity: oppression, exploitation, extreme poverty. I am privileged" (*Toute compte fait* [*All Said and Done*, 1972]). No doubt the paradox of privileged revolt—a paradox that engaged not only the course of her own life, but also the political fate of an entire generation of intellectuals—arose from the conditions of her time. But for her the paradox had a special urgency: it was the paradox of being both a writer and a woman. Understanding this paradox, and thereby the limits of freedom and responsibility drawn within it, became the single preoccupation of her life.

Some time must therefore be spent on the meaning of these special conditions, for she consecrated her life to the search for their meaning. To answer the apparently naive question: "Being a woman, French, a writer . . . what does it mean?" one would, as she herself knew, "first have to know the historical meaning of the moment in which I am actually living" (*All Said and Done*). Finding the uncertain and obscure answer to this question became the "grand project" that enflamed her life and all her writings. One might call this project the scandal of identity.

Why should the identity of a female writer be a scandal? In the false, autumnal calm before the outbreak of World War II, at the age of thirty, de Beauvoir had started her first novel, *L'Invitée* (*She Came to Stay*, 1943). Her literary output until then comprised a slim bundle of short stories. Discussing the fate of this new work, Sartre had suggested with sudden vehemence, "Why don't you put *yourself* into your writing?" (*La force de l'âge* [*The Prime of Life*, 1960]). De Beauvoir recalled receiving the suggestion with the force of a blow to the head: "I'd never dare do that. . . . It seemed to me that from the moment I began to nourish literature with the stuff of my own personality, it would become something as serious as happiness or death." Furthermore, we learn from her autobiography that for some time crime had been featuring insistently in de Beauvoir's dreams and fantasies. In these dreams she found herself standing on trial before a crowded courtroom, perpetrator of an unmentionable deed for which she alone was responsible: "I saw myself in the dock, facing judge, prosecutor, jury, and a crowd of spectators, bearing the consequences of an act which I recognized as my own handiwork, and bearing it alone." The dream played out the obscure and perilous intuition that the crime for which she stood accused was nothing other than female independence:

> Ever since Sartre and I had met, I had shuffled off responsibility for justifying my existence on to him. I felt that this was an immoral attitude, but I could not envisage any practical way of changing it. The only solution would have been to accomplish some deed for which I alone, and no one else, must bear the consequences. . . . Nothing in fact, short of an aggravated crime could bring me true independence.
>
> (*The Prime of Life*)

The dream unveiled the insurrectionary cast of a female identity fashioned apart from the sanction of men. Female autonomy is seen as an unpardonable condition that carries the stigma of a crime and erupts with the force of an insurrection. The discovery that the handiwork of autonomy was itself a deed tantamount to murder subsequently entered *She Came to Stay* as its founding theme and became, in metaphysical clothing, the stuff of much of her early fiction and philosophical thought.

Nevertheless, the fact that de Beauvoir could commit the "aggravated crime" of female independence on paper relieved her for a long time of the necessity of doing so in life. By choosing to be an intellectual she escaped the social fate decreed by class and birth, her mother's "dull, grey kind of existence." The solitary role of intellectual safeguarded her personal autonomy. As she declared, "Writing guaranteed my moral autonomy; in the solitude of risks taken, of decisions to be made, I made my freedom much more real than by accommodating myself to any money-making practice." In so doing she escaped for a long time the imperative of a more arduous and dangerous revolt: "For me, my books were a real fulfilment, and as such they freed me from the necessity to affirm myself in any other way" (*Force of Circumstance*). Nevertheless, de Beauvoir's great power and distinction are that by exploring with the utmost seriousness, integrity, and passion what it meant to be a female writer in her time, she drove the possibilities of her life beyond its limits and left us with an exemplary testimony of the conditions of the female life.

What is at stake, then, in all de Beauvoir's writing is not simply the scandal of female identity—"How does a woman adjust herself to her womanly state"—but also how she represents it. Here one comes directly upon the autobiographical nature of so much of de Beauvoir's writing. One of the first things to notice about her work is that it is a sustained circling around the creation of a female persona: Simone de Beauvoir. Most of her writing is in some form or other a radical project of self-justification: "I wanted to realise myself in books that . . . would be existing objects for others, but objects haunted by a presence—my presence. . . . Above all I wanted my contemporaries to hear and understand me" (*All Said and Done*). "I wanted to be widely read in my lifetime, to be understood, to be loved" (*Force

of Circumstance*). This desire to haunt the memory of her contemporaries inspired her fiction with no less urgency. As she said of *Les mandarins* (*The Mandarins,* 1954), "I wanted it to contain all of me—myself in relation to life, to death, to my times, to writing, to love, to friendship, to travel."

Any autobiography, as George Gusdorf has said, is not so much the vivid and truthful portrait of a life as it is a work of "personal justification." This is part of what de Beauvoir meant when she announced that art was "a means of protecting my life." As she herself so well knew, "a man would never get the notion of writing a book on the peculiar situation of the human male. But if I wish to define myself, I must first of all say: 'I am a woman'; on this truth must be based all further discussion" (*The Second Sex*). More than this, a woman who lives a life that flies in the face of convention and authority is already a scandal. To justify that life in public (to publish: *publicare simulacrum*—to erect a statue in a public place) is, as Nancy Miller has remarked, "to *reinscribe* the original violation." The autobiography of an exceptional woman is therefore a double scandal; it is to stand defiant in the dock.

For precisely this reason de Beauvoir wanted to be the one to "rummage through my past. . . . So long as it is I who paints my own portrait, nothing daunts me." As with Colette, the urgency that enflamed her art, "a passion, a madness," came from the knowledge that if she left the painting of her portrait to any other, her life would "trickle into the sand," and nothing would remain of her childhood self except "a pinch of ashes."

Autobiography as a form scarcely exists before the seventeenth century. It is commonly accepted that its rise has something to do with the historical discovery of the self-conscious individual during the Renaissance. Estelle Jelinek has also pointed out that "autobiography must share with the novel the distinction of being one of the first literary genres shaped with the active participation of women." Nevertheless, there are a number of clear differences between autobiographies written by women and those written by men. Women's autobiographies do not flourish at the high points of male history—revolutions and battles and national upheavals and so on. They wax according to the climactic changes of another history. Male autobiographies are also characteristically embellished and gracefully shaped into chronologically elegant wholes. Female autobiographies are typically fragmentary, irregular, anecdotal, and oblique, eloquent of the ingenuity and effort taken in negotiating a female life past the magisterial forms of male selfhood. As a result de Beauvoir always chafed against the elegant restraints and mannered symmetries of fictional form, for these turned art into a collector's item, "a statue dying of boredom in a villa garden." Events in an autobiography, on the other hand, "retain all the gratuitousness, the unpredictability, and the often preposterous complications that marked their original occurrence" (*Force of Circumstance*).

At the same time de Beauvoir was temperamentally and politically averse to the idea of autobiography as the heroics of an inner life, the unfolding saga of a single mind. If she wanted to voice the originality of her own experience, it was only to the extent that it was also illuminated by the incandescence of her epoch. As she insisted, "The background, tragic or serene, against which my experiences are drawn gives them their true meaning and constitutes their unity" (*Force of Circumstance*). She was impatient of the "pointless and in any case impossible undertaking" of building up a single portrait of herself. "What I should like to do above all is provide myself an idea of my place, my locus in the world" (*All Said and Done*). For this reason it is necessary to spend some time on the difficult, unruly, and elusive conditions that gave her life its meaning. To write her autobiography and keep faith with her deep commitment to veracity, de Beauvoir ransacked libraries, newspapers, diaries, letters, and memoirs, and conferred lengthily with friends and with Sartre. Yet she well knew that autobiography involves a "welter of caprice," whimsical omission, and crafted evasions, governed overall by the contrivances of artistic convention. Autobiographies are, as she put it, "fictions of selfhood." It is therefore well to bear in mind that one is dealing not only with the portrait of a real life, but with a fiction of selfhood—what Colette called a fabulation of "rearranged fragments."

II

On her return from China in 1956, at the age of forty-eight, de Beauvoir set out to write the story of her childhood. This story swelled to four fat volumes, some 2,200 pages in all, engaging more than sixty years of her life, and was some sixteen years in the writing. *Memoirs of a Dutiful Daughter,* the evocative first volume of her autobiography, covers the years 1908–1929, from her birth to the death of her beloved friend Zaza.

Daughter of Françoise and George de Beauvoir, a disappointed Catholic woman from a rich Verdun banking family and a well-off Parisian attorney, de Beauvoir faced a predictable future: "It was laid down what this child's state should be—French, bourgeois and Catholic; only its sex was unforeseen" (*All Said and Done*). She was raised in Paris in the "big village" that stretched from the Lion de Belfort to the rue Jacob, and from the boulevard Saint-Germain to the boulevard Raspail. Except for some years as a teacher in Marseilles and Rouen, and despite an insatiable appetite for travel, she always lived in more or less the same district in Paris.

Her childhood was the perfectly commonplace story of a girl born to an upper bourgeois French family of the years before the war. A "madly gay little girl," de Beauvoir had until the age of eleven "virtually no problems." Safely cushioned in the red velvets and silk drapes of her boulevard Raspail apartment, she indulged to her heart's content her fierce yearning for happiness, becoming apprenticed thereby, as was only fitting, to the bourgeois promise of individual happiness that was to enchant her for so long. In the *Memoirs* de Beauvoir discharges a debt: more than anything else it was to the "calm gaze" of the young female maidservant Louise that she owed the sense of "unalterable security" which was her class birthright until the outbreak of war. From the comforting security of this gaze sprang the "vital optimism" and unswerving will to happiness that de Beauvoir felt was her own peculiar gift: "I have never met anyone, in the whole of my life, who was so well equipped for happiness as I was, or who labored so stubbornly to achieve it" (*The Prime of Life*).

To Louise's calm gaze was added another comforting dimension: a whole race of supernatural beings bent over her from a Catholic heaven their "myriad benevolent eyes." A more mundane race of aunts and uncles in ostrich plumes and panamas played "the role of a kindly mirror," their flattering solicitude safeguarding de Beauvoir's illusion of standing in the privileged center of the world. Only the "black looks" of her unswervingly pious mother were capable of troubling these early years. She had difficulty distinguishing her mother's look from the eye of God.

Mirrors, eyes, and glances flash everywhere in de Beauvoir's writing, and the power of the gaze to shape identity figures powerfully in her existentialism and feminism. The crystalline certainties of class, religion, and family that graced her childhood with their special radiance, only to become the dark figures of her betrayal, were unveiled within what can be called the metaphysical tradition of the gaze. As she wrote, "A child receives its image and even its very being from others. . . . It perceives itself as something that is *seen*" (*The Second Sex*). The intellectual tradition of the gaze reaches back to G. W. F. Hegel and has been taken up in recent times by Sartre, the

French psychoanalyst Jacques Lacan, and a certain tradition of feminism. But it is de Beauvoir's special distinction in *The Second Sex* to have been the first to flesh out the geometry of the gaze and transform the idealist Hegelian ontology of self and other, frozen in faceless combat, into a politics of seeing and being seen, governed by socially consecrated rituals of dominance and submission and violently scored by history and gender.

By all accounts de Beauvoir inherited something of her early talent for impersonation from her father. Her paternal grandfather had enjoyed a sizable fortune and a 500-acre estate, but had chosen instead to take up an administrative post in the Town Hall in Paris. As a consequence his son, de Beauvoir's father, grew up lodged comfortably, if somewhat ambiguously, "halfway between the aristocracy and the bourgeoisie, between the landed gentry and the office clerk," and came to feel himself "neither completely integrated with society nor burdened with any serious responsibility." Attracted by the stability of the legal profession and eventually joining a law firm, his first passion remained the theater. Possessing the name but not the means to swim with the aristocracy, he contented himself with a theatrical impersonation of their manner of living.

In all other respects de Beauvoir's father was "a true representative of his period and his class." Fiercely patriotic, anti-Dreyfus, and anti-Republican, respecting but not believing in the church, his only religion was nationalism and his only private morality "the cult of the family." Epicurean, pagan, and vital, his neglect of his daughters' spiritual well-being stood in direct contrast to his wife's strict supervision. Françoise de Beauvoir, made bitterly resentful as a child by the whalebone collars and narrow spaces of her female upbringing, was diffident in society but passionately overbearing with her daughters, Simone and Poupette, in private. Her convent morality seeped into every recess of their life. From her de Beauvoir inherited the ethical fervor that infuses her early thought, her hunger for the absolute, her passion for travel, her faith in and enormous capacity for work, her dogmatism, and the lessons in self-abnegation that were to mark her early relation to her body.

As a consequence de Beauvoir lived out in her childhood the cultural contradictions of her period. To her father she was "simply a mind"; it was his duty to give his daughter the education that would be a discreet adornment to her role as wife and mother. Her body and her spiritual education were in the sole charge of her mother. Thus her being fell into two: "I grew accustomed to the idea that my intellectual life—embodied by my father—and my spiritual life—expressed by my mother—were two radically heterogeneous fields of experience which had absolutely nothing in common" (*Memoirs*).

This division had a profound effect on de Beauvoir's future. Her desire to be an intellectual was not a whimsical determination but rather the outcome of the jostling forces of her world. Her cultural inheritance was rife with contradictions: "My father's individual and pagan ethical standards were in complete contrast to the rigidly moral conventionalism of my mother's teaching." Suspended as she was between the aristocratic skepticism of her father and the bourgeois sobriety of her mother, her attempt to make sense of these ambiguities turned de Beauvoir's inner life into "a kind of endless disputation" and became, as she claims, the main reason she became an intellectual.

In 1914 her parents became the victims of calamity. As was the fashion of their class, her family spent their summers in the ancient province of Limousin on her grandfather's estate. Not only did the expansive property of Meyrignac give de Beauvoir material grounds for her mystical yearning for the infinite, but it was there among the water lilies and the peacocks, at the age of six, that she heard the news that war had been declared. The war did little to cloud her small horizon, but by the end of it her father's Russian stocks had plummeted,

and the family plunged with them into the newly poor.

Her father's legal career finished, the family in near poverty, they moved to the rue de Varennes. De Beauvoir lost Louise, her plush red and black apartment, space, and solitude: "I didn't even have a desk to put my things in. . . . I found it painful to never be on my own." She had in effect fallen into a different class. It was at this time that books came to play a more and more vital role in her life.

In 1913 de Beauvoir had been sent to a private Catholic school with the beguiling name of Le Cours Desir. There she was fed the "ersatz concoction" that was her allotted fare as a girl, and there she learned to hide her intellect "as though it was a deformity." Crimped and curtailed, hers was the typical inferior training of a caste firmly destined to live in exclusion within its own culture. Her education was in every respect a limitation, differing markedly from that enjoyed by, say, a Sartre or an André Gide.

The act of reading is therefore central to the *Memoirs*, as it is to any autobiography. The autobiographer, in what amounts to a ritual gesture, conjures up the reader, in order that the reader may in turn conjure the autobiographer's self into being: without this collaboration the voluble "I" would fall silent. But above and beyond this, reading played a peculiarly poignant role in de Beauvoir's childhood: she began to feel most urgently the ambiguity and uncertainty of her sexual identity.

Reading was from the outset linked to transgression. In the very first remembered action of the *Memoirs* she had crept under her father's desk in "the awful sanctum" of his black-pearwood study: a willful self-insertion into the seat of cultural and paternal power, and thus a small mimicry of the act of female autobiography itself. For de Beauvoir reading was a solemn rite promising a sorcerer's power and autonomy, and relief from the galling tedium of domesticity; it was also the punishing reminder of an exclusion that she could barely begin to comprehend.

"Impassable barriers," for example, prohibited her entry into the library in the rue Saint-Placide. Her books were carefully disfigured by her mother's censoring hand, and her reading was constantly and strictly circumscribed: "You *must not . . . you must not touch* books that are not meant for you" (*Memoirs*). This ban she recalls shuddering through her body with the same punitive and obscure jolt she had received when she had stuck her finger into the black hole of an electric socket. On both occasions she had been sitting in her father's black armchair. Here reading, transgression, and a forbidden eroticism merge in a scene that played itself out again and again in her adolescence. The overdetermined metaphor of forbidden holes, the furtive and secret touchings, the barred entry into places of obscure pleasure and power, disobedience answered by a swift and annihilating punishment—these profoundly colored her view of books as the place of a secret, libidinous insurrection. For this reason she always saw the act of female writing, and therefore the intellectual life, as a sexual and political revolt in itself.

At the same time de Beauvoir had inherited from her parents a "deep reverence for books." This was a cultural value typical of her father's background, but it had become raised to a family fetish by their loss of social face. For M. de Beauvoir the elite of the earth were those who had "intelligence, culture, and a sound education," but this was strictly an upper-middle-class prerogative. As Sartre has pointed out, the generation of writers before the war could not support themselves by literature alone. Gide had property, Proust independent means; Claudel was in the diplomatic service. In short, they had deep loyalties to the state; they were, as Sartre says, "integrated into the bourgeoisie."

Contemptuous of the kind of material wealth and success that took effort, M. de Beauvoir consoled himself for his social dishonor by an exaggerated attachment to culture. Nevertheless, it was indecorous for a woman to have too much of that magical ingredient which distinguished his class from all others. As de Beauvoir grew older and began to make her ungainly entry into puberty, she found it more and more difficult to play the role of "dutiful daughter," particularly with respect to curtailing the precocious mind of which her father was alternately proud and resentful. If, for de Beauvoir, identity is shaped by the male gaze, it did not help matters that her father, like her culture, had double vision. As she entered puberty, with all the reluctance a Catholic upbringing could induce, she came to live in her father's eyes as the vivid emblem of his failure. Without a dowry, she would never marry; she would have to work for a living. His attitude to de Beauvoir became more and more acrimonious, and her sense of his withdrawal plunged her into despair. The recriminating gaze of the "sovereign judge" began to hold all kinds of dangers for her.

If her father's pride had once been her "man's mind," it was a mind now discovered to inhabit a very female body, and she could not help but regard the "silent upheaval" of her importunate body as the culprit and cause of his disgust. Her femininity itself became a blemish and a malady: "I thought of myself in relation to my father as a purely spiritual being: I was horrified at the thought that he suddenly considered me a mere organism. I felt as if I could never hold up my head again" (*Memoirs*).

Her body became an embarrassment. She regarded the delirious and obscure desires that shook her with much the same "sickening curiosity" that forbidden books had formerly elicited. Shamed by the displeasure of the male eye, she directed the full arsenal of her lessons in Catholic self-abnegation to her body's defeat. She began to develop phobias. Clearly the paroxysms of dizziness, nausea, and anemia she began to suffer served as a hysterical protest against the incomprehensible paradoxes of her situation. Her horror at the "tyranny of the flesh" was more than anything else a fierce resistance to the social denigration of the female body. Her later rejection of maternity and marriage—which brought a great deal of fire on her head—was the most extreme revolt she could envisage against the imposed ignominy of her female situation. In an era with no legal contraceptives and no legal abortion, this revolt was the only recourse she had to protecting the autonomy she glimpsed in the vocation of writer.

One may note here an important discrepancy in the *Memoirs*. She often made the brave announcement: "I felt no disappointment at being a girl." Yet she could also recall: "My father's attitude towards the 'fairer sex' wounded me deeply." And again, later: "If he had continued to interest himself in me . . . I should certainly not have felt rejected, thrust out and betrayed." Her peculiarly willful blindness to the hobbling restraints of her femininity constituted a protest of its own and remained a defining feature of her identity until she wrote *The Second Sex*.

Her cousin Jacques, notable otherwise only as her first adolescent love, awakened her fully to the existing plenitude of her cultural heritage and at the same time to the baffling fact that she was exiled from this plenitude:

> He knew a host of poets and writers of whom I knew nothing at all, the distant clamor of a world that was closed to me used to come into the house with him: how I longed to explore that world! Papa would say with pride: "Simone has a man's brain, she thinks like a man; she *is* a man." And yet he treated me like a girl. Jacques and his friends read real books and were abreast of all current politics, they lived out in the open; I was confined to the nursery.
>
> *(Memoirs)*

How far removed from this passionate resentment is Sartre's memory (in *Qu'est-ce que la littérature? [What Is Literature?, 1948]*) of his confident childhood accession to the patrimony of books:

> We were used to literature long before beginning our first novel. To us it seemed natural for books to grow in a civilized society, like trees in a gar-

den. It is because we loved Racine and Verlaine too much that when we were fourteen years old, we discovered, during the evening study period or in the great court of the lycée, our vocation as a writer.

For de Beauvoir books became the occasion of a secret revolt and a double life. She began to trespass clandestinely on the "forbidden territory" of male culture; curling up in her father's leather armchair, she dipped "quite freely into all the books in the bookcase."

It was also fitting that her primordial act of disobedience—the unseating of God—should engage the three most tortuously entangled forces in her life: sex, books, and religion. Sitting under a tree devouring forbidden apples and reading "in a book by Balzac—also forbidden—the strange idyll of a young man and a panther," she decided that she was too attached to sensual joys to be able to live any longer under "the eye of God." She summarily emptied heaven of its occupants and inherited at once the "haunting anxiety about death" which never left her, and which she struggled unremittingly to conquer in her fiction. Death as the absence of God, a kind of spectral, ever-present black electric socket, never ceased threatening to suck her being into the void.

I have spent some time on de Beauvoir's relation to books, since her early experience of reading as a libidinous insurrection deeply marked not only her choice of career and her motivation to write, but also much of her fictional and philosophical thought about the nature of desire, freedom, and limitation.

De Beauvoir thus fell between two stools: books, she was constantly reminded, were the only precious things; yet, as a female, she could touch but not possess them. She was faced with two options: either to take blind refuge under the wing of authority and submit, or to rebel.

In 1925, in violation of paternal and class decree, she chose to become a teacher, betraying herself at once, as far as her father and the scandalized matrons at Le Cours Desir were concerned, to be "a traitor to her class." If writers elicited her father's ardent approval, intellectuals were a "dangerous sect" bent on peddling incendiary ideas about socialism, equality, and democracy. Moreover, it was decidedly indecorous for a woman of her station, however reduced, to enter the professions. Thus the first watershed of de Beauvoir's identity was marked by the resolute denial of her femininity as difference. Instead she placed all her hope in riding with the renegade class of the intellectuals. At roughly the same time she began to write. She was seventeen.

III

I am an intellectual, I take words and the truth to be of value.

(*The Prime of Life*)

In 1925 de Beauvoir took her *baccalauréat* and enrolled at the Institut Saint-Marie at Neuilly, where she studied literature and philosophy under R. Garric. Garric was a spellbinding Catholic socialist and founder of the Équipes Sociales, an experiment to unite students and the working class. He offered de Beauvoir her first glimpse of working-class life, but despite a delirious crush on him, this encounter did little to cure her itch for the metaphysical: she did not identify with the working-class youths she met, and she was still nurturing exalted dreams of the inner life. Nevertheless, her brief exposure to this radical environment had one decisive effect: she made the brutal discovery that the class values she held most precious (progress, eternal peace, universalism) were being betrayed by the very class which exalted them. The bourgeois promise of universal humanity and happiness was a lie: universalism cloaked a niggardly class interest and a narrow materialism that excluded most of humanity, including herself.

These years were marked by a sense of exile that could only be compensated for by dreams of lonely defiance. She took refuge in the solace

of a radical individualism, in a rationalistic self-sufficiency that she believed would distinguish her from her hated class but that was, in fact, a direct cultural inheritance: "I existed only through myself and for myself." She decided to "be a soul; a pure, disembodied spirit. . . . I found escape in the clouds." Her solitude bred a dogged pride that flowed directly into her aspirations to write. Her path was marked. The lofty vocation of the genius would assuage her loneliness: "I felt I should already be trying to communicate the experience of solitude. . . . In April I wrote the first pages of a novel" (*Memoirs*).

The main force of her fierce repudiation of family and class, and her turn to writing as a refuge, came from this deeply felt sense of exile, a dark leitmotif coursing through the latter half of the *Memoirs:* "I am alone. One is always alone. I shall always be alone. . . . I'm not like other people. . . . I was 'outside life.' . . . Loneliness continued to lower my spirits. . . . I felt shut out. . . . I shall always be ostracised," and so on. She had interrupted the Catholic hosts in their consoling progress across the heavens and had swept them away; henceforth she would be a pariah, an outcast. Her anxious accession to adolescence had doubly exiled her from her body and from her father. Her secret trespass on forbidden books left her morally alienated from her mother and, indeed, from the entire moral climate of her childhood. The niggardly habits of her society refused her entry into the world of men. There was only one recourse: "I felt myself an exile, whose one remedy against solitude lay in self-expression."

The act of writing became a radical project of self-creation and self-justification. On the other hand, it was also clearly a plea for social legitimacy: "above all I wanted my contemporaries to hear and understand me." Writing was, into the bargain, the sole path that a few women had trodden before her. Literature would be her calling, because there she glimpsed the shimmering promise of autonomy. Already, it is clear, the project was scored with contradictions. The lonely vocation of the genius immured de Beauvoir from the dangers of the world. Yet what she wanted above all was social recognition: "I wanted to be loved." Her desire to write expressed a stubborn will to impress herself on the public memory and insinuate herself into the records of the scribes. But in this way she fell at once into the quandary of seeking recognition, even confirmation, of her very identity in the eyes of the established order she had vowed to despise. She could win authenticity only if she fled the world, but the flight would have meaning only if it was remarked and approved by the world. Driving through these contradictions, de Beauvoir came to represent the fundamental social difficulty of writing in her period, a general difficulty, but one deeply complicated for women.

De Beauvoir's early, steadfast individualism left its unmistakable mark on her thinking for a very long time. But hers was not a singular unease. If the fact that she was female was the first cause of her alienation, she also inherited a particular literary crisis that was part of a more general social crisis deepening at just the time she started to write. The discovery she soon made—that to write about herself meant more than anything else giving "an idea of my place, my locus in the world"—permits one to ask the question Raymond Williams asked of George Orwell: What did it mean, in that particular generation, to be a writer?

De Beauvoir, like Orwell, began to write in a period of literary crisis, at a time when the act of writing, the legitimacy of representation itself, was in serious trouble. Earlier writers of the fin-de-siècle avant-garde, like Charles Baudelaire and Arthur Rimbaud, out of key with the general social and political climate of their period, had run amok among the canons of literary and social authority, flinging the relics of tradition into violent, unholy patterns. The rage for modernity, the "shock of the new," had discredited any appeal to the ancestral shibboleths of order and proportion, harmony, beauty, and perfection. As Williams points out, the antagonistic relation between artist and society had reached its first climax throughout most of Europe in the 1880's and 1890's, and had by the 1920's become more embattled and more polarized. For the stolid middle class, the successful writer was one who made money: in violent reaction to this and to their slow disinheritance from cultural authority, a postwar generation of artists came to define themselves in terms of their distance from society. As Williams describes it, "The 'writer,' the true writer, had no commercial aims, but also at root, no social function and by derivation, no social content. He just 'wrote.' And then as a self-defined recognizable figure, he lived 'outside' society— unconventional, the 'artist.' " Paris became the spiritual home for these artistic exiles and emigrés, the self-styled pariahs and bohemians, the peddlers of decadence, the dilettantes, aesthetes, and voyeurs of derangement who plied their wares in the smoky cafés and bars of the 1920's.

It was to these "disciples of disquiet" that de Beauvoir became drawn in her years at the École Normale and the Sorbonne (1927–1929). She read feverishly, intoxicated by the possibility that her loneliness was not a personal affliction, but the mark of an exalted breed of thinkers, who could, with Gide, shout: "Family, I hate you! Your dead homes and shut doors." These conspirators in cultural unease also wanted to set a bonfire in the family house, to murder their father the landlord, their brother the cardinal, and their cousin the imperial colonel. Her cousin Jacques had already introduced her to "the poetry of the bars," and de Beauvoir began to haunt them with deliberate intent, indulging in drinking bouts, aping the dress and manners of the prostitutes, and from time to time knocking off people's hats or breaking a glass or two. She delighted in the excesses of the avant-garde, "the outrageous jokes of pure negation . . . the systematic derangement of the senses, suicidal despair." At the same time, as she admits in the *Memoirs* with a self-irony colored with nostalgia, "since they had no intention of overturning society, they contented themselves with studying the states of their precious souls in the minutest detail." Nevertheless, the bar, like the café, became emblematic in her fiction of her fixation with the dark, liminal places that lay on the threshold of social respectability and social alienation. Characteristically, her imagination was always pitched at the places of the shadowy commerce between self and other, crime and authority, desire and law.

De Beauvoir was an extravagantly talented academic. She subjected herself to a taxing regimen of reading, and began to grope her way through Descartes, Spinoza, Kant, Bergson, Schopenhauer, and Nietzsche, accepting with exhilaration, as she did for the rest of her life, Gide's challenge "assumer le plus possible d'humanite," to take voracious possession of the immense emporium of created things. During this time her political ideas remained hazy and her sense of history muddled. The "incomprehensible uproar" of world affairs held small attraction for her. All forms of conformity and obscurantism elicited her untempered scorn. Temperament and the happenstances of her life inclined her to the Left: "One thing I knew. I detested the extreme right"; but it was a political Manichaeism that had little form or content and was in many ways a quasi-religious relic of her Catholic morality. Her vehement denunciations of society remained very much a rebellion of the mind, and she continued to exalt metaphysics and morals over the humdrum of social matters.

De Beauvoir was initiated during this period into the elite triumvirate of Sartre and his friends André Herbaud and Paul Nizan, three exceptional philosophy students who had formed a tight coterie. The sheer virtuosity of de Beauvoir's mind attracted their attention, and they gradually opened their ranks to her. This was a momentous event for her. Not only did she quickly form with Sartre the relationship she called the one "unquestioned success of my life," but she had for the first time found a community of intellectuals. The cost was that for a long time she could not admit that her femininity set her apart from them in the world's eyes, for then she would have had to grant that having been "expelled from the paradise of childhood, [she] had not yet been admitted into the world of men."

De Beauvoir called these years before the war her "golden age." By her own account she and Sartre lived like "elves" in the enchanted circle of their own company. Consciously repudiating the "discreet trafficking in betrayal" of middle-class monogamy, they contracted an open relationship in which each was free to have deep and lasting liaisons with others, founded on a scrupulous honesty. Their loathing of bourgeois society was their first premise: they had, they believed, jettisoned every craven evasion of family, class, and tradition. Society, they were confident, "could change only as a result of a sudden cataclysmic upheaval on a global scale," and capitalism was already being "shaken by a crisis of the utmost gravity." They were all for revolution and the overthrow of the ruling class, but they remained resolutely dubious of both Marxism and socialism, which, they felt, demanded the surrender of autonomy and of individual judgment.

In *The Prime of Life*, the second volume of her autobiography, covering the years 1929–1944, de Beauvoir lashes herself and Sartre with characteristically inclement honesty for the airy insouciance with which they prided themselves on their "radical freedom." Their circumstances as young petit-bourgeois intellectuals gave them a great deal of independence, leisure, and license. This specifically privileged social circumstance they confused with an ontological "sovereign freedom," which they identified as the fundamental condition of all human existence; those who genuflected to circumstance were morally complicit with the forces that trammeled them. They believed themselves, on the other hand, to "consist of pure reason and pure will" and raised the idea of freedom to a ghostly fetish that served as a spectral image of their disembodied role as intellectuals.

As de Beauvoir later attested, their notions of radical individual freedom served simply to conceal and protect their interests as members of an intellectual caste: "We fondly supposed that we were representative of mankind as a whole; and thus, all unknown to ourselves, we demonstrated our identity with the very privileged class that we thought to repudiate" (*The Prime of Life*). Bathed in the radiance of their own magic circle, they were deaf and blind to the insistent tramp of history. The fascists were massing, the world was on the move, but they remained spectators.

All the elements that flowed into de Beauvoir's aspirations to write and gave shape to the aesthetic form they would take were now in place. The relics of her Catholicism, her hankering for the infinite, her sense of exclusion as a female, her ambiguous class inheritance, her contact with sympathetic artistic movements—all conspired in a flight into aestheticism. But this was really an aesthetics of escape. De Beauvoir longed for an art of "inhuman purity," a cold, entranced art: faceless statues, landscapes bare of human figures, oceans caught in the immobility of a pure moment, men turned into salt, public squares scorched with the fire of death—the aesthetics of absence she would question and abandon in her second novel, *Le sang des autres* (*The Blood of Others,* 1945). She wanted "literature to get away from common humanity" and was drawn as a result to "hermetic poems, surrealist films, abstract art, illuminated manuscripts and ancient tapestries, African masks." Completed works of great beauty broke free of humanity: "dumb, inscrutable, like huge abandoned totems: in them alone I made contact with some vital, absolute element." Reading Katherine Mansfield, she consoled herself that she, too, was a romantic personification of Mansfield's "solitary woman."

The logic of this asocial stance was, nevertheless, a social logic, and began to reveal itself as just that as the darkening cataclysm of war descended on the world. As Williams put it:

The "aesthetic attitude towards life" was a displaced consciousness relating to one of many possible artistic decisions, but above all related to a version of society: not an artistic consciousness but a disguised social consciousness in which the real connections and involvements with others could be plausibly overlooked and then in effect ratified: a definition of "being a writer" that excluded social experience and social concerns.

But de Beauvoir's writing moved, in fact, in quite the opposite direction. What happened was the intervention of a historical crisis of such magnitude that it fundamentally discredited an entire way of thinking about literature and became thereby an example of what Orwell, living in Paris at the time, called "the invasion of literature by politics," the dramatic shift from the aestheticism of the 1920's to the socially committed writing of the 1930's.

In 1931 de Beauvoir was appointed to a teaching post in Marseilles, and Sartre received a similar position in Le Havre. In 1932 she moved to Rouen to teach literature at a *lycée* for girls. During these years she began to write in earnest, beginning and abandoning two novels, both of which evoked the memory of a "beloved face." The *Memoirs* were originally composed, we know, in order to lay two ghosts to rest: de Beauvoir's childhood self and the pale yellow face and black, brittle hair of her dead friend Zaza. Zaza—Elizabeth Mabille—was murdered, as far as de Beauvoir was concerned, by a class—the "monstrous alliance" of upper-middle-class families, with their Sunday-afternoon tea parties and croquet, the sham decor of their sobriety, their lethal decorum, and, most unforgivably, their disfiguring of the female life.

De Beauvoir had met Zaza at the age of ten as a fellow student at Le Cours Desir. Zaza's fire and temerity, her talent for cocking a snook at every propriety while playing the cool role of dutiful daughter, her easy mastery of ideas, books, and social graces, plunged de Beauvoir into the ignominy and delirium of an inadmissible passion. It was an (assiduously repressed) homoerotic love that lay outside the city of language as de Beauvoir knew it, a "flood of feeling that had no place in any code." She and Zaza quickly became conspirators in defiance against the suffocating tedium of domesticity, secreting themselves in M. Mabille's study to discuss forbidden ideas and books. The "tribal rites" of arranged marriage, the bartering of female bodies to cement familial prestige and property, elicited their particular loathing and fear, a fear much more pressing in Zaza's case. De Beauvoir planned to work for a living; in Zaza's class "a woman had to get married or become a nun." Zaza's mother, by all accounts a "perfect specimen of a right-minded bourgeois upbringing," hailed from "a dynasty of militant Catholics" and spent most of her waking hours in the commerce of arranging marriages. Her amiability cloaked an unrelenting fealty to Catholic propriety; as time went by and de Beauvoir began her studies, she came to recognize Zaza's friend, not inaccurately, as the enemy within, an ungracious, self-righteous, and stubborn-minded little atheist who planned to be an intellectual and work for a living.

Zaza differed from de Beauvoir in that her background was virtually airtight: it lacked the vivid contradictions that had pushed de Beauvoir's early attempts at understanding to the point of exhaustion and revolt. Zaza had been taught by a Catholic upbringing that brooked no argument to kneel before suffering as her natural female condition. In any event, the forces ranged against her were too strong: her beloved mother, bent on marrying her profitably, refused to countenance Zaza's love for de Beauvoir's friend "Herbaud," who for various family reasons could not immediately propose marriage, and Zaza after months of a deadly struggle to escape, surrendered to the impossibility of her situation, contracted brain fever, and died.

De Beauvoir never forgave the bourgeoisie for Zaza's death or herself for not being able to save her. The unacceptable fact of Zaza's death

became the theme in all de Beauvoir's early attempts to write. In her first fictional false starts she stalks restlessly around it, again in *Quand prime le spirituel* (*When Things of the Spirit Come First*, 1979), in *La femme rompue* (*The Woman Destroyed*, 1967), and in *Les belles images* (1966). Her autobiography breaks chronology in the final volume, returning obsessively to begin again the process of understanding. It was, by her own account, only when her political thinking had matured to the point where she could finally root Zaza's death in its full social context that the ghost would return to haunt her no more. This long attempt to account for the death of a friend involved in the process the dismantling of some of the more revered shibboleths of Western culture, the elaboration of an alternative ideology, and the writing of the first classic account of the social meaning of the female condition.

During the 1930's de Beauvoir struggled to find her literary feet. She produced two derivative novels that eventually, by her own account, degenerated into a mere hodgepodge and a bundle of short stories, *When Things of the Spirit Come First*, which borrowed its title, ironically, from Jacques Maritain and much of its tone, "a certain concealed irony," from John Dos Passos. The book, written over the years 1935–1937, though published only in 1979, is neither a novel nor independent stories, but a collection that orbits around the central ambition of unveiling the "multitude of crimes, both petty and great" which hide behind the "spiritual hocus-pocus" of bourgeois Catholicism.

Each story is concerned with a central female protagonist who falls victim in a different way to the intrigues, mortifications, and lethal charades of religion. The protagonist of the fourth story, Anne, is the first of a number of concealed Zazas who make their progress through de Beauvoir's fiction. Her murder in this virtually autobiographical tale serves as a vivid exemplum of all the themes that fascinated de Beauvoir: death, the scandal of otherness, the despised bourgeoisie, the conflict between crime and desire, freedom and responsibility, and the overwhelming question of how a woman comes to lead her life. Zaza's death became an exaggerated symptom of the difficulties besetting de Beauvoir's own life and inaugurated the twin obsessions round which almost all her writing revolved: the "black enlightenment" of death and "the mirage of the Other."

Indeed, it may be said that the nub around which all de Beauvoir's fiction turns, melding her political, metaphysical, and aesthetic concerns, is the paradox of death, the problem that "life contains two main truths that we must face simultaneously, and between which there is no choice—the joy of being, the horror of being no more." Almost all her novels are in some sense a "stratagem against death." Her first novel, *She Came to Stay*, ends with a murder, commited a moment before the collective debauch in death of World War II. Her second novel, *The Blood of Others*, set during the French Resistance, "attempted to show death laying siege in vain to the fullness of life." Her third novel, *Tous les hommes sont mortels* (*All Men Are Mortal*, 1946), was envisaged as a kind of "protracted wandering around the central theme of death," and much the same can be said of her nonfictional requiem to her mother, *Une mort très douce* (*A Very Easy Death*, 1964), and her exploration of old age, *La vieillesse* (*Old Age.*)

Many of of her novels open from an aboriginal darkness: the deathbed of a woman, a concierge's dead baby, a theater full of blackness. All her writing is in some sense a refusal of this void, a defiance in the face of all the evidence of the black electric socket, the metro rail, Louise's dead baby, Zaza's yellow face. Paradoxically, her writing springs in turn from this void; in defiance of the void it finds its meaning, an ambiguity she pursued tenaciously in her existentialism. Death exemplified in this way, more than anything else, the metaphysical ambiguity to which de Beauvoir was disposed.

This metaphysical ambiguity, that "all absences are contradicted by the immutable plenitude of the world," is one of the main themes of *All Men Are Mortal.* Fosca, a fifteenth-century Italian prince, bound by an elixir to immortality and condemned to witness to infinity the farcical repetition of wars, crises, and revolutions across the centuries, discovers that death gives life its savor and its import; without it there would be no stubborn "projects" to surpass it, no will to transcendence, and hence no human value. This is also one of the chief arguments in *Pyrrhus et Cinéas,* her first existentialist tract, written in 1943. Death serves as a kind of metaphysical syntactic structure, a dark invisibility on which depends the living tenses of past and future: without this differentiation time would be an unbroken monotone and would in effect cease to exist. It is in this sense that she asserts: "Our death is inside us, but not like the stone in the fruit, like the meaning of our life . . ." (*Force of Circumstance*).

De Beauvoir was in many respects breathing the tragic sigh of agnosticism of her generation. Having toppled God from the altar of the Absolute, death now designated a void that had all the "splendor of the plenitude of grace." Death was not simply an absence; it was a negative manifestation of God. This was almost necessarily so, considering the epoch, for the historical death of God was still too fresh for it to be felt in any other way. Her fascination with death was in part a historical response to the climate of anguish in a disenchanted world. War had exposed the visceral nakedness and organic vulnerability of the human body. Death, like sexuality, was a reminder of the body's animality, proof against all the immortal urges and lucid ambitions of the mind. A "secret and appalling organic disorder," death had the power to flagrantly flout the ideal of rational individual autonomy that de Beauvoir clung to so tenaciously.

Elaine Marks has, therefore, pointed correctly to a recurrent, almost ritualistic moment in de Beauvoir's fiction: a *divertissement,* an abrupt turning away from the evidence of death into a sunlit garden. The significant image is the old jacket, which occurs first in the unpublished *recit* of the childhood of Françoise Miquel, again in *Memoirs,* and again in *She Came to Stay.* In each variation a child stands alone in her mother's room, hemmed in by furniture that is suddenly felt to have a threatening opacity: "thick and heavy and secret; under the bookcase and under the marble console there lurked an ominous shadow" (*She Came to Stay*). The child's anxious gaze lights on an old jacket flung over a chair, enclosed about an enigmatic stillness. Emblematic of the ancient, black root of the chestnut tree in Sartre's *Nausea* (1938), the jacket remains stubbornly itself and utterly strange. Imprisoned in this mute indifference, the jacket neither emits nor admits any consoling word, rebutting thereby the ancient wisdom that the world is the word made flesh, and, by condemning the child to a radical silence, yields dire intimations of her own extinction. Turning in fright, the child dashes downstairs and out into a sunlit garden.

But the flight into the garden, as Elaine Marks notes, is not a "significant evasion." De Beauvoir brilliantly argued in *Faut-il brûler Sade?* (*Must We Burn Sade?,* 1953) that death, like sexuality, is not a biological matter. It is a social fact. If death exudes in some sense the vertiginous quality of nothingness, it is more importantly for de Beauvoir a material presence. In her novels and in her nonfiction, death's force is felt as a material and a social force. It is felt tangibly in the body: it is an odor; it is fluid and viscous; it is the blackish stuff vomited up by Uncle Gaston; it is Hélène's red blood on cotton wool. It is an organic fate, "the utter rottenness hidden in the womb of all human destiny," but more than anything else this organic secretion that leaks into the world smelling of the void insinuates itself into human lives in a social form and a social shape.

In *The Blood of Others,* written during the war and hailed as the first Resistance novel, the odor of death is indistinguishable from the odor of social guilt. For Jean Blomart, son of a wealthy industrialist, the smell of guilt seeps up through the floorboards from the dark printing workshops below, sousing the whole house, the blue velvet upholstery, the shining copper, the summer flowers. At the age of eight, like de Beauvoir, he had learned of the death of their servant Louise's baby and had inherited at once the "original curse" of the guilt of being consolable, of surviving another's death, the "sin of being another being." Shunning his class future, Blomart enters a factory and joins the Communist party. Events entrap him in responsibility for the deaths of a friend and of a lover, yet he decides in the end that no one can escape being tainted by social injustice and that the only moral recourse is to act— the same morganatic gift of responsibility bequeathed to de Beauvoir by the war.

In the same way that Michel Foucault challenged the traditional view of sexuality as a spontaneous upwelling within the body, replacing it with the idea of sexuality as *produced* by society, a creation of unstable social institutions and discourses that give it historical shape within practices of confinement, exclusion, and domination, so does de Beauvoir unfold within her fiction the idea that death is not an anonymous scandal, but rather a social and institutional force that polices garrets, workshops, and hospitals, an instrument for managing poverty, social difference, and political power. This is not to deny that death and sexuality are bodily matters, but rather to insist that they are never experienced in naked organic form. They are always social scripts, carved on the body in different ways in different historical times.

Encounters with death in de Beauvoir's novels are therefore always encounters with social reality, and death is made meaningful in collective action, revolt, and resistance— hence the sustained importance in her work of the *fête* as a collective, celebratory defiance. Death in itself is not a scandal. Only when humans deny other humans the right to exist does it become a social outrage. Clarice, in de

Beauvoir's only play, *Les bouches inutiles* (*Useless Mouths*, 1945), vows to kill herself rather than be returned to slavery: "They have not allowed me to live. But they will not steal my death from me."

De Beauvoir's prolonged combat with death finds its double in the theme that recurs in every plot line she sketched out: the "mirage of the other." The phantasmagoric other has haunted philosophy ever since the seventeenth century, when, as Hegel pointed out, Western thought began the long attempt to reinterpret history in terms of the individual subject. In Western philosophy the Cartesian Cogito became a kind of *Kaspar Hauser*, found standing alone in the marketplace, without origin or social history, heir without parents to the reshaping of history. But at the same time as the individual stepped into history as a cultural idea, the other stepped out with it, an unbidden Frankenstein's monster that would shadow the luminous progress of the individual self well into the twentieth century.

As a philosopher trained in the French academy, de Beauvoir was heiress to the powerful legacy of Cartesian dualism. In addition, at much the same time that she discovered Hegel, the problem of the other presented itself to her in personal terms, in the figure of a former student of hers, Olga Kosakiewicz. Chafing with ennui in the provinces, de Beauvoir and Sartre had drawn Olga into their magic circle, both seduced by the iridescent glamour the much younger woman cast over their lives. Capricious, moody, generous, in constant revolt against every social arrangement, Olga thumbed her nose at convention and propriety and became for them the passionate incarnation of the cult of youth and rebellion. She served for them as "Rimbaud, Antigone, every *enfant terrible* that ever lived, a dark angel judging us from her diamond-bright heaven." Passionately attached to both de Beauvoir and Sartre, Olga turned their magic circle into an intolerable triangle, and de Beauvoir, "led [in] a terrible dance by this quietly infernal machine we had set in motion," discovered for

herself the "curse of the other." She readily interpreted her dilemma within the ideology of the other that she had inherited. "The curse of the other" entered *She Came to Stay* as its founding theme.

In 1936 de Beauvoir was appointed, as was Sartre, to a *lycée*—he to Lyons, she to Paris. There, in the autumn before the war, she began *She Came to Stay*. Though she claims she discovered Hegel when she was well into the novel, it opens with the Hegelian epigraph "Each consciousness seeks the death of the other." For Hegel consciousness emerges only in opposition to another self. The self comes to consciousness only when it sees itself reflected in the eyes of another self-consciousness. The paradox of consciousness is that this alien being is immediately experienced as being outside the self, unknowable and malign. The primal relation between self and other is thus one of inescapable hostility and estrangement. As each self sees the alien other standing before it, it struggles to manifest the sovereignty of its own will by the subjection of the other. So the tragic paradox of consciousness is that it is founded on a life-and-death struggle between two beings, each trying to escape the sorrowful state of self-estrangement by the subjugation of the other, the very being on whom its own consciousness depends.

She Came to Stay opens at night with Françoise, a writer, cupped in the rosy light of her theater office. Enfolding this luminous center is the darkened theater, inhuman and black. As Françoise steps out into the office, objects spring to life, materializing before the conjuring glance of her eye: "when she was not there, the smell of dust, the half-light, the forlorn solitude, all this did not exist for anyone; it did not exist at all." This scene captures in miniature the grandiose illusion of individual autonomy—Françoise's fantasy of being her own cause and her own end, and philosophy's long dream that the rational, individual mind might illuminate at a glance the entire world. When Xaviere Pages intrudes into Françoise's long-standing relationship with her lover, Pierre, this crystal illusion shivers into pieces. Passionate, elusive, and unfathomable, Xaviere occasions for Françoise the shattering and unacceptable discovery of the other, the opacity of another being spellbound in the solitude of its own self. Xaviere becomes a "living question mark," an intolerable affront to Françoise's fierce will to autonomy: "Other people could not only steal the world from her, but also invade her personality and bewitch it." Expelled from her sovereign position at the center of the world, Françoise's answer to the ethical problem of coexistence is to defend herself against the invasion of the other in the most violently decisive way. At the end of the novel she turns on the gas in Xaviere's room, murdering her while she sleeps. Released at the same time from her bondage to Pierre, Françoise becomes the triumphant possessor of her own autonomy: "It was her own will which was being fulfilled. Now nothing separated her from herself. At last she had chosen. She had chosen herself."

Through Françoise, de Beauvoir was exploring the virtually demonic urge to devour the world that had bewitched her from her childhood, the will to imperialism of the human consciousness that she explores in social terms in *The Second Sex*. With the murder of Xaviere, de Beauvoir unfolds, though at this stage uncritically, the murderous and fatal logic of radical individualism. The barbaric simplicity of the metaphysics of individual freedom, as de Beauvoir later attests, reveals as its dark underbelly a vision of primordial conflict.

With the outbreak of war in 1939, de Beauvoir's life was invaded by a much more brutal and tragic intruder: "Suddenly History burst over me, and I dissolved into fragments. I woke to find myself scattered over the four corners of the globe." She made the radical discovery of solidarity and dependence on others. If until then her thought had been "riddled with bourgeois idealism and aestheticism," the spring of 1939 "marked a watershed. . . . I renounced my individualistic, anti-humanist way of life. I

learned the value of solidarity. . . . I now came to know that in the very marrow of my being I was bound up with my contemporaries."

Sartre had been mobilized in 1939 and taken prisoner of war in Lorraine in 1940. With Sartre snatched away from her, her life in turmoil, she learned for the first time what it was to live "under the domination of events." She now embarked on what she called "the moral period of my literary career." Her immediate postwar writings were thus more than anything a response to one inescapable lesson of the war: "the ghastly uncertainty of our moral state." Nevertheless, she could not jettison her individualism overnight; first she had to pass through existentialism, which can in many respects be seen as a last-ditch attempt to save the individual in a historical context.

Existentialism is a philosophy of crisis. Violently born into the political cradle of the French Resistance, it rapidly became, in Mark Poster's phrase, the "continental sensation" of the postwar 1940's and 1950's. Although de Beauvoir and Sartre originally protested the use of Gabriel Marcel's label to describe their work, existentialism was fully inaugurated in 1943 with the publication of Sartre's *L'Être et le néant* (*Being and Nothingness*). This huge, often impenetrably difficult work was at first reluctantly received but came to enjoy a phenomenal success, traveling rapidly from the corridors of philosophy into every nook and cranny of the cafés and nightclubs of Saint-Germain-des-Prés, where a mélange of discontented and iconoclastic artists and *poets maudits* flirted with fashionable versions of nausea, futility, and disenchantment.

The austerity and discipline of existential atheism, its combatant refusal of every traditional solace, and its loyalty to freedom and authenticity caught the mood of a bereft world. Fascism had triumphed and stalled, France had felt the German boot on its soil, and western civilization had been ransacked by its own fascist offspring and was in disarray. French culture cast about for a faith that could help it make sense of its world.

The existentialist climate for consciousness was as a result anxiety and introspection, negativity and frustration. Nevertheless, both de Beauvoir and Sartre always denied, against their critics, that existentialism was a doctrine of despair. They protested that it offered instead a sturdy and vital anxiety which did, indeed, snatch away every traditional strut, but replaced these with the challenge to accept full responsibility for living in a world without appeal. Still, between the years 1945 and 1950 existentialism faced a barrage of Marxist denunciation. Henri Le Febvre condemned it as a "neurosis of interiority," a pathological narcissism that arose from the morbid symptoms of petit-bourgeois anxiety. Existentialism was accused of fostering as a result a morose decadence and an infantile regression to anxious abandonment. The Right, in turn, viewed Sartre as the *poet maudit* of the sewers, peddling a godless credo of nothingness and futility.

Existentialism had, in fact, begun for Sartre during the war as an attempt to reconcile the German idealist tradition—and his freedom of intellectual judgment—with the political lessons of solidarity and commitment he had learned as a prisoner of war. The central tenor of all his writing in the 1950's and 1960's is the attempt to fuse into a livable doctrine a system that would unite the intelligentsia and the working class in an alliance against the old ruling classes of the world. His appointed role was that of mediator: "Coming from the middle-class, we tried to bridge the gap between the intellectual petite-bourgeoisie and the Communist intellectuals." Later he defined the writer's role in much the same way: "The writer is, par excellence, a mediator and his commitment is to mediation."

The original tenet of existentialism is freedom. Over the years de Beauvoir and Sartre both constantly revised their formulations of freedom and eventually abandoned altogether the notion of absolute freedom—in 1977 Sartre confessed the absurdity of such an illusion and wondered how he could ever have entertained it. But freedom nevertheless remains the founding principle of their thought. For both of them God had been emptied from the world. The roar of meaning the Greeks had heard in a torrential sky was a nostalgia for unity without foundation. Humanity no longer lived in a place in which stones and blossoms spoke of God. For de Beauvoir and Sartre the appetite for religious transcendence became an illusion as remote as a lost paradise; and having faded, it exposed the unending task of creating meaning from the ordinary heroics of human effort. In the early formulation of existentialism, humans are flung at birth into the paradox of an inescapable freedom; or as the famous slogan has it, "Man is condemned to be free." For de Beauvoir, as for Sartre, humans are nothing other than what they make of themselves. As Blomart chides Hélène in *The Blood of Others,* "I think that where you go wrong is that you imagine that your reasons for being ought to fall on you, ready-made from heaven, whereas you have to find them."

From this radical assertion of freedom sprang the ethics of authenticity through action: "From the point of view of freedom, all situations could be salvaged if one assumed them as a project" (*Force of Circumstance*). As Blomart says: "We only exist if we act." Any evasion of authenticity—the lucid defiance of things as they are—smells of the sin of *mauvais foi,* of bad faith against the *réalité humaine* of freedom. Hélène's attempt in *The Blood of Others* to use "the infinity of the future as an alibi" to escape from the intolerable present is just such an evasion.

Existentialism thus contains within it a political agenda and an ethics of action. As de Beauvoir puts it in *Force of Circumstance,* the third volume of her autobiography, "Existentialism was a definition of humanity through action; if it condemned one to anxiety it did so only in so far as it obliged one to accept responsibility. The hope it denied one was the idle reliance on anything other than oneself; it was an appeal to the human will." The ethics of authenticity entails in turn the politics of *engagement,* the moral obligation to intervene directly in changing the world. Moreover, the refusal to act politically is itself a political action. Freedom is authentic only if it is *engagé,* pitted against the unacceptable conditions of the present.

The abiding dilemma of existentialism now begins to make itself felt. Sartre defines existentialism as a philosophy according to which "existence precedes and perpetually creates the essence." But this apparently radical rejection of "natural humanity" still cloaks a faith in human essences. In existentialism the absurd adventure of freedom plays itself out more as a state of mind than anything to do with prisons, armies, asylums, or factories. The human being is willy-nilly identified with freedom and the politics of *engagement,* but this is strictly an affair of the individual and of individual will. For Sartre responsibility is "total responsibility in total solitude." As he defines it, "The basic idea of existentialism is that even in the most crushing situations, the most difficult circumstances, man is free. Man is never powerless except when he is persuaded that he is, and the responsibility of man is immense because he becomes what he decides to be." Existentialism was still haunted by its idealistic origins.

The plantation slave, the harem chattel, and the tyrant possess in these terms an identical potential for freedom, and hence the same moral culpability for resignation. Into the bargain, each choice is random and without prior foundation, a hazardous leap into the future. At the same time, the radical severance from history cripples any attempt to explain the tenacity of certain systems of power and authority; why, for example, some groups rather than others control the pathways of freedom. As a result, despite its radical promise and its exhilarating appeal to action, early Sartrean morality remains what Mary Evans calls "the morality of the free market."

De Beauvoir shed the ethic of absolute freedom more rapidly than Sartre; yet Sartre's actual political involvement was much in advance of hers. She admitted much earlier that Sartrean freedom is the abstract fantasy of intellectuals privileged to be able to intervene only sporadically in history. It might be said that the great arc of de Beauvoir's thinking describes a veering away from this Sartrean vision to a much more somber recognition of the dense historical limits to freedom. Out of this recognition evolved a persistently more radical view of social relations, perhaps best articulated in the words of her friend Colette Audry: "Relations with the Other . . . are transcended; they become relations with others."

There is no doubt that de Beauvoir's vision was initially more optimistic than Sartre's. *Pour une morale de l'ambiguité* (*The Ethics of Ambiguity*), first published in 1947 in *Les temps modernes,* a journal that Sartre and de Beauvoir founded, was undertaken to defend existentialism against the charges that it was a "sterile anguish." Sartre had insisted on the "abortive aspect of the human adventure"; as Anne Whitmarsh points out, it is "the positive, optimistic side of his philosophy, well hidden and often ignored, which she attempts to explore" (*Simone de Beauvoir*). For de Beauvoir existentialism defined itself as "a philosophy of ambiguity." The fundamental condition of being is lack-of-being, the frustration of potential: humanity is *manqué* from the start. But each person can "deny the lack as lack and confirm itself as a positive existence."

The example de Beauvoir gives is suggestive, for it captures her old affliction of loneliness, identified here as a metaphysical frustration before the "otherness" of a landscape: "I should like this sky, this quiet water to think themselves within me, that it might be I whom they express in flesh and bone, and I remain at a distance." The stubborn will to appropriate the landscape unfolds the lust for transcendence that sets humans apart, even in opposition, to nature: "I cannot appropriate the snowfield where I slide. It remains foreign, forbidden, but I take delight in this very effort toward an impossible possession. I experience it as a triumph, not as a defeat" (*The Ethics of Ambiguity*).

2719

De Beauvoir sets herself deliberately at odds with Hegel, who sought to reconcile all ambiguity in a final flowering of reason, but here she acquiesces at the same time in a specifically Hegelian tradition of defining the very ground of identity in terms of violence, appropriation, conflict, and possession, a metaphysics of violence she does not fully abandon even in *The Second Sex*. She later repudiated *The Ethics of Ambiguity* as her least satisfying book: "Of all my books, it is the one that irritates me the most today. . . . I was in error when I thought I could define a morality independent of a social context." As she puts it in a different context, at the very moment she was rejecting the language of her class, she was still using their language to do so: "The fact remains that on the whole I went to a great deal of trouble to present inaccurately a problem to which I then offered a solution quite as hollow as the Kantian maxims." "Why," she asks, "did I write *concrete liberty* instead of *bread*?" (*Force of Circumstance*).

In May 1946 de Beauvoir had finished *The Ethics of Ambiguity* and was casting about for a new subject. *The Blood of Others* had been very well received, *All Men Are Mortal* less so. Her play *Les bouches inutiles* strode rather baldly around the existential problem of whether the male council of a besieged town, Vauxcelles, should expel all the "useless mouths"—the women, the elderly, children, and the infirm—to die in the gullies beyond the town. It had a brief and disappointing season, and she never again tried her hand at drama. Now what she wanted above all was to write about herself. But this meant first of all answering the question that had been plaguing her for so long and to which she had turned a stolidly deaf ear: "What has it meant to me to be a woman?"

For nearly forty years de Beauvoir had pretended that being female made no difference: she was an intellectual and that was that. One might say therefore that the first forging of her adult identity was a negative one: a refusal of family, class, and the specifically female fate that had dragged Zaza down. She had fashioned her adult identity in deliberate opposition by becoming an intellectual. As an intellectual she could staunch her acutely feminine sense of exile by taking refuge, not as a woman, but as an individual within the tradition of radical individualism: "Just as previously I had refused to be labelled 'a child,' now I did not think of myself as a 'woman.' I was *me*." For quite a while, it worked: "Since I was twenty-one, I have never been lonely."

Yet through all her novels and writings there courses a very deep problem: that other identity, that other self, which *was* her, whether she liked it or not, and which remained an obscure and nagging obsession until she herself wrote about it, for the simple reason that her culture was not going to do it for her. So that the very choice she had made to be an intellectual ("writing would reconcile everything") inexorably returned her to the riddle of feminine identity from which it had originally promised a refuge.

One of the reasons she balked so long at the obvious was that it meant abandoning the morality of individualism which embued her entire life and bound her to Sartre. It meant accepting the intolerable and tragic fact that in the world's eyes being a woman was not the same as being an individual. Her position in the collective "we" of her relation to Sartre had in any case been presenting her for some time with a dilemma that arose out of the very individualism which buoyed her up. How could she define herself in relation to others within a philosophy that defined the other as the thief and enemy of selfhood and that, moreover, excluded her as a woman from its privileges? Specifically, how could she express fealty to a man without entering into vassalage: "Is there any possible reconciliation between fidelity and freedom? And if so, at what price. . . . To accept a secondary status in life, that of a mere ancillary being, would have been to degrade my own humanity"—a puzzle that is one of the founding themes of *The Mandarins*. For years she had shrugged off the discomfiting fact that "the only reason for the problem presenting itself to me in these terms was because I happened to be a woman. But it was qua individual that I attempted to resolve it. The idea of feminism and the sex war made no sense whatsoever to me."

Now, in May 1946, with an itch to write a personal confession, she followed Sartre's suggestion to explore what difference growing up female had in fact made: "I looked, and it was a revelation: this was a masculine world, my childhood had been nourished by myths forged by men, and I hadn't reacted to them in at all the same way I should have done if I had been a boy." This revolution in personal identity was summed up in one simple sentence: "Wanting to talk about myself, I became aware that to do so I should first have to describe the condition of women in general" (*Force of Circumstance*). The shock of identity was a genuine breakthrough, and with it de Beauvoir's life and thought moved into a new dimension. She was forty years old.

IV

Today I know that the first thing I have to say if I want to describe myself, is that I am a woman.
(*All Said and Done*)

The Second Sex was written out of its time. Published in 1949, it stood on an empty horizon, years after the suffrage movement at the turn of the century, years before the feminism of the 1970's. But it could not conceivably have been written at any other time. Its very untimeliness bears witness, in fact, to its paradoxical origins. Written by a woman who was also an existentialist intellectual, *The Second Sex* is scored through and through with the eddies and crosscurrents that arose from this special position. Quickened into life by the founding tenets of existentialism, the book came to reveal their phantasmic nature and delivered the *coup de grâce* to the alluring vision of individ-

ual autonomy and will that had enchanted de Beauvoir for so long.

The Second Sex is a remarkable document not only because many of its denunciations of the male management of the world remain tragically valid, but also because it records the fascinating record of the demise of an old way of thinking and the turbulent upheaval of a new—the emergence of a radical feminism that was in turn deeply colored, some would say blemished, by the very existentialist climate which had nourished it. In this respect it is what de Beauvoir would call an "epochal" book.

It has become easy to dismiss *The Second Sex* as an "unread classic." There is no doubt that it is a demanding book, an exhaustive thousand-page raid on biology, history, mythology, cosmology, politics, medicine, and literature to answer the single question of women's subjection. In its form it is turbulent, cataclysmic, and self-contradictory, virtually buckling under the stress of its innovatory brilliance and erudition. So it is important to remember how extraordinary a book it was in its time. The first volume, published in *Les temps modernes,* was read politely. The second met a storm of abuse and outrage, which did not abate. De Beauvoir had trampled publicly on very hallowed ground: the cult of the family, the mystique of maternity, the economy of domestic production, the cultural denigration of the female, the plundering and policing of female sexuality, lesbianism, and abortion. Ultimately, the revolution she was calling for would mean the most extensive redistribution of property and privilege in the history of the world.

The enabling idea of *The Second Sex* is existentialist freedom. For de Beauvoir, as for Sartre, there is no human nature, since there is no God to see it. Since there is no human nature, there is no fountain of the "eternal feminine," no feminine essence, no female fate. Women's subjection has nothing to do with the moon's drag or the flow of the tides. In the now famous terms that open Book II of *The Second Sex,* "One is not born, but rather becomes a woman." If everywhere women are subdued, beset, and distressed, the blame lies at the door of culture, which can be broken down. For de Beauvoir, dismantling the cities of custom erected by men to barricade their privilege will be an incendiary, revolutionary development. Moreover, this liberation "must be collective, and it requires first of all that the economic evolution of women's development first be accomplished."

At the same time feminists themselves have been dismayed by some of the arguments in *The Second Sex*. De Beauvoir was deeply indebted to existentialism, which nevertheless dragged in its train certain consequences that cast their ambiguous influence over the book. In *Being and Nothingness,* Sartre defines the origin of consciousness as the consequence of being seen by another: "On principle, the Other is he who looks at me." The glance of the other becomes the fundamental category of human consciousness and is, therefore, also the foundation of human relations. For Sartre the gaze of the other steals the world from me and turns me into an object: the other is the death of my possibilities and my "original sin." Here the gaze is a social idea, since it binds people and shapes identity, but it remains barren of social content, dramatizing social relations as a hostile clashing of equal and fleshless selves. In *The Second Sex* de Beauvoir discovers that the Sartrean idea of conflict as the crucible of consciousness becomes radically unstable when applied to women: by tradition and decree it is the man who gazes, it is the woman who is other. On her "journey into history," de Beauvoir was everywhere returned to a stark revelation: "What peculiarly signals the subjection of woman is that she—a free and autonomous being like all human creatures—nevertheless finds herself living in a world where men compel her to assume the status of the Other."

Rifling through anthropology, history, mythology, and culture, de Beauvoir finds that "Otherness is a fundamental category of human thought." In other words, self and other is a primordial division in all consciousness. It was therefore "not originally attached to the division of the sexes." De Beauvoir retains in this way the idea of consciousness as conflict, but makes the radical discovery that everywhere in history "man put himself forward as the Subject and considered the woman as an object, as the Other" (*Force of Circumstance*). At once the formal Sartrean categories of freedom, the autonomous individual, and the other are flooded with history and capsize, and the existentialism that quickens *The Second Sex* slowly begins to subvert itself.

The fundamental question of *The Second Sex* is historical. What is the origin of woman as the other? Jews, blacks, foreigners, proletarians are also periodically condemned to the ghetto of otherness. Yet de Beauvoir finds a crucial difference: "Proletarians say 'we'; Negroes also. Regarding themselves as subjects, they transform the bourgeois, the whites, into 'others.' But women do not say 'we.' " (Neither in fact does de Beauvoir; women in *The Second Sex* are "they.") For de Beauvoir, women are alone among the oppressed in that we have never risen up to dispute men's thrall; there is something in the condition of otherness that seduces us, and we become complicit in our own enchainment. This position has been fiercely disputed, and we will return to it shortly, but for the moment it is enough to say that de Beauvoir begins to answer the question of the origin of women's submission by importing into *The Second Sex* the existentialist distinction between immanence and transcendence.

For de Beauvoir, all humans, women and men, harbor within themselves a primitive conflict between immanence and transcendence. Immanence is a condition of blind submission to existence, torpid, submerged, and organic. Transcendence, on the other hand, expresses the insatiable will to "imperialism of the human consciousness, seeking always to exercise its sovereignty in objective fashion." Transcendence leaps up out of immanence into the realm of aggression, revolt, art, culture, and the risking of life: "Every time transcendence falls back into immanence, stagnation, there is a degradation of existence into the *en-soi*—the brutish life of subjection to given conditions."

As de Beauvoir sees it, there are powerful inducements to surrender to immanence. The ethical urge to liberty is challenging and fearful; alongside this there is a deep-seated temptation to "forgo liberty and become a thing," to acquiesce in the ruinous inertia of immanence. The anxiety of liberty is so tormenting and fundamental that "immediately after weaning, when the infant is separated from the whole, it is compelled to lay hold upon its alienated existence in mirrors and the gaze of its parents" to escape the heaviness of its own selfhood. Women, in particular, have been tempted to enshrine themselves in immanence, beguiled by the promise of security. This is their "original treason." Woman, for de Beauvoir, is "often well pleased with her role as the Other."

Certainly feminists have been most alarmed by those parts in *The Second Sex* where de Beauvoir treats the female body. At certain moments in the text the female body appears to serve as the incarnation of immanence itself: "Woman is doomed to the continuation of the species and the care of the home—that is to say, to immanence." The pregnant female is "victim of the species," which gnaws at her vitals. Her maternal fate is to be "prey to a stubborn and foreign life that each month constructs and tears down a cradle within her body . . . aborted in the crimson flow." Pregnant, she is "tenanted by another, who battens upon her substance."

Sexually, woman exists for man as inwardness, enclosure, a resistance to be broken through; in penetrating her the male bursts forth into transcendence and manifests the power of life. Her sexuality, on the other hand, conveys the essence of a mysterious, threatening passivity: female sexuality is "the soft throbbing of a mollusc," mucous, humid, and secretive. De Beauvoir consistently reaches for an array of what might be seen as perverse, neurotic metaphors that identify female eroticism as an organic degeneration to primitive life forms: "Woman lies in wait like the carnivorous plant, the bog in which insects and children are swallowed up." This metaphoric consistency reaches beyond *The Second Sex* into her fiction. In *The Blood of Others* Hélène abandons herself voluptuously in a sensual delirium that takes on all the appearance of an evolutionary metamorphosis to a primordial organic state: enveloped in sticky vapors, her flesh turns to plant, then to "a humid and spongy moss . . . forever enclosed in that viscid darkness," then to "an obscure and flabby jellyfish lying on a bed of magic sea-anemones."

It is not surprising that feminists have reacted with dismay to this depiction of female sexuality as submerged in a viscid, erotic night. It has, however, been pointed out that de Beauvoir inherited the nightmarish metaphors of "slimes and holes" from none other than Sartre, who devoted a portion of *Being and Nothingness* to an analysis of the "slimy": "The slimy is docile. . . . Slime is the revenge of the In-itself. A sickly-sweet, feminine revenge." The slimy reveals the threat of the "envenomed possession" of the male by the female. So does the "hole," which serves for Sartre as a fundamental, existential quality expressive of the "obscenity of the feminine, . . . that of everything which gapes open." For Sartre the tendency to fill, to plug holes, is a fundamental tendency of the human psyche: "The experience of the hole envelops the ontological presentiment of sexual experience in general; it is with his flesh that the child stops up the hole." It is important to note here, as Michèle Le Doeuff does, that this fundamental "human" tendency is suddenly revealed to be male: "The female child will no doubt have to trade in her . . . fundamental human tendency," which is to fill, in order to be filled. The subject is suddenly and forever male; the female is banished beyond the frontiers of subjectivity.

Sartre needed the metaphors of knowledge as penetration, of the female as a slimy, gaping immanence, in order to give closure to his system. The Sartrean transcendental self needs the sticky, threatening female to guarantee (male) identity through conflict and conquest. In *The Second Sex* de Beauvoir unfolds this timeless scenario as an epochal point of view, a cultural attitude so fashioned as to perpetuate the intolerable condition of women. There in fact runs alongside the troubling nightmare of the female as organic regression another quite different vision, often overlooked or ignored, a lyrical panegyric to the silky beauty and magnificence of the female body.

It is therefore important at this stage to read de Beauvoir's text very carefully. For accompanying, and in opposition to, her account of immanence and transcendence, runs a far more radical explanation of women's subjection. One of the reasons for the widely contradictory interpretations of *The Second Sex* is the intricacies of its tone. It is deeply ironic, an often satirical, dramatic tissue of many voices. De Beauvoir has, as a consequence, been hauled over the coals for pronouncements that, if read carefully in context, are experiments in ventriloquism, the ironic voicing of a view which she rapidly proceeds to demolish.

Her notions of immanence and transcendence appear to signal a fall back into "human nature," as does her account of the female body helpless in the iron grip of the species. There is little doubt that de Beauvoir's sense of "the primitive misery of being a body" was in part a relic of the Catholic denigration of the flesh, compounded by her fear that her own flesh would eventually plunge her into extinction. The body threatened in every way the lucid rationality she so treasured. As she saw it, women in orgasm, for example, literally "lost their minds." Yet while she insists on biological differences between men and women, she states clearly: "I deny that they establish for her a fixed and inevitable destiny. They are insufficient for setting up a hierarchy of the sexes; they fail to explain why woman is the Other; they do not condemn her to remain in this subordinate role forever. . . . I categorically reject the notion of psychophysiological parallelism."

Indeed, *The Second Sex* appears to describe a sporadic zigzag course: affirmation of a primordial conflict between transcendence and immanence as the origin of all action, and a categorical insistence on the primacy of the "situation." This is one of the reasons why the book is so variously interpreted. In fact, for her it is neither one nor the other, which is why it is so important to read her dialectically, in the full sense of the word. Part of what is happening in the book is the settling of a long debate with Sartre. We learn from her autobiography that for some time she had been disagreeing with him on the nature of freedom: "I maintained that from the angle of freedom as Sartre defined it—that is, an active transcendence of some given context rather than mere stoic resignation—not every situation was equally valid: what sort of transcendence could a woman shut up in a harem achieve?" (*The Prime of Life*). In the end, she says, she made a "token submission" to Sartre's point of view, even though she remained sure: "Basically I was right." Why this token submission? To defend her position would have meant abandoning the entire intellectual basis of all their work, "the plane of the individual, and therefore idealistic, morality on which we set ourselves." *The Second Sex* amounts to a tremendous, contorted, incendiary effort to wrest from this precious heritage of the individual an alternative, fully social history of the female condition.

What is the "situation" of women? It is not biology. Muscular force cannot be the basis for domination, since violence itself is a social category. Human privilege rests on anatomical privilege only by virtue of the total social situation. It is not psychology. De Beauvoir respects the fertile insights of psychoanalysis but rejects its portrayal of humans as the playthings of subterranean drives. Psychoanalysis robs humans of the responsibility for choice, and, far more damagingly, it fails to explain why woman is the other: "The phallus assumes the value it does because it symbolizes a sovereignty realized in other domains." Yet psychoanalysis is bankrupt when it comes to explaining the social sovereignty of the male.

Finally, it is not economy that ensures men their thrall over women. Despite the fact that *The Second Sex* owes so much to Marxism, de Beauvoir remained skeptical of its easy promises to women. For Friedrich Engels the arrival of private property ushered in the "world-historical defeat of the female sex." Maternal right yielded to patriarchy as property was handed down from father to son and no longer from mother to clan. Women became subsumed in property, passing from father to husband. Yet although de Beauvoir is deeply sympathetic and indebted to Engels, what she found missing was, firstly, an account of how the institution of private property came about, secondly, how this entailed the enslavement of women, and, thirdly, where the *interest* lay in the passing of inheritance from father to son, rather than from father to daughter, or to the clan. In the last analysis de Beauvoir faults Engels for his neglect of the original imperialism of the human will: "If the human consciousness had not included the original category of the Other and an original aspiration to dominate the Other, the invention of the bronze tool could not have caused the oppression of women."

There is, ultimately, only one reason why woman remains enchained: "Woman does not assert her demands as a subject because she lacks the concrete means." These concrete means have been stolen from her and are scrupulously denied her during her passage from infancy, to adolescence, to womanhood. It is to woman's "situation," the key word of *The Second Sex,* that de Beauvoir returns again and again: "It is said that woman is sensual, she wallows in immanence; but she has first been shut up in it." This, then, is the project of the book: "We shall study woman in an existentialist perspective with due regard to her total situation."

Since there is no founding, aboriginal cause of women's abjection, de Beauvoir employs her expansive intelligence to expose the "forest of props" that men have erected to barricade their privileges. As Le Doeuff puts it, "Daily life is all the more narrowly policed because the subjection of women has at each moment to be reinvented." The cultural invention of woman's lot begins at infancy, which is embattled by the capricious magic of the adult gaze. The arduous and dangerous accession to female adolescence is shaped by a host of damaging conventions: our crimped education, our enshrinement in the family, the theft of our sexuality, our economic servitude. Everything conspires against the young girl, but, for de Beauvoir, our vassalage is ultimately secured by two major institutions: marriage and maternity.

Marriage inspires nothing but de Beauvoir's unrestrained animosity. Following Claude Lévi-Strauss, she views matrimony as an institution whereby women become a fleshly coinage exchanged from man to man: "Woman, as slave or vassal, is integrated within families dominated by fathers and brothers, and she has always been given in marriage by certain males to other males." Marriage is an organized plundering of women's labor and sexuality. Women perform two-thirds of the world's work, yet own only one percent of the world's property. This situation is perpetuated by restricting a woman's aspirations to a career that reduces her to virtually total financial dependency and all her ambitions to the Sisyphian torture of housework.

Even granting, as de Beauvoir does, the different historical shapes that marriage has taken, much of her criticism remains valid. But her bleak portrayal of motherhood has drawn particularly hostile fire. For de Beauvoir the mother is "confined in a limbo of immanence and contingence"; doomed to repetition and futility, "she is occupied without ever *doing* anything." Moreover, for de Beauvoir, woman in the early history of the world was "nourishing, never creative. In no domain whatever did she create." Her picture of women as victims of their own seething, organic fecundity collapses the rich and historically diverse sphere of women's activities into the single "natural function" of maternity.

In fact, women were for the most part the gatherers and horticulturists in early societies and were thus in all likelihood responsible for the major cultural and technological advances in horticulture, medicine and healing, pottery, weaving, and so on. By way of dealing with the early history of the world de Beauvoir echoes Lévi-Strauss in claiming that "this has always been a man's world." But a rich body of knowledge has now been made available by anthropology and history that testifies to the paramount political and cultural authority women held in the myriad egalitarian, or matrilineal-matrilocal societies that have been documented (Eleanor Leacock, *Myths of Male Dominance*). Moreover, de Beauvoir's notion that women have never risen up to resist men's thrall is refuted by much historical evidence to the contrary. Throughout history, women have revolted individually or in groups, sporadically or for sustained periods, successfully or futilely, in different ways in different periods, but yielding overall a long and intricate history of stubborn refusal to genuflect before their fate.

It is hard to escape the fact that de Beauvoir's denunciation of maternity, if perfectly legitimate as a personal though privileged choice, is unrealistic as a general exhortation and connives ultimately with the male denigration of domestic life that produces precisely the crippling dependence of women she was combating. Her nausea of the flesh can, however, also be seen as a fierce protest against the socially conspired denial of female reproductive rights in an era with no legal abortion and no legal contraceptives. As she says: "There are many aspects of feminine behavior that should be interpreted as forms of protest."

What matters, therefore, is not to judge de Beauvoir from an absolute point of view, but rather to understand her in her time. The current renaissance in the industrial West of freely chosen motherhood is in fact a privileged heritage of the fight for abortion rights that de Beauvoir herself ignited, and remains, sadly, the privilege of a small number of the world's women. In her time de Beauvoir's unveiling of the glamorous cult of the family, the hypocrisy of middle-class monogamy and its historical alliance with prostitution, the grueling monotony of domestic labor and the economic servitude of the housewife, her assault on marriage as a "surviving relic of dead ways of life," and her call for full control by women over their bodies—all this was extraordinarily radical, and still is, to which the fury of public response is sufficient testimony.

De Beauvoir maintained that she was never hostile to motherhood as such, only to the suffocating cultural myths in which it has been swaddled and the social circumstances that make it a special burden to women. She also said that if she were to write *The Second Sex* today, she would root the oppression of women not in a primitive and Manichaean struggle between consciousness, but in a materialist analysis of the economic vicissitudes of scarcity and a struggle over vital resources. Nevertheless, she called *The Second Sex* "possibly the book that has brought me the deepest satisfaction of all that I have written."

One personal outcome of *The Second Sex* for de Beauvoir was that it loosed a flood of autobiographical creativity that did not abate until she ceased writing altogether. In October 1950 she began writing *The Mandarins,* for which she won the Prix Goncourt (1954) and the admiration of France. In her autobiography she has this to say of the novel: "I started a vast novel, the heroine was to live through all my own experiences. . . . I wanted it to contain all of me—myself in relation to life, to death, to my times, to writing, to love, to friendship, to travel." That is to say, in it would finally flower the autobiographical stirrings so long denied and now quickened into bud by *The Second Sex.* Like almost all of her writing after *The Second Sex, The Mandarins* amounts to the creation of a persona, Simone de Beauvoir: the bold assertion of a female figure stubbornly determined to haunt her epoch, in person and in public. For *The Mandarins* unites the three impulses—the autobiographical, the social, and the political—that had always dominated her life but that had been held apart until now: "I also wanted to depict other people, and above all to tell the feverish and disappointing story of what happened after the war" (*Force of Circumstance*).

The Mandarins explores de Beauvoir's own very special, paradoxical milieu: the heady, conflicted world of the French intellectual Left after the war. France has often been called the paradise of the intellectuals, and great weight is traditionally given intellectuals' writings. (Charles de Gaulle, for example, stung by Sartre's fierce public opposition to the attempts to crush the Algerian war of independence, nevertheless declined to arrest him: "One does not arrest Voltaire.") But the aftermath of World War II found the French intelligentsia standing unsteadily in a new and difficult world. The political system had capsized in 1940; the Third Republic, after defeat, occupation, and collaboration, had proved itself bankrupt of all credibility and became a political fatality. The nineteenth-century capitalist order had entered its dog days in the 1930's. The aftermath of war inspired as a result a great flaming of intellectual activity in politics. As de Beauvoir put it, "Politics had become a family affair, and we expected to have a hand in it."

In 1945 de Beauvoir had helped found *Les temps modernes*, which was consistently anticolonialist, independently socialist, and anti-Gaullist, with a largely intellectual rather than populist readership. In 1948 a group of intellectuals, activists, trade unionists, and journalists formed the Rassemblement Democratique Revolution, which "wanted to unite all the socialist forces in Europe behind a definite policy of neutralism." The Communists had consistently spurned Sartre's overtures of friendship, so he joined the RDR, which reflected his own unsteady class position "astride two classes, the bourgeoisie and the

proletariat." Sartre resigned from the RDR in 1949 to protest its listing toward the Right; the RDR soon collapsed and with it hope in a middle way. Sartre left the RDR convinced that the individual was powerless to effect change; the individual can be defended as an end in itself, but an effective political organization cannot be founded on the principle of radical individualism, which by definition cripples all collective action and renders political organizations inoperable. De Beauvoir voiced the bleak sense of disillusionment this occasioned: "History was no longer on my side. There was no place for those who refused to become part of either of the two blocs" (*Force of Circumstance*).

According to de Beauvoir, "Before the war few intellectuals had tried to understand their epoch." One notable and celebrated exception was Julien Benda, whose *La trahison des clercs* (*The Treason of the Intellectuals*, 1928) was a passionate defense of the intellectual vocation as a tradition of detachment. For Benda the intellectual life was a monkish calling, inspired only by "a pure passion of the intelligence, implying no terrestrial love," a position not at all remote from De Beauvoir and Sartre's early vision of themselves as ordained to be celestial "hunters of truth." Benda fulminated against the sight of intellectuals tramping in the marketplace and raising their voices in the political hubbub. But postwar France had moved irrevocably into a world in which cultural clout was passing from the hands of the traditional intellectuals into those of a new breed of media technocrats.

Regis Debray discerns three stages in French intellectual history: the academic (1880–1930), the publishing (1920–1960), and the reign of the media, on the ascendant since 1968. (In *Les belles images* de Beauvoir evokes the atmosphere of commercial peddling, the counterfeit images, the trafficking in banalities, and particularly the deleterious effect on how women are seen and see themselves in the impact of the media on the lives of two women: Laurence, who works in advertising, and her mother, Dominique, a powerful radio figure.) *The Mandarins,* written soon after Sartre resigned from the RDR, stands on the brink of the changing of the guard from the publishing era to that of the media.

De Beauvoir, standing on a "ground littered with smashed illusions," once more decided to turn failure to good purpose by redeeming it in words. Set in Paris between 1944 and 1947, *The Mandarins* follows the fate of an intimate group of Left intellectuals, loosely based on de Beauvoir's friends and associates, Sartre, Maurice Merleau-Ponty, Raymond Aron, Albert Camus, and others. The book opens into the jubilant "orgy of brotherhood" of the Liberation and travels a darkening trajectory from solidarity through a slow splintering into factions, internal dissent, and disillusionment, and then out into a glimmering of optimism.

The novel circles round the central intellectual debate at the time of how to act and write politically in a world that had been cloven into two imperialist blocs: the Soviet Union and the United States. Much of *The Mandarins'* momentum springs from a quarrel between two close friends, Henri Perron, a writer and editor of a paper called *L'Espoir,* and Robert Dubreuillh, a writer and founder of an independent, leftist political group, the SRL. At issue is whether to publish the news of the Soviet labor camps and thereby keep faith with the intellectual vocation of truth-telling, as Henri would, while at the same time knowing full well that doing so would be politically and strategically disastrous, fanning the dangerous fires of the Right and alienating the SRL from the French Left. The personal undertow of the novel is chiefly fed by the love affair between Anne, a psychoanalyst and Debreuillh's wife, and an American, Lewis Brogan. Brogan takes most of his life and veracity from de Beauvoir's own four-year affair with the American writer Nelson Algren, and occasions thereby the full fictional attempt to come to terms with the simultaneously tormenting and exhilarating consequences of her open relationship with Sartre.

The great distinction and power of the book stem from de Beauvoir's fiercely honest efforts to answer the political and aesthetic question that had begun to plague her and that can perhaps best be summed up in Franz Fanon's question to Sartre during the Algerian war: "We [that is, the Algerians, the Third World, the dispossessed] have claims on you. How can you continue to live normally, to write?" Sartre spoke of de Beauvoir's "staggering" reluctance to become fully embroiled in the "sordid manoeuvres of politics." She herself openly admitted that despite her lifelong hatred of her class and of the Right (which deepened to loathing as France waged brutal and futile wars in Indochina, Algeria, and at home), despite her "furious solidarity with the poverty of France," and despite her extensive and passionate political involvement, "I am not a woman of action; my reason for living is writing."

Podium politics waged in the glare of publicity was constitutionally abhorrent to de Beauvoir. She was temperamentally impatient with the tedium and bureaucratic squabbles of endless rounds of committee meetings, but at the same time, as she was well aware, her choice to avoid them was a privileged one. As Anne Whitmarsh has pointed out, her political activity was characteristically pitched behind the scenes in small, intimate groups. During the Algerian war she became more active, at demonstrations, speaking, and writing articles, campaigning in particular on behalf of Djamila Boupacha, an Algerian woman tortured by the French.

In 1971 the Mouvement de liberation des femmes (MLF) was founded, emerging from the clandestine *gauchiste* groups of 1968. The MLF soon appealed to de Beauvoir to intercede against the new and inadequate abortion bill. She joined the MLF soon afterward and was a signatory to the famous Manifeste des 343, a public declaration by 343 women, many of them prominent, that they had undergone abortions. The MLF subsequently split into two factions, the Groupes de quartier (community groups) and Psychoanalyse et politique (Psych et Po), a non-Marxist, largely semiotic and psychoanalytic group that rapidly became a flourishing publishing business. It alienated itself from the other French feminist groups by appropriating the name "mouvement de liberation des femmes" for itself, by its hierarchical structure, and by its divisive legal battles with the other groups. De Beauvoir publicly disassociated herself from Psych et Po, as well as from the privileging of *gynesis,* an essentially feminine form of writing, defined without reference to history.

In June 1972 de Beauvoir and the lawyer Gisèle Halimi founded Choisir to fight for abortion rights at the judicial level. In 1974 de Beauvoir was elected president of the Ligue du droits des femmes, which wages legal battles for women and publishes a monthly journal, *Questions Feministes.* For de Beauvoir the politics of reproduction, rape, and violence to women were the fundamental concerns of feminism. If in *The Second Sex* she left the feminist revolution to follow willy-nilly from the socialist revolution, from the 1960's she lost faith in Marxist promises to take care of the feminist cause: "Now when I speak of feminism I mean the fact of struggling for specifically feminine claims at the same time as carrying on the class war." In other words, Marxism is necessary but not sufficient. In the final analysis she summed herself up as an activist, Marxist feminist, committed to dismantling the present management of society by a vigilant, sustained, and cataclysmic disruption. But she was resolutely skeptical of all existing political parties and vehemently insistent that feminism remain unhierarchical and flexible, generously open to anomaly and indecision, contradiction, unpredictability, and change.

De Beauvoir's life described in this way a great arc from her first allegiance to the solitary vocation of intellectual to a passionate solidarity with the collective, incendiary progress of feminism. But, finally, it was writing that inspired her deepest commitment and melded the two great tendencies in her life: "Writing has remained the great concern of my life." De

Beauvoir remained as wary in her fiction as in her politics of easy solutions. Often scathingly impatient with the didactic strains in her early work, she saw the ultimate task of art as conveying the "perpetual dance" of nuance and ambiguity, anomaly and an often preposterous unpredictability in human lives. Irritated by well-proportioned plots (in fiction as in politics), she wanted above all to imitate "the disorder, the indecision, the contingency of life." The elusive ambiguity of language, "the black sorcery" of words that had bewitched her as a child, spilled out from her fiction to include her ambiguous relation to her public. Often misread, praised when she wanted to give offense, condemned when she thought she would please, she was acutely aware of the uncertain fate of a book once it left her hands. She always saw writing as a collaboration; for this reason, and motivated perhaps by a deep-seated sense of incompletion, she ended her autobiography with an open hand: "This time I shall not write a conclusion to my book. I leave the readers to draw any they may choose" (*All Said and Done*). She died in Paris on 14 April 1986 at the age of seventy-eight.

Selected Bibliography

EDITIONS

L'Invitée. Paris, 1943.
Pyrrhus et Cinéas. Paris, 1944.
Le sang des autres. Paris, 1945.
Les bouches inutiles. Paris, 1945.
Tous les hommes sont mortels. Paris, 1946.
Pour une morale de l'ambiguité. Paris, 1947.
L'Amerique au jour le jour. Paris, 1948.
L'Existentialisme et la sagesse des nations. Paris, 1948.
Le deuxième sexe. Paris, 1949.
Faut-il brûler Sade? Paris, 1953.
Les mandarins. Paris, 1954.
Privilèges. Paris, 1955.
La longue marche. Paris, 1957.
Mémoires d'une jeune fille rangée. Paris, 1958.
La force de l'âge. Paris, 1960.

Brigitte Bardot and the Lolita Syndrome. London, 1960.

La force des choses. Paris, 1963.

Une mort très douce. Paris, 1964.

Les belles images. Paris, 1966.

La femme rompue. Paris, 1967.

La vieillesse. Paris, 1970.

Tout compte fait. Paris, 1972.

Quand prime le spirituel. Paris, 1979.

La cérémonie des adieux. Paris, 1981.

Simone de Beauvoir heute. West Germany, 1983.

TRANSLATIONS

Adieux. Translated by Patrick O'Brian. 1984.

After "The Second Sex": Conversations with Simone de Beauvoir. Interviewed by Alice Schwarzer. Translated by Marianne Howarth. London, 1984.

All Men Are Mortal. Translated by Leonard M. Friedman. Cleveland, 1955.

All Said and Done. Translated by Patrick O'Brian. New York, 1974.

America Day by Day. Translated by Patrick Dudley. London, 1952.

Les belles images. Translated by Patrick O'Brian. New York, 1968.

The Blood of Others. Translated by Yvonne Moyse and Roger Senhouse. New York, 1948.

The Ethics of Ambiguity. Translated by Bernard Frechtman. New York, 1948.

Force of Circumstance. Translated by Richard Howard. London, 1964.

The Long March. Translated by Austryn Wainhouse. New York, 1958.

The Mandarins. Translated by M. Friedman. London, 1960.

Memoirs of a Dutiful Daughter. Translated by James Kirkup. New York, 1959.

Must We Burn Sade? Translated by Annette Michelson. London, 1953.

Old Age. Translated by Patrick O'Brian. London, 1972.

The Prime of Life. Translated by Peter Green. New York, 1962.

The Second Sex. Translated by H. M. Parshley. New York, 1953.

She Came to Stay. Translated by Yvonne Moyse and Roger Senhouse. London, 1966.

A Very Easy Death. Translated by Patrick O'Brian. New York, 1966.

When Things of the Spirit Come First. Translated by Patrick O'Brian. London, 1982.

The Woman Destroyed. Translated by Patrick O'Brian. London, 1968.

BIOGRAPHICAL AND CRITICAL STUDIES

L'Arc 61 (1975). Special issue on Simone de Beauvoir and the Women's Movement.

Armogathe, Daniel. *Le deuxième sexe: Beauvoir.* Paris, 1977.

Benda, Julien. *The Treason of the Intellectuals.* Translated by Richard Aldington. London, 1928.

Bieber, Konrad. *Simone de Beauvoir.* Boston, 1979.

Blair, Deirdre. *Simone de Beauvoir.* New York, 1990.

Brée, Germaine. *Women Writers in France.* New Brunswick, N.J., 1973.

————. "The Fictions of Autobiography." *Nineteenth-Century French Studies* 4 (1976):446.

Brombert, Victor. *The Intellectual Hero.* London, 1960.

Cayron, Claire. *La nature chez Simone de Beauvoir.* Paris, 1973.

Cottrell, Robert D. *Simone de Beauvoir.* New York, 1975.

Collins, Margery, and Pierce Christine. "Holes and Slime: Sexism in Sartre's Psychoanalysis." In *Women and Philosophy,* edited by Carol C. Gould and Marx W. Wartofsky. New York, 1976.

Debray, Regis. *Teachers, Writers, Celebrities.* London, 1981.

Dijkstra, Sandra. "Simone de Beauvoir and Betty Friedan: The Politics of Omission." *Feminist Studies* 6 (2):291–303 (1980).

Epstein, Cynthia Fuchs. "Guineas and Locks." *Dissent* 4:581–586 (1974).

Evans, Mary. *Simone de Beauvoir.* London, 1985.

Felstiner, Mary Lowenthal. "Seeing *The Second Sex* Through the Second Wave." *Feminist Studies* 6 (2):247–275 (1980).

Fuchs, Jo-Ann P. "Female Eroticism in *The Second Sex.*" *Feminist Studies* 6 (2):305–313 (1980).

Gagnebin, Laurent. *Simone de Beauvoir; ou, Le refus de l'indifférence.* Paris, 1968.

Gusdorf, George. "Conditions et limites de l'autobiography." In *Formen der Selbstdarstellung.* Berlin, 1956.

Harth, Erica. "The Creative Alienation of the Writer: Sartre, Camus, and Simone de Beauvoir." *Mosaic* 8:177–186 (1975).

Hourdin, Georges. *Simone de Beauvoir et la liberté.* Paris, 1962.

Jardine, Alice. "Interview with Simone de Beauvoir." *Signs* 5 (2):224–236 (1979).

Jelinek, Estelle C., ed. *Women's Autobiography.* Bloomington, Ind., 1980.

Leacock, Eleanor. *Myths of Male Dominance.* New York, 1981.

Le Doeuff, Michèle. "Simone de Beauvoir and Existentialism." *Feminist Studies* 6, 2:277–289 (1980).

Marks, Elaine. *Simone de Beauvoir: Encounters with Death.* New Brunswick, N.J., 1973.

McCall, Dorothy Kaufmann. "Simone de Beauvoir, *The Second Sex,* and Jean-Paul Sartre." *Signs* 2:209–223 (1979).

Miller, Nancy. "Women's Autobiography in France: For a Dialectics of Identification." In *Woman and Language in Literature and Society,* edited by Sally McConnell-Ginet, Ruth Borker, and Nelly Furman. New York, 1980.

Poster, Mark. *Existential Marxism in Postwar France.* Princeton, 1975.

The Second Sex—Thirty Years Later. A Commemorative Conference on Feminist Theory. New York Institute for the Humanities. New York University, 1979.

Whitmarsh, Anne. *Simone de Beauvoir.* Cambridge, 1981.

ANNE McCLINTOCK

ELIO VITTORINI

(1908–1966)

FOR MORE THAN thirty years, from the early 1930's to 12 February 1966, when he died after a heroic struggle against cancer, the star of Elio Vittorini was among the brightest and most promising in the Italian literary firmament. For years every book he published was an event not to be missed, certain to be followed by spirited discussions about the achievement of his new novel and the particular direction Vittorini was proposing for a truly contemporary work of the creative imagination. To the end, his imaginative, sensitive, poetic mind remained receptive to the changes of techniques he perceived would make his novels not just mirrors of life in our hectic era but also living testimonials to an artist's search for "truth." His good friend and collaborator, Italo Calvino, once identified the elements of such a novel in these words: "Its mythical form is the journey, its stylistic form is the dialogue, its conceptual form is the Utopia."

Life, as Vittorini conceived it, was precisely this: a journey to a better understanding through a dialogue with his readers in the pursuit of a dream of freedom, justice, and peace without which life would be intolerable and even absurd. In this respect Vittorini sided with those writers who, with considerable justification, hold that, to be truly meaningful, everything one does must be an inseparable part of the human and creative self, a reflection of the growth of the total being. In Vittorini's case this was true whether he was working with a construction gang building a bridge in the Veneto region, correcting proofs for a newspaper, writing criticism or fiction, translating, fighting as a member of the underground during World War II, editing the sociopolitical cultural journal *Il Politecnico* (1945–1947), making important or even controversial decisions (such as rejecting Tomasi di Lampedusa's *The Leopard* because of its backward ideological position and its awkwardly archaic structure) as a senior editor of Mondadori Publishing Company, or running for political office.

Vittorini was thus an intellectual on the order of Jean-Paul Sartre: a person highly conscious of his position in society, a privileged citizen who, precisely because of his privileges, has a special responsibility to his craft and to history. The state of the world could, and did, make changes in his strategy necessary; but Vittorini hung on to his fundamental belief in the dignity and worth of the individual, in the ability of people to recognize the fight against evil and work together with others for a better world.

Vittorini was, despite his deceptively simple personality, a complex man and an equally complex artist. Measured by the usual standards, his literary output is hardly impressive: a small number of short stories; eight novels and novellas (one of which was left unfinished and published posthumously); a book recording his personal discovery of the character of an island in so many ways very similar to his native Sicily; an absorbing volume entitled *Diario in pubblico* (Public Diary, 1957), in which he collected the bulk of his articles, reviews, notes, and comments on a broad variety of cultural, political, and literary matters (all previously published in reviews and newspapers); sections of his novels not included in the final versions, and clarifications of his ideas written shortly before publication of the diary. Nonetheless, as Donald Heiney suggested in his study, Vittorini will probably be remembered "primarily [as] the author of one novel. But he is that kind of one-book author, like Rabelais and Cervantes, who adds a new artistic dimension to the history of literature" (*Three Italian Novelists,* p. 151).

As is almost inevitable in the case of great and influential writers, there is in Vittorini's oeuvre an exceptional degree of thematic coherence and a similarly fascinating and equally erratic progression toward "his" book. Whatever Vittorini wrote, and however the reader may wish to label it—allegories, fables, realistic, or symbolic tales, perhaps, written in a highly imaginative and poetic style—should be regarded as parts of an intriguing work in progress cut short by his death. And here is the rub: despite their achievements, none of Vittorini's books except *Il garofano rosso* (*The Red Carnation,* 1948)—the one work he all but completely rejected when it was published in book form—can claim to be what could be called "well-made novels."

Part of Vittorini's difficulties may be traceable to his constant dissatisfaction with practically every book he wrote, which led to furious revisions and the elimination of chapters or episodes. Nowhere can this be seen more clearly than in *Le donne di Messina* (*The Women of Messina,* 1949). Begun in 1946, published in 1947 and 1948 under the title "Lo zio Agrippa passa in treno" (Uncle Agrippa Goes by in a Train) in serial form in the review *La Rassegna d'Italia,* it was revised some fourteen times and published in book form in 1949, and then completely rewritten and published in

1964. Hence the dilemmas of technique and form, the inevitable dissatisfaction with the finished product:

> I have never aspired to write books, I have always sought to write *the* book. . . . I write because I believe there is "one" truth to be said; and if I turn from one thing to another it is not because I have "more" or "something else" to say, but because it seems to me that something constantly changing in the truth requires that the way of expressing it be constantly renewed.
>
> ("Prefazione alla I edizione del 'Garofano rosso,'" in *Le opere narrative,* 1.428–429)

To this end Vittorini dedicated the better part of his creative efforts, but not in a regular, "disciplined" manner. It is, in fact, the astonishing diversity of his activities (translations, editorial work, creative writing, and so forth) that led one of his critics to underscore the fact that Vittorini's way of reasoning is like a small jungle: to confirm, to consolidate an idea that has just struck him, Vittorini loses himself in other arguments, at first parallel and similar, then increasingly more disparate, and finally opposed to one another. As though he were answering his critics, Vittorini confessed, in a "Note" to *Erica e i suoi fratelli:*

> I envy those writers who have the capacity to remain interested in their own work while pestilences and war are raging in the world. . . . A big public event can unfortunately distract me and cause a change of interests in my own work just as, no more no less, can a personal happy event or a misfortune. Thus the outburst of the Spanish Civil War, in July of 1936, made me suddenly indifferent to the developments of the story [*Erica*] on which I had been working for six months in a row.
>
> (*Le opere narrative,* 1.566)

Like traditional novelists, such as Alberto Moravia or Vasco Pratolini, Vittorini drew the subjects for his books from reality; unlike them, however, he was less interested in telling a "good story" than in recapturing deep and universal feelings about life. In his books everyday events are magically transformed into a timeless, "mythical" reality, far more real and effective than reality itself, stripped of its banalities, but where even commonplaces become poetry. It is unquestionably true that, compared with his contemporaries, Vittorini's range, in terms of both situations and themes, is considerably more limited and much more special. The main problem with which he struggled during much of his creative years was to find a suitable language to objectify his vision of the world, which meant to translate his ideology into poetry.

In all his books after *Conversazione in Sicilia* (*In Sicily*, 1941)—which was a turning point in his development as an artist—Vittorini presents a world that has a fragile, though vital, connection with the "real" world we know but is far more deeply connected with the world of our dreams, hopes, and aspirations. Justice, freedom, communion, peace—human and political concepts—are what his stories are all about. To accomplish his objective, Vittorini's books transport the reader into a no-man's-land where people feel intensely and suffer, to be sure, but don't work or play or make love. It is not for nothing that his finest tales take place in a mythical Sicily (*In Sicily*) or on a train, as in *The Women of Messina* and *La Garibaldina* (1956), or anywhere in postwar Italy (but is it really Italy?), as in *Il Sempione strizza l'occhio al Fréjus* (1947, translated as *The Twilight of the Elephant*), rather than in the realistic cities in which the action of *The Red Carnation* and *Uomini e no* (*Men and Not Men*, 1945) is set.

Vittorini was born in Syracuse, Sicily, on 23 July 1908. His father was a stationmaster for the state railroad and, being a southerner and a blue-collar worker, he wished his son to be a white-collar worker. His four sons traveled daily to a nearby town, where they completed their elementary schooling. Vittorini then enrolled in a technical school to learn accountancy. He did not obtain a diploma, however, realizing at the age of seventeen what he had long suspected: that studies did not suit him, and that it was better to give them up once and for all. Using his father's railroad pass, he traveled frequently, sometimes leaving home for weeks at a time. One day in 1924 he left—for the fourth time in three years—with his mind made up not to return. He went to the "Continent," hoping to begin a new life away from home.

Vittorini settled in Gorizia, a small city in the extreme northeastern part of Italy. The years there proved to be very important for him: his job as a construction worker revealed to him a world wholly different from that of the petite bourgeoisie into which he had been born. Most of the characters who were to people his fiction came from the working class and, more often than not, were the dispossessed, the exploited, the poor. But this discovery might have been less significant had it not gradually been accompanied by an intense and vital discovery of a nucleus of writers (mostly novelists but some poets as well) who were either in the avant-garde of continental European letters or from a world quite different (and in this sense ripe for a true discovery at the human and cultural level) from his own: Italo Svevo, Eugenio Montale, Stendhal, Proust, Mallarmé, Defoe, Kipling, Stevenson, Katherine Mansfield.

It is important to stress here that, much like Moravia, Vittorini was an autodidact; and though this process of educating oneself is not without its share of pitfalls, it has the distinct advantage of bypassing the backward bourgeois educational scheme that only rarely encourages a periodic reassessment of the worth of its writers, particularly of the so-called sacred cows. It should come as no surprise, therefore, that the first piece in *Diario in pubblico*, "Maestri cercando" (Looking for Masters), should focus on the necessity to search for something better (more responsive to the contemporary sensibility) than Giosuè Carducci, Giovanni Pascoli, Gabriele d'Annunzio, and Benedetto Croce, then the solid and respected pillars of modern Italian literature and philosophy.

By 1930 Vittorini was ready for the next move—to Florence, in those years the cultural capital of Italy. A few months earlier he had published his first essay in *Solaria,* the Florentine review that, under the editorship of its founder, Alberto Carocci, dedicated its best efforts to translating and commenting on the finest narrative and poetry being produced on both sides of the Atlantic. *Solaria* opened its doors to Vittorini and won him over completely: "I became *solariano,*" he wrote in *Diario in pubblico,* "and *solariano* was a word that in the literary circles of those days meant to be anti-Fascist, European, internationalist, anti-traditionalist." For some years he worked as proofreader on the newspaper *La Nazione,* and, with the help of a co-worker, he began learning English, practicing his skill on *Robinson Crusoe.*

In 1931 Vittorini published his first book, *Piccola borghesia* (Petite Bourgoisie), a slim collection of eight short stories. They are exercises of sorts, competent tales in which the author manages to transcribe, in a humorous, slightly ironical style, the monotonous life of middle-class bureaucrats. Shortly afterward Vittorini decided to earn his bread through intellectual activities. In 1933 the first of his translations of three novels by D. H. Lawrence was published by Mondadori, and three years later Vittorini's second book, *Viaggio in Sardegna* (Voyage in Sardinia), a curious work that is not the travelogue it may seem from the title, appeared. The setting is especially central. The best of Vittorini's subsequent fiction is set in places undisturbed by bourgeois civilization, chosen not for their color but for their stark simplicity, the primordial quality that encourages the effort to recover something precious and long lost with a maximum degree of effectiveness and a minimum degree of distraction.

Two books seem to have left an indelible impression upon Vittorini's sensibility: *The Thousand and One Nights,* with its Oriental charm, and Daniel Defoe's *Robinson Crusoe,* a novel that prefigures so much of Vittorini's own work, with flights to semi-deserted places, his desire to regain touch with nature and to begin all over the human discovery of the world, and of the place and meaning of the human race in it. From his first full-length book—*Viaggio in Sardegna*—to his last completed novel—*The Women of Messina*—we witness a voyage of one sort or another, either to an island that is "like a boyhood" (and therefore replete with a sense of magic discovery) or to a place where men and women dislocated by war may begin anew a life of fellowship and trust, as in *The Women of Messina.* It was only in the early 1930's that the importance of his early reading began to make itself manifest.

In the meantime—early in 1932—Vittorini's first novel, *The Red Carnation,* began to take shape. By 1933 the novel was well under way. With half of the book completed, as is customary in many European and Latin American countries, installments of the book began appearing in magazine form in *Solaria.* But Vittorini's handling of certain aspects of the story, and his candid, graphic language, met with serious objections from the censor, who decided that its language and content clearly were contrary to "morals and good customs," and ordered the March/April 1934 issue of the magazine withdrawn from circulation even though it had already reached its subscribers. Quite a similar fate awaited the work when the manuscript was submitted for publication in book form. Although many of the passages to which the censor had originally objected had been rewritten or deleted, and other changes had been made to preserve the novel's integrity, permission to publish was flatly denied.

In 1945, with the war over and the Fascists out of power, Vittorini's publisher saw no reason why the novel could not appear, and appear it did in 1948. In view of the fact that some fifteen years had elapsed between the original writing of the novel and its publication in book form, Vittorini felt obliged to discuss his changed attitude toward his work and its particular position in the context of his literary production. The discussion took the form of a lengthy essay that ranks as a major pronounce-ment on the art of the novel, the author's poet-ics, the special historical circumstances in which *The Red Carnation* was written, and its position in the author's work. As such it is a compelling statement that calls for scrutiny.

But let us first turn our attention to the novel itself. The story it tells is seemingly pedes-trian: Alessio Mainardi is in love with a fellow student, Giovanna, from whom he receives a red carnation. He speaks of his love to his friend Tarquinio, who in turn boasts of an af-fair with a more mature, somewhat mysterious woman, Zobeida, who, if not a prostitute, is "a lady of easy virtue" and is involved in a nar-cotics ring. Tarquinio, who is not exactly a good and generous friend, proceeds to seduce Giovanna, presenting his bloodstained hand-kerchief as evidence of his sexual prowess, while Alessio becomes involved in Zobeida's life. Intermingled with the narrative are several letters by Alessio's friend Tarquinio and sec-tions of the hero's diary. Nothing much hap-pens as the story unfolds. Alessio does well on his written examinations but misses his orals, and thus is not promoted. At that time he learns from Tarquinio of Giovanna's affair with him, and the book comes to an end.

The novel, which belongs to the tradition of middlebrow European fiction, could be dis-missed as trite, were it not for certain aspects that make it a much better and more interesting book than it might appear at first reading. For one thing, the underlying two-headed theme of sexual and idealistic love is linked with the violence of fascism: there is the bloodstained handkerchief boldly shown by Tarquinio as proof of his virility, and the anger shown by Alessio when he cries out to his friend, "I wish you were another Matteotti, and I would make you understand!" His words reflect the temptation to translate sexual frustration into positions on the extreme ends of the political spectrum.

Another interesting aspect of the novel is its hints that the regime has the support, perhaps indirect, of the liberal middle class: Alessio's father is a businessman, formerly a socialist, who, in his son's eyes, has saved himself at the expense of his workers. The air echoes with familiar names, events, and contemporary po-litical movements: Giovanni Matteotti's mur-der, Rosa Luxemburg, fascism and socialism, Lenin, and, ever present in the background, Mussolini. The restlessness of the students and young intellectuals and their "ambivalent" political attitude (as Vittorini rightly defines it) are persuasively dramatized. The theme of politics gradually proves to be, in Vittorini's later fiction, progressively more pervasive, ur-gent, and deeply felt, always connected with a tireless search for a better, less repressive, fairer sociopolitical order. And it is when seen in retrospect, as it were, that *The Red Car-nation*, for all its apparent confusion (or, at the very least, its ambiguity), most decisively marks the transition between its author's first and second (or more mature) periods.

A change in a writer's way of looking at the world and his view of life necessarily calls for a change in style and structure. Such a change, to be sure, did not occur overnight. Certain events were to hasten and encourage it. During the first months of writing *The Red Carnation*, Vittorini took a trip to Milan:

> If I ever write my autobiography, I will explain what a great importance this trip to Milan had for me. I came back enamored of places and names, of the world itself, as I had never been except in my childhood. This state of mind had not come of itself; I had sought it out. Yet it came in an ex-traordinary way, after a period of five or six years during which it seemed to me that only as a child had I had spontaneous relations with the mater-nal things of the earth. It came at a time when I looked only to the past, when I wrote with my eyes to the rear.
>
> ("Prefazione alla I edizione del 'Garofano rosso,'" in *Le opere narrative*, 1.426)

The Red Carnation had cost Vittorini "cold sweats of study." When confronted with the book as it was taking shape, he discovered its "technical mistakes," the incoherence and immaturity of its point of view, and, above all, his inability to identify himself with the characters he had created or with the book's view of the world: "The power of contact, the passion I had recaptured in March '33 had little by little worked its way into every aspect of my environment, and now I could 'feel passion' for political events as well. I felt that the wrong of fascism against others now offended me personally" (*Le opere narrative,* 1.430). Vittorini's changed attitudes toward a world he had more or less accepted lessened his belief in his manner of writing. While engaged in writing his novel, he began to feel uneasy and unhappy with the fundamental vehicle of a writer's expression, the kind of language that was available to the contemporary Italian novelist working within his tradition:

> Such a language constituted a century-old tradition that every novelist, Italian or otherwise, could bring up to date. One could bring to it those variations suggested by his sensibility as a writer . . . but in practice he had to respect its structure and no one could be called a novelist unless he did so. [Such a language] was excellent to gather the explicit facts of a reality, and to connect them with each other explicitly; to show them, explicitly, in their conflicts, but today it is inadequate for a type of representation in which someone wishes to express a total sentiment or a total idea, an idea that might synthesize the hopes and sufferings of men in general, all the more if [they were] secret.
>
> (*Le opere narrative,* 1.431)

This problem obsessed Vittorini and continued during the months following the completion of *The Red Carnation,* right to the next novella, *Erica e i suoi fratelli* (literally Erica and Her Siblings, 1956; published in English in *The Dark and the Light*). He wrote the tale between January and July 1936, interrupting it because of external circumstances ("I envy those writers who have the capacity of remaining interested in their own work while pestilences and wars are ravaging the world"). He

put aside the manuscript and forgot about its existence until 1953, when it was found by his elder son Giusto in a trunk packed with personal papers left with his family for over a decade. One year later it was published in the Roman review *Nuovi Argomenti,* accompanied by a letter from the author addressed to the editors, Moravia and Carocci. In a note appended to the novella, Vittorini once again told why he had been both unwilling and unable to finish the work, even when the manuscript had been retrieved:

> The manner in which I have been accustomed to write from *Conversazione* on, is not exactly the same in which the present story is told. Today I have become used to refer to my characters' feelings and thoughts only through their exterior manifestations. . . . It no longer comes naturally for me to write that such and such character "felt" that, or that "he thought" that. . . . But when I wrote this book it was still natural for me (as it had been in *Piccola borghesia,* or in *Sardegna,* or in *Il garofano rosso*) to say directly what one felt and what one thought. The book is, in fact, replete with "she thought," "she felt," "she used to think."
>
> (*Le opere narrative,* 1.566–567)

Traditional in structure, *Erica* is clearly Vittorini's first work that is not truly autobiographical, the first experience of handling the theme of poverty in a world of cruelty and hypocrisy. The story revolves around the experiences of a fourteen-year-old girl placed in charge of her younger brother and sister so that her mother can join her husband, who is working in a distant locality. Erica shows her maturity and good sense by assuming the role of the mother, and the three manage well as long as they have the pasta, coal, beans, and oil left by their parents. Even when she is under the pressure of repeated offers of help from her neighbors, Erica insists on living her own life. One day, however, when the provisions are exhausted, she realizes that she has reached an impasse. She becomes a prostitute, for it is the only thing she can do without feeling that she is begging others to help her. Erica's decision is readily accepted by her neighbors:

> Indeed just because she was little more than a child, and because they had witnessed the long agony which debouched in this misfortune, they were silent more than ever. . . . In a certain sense, they also felt grateful to Erica for having freed them of their preoccupation about what she should do.
>
> (*The Dark and the Light,* p. 69)

Despite the numerous wounds she suffers—wounds that only time and affection can heal—Erica is proud that she can continue to take care of her little family and face life with courage and serenity.

The novella is left unfinished at the point when the young girl, Vittorini projected, was supposed to enter the world and find a partial solution to her problems. Written in a simple style defined by Sergio Pautasso as almost "a watershed between the [artistic] experience of his youth and his maturity," the novella is particularly notable for the depth with which the author explores the complex feelings and social situations, reducing them to understatements in order to heighten their effect. To be sure, the importance of *Erica* is clearly thematic rather than purely stylistic. And while we are not quite at the threshold of that special richly symbolic language capable of expressing basic, profound truths about life, we begin to sense that both the texture and the substance of the narrative are indeed different from *The Red Carnation.*

The theme and preoccupations of *Erica* may well betray something nineteenth-centuryish (no doubt reminiscent of Dickens, Zola, and the work of many Italian *veristi*), and the language is more lyrical, more delicate, less restrained by realistic considerations. In fact, we might even speak of two tones, that of Erica and that of the objective narrator-observer. Of the two it is the former's that stands out; it is a

language Vittorini always preferred: the language of poetry, childlike in its simplicity, rich in its evocative power, capable of expressing what really matters in a human discourse—feelings, states of mind, in short, the "truth" about ourselves. The kind of book *Erica* turns out to be made this possible; after all, it is a kind of fable (in its original meaning) within which the story of its heroine unfolds.

Erica is raised in a city, in the gloomy years of the depression following "a war," haunted by the fear of being abandoned in the woods (or the jungle of the unknown) by her parents, just as happens in the fairy tales that, for most of her girlhood, constitute the sole source of her knowledge about life. The fairy tale turns out to be prophetic, and for once there will not be any possibility of being saved by Prince Charming. Erica's dread of tomorrow proves to be justified, as she finds herself surrounded by "witches" and "wolves" that threaten her existence. This makes the need for companionship, or camaraderie, more vital to her survival, for she needs understanding, help, and solace. But the world of Erica—our world—is all too frequently selfish, insensitive, manipulative. And when people give the appearance of wanting to help her, it is exploitation they have in mind, and to this Erica will not subject herself. When she turns to prostitution as a means to survive in a cruel world and support her younger brother and sister, what we have is an implicit indictment of the injustice of the social order that breeds such a monstrous situation.

While in Moravia's fiction money is presented as an instrument of power and control, in Vittorini's *Erica* money is what buys the staples that allow us to live as well as to gain the acceptance of the bourgeois world of traders. Unfortunately Erica herself will, in a way, become the victim of the same mentality, finding in "things" the companionship, security, and stability she was unable to find among human beings, including, shockingly enough, those who belong to the working class. It is only natural that Vittorini, perfectly conscious of this condition, should channel his artistic search in a direction that would yield some of the answers to the riddle of human misery and alienation.

In retrospect, and taking into account the position of the book in Vittorini's production, it becomes clear that *Erica* contains the first fruits of a seed planted in *The Red Carnation,* a seed that eventually blossomed into Vittorini's total identification with the aspirations of the masses. The identification was to occur through his lyrical concern for the "doomed human race"—a race divided into "men and not men." At the time Vittorini was writing *Erica,* however, he was still working within the limitations of the modes of expression and structure imposed by his native literary tradition, not particularly known for its daring. Only in scattered sections of the novel do we find the first hints of a style soon to develop into a coherent, personal, poetic means of communication; seldom in *Erica* does an attentive reader sense that it is endowed with a magical quality of myth and fable. By the end of 1936—the year of the Spanish Civil War and of an intensive period of translation—Vittorini was no longer interested in the facts of the day and in a realistic diction and vision. He had reached a spiritual and artistic crisis, out of which he was to produce his truly significant novels.

In Sicily is without doubt Vittorini's most significant book—even though he seemed to prefer *The Twilight of the Elephant*—and most original contribution to the novel as an art form. Better than any of the works written before or after, it recaptures in a cryptic form not only the spirit of the Fascist tyranny in Italy but also the anguish, expectations, and frustrations of modern man, fighting desperately to overcome despair. *In Sicily* is a unique book: born out of hopelessness, it led its author back to hope.

The writing of "his" book was taking place at a time when Vittorini had critically confronted American literature as a translator whose task was not a mere mechanical labor of changing into his native language images, thoughts, and feelings of other writers but a searching for a style that would "repeat" in Italian the stylistic quality of the original text. The exposure to a writer like William Saroyan, for example, proved extremely useful to Vittorini's linguistic search, particularly in terms of the effects possible through the insistent repetition of words, or even entire sentences, at times only slightly changed by the addition of a single word, a technique that Bruce Merry claims assumes "a liturgical, certainly a musical, function in the novel." But it was a fortunate coincidence that Vittorini's encounter with Saroyan, among others, should take place just as his own dissatisfaction with "the way" he had been writing his books, with " 'the way' it was then thought novels should be written," had reached a critical stage.

The intellectual experience that served as a catalyst to Vittorini's rethinking the whole question of the novel was his new, sudden, and complete love of opera, Verdi's *Traviata* first of all, as he recalls in his lengthy statement that serves as the introduction to *The Red Carnation.* What struck him, among other things, was the fact that

musical drama has the power denied to the novel, of expressing through its complexity some splendid general emotion undefinable by nature and independent of the action, the characters, and the emotions portrayed by the characters.

The novel and the opera are alike in that they are both composite things. But, while the opera is in a position to resolve its problems of scenic representation poetically, the novel is not yet in a position to solve poetically all its problems of the novelistic representation of reality. The opera can sustain and convey through music the very mental reactions of its characters. The novel has not, yet, or has no longer, the something to sustain and convey the particular elements of reality that it analyzes and presents. The opera can thus go beyond the realistic level of its events to arrive at the expression of a higher reality. But the novel, at least in the hands of the conventional realistic novelist of today, cannot, without turning into philosophy, transcend its own preoccupation with a reality of a lower order. . . . The opera began in pure music just as the novel began in pure poetry. The opera has taken on, in its formation, a something else that is not music, just as the novel has taken on something that is not poetry. But the opera has remained music, while the novel has not remained essentially poetry. The opera has assimilated and reabsorbed into music, and re-expressed through music, all its original nonmusical elements. The opera has knitted together and the novel has split apart.

(Le opere narrative, 1.434–436)

Could poetry and novel, once a single genre, be joined again into an inseparable whole? Could the novel shed its pretensions of closely imitating reality in order to mirror and reproduce it and, without losing its credibility, be "poetic"? These were the questions facing Vittorini in the mid 1930's as he began writing *In Sicily*. Only in retrospect was it to become clear how these thoughts were to lead him into new, virgin territory and place him in a slim nucleus of experimental novelists.

Vittorini began writing *In Sicily* toward the end of 1937, publishing it in five installments in the Florentine review *Letteratura* between April 1938 and April 1939. In 1941 the Florentine publishing house Parenti brought out a limited edition of 355 copies of the novel, accompanied by a short story that gave the book its title, *Nome e lacrime* (Name and Tears). Later that year, and in 1942, Bompiani of Milan (where Vittorini had moved) published the work with its present title. The press, which had given the novel a warm reception in 1941, now attacked it, having become aware of its subtle anti-establishment stance. The censor could hardly remain insensitive to its implications and references, and consequently ordered it withdrawn from circulation.

For years copies of the work circulated freely among the partisans, becoming symbolic of the intellectuals' opposition to fascism. Read in many of the Nazi-dominated countries, it reminded people of their elementary obligations to each other, of the necessity of working for peace and justice; and it dramatized the great insults perpetrated by people upon each other.

The book makes few concessions to the sort of formal structure we are accustomed to expect from a novel. Indeed, one cannot say much more than that *In Sicily* is a book about a journey undertaken by the narrator-protagonist-author named Silvestro, a thirty-year-old Linotype operator who works in Milan, to his native town of Syracuse, Sicily. When it is read more carefully, however, what may give the impression of being a rather loosely written, even puzzling narrative that starts with the depiction of a "state of mind" has the calculated structure of a great symphonic work, orchestrated around a main theme and complemented by other sub-themes or motifs, such as the "dark mice" (chapter 2), oranges (chapter 4), the "stink" (chapter 6), and so on. Marilyn Schneider has persuasively described the musical structure of the novel in terms of the "density and organic interdependence of a four-part Baroque fugue: from its tiny word patterns to its parade of diverse characters, to its all-encompassing image of the journey, each part thrusts backwards and forwards, weaving a matrix of themes, variations, crescendos and diminuendos, movement and rest that are at once form and content" ("Circularity as Mode and Meaning in *Conversazione in Sicilia,*" p. 93).

Part 1, which serves as a prologue that sets the mood and states the reason for the action that is about to unfold, begins with the description of Silvestro's state of mind: "haunted by abstract furies," paralyzed by what Sergio Pautasso called "an existential anguish," and his sudden decision to deliver a birthday card to his mother in Sicily after having heard from his father that he has left home. During the long train trip Silvestro meets a number of eccentric characters (notably Mustache and No Mustache, quite obviously police spies, and the Great Lombard, who speaks of "higher duties" mankind must accept). Part 2 begins with the protagonist's arrival in Syracuse and his meeting with his mother, Concezione, in what is a symbolic return to the womb, and extends through their Proustian conversation about the past and more particularly about Silvestro's father and grandfather, whose qualities and flaws are delightfully confused to the point where it is seldom clear about which of the two they are speaking. Part 3 follows Silvestro, who has decided to accompany his mother on her daily round of giving injections (she supports herself through this activity), an experience that sharpens his consciousness of the "offended world."

Part 4, the central and most moving section of the book, describes Silvestro's encounter with a number of characters (Calogero, Porfirio, Ezechiele, and Colombo), all of them from the working class, who discuss with him the ways in which the "offended world" can and must be saved from further suffering by those who are conscious of "other duties" and are ready to wash the woes of mankind "with live water." There is much drinking during their discussions, and in Part 5 Silvestro, drunk but still in possession of his faculties, stumbles into a cemetery, where the ghost of his brother Liborio, who (unknown to the family) has lost his life on the battlefield, appears and speaks to him. When Silvestro tells his mother about his experience, she dismisses it by pointing out that he was drunk. One more day will pass before the news of Liborio's death, preannounced by the crows flying "unscathed through the ash high up in the sky . . . cawing, laughing," reaches the family. In a very brief epilogue Silvestro's conversation in Sicily, which lasted three days and three nights, comes to an end. As he takes leave of his mother, he sees her washing the feet of a crying man, his father, to whom he does not speak.

These events, sparse and seemingly disconnected, allow the narrator-protagonist Silvestro to give vent to the "abstract furies" obsessing him at the beginning of his journey.

The trip to his native land proves to be a salutary spiritual and human experience: the people he meets (first on the train, then in his *paese,* the landscape he so deeply loves despite its rockiness and harshness, which remind us of Montale's *Ossi di seppia*), the thoughts that come upon him, conjure up a vision of anguish—anguish that is trepidation and sorrow for mankind that for centuries has been abused, vilified, and exploited by a few cruel men.

The voyage that began on a note of despair and hopelessness ends with at least a hint that things will—nay, *must*—change if only people, perpetrators and victims of their mistakes, can learn from history and chart a new route that will bring *salute* (well-being) to mankind. Silvestro's journey, in short, becomes a denial of the apathy, lethargy, and indifference from which he suffered, and signals a new resolution to become engaged by recognizing the ills and injustices of the past, and by calling for new bonds with the repressed poor—of Sicily and everywhere.

Both linguistically and structurally *In Sicily* marks a dramatic break with the tradition of the novel in Italy as it had been written during the previous hundred years. The linguistic fabric of the book, for example, is woven of words chosen for their simplicity and evocative power: through frequent repetitions a melodic, almost mesmerizing effect is created, almost as though we were reading poetry rather than prose. We forget time, accept a continuity based on tone, and no longer look for a strict sequence of events, willingly accepting the symbolic dimension of the characters who appear, one by one, almost magically out of nowhere and everywhere. We accept them readily because they seem to be so very "real," even though we are told very little about them. Even Silvestro is barely sketched out for us: we know that he is thirty years old, that he is a Linotype operator working in Milan, that he is married (or is the woman his "girl"?), and that he is going home, ostensibly at the request of his father, to bring greetings to his mother, whom he has not seen for several years. What in the hands of another writer might have well been a regional-realistic story is turned by Vittorini's artistry into a haunting allegory of a man's, and a nation's, suffering and of the need to rekindle human hope in freedom and justice.

There are several points that demand to be clarified. The first is that *In Sicily* was no mere accident, no product of fortuitous circumstances. On the contrary, it was the result of a spiritual-intellectual and political crisis that had begun several years earlier. Along with several intellectuals and writers—such as Alberto Moravia, Cesare Pavese, and Vasco Pratolini—Vittorini had come to understand the moral bankruptcy of a government that had gained power thanks to revolutionary promises it could not keep without severely damaging the interests of the middle class, that together with the church had helped and sanctified Mussolini's ascendancy to ultimate control over the destiny of the nation.

As Vittorini's ideological consciousness increased, so did his awareness that the "one truth" he aspired to express could no longer, for practical and artistic reasons, be told by using conventional structures. This eliminated the possibility of a realistic treatment, which would never receive the approval of the censor's office. Thus, the "woes of the outraged world," a theme that recurs throughout the book, together with the allusions to certain key political and historical events of the time (notably the Abyssinian war and the Spanish Civil War), are somewhat clouded by Vittorini, who "had to express himself without actually saying it." Hence the choice of a highly symbolic, and at times hermetic, form. Abstraction and realism, however, are subtly fused and balanced. And, while there is at least a semblance of action, *In Sicily* resembles less a traditional novel than a "romance" as described by Richard Chase in *The American Novel and Its Tradition* (New York, 1978):

By contrast [with the novel] the romance, following distantly the medieval example, feels free to render reality in less volume and detail. . . . The romance can flourish without providing much intricacy of relation. The characters, probably rather two-dimensional types, will not be complexly related to each other or to society or to the past. Human beings will on the whole be shown in ideal relation—that is, they will share emotions only after they have become abstract or symbolic. . . . Character itself becomes, then, somewhat abstract and ideal. . . . The plot we may expect to be highly colored. Astonishing events may occur, and these are likely to have a symbolic or ideological, rather than a realistic, plausibility. Being less committed to the immediate rendition of reality than the novel, the romance will more freely veer toward the mythic, allegorical, and symbolistic forms.

(p. 13)

The story of Silvestro's coming to grips with the world takes the shape of a voyage or, better still, a Dantesque pilgrimage to Syracuse. Like Dante's *Divine Comedy* the book begins when its narrator-hero has reached the bottom of despair; as with Dante's pilgrim, Silvestro's understanding of what is wrong with the world will be revealed, or illuminated, by his "guides" and the people with whom he comes in contact during his three-day visit. At the end of his haunting experience, having successfully connected with other human beings, he derives the strength, understanding, and hope that enable him to go home to Milan, to his family, his friends, and his job, and face life anew. More important, this is accomplished in a way which implies that the salvation of the individual can, and will, lead the way to the redemption of a whole society that has at last recognized, and is willing to combat, the inequities of a repressive political and economic system.

The opening chapter sets the stage and mood for the novel in its portrayal of what R. W. B. Lewis felicitously calls "the loss of reality as a result of disturbances on a lower or historical level," another way of saying alienation. It is an exceptionally effective piece of narrative that deserves to be quoted in full:

ELIO VITTORINI

That winter I was haunted by abstract furies. I won't try and describe them, because they're not what I intend to write about. But I must mention that they were abstract furies—not heroic or even live; some sort of furies concerning the doomed human race. They had obsessed me for a long time, and I was despondent. I saw the screaming newspaper placards, and I hung my head. I would see my friends and pass an hour or two with them in silence and dejection. My wife or my girl would be expecting me, but, downcast, I would meet them without exchanging a word. Meanwhile it rained and rained as the days and months went by. My shoes were tattered and soggy with rain. There was nothing but the rain, the slaughters on the newspaper placards, water in my dilapidated shoes and my taciturn friends. My life was like a blank dream, a quiet hopelessness.

That was the terrible part: the quietude of my helplessness; to believe mankind to be doomed, and yet to feel no fever to save it, but instead to nourish a desire to succumb with it.

I was shaken by abstract furies, but not in my blood; I was calm, unmoved by desires. I did not care whether my girl was expecting me, whether or not I met her, glanced over the leaves of a dictionary, went out and saw my friend, or stayed at home. I was calm, as if I had not lived a day, nor known what it meant to be happy; as if I had nothing to say, to affirm or deny, nothing to hazard, nothing to listen to, devoid of all urge; and as if in all the years of my life I had never eaten bread, drunk wine or coffee, never been to bed with a woman, never had children, never came to blows with anyone; as if I had not thought all such things possible; as if I had never been a man, never alive, never a baby spending my infancy in Sicily, among the prickly pears, the sulfur mines and the mountains.

But the abstract furies stirred violently within me, and I bowed my head, pondering mankind's doom; and all the while it rained and I did not exchange a word with my friends, and the rain seeped through my shoes.

(*A Vittorini Omnibus,* pp. 3–4)

Silvestro's story, of course, does not remain on the abstract level; it becomes realistic and, toward the end, even surrealistic. It has both

movement (the long train ride to Sicily, the nursing rounds the protagonist makes with his mother) and stillness (as in the brief scene at the cemetery in the last pages of the book). There is the visual confrontation with poverty and despair (beginning with the sight of the men traveling to Sicily, one of whom offers an orange to his wife and, when she refuses it, eats the orange himself, "as though he were swallowing curses"), and the articulation, first by the Great Lombard and then by Ezekiel, of the devastating effect social and economic injustice has had on mankind. The Great Lombard speaks these words:

> I believe that man is ripe for something else. . . . Not only for not stealing, not killing, and so on, and for being a good citizen. . . . I believe, the want of other duties, other things to accomplish. Things to accomplish for the sake of our conscience in a new sense.
>
> . . .
>
> Ah, I think it is precisely this. . . . We feel no satisfaction any longer in performing our duty, our duties. . . . Performing them is a matter of indifference, and we feel no better for having performed them. And the reason is this: those duties are too old, too old and they have become too easy. They don't count any longer for the conscience.
>
> (pp. 21, 22)

Silvestro's faith in humanity, his confidence in man, who will ultimately begin to redeem himself of the shame of his past misdeeds, is balanced, at the end of the book by the activism of the knife grinder Calogero, who is looking everywhere for anything to grind: blades, knives, swords. "Haven't you a cannon to grind?" he asks Silvestro. "Knives? Scissors? D'you think that knives and scissors still exist in the world? . . . Sometimes I think that it will be enough for everyone to have their teeth and nails ground. I'd grind them into viper fangs and leopard claws" (pp. 91, 92).

If the Great Lombard is the moral conscience of the book, Calogero is the militant proponent of armed struggle. Ezekiel, the prophet-like personage who works in a shop located at a very high point in the village, speaks to Silvestro (who by now has become more involved in the story itself) first through Calogero, who has led him there:

Tell him that I spend my day like an ancient hermit with these papers, writing the history of the insulted world. Tell him that I suffer but I go on writing; that I wrote about all the outrages one by one, and about the outrageous faces that laugh at the outrages they have inflicted and are going to inflict.

(pp. 98–99)

With all its simplicity and directness it is a beautiful statement, and it is foreshadowed by a passage describing Silvestro's perception of just what makes one man more of a man than others:

But perhaps every man is not a man; and the entire human race is not human. . . . One man laughs and another cries; both are human, the one who laughs has also been ill, is ill; yet he laughs *because* the other cries. He is a man who persecutes and massacres. . . . Not every man, then, is a man. One who persecutes and another is persecuted. Kill a man, and he will be something more than a man. Similarly, a man who is sick or starving is more than a man; and more human is the human race of the starving.

(p. 73)

If there is a problem with *In Sicily,* it is that, whether because of the particular political situation in which the book was written or because of Vittorini's ambition to endow his story with universal application, its characters at times tend to be a little too abstract and obscure, particularly in their pronouncements. They do not always translate their noble ideals of justice, fairness, and compassion into dramatic action. Silvestro's mother, Concezione, is an exception: she naturally embodies her goodness, and her understanding of the raw elements of life in her town—poverty and exploitation—is effectively understated. The fact that she earns her livelihood by giving injections to the ill in their homes is never allowed to disturb her kinship with those who need her help. She is a wonderful mixture of pride and humility, of seriousness and humor. Her love of life and her candid view of sex are the sources of the strength that enables her to lead her son back to life. Her example is a fundamental factor in the changes Silvestro undergoes in the few precious days in his native town. In a sense Concezione represents commitment and involvement, and as such she becomes the precursor, if not the direct prototype, of many of Vittorini's "engaged" characters.

Earlier it was noted how difficult it is to separate Vittorini's private life from his art. For him art and all creative activities are the conscious offspring of his human commitments, at once indivisible and mutually sustaining. "The time that interests me," he asserted in the course of an interview, "is the one in which I am living." His growing opposition to fascism and to all forms of repression and tyranny, coupled with his utter contempt for bourgeois values, made inevitable his decision to participate actively in the struggle of his nation against Nazism. In 1943 he joined the Italian Resistance, and out of his experience he wrote *Men and Not Men,* a title quite likely inspired by John Steinbeck's *Of Mice and Men.*

The novel, written between 1944 and 1945, whenever Vittorini's political activities permitted, was published shortly after the liberation. Its links with *In Sicily,* both thematically and stylistically, are at once evident. Once again the focus is on the sufferings of the exploited and persecuted—with a difference: the characters of *Men and Not Men* are activists. The philosophical musings of *In Sicily* have been replaced by the bullets and hand grenades of the partisans, who know that only through action can they bring change to an intolerable situation.

The 136 short chapters that make up the book recount the events of a few days in the winter of 1944—one of the mildest winters in Milan's history. The mildness of the weather is contrasted with the bloody action that rapidly unfolds.

The story is simple. Enne (N-2), the hero of the book, and a small group of Milanese workers are committed to kill German officers of the occupation troops. Their plot will, as usual, be followed by reprisals. Several Fascists, named to a special tribunal, are given the responsibility of selecting the 110 people (including women and children) who will pay with their lives for the German losses. The members of the underground again plan a raid against the Fascists, but their mission fails, with serious loss of lives, including that of N-2.

The narrative, far from flowing in a traditional fashion, is interrupted several times by passages printed in italics. In them the narrator of the story, who occasionally identifies himself with the "Io" (I) of the book, evokes his childhood years in Sicily in a language that has much of the lyricism and magic of *In Sicily*. The critic Sergio Pautasso notes that such chapters form a block

> that is not only a diversifying element, a technical artifice that characterizes moments of pause and reflection. [It also] presupposes another book, a different search for meaning to be given to one's own life, beyond the evil that offends man, but that is [also] part of man himself and [as such] indivisible from human nature.

As in *In Sicily*, the characters are identified primarily by monograms (as in the case of the protagonist, N-2), by simple names (Selva, Berta), by their status or nationality (the soldier, the German), by physical or moral characteristics (Grey Moustache, Cat-Eyes, Shaved Head, Black Dog), and so on. With the exception of N-2 and Berta, very little, if anything, is revealed about their pasts. Only through their conversations do we get to know them.

Stylistically Vittorini relies more than ever on dialogue (narrative or descriptive passages are very rare) and experiments with the poetic effects possible through the repetition of the same phrase, only slightly changed, in a man-

ner that recalls Gertrude Stein's famous "A rose is a rose is a rose." There is evidence that at least some of the story, particularly its ending, was fashioned after Ernest Hemingway's *For Whom the Bell Tolls*. Examples of Vittorini's technique are found in practically every page: "'He does not have much to do with many companions.' 'Has he much to do with other companions?' 'He has nothing to do with other companions.'"

Unfortunately it is hard to quarrel with the objections of some of Vittorini's most severe critics, Mario Praz among them, that technique is not, in *Men and Not Men*, subservient to poetry. Thus, what could have served, if used with moderation, to increase the ever-mounting tension of the story, becomes something that detracts from the drama of the action and distracts us to the point of annoyance. Indeed, after the first few chapters, the choral effect wears off and becomes another negative element that, together with the facelessness of the novel's nameless characters, contributes to the general weakness of the book.

Vittorini himself was apparently not completely happy with the book (a dissatisfaction he experienced with most of the books he wrote) and retouched it several times as it went through four editions. Thus, the definitive edition (1965) of *Men and Not Men* changes the status of the "I" that in the original (1945) version was associated with the writer of the book, and his relationship with Berta. In the later version, the "I" is no longer superimposed on the figure of the author—a situation that makes for a certain ambiguity when the love between N-2 and Berta is described. After all, the reader suspects from the beginning that N-2 and the author are one and the same person. Such a technical flaw may ultimately be traceable to the vagueness or ambiguity of Vittorini's ideological position.

Throughout the unfolding of the plot, it is difficult for the reader not to admire the general premises of the struggle in which N-2, Selva, and all the other partisans are engaged. ("We work," asserts Selva early in the novel, "in order that men may be happy.") But beyond this humane, reasonable statement there is little that sharply defines the ideological reasons for the struggle against fascism and Nazism. We are legitimately shocked by the spectacle of seeing men being lacerated by vicious dogs set against them by the Nazis, or the ruthlessness with which women and children are regularly shot to death and left in the streets as grim reminders of the Fascists' determination to retaliate most forcefully against the guerrillas. But, with Carlo Salinari, one finds it difficult, at least initially, to accept fascism "as a moral category evil" rather than as a "product of society and of one of its particular ways of organizing itself."

Some of the structural problems of the novel are intricately connected with Vittorini's undeclared ambition to shift the emphasis, firmly embedded in the tradition, from the individual to the collective, from the "I" to the "us," an effort that was to culminate in his last completed novel, *The Women of Messina*. The protagonist, N-2, is delineated in rather general terms, and the reader is led to assume, from his general behavior and from the kind of confidence he inspires among his fellow fighters, that he is just, brave, courageous, and deceptively simple. In this sense, at least, he is a character closest to Vittorini himself, for whom the struggle for peace, liberty, and dignity has to be fought both individually and collectively by all "simple" men everywhere.

Thus, the discourse begun in *In Sicily* concerning "the insults" endured by "the doomed human race," and the depiction of "the sorrows of the outraged human race," are extended in *Men and Not Men*, this time without being couched in ambiguous, symbolic, and "coded" language. It is true, of course, that the clipped, mater-of-fact style of *Men and Not Men* is more consonant not merely with the demands of the story but also with the changing political and historical reality: fascism and Nazism and their sordid designs for a new order are constantly resisted with bombs and sabotage, and, at long last, there is new hope for a radical reshaping of the social order. Much of Vittorini's creative as well as critical work in the last twenty years of his life reflects his vision of what society can accomplish collectively in order to realize its objectives of justice, peace, and well-being.

Il Sempione strizza l'occhio al Fréjus (The Simplon Winks at the Fréjus; translated as *The Twilight of the Elephant*), written in 1946 and published a year later, was composed, to put it in Vittorini's own words, "con piacere" (with pleasure). Much like *In Sicily,* this book seeks to recapture universal problems and feelings rather than to recount a story. There is, of course, a story to be told, but it is made up of small events that do not by themselves hold our attention. *Twilight* is about a family, a very unusual family:

> In our family we are a houseful of people, and the only one who works and earns anything is my brother, Euclid. For a long time I have been out of a job. My mother's new husband was already out of work when she married him and brought him home last autumn. My sister, a store clerk, was fired this summer; so, along with my grandfather, we all depend on the little my brother earns at repairing bicycles for his boss, who is a mechanic.
>
> (*A Vittorini Omnibus*, p. 137)

The central figure of the novella is the grandfather; a mason in his younger days, he used to be unbelievably strong. He had helped to build the Simplon, the Fréjus, and, as the mother claims in what is surely a symbolic assertion, all of the world's imposing monuments: the Duomo in Milan, the Colosseum in Rome, the Great Wall of China, the Pyramids. Now he is old, tired, silent. Beloved and respected by the whole family, he is the cause of great hardship in very difficult times. A voracious eater, he consumes more than three pounds of bread every day—a mere trifle compared with the twenty-two pounds he could eat when he worked! The family is forced, therefore, to purchase bread on the black market (bread is still rationed) and is deprived of all other necessities. Euclid's earnings are barely sufficient to purchase the bread, which, along with some chicory picked in the nearby woods, serves to satiate their continuous hunger.

One day a man with a smutty black face (he is thereafter called Muso-di-Fumo, Smut-Face) walks in. Grateful for the welcome extended by the family, he shares their poor meal. But what was ordinarily a meager repast is transformed into a sumptuous dinner when everyone agrees, without thinking about it, to "make believe" that they are to have chicken, wine, and other delicacies. The money Smut-Face gives the father will purchase some real wine, chestnuts, and even anchovies, and the feast can be repeated all over again, without having to "make believe." The members of the family are provided with the occasion to talk about man's poverty and wretchedness, and they listen to Smut-Face talk of how he wanted to be a sorcerer. Having obtained a fife, he had found a tune. But the tune, he explains, is not yet perfect, and in order to perfect it, he goes every day into the woods to practice. With the perfect tune he will be able to enchant elephants. When he shows them the fife, they notice that a piece of red rag hangs from the end of the instrument.

The music apparently is quite effective, for the grandfather, who has been a silent witness to what has been taking place, begins to mark time to the music with his fingers. After telling the amazed little audience how elephants die (they go to a secluded place, which man never sees, to lie down and die), Smut-Face departs. Early one morning some days later the grandfather, who is called "the elephant," disappears into the forest, presumably to die, although the mother states that the workers will no doubt bring him home.

While the story told by *Men and Not Men* is both original and unique, the reader of Vittorini's work should have little trouble recognizing the connections of this novella with his previous books, particularly *In Sicily*. The language is still simple and repetitive, the action quite modest, and the division into short chap-

ters prevails. The characters are few, usually identified with generic terms or nicknames. Three stand out: the mother, with her constant interventions; Smut-Face, whose smile reveals white teeth in a dark face; and the grandfather—biblical, majestic, and profoundly human—who seems to embody the *più uomo* (more man) quality typifying the exploited, persecuted peasants of *In Sicily*, and is endowed with the moral wisdom of the Great Lombard. Again, the book is in essence a "conversation" about people, their condition, and their fate.

What is changed is the general climate. We are no longer in Fascist Italy, subject to the tyranny of a dictator, but in postwar Italy, with different social and political problems. But what has not changed—indeed, becomes evident through whatever action there is in the book, and through the stance and conversations of the characters—is the humanity of the *povera gente* (poor people), the persuasion, as Piero de Tommaso has noted, "that, differently from the corrupt ruling classes, the people are naturally disposed to entertain noble feeling and thoughts."

In *The Twilight of the Elephant* there is more than a hint that a greater awareness of the issues, of ideologies, and of the various methods of struggle will inevitably help the proletariat to overcome the ruling class. Yet the novella, for all its allegory and suggestiveness, cannot be read as a political tract heralding the coming of communism. There is, of course, some naïveté in the symbol of the fife played by Smut-Face, the red flag hanging from it, and the overt declaration of a future revolution. What I find more significant is the human attitude of the author, who is actually pleading for a new condition that will bring dignity to mankind. Such a condition can only mean the death of the ideologies and social divisions that are out of step with modern times. Thus, Vittorini has great feeling for the grandfather, the old man who incarnates the accomplishments of unorganized, exploited labor. The fact that he is now old, worn out, and silent (he never speaks in the story) means little, for he can, when the opportunity presents itself, respond to the call of history. When Smut-Face plays the fife, the grandfather suddenly comes to life again and ceases being a mere spectator. Never are we allowed to forget that he built "tunnels and buildings, bridges and railroads, aqueducts, dikes, power plants, highways, and, of course, the Duomo, the Colosseum, the Wall of China and the Pyramids!" The trouble with him is that he is heavy, burdensome, and inert. No one is trying to minimize his past accomplishments. But what of the present, and what of the future? Has he, perchance, outlived his usefulness, becoming in the last years of his life an additional burden to his family?

Both *Men and Not Men* and *Twilight* were written in the last months of the war and the years immediately afterward, when Vittorini, through his role in the Resistance and, between 1945 and 1947, through his editorship of the leftist journal *Il Politecnico,* was actively working to change a traditional concept of culture, in its broadest forms, into a classless society under communism. Vittorini's perceptions of the role of the artist were doomed to clash with those of the party's more orthodox leaders, particularly Palmiro Togliatti, with whom Vittorini began a "dialogue" in the form of letters published in *Il Politecnico* and the Communist review *La Rinascita.* Vittorini's liberal views, particularly with regard to the necessity that the artist enjoy a maximum degree of autonomy while creating something that "enriches" politics by its constant search for truth, were rejected by the Communist leadership. By 1947 the dialogue had reached an impasse due to the irreconcilable views of the two sides, and Vittorini turned his attention to writing and other intellectual pursuits. While he remained fairly active in politics (in 1960 he was elected member of the City Council of Milan, a post from which he resigned shortly thereafter), his enthusiasm for communism diminished visibly in the last years of his life.

The political experience of 1943–1945, coupled with his ambition to write an epic of Italy freed from the shackles of the past, ready to begin a radical social transformation, led Vittorini to write what was to be his most ambitious work, *The Women of Messina,* a complex and not altogether successful book that cost him "cold sweats of study." Begun in 1946, it appeared in book form in 1949 in a version that left the author sufficiently dissatisfied to withhold permission to translate it into English, a translation that was eventually made from the second, definitive edition of 1964, itself some seventeen years in the making.

The sprawling tale, the longest Vittorini wrote, is definitely linked with his previous novels, and attempts to take its author's search for "truth" one step further. *In Sicily* represents the discovery of the insults to which the human race has been subjected, and the beginning of a journey that will eventually put its despondent hero, Silvestro, back in touch with reality. *Men and Not Men* shows the spirit of sacrifice necessary for the ultimate freedom of the people, while *The Twilight of the Elephant* dramatizes the dire need to move from economic-political structures that tolerate the exploitation of the working class to the acceptance of an ideology that will open the door to a more just and equitable enjoyment by all people of the labor of the people. *The Women of Messina* proposes to show how, after a period of conflict and destruction, mankind has within its grasp the possibility of beginning anew. The assumption, movingly articulated by the Great Lombard in *In Sicily,* was that man was ripe for something else, for "things to be done for our conscience." *The Twilight of the Elephant* looked forward to the time "when men would really be like elephants, serene like elephants. . . . But they must be free and not belong to somebody else, not from a menagerie. . . . Such a time can never have been. But perhaps it may come. And when it comes, I don't want to be alone" (*A Vittorini Omnibus,* p. 141).

The Women of Messina, with all its flaws, represents the ultimate extension of a world-view first sketched out in *In Sicily.* Starting from ground zero, it is a carefully and poetically worked-out book that shows what the structure of society may be when certain basic premises of goodwill, tolerance, love, and dignity are accepted. This was Vittorini's intention in the 1940's when he began writing his novel. The problem is that in the period from 1952 to 1954, during which Vittorini dedicated himself to revising it, he had changed, and the changes in his political outlook had considerable impact upon the novel and its quality as a work of art.

In *The Picaresque Saint* (New York, 1959), R. W. B. Lewis comments on John Steinbeck's *The Grapes of Wrath,* calling it a "picaresque novel in the modern manner, an episodic long tale of encounters along the way of a harried and difficult journey—the journey of dispossessed Oklahomans toward and into the deceptively promising land of California" (p. 183). It is a definition that applies remarkably well to the spirit and tone of *The Women of Messina,* which tells of the search by a group of "dispossessed" Italians at the end of the war for land on which to settle while they are engaged in the painful task of reuniting their families, separated by the misfortunes of war. The country has been defeated, much of its network of roads and railroads has been seriously damaged—that is tragic enough. Confusion and anarchy reign supreme. Yet, in the midst of so much chaos, there is one heartening note: the desire and willingness to make a new start, to piece together what the war has not destroyed, and to build something more genuinely meaningful because it responds to, and emerges from, the basic human desire for peace and goodwill.

That the novel should open with the description of the breakdown of a truck in which the group is traveling north is no accident, but a metaphor that proves to control the whole work. The truck represents, after all (at least in the context of the story), an advanced means of transportation symbolic of a fairly advanced technological stage of development; but now it has broken down and is incapable of performing the task for which it was built. It must be not only repaired but also completely overhauled, many of its parts taken from other vehicles so it can function again. Vittorini's perceptions as a social being and as a novelist have reached a similar situation. Like a radical concept of how society is to be structured so all can live in peace and well-being, the novel must depart radically from traditional forms if it is to depict a new society while responding to an intellectual need of the observer and the reader.

The structure of the novel, and not just its theme, reflects as closely as possible Vittorini's ideological stance. A description of a collective society, such as he envisaged as the goal to be achieved, must be written in a "collective" manner. In this respect Vittorini's attempt is quite similar to Giovanni Verga's equally ambitious technical attempt (beginning with *I malavoglia*) to compose a truly objective, impersonal novel that would give the illusion of "hav[ing] grown spontaneously, like a fact of nature, without maintaining any point of contact with its author." A "collective novel" must avoid the trappings of what, for want of a better term, we may call the "bourgeois novel," with the individualism of its form and the paternalism of its attitude. This means a kind of "authorless" book in which the collective effort is to be channeled toward the depiction of the making of the "classless" society. Thus, the task and responsibility to tell the story shift from the traditional narrator (whether the protagonist or an anonymous third person) to a number of other devices.

In *The Women of Messina,* Vittorini uses a variety of techniques to present the story: the first, and perhaps the most innovative and original, is a so-called *registro,* a log in which the events of the community are recorded. The second is the voice of what one could call a "commentator" who occasionally offers his observations on the material in the *registro.* Toward the middle of the book (chapters 44–48) a small number of characters intervene directly to recount a slice of their experience. The last is bits and pieces contained in the epilogue, recording the changes that have taken place since the end of the war.

Vittorini's technique is a curious mixture of different elements, and may even recall Alessandro Manzoni's handling of his masterpiece *I promessi sposi* (1842). In that novel Manzoni is at once the transcriber, editor, commentator, researcher, and moralist of a story he claims he has found in a seventeenth-century manuscript. But this technique is modified by Vittorini's desire not to intrude into the telling of the story, and the comments take the form of observations made by the characters themselves, in a way that recalls the strategy used by Vittorini in his diary, in which the notes, essays, and other material published between 1929 and 1956 are frequently followed by the author's reflections prepared especially for the appearance of the material in book form. The result is a multilevel perspective with a choral quality that is in perfect tune with the "communal" society Vittorini visualized as his Utopia.

There are three major parts in *Women:* the story of Uncle Agrippa, a retired worker with the state railroad who travels up and down Italy looking for his daughter Siracusa, missing since the day she left home; the love story of Siracusa and Ventura; and the story of the development of a community bound together by its needs and aspirations. It is important to note that there are substantial differences— stylistic, thematic, and ideological—between the first and second versions of the book, and that their significance must not be underestimated. While in the original version the travels of Uncle Agrippa give the novel its particular rhythm and control its movement, in the second version the emphasis is shifted to the villagers, intent on building a utopian society in miniature where differences between members, whether due to training, profession, private wealth, or lineage, no longer exist. How deeply Vittorini felt about such a society is seen in his efforts to present the various stages

through which it moves, each symbolized by the wheelbarrow, the mule-drawn cart, and finally the motorized vehicle—the broken-down truck patiently restored to working order, thus making the tasks to be performed at once easier and more efficient. But this "progress" has, like anything else, its price: the mechanization of work, while increasing productivity, leads to an alienation of the individual from society that stems from his lack of identification with the things he makes.

Not surprisingly, the premises of Vittorini's ideology greatly minimize the traditional necessity of the "hero" of the tale. Nevertheless, aside from Uncle Agrippa, two other characters manage to emerge as central points of reference: Carlo the Bald, who appears in the opening section of the book, traveling on Uncle Agrippa's train, and Ventura or "Ugly Mug." Both had been Fascists. Now that the war is over and fascism has been toppled from power, Carlo the Bald has shifted his allegiance to the new government and has become a sort of informer–special agent, keeping the government briefed on the activities of the settlers. His basic mission is unchanged: he merely works for one type of government instead of another. Ventura, on the other hand, has truly repented his past misdeeds and atrocities committed during the reign of fascism, and has become totally involved in planning the structure of the new village, earning the trust and respect of his comrades through his actions. Carlo the Bald, perhaps out of his sense of guilt or out of his envy of Ventura, is unable to accept the new situation. He is instrumental in the formation of an action group called the "hunters," charged with the task of tracking down anyone alleged to have committed crimes against the people under fascism, and sets them on Ventura's trail.

In the original version Ventura manages to hide for a while and contemplates the possibility of avoiding the ordeal by escaping. Terrified by the prospect of being captured and incapable of bearing Siracusa's condemnation, he kills her in a stable. Half of the third part of the book consists of the reconstruction of the murder and the events that follow it—the actions of the members of the community—and how Ventura is finally shot by the "hunters." The tale ends when the author realizes that the actions he has just described have taken place in the village almost simultaneously with his writing: "We have arrived in an identical present: the village and myself. . . . And to want to continue writing would mean to continue our story in the guise of a diary."

And so the tale is finished without a "conclusive word" about either the uncle or the village. What of the town, its people, their struggle against the lawful owners of the land, which they have cleared of mines, cultivating it and giving new life to it? What of the freedom of the individual citizen of the community? And what of the possibility of a society capable of leading an orderly life without the supervision and control of a merciless, bureaucratic government or an exploitative capitalistic structure? These questions are left unanswered. Vittorini is too aware that the poet may touch upon and delve into human problems and human possibilities, but the individual alone must try to resolve the conflicts inherent in life; the individual alone has the supreme potential ability to bring about any improvement in his or her social or spiritual life.

In the second version of the novel, Vittorini's extensive rewriting radically changed the denouement of the tale and, in a very distinct way, brought it up to date, so to speak. Since the original writing of the novel, events had drastically changed the nature of Italian and, for that matter, European society. Thus Ventura is not killed by the "hunters," because, in what the reader must see as an allegory of contemporary Italian (and, in a larger sense, European) history, the enemies of yesterday have become part of the fabric of today's society. The "hunters," the valiant fighters of the Resistance during World War II, no longer have dreams different from "ours." Life in the village has been transformed in a way that makes it pretty much indistinguishable from life in any other part of the country: commercial, crass, bitten by the bug of the profit motive of capitalistic society. Gone is the spirit of self-reliance (which reminds us of the successful Chinese policy), and gone, too, is the spirit of adventure and self-sacrifice; gone are the "hunters," who have moved on to more civilized places where they can enjoy the fruits of the "economic miracle," and with them are Red Kerchief and Toma, two of the most enthusiastic settlers of the village:

> Time passes, time has gone by—autumn, winter, March, June, August, and autumn is here again— 1947, 1948, the Cold War, the Marshall Plan, a Christian Democrat government, the Berlin Airlift. . . . Rita Hayworth has come and gone, and so has *The Third Man* with Orson Welles; faster planes than the Dakota fill the skies, Vespas and Lambrettas obstruct the roads; three crops of wheat have been reaped, workers in heavy industries have a new national wage scale, an attempt on the life of Togliatti has been followed by a general strike and the general strike by police repression; a new body of police, the *Celere,* is rough-riding over the sidewalks in jeeps, capital has flowed back from abroad, millionaires have reopened their villas on the lakes, supermillionaires come off their Panama-registered yachts to dine in the night clubs of what used to be fishing villages, young people are dancing the samba instead of the boogiewoogie, and the beaches are crowded with girls in bikinis.
>
> (p. 293)

A few things are still the same, as we see in the epilogue: Uncle Agrippa "is still riding the trains, just as he did in 1946." Carlo is still overseeing the affairs of the village, but the pattern of life there has changed so much that there is little to report to the authorities: even Ventura can no longer be considered dangerous. Although he spends a few hours a day in the fields, he has "turned out to be just the contrary [of a hard nut to crack]—soft, lazy, a sort of Bohemian, without any wish to get away." Today he is known as "Teresa's husband"—Teresa being Siracusa's new name:

> When I go there and ask for him, they seem hardly to know who he is. . . . Nobody sees him every day. . . . He's gone to seed, but he doesn't know how to be a genuine peasant or how to be a nonentity. Because that's what he is, a nonentity wasting his life in a mountain village, with a wife who supports him.
>
> . . . He never thinks of improving the land. Of terracing the hillsides, and growing vines and irrigating them in the dry season, of trying out a new crop and new ways of making it flourish.
>
> Once upon a time, nobody was his equal in all these things. When he was an engineer during the war, and in the early days of the village. As long as the land was worked in common, until August of 1946, he was the guiding spirit, commanding the rest of them like an orchestra director. While now that he has only the one field that belongs to him and his wife, a vision purely of his own of today and tomorrow, he floats like a half-collapsed balloon on a sea of indifference. Just the contrary of what usually happens.
>
> . . .
>
> Of what then is the contrary? I'm angry enough to say what I think—that he *is* the contrary. But the contrary of what? Tell me that, if you can.
>
> (pp. 305–306)

The concluding pages of the novel are full of irony, of an almost bitter yet inevitable realization of the way things have turned out: the hopes and high ideals of brotherhood, peace, and justice of the Resistance have evaporated; the strivings toward equality and a government based on the genuine consensus of the working people—the proletariat and the peasantry—have been dashed. To be sure, much has changed everywhere in the country: the rubble has been cleared away; the network of communications has been restored and improved; railroad stations, schools, churches, and public, as well as private, buildings have been rebuilt. Commerce is thriving. There is peace and many obvious signs of prosperity: the bars are crowded, the consumption of coffee and Coca-Cola (the new yardstick to measure economic well-being) has shot upward. The poverty of the postwar years is now a memory; the affluence of the "economic miracle" of the new times surrounds everyone. Things are good, to be sure. But what of the soul of mankind, what of the yearnings of yesteryear? The epilogue of the book, with its biting irony, is nothing less than Vittorini's commentary on the end of a dream. A balance sheet is unnecessary: the ways in which life has changed yield the answers to our queries:

> The land, as land, has lost its importance. The neon lights and the Motta ice cream don't conceal the reality of the situation. It's funny, isn't it, that there shouldn't be a single example of what you might call the usual and expected thing. Not even the women of Messina, who grow fat and plant grapevines. Not even Teresa, who pulls Ventura along like a wagon. She's not the Siracusa that she used to be; she's a housewife, trying to get a good price for her milk and putting up preserves for the winter.
>
> (pp. 306–307)

La Garibaldina (the last full-length work published in book form) reads much like an extension of, or a concluding note to, *In Sicily* and *The Women of Messina*. Written between December 1949 and May 1950, *La Garibaldina* was originally brought out in installments in the Florentine review *Il Ponte*. It is appropriate and revealing that the novella should have appeared (with two central chapters added) in the same volume with *Erica*, written fourteen years earlier, thus offering a valid yardstick to measure the long road Vittorini had traveled in his poetic quest. It becomes even clearer, too, that the novelist's sense of, and feeling for, reality had increased at the same pace as his interest in depicting contemporary reality in a realistic manner had decreased.

Structurally and stylistically, *La Garibaldina's* affinities with, and differences from, Vittorini's earlier work are evident to a careful reader. To begin, there is hardly a plot, and what there is, is sketchy and unimpressive. The time of the action is the early twentieth century, and much of the story takes place on a train, on which the passengers find themselves on their way not so much to a specific destination but, as in *In Sicily*, toward the past. The novella lacks the complex apparatus of *The Women of Messina*, the intense, extremely personal sensitivity of *In Sicily* (although it preserves, particularly in its baffling ending, its obscure symbolism), and the almost icy objectivity of *Men and Not Men*. There are only two central figures in the novella: a *bersagliere* (a member of the elite corps famous for its daring exploits and its colorful plumed hats) and a woman, vivacious, assertive, articulate. The soldier is a simple young man named Innocenzo, on his way home to Terranova on a brief leave. The woman is the eccentric Baronessa Leonilde (whose destination is also Terranova). Her past exploits (if we are to believe everything she says, she would be about one hundred years old!) include her having been a sort of camp follower during the Risorgimento and having inspired Garibaldi. Whether or not her claims are true, there is no denying that her presence and her authority are extraordinary. Witness the way she dismisses the protestations of the train conductors who attempt to collect from the soldier the difference between the third-class ticket he holds and the first-class coach seat he occupies. But the Baronessa, accompanied by a large dog, Don Carlos, does more than chastise the conductors: she hurls epithets and biting criticism at the government, institutions, and past historical figures while Innocenzo (whom she has named her orderly, and whose name she will change to Fortunato at the end of the story) serves as a semi-silent, increasingly amused listener.

Ultimately *La Garibaldina* is an effective tale less for what it says than for what it succeeds in evoking. Its style is typical of the linguistic agility we have come to expect of Vittorini, and the feeling for situations and sentiments is, as always, profound and amazing.

And one can always rely on the amusing combination of encounters and confrontations as an instrument of aesthetic pleasure. There are many wonderful scenes in the book: the first meeting of the Baronessa with Innocenzo, their meanderings in the town after they have gotten off the train, and the strange finale. What is most instructive, however, is the author's method, used with considerable subtlety, to fuse the real with the unreal, the present with the past, the immediate with the timeless, as in the description of the town and the impact it makes on the unsophisticated soldier:

> The tolling of a bell whose tone fell suddenly, reverberating against the paving stones, reminded them both of the task they had in common but it frightened Don Carlos who ran out of one of the alleys. They looked back at the dark town whose bronze throat had given voice. Was it one o'clock or did the sound mark a quarter after an unpredictable hour?
>
> The town too had something that was undefinable. There were wide-open doors, dark wells of emptiness, wide-open windows, wells of emptiness too: and there were other doors and windows closed as if they had been blacked out for centuries upon centuries in a far distant age, before the flood.
>
> The walls were covered with cracked dust and the northwest wind, blowing full strength, raised a yellowish clay of grit from the façades; even the houses with some sort of attempt at a style appeared shapeless with their outlines frayed, their corners rounded and their cornices nibbled away.
>
> The town might have witnessed the coming of Abraham, the pilgrimage of the Three Kings, Roland's passage on his way to Roncesvalles, and Garibaldi's passing. . . . The soldier and the old woman were somehow reconciled. They stopped and decided to rest.
>
> (*A Vittorini Omnibus*, p. 270)

Things are made to speak for themselves and questions are made to contain the answer to what is being asked. And that answer, in the last analysis, is the truth of the Great Lombard in *In Sicily*: "I believe that man is ripe for something else. . . . Not only for not stealing, not killing, and so on, and for being a good citizen. . . . I believe he's ripe for something else, for new and different duties" (*A Vittorini Omnibus*, p. 21). Hence the insults in *La Garibaldina* heaped upon the train conductors who insist that the poor soldier traveling in the wrong class pay the difference in fare; hence the heroine's magnificent rebellion and condemnation of old and useless rules, and of human folly.

People speak in this extraordinarily imaginative book, frequently censuring the Baronessa's past experiences, which she so candidly discusses—including her love affair with Garibaldi. Houses speak also, as do ghosts. And after we are through reading the tale, and manage to find stillness again (after so much, and such astonishing, *coralità* [choral quality]), we realize that it is not a "novel" we have been reading; it is a cry against despair, or a hymn to man's dignity and hope, and to the vitality, courage, and humor of a race not yet totally doomed and certainly not yet ready to surrender.

Earlier I suggested that the various roles Vittorini played—translator, editor, critic, *homme engagé*—make problematic an assessment based strictly on his creative writing, without taking into account the totality of his activities. Once the "wholeness" of Vittorini's work has been broken, the critical consensus has almost unanimously hailed the "man of culture" while minimizing his worth as a novelist.

A careful reading of Vittorini's fiction is bound to reveal his strength and uniqueness: his unusual mastery of the language, coupled with an extraordinary feeling for its possibilities, can hardly be overstressed. It would be difficult to think of another contemporary Italian novelist, with the exception of, say, Cesare Pavese or Carlo E. Gadda, who can match the originality and hypnotic character of his style. Indeed, in a sense Vittorini might well be remembered for having done for prose what Giuseppe Ungaretti did for poetry: restoring purity, meaning, and dignity to a language debased by artificiality, pompousness, and vulgarity. Better than most of his contemporaries, Vittorini has shown an uncanny ability to handle words, always remaining supremely conscious that ultimately the value of words rests on their capacity to uncover and illuminate "new" or hitherto unexplored facets of the human condition. "A word," he remarked once, "may give to a fact not-new, a new meaning." Commenting on Montale's collection of poetry *Le occasioni,* he noted: "A fact counts only when in some way, it is new for man's consciousness. Only in this circumstance is a fact truly a new fact: it enriches the [human] consciousness, if it adds a new meaning to the long chain of meanings of which such a consciousness is composed."

Words, then, are chosen carefully for their power to evoke and depict, in fable-like books, the loneliness and courage of human beings, their yearnings, their determination to work together to build a world cleansed at long last of the suffering mercilessly inflicted by the human race upon its fellows. In Vittorini's hands words become precious things, elements that allow us to keep in touch with our inner selves and the world. Words translate the artist's dream onto the page and in history: strange words at times, to be sure, highly charged with allusions and symbolic references. When he is successful, as in *In Sicily*, Vittorini's novels take on an extra dimension, and indeed sound like the operas he loved so deeply, to the point of duplicating their patterns in his books. The emotions at the center of his world are strong, timeless, and universal. What makes them unusually revealing is the manner in which they are expressed through a style that Vittorini created patiently and methodically, after experimenting and reflecting about his own work and that of the foreign authors he read and, at times, translated. His stylistic virtuosity is, by itself, an important element in what constitutes Vittorini's special artistry. What matters is that his style should be so persuasively capable of projecting the hopes, and not just the despair, of life in the twentieth century.

Selected Bibliography

EDITIONS

INDIVIDUAL WORKS

SHORT STORIES

Piccola borghesia. Florence, 1931; 2nd ed., Milan, 1953.

Nei Morlacchi. Viaggio in Sardegna. Florence, 1936. 2d ed., *Sardegna come un'infanzia.* Milan, 1952, 1969. *Viaggio* was first published in *L'Italia Letteraria* (25 December 1932) with the title *Quaderno sardo. Nei Morlacchi* was first published in *L'Italia Letteraria* (1 October 1933).

NOVELS

Il garofano rosso. Milan, 1948, 1970. First published in *Solaria* between February–March 1933 and September–December 1934.

Conversazione in Sicilia. Milan, 1942, 1972. First published in book form as *Nome e lacrime.* Florence, 1941. First published in *Letteratura* between April 1938 and April 1939.

Uomini e no. Milan, 1945; definitive ed., 1965.

Il Sempione strizza l'occhio al Fréjus. Milan, 1947, 1969.

Le donne di Messina. Milan, 1949; rev. ed., 1964. First published in *La Rassegna d'Italia* between February 1947 and September 1948.

Erica e i suoi fratelli. La Garibaldina. Milan, 1956.

Le città del mondo. Milan, 1969. A few unpublished pages of the novel are in *Le opere narrative,* vol. 2, pp. 873–884.

NONFICTION

La tragica vicenda di Carlo III (1848–1959). Milan, 1939. Reprinted as *Sangue a Parma.* Milan, 1967. Written with Giansiro Ferrata.

Guttuso. Milan, 1942. Reprinted as *Storia di Renato Guttoso e nota congiunta sulla pittura contemporanea.* Milan, 1960.

Diario in pubblico. Milan, 1957. 2nd ed., updated with writings published between 1961 and 1965, in *Il Menabò di Letteratura,* vol. 10. Milan, 1967. It has the subtitle *La ragione conoscitiva.* Also rev. and enl. ed., Milan, 1970.

"Il Politecnico" . . . : Antologia critica. Edited by Marco Forti and Sergio Pautasso. Milan, 1960.

Le due tensioni: Appunti per una ideologia della letteratura. Edited by Dante Isella. Milan, 1967, 1981.

ANTHOLOGIES

Scrittori nuovi. Edited with Enrico Falqui. Lanciano, 1930.

Americana: Raccolta di narratori dalle origini ai nostri giorni. Edited by Vittorini. 2 vols. Milan, 1941; repr. 1968.

Teatro Spagnolo: Raccolta di drammi e commedie dalle origini ai giorni nostri. Verona, 1941; Milan, 1944.

COLLECTED WORKS

Le opere narrative. Edited by Maria Corti. 2 vols. Milan, 1974. Vol. 1: *Piccola borghesia, Sardegna come un'infanzia, Il garofano rosso, Giochi di ragazzi, Erica e i suoi fratelli, Conversazione in Sicilia, Uomini e no, Il Sempione strizza l'occhio al Fréjus, Il barbiere di Carlo Marx, La Garibaldina.* Vol. 2: *Le donne di Messina, Le città del mondo, Racconti.*

LETTERS

Gli anni del "Politecnico": Lettere, 1945–1951. Edited by Carlo Minola. Turin, 1977.

I libri, la città, il mondo: Lettere 1933–1943. Edited by Carlo Minoia. Turin, 1985.

TRANSLATIONS

Erica. In *The Dark and the Light.* Translated by Frances Keene. New York, 1960.

La Garibaldina. In *The Dark and the Light.* Translated by Frances Keene. New York, 1960. Also in *A Vittorini Omnibus.*

In Sicily. Translated by Wilfrid David. London, 1948; New York, 1949. Also in *A Vittorini Omnibus.*

Men and Not Men. Translated by Sarah Henry. Marlboro, Vt., 1985.

The Red Carnation. Translated by Anthony Bower. New York, 1952, 1961.

The Twilight of the Elephant. Translated by Cinina Brescia. Norwalk, Conn., 1951. Also in *A Vittorini Omnibus.*

A Vittorini Omnibus. New York, 1973. Contains *In Sicily, The Twilight of the Elephant, La Garibaldina.*

The Women of Messina. Translated by Frances Frenaye and Frances Keene. New York, 1973.

BIOGRAPHICAL AND CRITICAL STUDIES

Aymone, Renato. *La manon a cavallo: Un'analisi di Vittorini.* Naples, 1975.

Barberi Squarotti, Giorgio. "Vittorini ed oltre." In *Scrivere la Sicilia: Vittorini ed oltre.* Syracuse, 1985. Pp. 13–25.

Bertacchini, Renato. "Elio Vittorini." In *Narratori italiani contemporanei,* vol. 2. Milan, 1963. Pp. 1507–1526.

Bianconi Bernardi, Franca. "Parola e mito in *Conversazione."* *Lingua e stile* 1:161–190 (1960).

———. "Simboli e immagini nella *Conversazione."* *Lingua e stile* 2:27–46 (1967).

Briosi, Sandro. *Elio Vittorini.* Florence, 1970.

———. *Invito alla lettura di Elio Vittorini.* 2nd ed. Milan, 1973.

Cambon, Glauco. "Elio Vittorini: Between Poverty and Wealth." *Wisconsin Studies in Contemporary Literature* 3:20–24 (Winter 1962).

Campana, John. "Techniche di ripetizione nella *Conversazione* vittoriniana." *Quaderni d'italianistica* 7:209–222 (Fall 1986).

Carducci, Nicola. *Gli intellettuali e l'ideologia americana nell'Italia letteraria degli anni trenta.* Manduria, 1973.

Catalano, Ettore. *La forma della coscienza: L'Ideologia letteraria del primo Vittorini.* Bari, 1977.

Corti, Maria. "Prefazione." In Vittorini's *Le opere narrative,* vol. 1. Milan, 1974.

Crovi, Raffaele. "I Gettoni." *Galleria* 6:1–31 (1956).

Di Grado, Antonio. "L'Isola nella bottiglia: La Sicilia di Vittorini." In *Scrivere la Sicilia: Vittorini ed oltre.* Syracuse, 1985. Pp. 27–33.

Falaschi, Giovanni. "La *Conversazione* anarchica di Vittorini." *Belfagor* 17:373–391 (July 1972).

———. "Vittorini senza lettere." *Belfagor* 41, no. 2:225–230 (31 March 1986).

Fernandez, Dominique. *Le roman italien et la crise de la conscience moderne.* Paris, 1958.

———. *Il mito dell'America negli intellettuali italiani dal 1930 al 1950.* Translated by Alfonso Zaccaria. Caltanisetta and Rome, 1969.

Girardi, Antonio. *Nome e lagrime: Linguaggio e ideologia di Elio Vittorini.* Naples, 1975.

Guizzi, Francesco. "Vittorini da Guernica a Budapest." *Il Mulino* 2:93–128 (February 1959).

Hanne, Michael. "Significant Allusions in Vittorini's 'Conversazione in Sicilia,'" *Modern Language Review* 70:75–83 (1975).

Heiney, Donald. *Three Italian Novelists: Moravia, Pavese, Vittorini.* Ann Arbor, Mich., 1968.

Longobardi, Fulvio. "Vittorini: La vita per la libertà." *Società* 8:709–729 (August 1957).

Merry, Bruce. "Vittorini's Multiple Resources of Style: *Conversazione in Sicilia."* *Mosaic* 5:107–116 (Spring 1972).

Orvieto, Paolo. "Elio Vittorini." In *Dieci poeti e dieci narratori italiani del novecento,* edited by Paolo Orvieto. Rome, 1984. Pp. 337–360.

Panicali, Anna. *Il primo Vittorini.* Milan, 1974.

Pautasso, Sergio. *Elio Vittorini.* Turin, 1967; rev. and enl. ed., 1977.

Potter, Joy H. "Patterns of Meaning in *Conversazione in Sicilia."* *Forum Italicum* 9:60–73 (March 1975).

———. *Elio Vittorini.* Boston, 1979.

Schneider, Marilyn. "Circularity as Mode and Meaning in *Conversazione in Sicilia."* *Modern Language Notes* 90:93–108 (1975).

Toscani, Claudio. *Come leggere "Conversazione in Sicilia" di Elio Vittorini.* Milan, 1975.

Zanobini, Folco. *Elio Vittorini: Introduzione e guida allo studio dell'opera vittoriniana.* Florence, 1974.

SERGIO PACIFICI

CESARE PAVESE

(1908–1950)

AUGUST 27, 1950, could have been a day like any other in late summer: hot, sultry, lazy. Most Italians are on vacation then, or getting ready to return to work at the factories, at the offices, at the stores. What made that day different and tragic, at least for the intellectual community, was the news that earlier that morning Cesare Pavese, age forty-two, essayist, poet, novelist, translator, and editor-in-chief of the prestigious Giulio Einaudi Publishing Company, had been found dead on the bed of Room 43 of the modest Hotel Roma in Turin. Cause of death: an overdose of sleeping pills.

The news was all the more bewildering in view of the popular and critical success Pavese had enjoyed during the months prior to his suicide. In 1948 he had received the Salento Prize for his *Prima che il gallo canti* (Before the Cock Crows, 1948); in 1950 he was awarded the prestigious Strega Prize for *La bella estate* (*The Beautiful Summer*), written in 1940 but brought out in 1949; and his last novel, *La luna e i falò* (*The Moon and the Bonfires,* 1950), had been greeted with lavish praise by the critics and the readers who had begun to appreciate the beauty and significance of his work. It was not clear then, as it was to be a few months later, when his diary, *Il mestiere di vivere* (*The Burning Brand: Diaries 1935–1950,* 1952), appeared, that his death, far from being due to a momentary state of depression, represented the culmination of a long, complex emotional

and intellectual preparation that had begun during his youth for the one act that he had come to value for its capacity to control one's destiny. Ironically, yet understandably, his suicide sparked an intense effort to begin assessing the achievement of his art and his position in Italian letters. Yet even at this date, that question has not been satisfactorily resolved. Much like Anguilla, the memorable protagonist of *The Moon and the Bonfires,* Pavese has proved to be as slippery as an eel, as mysterious as a sphinx, as elusive as some of the mythological figures of what he considered to be his best work, *Dialoghi con Leucò* (*Dialogues with Leucò,* 1947).

Cesare Pavese was born on 9 September 1908 in the small town of Santo Stefano Belbo in the Piedmont region. His father was a clerk in the city court of Turin; his mother, Consolina Mesturini, came from a moderately well-to-do middle-class family. His birth in the Langhe province proved to be significant: from his very first years Cesare developed a deep love for the countryside, and practically everything he wrote bears witness to his attachment to the hills, the farmlands, the places so rich in "primitive," highly symbolic meanings, the welcome alternatives to the anonymity and alienation of modern city living.

In 1914 Pavese's father died of a brain tumor, bringing more grief to a family that had already suffered the deaths of three children born before Cesare. Signora Consolina, from all available evidence, seems to have been a rigid and strict person, incapable of giving her son the warmth and understanding he needed. Quite likely their relationship was a central element in Pavese's own frustrating sexual life, a part of his experience he used again and again in his fiction.

In 1923 Pavese completed his middle school and entered the Liceo Massimo d'Azeglio, where he was fortunate to have Augusto Monti as one of his teachers. Himself a writer, a learned and understanding teacher, and a splendid mentor, Monti was able to challenge his students without losing their trust and respect, instilling in them a deep love of literature that embraced all periods, from the classical to the contemporary. In 1927 Pavese was enrolled at the School of Letters of the University of Turin, from which he graduated in 1930 after writing a dissertation on Walt Whitman. There he made his first important friends: the Slavicist Leone Ginzburg; the philosopher Norberto Bobbio; the future publisher Giulio Einaudi, with whom Pavese was associated until his death; the musicologist Massimo Mila. Even before receiving his degree, Pavese began undertaking what were to become lasting contributions to Italian culture: his translations, at once faithful and felicitous, of such American and English writers as Sinclair Lewis and Sherwood Anderson, followed by Herman Melville, O. Henry, Theodore Dreiser, Walt Whitman, John Dos Passos, James Joyce, Gertrude Stein, and William Faulkner. His activity as translator sustained him financially and left an indelible mark upon his creative work as well.

In 1932, out of strict necessity and not out of conviction, Pavese joined the Fascist party, the membership card being an absolute prerequisite for most jobs, especially teaching. His translations and contributions to literary reviews attracted the attention and respect of several people with connections in the publishing industry. In 1934 Giulio Einaudi bought the magazine *La Cultura* and asked Pavese to assume its directorship, even though the major editorial policy decisions were made by a trusted friend of Einaudi's, Arrigo Cajumi. Meanwhile, with Einaudi, Cajumi, and several other intellectuals, Pavese had joined a political group called Giustizia e Libertà (Justice and Freedom), which was frequently critical of official government policies. Reprisals were not long in coming; on 13 May 1935 Pavese's apartment was searched for evidence that could make a case against him, particularly one of "conspiracy against the regime." The police found several letters written by the well-known political agitator Altiero Spinelli. Together with Carlo Levi (of *Christ Stopped at Eboli* fame) and others, Pavese was accused of associating with, supporting, and sympathizing with leftists, a "crime" that was punishable by a jail sentence. Along with some two hundred people, including the entire staff of *La Cultura*, Pavese was brought to trial, found guilty, and sentenced to three years of political confinement (rather like house arrest) in Brancaleone, a town in Calabria.

The story has a strange and ironic twist: Although guilty by reason of circumstances, Pavese was in fact innocent; the letters found in his apartment were addressed to a young woman named Battistina (Tina) Pizzardo, a member of the Communist party whom he had met several years earlier and with whom he was hopelessly in love. It was Tina for whom Pavese wrote several poems of his collection *Lavorare stanca* (literally, Work Is Tiring, translated as *Hard Labor: Poems*, 1936), identifying her only as "the woman with the hoarse voice," and it was she who changed the course of his life. Paroled after spending less than one third of his sentence in Calabria, Pavese returned to Turin. A friend met him at the railroad station to prepare him and sustain him in one of the worst crises of his life: Tina, the woman he so deeply loved, had become engaged the day before Pavese's return home. Some biographers have expressed doubts about this account. Whatever the case, however, the breakup was a shock from which Pavese never completely recovered, and it was largely responsible for his depicting "women with a vengeance," in the words of his distinguished biographer, Davide Lajolo.

"A woman, unless she is an idiot," Pavese wrote in his diary, "sooner or later meets a piece of human wreckage and tries to rescue him. . . . But a woman, unless she is an idiot, sooner or later finds a sane, healthy man and makes a wreck of him. She always succeeds" (*The Burning Brand,* p. 65 [3 August 1937]). "The only women worth the trouble of marrying," he noted a few weeks later, "are those a man cannot trust enough to marry. But this is the most terrible thing: the art of living consists in not letting our loved ones know the pleasure it gives us to be with them, otherwise they leave us" (ibid. [30 September 1937]).

His intellectual activities gave Pavese renewed hope. The publication in 1936 of his first volume of poetry was followed by his translations of four American novels and a marked increase in his work as private tutor in literature and composition. His fiction—none of which was to appear until 1941—began receiving more and more of his attention. In 1942 he was promoted to the post of editor at Einaudi; one year later he left Turin for Rome on a special assignment whose main objectives were the opening of a new branch of Einaudi and the recruitment of the best new writers with roots in the south.

Called to serve in the Italian army, Pavese was discharged because of asthma, from which he had suffered for many years. In 1943, after the fall of Mussolini and the declaration of the so-called Republic of Salò, with Mussolini again at the helm, Pavese, alarmed by the prospect of the inevitable German occupation of Rome, joined his sister, Maria, in the hamlet of Serralunga near Casale in the province of Monferrato. At the end of the war he returned to Turin and to Einaudi with increased responsibilities. In 1945, perhaps out of guilt for not participating in the underground, he joined the Communist party and wrote several essays highly critical of the United States and its imperialistic-capitalistic policies. Pavese acknowledged the debt Europe owed to America during the trying years between 1930 and 1945, years during which America was the "only gigantic theater where with greater freedom than elsewhere the drama of us all was being acted out." "In brief," he concluded, "I honestly think that American culture has lost its mastery, its innocent and knowing intensity that put it in the vanguard of our intellectual world. Nor can I but remark that the loss coincides with the end, or suspension, of its fight against fascism" ("Ieri e oggi," in *La letteratura americana e altri saggi,* p. 196).

In the years that followed the end of the war, Pavese's prestige and popularity increased rapidly. By 1950 he had a distinguished corpus to his credit: nine short novels (a tenth was coauthored and left incomplete), most of which were completed during the last fifteen years of his life; a large number of short stories; a small number of highly original poems; several critical essays, noteworthy for their sensitivity and depth; a book on myths, *Dialogues with Leucò;* and a diary that remains one of the primary documents for understanding Pavese's private and creative life. His curriculum vitae is both diversified and unusually brilliant. A translator at the age of twenty, a poet at twenty-two, a novelist shortly thereafter, he never allowed himself to stop growing, venturing into new fields of knowledge and creativity.

Pavese was a loner, a man estranged from the world whose very awareness of his condition contributed to the pain he endured. Writing to his friend Tullio Pinelli, he commented:

I am one of the many decayed sons of the nineteenth century. That century was too great in thought, feeling, and action; and by the laws of history, equally great must be the dejection of those who can no longer believe in its ideals and cannot resolutely find new ones. That is the way I am.

(*Lettere,* 1.40)

Natalia Ginzburg, one of his closest friends and most perceptive associates, wrote in her moving tribute, "Ritratto d'un amico" ("Portrait of a Friend"):

> Conversation with him was never easy, even when he seemed happy. . . . Over the years he had built up such a tangled and inexorable system of ideas and principles that he was unable to carry through the simplest project, and the more forbidden and impossible he made the attainment of some simple reality the deeper his desire to master it became, twining itself in ever more complicated tangles like some suffocating species of vegetation.
>
> (*The Little Virtues,* pp. 16–18)

No factual summary of Pavese's life, however detailed, can do justice to his complex personality. Facts generally omit the feelings of a sensitive person and they fail to pinpoint the contradictions, the inexplicable sides of a person's actions and attitudes. In some ways Pavese had qualities in common with the nineteenth-century poet Giacomo Leopardi: sensitive, afflicted by a physical illness, unloved and not understood by his parents and family, Leopardi was, for a variety of reasons, unhappy with his life—and yet, out of his devastatingly deep unhappiness sprang some of the most lovely, tender lyrics ever written.

Much like Leopardi, Pavese remained essentially provincial in terms of his travels: he seldom left his native Piedmont, living in Turin and, for a few months, in Milan and Rome (and then only for business reasons); with the exception of Paris, he was never abroad. Yet what he lacked in practical experience and wide travels was more than balanced by an extraordinary intellect that embraced several disciplines and literatures (Greek, Latin, European, and American). At an age when most young men have little on their minds besides fun and sex, Pavese was producing translations of Lewis and Melville that were destined to become classics sui generis, even though, by his own admission, his knowledge of American slang was far from complete. Aside from his artistic creativity and his editorial work, little else received his attention and his com-

mitment: not politics (his involvement with communism is insignificant, if not downright trivial), not personal relationships, except in rare cases.

Among his contemporaries in Italy, the novelist, critic, and translator Elio Vittorini (1908–1966) must certainly be singled out as the person who, by virtue of his work and interest, was his peer. Aside from the similarity of their political views (both were Fascists for a while, both turned to the left and eventually became card-carrying Communists), they both dedicated themselves to a veritable revolution in the art of writing: in Pavese's case, grafting a local dialect onto the standard literary language; in Vittorini's case, developing a style that was a truly original expression of the themes closest to his sensibility. Both strove to represent less the factual than the rhythmical, or musical, quality of the experience. Both Vittorini and Pavese eventually emerged as masters of the novel as an art form, widely read, admired, and imitated by the younger generation of writers. Like Vittorini, Pavese devoted much of his time and talent, at least at the beginning of his career, to the study, translation, and explanation of American literature. Turning to American letters, however differently motivated, ultimately acquired a practical and a symbolic meaning for both writers, signifying their conscious attempt to free themselves from the shackles of their native tradition and of official culture.

Much has been written, and much more remains to be said, about the American influence on Pavese. From our still limited perspective it is reasonable to suggest that the gravitation toward American letters was motivated by such factors as the award of the Nobel Prize to Sinclair Lewis in 1930 and the fact that the whole field was relatively unexplored. But perhaps what captivated the new writers at once was the freedom with which American writers made contemporary life and its vast social problems the basic substance of their work, and the manner in which they were able to mold literary language, enriching it with slang and making it capable of capturing the reality and color of their characters and situations. "Anderson's style!" Pavese commented enthusiastically in one of his very first critical essays. "Not a crude dialect . . . but a texture of English, entirely constructed of American idioms, a style no longer *dialect* but *language,* reworked in the mind, re-created, *poetry.* In a tale written by Anderson there is always heard an American speaker, the *living man"* ("Sherwood Anderson," in *La letteratura americana e altri saggi,* p. 42).

Pavese's encounter with American literature was unquestionably the single most important intellectual experience of his life: it not only enabled him to achieve a profound understanding of his own culture but it also suggested to him the path to the discovery of his own style and of the fundamental theme of his poetic world, "a contrast between the natural and the civilized, the rejection of the *città* [city] for the *paese* [country]" (Heiney, p. 86).

Suicide (or what his biographer Davide Lajolo called "the absurd vice") haunted Pavese for much of his life, receiving constant attention in his diary from 1935 to 1950. "I am not a man for a biography," Lajolo recalls Pavese asserting in 1946. "The only things I shall leave are a few books, in which there is all or almost all [to be known] about me." Events proved him to be right, for he led an unusually sheltered existence, monotonous in its routine. Like many intellectuals with creative aspirations, he worked hard at several jobs: evening-school teaching, private tutoring, translating for commercial publishers, literary consultantships. Although he yearned for literary glory, he always felt embarrassed by praise and chose to remain a private, simple person. His diary confirms his unpretentiousness and his embarrassment about the thought of money. He lived and worked simply, trying to cope with what he called "the business of living," and writing, which he called "a métier like any other, like selling bottles or working the earth."

In his youth Pavese was somewhat skeptical about his creative ability. As he grew older and more experienced in the demanding craft of literary writing, he acquired a confidence in himself fully justified by his wide knowledge of contemporary letters. Throughout his life he maintained a view of success that was puzzling, if not altogether contradictory. If, on the one hand, he seemed to be modest and almost embarrassed by praise, for much of his youth he really coveted glory and success. One of the last entries in his diary offers this startling self-assessment: "In my work, then, I am king" (*The Burning Brand,* p. 366 [17 August 1950]). But even fame could not fill certain needs and cravings he had. Pavese's longtime personal friend Natalia Ginzburg noted:

> But because he had always expected [fame], it gave him no pleasure . . . , since as soon as he had something he was incapable of loving or enjoying it.
>
> He used to say he knew his art so thoroughly that it was impossible he should discover any further secret in it, and because it could not promise him any more secrets it no longer interested him.
>
> (*The Little Virtues,* p. 18)

To the end of his life, Pavese suffered from having chosen the relative tranquillity of his profession over what he saw as the turbulence, pressure, and responsibility of most other occupations. He considered the process of writing "monotonous," and, comparing it with swimming, he wrote:

> The beauty of swimming, like any other of life's activities, is the monotonous recurrence of a position. To narrate is to feel in the diversity of reality a significant cadence, an unresolved cipher of mystery, the seduction of a truth always about to reveal itself and always fleeting. Monotony is a token of sincerity.
>
> ("Raccontare è monotono," in *La letteratura americana e altri saggi,* p. 338)

That Pavese, for a number of complicated reasons (one of which was his failure with women), suffered from a bad conscience (his lack of commitment to the cause of his country's freedom is part of it) makes a psychological interpretation of his work tempting, to say the least. And in recent years that has been made by a brilliant French Italophile, Dominique Fernandez, in *L'Échec de Pavese* (The Failure of Pavese, 1967). Speculations about Pavese's ambivalences and ambiguities, however, have led us, as Donald Heiney anticipates in his excellent study of Pavese,

> to assertions that can be neither proved nor disproved and do not really throw very much light on the technical aspects of his work. For the purposes of literary criticism it is perhaps more valuable to approach the problem in another way: in what form, in what precise guises, does the theme of bad conscience appear in his work?
>
> (Heiney, p. 87)

Pavese's flaws, his feelings, his doubts are ultimately the flesh and blood of his art. While we are cognizant of some of the personal events that gave birth to his vision of life, it is his creative production and achievement that constitute the subject for critical discussion.

Pavese's entrance into the world of literature is marked by the publication of a slim volume of poems, *Lavorare stanca* (1936), a collection of some forty-five lyrics. Ordinarily there is nothing particularly unusual in commencing a literary career in Italy by writing poems, for that is the route taken by many novelists. But what is unusual, and therefore important, is that *Hard Labor* indicates a definite positioning with respect to Pavese's predecessors and contemporaries, and at the same time presents some of the main, recurrent themes of his later novels.

Every poet is born into a tradition that, if he is endowed with imagination and originality, he will seek to rejuvenate, to change, both to mold it into an adequate instrument of self-revelation and to make it reflect life as he sees it. The poetry of the early Pavese shows the debt he owes to, say, Gabriele d'Annunzio and some of the more distinguished "poets of the Twilight." But there is also an indication of the poet's genius, striving to depict the fascination

with city and country life, the clashes and tensions of the respective settings, all told in a style, as at least one critic has pointed out, strongly reminiscent of Cézanne, Renoir, and Manet in its color and tone. Attitudes or events or moods are presented with a simplicity that never lacks depth—a rare achievement in times of Fascist rhetoric and bombast. It is difficult to think of many other poets (with the exception of Eugenio Montale) whose special perceptiveness allowed them to be both excellent poets and excellent critics.

Pavese was deeply conscious of the importance of his lyrics, to the point of declaring in a brief essay written in 1934 and published in the second, enlarged edition of *Hard Labor* (1943) that his poetry was "among the best being written in Italy." In yet another essay, "A proposito di certe poesie non ancora scritte" (Regarding Certain Poems as Yet Unwritten), he pointed out what is one of the basic themes of his writing:

> . . . the adventures of an adolescent who is proud of his *paese* [native town] and imagines the city to be the same, but finds loneliness there and turns to sex and passion for comfort. This merely uproots him and increases the distance between him and both the *paese* and the city, driving him into a more tragic solitude, which is the end of adolescence.

The theme of the return home pervades much of Pavese's work: "A village has its purpose, even if it's only the fun of leaving it. A village also means that you're not alone, that you know that in those people, those trees, and that soil, there is a part of you; that even when you aren't there it stays there waiting for you," says the narrator of *The Moon and the Bonfires* (p. 7). Going away, of course, is also a refusal to be committed to something or someone: a cause, a woman, a country. Running away from the things that usually connect us with the kind of life we may perceive to be unattractive or even impossible to tolerate frequently leads to further estrangement and loneliness.

Pavese's poetry is a first, but fundamental, statement about his feelings toward art and life; its unpretentious language moves toward a goal of a "clear, objective and essential" poetry, composed in an effective mixture of the styles known as "veristic" and "crepuscular" (the latter referring to an early-twentieth-century Italian school characterized by melancholy and irony), with emphasis on clarity. He called the results of his labors "*poesia-racconto*" (poetry-narrative), a form that, while free from formal metrical requirements, retains its internal rhythm and power of synthesis. The subjects of his poems are drawn from the *paese*, its hills, its beauty, and, above all, its everyday life. The first of a number of myths to come to life is the hill, with its remarkable beauty and its mysteries. In contrast with this is the city, with its unique landmarks and tension, and its anguish and solitude. Simplicity of language detracts not at all from the directness and forcefulness of such lyrics. Although intensely personal, Pavese's poetry conspicuously rejects the traditional efforts to make the self its central preoccupation and instead focuses on others. The characters who appear in his poems are largely drawn from the working class. They are common people: "peasants, prostitutes, prisoners, working women, youths," as he states in his diary:

If there is any human figure in my poetry, it is that of a truant running back, full of joy, to his own village, where to him everything is picturesque and full of color; a man who likes to work as little as he can; finding great pleasure in the simplest things; always expansive, good natured, set in his views; incapable of deep suffering; happy to follow nature and enjoy a woman, but also glad to be free and on his own; ready every morning to start life afresh. As in *Mari del Sud*.

(*The Burning Brand*, p. 34 [10 November 1935])

In Pavese's early poetry we find the theme that eventually became one of the central motifs of his entire corpus—solitude, one of life's conditions that most afflicted him and that he never tired of depicting. Communication and love are two of the strongest experiences by which we establish, or reestablish, human contact, but Pavese, for emotional and psychological reasons, had difficulties in this area. In *The Burning Brand* he observes:

The greatest misfortune is loneliness. . . . Work is an equivalent to prayer, since ideally it puts you in contact with something that will not take advantage of you. The whole problem of life, then, is this: how to break out of one's loneliness, how to communicate with others. That explains the persistence of marriage, fatherhood, friendship, since they might bring happiness! But why it should be better to be in communication with another than to be alone is a mystery.

(p. 151 [15 May 1939])

Here Pavese's ambivalence is quite clear: his *thinking* that love, friendship, concern, commitment (social or political) would bridge the gap that keeps people isolated did not mean that he was ready to experience or capable of experiencing such "communication" then or at any time in his life. "We are frightened of being alone," comments Deola in the poem "Ritorno di Deola" ("Deola's Return"), "but we want to be alone."

Although Pavese continued to write poetry until the last months of his life, by the late 1930's his need to "narrate in [verse] form" was satisfied. He no longer felt challenged by the difficulties of his chosen medium—to the point, as he wrote in the opening pages of his diary, that

I no longer troubled to seek for deeper poetic discoveries, as though it were merely a question of applying a skillful technique to a state of mind. Instead, I was making a poetic farce of my poetic vocation. . . .

So far, I have confined myself, as if by caprice, to poetry in verse. Why do I never attempt a different genre? There is only one answer, inadequate though it may be. It is not out of caprice, but from cultural considerations, sentiment, and not habit, that I cannot get out of that vein, and the crazy idea of changing form to renovate the substance would seem to me shabby and amateurish.

(*The Burning Brand,* pp. 24–25 [October 1935])

These doubts, however carefully worded, strongly point to Pavese's decision to turn to fiction. On 15 October 1935 he added:

If I have truly lived these four years of poetry, so much the better: that cannot but help me towards greater incontestability and a better sense of expression. . . . I must not forget how much at a loss I felt before *Mari del Sud,* and how, as I went along, I grasped an understanding of my world that I had created. . . . Now that I have exhausted that vein, I am too worn-out, too circumscribed, to be still strong enough to throw myself with high hopes into making a new excavation.

(p. 29)

Two days later he wrote:

It really seems to me that my technique has become automatic, so that, without deliberately thinking about it, my ideas now come out in the form of images, as if in obedience to that fanciful law [where the image ends and logic begins] I mentioned on the 10th [actually it was the 9th]. And I am very much afraid that this means it is time to change the tune, or at least the instrument. . . .

So my formula for the future is discovered: if once I tormented my mind to create a blending of my lyrical forms . . . the result was *Mari del Sud,* with all the works that followed it; now I must find the secret of fusing the fantastic, trenchant vein of *Lavorare stanca* with that of the *pornoteca* [collection of pornographic writings]: slapstick, realistically declaimed to its public. And, beyond all doubt, that will mean prose.

(pp. 30–31)

The short stories are a kind of transition genre between the early poetry and the later novels and frequently treat themes that are dealt with more extensively in the novels. As early as 1928, Pavese was trying his hand at fiction, writing stories, most of which appeared only after his death. But it was only in the summer of 1936 that his efforts reached the promising stage with the completion of "Terra d'esilio" ("Land of Exile"), the first of some sixty short stories. Toward the end of 1938, while he was working for Einaudi in Turin, Pavese began *Il carcere* (literally, The Prison [or The Cell], translated as *The Political Prisoner,* 1948), the first of nine novels of which he was sole author, all fairly brief (running an average of one hundred printed pages), generally completed within a three-month period, and all uniformly divided into short chapters. The shift in genre, however, in no way diminished Pavese's seriousness of approach and high creative consciousness. He brought to the art of fiction the same care he had given to poetry. Indeed, he regarded fiction as a logical extension of what he had tried to do in poetry: to poetize prose, without (and this is what separates him from the school of the *prosa d'arte* of the 1910's and 1920's) losing the story, the events of a novel. In this sense his concern with writing a poetic novel was shared by Elio Vittorini, whose *Conversazione in Sicilia* (*In Sicily,* 1941) signaled an important new direction in the genre.

One of the most striking aspects of Pavese's novels, poetry, and nonfiction is that they were all conceived, in his own words, as integral parts of a "monolith," all, whatever their artistic merit or deficiencies, connected to each other in subtle, symbolic ways. Much like other great writers he admired enormously—Thomas Mann, Marcel Proust, Luigi Pirandello, and Samuel Beckett—Pavese built a circular world in which every part is at once its beginning and its end. In a radio interview (6 February 1946) Pavese declared:

I feel sure of the fundamental and lasting unity of all that I have written or will write—and I am talking not of an autobiographical unity or unity of taste, which are trivialities, but of one unity of the vital interest, the monotonous obstinacy, of someone who feels certain of having found his true, his eternal world on the very first day [of his writing] and can do nothing but revolve around the great monolith and takes off chunks [from it] and studies them in every possible light.

("L'influsso degli eventi [The Influence of Events], in *La letteratura americana e altri saggi*, p. 248)

Pavese's novels are set either in the country or in the city, the former symbolizing innocence and beauty, the latter the prison of contemporary life. His themes are always similar and yet always different, facets of the same stone their creator never tired of polishing and holding to the light. The people summoned by Pavese's imagination to recite their unique role, where death is the only certainty, constitute an odd lot indeed: men and women drawn from the middle class, boring and bored professionals, teachers and students, disillusioned intellectuals, shopkeepers, peasants, seamstresses, fashion models, would-be artists, prostitutes, workingmen from the blue-collar sector—people frequently spineless and at times dead to feelings, uninteresting and even banal, all seeking to cope in a world where little happens, where existence, as Pavese once wrote about himself, is an escape "from the damnation of daily sadness." Among them the figures of the adolescent, the wanderer, and the unemployed receive the special attention of the novelist, perhaps because he sees in the first the symbol of hope, in the second the symbol of the man searching with diminishing hope, and in the third the person who no longer has a constructive place in society, to which he has become a burden and a threat.

The space in which such characters live is limited to the street, the cafés, or the inn, where they can drink their wine and talk about things. These are "places," as the critic Fernandez remarks, "where we can go anytime, metaphors of a possibility without limit." "Pavese's hero," adds Fernandez, "is ready for all possible experiences because he is touched by none of them,

and because he is certain of being retrieved by his myths and by his deep nature at any time he wishes." A few friends, maybe a woman, a few excursions to the hills to dance, and sometimes a few discussions about the past, their love affairs, their feelings, fill the existence of Pavese's characters; more often than not, they share a reluctance, or perhaps an incapacity, to connect with other human beings. They live a life without fire, with few (if any) emotions or deep commitments, lost birds in unfriendly skies, true antiheroes in a world with no possibility of tragedy. Stability, tranquillity, and peace are clearly denied to them. The world being what it is, it is difficult to sink roots, however vital; solid relationships are rare, evasion common, genuine love almost unknown.

In some ways Pavese's characters resemble Albert Camus's Meursault of *L'Étranger* (*The Stranger*), or some of Jean-Paul Sartre's existential characters. What impresses us is how frequently they are, really or symbolically, "strangers," away from their home for a variety of reasons—in political confinement, like Stefano in *The Political Prisoner;* in jail, like Berto and Talino in *Paesi tuoi* (*The Harvesters*, 1941); on vacation, like the unnamed narrator of *La spiaggia* (*The Beach*, 1942), as well as his hosts; the three main characters of *Il diavolo sulle colline* (*The Devil in the Hills*, 1949); or returning home, after many years, like Anguilla in *The Moon and the Bonfires*. They are all painfully dislocated, searching for their identity, trying to make sense out of the imponderables and baffling mysteries of life. Whether by chance or by design, they begin reassessing things, although seldom in a planned manner. Almost invariably we are given few details about their past because it is so undramatic. The characters themselves seem uninteresting, at least when we first meet them. All this, far from being an artistic weakness, is very much part of Pavese's strategy, which calls for devaluing certain traditional techniques of novel writing so as to move the novel in other directions, yielding new, more serious insights, lessening the importance of facts and concentrating instead on creating moods.

In a radio interview shortly before his death, Pavese, speaking in an objective fashion about himself, described his purpose:

> When Pavese begins a story, a fable, a book, he never has in mind a socially defined milieu, a character or characters, a thesis. What he has in mind is almost always an indistinct rhythm, a play of events that more than anything are sensations and atmospheres. . . . From this comes the fact, never sufficiently noted, that Pavese does not care "to create characters." Characters are for him means, not an end. Characters serve him simply to construct intellectual fables, whose theme is what takes place. . . . His tales are not descriptions but fantastic judgments of reality. . . . The characters in [his] stories are all tersely defined; they are names and types, nothing more: they are on the same plane as a tree, a storm or an air raid.
>
> ("Intervista alla radio," in *Letteratura americana ed altri saggi,* p. 294)

Pavese's novels also show a marked decline in the importance of plot, consonant with his views about fiction. He notes in his diary:

> The art of the nineteenth century was centered on the development of situations (historic cycles, careers, etc.); the art of the twentieth on static essentials. In the first, the hero was not the same at the beginning of the story as he was at the end; now he remains unchanged. Childhood as a preparation for manhood (nineteenth century); childhood viewed only as such (twentieth).
>
> (*The Burning Brand,* p. 330 [21 December 1948])

"Terra d'esilio" ("Land of Exile," in *Notte di festa,* 1953) revolves around Corrado, an engineer whose job has taken him to southern Italy. In the course of his stay, he meets Otino, a young political "undesirable" who befriends him and is eventually killed by another man. At least two factors make the story less than successful: it is written too close to experience, and too much attention is given to local color.

The Political Prisoner, on the other hand, has at least the advantage of some perspective that Pavese was able to bring to his own painful experience.

The novel was completed in five months (27 November 1938–16 April 1939), but it did not appear in print until almost a decade later. The novel's protagonist, Stefano, is an engineer and, like the author, a political prisoner in a remote village of southern Italy. The setting is in at least one way symbolic: it evokes loneliness and a sense of dislocation that pervades so much of Pavese's fiction. The mood of the story is similarly remote, detached: there is a marked lack of concern about a certain segment of the population, which is made to feel inferior, unworthy of understanding and help, and therefore alienated—thus reflecting obliquely the traditional historical stance of fascism toward the *Mezzogiorno* (South).

Unlike another intellectual from Turin, Carlo Levi, also a political prisoner in Lucania, Pavese is hardly interested in the whole range of social, economic, and human problems of the south. He is ready, however, to accept and use, for his own fictional purposes, the solitude that stems from Stefano's refusal to come to terms with the condition of the villagers because he is absorbed in his own existential problems. This helps to make *The Political Prisoner* a severe, unsparing account of the author's situation and a reflection upon it, achieved primarily through Stefano's relationships with two women: Concia, a servant girl who embodies the sexual, almost primitive, force that cannot be bent, much less tamed (and who emerges as the "she-goat" of Pavese's early poems), desirable but unattainable, ever present in his dreams but very elusive; and Elena, the landlady's daughter, who embodies maternal love and actually encourages him to look upon her as his *mammina* (little mother), reassuring, mature, understanding but also potentially castrating. When Elena does indeed take on this role, Stefano proceeds to end a relationship with which he never felt comfortable.

The confusion besetting Stefano bears close similarity to Pavese's, who, as his diary shows, was aware that no meaningful human relationship can exist in a vacuum: indeed, friendships and understanding can pierce and eventually knock down the walls that imprison people. Yet, particularly during his youth, Pavese stubbornly regarded solitude as a sign of self-sufficiency and saw love (unconsciously, perhaps) as a threat, in that it implies opening and giving oneself to others, accepting the risks as well as the benefits. The natural need for love, however, clashed with the fear that it might increase his dependence on someone, and love became a nightmarish paradox defying solution.

The main theme of *The Political Prisoner* is the discovery that the world is always a "jail," a metaphor, as Donald Heiney perceptively notes, for "the very immensity of a world in which the individual feels himself in some elusive way an exile, longing to establish contact with other men yet cut off from them by mysterious and invisible walls." On every front Stefano behaves in a way that is alienating and ultimately destructive: he uses Elena's body (although it is Concia he really wants), indirectly and directly making his relationship with his mistress oedipal; he refuses to make any connection with the local folk and tells Giannino (the only person he befriends) about his affair with Elena, who, unable and unwilling to continue a seriously tainted relationship, vanishes. The final pages of the book acquire a new meaning through the implicit symbolism of the actions and words spoken by the characters. Thus, through a trusted friend, Pierino, Stefano sends a message to Giannino, who has been arrested for "carnal offenses" (raping a minor). "Tell him," Stefano asks Pierino, "one gets more satisfaction from leaving prison than from being shut up inside. The world on the other side of the bars is beautiful, while the prisoner's life is like life outside only somewhat more squalid" (p. 127).

At the center of the novel, there is a problem that has to do with the idea and the reality of solitude, on the one hand, and of liberty, on the other. Is it possible to be genuinely free and happy at the same time? Is not mankind ultimately condemned to endure the loneliness of togetherness (the fact that being with others does not diminish the sense of alienation)? It is no shock that those whom we love by necessity restrict our freedom: But would we prefer being alone, without commitments, or obligations, or concerns? Stefano makes his choice and must ultimately pay the price for it. He rejects Elena because he has her and wants Concia (who has been the mistress of Spano, a "foul old man," as he discovers) because she eludes him.

Stefano plays the game as best he can, avoiding at all costs any action that might hurt him, however accidentally, and shuts out every pleasure and every emotion. Love, therefore, is unacceptable, since in an indirect way it poses the danger of dependence, just as solidarity (political or human, which means commitment, involvement, and more—and therefore can be, and is, risky) is to be shunned because it presents practical dangers, as Stefano knows all too well, having already spent some time in a conventional jail. When Giannino is arrested, he proceeds to burn a message (from a political prisoner, an anarchist) at once, lest it should cause difficulties with the authorities, and instructs Barbariccia (who has acted as the go-between) not to bring him any more messages. Soon thereafter, Stefano receives the official notification of a reprieve. He sees Elena for the last time, proposes that she visit him that night (she does not), and leaves the next afternoon for the North, "home."

Some of Pavese's most informed critics, Armanda Guiducci among them, have called *The Political Prisoner* "ambitious, ambiguous, desperately and narcissistically literary; all told, inferior to its ambition." It is a harsh assessment but in many ways correct. The novel's imperfections—ranging from the shallow manner in which the excessively numerous characters are depicted, to the unclear political stance of Stefano, to the unfelicitous choice of a third-person narrative form (inappropriate in the light of such a highly personal story)—do not take away the reasons for its significance. In his first sketching-out of the condition of man as prisoner of life, Pavese succeeds both in translating some of his experiences into universal symbols through literature and in creating what is possibly one of the most vital metaphors of his entire novelistic output. Even if not a masterpiece (as Franco Mollia claims), *The Political Prisoner* occupies a prominent place in our understanding of Pavese. In his very first novel, he is able to perceive with great clarity the heavy price one must be prepared to pay when, threatened emotionally or politically, one wishes to retain one's identity: that price is solitude, withdrawal from the turmoil of existence.

Pavese's second novel, *Paesi tuoi* (*The Harvesters*), belongs to the other side of his interest: the *paese,* sex, and violence. Written between 3 June and 16 August 1939, and published two years later, the book's title derives from an old, widely known Italian adage, "Donne e buoi dai paesi tuoi" or "Pick your wife and your oxen from the people and places you know and trust." When Pavese sat down to compose his novel, he already had behind him considerable experience with American literature, as a translator and commentator, and his critical perception of the problems of the novel was increasingly sharper.

The short novel was received with mixed feelings by the critics, who objected to the violent nature of the story and its rough, ungrammatical, unliterary style. The history of Italian literature, particularly in the last century, is replete with examples of works (by such writers as Giovanni Verga, Federigo Tozzi, Italo Svevo, and Alberto Moravia) whose grammatical "impurities" have earned them a hostile critical reception. In a country where literary tradition is so deeply venerated, linguistic experimentation is all but frowned upon. Doing violence to language, however irreproachable the reason may be, carries a price—censure and possibly the end of what could be a suc-

cessful career—that few writers can afford, yet must be prepared to pay. Thus, by tradition, the art of the *bello scrivere* (fine style) has always been the uppermost preoccupation of most Italian poets and novelists, a tradition not broken until the work of Carlo Emilio Gadda (1893–1973). Pavese's reading of certain American novelists—particularly Sherwood Anderson, James M. Cain, and John Steinbeck—had persuaded him that no serious writer could avoid experimenting with language and technique. A few months after completing his second novel, he wrote in his diary: "The story of an artist is the successive improvement upon the technique employed in his previous work, with a fresh creation that imposes a more complex aesthetic law" (*The Burning Brand,* p. 161 [12 December 1939]).

How effectively Pavese applied his concepts to the art of the novel can be measured in *The Harvesters.* This time the story is set in the author's native region, Piedmont, and is narrated by its protagonist, Berto. As the book opens, we find Berto, who has decided to accompany Talino, with whom he has shared a jail cell for about a month, to Monticello, a hamlet in Piedmont. They have just been released from jail, where Berto has served time for a minor crime, Talino for arson. In a sense the story begins where *The Political Prisoner* left off. Berto's decision to join Talino springs from his desire to reconnect with life. Both men long for "home," which means the love and security of family life and affection, loyal friends, and roots; both men look forward to a new beginning, a new life. But their expectations are soon dashed. And readers, steeped in a tradition in which the *campagna* [countryside or farm] is supposed to be an idyllic place of beauty and tranquillity, a healthy antidote to the pressure and alienating ways of urban living, suddenly confront not a place of peace but one of strife and conflict, not a spot where gentle love reigns supreme but one where violent, bloody lust prevails.

At first Berto is content with his situation. Working for Vinverra, the owner of the farm, is not easy, but Berto's skill as a mechanic gives him a special status. Moreover, courting the town's girls and Gisella, Talino's beautiful, sensuous sister, makes life considerably more interesting—until several potentially ominous signs begin to surface. The most serious of these is that Gisella's informing the police sends her brother to jail for arson; his crime had been motivated by his jealousy of Ernesto Del Prato, who was in love with Gisella, who in turn has been a victim of her brother's incestuous love. The scar on her abdomen, which Berto had been told was the result of an accident suffered while she was working in the fields, is in reality the permanent reminder of an abortion undergone when she was fourteen.

Berto is greatly frightened by Gisella's confession, and advises her not to irritate or provoke her brother in any way—advice that does not stop the tragedy from running its course. One day during the harvest, Talino, angered by a trivial act, thrusts his pitchfork into his sister's throat, then flees. A few hours later, despite medical care, Gisella dies. The hunt for the murderer begins, without the lack of cooperation traditional among Italian families during police investigations of this particular type of crime. Deeply grieved by Gisella's death and now aware that the *paese,* where he had hoped to find peace, is no better or safer than the city, Berto leaves for his home in Turin.

If Pavese's first novel was marred by a pervasive intellectualism in subject and treatment, *The Harvesters* represents an intriguing, radical change in direction. For one thing, there are no intellectuals in the book. But, what is even more pivotal in terms of the gradual growth of Pavese as an artist, the construction of the novel is such that the events narrated and the characters created may be seen as what they are *and* as symbols of a universal condition. Thus, the fact that Berto is a mechanic is important in the story itself but also underscores the conflict between two kinds of society, the city dwellers and the farmers. People in the city are closer to machines, to mechanisms; people who live in the *campagna* (countryside) are closer to primordial feelings and to nature. The elements play a significant role in the lives of the *contadini* (peasants): too much sun or too much rain can ruin a harvest, too much wind can damage it, and insects can destroy it. Traditions are stronger in the country than in the city, where they are frequently turned into "festivals" whose only value is commercial, and whose object therefore is generating business and improving the economy. The setting of the novel, its characters, and its plot required a language consonant with, and capable of expressing, its characters' passions, needs, and fears.

Pavese was quite conscious of the impact the style of his novel would have, particularly his subtle blending of Piedmontese and the standard literary language. In his diary he noted:

> My language is very different from a naturalistic impression. I did not write in imitation of Berto— the only one who says anything—but translating his meditations, his wonderment, his raillery, as he would have expressed them himself, *had he spoken Italian.* I introduced errors of syntax only to indicate occasions when his own spirit grew scornful, involved or tedious. I wanted to show, not how Berto would write had he forced himself to speak Italian (that would have been dialectic impressionism), but what his own words would be, had they been changed into Italian by some new Pentecost. In short, his thoughts.
> (*The Burning Brand,* p. 160 [4 December 1939])

The narrative sections of the book are not less successful, particularly in conjuring up the tense atmosphere for the powerful drama that is about to explode: the intense heat that generates both sweat and lust; the smell of the animals on the farm; the sounds of the crickets and the birds; the scent and taste of the fruits, particularly the apples (with their sexual and biblical reference), and their connection with Gisella, depicted as "made of fruit." The gestures, actions, and words of Talino's father, Vinverra—a tough, crude, earthy authoritarian who does not hesitate to give Gisella a good thrashing—and his son's personality, so deeply shaped by his father's (added to his incestuous relationship with his sister and his pent-up anger), all contribute to an ugly climate of personal relationships that ultimately lead to the bloody murder of Gisella, a tragedy that the critic Elio Gioanola describes as breaking out like "a furious summer storm whose water is quickly soaked up by the parched earth."

Apart from the thematic interests of its author, *The Harvesters* breaks new ground in the gradual "sexualization" of the landscape: the hill is time and again called, or compared to, a woman's breast, and the bushes on its top are seen as the nipple. The interest in myth, dating back to the 1930's, and to such ethnological studies as James G. Frazer's *The Golden Bough,* begins to yield its first results in Pavese's second novel, in which realism harmoniously coexists with symbolism. Hence the increasing importance of the many rituals associated with country life, ranging from the tilling of the soil to the harvests, presented not as rituals that are merely interesting bits of coloristic folklore, but as elements that add a new dimension to the story. In short *The Harvesters* offers Pavese's first attempt to enrich a story by mythicizing its events much as Dante had sought to do when he expressed his journey in allegorical terms.

The question of symbols and myth was one that occupied Pavese's attention and study for much of his literary career. For example, referring to "the 'breast' in *Paesi tuoi*—a true epithet expressing the sexual reality of that countryside," he adds that it is "no longer an *allegorical symbol,* but an *imaginative symbol*—an additional means of expressing the 'fantasy,' the story." Several years later he wrote in his diary:

But we are convinced that myths are a language, a means of expression; not arbitrary, but pregnant with symbols that, like all languages, have a special significance which can be expressed in no other way. When we introduce a proper name, an action, some legendary marvel, we are expressing, between the lines and in a syllable or two, something comprehensive, all-embracing; the pith and marrow of a reality that will vitalize and nourish a whole living structure of passion, a complex conception of human existence.

(*The Burning Brand,* pp. 286–287 [20 February 1946])

In *The Harvesters* Pavese is quite successful in depicting the *campagna* in a manner that serves the development of the tense, erotic, and basically primitive plot. We learn to see and hear and smell the land, the trees, the animals; we feel the almost unbearable heat; we appreciate the coolness of the water; we almost experience what it means to go barefoot, or to be bothered by flies, or to taste the dust of country roads. The country is created by Pavese for us to discover. Only in his later novels, however, does he make full and appropriate use of the myths and symbols so richly stored in the *campagna* in a more genuinely "unliterary" (or spontaneous) representation of his worldview.

Originally entitled "La tenda" (The Curtain), *La bella estate* (*The Beautiful Summer*) was written between 2 March and 6 May 1940. It was published in Italy in 1949 and was warmly received. *The Beautiful Summer* (the title is not without irony) is the first of Pavese's novels to deal with the petite bourgeoisie and the first to be told from the point of view of its heroine. It is also the first to be set not in the desolate Calabrian hamlet of *The Political Prisoner* or in the fields and hills of the Langhe region, but in the city, Turin, and more precisely in the quarters and studios of artists and bohemians. It is not difficult to appreciate why such places should have a certain magnetism for a girl who, like the protagonist-narrator, comes from the *paese* to the city, lured by a place that offers the anonymity and freedom often necessary to control one's own life. The name of the girl is Ginia: she is just sixteen years old and works as a seamstress. The theme of the book, and the substance of the story, is her initiation into life.

In Turin, Ginia shares a flat with her unmarried brother, Severino, an electrician. Her best friends are Rosa, a factory worker, and, a bit later, Amelia, a sophisticated model who spends much of her free time at the cafés. Through her Ginia is introduced to the world of so-called artists and would-be intellectuals: Barbetta (Little Beard), an artist who sketches her face; Guido, a mediocre painter; and Rodrigues, whose association with artists is a means to bolster his own ego. Ginia, at first shocked and even dismayed that her friend Amelia poses in the nude, soon realizes that this need not degrade her body or her humanity. Like Alberto Moravia's Carla of *Gli indifferenti* (*The Time of Indifference*), Ginia thinks that her affair with Guido, with whom she has fallen in love, will drastically change the course of her life, a belief that soon proves to be totally mistaken. The other shock comes when Amelia confesses that she is a bisexual and that she contracted syphilis when she had an affair with another woman. Disappointed by her experiences, Ginia nevertheless gains some understanding of the mediocre, self-indulgent world in which she, too, will be doomed to live. Yet she accepts this fact and asks Amelia to "lead the way."

It has frequently been noted that Pavese's novels are largely autobiographical, but such is not the case with *The Beautiful Summer*, which is the author's effort to re-create a world that was largely alien, yet was strangely attractive to him. Seen from another vantage point, the book revolves around what has emerged as Pavese's special interests: the themes of love and sex, the sexual experience as the principal element in the transition to maturity; the themes of city life, work, and friendship; and, of course, the rather pitiless examination of bourgeois economic values. In *The Beautiful Summer* Pavese enters the world of women, reporting their conversations, their ways of thinking, their fears and aspirations—a considerable imaginative leap for him. The shift in setting from the *campagna* to the city is accompanied by other changes: violence, so pervasive in *The Harvesters*, gives way to apathy, lust to bourgeois "love"; primitive instincts and mythicized passions turn into superficial sentiments. If there is something horrifying about the cruelty and violence of *The Harvesters*, there is only something contemptible in the hollow and dissolute existence portrayed in *The Beautiful Summer*.

Is the novel successful? The answer, as always, is bound to vary from reader to reader. Armanda Guiducci, one of Pavese's sensitive critics, praises the "extraordinary index of the writer's stunning capacity to identify himself with the feminine psyche." If it is true that Pavese's heroine Ginia is well drawn, it is also true that the major weakness of the novel is in the limitations of her character, which lacks depth and sensitivity. The action, or what there is of it, is slow-moving if not downright dull. As for the ambience, it is too pervasively fraudulent to be completely convincing. And the male characters prove once again to be far more weakly portrayed than their female counterparts.

The book raises another problem: As an intellectual, Pavese had no trouble "knowing" how people like himself behaved. But all his life he was challenged by "the others": the workers, farmers, outcasts, derelicts of society, servants, pseudo artists. Much of his fiction is about them and how they reach out for the happiness or contentment that eluded him with a frightening regularity. How to bridge the enormous intellectual gap between them and himself, and how to make them interesting and articulate without robbing them of their independence, remained one of the greatest obstacles Pavese had to confront and did not always completely overcome.

The Beautiful Summer ends on a note of pathos: there is tacit acknowledgment that things did not turn out quite as Ginia would have wished; and appropriately enough, the story, which begins in the summer, ends in the winter. The warmth, the brightness of the sun, the sensuous garments worn in the summertime, give way to the cold of the winter, a season that forces people to take refuge in their homes and turn inward after the promises of the summer. For many people summer is carefree living, vitality, hope—but in Pavese's third novel hopes are dashed, and Ginia's acceptance of being led by Amelia (at the end of Ginia's short-lived affair with Guido) is a symbolic surrender of her freedom and individuality, her acceptance of a corrupt life she had always hoped to avoid.

In some respects *La spiaggia* (*The Beach*, 1942) continues, in a different direction, the mood of the previous novel, but without resolving the thematic and stylistic problems of *The Beautiful Summer.* There is evidence that Pavese was not very happy with it. Why should a writer of his sensitivity allow the publication of a work he himself acknowledged was "not a chip from the monolith"? The answer is quite simple, and surprising as well: Giambattista Vicari, the editor of the literary magazine *Lettere d'oggi* (Contemporary Literature), requested a contribution from Pavese; as a loyal friend, Pavese could not refuse. Written between 6 November 1940 and 18 January 1941, the work was serialized in *Lettere d'oggi* and appeared in book form in a very limited edition under the magazine's imprint. Only in 1956, six years after Pavese's death, did *The Beach* become widely available in book form.

The structure of the novel, with the exception of a short section at the beginning, is, like the story it tells, fairly linear. As Donald Heiney notes:

> Yet, taken simply as an exercise in construction and technique it represents a considerable step beyond the three novels that preceded it. It is the first treatment of the theme of producing vs. consuming that dominates *Tra donne sole,* and it forms an obvious bridge between his early "naturalism" and his later symbolistic style.
>
> (*Three Italian Novelists,* p. 119)

Doro, a friend of the anonymous thirty-five-year-old professor-narrator, is married to a tomboy, Clelia. At first the narrator resents their marriage (he refuses the invitation to their wedding), but he makes up with them and agrees to be their guest one summer at their little villa on the Genovese Riviera, a plan postponed for purely personal reasons. An unexpected visit by Doro startles the narrator: the two friends decide to go to the country, the Langhe region, for a bit of fun in what turns out to be an excursion into the past. They indulge in a little drinking and singing, and their escapade culminates in an incident in which a vase of flowers, accidentally pushed by an irate woman annoyed by their loudness, barely misses their heads.

The purpose of what at first may seem to be a purposeless diversion is less a Proustian attempt to recover the past than a way to dramatize how the friendship of two men has been changed by their new condition: the duties and obligations of marriage have indeed altered the delicate balance of feelings and commitment that once existed. The choice of summer is similarly part of the overall strategy of the novel: What better time than summer to engage in an attempt to reassess their lives during a period of vacation, when the weather itself seems to encourage men and women to disrobe, exposing themselves to the light of truth? On the other hand, vacations relax people, distract them, and the light of the sun blurs their vision, altering their perceptions, even inviting them to look at life from an unusual, not to say exceptional, vantage point. Doro and Clelia understand, and accept this reality—he indulging in little escapades from marital fidelity, she allowing Guido, a well-to-do young man, to court her. One day, while sunning himself at the beach, the narrator meets one of his former students, Berti, who wants someone in whom to confide. A sensitive, shy person, Berti is vacationing and, in a sense, trying to learn about life and people, particularly the narrator and his small circle. He also is attracted to Clelia and to the young Ginetta.

Nothing much happens in the book; indeed, we are kept waiting, page after page, for a surprise, for the introduction of a new element that might inject a touch of vitality into a sagging tale. The dull pace of *The Beach* is, of course, planned: what its author intended to write was a sort of commentary on the values and relationships of his middle-class characters. The gray sand of the beach is a major factor in the sameness of the landscape. The affluent vacationers spend much of their time sunning their bodies, at "the empty sea," incapable of appreciating the beauty of nature surrounding them, indulging in empty conversations. Even their friendships are based on the coincidence of being at the same vacation spot. In all this, there is a hint of F. Scott Fitzgerald's work. The decadent scenes in Pavese's portrayal of boring and bored characters might well have been created by Alberto Moravia. The ending finally provides the one surprise we almost wish had come sooner: Clelia is expecting a child, and Doro looks forward to his new role as a father. Their relationship finally gives signs of maturity. The narrator, accompanied by Berti, leaves for Turin, and with that the book comes to an end.

The parenthesis of the summer is concluded: everyone returns home, including the narrator, who, perhaps a little more mature, will once again take up his role of professor. But it is only at the end that we perceive that the book is, among other things, a study of what makes marriage work, seen from the perspective of an intellectual who, like Pavese, remains skeptical, ambivalent, ungenerous, and envious of his best friend's attachment to his wife. The questions the book raises, if only indirectly, recur time and again in Pavese's fiction: How can one break through the walls of loneliness? How can one communicate to other human beings one's fears and trepidations? Can a man experience some kind of happiness, at least, in his relationship with a woman? Is there any way, other than artistic creativity, that allows one to give of oneself to others generously and freely? The answers would have to wait for Pavese's last novels.

Il compagno (*The Comrade,* 1947) was written between 4 October and 22 December 1946, five years after *The Beach*—five long, hard, painful years during which World War II raged. The reader of Pavese's diary may be shocked to find only a few casual references to a war that destroyed hundreds of cities and killed millions of people on the battlefields and in the concentration camps, including some of Pavese's best friends, among them Leone Ginzburg and Giaime Pintor. Between 1941 and 1945 Pavese lived in Turin and Rome, where he had been sent by Giulio Einaudi to lay the foundations for a gradual expansion of the activities of his publishing house. For a few months during that period Pavese took refuge in the hamlet of Serralunga, in the hills of Piedmont, with his sister Maria, thus avoiding the danger of being arrested by the police for his political views. While the bombs were relentlessly falling on the industrial targets of Turin and other cities, Pavese read and studied, taking no part in the underground activities that were intensifying. He was to suffer for his lack of involvement and to be criticized by many of his intellectual friends, including his future biographer (and future member of the Chamber of Deputies), Davide Lajolo.

The book's title, with its strong Marxist connotation, should not lead one to think that *The Comrade* is either a tract or an opinionated tale. In fact it is hardly a political novel, although it is fair to characterize it as one that carefully follows the gradual political awareness of its main character. The name of the hero is Pablo. "They called me Pablo because I played the guitar" is an opening strongly reminiscent of Herman Melville's *Moby-Dick,* which Pavese had felicitously translated into Italian a few years earlier. Briefly, the story narrated by Pablo, a young man who works in his family's salt and tobacco shop, pivots at first on his relationship with the girlfriend of his best friend, Amelio, who is bedridden (perhaps permanently) after a serious motorcycle accident. This relationship with Linda, a well-known seamstress and a strikingly independent woman insofar as her private life is concerned, troubles Pablo considerably because he feels guilty for betraying his best friend, who happens to be a fine young man, a positive character whose role, as is frequently the case in Pavese's novels, is doomed to remain marginal. The encounter with Linda plays a large part in Pablo's life: for one thing he is introduced to the group of seedy entertainers who form the entourage of a small-time yet wealthy impresario (Lubrani), with whom Linda has an affair. Deeply hurt by the affair and no longer willing to continue leading a purposeless existence, Pablo decides to leave for Rome, accompanied by his friend Carletto, in search of a new, meaningful life.

Rome offers him new friendships, a new girl (Gina), and, what is more important, a new political consciousness. "I worked during the day and read in the evening," he says. Slowly, guided by his new friends, he begins to discover new and forbidden literature on fascism, Marxism, and socialism. He also begins to understand the necessity of actively fighting, not merely opposing, fascism, a cancer that must be eliminated if people are to be free again, since the politics of fascism can only result in a system of life based on a continuing exploitation of the working class by the bourgeoisie and the landowners. The destruction of such a repressive system must therefore become the ultimate commitment of the working class. At the same time, there must be an effort to develop leaders from within the working class: "You yourself need to study," says Pablo, "before you can have confidence in those who do" (p. 133). And "You've got to study to be able to dispense with those who study now. So you don't get cheated" (p. 134). What Pablo is insisting on is a culture that is relevant to the needs of the people, training them not only for a job but also for an understanding of political issues and of the governing structure.

In Rome, Pablo finds a job in a bicycle shop, and he is introduced to the underground and to

some of its most respected leaders, such as Scarpa, a veteran of the Spanish Civil War, and his friends. He becomes politically involved, his activities come to the attention of the police, and he is arrested. After several weeks in jail, he is released for lack of evidence and ordered back to Turin and to a period of police surveillance.

The problem of the novel seems to spring, on the one hand, from its having been written in order to acknowledge Pavese's belief in the soundness and worth of the Communist program, and, on the other hand, as a substitute for an experience and a genuinely personal (and not merely intellectual) commitment that Pavese, for a variety of complex reasons, was unable to make. As a result the unevenness of the second part of the book, despite some excellent pages depicting Pablo's Roman sojourn, is due to the obvious and unexplained lack of motivation of Pablo's political position, now anti-Fascist. But the political theme is an important one in Pavese's work, and he returns to it, this time with greater sensitivity and precision, in *La casa in collina,* written a few months later.

La casa in collina (*The House on the Hill,* 1948) and *The Moon and the Bonfires* are perhaps the best novels Pavese wrote. Composed between September 1947 and February 1948, *The House on the Hill* was published with *The Political Prisoner* in an omnibus volume, *Prima che il gallo canti* (*Before the Cock Crows,* 1948). The title is an allusion to Christ's announcement that before the cock crowed three times, Peter would betray him. As is often the case with Pavese, the genesis of *The House on the Hill* goes back to several short stories, particularly "La famiglia" ("The Family") and "Il fuggiasco" (The Fugitive), written in 1941 and 1944, respectively. The novel was written out of Pavese's innermost and most troubled feelings: it tells, with unusual clarity and perception, a great deal about the distanced and uninvolved role Pavese chose to play during the war. Its hero, Corrado, as Lajolo observes in his biography of Pavese, is "the character into which Pavese poured the most of himself." Because the author achieved a perfect blend of autobiography and fiction, and because he was, at last, truly honest about himself, the resulting book is not only one of the best tales to have been inspired by the Resistance but also a deeply personal statement about the futility of war, and the destruction, chaos, and misery it brings to mankind—a judgment lived, not just spoken or intellectualized, by the protagonist of the story.

The title of the book is symbolic: the house on the hill, where the protagonist lives in a rented room, is a safe place, away from Turin, a target of constant air raids in the final months of World War II; it is also a convenient place to which he can withdraw to avoid responsibilities and commitment. Like so many other of Pavese's characters, Corrado is an intellectual, a *liceo* (junior college) professor, with a special fondness for the hills with which he associates his childhood happiness. He also, like them, is unable to establish meaningful relations with anyone: not with Elvira, the daughter of his landlady; not with Cate, a young woman whom he meets in a tavern (she is a war refugee), and with whom some years before he had had an affair; not with her offspring, Dino, whose father is unknown but might well be Corrado himself. Much has happened since Cate disappeared from his life: she has matured emotionally and politically, has become a fierce anti-Fascist, and has had a child. Corrado, on the other hand, has become even more cautious, uncommitted, and estranged, apparently satisfied with looking at life from the sidelines.

The novel begins with this remarkably straightforward statement by the narrator-protagonist:

I should say—as I begin this story of a long illusion—that blame for what happened to me cannot be laid to the war. On the contrary, the war, I am certain, might still save me. . . . All the war did was to remove my last scruple about keeping to myself, about consuming the years and my heart alone; . . . The war had made it legitimate to turn in on oneself and live from day to day without regretting lost opportunities.

(*Selected Works,* p. 60)

What follows is the frank study of how Corrado tries to achieve some sort of perspective on his "extreme scruples" about being apart from the others during the war, avoiding death or physical harm without changing much and yet never feeling good about his survival. The fact that Pavese chose to publish the novel with the earlier *The Political Prisoner* must be viewed as part of his strategy of showing how the heroes of the two stories deal with their lifelong efforts to come to grips with themselves and their rapport with the world. Thus the titles themselves are symbolic: whereas in his first period of writing Pavese uses the metaphor of jail to express his conviction that it is impossible to free ourselves from our fate, in his mature years he acknowledges the incapacity or impossibility for us to take a hand in the process of history.

There is ample justification to support the widely held belief that Pavese's novels were written out of guilt feelings rooted in his sexual and political lives. Yet in his best novels, his bad conscience becomes our bad conscience, certainly insofar as politics is concerned. The forty-year-old Corrado, safe in his ivory tower at first and in his family's house later, tries to explain his unwillingness to accept an active role in the war, possibly with the Underground:

It was as if I had been waiting for the war a long time and had been counting on it, a war so vast and unprecedented that one could easily go home to the hills, crouch down, and let it rage in the skies above the cities. Things were happening now that justified a mere keeping alive without complaining. That species of dull rancor that hemmed in my youth found a refuge and a horizon in the war.

(*Selected Works,* p. 60)

The critic Fernandez further explains:

> Blood and fire: here the experience of the war is substituted for the experience of women and love. . . . *The House on the Hill* is the novel that sets the historical necessity of participating in the political and military action, of enlisting in the ranks of the Resistance, against the mythical necessity of living in the hills.
>
> (*Le roman italien et la crise de la conscience moderne*, pp. 189–190)

As in many of his earlier novels, Pavese makes the contrast between the city and the country one of the central motifs of his book. Turin (where some of the action is set) is presented as the place where the terror of the war is felt in every way, particularly through the air raids whose targets are the factories. The hills, and more specifically the room where Corrado lives, allow him to view the spectacle of war in relative safety. City and country become the two diametrically opposed loci of his experience. The hills now seem to symbolize the regularity of nature, while the city represents the upheavals, uncertainties, and unpredictability of human institutions.

Corrado's feeble attempt to make some sort of life for himself evaporates suddenly one day in early spring when Cate, along with a number of partisans, is arrested while he watches, petrified by fear, from the relative safety of the woods. After Cate's arrest Corrado leaves Dino to his fate (although a youngster of seven, he apparently joins the Resistance), and he never sees Cate or Dino again. For a while Corrado finds refuge in a seminary. But the fear of being found, compounded by his guilt over his non-participation in the struggle against Fascism, leads him to make his way home in a symbolic journey through memory of the innocence and happiness of his childhood. Protected by his mother and his sister, Corrado finds safety but not peace.

The last chapter is a fitting epilogue for the book: Corrado has been home for six months, but the horror of the war and what it means not only to him but also to Cate, to Dino, to his friends and family, and to the enemy, haunts him every day of his life. We know, of course, that he may be safe, but in many ways he is as good as dead; he will never learn to be a father, or a husband, or a brother. His selfishness, his egocentricity, his cowardice have spared his life, but they have robbed it of any significance. His incapacity for becoming involved has killed most of his decent feelings. He is left wondering about the war, life and death, humanity and inhumanity, cruelty and compassion:

> Looking at certain dead is humiliating. They are no longer other people's affairs: one doesn't seem to have happened there by chance. One has the impression that the same fate that threw these bodies to the ground holds us nailed to the spot to see them, to fill our eyes with the sight. It's not fear, not our usual cowardice. One feels humiliated because one understands—touching it with one's eyes—that we might be in their place ourselves: there would be no difference, and if we live we owe it to this dirtied corpse. That is why every war is a civil war; every fallen man resembles one who remains and calls him to account.
>
> (*Selected Works*, pp. 170–171)

Throughout the story Corrado, much like Pavese himself, lives accepting everything, including his own solitude, which he describes as "the courage of being alone as if nobody else were alive, thinking only of what you do, and thus accepting yourself and the others." Yet such indifference toward life ultimately leads Corrado to realize that "living by accident is not living, and I wonder if I have really escaped." The book ends on a philosophic meditation about the experience Corrado has gone through:

> Now that I've seen what war is, what civil war is, I know that everybody, if one day it should end, ought to ask himself: "And what shall we make of the fallen? Why are they dead?" I wouldn't know what to say. Not now, at any rate. Nor does it seem to me that the others know. Perhaps only the

dead know, and only for them is the war really over.

(*Selected Works*, p. 171)

In his diary, Pavese wrote:

On 4th October, *Diavolo sulle colline* was finished. It has the air of something big. It is a new language; dialectic, written with an atmosphere of culture and introducing "student discussions." For the first time you have really set up symbols. You have revitalized *La Spiaggia,* putting into it young men who make discoveries, the liveliness of debates, mythical reality.

(*The Burning Brand,* pp. 325–326
[4 October 1948])

Il diavolo sulle colline (*The Devil in the Hills,* 1949) is probably the most difficult and intellectually intricate of Pavese's novels. It is a cool portrait of bourgeois decadence, emptiness, and boredom, as well as an incisive treatment of one of the most painful themes of Pavese's work—man's incapacity to communicate with other human beings and the resulting estrangement from reality. All this is set, once again, in a manner calculated to bring out the dichotomy between the country and the city. The main characters, all young men, are the narrator and his friend Pieretto, both law students, and Oreste, a medical student. The three spend much of their time meandering in the streets of Turin or in the nearby hills, attempting to evade their responsibilities as students. One night they meet Poli, a wealthy young man, and join him in his frequent escapades with his mistress, an aging woman named Rosalba. Poli is hardly satisfied with his existence. In fact, he is nauseated by his constant escape into sex, liquor, and drugs in his search for whatever meaning life may have. One day Rosalba, sensing that their relationship has run its course, shoots and nearly kills him. Hastily summoned by Oreste, Poli's father, wishing to avoid a scandal, uses his influence to have the incident dismissed as an accident and places Rosalba in a convent.

The action then shifts to a small village in Piedmont, to the country house of Oreste's family, by whom the narrator and Pieretto have been invited to spend the rest of the summer. The sojourn affords them the opportunity to come into closer contact with the earth. Indeed, many of the descriptions of nature and of the activities of the three friends become integral to Pavese's determination to build into the work a number of symbolic myths that give intellectual substance to the story.

The three friends decide to pay a call on Poli, who is convalescing in a nearby town. Much to their surprise, they find him living with Gabriella, his estranged wife, who has returned home to help him recover. The group resumes a rather dissolute life, which includes a short love affair between Oreste and Gabriella, with Poli aware of, but unconcerned about, their relationship. The book ends with Poli being driven to the hospital in Milan, suffering from tuberculosis.

In a letter to his teacher and mentor, Augusto Monti, Pavese remarks that the novel was meant to be

. . . a youthful hymn of discovery of nature and society: everything seems beautiful to the three boys, and only little by little, each in his own way, do they establish contact with the sordidness of a "futile" world—a certain bourgeois world that does nothing, believes in nothing, [a world] which I see no reason to hide under a veil.

(*Lettere,* 2.460)

As in some of Pavese's earlier novels, what is portrayed in *The Devil in the Hills* is yet another treatment of the theme of the return. This time it is not the protagonist-narrator who is going home but his friend Oreste, accompanied by Pieretto and the narrator. Moreover, their experience seeks to recapture something of the mythical dimension of the country, with its magnetic power. What was to be a discovery of the earth turns out to be a confrontation between the *civiltà contadina* (peasant civilization) and the *civiltà cittadina* (urban civilization)—the former raw and violent but basically healthy, the latter sophisticated but thoroughly decadent and corrupted by vice, drugs, and an absence of a sense of purpose. The book, with its attempts to deal forcefully with the symbolism of its themes, is also about the evasion of responsibility displayed by the three young friends and the metaphorical illness of Poli and Gabriella. According to the critic Gianni Venturi:

> Just as in [Thomas] Mann's *The Magic Mountain,* the illness is not merely physical, so in the story of Poli and Gabriella the vice of the former and [his] relationship with the latter alludes to hidden truths, that is to say the impossibility of retrieving the sense of life without cherishing the sense of death.
>
> (p. 98)

As is often the case with Pavese, the story begins in the summer, and this makes possible an uninhibited exposure of the naked bodies of the three friends to the sun, basking in its heat in what is presented as a ritual, a "vice" sui generis. When the narrator asks Poli whether "cocaine could add to the peace of the soul," the answer is "that everyone took some kind of drug, from wine to sleeping pills, from nudism to the cruelty of the hunt. 'What has nudism to do with it?' Oh yes, it was part of the picture: people go naked into company to brutalize themselves and defy convention" (*Selected Works,* p. 364).

The search for meaning in a world that seems coherent and rational only to the insensitive or superficial person becomes more intense when the action moves to the Greppo hill. After a highly symbolic thunderstorm the narrator says: "You could hear the almost solid mass of water falling and rumbling. I imagined the steaming and running landscape, our cleft boiling over, roots laid bare, the most private cracks in the earth penetrated and violated" (*Selected Works,* p. 330). But the search ultimately proves fruitless: the devil is in the hills, and there can be no peace. Humans are his easy prey; their only hope is to be spared the tragic end of Poli and the sufferings of an implacable, savage, unforgiving nature.

Among Pavese's novels *Tra donne sole* (*Among Women Only,* 1949) is probably the most unusual for several reasons: it is told in the first person, is set in Turin's world of haute couture, and has a cast composed almost entirely of women. What attracted Pavese to such a world has not been satisfactorily explained. If our reading of Pavese is correct, he preferred situations that do not require much action (as *The Political Prisoner, The Beautiful Summer, The Beach,* and *The Devil in the Hills* indicate), and where time is of no immediate consequence. In this sense the choice of the world of haute couture was felicitous, in that it is frequented by the affluent upper middle class, with ample money to spend and ample time to waste, untouched by the pressures of earning a living. In addition, clothing is connected not with the substance, but with the appearance, the outer shell, as it were, of what one is. And because we know how much the middle class cares about the way first impressions are made by clothes, we sense why Pavese exploits this side of bourgeois behavior: in order to emphasize the contrast between appearance and substance.

As he did of *The Devil in the Hills,* Pavese thought highly of his eighth novel. In his diary he noted:

> Discovered today that *Tra donne sole* is a great novel; that the experience of being engulfed in the false, tragic world of high society is broad and incongruous, and blends well with Clelia's wistful memories. Starting from her search for a childish, *wistful* world that no longer exists, she discovers the grotesque, sordid tragedy of those women of Turin as it is, of her own realized dreams. Her discovery of herself, and the emptiness of her own world, which saves her ("I've got everything I wanted").
>
> (*The Burning Brand,* p. 338 [17 April 1949])

The central character of this short novel is Clelia Oitana, an exceedingly capable and mature businesswoman, of humble origin, who has just come from Rome to speed up the construction of a branch of a Roman fashion house. She arrives at her hotel shortly before a woman (Rosetta Mola) who has tried, unsuccessfully, to take her own life is removed on a stretcher. The nature of Clelia's interests brings her into contact with the "woman's world" of Turin, as well as with well-to-do friends and prospective clients. One of the problems besetting the protagonist is that her social origin makes difficult, not to say impossible, her being accepted by the affluent bourgeoisie. At one point she admits that she respects prostitutes, although she is not always sensitive to the hardships of those who, like herself, have had a tough struggle to gain a certain position in society.

Much of the story revolves around four women: Clelia, ambitious, torn by her past and present love affairs; Momina, a hard, cynical, abrasive woman, who is one of Pavese's most profoundly existential characters, experiences "nausea" toward so much of what she does, and is ultimately fed up with life itself; Rosetta, a sensitive, weak, tormented creature controlled by Momina; and Nene, the twenty-eight-year-old companion of a mediocre painter (Loris), who has preserved, despite her situation, an unusual degree of naïveté and shyness. In all cases there is a stubborn rejection of a meaningful relationship that could have eased the women's pain of living. For example, Clelia is unwilling to engage in a serious relationship with Becuccio, the architect who is supervising the remodeling of what will be a branch of a Roman fashion house, or Guido, her lover of some years earlier. Success proves not to be the key to happiness either, and here Pavese touches deeply on his experience as an esteemed editor and a respected, successful novelist.

"To be somebody" or "to be something"— two yearnings expressed in *The House on the Hill*—prove to be illusions, like much that life seems to offer or that man wants to achieve, in *Among Women Only*. This novel becomes the story of the particular condition in which

women, bearing the burden of discrimination, stereotyping, and male chauvinism, have to resolve their dream of what life ought to be for them.

Perhaps the salient features of this unusual novel are in the struggle Clelia fights to enter the world of the well-to-do, decadent middle class (her prospective clientele) and in her stubborn self-confidence in business matters, matched by a marked confusion when it comes to her feelings, as well as in the way that Pavese focuses on the particular manner in which the heroines of the story deal with their conditions. The book opens with a suicide manqué and closes with the death of the same person, Rosetta. Her suicide (which she is almost goaded to commit by Momina) represents the price some may have to pay when, unable to live a lonely existence, they perceive that life is unbearable, too ugly to be endured for long. Clelia, a businesswoman, can accept the compromises required to retain her sanity. Not so in Rosetta's case; and for her, death becomes liberation from the loneliness and sadness of existence.

If it is true that only exceptionally do literary critics find themselves in agreement in their assessment of literary texts, then the proverbial exception to the rule is Pavese's last novel, *La luna e i falò* (*The Moon and the Bonfires*). Written in less than two months (18 September–9 November 1949), it was published in April 1950, about four months before Pavese's suicide. Not without some flaws, and lacking the sensitivity toward human sufferings shown in *The House on the Hill, The Moon and the Bonfires* is unquestionably an impressive, hauntingly poetic novel. But the virtues of the book are not only in the story it tells nor in the superb handling of its characters and motifs, but also in the masterful manner in which so many of Pavese's themes are brought together, and the way his poetics are lucidly translated into practice. Thus, for example, Pavese's deep feelings for the country—especially the hills of the Langhe region—and his love for his native Piedmont—its rites, its mores, and its myths—are fused with the motif of the return home. This time, however, the protagonist comes back from a faraway, almost fabled land, America, where he has lived for many years in what is essentially a forced exile because of lack of work in his own country. The prolonged stay and the distance add an extra perspective to the experience, and the feeling of being home once more is both deeper and more complex.

The protagonist of the novel is a forty-year-old man, known only by his nickname of Anguilla (Eel), who has recently returned from California. He is now well off, thanks to his thrift and his work, and has settled in Genoa, where he operates a small business. As often as possible he goes home to his town in the Langhe hills. His *paese* is in his blood: he cannot forget it, nor can he live without it. His travels, his long period away from his native town, have taught him a great deal, for he has led a varied existence, experiencing new values. Although he has achieved considerable success, he knows that going back to his *paese* is essential if he is to understand the meaning of what has happened to him. Moreover, he does not know where he was born, nor does he know his biological parents, because he was raised by foster parents. And so he comes as a stranger, as someone who actually never lived there, who is eager to put together the pieces of his life: his boyhood, his years in America, the present, and eventually the time of the Italian Resistance during World War II. For the time being he has to acknowledge that the faces, the voices, and the hands that were supposed to touch him and recognize him are no longer there.

The question posed indirectly by the novel is fundamental to Pavese's world: Can we go home again? Thomas Wolfe answers in the negative. And no wonder: We can stand on familiar ground and find our bearings, remember the past, and recapture many lovely or sad memories. But time has passed; we have lived and experienced much; we have been hurt by life, and if we are fortunate, we have been blessed by some happiness. As time passes, we change, molded by life, and find the values that will guide us in our adult years.

Coming back to a place left long ago, particularly when still young, makes our understanding of places and people left long ago more difficult. Yet this gives Anguilla some sort of perspective: having lived away for many years ultimately enables him to understand much of what would otherwise have remained an enigma for him. And so Anguilla finds himself home (but a home he never really knew) after many years spent abroad, in a country he could never call his own, uprooted by necessity from what was the closest thing to a family he could have, happy to return if for no other reason than because it is comforting "to know that in the people, in the trees, the land, there is something that remains waiting for you, even when you have gone away" (*La luna e i falò*, in *I romanzi*, vol. 2, p. 387). The quest for his roots begins with a frank admission:

> I came back to this village and not to Canelli, Barbaresco or Alba, because I had a reason to. I wasn't born here, that's almost certain. I don't know where I was born. Around here there isn't a house or a piece of land or any bones that could make me say, "This is what I was before I was born."
>
> (*The Moon and the Bonfires*, Ceconio trans., p. 3)

The story itself is constructed as a relived, remembered experience. Memories of a life full of events and doings, both in Anguilla's native town and abroad, become the elements he tries to sort out in his search for his roots and his identity. Padrino and Virgilia, his foster parents, are no longer at the Gaminella farm, which is now rented to Valino, a surly type who resembles Talino (of *The Harvesters*), and his crippled son, Cinto, who is befriended by Anguilla and by Nuto, the protagonist's best friend. The three characters play the central roles of the story, while the women occupy a less central position. Anguilla, who narrates the story, is, as is often the case in Pavese's novels, largely passive. Nuto, on the other hand, although not a principal figure in the events narrated, assumes the part of the guide into the past and the commentator on many of the special characteristics, particularly the rites and symbols, of country life. His friendship with Anguilla goes back to their boyhood, and though many years have passed, he has retained his respect, affection, and loyalty.

Nuto becomes a sort of historian of the town's events during the last twenty years. This is, in a sense, an extension of the role of mentor he played during Anguilla's boyhood, when he encouraged him to study a musical instrument and to read books in order to widen his knowledge of the world. Unlike Anguilla he remained in his *paese,* growing up and participating in, though in a limited manner, the events of his country in the closing months of the war. A cordial, peaceful man who abhors violence, he has nevertheless taken part in at least one violent incident. He is basically an optimist, and he truly believes in man's ability to change his life, thus emerging as one of Pavese's few positive characters.

Nuto is a carpenter now and an artist in his trade. Once a gifted clarinet player, he hung his instrument on the wall when his father passed away, an act that suggests his seriousness and his realization that he could never support himself with his music, which gave him so much joy. It is Nuto, finally, who explains the meaning of the elements of nature in a rural civilization, and how the symbols of the kind we normally associate with the country are parts of the structure that, to a considerable degree, shapes the beliefs and the actions of the peasants.

We have seen how in his previous novels Pavese sought, with sporadic and uneven results, to achieve a fusion of the realistic and symbolic elements of his fiction. Generally, his failure can probably be ascribed to the intellectual nature of his characters, or to unwarranted or inappropriate superimposition of symbolism on persons and events. In *The Moon and the Bonfires* these difficulties are resolved in the natural way the characters speak (a kind of Piedmontese "italianized," as it were), and in their capacity to sustain a symbolic significance appropriate to their real, lived experience of the earth. It is through his understanding of the myths and symbols that Anguilla ultimately comes to grips with the meaning of life.

In his efforts to find the pieces of his past and fit them into the puzzle of his existence, some of the main events of Anguilla's boyhood are reviewed: his brief stint as a servant and later as a laborer at La Mora, Sor Matteo's farm; his first attachment and sexual attraction to Matteo's youngest daughter, Santina, one of three women who, by reason of their highly symbolic meaning, play an important part in the tale. The women's wealth and beauty in no way bring them happiness: Irene is brutally beaten by her husband, Arturo, a mediocre man who has squandered her dowry; Silvia leads a promiscuous life and becomes pregnant. Her father, unable to bear the shame, dies after a stroke; Silvia dies after an abortion, uttering the word "Papa" just before passing away. An even more tragic fate awaits the youngest of the sisters, Santina, remembered by Anguilla as being all dressed in silk at Irene's wedding, when she was six years old. During the war she betrays first the Fascists, then the Partisans, by whom she is captured. As she attempts to escape, she is killed by a rapid burst of submachine-gun fire in an incident remarkable for its economy and effectiveness of details. Still clad in her white dress, her body is covered with branches, over which gasoline is poured and set afire by two men who loved her, Baracca (who had read her death sentence) and Nuto, in a scene that is presented as a frighteningly impressive ritual: her ashes will fertilize the earth.

The theme of violence is realized dramatically through the actions of another character, the farmer Valino. In a moment when he can no longer control his anger, he beats his sister-in-law Rosina to death; threatens to kill Cinto, who runs away; sets fire to the haystacks, the stalls, and the farmhouse (the old grand-mother, unable to move, is burned to death); and then hangs himself in the vineyard. After his death Anguilla and Nuto agree to assume the responsibility of raising Cinto.

Woven into the fabric of the narrative, a new theme emerges with extraordinary force. Three chapters (3, 11, and 21) are devoted to Anguilla's American experience. It is a tribute to Pavese that although he had never set foot on American shores, he convincingly captures the spirit of a life so different from that of his native country. But what is also remarkable is the manner in which an imaginary experience is made so real and so much a part of the story itself. As Gian-Paolo Biasin perceptively notes, the three chapters "emphasize the fundamental difference between America and Piedmont, between valleys and hills, between artificiality and nature, between chaos and custom; and yet, in their similarity they emphasize the fundamental analogies between Anguilla and Santa, between terror and death" (p. 224). The story, set in 1948, approximately the time of its composition, stretches back some twenty years to a date that coincides almost exactly with the beginning of Pavese's intense and fruitful experience with American literature. This was a time when, as he wrote in one of the post–World War II essays printed in *La letteratura americana e altri saggi* (regrettably not included in the English translation), he saw America as "something serious and precious," a country that was free, unhampered by traditions, whose "culture enabled us to see our drama unfolding as though on a gigantic stage."

The rejection of America took place in the immediate postwar years, when Pavese realized that once the United States had ceased to be the bastion against fascism, it could no longer demand the attention, respect, and loyal affection it had once received, at least from many European and Asian nations. Pavese's rejection of America is parallel to Anguilla's, the author's emotions having become integral in the world of his art. Two ways of life and two different worlds are placed squarely before us. The contrast between Piedmont and the almost endless landscape of California (where Anguilla lived and worked) could hardly be more sharply and effectively dramatized. An alienating land, bare as the moon ("There is nothing, it's like the moon," Anguilla remarks at one point), with no real women and no wine, plenty of sex but no love, America is depicted as an illusory heaven ultimately to be rejected. Despite the opportunity it offers to hardworking individuals to make money so that they can go back to their *paese* and enjoy their mature years, it actually increases their rootlessness once they have returned, because they now feel even more alienated, having spent their lives away from their native town. Having come back to it, they have only the dimmest memories of their experiences there, and are unable to make their experiences abroad meaningful to their childhood friends. The moon of the title takes on a double meaning—the sterility of America and the magic, awesome power that influences so much of life in Piedmont—and mirrors the novelist's own ambivalence toward a nation whose generosity could give so many people a chance for a life of dignity and work, and whose power, with its atomic bombs, could threaten the future of the world—a conflict that still haunts young and mature people alike.

Selected Bibliography

EDITIONS

INDIVIDUAL WORKS

NOVELS

Paesi tuoi. Turin, 1941.

La spiaggia. Rome, 1942.

Il carcere. Published with *La casa in collina* under the title *Prima che il gallo canti.* Turin, 1948.

La casa in collina. Published with *Il carcere* under the title *Prima che il gallo canti.* Turin, 1948.

La bella estate. Turin, 1949.

Il diavolo sulle colline. Published in *La bella estate.* Turin, 1949.

Tra donne sole. Published in *La bella estate.* Turin, 1949.

La luna e i falò. Turin, 1950.

Il compagno. Turin, 1947.

SHORT STORIES

Feria d'agosto. Turin, 1946.

Notte di festa. Turin, 1953.

POETRY

Lavorare stanca. Florence, 1936; new, enl. ed., Turin, 1943.

Verrà la morte e avrà i tuoi occhi. Turin, 1951.

Poesie edite e inedite. Edited by Italo Calvino. Turin, 1962.

ESSAYS

Dialoghi con Leucò. Turin, 1947.

La letteratura americana e altri saggi. Turin, 1951.

COLLECTED WORKS

Racconti. Turin, 1960.

Romanzi. 2 vols. Turin, 1961. Vol. 1: *Il carcere, Paese tuoi, La bella estate, La spiaggia, Il compagno;* vol. 2: *La casa in collina, Il diavolo sulle colline, Tra donne sole, La luna e i falò.*

Opere. 14 vols. Turin, 1968.

LETTERS AND DIARIES

Il mestiere di vivere. Turin, 1952.

Lettere. 2 vols. Turin, 1966. Vol. 1, *1924–1944,* edited by Lorenzo Mondo. Vol. 2, *1945–1950,* edited by Italo Calvino.

TRANSLATIONS

NOVELS

Among Women Only. Translated by D. D. Paige. London, 1953; New York, 1959.

The Beach and *A Great Fire.* Translated by W. J Strachan. Published under the title *The Beach.* London, 1963.

The Comrade. Translated by W. J. Strachan. London, 1959.

The Devil in the Hills. Translated by D. D. Paige. London, 1954; New York, 1959.

The Harvesters. Translated by E. A. Murch. London, 1961.

The House on the Hill. Translated by W. J. Strachan. London, 1956; New York, 1959.

The Moon and the Bonfires. Translated by Louise Sinclair. London, 1952. Translated by Marianne Ceconio. New York, 1953.

The Political Prisoner and *The Beautiful Summer.* Translated by W. J. Strachan. Published under the title *The Political Prisoner.* London, 1955.

The Selected Works of Cesare Pavese. Translated, with an introduction, by R. W. Flint. New York, 1968. Contains *The Beach, The House on the Hill, Among Women Only,* and *The Devil in the Hills.*

SHORT STORIES

Festival Night, and Other Stories. Translated by A. E. Murch. London, 1964.

Stories. Translated by A. E. Murch. New York, 1987.

Summer Storm, and Other Stories. Translated by A. E. Murch. London, 1964.

POETRY

Hard Labor: Poems. Translated by William Arrowsmith. New York, 1976.

ESSAYS

American Literature: Essays and Opinions. Translated by Edwin Fussell. Berkeley, Cal., 1970.

Dialogues with Leuco. Translated by William Arrowsmith and D. S. Carne-Ross. Ann Arbor, Mich., 1966.

DIARIES

The Burning Brand: Diaries 1935–1950. Translated by A. E. Murch with Jeanne Molli. New York, 1961.

BIOGRAPHICAL AND CRITICAL STUDIES

Biasin, Gian-Paolo. *The Smile of the Gods: A Thematic Study of Cesare Pavese's Works.* Ithaca, N.Y., 1968.

Catalano. Ettore. *Cesare Pavese: Fra politica e ideologia.* Bari, 1976.

Fernandez, Dominique. *Il romanzo italiano e la crisi della consciencza moderna.* Milan, 1960. Pp. 117–167.

——— . *L'Échec de Pavese.* Paris, 1967.

——— . *Le roman italien et la crise de la conscience moderne.* Paris, 1968. Pp. 141–211.

Freccero, John. "Mythos and Logos: *The Moon*

and the Bonfires." *Italian Quarterly* 4(16):3–16 (1961).

Ghezzi, Aurelia. "Life, Destiny, and Death in Cesare Pavese's *Dialoghi con Leuco.*" *South Atlantic Bulletin* 45:31–39 (1980).

Ginzburg, Natalia. "Portrait of a Friend." In her *The Little Virtues.* Translated by Dick Davis. New York, 1986.

Gioanola, Elio. *Cesare Pavese: La poetica dell'essere.* Milan, 1971.

Guiducci, Armanda. *Il mito Pavese.* Florence, 1967.

———. *Invito alla lettura di Cesare Pavese.* Milan, 1972.

Heiney, Donald. *Three Italian Novelists: Moravia, Pavese, Vittorini.* Ann Arbor, Mich., 1968.

Hutcheon, Linda. "Pavese's Intellectual Rhythm." *Italian Quarterly* 16(61):5–26 (1972).

King, Martha. "Silence, an Element of Style in Pavese." *Modern Language Notes* 87:60–77 (1972).

Lajolo, Davide. *An Absurd Vice: A Biography of Cesare Pavese.* Translated and edited, with an introduction, by Mario Pietralunga and Mark Pietralunga. New York, 1983.

Mollia, Franco. *Cesare Pavese: Saggio su tutti le opere.* Florence, 1963.

Mondo, Lorenzo. *Cesare Pavese.* Milan, 1961.

Musumeci, Antonino. "Pavese: Stylistics of a Mythology." *Symposium* 34:260–269 (1980).

Norton, Peter M. "Cesare Pavese and the American Nightmare." *Modern Language Notes* 77:24–36 (1962).

Pacifici, Sergio. *The Modern Italian Novel from Pea to Moravia.* Carbondale, Ill., 1979. Pp. 118–159. The source for most of the present essay.

Pulleti, Ruggero. *Cesare Pavese: La maturità impossibile.* Padua, 1961.

Thompson, A. D. " 'Slow Rotation Suggesting Permanence': History, Symbol, and Myth in Pavese's Last Novel." *Italian Studies* 34:105–121.

———. *Cesare Pavese: A Study of the Major Novels and Poems.* Cambridge, 1982.

Venturi, Gianni. *Pavese.* Florence, 1967.

SERGIO PACIFICI

SIMONE WEIL

(1909–1943)

ONE OF THE most controversial figures of our time, Simone Weil has been variously described as genius, saint and martyr, anti-Semite, social prophet, political theorist, revolutionary anarchist, mystic, and victim of paranoia. Having gained notoriety as a radical, she was vilified in turn by both conservatives and Communists in France. Charles de Gaulle dismissed her wartime proposals as those of a fool or madwoman. In 1943, at age thirty-four, she died of self-imposed starvation in an English sanatorium, convinced she was a vessel of truth, the possessor of "a deposit of pure gold" that "ought to be passed on" but that would instead be buried with her. She feared that no one would give serious attention to her thoughts precisely because they had "settled in so inadequate a being."

During her lifetime Weil was unknown in literary circles. Her publications consisted of a number of articles that appeared in periodicals, often obscure and with limited circulation; they dealt with such subjects as the quantum theory, the foreign policy of France, the revolutionary syndicalist (trade unionist) movement, the extinct civilization of the Cathars, and the causes of liberty and oppression. There was also her profound reflection on the *Iliad,* which she published in the *Cahiers du Sud,* the most important literary magazine in unoccupied France.

It wasn't until after the war that her thoughts, jotted down for the most part in notebooks (fragmentary and sometimes incomplete), first gained general public attention with the posthumous publication in 1947 of *La pesanteur et la grâce* (*Gravity and Grace*), a collection of aphorisms and *pensées* that contains some of her most arresting and provocative metaphysical perceptions. The publication of her social and political writings followed. T. S. Eliot—who recognized the importance of withholding "premature judgment and summary classification" of Weil's thought—wrote the introduction to the English translation of *L'Enracinement* (*The Need for Roots,* 1949), her main political work of later years; he characterized Weil as a "complex personality . . . a woman of genius . . . akin to that of the saints . . . a passionate champion of the common people and especially of the oppressed, . . . a stern critic of both Right and Left" who "cannot be classified either as a reactionary or as a socialist." Some of her work was compiled and published in *Collection Espoir,* founded and edited by Albert Camus, who, like Weil, was attracted to the philosophy of the Stoics and the political theories of the syndicalist movement.

In spite of Weil's desire that her ideas be considered independently of her person, a certain mystique has developed and continues to grow around her personality. Since her integrity required that she put her beliefs into practice, it has been speculated that her unusual life would have brought her renown even if she had not left political, philosophical, and spiritual writings of remarkable originality. In fact, as some scholars have observed, Weil studies, at least in English-speaking countries, tend to focus on biographical issues. Nevertheless the key to her extraordinary life can only be found in her oeuvre. Both may be viewed as obsessive expressions of a message.

LIFE

Simone Weil was born in Paris on 3 February 1909. Her father, Bernard Weil, a physician, and her mother, Selma (a diminutive of Salomea) Reinherz Weil, were solidly middle-class and devoted to their two children. André, her older brother, proved to be a child prodigy in mathematics, often compared to Pascal; he later joined the Institute for Advanced Study in Princeton, New Jersey. Simone always felt that her own intellectual powers were lacking when compared to her brother's genius. In her adolescence, owing to a deep sense of inferiority and perhaps envy, she experienced a profound period of depression. In a letter of 1942 that is included in the posthumous collection *Attente de Dieu* (*Waiting for God,* 1950), she explains that it was not the absence of visible success that distressed her but rather the thought of being excluded from "that transcendent realm of truth to which only the truly great have access." She thought she preferred death to life without truth. Eventually, however, she came to the realization that all human beings, even the least gifted, can penetrate that realm, reserved for genius, if only they long for truth and continually direct their attention toward its attainment. Echoing the Gospel, she comments retrospectively: "When one hungers for bread, one does not receive stones."

If one applies Jean-Paul Sartre's definition that a Jew is one who is regarded as such by others (regardless of whether he freely chooses to remain one or not), then it may be said that the family was Jewish. Bernard Weil, however, was a confirmed atheist, and the children were brought up as agnostics without any religious training whatsoever. Simone preferred not to think of herself as Jewish and wrote many harsh invectives against Israel. Prevented from teaching by an anti-Semitic Vichy decree, she wrote a letter of protest in 1941 to the commissioner of education, in which she declared:

> I do not consider myself a Jew, because I have never been in a synagogue; I was raised without religious practice of any kind by parents who are freethinkers. I have no attraction for the Jewish religion . . . and have been brought up from infancy on Hellenic, Christian, and French traditions.

A delicate, sickly child, she was plagued by poor health most of her life. Eating, for her, was to become more of an effort than a pleasure. Headaches, sometimes so disabling that they caused, in her words, a "paralysis of the faculties"—variously described as migraines, sinusitis, psychosomatic symptoms, or simply a mystery—began about the age of twelve and continued to torment her intermittently for the rest of her life.

She developed a Franciscan-like moral conscience, a profound compassion for and identification with those who have not. Below the secure and comfortable bourgeoisie in a France rigidly stratified by class, there existed the proletariat—bitter workers, miserable and often illiterate—to whom Weil was to become passionately devoted. To the bewilderment of many and the admiration of others, she was to reject the comfort of her own class and align herself with the poor and oppressed, convinced that personal contact and not just an intellectual grasp was essential for the complete understanding of their problems. Yet her motivation was not engendered simply by a sense of pity or justice. "I have a natural love for them [laborers]," she remarks. "I find them more beautiful than the bourgeois." Foreshadowing her later concern with political and social issues, at age eleven she attended a meeting of striking workers to help prepare for a demonstration. As a teenager, she became more deeply involved in social action of various kinds and the syndicalist movement in particular, convinced that collaboration between the classes was a deception.

In 1928, as a result of the *concours,* a highly competitive nationwide examination, Weil was accepted into the prestigious École Normale Supérieure (Simone de Beauvoir following in second place), which prepares its students, the intellectual élite of their generation, to teach in the lycées and the universities. Its emphasis on philosophy and logic reinforced Weil's natural bent for abstract reasoning. At the same time, she continued to study under the renowned and brilliant Alain (the pen name of Émile-Auguste Chartier), who had been her teacher at the Lycée Henri IV between 1925 and 1928 and who exerted a deep influence on her thinking. The other students at the École Normale took to calling her the Red Virgin, because of her strong sympathy for left-wing and pacifist movements, and the Categorical Imperative in Skirts, owing to her constant and somewhat irritating propensity for philosophical disputation.

In her *Mémoires* (1958), Simone de Beauvoir relates the only discussion she ever had with Weil. To Weil's insistent declaration that the only thing of any consequence was the revolution that was to feed the whole world, de Beauvoir countered that the main problem was not so much how to improve man's well-being as to discover the meaning of existence. To which Weil replied disdainfully: "It's easy to see you don't know what it's like to go hungry."

Much has been written about Weil's conscious or unconscious suppression of sexuality and apparent rejection of her femininity with the adoption of a somewhat masculine attire. The beautiful child, somewhere along the way, was transformed into a plain-looking woman who, fingers stained with nicotine and ink, peered out intently from behind thick glasses. Careless of her appearance, she made little effort to conform to the styles of the time. There are those who interpret her dress and other eccentricities—such as occasionally signing letters to her parents as "Your son, Simon" (they, in return, would sometimes address her as such)—as a denial of her own sexual identity.

John Dunaway argues that "the masculine tendencies are probably best explained as growing out of her stoic temperament, her lack of self-regard, and her conscious acceptance of a vocation of heroic self-sacrifice. Her acquaintances . . . were of the opinion that her work left her no time to be concerned with such matters." Simone Pétrement, Weil's friend and biographer, records that her appearance became more and more that of a poor person or a monk "who dresses as inexpensively as he can and devotes as little time as possible to it." She also notes that in pursuit of her life's work, which obliged Weil at times to enter a man's world (for example, to ride the cage to the bottom of a mine shaft), it was—as Weil herself later remarked—"a great misfortune to have been born a woman." So she made the decision to minimize this handicap as best she could by ignoring it.

Weil has been described as uncoordinated, clumsy, almost never without a cigarette in her mouth, and incapable of demonstrative expressions of affection. She spoke her insistent monologues in a monotone that was punctuated by a persistent cough. Many found her relentless curiosity and her incessant and insensitive questioning intolerable. This lack of both physical and social graces, it has been suggested, caused her to sublimate her emotional and sexual development, her mode of dress being a conscious or unconscious means of discouraging amorous advances. "There are so many ways of saying what I am does not satisfy me and has become me without my consent," she writes. "What I am, I endure." It should be noted that, while her mannerisms and her indifference to her appearance amused some and alienated others, there were those who readily overlooked these superficialities and found in Weil a stimulating companion and a devoted friend whom they admired and respected.

In any case, Weil herself offers other explanations. In a letter, she reveals that, while contemplating a mountain landscape at the age of sixteen, the idea of Christian purity took possession of her. Years later, she indicated to Pétrement that, although she had not categorically ruled love out of her life (she admitted having felt a strong attraction for one of the men in their circle of friends), she had for the time being other more important priorities. And at age twenty-six, she advised a student that love is not something to be taken lightly, since it entails the mutual pledging of two lives forever; otherwise, in her view, it is reprehensible. The problem, then, is to reconcile the demands and constraints of love with freedom. She admits having been tempted several times over the years to learn of love but decided against it, wishing first to be certain what it was she desired from life.

The completion of the *agrégation* in 1931 entitled her to a post in a lycée. She taught philosophy and sometimes Greek as well as literature in five different schools during the years 1931 through 1937. Almost immediately she acquired a reputation as a revolutionary activist, scandalizing the municipal authorities, who were outraged that a functionary of the government should accompany a delegation of quarry workers to the city council meeting to air their grievances, actually seek out and prefer the company of manual laborers, and be seen regularly with a copy of the Communist newspaper. Nor did she endear herself to the Ministry of Education when, carrying a big red flag, she participated in a protest march of 3,000 miners.

Since she showed an interest in acquiring some of their basic skills, her comrades taught her how to solder a joint and operate a pneumatic drill. Wishing to eradicate the intellectual contempt for the laborer and desirous of giving manual labor the dignity she felt was its due, Weil attempted to bring the proletariat into contact with humanistic studies and culture by organizing courses for workers, who,

she writes, are even more in need of poetry than bread. One of Weil's tenets is that the ideal person, the most accomplished and most truly human, is one who is simultaneously both manual laborer and intellectual.

Although her students respected and supported her, Weil's teaching methods were considered unorthodox in that she generally refused to comply with the prescribed curriculum, often neglecting to prepare her students for the *baccalauréat* (essential for admittance into the French university system). Her emphasis was on the development of sound critical judgment through the writing of numerous short compositions on philosophical questions, which she conscientiously and carefully corrected, in the belief that insights develop more naturally through disciplined writing. The negative results of her students in the *baccalauréat* exams quite naturally brought about the disapproval of her superiors.

In the summer of 1932, Weil visited Germany to observe and report on the political situation prior to Hitler's rise to power and the weaknesses she perceived in the Social Democratic and Communist parties.

Her lifestyle became one of austerity. She could not remember, she writes, ever having been without "the spirit of poverty." She adopted the practice of sleeping on the floor or on a table, thus limiting herself to a maximum of three or four hours' sleep. Determined to subsist on the same amount of money as the dole distributed to unemployed workers, she gave the remainder of her salary to the needy. Her one luxury was cigarettes. Since she continued to eat little, her health, which had never been good, became progressively worse. The headaches were sometimes so severe that at one time she contemplated suicide as the only possible relief.

Gradually Weil came to the realization that the formation of an effective political and social plan to improve the working conditions of the proletariat required a more intimate knowledge of their daily lives, not just a marginal participation. With this in mind, in 1934 she took a year's leave of absence from teaching ("for personal research") in order to study first-hand the social problems resulting from advanced technology in our modern industrial society.

To gain insight through personal experience, Weil began working in a factory in Paris that manufactured large-scale electrical machinery. The din from the machines exacerbated her headaches, and she found herself in a constant state of exhaustion. Lacking the energy and the strength required for this kind of manual labor, she was unable to perform satisfactorily. While operating dangerous machines and tending furnaces, she received lacerations and burns on her hands and arms. It was only on Saturday and Sunday, she notes in the journal she kept, that she would become conscious once again that she was a rational being and not a docile and resigned slave.

After four months of factory work, Weil contracted pleurisy and was obliged to leave for a short rest. She found employment again, this time in a "filthy," dismal, small workshop, running a huge press, but she was dismissed at the end of the month because she had been unable to meet the minimum production demands. Following a month of unemployment, she was hired at the Renault works until the beginning of the school year. Having refused to accept financial assistance from her family, she relied exclusively on her earnings for her subsistence. What others had theorized about abstractly, Weil had experienced concretely: persistent hunger, the tension of trying to meet production levels, subjection to the monotony of the assembly line, the humiliation of waiting on unemployment lines. "The capital fact is not the physical suffering," she observes, "but the humiliation." She warns that no society can be stable in which a whole stratum of the population labors day after day with intense loathing for their work. This loathing colors their outlook on life. Factory work, she says, creates a gaping "void that cries out to be filled," and

the violent gratifications that fill this void, together with the resulting corruption, contaminate all classes of society.

It has been said that Weil never truly learned what it is to be a laborer—oppressed, dehumanized, socially debased, desperate for work—in that she remained what she always had been, a bourgeois; she suffered not as a member of the proletariat, but as an *agrégée de philosophie* desiring to suffer like a member of the proletariat. One thinks of John Howard Griffin, who by ingesting chemicals temporarily changed the pigmentation of his skin in order to write *Black Like Me* (1961), a book about what it is like to be black, but who never really did find out, since he always knew that he could, and eventually would, return to the world of the white man. Weil, too, always knew that the humiliation, the indignities, and the suffering she endured could be removed instantly by a simple act of her will. The degradation that she shared and that she describes as being inherent in the daily life of the factory worker was, in her case, self-imposed. There is a difference.

But, as John Hellman has asked, how many intellectuals who speak with authority about the proletariat have ever worked alongside their subjects on assembly lines, farms, or boats? In any case, Weil's nine-month factory experience plunged her into the world of the suffering poor and marked her for life. The compassion she had always evidenced for the oppressed deepened and became an obsession with—or, depending on one's point of view, a vocation for—what she calls *malheur*. (There being no exact equivalent in English, the term is generally translated as "affliction.")

Weil makes a sharp distinction between suffering and affliction; we eventually grow indifferent to the suffering we have experienced, she says, as inexplicable as that may be, but affliction, which entails physical pain accompanied by anguish of soul and social degradation, marks the body and the soul for life. In an autobiographical letter, she reflects on the effects of her factory work, which became the focal point of many of her later writings:

> This contact with affliction had destroyed my youth. . . . I knew very well that there was much affliction in the world; I was obsessed with it, but I had never experienced it over a prolonged period of time. In the factory . . . the affliction of others entered my flesh and my soul. . . . There I received for all time the brand of the slave, like the mark of the red hot iron that the Romans put on the foreheads of their most despised slaves. From that time on I have always regarded myself as a slave.
>
> (*Waiting for God,* pp. 74–75)

She identifies Christianity as preeminently the religion of slaves, to which, therefore, she feels she belongs. Pétrement remarks that the trials Weil endured during her nine months in the factories mellowed her personality. She became less abrasive and scornful, less strident and judgmental, more patient.

A pessimism regarding Karl Marx's belief in "the liberating power of the revolution" had been evolving in Weil's thought for some time. Revolution and not religion, she writes, is the opium of the people. She had already disassociated herself from the trade unionist movement. Now she resolved to abandon politics, which she describes as "a sinister farce." The Bolshevik leaders had proposed to create a free working class, but had probably never set foot inside a factory; not one of them had any real idea of the oppressive conditions of the workers. In *Oppression et liberté* (*Oppression and Liberty,* 1955), she remarks that oppression results when there is, as Marx put it, a "degrading division of labor into intellectual and manual labor," where workers and technicians amount to passive drudges, "ignorant of the theoretical basis of the knowledge that they use." The ideal society, she concludes, would be one in which manual labor represents the highest value. In the last year of her life, speaking of "the spirituality of labor," she wrote that the purpose of all work is to lead man to an encounter with God.

Weil now returned to teaching but with less enthusiasm, and continued to work on neighboring farms without remuneration. Jacques Cabaud reports her having confessed to a farm laborer: "I want to live the life of the poor, to participate in their work, to share their troubles, to eat at their table."

With the outbreak of the Spanish Civil War in the summer of 1936, she took the train to Barcelona and made her way to the Aragon front, offering her support to the anarchist forces. Her intention had been to participate in a fight for justice. She soon learned, however, that what had appeared to be simply a struggle between starving peasants and their landed proprietors was in actuality a strategic war between world powers that used the Spanish people as pawns, and, further, that the Loyalists committed atrocities as freely and with as little compunction as Generalissimo Francisco Franco's troops. Having accidentally scalded herself with boiling oil and severely burned her leg, she returned to Paris with her wounds unhealed. She concluded that no war promotes the cause of freedom.

Her health, always poor and worsened by her work in the factories, was now further weakened by the injury she had sustained in Spain. She was obliged to apply twice for a medical leave of absence from teaching and finally had to abandon it altogether. Yet she continued to write articles on subjects of social and political interest, predicting World War II and condemning all forms of totalitarianism, in addition to filling notebook after notebook with fragmentary reflections on numerous topics.

Weil had always shown an interest in Christianity, an admiration for Christ, and an affinity for the Catholic Church in particular, but her faith had been the *amor fati* of the Stoics: a love of the universe for its order and beauty and the impersonal providence that governs it. Because she held "the problem of God" to be one that could not be resolved, her method of dealing with it was to neither affirm nor deny anything. While vacationing in Italy during the summer of 1937, she visited the little twelfth-century Romanesque chapel of Santa Maria degli Angeli in Assisi, where Saint Francis often prayed. She writes that, inexplicably, a sudden and powerful feeling overwhelmed her: "Something stronger than I compelled me for the first time in my life to go down on my knees."

In 1938 Weil spent Easter Week at the Benedictine monastery of Solesmes, where she went to hear the Gregorian plainchant for which Solesmes is renowned. Her headaches were devastating, but by making an intense effort she was able to leave her miserable body to suffer alone, "crumpled in a corner," while she found what she describes as a "pure and perfect joy" in the beauty of the liturgy. It was then, by analogy, she says, that she arrived at a clearer understanding of Christ's passion: the possibility of loving God in the midst of affliction. Throughout her work, Weil insists on the strange affiliation between suffering and divine love. Affliction is a manifestation of God's mercy and can lead to joy, providing that love is not abandoned.

A young man who was visiting the monastery at the same time introduced her to the English metaphysical poets of the seventeenth century. She was particularly struck by George Herbert's poem "Love" (1633), which she memorized and made a practice of reciting, meditating on the moving words of God's invitation to the sinner. She had thought she was merely reciting a beautiful poem, but, as she puts it, without her intending it the recitation had become a prayer, in the course of which "Christ himself came down and took possession of me." Neither the senses nor the imagination played a role in this experience, she explains. She only felt, in the midst of her suffering, the presence of a love, "much like that which one senses in the tender smile on the face of a loved one," yet more personal and more real than that of any human being.

Weil had never conceived of the possibility of an actual contact, person to person, between a human being and the Deity, of an intimate relationship between creature and Creator. God, she later records, had prevented her from reading the mystics, so that she should not erroneously conclude that her encounters with him were illusory. She now had the deep conviction that she belonged to Christ. She considered herself a convert to Christianity, but a modified Christianity, one that she refused to see as a development of Judaism, conceiving of it instead as an evolution of Greek thought.

As time passed, a conflict arose in Weil's mind between the certitude of her mystical experience and the philosophical mentality that continued to inform all of her thinking. Her intellect only half accepted what had taken place. One can never struggle enough against God, she states, if one does so in the quest for truth. Christ wants us to prefer truth to him, because before being Christ he is truth: "If one turns away from him to move toward truth, one won't go far before falling into his arms." (One is reminded of Nicholas of Cusa, who remarked that truth is not an abstraction, a substance, or a thing but a person.)

In *La connaissance surnaturelle* (Supernatural Knowledge, 1950), there is a fragment which, as Richard Rees points out in *Simone Weil: A Sketch for a Portrait,* offers an explanation acceptable to any conventional rationalist: "If love finds no object, the lover must love his love itself, perceived as something external. Then one has found God." In any case, her subsequent writings reveal a preoccupation with drawing analogies between Christianity and Eastern philosophies, in the Vedas and the Upanishads, in Osiris, and in Plato. In reading the sacred literature of ancient India, she notes that the *Bhagavad Gita* complements the Gospels and that certain Buddhist teachings strongly resemble those of Christ.

Hitler's invasion of Czechoslovakia caused Weil, not without some hesitation, to renounce her pacifist position altogether. With the outbreak of war and the division of France into two zones, she left Paris after it was declared an open city in 1940 and went to Marseilles, where she became associated with a group of writers who expressed their views in a literary magazine known as the *Cahiers du Sud.* Under the anagrammatic pseudonym Émile Novis, she published several poems as well as a number of articles, including her intriguing essay "L'*Iliade; ou, Le poème de la force*" (*The "Iliad"; or, The Poem of Force,* 1940). It was at this time that she wrote *Venise sauvée* (Venice Preserved, 1955), an unfinished tragedy, partly in verse, based on a seventeenth-century story by Abbé de Saint-Réal and dealing with the Spanish conspiracy against the republic of Venice.

Metaphysical questions continued to preoccupy Weil during this period. She sought answers in the sacred books of the Egyptians, the works of Thomas Aquinas, Meister Eckhart, Theresa of Ávila, and John of the Cross, and the spiritual writings of the East. "Only God is worth concern," she writes. "Nothing else is." She felt herself drawn to Catholicism. Convinced of Christ's presence in the Eucharist, she began a serious study of the dogmas of the Church, but certain tenets troubled her.

At this time two men entered her life whose counsel, friendship, and understanding of her personal quest were comforting to her. A friend directed her to Father Joseph-Marie Perrin, a learned Dominican priest, who became her confidant and spiritual director. When she expressed a desire to become acquainted with the agricultural proletariat, he sent her to Gustave Thibon, a self-educated farmer in the Ardèche, who found her work as a grape harvester. She desired to become "empty of self," Thibon writes, by abandoning herself totally to earth and nature, to experience what soul and thought become in one who is ceaselessly subject to hard, mandatory work on the land, which, she hoped, would give itself in turn to her, "filling her emptiness with its plenitude."

Weil labored hard in the fields, even managing, despite her frailty, to acquire some competence. Excessive fasting continued to undermine her health; it was not uncommon for her to miss meals, satisfying herself with the berries she picked in the countryside. In the evening, she read Greek with Thibon, discussed philosophy, and worked late into the night on her writings. A warm friendship and mutual respect developed between them, in spite of the fact that initially she had irritated Thibon, causing his family considerable inconvenience by rejecting the quarters offered her on the grounds that they were too comfortable. She was detached from everything, he writes, but her own detachment: "Her ego was like a word she had, perhaps, managed to erase but left underlined."

It was at this time that Weil first experienced the desire to pray. Previously she had refrained from doing so, fearing the power of suggestion that prayer might have on her. While harvesting grapes it had become her practice to meditate on the spiritual value of labor and to repeat with "absolute attention" the Greek text of the Pater Noster, which she had committed to memory. These recitations, she comments, brought with them the certainty of Christ's presence. At times she felt that her soul was torn from her body and carried "to a place outside space where there is neither perspective nor point of view." Space opened up. This infinity of space was permeated by a dense silence, "which was not an absence of sound, but the object of a positive sensation, more real than sound."

These mystical experiences, Cabaud points out, should not be confused with the revelation described on the two loose pages, found after Weil's death, inserted in the middle of a notebook; it is this text Camus chose as the prologue for *La connaissance surnaturelle:*

He entered my room and said: "You poor creature, you understand nothing and know nothing; come with me and I will teach you things of which you have no idea." I followed him.

He led me into a church; it was new and ugly. He took me up to the altar and told me to kneel down. I said: "I have not been baptized." He answered: "Fall on your knees before this place with love, as you would before the place where truth exists." I obeyed.

He led me out and up to an attic room; through the open window we could see the whole city, wooden scaffolding, the river with boats discharging their cargo. He invited me to sit down.

We were alone. He talked. Occasionally someone would come in, join in our conversation, and then leave.

It was no longer winter. Nor was it yet spring. The branches of the trees were bare, without buds, in a cold air bathed in sunlight.

The light grew stronger, became dazzling bright, then faded; the stars and the moon could be seen clearly through the window. Then once more dawn broke.

At times he would fall silent and take some bread from a cupboard, which we shared between us. That bread truly tasted like bread. I have never since tasted anything like it.

He poured wine for me and for himself, which had the taste of the sun and the earth upon which that city had been built.

Sometimes we would stretch out on the floor, and the sweetness of sleep would fall upon me. Then I would awake and drink in the sunlight.

He had promised to teach me something, but he taught me nothing. We talked about anything and everything, without reserve, as old friends do.

One day he said: "Now, go." I fell on my knees, put my arms around his legs, and begged him not to send me away. But he put me out on the stairs. I went down, bewildered and broken-hearted. I wandered about the streets. Finally I realized that I had no idea where that house was.

I have never tried to find that attic room again. He made a mistake in coming for me. My place is not in that garret. It's anywhere else, in a prison cell, in one of those bourgeois rooms full of bric-a-brac and red plush, in a station waiting room. Anywhere, but not in that attic room.

Sometimes, despite fear and remorse, I can't resist repeating to myself some of the things he told me. But how can I be sure my memory is accurate? He is not here to assure me.

I know very well that he does not love me. How could he love me? And yet, deep inside, though I tremble with fear the while, something within me cannot help thinking that perhaps he does love me after all.

(pp. 9–10)

This text can be read as an allegory of Weil's spiritual progression: the encounter with the divine lover, the happiness and peace in this intimacy, and finally the classic "dark night of the soul," complete with apparent abandonment, doubts, anguish, and near despair. E.W.F. Tomlin suggests that "this passage is a happy hunting ground for the psychiatrist" but clearly rejects the hasty conclusion on the part of some that Weil was a neurotic whose transports were nothing more than a veiled form of eroticism. Tomlin notes that her writings are "remarkably free from any sentimental, yearning quality" and, further, that she manifests none of the self-deception of the neurotic.

That men and women fall in love with each other is an incontestable fact. That some fall in love with the Infinite is not universally acknowledged. That the Creator so passionately loves his creatures as to enter into intimate communion with them is considered by many, if not most, to be a delusion. Interpretations of Weil's revealed mystical encounters naturally depend, to a large extent, on one's *a priori* metaphysical or philosophical perspective on existence, the nature of man, and the supernatural. The modern secular reader who professes a repudiation of all transcendentals will deny the possibility of establishing communication between the spirit of man and That Which Is, the "Wholly Other," which some philosophers call the Absolute and most theologians God. Evelyn Underhill, one of the most highly respected scholars of mystical literature, insists in *Mysticism* (1911) that the reports of the mystics are given with "a strange accent of certainty and good faith" and recommends, therefore, that we give to them "the same attention" that we allow "to other explorers of countries in which we are not competent to adventure ourselves."

Weil next returned to Marseilles, having decided after much vacillation to accompany her parents to the United States, a decision she was later to regret bitterly. Her concern was to see them settled safely in New York; then she intended to leave for England to join the Free French movement. Before her departure in May 1942, she made a formal protest on behalf of the demobilized Annamite troops newly arrived from Indochina—who, she felt, were being poorly housed, pending repatriation—and succeeded in having the commandant of the camp transferred. She entrusted her papers, about twelve thick notebooks, to Thibon and wrote a long letter to Father Perrin (published in *Waiting for God*), containing an account of the evolution of her spiritual life and her credo; the last sentence reveals in full what has been called Weil's vocation for suffering: "Every time I reflect on the crucifixion of Christ, I commit the sin of envy."

Along with her parents, she was obliged to spend three weeks in a refugee camp in Casablanca before embarking for America. During this time she hurriedly revised and completed some of her notes, which were published posthumously as *Intuitions préchrétiennes* (included in *Intimations of Christianity Among the Ancient Greeks*, 1951).

Arriving in New York City in July 1942, the Weils rented an apartment near Columbia University. Simone attended mass regularly and also assisted at Sunday services of the Harlem Baptist Church, where she was the only white person in attendance. Pursuing her interest in establishing analogies between various myths and folklores and Christianity, she frequented the New York Public Library. And in preparation for the mission she hoped to obtain in occupied France, she took a course in first aid.

However, with increased political tension in Europe, travel to England had become severely restricted. Weil had never wanted to leave France, and now she was overwhelmed with feelings of guilt: she had abandoned her country in time of need; she should be sharing the suffering of her countrymen. She wrote urgent letters expressing her anguish to a former classmate, Maurice Schumann, whose intervention finally succeeded in gaining her passage on a Swedish ship bound for Liverpool in mid November. Of particular interest is her confession to him of her obsession with affliction: "The affliction spread over the surface of the earth obsesses me . . . , and I can only . . .

free myself from this obsession if I myself have a large share of danger and suffering."

By the end of November, Weil was in London at the Free French headquarters, analyzing proposals for the future constitution of the French republic and composing a number of studies on the postwar rehabilitation of France. She had asked for a more dangerous assignment, such as being parachuted into occupied France as a courier or for purposes of sabotage, but this was wisely deemed impracticable by the authorities. Continuing her entreaties for a perilous mission, she explained: "I can't remain here while Christ is suffering elsewhere." Extremely disappointed, she nonetheless devoted herself to her work. The essays in *Écrits de Londres et dernières lettres* (Writings from London and Last Letters, 1957; selections in *Selected Essays*, 1962) and *The Need for Roots* reflect the outcome of this political theorizing and philosophical speculation.

Weil's health deteriorated further as her asceticism increased. Upon leaving Marseilles, she had resolved to eat no more than the amount allotted in her countrymen's wartime rations. Now she drastically reduced her diet even more. It was not uncommon for her colleagues on arriving in the morning to find that, after working late into the night, she had fallen asleep at her desk or on the floor. In letters to friends, she speaks of an all-pervading fatigue and general weakness. As if aware that death was imminent, Weil accelerated her creative output, seemingly desperate to put down on paper the thoughts that "settled" in her mind on various subjects.

Succumbing finally to extreme exhaustion and pulmonary tuberculosis, she was hospitalized in April 1943. The prognosis was good, but she refused both the pneumothorax and adequate nourishment, murmuring that her compatriots in France were starving. Cabaud and others offer the opinion that Weil, unaware of an anorexic condition (as it was later diagnosed), supplied moral reasons for her refusal to eat. "It seemed to her," Cabaud writes, "that a divine law of compensation was in operation," that the unfortunate were, in some arcane way, able to benefit from the food which she deprived herself of. It is of interest to note that this thought is not alien to Catholic tradition.

Some critics, commenting on her affinity for the Cathars (the heretical Albigensian sect that flourished in the Languedoc of southern France during the twelfth century), suggest that Weil willingly induced death by starvation in conformity with "the most religious death" of the Perfecta, the spiritual leaders of the community. This seems unlikely, given Weil's forthrightness and penchant for the truth; had this been her motivation, she would have labeled it as such. Further, as her biographers have recorded, there were times when she made a genuine effort to eat, even requesting particular foods, but simply could not bring herself to swallow them. There seems to be no doubt that anorexia did indeed play a part in her excessive fastings, but this psychological disorder does not explain other ascetic practices. She was seeking detachment from more than food.

Weil has been accused of masochism and dolorism. In this regard, the notation that appears in her prewar notebooks is of capital importance: "I believe in the value of suffering, providing one makes every effort to avoid it." To desire affliction, she records elsewhere, is against nature: a perversion. At the same time, like all mystics, Weil welcomed suffering, regarding it as a kind of sacrament where the finite and the Infinite meet. "God uses suffering," she writes, "as a decreation to pull us toward him." God has suffered, she reasons; therefore, "suffering is something divine." No compensation or consolation should be sought; suffering will bear fruit in "attentive patience." She rejoiced in her discovery that Christianity doesn't seek a spiritual remedy for suffering, but rather makes a supernatural use of it. Like Pierre Teilhard de Chardin, she believed one should not brace oneself against pain but surrender to it, as to a great loving energy. "How can a human being whose essence it is to love God and who finds himself existing in time and space," she asks, "have any other vocation than the cross?" She wished to "become nothing," because as soon as she became nothing, God would love himself through her: "If we become nothing, Christ comes to fill our void."

Mystical literature offers considerable difficulty to the uninitiated; only mystics, it would seem, understand mystics. And no philosophy has ever satisfactorily explained pain, deprivation, and anguish; they can only be grasped intuitively by the religious spirit. "Suffering is the ancient law of love," the Eternal Light says to the German mystic Suso, and Récéjac declares that in order to approach the absolute, mystics must withdraw from everything, even from themselves. Examples can be multiplied from the writings of mystics of all cultures. Before leaving New York City, Weil recorded in her notebook the following awesome prayer, which has troubled many who have since read it:

Father, in the name of Christ, grant me this. That my will be incapable of bringing about any movement of my body, not even the slightest, like that of a total paralytic. That I may be blind, deaf, and incapable of receiving any sensation, like someone devoid of all his senses. That I be unable to make any connection whatsoever between two thoughts, even the simplest, like one of those complete idiots, who not only cannot count or read, but who have never even been able to learn to speak. That I may be insensible to sorrow or joy of any kind, to love for anyone or anything, even for myself, like the aged in the last stages of senility.

. . . May this body move or be immobile, with perfect suppleness or rigidity, always in conformity with your will. May these faculties of hearing, sight, taste, smell, and touch register perfectly the exact impress of your creation. May this intellect, in fullest lucidity, connect all ideas in perfect conformity with your truth. May this sensibility experience as intensely as possible and in all its purity, all the nuances of sorrow and joy. May this love be an all-consuming flame of love of God for God. May all this be stripped from me, devoured by God, transformed into the substance of Christ, and fed to the afflicted whose bodies and souls lack every kind of nourishment. And let me be a paralytic, blind, deaf, witless, and in a state of senile decay.

(*La connaissance surnaturelle*, pp. 204–207)

One key to this petition for self-immolation is what is called the "reversibility of sufferings," whereby it is believed possible to alleviate one suffering through another—a mystery of communion. Weil is asking to be offered up as a sacrificial victim, that her pain and deprivation be united with those of Christ, and through his to others in a dynamic network. She stresses absolute obedience to the divine will, one of her principal tenets. But the extremity of such a prayer goes beyond the desire for self-sacrifice.

The second key is her belief in the need for what she has termed "decreation," the stripping away of empirical personality in anticipation of God's ensuing action. She is expressing a longing for dissolution, so that she may finally be united with "the living flame of love." The mystical fulfillment of love, it is said, requires the annihilation of selfhood, the entire surrender of self. Scattered throughout her writings are aphorisms such as the following: "We must become nothing, we must descend to a vegetative level; it is then that God becomes bread" and "Renunciation requires that we experience anguish equivalent to the loss of all loved ones and all possessions, including our faculties. . . . And we must not renounce these things ourselves; they must be taken from us— like Job." This terrible prayer, as Pétrement and others refer to it, is not Weil's but that of the Holy Spirit. One does not voluntarily ask such things, she explains; one reaches this point in spite of oneself. But then one consents completely, without reserve. The mystic experience, Récéjac observes, echoing Saint Paul, ends with the words: "I live, yet not I, but God in me" (*cf.* Galatians 2:20).

Weil had written, "I am separated from Truth," and Father Perrin suggests that it was this separation that was at the heart of her de-

sire for death. It has often been noted that a "death wish" is not uncommon among mystics. The term, as used by contemporary psychologists, has strong negative overtones, suggesting a pathological condition. On the other hand, Jacques Maritain explains in *The Range of Reason* (1952) that man has aspirations that transcend human nature; these "transnatural aspirations" are a longing for a state in which man would finally "know things completely and without error, . . . in which he would inhabit a realm of unfading justice, in which he would have the intuitive knowledge of the First Cause of being." It is important to note, however, that with Weil, as with all mystics, there was, first and foremost, the desire to conform to the divine will. Saint Paul expresses this dual longing in Philippians 2:21, and the apostle's desire for death has always been given a positive evaluation by Christian tradition.

A week before her death, extremely weak and with both lungs seriously infected, Weil was transferred to Grosvenor Sanatorium in Ashford, Kent. On 24 August 1943 she fell into a coma and died. In his literary portrait of Weil, Rees makes the poignant comment, "As for her death, whatever explanation one may give of it will amount in the end to saying that she died of love."

SELECTED THOUGHTS

A team of scholars, under the auspices of the Association pour l'étude de la pensée de Simone Weil, is currently engaged in the compilation of the manuscripts and correspondence of Weil for a projected complete edition of her works. In addition, the American Weil Society, which is affiliated with the French organization, holds annual meetings and publishes a newsletter with bibliographical and scholarly information. Her manuscripts are on file at the Bibliothèque Nationale in Paris, and a complete microfilm of her oeuvre is on deposit at the Institute for Advanced Study in Princeton, New Jersey. With the exception of *The Need for*

Roots, which the author regarded as a rough draft, the books that have been brought out under Weil's name are actually collections of letters; notes; articles, published and unpublished; reviews; and meditations in the form of single words, phrases, or paragraphs—fragments, sometimes repetitious, unsystematic, contradictory, or obscure, that were often written with no intent of publication.

Weil's thought is (to use Dunaway's term) holistic; that is, all of her views, without exception, are directly related to her metaphysics, transcendentally oriented. The profundity of her reflections, however, can be fully appreciated only by a global reading, as her perspectives evolved with the passage of time, and themes that preoccupied her are scattered throughout her writings in various stages of development. Statements without reference to the corpus of her work are apt to lead to erroneous interpretations. According to her own testimony, as soon as she arrived at any conclusion, her modus operandi was to make every effort to discover in what sense the contrary was true. All of her speculations on a given topic are not to be found in a single text.

The English reader has an additional problem, in that translations do not always correspond exactly to the French editions. For example, *Intimations of Christianity* is a collection of Weil's writings on Greek thought, which includes all of *Intuitions préchrétiennes* and part of *La source grecque* (The Greek Source, 1953); *La connaissance surnaturelle* is contained, along with other works, in *First and Last Notebooks* (1970); this is the case with several other collections. Thus in considering her thought, one generally encounters a history or development of her ideas rather than analyses of individual texts.

"The Great Beast Is Always Repulsive"

Rome: The "Great Beast of the Apocalypse." Weil employs the Platonic metaphor throughout her writings to denounce transcendent social idolatry. The "we," the collective, when it becomes the object of idolatry, when it is taken as an end, chains us to the earth, she says. She writes of Rome, the "great beast of atheism and materialism, adoring only itself," as the early Christians spoke of Babylon. It represented, for her, all that she most abhorred: conquest and cruelty, colonialism, nationalism.

In *Écrits historiques et politiques* (Historical and Political Writings, 1960; selections in *Selected Essays*), she draws a parallel between the Roman Empire and Hitler's regime. What menaces the world is not, as some maintain, a perpetually aggressive German nation, but rather a mentality that encourages tyranny, a mentality that pervades our contemporary civilization. We have been taught to admire the Roman Empire; yet when that very same process of imperialistic conquest, subjugation, and exploitation is reproduced before our eyes, we recoil in horror. She rejects the traditional argument that Roman atrocities be excused on the grounds that there was a different moral code in antiquity, insisting that there is no reason to believe morality ever changes and citing in support of her thesis ancient Egyptian and Greek texts. And even if morality had changed, she adds, that does not justify our speaking in glowing terms of the Rome that totally abolished several civilizations and eradicated ideas that made up "the grandeur of what we term antiquity," that morally and spiritually uprooted and enslaved conquered nations, and that had a corrupting influence on western culture, on Christianity in particular. For the Beast of the Apocalypse, she writes, is almost certainly the empire. And again: "Such a terrible thing as Christ's crucifixion could only occur in a place in which evil far outweighed good. The Church, conceived and nurtured in such an atmosphere, must needs be impure from its inception."

She expresses the opinion that Rome introduced into history an insidious and pernicious notion of patriotism. The Romans were an idolatrous people, she asserts, not with regard to images, but with regard to themselves. And it is this idolatrous form of patriotism that the West has inherited: the need to humiliate the vanquished in addition to subjugating them. In Gaul and wherever they went, the Romans instituted the public spectacle of putting to death, in the most barbarous ways, thousands of innocent people to amuse the mob, and yet we call them civilizers.

French culture, Weil claims, has been impregnated with the Roman ideal. The literary heroes of Pierre Corneille and Jean Racine and the verses of Victor Hugo and Jean de La Fontaine, for instance, reflect the glory of conquest and subjugation, rather than that of serving justice and the public good. The leaders who have governed France and who, even today, are held up for our admiration, Louis XIV and Napoleon in particular, are products of this Roman mentality: "To look upon one's country as an absolute value that cannot be corrupted by evil is manifestly absurd."

The Roman Empire turned Christianity, she comments, into a state religion, and in the twentieth century religious life has been subordinated to adoration of the fatherland. Some French writers of the Catholic Renaissance movement, Charles Péguy, for example, have written moving works—which Weil labels blasphemous—on themes such as "eternal France," the vocation of France, and the cult of Joan of Arc. The idea of a nation set apart, "elected," she insists, belongs to the Mosaic law: "There is no such thing as a holy nation." A nation has no soul, no eternal destiny. France is not divine; she is finite, temporal, imperfect, and fragile. Some love France, she notes, for the glory they imagine ensures for her an extended existence in time and space, instead of for her earthliness and vulnerability, for which she is all the more precious. Compassion, she argues, is what France needs, and this same compassion should extend itself to all countries in misfortune; for all experience the misery of the human condition, whereas pride in national glory is by its very nature exclusive.

It was the Roman kind of arrogant patriotism that was responsible for imperialistic colonialism. Manifesting a certain pride in France as the cradle of liberty, equality, and fraternity, Weil admonishes her countrymen in *A Need for Roots:*

> Every other nation might conceivably have the right to carve out an empire for itself, but not France, for the same reason which made the temporal sovereignty of the pope a scandal in Christendom. When one takes upon oneself, as France did in 1789, the responsibility of thinking on behalf of the world, that is, of defining justice for the world, one does not then become an owner of human flesh.
>
> (p. 146)

Let the new French republic, she pleads, become a model of justice among nations.

Christians do not want to face the issue, she writes, as to the priority of their loyalties: God or country. The German bishops terminated one of their protests by declaring that they refused ever to choose between God and country. Circumstances can always occur, she insists, which may require that a choice be made between God and something else; and the choice must never be in doubt. The French bishops, she adds, would have expressed themselves no differently.

Israel: The "Great Beast of Religion." Weil has been accused by some of anti-Semitism. Passionately solicitous of human suffering, supporter and defender of the oppressed, evoking in her writings the horrors experienced by thousands of workers in concentration camps, her voice was strangely muted when it came to the persecution of the Jews who suffered in those same camps and elsewhere. Deeply devoted to the passion and cross of Christ, with which she personally identified, it has been noted that she could have—but did not—like Jacques Maritain, view Israel in affliction as coming to resemble more and more the body of Christ crucified. Some suggest that, consumed with the desire for self-effacement, she could never place herself in the position of speaking out in her own defense.

On the other hand, a deluge of invectives poured forth from her pen against her own heritage (perhaps, as some maintain, precisely because it was her heritage): "Israel. All from Abraham on inclusively (except for some of the prophets) is tainted and monstrous, as if by design. . . . As if to point out with absolute clarity: 'Take note: Here is evil!' A people chosen for their moral blindness, chosen to be the executioners of Christ." Or "The Jews, that handful of uprooted people, have caused the uprooting of the whole planet. The atrocities, the Inquisition, the liquidation of heretics and infidels, this was Israel. Capitalism is Israel. . . . Totalitarianism is Israel. . . ." Or "Jahveh made the same assurances to Israel as the devil did to Christ."

Eliot expresses the opinion that her castigation of Israel (the term is being used as Weil and other religious writers employ it, and not with reference to the modern state) is that of a Hebrew prophet, and reminds us that, though she was clearly drawn to the Church of Rome, much of what she wrote constitutes a formidable criticism of the Church; further, as a passionate patriot who would gladly have suffered and died for her country, she was outspoken about the faults and weaknesses of France. Still, one cannot help but lose tolerance for her position upon learning that she favored a law for postwar France by which the number of Jews in administrative posts would be limited, and that she proposed that mixed marriages be encouraged and the children of such unions be brought up in the Christian faith. Taking the stance that the world has "endured enough from the birth of new nations," she protested against Jewish immigration to Palestine: "Why create a new nationality?"

Remarkably erudite, Weil was well acquainted with religious and philosophic systems, ancient and modern, of both the East and the West, yet she ignores the profundity of the Hebrew writings and Jewish mysticism. Despite the fact that this forceful antipathy is an obsessive theme that recurs throughout her works, strongly suggesting the possibility of a complex, many scholars on Weil seem to neglect, minimize, or excuse this disturbing aspect of her thought. Leslie A. Fiedler feels that a more accurate description of Weil's antagonistic "doctrines" might be better termed "anti-Israelism" or "anti-Judaism," since it was the beliefs of the Jews, as she understood them, that she found so intolerable.

According to Weil, Israel was the embodiment of evil, in that it, too, worshiped what Plato calls "the great beast." In contrast to atheistic Rome, Israel's form of idolatry was "the tribal God," a national God of power, a concept, she writes, that caused the Hebrews to lose their sense of good and evil. Like the Romans, Israel could only recognize collective values: "The idol of the Hebrews was not something made of metal or wood, but a race, a nation. . . . Because of their belief in themselves as the 'chosen people,' their religion was essentially idolatry."

Yahweh was the cruel God of battles. No reasonable person, she states, could possibly regard the pitiless God of the Hebrew armies and the Father of the New Testament as one and the same. Israel and its religious tradition, she declares, have contaminated and distorted the true Christian spirit.

Weil appreciated some of the prophets, the Book of Job, and the psalms, and especially the Song of Songs, but was confirmed in her opinion that there was very little spirituality in Israel until the exile, that the Hebrews rejected the supernatural revelation because they did not want a God who spoke to the individual soul in secret, but one who presented himself to the nation as a whole and protected them on the battlefield: "What they desired was power and prosperity. . . . No wonder such a people was able to give scarcely anything good to the world."

Catholicism, she urges, must purify itself of the abomination of Israel. Drawn to the Catholic Church, she would not cross the threshold, partly because she saw it as "too Jewish." Maintaining that the Gospels were a product of Greek thought and not, as Christians hold, a fulfillment of the Old Testament, she was disturbed to find that the Church confirmed the Hebrew belief that the Jews were a chosen people.

The Church: "That Great Totalitarian Beast." The dual influence of the Old Testament and the Roman Empire, whose tradition the papacy continued, was, according to Weil, the essential cause of the corruption of Christianity. Against Roman Catholicism she brings the charge of exclusivism, suggesting that it denies validity to other approaches to God. The Church, she holds, is Catholic de jure, but not de facto, and it would cause her considerable anguish, she says, to be separated from the vast mass of unbelievers, whom she loves.

Even though she states repeatedly that she "belongs to Christ," Weil argues the possibility of prior incarnations of the Word: Melchizedek, Osiris, and Krishna, for example. Being of the opinion that the various religious traditions all reflect in essence the same truth, she saw herself as situated at "the intersection of Christianity and everything that is not Christian." Christianity, she writes, holds explicitly a number of truths that other religions contain implicitly, and conversely, other religious traditions contain explicitly what is implicit in Christianity. Cabaud observes that Weil subscribes to a *religio perennis,* whose teachings might be simultaneously present in several different traditions and which are assured of ultimate survival.

Weil notes that the mystical experience is identical in all cultures and that the only hope for purifying Christianity lies in the mystic consciousness. It was because of her affinity for mystical spirituality as well as her detestation of power that Weil was attracted to the Cathars; she never forgave the Church for the part it played in the persecution and annihilation of what she looked upon as an ideal spiritual civilization.

Weil's syncretistic leanings account only in part for her rejection of baptism. She was convinced that it was her vocation to remain a Christian outside the Church. If it had been otherwise, she writes, she would have been driven by an irresistible inner compulsion to ask for the sacrament, in which case she would have eagerly obeyed, for it was her ardent desire to receive the Eucharist. She thought of herself, Cabaud remarks, as the bell that calls others into the Church, while she herself was obliged to remain outside.

Insisting on the right to intellectual freedom, Weil objected to the Church's use through the centuries of the words *anathema sit* in its pronouncements of excommunication. While revering it as the guardian of truth and dispenser of the sacraments, she rejected the institutional Church, the social structure that invariably tended toward totalitarianism, "something oppressive and tyrannical." Dogmas, she claims, are not to be affirmed but to be contemplated with love. Still, in her own way, she herself affirmed the Trinity, the Incarnation, the Redemption, and the Eucharist. Toward the end of her life, though she continued to be its uncompromising critic, she declared that she was outside the Church only insofar as it was a social entity; she belonged to what has been called "the invisible Church."

Deus Absconditus

According to Weil's metaphysics, the act of creation involves a simultaneous act of abandonment on the part of the Deity. God has withdrawn from the world and, to give his creation some degree of independence, has renounced his sovereignty to what she calls the law of "necessity," the law of cause and effect. She does not mean that God is totally absent; she affirms that the creative hand continues to support and sustain all in existence, that the Creator is profoundly present in the order and beauty of the world and even abides among us in other more intimate and arcane ways.

Echoing the fourth Evangelist, she declares that God is love, and it is this definition of the Transcendent that forms the basis of her philosophy. "He loves," she writes in *La connaissance surnaturelle,* "not as I love, but as an

2802

emerald is green. He *is* 'I love.'" Along with most contemporary philosophers, she regards the traditional proofs of the existence of God as being, at best, highly questionable, but declares:

> I am totally convinced that there is a God in that I am absolutely sure that my love is not an illusion. I am totally convinced that there is no God in that I am absolutely sure that nothing real resembles what I could conceive of when I pronounce this word. But that of which I cannot conceive is not an illusion.
>
> (*Gravity and Grace,* p. 116)

Like Blaise Pascal, she felt that a loving intuition is more trustworthy than dialectic proofs. She points out that many, unknowingly, are idolatrous, adoring under the name of God a product of their imagination, a projection of themselves, so that the atheist's view is perhaps closer to the truth. God has withdrawn from the world in order that man may not love him in the way that he loves everything else, as an expansion of his ego.

Weil conceives of the Deity in both impersonal and personal terms. On the one hand, she is in agreement with certain early Greek philosophers and the Pythagorean doctrine of relations in particular, insisting that the Reality governing the cosmos is an impersonal one. Hence she rejects Jacques-Bénigne Bossuet's view of the providential ordering of history, Teilhard de Chardin's eschatological outlook of the entire cosmos moving toward a preordained Omega point, and the concept of miracles, since she finds it capricious that God would contravene the laws of nature that he has established. On the other hand, she sees in nature an arcane reflection of the supernatural, "a mysterious complicity, as regards the Good, on the part of the matter that makes up the world." Further, in *Intimations of Christianity,* she attenuates her position on miracles and declares that, though autonomous, nature is nonetheless changed by the presence of the supernatural:

> We are like shipwrecked people, who, clinging to logs floating in the ocean, are tossed about by every wave that comes their way and over which they have no control. From Heaven, God throws down a lifeline to each one of us. He who grabs hold of the lifeline and does not let go, in spite of pain and fear, continues to be buffeted, along with the others, by the waves. For him, however, these buffets merge with the tension of the rope to create a different mechanical whole.
>
> (p. 194)

Weil reiterates the message of Pascal, that the Creator is not merely the "all" of the philosophers, nor the utter transcendence of extreme absolutism, but a personal object of love, "a living flame of love" who evades the intellect but reveals himself to the heart in intimate communion.

The act of creation, for Weil, is not one of self-expansion on the part of the Creator but one of retreat and renunciation. All nature obeys its Creator in passive submission. God desires that man obey and love him, but freely, not under compulsion. It is because he seeks our love that he hides himself; his overt presence—"without the protection of space, time, and matter"—would overwhelm and deprive us of our freedom, would, in fact, annihilate us "as a flame kills a butterfly." His retreat is in itself an act of love. He, all-powerful, humbles himself, "empties himself of his divinity," leaving the universe subject to "necessity," a blind determinism in space and time ("God is not in time"), allowing autonomy to reign in the individual soul. He elects not to interfere in the operations of nature's laws.

Because the blind, "hard, and metallic-cold" mechanism that rules the universe is indifferent to man's desires and well-being, "causing the sun to rise and the rain to fall on the just and the unjust alike," it results in suffering and thus forms a barrier between man and the Infinite, whose governing power is not manifest. Since God is hidden, man seeks absolute happiness in worldly delights, tending to look upon these terrestrial attachments as an end; so that this too becomes a "screen" between

Creator and creature. But it is also an intermediary, a means by which man may come to him: "The world is a closed door, a barrier, but at the same time it is a passage." Without desire for what is illusory, we would not seek for that which is absolute.

Writing in a voice that is reminiscent of Saint Augustine and Pascal, Weil says that if we focus our attention on the disturbing truth that the world and the finite goods it has to offer are radically incapable of satisfying "the desire which burns perpetually within for an infinite and perfect Good," then our awareness of this fact brings about a degree of detachment from the world, which in turn creates a "void" in us, a "passage" through which God enters into us in secret. Without making his presence known, he plants a seed of love in us, she says, which grows into a persistent hunger for the Infinite. In fact, "this divine semen" is God's Spirit. For "only God can love God." He loves himself through us. (Weil is espousing the doctrine of the Trinity.)

To illustrate her thought, she employs an ancient symbol. The egg is the visible world, and the chick inside is Love, God himself, who abides deep within every person, though initially imperceptibly as a tiny seed. When the chick breaks through the shell, the world is still there, but, she explains, he is no longer inside it, and now he loves the whole universe indiscriminately. The growth of the seed within us is painful. We have to "pull up the weeds, cut the grass." This gardening is an arduous operation.

What we must offer to God, writes Weil, is the power to say "I." The "I" must be annihilated, "decreated." Stripping ourselves of the false perspective that we are located at the center of the universe and that all others exist only insofar as they are our aims, our pleasures, or our pain is a kind of death, "more radical than that of the body," but one that leads to a resurrection; only at the time of our renunciation, it is not recognized as such. Although the term "decreation" is a neologism (borrowed from Charles-Pierre Péguy, who gives it a different

sense), this giving up of the "I"-hood or the ego, this process of self-stripping, finds its parallel in the purgative phase of all mystics. He who gives us our being, she declares, loves in us our acceptance of not being: "He is perpetually begging from us that existence which he gives." Our longing for God becomes more intense as our awareness of the natural world's indifference to our pursuits increases.

We know very well, she writes, that the good things we possess at present—wealth, power, respect, love—are not sufficient for our happiness. We delude ourselves into thinking that if the future brings us this or that we shall be fulfilled. But if all our desires were satisfied, we would long for something else and be miserable from not knowing what it is. "We accept stones," she says, "in place of the bread for which the soul hungers"; "we are like the prince who makes love to the handmaiden instead of the mistress." On the other hand, the soul detached from the world and oriented toward God is illumined by truth and filled with felicity. Love of God is the very essence of our being, she explains; when we focus this love on anything else, "we are like someone who runs joyfully down the street toward a stranger whom at a distance he has mistaken for a friend."

It is detachment from worldly things that produces growth in the love-seed within us, purifying and perfecting our love of neighbor and the universe. But even though every man recognizes, at least momentarily, that the finite cannot satisfy his inner longing for the Infinite, rather than face the facts of the human condition he resorts once again to self-deception. This natural tendency in man toward "false gods," which Weil defines metaphorically as "gravity" can be overcome only by grace, not by willpower: "We cannot take one step vertically; God crosses the universe and comes to us."

Weil maintains that the Deity is secretly present in our neighbor, in the beauty and order of the universe, in religious ceremonies, and in friendship. It is in loving these for their own sake that we indirectly love the Father, even though we are unaware that it is he whom we love. And this "implicit" love prepares us for an "explicit" love of God, which we attain when we have reached a high degree of purity. It is God's love, the seed planted within us, that loves our neighbor. By our consent to its growth in us, however, it becomes by a mysterious fusion ours too. We love with a divine love, and our entire being is guided by this love. Christ, reincarnated in us, loves Christ, reincarnated in others. The key to the alleviation of the afflicted, she declares, can be found in the parable of the Good Samaritan, who in giving "loving attention" to a dehumanized, little piece of flesh, naked, bleeding, a mere "thing," enables this inert, passive example of affliction to return to a human state. The act of "decreative" renunciation on the part of the Samaritan (his care for the "thing" amounts to a denial of self), in that it restores existence to another being, is a creative act, paralleling God's creation.

Weil distinguishes friendship from love of neighbor, which she equates with charity. Whereas charity does not discriminate, friendship means preference for some individual. It is a miracle of sorts by which one person, out of respect for human autonomy and affection for another, consents to view from a certain distance the very being "who is as necessary to him as food." Pure friendship, she says, images the relationship that unites the persons of the Trinity and is the very essence of God.

The arbitrary destruction that is the result of nature's laws is an indication that God is elsewhere; in his love, he "restricts himself." Just as Christ submitted to the laws of creation, we are asked to consent to the rule of "necessity" in matter. This necessity, to which the universe has been entrusted and which tends, on one level, to alienate us from the Almighty, at the same time reveals the Creator's presence in the beauty that is its order, "in the fleeing folds of the waves of the sea or in the almost eternal folds of the mountains." Beauty, the relation between the world and our sensibility, attracts our attention and commands our contemplation of it, as though it contained an inherent value that might answer our inner longings, but it is only a promise that is never fulfilled: "We long to consume it, but it is only for looking at." It points, as Plato indicated, to an absolute beauty. This painful, "tantalizing mystery," this "snare," which "stimulates hunger" but does not satisfy it, is a *metaxu,* a means to an end. Unlike so much in nature, beauty has no apparent function, yet it nourishes the seed of love.

Weil compares the world's beauty, "Christ's tender smile for us coming through matter," to the opening of a labyrinth. After taking a few steps within, man is unable to find his way back to the entrance; but, if he keeps his courage and continues to walk, he will finally arrive at the center, where God is waiting "to eat him." Later he will find his way out, but he will be forever changed. After having been "eaten and digested by God," he can no longer be the same. He will remain near the mouth of the labyrinth, gently pushing all who approach through the opening. This oblique reference to the Greek myth, which functions as a metaphor for alchemists, can be seen as an allegory of man's spiritual transmutation in what mystics call the "unitive life."

Men seek riches, power, and social consideration in order to reinforce the false perspective of themselves as occupying the central position of the universe. But they also love riches, Weil observes, because wealth permits them to luxuriate in beautiful surroundings; poverty is repugnant precisely because it prevents the soul from appreciating the beauty of the world. Ambition for power is in essence the desire to establish order of a kind; and order, for Weil, is beautiful. A true work of art reflects the beauty of the cosmos and is divinely inspired, of the nature of a sacrament. Scientists study the order of the world, the presence of God in matter. Men consume drugs of all kinds in an attempt to make beauty tangible. What all men everywhere are seeking is universal beauty.

Carnal love, in all its forms, albeit unknowingly, has as its object universal beauty. Whereas there is a tendency today to view the love for God as a deviation of sexual desire, following the thought of Plato, Weil states that, on the contrary, carnal love is a corruption of the love for God, the hunger for his plenitude. What makes carnal love so imperious, she remarks, is the transcendental élan that informs it. Man yearns for the Infinite in the finite. (In twentieth-century literature, this concept of carnal love is dominant in the writings of Paul Claudel, François Mauriac, Graham Greene, and Marguerite Yourcenar, among others.)

This is what love literature always expresses, she says, from the most ancient to the subtle analyses of Proust. It is therefore wrong to deride mystics, as is sometimes done, for their use of the language of love: "It is theirs by right; others only borrow it." And this is why, she adds, sexual transgressions are considered so serious; they are sins precisely because the soul is by this act, though unknowingly, searching for God. The Absolute is present in sexual temptation. Beauty cannot be possessed by taking possession of the object in which it is housed. It is meant to be contemplated, not "eaten." She suggests that vice, depravity, and crime are essentially attempts to eat what should only be looked at. The person who locates the Absolute in pleasure commits the sin of idolatry.

To reprove mystics on the grounds that there is sexuality in their love of God, she comments, is tantamount to reproaching an artist for employing a material pigment to paint his picture: "What else does he have to paint with? What else does he have to love with?" If we are going to make this kind of reproach, we might as well say that the ordinary love between men and women is impure. Freudianism is permeated with the very prejudice it professes to oppose, says Weil: that is, that sexuality is vile.

Religious rites are yet another way by which we can make contact, an indirect one, with God. By focusing our attention on something tangible and pure, "some of the evil or mediocrity in us is destroyed." But love and respect for religious ceremonies are rare, Weil remarks, even among those who profess to practice them. Yet all that is required to draw God to the soul is attentiveness to where he is secretly present.

These "supernatural loves" of one's neighbor, of friends, of beauty and order, and of religious ceremonies constitute "the period of preparation when the soul loves in the void without knowing whether anything real responds to its love." If man tries to believe, he only succeeds in labeling something else as God: idolatry. Or else his belief is "abstract and verbal"; it doesn't penetrate the soul. Distinguishing between faith and belief, Weil states that faith is a gift, the result of an experience of God. Until God elects to reveal his reality, there can be no certitude, only belief. And belief, she maintains, is not sufficient. "Only certitude is worthy of God."

The implicit loves, however, orient the soul toward a divine encounter. Because of them the soul falls prey to an insatiable hunger. When the love of God becomes explicit, they grow more intense and unite to form one single love. With many people, she conjectures, the implicit love of God may be all that they ever experience; nevertheless this kind of love can attain a high degree of purity and power. It is this concern with giving a transcendental dimension to all aspects of life, while refusing to subscribe to any one religion, that has motivated some to describe Weil as a "secular saint."

Sociopolitical Reflections

It is clear that Weil's sociopolitical views are informed by a spiritual perspective. In her reflections on the regeneration of a free France after the Liberation, she denounces the separation of public affairs from morality and urges her countrymen to base all their actions always on what is purely and truly good and just with total disregard for expediency, as the only feasible principle of social progress. The purpose of religion, she holds, is to enlighten, without dominating, all aspects of secular life.

She notes that Cardinal Richelieu, "the true

precursor of Hitler," to whom the modern state owes its origin, without concern for the common good or moral precepts of any kind, built a "blind and anonymous machine for producing order and power," capable of being worshiped. She quotes the cardinal as declaring that the same rules should not be applied to the welfare of the state as to that of the soul, since the salvation of the soul has to do with another world. Her ironic response to this espousal of a utilitarian ethics is that the Christian should conclude from this that, whereas a total, absolute, and unconditional loyalty is owed to the soul, or in other words, to the divine will, the state is an entity to which only a limited and conditional allegiance is due. Man's original intent in organizing a society, she points out, was to free himself from the constraints and caprices of the indifferent, mechanical laws of the universe, but now he is threatened or oppressed by this "collective humanity," whose chief concern is power. Added to this is the lust for riches, for wealth translates into power. All this leads to theft, intrigue, and corruption.

While affirming man's need to feel a part of a physical, cultural, and social community that preserves values and traditions of the past, a need she calls "rootedness," Weil warns against holding up the collectivity in adoration. An anarcho-syndicalist early on, she always maintained an opposition to the view of the state as the ultimate center and envisioned a political organization, one that was not too centralized or arbitrary, that would foster submission without humiliation in an atmosphere devoid of fear and hate and, more important, nurture the development of the spiritual needs of man.

Marx has judiciously observed, she writes, that France became a state machine with totalitarian tendencies which not only survived all changes of regime but were strengthened and perfected by each successive change. The obedience demanded by such a state must be backed up by force, the ensuing result being the loss of much of the moral life of the people. Our entire civilization, according to Weil, is corrupted by man's rejection of the spiritual, by his physical and cultural uprootedness, and by his contact with force.

In her effort to envision a new French order, in the opening pages of *A Need for Roots* Weil argues for the priority of obligations over rights. The concept of the natural rights of man, as embodied in the American and French republics, is only meaningful in relation to corresponding obligations and is dependent upon force for its effectiveness: "An obligation that goes unrecognized loses none of the full power of its reality, but a right that goes unrecognized is of little value." To illustrate, she remarks that the rights of fetuses, the insane, the poor, or the weak are effective only when others exercise their obligation toward them. Her understanding of obligation is based on a firm belief in a "Reality outside the world" and in an innate human élan toward this Reality. Our obligation to God, she insists, is best fulfilled by "loving attention" to natural necessity and the needs of our fellow men. Her ideal society is founded on nobility of intention and selfless love.

In contrast to Marx, who postulated that revolution is the only valid transforming social agent, Weil insists that our materialistic world can only throw off the yoke of oppression and attain a semblance of justice through the supernatural force of grace, "quite a different kind from that which is wielded by the powerful." Only those who surrender to this divine power can truly understand and generously respond, she holds, to the physical and spiritual needs of men. Everything underlines the fact, she writes, that unless grace intervenes, there is no form of cruelty or disparity of which ordinary, respectable people are not capable, once the corresponding psychological mechanisms have been set in motion.

"The *Iliad*; or, The Poem of Force"

In "The *Iliad*; or, The Poem of Force," unquestionably her best-known essay, Weil treats her belief that one of the keys to understanding history or human relations is the concept of might. "The real protagonist," she begins in a simple and lucid prose, "the true subject, the matrix of the *Iliad* is force. That force which is wielded by men enslaves them; before it man's flesh recoils." The human soul is always modified by its encounter with force, which is capable of transforming a being into a "thing," while it is still alive, dragging him down to the level of inert matter. When exercised to the limit, force changes an individual into a thing in the most literal sense; it makes him into a corpse. The soul, she continues, was not meant to inform a thing; when obliged to do so, it suffers violence. That thing longs to regain its lost humanity, but never succeeds: "This is a death drawn out for the duration of a life, a life that death has frozen long before it has terminated it."

Weil analyzes the psychological and spiritual effects of impending death, of cruelty and slavery, of violence and affliction—in short, of the world of force, which no one on earth, she asserts, escapes. The strong and the weak alike are ignorant of the fact that they are members of the same species, both destined in turn to be subjected to might, which is as merciless and indifferent to the one who possesses it as to its victims; the latter it obliterates, the former it intoxicates and maddens. The truth is, she notes; it is not possessed by anyone. It changes from one to another so easily that it takes on an air of independence and reveals a blind, automatic justice that destroys those who destroy, a kind of retribution, of geometric precision, that penalizes the abuse of power. This concept of an equilibrium of powers, common to Greek and Oriental tradition, is found not only in the *Iliad* but also in life itself. It never occurs to the powerful that the consequences of their actions will turn against them. No one is spared the subordination of the soul as well as the body to might. Even the incarnate God, she points out, could not regard his suffering and death without anguish. Grace can protect the soul against the corrupting power of force, but not against its searing effects.

Moral Perspectives on Literature

Sensitive to the reality that the public has been inundated by bad literature for which the religious impulse has been responsible, Graham Greene, Shūsaku Endō, François Mauriac, Julien Green, Georges Bernanos, and Flannery O'Connor, among others, have all affirmed that they are writers who happen to be Catholic. This affirmation is an effort on their part to underline the fact that they are artists, not evangelists. It does mean nonetheless that they view life through a special lens; hence the natural world that they portray contains the added dimension of the supernatural. For, as O'Connor has remarked, "To try to disconnect faith from vision is to do violence to the whole personality, and the whole personality participates in the act of writing." The writer need not think in explicit theological terms or subscribe to a particular ideology to depict a spiritual overview. Camus has been called a religious novelist in that his imaginative world puts in relief the absence of God, the general mystery and anguish of incompleteness.

For her part, Weil expresses her regret that twentieth-century literature lacks this added dimension. Contemporary fiction is largely psychological, and the concern of psychology, she notes, is to describe the states of the soul without making value judgments. Proust's mammoth novel, for instance, deals with the analysis of non-oriented states of the soul, "as though good and evil were extraneous to them."

Writers who refuse to give value to human actions manifest a fundamental breach of responsibility, writes Weil. The surrealists, proponents of total license, "the literary equivalent of the sacking of towns," have chosen "the complete absence of value as their supreme value." She censures André Gide, in particular, for the publication of books that posit an openness to any and all experiences with total disregard for moral precepts of any kind. All serious writers, she says, express the human condition, of which good and evil are an essential part. Literature that ignores this polarity "betrays its function and forfeits all claim to excellence." Creative writers, she maintains, should be held accountable for the influence of their works. They should not be acquitted on the grounds of "the sacred privilege of art for art's sake." Whereas most will argue that immorality is not an aesthetic criterion, Weil insists that aesthetic criteria are not the only ones applicable to literature, that works, whether written well or badly, may have as their source good or evil.

But how can a writer be true to his art and to his moral principles both? This issue was raised in the first half of the twentieth century by Jacques Maritain and others. Does it mean, Friedrich von Hügel asked, that the creative writer must "tidy up reality"? O'Connor's answer was that if the writer's attention is on producing a work of art, then the responsibility lies solely with God, for the basis of art is truth. And Maritain's famous counsel to Mauriac, who anguished over this apparent conflict, was simple: "Purify the source."

Nothing, Weil points out (as others have also observed), is so beautiful, so marvelous, so fresh and surprising, so enticing as the good, and nothing so tedious, so monstrous and boring as evil. In fiction, however, where the values are reversed, the good is dreary and insipid, while evil becomes appealing and intriguing, diverse and profound. The reason for this, she explains, is that there exist necessities and impossibilities in reality that do not obtain in fiction. One must conclude therefore that immorality is an integral part of fiction.

It is wrong to reproach writers for being immoral, says Weil, unless we criticize them at the same time for being writers, as some in the seventeenth century were courageous enough to do. Writers of genius, however, such as Homer, Aeschylus, Sophocles, the Racine of *Phèdre,* François Villon, the Shakespeare of *King Lear,* and Molière, are capable of producing fictional worlds comparable to reality, where good and evil appear in their full truth. Consequently, literature of this order is moral: "All true artists have had a real, direct, and immediate contact with the beauty of the world; this contact is a kind of sacrament." The contemplation of their works inspires us, as Plato said, to "grow wings to overcome gravity."

Although we are not all writers, we are all, according to Weil, creators of fiction and therefore of immorality. To avoid facing the misery of the human condition, we live with self-delusion and falsehood, and these inevitably precede and accompany submission to evil. Reveries are dangerous. We fictionalize our future; and, with the exception of those who are dedicated to truth, we remake the past to please us. We do not give true attention to others, she continues, to discover who and what they are; we fabricate their thoughts, words, and actions. Just as novelists often take a theme from a news story, we refashion reality, enveloping it in a mist, in which—as in literary fiction—the values of good and evil are reversed. Occasionally we are momentarily shocked into facing the truth by an experience of some kind: an encounter with a saint, perhaps, or a contact with depravity or affliction. But we quickly resume our waking dream state with its fictionalized scenario. Still, she maintains, works of genius, where good and evil are revealed as they truly are, have the power to release us from our self-deceptions.

Doctrine of Attention

The faculty of attention is central to the writings of Weil, where the term has several different but related meanings. Sometimes it is synonymous with meditation. For example, to acquire the proper spiritual orientation, she urges us to "fix our attention" upon various truths: that detachment confers liberty; that suffering, which forms an integral part of the experience of all, if embraced, is the kindly instructor of immortal secrets, the complement of love, and the door through which we may go toward the Absolute; that finite goods are incapable of satisfying the innate longing for the Infinite; that the Unknowable, who cannot be gotten by the senses or by reason, may nonetheless be chosen and loved.

More often, however, the word "attention" takes on the meaning of looking at with profound interest and expectation, even longing, while passively and patiently waiting. As Eric O. Springsted astutely points out, "Waiting (*attente*) implies an orientation of our desire and a direction of our sight to the place where we are to look while waiting (*attention*). Our souls are so made that they desire good and direct their attention towards that which they believe will provide it." We cannot make a single move toward God, says Weil; if, however, we direct our attention heavenward for a long time, he comes down and raises us up to him.

Weil contends that we project "a part of the evil within us" into the objects of our attention and desire, and "they reflect it back to us," unless they are completely pure (as, for example, liturgical rites, certain sacred texts, the beauty of the world, and individuals "in whom God resides"), in which case the evil is absorbed by them, and we are delivered of it. But "the mediocre parts of the soul" resist and "fabricate all kinds of delusions to divert our attention," usually by presenting to the imagination the finite as the Infinite, a temporal good as the Ultimate Good, a means as an end. It is the function of the will to sweep away these distractions; for lack of attention, according to Weil, is in some arcane way linked to evil:

In "Reflections on the Right Use of School Studies with a View to the Love of God" (in *Waiting for God*), an essay written presumably for Father Perrin's students, she notes, "There is something in the soul that has a far more violent revulsion for true attention than the flesh has for bodily fatigue. This something is much more clearly related to evil than is the flesh." That is why, she continues, absolute attention destroys evil and is of greater value than many good works. It is because of our lack of attention that we live in a dream world, she comments elsewhere, unaware of reality, allowing our fantasies to distort the truth, resorting to self-deception for fear of not being able to live with the facts of the human situation.

We conjure up false images of others to complement our personal needs, instead of emptying ourselves of self in order to take into ourselves the being confronting us, just as he is, in his own truth.

"The unfortunate have no need of anything this world has to offer except people capable of giving them their attention," she insists. But the capacity to give true attention to the afflicted is a rare and most difficult thing, because we recoil from attending to the afflicted. They are subhuman, mere "things" that only inspire us with loathing and disgust. True love of our neighbor consists of being able to ask him, "What are you going through?" It is a question that reinstates him as another human being. No one asks the factory worker, the miner, the agricultural laborer, or the fisherman, she remarks in *The Need for Roots*, "What are you enduring?"—not employers, not union leaders, not the "experts," not revolutionaries like Leon Trotsky, not even the workers themselves one of another. This lack of sensitivity, she finds, is the crux of all social problems. The Good Samaritan first looked with attention ("the rarest and purest form of generosity") at the beaten man at the side of the road, the crumpled "thing" from which others had quickly averted their eyes.

As already mentioned, it is by directing our attention toward "implicit loves" that we make intermediate contact with the Infinite. This attention takes us out of self and engenders in us a transformation: an increased renunciation of the "I." What is thought of by most as simply an intellectual faculty takes on, for Weil, mystical qualities. For this reason it is of capital importance that this faculty be assiduously developed: "No real effort of attention is ever wasted, even though there may never be any visible result." Paradoxical as it may seem, she contends, a Latin text or a geometry problem, even done incorrectly, may one day make us better able to give someone precisely the assistance he needs.

Weil emphasizes the importance of the

"lower form of attention" required in the performance of school exercises, the development of which, she states, should be the real object of studies. The intrinsic interest of academic assignments is secondary to their effectiveness in increasing the power of attention. If we struggle in earnest to solve a problem of geometry and are unsuccessful, in a way it matters little; for our efforts will be rewarded on the spiritual level and, consequently, on the lower one of the intelligence. We have made progress in another dimension; this apparently fruitless effort has brought more "light into the soul," which one day will be revealed in prayer. In addition, the result may very likely manifest itself in some area totally unrelated to mathematics. Perhaps he who failed to solve the geometry problem will at some future time, on account of this seemingly barren effort, be able to grasp more intuitively the beauty of a line of Racine. For this reason, the primary motivation of students, she contends, should not be high grades, academic honors, or even an affinity for a particular discipline. Instead, applying themselves equally in all areas, their efforts should be directed to the formation of habitual attention, which, she insists, is the essence of prayer: the orientation of total attention toward God.

Weil distinguishes between what she describes as a "muscular effort," an active application that is an act of the will, and a concentrated "negative effort," a passive action that involves an openness or receptivity. Attention means suspending thought, leaving the mind in a state of "emptiness" and readiness to be permeated by the object of interest. It also consists of holding in our peripheral intellectual vision, on a lower plane, the diverse knowledge we have acquired and which we need, just as "a man on a mountain who, looking straight ahead, sees below him, without actually looking at them, numerous forests and plains. Our mind should be empty of thought, waiting, not seeking anything, but ready to be penetrated by the object in its naked truth." Errors of all kinds, she maintains, as well as stylistic awkwardness, are due to the fact that we have rushed forward hastily, thus blocking truth, which instead we should await patiently. It is because man erroneously believes that he can, by his own power, discover truths that he obtains counterfeits, which he is unable to perceive as false. According to Weil, intuition, resulting from intense attention, plays a capital role in the discovery of truth.

Incorrect translations, faulty solutions to problems, illogical connections of ideas, and the like, belong to falsity, and falsity is opposed to truth. Truth, along with beauty and good, is divine. Therefore the correct answer to a geometry problem is the "image of something precious." It is a fragment of the truth, a reflection of "the unique, eternal, and living truth, this same truth that once proclaimed in a human voice: 'I am the truth.'" All knowledge, as Augustine has said, leads to God. For this reason, Weil perceives the efforts of the intellectual as a spiritual quest, though one that must be undertaken with humility; this is one reason why she sought to deepen the spirituality of the manual laborer with academic interests.

In stating that "only the highest part of the attention makes contact with God," Weil is equating the term "attention" with what mystics usually call the state of recollection, the required prelude to contemplation, where the soul enters into communion with the Transcendent Personality. It consists of (to use Underhill's words) "the movement of desire passing over . . . into the act of concentration . . . , the passionate focusing of self upon one point . . . : a condition, peculiarly characteristic of the mystical consciousness," which results in a "shift" of the "field of perception." God rewards the soul, Weil remarks in *Waiting for God,* that focuses its attention on him with love by offering it direction; it must then abandon itself to this guiding impulse, hastening to wherever it is led, "but not taking one step beyond, even if that be toward the good."

All forms of the concept of attention are, for

Weil, interrelated and possess a spiritual filiation. Thus she looks upon this faculty as a basic human requirement, one that unites all segments of society, regardless of personal faith or ideological persuasion: "The only faculty of the soul that provides access to God is attention."

As if in defiance of her philosophical formation, there was imposed on Simone Weil, according to her own testimony, a mystical conception of the Infinite as a personal object of love, which is neither the utter transcendence of extreme Absolutism nor the utter immanence of the Vitalists. She was driven, it would seem from all that is known of her life and thought, by two intense aspirations (aspirations that are active or dormant in all, she claims): to attain both knowledge of and actual contact with the suprasensible Reality. In pursuit of these goals, she rejected the pleasures of the sense world, looking upon them as obstacles to the total surrender of self, and assiduously pursued a course of asceticism with a view to annihilation of the "I"-hood, perceiving suffering as the tender "caress of God."

Consequently, Weil has been accused of being a masochist who exalted pain and anguish as supreme values. In actual fact, however, she saw them not as ends but as means. With the very same urgent motivation to mortify the senses by deliberately opposing them, Saint Catherine of Genoa forced herself to eat lice and Saint Francis embraced lepers. "Let me suffer or die!" said Saint Theresa. "Strange alternatives," comments Underhill, "but a forced option in the spiritual sphere." The general reader who comes to mystical accounts without adequate preparation finds himself in considerable difficulty. It is a commonplace that only mystics can understand mystics. Still, the possibility, even the likelihood, of unbalanced tendencies existing alongside mystical experiences cannot be overlooked.

Those to whom the Transcendental Personality is nonexistent or unattainable can only conclude (without ever questioning her integrity) that Weil labored under a series of delusions. Be that as it may, her life and her thought, at every level, were dominated by her deep conviction that there is a Reality, which she defined as Love, "outside the world, beyond space and time." Whatever evaluation one makes of her aberrant behavior, her thoughts can nonetheless be examined in their own right, which is precisely what she so ardently desired.

Weil's metaphysics pervade her entire oeuvre. All her views are based on the belief that man's welfare depends on his fundamental orientation. She believed that unless science espouses some conception of human destiny, it will lose its validity; that all great artists are divinely inspired (a true painter's hand is "impelled to move with the brush suspended from it"); that a just society must be based on actions stemming from motives that are pure and not dependent on the fruits of those actions; that genius is necessarily affiliated with sanctity; that work embodies a spiritual dimension.

An unorthodox, challenging writer, Weil did not produce a philosophical system and cannot be summarily classified. Her ideas on diverse subjects, sometimes difficult to grasp, are always expressed in a very simple and elegant French, free of technical jargon; though she professed to be indifferent to style, her images are arresting, her prose often poetic.

The responses to her work extend from an uncritical adulation that labels her saint and genius, the author of infallible pronouncements, to a critical questioning of the validity of every aspect of her thought, reflecting incredulity about both the authenticity of her mystical revelations and the extreme and provocative exaggerations of her polemics. As T. S. Eliot has written, "I cannot conceive of anybody's agreeing with all of her views or of not disagreeing violently with some of them." Yet the importance of Weil's thought cannot be denied, and her feverish pursuit of self-effacement, as Father Perrin points out, has only resulted in a heightened interest in her as a person.

Selected Bibliography

EDITIONS

La pesanteur et la grâce. Paris, 1947.

L'Enracinement, prélude à une déclaration des devoirs envers l'être humain. Paris, 1949.

Attente de Dieu. Paris, 1950.

La connaissance surnaturelle. Paris, 1950.

La condition ouvrière. Paris, 1951.

Intuitions préchrétiennes. Paris, 1951.

Lettre à un religieux. Paris, 1951.

Cahiers I. Paris, 1951; revised and expanded, Paris, 1970.

Cahiers II. Paris, 1953; revised and expanded, Paris, 1972.

La source grecque. Paris, 1953. Includes "L'Iliade; ou, Le poème de la force" (1940).

Oppression et liberté. Paris, 1955.

Venise sauvée. Paris, 1955.

Cahiers III. Paris, 1956; revised and expanded, Paris, 1975.

Écrits de Londres et dernières lettres. Paris, 1957.

Leçons de philosophie de Simone Weil. Paris, 1959.

Ecrits historiques et politiques. Paris, 1960.

Pensées sans ordre concernant l'amour de Dieu. Paris, 1962.

Sur la science. Paris, 1966.

Poèmes suivis de Venise sauvée, Lettre de Paul Valéry. Paris, 1968.

TRANSLATIONS

First and Last Notebooks. Translated by Richard Rees. London, 1970. Includes *La connaissance surnaturelle.*

Formative Writings, 1929–1941. Translated by Dorothy Tuck Mc Farland and Wilhelmina Van Ness. Amherst, Mass., 1987.

Gravity and Grace. Translated by Arthur Wills. New York, 1952.

The "Iliad"; or, The Poem of Force. Translated by Mary McCarthy. Wallingford, Pa., 1956.

Intimations of Christianity Among the Ancient Greeks. Translated by Elisabeth Chase Geissbuhler. London, 1957; Boston, 1958. Includes *Intuitions préchrétiennes* and portions of *La source grecque,* among them "The *Iliad;* or, The Poem of Might."

Letter to a Priest. Translated by Arthur Wills. London, 1953; New York, 1954.

The Need for Roots: Prelude to a Declaration of Duties Toward Mankind. Translated by Arthur Wills. Preface by T. S. Eliot. New York, 1952.

The Notebooks of Simone Weil. 2 vols. Translated by Arthur Wills. London and New York, 1956.

On Science, Necessity, and the Love of God. Translated by Richard Rees. London, 1968. Includes major portions of *La source grecque* and most of *Sur la science.*

Oppression and Liberty. Translated by Arthur Wills and John Petrie. London, 1958.

Selected Essays, 1934–1943. Translated by Richard Rees. London, 1962. Includes portions of *Écrits de Londres et dernières lettres* and *Écrits historiques et politiques.*

Simone Weil: Lectures on Philosophy. Translated by Hugh Price. London, New York, and Melbourne, 1978.

Simone Weil: Seventy Letters. Translated by Richard Rees. London, 1965. Includes part of *La condition ouvrière* and portions of *Pensées sans ordre concernant l'amour de Dieu.*

Waiting for God. Translated by Emma Craufurd. Preface by Leslie A. Fiedler. London, 1951.

BIOGRAPHICAL AND CRITICAL STUDIES

Allen, Diogenes. *Three Outsiders: Pascal, Kierkegaard, Simone Weil.* Cambridge, Mass., 1983.

Anderson, David. *Simone Weil.* London, 1971.

Balla, Borisz de. "Simone Weil, Witness of the Absolute." *The Catholic World* 179, no. 1070 (May 1954):101–109.

Buber, Martin. "The Silent Question: On Henri Bergson and Simone Weil." In his *At the Turning: Three Addresses on Judaism.* New York, 1952.

Cabaud, Jacques. *L'Expérience vécue de Simone Weil.* Paris, 1957.

———. *Simone Weil: A Fellowship in Love.* London, 1964.

———. *Simone Weil à New York et à Londres.* Paris, 1967.

Cohen, Robert S. "Parallels and the Possibility of Influence Between Simone Weil's *Waiting for God* and Samuel Beckett's *Waiting for Godot.*" *Modern Drama* 6 (February 1964):425–436.

Coles, Robert. *Simone Weil: A Modern Pilgrimage.* Reading, Mass., 1987.

Cook, Bradford. "Simone Weil: Art and the Artist Under God." *Yale French Studies* 12 (Autumn 1953):73–80.

Davy, M. M. *Introduction au message de Simone Weil.* Paris, 1954.

———. *Simone Weil.* Paris, 1956.

Debidour, Victor-Henry. *Simone Weil; ou, La transparence.* Paris, 1963.

Dunaway, John. *Simone Weil.* Boston, 1984.

Fiedler, Leslie A. "Simone Weil: Prophet Out of Israel." *Commentary* 11(January 1951):36–46.

Fiori, Gabriella. *Simone Weil: An Intellectual Biography.* Athens, Ga., 1989.

Fleuré, Eugène. *Simone Weil ouvrière.* Paris, 1955.

Giniewski, Paul. *Simone Weil; ou, La haine de soi.* Paris, 1978.

Goldschlager, Alain. *Simone Weil et Spinoza: Essai d'interprétation.* Quebec, 1982.

Greene, Graham. "Waiting for God." In *Collected Essays.* London, 1969.

Hautefeuille, François. *Le tourment de Simone Weil.* Paris, 1970.

Heidsieck, François. *Simone Weil.* Paris, 1965.

Hellman, John. *Simone Weil: An Introduction to Her Thought.* Ontario, 1982.

Jennings, Elisabeth. "A World of Contradictions: A Study of Simone Weil." *The Month* 22, no. 6 (December 1959):349–358.

Kempfner, Gaston. *La philosophie mystique de Simone Weil.* Paris, 1960.

Little, Janet Patricia. *Simone Weil: A Bibliography.* London, 1980.

McClellan, David. *Utopian Pessimist: The Life and Thought of Simone Weil.* New York, 1990.

Mc Farland, Dorothy Tuck. *Simone Weil.* New York, 1983.

Malan, Ivo. *L'Enracinement de Simone Weil.* Paris, 1961.

Marcel, Gabriel. "Simone Weil." *The Month* 2, no. 1 (July 1949):9–18.

Ottensmeyer, Hilary, OSB. *Le thème de l'amour dans l'oeuvre de Simone Weil.* Paris, 1958.

———. "Simone Weil: 'Mystic' and Lover of the Poor." *American Benedictine Review* 15 (1964): 504–514.

Perrin, Joseph-Marie, and Gustave Thibon. *Simone Weil telle que nous l'avons connue.* Paris, 1952. Translated as *Simone Weil as We Knew Her* by Emma Craufurd. London, 1953.

Pétrement, Simone. *La vie de Simone Weil, avec des lettres et d'autres textes inédites.* 2 vols. Paris, 1973. Translated as *Simone Weil: A Life* by Raymond Rosenthal. New York, 1976.

Piccard, E. *Simone Weil: Essai biographique et critique, suivi d'une anthologie raisonnée des oeuvres de Simone Weil.* Paris, 1960.

Pierce, Roy. *Contemporary French Political Thought.* London, 1966.

Rees, Richard. *Brave Men: A Study of D. H. Lawrence and Simone Weil.* London, 1958; Carbondale, Ill., 1959.

———. *Simone Weil: A Sketch for a Portrait.* Carbondale, Ill., 1966.

Reinhold, H. A. "Simone Weil, Saint of the Churchless." *Commonweal* 55 (October 1951):65–69.

Schumann, Maurice. *La mort née de leur propre vie: Péguy, Simone Weil, Gandhi.* Paris, 1974.

Sontag, Susan. "Simone Weil." In her *Against Interpretation.* London, 1967.

Springsted, Eric O. *Christus Mediator: Platonic Mediation in the Thought of Simone Weil.* Princeton, 1983.

———. *Simone Weil: The Suffering of Love.* Cambridge, Mass., 1986.

Sulzbach, F. "Simone Weil: Primitive Christian." *Theology Today* 8, no. 3 (October 1951):345–353.

Thiout, Michel. *Jalons sur la route de Simone Weil.* Vol. 1: *La recherche de la verité chez Simone Weil.* Vol. 2: *Essai de bibliographie des écrits de Simone Weil.* Paris, 1959.

Tomlin, E. W. F. *Simone Weil: A Critical Study.* New Haven, Conn., 1954.

Vetö, Miklos. "Simone Weil and Suffering." *Thought* 40, no. 157 (Summer 1965):275–286.

———. *La métaphysique religieuse de Simone Weil.* Paris, 1971.

Watkins, Peter. "Simone Weil: Anti-Semitism and Syncretism." *Church Quarterly Review* 163 (1962):463–473.

White, George Abbott, ed. *Simone Weil: Interpretations of a Life.* Amherst, Mass., 1981.

Whitehead, Alfred North. *Science and the Modern World.* New York, 1925.

ANN M. BEGLEY

YANNIS RITSOS

(b. 1909)

THE CONTEMPORARY GREEK poet Yannis Ritsos belongs to the longest literary tradition of the Western world. Greek poetry began with the Homeric epics around 800 B.C. and has continued uninterrupted to modern times. It is this three-thousand-year tradition that has become for Ritsos the reference point for his observations on the Greece of his own times and, by extension, the human condition.

The poetic tradition of which Ritsos is a part can be divided into five stages: the ancient Greek period (ca. 2000–323 B.C.); the period of Hellenistic literature (323 B.C.–A.D. 641); the Byzantine period (641–1204); the Franco-Turkish period (1204–1829); and the period to which Ritsos and his contemporaries belong, the modern Greek period (1829–present).

Within modern Greek literature three separate schools are easily identifiable. They are the Old School of Athens (1829–1880), the School of the Ionian Islands (1821–1912), and the New School of Athens (1880–present). The latter, to which Ritsos belongs, itself has a developed tradition over a hundred years old. Even within this school, which is but one part of one stage of a five-stage poetic tradition, Greek poetry has experienced a number of movements and directions. Perhaps the most crucial is that which brought Greek poetry into closer contact with the poetic experimentation of the rest of Europe. The publication in 1930 of the first work of Greece's first Nobel Prize winner (1963), George Seferis' *Strofi* (Turning

Point), initiated this new direction. Seferis' work defied traditional forms, opened the way for free verse, and established in Greece the influence of France's symbolist poets. It was shortly followed by the surrealist experimentation of Greece's second Nobel Prize winner (1979), Odysseus Elytis, and the new poetry of the journal *Nea ghrammata* (New Letters), the mouthpiece of Greece's avant-garde. It was at this time and in this context that the young Ritsos was first heard, in a work entitled *Trakter* (Tractor), in 1931.[1]

Ritsos was born on 1 May 1909 in Monemvasia in the district of Laconia, on the southeastern tip of the Peloponnesos. He was the youngest of four children, two boys and two girls, born to a well-to-do landowner, Eleferios Ritsos. The poetry Ritsos started writing at the early age of eight shows him to be a lonely boy who loathed his father. Young Ritsos attended primary school in Monemvasia and saw some of his poetry published in a children's collection, *Dhiaplasi ton pedhon* (Bringing Up Children), when he was twelve. At about this time, in August 1921, Ritsos' older brother, Dimitri, died of tuberculosis, a disease that has plagued the poet himself all of his life. Three months later, in November 1921, Ritsos' forty-two-year-old mother died of the same disease

---

[1] Dates given in the text generally refer to the *composition* of individual works. See bibliography for dates of publication in book form.

in a sanatorium. His attachment to his mother remained with Ritsos throughout his life, appearing again and again in his poetry in an emphasis on domestic objects and attention to everyday details. The same year Ritsos entered high school in Yithion, a seaside town near his home; he graduated in 1925 at the age of sixteen and immediately left for Athens, where he enrolled at the university. His arrival coincided with the flow of one million refugees from Anatolia, who doubled the population of Athens in their flight from the Asia Minor disaster of August 1922, when Turkey mounted an overwhelming and victorious ten-day offensive against the Greek army, forcing the Greek residents of Smyrna (present-day İzmir) to escape into the sea.

In Athens Ritsos secured a job as a typist and then as a copyist for a notary public at the National Bank. Within the year he contracted tuberculosis and was forced to return to Monemvasia. On arriving, he found his father in so desperate a mental state that the family committed him to an asylum in Daphni near Athens. Ritsos remained at home to write poetry, some of which was included in a supplement to a children's encyclopedia under the title *To palio mas spiti* (Our Old House), a phrase that preoccupied Ritsos throughout his long career.

In the autumn of 1926, the poet returned to Athens and worked as a librarian's aide at a lawyers' association. In the following year, at the age of eighteen, several of his poems were printed in *Meghali Elliniki egkyklopedhia* (The Large Greek Encyclopedia) published by Pyrsos Publishers. Unfortunately, in January Ritsos suffered a relapse of tuberculosis. Hospitalized at the Papademetriou clinic, he was later transferred to the Sotiria sanatorium in Athens, where he remained until September 1930. This period saw the refugees from Asia Minor establish a large working class in Athens and witnessed the rise of the Communist party, which was established in 1929.

Hospitalized with the "poor man's disease,"

as tuberculosis was called, Ritsos was placed in the sanatorium's public ward. Here he became acquainted with the work of Kostas Varnalis, the first Greek poet to openly join the Communist party; it was Varnalis' influence that later led Ritsos to become a Communist.

In 1930 Ritsos was transferred from Sotiria to the Kapsalona sanatorium in Crete. Because of a letter he published criticizing conditions in the sanatorium, he and his fellow patients were retransferred to the Saint John sanatorium in Hania, Crete. Both institutions were for paupers. Ritsos remained at Saint John's until October 1931, when, at the age of twenty-one, he was released and returned to Athens. For the first time in five years he was free of the sanatorium. In Athens the intercession of a leftist political organization, the Protopori, placed Ritsos in charge of the literary department of the left-wing Workers' Club. He remained there for two years, aided financially by his older sister, Loula. His job at the Workers' Club brought him in contact with a publisher of Marxist literature, Constantine Govostis, who brought out many of Ritsos' early poetic works. In 1934 Govostis hired Ritsos as a reader and proofreader, a position he held at various intervals until 1956. Continuing work on his poetry, Ritsos studied acting and directing and performed as a supporting actor and dancer at the professional theater of Kypselis from 1933 until war was declared.

During this period, in 1936, Ritsos wrote one of his best-loved poems, *Epitafios,* the lament of a mother whose son is killed by police during a workers' strike. Published initially in installments by the newspaper *Rizospastis* (Radicalist), the organ of the Communist party of Greece, *Epitafios* was subsequently issued in a ten-thousand-copy edition. When all civil liberties were suspended by the dictator General Yiannis Metaxas on 4 August 1936, Ritsos was included in an arrest that swept up fifty thousand people. All existing copies of *Epitafios* were confiscated by the authorities and, together with other of his works and the works of other dissenters, burned before the columns of the Temple of Olympian Zeus in downtown Athens.

The poet's personal life proved equally stressful. Not only was his sister, Loula, committed to the same asylum in Daphni as his father, but in the following year, 1937, Ritsos suffered yet another relapse; he entered the sanatorium of Mount Parnitha, where he remained until 1938. Upon his release, he joined the Lyrical Stage, a branch of the National Theater, to take a part in a play, *Nyhteridha* (The Bat), and to perform in the choruses of ancient drama.

This respite was brutally disrupted on 6 April 1941 with the German declaration of war against Greece. The declaration was followed in quick succession by the organization of EAM (Ethnikon Apeleftherotikon Metopon), the National Liberation Front, on 27 September and the formation of ELAS (Ellinikos Laikos Apeleftherotikos Stratos), the Greek National Liberation Army, on 10 April 1942. Ritsos joined the cultural section of EAM, became the artistic director of EDES (Ellinikos Dimokratikos Ethnikos Syndesmos), the National Democratic Greek League, and joined the central committee of a crypto-communist party known as EDA (Eneia Dhimokratiki Aristera), or the Union of the Democratic Left. During the war years, 1943–1945, he continued his involvement with EAM–ELAS in Kozani in northern Greece, where he was sent with other actors and writers to set up the Popular Theater of Macedonia. Here Ritsos wrote his one-act play "Athina sta opla" (Athens in Arms; unpublished), which was later rewritten as the play *Pera ap ton iskio ton kyparission* (Beyond the Shadow of the Cypress Trees, 1958). This play was dedicated to the events of 3 December 1944, which led to the Greek Civil War. During the German occupation of Greece a vigorous resistance movement arose to contest the Axis occupation. This organization, formed in September 1941, was EAM, whose membership at its height included one-fifth of the Greek population and which was responsible for 90 percent of the resistance against the Germans. In 1944 EAM refused to obey Prime Minister George Papandreou's orders to disarm, fearing the restoration of a right-wing dictatorship. EAM would not disarm unless a corresponding disarmament of the royalist segment of the Greek armed forces occurred. However, at the instigation of Winston Churchill, Papandreou forced the issue. Demonstrations followed in which the police opened fire and killed many civilians. After this, EAM supporters began to attack various police stations in Athens, paving the way for the civil war that was to follow.

Following the collapse of the Left in 1944, Ritsos went into hiding. With the declaration of amnesty for members of EAM, he returned to Athens, only to be rejected by the National Theater. Of those EAM members who returned to Athens, many were arrested and harassed; others went to the mountains. Countering the prevailing climate, Ritsos wrote a stirring hymn, *Romiosini* (first published in a collection, *Aghrypnia* [Vigilance], in 1954; first issued in book form in 1966), exalting the courage of the partisans and comparing them to the great heroes of the Byzantine, Ottoman, and classical past. Fleeing Athens himself, he lost his only novel, "Stous propodhes tis siopis" (At the Base of Silence), a work of some thousand pages that he never reconstructed. Once again he suffered a relapse of tuberculosis.

In July 1948 Ritsos was apprehended in a general round-up of one hundred thousand partisans. Incarcerated in various detention camps until August 1952, he was first deported to the prison camp of Kontopouli on the Aegean island of Lemnos. In May 1949 he was transferred to Makronisos, a rock island without drinking water where some of the worst atrocities against the leftists and leftist sympathizers occurred. Here Ritsos refused to sign a statement renouncing his leftist activities and pledging his obedience to the postwar Greek government. Following international protests by such figures as the French poet Louis Aragon, Ritsos was finally transferred in 1952 to a prison camp on Saint Stratis, a small island near Lemnos, where he remained until his release at the end of that year.

From 1952 to 1967, living in Athens, Ritsos enjoyed a degree of physical, mental, and spiritual comfort. During this period he wrote and published a number of poems dealing with the occupation, the civil war, and his period of exile. In 1954 he married Falitsa Gheorghiadis, a medical doctor and fellow activist known for her resistance work on the island of Samos. They had first met as students at the University of Athens. One year later, his daughter and only child, Eleutheria (Freedom), was born, for whom he wrote and dedicated a book of poems, *Proino astro* (Morning Star). In the year following the appearance of *Proino astro* (1955), Ritsos published *I sonata tou selinofotos* (*The Moonlight Sonata*), a work for which he received the National Prize for Poetry.[2] As a further indication of his newly won freedom, he was allowed for the first time to leave Greece. Visiting the Soviet Union with a group in which he was the sole representative of the left, he recorded his impressions of the trip and on his return published them in thirty-three articles that appeared in the daily newspaper *Ayghi*.

The years between Ritsos' release from the detention camps and his re-arrest after the Papadopoulos coup in 1967 represent his most productive period, resulting in twenty-nine published works. In 1957 alone he published six books of poetry. In 1958 the poet left the country for the second time, to visit Bulgaria, Czechoslovakia, the Soviet Union, and Romania. He remained in Prague for three months, suffering another tubercular relapse. Once again he recorded his impressions, publishing them as *I arhitektoniki ton dhentron* (The Ar-

chitecture of Trees, 1958). This period saw the poet's use of Greek myth as the basis for some of his greatest poetry, written in his most distinctive form, the dramatic monologue, and resulting in the first two works of his classical cycle, *To nekro spiti* (*The Dead House*) and *Kato ap ton iskio tou vounou* (*Beneath the Shadow of the Mountain*), both published in 1962.

On 21 April 1967 at 5:00 A.M. Ritsos was arrested by the Papadopoulos government, which had risen to power as the result of a military coup. After being held for three days, he was removed to the hippodrome in Neo Faliro outside Athens, where thousands of those arrested were gathered. From here he was sent with 6,500 others to the prison camp of Yiaros, "the island of the devil" as it came to be known. He had just turned fifty-eight. In September the Yiaros detention camp was shut down as a result of its intolerable conditions. On Leros two camps were set up, Lakki and Partheni; Ritsos was assigned to the latter. The poet's experiences on Leros are reflected in his collection of poetry *O tihos mesa ston kathrefti* (*The Wall in the Mirror*), published in 1974.

At Leros, Ritsos was diagnosed by army doctors as having cancer and was transferred to Saint Savvas, a cancer clinic in Athens. Rejecting the original diagnosis, the clinic returned him to Leros. Within a month he was permitted to go into internal exile on the island of Samos, where he joined his wife. Arriving in December 1968, Ritsos was forbidden to approach anyone on the island, to receive mail, or to communicate with the mainland. When he fell ill and needed medical treatment, his trip to Athens for an operation was delayed until January 1970. Later that year, in April, he was ordered to return to Athens by one of the three junta leaders, Stelios Pattakos, who advised him to accept the government. His refusal was met by the denial of his remaining freedoms on his return to Samos, and he was put under house arrest. In 1971 Ritsos was finally released and permitted to live in Athens. His ex-

---

[2] Ritsos' works are generally referred to here under their original Greek titles, with English translations appended for convenience at first mention. If the English title appears in italics or quotation marks, a translation of the work has appeared in print—usually in a collection bearing some other name. See the bibliography following this essay for the locations of individual translations.

periences from these years inform the poetry collected in *Dhiadhromos kai skala* (*Corridor and Stairs*), published in 1973.

In the late 1980's Ritsos spent his time alternately at his winter home in Athens and at his summer home on the island of Samos, where his wife continued to practice medicine. Writing and painting, he worked incessantly, a habit he developed in confinement as a means of preserving both his art and his sanity. His paintings and sketches on stones, bone, bits of wood and glass, in varied materials, have been well received in a number of European art shows.

Ritsos is one of Greece's most honored poets. Since first publishing in 1934, he has written over one hundred fifty poetic works published in over ninety books of poetry, two dramatic works, three works of prose, a collection of essays, and eleven books of translations (from the Russian poetry of Vladimir Mayakovsky, Alexander Blok, and Ilya Ehrenburg; the Hungarian of Attila József; the Turkish of Nazim Hikmet; the Spanish of Nicolás Guillén; and the Bulgarian of Dora Gabe; and anthologies of Romanian and Czechoslovakian poetry). His output by the end of 1984 registered a total of one hundred seven published works.

Nominated for the Nobel Prize ten times (by a group of French authors, the PEN Club of Sweden, and Konstantinos Karamanlis' New Democracy Party), Ritsos has been honored with the highest awards of many European nations, among them the First State Prize in Poetry (Greece, 1956); the Great International Prize in Poetry of the Bienniale of Knokke Het Zoute (Belgium, 1972); the International Award "Georgi Dimitrof" (Bulgaria, 1974); the Great French Award in Poetry "Alfred de Vigny" (France, 1975); the International Award in Poetry "Etna-Taormina" (Italy, 1976); the Lenin Prize (USSR, 1977); as well as memberships in the Academy of Arts and Sciences, Mainz (1970), and the Mallarmé Academy (1977), and honorary doctorates from the School of Philosophy, University of Thessaloniki, Greece (1975), and the University of Birmingham, England (1978).

Ritsos' poetry has been translated into forty-four languages, among them Bulgarian, Chinese, Czech, Danish, Dutch, English, French, German, Hungarian, Italian, Polish, Romanian, Russian, Slovak, Spanish, Swedish, and Ukrainian. Since 1970 more than sixteen book translations of his poetry have appeared in English alone.

The full range of Yannis Ritsos' poetry divides easily into long and short poems, the former ranging from no more than two pages ("Psyhosavvato" [All Soul's Day] in *Ydhria* [Pitcher], 1957) to 135 pages (*I ghitonies tou kosmou* [The World's Neighborhoods], 1957). His short poems, by contrast, range from two lines to a page in length. The shortest collection in this group contains five poems (*Ymnos kai thrinos ghia tin Kypro* [A Hymn and Lamentation for Cyprus], 1974), while the longest contains 204 poems (*Nyxis* [Allusions] in *Piimata IV* [Poems IV], 1975). In all we are faced with a body of work approaching three thousand poems of varying length, covering over five thousand pages of print, and growing each day at a prodigious rate. It is not unusual, for example, for Ritsos to write two or three poems a day; indeed, for his collection *To roptro* (Doorbell, 1977) he wrote 126 of the 135 poems collected in a two-to-three-week period, composing in one day sixteen poems. At any given moment, Ritsos may have in his possession twenty to thirty unpublished texts. These he customarily revises three and four times before releasing them to the public. Often his revisions occur over a period of many years, so that poetry written in the 1940's might still be under revision. Thus, his anthology *Piimata IV*, published in 1975, contains pieces composed as early as 1938 and as late as 1971. Several of his collections have appeared in foreign bilingual editions before being published in Greek (*Parentheses*, 1950–1961, *Ghrafi tiflou* [*Scripture of the Blind*], 1979).

Ritsos' method of publication further confounds a clear picture of his many works. He is apt, for example, to publish a collection by itself (*I Eleni* [Helen], 1972) or in combination with other collections (*I Eleni* is also included as one unit in a group of seventeen poems in *Tetarti dhiastasi* [*The Fourth Dimension*], 1972). Smaller collections of poems might be published in combination with other collections under one title (*Trakter*). A larger collection written over a long period of time (*Martyries* [*Testimonies*]) might be published in different volumes at various times (*Martyries: Sira Proti*, 1963; and *Martyries: Seira Dhefteri*, 1966). A single short poem that has been part of one collection ("Paramones iliou" [Sun's Eve], in *Dhokimasia* [Trial], 1943) might become part of another collection (it reappears in *Aghrypnia*, 1954); or a single short poem ("Septiria kai dhafnforia" [Laureled Septeria]) from a collection of short poems (*Epanalipsis* [*Repetitions*]) published in an anthology (*Petres, Epanalipsis, Kigklidhoma* [*Stones, Repetitions, Barriers*], 1972) might be published separately as well (*Septiria kai dhafniforia*, 1973).

FORMS

Long Poems

Narrative Poems. Ritsos' long poems can be divided into three types: narrative poems, dramatic monologues, and choral poems. The narrative is the largest group (fifty-one long poems and seventeen works of six to twelve pages) and includes the earliest of his long compositions, "Polemos" (War), composed between 1930 and 1932. Many of these poems are over twelve pages, although several are considerably longer and a few are as short as six pages. Treating a single theme, they are divided into movements or parts and, except for the earliest ones, which are rhymed, are written in long, convoluted lines of free verse. By themselves, the movements resemble Ritsos' short poems in their laconic statements, their disjointed visual images of everyday objects strung together in what might seem to be purposeful disorder, in their short, iconic scenes that create specific moods or feelings, and in their reflective quality.

For the most part, the earlier long poems were written during the years of Ritsos' active political involvement with the left and are committed to a struggle that makes art subservient to political purpose. Art acts as an outlet in a situation in which physical resistance is not possible. Poetry becomes a means of survival, releasing the poet's pent-up anger and uniting his voice with those who struggle less eloquently, to become part of a larger suffering that minimizes his own and places it in context. This is not a poetry of colors and images, but one of hyperbole that deifies its subjects, a poetry that sometimes exceeds the believable and displays a loss of perspective. One such poem is *I ghitonies tou kosmou* (The World's Neighborhoods), a paean to ELAS–EAM partisans written in 1949–1951. Holding the distinction of being Ritsos' longest single work, it is characterized by a Whitmanesque reiteration of domestic detail that all too soon degenerates into a monotonous catalog—qualities shared by "Ghramma sto Zolio Kioyri" (Letter to Joliot-Curie, in *Piimata III* [Poems III], 1964), *Anipotahti politia* (Unsubdued City, 1958), and other poems written in the detention camps where Ritsos was held from 1948 to 1952. Some of the poems composed during the period 1930 to 1953, however, are Ritsos' best-loved and most successful. Among them is *Epitafios*, which has already exceeded its twentieth edition. This long revolutionary poem in rhymed couplets is modeled on the folk *miroloi* (an eight-syllable-line demotic lament sung by professional mourners) and expresses a mother's sorrow for her worker-son killed by police during the breaking up of a strike in Salonica.

A second widely popular piece, *Romiosini*, written in 1945–1946, eulogizes anti-Fascist Greek partisans in a poem of universal interest linking the Greek present to the Greek past. The later poems of this narrative group (those written during and after the Papadopoulos dictatorship of 1967–1974) control their political voice through a montage of images that can be compared to mental shocks. These poems offer us a direct and open confession of Ritsos' feelings about Greece under the colonels (in *Gkragkanta,* 1973, and *Kodhonostasio* [Belfry], 1974) and celebrate those who fell in the struggle to oust the regime (*To soma kai to ema* [Body and Blood], 1978). In these later poems the poetic voice overshadows the rhetorical and the literal, as the need for emotional release is sufficiently controlled to serve, not overwhelm, art. On the other hand, the role of the poet has not changed, for he offers in these poems his active belief that poetry calls up this role as an *agent provocateur:* "The true act is the just word, the just / and it will be heard and it will be done. I no longer have anything to hide" (*Volidhoskopos* [The Sounder], 1978).

Choral Poems. Ritsos' choral poems, of which he has written ten to date, constitute his smallest group of long works. They range in length from 200 to 1,700 lines, use a three-part form—prose prologue, poem proper, prose epilogue—and are divided, like a dramatic work, into spoken parts. In some choral poems, as in *Tria horika* (Three Chorals, in *Piimata II* [Poems II], 1961), composed between 1944 and 1947, brief prose stage directions describing some small movement or action permeate the work.

The spoken parts of the choral poem are identified by number, the characters as old peasant women (in five of them) or old peasant men (in two others). The voices are essentially indistinguishable from each other and, taken collectively, function as members of a Greek tragic chorus commenting on events and issues that affect their existence. That the voices are meant to function as a tragic chorus is made clear by the poet in the prologue to the choral poem *To dhentro tis fylakis kai i ghinekes* (The Prison Tree and the Women, 1963): "The women sit in a semicircle on the ground, as though around an invisible well, and con-

verse softly, almost inaudibly. Though they remain there motionless, they seem to be moving rhythmically as in the chorus of an ancient tragedy." Taken together the separate parts of the poem constitute a unit that is essentially a monologue in the first-person plural. In many cases one voice stops in the middle of a line and must be completed by the next voice. No identifying characteristics are provided for the various parts, nor are the characters ever developed beyond age, sex, or occupation. The choruses are only regarded as heterogeneous units in two of the works, in which an assortment of characters of both sexes, young and old, are characterized by occupation. The poet's interest is in the continuity of a single thought progressively developed by any of a number of voices.

Ritsos' choral poems (1944–1973) originated in his early one-act play, "Athina sta opla." Written for the Popular Theater of Macedonia and performed in Kozani, a northern Greek city, on 9 February 1945, its purpose was to recruit partisans and gain support from the average Greek by propagating the resistance message. With the breakdown of order that followed the war, the play was abandoned by the poet, who felt its purpose had been muted by the imminence of a civil war. Ritsos later reworked the play, expanding it into a three-act work, *Mana* (Mother), that subsequently reappeared in his eleventh book of poetry, *Aghrypnia,* as a dramatic poem entitled *Tria horika* (Three Chorals). Thereafter, Ritsos published *Pera ap ton iskio ton kyparission,* which once again reworked the one-act "Athina sta opla" text into a three-act play. This interchangeability of poetry and drama demonstrates Ritsos' desire to combine the realism of the theater with the lyricism of poetry; the prevailing force, however, is lyricism, as he indicates in a letter of 2 October 1957 written to Yannis Veakis, the director of his only two plays. The director is encouraged in this letter to bring out the lyric element of the drama: "Great care is needed in the interpretation in order for the lyric quality of the play to shine forth and in order that the play not appear bastardized and sweet." According to Ritsos, the inability of the theater to bring out the lyric quality he sought turned his attention away from writing drama for the stage after one additional attempt, *Mia ghineka plai sti thalassa* (A Woman Beside the Sea, 1959), written during the occupation but, like *Pera ap ton iskio ton kyparission,* not published until many years later.

In the choral poem Ritsos found access to a dramatic form while retaining control over his medium; once the piece was staged, he would lose this control to the director of the performance. Ritsos was concerned as well that the theater was not personal or private enough for the confessional aspect of his poetry. Thus, he turned to the choral poem, which allowed him to combine poetry and drama and yet emphasize the private, lyric voice of its creator.

Thematically, the choral poems differ little from Ritsos' other poems. Basically narrative poems whose lines are distributed among anonymous members of a chorus, they differ from the narrative group only in their less direct political tone and less autobiographical quality. The choral poems eventually led to another, more significant format in Ritsos' poetry, although he never really abandoned the form, just as he never abandoned the narrative or short poem for the chorals. He merely expanded the number of forms he would work into four different types—the narrative, the choral, the dramatic monologue (as the new form was called), and the short poem. In the dramatic monologue the poet stripped away all the external signs of the dramatic and left only its "sense" or tone. Thematically, he turned to the Greek myths and the protagonists of the Greek tragedies, in particular the figures of the *Oresteia,* as masks through which he could more intimately talk about himself.

The Dramatic Monologue. The appearance of a transitional form signaling Ritsos' movement from the choral poem to the dramatic monologue occurred in 1956 with the publication of *I sonata tou selinofotos.* In form it is like a choral poem in which a single voice, introduced in an expanded (though still short) prose prologue, performs all parts.

The thirty-four pieces Ritsos has produced in this form to date open with a short prose prologue in which the poet introduces his main characters, sketches the scene of the action, and sets the time of day or year. The poem's prose epilogue concludes the action initiated in the prologue. Set between the two prose sections is a dramatic monologue in free verse spoken in the first person singular.

The dramatic monologue enables the poet to deal more completely with the intense meditation that long years of imprisonment forced on him. It treats the contemplation of action rather than dramatic action itself; it represents the unfolding of the inner worlds of men faced with complex choices. Caught in a labyrinth of images and memories, thoughts emerge from the depths of the inner self. Characters' identities are kept purposefully ambiguous, and their place in time is vague; the myths with which most of these monologues are associated serve as flickering shadows across the poem. Suspended in time, throwing the light of the past on the darkness of the present, the figures of these poems proclaim no truth, affirm no path. In many of these poems, the poet works contemporary variations on ancient myths.

Dramatic monologues such as *I sonata tou selinofotos, To nekro spiti,* and *I ghefira* (The Bridge, 1960), the poems of the classical cycle *Orestis* (Orestes, 1966), *Filoktitis* (Philoctetes, 1965), *Ismini (Ismene,* 1972), *Hrysothemis* (Chrysothemis, 1972), *I Eleni* (Helen, 1972), *I epistrofi tis Ifighenias* (The Return of Iphigenia, 1972), and *Fedhra* (Phaedra, 1978), and *Persefoni* (Persephone), *Aghamemnon* (Agamemnon), and *Aias* (Ajax; all three published in *Tetarti dhiastasi* [*The Fourth Dimension,* 1972]) hold a rare place among Ritsos' works, for they can be studied individually as microcosms of the poet's corpus. Serving a unifying function, they deal with those questions most characteristic of his poetry: the irresistible force of life in the face of death; archetypal feminine tenderness and the concomitant threat of sterility; the ravaged, nightmarish home to which men are tied by an umbilical cord; and the carnal bonds with which men are united to those objects which express our selves.

In the mythic monologue the speaker is identified in the prologue, and stage directions are confined to either the prologue or the epilogue; the poem in its center section thus appears no different from any other of Ritsos' long poems. The free verse of the monologue proper effectively sets off the central section from the flanking prose prologue and epilogue, which average a few lines to a page each; by contrast, the central section averages around four hundred lines. The two framing pieces, moreover, are enclosed in parentheses, further separating them from the main part of the poem and stressing their function as asides that, like stage directions and decorations, provide the backdrop and set the stage for the real drama. Finally, the prose sections are voiced in the third person as distinct and separate comments on the first-person narration of the central piece and its actual drama. One way of looking at the two prose pieces is to see them as curtain-raiser and after-piece to the main performance, for while they serve to set the stage and to initiate and close off the action of the "play," they are also independent creations that render the original myths of each poem in modern dress. The central monologue, by contrast, utilizes the mythic persona introduced in the prologue as a voice through which to express a separate experience that does not require verification by the myth. The more concrete and familiar prose parts thus frame and inform the abstract and less familiar monologue that constitutes the "play" part of the whole.

Ritsos' most recent mythic monologue, *Fedhra,* provides us with just such an example of the poet's use of the prologue and epilogue. Here the prose sections suggest the Hippolytus-Phaedra story; the figures are nowhere mentioned by name but their identities are im-

plied by their actions and the actions of others. Complete identification of the myth, however, requires the epilogue, as if the poet wishes his audience to hang suspended in uncertainty until he closes off his action. Only then is he willing to display the unmistakable signs of the myth—the hanged Phaedra, the note, the curse, the nurse, Antiope, the statues of Aphrodite and Artemis.

The initial setting is also typically vague and undetermined. The action occurs in a large room of a great old house, a common setting for the monologues. A rapid montage of images—a chair, a couch, a room, a silence—is built up by the omniscient narrator, creating a concrete and definite mood that is really no more than a spring afternoon in some large old room where a woman, "perhaps over forty," rhythmically sways in a rocking chair. Like his interjected "perhaps," a word common to Ritsos' prologues and epilogues, the concreteness of the images is imbedded in indefiniteness or pseudo-precision. While immediacy is suggested by "the young man who comes out of the shower, naked, dripping wet, with a towel around his waist," the reality of present time is ultimately compromised by interjected references to a supposed past of slaves, carriages, and classical gods, among other general references to the Hippolytus-Phaedra story. In spare and taut style, Ritsos sketches pictures in his prologues and epilogues that seem far more substantial and rooted than what we are actually provided with. Focusing on minute details of little immediate interest to the drama, he creates a mood of concrete intangibility. This is the mood that is not only to envelop the imaginary stage of the prologue and epilogue, but that will later give expression to the inexpressibly abstract, that which weighs so heavily on the speakers.

Reducible ultimately to an ephemera, the world of the prologue and epilogue is thus in keeping with that of the more abstract center of the poem. The essential continuity of realms enables the poet to engage his audience at a point close to its own external world before descending into the inner world of the monologue; we emerge again in the epilogue into an external world somewhat familiar to us, drawing tight the circle of our experience seemingly on solid ground. Because the epilogue states what was left unstated in the prologue, it has moved us one step closer to certainty; because both prose parts keep us within easy reach of the touchstone of myth, they provide us with a stable story component; finally, the use of contemporary reality as a backdrop to both prose parts provides an element of familiarity. The poet has created in us the sense of having witnessed a completed drama, when in fact we have only attended a clever reading through a mask. The various characters who people the *Fedhra* epilogue—the hanged woman, the older man, the young man, the nurse, the two statues, the slaves, the carriage drivers, and the servants—reflect back on the monologue to fill his stage. And yet in the monologue itself only one voice speaks for over five hundred lines. It is not what we see, but what the poet suggests to us, that is Ritsos' stage.

Once the monologue begins, the speaker's words flow in an uninterrupted stream creating the internal mood of the speaker. The dramatic method in this section is made up of a dialectic play between the internal and the external. Set into an external and concrete frame that gives it context, the internal and abstract monologue is like a volcano whose activity is triggered by yet another external reality, the temporal events that affected the poem's composition. In the ten mythic monologues Ritsos has produced, these are the events surrounding the Papadopoulos dictatorship of 1967–1974. The mask of a mythic figure allows the poet to distance himself from these events, not only objectifying them but also universalizing them, exploring their confluence with similar events in past history. Internalized, these events become the proper study of poetry, given shape by the mythic persona and given reality by their expression through concrete objects.

The dramatic effect of the monologue results partly from the reader's recognition that the lines spoken are those of a character whom he has imagined called on stage. In *Fedhra,* for example, the reader is introduced to a visitor, a "young man," seeking a middle-aged woman. Their meeting results in the hostess' soliloquy. The presence of a "stage" is kept before the reader through the speaker's references and asides. The speaker may address the listener directly, as when Phaedra asserts, "I invited you. I don't know where to begin." She may ask a question, reminding the reader of the visitor's continued presence: "Truly, how did the hunting go today?" She may command, directing her fellow actor to some action: "Go now, / and wash off the sweat and dirt of your glorious solitary hunt." Or she may turn our attention to some offstage sound that she assumes we, too, must have heard: "Listen, the frogs have gone crazy down at the lake; they too must know something." But the dramatic effect resides just as strongly in the casual references to the characters and objects that fill this poet's imagined stage like so many supernumeraries and stage properties.

Ritsos' monologues, finally, are "confessions," a term that carries for this poet a theatrical meaning, as we find in his essay "On Rereading the Poetic Selections 'The Wall in the Mirror' and 'Caretaker's Desk.' " (The essay appears in the volume *Thyrorio* [1976], which has been rendered as both "Caretaker's Desk" and "Porter's Lodge." A translation of the essay appears in *The Falcon* 9, no. 16:131–132 [Spring 1978].)

> Only before many friends (or is it perhaps before many strange and unknown people?) can we disarm ourselves of seriousness or superficial importance, defensive or offensive, and "joke" with them. Only before them can we openly disguise ourselves (like actors in a tragedy or comedy), or undress ourselves, revealing one by one our garments, our wigs, our beards, our disguises; actors of a true-to-life, unwritten play, actors, perhaps, who remove their makeup and change their costumes after the *performance,* allowing others to suppose consolingly that the previous "work of life" was simply a "theatrical work" which, end-

ing, cannot be restaged, but can be reproduced more effectively.

(*Thyrorio*, pp. 107–108)[3]

These strange and unknown "friends" are the audience of the monologues; the speaker, the poet; the visitor who provides the occasion is fate, poetic creation, perhaps the pressure of temporal events. The "confession" is thus so revealing that it intersects with the poet's private life; it requires the mask, the persona, the mythic distance to make so intimate a disclosure of the self possible. Thus, in *O tihos mesa ston kathrefti* and *Thyrorio*, Ritsos is not speaking merely of a created theatrical illusion, but of a psychic distance necessary to make possible the poetic revelation of personal events. The imaginary stage with its classical setting provides that distance between the poet and the present. The idea of a theatrical production, by raising the material to the level of make-believe, aids in distancing the present so it can be viewed objectively. It is not the weak, moreover, who must confess themselves, but those with courage, those with the willingness to risk intimate contact with "unknown friends," as Nikos Papandreou, the editor of the 1979 edition of *Pera ap ton iskio ton kyparission*, reveals in the preface, where he explains: "The greater the event, the longer the distance between this event and the poet's creation. But whereas weak poets sit waiting for this distance to naturally come about, strong poets create this distance in their minds" (p. 10).

With this more expanded meaning of the word "confession," we come to Ritsos' final sense of the value of his dramatic form: it functions for him as a catharsis, a purging of the personal soul for the larger good; the expression of the poetic arises out of reality and ultimately refers to reality for its meaning as well as its source. The process is that of spiritual liberation rather than purification, a refinement that for Ritsos explains the contempora-

neity of the experience. Thus Phaedra's confession to Hippolytus liberates her from the guilt of loving him and as a result makes inevitable the outcome that follows—her death. The catharsis arises from the nobility of Phaedra's character and is expressed through her soliloquy, an inner song sung against despair.

The prologue and epilogue, summarizing the Phaedra-Hippolytus myth as it has come down to us, make clear the consequences of Phaedra's confession. The monologue proper, the confession itself, is delivered against the background of a predetermined fate (Phaedra's death if ever she reveals her secret). It is this unwavering purpose of Ritsos' persona to reveal all in the face of inevitable doom that exalts the reader, that gives pride and assurance; while at the same time, like Greek tragedy, the poem engulfs itself in the universal questions of the human dilemma, as when toward the end of her monologue Phaedra says:

> [The injustice]
> of one man toward another can be fought, and
>   at times vanquished
> But the injustice of nature—what can we say?
>   —is indomitable,
> vain, and unjustified—(Why injustice, I
>   wonder?). The only injustice
> is life itself. And death is the only
> decisive justice, even though it always
>   arrives late. Perhaps even this
> might be one of our own contrivances, a
>   comforting lie—
> the final consolation for he who will no
>   longer have any need for one.

Short Poems

Ritsos' short poems make up forty-three collections published separately or in combination. Whereas their publishing history suggests a division into four periods (socialist poetry, 1930–1945; poetry of the occupation and civil war, 1945–1952; prison poetry, 1948–1971; post-junta poetry, 1972–present), developmentally the short poems can be conceived of as part of a larger whole that finds a stable

---

[3] Except as noted, all translations of Ritsos' works are by the present writer.

form in *Simiosis sta perithoria tou hronou* (*Notes on the Margins of Time*, in *Piimata I* [Poems I], 1961), written between 1938 and 1941. Brief, objective poems, at first symbolic and later bordering on the surrealistic, the most characteristic appear in such collections as *Parentheses* (in *Piimata II*), *Askisis* (*Exercises*, in *Piimata III*), *Martyries*, *Hironomies* (*Gestures*, 1972), *Diadhromos kai skala*, and *Ghrafi tiflou*. The poet himself explains these poems in his *Meletimata* (Studies, 1974) as "laconic and frequently epigrammatic." They arise, he asserts,

> perhaps from a proclivity to prove to myself and others that I am able to express myself in a concise and dense language; perhaps from a disposition to rest after the sleepless tensions of long creative periods; perhaps from the need to exercise myself in the perfecting and preparing of my craft so that I might, with immediacy and as faultlessly as possible, give value in art to life experiences constantly renewed; perhaps from an attempt to condense expression in reaction to the dangers of verbosity and rhetoric that often lurk in ambush behind long poems; perhaps from the need to respond instantaneously to the grave and urgent problems of our times; perhaps even from the desire to detach and pin down *a moment* of time that would permit a microscopic examination of it in depth and thus to discover all those elements of time that probably would have scattered to the winds on a limitless horizon—that is to say, to conceive of the indivisible by what is divisible, to conceive of everlasting motion by what is immobile.
>
> (p. 98)

In the short poem the poet relies on his skill as a montagist, combining seemingly familiar images in such a way that they become strange and creating through their arbitrary combination and its attendant shock effect distinct impressions, largely those of loneliness, alienation, and displacement. The point of view that permeates these collections is impersonal and abstract, that of the observer; the subject matter is the everyday, but seen as the unusual, attuned in later collections to an urban setting and in earlier ones to that of a rural one. The most poignant quality of the short poems as they mature in a later collection such as *Hironomies* is their increasing sparseness, their abandonment of the overtly political qualities exhibited by some of Ritsos' poetry of the 1940's and 1950's. At the same time they share with the earlier poetry their roots in the earth and in people of the earth. The peasants, the huts, the vineyards of Ritsos' later poetry express a deepening appreciation of domestic details that are here associated with a ripened style, with the poet's mature, most direct and unencumbered reflections.

In more recent collections of short poems such as *Thyrorio* and *Ghrafi tiflou*, the poet leaves the world of actuality to enter the realms of dream and the absurd, and thus gains the freedom to dominate rather than be dominated by his fate. As he objectifies his approach in this world of fluid vision, he detaches himself from his poetry and universalizes it. His purpose: to express and relieve the pain of his waking world. In *Thyrorio*, for example, natural, everyday occurrences are juxtaposed to unnatural, absurd events simply stated, as if they were as common as the obviously natural images with which they are linked. The poetry itself becomes a caricature of life, a slice of unreality that strikes us as too real and too natural. But beneath the images, which are as alive to the eye as their sounds are to the ear, lies Ritsos' world of totalitarian regimes inflicting torture and agony:

> He spread his palms. No marks were visible.
> Wounds heal. The nails remain within.
> Deep inside. Nothing can be seen.
> He is smoking.
> He exhales the smoke. His teeth are copper.
> Could
> they be the nails? Can he chew with them?
> Or are they
> perhaps the others beneath the soldier's
> boots?
>
> ("Exallaghi" [Exchange])

2826

This combination of simplicity of presentation and equally simple images tinged with the absurd or unreal, subtexted with private suffering in a very real world of arbitrary totalitarianism, shows Ritsos at his most powerful.

In *Petres Epanalipsis Kigklidhoma,* a volume containing three separate collections of short poems, Ritsos presents dry wells and withered trees, a wasted landscape of limping old women with rotted teeth and old sea captains in decaying taverns. This work develops the political landscape in images of torture and darkness, of men painting themselves with blood while others watch unconcerned and smiling. In *Epanalipsis* classical themes comment on contemporary suffering. Agamemnon becomes all men who give no credence to their Cassandras. The poet himself, like Philomela of the myth, must turn to his art to weave his vision when his poetic tongue is cut by censorship.

In *Hironomies,* as in *Petres* and *Kigklidhoma,* the poet's visions touch hidden wells of existence. His imagery, sometimes metaphysical and ingrown, opens up here to life, taking its inspiration from the most unlikely, and yet for Ritsos the richest, of sources—an old woman excreting in a flowerpot, a mirror emptying its images like a river, swaying lamps, copper-green and drowned, a man searching among many faces for his own. The poet's country becomes in "Elladha" (Greece, in *Kigklidhoma*) ruined fields deserted during hard times by their owner; returning themselves to nature, they are inhabited now by an old woman: "'With things like this, my son, falsehoods,' she said, 'we hack out our existence.'" In *Dhiadhromos kai skala,* the poet speaks of the precedence that freedom must take over death; he warns of false heroism and the indifference of man to man. In this collection Ritsos presents the dark drudgery of his fellow men in vignettes of deadening impact. He depicts mechanical lives of self-deception, offering figures whose lives are neither heroic nor meaningful, people who go through the motions of eating when there is nothing to eat because the pattern of their lives requires them to do so. He treats the poor, the disinherited, and the despised without illusions. These souls will join the struggle with what little has been given them. We must do what we do, the poet reminds us; we cannot do otherwise.

Figures that appear in *Hironomies* and *Petres Epanalipsis Kigklidhoma* appear again: fishermen, farmers, black-clad old women. The poet neither extols nor condemns them; those who live on are victims as much as those who are called on to suffer. Still, as he moves from image to image, creating the moods and tones of painting and music in the worlds of words he builds, Ritsos' pictures act as pricks to the conscience. Those who do not hear the cry for help do not belong to life:

> the cry
> of a lonely bird
> in the hollow sky
> seeking us one more time
> understanding again
> (what "yes" does it imply?)
> falling from high
> on top parked buses
> with their centuries-old dead travelers.
>> ("Sto keno" [In the Void],
>> in *Corridor and Stairs*)

Dealing with concretely visual images, Ritsos moves in this collection from the coldly objective to the highly personal and subjective. His poems here begin by distancing the reader, but end by trapping him in terror-filled images that grip and rend. In this collection Ritsos creates a realm in which he has become a practiced traveler and of which he is a profound expositor.

Ritsos' collection *Ghrafi tiflou* not only is most characteristic of his short poems but also represents his poetry at its most incisive and richly metaphorical. Here an oppression invades the work with a characteristic totality seen also in *Dhiadhromos kai skala, O tihos mesa ton kathrefti,* and *Thyrorio.* This poetry is preoccupied with the presence of an enemy, betrayal and arrest, reactions to oppression, guards, gallows, death, exile, surgeons and rubber hoses, confessions, identity cards, desertions, revolts, and the bitterness and emptiness of a menaced land. The poetry reveals itself as well in details of domestic life: the pall that hangs over the simplest family gathering, unmatched shoes, red eggs against bread perforated by bullets on a white napkin, a vacuum cleaner run to cover the sound of shots, a knife wrapped in bandages. At this domestic level pain is neither avoidable nor resistible. It is so pervasive that it can no longer be considered abnormal. Rather, oppression becomes its own norm, that which is now natural to humankind. Heroics, like heroes, are lost and useless in these mundane lives.

A figure of existential despair, man in *Ghrafi tiflou* is faceless, an image lacking form. One's sense of identity is confused in poems in which women are denied their mirror images and in which nameless coffins, masks, wigs, and disguises proliferate. When a mask will not come unstuck, the reality of the face becomes that of the mask. Many of the faces are viewed through a window or against it, a suggestion that the face may itself be transparent. Here it is the reflecting surface that controls the reality of the face; mirrors hold the image, multiply it, distort it, partially return it, make it more real than its original, or refuse it altogether. When the mirror is present, bullets cannot shatter its reflecting surface; they merely pass through it, leaving holes through which the dead reach out and steal the bread of the living—a two-way mirror from past to present, life to death. Death itself is described as "without a mirror any longer," implying that life is death's mirror image. Uncontrollable reflections, human images in *Ghrafi tiflou* serve as warnings, a presence of possibilities like a pocketed newspaper that a mute customs officer does not read. Yielding to his masks and to his statues (images of himself), man ceases to live. Trapped thus between the living and the dead, between identity and facelessness, the protean image

explodes, multiplying itself in one instance, dissolving in another. Only because the monstrous in *Ghrafi tiflou* is treated as commonplace does wonder occur. Miracles exist in simple, everyday elements, in domestic details—a large tray of potatoes, a warm loaf of bread.

"Normal" people, it appears, are less interesting and less decisive than the eccentric, the deformed, the heroic (those at the fringes and pressing the limits of normality). They are depicted largely as bystanders who watch figures pass by. They rarely do more than report a situation or suffer from it; their lives do not appear to be structured by their own intent but by that which is inflicted upon them. They live through reflected images and not directly, as if "through a mirror, darkly," without self-knowledge.

In *Ghrafi tiflou,* the most ordinary details—a blurred windowpane, the fragrance of myrtle—are presented not because they are the most essential (indeed, they may only have accidentally caught the poet's eye), but because they are merely there. They are not planted by the poet to mislead or to surprise. It is not necessary, as a result, to make sense of the vision or to insist on their inexplicableness. Caterpillars, ugly many-legged creatures crawling low against the ground, are viewed from above as they pass along the wings of the statue of Victory, while maddened ladies with unwashed hair celebrate a triumph of female over male, a triumph like that of the insects over cold, unresisting marble. Such things happen, and we condone them by our acquiescence.

Ghrafi tiflou contains a poetry once again rooted in instinct and inspiration. Throughout this work Ritsos seems to warn the reader to rely for understanding on his own instinct for poetry; the source of poetry is described in terms of a woman's necklace that lies in "an untouched suspension of studied silence—there where poetry always waits to be detected." Passing from the wonderful to the commonplace, inspiration exists independent of the craft of shaping a poem.

THEMES

Sociohistorical

Poetry in Ritsos' view is, in a critical sense, a mission. Indeed, as he has said, it

> fulfills the poet's highest priority, which is to bring together fraternally human strengths and to organize them against tyranny, injustice, and vileness. Such a mission always leads the true poet. And the greatest honor for such a poet is to carry his social responsibility on his own shoulders to the end. It is in this way that the masses find worthy spokesmen and leaders.
>
> (quoted in S. Gheranis, *Ta mikra mou thavmata* [Small Miracles], p. 1)

What Ritsos insists must be accepted without question and without expectation of gratitude is the poet's duty to serve the people as one of their own and to purge egocentricity and personalism from his work. He makes ours what is already ours, unhurriedly and simply, Ritsos asserts. Thus he seems to downplay the importance of his own art, as if he expects no more recognition than that received by a mother, who, like the poet with his poetry, gives birth to and nurtures her progeny. Ritsos suggests in his essay on Ilya Ehrenburg in *Meletimata* that the poet subordinates himself to the people because the individual cannot be saved alone and for himself, and even if he could, it would not make any difference. This would be an exception without meaning, an exception without consequence for the wholeness of things. Thus the poet must become more substantial for society, for the historical period in which he finds himself, for his nation, and for the problems that afflict that nation. In the end the poet who turns out of his private world into the social realm has, for Ritsos, achieved universality, while the poet who sings of the self only wails of his misfortunes. To lay aside the private and take on society's burdens, Ritsos says in his essay on Paul Eluard (also in *Meletimata*) is to speak with the voice of one's people and, ultimately, with the world's voice. "The entire world begins to speak through [the poet's] mouth. That is why his voice deepens, widens, and strengthens. Isolated, specific, and private feelings are not served by a strong voice. They are only ridiculed by it" (p. 85).

Of the roles the poet assumes in his poetry, the most pervasive is the sociohistoric. The characters, the settings, and the subject matter of the whole corpus of Ritsos' poetry stress social concerns, particularly those of the common man. Indeed, at the time Ritsos began to write poetry, few Greek poets of any stature, with the exception of Varnalis, were preoccupied with themes arising from the life of the working man or the common peasant. Yet Ritsos' first collection of poetry, pragmatically titled "Tractor," clearly showed his concern for the worker. In this collection, such titles as "Sto Marx" (To Marx), "ESSD" (To the Soviet Union), "Atomikistis" (The Individualist), and "Epanastates" (Revolutionaries) are indicative of the poet's continuing identification with the working class. Comparing Ritsos' *Epitafios* to Varnalis' "I mana tou Hristou" (Mother of God, 1922), both demotic lamentations treating social themes, one is struck by Ritsos' less personal, less private tone. The social situation in Ritsos' poem is quite different. Varnalis' mother is concerned for her own child's welfare, while Ritsos' mother adopts a collective spirit. This spirit is emphasized throughout Ritsos' poetry by the predominance of the pronoun "we," especially apparent in his long poems of the 1940's and 1950's, "Letter to Joliot-Curie" and "Neighborhoods of the World." Even in his most recent poetry, his poems are peopled with peasants—from the old village women of *Monemvasiotises* (Women of Monemvasia, 1978) to the forty-eight speaking voices of *Volidhoskopos*, which offer a cross-section of the common people, represented by the young, the old, the ugly, the beautiful, and the lame. In *Ghrafi tiflou* the marginal and the dejected, the main figures of the work, displace "normal" people, who are regarded as less interesting and less decisive than the eccentric, the deformed, the heroic—those at the fringes, who press the limits of normality.

Ritsos' characters either are of the masses or are laic heroes, those who in the poet's view fought for a more democratic Greece: the young worker of the May 1936 demonstration in Salonika in *Epitafios*; the resistance fighters in *Romiosini*; Aris Velouchiotis, leader of ELAS, in *To isteroghrafo tis dhoxas* (Postscript to Praise, 1975); Nikos Velogiannis, the assassinated Marxist, in *O anthropos me to gharyfallo* (The Man with the Carnation, 1952); Grighoris Lambrakis, the Socialist deputy assassinated in Salonica in 1963, in *Thrinos tou mai* (May Lamentation, in *Ta Epikerika* [The Timely], 1975); and Nikos Zahariadis, secretary general of the Greek Communist party, in *O syntrofos mas. Nikos Zahariadhis* (Our Comrade. Nikos Zahariadhis, 1945).

The poet's historical interest is not limited solely to contemporary Greek history; his praise turns as well to those he considers have furthered international leftist causes—Patrice Lumumba, the African revolutionary leader, in *O Mavros Aghios* (The Black Saint, 1961), Marx and Christ in *Meghali ora* (Great Hour, in *Trakter*). His interests, nevertheless, focus most sharply on events that have shaped recent Greek history—the Polytechnic University student unrest in 1974 in *Imerologhio mias vdhomadhas* (A Week's Diary, in *Ghignesthe* [Becoming], 1977) and in *To soma kai to ema*; American involvement in Greece and Vietnam in *Kodhonostasio*. Even his most difficult and abstract verse, whether in long poems like *I Eleni, Filoktitis, Orestis,* and *Aghamemnon* or in short collections like *Thyrorio, O tihos mesa ston kathrefti,* and *Diadhromos kai skala,* interpret events current at the time of the poem's composition.

The dates of composition noted at the end of the poems serve as the poet's reminder to the reader to remain aware of the events of the times. Indeed, Ritsos' poetry follows the most

important stages of Greek political history and witnesses its effects on the lives of the populace. Thus, not only such early poems as "Ghermania" (Germany, in *Trakter*), written between 1930 and 1934, which documents the cruelty and the brutality of pre–World War II German ideology, but also much of the difficult and abstract poetry of *Tetarti dhiastasi,* which speaks of the events surrounding the Papadopoulos regime of 1967–1974, is of historical interest. The poems speak of the horror of war, where the suffering inflicted becomes one for man, tree, and stone. The pain felt by both animate and inanimate objects is described by Ritsos in *I teleftea pro Anthropou ekatontaetia* (The Last One Hundred Years Before Man, 1975), a hymn written in 1942 to the common man's struggle against the oppression and hardship caused by the seemingly interminable wars experienced by modern Greece.

In *Tria horika* Ritsos laments the pain of a mother who raises children only to see them snatched away by war. In "To dhihty" (The Net), composed in 1970, he calls on the populace to take arms for freedom and democracy. Throughout his work Ritsos speaks for those who suffer the greatest injustices of all. The oppressed, the enslaved, must, more than others, keep their freedom of identity and their dignity, for people truly exist only if they keep alive within them a sense of who they are. Keeping alive the thought of rising against his master, in *O afanismos tis Milos* (The Annihilation of Milos, 1974), the slave becomes a man. At times this freedom exists only in thought: "Only in our memories does a little air remain / only in our memories can we breathe" (*Mantatofores* [News-Bearing Women, 1975]); elsewhere, in death itself: "Death in this life is our only freedom / soothing oil of freedom on our open wounds" (*To horiko ton sfouggaradhon* [Sponge Diver's Chorale, 1983]).

The dignity that comes with freedom has itself a liberating quality. The father in *To horiko ton sfouggaradhon* can accept his son's drowning only after he realizes that *leventia,* the quality that renders one heroic, requires not sorrow but celebration. In *Kodhonostasio* those who are of the earth, even an earth ravished by suffering and pain, endure like the classical statues of the surrounding landscape; though maimed, they are still white and remain immovable, holding high their heads. In "Kina thaymata" (Common Miracles), a poem typical of the collection *Ghrafi tiflou,* the dignity of man is presented through a parable of a dog (the common man) denied water from a bucket at the church door (society):

They took out the candelabra into the open air under
  the trees
and scrubbed the church. From the large door
a dark humidity spread out over the steps
and over the white sunwashed tiles. The beadle
kicked a limping dog that had drawn near
to drink water from the bucket. Then, from the
  beautiful altar door,
the Archangel with his large red wings came out,
stooped to the dog, and gave it to drink out of his
  cupped hands.
And so the next day the five paralytics walked.

Inequality exists only among men. In the eyes of the universe all are equal and have an equal right to dignity and self-worth. Material wealth is not requisite to freedom, says Ritsos, and men should therefore not seek it. The peasant women of *Mantatofores* ask only for a greeting from their neighbors, a smile, a pot of flowers, the silence of an old man, to enjoy life as they know it. Constant struggle undertaken in a harsh environment and with heads held high transforms Ritsos' peasants into existential figures who perform their tasks with the persistence of a Sisyphus, knowing, like him, that their efforts are useless.

Mythic

But Ritsos' poetry is not merely sociohistorical; it is also significantly preoccupied with themes deriving from classical mythology. In his long poems, primarily the dramatic monologues and many of the choral poems, Ritsos presents ancient myths as themes on which the poet works contemporary variations. *Filoktitis* places its figures in a world of appearances: a young man with "Achilles' features but slightly more spiritualized, as though he were his son, Neoptolemus"; Philoctetes stranded on an island, "perhaps Lemnos." The hero's companion in "Orestes" is someone "like Pylades." The pair arrive in the prologue "with an air about them as though they were trying to remember or recognize something, even though everything was incredibly familiar and moving, though somewhat smaller—much smaller—than they had thought when they had been in exile, in another land, another time." Neither Orestes nor Philoctetes is permitted to escape his fated role:

How is it that others can little by little determine our fate, inflict it on us, and we accept? How is it that with the smallest threads from part of our own moments they can weave our entire life for us, coarse and dark, cast it like a veil upon us from head to foot, covering every part of our faces and hands?

A man prepared to acknowledge past misdeeds and make amends, the hero of *Aghamemnon* finds, too, that fate has a reality that reality itself lacks:

A man, handsome, bare-headed, in battle dress, with a large, bloodstained sword in his hand, enters the empty hall. With his left hand, he takes the helmet from the console. He puts it on backwards. The horsetail in his face. Like a mask. He leaves. The voice of the raving woman: "Citizens of Argos, it's already too late, too late, citizens of Argos—"

In *I Eleni,* a poem for which Ritsos admits a special affection, the pointlessness of the past as a model for the present is brought home. Now an "old, old woman—one, two hundred years old," whose servants fight over her possessions as they wait for her to die, she was once the most handsome woman in the world, over whose favors the strongest fought:

How pointless everything was,
without purpose, stability, substance—riches, wars,
glory and murder, jewels, even my own beauty.
        What foolish legends,
swans, Troys, loves, and brave deeds.

Like her male counterparts of the other classical monologues, Helen is closed up in the confines of her memories. She is decaying, like the house she occupies, her past a void. The face that launched a thousand ships is overgrown with warts; her body is ravaged by death, her home looted by greedy neighbors:

"Ah, ah," they shouted and hid things under their dresses. Another phone call. The police were already coming up. They sent away the servants and women, but the neighbors just had time to grab the birdcages with the canaries, some flowerpots with exotic plants, a transistor, an electric heater. One of them was holding a gold picture frame.

O afanismos tis Milos, reminding us of Helen, treats three old women who have lost their sense of time and live in their memories on a lonely and isolated present-day Milos. Loosely based on the massacre of the inhabitants of Milos by their Athenian allies (as described in Thucydides' *Peloponnesian War*), the poem tells us, "Yes, they are women of Milos, but on another island now." In *To nekro spiti* vague references—to a bath, to a mistress as a murderess, to words such as "slaughtered," to the dead house of the title—evoke the Mycenaean past and the myth of the House of Atreus. But the references are not specifically to one period or to one myth. The mistress, the children, the bath could refer to Medea as well as to Clytemnestra, to present as well as to past horrors. Time and space are here dissolved so that the poet may extend through time the psychology and suffering of these figures.

In many of his shorter poems, as in *Epanalipsis,* Ritsos' use of myth is quite different from that in his longer dramatic works. Here he does not strip the classical myths of their antiquity but clothes the modern age in classical garb, commenting on classical figures to render judgements on the actions and concerns of men of his own time and place. In "Mnimosyno ston Poro" (Memorial Service at Poros), we are transported to the village of Kalavrita on a particular evening in July, to a shore where once Poseidon roamed, near a "sacred wood" where "ivy-crowned youths" once played. Evoking the past, the poet prepares the reader for Demosthenes, the orator who

        took poison—
he, the stutterer, who labored till he became the first orator of the Greeks,
and then condemned by Macedonians and Athenians, in one night,
learnt the most difficult, the greatest art: to be silent.

The focus of the poem is on the artist, the poet who labors to perfect his art, to speak the truth, only to learn that the truth can destroy him. Written under the military junta in 1969, the poem treats that function of the poet which had been denied Ritsos.

In "O Talos" (Talos) Ritsos' central image is the giant Talos, whose single vein was plugged at the end with a bronze pin that when pulled would spill his life blood. While the past is recalled here in classical names—Jason, Odysseus, Colchis, Troy, the Minotaur—the single nail clearly belongs as much to the present:

        And perhaps, I say,
we all have but one vein, sealed with a nail,
and all of us have the same fear.
   Opposite, on the great whitewashed wall,
on nails hammered in a row (from unplugged veins perhaps?) we hang
our coats, hats, umbrellas, underpants, and masks.

Only here in the final lines does the retelling of the myth become apparent. We, like Talos, have given our lives to causes we believed in and yet, Ritsos suggests, to no effect. On the whitewashed walls on which the peasants hang their clothes, the nails stand for fallen warriors who, like Talos, Odysseus, and Jason, have been forgotten. The sacrifice of those who fought to change Greece is forgotten.

Ritsos uses the classical myth as a yardstick against which to measure the actions of present-day man. Borrowing from the classical past, the poet has at his disposal a wealth of characters whose lives, being complete, comment on our own similar, if incomplete, lives. Ritsos speaks of the misunderstood, the sensitive, the weak, those who stand for a purer truth or greater knowledge. In "Niovi" (Niobe) the poet's mythic material speaks to the modern insensitivity toward people's inner feelings and thoughts. Viewing the state of Niobe, the poet speaks of the magic, the wonder, the miracle of her tears and recalls the loss of her seven butchered sons. Today, he says, we do not seek the suffering that produced the statue's tears. Today we seek explanations, rationalizations. Unsatisfied with the beauty of the message the statue sends us, we exchange the aesthetic for the analytical.

In other of Ritsos' short and long narrative poems, myth is used to underline a comment, to draw a contrast, or to demonstrate continuity between the past and the present. In "Arheo theatro" (Ancient Theater), in *Martyries: Sira Proti,* a Greek youth in the center of an ancient amphitheater lends the echo of his voice to the uninterrupted thread of history:

> From across
> the precipitous mountain, the echo answered—
> the Greek echo, which neither imitates nor repeats
> but merely continues to a height immeasurable
> the eternal cry of the dithyramb.

Far from imitating or repeating the splendor of the original (the past), the echo (the present) intensifies it, illuminating and extending the eternal cry of the human condition. In *Romiosini* the future depends on the continued existence of the past; *romiosini* is the presence of continued Greekness. Necessary to the very being of the modern Greek, it is that without which by definition "Greek" may not exist. Thus the contemporary sailor "drinks the bitter sea from the wine cup of Odysseus" or the guerrillas meet "with Dighenis on those same threshing-floors"—a reference to the legendary Greek folk hero Dighenis Akritas, who guarded the eastern frontiers of Byzantium and who for three days fought death on a marble threshing floor. When the poet asks, "How much longer must the mother wring her heart-strings / for her seven butchered sons," the mother is all Greek mothers, ancient and modern, who like the mythic Niobe have experienced that suffering which follows great loss.

Autobiographical

The third thematic strand of Ritsos' work is autobiographical, for the poet's concern for the sociohistorical and the mythic ultimately emerges out of his own rich personal history. These themes express his tragic family experiences, his personal involvement in his country's recent political history, and his sense of poetic purpose. Autobiographical references are found interspersed throughout Ritsos' poetry, alongside social and mythic themes. In some instances entire collections are almost exclusively autobiographical. *Monovasia* (Monovasia, 1982), for example, deals with the poet's ancestral village; *Makronisiotika* (From Makronisos, 1957), with his experiences in political detention camps; *I arhitektoni ton dhentron,* with his visit to Romania; *Anthropi kai topia* (People and Places, in *Ta Epikerika* [The Timely], 1975), with his visit to Bulgaria; *Italiko triptyho* (Italian Triptych, 1982), with his trips to Italy; and *Hartina* (*Paper Poems,* 1974), a series of haiku-like poems, explores the poet's view of his art.

In most of Ritsos' work, the autobiographical becomes so intermingled with his other major themes that the poet's presence can be detected only behind a mask through which he speaks and whose persona is, in part, a reflection of his private self. Ritsos is like Phaedra, trapped by passion and forced to internalize feelings, to feed that passion on memories or externalize it through cold and unfeeling objects (a necklace, the chair Hippolytus sat on). Ritsos, incarcerated for so many years in camps and hospitals, internalized and expressed his feelings through his poetry. In *Ismene* the mask muses on the fates of Antigone and Haemon, touching by extension on the worth of causes for which the poet had himself been exiled for so many years: "What good did it do them, my God? What did they gain?" Elsewhere, as in *Tiresias* (1983) or *I Eleni,* the poet justifies past actions or reassesses them, surfacing unexpectedly, always fleetingly, and eternally separated from his reader by the mask.

Through his poetry Ritsos carries on a dialogue with himself on contemporary society and man. Clothing his private views in his heroes, not only does he objectify his material but he also universalizes it. Protected behind his mask from prying eyes, in such monologues as *Aias* the poet is distanced from his own emotions, lucid, revealing, and yet safe from the government censors who seek him out. Writing in exile first on Leros and later on Samos, the poet becomes Ajax, a man punished by the very nation he had fought as both a soldier and a poet to protect. Thus when in *Aias* the hero says, "I cast into the helmet not fresh lumps of earth / but my big, clear, nuptial ring and came forth first / against the enemy body to body," it is Ritsos speaking to fellow Greeks who fled into hiding and self-imposed exile to await the war's end; the poet, at the same time, remained behind offering his life. It was he who stood before Hector, the enemy's best, as others amassed wealth from the destruction of their fellow men. "In nothing will the stolen shield be of use, no matter how / beautiful and big," he concludes. This is the lesson learned by standing "naked before the night and its lengthy road," divesting oneself of all hate, prejudice, and material needs, and accepting forthrightly life's true meaning—the presence and realization of death.

Elsewhere, as in *To nekro spiti,* the poet objectifies personal tragedy, that of his own fam-ily life. In that poem an aged Electra in Argos speaks of her two brothers and two sisters, a deviation from the myth, which tells of one brother and three sisters: "And the house—not Agamemnon's. And the younger brother with the artistic inclinations—who was he? There was no second brother. Then? What was this house for?" The house is the poet's own, the family his two brothers and two sisters. Ritsos, taking on the persona of Electra, can express through her alienation his own suffering.

The same approach is used to explore autobiographical themes that comment on the poet's art in the short-poem collections *Epanalipsis, Thyrorio,* and *To roptro.* In the poem "Filomila" ("Philomel" in *Epanalipsis*), Ritsos draws tight the connection between his art and life. The raped Philomel, her tongue severed, embroiders her torments on a cloth. Today while we have the cloth—the poem—we forget the suffering that produced it. But without this experience, "Would there perhaps have been this superb tunic and the nightingale?" In the end the cloth itself both receives the poet's imprint and stands for him, making complete the intersection of life and art, as we see in the *To horiko ton sfouggaradhon:*

> 1ST OLD MAN: A song can see.
> 2ND OLD MAN: It looks inward.
> 3RD OLD MAN: It can look outward also.
> ALL: It sees everything like a dry sponge with its thousand eyes.

TECHNIQUES

Whether long or short, sociohistorical, mythic, or autobiographical, Ritsos' poetry constitutes a world of highly visual concrete objects rooted in the life of the Greek peasant. In "Irini" (Peace in *Aghrypnia*) it is through the images of daily life—a father returning from the fields, a basket of fruit in his arms; a worker emerging freshly shaven from a neighborhood barber shop; the odor of "warm bread on the world's table"—that the sensation of a world at rest is created. The feeling for domestic detail, found early in Ritsos' poetry, deepens in late collections as it opens to a wider range of human experience. A reading of the whole body of Ritsos' work impresses us with an increasing sparseness, an abandonment of philosophizing and politicizing, and an insistence on the objects of present reality that contribute to the immediacy of the poetry as well as to its folk quality. Produced by unusual and striking juxtapositions, it is an effect that holds the reader. Where animate and inanimate objects are juxtaposed, the lifeless is given life and the living becomes lifeless.

Sometimes incongruity is achieved with the unusual placement of an adjective, as in "stone sun" or "sick houses" ("Mesimvrina parathyra" [Southerly Windows], in *Dhokimasia* [Trial], 1943). Elsewhere, personification gives unexpected life: "forehead of autumn;" "almond trees pull their curtains"; "fruits show their clenched fists"; "a stalk of wheat to bend its knee to the sky"; "the afternoon stood at the edge of the sea"; "night's dustless tail in thorns." Incongruity may come from striking similes: "My good ladies with your white thighs, your white buttocks like boiled cauliflower" ("The Sounder"); "Two thin clouds / hung over the mountain like two braids of garlic" ("The Last One Hundred Years Before Man"). The images created by such combinations are born of the collision of juxtaposed objects in which, like the Eisensteinian explanation of montage, one object combines with a second unrelated object to create a meaning not found in either. In Ritsos this third "meaning" constitutes the mood of the poem, frequently one of loneliness and nostalgia.

An examination of the body of Ritsos' poetry shows that his maturity as a poet rests primarily in the sophisticated complexity with which he handles these juxtapositions. The incongruity he achieves increases as his poetry develops; striking images appear infrequently in the earlier poetry, while in the post-sixties period they constitute whole poems. Particularly where Ritsos' early poetry extols the virtues of his leftist comrades, its pathos diminishes the impact that juxtaposition creates:

> Ari
> trees weep
> mountains weep
> rivers weep
> and your shadow darkens the valleys
> it darkens the air
> Greece beats her breast
> Freedom beats herself
>> ("Ston Ari" [To Ari], in
>> *To ysterografo tis dhoxas*
>> [Postscript to Praise], 1945)

His later work, by contrast, exploits an abstracted world of displacement and disjointedness, a nightmarish world of dislocated objects displayed across an expanse of undifferentiated time. It is the unlikeliness of the things described and the cinematic "jump-cuts" from topic to topic that condition the reading of the poem:

One disappeared into a corner. Three were asleep.
The woman on the bench had an umbrella.
It wasn't raining. The others were having sex
behind the hedge. Night fell daily.
They wrapped the bones in flags.
"What are they carrying?"—we asked. They didn't
  answer.
They were climbing the hill. They didn't turn their
  heads.
The bones, the flags, a lizard on a rock.
It isn't anything, I tell you. It's already gone.
How well you look in the yellow dress.
Especially if you wear a gold belt.
>> ("Vradhinos ponokefalos"
>> [Nighttime Headache], in "Porter's Lodge")

Here a progression of events is suggested but devoid of cause and effect. Objects and events, introduced suddenly with little relation to what precedes or follows, are nevertheless connected in a broad sense. The poems are characterized by the interchangeability of their lines.

Rearranged, the poems are not affected in their continuity or meaning. In the longer poems, whole speeches, even sections, can be interchanged without apparent disruption to the flow of the whole. Indeed, these long works are themselves composed of imagery that does not follow conventional ideas of "narrative" and seeks to create individual effects. Thus passages easily isolated as separate small poems are fitted into larger poems that, as a result, are free of any "plotted" quality.

In one sense all Ritsos' poetry is a poetry of memories and thoughts. Reading his poetry is like reviewing a parade that emanates from the poet's subconscious and passes before the reader as a series of ancient and contemporary masks displayed in tableaux that come to life at the touch of some unknown stimuli. *Mantatofores* shows the poet's various voices being pulled together to converge in one exasperated voice. Elsewhere, images, sometimes abstract, sometimes lucid, race before the reader, who finds himself invited to a feast of disembodied thoughts. In the long narrative poem "The Net," disturbed thoughts jump, fragmented, from subject to subject in nightmarish confusion interspersed only periodically with moments of sober clear-headedness. In *Ismini* these memories pile atop one another to create an almost Dionysian frenzy of sensuality and violence.

The more internal the themes of Ritsos' poetry, the greater their effect. When it deals with the external, as does his early political poetry, and such isolated later works treating broad topics as the *To horiko ton sfouggaradhon,* his poetry generalizes without universalizing. His most intimate or confessional poetry serves as a personal testimony (as the titles to his impressive short poems in *Martyries* suggest) that relieves the poet of his role as an outside observer and places him squarely within the world of experience.

Even as an insider, however, the poet assumes an objective stance that distances him from the highly personal and private themes he explores, a stance clearly seen in the multitude of voices with which he speaks to his readers. In the longer dramatic poems the speakers provide that distance, while in the short poems it is achieved by the introduction of a third-person singular or plural—"he said," "they said," "he used to say"—which punctuates the poems. The introduction of the third-person "he says" lends the short poems a dramatic quality as well, for we are conscious not only of the recording voice of the poet, but also of a second voice who addresses either the reader, a figure in the poem, or the poet. When the speaking voice is clearly Ritsos' own, we are faced with either a dramatic confrontation between poet and reader or an internal debate between the poet and himself.

In the monologues dramatic tension is created through the reader's recognition that the lines spoken are those of a character he has witnessed being called upon a "stage." In *Aghamemnon* the prologue "sets" the "stage" on which appear a warlord and his wife: "He places his left hand on her hair, careful lest he spoil her beautiful coiffure. She pulls away. She stands upright, a little further away. His smile appears distant, weary. He speaks to her. You don't know if she is listening."

Setting the stage, the poet suggests an interaction between two characters with complex motives; the reader's knowledge of the myth of the House of Atreus further specifies expectations. In *Filoktitis,* too, the poem is set like the opening scene of a play revealed by a rising theater curtain: "Two men are seated before a stony cavern on some remote island." In each instance a dialogue is implied, a dramatic interaction is anticipated.

Continued reference to the presence of a stage in the monologue proper reinforces this created sense of the dramatic. A speaker may himself refer to the stage, or, as in the choral poems, actual stage directions may appear. In *I Eleni,* for example, the speaker continually refers us to the immediate audience of her "stage," the ever-silent young man to whom she speaks. "Yes, yes, it's me. Sit down a while," she says. Elsewhere she implores, "Don't go away. Stay a while longer."

In the choral poems the staccato and rapid movement of the voices suggests the movements of a chorus. In *Mantatofores,* for example, the long lines with which the poem opens shorten progressively as the end of the poem approaches; and in the body of the poem the refrain "Bone, rock, iron—iron, rock" is that of the performance ritualistically repeated by seven old women. In *Tiresias* the cadence of ritual is achieved by repetition with variation:

> and the knife is hidden in the broad, green leaves
> or in the basket with its purple grapes
> or behind the jugs of wine and honey.

In Ritsos' earlier poetry the repetition of words or phrases is incantational and improvisational, almost like oral poetry. But once the poet opens a subject, a flood of emotion overtakes him and cannot be contained:

> Freedom or death
> freedom or death—the people
> in the open cars shouting—and the leaflets
> and the people chasing the leaflets and shouting
>   hurrah
> stumbling over the tanks and shouting hurrah
> hurrah, hurrah, hurrah,
> freedom or death, freedom or death—the people
> in the open cars shouting
> freedom or death, freedom or death
> the people who fought and fell
> who fell and smiled
> who kissed the people and smiled
> who pulled the wedged bullet out of their chests
>   with their fingers
> and came back among us and fought
> and fought and smiled.
>   (The World's Neighborhoods)

In later poems the repetition becomes more controlled, more balanced and musical. In *Khodonostasio* the repetition of "house" (a favored Ritsos image) at the beginning of each of four lines recalls the balance and tone of Ecclesiastes:

> House with a garden, with red shirts on
>   the washline,
> house with a balcony, with plaster statues,
> house without a balcony, itinerant knife grinders
>   piss in the corner
> house with a lank Crucifixion outside the door, with
>   the paralyzed woman on the bed.

In a poem like *Epitafios* the repetition is built around specific letters with musical qualities, "r" and "l." Here the poet capitalizes on an affection for music that is reflected in the titles as well as in the structure of a number of his poems, including *To traghoudi tis adhelfis mou* (Song of My Sister, 1937); *Earini symfonia* (Spring Symphony, 1938); "I rapsodhia toy gymoy fotos" (Rhapsody of Naked Light in *Phokimasia*); *Palia mazourka se rythmo vrohis* (An Old Mazurka Set to the Rhythm of Rain, 1943); *To emvatirio tou okeanou* (The Ocean's Musical March, 1940); *I sonata tou selinofotos; Exercises; Thrinos tou mai* (May Lamentation in *Ta Epikerika*); *Dhekaohto lianotraghoudha tis pikris patridhas* (Eighteen Short Songs of the Bitter Motherland, 1973); and *Ymnos kai thrinos ghia tin Kypro* (A Hymn and Lament for Cyprus, 1974).

OTHER WORKS

Translations and Criticism

Of the more than one hundred published works of Ritsos only seventeen consist of anything other than original poems—chiefly prose, poetic translations, and drama. The bulk of this group comprises eleven translations of the poets of Russia, Romania, France, Turkey, and Czechoslovakia. The first, Alexander Blok's *I dhodheka* (The Twelve), was published in 1957 and the last, Sergei Essenin's *Piimata* (Poems), in 1981. In the 1960's and 1970's Ritsos translated selected poetry from France and works by Attila József, Vladimir Mayakovsky, Nazim Hikmet, Ilya Ehrenburg, and Nicolás Guillén, two anthologies of Romanian and Czechoslovakian poetry, a short story by Tolstoy, and a children's story by Dora Gabe.

Of special interest to the student of Ritsos' work are the introductions to the poet's translations, several of which have been collected in the volume entitled *Meletimata* (Studies), published in 1974. This volume of six essays—four on translated poets (Mayakovsky, Hikmet, Ehrenburg, Éluard) and two on his own works (*Martyries, O tihos mesa ston kathrefti,* and *Thyrorio*)—written between 1961 and 1963 is Ritsos' single work of criticism. His affection for the four foreign poets, particularly Hikmet, is tied to their devotion to the people, their simplicity, and their insistence on the present. In Ritsos' view they are people's artists of an advanced state; extensions of the era in which they live, they move in time with those about them and express in the language of the people that which is felt and seen at the moment it is occurring. This concern for the immediate present and the expression of that concern in terms of the mode of the times constitute "modernity" in Ritsos' view. It is an insistence on the common folk (*laic*) that breeds modernity and an interest in modernity that leads to the *laic.* Greatness in poetry, Ritsos insists, rests on its immediacy, its directness, and its usefulness to the masses.

Ritsos finds the importance of these four leftist poets in the message of their poetry and not in their technique or style. Acknowledging that a poet can limit himself too strictly to his own times, Ritsos nevertheless finds in the immediate present and in material reality a springboard to leap the gap to the realm of the universal. In the central, seminal essay of the collection, that on Mayakovsky, he explains that it takes a great poet to root himself in the persistence and pain of the people and still create the wonder that is

> if not a synthesis and a union of natural, ethical, and social contrasts, at least a bridge between the present and the future, between that which is and the fantastic, between the individual and the masses, between man and world, between life and dream, in each case of hardship and personal drama.

Ritsos admires in Mayakovsky just such mastery of the "wonder" of poetry, for Mayakovsky inspires an amazement that envelops the reader and obscures the critical faculty. This quality, according to Ritsos, stems from Mayakovsky's enthusiasm, his futurism, and his love of people. In understanding such a poet, he claims, analytical criticism is at a loss. What is required—and it is the path that Ritsos follows—is criticism that is "journalistic, autobiographical, investigative, and confessional" at the same time.

Ritsos' essays on his own poetry remind us, as the poetry itself does, how reluctant he is to act as an intermediary between the reader and the poem. In any case, he refuses to comment at any length on his own work: "Poetry, to the degree that it is exactly poetry, always tells us a great deal more and in a much better way than that which we might be able to say about it." He reveals, nevertheless, that his later body of work, in particular *Martyries,* expresses a silent gratitude toward human life, its trials, death, and art. He recognizes that his work, as time passed, tended more and more toward what he calls "komikopiisi," an uplifting or positive poetry that diminishes and exploits the nightmare of death.

In this criticism Ritsos is not wholly satisfying as either a critic or a theorist; the essays cannot by any means be said to suggest a complete aesthetic. But as revealing poetic influences (those of Aristotle, G. W. F. Hegel, and John Ruskin in his critical approach), expressing his appreciation of other bodies of poetry (Turkish, Russian, and French), and allowing access to the private world of his judgments about the value and function of poetry, they deserve close attention.

Prose

The remainder of Ritsos' nonpoetic works make up five published volumes; three are books of prose and two are dramatic works already discussed. The prose was only published in the 1980's (*Ariostos o prosehtikos afighite stighmes tou viou tou kai tou ipnou tou* [Ariostos the Mindful Narrates Moments from His Life and Sleep], 1982; *Ti paraxena pramata* [What Strange Things], 1983; *Me to skountima tou agkona* [With a Nudge of the Elbow], 1984), although *Ariostos* was written as early as 1942. The poet calls these works "novels," a term with which he does not appear comfortable. Indeed, on the title page of *Ti paraxena pramata* he adds a question mark after the word "novel." The three works are in reality prose poems broken into parts, several pages in length, that are individually titled. Entries in the ongoing diary of Ritsos' confessional writings, these works continue to explore the same themes as his poetry and share the same language. In a note included at the end of the most recent of these works, *Me to skountima tou agkona,* Ritsos emphasizes the similarity of their content: "One could consider [this book] a continuation of the last—the same faces, about the same places at different times." He adds that each volume continues the one before it and suggests they might eventually be published as a trilogy under the title, "Imitelis kai ypotypodhis triloghia" (The Unfinished and Undeveloped Trilogy). In another breath he suggests that, should he live long enough, the trilogy might become a five- or even a ten-volume work.

CONCLUSION

Ritsos' place as a poet is not to be found merely in a study of the techniques, forms, and themes of his poetry and prose, but in his ability to see through his role as a poet of the sociohistoric, the mythic, and the autobiographical to a poetry of instinct and inspiration that controls without inhibiting, a poetry to be detected "in an intangible position of studied silence—there / where poetry always waits to be discovered" (*Ghrafi tiflou*). In much of Ritsos' early verse, the reader is led to expect a poetry of politics and pain of a literal and direct nature but finds instead, in the poet's maturity, a poetry whose attitude of resistance to the confining, the quelling, the humiliating, and the enslaving passes through all aspects of life; a poetry that goes far beyond the merely literal to touch on the concerns of men of all ages; a poetry that penetrates into the fantastic and the grotesque, that uses for its material the mundane grown monstrous, inescapable because it is so much a part of the everyday. Ritsos has created works that speak of modern man's most basic concerns; a poetry built on suffering that detaches itself from its most immediate meaning to permit a universal statement; a poetry that, as he states in *Ghrafi tiflou,* is like

> the tigress' tongue
> in the cage—a red tongue, venomous, between
> her pointed gleaming teeth.

His poetry is an inspiration that provides relief by rising from the common to the wonderful.

Selected Bibliography

EDITIONS

INDIVIDUAL WORKS

POETRY

Trakter (Tractor). Athens, 1934.

Pyramidhes (Pyramids). Athens, 1935.

Epitafios. Athens, 1936.

To traghoudi tis adhelfis mou (The Song of My Sister). Athens, 1937.

Earini symfonia (Spring Symphony). Athens, 1938.

To emvatirio tou okeanou (The Ocean's Musical March). Athens, 1940.

Dhokimasia (Trial). Athens, 1943.

Palia mazourka se rythmo vrohis (An Old Mazurka Set to the Rhythm of Rain). Athens, 1943.

O syntrofos mas, Nikos Zahariadhis (Our Comrade, Nikos Zahariadhis). Athens, 1945.

O anthropos me to gharyfallo (The Man with the Carnation). Athens, 1952.

Aghrypnia (Vigilance). Athens, 1954.

Proino astro (Morning Star). Athens, 1955.

I sonata tou selinofotos (Moonlight Sonata). Athens, 1956.

Apoheretismos (Farewell). Athens, 1957.

I ghitonies tou kosmou (The World's Neighborhoods). Athens, 1957.

Himerini dhiavghia (Winter Clarity). Athens, 1957.

Hroniko (Chronicle). Athens, 1957.

Makronisiotika (From Makronisos). Athens, 1957.

Ydhria (Pitcher). Athens, 1947.

Anipotahti politia (Unsubdued City). Athens, 1958.

I arhitektoniki ton dhentron (The Architecture of Trees). Athens, 1958.

Otan erhete o xenos (When the Stranger Comes). Athens, 1958.

I gherontisses k'i thalassa (The Old Women and the Sea). Athens, 1959.

I ghefira (The Bridge). Athens, 1960.

To parathiro (The Window). Athens, 1960.

O mavros aghios (The Black Saint). Athens, 1961.

Piimata I (Poems I). Athens, 1961.

Piimata II (Poems II). Athens, 1961.

Kato ap ton iskio tou Vounou (Under the Mountain's Shadow). Athens, 1962.

To nekro spiti (The Dead House). Athens, 1962.

To dhentro tis fylakis kai i ghinekes (The Prison Tree and the Women). Athens, 1963.

Dhodheka piimata ghia ton Kavafi (Twelve Poems for Cavafy). Athens, 1963.

Martyries: Sira proti (Testimonies I). Athens, 1963.

Paihnidhia t'ouranou kai tou nerou (Games of the Sky and Water). Athens, 1964.

Piimata III (Poems III). Athens, 1964.

Filoktitis (Philoctetes). Athens, 1965.

Martyries: Seira dhefteri (Testimonies II). Athens, 1966.

Orestis (Orestes). Athens, 1966.

Romiosini (Romiosini). Athens, 1966.

Ostrava (Ostrava). Athens, 1967.

I Eleni (Helen). Athens, 1972.

I epistrofi tis Ifighenias (The Return of Iphigenia). Athens, 1972.

Hironomies (Gestures). Athens, 1972.

Hrysothemis (Chrysothemis). *Athens, 1972.*

Ismini (Ismene). Athens, 1972.

Petres Epanalipsis Kigklidhoma (Stones, Repetitions, Railings). Athens, 1972.

Tetarti dhiastasi (Fourth Dimension). Athens, 1972.

Dhekaohto lianotraghoudhia tis pikris patridhas (Eighteen Songs for the Bitter Motherland). Athens, 1973.

Dhiadhromos kai skala (Corridor and Stairs). Athens, 1973.

Gkragkanta (Gkragkanta). Athens, 1973.

Kapnismeno tsoukali (Smoked Earthen Pot). Athens, 1973.

Septiria kai dhafniforia (Laureled Septeria). Athens, 1973.

O afanismos tis Milos (The Annihilation of Milos). Athens, 1974.

Hartina (Paper Poems). Athens, 1974.

Kodhonostasio (Belfry). Athens, 1974.

O tihos mesa ston kathrefti (The Wall in the Mirror). Athens, 1974.

Ymnos kai thrinos ghia tin Kypro (Hymn and Lament for Cyprus). Athens, 1974.

Ta Epikerika (The Timely). Athens, 1975.

Imerologhia exorias (Chronicle of Exile). Athens, 1975.

To isteroghrafo tis dhoxas (Postscript to Praise). Athens, 1975.

I kyra ton ampelion (The Lady of the Vineyards). Athens, 1975.

Mantatofores (News-Bearing Women). Athens, 1975.

Piimata IV (Poems IV). Athens, 1975.

I teleftea pro Anthropou ekatontaetia (The Last One Hundred Years Before Man). Athens, 1975.

Thyrorio (Porter's Lodge). Athens, 1976.

Ghignesthe (Becoming). Athens, 1977.

To makrino (The Distant). Athens, 1977.

Ta paidia tis KNE (The Children of KNE). Athens, 1977.

To roptro (Doorbell). Thessaloniki, 1977.

Fhedra (Phaedra). Athens, 1978.

Lipon; (So?). Athens, 1978.

Monemvasiotises (Women of Monemvasia). Athens, 1978.

I pili (The Gate). Athens, 1978.

Mia pygholampidha fotizi ti nichta (A Firefly Illuminates the Night). Athens, 1978.

To soma kai to ema (Body and Blood). Athens, 1978.

To teratodhes aristourghima (The Monstrous Masterpiece). Athens, 1978.

Tihokollitis (Billposter). Athens, 1978.

Trohonomos (Traffic Cop). Athens, 1978.

Volidhoskopos (The Sounder). Athens, 1978.

Ghrafi tiflou (Scripture of the Blind). Athens, 1979.

Dhiafania (Transparency). Athens, 1980.

Monohordha (Monochords). Athens, 1980.

Oniro kalokerinou mesimeriou (A Mid-Spring-Day Dream). Athens, 1980.

Parodhos (Side Street). Athens, 1980.

Ta erotika (Erotic Poems). Athens, 1981.

Syntrofika traghoudhia (Common Songs). Athens, 1981.

Italiko triptyho (Italian Triptych). Athens, 1982.

Monovasia (Monovasia). Athens, 1982.

Ypokofa (Muffled). Athens, 1982.

To horiko ton sfouggaradhon (Sponge Divers' Choral). Athens, 1983.

Tiresias (Tiresias). Athens, 1983.

Epinikia (Victory Songs). Athens, 1984.

Tanagrees (Tanagra Figurines). Athens, 1984.

Antapokrisis (Correspondences). Athens, 1987.

3 × 111 Tristiha (3 × 111 Tercets). Athens, 1987.

PLAYS

Pera ap ton iskio ton kyparission (Beyond the Shadow of the Cypress Trees). Athens, 1958.

Mia ghineka plai sti thalassa (A Woman Beside the Sea). Athens, 1959.

PROSE

Ariostos o Prosehtikos afighite stighmes tou viou tou kai tou ipnou tou (Ariostos the Mindful Narrates Moments from His Life and Sleep). Athens, 1982.

Ti paraxena praghmata (What Strange Things). Athens, 1983.

Me to skountima tou agkona (With a Nudge of the Elbow). Athens, 1984.

O gerontas me tous hartaitous (The Old Man with the Kites). Athens, 1985.

Isos na'ne kai etsi (Perhaps It's Also That Way). Athens, 1985.

Ohi monaha gia sena (Not Only for You). Athens, 1985.

Sfragismena m'ena hamogelo (Sealed with a Smile). Athens, 1986.

O Ariostos arnite na gini agios (Ariostos Refuses Sainthood). Athens, 1986.

Ligostevoun e eroteseis (Diminishing Questions). Athens, 1986.

CRITICISM

Meletimata (Studies). Athens, 1974.

TRANSLATIONS BY RITSOS

Nazim Hikmet, Piimata (Nazim Hikmet: Poems). Athens, 1953.

Alexi Tolstoi, I gkriniara katsika kai alla rosika laika paramythia (Leo Tolstoy: The Complaining Goat and Other Russian Laic Myths). Athens, 1956.

Alexandhrou Blok, I dhodheka (Alexander Blok: The Twelve). Athens, 1957.

Antologhia Roumanikis Piisis (Anthology of Romanian Poetry). Athens, 1961.

Attila Josef, Piimata (Attila József: Poems). Athens, 1963.

Vladimir Mayakovsky, Piimata (Vladimir Mayakovsky: Poems). Athens, 1964.

Dora Gabe, Egho. I mitera mou kai o kosmos (Dora Gabe: I. My Mother and the World). Athens, 1965.

Ilya Ehrenburg, To dhentro (Ilya Ehrenburg: The Tree). Athens, 1966.

Antologhia Tsehon kai Slovakon piiton (Anthology of Romanian and Czechoslovak Poetry). Athens, 1966.

Nicholas Guillén, O meghalos zoologhikos kipos (Nicolás Guillén: The Big Zoo). Athens, 1966.

Sergei Gesenin. Piimata (Sergei Essenin: Poems). Athens, 1981.

TRANSLATIONS

Most Ritsos poems have appeared in English not under their own titles but as part of larger collections. The following list includes the chief book-length translations and the major works contained therein. To associate the English titles given here with the Greek originals, the reader should consult the primary bibliography above.

Chronicle of Exile. Translated by Minas Savvas. San Francisco, 1977. Includes selections from *Testimonies, Corridor and Stairs,* and other works.

Corridor and Stairs. Translated by Nikos Germanacos. Curragh, Ireland, 1976.

Eighteen Short Songs of the Bitter Motherland. Translated by Amy Mims. Minneapolis, 1974.

Exile and Return: Selected Poems, 1967–1974. Translated by Edmund Keeley. New York, 1985. Selections from *The Wall Inside the Mirror, Stones, Repetitions, Railing, Doorman's Desk, Sidestreet, Muted Poems,* and *Paper Poems.*

The Fourth Dimension: Selected Poems of Yannis Ritsos. Translated by Rae Dalven. Boston, 1977.

YANNIS RITSOS

Selections from *Notes in the Margin of Time, Parentheses, Exercises, Testimonies I, Twelve Poems for Cavafy, The Wall in the Mirror,* and the long poems *The Blackened Pot, The Moonlight Sonata, The Window, Beneath the Shadow of the Mountain,* and *Ismene.*

Gestures and Other Poems, 1986–1970. Translated by Nikos Stangos. London, 1971. Selections from *Stones, Repetitions, Gestures,* and *Corridor and Stairs.*

The Lady of the Vineyards. Translated by Apostolos N. Athanassakis. New York, 1978.

Monovasia and The Women of Monemvasia. Translated by Kimon Friar and Kostas Myrsiades. Minneapolis, 1987.

Ritsos in Parentheses. Translated by Edmund Keeley. Princeton, N.J., 1979. Selections from *Parentheses, 1946–1947, Parentheses, 1950–1961,* and *The Distant.*

Scripture of the Blind. Translated by Kimon Friar and Kostas Myrsiades. Columbus, Ohio, 1979.

Selected Poems. Translated by Nikos Stangos. Baltimore, 1974. Selections from *Testimonies I, Testimonies II, Testimonies III, Tanagra Women, Stones, Repetitions, Railings, Gestures, Corridor and Stairs, Papermade, Muffled,* and the long poem *The Dead House.*

Selected Poems, 1938–1975. Edited by Kimon Friar and Kostas Myrsiades. Mansfield, Penn., 1978. Selections from *The Distant, Scripture of the Blind, The Wall in the Mirror, Gestures, Testimonies I, Testimonies II, Exercises, Petrified Time, Parentheses, The Swaying of the Scale, Notes on the Margins of Time,* and the long poem *The Prison Tree and the Women.*

Subterranean Horses. Translated by Minas Savvas. Athens, Ohio, 1980. Fifty-seven short poems from various collections.

Yannis Ritsos: Selected Poems, 1938–1988. Edited by Kimon Friar and Kostas Myrsiades. Translated by Friar, Myrsiades, et al. New York, 1989. Selections from 43 volumes of poetry (440 poems). Includes two critical studies.

BIOGRAPHICAL AND CRITICAL STUDIES

Aragon, Louis. *Yiannis Ritsos. Meletes ghia to ergho tou.* Athens, 1975.

Bien, Peter. "Myth in Modern Greek Letters with Special Attention to Yannis Ritsos' 'Philoctetes.' " *Books Abroad* 48:15–19 (1974).

Dhialismas, Stefanos. *Isaghoghi stin piisi tou Yianni Ritsoy.* Athens, 1984.

Ghinis, Spyros. *Ghia ton Yianni Ritso.* Athens, n.d.

Keeley, Edmund. "Ritsos: Voice and Vision in the Shorter Poems." In *Modern Greek Poetry: Voice and Myth.* Princeton, N.J., 1983.

Myrsiades, Kostas. "The Classical Past in Yannis Ritsos' Dramatic Monologues." *Papers on Language and Literature* 14, no. 4:450–458 (Fall 1978).

———. "The Poetry of Oppression: Yiannis Ritsos' 'Scripture of the Blind.' " *The Literary Review* 21, no. 4:457–464 (Summer 1978).

———. "Yannis Ritsos and Greek Resistance Poetry." *Journal of the Hellenic Diaspora* 5, no. 3:47–56 (Fall 1978).

Prevelaki, Panteli. *O piitis Yiannis Ritsos.* Athens, 1981.

Prokopaki, Chrysa. *I poria pros ti Gkragkanta i i peripeties tou oramatos.* Athens, 1981.

———. *Yannis Ritsos.* Paris, 1973.

Ritsou-Glezou, Loula. *Ta pedhika hronia tou adhelfou mou Yianni Ritsou.* Athens, 1981.

Spanos, William V. "Yannis Ritsos' 'Romiosini': Style as Historical Memory." *The American Poetry Review* 2, no. 5:18–22 (1973).

KOSTAS MYRSIADES